Prepare, Apply, and Confirm

- **Auto-Graded Excel Projects**—Using proven, field-tested technology, MyAccountingLab's new auto-graded Excel Projects allow instructors to seamlessly integrate Excel content into their course without having to manually grade spreadsheets. Students have the opportunity to practice important Accounting skills in Microsoft Excel, helping them to master key concepts and gain proficiency in Excel. Students simply download a spreadsheet, work live on an accounting problem in Excel, and then upload that file back into MyAccountingLab, where they receive reports on their work that provide personalized, detailed feedback to pinpoint where they went wrong on any step of the problem. Available with select titles.

- **Enhanced eText**—The Pearson eText gives students access to their textbook anytime, anywhere. In addition to note-taking, highlighting, and bookmarking, the Pearson eText offers interactive and sharing features. Students actively read and learn through auto-graded practice, author videos, and more. Instructors can share comments or highlights, and students can add their own, for a tight community of learners in any class.

- Keep students engaged in learning on their own time, while helping them achieve greater conceptual understanding of course material through author-created solutions videos, opportunities to Try It!, and live exhibits.

- **Accounting Cycle Tutorial**—Accessed by computer, smartphone, or tablet, the ACT provides students with brief explanations of each concept in the Accounting Cycle through engaging, interactive activities.

with MyAccountingLab®

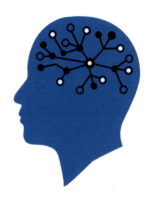

- **Dynamic Study Modules**—With a focus on key topics, these modules work by continuously assessing student performance and activity in real time and, using data and analytics, provide personalized content to reinforce concepts that target each student's particular strengths and weakness.

- **Hallmark Features**—Personalized Learning Aids, like Help Me Solve This, Demo Docs, and instant feedback are available for further practice and mastery when students need the help most!

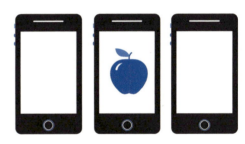

- **Learning Catalytics**—Generates classroom discussion, guides lecture, and promotes peer-to-peer learning with real-time analytics. Now, students can use any device to interact in the classroom.

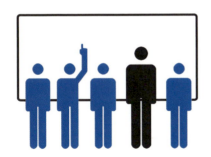

- **Personalized Study Plan**—Assists students in monitoring their own progress by offering them a customized study plan based on Homework, Quiz, and Test results. Includes regenerated exercises with unlimited practice, as well as the opportunity to earn mastery points by completing quizzes on recommended learning objectives.

- **Worked Solutions**—Provide step-by-step explanations on how to solve select problems using the exact numbers and data that were presented in the problem. Instructors will have access to the Worked Out Solutions in preview and review mode.

Prepare, Apply, and Confirm with MyAccountingLab®

General Ledger—Students can launch General Ledger software in MyAccountingLab, where they will be able to record transactions and adjusting entries, post to the ledger, close periods, and see the effects in the ledger accounts. Their work will be auto-graded, and grades will then automatically flow to the MyAccountingLab Gradebook.

Algorithmic Test Bank—Instructors have the ability to create multiple versions of a test or extra practice for students.

Reporting Dashboard—View, analyze, and report learning outcomes clearly and easily. Available via the Gradebook and fully mobile-ready, the Reporting Dashboard presents student performance data at the class, section, and program levels in an accessible, visual manner.

LMS Integration—Link from any LMS platform to access assignments, rosters, and resources, and synchronize MyLab grades with your LMS gradebook. For students, new direct, single sign-on provides access to all the personalized learning MyLab resources that make studying more efficient and effective.

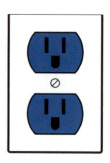

P Pearson

ALWAYS LEARNING

Vice President, Business Publishing: Donna Battista
Director of Portfolio Management: Adrienne D'Ambrosio
Specialist Portfolio Management: Lacey Vitetta
Vice President, Product Marketing: Roxanne McCarley
Director of Strategic Marketing: Brad Parkins
Strategic Marketing Manager: Deborah Strickland
Product Marketing Manager: Tricia Murphy
Field Marketing Manager: Natalie Wagner
Field Marketing Assistant: Kristen Compton
Product Marketing Assistant: Jessica Quazza
Vice President, Production and Digital Studio, Arts and Business: Etain O'Dea
Director of Production, Business: Jeff Holcomb
Managing Producer, Business: Ashley Santora
Content Producer: Mary Kate Murray
Operations Specialist: Carol Melville
Creative Director: Blair Brown

Manager, Learning Tools: Brian Surette
Digital Strategist: Sarah Peterson
Managing Producer, Digital Studio, Arts and Business: Diane Lombardo
Digital Studio Producer: Regina DaSilva
Digital Studio Producer: Alana Coles
Senior Tech Manager: James Bateman
Digital Content Team Lead: Noel Lotz
Digital Content Project Lead: Martha LaChance
Full-Service Project Management and Composition: SPi Global
Interior Designer: Jon Boylan/SPi Global
Cover Designer: Jon Boylan
Cover Art: mbbirdy/Getty Images; Lisa Thornberg/Getty Images; 9comeback/Shutterstock; Kritchanut/Getty Images
Printer/Binder: LSC Communications
Cover Printer: LSC Communications
Typeface: Garamond MT Pro

Library of Congress Cataloging-in-Publication Data:

Cataloging-in-Publication Data is on file with the Library of Congress.

6   17

ISBN-13: 978-0-13-448685-7
ISBN-10:   0-13-448685-4

HORNGREN'S
Financial & Managerial
Accounting
THE MANAGERIAL CHAPTERS

SIXTH EDITION

Tracie Miller-Nobles
Austin Community College

Brenda Mattison
Tri-County Technical College

Ella Mae Matsumura
University of Wisconsin-Madison

 Pearson

About the Authors

Tracie L. Miller-Nobles, CPA, received her bachelor's and master's degrees in accounting from Texas A&M University and is currently pursuing her Ph.D. in adult education also at Texas A&M University. She is an Associate Professor at Austin Community College, Austin, TX. Previously she served as a Senior Lecturer at Texas State University, San Marcos, TX, and has taught as an adjunct at University of Texas-Austin. Tracie has public accounting experience with Deloitte Tax LLP and Sample & Bailey, CPAs.

Tracie is a recipient of the following awards: American Accounting Association J. Michael and Mary Anne Cook prize, Texas Society of CPAs Rising Star TSCPA Austin Chapter CPA of the Year, TSCPA Outstanding Accounting Educator, NISOD Teaching Excellence and Aims Community College Excellence in Teaching. She is a member of the Teachers of Accounting at Two Year Colleges, the American Accounting Association, the American Institute of Certified Public Accountants, and the Texas State Society of Certified Public Accountants. She is currently serving on the Board of Directors as secretary/webmaster of Teachers of Accounting at Two Year Colleges and as a member of the American Institute of Certified Public Accountants financial literacy committee. In addition, Tracie served on the Commission on Accounting Higher Education: Pathways to a Profession.

Tracie has spoken on such topics as using technology in the classroom, motivating non-business majors to learn accounting, and incorporating active learning in the classroom at numerous conferences. In her spare time she enjoys camping and hiking and spending time with friends and family.

Brenda L. Mattison, CMA, has a bachelor's degree in education and a master's degree in accounting, both from Clemson University. She is currently an Accounting Instructor at Tri-County Technical College in Pendleton, South Carolina. Brenda previously served as Accounting Program Coordinator at TCTC and has prior experience teaching accounting at Robeson Community College, Lumberton, North Carolina; University of South Carolina Upstate, Spartanburg, South Carolina; and Rasmussen Business College, Eagan, Minnesota. She also has accounting work experience in retail and manufacturing businesses and is a Certified Management Accountant.

Brenda is a member of the American Accounting Association, Institute of Management Accountants, South Carolina Technical Education Association, and Teachers of Accounting at Two Year Colleges. She is currently serving on the Board of Directors as Vice President of Conference Administration of Teachers of Accounting at Two Year Colleges.

Brenda previously served as Faculty Fellow at Tri-County Technical College. She has presented at state, regional, and national conferences on topics including active learning, course development, and student engagement.

In her spare time, Brenda enjoys reading and spending time with her family. She is also an active volunteer in the community, serving her church and other organizations.

Ella Mae Matsumura, Ph.D. is a professor in the Department of Accounting and Information Systems in the School of Business at the University of Wisconsin–Madison, and is affiliated with the university's Center for Quick Response Manufacturing. She received an A.B. in mathematics from the University of California, Berkeley, and M.Sc. and Ph.D. degrees from the University of British Columbia. Ella Mae has won two teaching excellence awards at the University of Wisconsin–Madison and was elected as a lifetime fellow of the university's Teaching Academy, formed to promote effective teaching. She is a member of the university team awarded an IBM Total Quality Management Partnership grant to develop curriculum for total quality management education.

Ella Mae was a co-winner of the 2010 Notable Contributions to Management Accounting Literature Award. She has served in numerous leadership positions in the American Accounting Association (AAA). She was coeditor of *Accounting Horizons* and has chaired and served on numerous AAA committees. She has been secretary-treasurer and president of the AAA's Management Accounting Section. Her past and current research articles focus on decision making, performance evaluation, compensation, supply chain relationships, and sustainability. She coauthored a monograph on customer profitability analysis in credit unions.

Brief Contents

Contents

Changes to This Edition

General

Revised end-of-chapter short exercises, exercises, problems, continuing problems, comprehensive problems, and critical thinking cases.

NEW! Using Excel. This end-of-chapter problem introduces students to Excel to solve common accounting problems as they would in the business environment.

NEW! Tying It All Together feature ties together key concepts from the chapter using the company highlighted in the chapter opener. The in-chapter box feature presents scenarios and questions that the company could face and focuses on the decision-making process. The end-of-chapter business case helps students synthesize the concepts of the chapter and reinforce critical thinking.

NEW! A Continuing Problem starts in Chapter 1 and runs through the financial chapters, exposing students to recording entries for a service company and then moving into recording transactions for a merchandiser later in the text. The managerial chapters' continuing problem has been revised for this edition and emphasizes the relevant topics for that chapter using a continuous company.

Chapter 16

Expanded the discussion of managerial accounting to include manager's role in the organization and managerial accounting functions.

Clarified and expanded the discussion of how companies classify costs used in managerial accounting.

Revised the discussion on manufacturing cost flows, including better explanation of how cost of goods manufactured and cost of goods sold are calculated.

Expanded discussion on business trends that are affecting managerial accounting.

Chapter 17

Expanded the discussion on cost accounting systems, including why companies choose either process or job-order costing.

Clarified the discussion on the allocation and adjustment of manufacturing overhead.

Chapter 18

REVISED! For consistency throughout the chapter, all company examples now use the same company, Puzzle Me, to better understand how costs flow through a process costing system and are reflected on the production cost report.

Expanded and clarified discussion on equivalent units of production.

REVISED! The discussion on preparing a production cost report was split into two learning objectives (first department and subsequent departments) allowing faculty to omit the discussion on subsequent departments.

REVISED! Discussion on preparing a production cost report for the first department now realistically reflects beginning inventory.

Updated the discussion on how the weighted-average method is different than the FIFO method when preparing the production cost report.

Chapter 19

Clarified the differences between the use of a single plantwide rate versus a multiple department rate when allocating overhead.

Expanded the discussion of how service companies can use activity-based management.

Chapter 20

Moved discussion of breakeven point before coverage of target profit for better student understanding.

Clarified the high-low method when determining a company's variable and fixed costs.

NEW! Discussion on how sensitivity analysis could be used and the differences between predicted cost behavior versus actual management behavior.

Chapter 21

Expanded discussion on the differences between absorption and variable costing and the impact on operating income.

Chapter 22

Expanded discussion benefits of budgets, including benchmarking.

NEW! Added discussion on types of budgets, including participative, zero-based, and continuous budgets.

Moved the coverage of merchandising budgets from the appendix into the chapter. This allows faculty to choose to cover both manufacturing and merchandising budgets or either. Each section is developed on a stand-alone basis.

Clarified the steps involved in the different budgets for better student understanding.

Chapter 23

Expanded the discussion on performance reports using static budgets, including advantages and disadvantages.

Chapter 26

NEW! Added discussion on future value, including determining the future value of a lump sum and of an annuity.

Appendix C

Modified the wording in Changes to Current Assets and Current Liabilities section of preparing the statement of cash flows, indirect method, to emphasize adjustments are made to net income to convert from accrual basis to cash basis.

Appendix D

Rearranged the liquidity ratios from most stringent to least stringent (cash ratio, acid-test ratio, current ratio).

NEW! Added problem (both A and B series) that has students complete a trend analysis and ratios to analyze a company for its investment potential.

http://www.pearsonhighered.com/Horngren

Financial & Managerial Accounting . . . Expanding on Proven Success

Accounting Cycle Tutorial

MyAccountingLab's interactive tutorial helps students master the Accounting Cycle for early and continued success in the Introduction to Accounting course. The tutorial, accessed by computer, smartphone, or tablet, provides students with brief explanations of each concept of the Accounting Cycle through engaging, interactive activities. Students are immediately assessed on their understanding and their performance is recorded in the MyAccountingLab Gradebook. Whether the Accounting Cycle Tutorial is used as a remediation self-study tool or course assignment, students have yet another resource within MyAccountingLab to help them be successful with the accounting cycle.

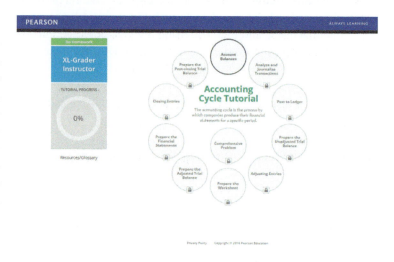

NEW! ACT Comprehensive Problem

The Accounting Cycle Tutorial now includes a comprehensive problem that allows students to work with the same set of transactions throughout the accounting cycle. The comprehensive problem, which can be assigned at the beginning or the end of the full cycle, reinforces the lessons learned in the accounting cycle tutorial activities by emphasizing the connections between the accounting cycle concepts.

Study Plan

The Study Plan acts as a tutor, providing personalized recommendations for each of your students based on his or her ability to master the learning objectives in your course. This allows students to focus their study time by pinpointing the precise areas they need to review, and allowing them to use customized practice and learning aids—such as videos, eText, tutorials, and more—to get them back on track. Using the report available in the Gradebook, you can then tailor course lectures to prioritize the content where students need the most support—offering you better insight into classroom and individual performance.

Dynamic Study Modules

help students study effectively on their own by continuously assessing their activity and performance in real time. Here's how it works: students complete a set of questions with a unique answer format that also asks them to indicate their confidence level. Questions repeat until the student can answer them all correctly and confidently. Once completed, Dynamic Study Modules explain the concept using materials from the text. These are available as graded assignments prior to class, and accessible on smartphones, tablets, and computers. NEW! Instructors can now remove questions from Dynamic Study Modules to better fit their course. Available for select titles.

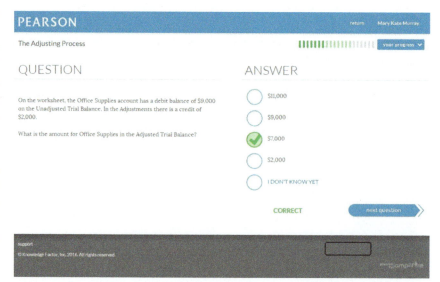

Learning Catalytics

Learning Catalytics helps you generate class discussion, customize your lecture, and promote peer-to-peer learning with real-time analytics. As a student response tool, Learning Catalytics uses students' smartphones, tablets, or laptops to engage them in more interactive tasks and thinking.

- **NEW!** Upload a full PowerPoint® deck for easy creation of slide questions.
- Help your students develop critical thinking skills.
- Monitor responses to find out where your students are struggling.
- Rely on real-time data to adjust your teaching strategy.
- Automatically group students for discussion, teamwork, and peer-to-peer learning.

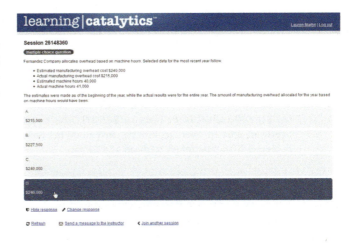

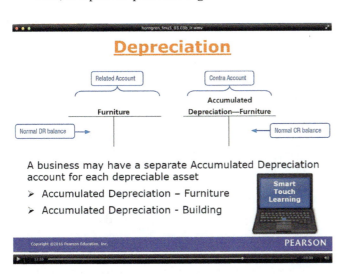

Animated Lectures

These pre-class learning aids are available for every learning objective and are professor-narrated PowerPoint summaries that will help students prepare for class. These can be used in an online or flipped classroom experience or simply to get students ready for lecture.

Chapter Openers

Chapter openers set up the concepts to be covered in the chapter using stories students can relate to. The implications of those concepts on a company's reporting and decision making processes are then discussed.

NEW! Tying It All Together

This feature ties together key concepts from the chapter using the company highlighted in the chapter opener. The in-chapter box feature presents scenarios and questions that the company could face and focuses on the decision-making process. The end of chapter business case helps students synthesize the concepts of the chapter and reinforce critical thinking.

TYING IT ALL TOGETHER

In the chapter opener, we introduced **Best Buy Co., Inc.** Best Buy is a leading provider of technology products and services. Managers of retail companies like Best Buy have to make decisions about which products to sell, how much to charge customers for those products, and how to control costs so that the company earns a profit that is acceptable to its investors. In 2015, Best Buy incurred $711 million in advertising expenses for digital, print and television advertisements and promotional events (Notes to Consolidated Financial Statements, Note 1) and is transforming how it advertises by moving to more digital and personalized marketing (Letter to Stockholders). The company had $40,339 million in sales in 2015. Therefore, its advertising costs were less than 2% of sales ($711 million / $40,339 million = 1.76%).

When advertising expenses are classified by behavior, are they variable, fixed, or mixed costs?
Advertising expenses are fixed costs because they do not vary in total when there is a change in sales volume.

When advertising expenses are classified by function, are they product or period costs?
Advertising expenses are selling costs, part of the Selling and Administrative Expenses, which are period costs.

What would most likely happen if Best Buy increased its advertising?
An increase in advertising will increase costs, which decreases profits. However, if increased digital and personalized advertising also results in increased sales, which will increase profits, then the cost may be justified.

How might a marketing manager use CVP analysis to make decisions about increasing or decreasing advertising costs?
The marketing manager will have to predict how increased advertising will affect sales volume and complete a CVP analysis to determine if the benefit resulting from the increased advertising will be greater than the cost. A decrease in advertising will most likely result in a decrease in sales. If customers are not as exposed to the Best Buy brand and are not as aware of special deals, they may shop elsewhere. Also, if Best Buy decreases its advertising and its competitors do not, then customers may become more aware of the competitors and choose to shop there. As with the decision to increase advertising, the marketing manager will complete a CVP analysis to determine if the cost savings outweighs the profits lost due to the decrease in sales.

> Tying It All Together Case 20-1

Before you begin this assignment, review the Tying It All Together feature in the chapter.

Best Buy Co., Inc. is a leading provider of technology products. Customers can shop at more than 1,700 stores or online. The company is also known for its Geek Squad for technology services. Suppose Best Buy is considering a particular HDTV for a major sales item for Black Friday, the day after Thanksgiving, known as one of the busiest shopping days of the year. Assume the HDTV has a regular sales price of $900, a cost of $500, and a Black Friday proposed discounted sales price of $650. Best Buy's 2015 Annual Report states that failure to manage costs could have a material adverse effect on its profitability and that certain elements in its cost structure are largely fixed in nature. Best Buy, like most companies, wishes to maintain price competitiveness while achieving acceptable levels of profitability. (Item 1A. Risk Factors.)

Requirements

1. Calculate the gross profit of the HDTV at the regular sales price and at the discounted sales price.

2. Assume that during the November/December holiday season last year, Best Buy sold an average of 150 of this particular HDTV per store. If the HDTVs are marked down to $650, how many would each store have to sell this year to make the same total gross profit as last year?

3. Relative to Sales Revenue, what type of costs would Best Buy have that are fixed? What type of costs would be variable?

4. Because Best Buy stated that its cost structure is largely fixed in nature, what might be the impact on operating income if sales decreased? Does having a cost structure that is largely fixed in nature increase the financial risk to a company? Why or why not?

5. In the Tying It All Together feature in the chapter, we looked at the cost of advertising. Is advertising a fixed or variable cost? If the company has a small margin of safety, how would increasing advertising costs affect Best Buy's operating income? What would be the effect of decreasing advertising costs?

Effect on the Accounting Equation

Next to every journal entry in both financial and managerial chapters, these illustrations help reinforce the connections between recording transactions and the effect those transactions have on the accounting equation.

the $169,000 direct labor costs, or $67,600. The journal entry to allocate manufacturing overhead cost to Work-in-Process Inventory increases Work-in-Process Inventory and decreases Manufacturing Overhead as follows:

Date	Accounts and Explanation	Debit	Credit
Trans. 8	Work-in-Process Inventory	67,600	
	Manufacturing Overhead		67,600

$$\left. \frac{A\uparrow}{WIP\uparrow} \right\} = \left\{ \frac{L}{} + \frac{E\uparrow}{MOH\downarrow} \right.$$

Instructor Tips & Tricks

Found throughout the text, these handwritten notes mimic the experience of having an experienced teacher walk a student through concepts on the "board." Many include mnemonic devices or examples to help students remember the rules of accounting.

Date	Accounts and Explanation	Debit	Credit
Trans. 9	Manufacturing Overhead	500	
	Cost of Goods Sold		500
	Adjusted MOH for overallocated overhead.		

$$\left. A \right\} = \left\{ L + \frac{E\uparrow\downarrow}{\substack{COGS\downarrow \\ MOH\uparrow}} \right.$$

The adjusting entry for overallocated or underallocated manufacturing overhead is usually prepared at the end of the year. We are showing it here at the end of the month so we can illustrate all journal entries for a process costing system.

Common Questions, Answered

Our authors have spent years in the classroom answering students' questions and have found patterns in the concepts or rules that consistently confuse students. These commonly asked questions are located in the margin of the text next to where the answer or clarification can be found highlighted in purple text.

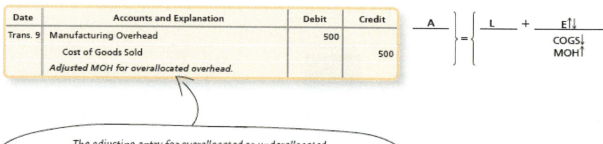

Why would the company use a subsidiary ledger for raw materials?

eral ledger account.

The raw materials subsidiary ledger includes a separate record for each type of material, so there is a separate ledger account (or record) for the batteries, processors, cases, and other materials used in producing the tablets. The subsidiary ledger records show the raw materials purchased (received), used in production (issued), and balance on hand (balance) at all times. **The use of a subsidiary ledger allows for better control of inventory because it helps track each type of material used in production.** Exhibit 17-3 shows the subsidiary ledger of one type of battery that Smart Touch Learning uses. The balance of the Raw Materials Inventory account in the general ledger should always equal the sum of the balances in the raw materials subsidiary ledger.

Try It! Boxes

Found after each learning objective, Try Its! give students opportunities to apply the concept they've just learned by completing an accounting problem. Links to these exercises appear throughout the eText, allowing students to practice in MyAccountingLab without interruption.

Try It!

Record the following journal entries for Smith Company:

6. Purchased raw materials on account, $10,000.
7. Used $6,000 in direct materials and $500 in indirect materials in production.
8. Incurred $8,000 in labor costs, of which 80% was direct labor.

Check your answers online in MyAccountingLab or at http://www.pearsonhighered.com/Horngren.

For more practice, see Short Exercises S17-2 through S17-4. MyAccountingLab

Try It! Solution Videos

Author-recorded and accompanying Try It! Exercises, these videos walk students through the problem and the solution.

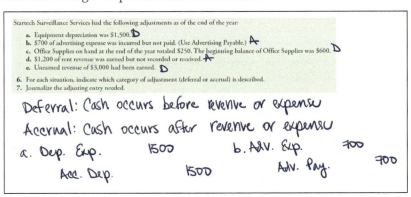

IFRS

Information on IFRS provides guidance on how IFRS differs from U.S. GAAP throughout the financial chapters.

Decision Boxes

This feature provides common questions and potential solutions business owners face. Students are asked to determine the course of action they would take based on concepts covered in the chapter and are then given potential solutions.

DECISIONS

What should the company charge?

Refer to the information for the service company example, Walsh Associates. Assume Jacob Walsh desires a profit equal to 50% of the firm's cost. Should Walsh consider only the direct costs when making pricing decisions? How much should the firm bill Client 367?

Solution

Walsh should consider more than just the direct labor costs when determining the amount to charge his clients. Client 367 incurred $700 in direct costs. At a 50% markup, Walsh would add $350 ($700 × 50%) and charge the client $1,050 ($700 + $350). That means Walsh would not cover the full cost of providing service to the client. The loss on the job would be $70 ($1,050 − $1,120). He left out the indirect costs. The markup should be 50% of the total cost, $560 ($1,120 × 50%). The amount charged to the client would be $1,680, which would generate a profit of $560 ($1,680 − $1,120).

> Things You Should Know

1. **Why is managerial accounting important?**
   - Managerial accounting focuses on providing information for internal decision makers.
   - Managerial accounting helps managers plan, direct, control, and make decisions about the business.

2. **How are costs classified?**
   - Manufacturing companies track costs using three inventory accounts: Raw Materials Inventory, Work-in-Process Inventory, and Finished Goods Inventory.
   - Direct costs such as direct materials and direct labor can be easily and cost-effectively traced directly to a cost object, whereas indirect costs such as indirect materials and indirect labor cannot be easily or cost-effectively traced to cost objects.
   - Manufacturing companies can classify product costs into three distinct categories: direct materials, direct labor, and manufacturing overhead.
     - Prime costs are direct materials and direct labor.
     - Conversion costs are direct labor and manufacturing overhead.
   - Product costs are all costs (direct materials, direct labor, and manufacturing overhead)

Things You Should Know

Provides students with a brief review of each learning objective presented in a question and answer format.

Using Excel Problems

This end of chapter problem introduces students to Excel to solve common accounting problems as they would in the business environment. Students will work from a template that will aid them in solving the problem related to accounting concepts taught in the chapter. Each chapter focuses on different Excel skills.

> Using Excel

P20-47 Using Excel for cost-volume-profit (CVP) analysis

Download an Excel template for this problem online in MyAccountingLab or at http://www.pearsonhighered.com/Horngren.

The Oceanside Garden Nursery buys flowering plants in four-inch pots for $1.00 each and sells them for $2.50 each. Management budgets monthly fixed costs of $2,100 for sales volumes between 0 and 5,000 plants.

Requirements

1. Use the contribution margin approach to compute the company's monthly breakeven point in units.
2. Use the contribution margin ratio approach to compute the breakeven point in sales dollars.
3. Use the contribution margin approach to compute the monthly sales level (in units) required to earn a target operating income of $5,000.
4. Prepare a graph of the company's CVP relationships. Include the sales revenue line, the fixed cost line, and the total cost line. Create a chart title and label the axes.

End-of-Chapter Continuing and Comprehensive Problems

> Continuing Problem

P16-42

This is the first problem in a sequence of problems for Piedmont Computer Company, a manufacturer of personal computers and tablets. During its first month of manufacturing, Piedmont Computer Company incurred the following manufacturing costs:

Balances:	Beginning	Ending
Direct Materials	$ 10,500	$ 9,700
Work-in-Process Inventory	0	17,000
Finished Goods Inventory	0	31,000

Other information:	
Direct materials purchases	$ 16,000
Plant janitorial services	500
Sales salaries expense	10,000
Delivery expense	1,600
Sales revenue	1,100,000
Utilities for plant	16,000
Rent on plant	9,000
Customer service hotline costs	19,000
Direct labor	210,000

Continuing Problem—Starts in Chapter 16 and runs through the financial chapters, exposing students to recording entries for a service company and then moving into recording transactions for a merchandiser later in the text. The managerial chapters' continuing problem has been revised for this edition and emphasizes the relevant topics for that chapter using a continuous company.

Comprehensive Problem for Chapters 16–20—Covers fundamental managerial accounting concepts: job order costing, process costing, cost management systems, and cost-volume-profit analysis.

Comprehensive Problem for Chapters 22–24—Covers planning and control decisions for a manufacturing company, including a master budget, flexible budget, variance analysis, and performance evaluation.

Comprehensive Problem for Chapters 25–26—Covers decision making, both short-term business decisions and capital budgeting decisions.

Comprehensive Problem for Appendix B—Uses special journals and subsidiary ledgers and covers the entire accounting cycle for a merchandise company. Students can complete this comprehensive problem using the MyAccountingLab General Ledger or Quickbooks™ software.

> **Comprehensive Problem for Chapters 16–20**

The Jacksonville Shirt Company makes two types of T-shirts: basic and custom. Basic shirts are plain shirts without any screen printing on them. Custom shirts are created using the basic shirts and then adding a custom screen printing design.

The company buys cloth in various colors and then makes the basic shirts in two departments, Cutting and Sewing. The company uses a process costing system (weighted-average method) to determine the production cost of the basic shirts. In the Cutting Department, direct materials (cloth) are added at the beginning of the process and conversion costs are added evenly through the process. In the Sewing Department, no direct materials are added. The only additional material, thread, is considered an indirect material because it cannot be easily traced to the finished product. Conversion costs are added evenly throughout the process in the Sewing Department. The finished basic shirts are sold to retail stores or are sent to the Custom Design Department for custom screen printing.

The Custom Design Department creates custom shirts by adding screen printing to the basic shirt. The department creates a design based on the customer's request and then prints the design using up to four colors. Because these shirts have the custom printing added, which is unique for each order, the additional cost incurred is determined using job order costing, with each custom order considered a separate job.

For March 2018, the Jacksonville Shirt Company compiled the following data for the Cutting and Sewing Departments:

Enhanced eText

The **Enhanced eText** keeps students engaged in learning on their own time, while helping them achieve greater conceptual understanding of course material. The worked examples, animations, and interactive tutorials bring learning to life, and algorithmic practice allows students to apply the very concepts they are reading about. Combining resources that illuminate content with accessible self-assessment, MyLab with Enhanced eText provides students with a complete digital learning experience—all in one place.

And with the **Pearson eText 2.0** mobile app (available for select titles) students can now access the Enhanced eText and all of its functionality from their computer, tablet, or mobile phone. Because students' progress is synced across all of their devices, they can stop what they're doing on one device and pick up again later on another one—without breaking their stride.

Dear Colleague,

Thank you for taking the time to review *Horngren's Financial and Managerial Accounting.* We are excited to share our innovations with you as we expand on the proven success of our revision to the Horngren franchise. Using what we learned from focus groups, market feedback, and our colleagues, we've designed this edition to focus on several goals.

First, we again made certain that the textbook, student resources, and instructor supplements are clear, consistent, and accurate. As authors, we reviewed each and every component to ensure a student experience free of hurdles. Next, through our ongoing conversations with our colleagues and our time engaged at professional conferences, we confirmed that our pedagogy and content represents the leading methods used in teaching our students these critical foundational topics. Lastly, we concentrated on student success and providing resources for professors to create an active and engaging classroom.

We are excited to share with you some new features and changes in this latest edition. First, we have added a new Tying It All Together feature that highlights an actual company and addresses how the concepts of the chapter apply to the business environment. A Using Excel problem has also been added to every chapter to introduce students to using Excel to solve common accounting problems as they would in the business environment. Chapter 5 (Merchandising Operations) has been updated for the newly released revenue recognition standard. The managerial chapters went through a significant review with a focus of clarifying current coverage and expanding on content areas that needed more explanation.

We trust you will find evidence of these goals throughout our text, MyAccountingLab, enhanced eText, and in our many new media enhanced resources such as the Accounting Cycle Tutorial with a new comprehensive problem and animated lectures. We welcome your feedback and comments. Please do not hesitate to contact us at HorngrensAccounting@pearson.com or through our editor, Lacey Vitetta, LaceyVitetta@pearson.com.

Tracie L. Miller-Nobles, CPA   *Brenda Mattison, CMA*   *Ella Mae Matsumura, PhD*

Instructor and Student Resources

Each supplement, including the resources in MyAccountingLab, has been reviewed by the author team to ensure accuracy and consistency with the text. Given their personal involvement, you can be assured of the high quality and accuracy of all supplements.

For Instructors

MyAccountingLab

Online Homework and Assessment Manager: http://www.myaccountinglab.com

Instructor Resource Center: http://www.pearsonhighered.com/Horngren

For the instructor's convenience, the instructor resources can be downloaded from the textbook's catalog page (http://www.pearsonhighered.com/Horngren) and MyAccountingLab. Available resources include the following:

Online Instructor's Resource Manual:

Course Content:

■ Tips for Taking Your Course from Traditional to Hybrid, Blended, or Online
■ Standard Syllabi for Financial Accounting (10-week & 16-week)
■ Standard Syllabi for Managerial Accounting (10-week & 16-week)
■ Sample Syllabi for 10- and 16-week courses
■ "First Day of Class" student handouts include:
  • Student Walk-Through to Set-up MyAccountingLab
  • Tips on How to Get an A in This Class

Chapter Content:

■ Chapter Overview
  • Contains a brief synopsis and overview of each chapter.
■ Learning Objectives
■ Teaching Outline with Lecture Notes
  • Combines the Teaching Outline and the Lecture Outline Topics, so instructors only have one document to review.
  • Walks instructors through what material to cover and what examples to use when addressing certain items within the chapter.
■ Handout for Student Notes
  • An outline to assist students in taking notes on the chapter.
■ Student Chapter Summary
  • Aids students in their comprehension of the chapter.
■ Assignment Grid
  • Indicates the corresponding Learning Objective for each exercise and problem.
  • Answer Key to Chapter Quiz
■ Ten-Minute Quiz
  • To quickly assess students' understanding of the chapter material.
■ Extra Critical Thinking Problems and Solutions
  • Critical Thinking Problems previously found in the text were moved to the IRM so instructors can continue to use their favorite problems.
■ Guide to Classroom Engagement Questions
  • Author-created element will offer tips and tricks to instructors in order to help them use the Learning Catalytic questions in class.

Online Instructor's Solutions Manual:

■ Contains solutions to all end-of-chapter questions, short exercises, exercises, and problems.
■ The Try It! Solutions, previously found at the end of each chapter, are now available for download with the ISM.
■ Using Excel templates, solutions, and teaching tips.
■ All solutions were thoroughly reviewed by the author team and other professors.

Online Test Bank:
- Includes more than 3,900 questions, including NEW multi-level questions.
- Both conceptual and computational problems are available in true/false, multiple choice, and open-ended formats.
- Algorithmic test bank is available in MyAccountingLab.

PowerPoint Presentations:

Instructor PowerPoint Presentations:
- Complete with lecture notes.
- Mirrors the organization of the text and includes key exhibits.

Student PowerPoint Presentations:
- Abridged versions of the Instructor PowerPoint Presentations.
- Can be used as a study tool or note-taking tool for students.

Demonstration Problem PowerPoint Presentations:
- Offers instructors the opportunity to review in class the exercises and problems from the chapter using different companies and numbers.

Clicker Response System (CRS) PowerPoint Presentations:
- 10 multiple-choice questions to use with a Clicker Response System.

Image Library:
- All image files from the text to assist instructors in modifying our supplied PowerPoint presentations or in creating their own PowerPoint presentations.

Working Papers and Solutions:
- Available in Excel format.
- Templates for students to use to complete exercises and problems in the text.

Data and Solutions Files:
- Select end-of-chapter problems have been set up in different software applications, including QuickBooks and General Ledger.
- Corresponding solution files are provided for QuickBooks.

For Students

MyAccountingLab

Online Homework and Assessment Manager: http://www.myaccountinglab.com

- Pearson eText
- Using Excel templates
- Animated Lectures
- Demo Docs
- Interactive Figures

- Working Papers
- Accounting Videos
- Student PowerPoint® Presentations
- Accounting Cycle Tutorial
- Flash Cards

Student Resource Web site: http://www.pearsonhighered.com/Horngren
The book's Web site contains the following:
- Data Files: Select end-of-chapter problems have been set up in QuickBooks software and the related files are available for download.
- Working Papers
- Try It! Solutions: The solutions to all in-chapter Try Its! are available for download.
- Links to Target Corporation's Annual Report and Kohl's Corporation's Annual Report

http://www.pearsonhighered.com/Horngren

Acknowledgments

Acknowledgments for This Edition:

Tracie Miller-Nobles would like to thank her husband, Kevin, her parents, Kipp and Sylvia, and her sister Michelle for their love and support. She would also like to express her gratitude to her many colleagues and friends. In addition, she would like to dedicate this book to her students who have shaped her teaching and love of this profession.

Brenda Mattison appreciates the loving support of her family, especially from her husband, Grant, and sons, Christopher and Dillon. Her family's faith in her, along with her faith in God, provided her the inspiration to follow her dreams. This book is dedicated to her students, who work hard to achieve their dreams, are a constant reminder of what's really important in our lives, and inspire her to continuously seek ways to improve her craft of teaching.

Ella Mae Matsumura thanks her family for their longstanding love and support in her endeavors: husband, Kam-Wah Tsui; son, David Tsui; sister and late parents, Linda, Lester, and Eda Matsumura. She would also like to express her appreciation to: the numerous colleagues and friends who have encouraged her and helped her grow as a scholar and a person; the many students who have provided constructive feedback that has shaped her teaching; and her faith community for its enduring love and affirmation.

The authors would like to sincerely thank Lacey Vitetta, Roberta Sherman, Mary Kate Murray, Tricia Murphy, Natalie Wagner, Adrienne D'Ambrosio, and Donna Battista for their unwavering support of this edition. They express their extreme pleasure in working with each of them and are appreciative of their guidance, patience, and belief in the success of this project.

Advisory Panels, Focus Group Participants, and Reviewers:

Samad Adams, *Bristol Community College*

Sharon Agee, *Rollins College*

Markus Ahrens, *St. Louis Community College*

Janice Akao, *Butler County Community College*

Anna Alexander, *Caldwell Community College and Technical Institute*

Sheila Ammons, *Austin Community College*

Sidney Askew, *Borough of Manhattan Community College*

John Babich, *Kankakee Community College*

Michael Barendse, *Grossmont College*

Robert Beatty, *Anne Arundel Community College*

Lana Becker, *East Tennessee State University*

Vikki Bentz, *Yavapai College*

Jeff Brennan, *Austin Community College*

Lisa Busto, *William Rainey Harper College*

Jennifer Cainas, *University of South Florida*

Anne Cardozo, *Broward College*

Elizabeth Carlson, *University of South Florida Sarasota-Manatee*

Martha Cavalaris, *Miami Dade College*

Donna Chadwick, *Sinclair Community College*

Colleen Chung, *Miami Dade College*

Tom Clement, *University of North Dakota*

Geoffrey Danzig, *Miami Dade College–North*

Judy Daulton, *Piedmont Technical College*

Michelle Davidowitz, *Kingsborough Community College*

Annette Fisher Davis, *Glendale Community College*

Anthony Dellarte, *Luzerne County Community College*

Crystal Drum, *Guilford Technical Community College*

Mary Ewanechko, *Monroe Community College*

Elisa Fernandez, *Miami Dade College*

Julie Gilbert, *Triton College*

Lori Grady, *Bucks County Community College*

Marina Grau, *Houston Community College*

Gloria Grayless, *Sam Houston State University*

Becky Hancock, *El Paso Community College*

Dawn D. Hart, *Darton State College*

Lori Hatchell, *Aims Community College*

Shauna Hatfield, *Salt Lake Community College*

Patricia Holmes, *Des Moines Area Community College*

Cynthia Johnson, *University of Arkansas, Little Rock*

Gina Jones, *Aims Community College*

Jeffrey Jones, *The College of Southern Nevada*

Thomas K. Y. Kam, *Hawaii Pacific University*

Naomi Karolinski, *Monroe Community College*

Anne Kenner, *Brevard Community College*

Stephanie (Sam) King, *Edison State College*

Emil Koren, *Saint Leo University*

Paul Koulakov, *Nashville State Community College*

Christy Land, *Catawba Valley Community College*

Suzanne Lay, *Colorado Mesa University*

Wayne Lewis, *Hudson Valley Community College*

Mabel Machin, *Valencia College*

Mostafa Maksy, *Kutztown University*

Richard Mandau, *Piedmont Technical College*

Christina Manzo, *Queensborough Community College*

Maria C. Mari, *Miami Dade College*

Cynthia J. Miller, *University of Kentucky*

Joanne Orabone, *Community College of Rhode Island*

Kimberly Perkins, *Austin Community College*

William Quilliam, *Florida Southern College*

Marcela Raphael, *Chippewa Valley Technical College*

Ryan Rees, *Salt Lake Community College*

Katheryn Reynolds, *Front Range Community College Larimer*

Alice Rivera, *Golden West College*

Cecile Robert, *Community College of Rhode Island*

Shani Nicole Robinson, *Sam Houston State University*
Carol Rowey, *Community College of Rhode Island*
Amanda J. Salinas, *Palo Alto College*
Sayan Sarkar, *University of Texas, El Paso*
Maurice Savard, *East Stroudsburg University*
Dennis Shea, *Southern New Hampshire University*
Jaye Simpson, *Tarrant County*
John Stancil, *Florida Southern*
Diana Sullivan, *Portland Community College*
Annette Taggart, *Texas A&M University–Commerce*
Linda Tarrago, *Hillsborough Community College*
Teresa Thompson, *Chaffey College*

Judy Toland, *Bucks County Community College*
Robin D. Turner, *Rowan-Cabarrus Community College*
William Van Glabek, *Edison State College*
Stanley Walker, *Georgia Northwestern Tech*
Christine Wayne, *William Rainey Harper College*
Deb Weber, *Hawkeye Community College*
Denise A. White, *Austin Community College*
Donald R. Wilke, *Northwest Florida State College*
Wanda Wong, *Chabot College*
Angela Woodland, *Montana State University*
Judy Zander, *Grossmont College*

Accuracy Checkers:
Carolyn Streuly
James L. Baker, *Harford Community College*
Nancy Emerson, *North Dakota State University*

Gail Hoover-King, *Purdue University Calumet*
Richard Mandau, *Piedmont Technical College*
Carol Hughes, *Asheville-Buncombe Technical Community College*

Supplements Authors and Reviewers:
Dave Alldredge, *Salt Lake Community College*
Sheila Ammons, *Austin Community College*
Sidney Askew, *Borough of Manhattan Community College, CUNY*
James L. Baker, *Salt Lake Community College*
Connie Belden, *Butler Community College*
Alisa Brink, *Virginia Commonwealth University*
Helen Brubeck, *Saint Mary-of-the-Woods College*

Kate Demarest, *Carroll Community College*
Lori Hatchell, *Alms Community College*
Carol Hughes, *Asheville-Buncombe Technical Community College*
Brett Killion, *Lakeland College*
Diane O'Neill, *Seattle University*
Teresa Stephenson, *The University of South Dakota*

The authors would like to express their gratitude for the diligent and exemplary work of all of our contributors, reviewers, accuracy checkers, and supplement authors. Each of you played a part in making this book successful! Thank you!

Introduction to Managerial Accounting 16

Which One Will They Buy?

Gerald is enjoying working at Starwood Campers, a recreational vehicle (RV) manufacturer, as a sales representative. He has met a lot of people who are looking at the various motor homes and camping trailers on display. He met one young couple who wants to purchase an RV to use during the summers as they explore the country while on break from their teaching jobs. He met a family looking for a way to spend quality time together on the weekends. He has also met a couple ready to retire, sell their home, and hit the road for a few years. The RV showroom has lots of models on display to meet all of these needs. There are many choices with different designs that make the small living spaces efficient and comfortable.

Gerald realizes that these potential customers are not just interested in comfort, however. They also want quality-built RVs that can be used for many years and travel many miles. As Gerald talks to the customers, he also shares information about the construction materials and manufacturing processes his company uses. He even invites interested parties to schedule a factory tour to get a better understanding of the manufacturing process.

Why Managerial Accounting?

Have you ever wondered how companies like **Winnebago Industries, Inc.** make their products? Winnebago is a leading manufacturer of recreational vehicles (RVs), including motorized and towable products. The company designs, develops, manufactures, and markets RVs, as well as supporting products and services. The RVs are sold to consumers through a dealer network. RV manufacturers begin with raw materials, such as steel, aluminum, and fiberglass, but motor homes include much more than the basic structure. If you purchase a Winnebago motor home, it may have a Ford engine, an Amana refrigerator, a Select Comfort Sleep Number bed, and a Sony entertainment center. There are so many components that go into the finished product that managers at Winnebago have to keep detailed records of inventory used and other costs incurred to build the RVs. In 2015, Winnebago reported net revenues of $977 million and cost of goods sold was $871 million. Cost of goods sold represented 89% of net revenues. How was the cost of goods sold calculated? Cost of goods sold includes not only the materials used in the manufacturing process, but also the costs of the labor of the men and women who built the RVs and the costs of operating the factory, such as utilities, insurance, and depreciation. Determining cost of goods sold for a manufacturer can be complicated. These companies use *managerial accounting* to help track costs and make decisions about production. Let's begin our study of managerial accounting to see how successful companies use accounting information to make good internal business decisions.

Chapter 16 Learning Objectives

1 Define managerial accounting and understand how it is used

2 Classify costs used in managerial accounting

3 Prepare financial statements for a manufacturer, including a balance sheet, income statement, and schedule of cost of goods manufactured

4 Describe business trends affecting managerial accounting

5 Describe how managerial accounting is used in service and merchandising companies

WHY IS MANAGERIAL ACCOUNTING IMPORTANT?

Learning Objective 1

Define managerial accounting and understand how it is used

Managerial Accounting

The field of accounting that focuses on providing information for internal decision makers.

Financial Accounting

The field of accounting that focuses on providing information for external decision makers.

Managerial accounting focuses on providing information for internal decision makers. This type of accounting concentrates on both financial and nonfinancial information for managers and other business users, such as supervisors, foremen, and directors. **Financial accounting** focuses on providing information for external decision makers. While managers use financial accounting to report monetary transactions and prepare financial statements, managerial accounting helps managers make decisions needed to be successful. Individuals in management roles, such as department heads, division managers, chief executive officers, and vice presidents, rely on managerial accounting to help them plan, direct, control, and make decisions about the business. Exhibit 16-1 illustrates the major differences between managerial and financial accounting.

Exhibit 16-1 | Financial Accounting Versus Managerial Accounting

	Financial Accounting	Managerial Accounting
Primary users	External—investors, creditors, and government authorities	Internal—the company's managers and employees
Purpose of information	Help investors and creditors make investment and credit decisions	Help managers and employees plan, direct, and control operations
Focus and time dimension of the information	Relevant and faithfully representative information and focus on the past Example: 2017 actual performance reported in 2018	Relevant information and focus on the future Example: 2018 budget prepared in 2017
Rules and restrictions	Required to follow Generally Accepted Accounting Principles (GAAP); public companies required to be audited by an independent CPA	Not required to follow GAAP
Scope of information	Summary reports prepared primarily on the company as a whole, usually on a quarterly or annual basis	Detailed reports prepared on parts of the company (products, departments, territories), often on a daily or weekly basis
Behavioral	Concern about adequacy of disclosures; behavioral implications are secondary	Concern about how reports will affect employee behavior

Managers' Role in the Organization

Managers occur in all different parts of a company's structure. Most companies structure their organization along departments or divisions. A company's **organizational chart** helps show the relationship between departments and divisions and the managers that are responsible for each section.

Exhibit 16-2 provides a partial organizational chart for Smart Touch Learning, a fictional company that we use to illustrate the concepts in each chapter. Smart Touch Learning began operations as a service company that specialized in providing online courses in accounting, economics, marketing, and management. The company later evolved into a merchandising company selling tablet computers that are preloaded with its e-learning software programs. The demand for Smart Touch Learning's tablets has grown because customers like the online courses offered as part of their tablet computer purchase. Smart Touch Learning has done well, but the competition is requiring Smart Touch Learning to once again look at its strategy. Smart Touch Learning has decided that in order to maintain its market share and to stay competitive, the company will begin manufacturing its own tablet rather than purchasing them. Smart Touch Learning believes that the company can manufacture a tablet at a cost lower than the current purchase cost and still offer customers the value they have come to expect. Later in this chapter, we will determine if this strategy did indeed pay off.

Organizational Chart
Shows the relationship between departments and divisions and managers responsible for each section.

Exhibit 16-2 | Organizational Chart for Smart Touch Learning (Partial)

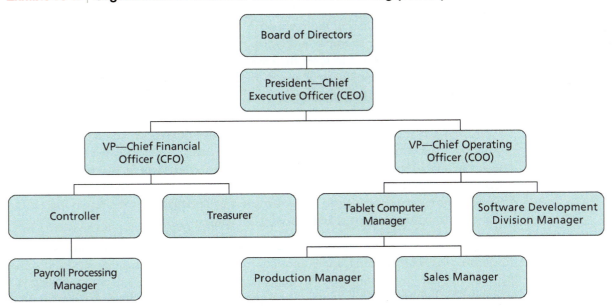

The decision to change Smart Touch Learning's business model is made by the board of directors. Notice that the board of directors is listed at the top of Smart Touch Learning's organizational chart. The **board of directors** is elected by the stockholders, the owners of Smart Touch Learning, and is responsible for developing the strategic goals of the corporation. The board also selects the president—chief executive officer.

The President—**chief executive officer (CEO)** of Smart Touch Learning is ultimately responsible for developing a plan to meet the company's short and long-term strategy as well as overseeing the implementation of the plans. The CEO is the liaison between the board of directors and the management of the company, and delegates the responsibility of implementing the plans to the vice presidents of the organization. The vice presidents of Smart Touch Learning are each responsible for a different area, such as finance and

Board of Directors
Elected by the stockholders and responsible for developing the strategic goals of a corporation.

Chief Executive Officer (CEO)
Officer of a company that has ultimate responsibility for implementing the company's short and long-term plans.

Line Position
Job that is directly involved in providing goods or services to customers.

Staff Position
Job that provides support for line positions.

operations. Each position in a company can be classified as either a line or staff position. **Line positions** are directly involved in providing goods or services to customers. Examples of line positions for Smart Touch Learning are vice president—chief operating officer (COO), tablet computer manager, software development division manager, production manager, and sales manager. **Staff positions** support the line positions. Vice president—chief financial officer (CFO), controller, treasurer, and payroll processing manager are examples of staff positions.

Managerial Accounting Functions

Business managers need information that will help them plan, direct, and control operations as they lead the business. This includes managing the company's plant, equipment, and human resources.

Planning
Choosing goals and deciding how to achieve them.

Strategic Planning
Involves developing long-term strategies to achieve a company's goals.

Operational Planning
Focuses on short-term actions dealing with a company's day-to-day operations.

Directing
Running the day-to-day operations of a business.

- **Planning** means choosing goals and deciding how to achieve them. Planning requires managers to look to the future and establish goals for the business. A business's goals could be varied. For example, a common goal of all businesses is to increase operating income. Another goal might be to develop a new product or begin operations in a new territory. Planning can be classified as strategic or operational. **Strategic planning** involves developing long-term strategies to achieve a company's goals. Strategic plans often span 3 to 10 years. **Operational planning**, on the other hand, focuses on short-term actions dealing with a company's day-to-day operations. Operational plans are most often one year in length, but may also span only a week, a month, or a quarter.

- **Directing** involves running the day-to-day operations of a business. Managers are responsible for coordinating the company's activities including purchasing, manufacturing, and selling. For example, a division manager must ensure that a company has enough materials on hand to meet the customers' demand. Managers are also responsible for motivating employees. A marketing manager's responsibilities might include coordinating the marketing plan and training sales representatives on the sale of a new product.

Controlling
Monitoring operations and keeping the company on track.

- **Controlling** is the process of monitoring day-to-day operations and keeping the company on track. Controlling involves comparing actual results to expected results. For example, managers can compare actual costs to expected costs to evaluate their performance. If actual costs fall below budgeted costs, that is usually good news. However, if actual costs exceed the expected costs, managers will evaluate why the results were different and if modifications or changes need to be made.

Businesses rely on managers to make decisions. Decision-making is a part of all three functions (planning, directing, and controlling) and good decision-making results in a prosperous company. Accounting plays an important role in a manager's decision-making. The Pathways Vision Model (see Exhibit 16-3) provides a visual way to understand the role of managerial accounting in making good decisions. Managers review information about economic activities and then use critical thinking and accounting judgment to create useful information. This useful information helps managers make good decisions that in turn have an impact on society and future economic activity, thus creating a circular flow of cause and effect.

Exhibit 16-3 | **Pathways Vision Model**

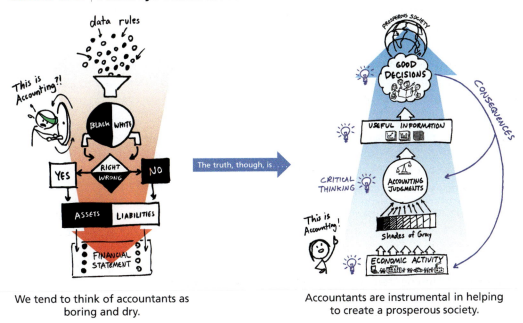

We tend to think of accountants as boring and dry.

Accountants are instrumental in helping to create a prosperous society.

This work is by The Pathways Commission. The Pathways Vision Model: AI artwork: AAA Commons. American Accounting Association.

Ethical Standards of Managers

Managers often face ethical challenges. The Institute of Management Accountants (IMA) has developed standards that managerial accountants are expected to uphold when faced with ethical challenges. The IMA standards remind us that society expects professional accountants to exhibit the highest level of ethical behavior. An excerpt from the IMA's Statement of Ethical Professional Practice appears in Exhibit 16-4 (on the next page). These standards require managerial accountants to do the following:

- Maintain their professional competence.
- Preserve the confidentiality of the information they handle.
- Act with integrity and credibility.

To resolve ethical dilemmas, the IMA suggests following organizationally established policies. If the policies do not result in a resolution, the IMA recommends discussing the ethical situation with: (1) an immediate supervisor; (2) an objective adviser; and, if necessary, (3) an attorney.

Exhibit 16-4 | **IMA Statement of Ethical Professional Practice (Excerpt)**

Management accountants have a commitment to ethical professional practice which includes principles of Honesty, Fairness, Objectivity, and Responsibility. The standards of ethical practice include the following:

I. COMPETENCE

1. Maintain an appropriate level of professional expertise by continually developing knowledge and skills.
2. Perform professional duties in accordance with relevant laws, regulations, and technical standards.
3. Provide decision support information and recommendations that are accurate, clear, concise, and timely.
4. Recognize and communicate professional limitations or other constraints that would preclude responsible judgment or successful performance of an activity.

II. CONFIDENTIALITY

1. Keep information confidential except when disclosure is authorized or legally required.
2. Inform all relevant parties regarding appropriate use of confidential information. Monitor subordinates' activities to ensure compliance.
3. Refrain from using confidential information for unethical or illegal advantage.

III. INTEGRITY

1. Mitigate actual conflicts of interest, regularly communicate with business associates to avoid apparent conflicts of interest. Advise all parties of any potential conflicts.
2. Refrain from engaging in any conduct that would prejudice carrying out duties ethically.
3. Abstain from engaging in or supporting any activity that might discredit the profession.

IV. CREDIBILITY

1. Communicate information fairly and objectively.
2. Disclose all relevant information that could reasonably be expected to influence an intended user's understanding of the reports, analyses, or recommendations.
3. Disclose delays or deficiencies in information, timeliness, processing, or internal controls in conformance with organization policy and/or applicable law.

Source: "IMA Statement of Ethical Professional Practice 2012" IMA, Montvale, New Jersey. www.imanet.org

ETHICS

Where do you draw the line?

As the staff accountant of Casey Computer Co., Sam Butler is aware of the company's weak financial condition. The company is close to signing a lucrative contract that should ensure its future. The controller, who is Sam's supervisor, states that the company *must* report a profit this year. He suggests: "Two customers have placed orders that are scheduled to be shipped on January 3, when production of those orders is completed. Let's record the goods as finished and bill the customer on December 31 so we can show the profit from those orders in the current year."

    What should Sam do? What would you do?

Solution

Sam could consider working with the production manager to get the orders completed and shipped in December. The orders could then be recorded in December, and the profits would be reflected in the current year's financial statements. However, if that is not possible, Sam should convince the controller that the income manipulation is not ethical and violates the revenue recognition principle—and that the company should not record these transactions in December. If Sam is unable to convince the controller, he has an obligation to report the situation to the controller's supervisor.

Try It!

HOW ARE COSTS CLASSIFIED?

How costs are classified depends on the type of business the company engages in. Businesses are generally classified as service, merchandising, or manufacturing companies. **Service companies** sell their time, skills, and knowledge. Examples of service companies include accounting firms such as Ernst & Young and law offices such as Baker & McKenzie. **Merchandising companies** resell products they buy from suppliers. Merchandisers keep an inventory of products, and managers are accountable for the purchasing, storage, and sale of the products. Companies such as Home Depot and Lowes are examples of merchandising companies.

Manufacturing Companies

Unlike service and merchandising companies, **manufacturing companies** use labor, equipment, supplies, and facilities to convert raw materials into finished products. Managers in manufacturing companies must use these resources to create a product that customers want at a price customers are willing to pay. Honda Motor Co., Ltd., The Coca Cola Company, and The Boeing Company are all examples of manufacturing companies.

In contrast with service and merchandising companies, manufacturing companies track costs using three kinds of inventory:

1. **Raw Materials Inventory (RM)** includes materials used to make a product. For example, Smart Touch Learning's raw materials include the processor, screen, tablet case, and glue.
2. **Work-in-Process Inventory (WIP)** includes goods that are in the manufacturing process but are not yet complete. Some production activities have taken place that transformed the materials, but the product is not yet finished and ready for sale. Smart Touch Learning's Work-in-Process Inventory could include tablets that only include the electronic components but not the screen.
3. **Finished Goods Inventory (FG)** includes completed goods that have not yet been sold. Finished goods are the products that the manufacturer sells, such as Smart Touch Learning's finished tablet.

Learning Objective 2

Classify costs used in managerial accounting

Service Company

A company that sells services—time, skills, and knowledge—instead of products.

Merchandising Company

A company that resells products previously bought from suppliers.

Manufacturing Company

A company that uses labor, equipment, supplies, and facilities to convert raw materials into finished products.

Raw Materials Inventory (RM)

Materials converted through the manufacturing process into a finished product.

Work-in-Process Inventory (WIP)

Goods that have been started in the manufacturing process but are not yet complete.

Finished Goods Inventory (FG)

Completed goods that have not yet been sold.

Direct and Indirect Costs

Direct Cost
Cost that can be easily and cost-effectively traced to a cost object.

Cost Object
Anything for which managers want a separate measurement of cost.

Manufacturing companies classify costs in many different ways. For example, costs can be classified as direct or indirect. A **direct cost** is a cost that can be easily and cost-effectively traced to a cost object. A **cost object** is anything for which managers want a separate measurement of cost and may be a product, department, sales territory, or activity. For example, the cost object for Smart Touch Learning would be the tablet and the direct costs of the tablet would be the cost of materials used, such as the processor, screen, and case.

Don't confuse prices with costs. <u>Price</u> *(or sales price) is the amount the company charges the customer for the goods or services provided.* <u>Cost</u> *is the amount the company incurs to acquire the goods or services. If a company purchases an item for $4 and sells it for $10, the cost is $4 and the price is $10.*

Indirect Cost
Cost that cannot be easily or cost-effectively traced to a cost object.

Costs that cannot be easily or cost-effectively traced directly to a cost object are **indirect costs**. For Smart Touch Learning, indirect costs might include the salary of the production supervisor. Although the production supervisor is involved in the factory, he or she is not directly responsible for producing the product.

Manufacturing Costs

In a manufacturing company, such as Smart Touch Learning, costs can be classified into three categories.

Direct Materials (DM)
The cost of raw materials that are converted into the finished product and are easily traced to the product.

Direct Labor (DL)
The cost of wages and salaries of employees who convert raw materials into finished products.

Manufacturing Overhead (MOH)
Manufacturing costs that cannot be easily and cost-effectively traced to a cost object. Includes all manufacturing costs except direct materials and direct labor.

1. **Direct materials (DM)** are the cost of raw materials that are converted into the finished product and are easily traced to the product. The cost of such materials are considered direct materials. Smart Touch Learning's direct materials would include the processor, the screen, and the tablet case.
2. **Direct labor (DL)** is the cost of wages and salaries of employees who convert the raw materials into the finished product. Direct labor is also a direct cost that can be easily traced to the finished product. Direct labor for Smart Touch Learning would include the wages of the employees who assemble the tablets.
3. **Manufacturing overhead (MOH)** refers to indirect manufacturing costs that cannot be easily traced to specific products. It includes all manufacturing costs other than direct materials and direct labor. These costs are created by all of the supporting production activities, including storing materials, setting up machines, and cleaning the work areas. Examples include costs of indirect materials, manufacturing factory managers' salaries and other indirect labor, repair and maintenance costs, and depreciation on manufacturing buildings and equipment. Other examples include the following costs for the factory: utilities, rent, insurance, and property taxes. Manufacturing overhead is also called *factory overhead* or *indirect manufacturing costs*.

Let's look at two of the components of manufacturing overhead more closely. It is important to be able to distinguish between direct and indirect materials and direct and indirect labor.

- **Indirect materials** are the cost of raw materials that are difficult or not cost-effective to trace directly to the product. For Smart Touch Learning, it may be the cost of glue used in assembling the tablets. The cost of tracing the drops of glue used on each tablet and then determining the cost of those drops exceeds the benefit of having this information.
- **Indirect labor** includes the cost of wages and salaries in the factory for persons not directly producing the product. Examples include production supervisors, factory janitors, workers who repair factory equipment, and factory groundskeepers.

Exhibit 16-5 illustrates the three different manufacturing costs and the difference between direct and indirect costs.

Exhibit 16-5 | Manufacturing Costs

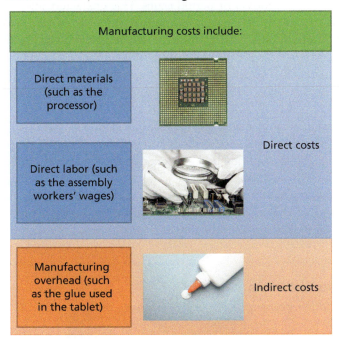

Indirect Materials
The cost of raw materials that cannot be conveniently traced directly to specific finished products or are not large enough to justify tracing to the specific product.

Indirect Labor
The cost of wages and salaries in the factory for persons not directly producing the product and cannot be conveniently traced directly to specific finished products or are not large enough to justify tracing to the specific product.

Prime and Conversion Costs

The purpose of managerial accounting is to provide useful information to managers. To make cost information more useful, manufacturing costs are sometimes combined in different ways, depending on the managers' needs.

Prime costs combine the direct costs of direct materials and direct labor. In a manufacturing process that is labor-intensive, the direct costs are the *primary* costs. *Labor-intensive* means people do most of the work, not machines. In that type of environment, managers may want to concentrate on these direct, or prime, costs. To be profitable, it is vital for the company to control these costs.

Conversion costs combine direct labor with manufacturing overhead. These are the costs to *convert* the direct materials into the finished product. In a manufacturing process that is machine-intensive, the cost of direct labor is minimal because machines do most of the work. Employees primarily set up and oversee the machine production. Overhead costs, however, can be substantial, including the cost of utilities and depreciation on the machinery. In that type of environment, managers may want to focus on the total conversion cost rather than tracking direct labor and manufacturing overhead separately.

Exhibit 16-6 (on the next page) illustrates the relationship between prime costs and conversion costs. Notice that direct labor is considered both a prime cost and a conversion cost.

Prime Costs
The direct costs of the manufacturing process: Direct materials plus direct labor.

Conversion Costs
The cost to convert direct materials into finished goods: Direct labor plus manufacturing overhead.

Exhibit 16-6 | Prime and Conversion Costs

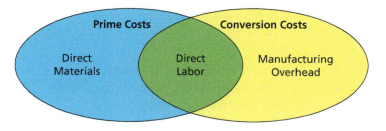

<table>
<tr><td>Prime Costs</td><td></td><td>Conversion Costs</td></tr>
<tr><td>Direct Materials</td><td>Direct Labor</td><td>Manufacturing Overhead</td></tr>
</table>

Product and Period Costs

Product Cost

The cost of purchasing or making a product. The cost is recorded as an asset (inventory) and then expensed (Cost of Goods Sold) when the product is sold.

Another way costs can be classified is as product or period costs. This characterization is required when preparing financial statements. **Product costs** include the costs of purchasing or making a product. Direct materials, direct labor, and manufacturing overhead are all examples of product costs. Product costs are recorded as assets in inventory accounts on the balance sheet when they are incurred. The cost does not become an expense until the company has sold the inventory. At that time, the cost is reported as Cost of Goods Sold on the income statement.

Period Cost

Operating cost that is expensed in the accounting period in which it is incurred.

Period costs, on the other hand, are non-manufacturing costs. Period costs are selling and administrative expenses and other expenses such as taxes and interest. These costs are matched with the revenue of a specific time period and expensed in the same accounting period. Examples of period costs might include the salaries and wages of the accounting staff, rent for the administrative building, sales commissions paid to sales representatives, or utilities paid for the marketing office. Exhibit 16-7 illustrates the difference between product and period costs and Exhibit 16-8 provides some examples of Smart Touch Learning's period and product costs.

Exhibit 16-7 | Period Versus Product Costs

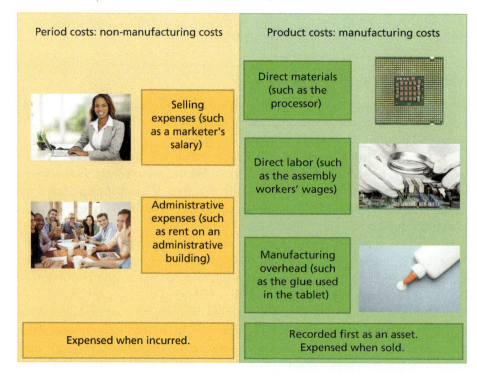

Period costs: non-manufacturing costs	Product costs: manufacturing costs
Selling expenses (such as a marketer's salary)	Direct materials (such as the processor)
Administrative expenses (such as rent on an administrative building)	Direct labor (such as the assembly workers' wages)
	Manufacturing overhead (such as the glue used in the tablet)
Expensed when incurred.	Recorded first as an asset. Expensed when sold.

Exhibit 16-8 | **Period and Product Costs for Smart Touch Learning**

Cost Incurred	Period Costs	Product Costs		
	Selling and Administrative	Direct Materials	Direct Labor	Manufacturing Overhead
Depreciation on manufacturing equipment				X
Depreciation on office equipment	X			
Advertising	X			
Property taxes and insurance on office	X			
Property taxes and insurance on factory				X
Production supervisor's salary				X
CEO's salary	X			
Wages for assembly line workers			X	
Batteries, processors, and other materials used in making tablets		X		
Manufacturing supplies				X
Freight costs on purchase of materials		X		
Delivery expense	X			

> *Overhead costs can be confusing. For example, for a service or merchandising company, the cost of rent is a period cost and is classified as a selling and administrative expense. For a manufacturing company, you must consider the reason for the cost. If the rent is for the corporate office, it is still a period cost. However, if the rent is for the factory, then it is a product cost because it is a cost incurred in the manufacturing process. Because the rent is neither direct materials nor direct labor, it is classified as manufacturing overhead.*

Try It!

Identify each cost as a period cost or a product cost. If it is a product cost, further indicate if the cost is direct materials, direct labor, or manufacturing overhead. Then determine if the product cost is a prime cost and/or a conversion cost.

6. Wages of assembly line workers for a factory

7. Wages of the office receptionist in an administrative office

8. Property taxes on the factory

9. Sugar and flour used to make cookies

10. Salary of the factory maintenance supervisor

11. Salary of the sales manager

Check your answers online in MyAccountingLab or at http://www.pearsonhighered.com/Horngren.

For more practice, see Short Exercises S16-3 through S16-5. MyAccountingLab

HOW DO MANUFACTURING COMPANIES PREPARE FINANCIAL STATEMENTS?

Learning Objective 3

Prepare financial statements for a manufacturer, including a balance sheet, income statement, and schedule of cost of goods manufactured

In financial accounting, you learned about the financial statements for service and merchandising companies. In this chapter, we will focus on how the financial statements are different for manufacturing companies.

Balance Sheet

Let's first begin by concentrating on the balance sheet. Service companies sell their time, skills, and knowledge and therefore carry no inventories on their balance sheet. Merchandising companies resell products they buy from suppliers and record the cost of inventory purchased as an asset, Merchandise Inventory, on their balance sheet. As you learned earlier, manufacturing companies keep track of costs using three inventory accounts, Raw Materials Inventory, Work-in-Process Inventory, and Finished Goods Inventory. On a manufacturing company's balance sheet the three inventory accounts will be listed in the asset section.

Exhibit 16-9 shows a comparison of balance sheets for service, merchandising, and manufacturing companies. Notice the accounts highlighted in blue, which illustrate the different kinds of inventory accounts used by various types of companies.

Exhibit 16-9 | **Balance Sheet Comparison**

Service Company Balance Sheet (Partial) December 31, 2019		Merchandising Company Balance Sheet (Partial) December 31, 2019		Manufacturing Company Balance Sheet (Partial) December 31, 2019	
Assets		**Assets**		**Assets**	
Cash	$ 10,500	Cash	$ 10,500	Cash	$ 10,500
Accounts Receivable	8,750	Accounts Receivable	8,750	Accounts Receivable	8,750
Equipment	60,000	Merchandise Inventory	2,200	Raw Materials Inventory	1,500
		Equipment	60,000	Work-in-Process Inventory	800
				Finished Goods Inventory	2,200
				Equipment	60,000
Total Assets	$ 79,250	Total Assets	$ 81,450	Total Assets	$ 83,750

Income Statement

On the income statement, because service companies do not have any product costs, they only record period costs such as salaries expense and rent expense. In contrast with service companies, merchandisers' income statements usually report Cost of Goods Sold as the major expense. Cost of Goods Sold represents the business's cost of the merchandise inventory sold. In a manufacturing company, as in a merchandising company, Cost of Goods Sold is usually the largest expense. However, because a manufacturer makes the product it sells the calculation of cost of goods sold is different. Exhibit 16-10 illustrates the difference between a merchandising company's calculation of cost of goods sold and a manufacturer's calculation of cost of goods sold. Notice that the differences are highlighted in blue.

Exhibit 16-10 | **Income Statement Comparison**

Service Company Income Statement Month Ended December 31, 2019			Merchandising Company Income Statement Month Ended December 31, 2019			Manufacturing Company Income Statement Month Ended December 31, 2019		
Revenues:			**Revenues:**			**Revenues:**		
Service Revenue		$ 7,600	Sales Revenue		$ 7,600	Sales Revenue		$ 7,600
Expenses:			Cost of Goods Sold:			Cost of Goods Sold:		
Salaries Expense	$ 3,800		Beginning Merchandise Inventory	$ 2,000		Beginning Finished Goods Inventory	$ 2,000	
Rent Expense	1,000		Purchases and Freight In	3,800		Cost of Goods Manufactured	3,800	
Utilities Expense	400		Cost of Goods Available for Sale	5,800		Cost of Goods Available for Sale	5,800	
Total Expenses		5,200	Ending Merchandise Inventory	(2,200)		Ending Finished Goods Inventory	(2,200)	
Operating Income		$ 2,400	Cost of Goods Sold		3,600	Cost of Goods Sold		3,600
			Gross Profit		4,000	Gross Profit		4,000
			Selling and Administrative Expenses		1,600	Selling and Administrative Expenses		1,600
			Operating Income		$ 2,400	Operating Income		$ 2,400

Product Costs Flow Through a Manufacturing Company

Understanding how to calculate cost of goods manufactured and ultimately cost of goods sold requires knowledge of how product costs flow through a manufacturing company. Exhibit 16-11 illustrates the flow of product costs.

Exhibit 16-11 | **Product Costs Flow through Manufacturing Company**

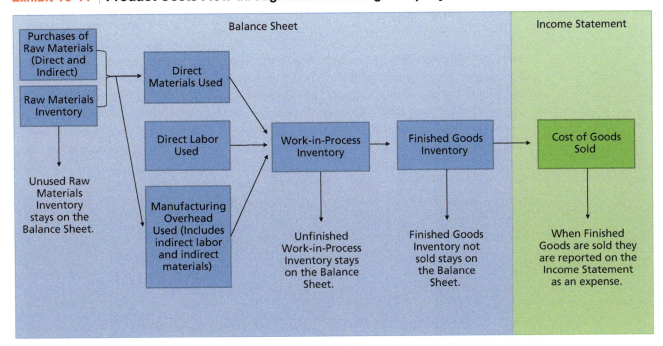

First, because manufacturing companies convert raw materials into a finished product, you will notice that the flow of costs starts with raw materials. Any raw materials purchased, along with any beginning raw materials inventory, gives the company raw materials available for use. The raw materials are either used in production or remain in the raw materials inventory and are reported on the balance sheet.

During production, the manufacturer uses direct labor and manufacturing overhead (including indirect labor and indirect materials) to convert direct materials into Work-in-Process Inventory. The cost of the beginning work-in-process units are added to the cost of direct materials, direct labor, and manufacturing overhead incurred during the period. This is the work-in-process inventory costs to account for. When the manufacturing process is complete, the costs are then transferred to Finished Goods Inventory. The cost of manufacturing the finished goods make up the **cost of goods manufactured**. If the work-in-process units are incomplete, the costs remain in Work-in-Process Inventory and are reported on the balance sheet. The cost of goods manufactured is used on the income statement to determine the cost of goods sold. Only when finished goods are sold will the costs be transferred from the balance sheet to the income statement as cost of goods sold.

Cost of Goods Manufactured

The manufacturing costs of the goods that finished the production process in a given accounting period.

Calculating Cost of Goods Manufactured

Let's use Smart Touch Learning to help illustrate the calculation of cost of goods manufactured using the following three steps:

Step 1: Calculate direct materials used. Assume Smart Touch Learning begins the period with a direct materials balance of $70,000. During the year, Smart Touch Learning purchased $350,000 of direct materials and the ending balance of direct materials was $65,000. Smart Touch Learning can calculate the cost of direct materials used as follows:

Beginning Direct Materials	$ 70,000
Purchases of Direct Materials (Including Freight In)	350,000
Direct Materials Available for Use	420,000
Ending Direct Materials	(65,000)
Direct Materials Used	$ 355,000

Step 2: Calculate total manufacturing costs incurred during the year. Smart Touch Learning will next determine the total manufacturing costs incurred during the year, which includes direct materials used (see Step 1), direct labor used ($169,000), and manufacturing overhead. Smart Touch Learning's manufacturing overhead includes indirect materials ($17,000), indirect labor ($28,000), depreciation on the plant and equipment ($20,000), and plant utilities, insurance, and property taxes ($18,000). The total manufacturing costs incurred is calculated as follows:

Direct Materials Used		$ 355,000
Direct Labor		169,000
Manufacturing Overhead:		
Indirect Materials	$ 17,000	
Indirect Labor	28,000	
Depreciation—Plant and Equipment	20,000	
Plant Utilities, Insurance, and Property Taxes	18,000	
Total Manufacturing Overhead		83,000
Total Manufacturing Costs Incurred during the Year		$ 607,000

Step 3: Calculate cost of goods manufactured. Smart Touch Learning will calculate cost of goods manufactured by adding the total manufacturing costs incurred during the year (see Step 2) to the beginning Work-in-Process Inventory ($80,000) to determine the total manufacturing costs to account for. The units that are represented by these costs will either be completed and transferred to Finished Goods Inventory or be partially completed and remain as ending Work-in-Process Inventory. Assume Smart Touch Learning has some tablets partially finished representing $27,000 of ending Work-in-Process Inventory. To determine the cost of goods manufactured, Smart Touch Learning will subtract the ending Work-in-Process Inventory from the total manufacturing costs to account for as follows:

Beginning Work-in-Process Inventory	$ 80,000
Total Manufacturing Costs Incurred during the Year	607,000
Total Manufacturing Costs to Account for	687,000
Ending Work-in-Process Inventory	(27,000)
Cost of Goods Manufactured	$ 660,000

Exhibit 16-12 shows a completed schedule of cost of goods manufactured for Smart Touch Learning, including all three steps. This schedule is prepared by companies to show detailed information about the costs of making its inventory and is part of the calculation of cost of goods sold.

Exhibit 16-12 | Schedule of Cost of Goods Manufactured

SMART TOUCH LEARNING Schedule of Cost of Goods Manufactured Year Ended December 31, 2020			
Beginning Work-in-Process Inventory			$ 80,000
Direct Materials Used:			
Beginning Direct Materials	$ 70,000		
Purchases of Direct Materials (including Freight In)	350,000		
Direct Materials Available for Use	420,000		
Ending Direct Materials	(65,000)		
Direct Materials Used		$ 355,000	
Direct Labor		169,000	
Manufacturing Overhead:			
Indirect Materials	17,000		
Indirect Labor	28,000		
Depreciation—Plant and Equipment	20,000		
Plant Utilities, Insurance, and Property Taxes	18,000		
Total Manufacturing Overhead		83,000	
Total Manufacturing Costs Incurred during the Year			607,000
Total Manufacturing Costs to Account For			687,000
Ending Work-in-Process Inventory			(27,000)
Cost of Goods Manufactured			$ 660,000

Calculating Cost of Goods Sold

Now that Smart Touch Learning has calculated cost of goods manufactured, the calculation of cost of goods sold is determined. Cost of goods sold represents the cost of the Finished Goods Inventory that has been sold. Assume Smart Touch Learning has beginning Finished Goods Inventory of $0 and its ending Finished Goods Inventory is $60,000. Smart Touch Learning will calculate cost of goods sold as follows:

Beginning Finished Goods Inventory	$ 0
Cost of Goods Manufactured	660,000
Cost of Goods Available for Sale	660,000
Ending Finished Goods Inventory	(60,000)
Cost of Goods Sold	$ 600,000

Exhibit 16-13 shows the completed income statement for Smart Touch Learning. Notice cost of goods sold is subtracted from net sales revenue to determine gross profit. Next, the period costs, selling and administrative expenses, are subtracted to determine operating income. Lastly, other income and expenses and income tax expense are subtracted to determine net income.

Exhibit 16-13 | **Income Statement—Manufacturing Company**

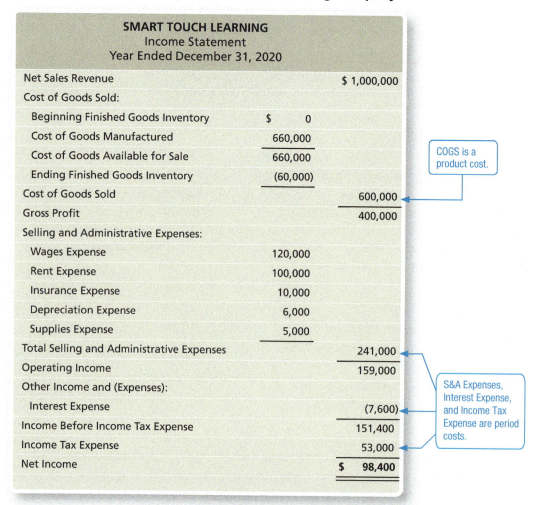

SMART TOUCH LEARNING Income Statement Year Ended December 31, 2020		
Net Sales Revenue		$ 1,000,000
Cost of Goods Sold:		
Beginning Finished Goods Inventory	$ 0	
Cost of Goods Manufactured	660,000	
Cost of Goods Available for Sale	660,000	
Ending Finished Goods Inventory	(60,000)	
Cost of Goods Sold		600,000
Gross Profit		400,000
Selling and Administrative Expenses:		
Wages Expense	120,000	
Rent Expense	100,000	
Insurance Expense	10,000	
Depreciation Expense	6,000	
Supplies Expense	5,000	
Total Selling and Administrative Expenses		241,000
Operating Income		159,000
Other Income and (Expenses):		
Interest Expense		(7,600)
Income Before Income Tax Expense		151,400
Income Tax Expense		53,000
Net Income		$ 98,400

COGS is a product cost.

S&A Expenses, Interest Expense, and Income Tax Expense are period costs.

Flow of Costs Through the Inventory Accounts

Exhibit 16-14 summarizes the flow of costs through Smart Touch Learning's inventory accounts. Notice that the format is the same for all three inventory accounts:

> Beginning balance + Additions − Ending balance = Amount used, manufactured, or sold

The final amount at each stage is added at the beginning of the next stage. Take time to see how the schedule of cost of goods manufactured in Exhibit 16-12 uses the cost flows of the Raw Materials and Work-in-Process stages, and the income statement in Exhibit 16-13 uses the cost flows of the Finished Goods stage. Understanding the flow of costs through a manufacturing company's accounts is very important and will be used in future chapters.

Exhibit 16-14 | **Flow of Costs Through Smart Touch Learning's Inventory Accounts**

Raw Materials Inventory*		Work-in-Process Inventory		Finished Goods Inventory	
Beginning Direct Materials	$ 70,000	Beginning WIP Inventory	$ 80,000	Beginning FG Inventory	$ 0
+ Purchases of Direct Materials (including Freight In)	350,000	+ Direct Materials Used	355,000	+ Cost of Goods Manufactured	660,000
= Direct Materials Available for Use	420,000	+ Direct Labor	169,000	= Cost of Goods Available for Sale	660,000
− Ending Direct Materials	(65,000)	+ Manufacturing Overhead	83,000	− Ending FG Inventory	(60,000)
		= Total Manufacturing Costs to Account For	687,000		
= Direct Materials Used	$ 355,000			= Cost of Goods Sold	$ 600,000
		− Ending WIP Inventory	(27,000)		
		= Cost of Goods Manufactured	$ 660,000		

*Direct materials portion only

Using the Schedule of Cost of Goods Manufactured to Calculate Unit Product Cost

Managers can use the schedule of cost of goods manufactured to calculate the unit product cost. Why would knowing the unit product cost be important to a manger? Knowing the unit product cost helps managers decide on the prices to charge for each product to ensure that each product is profitable. They can then measure operating income and determine the cost of Finished Goods Inventory. Smart Touch Learning produced 2,200 tablets during 2020. What did it cost to make each tablet?

Cost of goods manufactured	/	Total units produced	=	Unit product cost
$660,000	/	2,200 tablets	=	$300 per tablet

During 2020, Smart Touch Learning sold 2,000 tablets, and the company knows each tablet cost $300 to produce. With this information, Smart Touch Learning can compute its Cost of Goods Sold as follows:

Number of units sold	×	Unit product cost	=	Cost of Goods Sold
2,000 tablets	×	$300 per tablet	=	$600,000

Keep in mind that knowing the unit product cost is only part of the information that is needed to determine the sales price to charge for each product. In addition to product costs, manufacturers still have period costs such as selling and administrative expenses that are reported separately on the income statement. The sales price of a product must cover both the product and period costs in order to make a profit.

TYING IT ALL TOGETHER

In the chapter opener, we introduced **Winnebago Industries, Inc.** Winnebago is headquartered in Forest City, Iowa, and is a leading manufacturer of recreational vehicles (RVs), including motorized and towable products. The company designs, develops, manufactures, and markets RVs as well as supporting products and services. The RVs are sold to consumers through a dealer network.

On the August 29, 2015, balance sheet, Winnebago reported total inventory of $112 million. What type inventory accounts would Winnebago have?

Winnebago is a manufacturer so it would have Raw Materials, Work-in-Process, and Finished Goods Inventory accounts.

For the year ended August 29, 2015, Winnebago reported cost of goods sold of $871 million and operating expenses of $45 million. Which costs are period costs? Which costs are product costs?

The operating expenses are period costs and the cost of goods sold is a product cost.

List some examples of product costs for Winnebago.

Product costs include direct materials, direct labor, and manufacturing overhead. For Winnebago, direct materials would include items such as steel, aluminum, and fiberglass. Direct materials would also include tires, engines, refrigerators, sinks, washers, and dryers. Direct labor would include the costs of the men and women working on the assembly lines. Manufacturing overhead would include indirect factory costs, such as plant utilities, plant insurance, indirect materials, indirect labor, and depreciation on plant buildings and equipment.

Try It!

12. ABC Manufacturing Company has the following data for 2019 (amounts in millions):

Direct Materials, January 1	$ 5
Direct Materials, December 31	7
Work-in-Process Inventory, January 1	12
Work-in-Process Inventory, December 31	16
Finished Goods Inventory, January 1	8
Finished Goods Inventory, December 31	6
Direct Materials Purchased, including Freight In	25
Direct Labor	36
Manufacturing Overhead	17

Prepare the schedule of cost of goods manufactured and the cost of goods sold section of the income statement for the year ended December 31, 2019.

Check your answers online in MyAccountingLab or at www.pearsonhighered.com/Horngren.

For more practice, see Short Exercises S16-6 through S16-10. MyAccountingLab

WHAT ARE BUSINESS TRENDS THAT ARE AFFECTING MANAGERIAL ACCOUNTING?

In order to be successful, managers of both large corporations and small, privately owned businesses must consider recent business trends and how managerial accounting can be used to help handle these future changes.

Learning Objective 4
Describe business trends affecting managerial accounting

Shift Toward a Service Economy

Service companies provide health care, communication, banking, and other important benefits to society. The United States Bureau of Labor Statistics predicts service-providing sectors will account for the majority of projected job growth from 2014 to 2024, especially in health care and social assistance and professional and business services sectors. The Bureau of Labor Statistics also reports that service industries account for four out of five U.S. jobs. Managers in the service industry need to understand the cost of providing services and supporting customers as well as planning for future customer and service needs.

Global Competition

To be competitive, many companies are moving operations to other countries to be closer to new markets. Other companies are partnering with foreign companies to meet local needs. For example, Toyota, a Japanese company, has 10 manufacturing plants located in North America. Managerial accounting concepts can be used to help managers make decisions about outsourcing portions of the production process and delivery of goods to customers in different geographic markets. Even the decision of moving operations requires an understanding of cost savings and the ability to plan such a move.

Time-Based Competition

The Internet, electronic commerce (e-commerce), and express delivery speed the pace of business. Customers who instant message around the world will not want to wait two weeks to receive merchandise they purchased online. Time is the new competitive turf for world-class business. To compete, companies have developed the following time-saving responses:

- **Advanced Information Systems**   Many companies use **Enterprise Resource Planning (ERP)** systems to integrate all their worldwide functions, departments, and data. ERP systems help to streamline operations and enable companies to respond quickly to changes in the marketplace.

- **E-commerce**   The Internet allows companies to sell to customers around the world by providing 24/7 access to company information and products.

- **Just-in-Time Management**   Inventory held too long may become obsolete. Stored goods take space and must be insured, which increases costs. The just-in-time philosophy helps managers cut costs by speeding the transformation of raw materials into finished products. Using a **Just-in-Time (JIT) Management** system means producing products *just in time* to satisfy needs. Ideally, suppliers deliver materials for today's production in exactly the right quantities *just in time* to begin production, and finished units are completed *just in time* for delivery to customers.

Enterprise Resource Planning (ERP)
Software system that can integrate all of a company's functions, departments, and data into a single system.

Just-in-Time (JIT) Management
A cost management system in which a company produces products just in time to satisfy needs. Suppliers deliver materials just in time to begin production, and finished units are completed just in time for delivery to the customer.

Total Quality Management

Companies must deliver high-quality goods and services in order to be successful. **Total Quality Management (TQM)** is a philosophy of continuous improvement of products and processes. Continuous improvement leads to fewer defects and higher customer satisfaction. TQM also emphasizes the importance of each person in the organization, creating

Total Quality Management (TQM)
A philosophy designed to integrate all organizational areas in order to provide customers with superior products and services, while meeting organizational goals throughout the value chain.

a culture of cooperation across all business processes: research and development, design, production, marketing and sales, distribution, and customer support. Each step in the process adds value to the end product. Therefore, these steps are referred to as the **value chain**. The value chain, as shown in Exhibit 16-15, includes both upstream and downstream activities in which a business engages. The upstream value added activities begin in the research and development activities through product design to the production process. Downstream refers to the activities of selling the product, delivering product to customers, and follow up customer support. Managerial accounting is involved in the decision making by helping with the planning and costing of each activity of the value chain.

Value Chain
Includes all activities that add value to a company's products and services.

Exhibit 16-15 | **Value Chain**

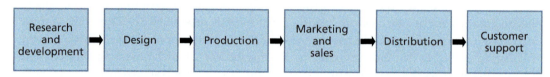

The Triple Bottom Line

Triple Bottom Line
Evaluating a company's performance by its economic (profits), social (people), and environmental (planet) impact.

The **triple bottom line** refers to profits, people, and the planet—the economic, social, and environmental impact of doing business. Companies are recognizing that they have multiple responsibilities and that generating profits for owners and investors is only one aspect of being a socially responsible organization. Increasingly, customers and stockholders are choosing to support companies based on their labor practices, community service, and sustainable environmental practices.

Try It!

Match the definition to the key term.

13. Triple bottom line	**a.** A cost management system in which a company produces products just in time to satisfy needs.
14. Value chain	**b.** A philosophy designed to integrate all organizational areas in order to provide customers with superior products and services, while meeting organizational goals throughout the value chain.
15. Just-in-time management	
16. Enterprise resource planning	**c.** Software system that can integrate all of a company's functions, departments, and data into a single system.
17. Total quality management	**d.** Evaluating a company's performance by its economic (profits), social (people), and environmental (planet) impact.
	e. Includes all activities that add value to a company's products and services.

Check your answers online in MyAccountingLab or at http://www.pearsonhighered.com/Horngren.

For more practice, see Short Exercise S16-11. MyAccountingLab

HOW IS MANAGERIAL ACCOUNTING USED IN SERVICE AND MERCHANDISING COMPANIES?

The previous sections of this chapter focused on manufacturing companies, but managerial accounting is used in all types of businesses. Even though service and merchandising companies don't manufacture a product, the managers are still interested in planning, directing, and controlling operations. We now know how to determine the cost of a manufactured product. Let's see how managerial accounting can be used to help service and merchandising companies.

Learning Objective 5

Describe how managerial accounting is used in service and merchandising companies

Calculating Cost per Service

Knowing the cost per service helps managers set the price of each service provided. Service companies do not have product costs, so they often consider *all* operating expenses as part of their cost of service. In larger, more advanced service companies, the period costs may be split between service costs and nonservice costs. Let's assume that in 2018, before Smart Touch Learning began buying or manufacturing tablets, the company incurred costs of $3,900 and provided 1,950 e-learning services. What is the cost per service? Use the following formula to calculate the unit cost per service:

Total costs	**/**	**Total number of services provided**	**=**	**Unit cost per service**
$3,900	/	1,950 services	=	$2 per service

Calculating Cost per Item

Merchandising companies need to know cost per item to be able to determine which products are most profitable. Knowing the unit cost per product helps managers set appropriate selling prices. Let's assume that in December 2019, Smart Touch Learning sold 260 tablets that cost $90,800 to purchase (this was before it expanded into manufacturing). What is the cost of each item sold? Use the following formula to calculate the average unit cost per item:

Total cost of goods sold	**/**	**Total number of items sold**	**=**	**Unit cost per item**
$90,800	/	260 tablets	=	$349.23 per tablet

Note that this further justifies Smart Touch Learning's decision to manufacture the tablets. The company was purchasing the tablets for $349.23 and was able to manufacture them for $300.

18. ABC Cleaning Company cleaned 45 offices and incurred costs of $2,340. What was the cost to clean each office?

Check your answers online in MyAccountingLab or at http://www.pearsonhighered.com/Horngren.

For more practice, see Short Exercise S16-12. MyAccountingLab

REVIEW

> Things You Should Know

1. Why is managerial accounting important?

- Managerial accounting focuses on providing information for internal decision makers.
- Managerial accounting helps managers plan, direct, control, and make decisions about the business.

2. How are costs classified?

- Manufacturing companies track costs using three inventory accounts: Raw Materials Inventory, Work-in-Process Inventory, and Finished Goods Inventory.
- Direct costs such as direct materials and direct labor can be easily and cost-effectively traced directly to a cost object, whereas indirect costs such as indirect materials and indirect labor cannot be easily or cost-effectively traced to cost objects.
- Manufacturing companies can classify product costs into three distinct categories: direct materials, direct labor, and manufacturing overhead.
  - Prime costs are direct materials and direct labor.
  - Conversion costs are direct labor and manufacturing overhead.
- Product costs are all costs (direct materials, direct labor, and manufacturing overhead) incurred in the manufacture of final products. Product costs are first recorded as inventory and not expensed until the product is sold.
- Period costs are all costs not considered product costs, such as selling and administrative costs. Period costs are expensed in the accounting period incurred.

3. How do manufacturing companies prepare financial statements?

- Manufacturing companies list the three inventory accounts (Raw Materials Inventory, Work-in-Process Inventory, and Finished Goods Inventory) on the balance sheet.
- The income statement for a manufacturing company involves the calculation of cost of goods manufactured and cost of goods sold.
- The calculation of cost of goods manufactured involves three steps.

  Step 1. Calculate direct materials used. Direct Materials Used = Beginning Direct Materials + Purchases of Direct Materials (including Freight In) − Ending Direct Materials.

  Step 2. Calculate total manufacturing costs incurred during the year. Total Manufacturing Costs Incurred during the Year = Direct Materials Used + Direct Labor + Manufacturing Overhead.

  Step 3. Calculate cost of goods manufactured. Cost of Goods Manufactured = Beginning Work-in-Process Inventory + Total Manufacturing Costs Incurred during the Year − Ending Work-in-Process Inventory.

- Cost of Goods Sold = Beginning Finished Goods Inventory + Cost of Goods Manufactured − Ending Finished Goods Inventory.

4. **What are business trends that are affecting managerial accounting?**

- There are many factors that influence how managers use managerial accounting, including a shift towards a service-based economy and global and time-based competition.

- Managers use strategies such as just-in-time management, total quality management, and triple bottom line to plan, direct, and control operations for a business.

5. **How is managerial accounting used in service and merchandising companies?**

- Service and merchandising companies also use managerial accounting to determine the cost per service and cost per item.

- Calculation of unit costs can help managers determine the sales price to charge customers.

  - Unit cost per service = Total costs / Total number of services provided.

  - Unit cost per item = Total cost of goods sold / Total number of items sold.

> Check Your Understanding

Check your understanding of the chapter by completing this problem and then looking at the solution. Use this practice to help identify which sections of the chapter you need to study more.

Requirements

1. For a manufacturing company, identify the following as either a product cost or a period cost (See Learning Objective 2):

   a. Depreciation on plant equipment

   b. Depreciation on salespersons' automobiles

   c. Insurance on plant building

   d. Marketing manager's salary

   e. Direct materials used

   f. Manufacturing overhead

   g. Electricity bill for human resources office

   h. Production employee wages

2. Show how to compute cost of goods manufactured. Use the following amounts: direct materials used, $24,000; direct labor, $9,000; manufacturing overhead, $17,000; beginning Work-in-Process Inventory, $5,000; and ending Work-in-Process Inventory, $4,000. (See Learning Objective 3)

3. Using the results from Requirement 2, calculate the cost per unit for goods manufactured assuming 1,000 units were manufactured. (See Learning Objective 3)

4. Beginning Finished Goods Inventory had 100 units that had a unit cost of $50 each. Ending Finished Goods Inventory has 200 units left. Using the results from Requirement 3, calculate cost of goods sold assuming FIFO inventory costing is used. (See Learning Objective 3)

> Solution

Requirement 1

Product costs: a, c, e, f, h

Period costs: b, d, g

Requirement 2

Cost of goods manufactured:

Beginning Work-in-Process Inventory		$ 5,000
Direct Materials Used	$ 24,000	
Direct Labor	9,000	
Manufacturing Overhead	17,000	
Total Manufacturing Costs Incurred during Period		50,000
Total Manufacturing Costs to Account For		55,000
Ending Work-in-Process Inventory		(4,000)
Cost of Goods Manufactured		$51,000

Requirement 3

Cost of Goods Manufactured	/	Total Units Produced	=	Unit Product Cost
$51,000	/	1,000 units	=	$51 per unit

Requirement 4

Beginning Finished Goods Inventory (100 units × $50 per unit)	$ 5,000
Cost of Goods Manufactured	51,000
Cost of Goods Available for Sale	56,000
Ending Finished Goods Inventory (200 units × $51 per unit)	(10,200)
Cost of Goods Sold [(100 units × $50 per unit) + (800 units × $51 per unit)]	$ 45,800

> Key Terms

Board of Directors (p. 861)

Chief Executive Officer (CEO) (p. 861)

Controlling (p. 862)

Conversion Costs (p. 867)

Cost Object (p. 866)

Cost of Goods Manufactured (p. 872)

Direct Cost (p. 866)

Direct Labor (DL) (p. 866)

Direct Materials (DM) (p. 866)

Directing (p. 862)

Enterprise Resource Planning (ERP) (p. 877)

Financial Accounting (p. 860)

Finished Goods Inventory (FG) (p. 865)

Indirect Cost (p. 866)

Indirect Labor (p. 867)

Indirect Materials (p. 867)

Just-in-Time (JIT) Management (p. 877)

Line Position (p. 862)

Managerial Accounting (p. 860)

Manufacturing Company (p. 865)

Manufacturing Overhead (MOH) (p. 866)

Merchandising Company (p. 865)

Operational Planning (p. 862)

Organizational Chart (p. 861)

Period Cost (p. 868)

Planning (p. 862)

Prime Costs (p. 867)

Product Cost (p. 868)

Raw Materials Inventory (RM) (p. 865)

Service Company (p. 865)

Staff Position (p. 862)

Strategic Planning (p. 862)

Total Quality Management (TQM) (p. 877)

Triple Bottom Line (p. 878)

Value Chain (p. 878)

Work-in-Process Inventory (WIP) (p. 865)

> Quick Check

1. Which is *not* a characteristic of managerial accounting information?

   Learning Objective 1

   a. Emphasizes the external financial statements
   b. Provides detailed information about individual parts of the company
   c. Emphasizes relevance
   d. Focuses on the future

2. A management accountant who avoids conflicts of interest meets the ethical standard of

   Learning Objective 1

   a. confidentiality.
   b. competence.
   c. credibility.
   d. integrity.

3. Dunaway Company reports the following costs for the year:

   Learning Objective 2

Direct Materials Used	$ 120,000
Direct Labor Incurred	150,000
Manufacturing Overhead Incurred	75,000
Selling and Administrative Expenses	175,000

   How much are Dunaway's period costs?

   a. $250,000
   b. $270,000
   c. $345,000
   d. $175,000

4. Which of the following is a direct cost of manufacturing a sport boat?

   Learning Objective 2

   a. Salary of an engineer who rearranges plant layout
   b. Depreciation on plant and equipment
   c. Cost of the boat engine
   d. Cost of the customer service hotline

5. Which of the following is *not* part of manufacturing overhead for producing a computer?

   Learning Objective 2

   a. Manufacturing plant property taxes
   b. Manufacturing plant utilities
   c. Depreciation on delivery trucks
   d. Insurance on plant and equipment

6. Which of the following accounts does a manufacturing company have that a service company does not have?

   Learning Objective 3

   a. Advertising Expense
   b. Salaries Payable
   c. Cost of Goods Sold
   d. Accounts Receivable

Questions 7 and 8 use the data that follow.

Suppose a bakery reports the following information:

Beginning Direct Materials	$ 6,000
Ending Direct Materials	5,000
Beginning Work-in-Process Inventory	3,000
Ending Work-in-Process Inventory	2,000
Beginning Finished Goods Inventory	4,000
Ending Finished Goods Inventory	6,000
Direct Labor	29,000
Purchases of Direct Materials	102,000
Manufacturing Overhead	20,000

Learning Objective 3

7. What is the cost of direct materials used?
   a. $101,000
   b. $103,000
   c. $114,000
   d. $102,000

Learning Objective 3

8. What is the cost of goods manufactured?
   a. $151,000
   b. $153,000
   c. $150,000
   d. $177,000

Learning Objective 4

9. World-class businesses use which of these systems to integrate all of a company's worldwide functions, departments, and data into a single system?
   a. Cost standards
   b. Enterprise resource planning
   c. Just-in-time management
   d. Items a, b, and c are correct.

Learning Objective 4

10. Today's business environment is characterized by
    a. global competition.
    b. time-based competition.
    c. a shift toward a service economy.
    d. Items a, b, and c are correct.

Check your answers at the end of the chapter.

ASSESS YOUR PROGRESS

> Review Questions

1. What is the primary purpose of managerial accounting?
2. List six differences between financial accounting and managerial accounting.
3. Explain the difference between line positions and staff positions.
4. Explain the differences between planning, directing, and controlling.
5. List the four IMA standards of ethical practice, and briefly describe each.
6. Describe a service company, and give an example.
7. Describe a merchandising company, and give an example.
8. How do manufacturing companies differ from merchandising companies?

9. List the three inventory accounts used by manufacturing companies, and describe each.

10. Explain the difference between a direct cost and an indirect cost.

11. What are the three manufacturing costs for a manufacturing company? Describe each.

12. Give five examples of manufacturing overhead.

13. What are prime costs? Conversion costs?

14. What are product costs?

15. How do period costs differ from product costs?

16. How is cost of goods manufactured calculated?

17. How does a manufacturing company calculate cost of goods sold? How is this different from a merchandising company?

18. How does a manufacturing company calculate unit product cost?

19. How does a service company calculate unit cost per service?

20. How does a merchandising company calculate unit cost per item?

> Short Exercises

S16-1 Comparing managerial accounting and financial accounting

Learning Objective 1

For each of the following, indicate whether the statement relates to managerial accounting (MA) or financial accounting (FA):

a. Helps investors make investment decisions.

b. Provides detailed reports on parts of the company.

c. Helps in planning and controlling operations.

d. Reports must follow Generally Accepted Accounting Principles (GAAP).

e. Reports audited annually by independent certified public accountants.

S16-2 Identifying ethical standards

Learning Objective 1

The Institute of Management Accountants' Statement of Ethical Professional Practice requires managerial accountants to meet standards regarding competence, confidentiality, integrity, and credibility. Consider the following situations. Which standard(s) is(are) violated in each situation?

a. You tell your brother that your company will report earnings significantly above financial analysts' estimates.

b. You see others take home office supplies for personal use. As an intern, you do the same thing, assuming that this is a "perk."

c. At a company-paid conference on e-commerce, you skip the afternoon session and go sightseeing.

d. You failed to read the detailed specifications of a new accounting software package that you asked your company to purchase. After it is installed, you are surprised that it is incompatible with some of your company's older accounting software.

e. You do not provide top management with the detailed job descriptions they requested because you fear they may use this information to cut a position in your department.

Learning Objective 2

S16-3 Distinguishing between direct and indirect costs

Granger Cards is a manufacturer of greeting cards. Classify its costs by matching the costs to the terms.

1. Direct materials	a. Artists' wages
2. Direct labor	b. Wages of materials warehouse workers
3. Indirect materials	c. Paper
4. Indirect labor	d. Depreciation on manufacturing equipment
5. Other manufacturing overhead	e. Manufacturing plant manager's salary
	f. Property taxes on manufacturing plant
	g. Glue for envelopes

Learning Objective 2

S16-4 Computing manufacturing overhead

Sunglasses Unlimited Company manufactures sunglasses. Following is a list of costs the company incurred during May. Use the list to calculate the total manufacturing overhead costs for the month.

Glue for frames	$ 250
Depreciation on company cars used by sales force	4,000
Plant depreciation	7,500
Interest Expense	1,500
Lenses	52,000
Company president's salary	24,500
Plant foreman's salary	3,500
Plant janitor's wages	1,300
Oil for manufacturing equipment	150

Learning Objective 2

S16-5 Identifying product costs and period costs

Classify each cost of a paper manufacturer as either a product cost or a period cost:

a. Salaries of scientists studying ways to speed forest growth.

b. Cost of computer software to track WIP Inventory.

c. Cost of electricity at the paper mill.

d. Salaries of the company's top executives.

e. Cost of chemicals to treat the paper.

f. Cost of TV ads.

g. Depreciation on the manufacturing plant.

h. Cost to purchase wood pulp.

i. Life insurance on the CEO.

S16-6 Computing cost of goods sold, merchandising company

Use the following information for The Windshield Helper, a retail merchandiser of auto windshields, to compute the cost of goods sold:

Web Site Maintenance	$ 7,900
Delivery Expense	400
Freight In	2,400
Purchases	47,000
Ending Merchandise Inventory	5,500
Revenues	63,000
Marketing Expenses	10,700
Beginning Merchandise Inventory	8,600

S16-7 Computing cost of goods sold and operating income, merchandising company

Consider the following partially completed income statements for merchandising companies and compute the missing amounts:

	Smith, Inc.	Allen, Inc.
Net Sales Revenue	$ 101,000	$ (d)
Cost of Goods Sold:		
Beginning Merchandise Inventory	(a)	29,000
Purchases and Freight In	50,000	(e)
Cost of Goods Available for Sale	(b)	89,000
Ending Merchandise Inventory	(2,200)	(2,200)
Cost of Goods Sold	61,000	(f)
Gross Profit	40,000	114,000
Selling and Administrative Expenses	(c)	84,000
Operating Income	$ 12,000	$ (g)

S16-8 Computing direct materials used

Tuscany, Inc. has compiled the following data:

Purchases of Direct Materials	$ 6,300
Freight In	400
Property Taxes	800
Ending Direct Materials	1,300
Beginning Direct Materials	4,100

Compute the amount of direct materials used.

Learning Objective 3

S16-9 Computing cost of goods manufactured

Use the following inventory data for Caddy Golf Company to compute the cost of goods manufactured for the year:

Direct Materials Used	$ 12,000
Manufacturing Overhead	21,000
Work-in-Process Inventory:	
Beginning Balance	1,000
Ending Balance	5,000
Direct Labor	9,000
Finished Goods Inventory:	
Beginning Balance	18,000
Ending Balance	4,000

Learning Objective 3

S16-10 Computing cost of goods sold, manufacturing company

Use the following information to calculate the cost of goods sold for The Ellis Company for the month of June:

Finished Goods Inventory:	
Beginning Balance	$ 30,000
Ending Balance	10,000
Cost of Goods Manufactured	165,000

Learning Objective 4

S16-11 Matching business trends terminology

Match the term with the correct definition.

1. A philosophy designed to integrate all organizational areas in order to provide customers with superior products and services while meeting organizational objectives. Requires improving quality and eliminating defects and waste.
2. Use of the Internet for business functions such as sales and customer service. Enables companies to reach customers around the world.
3. Evaluating a company's performance by its economic, social, and environmental impact.
4. Software system that integrates all of a company's functions, departments, and data into a single system.
5. A system in which a company produces products just when they are needed to satisfy needs. Suppliers deliver materials when they are needed to begin production, and finished units are completed at the right time for delivery to customers.

a. ERP
b. JIT
c. E-commerce
d. TQM
e. Triple bottom line

S16-12 Calculating unit cost per service

Marx and Tyler provides hair-cutting services in the local community. In February, the business cut the hair of 190 clients, earned $4,800 in revenues, and incurred the following operating costs:

Hair Supplies Expense	$ 950
Wages Expense	548
Utilities Expense	190
Depreciation Expense—Equipment	60

What was the cost of service to provide one haircut?

> Exercises

E16-13 Comparing managerial accounting and financial accounting

Match the following terms to the appropriate statement. Some terms may be used more than once, and some terms may not be used at all.

Directing	Managerial
Creditors	Managers
Controlling	Planning
Financial	Stockholders

a. Accounting systems that must follow GAAP.

b. External parties for whom financial accounting reports are prepared.

c. The role managers play when they are monitoring day-to-day operations and keeping the company on track.

d. Internal decision makers.

e. Accounting system that provides information on a company's past performance.

f. Accounting system not restricted by GAAP.

g. The management function that involves choosing goals and deciding how to achieve them.

E16-14 Making ethical decisions

Sue Peters is the controller at Vroom, a car dealership. Dale Miller recently has been hired as the bookkeeper. Dale wanted to attend a class in Excel spreadsheets, so Sue temporarily took over Dale's duties, including overseeing a fund used for gas purchases before test drives. Sue found a shortage in the fund and confronted Dale when he returned to work. Dale admitted that he occasionally uses the fund to pay for his own gas. Sue estimated the shortage at $450.

Requirements

1. What should Sue Peters do?

2. Would you change your answer if Sue Peters was the one recently hired as controller and Dale Miller was a well-liked, longtime employee who indicated he always eventually repaid the fund?

Learning Objective 2

E16-15 Classifying costs

Wheels, Inc. manufactures wheels for bicycles, tricycles, and scooters. For each cost given below, determine if the cost is a product cost or a period cost. If the cost is a product cost, further determine if the cost is direct materials (DM), direct labor (DL), or manufacturing overhead (MOH) and then determine if the product cost is a prime cost, conversion cost, or both. If the cost is a period cost, further determine if the cost is a selling expense or administrative expense (Admin). *Cost (a) is answered as a guide.*

Cost	Product					Period	
	DM	DL	MOH	Prime	Conversion	Selling	Admin.
a. Metal used for rims	X			X			
b. Sales salaries							
c. Rent on factory							
d. Wages of assembly workers							
e. Salary of production supervisor							
f. Depreciation on office equipment							
g. Salary of CEO							
h. Delivery expense							

Use the following data for Exercises E16-16, E16-17, and E16-18.

Selected data for three companies are given below. All inventory amounts are ending balances and all amounts are in millions.

Company A		Company B		Company C	
Cash	$ 6	Wages Expense	$ 12	Administrative Expenses	$ 4
Net Sales Revenue	48	Equipment	32	Cash	25
Finished Goods Inventory	10	Accounts Receivable	8	Net Sales Revenue	75
Cost of Goods Sold	23	Service Revenue	65	Selling Expenses	8
Selling Expenses	4	Cash	34	Merchandise Inventory	12
Equipment	67	Rent Expense	12	Equipment	55
Work-in-Process Inventory	9			Accounts Receivable	19
Accounts Receivable	14			Cost of Goods Sold	25
Cost of Goods Manufactured	23				
Administrative Expenses	7				
Raw Materials Inventory	6				

Learning Objective 3

E16-16 Identifying differences between service, merchandising, and manufacturing companies

Using the above data, determine the company type. Identify each company as a service company, merchandising company, or manufacturing company.

E16-17 Identifying differences between service, merchandising, and manufacturing companies

Using the data on the previous page, calculate operating income for each company.

Learning Objective 3

Company B: $41

E16-18 Identifying differences between service, merchandising, and manufacturing companies

Using the data on the previous page, calculate total current assets for each company.

Learning Objective 3

Company C: $56

E16-19 Computing cost of goods manufactured

Consider the following partially completed schedules of cost of goods manufactured. Compute the missing amounts.

Learning Objective 3

	Banner, Inc.	Larry's Bakery	Sports Gear
Beginning Work-in-Process Inventory	$ (a)	$ 40,800	$ 2,200
Direct Materials Used	14,400	35,900	(g)
Direct Labor	10,300	20,100	1,900
Manufacturing Overhead	(b)	10,000	900
Total Manufacturing Costs Incurred during the Year	45,200	(d)	(h)
Total Manufacturing Costs to Account for	55,400	(e)	8,300
Ending Work-in-Process Inventory	(c)	(25,500)	(2,600)
Cost of Goods Manufactured	$ 50,500	$ (f)	$ (i)

E16-20 Preparing a schedule of cost of goods manufactured

Wilson Corp., a lamp manufacturer, provided the following information for the year ended December 31, 2018:

Learning Objective 3

1. COGM: $444,000

Balances:	Beginning	Ending
Direct Materials	$ 59,000	$ 23,000
Work-in-Process Inventory	109,000	62,000
Finished Goods Inventory	41,000	44,000

Other information:	
Depreciation, plant building and equipment	$ 16,000
Direct materials purchases	151,000
Insurance on plant	24,000
Sales salaries	47,000
Repairs and maintenance—plant	10,000
Indirect labor	39,000
Direct labor	121,000
Administrative expenses	60,000

Requirements

1. Use the information to prepare a schedule of cost of goods manufactured.
2. What is the unit product cost if Wilson manufactured 3,700 lamps for the year?

CHAPTER 16

Learning Objective 3

COGM: $211,000

E16-21 Computing cost of goods manufactured and cost of goods sold

Use the following information for a manufacturer to compute cost of goods manufactured and cost of goods sold:

Balances:	Beginning	Ending
Direct Materials	$ 27,000	$ 28,000
Work-in-Process Inventory	40,000	32,000
Finished Goods Inventory	18,000	25,000
Other information:		
Purchases of direct materials		$ 73,000
Direct labor		88,000
Manufacturing overhead		43,000

Learning Objective 4

E16-22 Understanding today's business environment

Match the following terms to the appropriate statement. Some terms may be used more than once, and some terms may not be used at all.

E-commerce	Just-in-time management (JIT)
Enterprise resource planning (ERP)	Total quality management (TQM)

a. A management system that focuses on maintaining lean inventories while producing products as needed by the customer.

b. A philosophy designed to integrate all organizational areas in order to provide customers with superior products and services while meeting organizational objectives.

c. Integrates all of a company's functions, departments, and data into a single system.

d. Adopted by firms to conduct business on the Internet.

Learning Objectives 3, 5

1. $9,304

E16-23 Calculating income and cost per service for a service company

Buddy Grooming provides grooming services for pets. In April, the company earned $16,300 in revenues and incurred the following operating costs to groom 660 dogs:

Wages Expense	$ 4,061
Grooming Supplies Expense	1,675
Building Rent Expense	900
Utilities Expense	305
Depreciation Expense—Equipment	55

Requirements

1. What is Buddy's operating income for April?
2. What is the cost of service to groom one dog?

E16-24 Calculating income and cost per unit for a merchandising company

Learning Objectives 3, 5

2. $12.42

Conway Brush Company sells standard hair brushes. The following information summarizes Conway's operating activities for 2018:

Selling and Administrative Expenses	$ 47,058
Purchases	85,800
Net Sales Revenue	151,800
Merchandise Inventory, January 1, 2018	7,920
Merchandise Inventory, December 31, 2018	11,748

Requirements

1. Calculate the operating income for 2018.
2. Conway sold 6,600 brushes in 2018. Compute the unit cost for one brush.

> Problems Group A

P16-25A Applying ethical standards

Learning Objective 1

Natalia Wallace is the new controller for Smart Software, Inc. which develops and sells education software. Shortly before the December 31 fiscal year-end, James Cauvet, the company president, asks Wallace how things look for the year-end numbers. He is not happy to learn that earnings growth may be below 13% for the first time in the company's five-year history. Cauvet explains that financial analysts have again predicted a 13% earnings growth for the company and that he does not intend to disappoint them. He suggests that Wallace talk to the assistant controller, who can explain how the previous controller dealt with such situations. The assistant controller suggests the following strategies:

a. Persuade suppliers to postpone billing $13,000 in invoices until January 1.

b. Record as sales $115,000 in certain software awaiting sale that is held in a public warehouse.

c. Delay the year-end closing a few days into January of the next year so that some of the next year's sales are included in this year's sales.

d. Reduce the estimated Bad Debts Expense from 5% of Sales Revenue to 3%, given the company's continued strong performance.

e. Postpone routine monthly maintenance expenditures from December to January.

Requirements

1. Which of these suggested strategies are inconsistent with IMA standards?
2. How might these inconsistencies affect the company's creditors and stockholders?
3. What should Wallace do if Cauvet insists that she follow all of these suggestions?

Learning Objective 2

P16-26A Classifying period costs and product costs

Lawlor, Inc. is the manufacturer of lawn care equipment. The company incurs the following costs while manufacturing weed trimmers:

- Shaft and handle of weed trimmer
- Motor of weed trimmer
- Factory labor for workers assembling weed trimmers
- Nylon thread used by the weed trimmer (not traced to the product)
- Glue to hold the housing together
- Plant janitorial wages
- Depreciation on factory equipment
- Rent on plant
- Sales commissions
- Administrative salaries
- Plant utilities
- Shipping costs to deliver finished weed trimmers to customers

Requirements

1. Describe the difference between period costs and product costs.

2. Classify Lawlor's costs as period costs or product costs. If the costs are product costs, further classify them as direct materials, direct labor, or manufacturing overhead.

Learning Objective 3

3. Company B: $217,800

P16-27A Calculating cost of goods sold for merchandising and manufacturing companies

Below are data for two companies:

	Company A	Company B
Beginning balances:		
Merchandise Inventory	$ 10,600	
Finished Goods Inventory		$ 15,000
Ending balances:		
Merchandise Inventory	13,100	
Finished Goods Inventory		11,700
Net Purchases	154,500	
Cost of Goods Manufactured		214,500

Requirements

1. Define the three business types: service, merchandising, and manufacturing.

2. Based on the data given for the two companies, determine the business type of each one.

3. Calculate the cost of goods sold for each company.

P16-28A Preparing a schedule of cost of goods manufactured and an income statement for a manufacturing company

Learning Objective 3

2. Operating income: $23,200

Gourmet Bones manufactures its own brand of pet chew bones. At the end of December 2018, the accounting records showed the following:

CHAPTER 16

Balances:	Beginning	Ending
Direct Materials	$ 13,500	$ 7,500
Work-in-Process Inventory	0	3,500
Finished Goods Inventory	0	5,200

Other information:	
Direct materials purchases	$ 36,000
Plant janitorial services	700
Sales salaries	6,000
Delivery costs	1,300
Net sales revenue	107,000
Utilities for plant	1,300
Rent on plant	17,000
Customer service hotline costs	1,200
Direct labor	23,000

Requirements

1. Prepare a schedule of cost of goods manufactured for Gourmet Bones for the year ended December 31, 2018.

2. Prepare an income statement for Gourmet Bones for the year ended December 31, 2018.

3. How does the format of the income statement for Gourmet Bones differ from the income statement of a merchandiser?

4. Gourmet Bones manufactured 17,900 units of its product in 2018. Compute the company's unit product cost for the year, rounded to the nearest cent.

CHAPTER 16

Learning Objectives 3

P16-29A Preparing a schedule of cost of goods manufactured and an income statement for a manufacturing company

COGM: $182,000

Certain item descriptions and amounts are missing from the monthly schedule of cost of goods manufactured and income statement of Elly Manufacturing Company. Fill in the blanks with the missing words, and replace the Xs with the correct amounts.

ELLY MANUFACTURING COMPANY

_____

_____ June 30, 2018

Beginning_____		$ 27,000
Direct _____ :		
Beginning Direct Materials	$ X	
Purchases of Direct Materials	56,000	
_____	84,000	
Ending Direct Materials	(20,000)	
Direct _____	$ X	
Direct _____	X	
Manufacturing Overhead	44,000	
Total _____ Costs _____		180,000
Total _____ Costs _____		X
Ending _____		(25,000)
_____		$ X

ELLY MANUFACTURING COMPANY

_____

_____ June 30, 2018

Net Sales Revenue		$ X
Cost of Goods Sold:		
Beginning_____	$ 110,000	
_____	X	
Cost of Goods _____	X	
Ending _____	X	
Cost of Goods Sold		232,000
Gross Profit		258,000
_____ Expenses:		
Selling Expenses	98,000	
Administrative Expenses	X	
Total _____		160,000
_____ Income		$ X

P16-30A Determining flow of costs through a manufacturer's inventory accounts

Learning Objective 3

Root Shoe Company makes loafers. During the most recent year, Root incurred total manufacturing costs of $26,300,000. Of this amount, $2,000,000 was direct materials used and $19,800,000 was direct labor. Beginning balances for the year were Direct Materials, $700,000; Work-in-Process Inventory, $1,500,000; and Finished Goods Inventory, $400,000. At the end of the year, balances were Direct Materials, $800,000; Work-in-Process Inventory, $1,200,000; and Finished Goods Inventory, $600,000.

3. $26,400,000

Requirements

Analyze the inventory accounts to determine:

1. Cost of direct materials purchased during the year.

2. Cost of goods manufactured for the year.

3. Cost of goods sold for the year.

P16-31A Preparing an income statement and calculating unit cost for a service company

Learning Objectives 3, 5

The Windshield Doctors repair chips in car windshields. The company incurred the following operating costs for the month of March 2018:

2. $37.72

Salaries and wages	$ 12,000
Windshield repair materials	4,600
Depreciation on truck	300
Depreciation on building and equipment	1,200
Supplies used	300
Utilities	460

The Windshield Doctors earned $23,000 in service revenues for the month of March by repairing 500 windshields. All costs shown are considered to be directly related to the repair service.

Requirements

1. Prepare an income statement for the month of March.

2. Compute the cost per unit of repairing one windshield.

3. The manager of Windshield Doctors must keep unit operating cost below $50 per windshield in order to get his bonus. Did he meet the goal?

Learning Objectives 3, 5

1. Operating income: $15,150

P16-32A Preparing an income statement and calculating unit cost for a merchandising company

Clyde Conway owns Clyde's Pets, a small retail shop selling pet supplies. On December 31, 2018, the accounting records of Clyde's Pets showed the following:

Merchandise Inventory on December 31, 2018	$ 10,100
Merchandise Inventory on January 1, 2018	15,900
Net Sales Revenue	56,000
Utilities Expense for the shop	3,300
Rent for the shop	4,100
Sales Commissions	2,650
Purchases of Merchandise Inventory	25,000

Requirements

1. Prepare an income statement for Clyde's Pets for the year ended December 31, 2018.

2. Clyde's Pets sold 3,850 units. Determine the unit cost of the merchandise sold, rounded to the nearest cent.

> Problems Group B

Learning Objective 1

P16-33B Applying ethical standards

Ava Borzi is the new controller for Halo Software, Inc. which develops and sells education software. Shortly before the December 31 fiscal year-end, Jeremy Busch, the company president, asks Borzi how things look for the year-end numbers. He is not happy to learn that earnings growth may be below 9% for the first time in the company's five-year history. Busch explains that financial analysts have again predicted a 9% earnings growth for the company and that he does not intend to disappoint them. He suggests that Borzi talk to the assistant controller, who can explain how the previous controller dealt with such situations. The assistant controller suggests the following strategies:

a. Persuade suppliers to postpone billing $18,000 in invoices until January 1.

b. Record as sales $120,000 in certain software awaiting sale that is held in a public warehouse.

c. Delay the year-end closing a few days into January of the next year so that some of the next year's sales are included in this year's sales.

d. Reduce the estimated Bad Debts Expense from 3% of Sales Revenue to 2%, given the company's continued strong performance.

e. Postpone routine monthly maintenance expenditures from December to January.

Requirements

1. Which of these suggested strategies are inconsistent with IMA standards?

2. How might these inconsistencies affect the company's creditors and stockholders?

3. What should Borzi do if Busch insists that she follow all of these suggestions?

P16-34B Classifying period costs and product costs

Learning Objective 2

Langley, Inc. is the manufacturer of lawn care equipment. The company incurs the following costs while manufacturing edgers:

- Handle and shaft of edger
- Motor of edger
- Factory labor for workers assembling edgers
- Lubricant used on bearings in the edger (not traced to the product)
- Glue to hold the housing together
- Plant janitorial wages
- Depreciation on factory equipment
- Rent on plant
- Sales commissions
- Administrative salaries
- Plant utilities
- Shipping costs to deliver finished edgers to customers

Requirements

1. Describe the difference between period costs and product costs.

2. Classify Langley's costs as period costs or product costs. If the costs are product costs, further classify them as direct materials, direct labor, or manufacturing overhead.

P16-35B Calculating cost of goods sold for merchandising and manufacturing companies

Learning Objective 3

3. Company 2: $218,600

Below are data for two companies:

	Company 1	Company 2
Beginning balances:		
Merchandise Inventory	$ 11,600	
Finished Goods Inventory		$ 15,400
Ending balances:		
Merchandise Inventory	12,400	
Finished Goods Inventory		11,300
Net Purchases	152,500	
Cost of Goods Manufactured		214,500

Requirements

1. Define the three business types: service, merchandising, and manufacturing.

2. Based on the data given for the two companies, determine the business type of each one.

3. Calculate the cost of goods sold for each company.

Learning Objective 3

P16-36B Preparing a schedule of cost of goods manufactured and an income statement for a manufacturing company

2. Operating income: $44,500

Chewy Bones manufactures its own brand of pet chew bones. At the end of December 2018, the accounting records showed the following:

Balances:	Beginning	Ending
Direct Materials	$ 13,400	$ 10,500
Work-in-Process Inventory	0	1,500
Finished Goods Inventory	0	5,400
Other information:		
Direct materials purchases		$ 39,000
Plant janitorial services		900
Sales salaries		5,100
Delivery costs		1,700
Net sales revenue		115,000
Utilities for plant		1,200
Rent on plant		9,000
Customer service hotline costs		1,600
Direct labor		16,000

Requirements

1. Prepare a schedule of cost of goods manufactured for Chewy Bones for the year ended December 31, 2018.

2. Prepare an income statement for Chewy Bones for the year ended December 31, 2018.

3. How does the format of the income statement for Chewy Bones differ from the income statement of a merchandiser?

4. Chewy Bones manufactured 17,500 units of its product in 2018. Compute the company's unit product cost for the year, rounded to the nearest cent.

P16-37B Preparing a schedule of cost of goods manufactured and an income statement for a manufacturing company

Learning Objective 3

COGM: $174,000

CHAPTER 16

Certain item descriptions and amounts are missing from the monthly schedule of cost of goods manufactured and income statement of Charlie Manufacturing Company. Fill in the blanks with the missing words, and replace the Xs with the correct amounts.

CHARLIE MANUFACTURING COMPANY

_____

_____ June 30, 2018

Beginning_____		$ 26,000
Direct _____ :		
Beginning Direct Materials	$ X	
Purchases of Direct Materials	51,000	
_____	81,000	
Ending Direct Materials	(26,000)	
Direct _____	$ X	
Direct _____	X	
Manufacturing Overhead	50,000	
Total _____ Costs _____		177,000
Total _____ Costs _____		X
Ending _____		(29,000)
_____		$ X

CHARLIE MANUFACTURING COMPANY

_____

_____ June 30, 2018

Net Sales Revenue		$ X
Cost of Goods Sold:		
Beginning_____	$ 118,000	
_____	X	
Cost of Goods _____	X	
Ending _____	X	
Cost of Goods Sold		232,000
Gross Profit		268,000
_____ Expenses:		
Selling Expenses	90,000	
Administrative Expenses	X	
Total _____		150,000
_____ Income		$ X

Learning Objective 3

3. $21,420,000

P16-38B Determining the flow of costs through a manufacturer's inventory accounts

True Fit Shoe Company makes loafers. During the most recent year, True Fit incurred total manufacturing costs of $21,900,000. Of this amount, $2,600,000 was direct materials used and $14,800,000 was direct labor. Beginning balances for the year were Direct Materials, $700,000; Work-in-Process Inventory, $1,500,000; and Finished Goods Inventory, $1,100,000. At the end of the year, balances were Direct Materials, $800,000; Work-in-Process Inventory, $2,000,000; and Finished Goods Inventory, $1,080,000.

Requirements

Analyze the inventory accounts to determine:

1. Cost of direct materials purchased during the year.
2. Cost of goods manufactured for the year.
3. Cost of goods sold for the year.

Learning Objectives 3, 5

2. $82.00

P16-39B Preparing an income statement and calculating unit cost for a service company

The Glass Doctors repair chips in car windshields. The company incurred the following operating costs for the month of July 2018:

Salaries and wages	$ 10,000
Windshield repair materials	4,100
Depreciation on truck	500
Depreciation on building and equipment	900
Supplies used	450
Utilities	4,550

The Glass Doctors earned $25,000 in service revenues for the month of July by repairing 250 windshields. All costs shown are considered to be directly related to the repair service.

Requirements

1. Prepare an income statement for the month of July.
2. Compute the cost per unit of repairing one windshield, rounded to the nearest cent.
3. The manager of The Glass Doctors must keep unit operating cost below $80 per windshield in order to get his bonus. Did he meet the goal?

P16-40B Preparing an income statement and calculating unit cost for a merchandising company

Learning Objectives 3, 5

1. Operating income: $15,450

Dillon Young owns Dillon's Pets, a small retail shop selling pet supplies. On December 31, 2018, the accounting records for Dillon's Pets showed the following:

Merchandise Inventory on December 31, 2018	$ 10,500
Merchandise Inventory on January 1, 2018	16,000
Net Sales Revenue	56,000
Utilities Expense for the shop	3,200
Rent for the shop	4,100
Sales Commissions	2,750
Purchases of Merchandise Inventory	25,000

Requirements

1. Prepare an income statement for Dillon's Pets for the year ended December 31, 2018.

2. Dillon's Pets sold 5,550 units. Determine the unit cost of the merchandise sold, rounded to the nearest cent.

CRITICAL THINKING

> Using Excel

P16-41 Using Excel to classify manufacturing costs and to determine the cost of manufactured products.

Download an Excel template for this problem online in MyAccountingLab or at http://www.pearsonhighered.com/Horngren.

Fremont Troll House Cookies has been baking coconut cookies for 27 years. Classify manufacturing costs, and prepare schedules for the Cost of Goods Manufactured and the Cost of Goods Sold for the month ended March 31, 2018.

Requirements

1. Use Excel to classify the costs

   a. Classify the costs as either period costs or product costs.

      i. To classify the cost, click in the cell. A drop down arrow will appear to the right. Click the arrow and select either Product or Period.

   b. Classify the product costs as direct materials, direct labor, or manufacturing overhead.

      i. To identify the classification, click in the cell. A drop down arrow will appear to the right. Click the arrow. If it's a product cost, select direct materials, direct labor, or manufacturing overhead. If it's a period cost, select expense.

2. Complete the Schedule of Cost of Goods Manufactured. Use the blue shaded areas for inputs. Use the following amounts: direct materials used, $2,500; direct labor, $3,000; manufacturing overhead, $11,000; beginning Work-in-Process Inventory, $1,500; and ending Work-in-Process Inventory, $1,200.

   a. Complete the heading

   b. To select the correct report caption, click in the cell. A drop down arrow will appear to the right. Click the arrow and select the appropriate caption from the alphabetical list.

   c. Indent the captions for Direct Materials Used, Direct Labor, and Manufacturing Overhead. Use the Increase Indent button on the Home tab in the Alignment section.

d. Complete the amounts to the right. Use the Excel function SUM to sum amounts on the schedule.

e. Format the cells requiring dollar signs.

f. Format underlines or double underlines as needed.

g. Boldface the total.

3. Using the results from Requirement 2, calculate the cost per unit for goods manufactured assuming 16,000 units were manufactured. Use the blue shaded areas for inputs. Use a formula to calculate the cost per unit.

4. Complete the Cost of Goods Sold schedule. Beginning Finished Goods had 500 units that had a cost of $0.98 each. Ending Finished Goods Inventory had 700 units.

a. Complete the heading.

b. Using the results from Requirement 3, calculate cost of goods sold assuming FIFO inventory costing is used.

c. To select the correct report caption, click in the cell. A drop down arrow will appear to the right. Click the arrow and select the appropriate caption from the alphabetical list.

d. Complete the amounts to the right. Use the Excel function SUM to derive the Cost of Goods Sold.

e. Format the cells requiring dollar signs.

f. Format underlines or double underlines as needed.

g. Boldface the total.

> Continuing Problem

P16-42

This is the first problem in a sequence of problems for Piedmont Computer Company, a manufacturer of personal computers and tablets. During its first month of manufacturing, Piedmont Computer Company incurred the following manufacturing costs:

Balances:	Beginning	Ending
Direct Materials	$ 10,500	$ 9,700
Work-in-Process Inventory	0	17,000
Finished Goods Inventory	0	31,000

Other information:	
Direct materials purchases	$ 16,000
Plant janitorial services	500
Sales salaries expense	10,000
Delivery expense	1,600
Sales revenue	1,100,000
Utilities for plant	16,000
Rent on plant	9,000
Customer service hotline costs	19,000
Direct labor	210,000

Prepare a schedule of cost of goods manufactured for Piedmont Computer Company for the month ended January 31, 2020.

> Tying It All Together Case 16-1

Before you begin this assignment, review the Tying It All Together feature in the chapter.

Winnebago Industries, Inc. is a leading manufacturer of recreational vehicles (RVs), including motorized and towable products. The company designs, develops, manufactures, and markets RVs as well as supporting products and services. The RVs are sold to consumers through a dealer network. On the August 29, 2015, balance sheet, Winnebago reported inventory of approximately $112 million. Of this amount, approximately $12 million, about 11%, was Finished Goods Inventory (Notes to Consolidated Financial Statements, Note 3). Suppose Winnebago motor homes have an average sales price of $96,000 and cost of goods sold is 89% of sales. Thor Industries, Inc., a major competitor, has an average cost of goods sold of 86% of sales. For year ending August 29, 2015, Winnebago sold 9,097 motor homes (Form 10-K, Item 1 Business).

Requirements

1. Why would the Finished Goods Inventory be such a relatively small portion of total inventory?

2. What is the average cost of goods sold (in dollars) for a Winnebago motor home? What is the average gross profit?

3. If Winnebago could reduce production costs so that the average cost of goods sold is equal to their competitor's average cost of goods sold, how much more profit would Winnebago earn on each motor home sold?

4. Based on 2015 sales, how much would operating income increase if the company reduced the average cost of goods sold to equal their competitor's average cost of goods sold?

5. How could managers at Winnebago use managerial accounting to reduce costs and increase profits?

> Decision Case 16-1

Power Switch, Inc. designs and manufactures switches used in telecommunications. Serious flooding throughout North Carolina affected Power Switch's facilities. Inventory was completely ruined, and the company's computer system, including all accounting records, was destroyed.

Before the disaster recovery specialists clean the buildings, Stephen Plum, the company controller, is anxious to salvage whatever records he can to support an insurance claim for the destroyed inventory. He is standing in what is left of the accounting department with Paul Lopez, the cost accountant.

"I didn't know mud could smell so bad," Paul says. "What should I be looking for?"

"Don't worry about beginning inventory numbers," responds Stephen, "we'll get them from last year's annual report. We need first-quarter cost data."

"I was working on the first-quarter results just before the storm hit," Paul says. "Look, my report is still in my desk drawer. All I can make out is that for the first quarter, direct material purchases were $476,000 and direct labor, manufacturing overhead, and total manufacturing costs to account for were $505,000, $245,000, and $1,425,000, respectively. Wait! Cost of goods available for sale was $1,340,000."

"Great," says Stephen. "I remember that sales for the period were approximately $1,700,000. Given our gross profit of 30%, that's all you should need."

Paul is not sure about that but decides to see what he can do with this information. The beginning inventory numbers were:

- Direct Materials, $113,000
- Work-in-Process, $229,000
- Finished Goods, $154,000

Requirements

1. Prepare a schedule showing each inventory account and the increases and decreases to each account. Use it to determine the ending inventories of Direct Materials, Work-in-Process, and Finished Goods.

2. Itemize a list of the cost of inventory lost.

> Ethical Issue 16-1

Becky Knauer recently resigned from her position as controller for Shamalay Automotive, a small, struggling foreign car dealer in Upper Saddle River, New Jersey. Becky has just started a new job as controller for Mueller Imports, a much larger dealer for the same car manufacturer. Demand for this particular make of car is exploding, and the manufacturer cannot produce enough to satisfy demand. The manufacturer's regional sales managers are each given a certain number of cars. Each sales manager then decides how to divide the cars among the independently owned dealerships in the region. Because of high demand for these cars, dealerships all want to receive as many cars as they can from the regional sales manager.

Becky's former employer, Shamalay Automotive, receives only about 25 cars each month. Consequently, Shamalay is not very profitable.

Becky is surprised to learn that her new employer, Mueller Imports, receives more than 200 cars each month. Becky soon gets another surprise. Every couple of months, a local jeweler bills the dealer $5,000 for "miscellaneous services." Franz Mueller, the owner of the dealership, personally approves payment of these invoices, noting that each invoice is a "selling expense." From casual conversations with a salesperson, Becky learns that Mueller frequently gives Rolex watches to the manufacturer's regional sales manager and other sales executives. Before talking to anyone about this, Becky decides to work through her ethical dilemma. Put yourself in Becky's place.

Requirements

1. What is the ethical issue?
2. What are your options?
3. What are the possible consequences?
4. What should you do?

> Communication Activity 16-1

In 100 words or fewer, explain the difference between product costs and period costs. In your explanation, explain the inventory accounts of a manufacturer.

MyAccountingLab   **For a wealth of online resources, including exercises, problems, media, and immediate tutorial help, please visit** http://www.myaccountinglab.com.

> Quick Check Answers

1. a **2.** d **3.** d **4.** c **5.** c **6.** c **7.** b **8.** b **9.** b **10.** d

Job Order Costing

Why Are We Losing Clients?

Melinda Duncan is deep in thought. Melinda works for a regional construction firm. A major part of the business is bidding on new construction projects, and Melinda really enjoys the work. She thinks cost projections for new projects are like puzzles and finds it challenging to put the pieces together, making sure she has considered all likely costs the company will incur during construction. Recently, her firm has lost clients to a competitor that is charging lower prices. Melinda is considering the situation and has lots of questions. Does Melinda's company need to lower its prices to stay competitive? If the company drops its prices, will it remain profitable?

Melinda knows the amount charged for a construction project has to cover all the costs associated with the project. The largest costs are construction materials and labor costs. But the company has other costs that have to be covered, too—for example, the costs of maintaining the construction machinery and the salary paid to the construction foreman. Before the construction firm can make a decision about lowering the prices charged to clients, it must first determine an accurate cost of each construction project. How can the firm determine the full cost of a job? Construction firms can use a *job order costing system* to track the costs of each job and then use the information to make pricing decisions.

What Does It Really Cost?

All companies need to know the cost of their products and services. Major construction firms, such as **Granite Construction Incorporated**, track the costs associated with each construction project so that they can correctly bid on projects and charge the right sales price to its customers. The firm's history goes back to 1900 and the founding of its predecessor, Granite Rock Company. Some of the company's historical projects include building a road to the top of Yosemite National Park, part of Highway 66 through the Mojave Desert, and approximately 100 miles of the California Aqueduct. One of the original founders of the company, Walter J. Wilkinson, was known as a stickler for detail. His cost estimates were so detailed he included the cost of hay for the work horses.

How do companies like Granite Construction determine the costs of its projects? Some costs, such as direct costs, are easy to determine. The accountants can record hours worked on a job site to determine the direct labor costs and track the costs of the building materials delivered to the construction site. Other costs, such as the construction foreman's salary and construction equipment depreciation, are indirect costs that apply to multiple jobs and cannot be easily traced to a specific job. This chapter shows how manufacturing and service companies determine the cost of their products and services.

Chapter 17 Learning Objectives

1   Distinguish between job order costing and process costing

2   Record materials and labor costs in a job order costing system

3   Record actual and allocated overhead costs in a job order costing system

4   Record the completion and sales of finished goods

5   Adjust for overallocated and underallocated overhead

6   Calculate job costs for a service company

HOW DO MANUFACTURING COMPANIES USE JOB ORDER AND PROCESS COSTING SYSTEMS?

Learning Objective 1

Distinguish between job order costing and process costing

Cost Accounting System

An accounting system that measures, records, and reports product costs.

Cost accounting systems measure, record, and report product costs. They are used to *accumulate* product cost information so that managers can measure how much it costs to produce each unit of product. Knowing these unit costs helps managers do the following:

- Determine which products to produce.
- Set sales prices that will lead to profits.
- Determine how many products to produce.
- Compute cost of goods sold for the income statement.
- Compute the cost of inventory for the balance sheet.

Remember that a manager's primary duties include planning, directing, and controlling. If a manager knows the cost to manufacture each unit of product, then the manager can plan for and control the cost of resources needed to create the product and deliver it to the customer. The information from cost accounting systems helps managers make planning, directing, and controlling decisions. There are two main types of traditional cost accounting systems: job order costing and process costing. This chapter concentrates on job order costing; process costing is covered in the next chapter. But before we begin our study of job order costing, you need to understand the differences between the two systems.

Job Order Costing

Job Order Costing System

An accounting system that accumulates costs by job. Used by companies that manufacture unique products or provide specialized services.

Job

The production of a single unique product or specialized service, or a batch of unique products.

Some companies manufacture batches of *unique products* or provide *specialized services*. A job order costing system accumulates costs for each unique batch or job. A job may be a single unique product or specialized service, or a batch of unique products. An example of a job for a building contractor might be the construction of a custom house. An accounting firm might classify a job as preparing a tax return for a client. An example of a batch for a custom baker might be three dozen specialty cupcakes made for a wedding reception. Companies that manufacture unique products or provide specialized services—such as accounting firms, music studios, health care providers, building contractors, and custom furniture manufacturers—use job order costing systems. In job order costing, the goal is to keep track of the costs associated with the job.

Process Costing

Other companies produce identical units through a series of production steps or processes. A **process costing system** accumulates the costs of each process needed to complete the product over a period of time instead of assigning costs to specific jobs. For example, a soft drink company's processes may include mixing, bottling, and packaging. A surfboard manufacturing company's processes may include sanding, painting, waxing, and packaging. A medical equipment manufacturer of a blood glucose meter may have processes that include soldering, assembling, and testing. Process costing is used primarily by companies that produce large quantities of similar products.

Some companies may use both job order and process costing. For example, an RV manufacturing company might use process costing for its standard units but would use job order costing for custom-made orders. Both job order and process costing systems use a four-step method to track product costs: *accumulate, assign, allocate,* and *adjust*. Look for the four steps as we track the product costs through the inventory accounts on the balance sheet to Cost of Goods Sold on the income statement.

Process Costing System
An accounting system that accumulates costs by process. Used by companies that manufacture identical units through a series of uniform production steps or processes.

Would the following companies most likely use a job order costing system or a process costing system?

1. Paint manufacturer
2. Print shop
3. Caterer
4. Soft drink bottler
5. Yacht builder

Check your answers online in MyAccountingLab or at http://www.pearsonhighered.com/Horngren.

For more practice, see Short Exercise S17-1. MyAccountingLab

HOW DO MATERIALS AND LABOR COSTS FLOW THROUGH THE JOB ORDER COSTING SYSTEM?

A job order costing system tracks costs as raw materials move from the storeroom to the production floor, where they are converted into finished products. Let's consider how a manufacturer uses job order costing. To illustrate the process, we will use our fictitious company, Smart Touch Learning. Remember that Smart Touch Learning manufactures touch screen tablet computers that are preloaded with its e-learning software programs. Most customers order a batch of customized tablets, and the company considers each customer order as a separate job (batch). Smart Touch Learning uses a **job cost record** to document the product costs for each job: direct materials, direct labor, and manufacturing overhead. Exhibit 17-1 (on the next page) provides an example of a completed job cost record for Job 27.

Learning Objective 2
Record materials and labor costs in a job order costing system

Job Cost Record
A document that shows the direct materials, direct labor, and manufacturing overhead costs for an individual job.

Exhibit 17-1 | **Job Cost Record, Job 27, Completed**

JOB COST RECORD

STL SMART TOUCH LEARNING

Job Number 27
Customer Central College Bookstore
Job Description 15 tablets with accounting e-learning software

Direct Materials			Direct Labor			Manufacturing Overhead		
Date	Requisition Number	Amount	Date	Labor Time Record Number	Amount	Date	Rate	Amount
1/14	342	$ 825	1/15	236	$ 90	1/31	40% of DL Cost	$500
1/16	345	650	1/15	237	450			
1/25	352	1,275	1/31	252	710			

Cost Summary

Direct Materials	$ 2,750
Direct Labor	1,250
Manufacturing Overhead	500
Total Cost	$ 4,500
Unit Cost	$ 300

In a job order costing system, companies must accumulate costs and then assign costs to each job. Costs are accumulated when the company purchases raw materials, incurs direct labor, and incurs manufacturing overhead. The company starts the job cost record when work begins on the job. As Smart Touch Learning incurs costs, the company adds costs to the job cost record, and the costs are added to the Work-in-Process Inventory (WIP). When Smart Touch Learning finishes a job, the company totals the costs and transfers the costs from Work-in-Process Inventory to Finished Goods Inventory (FG). The costs transferred to Finished Goods Inventory are called *Cost of Goods Manufactured (COGM)*. When the job's units are sold, the costing system moves the costs from Finished Goods Inventory, an asset, to Cost of Goods Sold (COGS), an expense.

Exhibit 17-2 diagrams the flow of costs for three jobs (Job 27, Job 28, and Job 29) that were worked on during the accounting period at Smart Touch Learning. Smart Touch Learning worked on many jobs in addition to these three jobs during the year. In Exhibit 17-2, notice that Jobs 27 and 28 were completed and their costs were transferred from WIP to FG. Job 27 was delivered to the customer, so those costs were transferred from FG to COGS. Job 29 is the only job that is not complete and still in process. Job 28 is complete but not delivered to the customer and Job 27 is the only job completed and sold.

Exhibit 17-2 | **Flow of Product Costs in Job Order Costing**

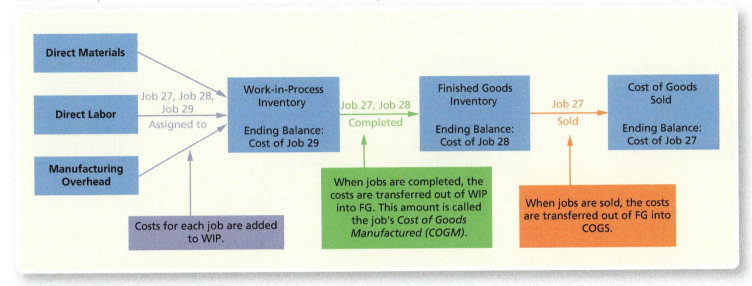

The next sections of the chapter show how Smart Touch Learning will record journal entries using job order costing. On December 31, 2019, Smart Touch Learning had the following inventory balances:

Raw Materials Inventory		Work-in-Process Inventory		Finished Goods Inventory	
Bal.	70,000	Bal.	80,000	Bal.	0

Materials

There are two aspects to accounting for raw materials: purchasing materials and using materials in production. Because raw materials do not have to be used immediately when purchased and can be stored for later use, materials purchased accumulate in the Raw Materials Inventory account until they are assigned to each job. Let's look at the recording of both activities: purchasing materials and using materials.

Purchasing Materials

Transaction 1—Materials Purchased: During 2020, Smart Touch Learning purchased raw materials of $367,000 on account. This is a product cost that *accumulates* in the Raw Materials Inventory account. To simplify the recording process, we are recording the materials purchases as a summary journal entry for the year, rather than showing each individual purchase. The purchase is recorded as follows:

Date	Accounts and Explanation	Debit	Credit
Trans. 1	Raw Materials Inventory	367,000	
	Accounts Payable		367,000

$$A\uparrow \atop RM\uparrow \Bigg\} = \Bigg\{ {L\uparrow \atop A/P\uparrow} + E$$

Raw Materials Inventory	
Bal.	70,000
Trans. 1	367,000

Raw Materials Inventory is a general ledger account. Smart Touch Learning also uses a subsidiary ledger for raw materials. A subsidiary ledger contains the details of a general ledger account, and the sum of the subsidiary ledger records equals the balance in the general ledger account.

The raw materials subsidiary ledger includes a separate record for each type of material, so there is a separate ledger account (or record) for the batteries, processors, cases, and other materials used in producing the tablets. The subsidiary ledger records show the raw materials purchased (received), used in production (issued), and balance on hand (balance) at all times. **The use of a subsidiary ledger allows for better control of inventory because it helps track each type of material used in production.** Exhibit 17-3 shows the subsidiary ledger of one type of battery that Smart Touch Learning uses. The balance of the Raw Materials Inventory account in the general ledger should always equal the sum of the balances in the raw materials subsidiary ledger.

> **Why would the company use a subsidiary ledger for raw materials?**

Exhibit 17-3 | Raw Materials Subsidiary Ledger

RAW MATERIALS SUBSIDIARY LEDGER

STL SMART TOUCH LEARNING

Item No. B-103   Description: STL Batteries

	Received			Issued				Balance		
Date	Units	Unit Cost	Total Cost	Mat. Req. No	Units	Unit Cost	Total Cost	Units	Unit Cost	Total Cost
2019										
12–05	200	$55	$11,000					200	$55	$11,000
12–10				334	50	$55	$2,750	150	$55	$ 8,250
2020										
1–14				342	15	$55	$825	135	$55	$ 7,425

Using Materials

Materials Used, Job 27: Smart Touch Learning started Job 27 in 2020. On January 14, the production team requested materials for the job. Exhibit 17-4 illustrates the **materials requisition** for batteries—the request to transfer raw materials to the production floor. Note that the subsidiary ledger in Exhibit 17-3 records the materials requisition number (342) along with the number of units requisitioned and their cost.

When the raw materials are issued to the production floor, the transfer is recorded in the raw materials subsidiary ledger, as shown in Exhibit 17-3. When they are received on the production floor, the direct materials are recorded on the job cost record. Exhibit 17-5 shows the job cost record for Job 27 after Materials Requisition 342 has been recorded.

Materials Requisition
A document that requests the transfer of raw materials to the production floor.

Exhibit 17-4 | Materials Requisition

MATERIALS REQUISITION #342

STL SMART TOUCH LEARNING

Date 1-14-20

Job Number 27

Requested by Hugh Patterson

Item	Quantity	Unit Cost	Total Cost
B-103 Batteries	15	$55	$825

Exhibit 17-5 | Job Cost Record—Direct Materials Recorded

JOB COST RECORD

STL SMART TOUCH LEARNING

Job Number   27

Customer   Central College Bookstore

Job Description   15 tablets with accounting e-learning software

Direct Materials			Direct Labor			Manufacturing Overhead		
Date	Requisition Number	Amount	Date	Labor Time Record Number	Amount	Date	Rate	Amount
1/14	342	$825						

Cost Summary
Direct Materials   _____
Direct Labor   _____
Manufacturing Overhead   _____
Total Cost   _____
Unit Cost   _____

The materials added to Job 27 from Materials Requisition 342 are considered *direct materials* because the batteries can be easily and cost-effectively traced directly to the finished product. The materials cost has been *assigned* to Job 27 which will result in a decrease on the raw materials subsidiary ledger and as an increase on the job cost record. However, Smart Touch Learning will not complete a journal entry at this time but will wait and record a summary journal entry at the end of the period for all materials used.

Transaction 2—Materials Used: Smart Touch Learning worked on many jobs during the year in addition to Job 27. In 2020, the company used materials costing $355,000, including batteries, processors, and cases. This amount includes the materials used in Job 27 as well as all other jobs the company worked on during the year. These materials can be easily traced to specific jobs and are all *direct materials*. The cost of direct materials is transferred out of Raw Materials Inventory and is *assigned* to Work-in-Process Inventory. The individual job cost records would indicate the amount of direct materials cost *assigned* to each job.

By contrast, the company used materials costing $17,000 that are difficult to trace to a specific job. These costs are *indirect materials*. The cost of indirect materials is transferred out of the Raw Materials Inventory account and is *accumulated* in the Manufacturing Overhead account. The following summary journal entry records the issuance of the raw materials used in production during the year:

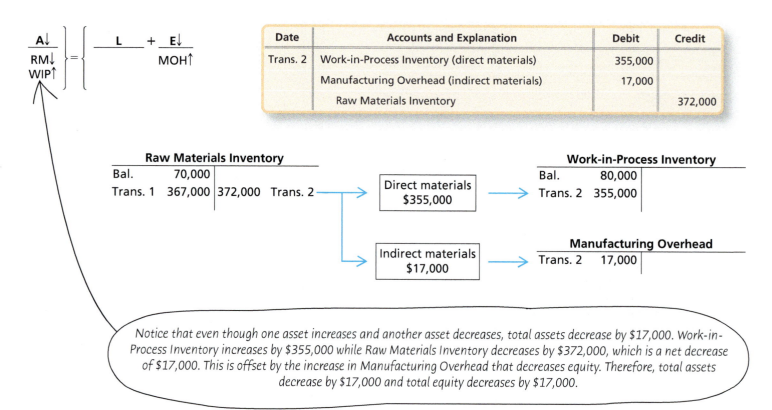

$$\frac{A\downarrow}{\begin{array}{c}RM\downarrow\\WIP\uparrow\end{array}} \Big\} = \Big\{ \frac{L \quad + \quad E\downarrow}{MOH\uparrow}$$

Date	Accounts and Explanation	Debit	Credit
Trans. 2	Work-in-Process Inventory (direct materials)	355,000	
	Manufacturing Overhead (indirect materials)	17,000	
	Raw Materials Inventory		372,000

Raw Materials Inventory

Bal.	70,000		
Trans. 1	367,000	372,000	Trans. 2

Direct materials $355,000

Work-in-Process Inventory

Bal.	80,000	
Trans. 2	355,000	

Indirect materials $17,000

Manufacturing Overhead

Trans. 2	17,000	

Notice that even though one asset increases and another asset decreases, total assets decrease by $17,000. Work-in-Process Inventory increases by $355,000 while Raw Materials Inventory decreases by $372,000, which is a net decrease of $17,000. This is offset by the increase in Manufacturing Overhead that decreases equity. Therefore, total assets decrease by $17,000 and total equity decreases by $17,000.

Manufacturing Overhead is a temporary account used to *accumulate* indirect production costs during the accounting period. Because it is a temporary account for accumulating costs, it is treated similar to an expense account and classified as an equity account. We will adjust Manufacturing Overhead later in the chapter.

For both direct materials and indirect materials, the production team completes materials requisitions to request the transfer of materials to the production floor. Because we showed a summary journal entry for these requisitions, we are not showing each document. Also, these requisitions are often in electronic form rather than on paper. Samples of these documents are shown for illustrative purposes only.

Labor

Direct Labor Incurred, Job 27: Most companies use electronic labor/time records to streamline the tracking of labor costs. Employees use ID cards to swipe and enter job information. The time is automatically added to the appropriate job cost record. If a manual system is used, each employee completes a **labor time record** that indicates the amount of time spent on each job. The labor time record for one assembly worker shows that one employee spent 5 hours on Job 27. The employee earns $18 per hour. The system then charged $90 to the job (5 hours × $18 per hour).

Labor Time Record
A record used to assign direct labor cost to specific jobs.

Exhibit 17-6 shows how Smart Touch Learning adds the direct labor cost to the job cost record for Job 27.

The employee's labor is considered direct labor, so the cost is *assigned* to the job. The cost is added to the job cost record. Smart Touch Learning will make summary journal entries for the labor costs each pay period.

Exhibit 17-6 | **Job Cost Record—Direct Labor Recorded**

JOB COST RECORD

Job Number 27
Customer Central College Bookstore
Job Description 15 tablets with accounting e-learning software

Direct Materials			Direct Labor			Manufacturing Overhead		
Date	Requisition Number	Amount	Date	Labor Time Record Number	Amount	Date	Rate	Amount
1/14	342	$825	1/15	236	$90			

Cost Summary
    Direct Materials   _____
    Direct Labor   _____
    Manufacturing Overhead   _____
Total Cost   _____
Unit Cost   _____

Transaction 3—Labor Costs Incurred: During 2020, Smart Touch Learning incurred total labor costs of $197,000, of which $169,000 was direct labor and $28,000 was indirect labor. These amounts include all the direct labor costs for Job 27 that we have been working with plus all the company's other jobs worked on during the year. Indirect labor is labor costs for employees working in the factory, but not directly on the products, including employees in supervision, maintenance, and janitorial positions.

The direct labor costs are *assigned* to individual jobs and recorded on the job cost records. The total direct labor amount is debited to Work-in-Process Inventory. The indirect labor costs are *accumulated* in Manufacturing Overhead. This is the same treatment as the direct and indirect materials illustrated in Transaction 2.

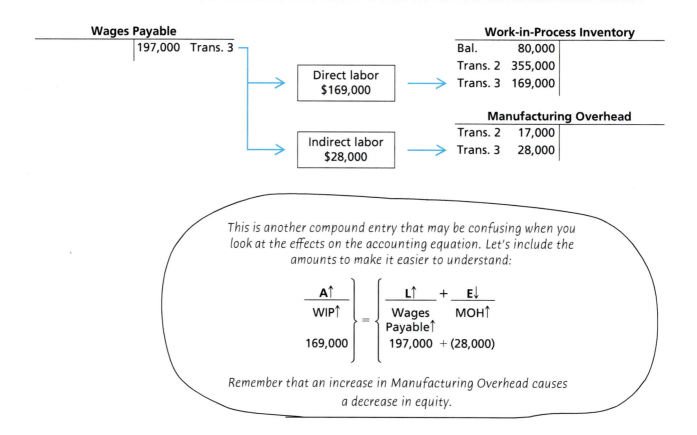

$$\frac{A\uparrow}{WIP\uparrow}\Bigg\}=\Bigg\{\frac{L\uparrow}{\substack{\text{Wages}\\\text{Payable}\uparrow}}+\frac{E\downarrow}{MOH\uparrow}$$

Date	Accounts and Explanation	Debit	Credit
Trans. 3	Work-in-Process Inventory (direct labor)	169,000	
	Manufacturing Overhead (indirect labor)	28,000	
	Wages Payable		197,000

Wages Payable

| | 197,000 | Trans. 3 |

Direct labor $169,000

Indirect labor $28,000

Work-in-Process Inventory

Bal.	80,000	
Trans. 2	355,000	
Trans. 3	169,000	

Manufacturing Overhead

| Trans. 2 | 17,000 | |
| Trans. 3 | 28,000 | |

This is another compound entry that may be confusing when you look at the effects on the accounting equation. Let's include the amounts to make it easier to understand:

$$\frac{A\uparrow}{\substack{WIP\uparrow\\169,000}}\Bigg\}=\Bigg\{\frac{L\uparrow}{\substack{\text{Wages}\\\text{Payable}\uparrow\\197,000}}+\frac{E\downarrow}{\substack{MOH\uparrow\\(28,000)}}$$

Remember that an increase in Manufacturing Overhead causes a decrease in equity.

We have now accounted for the direct and indirect materials costs and labor costs; it is time to take a closer look at additional indirect costs.

Try It!

Record the following journal entries for Smith Company:

6. Purchased raw materials on account, $10,000.
7. Used $6,000 in direct materials and $500 in indirect materials in production.
8. Incurred $8,000 in labor costs, of which 80% was direct labor.

Check your answers online in MyAccountingLab or at http://www.pearsonhighered.com/Horngren.

For more practice, see Short Exercises S17-2 through S17-4. MyAccountingLab

TYING IT ALL TOGETHER

Granite Construction Incorporated is one of the largest construction contractors in the United States. The company's jobs including providing construction services in the area of transportation, mining, tunnels, and oil and gas. A recent project for Granite Construction involved building the International Airport Terminal for the Dallas/Fort Worth airport.

Would Granite Construction Incorporated likely use a job order costing system or a process costing system?

Most likely Granite Construction Incorporated would use a job order costing system. Companies that manufacture unique products, such as building a new international airport terminal, would need to keep track of costs separately for each project. For example, Granite Construction will handle many different projects at the same time, but the costs associated with each project need to be separate from each other. Granite Construction would be less likely to use a process costing system. This type of cost accounting system is used when a company manufactures similar or identical units and there is no need to accumulate cost by jobs. Examples of companies that might use a process costing system include PepsiCo, Inc. and The Sherwin-Williams Company (a manufacturer of high-quality paint).

What would be examples of direct materials, direct labor, and manufacturing overhead costs that would be recorded in building an international airport terminal?

Direct materials would include the cost of steel and lumber used in the construction of the terminal. Direct labor would include the

cost of wages for the construction workers. Manufacturing overhead would include indirect materials such as the screws, glue, and nails used in the airport terminal. Manufacturing overhead also includes the cost of indirect labor, such as the construction foreman's salary, and depreciation on the equipment used at the job site.

When would raw materials associated with the building of an international airport terminal be assigned to the job?

Raw materials are assigned to the job when they are transferred from the Raw Materials Inventory storeroom or warehouse to the job site to be used in the construction of the airport terminal. When a company assigns the cost of raw materials to a job, the company would record a debit to Work-in-Process Inventory and a credit to Raw Materials Inventory.

When would direct labor associated with the building of an international airport terminal be assigned to the job?

Direct labor is assigned to the job when the labor is incurred. Employees will keep track of their time spent on each job and the costs will be recorded on the job cost record. The direct labor will be assigned to the Work-in-Process Inventory as a debit and Wages Payable will be credited.

HOW DO OVERHEAD COSTS FLOW THROUGH THE JOB ORDER COSTING SYSTEM?

Next we look at how overhead costs flow through the job order costing system.

Transactions 4–7—Actual Overhead Costs Incurred: All actual manufacturing overhead costs are *accumulated* as debits to a single general ledger account—Manufacturing Overhead. We have already *accumulated* the costs of indirect materials (Transaction 2, $17,000) and indirect labor (Transaction 3, $28,000) to Manufacturing Overhead. In addition to indirect materials and indirect labor, Smart Touch Learning also incurred the following overhead costs:

- Depreciation on manufacturing plant and equipment, $20,000
- Plant utilities paid now, $7,000
- Plant insurance previously paid, $6,000
- Plant property taxes incurred but not yet paid, $5,000

Transactions 4 through 7 record these manufacturing overhead costs. The actual manufacturing overhead costs are debited to Manufacturing Overhead as they occur throughout the year. By the end of the year, the Manufacturing Overhead account has *accumulated* all the actual overhead costs as debits.

Learning Objective 3

Record actual and allocated overhead costs in a job order costing system

$$\left. \underbrace{A\downarrow}_{\text{Accumulated Depreciation}\uparrow} \right\} = \left\{ \begin{array}{c} L + \underbrace{E\downarrow}_{\text{MOH}\uparrow} \end{array} \right.$$

$$\left. \underbrace{A\downarrow}_{\text{Cash}\downarrow} \right\} = \left\{ \begin{array}{c} L + \underbrace{E\downarrow}_{\text{MOH}\uparrow} \end{array} \right.$$

$$\left. \underbrace{A\downarrow}_{\text{Prepaid Insurance}\downarrow} \right\} = \left\{ \begin{array}{c} L + \underbrace{E\downarrow}_{\text{MOH}\uparrow} \end{array} \right.$$

$$\left. \underbrace{A}_{} \right\} = \left\{ \begin{array}{c} \underbrace{L\uparrow}_{\substack{\text{Property}\\\text{Taxes}\\\text{Payable}\uparrow}} + \underbrace{E\downarrow}_{\text{MOH}\uparrow} \end{array} \right.$$

Date	Accounts and Explanation	Debit	Credit
Trans. 4	Manufacturing Overhead	20,000	
	Accumulated Depreciation		20,000
Trans. 5	Manufacturing Overhead	7,000	
	Cash		7,000
Trans. 6	Manufacturing Overhead	6,000	
	Prepaid Insurance		6,000
Trans. 7	Manufacturing Overhead	5,000	
	Property Taxes Payable		5,000

Manufacturing Overhead

Trans. 2	17,000	
Trans. 3	28,000	
Trans. 4	20,000	
Trans. 5	7,000	
Trans. 6	6,000	
Trans. 7	5,000	
Bal.	83,000	

As you can see, overhead includes a variety of costs that the company cannot easily trace to individual jobs. For example, it is impossible to say how much of the cost of plant utilities is related to Job 27. Because manufacturing overhead cannot be easily traced to each job, companies treat manufacturing overhead differently than direct materials and direct labor. Companies such as Smart Touch Learning *allocate* overhead costs to specific jobs. The accounting for the *allocation* of overhead costs is a three-step process and occurs at three different points in the accounting cycle:

1. Calculating the predetermined overhead allocation rate before the period
2. Allocating overhead during the period
3. Adjusting overhead at the end of the period

Before the Period—Calculating the Predetermined Overhead Allocation Rate

The most accurate allocation can be made only when total overhead costs are known—and that is not until the end of the period. But managers cannot wait that long for product cost information because it is important that they have an understanding of how much each product is costing. So the **predetermined overhead allocation rate** is calculated before the period begins. Companies use this predetermined rate to allocate estimated overhead costs to individual jobs.

Predetermined Overhead Allocation Rate

Estimated overhead cost per unit of the allocation base, calculated at the beginning of the accounting period. Total estimated overhead costs / Total estimated quantity of the overhead allocation base.

$$\text{Predetermined overhead allocation rate} = \frac{\text{Total estimated overhead costs}}{\text{Total estimated quantity of the overhead allocation base}}$$

The predetermined overhead allocation rate is based on two factors:

- Total *estimated* overhead costs for the period (in Smart Touch Learning's case, one year)
- Total *estimated* quantity of the overhead allocation base

The key to *allocating* indirect manufacturing costs to jobs is to identify a workable manufacturing overhead allocation base. The **allocation base** is a denominator that links overhead costs to the products. Ideally, the allocation base is the primary cost driver of manufacturing overhead. As the phrase implies, a **cost driver** is the primary factor that causes (drives) a cost. For example, the cost of electricity to operate machinery increases with increased machine use. Therefore, the cost driver for electricity is the amount of machine usage, and the allocation base would be machine hours (the number of hours the machine runs). There is a relationship between the overhead cost and the allocation base; that is, the higher the quantity of the allocation base, the higher the overhead costs, and vice versa.

Traditionally, manufacturing companies have used the following as cost drivers:

- Direct labor hours (for labor-intensive production environments)
- Direct labor costs (for labor-intensive production environments)
- Machine hours (for machine-intensive production environments)

Smart Touch Learning uses only one allocation base, direct labor costs, to *allocate* manufacturing overhead to jobs. In later chapters, we will look at other ways to allocate overhead using different overhead allocation rates for each type of overhead activity. For right now, though, we will assume that Smart Touch Learning allocates manufacturing overhead using only direct labor costs.

At the end of 2019, Smart Touch Learning estimated that total overhead costs for 2020 would be $68,000 and direct labor costs would total $170,000. Using this information, we can compute the predetermined overhead allocation rate as follows:

> **Allocation Base**
> A denominator that links indirect costs to cost objects. Ideally, the allocation base is the primary cost driver of the indirect costs.

> **Cost Driver**
> The primary factor that causes a cost to increase or decrease.

$$\text{Predetermined overhead allocation rate} = \frac{\text{Total estimated overhead costs}}{\text{Total estimated quantity of the overhead allocation base}}$$

$$= \frac{\$68,000}{\$170,000} = 0.40 = 40\% \text{ of direct labor costs}$$

During the Period—Allocating Overhead

As we have seen, Smart Touch Learning assigns direct costs directly to each job. But how does the company *allocate* overhead costs to jobs? As jobs are completed in 2020, Smart Touch Learning will *allocate* overhead costs using the predetermined overhead allocation rate and assign 40% of each direct labor dollar incurred for the job as manufacturing overhead costs. Smart Touch Learning uses the same predetermined overhead rate to allocate manufacturing overhead to all jobs worked on throughout the year, including jobs still in process at the end of the accounting period. Let's use Job 27 as an example. The total direct labor cost for Job 27 is $1,250, and the predetermined overhead allocation rate is 40% of direct labor costs. Therefore, Smart Touch Learning *allocates* $500 ($1,250 × 0.40) of manufacturing overhead to Job 27. The $500 of overhead is recorded on the job cost record.

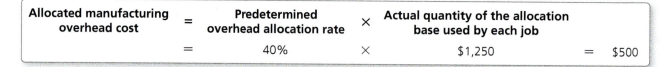

Allocated manufacturing overhead cost	=	Predetermined overhead allocation rate	×	Actual quantity of the allocation base used by each job		
	=	40%	×	$1,250	=	$500

Exhibit 17-7 shows the allocated manufacturing overhead costs of $500 on the job cost record. The Cost Summary section of the completed job cost record for the Central College Bookstore order shows that Job 27 cost Smart Touch Learning a total of $4,500, composed of $2,750 for direct materials, $1,250 for direct labor, and $500 of allocated manufacturing overhead. Job 27 produced 15 tablets, so Smart Touch Learning's cost per tablet is $300 ($4,500 / 15 tablets).

Cost of goods manufactured	/	Total units produced	=	Unit product cost
$4,500	/	15 tablets	=	$300 per tablet

Exhibit 17-7 | Job Cost Record, Job 27, Completed

JOB COST RECORD

STL SMART TOUCH LEARNING

Job Number   27
Customer   Central College Bookstore
Job Description   15 tablets with accounting e-learning software

Direct Materials			Direct Labor			Manufacturing Overhead		
Date	Requisition Number	Amount	Date	Labor Time Record Number	Amount	Date	Rate	Amount
1/14	342	$ 825	1/15	236	$ 90	1/31	40% of DL Cost	$500
1/16	345	650	1/15	237	450			
1/25	352	1,275	1/31	252	710			

Cost Summary

Direct Materials	$ 2,750
Direct Labor	1,250
Manufacturing Overhead	500
Total Cost	$ 4,500
Unit Cost	$ 300

Transaction 8—Overhead Allocation: Smart Touch Learning worked on many jobs, including Job 27, during 2020. The company allocated manufacturing overhead to each of these jobs, including jobs still in process at the end of 2020. Smart Touch Learning's total direct labor costs for 2020 were $169,000, so total overhead allocated to all jobs is 40% of

the $169,000 direct labor costs, or $67,600. The journal entry to allocate manufacturing overhead cost to Work-in-Process Inventory increases Work-in-Process Inventory and decreases Manufacturing Overhead as follows:

Date	Accounts and Explanation	Debit	Credit
Trans. 8	Work-in-Process Inventory	67,600	
	Manufacturing Overhead		67,600

$$\left.\frac{A\uparrow}{WIP\uparrow}\right\} = \left\{\frac{L \quad + \quad E\uparrow}{MOH\downarrow}\right.$$

Manufacturing Overhead

Trans. 2	17,000	67,600	Trans. 8
Trans. 3	28,000		
Trans. 4	20,000		
Trans. 5	7,000		
Trans. 6	6,000		
Trans. 7	5,000		
Bal.	15,400		

Overhead Allocated

Work-in-Process Inventory

Bal.	80,000
Trans. 2	355,000
Trans. 3	169,000
Trans. 8	67,600

Before moving on, take a moment to review the manufacturing overhead T-account and note the following:

- manufacturing overhead is debited (increased) for *actual* overhead costs.
- manufacturing overhead is credited (decreased) for *allocated* overhead costs.

Try It!

Smith Company expected to incur $10,000 in manufacturing overhead costs and use 4,000 machine hours for the year. Actual manufacturing overhead was $9,700, and the company used 4,250 machine hours.

9. Calculate the predetermined overhead allocation rate using machine hours as the allocation base.
10. How much manufacturing overhead was allocated during the year?

Check your answers online in MyAccountingLab or at http://www.pearsonhighered.com/Horngren.

For more practice, see Short Exercises S17-5 through S17-7. MyAccountingLab

WHAT HAPPENS WHEN PRODUCTS ARE COMPLETED AND SOLD?

Now you know how to *accumulate, assign,* and *allocate* the cost of direct materials, direct labor, and overhead to jobs. To complete the process, we must do the following:

- Account for the completion of jobs.
- Account for the sale of jobs.
- Adjust Manufacturing Overhead at the end of the period.

Learning Objective 4

Record the completion and sales of finished goods

Transferring Costs to Finished Goods Inventory

When a job is completed, the costs must be transferred from the Work-in-Process Inventory account to the Finished Goods Inventory account.

Transaction 9—Jobs Completed: Assume Smart Touch Learning completed jobs that cost $644,600 during 2020. This represents the completion of Job 27, Job 28, and additional jobs that were completed throughout the year. Normally, this entry would be made as each individual job is completed, but we are showing it as one summary journal entry. The amount is transferred from Work-in-Process Inventory to Finished Goods Inventory as jobs are completed and moved into the finished goods storage area. Smart Touch Learning records goods completed in 2020 as follows:

$$\left.\begin{array}{c} A\uparrow\downarrow \\ \hline FG\uparrow \\ WIP\downarrow \end{array}\right\} = \left\{\begin{array}{c} \underline{\quad L \quad} + \underline{\quad E \quad} \end{array}\right.$$

Date	Accounts and Explanation	Debit	Credit
Trans. 9	Finished Goods Inventory	644,600	
	Work-in-Process Inventory		644,600

Transferring Costs to Cost of Goods Sold

Transactions 10 and 11—Jobs Sold: As the tablets are sold on account, Smart Touch Learning will need to record the Sales Revenue and associated Cost of Goods Sold. This represents the sale of Job 27 and additional jobs that were sold throughout the year. Assume Smart Touch Learning sells jobs with a sales price of $1,200,000 and a cost of $584,600. Smart Touch Learning will record two entries, one for the sale and the other to recognize the Cost of Goods Sold.

$$\left.\begin{array}{c} A\uparrow \\ \hline A/R\uparrow \end{array}\right\} = \left\{\begin{array}{c} \underline{\quad L \quad} + \underline{\quad E\uparrow \quad} \\ Sales \\ Revenue\uparrow \end{array}\right.$$

$$\left.\begin{array}{c} A\downarrow \\ \hline FG\downarrow \end{array}\right\} = \left\{\begin{array}{c} \underline{\quad L \quad} + \underline{\quad E\downarrow \quad} \\ COGS\uparrow \end{array}\right.$$

Date	Accounts and Explanation	Debit	Credit
Trans. 10	Accounts Receivable	1,200,000	
	Sales Revenue		1,200,000
Trans. 11	Cost of Goods Sold	584,600	
	Finished Goods Inventory		584,600

The T-accounts for Smart Touch Learning's manufacturing costs now show:

BALANCE SHEET

Work-in-Process Inventory				Finished Goods Inventory				Cost of Goods Sold	
Costs Incurred	COGM			COGM	COGS			COGS	
Bal. 80,000	644,600 Trans. 9			Bal. 0				Trans. 11 584,600	
Trans. 2 355,000				Trans. 9 644,600	584,600 Trans. 11				
Trans. 3 169,000				Bal. 60,000					
Trans. 8 67,600									
Bal. 27,000									

INCOME STATEMENT

As jobs are completed, their costs are transferred to Finished Goods Inventory. We end the period with other jobs started but not finished, which are represented by the $27,000 ending balance of Work-in-Process Inventory. We also have jobs completed and not sold, which are represented by the $60,000 ending balance of Finished Goods Inventory.

> Remembering the journal entries is easier if you concentrate on the account you are transferring the costs into. The transfer is always to either an asset account or an expense account. Both account types are increased by debits, so the Transfer *To* account is Debited. Therefore, the Transfer *From* account is Credited.

Try It!

The following information pertains to Smith Company, which you worked with previously in this chapter:

11. Smith Company completed jobs that cost $25,000 to manufacture. Record the journal entry.
12. Smith Company sold jobs to customers on account for $52,000 that cost $22,000 to manufacture. Record the journal entries.

Check your answers online in MyAccountingLab or at http://www.pearsonhighered.com/Horngren.

For more practice, see Short Exercise S17-8. MyAccountingLab

HOW IS THE MANUFACTURING OVERHEAD ACCOUNT ADJUSTED?

The last step of recording costs in a job order costing system is to *adjust* the Manufacturing Overhead account for the amount of overallocated or underallocated overhead.

At the End of the Period—Adjusting for Overallocated and Underallocated Overhead

After *allocating* manufacturing overhead to jobs for 2020, a $15,400 debit balance remains in the Manufacturing Overhead account. This means that Smart Touch Learning's actual overhead costs of $83,000 were greater than the overhead allocated to jobs in Work-in-Process Inventory of $67,600. We say that Smart Touch Learning's Manufacturing Overhead is *underallocated*. **Underallocated overhead** occurs when the actual manufacturing overhead costs are more than allocated manufacturing overhead costs because the company allocated less costs to jobs than actual costs incurred. **Overallocated overhead**, on the other hand, occurs when the actual manufacturing overhead costs are less than allocated manufacturing overhead costs.

Recall that Manufacturing Overhead is a temporary account used to *accumulate* indirect production costs during the accounting period. At the end of the accounting year, the Manufacturing Overhead account must have a zero balance. Therefore, an adjustment is required if overhead is underallocated or overallocated at the end of the period.

Transaction 12—Adjust Manufacturing Overhead: During the year, the Manufacturing Overhead account is debited for actual overhead costs incurred and credited for overhead costs allocated to jobs.

Learning Objective 5
Adjust for overallocated and underallocated overhead

Underallocated Overhead
Occurs when the actual manufacturing overhead costs are more than allocated manufacturing overhead costs.

Overallocated Overhead
Occurs when the actual manufacturing overhead costs are less than allocated manufacturing overhead costs.

	Manufacturing Overhead	
Total Actual Costs →	83,000	67,600	← Total Allocated Costs
Unadj. Bal.	15,400	

Why does the Manufacturing Overhead account have a balance after allocating manufacturing overhead to jobs?

The total debits to the Manufacturing Overhead account rarely equal the total credits. Why? **Because companies allocate overhead to jobs using a *predetermined* overhead allocation rate that is based on *estimates*.** The predetermined overhead allocation rate represents the *expected* relationship between overhead costs and the allocation base. In our example, the $15,400 debit balance of Manufacturing Overhead represents underallocated overhead because the manufacturing overhead allocated to Work-in-Process Inventory was *less* than the actual overhead cost. If it had been overallocated overhead instead, the Manufacturing Overhead account would have had a credit balance.

Accountants *adjust* for underallocated and overallocated overhead at the end of the period when closing the Manufacturing Overhead account. Closing the account means zeroing it out. So, when overhead is underallocated, as in our example, a credit to Manufacturing Overhead of $15,400 is needed to bring the account balance to zero. What account should we debit? The underallocated overhead indicates that Smart Touch Learning *undercosted* jobs by $15,400 during the year. The costs flowed through Work-in-Process Inventory and Finished Goods Inventory and ultimately were transferred to Cost of Goods Sold. Therefore, the *adjustment* should increase Cost of Goods Sold. Cost of Goods Sold is an expense account, so it is increased with a debit:

$$A = \left\{ \begin{array}{l} L + E\uparrow\downarrow \\ \text{COGS}\uparrow \\ \text{MOH}\downarrow \end{array} \right.$$

Date	Accounts and Explanation	Debit	Credit
Trans. 12	Cost of Goods Sold	15,400	
	Manufacturing Overhead		15,400

Manufacturing Overhead

Trans. 2	17,000	67,600	Trans. 8
Trans. 3	28,000		
Trans. 4	20,000		
Trans. 5	7,000		
Trans. 6	6,000		
Trans. 7	5,000		
Unadj. Bal.	15,400		
		15,400	Trans. 12
Adj. Bal.	0		

Cost of Goods Sold

Trans. 11	584,600	
Trans. 12	15,400	
Adj. Bal.	600,000	

The Manufacturing Overhead account balance is now zero, and the Cost of Goods Sold account reflects the actual cost of producing the product.

If the manufacturing overhead account was instead overallocated, the jobs would be *overcosted*. The adjustment should then decrease Cost of Goods Sold. The company would record an adjustment that debits Manufacturing Overhead and credits Cost of Goods Sold.

Exhibit 17-8 summarizes the accounting for Manufacturing Overhead.

Exhibit 17-8 | **Accounting for Manufacturing Overhead**

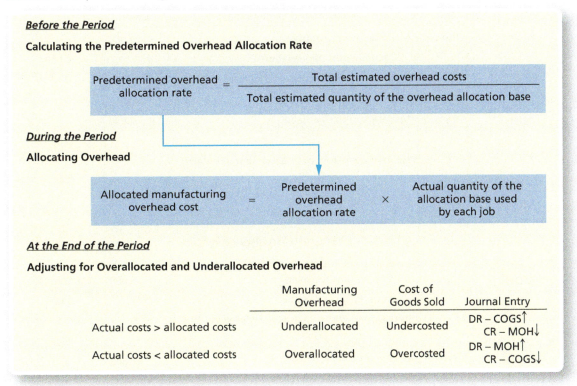

Summary of Journal Entries

As costs flow through the job order costing system, we go through a four-step process to *accumulate, assign, allocate,* and *adjust.* Exhibit 17-9 is a list of all journal entries illustrated in the chapter with notations on the four steps.

Exhibit 17-9 | **Summary of Journal Entries**

Date	Accounts and Explanation	Debit	Credit
Trans. 1	Raw Materials Inventory	367,000	
	Accounts Payable		367,000
	Purchased materials, **accumulated** *in RM.*		
Trans. 2	Work-in-Process Inventory	355,000	
	Manufacturing Overhead	17,000	
	Raw Materials Inventory		372,000
	Used materials, direct materials **assigned** *to WIP, indirect materials* **accumulated** *in MOH.*		
Trans. 3	Work-in-Process Inventory	169,000	
	Manufacturing Overhead	28,000	
	Wages Payable		197,000
	Incurred labor, direct labor **assigned** *to WIP, indirect labor* **accumulated** *in MOH.*		

$$A\uparrow \left\}\right. = \left\{\right. \quad L\uparrow + E$$
$$RM\uparrow \qquad A/P\uparrow$$

$$A\downarrow \left\}\right. = \left\{\right. \quad L + E\downarrow$$
$$RM\downarrow \qquad\qquad MOH\uparrow$$
$$WIP\uparrow$$

$$A\uparrow \left\}\right. = \left\{\right. \quad L\uparrow + E\downarrow$$
$$WIP\uparrow \qquad \text{Wages} \quad MOH\uparrow$$
$$\text{Payable}\uparrow$$

(Exhibit continued on next page.)

Exhibit 17-9 | **Continued**

$$\dfrac{A\downarrow}{\text{Accumulated}\atop\text{Depreciation}\uparrow}\Bigr\}=\Bigl\{\dfrac{L}{}+\dfrac{E\downarrow}{\text{MOH}\uparrow}$$

$$\dfrac{A\downarrow}{\text{Cash}\downarrow}\Bigr\}=\Bigl\{\dfrac{L}{}+\dfrac{E\downarrow}{\text{MOH}\uparrow}$$

$$\dfrac{A\downarrow}{\text{Prepaid}\atop\text{Insurance}\downarrow}\Bigr\}=\Bigl\{\dfrac{L}{}+\dfrac{E\downarrow}{\text{MOH}\uparrow}$$

$$\dfrac{A}{}\Bigr\}=\Bigl\{\dfrac{L\uparrow}{\text{Property}\atop\text{Taxes}\atop\text{Payable}\uparrow}+\dfrac{E\downarrow}{\text{MOH}\uparrow}$$

$$\dfrac{A\uparrow}{\text{WIP}\uparrow}\Bigr\}=\Bigl\{\dfrac{L}{}+\dfrac{E\uparrow}{\text{MOH}\downarrow}$$

$$\dfrac{A\uparrow\downarrow}{\text{FG}\uparrow\atop\text{WIP}\downarrow}\Bigr\}=\Bigl\{\dfrac{L}{}+\dfrac{E}{}$$

$$\dfrac{A\uparrow}{\text{A/R}\uparrow}\Bigr\}=\Bigl\{\dfrac{L}{}+\dfrac{E\uparrow}{\text{Sales}\atop\text{Revenue}\uparrow}$$

$$\dfrac{A\downarrow}{\text{FG}\downarrow}\Bigr\}=\Bigl\{\dfrac{L}{}+\dfrac{E\downarrow}{\text{COGS}\uparrow}$$

$$\dfrac{A}{}\Bigr\}=\Bigl\{\dfrac{L}{}+\dfrac{E\uparrow\downarrow}{\text{COGS}\uparrow\atop\text{MOH}\downarrow}$$

Date	Accounts and Explanation	Debit	Credit
Trans. 4	Manufacturing Overhead	20,000	
	Accumulated Depreciation		20,000
	*Incurred overhead, costs **accumulated** in MOH.*		
Trans. 5	Manufacturing Overhead	7,000	
	Cash		7,000
	*Incurred overhead, costs **accumulated** in MOH.*		
Trans. 6	Manufacturing Overhead	6,000	
	Prepaid Insurance		6,000
	*Incurred overhead, costs **accumulated** in MOH.*		
Trans. 7	Manufacturing Overhead	5,000	
	Property Taxes Payable		5,000
	*Incurred overhead, costs **accumulated** in MOH.*		
Trans. 8	Work-in-Process Inventory	67,600	
	Manufacturing Overhead		67,600
	***Allocated** overhead to WIP.*		
Trans. 9	Finished Goods Inventory	644,600	
	Work-in-Process Inventory		644,600
	*Completed jobs, costs **assigned** to FG.*		
Trans. 10	Accounts Receivable	1,200,000	
	Sales Revenue		1,200,000
	Sold jobs, entry reflects sales price, not costs.		
Trans. 11	Cost of Goods Sold	584,600	
	Finished Goods Inventory		584,600
	*Sold jobs, costs **assigned** to COGS.*		
Trans. 12	Cost of Goods Sold	15,400	
	Manufacturing Overhead		15,400
	***Adjusted** MOH for underallocated overhead.*		

(Exhibit continued on next page.)

Exhibit 17-9 | **Continued**

Raw Materials Inventory			
Beg. Bal.	70,000		
Trans. 1	367,000	372,000	Trans. 2
End. Bal.	65,000		

Work-in-Process Inventory			
Beg. Bal.	80,000		
Trans. 2	355,000	644,600	Trans. 9
Trans. 3	169,000		
Trans. 8	67,600		
End. Bal.	27,000		

Finished Goods Inventory			
Beg. Bal.	0		
Trans. 9	644,600	584,600	Trans. 11
End. Bal.	60,000		

Manufacturing Overhead			
Trans. 2	17,000	67,600	Trans. 8
Trans. 3	28,000		
Trans. 4	20,000		
Trans. 5	7,000		
Trans. 6	6,000		
Trans. 7	5,000		
Unadj. Bal.	15,400		
		15,400	Trans. 12
Adj. Bal.	0		

Cost of Goods Sold		
Trans. 11	584,600	
Trans. 12	15,400	
Adj. Bal.	600,000	

Cost of Goods Manufactured and Cost of Goods Sold

At the end of the accounting period, Smart Touch Learning will prepare financial statements that show the costs for all jobs manufactured and sold. Exhibit 17-10 shows the schedule of cost of goods manufactured for Smart Touch Learning for 2020. Notice that in calculating the cost of goods manufactured, Smart Touch Learning uses manufacturing overhead allocated instead of actual manufacturing costs. This is because the allocated manufacturing overhead costs are used when determining the cost of work-in-process.

Exhibit 17-10 | **Schedule of Cost of Goods Manufactured**

SMART TOUCH LEARNING
Schedule of Cost of Goods Manufactured
Year Ended December 31, 2020

Beginning Work-in-Process Inventory		$ 80,000
Direct Materials Used	$ 355,000	
Direct Labor	169,000	
Manufacturing Overhead Allocated	67,600	
Total Manufacturing Costs Incurred during the Year		591,600
Total Manufacturing Costs to Account for		671,600
Ending Work-in-Process Inventory		(27,000)
Cost of Goods Manufactured		$ 644,600

Exhibit 17-11 (on the next page) shows the income statement for the same period. Notice on the income statement that the underallocated overhead is added in the cost of goods sold calculation so that the cost of goods sold on the income statement matches the amount in the T-account. If overhead had been overallocated, the adjustment amount would have been subtracted.

Exhibit 17-11 | **Income Statement**

SMART TOUCH LEARNING Income Statement Year Ended December 31, 2020		
Net Sales Revenue		$ 1,000,000
Cost of Goods Sold:		
Beginning Finished Goods Inventory	$ 0	
Cost of Goods Manufactured	644,600	
Cost of Goods Available for Sale	644,600	
Ending Finished Goods Inventory	(60,000)	
Cost of Goods Sold Before Adjustment	584,600	
Adjustment for Underallocated Overhead	15,400	
Cost of Goods Sold		600,000
Gross Profit		400,000
Selling and Administrative Expenses:		
Wages Expense	120,000	
Rent Expense	100,000	
Insurance Expense	10,000	
Depreciation Expense	6,000	
Supplies Expense	5,000	
Total Selling and Administrative Expenses		241,000
Operating Income		159,000
Other Income and (Expenses):		
Interest Expense		(7,600)
Income Before Income Tax Expense		151,400
Income Tax Expense		53,000
Net Income		$ 98,400

Try It!

The following information pertains to Smith Company for the year:

Estimated manufacturing overhead	$ 500,000	Actual manufacturing overhead	$ 550,000
Estimated direct labor hours	10,000 hours	Actual direct labor hours	10,500 hours

13. Calculate the predetermined overhead allocation rate using direct labor hours as the allocation base.
14. Determine the amount of overhead allocated during the year. Record the journal entry.
15. Determine the amount of underallocated or overallocated overhead. Record the journal entry to adjust Manufacturing Overhead.

Check your answers online in MyAccountingLab or at http://www.pearsonhighered.com/Horngren.

For more practice, see Short Exercises S17-9 through S17-12. MyAccountingLab

HOW DO SERVICE COMPANIES USE A JOB ORDER COSTING SYSTEM?

Learning Objective 6

Calculate job costs for a service company

As we have seen, service firms have no inventory. These firms incur only noninventoriable costs. But their managers still need to know the costs of different jobs in order to set prices for their services. We will use a law firm to illustrate how service firms *assign* and *allocate* costs to jobs.

The law firm of Walsh Associates considers each client a separate job. Walsh's most significant cost is direct labor—attorney time spent on clients' cases. How do service firms trace direct labor to individual jobs?

Walsh's employees fill out a weekly electronic labor time record and the software totals the amount of time spent on each job. For example, attorney Lois Fox's electronic time record shows that she devoted 14 hours to Client 367 and 26 hours to other clients during the week of June 10, 2018.

Fox's salary and benefits total $100,000 per year. Assuming a 40-hour workweek and 50 workweeks in each year (which allows for a standard two-week vacation), Fox has 2,000 available work hours per year (50 weeks × 40 hours per week). Fox's hourly pay rate is as follows:

$$\text{Hourly rate to the employer} = \frac{\$100,000 \text{ per year}}{2,000 \text{ hours per year}} = \$50 \text{ per hour}$$

Fox worked 14 hours for Client 367, so the direct labor cost *assigned* to Client 367 is 14 hours × $50 per hour = $700. This direct labor cost would be recorded on the job cost record for Client 367.

Founding partner Jacob Walsh wants to know the total cost of serving each client, not just the direct labor cost. Walsh Associates also *allocates* indirect costs to individual jobs (clients). The law firm develops a predetermined overhead allocation rate, following the same approach that Smart Touch Learning used. In December 2017, Walsh estimates that the following indirect costs will be incurred in 2018:

Office rent	$ 200,000
Office support staff	70,000
Maintaining and updating law library for case research	25,000
Advertisements	3,000
Office supplies used	2,000
Total indirect costs	$ 300,000

Walsh uses direct labor hours as the allocation base because direct labor hours are the main driver of indirect costs. He estimates that Walsh attorneys will work 10,000 direct labor hours in 2018.

Step 1: Compute the predetermined overhead allocation rate.

$$\text{Predetermined overhead allocation rate} = \frac{\$300,000 \text{ estimated indirect costs}}{10,000 \text{ estimated direct labor hours}}$$
$$= \$30 \text{ per direct labor hour}$$

Step 2: Allocate indirect costs to jobs by multiplying the predetermined overhead allocation rate (Step 1) by the actual quantity of the allocation base used by each job. Client 367, for example, required 14 direct labor hours of Fox's time, so the indirect costs are allocated as follows:

$$14 \text{ direct labor hours} \times \$30 \text{ per hour} = \$420$$

To summarize, the total costs *assigned* and *allocated* to Client 367 are as follows:

Direct labor: 14 hours × $50 per hour	$ 700
Indirect costs: 14 hours × $30 per hour	420
Total costs	$ 1,120

As you can see from the above example, just like a manufacturing company, a service company can use a job order cost system to *assign* direct costs and *allocate* indirect costs to jobs.

Now that the service company has a good estimate for total job costs, it is better prepared to make pricing decisions. The total hourly rate for the company is $80, which is $50 per hour for direct labor plus $30 per hour for indirect costs. The firm can use cost-plus pricing to set the rate charged to clients. For example, if the firm desires a profit equal to 75% of the firm's cost, then the price would be calculated as follows:

> Markup = Total cost × Markup percentage
> = $80 per hour × 75% = $60 per hour
>
> Price = Total cost + Markup
> = $80 per hour + $60 per hour = $140 per hour

Based on the above calculations, the firm should charge clients $140 per hour.

DECISIONS

What should the company charge?

Refer to the information for the service company example, Walsh Associates. Assume Jacob Walsh desires a profit equal to 50% of the firm's cost. Should Walsh consider only the direct costs when making pricing decisions? How much should the firm bill Client 367?

Solution

Walsh should consider more than just the direct labor costs when determining the amount to charge his clients. Client 367 incurred $700 in direct costs. At a 50% markup, Walsh would add $350 ($700 × 50%) and charge the client $1,050 ($700 + $350). That means Walsh would not cover the full cost of providing service to the client. The loss on the job would be $70 ($1,050 − $1,120). He left out the indirect costs. The markup should be 50% of the total cost, $560 ($1,120 × 50%). The amount charged to the client would be $1,680, which would generate a profit of $560 ($1,680 − $1,120).

Try It!

Wesson Company is a consulting firm. The firm expects to have $45,000 in indirect costs during the year and bill customers for 6,000 hours. The cost of direct labor is $75 per hour.

16. Calculate the predetermined overhead allocation rate for Wesson using estimated billable hours for the allocation base.
17. Wesson completed a consulting job for George Peterson and billed the customer for 15 hours. What was the total cost of the consulting job?
18. If Wesson wants to earn a profit equal to 60% of the cost of a job, how much should the company charge Mr. Peterson?

Check your answers online in MyAccountingLab or at http://www.pearsonhighered.com/Horngren.

For more practice, see Short Exercises S17-13 and S17-14. MyAccountingLab

REVIEW

> Things You Should Know

1. **How do manufacturing companies use job order and process costing systems?**

   ▪ All businesses need to know the cost of their products or services.

   ▪ Job order costing accumulates costs by jobs and is used by companies that manufacture unique products or provide specialized services.

   ▪ Process costing accumulates costs by processes and is used by companies that produce identical units through a series of uniform processes.

2. **How do materials and labor costs flow through the job order costing system?**

   ▪ Purchases of materials on account *accumulate* the cost into the Raw Materials Inventory account, which is an increase.

Date	Accounts and Explanation	Debit	Credit
	Raw Materials Inventory	XXX	
	Accounts Payable		XXX

   ▪ The use of materials decreases Raw Materials Inventory. The use of direct materials are *assigned* to Work-in-Process Inventory, which is an increase. The use of indirect materials are *accumulated* in Manufacturing Overhead, which is also an increase.

Date	Accounts and Explanation	Debit	Credit
	Work-in-Process Inventory	XXX	
	Manufacturing Overhead	XXX	
	Raw Materials Inventory		XXX

   ▪ Labor incurred increases Wages Payable. Direct labor is *assigned* to Work-in-Process Inventory, which is an increase. Indirect labor is *accumulated* in Manufacturing Overhead, which is also an increase.

Date	Accounts and Explanation	Debit	Credit
	Work-in-Process Inventory	XXX	
	Manufacturing Overhead	XXX	
	Wages Payable		XXX

3. **How do overhead costs flow through the job order costing system?**

   ▪ Before the period: Calculate the predetermined overhead allocation rate.
   - Predetermined overhead allocation rate = Total estimated overhead costs / Total estimated quantity of the overhead allocation base
   ▪ During the period: Use the predetermined overhead allocation rate to allocate overhead to jobs.
   - Allocated manufacturing overhead cost = Predetermined overhead allocation rate × Actual quantity of the allocation base used for each job

■ Manufacturing overhead is *allocated* to the Work-in-Process Inventory account using the predetermined overhead allocation rate.

Date	Accounts and Explanation	Debit	Credit
	Work-in-Process Inventory	XXX	
	Manufacturing Overhead		XXX

4. What happens when products are completed and sold?

■ The cost of completed jobs is *assigned* to Finished Goods Inventory by transferring the cost from Work-in-Process Inventory to Finished Goods Inventory.

Date	Accounts and Explanation	Debit	Credit
	Finished Goods Inventory	XXX	
	Work-in-Process Inventory		XXX

■ Jobs are sold on account.

Date	Accounts and Explanation	Debit	Credit
	Accounts Receivable	XXX	
	Sales Revenue		XXX

■ The cost of sold jobs is *assigned* to Cost of Goods Sold by transferring the cost from Finished Goods Inventory to Cost of Goods Sold.

Date	Accounts and Explanation	Debit	Credit
	Cost of Goods Sold	XXX	
	Finished Goods Inventory		XXX

■ The transfer from Finished Goods Inventory to Cost of Goods Sold moves the product costs from the balance sheet to the income statement.

5. How is the manufacturing overhead account adjusted?

■ At the end of the period: *Adjust* Manufacturing Overhead for any underallocated or overallocated overhead.

• If actual costs > allocated costs, overhead is underallocated

Date	Accounts and Explanation	Debit	Credit
	Cost of Goods Sold	XXX	
	Manufacturing Overhead		XXX

• If actual costs < allocated costs, overhead is overallocated

Date	Accounts and Explanation	Debit	Credit
	Manufacturing Overhead	XXX	
	Cost of Goods Sold		XXX

6. **How do service companies use a job order costing system?**

   - Service companies also have direct and indirect costs associated with providing the service.
   - Direct costs are *assigned* to jobs.
   - Indirect costs are *allocated* to jobs using the predetermined overhead allocation rate.
   - Knowing the full cost of the job allows for better pricing decisions.

> Check Your Understanding

Check your understanding of the chapter by completing this problem and then looking at the solution. Use this practice to help identify which sections of the chapter you need to study more.

Skippy Scooters manufactures motor scooters. The company has automated production, so it allocates manufacturing overhead based on machine hours. Skippy expects to incur $240,000 of manufacturing overhead costs and to use 4,000 machine hours during 2018. At the end of 2017, Skippy reported the following inventories:

Raw Materials Inventory	$ 20,000
Work-in-Process Inventory	17,000
Finished Goods Inventory	11,000

During January 2018, Skippy actually used 300 machine hours and recorded the following transactions:

a. Purchased materials on account, $31,000

b. Used direct materials, $39,000

c. Manufacturing wages incurred totaled $40,000, of which 90% was direct labor and 10% was indirect labor

d. Used indirect materials, $3,000

e. Incurred other manufacturing overhead on account, $13,000

f. Allocated manufacturing overhead for January 2018

g. Cost of completed motor scooters, $100,000

h. Sold scooters on account, $175,000; cost of scooters sold, $95,000

Requirements

1. Compute Skippy's predetermined overhead allocation rate for 2018. (See Learning Objective 3)

2. Journalize the transactions in the general journal. Use the following accounts: Accounts Receivable, Raw Materials Inventory, Work-in-Process Inventory, Finished Goods Inventory, Accounts Payable, Wages Payable, Sales Revenue, Manufacturing Overhead, and Cost of Goods Sold. (See Learning Objectives 2, 3, and 4)

3. Set up T-accounts for the accounts listed in Requirement 2. Enter the beginning balances for the inventory accounts and assume the remaining accounts have a beginning balance of $0. Post the transactions to the T-accounts and determine the ending balances. (See Learning Objectives 2, 3, and 4)

4. Prepare the journal entry to adjust Manufacturing Overhead for the overallocated or underallocated overhead. Post your entry to the T-accounts. (See Learning Objective 5)

5. What are the ending balances in the three inventory accounts and in Cost of Goods Sold? (See Learning Objectives 2, 3, 4, and 5)

> Solution

Requirement 1

Compute Skippy's predetermined overhead allocation rate for 2018.

$$\text{Predetermined overhead allocation rate} = \frac{\text{Total estimated overhead costs}}{\text{Total estimated quantity of the overhead allocation base}}$$

$$= \frac{\$240,000}{4,000 \text{ machine hours}} = \$60 \text{ per machine hour}$$

Requirement 2

Journalize the transactions in the general journal.

Date	Accounts and Explanation	Debit	Credit
(a)	Raw Materials Inventory	31,000	
	Accounts Payable		31,000
(b)	Work-in-Process Inventory	39,000	
	Raw Materials Inventory		39,000
(c)	Work-in-Process Inventory ($40,000 × 0.90)	36,000	
	Manufacturing Overhead ($40,000 × 0.10)	4,000	
	Wages Payable		40,000
(d)	Manufacturing Overhead	3,000	
	Raw Materials Inventory		3,000
(e)	Manufacturing Overhead	13,000	
	Accounts Payable		13,000
(f)	Work-in-Process Inventory (300 machine hours × $60/hr.)	18,000	
	Manufacturing Overhead		18,000
(g)	Finished Goods Inventory	100,000	
	Work-in-Process Inventory		100,000
(h)	Accounts Receivable	175,000	
	Sales Revenue		175,000
	Cost of Goods Sold	95,000	
	Finished Goods Inventory		95,000

Requirement 3

Post the transactions.

Accounts Receivable		
(h)	175,000	

Raw Materials Inventory			
Bal.	20,000	39,000	(b)
(a)	31,000	3,000	(d)
Bal.	9,000		

Work-in-Process Inventory			
Bal.	17,000	100,000	(g)
(b)	39,000		
(c)	36,000		
(f)	18,000		
Bal.	10,000		

Finished Goods Inventory			
Bal.	11,000	95,000	(h)
(g)	100,000		
Bal.	16,000		

Accounts Payable		
	31,000	(a)
	13,000	(e)
	44,000	Bal.

Wages Payable		
	40,000	(c)

Sales Revenue		
	175,000	(h)

Manufacturing Overhead			
(c)	4,000	18,000	(f)
(d)	3,000		
(e)	13,000		
Bal.	2,000		

Cost of Goods Sold		
(h)	95,000	

Requirement 4

Adjust Manufacturing Overhead.

Date	Accounts and Explanation	Debit	Credit
(i)	Cost of Goods Sold	2,000	
	Manufacturing Overhead		2,000

Manufacturing Overhead			
(c)	4,000	18,000	(f)
(d)	3,000	2,000	(i)
(e)	13,000		
Bal.	0		

Cost of Goods Sold		
(h)	95,000	
(i)	2,000	
Bal.	97,000	

Requirement 5

Ending balances:

Raw Materials Inventory (from Requirement 3)	$ 9,000
Work-in-Process Inventory (from Requirement 3)	10,000
Finished Goods Inventory (from Requirement 3)	16,000
Cost of Goods Sold (from Requirement 4)	97,000

CHAPTER 17

> Key Terms

Allocation Base (p. 919)

Cost Accounting System (p. 908)

Cost Driver (p. 919)

Job (p. 908)

Job Cost Record (p. 909)

Job Order Costing System (p. 908)

Labor Time Record (p. 914)

Materials Requisition (p. 912)

Overallocated Overhead
 (p. 923)

Predetermined Overhead Allocation
 Rate (p. 918)

Process Costing System
 (p. 909)

Underallocated Overhead (p. 923)

> Quick Check

Learning Objective 1

1. Would an advertising agency use job order or process costing? What about a cell phone manufacturer?

   a. Advertising agency—process costing; Cell phone manufacturer—process costing
   b. Advertising agency—job order costing; Cell phone manufacturer—job order costing
   c. Advertising agency—process costing; Cell phone manufacturer—job order costing
   d. Advertising agency—job order costing; Cell phone manufacturer—process costing

Learning Objective 2

2. When a manufacturing company *uses* direct materials, it *assigns* the cost by debiting

   a. Direct Materials.
   b. Work-in-Process Inventory.
   c. Manufacturing Overhead.
   d. Raw Materials Inventory.

Learning Objective 2

3. When a manufacturing company *uses* indirect materials, it *accumulates* the cost by debiting

   a. Work-in-Process Inventory.
   b. Indirect Materials.
   c. Raw Materials Inventory.
   d. Manufacturing Overhead.

Learning Objective 2

4. When a manufacturing company *uses* direct labor, it *assigns* the cost by debiting

   a. Work-in-Process Inventory.
   b. Manufacturing Overhead.
   c. Direct Labor.
   d. Wages Payable.

Questions 5, 6, 7, and 8 are based on the following information:

Gell Corporation manufactures computers. Assume that Gell:

- allocates manufacturing overhead based on machine hours
- estimated 12,000 machine hours and $93,000 of manufacturing overhead costs
- actually used 16,000 machine hours and incurred the following actual costs:

Indirect labor	$ 11,000
Depreciation on plant	48,000
Machinery repair	11,000
Direct labor	75,000
Plant supplies	6,000
Plant utilities	7,000
Advertising	35,000
Sales commissions	27,000

Learning Objective 3

5. What is Gell's predetermined overhead allocation rate?

    a. $7.75/machine hour   c. $6.92/machine hour

    b. $5.81/machine hour   d. $5.19/machine hour

Learning Objective 3

6. What is Gell's actual manufacturing overhead cost?

    a. $158,000   b. $83,000   c. $145,000   d. $220,000

Learning Objective 3

7. How much manufacturing overhead would Gell allocate?

    a. $83,000   b. $93,000   c. $124,000   d. $220,000

Learning Objective 5

8. What entry would Gell make to adjust the manufacturing overhead account for overallocated or underallocated overhead?

Date	Accounts and Explanation	Debit	Credit
a.	Manufacturing Overhead	10,000	
	Cost of Goods Sold		10,000
b.	Manufacturing Overhead	41,000	
	Cost of Goods Sold		41,000
c.	Cost of Goods Sold	41,000	
	Manufacturing Overhead		41,000
d.	Cost of Goods Sold	10,000	
	Manufacturing Overhead		10,000

Learning Objective 4

9. A manufacturing company completed work on a job. The cost of the job is transferred into _____ with a _____.

    a. Work-in-Process Inventory; debit   c. Finished Goods Inventory; debit

    b. Finished Goods Inventory; credit   d. Cost of Goods Sold; credit

Learning Objective 6

10. For which of the following reasons would David Laugherty, owner of the Laugherty Associates law firm, want to know the total costs of a job (serving a particular client)?

    a. For inventory valuation   c. For external reporting

    b. To determine the fees to charge clients   d. a, b, and c are correct

Check your answers at the end of the chapter.

ASSESS YOUR PROGRESS

> Review Questions

1. Why do managers need to know the cost of their products?

2. What types of companies use job order costing systems?

3. What types of companies use process costing systems?

4. What is the purpose of a job cost record?

5. Explain the difference between cost of goods manufactured and cost of goods sold.

6. A job was started on May 15, completed on June 27, and delivered to the customer on July 6. In which accounts would the costs be recorded on the financial statements dated May 31, June 30, and July 31?

CHAPTER 17

7. Give the journal entry for raw materials purchased on account. Explain how this transaction affects the accounting equation.

8. What is the purpose of the raw materials subsidiary ledger? How is it related to the general ledger?

9. How does the use of direct and indirect materials in production affect the accounts?

10. Give the journal entry for direct and indirect labor costs incurred. Explain how this transaction affects the accounting equation.

11. Give five examples of manufacturing overhead costs. Why are they considered indirect costs?

12. What is the predetermined overhead allocation rate?

13. What is an allocation base? Give some examples.

14. How is manufacturing overhead allocated to jobs?

15. A completed job cost record shows the unit cost of the products. How is this calculated?

16. Explain the journal entry for the allocation of overhead. What accounts are affected? Are they increased or decreased?

17. Give the journal entry for the completion of a job. How is the accounting equation affected?

18. Why does the sale of a completed job require two journal entries? What are they?

19. Explain the difference between underallocated overhead and overallocated overhead. What causes each situation?

20. If a company incurred $5,250 in actual overhead costs and allocated $5,575 to jobs, was the overhead overallocated or underallocated? By how much?

21. Refer to the previous question. Give the journal entry to adjust the Manufacturing Overhead account for overallocated or underallocated overhead.

22. Explain the terms *accumulate, assign, allocate,* and *adjust* as they apply to job order costing.

23. Why would the manager of a service company need to use job order costing?

24. How is the predetermined overhead allocation rate used by service companies?

> Short Exercises

Learning Objective 1

S17-1 Distinguishing between job order costing and process costing

Would the following companies most likely use job order costing or process costing?

a. A manufacturer of refrigerators

b. A manufacturer of specialty wakeboards

c. A manufacturer of luxury yachts

d. A professional services firm

e. A landscape contractor

f. A custom home builder

g. A cell phone manufacturer

h. A manufacturer of frozen pizzas

i. A manufacturer of multivitamins

j. A manufacturer of tennis shoes

CHAPTER 17

S17-2 Accounting for materials

Learning Objective 2

Back Country manufactures backpacks. Its plant records include the following materials-related data:

Raw Materials Inventory, beginning balance	$ 38,000
Purchases of canvas, on account	72,000
Purchases of sewing machine lubricating oil, on account	1,200
Materials requisitions:	
Canvas	59,000
Sewing machine lubricating oil	450

Journalize the entries to record the transactions, post to the Raw Materials Inventory account, and determine the ending balance in Raw Materials Inventory.

S17-3 Accounting for materials

Learning Objective 2

Analyze the following T-accounts to determine the amount of direct and indirect materials used.

Raw Materials Inventory				
Bal.	35			
Purchased	215	???	Used	
Bal.	10			

Work-in-Process Inventory				
Bal.	25			
Direct Materials	???	505	Cost of Goods Manufactured
Direct Labor	280		
Manufacturing Overhead	150		
Bal.	40		

S17-4 Accounting for labor

Learning Objective 2

Journalize the following labor-related transactions for Portland Glass Creations at its plant in Portland, Oregon. Assume that the labor has been incurred, but not yet paid.

Plant janitor's wages	$ 620
Plant furnace operator's wages	860
Glass blower's wages	74,000

S17-5 Accounting for overhead

Learning Objective 3

Oak Outdoor Furniture manufactures wood patio furniture. If the company reports the following costs for June 2018, what is the balance in the Manufacturing Overhead account before overhead is allocated to jobs? Assume that the labor has been incurred, but not yet paid. Prepare journal entries for overhead costs incurred in June.

Wood	$ 270,000
Nails, glue, stain	18,000
Depreciation on saws	5,300
Indirect manufacturing labor	45,000
Depreciation on delivery truck	1,700
Assembly-line workers' wages	51,000

CHAPTER 17

Learning Objective 3

S17-6 Allocating overhead

Job 303 includes direct materials costs of $550 and direct labor costs of $400. If the predetermined overhead allocation rate is 40% of direct labor cost, what is the total cost assigned to Job 303?

Learning Objective 3

S17-7 Calculating predetermined overhead allocation rate, allocating overhead

Rosco Company estimates the company will incur $80,750 in overhead costs and 4,750 direct labor hours during the year. Actual direct labor hours were 4,600. Calculate the predetermined overhead allocation rate using direct labor hours as the allocation base, and prepare the journal entry for the allocation of overhead.

Learning Objective 4

S17-8 Completing and selling products

Lincoln Company completed jobs that cost $38,000 to produce. In the same period, the company sold jobs for $88,000 that cost $42,000 to produce. Prepare the journal entries for the completion and sales of the jobs. All sales are on account.

Learning Objective 5

S17-9 Comparing actual to allocated overhead

Columbus Enterprises reports the following information at December 31, 2018:

Manufacturing Overhead	
3,500	50,600
19,000	
34,500	

Requirements

1. What is the actual manufacturing overhead of Columbus Enterprises?
2. What is the allocated manufacturing overhead?
3. Is manufacturing overhead underallocated or overallocated? By how much?

Learning Objective 5

S17-10 Calculating under/overallocated overhead

The T-account showing the manufacturing overhead activity for Aliyah Corp. for 2018 is as follows:

Manufacturing Overhead	
195,000	203,000

Requirements

1. What is the actual manufacturing overhead?
2. What is the allocated manufacturing overhead?
3. Is manufacturing overhead underallocated or overallocated? By how much?

Learning Objective 5

S17-11 Adjusting Manufacturing Overhead

Justice Company's Manufacturing Overhead account is given below. Use this information to prepare the journal entry to adjust for overallocated or underallocated overhead.

Manufacturing Overhead	
148,000	147,000

S17-12 Determining the flow of costs in job order costing

For the following accounts, indicate what causes the account to increase and decrease. The first account is completed as an example.

Account	Is increased by:	Is decreased by:
Raw Materials Inventory	Materials purchased	Materials used
Work-in-Process Inventory		
Finished Goods Inventory		
Cost of Goods Sold		

S17-13 Using job order costing in a service company

Roth Accounting pays Jack Smith $90,000 per year.

Requirements

1. What is the hourly cost to Roth Accounting of employing Smith? Assume a 30-hour week and a 50-week year.

2. What direct labor cost would be assigned to Client 507 if Smith works 15 hours to prepare Client 507's financial statements?

S17-14 Using job order costing in a service company

Assume that Roth's accountants are expected to work a total of 8,000 direct labor hours in 2018. Roth's estimated total indirect costs are $96,000 and the allocation base used is direct labor hours.

Requirements

1. What is Roth's predetermined overhead allocation rate?

2. What indirect costs will be allocated to Client 507 if Jack Smith, an accountant at Roth Accounting, works 15 hours to prepare the financial statements?

> Exercises

E17-15 Distinguishing between job order costing and process costing

Following is a list of cost system characteristics and sample companies. Match each to either job order costing or process costing.

a. Companies that produce small quantities of many different products.

b. A company that pulverizes wood into pulp to manufacture cardboard.

c. A company that manufactures thousands of identical files.

d. Companies that produce large numbers of identical products.

e. A computer repair service that makes service calls to homes.

f. A company that assembles electronic parts and software to manufacture millions of portable media players.

g. A textbook publisher that produces copies of a particular book in batches.

h. A company that bottles milk into one-gallon containers.

i. A company that makes large quantities of one type of tankless hot water heaters.

j. A governmental agency that takes bids for specific items it utilizes where each item requires a separate bid.

Learning Objectives 1, 2

E17-16 Defining terminology

Match the following terms to their definitions.

a. A record used to assign direct labor cost to specific jobs.

b. A document that requests the transfer of materials to the production floor.

c. A document that shows the direct materials, direct labor, and manufacturing overhead costs for an individual job.

d. An accounting system that accumulates costs by process.

e. The production of a unique product or specialized service

f. Used by companies that manufacture unique products or provide specialized services.

1. Job
2. Job Cost Record
3. Job Order Costing System
4. Labor Time Record
5. Materials Requisition
6. Process Costing System

Learning Objective 2

c. COGS $17,100

E17-17 Accounting for job costs

Root Trailers' job cost records yielded the following information:

Job No.	Started	Finished	Sold	Total Cost of Job at July 31
1	June 21	July 16	July 17	$ 3,400
2	June 29	July 21	July 26	13,700
3	July 3	August 11	August 13	6,000
4	July 7	July 29	August 1	4,400

Use the dates in the table to identify the status of each job. Compute the following balances for Root:

a. Work-in-Process Inventory at July 31

b. Finished Goods Inventory at July 31

c. Cost of Goods Sold for July

Learning Objective 2

E17-18 Recording materials and labor costs

Goldenrod Company makes artificial flowers and reports the following data for the month:

Purchases of materials, on account	$ 51,000
Materials requisitions:	
Direct materials	42,300
Indirect materials	500
Labor incurred (not yet paid):	
Direct labor	20,300
Indirect labor	1,340

Journalize the entries relating to materials and labor.

E17-19 Allocating and adjusting manufacturing overhead

Learning Objectives 3, 5

3. Underallocated by $8,800

Selected cost data for Classic Print Co. are as follows:

Estimated manufacturing overhead cost for the year	$ 125,000
Estimated direct labor cost for the year	78,125
Actual manufacturing overhead cost for the year	116,000
Actual direct labor cost for the year	67,000

Requirements

1. Compute the predetermined overhead allocation rate per direct labor dollar.
2. Prepare the journal entry to allocate overhead costs for the year.
3. Use a T-account to determine the amount of underallocated or overallocated manufacturing overhead.
4. Prepare the journal entry to adjust for the underallocated or overallocated manufacturing overhead.

E17-20 Allocating and adjusting manufacturing overhead

Learning Objectives 3, 5

1. $12 per MHr

Young Foundry uses a predetermined overhead allocation rate to allocate overhead to individual jobs, based on the machine hours required. At the beginning of 2018, the company expected to incur the following:

Manufacturing overhead costs	$ 840,000
Direct labor costs	1,480,000
Machine hours	70,000 hours

At the end of 2018, the company had actually incurred:

Direct labor costs	$ 1,230,000
Depreciation on manufacturing plant and equipment	620,000
Property taxes on plant	35,500
Sales salaries	26,000
Delivery drivers' wages	22,500
Plant janitor's wages	17,000
Machine hours	60,000 hours

Requirements

1. Compute Young's predetermined overhead allocation rate.
2. Prepare the journal entry to allocate manufacturing overhead.
3. Post the manufacturing overhead transactions to the Manufacturing Overhead T-account. Is manufacturing overhead underallocated or overallocated? By how much?
4. Prepare the journal entry to adjust for the underallocated or overallocated manufacturing overhead. Does your entry increase or decrease Cost of Goods Sold?

Learning Objectives 3, 5

2. Underallocated by $22,800

E17-21 Allocating and adjusting manufacturing overhead

The manufacturing records for Sporty Kayaks at the end of the 2018 fiscal year show the following information about manufacturing overhead:

Overhead allocated to production	$ 409,200
Actual manufacturing overhead costs	432,000
Predetermined overhead allocation rate	$ 44 per machine hour

Requirements

1. How many machine hours did Sporty Kayaks use in 2018?

2. Was manufacturing overhead overallocated or underallocated for the year, and by how much?

3. Prepare the journal entry to adjust for the underallocated or overallocated manufacturing overhead.

Learning Objective 4

4. Gross profit $15,000

E17-22 Completing and selling jobs

June production generated the following activity in Bentley Chassis Company's Work-in-Process Inventory account:

June 1 balance	$ 36,000
Direct materials used	32,000
Direct labor assigned to jobs	40,000
Manufacturing overhead allocated to jobs	28,000

Additionally, Bentley Chassis has completed Jobs 142 and 143, with total costs of $37,000 and $48,000, respectively.

Requirements

1. Prepare the journal entry for production completed in June.

2. Open a T-account for Work-in-Process Inventory. Post the journal entry made in Requirement 1. Compute the ending balance in the Work-in-Process Inventory account on June 30.

3. Prepare the journal entry to record the sale on account of Job 143 for $63,000. Also, prepare the journal entry to record Cost of Goods Sold for Job 143.

4. What is the gross profit on Job 143?

E17-23 Preparing a schedule of cost of goods manufactured and an income statement

Learning Objective 5

Operating Income $69

Jordan Company has the following information for the year ended December 31, 2018. Use the information to prepare a schedule of cost of goods manufactured and an income statement. Assume no indirect materials are used and all amounts are shown in millions.

Inventory Balances:	Beginning	Ending
Work-in-Process	$ 5	$ 16
Finished Goods	12	15
Other information:		
Sales Revenue		$ 253
Selling and Administrative Expenses		85
Direct Labor		62
Manufacturing Overhead; actual and allocated		20
Direct Materials Used		31

E17-24 Preparing job order costing journal entries

Learning Objectives 2, 3, 4, 5

i. Underallocated by $9,650

Journalize the following transactions for Marge's Sofas. Explanations are not required.

a. Incurred and paid Web site expenses, $2,000.

b. Incurred manufacturing wages of $15,000, 75% of which was direct labor and 25% of which was indirect labor.

c. Purchased raw materials on account, $24,000.

d. Used in production: direct materials, $7,500; indirect materials, $5,000.

e. Recorded manufacturing overhead: depreciation on plant, $18,000; plant insurance (previously paid), $1,500; plant property tax, $3,900 (credit Property Tax Payable).

f. Allocated manufacturing overhead to jobs, 200% of direct labor costs.

g. Completed production on jobs with costs of $40,000.

h. Sold inventory on account, $22,000; cost of goods sold, $18,000.

i. Adjusted for overallocated or underallocated overhead.

E17-25 Identifying job order costing journal entries

Learning Objectives 2, 3, 4, 5

Analyze the following T-accounts, and describe each lettered transaction. Note that some transactions may be compound entries.

Raw Materials Inventory		Work-in-Process Inventory		Finished Goods Inventory		Prepaid Insurance
(a)	(b)	(b)	(f)	(f)	(g)	(d)
		(c)				
		(e)				

Accounts Payable		Wages Payable		Manufacturing Overhead		Cost of Goods Sold
	(a)		(c)	(b)	(e)	(g)
				(c)	(h)	(h)
				(d)		

Learning Objectives 2, 3, 4, 5

E17-26 Determining missing amounts

Analyze the following T-accounts, and determine the missing amounts.

Raw Materials Inventory			Work-in-Process Inventory			Finished Goods Inventory			Accumulated Depreciation	
	28,000	(a)		(b)	37,000		(c)	(d)		12,000
Bal.	9,000			8,000		Bal.	13,000			
				13,500						
			Bal.	1,500						

Accounts Payable			Wages Payable			Manufacturing Overhead			Cost of Goods Sold	
		28,000			(e)		2,000	13,500		(g)
							1,000	(f)		1,500
							12,000		Bal.	25,500
						Bal.	0			

Learning Objective 6

2. Total cost $54,720

E17-27 Using job order costing in a service company

Chance Realtors, a real estate consulting firm, specializes in advising companies on potential new plant sites. The company uses a job order costing system with a predetermined overhead allocation rate, computed as a percentage of direct labor costs.

At the beginning of 2018, managing partner Andrew Chance prepared the following budget for the year:

Direct labor hours (professionals)	13,750 hours
Direct labor costs (professionals)	$ 2,200,000
Office rent	330,000
Support staff salaries	1,200,000
Utilities	450,000

Maynard Manufacturing, Inc. is inviting several consultants to bid for work. Andrew Chance wants to submit a bid. He estimates that this job will require about 180 direct labor hours.

Requirements

1. Compute Chance Realtors' (a) hourly direct labor cost rate and (b) predetermined overhead allocation rate.

2. Compute the predicted cost of the Maynard Manufacturing job.

3. If Chance wants to earn a profit that equals 25% of the job's cost, how much should he bid for the Maynard Manufacturing job?

> Problems Group A

P17-28A Analyzing cost data, recording completion and sales of jobs

Learning Objectives 1, 2, 4

5. Gross profit $400

Clement Manufacturing makes carrying cases for portable electronic devices. Its costing records yield the following information:

Job No.	Date Started	Date Finished	Date Sold	Total Cost of Job at October 31	Total Manufacturing Costs Added in November
1	10/03	10/12	10/13	$ 1,300	
2	10/03	10/30	11/01	1,400	
3	10/17	11/24	11/27	1,000	$ 900
4	10/29	11/29	12/03	1,200	1,200
5	11/08	11/12	11/14		650
6	11/23	12/06	12/09		500

Requirements

1. Which type of costing system is Clement using? What piece of data did you base your answer on?

2. Use the dates in the table to identify the status of each job at October 31 and November 30. Compute Clement's account balances at October 31 for Work-in-Process Inventory, Finished Goods Inventory, and Cost of Goods Sold. Compute, by job, account balances at November 30 for Work-in-Process Inventory, Finished Goods Inventory, and Cost of Goods Sold.

3. Prepare journal entries to record the transfer of completed jobs from Work-in-Process Inventory to Finished Goods Inventory for October and November.

4. Record the sale of Job 3 for $2,300 on account.

5. What is the gross profit for Job 3?

P17-29A Preparing and using a job cost record to prepare journal entries

Learning Objectives 2, 3, 4

1. Cost per DVD $0.38

Ki Technology Co. manufactures DVDs for computer software and entertainment companies. Ki uses job order costing.

On April 2, Ki began production of 6,000 DVDs, Job 423, for Paradigm Pictures for $1.20 sales price per DVD. Ki promised to deliver the DVDs to Paradigm Pictures by April 5. Ki incurred the following direct costs:

Date	Labor Time Record No.	Description	Amount
4/02	655	10 hours @ $16 per hour	$ 160
4/03	656	20 hours @ $15 per hour	300

Date	Materials Requisition No.	Description	Amount
4/02	63	31 lbs. polycarbonate plastic @ $11 per lb.	$ 341
4/02	64	25 lbs. acrylic plastic @ $29 per lb.	725
4/03	74	3 lbs. refined aluminum @ $45 per lb.	135

Ki Technology allocates manufacturing overhead to jobs based on the relation between estimated overhead of $574,000 and estimated direct labor costs of $410,000. Job 423 was completed and shipped on April 3.

Requirements

1. Prepare a job cost record for Job 423. Calculate the predetermined overhead allocation rate (round to two decimal places); then allocate manufacturing overhead to the job.

2. Journalize in summary form the requisition of direct materials and the assignment of direct labor and the allocation of manufacturing overhead to Job 423. Wages are not yet paid.

3. Journalize completion of the job and the sale of the 6,000 DVDs on account.

Learning Objectives 2, 3, 4

3. WIP Bal. $254,800

P17-30A Accounting for transactions, construction company

Superior Construction, Inc. is a home builder in Arizona. Superior uses a job order costing system in which each house is a job. Because it constructs houses, the company uses an account titled Construction Overhead. The company applies overhead based on estimated direct labor costs. For the year, it estimated construction overhead of $1,150,000 and total direct labor costs of $5,750,000. The following events occurred during August:

a. Purchased materials on account, $400,000.

b. Requisitioned direct materials and used direct labor in construction. Recorded the materials requisitioned.

	Direct Materials	Direct Labor
House 402	$ 58,000	$ 44,000
House 403	62,000	32,000
House 404	61,000	58,000
House 405	86,000	57,000

c. The company incurred total wages of $300,000. Use the data from Item b to assign the wages. Wages are not yet paid.

d. Depreciation of construction equipment, $6,700.

e. Other overhead costs incurred: Equipment rentals paid in cash, $30,000; Worker liability insurance expired, $7,000.

f. Allocated overhead to jobs.

g. Houses completed: 402, 404.

h. House sold on account: 404 for $250,000.

Requirements

1. Calculate Superior's predetermined overhead allocation rate for the year.

2. Prepare journal entries to record the events in the general journal.

3. Open T-accounts for Work-in-Process Inventory and Finished Goods Inventory. Post the appropriate entries to these accounts, identifying each entry by letter. Determine the ending account balances, assuming that the beginning balances were zero.

4. Add the costs of the unfinished houses, and show that this total amount equals the ending balance in the Work-in-Process Inventory account.

5. Add the costs of the completed house that has not yet been sold, and show that this equals the ending balance in Finished Goods Inventory.

6. Compute gross profit on the house that was sold. What costs must gross profit cover for Superior Construction?

P17-31A Accounting for manufacturing overhead

Prestige Woods manufactures jewelry boxes. The primary materials (wood, brass, and glass) and direct labor are assigned directly to the products. Manufacturing overhead costs are allocated based on machine hours. Data for 2018 follow:

Learning Objectives 3, 5

1. $8.24 per machine hour

CHAPTER 17

	Estimated	Actual
Machine hours	27,000 hours	32,100 hours
Maintenance labor (repairs to equipment)	$ 17,000	$ 23,500
Plant supervisor's salary	48,000	50,000
Screws, nails, and glue	28,000	45,000
Plant utilities	44,000	92,850
Freight out	37,000	49,500
Depreciation on plant and equipment	85,400	83,000
Advertising expense	46,000	53,000

Requirements

1. Compute the predetermined overhead allocation rate. Round to two decimal places.

2. Post actual and allocated manufacturing overhead to the Manufacturing Overhead T-account.

3. Prepare the journal entry to adjust for underallocated or overallocated overhead.

4. The predetermined overhead allocation rate usually turns out to be inaccurate. Why don't accountants just use the actual manufacturing overhead rate?

Learning Objectives 2, 3, 4, 5

4. COGM $47,430

5. Operating Income $18,950

P17-32A Preparing comprehensive accounting for manufacturing transactions

Mighty Stars produces stars for elementary teachers to reward their students. Mighty Stars' trial balance on June 1 follows:

MIGHTY STARS Trial Balance June 1, 2018		
	Balance	
Account Title	**Debit**	**Credit**
Cash	$ 14,000	
Accounts Receivable	160,000	
Inventories:		
Raw Materials	6,000	
Work-in-Process	40,000	
Finished Goods	20,400	
Property, Plant, and Equipment	220,000	
Accumulated Depreciation		$ 75,000
Accounts Payable		134,000
Wages Payable		2,600
Common Stock		139,000
Retained Earnings		109,800
Sales Revenue		0
Cost of Goods Sold	0	
Manufacturing Overhead	0	
Selling and Administrative Expenses	0	
Totals	$ 460,400	$ 460,400

June 1 balances in the subsidiary ledgers were as follows:

- Raw Materials Inventory subsidiary ledger: Paper, $4,000; indirect materials, $2,000
- Work-in-Process Inventory subsidiary ledger: Job 120, $40,000; Job 121, $0
- Finished Goods Inventory subsidiary ledger: Large Stars, $9,900; Small Stars, $10,500

June transactions are summarized as follows:

a. Collections on account, $145,000.

b. Selling and administrative expenses incurred and paid, $32,000.

c. Payments on account, $39,000.

d. Materials purchases on account: Paper, $24,000; indirect materials, $4,200.

e. Materials requisitioned and used in production:

Job 120: Paper, $950

Job 121: Paper, $7,900

Indirect materials, $1,200

f. Wages incurred during June, $39,000. Labor time records for the month: Job 120, $3,600; Job 121, $17,000; indirect labor, $18,400.

g. Wages paid in June include the balance in Wages Payable at May 31 plus $36,100 of wages incurred during June.

h. Depreciation on plant and equipment, $2,500.

i. Manufacturing overhead allocated at the predetermined overhead allocation rate of 80% of direct labor costs.

j. Jobs completed during the month: Job 120 with 700,000 Large Stars at a total cost of $47,430.

k. Sales on account: all of Job 120 for $104,000.

l. Adjusted for overallocated or underallocated manufacturing overhead.

Requirements

1. Journalize the transactions for the company.

2. Open T-accounts for the general ledger, the Raw Materials Inventory subsidiary ledger, the Work-in-Process Inventory subsidiary ledger, and the Finished Goods Inventory subsidiary ledger. Insert each account balance as given, and use the reference *Bal*. Post the journal entries to the T-accounts using the transaction letters as a reference.

3. Prepare a trial balance at June 30, 2018.

4. Use the Work-in-Process Inventory T-account to prepare a schedule of cost of goods manufactured for the month of June.

5. Prepare an income statement for the month of June.

P17-33A Using job order costing in a service company

Learning Objective 6

2. Delightful Treats $148,500

Bluebird Design, Inc. is a Web site design and consulting firm. The firm uses a job order costing system in which each client is a different job. Bluebird Design assigns direct labor, licensing costs, and travel costs directly to each job. It allocates indirect costs to jobs based on a predetermined overhead allocation rate, computed as a percentage of direct labor costs.

At the beginning of 2018, managing partner Sally Simone prepared the following budget estimates:

Direct labor hours (professionals)	7,500 hours
Direct labor costs (professionals)	$ 1,500,000
Support staff salaries	464,000
Computer leases	45,000
Office supplies	29,000
Office rent	62,000

In November 2018, Bluebird Design served several clients. Records for two clients appear here:

	Delightful Treats	Melva Chocolates
Direct labor hours	500 hours	400 hours
Software licensing costs	$ 3,500	$ 200
Travel costs	5,000	0

Requirements

1. Compute Bluebird Design's direct labor rate and its predetermined overhead allocation rate for 2018.

2. Compute the total cost of each job.

3. If Simone wants to earn profits equal to 50% of service revenue, what fee should she charge each of these two clients?

4. Why does Bluebird Design assign costs to jobs?

> Problems Group B

Learning Objectives 1, 2, 4

5. Gross profit $100

P17-34B Analyzing cost data, recording completion and sales of jobs

Sutherland Manufacturing makes carrying cases for portable electronic devices. Its costing records yield the following information:

Job No.	Date Started	Date Finished	Sold	Total Cost of Job at October 31	Total Manufacturing Costs Added in November
1	10/03	10/12	10/13	$ 1,400	
2	10/03	10/30	11/01	1,900	
3	10/17	11/24	11/27	1,000	$ 1,100
4	10/29	11/29	12/03	600	1,400
5	11/08	11/12	11/14		750
6	11/23	12/06	12/09		1,100

Requirements

1. Which type of costing system is Sutherland using? What piece of data did you base your answer on?

2. Use the dates in the table to identify the status of each job at October 31 and November 30. Compute Sutherland's account balances at October 31 for Work-in-Process Inventory, Finished Goods Inventory, and Cost of Goods Sold. Compute, by job, account balances at November 30 for Work-in-Process Inventory, Finished Goods Inventory, and Cost of Goods Sold.

3. Prepare journal entries to record the transfer of completed jobs from Work-in-Process Inventory to Finished Goods Inventory for October and November.

4. Record the sale of Job 3 for $2,200 on account.

5. What is the gross profit for Job 3?

P17-35B Preparing and using a job cost record to prepare journal entries

Learning Objectives 2, 3, 4

1. Cost per DVD $0.41

Ye Technology Co. manufactures DVDs for computer software and entertainment companies. Ye uses job order costing.

On November 2, Ye began production of 5,200 DVDs, Job 423, for Prototype Pictures for $1.70 sales price per DVD. Ye promised to deliver the DVDs to Prototype by November 5. Ye incurred the following direct costs:

Date	Labor Time Record No.	Description	Amount
11/02	655	10 hours @ $16 per hour	$ 160
11/03	656	20 hours @ $13 per hour	260

Date	Materials Requisition No.	Description	Amount
11/02	63	31 lbs. polycarbonate plastic @ $11 per lb.	$ 341
11/02	64	25 lbs. acrylic plastic @ $28 per lb.	700
11/03	74	3 lbs. refined aluminum @ $42 per lb.	126

Ye Technology allocates manufacturing overhead to jobs based on the relation between estimated overhead of $550,000 and estimated direct labor costs of $440,000. Job 423 was completed and shipped on November 3.

Requirements

1. Prepare a job cost record for Job 423. Calculate the predetermined overhead allocation rate (round to two decimal places); then allocate manufacturing overhead to the job.

2. Journalize in summary form the requisition of direct materials and the assignment of direct labor and the allocation of manufacturing overhead to Job 423. Wages are not yet paid.

3. Journalize completion of the job and the sale of the 5,200 DVDs on account.

P17-36B Accounting for transactions, construction company

Learning Objectives 2, 3, 4

3. WIP Bal. $260,600

Meadow Construction, Inc. is a home builder in Arizona. Meadow uses a job order costing system in which each house is a job. Because it constructs houses, the company uses an account titled Construction Overhead. The company applies overhead based on estimated direct labor costs. For the year, it estimated construction overhead of $1,150,000 and total direct labor costs of $5,750,000. The following events occurred during August:

a. Purchased materials on account, $450,000.

b. Requisitioned direct materials and used direct labor in construction. Recorded the materials requisitioned.

	Direct Materials	Direct Labor
House 402	$ 52,000	$ 47,000
House 403	67,000	36,000
House 404	63,000	54,000
House 405	88,000	52,000

c. The company incurred total wages of $240,000. Use the data from Item b to assign the wages. Wages are not yet paid.

d. Depreciation of construction equipment, $6,300.

e. Other overhead costs incurred: Equipment rentals paid in cash, $40,000; Worker liability insurance expired, $5,000.

f. Allocated overhead to jobs.

g. Houses completed: 402, 404.

h. House sold on account: 404 for $250,000.

Requirements

1. Calculate Meadow's predetermined overhead allocation rate for the year.

2. Prepare journal entries to record the events in the general journal.

3. Open T-accounts for Work-in-Process Inventory and Finished Goods Inventory. Post the appropriate entries to these accounts, identifying each entry by letter. Determine the ending account balances, assuming that the beginning balances were zero.

4. Add the costs of the unfinished houses, and show that this total amount equals the ending balance in the Work-in-Process Inventory account.

5. Add the cost of the completed house that has not yet been sold, and show that this equals the ending balance in Finished Goods Inventory.

6. Compute gross profit on the house that was sold. What costs must gross profit cover for Meadow Construction?

Learning Objectives 3, 5

1. $8.44 per machine hour

P17-37B Accounting for manufacturing overhead

Elegant Woods manufactures jewelry boxes. The primary materials (wood, brass, and glass) and direct labor are assigned directly to the products. Manufacturing overhead costs are allocated based on machine hours. Data for 2018 follow:

	Estimated	Actual
Machine hours	24,500 hours	32,200 hours
Maintenance labor (repairs to equipment)	$ 19,000	$ 27,500
Plant supervisor's salary	41,000	46,000
Screws, nails, and glue	21,000	41,000
Plant utilities	42,000	97,850
Freight out	39,000	44,500
Depreciation on plant and equipment	83,800	82,000
Advertising expense	46,000	60,000

Requirements

1. Compute the predetermined overhead allocation rate. Round to two decimal places.

2. Post actual and allocated manufacturing overhead to the Manufacturing Overhead T-account.

3. Prepare the journal entry to adjust for underallocated or overallocated overhead.

4. The predetermined overhead allocation rate usually turns out to be inaccurate. Why don't accountants just use the actual manufacturing overhead rate?

P17-38B Preparing comprehensive accounting for manufacturing transactions

Hero Stars produces stars for elementary teachers to reward their students. Hero Stars' trial balance on June 1 follows:

Learning Objectives 2, 3, 4, 5

4. COGM $45,900
5. Operating Income $25,200

HERO STARS
Trial Balance
June 1, 2018

Account Title	Balance	
	Debit	Credit
Cash	$ 25,000	
Accounts Receivable	190,000	
Inventories:		
Raw Materials	6,300	
Work-in-Process	39,400	
Finished Goods	21,300	
Property, Plant, and Equipment	270,000	
Accumulated Depreciation		$ 71,000
Accounts Payable		129,000
Wages Payable		1,800
Common Stock		138,000
Retained Earnings		212,200
Sales Revenue		0
Cost of Goods Sold	0	
Manufacturing Overhead	0	
Selling and Administrative Expenses	0	
Totals	$ 552,000	$ 552,000

June 1 balances in the subsidiary ledgers were as follows:

- Raw Materials Inventory subsidiary ledger: Paper, $5,000; indirect materials, $1,300
- Work-in-Process Inventory subsidiary ledger: Job 120, $39,400; Job 121, $0
- Finished Goods Inventory subsidiary ledger: Large Stars, $9,900; Small Stars, $11,400

June transactions are summarized as follows:

a. Collections on account, $141,000.

b. Selling and administrative expenses incurred and paid, $22,000.

c. Payments on account, $35,000.

d. Materials purchases on account: Paper, $25,500; indirect materials, $4,100.

e. Materials requisitioned and used in production:

> Job 120: Paper, $800
> Job 121: Paper, $7,900
> Indirect materials, $1,700

f. Wages incurred during June, $40,000. Labor time records for the month: Job 120, $3,800; Job 121, $18,800; indirect labor, $17,400.

g. Wages paid in June include the balance in Wages Payable at May 31 plus $37,200 of wages incurred during June.

h. Depreciation on plant and equipment, $3,100.

i. Manufacturing overhead allocated at the predetermined overhead allocation rate of 50% of direct labor cost.

j. Jobs completed during the month: Job 120 with 700,000 Large Stars at a total cost of $45,900.

k. Sales on account: all of Job 120 for $104,000.

l. Adjusted for overallocated or underallocated manufacturing overhead.

Requirements

1. Journalize the transactions for the company.

2. Open T-accounts for the general ledger, the Raw Materials Inventory subsidiary ledger, the Work-in-Process Inventory subsidiary ledger, and the Finished Goods Inventory subsidiary ledger. Insert each account balance as given, and use the reference *Bal.* Post the journal entries to the T-accounts using the transaction letters as a reference.

3. Prepare a trial balance at June 30, 2018.

4. Use the Work-in-Process Inventory T-account to prepare a schedule of cost of goods manufactured for the month of June.

5. Prepare an income statement for the month of June.

Learning Objective 6

2. Tasty Co-op $312,500

P17-39B Using job order costing in a service company

Skylark Design, Inc. is a Web site design and consulting firm. The firm uses a job order costing system in which each client is a different job. Skylark Design assigns direct labor, licensing costs, and travel costs directly to each job. It allocates indirect costs to jobs based on a predetermined overhead allocation rate, computed as a percentage of direct labor costs.

At the beginning of 2018, managing partner Judi Jacquin prepared the following budget estimates:

Direct labor hours (professionals)	8,000 hours
Direct labor costs (professionals)	$ 2,000,000
Support staff salaries	866,000
Computer leases	49,000
Office supplies	24,000
Office rent	61,000

In November 2018, Skylark Design served several clients. Records for two clients appear here:

	Tasty Co-op	Maynard Chocolates
Direct labor hours	800 hours	300 hours
Software licensing costs	$ 1,500	$ 500
Travel costs	11,000	0

Requirements

1. Compute Skylark Design's direct labor rate and its predetermined overhead allocation rate for 2018.

2. Compute the total cost of each job.

3. If Judi wants to earn profits equal to 50% of service revenue, what fee should she charge each of these two clients?

4. Why does Skylark Design assign costs to jobs?

CRITICAL THINKING

> Using Excel

P17-40 Using Excel to calculate a predetermined overhead allocation rate, journalize and post manufacturing entries, and adjust for overallocated or underallocated overhead.

Download an Excel template for this problem online in MyAccountingLab or at http://www.pearsonhighered.com/Horngren.

Cedar River Trikes manufactures three-wheeled bikes for adults. The company allocates manufacturing overhead costs based on machine hours. Cedar River expects to incur $250,000 of manufacturing overhead costs, and to use 10,000 machine hours during fiscal year 2018. Cedar River reported the following inventory balances at May 31, 2018:

Raw Materials Inventory	$ 25,000
Work-in-Process Inventory	18,000
Finished Goods Inventory	43,000

During June 2018, Cedar River actually used 1,100 machine hours.

Requirements

1. Compute the predetermined overhead allocation rate for fiscal year 2018. Use the blue shaded areas for inputs.

2. Use Excel to journalize the transactions in the general journal. The account titles are available when you click the down-arrow. Use the Increase Indent button on the Home tab to indent items.

3. Enter the beginning balances for the inventories. Assume the rest of the accounts do not have beginning balances. Post the transactions to T-accounts. The balances in the T-accounts are automatically updated.

4. Adjust the manufacturing overhead.
   a. Prepare the journal entry.
   b. Post to T-accounts.

5. List the ending balances for Raw Materials Inventory, Work-in-Process Inventory, Finished Goods Inventory, and Cost of Goods Sold.

> Continuing Problem

P17-41 Accounting for manufacturing overhead

This problem continues the Piedmont Computer Company situation from Chapter 16. Piedmont Computer Company uses a job order costing system in which each batch manufactured is a different job. Piedmont Computer Company assigns direct materials and direct labor to each job. The company assigns labor costs at $25 per hour. It allocates manufacturing overhead to jobs based on a predetermined overhead allocation rate, computed as a percentage of direct labor costs.

At the beginning of 2020, the controller prepared the following budget:

Manufacturing overhead	$ 290,000
Direct labor costs	$ 1,160,000

In November 2020, Piedmont Computer Company worked on several jobs. Records for two jobs appear here:

	Job 721	Job 722
Direct labor hours	780 hours	60 hours
Direct materials	$ 23,400	$ 2,500

Requirements

1. Compute Piedmont Computer Company's predetermined overhead allocation rate for 2020.

2. Compute the total cost of each job.

3. Why does Piedmont assign costs to jobs?

> Tying It All Together Case 17-1

Before you begin this assignment, review the Tying It All Together feature in the chapter.

Granite Construction Incorporated is a major construction firm whose projects include roads, highways, bridges, dams, tunnels, mass transit facilities, and airports. Suppose Granite Construction wants to bid on a project to construct a bridge in Nevada. Estimators have projected the expected direct materials costs to be $55 million and the direct labor costs (including design and construction) to be $30 million. The company uses a predetermined overhead allocation rate of 50% of direct labor costs and a markup of 20% of total costs.

Requirements

1. What items would most likely be included in direct materials?

2. Calculate the estimated direct costs, the indirect costs, and the total costs for the project.

3. What amount should Granite Construction bid for the project?

4. Why does Granite Construction include both direct and indirect costs when calculating the markup?

> Decision Case 17-1

Hiebert Chocolate, Ltd. is located in Memphis. The company prepares gift boxes of chocolates for private parties and corporate promotions. Each order contains a selection of chocolates determined by the customer, and the box is designed to the customer's specifications. Accordingly, Hiebert uses a job order costing system and allocates manufacturing overhead based on direct labor cost.

One of Hiebert's largest customers is the Goforth and Leos law firm. This organization sends chocolates to its clients each Christmas and also provides them to employees at the firm's gatherings. The law firm's managing partner, Bob Goforth, placed the client gift order in September for 500 boxes of cream-filled dark chocolates. But Goforth and Leos did not place its December staff-party order until the last week of November. This order was for an additional 100 boxes of chocolates identical to the ones to be distributed to clients.

Hiebert budgeted the cost per box for the original 500-box order as follows:

Chocolate, filling, wrappers, box	$ 14.00
Employee time to fill and wrap the box (10 min.)	2.00
Manufacturing overhead	1.00
Total manufacturing cost	$ 17.00

Ben Hiebert, president of Hiebert Chocolate, Ltd., priced the order at $20 per box.

In the past few months, Hiebert has experienced cost increases for both dark chocolate and direct labor. All other costs have remained the same. Hiebert budgeted the cost per box for the second order as follows:

Chocolate, filling, wrappers, box	$ 15.00
Employee time to fill and wrap the box (10 min.)	2.20
Manufacturing overhead	1.10
Total manufacturing cost	$ 18.30

Requirements

1. Do you agree with the cost analysis for the second order? Explain your answer.

2. Should the two orders be accounted for as one job or two in Hiebert's system?

3. What sales price per box should Ben Hiebert set for the second order? What are the advantages and disadvantages of this sales price?

> Fraud Case 17-1

Jerry never imagined he'd be sitting there in Washington being grilled mercilessly by a panel of congressmen. But a young government auditor picked up on his scheme last year. His company produced high-tech navigation devices that were sold to both military and civilian clients. The military contracts were "cost-plus," meaning that payments were calculated based on actual production costs plus a profit markup. The civilian contracts were bid out in a very competitive market, and every dollar counted. Jerry knew that because all the jobs were done in the same factory, he could manipulate the allocation of overhead costs in a way that would shift costs away from the civilian contracts and into the military "cost-plus" work. That way, the company would collect more from the government and be able to shave its bids down on civilian work. He never thought anyone would discover the alterations he had made in the factory workers' time sheets, but one of his accountants had noticed and tipped off the government auditor. Now, as the congressman from Michigan rakes him over the coals, Jerry is trying to figure out his chances of dodging jail time.

Requirements

1. Based on what you have read above, what was Jerry's company using as a cost driver to allocate overhead to the various jobs?

2. Why does the government consider Jerry's actions fraudulent?

3. Name two ways that reducing costs on the civilian contracts would benefit the company and motivate Jerry to commit fraud.

MyAccountingLab **For a wealth of online resources, including exercises, problems, media, and immediate tutorial help, please visit http://www.myaccountinglab.com.**

> Quick Check Answers

1. d **2.** b **3.** d **4.** a **5.** a **6.** b **7.** c **8.** b **9.** c **10.** b

Process Costing

Soft Drink, Anyone?

Carl Marino watched the plastic bottles go by. His machine was running smoothly, and it looked like it was going to be a good shift. Carl works at the Drake Drink Company. The company runs two 10-hour shifts for full-time employees and a four-hour mini-shift for part-timers. The mini-shift is perfect for Carl, a college student. It gives Carl the opportunity to earn some money without cutting into his study time. But the best part of the job is the management. The managers at Drake are always willing to answer Carl's questions. And as a business student, Carl has lots of questions about managing a business.

Lately, Carl has been wondering about the cost of producing a bottle of Drake's soft drink. With the company producing a large quantity of soft drinks, how does the company know the cost of one bottle of a particular soft drink? Carl's managers have been explaining their costing system to him. Drake uses a process costing system, where the company determines the cost of each manufacturing process, such as mixing, bottling, and packaging. Then, at the end of the month, the company uses the costing system to determine the average cost of producing one bottle of soft drink. Knowing the cost per bottle allows the managers to make good pricing decisions and stay competitive in the market.

As Carl watches the bottles go by, he decides to find out more about the company's process costing system.

How Much Does That Soft Drink Cost?

You stop at a convenience store to buy a soft drink. As you pay for your purchase, you may wonder about the cost of producing such a product. **PepsiCo, Inc.** has 22 billion-dollar brands, which means it has 22 brands, such as Pepsi, Lay's, Mountain Dew, and Gatorade, that generate more than $1 billion in sales each year. With that volume of production and sales, how does the company track its production costs? Many food and beverage companies mass-produce their products. Production consists of a series of processes and there are costs associated with each process. In this chapter, you will learn how companies such as PepsiCo keep track of their production costs for each process. By tracking costs by process, the company can determine the total product cost at the end of the accounting period.

Chapter 18 Learning Objectives

1   Describe the flow of costs through a process costing system

2   Calculate equivalent units of production for direct materials and conversion costs

3   Prepare a production cost report for the first department using the weighted-average method

4   Prepare a production cost report for subsequent departments using the weighted-average method

5   Prepare journal entries for a process costing system

6   Use a production cost report to make decisions

7   Prepare a production cost report using the first-in, first-out method (Appendix 18A)

HOW DO COSTS FLOW THROUGH A PROCESS COSTING SYSTEM?

Learning Objective 1

Describe the flow of costs through a process costing system

In the previous chapter, you learned the importance of using a costing system to determine the cost of products and services. Managers use cost information in their primary duties of planning, directing, and controlling. The focus in the previous chapter was on job order costing systems. This chapter concentrates on process costing systems. Let's review the differences and similarities between the two systems.

Job Order Costing Versus Process Costing

In the previous chapter, you learned that companies like Smart Touch Learning, our fictitious company that manufactures touch screen tablet computers that are preloaded with its e-learning software programs, use a **job order costing system** to determine the cost of its custom goods and services. Job order costing is appropriate for companies that manufacture batches of unique products or provide specialized services. Other examples of companies that use job order costing systems include accounting firms, building contractors, and custom furniture manufacturers.

Job Order Costing System
An accounting system that accumulates costs by job. Used by companies that manufacture unique products or provide specialized services.

In contrast, other companies use a series of steps, which are called **processes**, to make large quantities of similar products. Examples of companies that manufacture homogenous products include soft drink bottlers, paint manufacturers, and gasoline refiners. These companies use a **process costing system**. There are two methods for handling process costing: weighted-average and first-in, first-out (FIFO). This chapter's focus is on the weighted-average method; however, you learn about the FIFO method in Appendix 18A at the end of the chapter.

Process
One of a series of steps in manufacturing production; usually associated with making large quantities of similar items.

Both job order and process costing systems track the product costs of direct materials, direct labor, and manufacturing overhead through the three inventory accounts on the balance sheet: Raw Materials Inventory, Work-in-Process Inventory, and Finished Goods Inventory. When the products are sold, both systems transfer the product costs to Cost of Goods Sold, an expense account on the income statement.

Process Costing System
An accounting system that accumulates costs by process. Used by companies that manufacture identical units through a series of uniform production steps or processes.

The primary differences between job order costing and process costing are *how* and *when* costs are recorded in Work-in-Process Inventory. Job order costing has one Work-in-Process Inventory account, with a subsidiary ledger containing individual job cost records for each job. Costs are transferred to Finished Goods Inventory when the jobs are completed. Process costing has a separate Work-in-Process Inventory account for each process or department. A production cost report is completed for each process or department, and costs are transferred at the end of each period. The cost transfer is from one Work-in-Process Inventory account to the next Work-in-Process Inventory account and eventually to Finished Goods Inventory.

Exhibit 18-1 summarizes the differences between job order costing systems and process costing systems.

Exhibit 18-1 | Job Order Costing Versus Process Costing

	Job Order Costing System	**Process Costing System**
Company Type	Manufactures batches of unique products or provides specialized services	Manufactures homogenous products through a series of uniform steps or processes
Cost Accumulation	By job	By process
Work-in-Process Inventory	One general ledger account with a subsidiary ledger containing individual job cost records	Separate Work-in-Process Inventory accounts for each process or department
Record Keeping	Job cost record for each job	Production cost report for each process or department
Timing of Cost Transfers	When each job is completed	At the end of the accounting period

Flow of Costs Through a Process Costing System

To gain an understanding of process costing, consider a company that manufactures jigsaw puzzles. Puzzle Me, a fictitious jigsaw puzzle manufacturing company, divides its manufacturing operations into two processes: assembly and cutting. The Assembly Department applies the glue to the cardboard and then presses a picture onto the cardboard. The Cutting Department cuts the cardboard into puzzle pieces and packages the puzzles in a box. The box is then moved to the finished goods storage. The jigsaw puzzles *accumulate* production costs during each process. The company then *assigns* these costs to the puzzles passing through that process. At Puzzle Me, each process is a separate department. Exhibit 18-2 illustrates Puzzle Me's manufacturing operations.

Exhibit 18-2 | Puzzle Me Manufacturing Operations

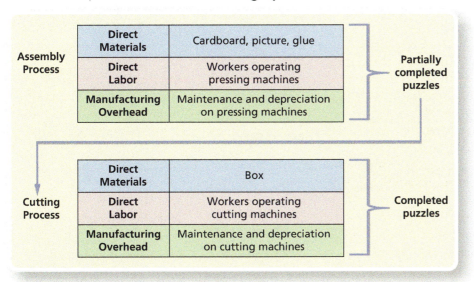

Suppose the company's production costs incurred to make 50,000 puzzles and the costs per puzzle are as follows:

	Total Costs	Cost per Puzzle
Assembly	$ 220,000	$ 4.40
Cutting	45,000	0.90
Total Cost	$ 265,000	$ 5.30

The total cost to produce 50,000 puzzles is the sum of the costs incurred for the two processes ($265,000). The cost per puzzle is the total cost divided by the number of puzzles, or

$$\$265,000 / 50,000 \text{ puzzles} = \$5.30 \text{ per puzzle}$$

Puzzle Me uses the cost per unit of each process to do the following:

- **Control costs.** The company can look for ways to cut the costs when actual process costs are more than planned process costs.
- **Set sales prices.** The company wants the sales price to cover the costs of making the puzzles, and it also wants to earn a profit.
- **Calculate account balances.** The company needs to know the ending balances in Work-in-Process Inventory and Finished Goods Inventory for the balance sheet and Cost of Goods Sold for the income statement.

At any moment, some puzzles are in the assembly process and others are in the cutting process. Computing the puzzles' cost becomes more complicated when the units are at different places in the production cycle.

Exhibit 18-3 compares cost flows in a job order costing system for Smart Touch Learning and a process costing system for Puzzle Me.

Exhibit 18-3 | Comparison of Cost Flows: Job Order Costing and Process Costing

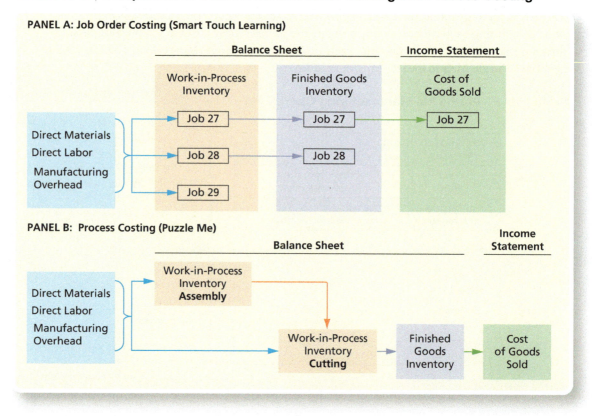

Panel A shows that a job order costing system has a single Work-in-Process Inventory supported by an individual job cost record for each job. Panel B summarizes the flow of costs for a process costing system. Notice the following:

1. Each process (assembly and cutting) is a separate department, and each department has its own Work-in-Process Inventory account.
2. Direct materials, direct labor, and manufacturing overhead are assigned to Work-in-Process Inventory for each process that uses them.
3. When the Assembly Department's process is complete, the unit moves out of the Assembly Department and into the Cutting Department. The Assembly Department's costs are also transferred out of the Assembly Department's Work-in-Process Inventory into Work-in-Process Inventory—Cutting.
4. When the Cutting Department's process is complete, the boxes of puzzles go into finished goods storage. The combined costs from both the Assembly and Cutting Departments flow into Finished Goods Inventory.
5. The total cost of the puzzles includes the costs of assembly and cutting. The costs incurred in the first process are transferred to the second process. The costs incurred in the first and second processes are then transferred to Finished Goods Inventory. When the puzzles are sold, the costs are transferred from Finished Goods Inventory to Cost of Goods Sold.

TYING IT ALL TOGETHER

In the chapter opener, we introduced **PepsiCo, Inc.**, a global food and beverage company that manufactures brands such as Frito-Lay, Gatorade, Pepsi-Cola, Quaker, and Tropicana. The original Pepsi-Cola product was created by a pharmacist, Caleb Bradham, who developed a flavored soda water that had a refreshing taste. PepsiCo, Inc. was incorporated in Delaware in 1919 and has now grown to a company that sells its products in more than 200 countries and territories.

One of the products PepsiCo, Inc. manufactures is Mountain Dew. What would be examples of direct materials, direct labor, and manufacturing overhead involved in manufacturing Mountain Dew?

The direct materials in a soft drink such as Mountain Dew would include carbonated water, sugar, and flavorings. Direct labor would include the wages of the factory workers who work on the assembly line. Manufacturing overhead might include the glue used to adhere the label to the bottle, the salary of the assembly line manager, and the depreciation on the machines used for production.

What would the manufacturing process look like when manufacturing Mountain Dew?

Soft drinks such as Mountain Dew are made at bottling and canning facilities. The first process involves clarifying the water to remove any impurities, such as organic matter and bacteria. Next, the manufacturer mixes the sugar and flavor concentrates with the clarified water. The liquid is then carbonated to give the product its fizziness. The liquid is then transferred to bottles or cans. Labels are affixed to the product and the bottles or cans are packaged into cartons.

Would PepsiCo, Inc. most likely use a job-order costing system or a process costing system to account for the manufacturing of Mountain Dew? Why?

PepsiCo, Inc. would most likely use a process costing system because it is manufacturing large quantities of similar products. The company could separate its production into four different processes: Clarification, Mixing, Carbonation, and Filling and Packaging. Each of these processes would be a separate department and each department would have its own Work-in-Process Inventory account. The total cost of manufacturing the Mountain Dew would include the costs of each department.

Try It!

WHAT ARE EQUIVALENT UNITS OF PRODUCTION, AND HOW ARE THEY CALCULATED?

Learning Objective 2

Calculate equivalent units of production for direct materials and conversion costs

The production process takes time, so companies may have products that are not completed and are still in process at the end of the accounting period. In process costing, production costs are *accumulated* by process. At the end of the period, the total production costs incurred in each process must be split between the following:

- The units that have been completed in that process and transferred to the next process (or to Finished Goods Inventory if it is the last process).
- The units not completed and remaining in Work-in-Process Inventory for that department.

Exhibit 18-4 illustrates the point that all costs must be accounted for. They must either remain in the department or be transferred to the next department.

Exhibit 18-4 | **Assignment of Department 1 Costs at the End of the Period**

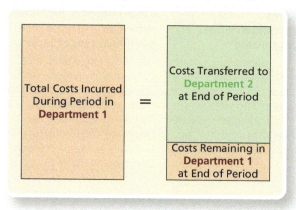

When the production costs have to be split between completed and uncompleted units, we cannot just divide the total cost by the number of units started to get a unit cost because some units are not complete and, therefore, have not incurred the same amount of costs. The unit cost of the completed units is more than the unit cost of the incomplete units. So how are the costs divided?

Equivalent Units of Production

The concept of **equivalent units of production (EUP)** allows businesses to measure the direct materials, direct labor, and manufacturing overhead incurred on a partially finished group of units during a period and to express it in terms of fully complete units of output.

Let's apply the concept of equivalent units of production to a manufacturing setting. Assume Puzzle Me has 40,000 units that the Assembly Department completed and transferred out, and 10,000 units in ending work in process which are 100% complete as to direct materials cost and 25% completed with respect to conversion costs. **Conversion costs** are the sum of direct labor and manufacturing overhead costs and represent the cost to convert direct materials into finished goods.

The 40,000 units that are completed and transferred out are 100% complete in regards to direct materials and conversion costs associated with the Assembly Department. Therefore, the equivalent units would be 40,000 units (40,000 units × 100% complete) for both direct materials and conversion costs. The 10,000 units in ending Work-in-Process Inventory, though, must be calculated separately in terms of direct materials (100% complete) and conversion costs (25% complete). The equivalent units for ending Work-in-Process Inventory with respect to direct materials would be

> 10,000 units × 100% complete = 10,000 EUP for Direct Materials

The equivalent units for ending Work-in-Process Inventory with respect to conversion costs would be

> 10,000 units × 25% complete = 2,500 EUP for Conversion Costs

> *Consider this example: A young boy is helping his father in the garden by carrying buckets of water for the plants. But the boy is small and the bucket is heavy, so the father only fills the bucket half full. At the end of the day, the boy tells his mother he carried 6 buckets of water. While he may have made 6 trips, he only carried the equivalent of 3 buckets of water because 6 buckets that are half full is the equivalent of 3 buckets that are completely full. In mathematical terms, 6 × 50% = 3 × 100%.*

In summary, Puzzle Me ended the accounting period with 10,000 units in the Assembly Department. The 10,000 units were 100% complete for direct materials and 25% complete for conversion. Expressed in terms of equivalent units of production, the 10,000 partially completed units are equal to 10,000 EUP for direct materials and 2,500 EUP for conversion costs.

> *This example illustrates an important point: The equivalent units of production can be different for direct materials and conversion costs and therefore must be calculated separately.*

Equivalent Units of Production (EUP)
Used to measure the direct materials, direct labor, and manufacturing overhead incurred on partially completed units and expressed in terms of fully completed units.

Conversion Costs
The cost to convert direct materials into finished goods: Direct labor plus manufacturing overhead.

Try It!

6. The Cutting Department has 6,500 units in process at the end of September that are 100% complete for direct materials and 85% complete for conversion costs. Calculate the equivalent units of production for direct materials and conversion costs.

Check your answers online in MyAccountingLab or at http://www.pearsonhighered.com/Horngren.

For more practice, see Short Exercises S18-3 through S18-6. MyAccountingLab

HOW IS A PRODUCTION COST REPORT PREPARED FOR THE FIRST DEPARTMENT?

For a comprehensive example of a process costing system, let's continue our example using Puzzle Me. Exhibit 18-5 illustrates the two major production processes:

- The Assembly Department applies glue to the cardboard and then presses a picture onto the cardboard.
- The Cutting Department cuts the cardboard into puzzle pieces and packages the puzzles in a box. The box is then moved to finished goods storage.

Exhibit 18-5 | **Flow of Costs in Producing Puzzles**

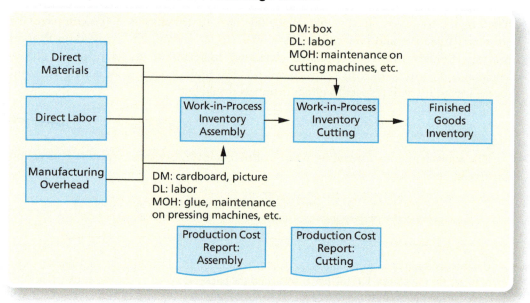

The production process uses materials, machines, and labor in both departments, and there are two Work-in-Process Inventory accounts: one for the Assembly Department and one for the Cutting Department.

> We are going to complete a lot of calculations in this chapter. As you work through the computations, keep the picture in Exhibit 18-5 in mind so you don't confuse inputs with outputs. The inputs are the materials, labor, and overhead. The outputs are the completed puzzles.

Production Cost Report

A report prepared by a processing department for equivalent units of production, production costs, and the assignment of those costs to the completed and in process units.

Puzzle Me must complete a **production cost report** for each department each month. The production cost reports show the calculations for the *physical flows* and the *cost flows* of the products. There are four steps to preparing a production cost report:

1. Summarize the flow of physical units.
2. Compute output in terms of equivalent units of production.
3. Compute the cost per equivalent unit of production.
4. Assign costs to units completed and units in process.

There are two unique terms used on a production cost report:

- *To account for* includes the amount in process at the beginning of the period plus the amount started or added during the period.
- *Accounted for* shows what happened to the amounts to account for. They are either still in process or completed and transferred out.

These terms are used for both units and costs. *To account for* and *accounted for* must always be equal. To illustrate the use of these terms, let's prepare a production cost report for Puzzle Me's Assembly Department for the month of July. A production report for the second process, Cutting Department, will be explained after we have completed the production cost report for the Assembly Department.

Production Cost Report—First Process—Assembly Department

The production cost reports prepared in the chapter use the weighted-average method. The first-in, first-out (FIFO) method is illustrated in Appendix 18A at the end of the chapter.

The Assembly Department applies glue to the cardboard and then presses a picture onto the cardboard. Operations for this department include two inputs:

- The Assembly Department's direct materials (glue and cardboard) are added at the beginning of the process.
- The Assembly Department's conversion costs are added evenly throughout the process.

The Assembly Department has the following data for July:

	Assembly Dept.
Units	
Beginning WIP	8,000
Started in production in July	42,000
Transferred out in July	40,000
Ending WIP:	
Units	???
Percent Complete:	
Direct materials	100%
Conversion costs	25%
Costs	
Beginning WIP:	
Direct materials costs	$ 9,800
Conversion costs	3,910
Direct materials costs added in July	130,200
Conversion costs added in July:	
Direct labor	22,090
Manufacturing overhead allocated	42,000
Total conversion costs added	$ 64,090

Step 1: Summarize the Flow of Physical Units The **physical units** are the actual units that the company will account for during the period. The Assembly Department had 8,000 units in process on July 1 and started 42,000 units during the month. Therefore, *to account for* is 50,000 physical units.

Physical Units
Actual units that the company will account for during the period.

To account for = Beginning balance + Amount started = 8,000 units + 42,000 units = 50,000 units

The Assembly Department completed the assembly process on 40,000 units of the 50,000 *to account for* and transferred those units to the Cutting Department. Therefore, the remaining 10,000 units must still be in process and we have *accounted for* all units.

> Accounted for = Transferred out + In process = 40,000 units + 10,000 units = 50,000 units

To account for equals *accounted for*, so we are ready to record this information on the production cost report. Exhibit 18-6 shows units to account for and units accounted for. Notice that we are completing the UNITS section of the report. At this point, we are not yet assigning costs to units.

Exhibit 18-6 | **Production Cost Report—Assembly Department—Physical Units**

PUZZLE ME
Production Cost Report—ASSEMBLY DEPARTMENT
Month Ended July 31, 2018

		Equivalent Units	
UNITS	**Physical Units**	**Direct Materials**	**Conversion Costs**
Units to account for:			
Beginning work-in-process	8,000	Step 1: Physical flow of units	
Started in production	42,000		
Total units to account for	50,000		
Units accounted for:			
Completed and transferred out	40,000		
Ending work-in-process	10,000		
Total units accounted for	50,000		

Step 2: Compute Output in Terms of Equivalent Units of Production The Assembly Department adds all direct materials at the beginning of the process. In contrast, conversion costs are incurred evenly throughout the process. Thus, we must compute equivalent units of production separately for direct materials and conversion costs. Equivalent units must be used instead of physical units because some units will be incomplete at the end of the period.

The Assembly Department worked on 50,000 puzzle boards during July. We have already determined that 40,000 puzzle boards are completed and have been transferred to the next department. If they are completed and transferred out, then they are 100% complete for both direct materials and conversion costs in this department. Another 10,000 puzzle boards are only 25% complete. How many equivalent units of production did the Assembly Department produce during July? Let's look at the calculation for each input.

Equivalent Units of Production for Direct Materials Equivalent units of production for direct materials total 50,000 because all the direct materials have been added to all 50,000 units worked on during July. Because the direct materials are added at the beginning of the process, if the units are started, then 100% of the materials have been added.

> Completed units: 40,000 units × 100% = 40,000 EUP for direct materials
> In process units: 10,000 units × 100% = 10,000 EUP for direct materials
> Total EUP for direct materials   = 50,000 EUP for direct materials

Equivalent Units of Production for Conversion Costs Conversion costs are 100% complete for the 40,000 puzzle boards completed and transferred out to the Cutting Department, but only 25% of the conversion work has been done on the 10,000 puzzle boards in ending Work-in-Process Inventory. To calculate the equivalent units of production for conversion costs

Completed units: 40,000 units × 100% = 40,000 EUP for conversion costs

In process units: 10,000 units × 25% = 2,500 EUP for conversion costs

Total EUP for conversion costs = 42,500 EUP for conversion costs

We can now add this information to the production cost report. Exhibit 18-7 shows the updated report.

Exhibit 18-7 | Production Cost Report—Assembly Department—EUP

PUZZLE ME
Production Cost Report—ASSEMBLY DEPARTMENT
Month Ended July 31, 2018

UNITS	Physical Units	Equivalent Units Direct Materials	Conversion Costs
Units to account for:			
Beginning work-in-process	8,000		
Started in production	42,000		
Total units to account for	50,000		
		Step 2: EUP	
Units accounted for:			
Completed and transferred out	40,000	40,000	40,000
Ending work-in-process	10,000	10,000	2,500
Total units accounted for	50,000	50,000	42,500

Step 3: Compute the Cost per Equivalent Unit of Production Now that we have completed the UNITS section of the report, it is time to complete the COSTS section. The Assembly Department has to account for costs associated with the following:

- Work done *last* month on the 8,000 partially completed units (beginning work-in-process)
- Work done *this* month to complete the 8,000 partially completed units
- Work done *this* month on the 42,000 units that were started into production

We will use the **weighted-average method** to account for costs. The weighted-average method combines the beginning work-in-process costs and the costs added during the period into one cost pool. A **cost pool** is an accumulation of individual costs. The total costs to be accounted for include direct materials and conversion costs and will be calculated as beginning work-in-process costs plus costs added during the period.

Weighted-Average Method (for Process Costing)
Determines the average cost of equivalent units of production by combining beginning inventory costs with current period costs.

Cost Pool
An accumulation of individual costs.

	Direct Materials	Conversion Costs	Total Costs
Beginning work-in-process	$ 9,800	$ 3,910	$ 13,710
Costs added during period	130,200	64,090	194,290
Total costs to account for	$ 140,000	$ 68,000	$ 208,000

To calculate the cost per equivalent unit of production, divide the total costs by the equivalent units of production. Computations are required for both direct materials and conversion costs.

$$\text{Cost per EUP for direct materials} = \frac{\text{Total direct materials costs}}{\text{Equivalent units of production for direct materials}}$$

$$\text{Cost per EUP for conversion costs} = \frac{\text{Total conversion costs}}{\text{Equivalent units of production for conversion costs}}$$

The Assembly Department has $208,000 of costs to account for: $140,000 in direct materials costs and $68,000 in conversion costs. In Step 2, we computed equivalent units of production for direct materials as 50,000 EUP and conversion costs as 42,500 EUP. Because the equivalent units of production differ, we must compute a separate cost per equivalent unit of production for direct materials and for conversion costs. The cost per equivalent unit of production for direct materials is $2.80, which is calculated as follows:

$$
\begin{aligned}
\textbf{Cost per EUP for direct materials} &= \frac{\textbf{Total direct materials costs}}{\textbf{Equivalent units of production for direct materials}} \\
&= \frac{\$140,000}{50,000 \text{ EUP}} \\
&= \$2.80 \text{ per EUP}
\end{aligned}
$$

The cost per equivalent unit of production for conversion costs is $1.60, which is calculated as follows:

$$
\begin{aligned}
\textbf{Cost per EUP for conversion costs} &= \frac{\textbf{Total conversion costs}}{\textbf{Equivalent units of production for conversion costs}} \\
&= \frac{\$68,000}{42,500 \text{ EUP}} \\
&= \$1.60 \text{ per EUP}
\end{aligned}
$$

Exhibit 18-8 shows these calculations added to the production cost report.

Exhibit 18-8 | **Production Cost Report—Assembly Department—Costs to Account For**

PUZZLE ME
Production Cost Report—ASSEMBLY DEPARTMENT
Month Ended July 31, 2018

UNITS	Physical Units	Equivalent Units Direct Materials	Equivalent Units Conversion Costs
Units to account for:			
Beginning work-in-process	8,000		
Started in production	42,000		
Total units to account for	50,000		
Units accounted for:			
Completed and transferred out	40,000	40,000	40,000
Ending work-in-process	10,000	10,000	2,500
Total units accounted for	50,000	50,000	42,500

COSTS		Direct Materials	Conversion Costs	Total Costs
Costs to account for:				
Beginning work-in-process	Step 3: Costs to account for	$ 9,800	$ 3,910	$ 13,710
Costs added during period		130,200	64,090	194,290
Total costs to account for		140,000	68,000	$ 208,000
Divided by: Total EUP		÷ 50,000	÷ 42,500	
Cost per equivalent unit		$ 2.80	$ 1.60	
Costs accounted for:				
Completed and transferred out				
Ending work-in-process				
Total costs accounted for				

Step 4: Assign Costs to Units Completed and Units in Process The last step on the production cost report is to determine where the $208,000 total costs to be accounted for by the Assembly Department should be assigned. The cost of each input must be assigned to each output or partially completed output. The costs must be divided between two outputs:

- The 40,000 completed puzzle boards that have been transferred out to the Cutting Department.
- The 10,000 partially completed puzzle boards remaining in the Assembly Department's ending Work-in-Process Inventory.

This is accomplished by multiplying the cost per equivalent unit of production (Step 3) times the equivalent units of production (Step 2). For example, to calculate the direct materials costs assigned to the 40,000 completed and transferred out units, Puzzle Me will multiply 40,000 units by $2.80 cost per equivalent unit.

> Costs accounted for = Equivalent units of production × Cost per equivalent unit
> = 40,000 equivalent units × $2.80 cost per equivalent unit
> = $112,000

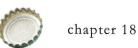
To assign the costs of the two inputs to the two outputs, this step must be repeated four times to assign:

- Direct materials costs to:
  - Completed units
  - In process units

- Conversion costs to:
  - Completed units
  - In process units

Direct Materials:

Completed	40,000 EUP × $ 2.80 per EUP =	$ 112,000
In Process	10,000 EUP × $ 2.80 per EUP =	28,000
Total		$ 140,000

Conversion Costs:

Completed	40,000 EUP × $ 1.60 per EUP =	$ 64,000
In Process	2,500 EUP × $ 1.60 per EUP =	4,000
Total		$ 68,000

We have accomplished our goal of splitting the $208,000 total cost between the completed units and the in process units and can record these costs on the production cost report. Exhibit 18-9 shows the completed production cost report for the Assembly Department.

Exhibit 18-9 | Production Cost Report—Assembly Department—Costs Accounted For

PUZZLE ME
Production Cost Report—ASSEMBLY DEPARTMENT
Month Ended July 31, 2018

		Equivalent Units	
UNITS	**Physical Units**	**Direct Materials**	**Conversion Costs**
Units to account for:			
Beginning work-in-process	8,000		
Started in production	42,000		
Total units to account for	50,000		
Units accounted for:			
Completed and transferred out	40,000	40,000	40,000
Ending work-in-process	10,000	10,000	2,500
Total units accounted for	50,000	50,000	42,500

COSTS	**Direct Materials**	**Conversion Costs**	**Total Costs**
Costs to account for:			
Beginning work-in-process	$ 9,800	$ 3,910	$ 13,710
Costs added during period	130,200	64,090	194,290
Total costs to account for	140,000	68,000	$ 208,000
Divided by: Total EUP	÷ 50,000	÷ 42,500	
Cost per equivalent unit	$ 2.80	$ 1.60	
Costs accounted for:			
Completed and transferred out	$ 112,000	$ 64,000	$ 176,000
Ending work-in-process	28,000	4,000	32,000
Total costs accounted for	$ 140,000	$ 68,000	$ 208,000

Step 4: Costs accounted for

Try It!

The Blending Department for CenTex Paints started October with 1,000 gallons in process and started in production 9,500 gallons. During the month, 7,000 gallons were completed and transferred to the next department. Ending work-in-process was 3,500 gallons (100% complete with respect to direct materials and 30% complete for conversion costs). The department uses the weighted-average method. The Blending Department incurred the following costs:

Beginning WIP—Direct materials costs	$ 500
Beginning WIP—Conversion costs	1,210
Direct materials added during the month	5,800
Conversion costs added during the month	5,230
Total	$ 12,740

7. Prepare a production cost report for the Blending Department for the month of October.

Check your answers online in MyAccountingLab or at http://www.pearsonhighered.com/Horngren.

For more practice, see Short Exercises S18-7 through S18-10. MyAccountingLab

HOW IS A PRODUCTION COST REPORT PREPARED FOR SUBSEQUENT DEPARTMENTS?

We have now *accounted for* all units and costs for the Assembly Department, and it is time to complete the same process for the Cutting Department.

> **Learning Objective 4**
> Prepare a production cost report for subsequent departments using the weighted-average method

Production Cost Report—Second Process—Cutting Department

The Cutting Department receives the puzzle boards from the Assembly Department and cuts the boards into puzzle pieces before inserting the pieces into the box at the end of the process. Operations for this department include three inputs:

- Glued puzzle boards with pictures are *transferred in* from the Assembly Department at the beginning of the Cutting Department's process.
- The Cutting Department's *conversion costs* are added evenly throughout the process.
- The Cutting Department's *direct materials* (boxes) are added at the end of the process.

Keep in mind that *direct materials* in the Cutting Department refers to the boxes added *in that department* and not to the materials (cardboard, pictures, and glue) added in the Assembly Department. The costs of the materials from the Assembly Department that are *transferred into* the Cutting Department are called **transferred in costs**. Likewise, *conversion costs* in the Cutting Department refers to the direct labor and manufacturing overhead costs incurred only in the Cutting Department. The conversion costs incurred in the Assembly Department are also transferred in costs for the Cutting Department.

> **Transferred In Costs**
> Costs that were incurred in a previous process and brought into a later process as part of the product's cost.

Listed below is the cost information for Puzzle Me's Cutting Department:

	Cutting Dept.
Units	
Beginning WIP	5,000
Transferred in from Assembly Dept.	40,000
Transferred out to Finished Goods	38,000
Ending WIP:	
Units	???
Percent Complete:	
Direct materials	0%
Conversion costs	30%
Costs	
Beginning WIP:	
Transferred in	$ 22,000
Direct materials costs	0
Conversion costs	1,200
Direct materials added in July	19,000
Conversion costs added in July:	
Direct labor	3,840
Manufacturing overhead allocated	11,000
Total conversion costs added	$ 14,840

The data show that Puzzle Me's Cutting Department started the July period with 5,000 puzzle boards partially completed through work done in the Cutting Department in June. During July, the Cutting Department started work on 40,000 additional puzzle boards that were received from the Assembly Department. Let's prepare a production cost report for the Cutting Department using the weighted-average method and the same four-step procedure we used for the Assembly Department.

> Remember: Units and costs that are transferred *out* for the Assembly Department become transferred *in* for the Cutting Department.

Step 1: Summarize the Flow of Physical Units The Cutting Department had 5,000 units in process on July 1 and received 40,000 units during the month from the Assembly Department. Therefore, *to account for* is 45,000 units.

> To account for = Beginning balance + Amount transferred in = 5,000 units + 40,000 units = 45,000 units

The Cutting Department completed the cutting and boxing process on 38,000 units of the 45,000 units *to account for* and transferred those units to Finished Goods Inventory. Therefore, 7,000 units must still be in process and we have *accounted for* all units.

> Accounted for = Transferred out + in process = 38,000 units + 7,000 units = 45,000 units

To account for equals *accounted for*, so we are ready to record this information on the production cost report. Just as we did with the Assembly Department, we start with completing the UNITS section of the report. At this point, we are not yet assigning costs to units. Exhibit 18-10 shows the units to account for and units accounted for. Notice that because this is a subsequent department we must account for units that are transferred in. We show this by having a Transferred In column on the production cost report.

Exhibit 18-10 | **Production Cost Report—Cutting Department—Physical Units**

PUZZLE ME
Production Cost Report—CUTTING DEPARTMENT
Month Ended July 31, 2018

| | | Equivalent Units | | |
| | Physical | Transferred | Direct | Conversion |
UNITS	Units	In	Materials	Costs
Units to account for:				
Beginning work-in-process	5,000			
Transferred in	40,000	Step 1: Physical flow of units		
Total units to account for	45,000			
Units accounted for:				
Completed and transferred out	38,000			
Ending work-in-process	7,000			
Total units accounted for	45,000			

Step 2: Compute Output in Terms of Equivalent Units of Production The Cutting Department would start with the units transferred in from the Assembly Department. The Cutting Department adds direct materials at the end of the process, and conversion costs are incurred evenly throughout the process. Thus, we must compute equivalent units of production separately for direct materials and conversion costs. Additionally, the units have costs that were transferred in with them that must be accounted for.

The Cutting Department worked on 45,000 puzzle boards during July. We have already determined that 38,000 puzzles are completed and have been transferred to Finished Goods Inventory. If they are completed and transferred out, then they are 100% complete for transferred in, direct materials, and conversion costs in this department. The remaining 7,000 puzzle boards are only 30% complete for conversion costs and 0% complete for direct materials. How many equivalent units of production did the Cutting Department produce during July?

Equivalent Units of Production for Transferred In The Cutting Department is the second department in the process system, so it receives units from the Assembly Department. These units are the *transferred in* units. The equivalent units of production for transferred in are always 100%. Why? **Because these units came in with costs assigned to them from the previous department, which was calculated on the production cost report for the Assembly Department. If they were not 100% complete with respect to the previous process, then they would not have been transferred in. They would still be in process in the previous department. Therefore, any costs associated with the work done in the Assembly Department stay with them at 100% EUP.**

Why is EUP for transferred in always 100%?

Completed units: 38,000 units × 100% = 38,000 EUP for transferred in	
In process units: 7,000 units × 100% = 7,000 EUP for transferred in	
Total EUP for transferred in = 45,000 EUP for transferred in	

Equivalent Units of Production for Direct Materials Equivalent units of production for direct materials total 38,000 for the completed units because they are 100% complete. However, the units that are in process do not yet have any direct materials added in this department because the box is added at the end of the process. Because they are still in process, the box has not yet been added. To calculate the equivalent units of production for direct materials:

Completed units: 38,000 units × 100% =	38,000 EUP for direct materials
In process units: 7,000 units × 0% =	0 EUP for direct materials
Total EUP for direct materials	= 38,000 EUP for direct materials

Equivalent Units of Production for Conversion Costs Conversion costs are complete for the 38,000 puzzles completed and transferred out to Finished Goods Inventory, but only 30% of the conversion work has been done on the 7,000 puzzle boards in ending Work-in-Process Inventory. To calculate the equivalent units of production for conversion costs:

Completed units: 38,000 units × 100% =	38,000 EUP for conversion costs
In process units: 7,000 units × 30% =	2,100 EUP for conversion costs
Total EUP for conversion costs	= 40,100 EUP for conversion costs

We can now add this information to the production cost report as shown in Exhibit 18-11.

Exhibit 18-11 | Production Cost Report—Cutting Department—EUP

		Equivalent Units		
PUZZLE ME Production Cost Report—CUTTING DEPARTMENT Month Ended July 31, 2018				
UNITS	**Physical Units**	**Transferred In**	**Direct Materials**	**Conversion Costs**
Units to account for:				
Beginning work-in-process	5,000			
Transferred in	40,000			
Total units to account for	45,000			
			Step 2: EUP	
Units accounted for:				
Completed and transferred out	38,000	38,000	38,000	38,000
Ending work-in-process	7,000	7,000	0	2,100
Total units accounted for	45,000	45,000	38,000	40,100

Step 3: Compute the Cost per Equivalent Unit of Production Now that we have completed the UNITS section of the report, it is time to complete the COSTS section. The formulas to compute the cost per equivalent unit of production are the same as used for the Assembly Department; we just need to add the calculation for the transferred in costs. The Cutting Department has three inputs and therefore must make three calculations for cost per equivalent unit of production.

$$\text{Cost per EUP for transferred in} = \frac{\text{Total transferred in costs}}{\text{Equivalent units of production for transferred in}}$$

$$\text{Cost per EUP for direct materials} = \frac{\text{Total direct materials costs}}{\text{Equivalent units of production for direct materials}}$$

$$\text{Cost per EUP for conversion costs} = \frac{\text{Total conversion costs}}{\text{Equivalent units of production for conversion costs}}$$

The Cutting Department has $233,040 of costs to account for, as illustrated in Exhibit 18-12.

Exhibit 18-12 | **Cutting Department: Costs to Account For**

	Transferred In	Direct Materials	Conversion Costs	Totals
Beginning balance in Work-in-Process Inventory—Cutting, July 1	$ 22,000	$ 0	$ 1,200	$ 23,200
Transferred in from Assembly Department during July	176,000			176,000
Additional added in Cutting Department during July		19,000	14,840	33,840
Totals	$ 198,000	$ 19,000	$ 16,040	$ 233,040

The beginning balances and the additional costs incurred were given in the original data. The amount transferred in from the Assembly Department, $176,000, is the amount calculated on the production cost report for the Assembly Department for July as the amount completed and transferred out in the costs accounted for section.

Our next task is to split these costs between the 38,000 completed puzzles transferred out to Finished Goods Inventory and the 7,000 partially complete puzzle boards that remain in the Cutting Department's ending Work-in-Process Inventory.

In Step 2, we computed equivalent units of production for transferred in as 45,000 EUP, direct materials as 38,000 EUP, and conversion costs as 40,100 EUP. Because the equivalent units of production differ, we must compute a separate cost per unit for each input.

The cost per equivalent unit of production for transferred in is $4.40, which is calculated as follows:

$$\text{Cost per EUP for transferred in} = \frac{\text{Total transferred in costs}}{\text{Equivalent units of production for transferred in}}$$
$$= \frac{\$198,000}{45,000 \text{ EUP}}$$
$$= \$4.40 \text{ per EUP}$$

The cost per equivalent unit of production for direct materials is $0.50, which is calculated as follows:

$$\text{Cost per EUP for direct materials} = \frac{\text{Total direct materials costs}}{\text{Equivalent units of production for direct materials}}$$
$$= \frac{\$19,000}{38,000 \text{ EUP}}$$
$$= \$0.50 \text{ per EUP}$$

The cost per equivalent unit of production for conversion costs is $0.40, which is calculated as follows:

$$\text{Cost per EUP for conversion costs} = \frac{\text{Total conversion costs}}{\text{Equivalent units of production for conversion costs}}$$
$$= \frac{\$16,040}{40,100 \text{ EUP}}$$
$$= \$0.40 \text{ per EUP}$$

These calculations are added to the production cost report as shown in Exhibit 18-13.

Exhibit 18-13 | **Production Cost Report—Cutting Department—Costs to Account For**

PUZZLE ME
Production Cost Report—CUTTING DEPARTMENT
Month Ended July 31, 2018

UNITS	Physical Units	Equivalent Units Transferred In	Direct Materials	Conversion Costs
Units to account for:				
Beginning work-in-process	5,000			
Transferred in	40,000			
Total units to account for	45,000			
Units accounted for:				
Completed and transferred out	38,000	38,000	38,000	38,000
Ending work-in-process	7,000	7,000	0	2,100
Total units accounted for	45,000	45,000	38,000	40,100

COSTS	Transferred In	Direct Materials	Conversion Costs	Total Costs
Costs to account for:				
Beginning work-in-process	$ 22,000	$ 0	$ 1,200	$ 23,200
Costs added during period	176,000	19,000	14,840	209,840
Total costs to account for	198,000	19,000	16,040	$ 233,040
Divided by: Total EUP	÷ 45,000	÷ 38,000	÷ 40,100	
Cost per equivalent unit	$ 4.40	$ 0.50	$ 0.40	
Costs accounted for:				
Completed and transferred out				
Ending work-in-process				
Total costs accounted for				

Step 3: Costs to account for

Step 4: Assign Costs to Units Completed and Units in Process The last step on the production cost report is to determine how the $233,040 total costs accounted for by the Cutting Department should be assigned to the following:

- The 38,000 completed puzzles that have been transferred out to Finished Goods Inventory.
- The 7,000 partially completed puzzle boards remaining in the Cutting Department's ending Work-in-Process Inventory.

This is accomplished by multiplying the cost per equivalent unit of production times the equivalent units of production. To assign the costs of the three inputs to the two outputs, this step must be completed six times to assign:

- Transferred in costs to:
  - Completed units
  - In process units
- Direct materials cost to:
  - Completed units
  - In process units
- Conversion costs to:
  - Completed units
  - In process units

Transferred In

Completed	38,000 EUP × $ 4.40 per EUP	=	$ 167,200
In Process	7,000 EUP × $ 4.40 per EUP	=	30,800
Total			$ 198,000

Direct Materials

Completed	38,000 EUP × $ 0.50 per EUP	=	$ 19,000
In Process	0 EUP × $ 0.50 per EUP	=	0
Total			$ 19,000

Conversion Costs

Completed	38,000 EUP × $ 0.40 per EUP	=	$ 15,200
In Process	2,100 EUP × $ 0.40 per EUP	=	840
Total			$ 16,040

We have accomplished our goal of splitting the $233,040 total cost between the completed units and the in process units and can record these costs on the production cost report. The completed report is shown in Exhibit 18-14.

Exhibit 18-14 | Production Cost Report—Cutting Department—Costs Accounted For

PUZZLE ME
Production Cost Report—CUTTING DEPARTMENT
Month Ended July 31, 2018

		Equivalent Units		
UNITS	**Physical Units**	**Transferred In**	**Direct Materials**	**Conversion Costs**
Units to account for:				
Beginning work-in-process	5,000			
Transferred in	40,000			
Total units to account for	45,000			
Units accounted for:				
Completed and transferred out	38,000	38,000	38,000	38,000
Ending work-in-process	7,000	7,000	0	2,100
Total units accounted for	45,000	45,000	38,000	40,100

COSTS	**Transferred In**	**Direct Materials**	**Conversion Costs**	**Total Costs**
Costs to account for:				
Beginning work-in-process	$ 22,000	$ 0	$ 1,200	$ 23,200
Costs added during period	176,000	19,000	14,840	209,840
Total costs to account for	198,000	19,000	16,040	$ 233,040
Divided by: Total EUP	÷ 45,000	÷ 38,000	÷ 40,100	
Cost per equivalent unit	$ 4.40	$ 0.50	$ 0.40	
Costs accounted for:				
Completed and transferred out	$ 167,200	$ 19,000	$ 15,200	$ 201,400
Ending work-in-process	30,800	0	840	31,640
Total costs accounted for	$ 198,000	$ 19,000	$ 16,040	$ 233,040

Step 4: Costs accounted for

Try It!

The Finishing Department started the month with 500 units in process, received 2,000 units from the Assembly Department, and transferred 2,100 units to the finished goods storage area. All direct materials are added at the beginning of the process. The units in process at the end of the month are 45% complete with respect to conversion costs. The department uses the weighted-average method. The Finishing Department incurred the following costs:

	Beginning WIP	Added this month	Total
Transferred In	$ 6,250	$ 25,000	$ 31,250
Direct Materials	500	2,000	2,500
Conversion Costs	1,250	5,590	6,840
Total	$ 8,000	$ 32,590	$ 40,590

8. How many units are still in process at the end of the month?
9. Compute the equivalent units of production for the Finishing Department.
10. Determine the cost per equivalent unit for transferred in, direct materials, and conversion costs.
11. Determine the cost to be transferred to Finished Goods Inventory.

Check your answers online in MyAccountingLab or at http://www.pearsonhighered.com/Horngren.

For more practice, see Short Exercises S18-11 and S18-12. MyAccountingLab

WHAT JOURNAL ENTRIES ARE REQUIRED IN A PROCESS COSTING SYSTEM?

Learning Objective 5

Prepare journal entries for a process costing system

As costs flow through the process costing system, we go through a four-step process to *accumulate, assign, allocate,* and *adjust.* This is the same process that was illustrated in the previous chapter for job order costing. Remember, the primary differences between the two costing systems are how costs are accumulated and when costs are assigned. In a process costing system, costs are accumulated in the following accounts: Raw Materials Inventory, the various Work-in-Process Inventory accounts, and Manufacturing Overhead. At the end of the month, when the production cost reports are prepared, the costs are assigned to units. The costs assigned to the units completed in each process are transferred from one Work-in-Process Inventory account to the next and eventually to Finished Goods Inventory and Cost of Goods Sold. Following is a description of the journal entries associated with Puzzle Me's process costing system for July.

Transaction 1—Raw Materials Purchased

During July, the company purchased materials on account for $175,000.

$$\frac{A\uparrow}{RM\uparrow} \Big\} = \Big\{ \frac{L\uparrow}{A/P\uparrow} + \underline{E}$$

Date	Accounts and Explanation	Debit	Credit
Trans. 1	Raw Materials Inventory	175,000	
	Accounts Payable		175,000
	Purchased materials, **accumulated** in RM.		

Transaction 2—Raw Materials Used in Production

During July, direct materials were *assigned* to the two production departments: $130,200 to the Assembly Department and $19,000 to the Cutting Department; $2,000 in indirect materials was *accumulated* in Manufacturing Overhead.

Date	Accounts and Explanation	Debit	Credit
Trans. 2	Work-in-Process Inventory—Assembly	130,200	
	Work-in-Process Inventory—Cutting	19,000	
	Manufacturing Overhead	2,000	
	Raw Materials Inventory		151,200
	Used materials, direct materials **assigned** *to WIP, indirect materials* **accumulated** *in MOH.*		

$$\left.\frac{A\downarrow}{\substack{RM\downarrow \\ WIP\text{—Assembly}\uparrow \\ WIP\text{—Cutting}\uparrow}}\right\} = \left\{ \frac{L}{} + \frac{E\downarrow}{MOH\uparrow} \right.$$

Transaction 3—Labor Costs Incurred

During the month, Puzzle Me *assigned* $22,090 in direct labor costs to the Assembly Department and $3,840 in direct labor costs to the Cutting Department. $1,500 in indirect labor costs were *accumulated* in Manufacturing Overhead.

Date	Accounts and Explanation	Debit	Credit
Trans. 3	Work-in-Process Inventory—Assembly	22,090	
	Work-in-Process Inventory—Cutting	3,840	
	Manufacturing Overhead	1,500	
	Wages Payable		27,430
	Incurred labor, direct labor **assigned** *to WIP, indirect labor* **accumulated** *in MOH.*		

$$\left.\frac{A\uparrow}{\substack{WIP\text{—Assembly}\uparrow \\ WIP\text{—Cutting}\uparrow}}\right\} = \left\{ \frac{L\uparrow}{\substack{Wages \\ Payable\uparrow}} + \frac{E\downarrow}{MOH\uparrow} \right.$$

Transaction 4—Additional Manufacturing Costs Incurred

In addition to the indirect materials and indirect labor costs, Puzzle Me incurred $30,000 in machinery depreciation and $19,000 in indirect costs that were paid in cash, which included rent and utilities. These costs are *accumulated* in the Manufacturing Overhead account.

Date	Accounts and Explanation	Debit	Credit
Trans. 4	Manufacturing Overhead	30,000	
	Accumulated Depreciation—Machinery		30,000
	Incurred overhead, costs **accumulated** *in MOH.*		
	Manufacturing Overhead	19,000	
	Cash		19,000
	Incurred overhead, costs **accumulated** *in MOH.*		

$$\left.\frac{A\downarrow}{\substack{Accumulated \\ Depreciation\uparrow}}\right\} = \left\{ \frac{L}{} + \frac{E\downarrow}{MOH\uparrow} \right.$$

$$\left.\frac{A\downarrow}{Cash\downarrow}\right\} = \left\{ \frac{L}{} + \frac{E\downarrow}{MOH\uparrow} \right.$$

Transaction 5—Allocation of Manufacturing Overhead

Puzzle Me used a predetermined overhead allocation rate to *allocate* indirect costs to the departments: $42,000 to the Assembly Department and $11,000 to the Cutting Department.

$$\left. \frac{A\uparrow}{\substack{\text{WIP—Assembly}\uparrow \\ \text{WIP—Cutting}\uparrow}} \right\} = \left\{ \underline{\quad L \quad} + \frac{E\uparrow}{\text{MOH}\downarrow} \right.$$

Date	Accounts and Explanation	Debit	Credit
Trans. 5	Work-in-Process Inventory—Assembly	42,000	
	Work-in-Process Inventory—Cutting	11,000	
	Manufacturing Overhead		53,000
	Allocated overhead to WIP.		

Transaction 6—Transfer from the Assembly Department to the Cutting Department

At the end of July, when the production cost report for the Assembly Department was prepared, Puzzle Me *assigned* $176,000 to the 40,000 units transferred from the Assembly Department to the Cutting Department.

$$\left. \frac{A\uparrow\downarrow}{\substack{\text{WIP—Assembly}\downarrow \\ \text{WIP—Cutting}\uparrow}} \right\} = \left\{ \underline{\quad L \quad} + \underline{\quad E \quad} \right.$$

Date	Accounts and Explanation	Debit	Credit
Trans. 6	Work-in-Process Inventory—Cutting	176,000	
	Work-in-Process Inventory—Assembly		176,000
	Transferred costs **assigned** to units transferred.		

Transaction 7—Transfer from Cutting Department to Finished Goods Inventory

At the end of July, when the production cost report for the Cutting Department was prepared, Puzzle Me *assigned* $201,400 to the 38,000 units transferred from the Cutting Department to Finished Goods Inventory. This is the cost of goods manufactured.

$$\left. \frac{A\uparrow\downarrow}{\substack{\text{FG}\uparrow \\ \text{WIP—Cutting}\downarrow}} \right\} = \left\{ \underline{\quad L \quad} + \underline{\quad E \quad} \right.$$

Date	Accounts and Explanation	Debit	Credit
Trans. 7	Finished Goods Inventory	201,400	
	Work-in-Process Inventory—Cutting		201,400
	Completed units, costs **assigned** to FG.		

Transaction 8—Puzzles Sold

During July, Puzzle Me sold 35,000 puzzles. The production cost report for the Cutting Department, Exhibit 18-13, shows that the total production cost of manufacturing a puzzle is $5.30 ($4.40 per EUP for transferred in, $0.50 per EUP for direct materials, and $0.40 per EUP for conversion costs). Therefore, the cost of 35,000 puzzles is $185,500 (35,000 puzzles × $5.30 per puzzle). The puzzles were sold on account for $8.00 each, which is a total of $280,000 (35,000 puzzles × $8.00 per puzzle).

Date	Accounts and Explanation	Debit	Credit
Trans. 8	Accounts Receivable	280,000	
	Sales Revenue		280,000
	Sold units, entry reflects sales price, not costs.		
	Cost of Goods Sold	185,500	
	Finished Goods Inventory		185,500
	*Sold units, costs **assigned** to COGS.*		

$$\frac{A\uparrow}{A/R\uparrow} \Big\} = \Big\{ \frac{L}{} + \frac{E\uparrow}{\text{Sales Revenue}\uparrow}$$

$$\frac{A\downarrow}{FG\downarrow} \Big\} = \Big\{ \frac{L}{} + \frac{E\downarrow}{\text{COGS}\uparrow}$$

Transaction 9—Adjust Manufacturing Overhead

The actual manufacturing overhead costs incurred were $50,500, which includes the indirect materials in Transaction 2, the indirect labor in Transaction 3, and the accumulated depreciation and other indirect costs in Transaction 4. The amount of manufacturing overhead allocated to the two departments was $53,000, as shown in Transaction 5.

Manufacturing Overhead

Trans. 2	2,000	53,000	Trans. 5
Trans. 3	1,500		
Trans. 4	30,000		
Trans. 4	19,000		
		500	Unadj. Bal.

The T-account for Manufacturing Overhead shows that the amount of manufacturing overhead allocated was $500 more than the actual costs incurred. This means the overhead was overallocated. To *adjust* for the overallocation, Manufacturing Overhead must be debited to bring the account to zero. The credit is to Cost of Goods Sold to decrease the expense account for the amount the puzzles were overcosted.

Date	Accounts and Explanation	Debit	Credit
Trans. 9	Manufacturing Overhead	500	
	Cost of Goods Sold		500
	Adjusted MOH for overallocated overhead.		

$$\frac{A}{} \Big\} = \Big\{ \frac{L}{} + \frac{E\uparrow\downarrow}{\begin{array}{c}\text{COGS}\downarrow \\ \text{MOH}\uparrow\end{array}}$$

The adjusting entry for overallocated or underallocated manufacturing overhead is usually prepared at the end of the year. We are showing it here at the end of the month so we can illustrate all journal entries for a process costing system.

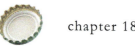

After posting, the key accounts appear as follows:

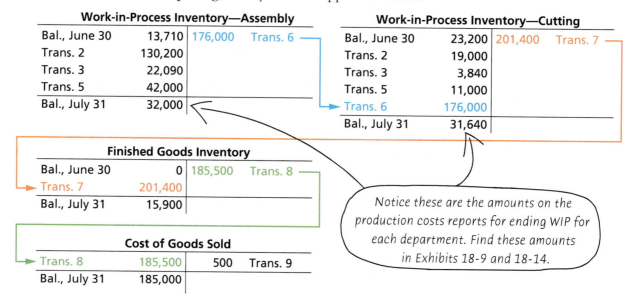

Work-in-Process Inventory—Assembly			
Bal., June 30	13,710	176,000	Trans. 6
Trans. 2	130,200		
Trans. 3	22,090		
Trans. 5	42,000		
Bal., July 31	32,000		

Work-in-Process Inventory—Cutting			
Bal., June 30	23,200	201,400	Trans. 7
Trans. 2	19,000		
Trans. 3	3,840		
Trans. 5	11,000		
Trans. 6	176,000		
Bal., July 31	31,640		

Finished Goods Inventory			
Bal., June 30	0	185,500	Trans. 8
Trans. 7	201,400		
Bal., July 31	15,900		

Notice these are the amounts on the production costs reports for ending WIP for each department. Find these amounts in Exhibits 18-9 and 18-14.

Cost of Goods Sold			
Trans. 8	185,500	500	Trans. 9
Bal., July 31	185,000		

Try It!

12. Castillo Company has three departments: Mixing, Bottling, and Packaging. At the end of the month, the production cost reports for the departments show the costs of the products completed and transferred were $75,000 from Mixing to Bottling, $50,000 from Bottling to Packaging, and $65,000 from Packaging to Finished Goods Inventory. Prepare the journal entries for the transfer of the costs.

Check your answers online in MyAccountingLab or at http://www.pearsonhighered.com/Horngren.

For more practice, see Short Exercises S18-13.   MyAccountingLab

HOW CAN THE PRODUCTION COST REPORT BE USED TO MAKE DECISIONS?

Learning Objective 6

Use a production cost report to make decisions

So far in the chapter, you have learned how to prepare the production cost report. Now let's consider how managers can use production cost reports to make decisions for their companies.

- **Controlling costs.** Puzzle Me uses product cost data to look for ways to reduce costs. A manager may decide that the company needs to change suppliers to reduce the cost of its direct materials. Or a manager may change a component in the production process to reduce direct materials costs. To reduce labor costs, a manager may need employees with different skill levels paid at different hourly rates. Perhaps more skilled employees would require a higher pay rate but be more efficient. The increase in cost per labor hour may be more than offset by the increased productivity of the workers. Managers may also evaluate the efficiency of the production equipment. Newer, more efficient equipment may reduce manufacturing overhead costs.

- **Evaluating performance.** Managers are often rewarded based on how well they meet the budget. Puzzle Me compares the actual direct materials and conversion costs with expected amounts. If actual costs are too high, managers look for ways to cut them. If actual costs are less than expected, the managers may receive a bonus.

DECISIONS

Can we cut these costs?

The management team of Puzzle Me is looking at the production cost reports for July, and discussing opportunities for improvement. The production manager thinks the production process is very efficient, and there is little room for cost savings in conversion costs. The purchasing manager tells the team that he was recently approached by a supplier with an excellent reputation for quality. This supplier submitted a bid for cardboard that was a little thinner but would allow the company to decrease direct materials costs by 5%. What should the team do?

Solution

The production cost reports for the Assembly and Cutting Departments show direct materials costs of $2.80 and $0.50 per puzzle, respectively, for total direct materials cost of $3.30 per puzzle. A decrease of 5% in direct materials costs would result in a savings

of $0.165 per puzzle ($3.30 × 5%) and decrease total costs from $5.30 to $5.135 per puzzle. Based on the completed production of 38,000 puzzles in July, the total cost savings would be $6,270 per month ($0.165 per puzzle × 38,000 puzzles). The purchasing manager recommends using the new supplier.

Alternate Solution

The marketing manager has a different perspective. He points out that most of the puzzles produced are for toddlers. Based on market research, the adults who purchase these puzzles like the sturdy construction. If Puzzle Me changes materials and the puzzles do not stand up well to the treatment they receive by young children, the company could rapidly lose market share. The marketing manager does not recommend using a thinner cardboard.

- **Pricing products.** Puzzle Me must set its sales price high enough to cover the manufacturing cost of each puzzle plus selling and administrative costs. The production cost report for the Cutting Department, Exhibit 18-13, shows that the total production cost of manufacturing a puzzle is $5.30 ($4.40 per EUP for transferred in, $0.50 per EUP for direct materials, and $0.40 per EUP for conversion costs). Obviously, the puzzle must be priced more than this for the company to be profitable.

- **Identifying the most profitable products.** Sales price and cost data help managers figure out which products are most profitable. They can then promote these products to help increase profits.

- **Preparing the financial statements.** Finally, the production cost report aids financial reporting. It provides inventory data for the balance sheet and cost of goods sold for the income statement.

13. Describe some ways managers use production cost reports to make business decisions.

Check your answers online in MyAccountingLab or at http://www.pearsonhighered.com/Horngren.

For more practice, see Short Exercise S18-14. MyAccountingLab

APPENDIX 18A: Process Costing: First-In, First-Out Method

The chapter illustrated how to complete the production cost reports for Puzzle Me using the weighted-average method. In the weighted-average method, the costs from the beginning balance in Work-in-Process Inventory are combined with the current period costs when determining the costs per equivalent unit of production. In this appendix, we will

First-In, First-Out Method (for Process Costing)

Determines the cost of equivalent units of production by accounting for beginning inventory costs separately from current period costs. It assumes the first units started in the production process are the first units completed and sold.

Learning Objective 7

Prepare a production cost report using the first-in, first-out method

APPENDIX 18A

look at another method for assigning production costs—the **first-in, first-out method (for Process Costing)**—in which the costs from the beginning balance in Work-in-Process Inventory that were incurred in the prior period are accounted for separately from the current period costs. The first-in, first-out method is also known as *FIFO*.

HOW IS A PRODUCTION COST REPORT PREPARED USING THE FIFO METHOD?

The data related to Puzzle Me's Assembly Department is listed below:

	Assembly Dept.
Units	
Beginning WIP:	
Units	8,000
Percent Complete:	
Direct materials	100%
Conversion costs	60%
Started in production in July	42,000
Transferred out in July	40,000
Ending WIP:	
Units	???
Percent Complete:	
Direct materials	100%
Conversion costs	25%
Costs	
Beginning WIP:	
Materials costs	$ 9,800
Conversion costs	3,910
Direct materials added in July	130,200
Conversion costs added in July:	
Direct labor	22,090
Manufacturing overhead allocated	42,000
Total conversion costs added	$ 64,090

We will use the same four-step procedure to complete the production cost report for the Assembly Department for July using the FIFO method:

1. Summarize the flow of physical units.
2. Compute output in terms of equivalent units of production.
3. Compute the cost per equivalent unit of production.
4. Assign costs to units completed and units in process.

Step 1: Summarize the Flow of Physical Units The Assembly Department had 8,000 units in process on July 1 and started 42,000 units during the month. Therefore, *to account for* is 50,000 units. This is the same as the weighted-average method.

> **To account for = Beginning balance + Amount started**
> = 8,000 units + 42,000 units
> = 50,000 units

Using the FIFO method creates three groups of units to be accounted for:

- Units in beginning inventory that were started in June and completed in July
- Units started in July and completed in July
- Units started in July but not completed in July. These units are still in process at the end of July and will be completed in August.

The information for the Assembly Department shows 8,000 units in beginning inventory and 40,000 units transferred out. If 40,000 units were completed and transferred, this would include the 8,000 units in beginning inventory plus another 32,000 units that were started in July. Remember, FIFO stands for first-in, first-out. Therefore, it is assumed that the first units in (those in beginning inventory) are the first units out. We must account for 50,000 units. If 40,000 were transferred out, then that leaves 10,000 still in process at the end of July. We have now *accounted for* all units.

> **Accounted for = Beginning balance + Started and completed + In process**
> = 8,000 units + 32,000 units + 10,000 units
> = 50,000 units

Exhibit 18A-1 illustrates the three groups of units accounted for.

Exhibit 18A-1 | July Units Accounted For

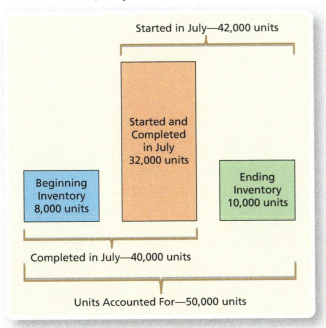

APPENDIX 18A

To account for equals *accounted for*, so we are ready to record this information on the production cost report. Just as we did with the weighted-average method, we start with completing the UNITS section of the report. At this point, we are not yet assigning costs to units. Exhibit 18A-2 (on the next page) shows the units to account for and units accounted for.

Exhibit 18A-2 | **Production Cost Report—Assembly Department—FIFO Method—Physical Units**

PUZZLE ME
Production Cost Report—ASSEMBLY DEPARTMENT
Month Ended July 31, 2018

	Physical Units	Equivalent Units for Current Period	
UNITS		Direct Materials	Conversion Costs
Units to account for:			
Beginning work-in-process	8,000		
Started in production	42,000		
Total units to account for	50,000	Step 1: Physical flow of units	
Units accounted for:			
Beginning work-in-process	8,000		
Started and completed	32,000		
Transferred to Cutting Department	40,000		
Ending work-in-process	10,000		
Total units accounted for	50,000		

Step 2: Compute Output in Terms of Equivalent Units of Production In the FIFO method, costs from the previous period are not merged with the costs from the current period. Therefore, the EUP calculation is for *the current period.* The Assembly Department adds direct materials at the beginning of the process, and conversion costs are incurred evenly throughout the process. Thus, we must compute equivalent units of production separately for direct materials and conversion costs.

Equivalent Units of Production for Direct Materials Because Puzzle Me adds materials at the beginning of the process, no additional direct materials will be added to complete the beginning work-in-process units. The completed units and ending WIP are 100% complete for direct materials.

Beginning WIP units: 8,000 units × 0% =	0 EUP for direct materials
Started and completed units: 32,000 units × 100% =	32,000 EUP for direct materials
In process units: 10,000 units × 100% =	10,000 EUP for direct materials
Total EUP for direct materials	= 42,000 EUP for direct materials

Equivalent Units of Production for Conversion Costs This is the section where the difference between the weighted-average and FIFO methods is most obvious.

- **Beginning WIP.** The 8,000 units that were in process at the beginning of July were 60% complete. That means 60% of the work was done in June. We are concerned with the work completed in July. If 60% of the work was done in June and the units were completed in July, then 40% of the work was done in July (100% − 60% = 40%). Therefore, the EUP for these units is 8,000 units × 40% = 3,200 EUP.

- **Started and Completed.** For the 32,000 units started and completed in July all (100%) of the work done on the units started and completed was done in July, so the equivalent units of production are 32,000 units × 100% = 32,000 EUP.

- **In Process.** Only 25% of the conversion work has been done on the 10,000 puzzle boards in ending Work-in-Process Inventory. Equivalent units of production are 10,000 units × 25% = 2,500 EUP.

To calculate the equivalent units of production for conversion costs:

Beginning WIP units: 8,000 units × 40% =	3,200 EUP for conversion costs
Started and completed units: 32,000 units × 100% =	32,000 EUP for conversion costs
In process units: 10,000 units × 25% =	2,500 EUP for conversion costs
Total EUP for conversion costs	= 37,700 EUP for conversion costs

Exhibit 18A-3 illustrates the timing of the incurrence of conversion costs. Exhibit 18A-4 shows the production cost report with the EUP calculations added.

Exhibit 18A-3 | Timing of Conversion Costs

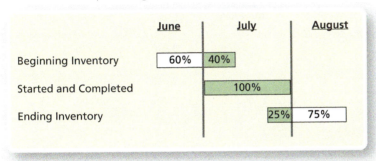

Exhibit 18A-4 | Production Cost Report—Assembly Department—FIFO Method—EUP

PUZZLE ME
Production Cost Report—ASSEMBLY DEPARTMENT
Month Ended July 31, 2018

| | | Equivalent Units for Current Period | |
UNITS	Physical Units	Direct Materials	Conversion Costs
Units to account for:			
Beginning work-in-process	8,000		
Started in production	42,000		
Total units to account for	50,000		
Units accounted for:			
Beginning work-in-process	8,000	0	3,200
Started and completed	32,000	32,000	32,000
Transferred to Cutting Department	40,000	32,000	35,200
Ending work-in-process	10,000	10,000	2,500
Total units accounted for	50,000	42,000	37,700

(Step 2: EUP)

Step 3: Compute the Cost per Equivalent Unit of Production Now that we have completed the UNITS section of the report, it is time to complete the COSTS section. The Assembly Department has two inputs and therefore must make two calculations for cost per equivalent unit of production.

$$\text{Current period cost per EUP for direct materials} = \frac{\text{Current period direct materials costs}}{\text{Equivalent units of production for direct materials}}$$

$$\text{Current period cost per EUP for conversion costs} = \frac{\text{Current period conversion costs}}{\text{Equivalent units of production for coversion costs}}$$

The Assembly Department has $208,000 of costs to account for, as illustrated in Exhibit 18A-5.

Exhibit 18A-5 | **Assembly Department: Costs to Account For**

	Direct Materials	Conversion Costs	Totals
Beginning balance in Work-in-Process Inventory—Assembly July 1	$ 9,800	$ 3,910	$ 13,710
Additional added in Assembly Department during July	130,200	64,090	194,290
Totals	$ 140,000	$ 68,000	$ 208,000

Our next task is to split these costs between the 40,000 completed puzzle boards transferred out to the Cutting Department and the 10,000 partially complete puzzle boards that remain in the Assembly Department's ending Work-in-Process Inventory.

In Step 2, we computed equivalent units of production for direct materials as 42,000 EUP, and conversion costs as 37,700 EUP. Because the equivalent units of production differ, we must compute a separate cost per unit for each input. Also, the numerator for each calculation is the cost incurred in the current period, not total costs, because of the FIFO method. We need to calculate the *cost per EUP for the current period.*

The cost per equivalent unit of direct materials is $3.10, which is calculated as follows:

$$\text{Current period cost per EUP for direct materials} = \frac{\text{Current period direct materials costs}}{\text{Equivalent units of production for direct materials}}$$
$$= \frac{\$130,200}{42,000 \text{ EUP}}$$
$$= \$3.10 \text{ per EUP}$$

The cost per equivalent unit of production for conversion costs is $1.70, which is calculated as follows:

$$\text{Current period cost per EUP for conversion costs} = \frac{\text{Current period conversion costs}}{\text{Equivalent units of production for conversion costs}}$$
$$= \frac{\$64,090}{37,700 \text{ EUP}}$$
$$= \$1.70 \text{ per EUP}$$

The costs to account for calculations are added to the production cost report as shown in Exhibit 18A-6.

Exhibit 18A-6 | **Production Cost Report—Assembly Department—FIFO Method—Costs to Account For**

PUZZLE ME
Production Cost Report—ASSEMBLY DEPARTMENT
Month Ended July 31, 2018

UNITS	Physical Units	Equivalent Units for Current Period	
		Direct Materials	Conversion Costs
Units to account for:			
Beginning work-in-process	8,000		
Started in production	42,000		
Total units to account for	50,000		
Units accounted for:			
Beginning work-in-process	8,000	0	3,200
Started and completed	32,000	32,000	32,000
Transferred to Cutting Department	40,000	32,000	35,200
Ending work-in-process	10,000	10,000	2,500
Total units accounted for	50,000	42,000	37,700

COSTS	Direct Materials	Conversion Costs	Total Costs	Cost per Unit
Costs to account for:				
Beginning work-in-process	$ 9,800	$ 3,910	$ 13,710	
Costs added during period	130,200	64,090	194,290	
Total costs to account for	$ 140,000	$ 68,000	$ 208,000	
Costs added during current period	$ 130,200	$ 64,090		
Divided by: EUP this period	÷ 42,000	÷ 37,700		
Cost per equivalent unit this period	$ 3.10	$ 1.70		
Costs accounted for:				
Beginning work-in-process				
Costs to complete beginning WIP				
Total costs for beginning WIP				
Started and completed				
Transferred to Cutting Department				
Ending work-in-process				
Total costs accounted for				

Step 3: Costs to account for (annotation next to Total costs to account for)

Step 4: Assign Costs to Units Completed and Units in Process The last step on the production cost report is to assign the $208,000 total costs to be accounted for by the Assembly Department to the following:

- The 8,000 puzzle boards from beginning inventory that have now been completed and transferred to the Cutting Department.
- The 32,000 started and completed puzzle boards that have also been transferred to Cutting Department.
- The 10,000 partially completed puzzle boards remaining in the Assembly Department's ending Work-in-Process Inventory.

This is accomplished by multiplying the cost per equivalent unit of production times the equivalent units of production. To assign the costs of the two inputs to the three groups of outputs, this step must be repeated six times to assign:

- Direct materials cost to:
  - Complete beginning units
  - Started and completed units
  - In process units

- Conversion costs to:
  - Complete beginning units
  - Started and completed units
  - In process units

- In addition, the costs in beginning WIP must be added to the above calculations for costs incurred in the current period.

Direct Materials		
Beginning WIP		$ 9,800
To complete beginning WIP	0 EUP × $3.10 per EUP =	0
Started and Completed	32,000 EUP × $3.10 per EUP =	99,200
Transferred to Cutting		109,000
In process	10,000 EUP × $3.10 per EUP =	31,000
Total		$ 140,000
Conversion Costs		
Beginning WIP		$ 3,910
To complete beginning WIP	3,200 EUP × $1.70 per EUP =	5,440
Started and Completed	32,000 EUP × $1.70 per EUP =	54,400
Transferred to Cutting		63,750
In process	2,500 EUP × $1.70 per EUP =	4,250
Total		$ 68,000

We have accomplished our goal of splitting the $208,000 total cost between the completed units and the in process units and can record these costs on the production cost report. The completed report is shown in Exhibit 18A-7.

Exhibit 18A-7 | Production Cost Report—Assembly Department—FIFO Method—Costs Accounted For

PUZZLE ME
Production Cost Report—ASSEMBLY DEPARTMENT—FIFO Method
Month Ended July 31, 2018

UNITS	Physical Units	Equivalent Units for Current Period Direct Materials	Conversion Costs
Units to account for:			
Beginning work-in-process	8,000		
Started in production	42,000		
Total units to account for	50,000		
Units accounted for:			
Beginning work-in-process	8,000	0	3,200
Started and completed	32,000	32,000	32,000
Transferred to Cutting Department	40,000	32,000	35,200
Ending work-in-process	10,000	10,000	2,500
Total units accounted for	50,000	42,000	37,700

COSTS	Direct Materials	Conversion Costs	Total Costs	Cost per Unit
Costs to account for:				
Beginning work-in-process	$ 9,800	$ 3,910	$ 13,710	
Costs added during period	130,200	64,090	194,290	
Total costs to account for	$ 140,000	$ 68,000	$ 208,000	
Costs added during current period	$ 130,200	$ 64,090		
Divided by: EUP this period	÷ 42,000	÷ 37,700		
Cost per equivalent unit this period	$ 3.10	$ 1.70		
Costs accounted for:				
Beginning work-in-process	$ 9,800	$ 3,910	$ 13,710	
Costs to complete beginning WIP	0	5,440	5,440	
Total costs for beginning WIP	9,800	9,350	19,150	$ 2.39[a]
Started and completed	99,200	54,400	153,600	4.80[b]
Transferred to Cutting Department	109,000	63,750	172,750	
Ending work-in-process	31,000	4,250	35,250	
Total costs accounted for	$ 140,000	$ 68,000	$ 208,000	

(a) Beginning WIP: $19,150 / 8,000 units = $2.3938 per unit
(b) Started and completed: $153,600 / 32,000 units = $4.80 per unit

Step 4: Costs accounted for

APPENDIX 18A

Notice the cost per unit for the units that were in beginning WIP is $2.39 ($19,150 / 8,000 units) and the cost per unit for the units started and completed in July is $4.80 ($153,600 / 32,000 units). This indicates that costs varied from June to July. Exhibit 18A-8 (on the next page) shows the completed production cost report for July for the Assembly Department using the weighted-average method. This is a duplicate of Exhibit 18-9 from the chapter. Take a moment to study the reports. Find the similarities and differences.

Exhibit 18A-8 | **Production Cost Report—Assembly Department—Weighted-Average Method**

PUZZLE ME
Production Cost Report—ASSEMBLY DEPARTMENT—Weighted-Average Method
Month Ended July 31, 2018

		Equivalent Units	
UNITS	**Physical Units**	**Direct Materials**	**Conversion Costs**
Units to account for:			
Beginning work-in-process	8,000		
Started in production	42,000		
Total units to account for	50,000		
Units accounted for:			
Completed and transferred out	40,000	40,000	40,000
Ending work-in-process	10,000	10,000	2,500
Total units accounted for	50,000	50,000	42,500

COSTS	**Direct Materials**	**Conversion Costs**	**Total Costs**
Costs to account for:			
Beginning work-in-process	$ 9,800	$ 3,910	$ 13,710
Costs added during period	130,200	64,090	194,290
Total costs to account for	140,000	68,000	$ 208,000
Divided by: Total EUP	÷ 50,000	÷ 42,500	
Cost per equivalent unit	$ 2.80	$ 1.60	
Costs accounted for:			
Completed and transferred out	$ 112,000	$ 64,000	$ 176,000
Ending work-in-process	28,000	4,000	32,000
Total costs accounted for	$ 140,000	$ 68,000	$ 208,000

Comparison of Weighted-Average and FIFO Methods

Notice the differences in the completed and transferred out costs and ending work-in-process costs under each method.

	Weighted-Average	**FIFO**
Completed and transferred out	$ 176,000	$ 172,750
Ending work-in-process	32,000	35,250
Total costs accounted for	$ 208,000	$ 208,000

The total costs are the same regardless of which method is used. The difference between the two methods relates to how the total costs of $208,000 is split between completed and transferred out and ending work-in-process. A company would choose to either use the weighted-average method or the FIFO method. How does a manager decide which method to use?

If a business operates in an industry that experiences significant cost changes, it would be to its benefit to use the FIFO method. The weighted-average method merges costs from the prior period with the current period. This creates a smoothing effect, where cost changes are not as exposed. The FIFO method would create better month-to-month cost comparisons. This would be especially evident when there are substantial quantities of units in process at the end of the period. The more detailed cost information obtained from the FIFO method would allow managers to make better pricing and product mix decisions.

If a business operates in an industry that does not experience significant cost changes, the weighted-average method would be appropriate. This method is easier to use, and the additional benefit derived from more detailed calculations would not outweigh the cost of obtaining them.

Which method is better: weighted-average or first-in, first-out? Why?

Try It!

Bishop Company uses the FIFO method in its process costing system. The Mixing Department started the month with 500 units in process that were 20% complete, started in production 2,000 units, and transferred 2,100 units to the finished goods storage area. All materials are added at the beginning of the process and conversion costs occur evenly. The units in process at the end of the month are 45% complete with respect to conversion costs. The department incurred the following costs:

	Beginning WIP	Added this month	Total
Direct Materials	$ 500	$ 2,000	$ 2,500
Conversion Costs	1,250	5,450	6,700
Total	$ 1,750	$ 7,450	$ 9,200

14A. How many units are still in process at the end of the month?
15A. Compute the equivalent units of production for the Mixing Department for the current month.
16A. Determine the cost per equivalent unit for the current period for direct materials and conversion costs.
17A. Determine the cost to be transferred to the next department.

Check your answers online in MyAccountingLab or at http://www.pearsonhighered.com/Horngren.

For more practice, see Short Exercises S18A-15 and S18A-16.   MyAccountingLab

APPENDIX 18A

REVIEW

> Things You Should Know

1. How do costs flow through a process costing system?

- Process costing systems accumulate costs by process and are most likely used in companies that manufacture large quantities of similar products.
- Process costing systems have multiple Work-in-Process Inventory accounts—one for each process or department.
- Costs flow from one Work-in-Process Inventory account to the next until production is complete.

- Costs flow from the last Work-in-Process Inventory account to Finished Goods Inventory.

- When the products are sold, costs flow from Finished Goods Inventory to Cost of Goods Sold.

2. What are equivalent units of production, and how are they calculated?

- Equivalent units of production are a way of expressing partially completed units in terms of completed units.

- For example, assuming conversion is uniform throughout the process, units that are halfway through a production process will have incurred half of the conversion costs. Therefore, 10 units that are one-half complete have the equivalent costs of 5 units that are complete: $10 \times 50\% = 5 \times 100\%$.

3. How is a production cost report prepared for the first department?

- The production cost report for the first department can be prepared by following four steps.

  - Step 1: Summarize the flow of physical units.
  - Step 2: Compute output in terms of equivalent units of production.
  - Step 3: Compute the cost per equivalent unit of production.
  - Step 4: Assign costs to units completed and units in process.

- Review Exhibit 18-9 for an example of a complete cost production report.

4. How is a production cost report prepared for subsequent departments?

- The production cost report for subsequent departments is the same as the first department with the exception of an additional Transferred In column. The production cost report is still completed using the four step process.

- Units that are received from a previous department are considered transferred in units. These units are always considered 100% complete in terms of equivalent units because the costs were assigned to them in the previous department.

5. What journal entries are required in a process costing system?

- Costs incurred during the period are added to *each* Work-in-Process Inventory account

Date	Accounts and Explanation	Debit	Credit
	Work-in-Process Inventory—Department 1	XXX	
	Work-in-Process Inventory—Department 2	XXX	
	Raw Materials Inventory (for amount of direct materials used)		XXX
	Wages Payable (for amount of direct labor incurred)		XXX
	Manufacturing Overhead (for amount of overhead allocated)		XXX

- Costs transferred to the next department are deducted (credited) from the Work-in-Process Inventory account of the department transferred from and added (debited) to the Work-in-Process Inventory account of the department transferred to.

Date	Accounts and Explanation	Debit	Credit
	Work-in-Process Inventory—Department (transferred in)	XXX	
	Work-in-Process Inventory—Department (transferred out)		XXX

- When costs are transferred from the last department, they are transferred using a debit to Finished Goods Inventory.

Date	Accounts and Explanation	Debit	Credit
	Finished Goods Inventory	XXX	
	Work-in-Process Inventory—Department (transferred out)		XXX

- When goods are sold, the sale is recorded and the cost is transferred from Finished Goods Inventory with a credit and transferred to Cost of Goods Sold with a debit.

Date	Accounts and Explanation	Debit	Credit
	Accounts Receivable (sales price)	XXX	
	Sales Revenue (sales price)		XXX
	Cost of Goods Sold (transferred in at cost)	XXX	
	Finished Goods Inventory (transferred out at cost)		XXX

6. How can the production cost report be used to make decisions?

- Controlling costs
- Evaluating performance
- Pricing products
- Identifying most profitable products
- Preparing financial statements

7. How is a production cost report prepared using the FIFO method? (Appendix 18A)

- The same four step process is used to prepared a production cost report using the FIFO method.
- The only difference is that prior period costs are not merged with current period costs.
- Equivalent units of production must be calculated for

  - Units in beginning inventory completed in current period
  - Units started and completed during current period
  - Units started and still in process at end of current period

CHAPTER 18

> Check Your Understanding 18-1

Check your understanding of the chapter by completing this problem and then looking at the solution. Use this practice to help identify which sections of the chapter you need to study more.

Santa Fe Paints provides the following information for the Mixing Department for the month of September 2018:

	Units	Costs
Beginning Work-in-Process Inventory	0	$ 0
Started in Production in September	18,000	38,000*
Total to Account For	18,000	38,000
Completed and Transferred to Finishing Department during September	14,000	?
Ending Work-in-Process Inventory (25% complete for direct materials; 50% complete for conversion costs)	4,000	?
Total Accounted For	18,000	$ 38,000

*Includes $6,000 direct materials and $32,000 conversion costs

Complete a production cost report for the Mixing Department for the month of September 2018 to determine the cost of the units completed and transferred out and the cost of the ending Work-in-Process Inventory–Mixing. Assume Santa Fe Paints uses the weighted-average method. (See Learning Objectives 2 and 3)

> Solution

SANTA FE PAINTS
Production Cost Report—MIXING DEPARTMENT
Month Ended September 30, 2018

		Equivalent Units	
UNITS	**Physical Units**	**Direct Materials**	**Conversion Costs**
Units to account for:			
Beginning work-in-process	0		
Started in production	18,000		
Total units to account for	18,000		
Units accounted for:			
Completed and transferred out	14,000	14,000	14,000
Ending work-in-process	4,000	1,000[a]	2,000[b]
Total units accounted for	18,000	15,000	16,000

COSTS	**Direct Materials**	**Conversion Costs**	**Total Costs**
Costs to account for:			
Beginning work-in-process	$ 0	$ 0	$ 0
Costs added during period	6,000	32,000	38,000
Total costs to account for	6,000	32,000	$ 38,000
Divided by: Total EUP	÷ 15,000	÷ 16,000	
Cost per equivalent unit	$ 0.40[c]	$ 2.00[d]	
Costs accounted for:			
Completed and transferred out	$ 5,600[e]	$ 28,000[f]	$ 33,600[g]
Ending work-in-process	400[h]	4,000[i]	4,400[j]
Total costs accounted for	$ 6,000	$ 32,000	$ 38,000

Calculations:	
(a)	4,000 units × 25% complete = 1,000 EUP
(b)	4,000 units × 50% complete = 2,000 EUP
(c)	$6,000 / 15,000 EUP = $0.40 per EUP
(d)	$32,000 / 16,000 EUP = $2.00 per EUP
(e)	14,000 EUP × $0.40 per EUP = $5,600
(f)	14,000 EUP × $2.00 per EUP = $28,000
(g)	$5,600 + $28,000 = $33,600
(h)	1,000 EUP × $0.40 per EUP = $400
(i)	2,000 EUP × $2.00 per EUP = $4,000
(j)	$400 + $4,000 = $4,400

The Mixing Department transferred 14,000 units with a cost of $33,600 to the Finishing Department in September. The ending balance in Work-in-Process Inventory—Mixing is $4,400.

> Check Your Understanding 18-2

Check your understanding of the chapter by completing this problem and then looking at the solution. Use this practice to help identify which sections of the chapter you need to study more.

This problem extends Check Your Understanding 18-1 into a second department, Finishing. During September, Santa Fe Paints reports the following in its Finishing Department:

UNITS	
Beginning Work-in-Process Inventory (20% complete for direct materials; 70% complete for conversion costs)	4,000 units
Transferred in from Mixing Department during September	14,000 units
Completed and transferred out to Finished Goods Inventory during September	15,000 units
Ending Work-in-Process Inventory (30% complete for direct materials; 80% complete for conversion costs)	3,000 units
COSTS	
Work-in-Process Inventory, August 31 (transferred in costs, $11,400; direct materials costs, $1,000; conversion costs, $1,800)	$ 14,200
Transferred in from Mixing Department during September (see Summary Problem 1)	33,600
Direct materials added during September	5,360
Conversion costs added during September	24,300

Complete a production cost report to assign the Finishing Department's September total costs to units completed and to units in process at the end of the month. Assume Santa Fe Paints uses the weighted-average method. (See Learning Objective 4)

> Solution

SANTA FE PAINTS
Production Cost Report—FINISHING DEPARTMENT
Month Ended September 30, 2018

		Equivalent Units		
UNITS	Physical Units	Transferred In	Direct Materials	Conversion Costs
Units to account for:				
Beginning work-in-process	4,000			
Started in production	14,000			
Total units to account for	18,000			
Units accounted for:				
Completed and transferred out	15,000	15,000	15,000	15,000
Ending work-in-process	3,000	3,000	900ª	2,400ᵇ
Total units accounted for	18,000	18,000	15,900	17,400

COSTS	Transferred In	Direct Materials	Conversion Costs	Total Costs
Costs to account for:				
Beginning work-in-process	$ 11,400	$ 1,000	$ 1,800	$ 14,200
Costs added during period	33,600	5,360	24,300	63,260
Total costs to account for	45,000	6,360	26,100	$ 77,460
Divided by: Total EUP	÷ 18,000	÷ 15,900	÷ 17,400	
Cost per equivalent unit	$ 2.50ᶜ	$ 0.40ᵈ	$ 1.50ᵉ	
Costs accounted for:				
Completed and transferred out	$ 37,500ᶠ	$ 6,000ᵍ	$ 22,500ʰ	$ 66,000ⁱ
Ending work-in-process	7,500ʲ	360ᵏ	3,600ˡ	11,460ᵐ
Total costs accounted for	$ 45,000	$ 6,360	$ 26,100	$ 77,460

Calculations:	
(a)	3,000 units × 30% complete = 900 EUP
(b)	3,000 units × 80% complete = 2,400 EUP
(c)	$45,000 / 18,000 EUP = $2.50 per EUP
(d)	$6,360 / 15,900 EUP = $0.40 per EUP
(e)	$26,100 / 17,400 EUP = $1.50 per EUP
(f)	15,000 EUP × $2.50 per EUP = $37,500
(g)	15,000 EUP × $0.40 per EUP = $6,000
(h)	15,000 EUP × $1.50 per EUP = $22,500
(i)	$37,500 + $6,000 + $22,500 = $66,000
(j)	3,000 EUP × $2.50 per EUP = $7,500
(k)	900 EUP × $0.40 per EUP = $360
(l)	2,400 EUP × $1.50 per EUP = $3,600
(m)	$7,500 + $360 + $3,600 = $11,460

The Finishing Department transferred 15,000 units with a cost of $66,000 to Finished Goods Inventory in September. The ending balance in Work-in-Process Inventory—Finishing is $11,460.

> Key Terms

Cost Pool (p. 971)

Conversion Costs (p. 967)

Equivalent Units of Production (EUP) (p. 967)

First-In, First-Out Method (for Process Costing) (p. 988) (Appendix 18A)

Job Order Costing System (p. 962)

Physical units (p. 969)

Process (p. 962)

Process Costing System (p. 962)

Production Cost Report (p. 968)

Transferred In Costs (p. 975)

Weighted-Average Method (for Process Costing) (p. 971)

> Quick Check

1. Which company is least likely to use a process costing system?

   a. Paper manufacturer

   b. Soft drink bottler

   c. Accounting firm

   d. Petroleum processor

Learning Objective 1

2. Which characteristic is the same in both job order costing systems and process costing systems?

   a. Types of product costs

   b. Flow of costs through the accounts

   c. Number of Work-in-Process Inventory accounts

   d. Method of record keeping

Learning Objective 1

3. Conversion costs are

   a. direct materials plus direct labor.

   b. direct labor plus manufacturing overhead.

   c. direct materials plus manufacturing overhead.

   d. indirect materials plus indirect labor.

Learning Objective 2

Use the following information for Questions 4–6:

Burton Company uses the weighted-average method in its process costing system. The Packaging Department started the month with 200 units in process, started 1,500 units, and had 150 units in process at the end of the period. All materials are added at the beginning of the process, and conversion costs are incurred uniformly. The units in process at the end of the month are 20% complete with respect to conversion costs. The department incurred the following costs:

	Beginning WIP	Added this month	Total
Direct Materials	$ 200	$ 3,200	$ 3,400
Conversion Costs	500	5,820	6,320
Total	$ 700	$ 9,020	$ 9,720

4. How many units were completed and transferred out?

   a. 150 units   **b.** 1,500 units   **c.** 1,350 units   **d.** 1,550 units

Learning Objective 3

Learning Objective 3

5. For conversion costs, the equivalent units of production are

    a. 1,700 units.   **b.** 1,580 units.   **c.** 1,500 units.   **d.** 1,550 units.

Learning Objective 3

6. The cost per equivalent unit for direct materials is

    a. $2.00.   **b.** $4.00.   **c.** $8.00.   **d.** $14.00.

Learning Objective 4

7. The Assembly Department had 4,500 units of beginning inventory in September, and 6,000 units were transferred to it from the Cutting Department. The Assembly Department completed 3,000 units during the month and transferred them to the Packaging Department. Determine the total number of units to account for by the Assembly Department.

    a. 3,000 units   **b.** 4,500 units   **c.** 7,500 units   **d.** 10,500 units

Learning Objective 5

8. The Mixing Department incurred the following costs during the month:

	Direct Materials	Direct Labor	Manufacturing Overhead Allocated
Beginning WIP	$ 50	$ 25	$ 80
Added this month	225	150	500
Total	$ 275	$ 175	$ 580

What is the journal entry to record the costs incurred during the month?

Date	Accounts and Explanation	Debit	Credit
a.	Work-in-Process Inventory—Mixing	1,030	
	Raw Materials Inventory		275
	Wages Payable		175
	Manufacturing Overhead		580
b.	Work-in-Process Inventory—Mixing	2,280	
	Transfer Costs		1,250
	Raw Materials Inventory		275
	Wages Payable		175
	Manufacturing Overhead		580
c.	Work-in-Process Inventory—Mixing	875	
	Raw Materials Inventory		225
	Wages Payable		150
	Manufacturing Overhead		500
d.	Work-in-Process Inventory—Mixing	875	
	Raw Materials Inventory		225
	Conversion Costs		650

9. Department 1 completed work on 500 units and transferred them to Department 2. The cost of the units was $750. What is the journal entry to record the transfer?

Learning Objective 5

Date	Accounts and Explanation	Debit	Credit
a.	Work-in-Process Inventory—Dept. 1	750	
	Work-in-Process Inventory—Dept. 2		750
b.	Work-in-Process Inventory—Dept. 2	750	
	Work-in-Process Inventory—Dept. 1		750
c.	Work-in-Process Inventory—Dept. 2	750	
	Cost of Goods Sold		750
d.	Cost of Goods Sold	750	
	Work-in-Process Inventory—Dept. 1		750

10. The manager of Gilbert Company used the production cost report to compare budgeted costs to actual costs and then based bonuses on the results. This is an example of using the reports to

Learning Objective 6

   a. prepare financial statements.
   b. control costs.
   c. evaluate performance.
   d. identify profitable products.

11A. Which statement is accurate concerning the FIFO method for assigning costs in a process costing system?

Learning Objective 7
Appendix 18A

   a. FIFO method assumes the first costs incurred are transferred out.
   b. FIFO method merges costs from prior periods with costs from current periods.
   c. FIFO method assumes the first costs incurred are still in process.
   d. FIFO method treats units in process at the beginning of the period in the same manner as units in process at the end of the period.

Check your answers at the end of the chapter.

CHAPTER 18

ASSESS YOUR PROGRESS

> Review Questions

1. What types of companies use job order costing systems?
2. What types of companies use process costing systems?
3. What are the primary differences between job order costing systems and process costing systems?
4. List ways in which job order costing systems are similar to process costing systems.
5. Describe the flow of costs through a process costing system.
6. What are equivalent units of production?
7. Why is the calculation of equivalent units of production needed in a process costing system?
8. What are conversion costs? Why do some companies using process costing systems use conversion costs?

9. What is a production cost report?

10. What are the four steps in preparing a production cost report?

11. Explain the terms *to account for* and *accounted for*.

12. If a company began the month with 50 units in process, started another 600 units during the month, and ended the month with 75 units in process, how many units were completed?

13. Most companies using process costing systems have to calculate more than one EUP. Why? How many do they have to calculate?

14. What is the weighted-average method for process costing systems?

15. How is the cost per equivalent unit of production calculated?

16. What is the purpose of the Costs Accounted For section of the production cost report?

17. What are transferred in costs? When do they occur?

18. Explain the additional journal entries required by process costing systems that are not needed in job order costing systems.

19. Department 1 is transferring units that cost $40,000 to Department 2. Give the journal entry.

20. Department 4 has completed production on units that have a total cost of $15,000. The units are ready for sale. Give the journal entry.

21. Describe ways the production cost report can be used by management.

22A. Describe how the FIFO method is different from the weighted-average method.

23A. Describe the three groups of units that must be accounted for when using the FIFO method.

24A. When might it be beneficial for a company to use the FIFO method? When is the weighted-average method more practical?

> Short Exercises

Learning Objective 1

S18-1 Comparing job order costing versus process costing

Identify each costing system characteristic as job order costing or process costing.

a. One Work-in-Process Inventory account

b. Production cost reports

c. Cost accumulated by process

d. Job cost sheets

e. Manufactures homogenous products through a series of uniform steps

f. Multiple Work-in-Process Inventory accounts

g. Costs transferred at end of period

h. Manufactures batches of unique products or provides specialized services

S18-2 Tracking the flow of costs

Learning Objective 1

The Jimenez Toy Company makes wooden toys. The company uses a process costing system. Arrange the company's accounts in the order the production costs are most likely to flow, using 1 for the first account, 2 for the second, and so on.

Order	Account
_____	Work-in-Process Inventory—Packaging
_____	Cost of Goods Sold
_____	Work-in-Process Inventory—Cutting
_____	Work-in-Process Inventory—Finishing
_____	Finished Goods Inventory

S18-3 Calculating conversion costs

Learning Objective 2

Evergreen Orange manufactures orange juice. Last month's total manufacturing costs for the Tampa operation included:

Direct materials	$ 450,000
Direct labor	32,000
Manufacturing overhead	125,000

What was the conversion cost for Evergreen Orange's Tampa operation last month?

S18-4 Calculating EUP

Learning Objective 2

Cadwell manufactures cell phones. The conversion costs to produce cell phones for November are added evenly throughout the process in the Assembly Department. The company uses the weighted-average method. For each of the following separate assumptions, calculate the equivalent units of production for conversion costs in the ending Work-in-Process Inventory for the Assembly Department:

1. 12,000 cell phones were 60% complete

2. 21,000 cell phones were 40% complete

S18-5 Calculating conversion costs and unit cost

Learning Objective 2

Spring Fresh produces premium bottled water. Spring Fresh purchases artesian water, stores the water in large tanks, and then runs the water through two processes: filtration and bottling.

During February, the filtration process incurred the following costs in processing 200,000 liters:

Wages of workers operating filtration equipment	$ 19,950
Manufacturing overhead allocated to filtration	20,050
Water	110,000

Spring Fresh had no beginning Work-in-Process Inventory in the Filtration Department in February and uses the weighted-average method.

Requirements

1. Compute the February conversion costs in the Filtration Department.

2. The Filtration Department completely processed 200,000 liters in February. What was the filtration cost per liter?

Note: Short Exercise S18-5 must be completed before attempting Short Exercise S18-6.

Learning Objective 2

S18-6 Computing EUP

Refer to Short Exercise S18-5. At Spring Fresh, water is added at the beginning of the filtration process. Conversion costs are added evenly throughout the process. Now assume that in February, 155,000 liters were completed and transferred out of the Filtration Department into the Bottling Department. The 45,000 liters remaining in Filtration's ending Work-in-Process Inventory were 80% of the way through the filtration process. Recall that Spring Fresh has no beginning inventories.

Compute the equivalent units of production for direct materials and conversion costs for the Filtration Department.

Learning Objective 3

S18-7 Computing costs transferred

The Finishing Department of Lee and Lewis, Inc., the last department in the manufacturing process, incurred production costs of $220,000 during the month of June. If the June 1 balance in Work-in-Process Inventory—Finishing is $0 and the June 30 balance is $70,000, what amount was transferred to Finished Goods Inventory?

Learning Objectives 2, 3

S18-8 Computing EUP

The Mixing Department of Complete Foods had 62,000 units to account for in October. Of the 62,000 units, 38,000 units were completed and transferred to the next department, and 24,000 units were 20% complete. All of the materials are added at the beginning of the process. Conversion costs are added evenly throughout the mixing process and the company uses the weighted-average method.

Compute the total equivalent units of production for direct materials and conversion costs for October.

Note: Short Exercise S18-8 must be completed before attempting Short Exercise S18-9.

Learning Objective 3

S18-9 Computing the cost per EUP

Refer to the data in Short Exercise S18-8 and your results for equivalent units of production. The Mixing Department of Complete Foods has direct materials costs of $46,500 and conversion costs of $23,540 for October.

Compute the cost per equivalent unit of production for direct materials and for conversion costs.

Note: Short Exercises S18-8 and S18-9 must be completed before attempting Short Exercise S18-10.

Learning Objective 3

S18-10 Assigning costs

Refer to Short Exercises S18-8 and S18-9. Use Complete Foods's costs per equivalent unit of production for direct materials and conversion costs that you calculated in Short Exercise S18-9.

Calculate the cost of the 38,000 units completed and transferred out and the 24,000 units, 20% complete, in the ending Work-in-Process Inventory.

Learning Objective 4

S18-11 Computing EUP, second department

The Packaging Department started the month with 600 units in process, received 1,200 units from the Finishing Department, and transferred 1,500 units to Finished Goods. Direct materials are added at the beginning of the process and conversion costs are incurred evenly. The units still in process at the end of the month are 60% complete for conversion costs. Calculate the number of units still in process at the end of the month and the equivalent units of production. The company uses the weighted-average method.

CHAPTER 18

S18-12 Computing the cost per EUP, second department

Learning Objective 4

The Finishing Department reports the following data for the month:

Equivalent Units of Production:

Transferred In	3,000
Direct Materials	3,000
Conversion Costs	2,250

Costs:	Beginning WIP	Added this Month	Total
Transferred In	$ 7,500	$ 15,000	$ 22,500
Direct Materials	3,250	6,500	9,750
Conversion Costs	6,125	13,000	19,125
Total	$ 16,875	$ 34,500	$ 51,375

Calculate the cost per equivalent units of production for each input. The company uses the weighted-average method.

S18-13 Preparing journal entry

Learning Objective 5

The Mixing Department's production cost report for May shows $12,500 in total costs, of which $2,500 will remain in the department assigned to the units still in process at the end of the month. Prepare the journal entry to record the transfer of costs from the Mixing Department to the Packaging Department.

S18-14 Making decisions

Learning Objective 6

Miller Company sells several products. Sales reports show that the sales volume of its most popular product has increased the past three quarters while overall profits have decreased. How might production cost reports assist management in making decisions about this product?

S18A-15 Calculating conversion costs and unit cost—FIFO method

Learning Objective 7
Appendix 18A

Spring Fresh produces premium bottled water. Spring Fresh purchases artesian water, stores the water in large tanks, and then runs the water through two processes: filtration and bottling.

During February, the filtration process incurred the following costs in processing 200,000 liters:

Wages of workers operating filtration equipment	$ 34,950
Manufacturing overhead allocated to filtration	19,050
Water	110,000

Spring Fresh had no beginning Work-in-Process Inventory in the Filtration Department in February.

Requirements

1. Use the FIFO method to compute the February conversion costs in the Filtration Department.
2. The Filtration Department completely processed 200,000 liters in February. Use the FIFO method to determine the filtration cost per liter.

CHAPTER 18

Note: Short Exercise S18A-15 must be completed before attempting Short Exercise S18A-16.

Learning Objective 7
Appendix 18A

S18A-16 Computing EUP—FIFO Method

Refer to Short Exercise S18A-15. At Spring Fresh, water is added at the beginning of the filtration process. Conversion costs are added evenly throughout the process. Now assume that in February, 130,000 liters were completed and transferred out of the Filtration Department into the Bottling Department. The 70,000 liters remaining in Filtration's ending Work-in-Process Inventory were 80% of the way through the filtration process. Recall that Spring Fresh has no beginning inventories.

Compute the equivalent units of production for direct materials and conversion costs for the Filtration Department using the FIFO method.

>Exercises

For all Exercises, assume the weighted-average method is to be used unless you are told otherwise.

Learning Objective 1

E18-17 Comparing job order costing versus process costing

For each of the following products or services, indicate if the cost would most likely be determined using a job order costing system or a process costing system.

a. Soft drinks

b. Automobile repairs

c. Customized furniture

d. Aluminum foil

e. Lawn chairs

f. Chocolate candy bars

g. Hospital surgery

h. Pencils

Learning Objectives 1, 2, 3, 4

E18-18 Understanding terminology

Match the following terms to their definitions.

1. Direct labor plus manufacturing overhead
2. Prepared by department for EUP, production costs, and assignment of costs
3. Equivalent units of production
4. Process costing system
5. Transferred in costs
6. Weighted-average method

a. Expresses partially completed units in terms of fully completed units
b. Used by companies that manufacture homogenous products
c. Previous costs brought into later process
d. Conversion costs
e. Combines prior period costs with current period costs
f. Production cost report

CHAPTER 18

E18-19 Tracking the flow of costs

Learning Objectives 1, 5

c. $13,000

Complete the missing amounts and labels in the T-accounts.

Work-in-Process Inventory—Cutting

Balance, May 1	0	(a)	Transfer out to _____
Direct Materials	57,000		
Direct Labor	5,000		
Manufacturing Overhead	39,000		
Balance, May 31	16,000		

Work-in-Process Inventory—Finishing

Balance, May 1	11,000	80,000	Transfer out to _____
Transfer in from _____	(b)		
Direct Materials	21,000		
Direct Labor	(c)		
Manufacturing Overhead	18,000		
Balance, May 31	68,000		

Work-in-Process Inventory—Packaging

Balance, May 1	4,000	(d)	Transfer out to _____
Transfer in from _____	(e)		
Direct Materials	1,000		
Direct Labor	9,000		
Manufacturing Overhead	14,000		
Balance, May 31	8,000		

Finished Goods Inventory

Balance, May 1	0	(f)	Transfer out to _____
Transfer in from _____	(g)		
Balance, May 31	2,000		

Cost of Goods Sold

Balance, May 1	0	
Transfer in from _____	(h)	
Balance, May 31	(i)	

E18-20 Computing EUP

Learning Objective 2

3. EUP for DM 2,100

Collins Company has the following data for the Assembly Department for August:

Units in process at the beginning of August	900
Units started in August	2,000
Units completed and transferred	2,100
Units in process at end of August	800

Conversion costs are added evenly throughout the process. The company uses the weighted-average method. Compute the equivalent units of production for direct materials and conversion costs for each independent scenario:

1. Units in process at the end of August are 20% complete; materials are added at the beginning of the process.
2. Units in process at the end of August are 80% complete; materials are added at the beginning of the process.

3. Units in process at the end of August are 20% complete; materials are added at the end of the process.

4. Units in process at the end of August are 80% complete; materials are added at the halfway point.

Learning Objectives 2, 3

1. Total EUP for CC 7,100

E18-21 Computing EUP, assigning costs, no beginning WIP or costs transferred in

Color Explosion prepares and packages paint products. Color Explosion has two departments: Blending and Packaging. Direct materials are added at the beginning of the blending process (dyes) and at the end of the packaging process (cans). Conversion costs are added evenly throughout each process. The company uses the weighted-average method. Data from the month of May for the Blending Department are as follows:

Gallons	
Beginning Work-in-Process Inventory	0 gallons
Started in production	8,500 gallons
Completed and transferred out to Packaging in May	6,500 gallons
Ending Work-in-Process Inventory (30% of the way through the blending process)	2,000 gallons
Costs	
Beginning Work-in-Process Inventory	$ 0
Costs added during May:	
Direct materials	5,525
Direct labor	1,500
Manufacturing overhead allocated	2,547
Total costs added during May	$ 9,572

Requirements

1. Compute the Blending Department's equivalent units of production for direct materials and for conversion costs.
2. Compute the total costs of the units (gallons)
   a. completed and transferred out to the Packaging Department.
   b. in the Blending Department ending Work-in-Process Inventory.

Note: Exercise E18-21 must be completed before attempting Exercise E18-22.

Learning Objectives 5, 6

2. WIP Balance $1,642

E18-22 Preparing journal entries, posting to T-accounts, making decisions

Refer to your answers from Exercise E18-21.

Requirements

1. Prepare the journal entries to record the assignment of direct materials and direct labor and the allocation of manufacturing overhead to the Blending Department. Also, prepare the journal entry to record the costs of the gallons completed and transferred out to the Packaging Department. Assume labor costs are accrued and not yet paid.
2. Post the journal entries to the Work-in-Process Inventory—Blending T-account. What is the ending balance?
3. What is the average cost per gallon transferred out of the Blending Department into the Packaging Department? Why would the company managers want to know this cost?

E18-23 Computing EUP, assigning costs, with beginning WIP, no costs transferred in

Learning Objectives 2, 3

1. EUP for CC 8,860

Shea Winery in Pleasant Valley, New York, has two departments: Fermenting and Packaging. Direct materials are added at the beginning of the fermenting process (grapes) and at the end of the packaging process (bottles). Conversion costs are added evenly throughout each process. The company uses the weighted-average method. Data from the month of March for the Fermenting Department are as follows:

Gallons	
Beginning Work-in-Process Inventory	500 gallons
Started in production	8,600 gallons
Completed and transferred out to Packaging in March	7,900 gallons
Ending Work-in-Process Inventory (80% of the way through the fermenting process)	1,200 gallons
Costs	
Beginning Work-in-Process Inventory:	
Direct materials	$ 540
Direct labor	195
Manufacturing overhead allocated	210
Costs added during March:	
Direct materials	9,288
Direct labor	3,305
Manufacturing overhead allocated	3,378
Total costs added during March	$ 15,971

Requirements

1. Compute the Fermenting Department's equivalent units of production for direct materials and for conversion costs.
2. Compute the total costs of the units (gallons)
   a. completed and transferred out to the Packaging Department.
   b. in the Fermenting Department ending Work-in-Process Inventory.

Note: Exercise E18-23 must be completed before attempting Exercise E18-24.

E18-24 Preparing journal entries, posting to T-accounts, making decisions

Learning Objectives 5, 6

2. WIP Balance $2,064

Refer to the data and your answers from Exercise E18-23.

Requirements

1. Prepare the journal entries to record the assignment of direct materials and direct labor and the allocation of manufacturing overhead to the Fermenting Department. Assume labor costs are accrued and not yet paid. Also prepare the journal entry to record the cost of the gallons completed and transferred out to the Packaging Department.
2. Post the journal entries to the Work-in-Process Inventory—Fermenting T-account. What is the ending balance?
3. What is the average cost per gallon transferred out of the Fermenting Department into the Packaging Department? Why would Shea Winery's managers want to know this cost?

Learning Objectives 2, 3

(p) $3.70

E18-25 Preparing production cost report, missing amounts

Complete the missing amounts in the following production report. Materials are added at the beginning of the process; conversion costs are incurred evenly; the ending inventory is 60% complete. The company uses the weighted-average method.

NATHAN COMPANY
Production Cost Report—FINISHING DEPARTMENT
Month Ended September 30, 2018

UNITS	Physical Units	Equivalent Units Direct Materials	Equivalent Units Conversion Costs
Units to account for:			
Beginning work-in-process	500		
Started in production	2,200		
Total units to account for	(a)		
Units accounted for:			
Completed and transferred out	(b)	(d)	(g)
Ending work-in-process	500	(e)	(h)
Total units accounted for	(c)	(f)	(i)

COSTS	Direct Materials	Conversion Costs	Total Costs
Costs to account for:			
Beginning work-in-process	$ 1,200	(j)	$ 2,140
Costs added during period	12,030	8,310	(k)
Total costs to account for	(l)	9,250	22,480
Divided by: Total EUP	(m)	(n)	
Cost per equivalent unit	(o)	(p)	
Costs accounted for:			
Completed and transferred out	(q)	(r)	(s)
Ending work-in-process	(t)	(u)	(v)
Total costs accounted for	(w)	(x)	$ 22,480

Learning Objectives 2, 3, 4

2. EUP for DM 92,800

E18-26 Computing EUP, first and second departments

Selected production and cost data of Laura's Caliper Co. follow for May 2018:

	Mixing Department	Heating Department
Units to account for:		
Beginning work-in-process, April 30	25,000	10,000
Started in May	90,000	
Transferred in during May		90,000
Total units to account for	115,000	100,000
Units accounted for:		
Completed and transferred out during May	90,000	82,000
Ending work-in-process, May 31	25,000	18,000
Total units accounted for	115,000	100,000

On May 31, the Mixing Department ending Work-in-Process Inventory was 80% complete for materials and 45% complete for conversion costs. The Heating Department ending Work-in-Process Inventory was 60% complete for materials and 35% complete for conversion costs. The company uses the weighted-average method.

Requirements

1. Compute the equivalent units of production for direct materials and for conversion costs for the Mixing Department.

2. Compute the equivalent units of production for transferred in costs, direct materials, and conversion costs for the Heating Department.

E18-27 Preparing production cost report, journalizing, second department

Refreshing Water Company produces premium bottled water. In the second department, the Bottling Department, conversion costs are incurred evenly throughout the bottling process, but packaging materials are not added until the end of the process. Costs in beginning Work-in-Process Inventory include transferred in costs of $1,400, direct labor of $700, and manufacturing overhead of $330. March data for the Bottling Department follow:

(Requirement 1 only)

Learning Objectives 2, 4, 5

3. WIP Balance $22,770

REFRESHING WATER COMPANY
Work-in-Process Inventory—Bottling
Month Ended March 31, 2018

		Dollars				
	Units	Transferred In	Direct Materials	Direct Labor	Manufacturing Overhead	Total Costs
Beginning inventory, Mar. 1 (40% complete)	15,000	$ 1,400		$ 700	$ 330	$ 2,430
Production started	160,000	135,100	$ 30,400	33,100	16,300	214,900
Transferred out	152,000					
Ending inventory, Mar. 31 (70% complete)	23,000					

Requirements

1. Prepare a production cost report for the Bottling Department for the month of March. The company uses the weighted-average method.

2. Prepare the journal entry to record the cost of units completed and transferred out.

3. Post all transactions to the Work-in-Process Inventory—Bottling T-account. What is the ending balance?

E18-28 Preparing journal entries—inputs

Oxford Company had the following transactions in October:

Learning Objective 5

1. Purchased raw materials on account, $70,000

2. Used materials in production: $26,000 in the Mixing Department; $14,000 in the Packaging Department; $1,000 in indirect materials

3. Incurred labor costs: $8,000 in the Mixing Department; $7,200 in the Packaging Department; $2,200 in indirect labor

4. Incurred manufacturing overhead costs: $3,500 in machinery depreciation; paid $2,300 for rent and $1,590 for utilities

Prepare the journal entries for Oxford Company.

CHAPTER 18

Learning Objective 5

E18-29 Preparing journal entries—outputs

Hartley Company has a production process that involves three processes. Units move through the processes in this order: cutting, stamping, and then polishing. The company had the following transactions in November:

1. Cost of units completed in the Cutting Department, $17,000
2. Cost of units completed in the Stamping Department, $30,000
3. Cost of units completed in the Polishing Department, $35,000
4. Sales on account, $50,000
5. Cost of goods sold is 80% of sales

Prepare the journal entries for Hartley Company.

Learning Objective 5

E18-30 Preparing journal entries—manufacturing overhead

Blue Ridge Mountain Manufacturing had the following transactions related to manufacturing overhead for the year:

1. Incurred manufacturing overhead costs
   a. $5,000 in indirect materials
   b. $12,500 in indirect labor (credit Wages Payable)
   c. $30,600 in machinery depreciation
   d. $20,400 in other indirect costs that were paid in cash
2. Allocated manufacturing overhead (use a compound entry)
   a. $30,000 to the Mixing Department
   b. $37,000 to the Packaging Department

Requirements

1. Prepare the journal entries for Blue Ridge Mountain Manufacturing.
2. Determine the amount of overallocated or underallocated manufacturing overhead by posting the transactions to the Manufacturing Overhead account. Assume the balance in Manufacturing Overhead on January 1 is $0. Prepare the adjusting entry.

Learning Objective 7
Appendix 18A

2. Prepping Dept. EUP for CC
51,750

E18A-31 Computing EUP—FIFO method

Brian's Frozen Pizzas uses FIFO process costing. Selected production and cost data follow for April 2018.

	Prepping Department
Units to account for:	
Beginning work-in-process, March 31	20,000
Started in April	45,000
Total units to account for	65,000
Units accounted for:	
Completed and transferred out during April:	
From beginning work-in-process inventory	20,000
Started and completed during April	30,000
Ending work-in-process, April 30	15,000
Total units accounted for	65,000

Requirements

1. Calculate the following:

   a. On March 31, the Prepping Department beginning Work-in-Process Inventory was 75% complete for materials and 55% complete for conversion costs. This means that for the beginning inventory ___ % of the materials and ___ % of the conversion costs were added during April.

   b. On April 30, the Prepping Department ending Work-in-Process Inventory was 60% complete for materials and 85% complete for conversion costs. This means that for the ending inventory ___ % of the materials and ___ % of the conversion costs were added during April.

2. Use the information in the table and the information in Requirement 1 to compute the equivalent units of production for direct materials and conversion costs for the Prepping Department.

> Problems Group A

P18-32A Preparing a production cost report, no beginning WIP or costs transferred in

Learning Objectives 2, 3

1. Cost per EUP for DM $3.99
2. WIP Balance $49,980

Dee Electronics makes game consoles in three processes: assembly, programming, and packaging. Direct materials are added at the beginning of the assembly process. Conversion costs are incurred evenly throughout the process. The Assembly Department had no Work-in-Process Inventory on October 31. In mid-November, Dee Electronics started production on 100,000 game consoles. Of this number, 90,000 game consoles were assembled during November and transferred out to the Programming Department. The November 30 Work-in-Process Inventory in the Assembly Department was 35% of the way through the assembly process. Direct materials costing $399,000 were placed in production in Assembly during November, direct labor of $139,000 was assigned, and manufacturing overhead of $130,280 was allocated to that department.

Requirements

1. Prepare a production cost report for the Assembly Department for November. The company uses the weighted-average method.

2. Prepare a T-account for Work-in-Process Inventory—Assembly to show its activity during November, including the November 30 balance.

P18-33A Preparing a production cost report, beginning WIP, no costs transferred in; journal entries

Learning Objectives 2, 3, 5

1. Cost per EUP for CC $1.45

Roan Paper Co. produces the paper used by wallpaper manufacturers. Roan's four-stage process includes mixing, cooking, rolling, and cutting. On March 1, the Mixing Department had 300 rolls of paper in process. During March, the Mixing Department completed the mixing process for those 300 rolls and also started and completed the mixing process for an additional 4,200 rolls of paper. The department started but did not finish the mixing process for an additional 500 rolls, which were 20% complete with respect to both direct materials and conversion work at the end of March. Direct materials and conversion costs are

CHAPTER 18

incurred evenly throughout the mixing process. The Mixing Department compiled the following data for March:

	Direct Materials	Direct Labor	Manufacturing Overhead Allocated	Total Costs
Beginning inventory, Mar. 1	$ 350	$ 245	$ 200	$ 795
Costs added during March	4,940	3,000	3,225	11,165
Total costs	$ 5,290	$ 3,245	$ 3,425	$ 11,960

Requirements

1. Prepare a production cost report for the Mixing Department for March. The company uses the weighted-average method.
2. Journalize all transactions affecting the company's mixing process during March. Assume labor costs are accrued and not yet paid.

Learning Objectives 2, 3, 5

1. Total EUP for CC 3,170
3. WIP Balance $981

P18-34A Preparing a production cost report, two materials added at different points, no beginning WIP or costs transferred in; journal entries

Bert's Exteriors produces exterior siding for homes. The Preparation Department begins with wood, which is chopped into small bits. At the end of the process, an adhesive is added. Then the wood/adhesive mixture goes on to the Compression Department, where the wood is compressed into sheets. Conversion costs are added evenly throughout the preparation process. January data for the Preparation Department are as follows:

UNITS	
Beginning Work-in-Process Inventory	0 sheets
Started in production	3,800 sheets
Completed and transferred out to Compression in January	2,900 sheets
Ending Work-in-Process Inventory (30% of the way through the preparation process)	900 sheets

COSTS	
Beginning Work-in-Process Inventory	$ 0
Costs added during January:	
Wood	2,888
Adhesives	1,914
Direct labor	987
Manufacturing overhead allocated	2,500
Total costs	$ 8,289

Requirements

1. Prepare a production cost report for the Preparation Department for January. The company uses the weighted-average method. (*Hint:* Each direct material added at a different point in the production process requires its own equivalent units of production computation.)
2. Prepare the journal entry to record the cost of the sheets completed and transferred out to the Compression Department.
3. Post the journal entries to the Work-in-Process Inventory—Preparation T-account. What is the ending balance?

P18-35A Preparing production cost report, second department with beginning WIP; journal entries

Learning Objectives 2, 4, 5

1. Cost per EUP DM $25.00

Carla Carpet manufactures broadloom carpet in seven processes: spinning, dyeing, plying, spooling, tufting, latexing, and shearing. In the Dyeing Department, direct materials (dye) are added at the beginning of the process. Conversion costs are incurred evenly throughout the process. Information for November 2018 follows:

UNITS	
Beginning Work-in-Process Inventory	70 rolls
Transferred in from Spinning Department during November	550 rolls
Completed during November	480 rolls
Ending Work-in-Process Inventory (80% complete for conversion work)	140 rolls
COSTS	
Beginning Work-in-Process Inventory (transferred in costs, $4,000; materials costs, $1,400; conversion costs, $5,300)	$ 10,700
Transferred in from Spinning Department	23,280
Materials costs added during November	14,100
Conversion costs added during November (manufacturing wages, $8,725; manufacturing overhead allocated, $43,991)	52,716

Requirements

1. Prepare the November production cost report for Carla's Dyeing Department. The company uses the weighted-average method.

2. Journalize all transactions affecting Carla's Dyeing Department during November, including the entries that have already been posted. Assume labor costs are accrued and not yet paid.

P18-36A Preparing production cost report, second department with beginning WIP; decision making

Learning Objectives 2, 4, 6

1. Total cost per EUP for CC $12.00

Ocean Worthy uses three processes to manufacture lifts for personal watercraft: forming a lift's parts from galvanized steel, assembling the lift, and testing the completed lift. The lifts are transferred to Finished Goods Inventory before shipment to marinas across the country.

Ocean Worthy's Testing Department requires no direct materials. Conversion costs are incurred evenly throughout the testing process. Other information follows for the month of August:

UNITS	
Beginning Work-in-Process Inventory	2,000 units
Transferred in from Assembling Department during the period	7,000 units
Completed during the period	4,000 units
Ending Work-in-Process Inventory (40% complete for conversion work)	5,000 units
COSTS	
Beginning Work-in-Process Inventory (transferred in costs, $93,000; conversion costs, $18,000)	$ 111,000
Transferred in from the Assembly Department during the period	672,000
Conversion costs added during the period	54,000

The cost transferred into Finished Goods Inventory is the cost of the lifts transferred out of the Testing Department. Ocean Worthy uses weighted-average process costing.

Requirements

1. Prepare a production cost report for the Testing Department.

2. What is the cost per unit for lifts completed and transferred out to Finished Goods Inventory? Why would management be interested in this cost?

Learning Objective 7
Appendix 18A

1. Total EUP for CC 5,320

P18A-37A Preparing production cost report, first department, with beginning WIP; journal entries; FIFO method

Cheerful Colors manufactures crayons in a three-step process: mixing, molding, and packaging. The Mixing Department combines the direct materials of paraffin wax and pigments. The heated mixture is pumped to the Molding Department, where it is poured into molds. After the molds cool, the crayons are removed from the molds and are transferred to the Packaging Department, where paper wrappers are added and the crayons are boxed.

In the Mixing Department, the direct materials are added at the beginning of the process and the conversion costs are incurred evenly throughout the process. Work in process of the Mixing Department on March 1, 2018, consisted of 800 batches of crayons that were 10% of the way through the production process. The beginning balance in Work-in-Process Inventory—Mixing was $32,800, which consisted of $14,000 in direct materials costs and $18,800 in conversion costs. During March, 5,200 batches were started in production. The Mixing Department transferred 3,000 batches to the Molding Department in March, and 3,000 were still in process on March 31. This ending inventory was 80% of the way through the mixing process. Cheerful Colors uses FIFO process costing.

At March 31, before recording the transfer of costs from the Mixing Department to the Molding Department, the Cheerful Colors general ledger included the following account:

Work-in-Process Inventory—Mixing	
Balance, Mar. 1	32,800
Direct materials	42,000
Direct labor	24,610
Manufacturing overhead	65,830

Requirements

1. Prepare a production cost report for the Mixing Department for March. Round equivalent unit of production costs to four decimal places. Round all other costs to the nearest whole dollar.

2. Journalize all transactions affecting the Mixing Department during March, including the entries that have already been posted. Assume labor costs are accrued and not yet paid.

Learning Objective 7
Appendix 18A

1. Cost per EUP for CC $1.3895

P18A-38A Preparing a production cost report, first department, with beginning WIP; journal entries; FIFO method

Work Problem P18-33A using the FIFO method. The Mixing Department beginning work in process of 300 units is 40% complete as to both direct materials and conversion costs. Round equivalent unit of production costs to four decimal places. Round all other costs to the nearest whole dollar.

> Problems Group B

For all Problems, assume the weighted-average method is to be used unless you are told otherwise.

P18-39B Preparing a production cost report, no beginning WIP or cost transferred in

Learning Objectives 2, 3

1. Total cost per EUP $5.50
2. WIP Balance $16,610

Mayhem Electronics makes game consoles in three processes: assembly, programming, and packaging. Direct materials are added at the beginning of the assembly process. Conversion costs are incurred evenly throughout the process. The Assembly Department had no Work-in-Process Inventory on March 31. In mid-April, Mayhem Electronics started production on 99,000 game consoles. Of this number, 95,000 game consoles were assembled during April and transferred out to the Programming Department. The April 30 Work-in-Process Inventory in the Assembly Department was 45% of the way through the assembly process. Direct materials costing $301,950 were placed in production in Assembly during April, direct labor of $100,960 was assigned, and manufacturing overhead of $136,200 was allocated to that department.

Requirements

1. Prepare a production cost report for the Assembly Department for April. The company uses the weighted-average method.
2. Prepare a T-account for Work-in-Process Inventory—Assembly to show its activity during April, including the April 30 balance.

P18-40B Preparing a production cost report, beginning WIP, no costs transferred in; journal entries

Learning Objectives 2, 3, 5

1. Cost per EUP for CC $1.40

Smith Paper Co. produces the paper used by wallpaper manufacturers. Smith's four-stage process includes mixing, cooking, rolling, and cutting. On March 1, the Mixing Department had 400 rolls in process. During March, the Mixing Department completed the mixing process for those 400 rolls and also started and completed the mixing process for an additional 4,100 rolls of paper. The department started but did not finish the mixing process for an additional 500 rolls, which were 20% complete with respect to both direct materials and conversion work at the end of March. Direct materials and conversion costs are incurred evenly throughout the mixing process. The Mixing Department compiled the following data for March:

	Direct Materials	Direct Labor	Manufacturing Overhead Allocated	Total Costs
Beginning inventory, Mar. 1	$ 475	$ 275	$ 300	$ 1,050
Costs added during March	5,045	2,900	2,965	10,910
Total costs	$ 5,520	$ 3,175	$ 3,265	$ 11,960

Requirements

1. Prepare a production cost report for the Mixing Department for March. The company uses the weighted-average method.
2. Journalize all transactions affecting the company's mixing process during March. Assume labor costs are accrued and not yet paid.

CHAPTER 18

Learning Objectives 2, 3, 5

1. Total EUP for CC 3,000
3. WIP Balance $1,269

P18-41B Preparing a production cost report, two materials added at different points, no beginning WIP or costs transferred in; journal entries

Bergeron's Exteriors produces exterior siding for homes. The Preparation Department begins with wood, which is chopped into small bits. At the end of the process, an adhesive is added. Then the wood/adhesive mixture goes on to the Compression Department, where the wood is compressed into sheets. Conversion costs are added evenly throughout the preparation process. January data for the Preparation Department are as follows:

UNITS	
Beginning Work-in-Process Inventory	0 sheets
Started in production	3,900 sheets
Completed and transferred out to Compression in January	2,700 sheets
Ending Work-in-Process Inventory (25% of the way through the preparation process)	1,200 sheets
COSTS	
Beginning Work-in-Process Inventory	$ 0
Costs added during January:	
Wood	3,120
Adhesives	1,836
Direct labor	990
Manufacturing overhead allocated	2,100
Total costs	$ 8,046

Requirements

1. Prepare a production cost report for the Preparation Department for January. The company uses the weighted-average method. (*Hint*: Each direct material added at a different point in the production process requires its own equivalent unit of production computation.)

2. Prepare the journal entry to record the cost of the sheets completed and transferred out to the Compression Department.

3. Post the journal entries to the Work-in-Process Inventory—Preparation T-account. What is the ending balance?

P18-42B Preparing a production cost report, second department with beginning WIP; journal entries

Learning Objectives 2, 4, 5

1. Cost per EUP DM $19.00

Casey Carpet manufactures broadloom carpet in seven processes: spinning, dyeing, plying, spooling, tufting, latexing, and shearing. In the Dyeing Department, direct materials (dye) are added at the beginning of the process. Conversion costs are incurred evenly throughout the process. Information for July 2018 follows:

UNITS	
Beginning Work-in-Process Inventory	75 rolls
Transferred in from Spinning Department during July	590 rolls
Completed during July	550 rolls
Ending Work-in-Process Inventory (80% complete for conversion work)	115 rolls
COSTS	
Beginning Work-in-Process Inventory (transferred in costs, $3,700; materials costs, $1,450; conversion costs, $4,950)	$ 10,100
Transferred in from Spinning Department	21,570
Materials costs added during July	11,185
Conversion costs added during July (manufacturing wages, $8,050; manufacturing overhead allocated, $45,422)	53,472

Requirements

1. Prepare a production cost report for Casey's Dyeing Department for July. The company uses the weighted-average method.

2. Journalize all transactions affecting Casey's Dyeing Department during July, including the entries that have already been posted. Assume labor costs are accrued and not yet paid.

P18-43B Preparing a production cost report, second department with beginning WIP; decision making

Learning Objectives 2, 4, 6

1. Cost per EUP CC $11.00

Sea Worthy uses three processes to manufacture lifts for personal watercrafts: forming a lift's parts from galvanized steel, assembling the lift, and testing the completed lift. The lifts are transferred to finished goods before shipment to marinas across the country.

Sea Worthy's Testing Department requires no direct materials. Conversion costs are incurred evenly throughout the testing process. Other information follows for October 2018:

UNITS	
Beginning Work-in-Process Inventory	2,300 units
Transferred in from Assembling Department during the period	6,800 units
Completed during the period	4,100 units
Ending Work-in-Process Inventory (40% complete for conversion work)	5,000 units
COSTS	
Beginning Work-in-Process Inventory (transferred in costs, $93,400; conversion costs, $18,100)	$ 111,500
Transferred in from the Assembly Department during the period	671,000
Conversion costs added during the period	49,000

CHAPTER 18

The cost transferred into Finished Goods Inventory is the cost of the lifts transferred out of the Testing Department. Sea Worthy uses weighted-average process costing.

Requirements

1. Prepare a production cost report for the Testing Department.
2. What is the cost per unit for lifts completed and transferred out to Finished Goods Inventory? Why would management be interested in this cost?

Learning Objective 7
Appendix 18A

1. Total EUP for CC 3,270

P18A-44B Preparing a production cost report, second department, with beginning WIP and transferred in costs; journal entries; FIFO method

Happy Colors manufactures crayons in a three-step process: mixing, molding, and packaging. The Mixing Department combines the direct materials of paraffin wax and pigments. The heated mixture is pumped to the Molding Department, where it is poured into molds. After the molds cool, the crayons are removed from the molds and are transferred to the Packaging Department, where paper wrappers are added and the crayons are boxed.

In the Mixing Department, the direct materials are added at the beginning of the process and the conversion costs are incurred evenly throughout the process. Work in process of the Mixing Department on April 1, 2018, consisted of 300 batches of crayons that were 30% of the way through the production process. The beginning balance in Work-in-Process Inventory—Mixing was $27,800, which consisted of $10,700 in direct materials costs and $17,100 in conversion costs. During April, 3,200 batches were started in production. The Mixing Department transferred 2,800 batches to the Molding Department in April, and 700 were still in process on April 30. This ending inventory was 80% of the way through the mixing process. Happy Colors uses FIFO process costing.

At April 30, before recording the transfer of costs from the Mixing Department to the Molding Department, the Happy Colors general ledger included the following account:

Work-in-Process Inventory—Mixing	
Balance, Apr. 1	27,800
Direct materials	22,400
Direct labor	21,330
Manufacturing overhead	44,070

Requirements

1. Prepare a production cost report for the Mixing Department for April. Round equivalent unit costs to four decimal places. Round all other costs to the nearest dollar.
2. Journalize all transactions affecting the Mixing Department during April, including the entries that have already been posted. Assume the labor costs are accrued and not yet paid.

Learning Objective 7
Appendix 18A

1. Cost per EUP for CC $1.3703

P18A-45B Preparing a production cost report, second department, with beginning WIP and transferred in costs; journal entries; FIFO method

Work Problem P18-40B using the FIFO method. The Mixing Department beginning work in process of 400 units is 80% complete as to both direct materials and conversion costs. Round equivalent unit costs to four decimal places. Round all other costs to the nearest dollar.

CRITICAL THINKING

> Using Excel

P18-46 Using Excel to prepare a production cost report.

Download an Excel template for this problem online in MyAccountingLab or at http://www.pearsonhighered.com/Horngren.

Salish Craft Beers provides the following information for the Malting Department for the month of August 2018:

	UNITS	COSTS
Beginning Work-in-Process Inventory	0	$ 0
Started in Production in August	26,000	54,000*
Total to Account For	26,000	$ 54,000
Completed and Transferred to Packaging Department during August	21,000	?
Ending Work-in-Process Inventory (30% complete for direct materials and 60% complete for conversion work)	5,000	?
Total Accounted For	26,000	$ 54,000

* Includes $18,000 direct materials and $36,000 conversion costs

Requirements

Complete a production cost report for the Malting Department for the month of August 2018 to determine the cost of the units completed and transferred out, and the cost of the ending Work-in-Process Inventory. Assume Salish Craft Beers uses the weighted-average method.

> Tying It All Together Case 18–1

Before you begin this assignment, review the Tying It All Together feature in the chapter.

PepsiCo, Inc. is a global food and beverage company that manufactures brands such as Frito-Lay, Gatorade, Pepsi-Cola, Quaker, and Tropicana. One of the products PepsiCo, Inc. manufactures is Mountain Dew. The first process in manufacturing Mountain Dew consists of clarifying the water to remove impurities such as organic materials and bacteria. The clarification process involves mixing the water with aluminum sulfate (an indirect material) to remove the impurities. Assume PepsiCo uses the weighted-average method of process costing.

Requirements

1. During the month of June, the Clarification Department incurred the following costs in processing 100,000 liters:

Wages of workers operating the clarification equipment	$ 20,000
Manufacturing overhead allocated to clarification	24,000
Water	160,000

    PepsiCo had no beginning Work-In-Process Inventory in the Clarification Department in June. Compute the June conversion costs in the Clarification Department.

2. Assume that water is added at the beginning of the clarification process and conversion costs are added evenly throughout the process. The Clarification Department completed and transferred out 60,000 liters during June. The 40,000 liters remaining in Clarification's ending Work-in-Process Inventory were 100% complete for direct materials and 60% complete for conversion costs. Compute the equivalent units of production for direct materials and conversion costs for the Clarification Department.

3. Compute the cost per equivalent unit for direct materials and conversion costs for the Clarification Department.

> Decision Case 18-1

Billy Davidson operates Billy's Worm Farm in Mississippi. Davidson raises worms for fishing. He sells a box of 20 worms for $12.60. Davidson has invested $400,000 in the worm farm. He had hoped to earn a 24% annual rate of return (net income divided by total assets), which works out to a 2% monthly return on his investment. After looking at the farm's bank balance, Davidson fears he is not achieving this return. To evaluate the farm's performance, he prepared the following production cost report. The Finished Goods Inventory is zero because the worms ship out as soon as they reach the required size. Monthly operating expenses total $2,000 (in addition to the costs below).

BILLY'S WORM FARM
Production Cost Report—BROODING DEPARTMENT
Month Ended June 30, 2018

UNITS	Physical Units	Equivalent Units Transferred In	Direct Materials	Conversion Costs
Units to account for:				
Beginning work-in-process	9,000			
Transferred in	21,000			
Total units to account for	30,000			
Units accounted for:				
Completed and transferred out	20,000	20,000	20,000	20,000
Ending work-in-process	10,000	10,000	6,000	3,600
Total units accounted for	30,000	30,000	26,000	23,600

COSTS	Transferred In	Direct Materials	Conversion Costs	Total Costs
Costs to account for:				
Beginning work-in-process	$ 21,000	$ 39,940	$ 5,020	$ 65,960
Costs added during period	46,200	152,460	56,340	255,000
Total costs to account for	67,200	192,400	61,360	$ 320,960
Divided by: Total EUP	÷ 30,000	÷ 26,000	÷ 23,600	
Cost per equivalent unit	$ 2.24	$ 7.40	$ 2.60	
Costs accounted for:				
Completed and transferred out	$ 44,800	$ 148,000	$ 52,000	$ 244,800
Ending work-in-process	22,400	44,400	9,360	76,160
Total costs accounted for	$ 67,200	$ 192,400	$ 61,360	$ 320,960

Requirements

Billy Davidson has the following questions about the farm's performance during June.

1. What is the cost per box of worms sold? (*Hint:* This is the unit cost of the boxes completed and shipped out of brooding.)

2. What is the gross profit per box?

3. How much operating income did Billy's Worm Farm make in June?

4. What is the return on Davidson's investment of $400,000 for the month of June? (Compute this as June's operating income divided by Davidson's $400,000 investment, expressed as a percentage.)

5. What monthly operating income would provide a 2% monthly rate of return? What sales price per box would Billy's Worm Farm have had to charge in June to achieve a 2% monthly rate of return?

> Ethical Issue 18-1

Rick Pines and Joe Lopez are the plant managers for High Mountain Lumber's particle board division. High Mountain Lumber has adopted a just-in-time management philosophy. Each plant combines wood chips with chemical adhesives to produce particle board to order, and all product is sold as soon as it is completed. Laura Green is High Mountain Lumber's regional controller. All of High Mountain Lumber's plants and divisions send Green their production and cost information. While reviewing the numbers of the two particle board plants, she is surprised to find that both plants estimate their ending Work-in-Process Inventories at 75% complete, which is higher than usual. Green calls Lopez, whom she has known for some time. He admits that to ensure their division would meet its profit goal and that both he and Pines would make their bonus (which is based on division profit), they agreed to inflate the percentage completion. Lopez explains, "Determining the percent complete always requires judgment. Whatever the percent complete, we'll finish the Work-in-Process Inventory first thing next year."

Requirements

1. How would inflating the percentage completion of ending Work-in-Process Inventory help Pines and Lopez get their bonus?

2. The particle board division is the largest of High Mountain Lumber's divisions. If Green does not correct the percentage completion of this year's ending Work-in-Process Inventory, how will the misstatement affect High Mountain Lumber's financial statements?

3. Evaluate Lopez's justification, including the effect, if any, on next year's financial statements.

4. Address the following: What is the ethical issue? What are the options? What are the potential consequences? What should Green do?

MyAccountingLab   **For a wealth of online resources, including exercises, problems, media, and immediate tutorial help, please visit** http://www.myaccountinglab.com.

> Quick Check Answers

1. c **2.** a **3.** b **4.** d **5.** b **6.** a **7.** d **8.** c **9.** b **10.** c **11A.** a

19 Cost Management Systems: Activity-Based, Just-in-Time, and Quality Management Systems

What Does It Cost to Groom a Dog?

Bryan Lamb looked at the report his controller gave him. Instinctively, he knew something was wrong. Bryan's company, Pet Care, had recently found a niche market, and the business was growing. Rather than have customers bring their pets into Pet Care for grooming, Bryan started sending his groomers out to some of the customers' homes. These customers love the special attention and are willing to pay extra for the convenience of in-home grooming. In fact, the business has grown so much that Bryan needs to hire an additional groomer. Or even two. So why does the controller's report show profits are down when business is booming?

A closer look at the report shows some costs have had substantial increases. For example, travel costs have tripled in the past few months, which makes sense considering the groomers are driving to the customers' homes and are reimbursed for mileage. But shouldn't the increased revenues more than cover the increased costs?

Bryan decides it is time to take a closer look at the cost of in-home grooming. Perhaps he has not considered all the costs incurred by this new service. If the indirect costs are not being allocated correctly, then the niche market that currently appears to be profitable may not be profitable after all.

What Are Cost Management Systems?

Cost management systems, such as activity-based management, just-in-time management, and quality management, help managers collect data, analyze it, and then make decisions that lead to customer satisfaction and increased profits. Consider **PetSmart, Inc.**, a large speciality pet retailer of services and solutions for the needs of pets. The company was founded in 1986 and has grown to more than 1,400 locations. In addition to selling pet food and pet products, PetSmart also offers dog training, pet grooming, pet boarding, and Doggie Day Camp day care services. Veterinary care is also available at more than 60% of its stores. Companies such as PetSmart can implement cost management systems to help employees improve efficiency and reduce costs while also increasing profits. In today's competitive business environment, even small improvements can have a major impact. Let's look at some cost management systems and how they are used to make decisions.

Chapter 19 Learning Objectives

1   Assign direct costs and allocate indirect costs using predetermined overhead allocation rates with single and multiple allocation bases

2   Use activity-based costing (ABC) to compute predetermined overhead allocation rates and allocate indirect costs

3   Use activity-based management (ABM) to make decisions

4   Use activity-based management (ABM) in a service company

5   Describe a just-in-time (JIT) management system and record its transactions

6   Describe quality management systems (QMS) and use the four types of quality costs to make decisions

In this chapter, we are going to look at three types of systems companies use to manage their businesses:

- Activity-based management systems (ABM)
- Just-in-time management systems (JIT)
- Quality management systems (QMS)

Managers use these systems to accumulate data and make informed decisions. Each system helps businesses be more productive, less costly, and more profitable. To get started with our study of these management systems, let's review some product cost information.

HOW DO COMPANIES ASSIGN AND ALLOCATE COSTS?

Learning Objective 1

Assign direct costs and allocate indirect costs using predetermined overhead allocation rates with single and multiple allocation bases

As you have learned, product costs consist of direct materials costs, direct labor costs, and manufacturing overhead costs. These costs must be traced to each product manufactured. Direct materials costs and direct labor costs can be easily traced to products. For example, Smart Touch Learning can trace the cost of installing a battery in a tablet because there is a logical relation between the number of tablets produced and the number of batteries needed for each tablet. Therefore, direct materials costs and direct labor costs are *assigned* to products.

Manufacturing overhead costs, also called *indirect costs*, cannot be cost-effectively traced to products. Examples of manufacturing overhead costs include rent, utilities, insurance, and property taxes on the manufacturing facility; depreciation on the manufacturing equipment; indirect labor, such as production supervisors' salaries; and indirect materials, such as glue, thread, or other materials that cannot be cost-effectively traced to products. For example, the cost of utilities on the manufacturing facility is not easily linked to the number of tablets made. Because of this manufacturing overhead costs are *accumulated* in cost pools and then *allocated* to products.

The most accurate overhead allocation can be made only when total overhead costs are known—and that is not until the end of the accounting period. But managers cannot wait that long for product cost information because knowing product cost information helps managers set a sales price for the product. Businesses must, instead, figure out a way to allocate these indirect costs during the accounting period.

In this chapter, we look at three different ways that businesses can allocate indirect costs: single plantwide rate, multiple department rates, and activity-based costing. We start with the simplest method and move to the more complex. With complexity comes more detailed information—which usually leads to better decisions. There are situations, however, when the cost of obtaining more detailed information outweighs the benefits received from the additional information. If that is the situation, then a simpler method may be appropriate.

Smart Touch Learning, the fictitious company we used in previous chapters, is used again here. Smart Touch Learning manufactures its own brand of touch screen tablet computers that are preloaded with the company's e-learning software. Its manufacturing operations have been successful, and the company is now expanding production by producing a premium model in addition to the standard model.

The premium model has several superior features, including a larger screen, faster processor, longer-lasting battery, and specialized software programs. The features included in the premium model trigger some differences in the manufacturing process. For example, smaller circuitry in the hardware components requires the use of refined tools that are capable of more precise calibration. Before beginning production on a batch of tablets, a calibration setup is required. (*Setup* is when the company prepares the manufacturing line—sets it up—to produce a different product.) The calibration setup for premium tablets is performed by workers with specialized skills. Due to their specialized skills, laborers working on the premium model are paid at a higher rate. Furthermore, the operating system on the premium model requires additional software components with a specialized configuration to support the superior hardware features. Due to the specialized configuration, testing the operating system of the premium model takes longer than testing the operating system of the standard model.

The management team has compiled the following information regarding its expectations for the next year:

		Standard Model	Premium Model
Number of units		2,000 units	500 units
Direct materials cost per unit		$ 150.00	$ 200.00
Direct labor cost per unit		$ 88.00	$ 148.00
Total manufacturing overhead	$ 100,000		

The challenge is to determine the best way to *allocate* the $100,000 in manufacturing overhead costs to the 2,500 tablets so the manufacturing cost per unit can be calculated. Managers need to know the product cost to make planning, directing, and controlling decisions.

Single Plantwide Rate

Using a single plantwide rate is the traditional method of allocating manufacturing overhead costs and is the simplest method. In this method, the company calculates the **predetermined overhead allocation rate** before the period begins by selecting one allocation base and using the same base to allocate overhead costs to all units. Exhibit 19-1 illustrates a single plantwide rate for manufacturing overhead costs. When Smart Touch Learning was producing only one model of tablets, direct labor cost was used as the allocation base. Retaining direct labor cost as the allocation base, let's calculate the predetermined overhead allocation rate, use the rate to allocate overhead, and determine the total unit cost.

Predetermined Overhead Allocation Rate
Estimated overhead cost per unit of the allocation base, calculated at the beginning of the accounting period. Total estimated overhead costs / Total estimated quantity of the overhead allocation base.

Exhibit 19-1 | **Single Plantwide Rate**

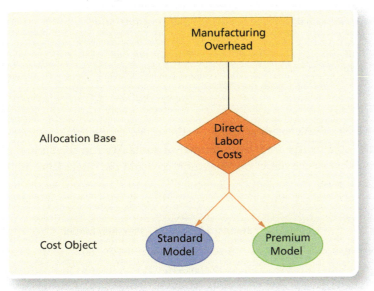

The total estimated overhead costs are given, $100,000. To determine the total estimated direct labor cost, multiply the direct labor cost per unit times the estimated number of units. This must be done for both models.

	Direct labor cost per unit	×	Number of units	=	Total direct labor costs
Standard	$ 88 per unit	×	2,000 units	=	$ 176,000
Premium	$ 148 per unit	×	500 units	=	74,000
Total					$ 250,000

We now have the amounts needed to calculate the predetermined overhead allocation rate.

$$\text{Predetermined overhead allocation rate} = \frac{\text{Total estimated overhead costs}}{\text{Total estimated quantity of the overhead allocation base}}$$

$$= \frac{\$100,000 \text{ total estimated overhead costs}}{\$250,000 \text{ total estimated direct labor costs}} = \frac{40\% \text{ of direct}}{\text{labor costs}}$$

The manufacturing overhead costs can now be allocated to each model by multiplying the predetermined overhead allocation rate by the actual quantity of the allocation base used by the product.

	Predetermined overhead allocation rate	×	Actual quantity of the allocation base used	=	Allocated manufacturing overhead cost
Standard	40%	×	$ 176,000 direct labor	=	$ 70,400
Premium	40%	×	$ 74,000 direct labor	=	29,600
Total					$ 100,000

Note that the predetermined overhead allocation rate is multiplied by the *actual* quantity of the allocation base used. In this illustration (and in the illustrations of the additional two methods discussed), we have made the assumption that the *estimated* quantity of the allocation base used and the *actual* quantity of the allocation base used are the same. This simplifies the illustration.

To determine the unit cost of the manufacturing overhead, we divide each product's total manufacturing overhead cost by the associated number of units. We can then add the manufacturing overhead unit cost to the direct materials unit cost and the direct labor unit cost to determine the total unit cost.

	Standard Model	Premium Model
Total manufacturing overhead	$ 70,400	$ 29,600
÷ Number of units	÷ 2,000 units	÷ 500 units
Manufacturing overhead cost per unit	$ 35.20	$ 59.20
Direct materials cost per unit	$ 150.00	$ 200.00
Direct labor cost per unit	88.00	148.00
Manufacturing overhead cost per unit	35.20	59.20
Total cost per unit	$ 273.20	$ 407.20

Because direct labor cost is the single allocation base for all products, Smart Touch Learning allocates far more *total* dollars of overhead cost to the standard model than to the premium model, $70,400 compared with $29,600. However, total dollars of overhead are spread over more tablets for the standard model, which is why the *per unit* cost of overhead is less for the standard model than for the premium model, $35.20 compared with $59.20.

Using a single plantwide rate is simple, but it may not be accurate. Using direct labor costs as the allocation base may distort the unit costs of the two models. For example, we know that the premium model requires workers with advanced skills who are paid at a higher rate. The higher labor cost for the premium model resulted in more overhead cost per unit being allocated to that model. Does the fact that the premium model workers earn more result in the premium model using more resources that would cause an increase in overhead costs? In other words, is there a relationship between labor cost and overhead cost? If so, then it is appropriate to use direct labor cost as the allocation base. If not, another allocation method is needed.

Multiple Department Rates

A modification of the overhead allocation method using a single plantwide rate is using multiple predetermined overhead allocation rates that have different allocation bases. This method is more complex, but it may be more accurate. The allocation process is the same, except now the Manufacturing Overhead is accumulated in multiple cost pools and allocated using multiple allocation bases. Exhibit 19-2 illustrates multiple department rates for manufacturing overhead costs.

Exhibit 19-2 | **Multiple Department Rates**

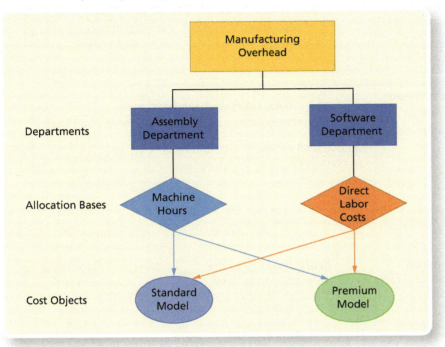

Smart Touch Learning has determined that the manufacturing process can be separated into two main departments. In the first department, Assembly, the tablet parts are assembled. In the second department, Software, the software is installed and tested. Management has further separated the overhead costs into two cost pools—one pool for the overhead costs associated with the Assembly Department and another pool for the overhead costs associated with the Software Department.

After careful analysis, Smart Touch Learning has decided that machine usage is the primary cost driver for the Assembly Department. In other words, the company feels there is a direct relationship between the number of hours the machines are used and the amount of overhead costs incurred. Therefore, it has decided to use machine hours for the allocation base for the Assembly Department. Smart Touch Learning has also decided that direct labor costs are the primary cost driver for the Software Department and has decided to use direct labor costs as the allocation base for that department.

Smart Touch Learning managers have compiled the following data for the Assembly Department for the next year:

	Standard Model	Premium Model	Total
Machine hours (MHr)	15,000 MHr	5,000 MHr	20,000 MHr

Management has also analyzed the expected overhead costs and separated them into two cost pools—one for each department. For example, depreciation on machinery used in the Assembly Department is accumulated in that department. The salary of the Software Department supervisor would be accumulated in that department. Smart Touch Learning has determined the expected $100,000 in overhead costs should be split with $80,000 accumulating in the Assembly Department cost pool and $20,000 accumulating in the Software Department cost pool. We are now ready to compute the predetermined overhead allocation rates for the two departments, allocate overhead costs, and calculate the total cost per unit.

Assembly Department

The total estimated overhead costs for the Assembly Department are given, $80,000. The department's total quantity of the allocation base, machine hours, is also given, 20,000 MHr. We have the amounts needed to calculate the predetermined overhead allocation rate.

$$\text{Predetermined overhead allocation rate} = \frac{\text{Total estimated overhead costs}}{\text{Total estimated quantity of the overhead allocation base}}$$

$$= \frac{\$80{,}000 \text{ total estimated overhead costs}}{20{,}000 \text{ total estimated machine hours}} = \$4.00 \text{ per MHr}$$

The manufacturing overhead costs for the Assembly Department can now be allocated to each model.

	Predetermined overhead allocation rate	×	Actual quantity of the allocation base used	=	Allocated manufacturing overhead cost
Standard	$4.00 per MHr	×	15,000 MHr	=	$ 60,000
Premium	$4.00 per MHr	×	5,000 MHr	=	20,000
Total					$ 80,000

Software Department

The total estimated overhead costs for the Software Department are given, $20,000. Smart Touch Learning's managers have compiled the following data for the Software Department's total quantity of the allocation base, direct labor costs, for the next year:

	Standard Model	Premium Model	Total
Direct labor costs	$22,000	$9,250	$31,250

We have the amounts needed to calculate the predetermined overhead allocation rate.

$$\text{Predetermined overhead allocation rate} = \frac{\text{Total estimated overhead costs}}{\text{Total estimated quantity of the overhead allocation base}}$$

$$= \frac{\$20{,}000 \text{ total estimated overhead costs}}{\$31{,}250 \text{ total estimated direct labor costs}} = \begin{array}{c} 64\% \text{ of direct} \\ \text{labor costs} \end{array}$$

The manufacturing overhead costs for the Software Department can now be allocated to each model.

	Predetermined overhead allocation rate	×	Actual quantity of the allocation base used	=	Allocated manufacturing overhead cost
Standard	64%	×	$22,000 direct labor	=	$ 14,080
Premium	64%	×	$ 9,250 direct labor	=	5,920
Total					$ 20,000

Total Cost

To determine the unit cost of the manufacturing overhead, we divide the total cost by the number of units. We can then add the manufacturing overhead unit cost to the direct materials and direct labor unit costs to determine the total unit cost.

	Standard Model	Premium Model
Manufacturing overhead—Assembly	$ 60,000	$ 20,000
Manufacturing overhead—Software	14,080	5,920
Total manufacturing overhead	$ 74,080	$ 25,920
÷ Number of units	÷ 2,000 units	÷ 500 units
Manufacturing overhead cost per unit	$ 37.04	$ 51.84
Direct materials cost per unit	$ 150.00	$ 200.00
Direct labor cost per unit (Assembly and Software Departments)	88.00	148.00
Manufacturing overhead cost per unit	37.04	51.84
Total cost per unit	$ 275.04	$ 399.84

Analysis

Now that we have computed an estimated cost per unit using two different methods, let's compare the results.

	Standard Model	Premium Model
Total estimated cost per unit:		
Multiple department allocation rates	$ 275.04	$ 399.84
Single plantwide allocation rate	273.20	407.20
Difference	$ 1.84	$ (7.36)

Using a more refined allocation system with multiple allocation rates shows the standard model costs slightly more than originally thought, whereas the premium model costs less than originally thought. The differences may not seem significant, but in today's competitive market, even slight differences can make an impact. For example, if there is a great deal of competition in the Premium Model market and consumers make decisions based on solely on price, because Smart Touch Learning has better costing information, the company has the opportunity to reduce the sales price, still make a profit, and remain competitive. Managers need better data to set prices and identify the most profitable products. Let's look at one more allocation method, activity-based costing, which refines the allocation process even more than using departmental allocation rates.

Try It!

The Santos Shirt Company manufactures shirts in two departments: Cutting and Sewing. The company allocates manufacturing overhead using a single plantwide rate with direct labor hours as the allocation base. Estimated overhead costs for the year are $500,000, and estimated direct labor hours are 200,000. In June, the company incurred 17,500 direct labor hours.

1. Compute the predetermined overhead allocation rate.
2. Determine the amount of overhead allocated in June.

The Santos Shirt Company has refined its allocation system by separating manufacturing overhead costs into two cost pools—one for each department. The estimated costs for the Cutting Department are $200,000. They will be allocated based on direct labor hours, which are estimated to be 125,000 hours for the year. The estimated costs for the Sewing Department are $300,000. Those costs will be allocated based on machine hours, which are estimated to be 150,000 hours for the year. In June, the company incurred 10,000 direct labor hours in Cutting and 12,500 machine hours in Sewing.

3. Compute the predetermined overhead allocation rates for each department.
4. Determine the total amount of overhead allocated in June.

Check your answers online in MyAccountingLab or at http://www.pearsonhighered.com/Horngren.

For more practice, see Short Exercises S19-1 and S19-2. MyAccountingLab

HOW IS AN ACTIVITY-BASED COSTING SYSTEM DEVELOPED?

Learning Objective 2

Use activity-based costing (ABC) to compute predetermined overhead allocation rates and allocate indirect costs

When companies produce few products and production is similar across product lines, managers could limit their focus to a broad business function, such as production, and use a single plantwide rate or multiple department rates to allocate manufacturing overhead costs to their inventory. But today's business environment involves complex production processes and personalization of products to customers' specifications which calls for more refined cost accounting. This is especially important when production includes manufacturing products that require different resources or different amounts of the various resources.

Smart Touch Learning is now facing this situation—its two primary products require different amounts of the resources. As we stated previously, the premium model of the touch screen tablet computer requires the calibration setup to be performed by higher-paid workers with specialized skills, and the operating system testing process takes longer than testing the standard model due to the specialized configuration. Additionally, the premium model is produced in smaller batches because the quantity of sales is lower than the standard model (500 units compared with 2,000 units).

Companies like Smart Touch Learning, with diverse products, can obtain better costing information by using activity-based costing and activity-based management. **Activity-based management (ABM)** focuses on the primary activities the business performs, determines the costs of the activities, and then uses the cost information to make decisions that will lead to improved customer satisfaction and greater profits. The costs of the activities (rather than the overhead costs of the plant or departments) become the building blocks for allocating indirect costs to products and services. An **activity** is a task, operation, or procedure such as quality inspection, warranty services, or shipping. The process of first determining the costs of the activities to then determine the cost of products and services is called **activity-based costing (ABC)**.

Activity-Based Management (ABM)
Using activity-based cost information to make decisions that improve customer satisfaction while also increasing profits.

Activity
A task, operation, or procedure.

Activity-Based Costing (ABC)
Focuses on the costs of activities as the building blocks for allocating indirect costs to products and services.

In ABC, each activity has its own (usually unique) allocation base, often called a *cost driver*. Exhibit 19-3 shows some representative activities and allocation bases.

Exhibit 19-3 | Examples of Activities and Allocation Bases

Activity	Allocation Base
Quality Inspection—Inspecting raw materials or finished products	Number of inspections
Warranty Services—Providing service for defective products	Number of service calls
Shipping—Shipping finished products to customers	Number of pounds of product shipped
Setup—Setting up machines for production	Number of batches
Machining—Machine usage	Number of machine hours
Purchasing—Purchasing raw materials	Number of purchase orders

You go to a restaurant with three of your friends, and the waiter brings one bill for $100. You had the special and ordered water to drink. The meal you ordered cost only $15. Your friends ordered appetizers and drinks with their meals. How do you split the bill? Because four of you had dinner together, do you pay 1/4 of the bill, $25, or do you pay based on the cost of what you ordered, $15? Paying based on what you ordered is the key to activity-based costing. Production costs are allocated based on the amount of each activity of production that the products use.

An activity-based costing system is developed in four steps. Let's look at these four steps for Smart Touch Learning.

Step 1: Identify Activities and Estimate Their Total Indirect Costs

The first step in developing an activity-based costing system is to identify the activities that will be used to allocate the manufacturing overhead. Analyzing all the activities required for a product or service forces managers to think about how each activity might be improved—or whether it is necessary at all.

The Smart Touch Learning management team has carefully analyzed the production process. It has determined there are three activities in the production process (setup, production, and testing) that incur the majority of the manufacturing overhead costs. Therefore, Smart Touch Learning will create three cost pools to accumulate the overhead costs. Cost pools are a collection of costs. The first activity is setup. Before a batch of tablets can be manufactured, the machines must be properly calibrated. After the setup activity is complete, the tablets can be produced. Production is the second activity. The third activity is testing the operating system of each tablet. The managers at Smart Touch Learning then looked at the manufacturing overhead costs incurred by these three activities and estimated each activity would incur the following overhead costs during the next year:

Activity	Estimated Overhead Costs
Setup	$ 15,000
Production	65,000
Testing	20,000
Total	$ 100,000

Exhibit 19-4 illustrates how manufacturing overhead is allocated to the tablets at Smart Touch Learning.

Exhibit 19-4 | **ABC System**

Step 2: Identify the Allocation Base for Each Activity and Estimate the Total Quantity of Each Allocation Base

Because there are multiple activities that require different resources, Smart Touch Learning will use a different allocation base for each activity. In ABC systems, ideally the allocation base is the primary cost driver, the factor that causes the cost to increase or decrease. For example, Smart Touch Learning has determined that the allocation base for setups is the number of batches. Step 2 must be completed for each activity.

Setup

Smart Touch Learning has determined that the allocation base for setup is the number of batches. The standard model is normally produced in batches of 50 units. Therefore, the production of 2,000 units would require 40 batches (2,000 units / 50 units per batch). The premium model is normally produced in batches of 25 units. Therefore, the production of 500 units would require 20 batches (500 units / 25 units per batch).

Production

Smart Touch Learning has determined that the allocation base for production is direct labor hours. Note that the company is not using direct labor *costs* but direct labor *hours*. Analysis of the process indicated that the overhead costs were related to the time it took to process the units through the activity, not how much the workers were paid. Both models require an average of five hours of labor to assemble. Therefore, the standard model is expected to require 10,000 labor hours during the next year (2,000 units × 5 hours per unit) and the premium model is expected to require 2,500 hours (500 units × 5 hours per unit).

Testing

Smart Touch Learning has determined that the allocation base for testing is the number of testing operations performed. Units are randomly selected for testing, with the premium units tested more often than the standard units due to their complexity. Based on the number of units to be produced, the production manager estimates the standard model units to have 7,750 tests during the year and the premium model to have 2,250 tests, for a total of 10,000 tests.

Exhibit 19-5 summarizes the data for each allocation base.

Exhibit 19-5 | **Smart Touch Learning—Allocation Base Summary**

Activity	Allocation Base	Standard Model	Premium Model	Total
Setup	Number of batches	40 batches	20 batches	60 batches
Production	Direct labor hours (DLHr)	10,000 DLHr	2,500 DLHr	12,500 DLHr
Testing	Number of tests	7,750 tests	2,250 tests	10,000 tests

Step 3: Compute the Predetermined Overhead Allocation Rate for Each Activity

The formula to compute the predetermined overhead allocation rate for each activity is the same as the formula used for the other methods. The process is repeated for each activity. The predetermined overhead allocation rates for Smart Touch Learning are:

$$\text{Predetermined overhead allocation rate} = \frac{\text{Total estimated overhead costs}}{\text{Total estimated quantity of the overhead allocation base}}$$

Setup: $\dfrac{\$15,000 \text{ total estimated overhead costs}}{60 \text{ batches}} = \$250.00 \text{ per batch}$

Production: $\dfrac{\$65,000 \text{ total estimated overhead costs}}{12,500 \text{ direct labor hours}} = \$5.20 \text{ per DLHr}$

Testing: $\dfrac{\$20,000 \text{ total estimated overhead costs}}{10,000 \text{ tests}} = \$2.00 \text{ per test}$

Step 4: Allocate Indirect Costs to the Cost Object

The fundamental cost pools of an activity-based costing system are the activities. Now that we have determined the cost of each activity and computed a predetermined overhead allocation rate for each activity, we can use the rates to *allocate* overhead costs from the cost pools to the units. The following table shows the allocation of overhead costs and the calculation of overhead cost per unit for each model:

	Predetermined overhead allocation rate	×	Actual quantity of the allocation base used	=	Allocated manufacturing overhead cost
STANDARD					
Setup	$250.00 per batch ×		40 batches	=	$ 10,000
Production	$ 5.20 per DLHr ×		10,000 DLHr	=	52,000
Testing	$ 2.00 per test ×		7,750 tests	=	15,500
Total manufacturing overhead					$ 77,500
÷ Number of units					÷ 2,000 units
Manufacturing overhead cost per unit					$ 38.75
PREMIUM					
Setup	$250.00 per batch ×		20 batches	=	$ 5,000
Production	$ 5.20 per DLHr ×		2,500 DLHr	=	13,000
Testing	$ 2.00 per test ×		2,250 tests	=	4,500
Total manufacturing overhead					$ 22,500
÷ Number of units					÷ 500 units
Manufacturing overhead cost per unit					$ 45.00

The total production cost of each model, including direct materials, direct labor, and manufacturing overhead costs, is shown below:

	Standard Model	Premium Model
Direct materials cost per unit	$ 150.00	$ 200.00
Direct labor cost per unit	88.00	148.00
Manufacturing overhead cost per unit	38.75	45.00
Total cost per unit	$ 276.75	$ 393.00

Traditional Costing Systems Compared with ABC Systems

Let's compare the estimated cost per unit calculated with the three different systems.

	Standard Model	Premium Model
Single plantwide allocation rate		
Direct materials cost per unit	$ 150.00	$ 200.00
Direct labor cost per unit	88.00	148.00
Manufacturing overhead cost per unit	35.20	59.20
Total cost per unit	$ 273.20	$ 407.20
Multiple department allocation rates		
Direct materials cost per unit	$ 150.00	$ 200.00
Direct labor cost per unit	88.00	148.00
Manufacturing overhead cost per unit	37.04	51.84
Total cost per unit	$ 275.04	$ 399.84
Activity-based allocation rates		
Direct materials cost per unit	$ 150.00	$ 200.00
Direct labor cost per unit	88.00	148.00
Manufacturing overhead cost per unit	38.75	45.00
Total cost per unit	$ 276.75	$ 393.00

With each refinement of the costing system, from a single plantwide allocation rate to multiple department allocation rates to activity-based allocation rates, the cost per unit of the standard model increased while the cost per unit of the premium model decreased. **Activity-based costs are more accurate because ABC considers the resources (activities) each product actually uses.** Allocating overhead based on labor costs distorted the cost of the premium units. This happened because the laborers working on premium units are paid more due to their advanced skills, which increased the cost of the direct labor on the premium models. However, the higher direct labor cost does not have a direct cause-and-effect relationship on the overhead costs. Other factors, such as the number of batches and the number of tests, do have an effect.

> *It is important to note that the total overhead cost did not change, only the allocation of the total overhead to the two different types of tablets. Total overhead allocated in all three methods is $100,000.*

Now that we know the indirect costs of the standard and premium models of touch screen tablet computers, let's see how Smart Touch Learning's managers *use* the ABC cost information to make better decisions.

Which cost calculation is most accurate?

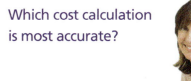

Newton Company has analyzed its production process and identified two primary activities. These activities, their allocation bases, and their estimated costs are listed below.

Activity	Allocation Base	Estimated Activity	Estimated Costs
Purchasing	Number of purchase orders	200 purchase orders	$ 10,000
Materials handling	Number of parts	15,000 parts	$ 7,500

The company manufactures two products: Regular and Super. The products use the following resources in March:

	Regular	Super
Number of purchase orders	5 purchase orders	7 purchase orders
Number of parts	600 parts	750 parts

5. Compute the predetermined overhead allocation rates using activity-based costing.
6. Determine the amount of overhead allocated to Regular products in March.
7. Determine the amount of overhead allocated to Super products in March.

Check your answers online in MyAccountingLab or at http://www.pearsonhighered.com/Horngren.

For more practice, see Short Exercises S19-3 through S19-8. MyAccountingLab

HOW CAN COMPANIES USE ACTIVITY-BASED MANAGEMENT TO MAKE DECISIONS?

Learning Objective 3
Use activity-based management (ABM) to make decisions

Activity-based management (ABM) uses activity-based costs to make decisions that increase profits while meeting customer needs. In this section, we show how Smart Touch Learning can use ABM in making two kinds of decisions:

- Pricing and product mix
- Cost management

Pricing and Product Mix Decisions

Smart Touch Learning now knows the ABC manufacturing overhead cost per tablet. To determine which products are the most profitable, the company controller recomputes each product's total manufacturing cost and gross profit. Last year, the manufacturing cost of the standard model tablet was $300 and the item sold for $500.

	Standard Model Last Year	Standard Model This Year, Traditional Allocation	Standard Model This Year, ABC Allocation
Net Sales Revenue	$ 500.00	$ 500.00	$ 500.00
Cost of Goods Sold	300.00	273.20	276.75
Gross Profit	$ 200.00	$ 226.80	$ 223.25
Gross Profit Percentage	40.00%	45.36%	44.65%

Compared with last year's production, Smart Touch Learning has predicted costs will decrease by $26.80 per unit this year using a traditional allocation method (from $300.00 to $273.20). The refinement of the costing system with ABC shows actual costs to be slightly higher than calculated with the traditional allocation method, but the company has still increased the gross profit margin by $23.25 per unit ($223.25 as compared with $200.00). If the company sells 2,000 units as expected, gross profits will increase by $46,500 (2,000 units × $23.25 per unit).

With the decrease in costs, Smart Touch Learning could consider lowering the sales price. With costs of $276.75, to maintain a 40.00% gross profit percentage (which means COGS is 60%), the sales price could drop to $461.25 ($276.75 / 60%). The decrease in sales price could lead to an increase in sales volume.

Now let's look at the premium model. Based on research conducted by the marketing department, the company expects the premium model to sell for $600.

	Premium Model, Traditional Allocation	Premium Model, ABC Allocation
Net Sales Revenue	$ 600.00	$ 600.00
Cost of Goods Sold	407.20	393.00
Gross Profit	$ 192.80	$ 207.00
Gross Profit Percentage	32.13%	34.50%

More accurate cost allocations using ABC indicate that the premium model will be more profitable than originally thought. The increase in gross profit from $192.80 to $207.00 is a difference of $14.20. When multiplied by the expected sales of 500 units, gross profit increases by $7,100 ($14.20 per unit × 500 units).

By comparing the expected gross profit of the two products, it is clear that the standard model is more profitable than the premium model. Therefore, to maximize profits, the company should continue to sell as many of the standard models as possible. This is a product mix decision. Product mix considers overall production capacity and focuses on producing the mix of products that is most profitable, considering limited production capabilities.

Cost Management Decisions

Most companies adopt ABC to get more accurate product costs for pricing and product mix decisions. However, they often benefit more by cutting costs. ABC and value engineering can work together. **Value engineering** means reevaluating activities to reduce costs while still meeting customer needs. It requires cross-functional teams that include the following:

Value Engineering
Reevaluating activities to reduce costs while satisfying customer needs.

- Marketers to identify customer needs
- Engineers to design products that can be produced more efficiently
- Production personnel to help improve manufacturing processes
- Accountants to estimate costs

Why are managers turning to value engineering? Because it gets results! Companies set sales prices based on **target prices**—what customers are willing to pay for the product or service. Exhibit 19-6 (on the next page) compares cost-based pricing with target pricing. Study each column separately.

Target Price
The amount customers are willing to pay for a product or service.

Exhibit 19-6 | **Cost-Based Pricing Versus Target Pricing**

Cost-Based Pricing	Target Pricing
Full Product Cost	Target Sales Price
+ Desired Net Profit	− Desired Net Profit
Sales Price	Target Cost

Full Product Cost

The cost to develop, produce, and deliver the product or service.

Target Cost

The maximum cost to develop, produce, and deliver the product or service *and* earn the desired net profit. Target sales price minus desired net profit.

Cost-based pricing (left column) starts with the **full product cost**, the cost to develop, produce, and deliver the product or service. The full product cost is added to the desired net profit to determine the sales price. Target pricing (right column) does just the opposite. Target pricing starts with the sales price that customers are willing to pay and then subtracts the company's desired net profit to determine the **target cost**, the maximum cost to develop, produce, and deliver the product or service *and* earn the desired net profit. Notice that the target cost includes all costs, not just manufacturing costs. Then the company works backward to develop the product at the target cost. The company's goal is to achieve the target cost.

Let's return to our Smart Touch Learning illustration. The ABC analysis shows the premium model has a gross profit percentage of only 34.50%, compared with the standard model gross profit percentage of 44.65%. This analysis prompts the sales team to focus its efforts on selling the standard model. Smart Touch Learning can use value engineering to look for ways to decrease the cost of producing the premium model, which will increase profits.

Target pricing considers full product costs in the analysis. Full product costs consider all production costs (direct materials, direct labor, and allocated manufacturing overhead) plus all nonmanufacturing costs (operating expenses, such as administrative and selling expenses). Smart Touch Learning desires a 20% net profit margin on its products. What is the company's target full product cost per premium model tablet? The following is the computation:

Target sales price per premium model tablet	$ 600.00
− Desired net profit ($600.00 × 20%)	(120.00)
Target cost per premium model tablet	$ 480.00

> *Notice that we used net profit here, not gross profit. Gross profit is net sales minus cost of goods sold. Net profit is gross profit less the period costs. Remember that period costs are also called selling and administrative expenses.*

Does Smart Touch Learning's current full product cost meet this target? Assuming nonmanufacturing costs related to the premium model tablet are $120 per unit, the current full product cost per premium model tablet is:

Current total manufacturing cost per premium model tablet	$ 393.00
+ Nonmanufacturing costs (operating expenses)	120.00
Current full product cost per premium model tablet	$ 513.00

Smart Touch Learning's current full product cost does not meet the target cost.

Because Smart Touch Learning's current full product cost, $513, exceeds the target cost of $480, CEO Sheena Bright can assemble a value engineering team to identify ways to cut costs. This team analyzes each production activity and considers how to do one or both of the following:

- Cut costs, given Smart Touch Learning's current production process.
- Redesign the production process to further cut costs.

If the team can find a way to reduce costs by $33 per unit, the difference between the target cost and the actual cost, the company will make its desired net profit.

8. Goodwin, Inc. manufactures children's sandals. Similar sandals manufactured by competitors sell for $12.50 per pair. Goodwin desires a 20% net profit margin. What is Goodwin's target cost?

Check your answer online in MyAccountingLab or at http://www.pearsonhighered.com/Horngren.

For more practice, see Short Exercise S19-9. MyAccountingLab

ETHICS

Why can't "they" leave me alone?

"Why do we have to change things?" mumbled Clayton Huff. "We've always done it this way. No need to change now." Clayton is returning to his workstation after a department meeting where the controller explained how an ABC system works. The controller wants all employees to help develop the system by documenting their activities and the time spent on each activity. Then the accounting department will determine cost drivers and create cost pools and compute allocation rates.

Clayton enjoys his job in production and is quite good at it. In fact, he is so efficient he can get as many units completed in a shift as the other workers and not work nearly as hard. Clayton is also smart enough to realize that if he reports his actual time spent on activities, management will find out how much he has been goofing off. Clayton decides the best thing

to do is fudge the numbers to make it look like he takes longer to make the product than he actually does. Should Clayton report his actual time or adjust it? What would you do?

Solution

Clayton has the responsibility to his employer to work efficiently and effectively in return for his pay. Failure to do so violates the ethical practice of integrity. Falsifying the data submitted to the accounting department could cause management to make pricing and product mix decisions that will have a negative impact on profits which could result in layoffs. On the other hand, presenting the accurate information may provide management with enough information to give him a raise and help the business improve processes for other employees.

HOW CAN ACTIVITY-BASED MANAGEMENT BE USED IN SERVICE COMPANIES?

Activity-based management is not just for manufacturing companies. Many service companies also use ABM. For example, a hospital may use activity-based costing to determine the cost of treating each patient. Activities could include admitting the patient, conducting procedures such as X-rays and MRIs, and providing care for patients in their hospital rooms. The hospital would follow the same four steps as the manufacturing company.

Learning Objective 4

Use activity-based management (ABM) in a service company

Step 1: Identify activities and estimate their total indirect costs.

Step 2: Identify the allocation base for each activity and estimate the total quantity of each allocation base.

Step 3: Compute the predetermined overhead allocation rate for each activity.

Step 4: Allocate indirect costs to the cost object.

Assume Get Well Hospital wishes to allocate overhead costs to Henry Whitestone, a patient at the hospital. Get Well Hospital decides to use ABM and decides to allocate overhead on the basis of three activities (admission, procedures, and care). The hospital has computed the predetermined overhead allocation rates as follows:

	Step 1	Step 2		Step 3
Activity	Estimated Overhead Costs	Allocation Base	Estimated Quantity of Allocation Base	Predetermined Overhead Allocation Rate
Admission	$ 80,000	Number of staff-hours	800 hours	$100 per staff-hour
Procedures	200,000	Number of tests	2,500 tests	$ 80 per test
Care	120,000	Number of nurse-hours	3,000 hours	$ 40 per nurse-hour
Total	$ 400,000			

Assume Henry Whitestone had the following activities performed while at the hospital:

Activity	Actual Quantity
Admission	1 staff-hour
Procedures	5 tests
Care	20 nurse-hours

Get Well Hospital can allocate total overhead costs to Henry Whitestone as follows:

	Step 4			
Activity	Predetermined Overhead Allocation Rate	×	Actual Quantity of the Allocation Based Used	Allocated overhead costs
Admission	$100 per staff-hour	×	1 staff-hour	$ 100
Procedures	$80 per test	×	5 tests	400
Care	$40 per nurse-hour	×	20 nurse-hours	800
				$ 1,300

At the end of each patient's stay, the hospital would have an accurate cost of providing health care to the patient. The hospital could then use the costing information to make decisions about prices to charge the patient and also evaluate its activities and look for ways to cut costs.

Activity-based management is also useful in other types of service companies, such as accounting firms wanting to know the cost of completing various tax returns, attorneys wanting to know the cost to represent various clients, and cleaning services wanting to know the cost to clean different residential and commercial buildings.

TYING IT ALL TOGETHER

In the chapter opener, we introduced **PetSmart, Inc.**, a large specialty pet retailer of services and solutions for the needs of pets. In addition to selling pet food and pet products, PetSmart also offers dog grooming services including bath, nail trim, teeth brushing, aromatherapy to reduce everyday stress, and nail polish and stickers. PetSmart even offers a Top Dog service that includes a premium shampoo, milk bath conditioner, scented cologne spritz, teeth brushing, and bandana or bow.

Assume PetSmart, Inc. uses activity-based costing, what type of activities might the company identify related to its Top Dog service?

PetSmart might identify the following three activities: admission, cleaning, and grooming. The admission activity would include checking the dog in and ensuring the proper vaccine requirements have been met. Cleaning would include the premium bath, blow-dry, and teeth brushing. The grooming activity would include applying the scented cologne spritz, nail polish, and finishing off with a decorative bandana or bow.

What activity cost drivers would PetSmart, Inc. most likely use for the activities identified?

Number of admissions might be used as a cost driver for the admission activity. The cleaning activity could use cleaning direct labor hours and grooming activities could use grooming direct labor hours as their cost drivers.

What are some benefits to using activity-based costing for services such as the Top Dog service?

Activity-based costing provides more accurate cost per service information for companies such as PetSmart, Inc. This is because the allocation of overhead is based on multiple activities and cost drivers as opposed to using a single allocation rate. Having accurate cost per service information can help PetSmart set the sales price for services in order to ensure a desired net profit.

9. Clancy's Carpet Cleaning Services uses ABC to allocate overhead costs and has computed the following predetermined overhead allocation rates:

Activity	Allocation Base	Allocation Rate
Supplies	Number of square feet	$ 0.05 per square foot
Travel	Number of customer sites	$ 20.00 per site

Clancy cleans the carpets for an apartment management firm. When a renter moves out, the apartment management firm contacts Clancy to clean the carpets in preparation for a new tenant. During the past month, Clancy cleaned the carpets of 23 apartments with 1,200 square feet each. What amount of indirect costs should Clancy allocate to the apartment firm for the month?

Check your answers online in MyAccountingLab or at http://www.pearsonhighered.com/Horngren.

For more practice, see Short Exercises S19-10 and S19-11. MyAccountingLab

HOW DO JUST-IN-TIME MANAGEMENT SYSTEMS WORK?

Learning Objective 5

Describe a just-in-time (JIT) management system and record its transactions

Just-in-Time (JIT) Management

A cost management system in which a company produces products just in time to satisfy needs. Suppliers deliver materials just in time to begin production, and finished units are completed just in time for delivery to the customer.

Competition is fierce, especially in technology-related manufacturing, where overseas companies are producing high-quality goods at very low costs. As we saw in the discussion of activity-based costing, there is a never-ending quest to cut costs.

The cost of buying, storing, and moving inventory can be significant for companies. To reduce inventory costs, many companies use a **just-in-time (JIT) management** system. Companies with JIT management systems buy raw materials and complete finished goods *just in time* for delivery to customers.

In traditional manufacturing systems, raw materials are ordered in large quantities to obtain volume discounts and to have surplus raw materials on hand in case some of the raw materials turn out to be defective. Under the JIT management system, the manufacturer contracts with suppliers to deliver small quantities of raw materials as needed. Deliveries are small and frequent, and the suppliers must guarantee a close-to-zero defect rate. Because of the zero defect rate and quick delivery, manufacturers can hold small amounts of raw materials in the warehouse and still be assured they won't run out of raw materials and have to shut down production. For JIT management to work, relationships with suppliers of raw materials must be very reliable to ensure that the company has raw materials just when they are needed to manufacture products. Because products are made as ordered, finished goods inventories are kept to a minimal amount. This reduces the company's cost to store and insure inventory. It also allows the company to minimize the resources it has invested in Raw Materials and Finished Goods Inventories. Lastly, because the inventories are low, the risk of the inventory becoming obsolete or unsalable is very small.

Production in JIT management systems is completed in self-contained work cells, as shown in Panel A of Exhibit 19-7. A work cell is an area where everything needed to complete a manufacturing process is readily available. Each work cell includes the machinery and labor resources to manufacture a product. Employees work in a team in the work cell and are empowered to complete the work without supervision. Workers complete a small batch of units and are responsible for inspecting for quality throughout the process. As the completed product moves out of the work cell, the suppliers deliver more raw materials to the work cell just in time to keep production moving along.

By contrast, traditional production systems (shown in Panel B of Exhibit 19-7) separate manufacturing into various processing departments that focus on a single activity. Work in process must be moved from one department to another. More movements waste time, and wasted time is wasted money.

Under JIT management, customer demand, in the form of a customer's order, triggers manufacturing. The sales order "pulls" materials, labor, and overhead into production. This "demand-pull" system extends back to the suppliers of raw materials. As noted previously, suppliers make frequent deliveries of defect-free materials *just in time* for production. Purchasing raw materials to meet customers' demands for final products reduces inventory. Less inventory frees floor space (and resources) for more productive use. Thus, JIT management systems help reduce waste. The traditional system requires more inventory and workers and costs more to operate than a JIT management system.

Exhibit 19-7 | **Production Flow Comparison: Just-in-Time Versus Traditional Production**

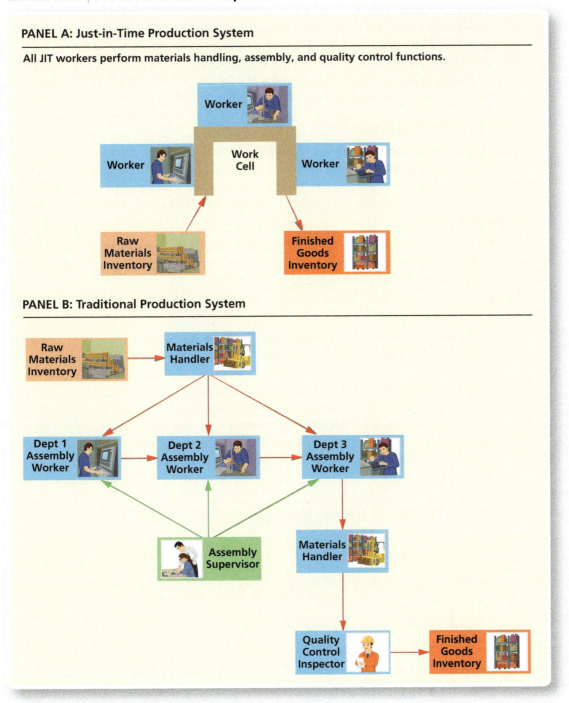

Many companies credit JIT management for saving them millions of dollars. But JIT management systems are not without problems. With little or no inventory buffers, JIT management users lose sales when they cannot get materials on time or when poor-quality materials arrive just in time. There is no way to make up for lost time. As a result, as noted earlier, strong relationships with quality raw materials vendors are very important to successfully implement a JIT management system. Additionally, many JIT management companies still maintain small inventories of critical materials.

Just-in-Time Costing

Just-in-Time Costing
A costing system that starts with output completed and then assigns manufacturing costs to units sold and to inventories.

JIT costing leads many companies to simplify their accounting. **Just-in-time costing**, also called *backflush costing*, seems to work backward. It starts with output that has been completed and then assigns manufacturing costs to units sold and to inventories. There are three major differences between JIT costing and traditional costing, as shown in Exhibit 19-8:

1. JIT costing does not track the cost of products from Raw Materials Inventory to Work-in-Process Inventory to Finished Goods Inventory. Instead, JIT costing waits until the units are completed to record the cost of production.

Raw and In-Process Inventory
A combined account for Raw Materials Inventory and Work-in-Process Inventory used in JIT management systems.

2. JIT costing combines Raw Materials Inventory and Work-in-Process Inventory accounts into a single account called **Raw and In-Process Inventory**.

Conversion Costs Account
A temporary account used in JIT management systems to accumulate direct labor and manufacturing overhead costs and then allocate the costs as units are completed.

3. Under the JIT philosophy, workers perform many tasks. Most companies using JIT combine direct labor and manufacturing overhead costs into a single account called *Conversion Costs*. The **Conversion Costs account** is a temporary account that works just like the Manufacturing Overhead account. Actual conversion costs *accumulate* as debits in the Conversion Costs account, and *allocated* conversion costs are credited to the account as units are completed. Accountants *adjust* any underallocated or overallocated conversion costs to Cost of Goods Sold at the end of the period, just as they do for underallocated or overallocated manufacturing overhead.

Exhibit 19-8 | **Comparison of Traditional and Just-in-Time Costing**

	Traditional	Just-in-Time
Production activity	Records the costs of products as they move through the manufacturing process	Records the costs of products when units are completed
Inventory accounts	Raw Materials Inventory Work-in-Process Inventory Finished Goods Inventory	Raw and In-Process Inventory Finished Goods Inventory
Manufacturing costs	Direct materials Direct labor Manufacturing overhead	Direct materials Conversion costs

Recording Transactions in JIT

To illustrate JIT costing, we'll continue with our Smart Touch Learning example. Smart Touch Learning purchases raw materials to be used in the production of touch screen tablet computers. These costs are recorded in the Raw and In-Process Inventory account. All other manufacturing costs—including labor, various indirect materials, and overhead—are indirect costs of converting the raw materials into finished goods (tablet computers). All these indirect costs are accumulated in the Conversion Costs account.

As noted previously, JIT does not use a separate Work-in-Process Inventory account. Instead, it uses only two inventory accounts:

- Raw and In-Process Inventory, which combines raw materials with work in process
- Finished Goods Inventory

Assume that on January 1, Smart Touch Learning had a beginning balance of $20,000 in Raw and In-Process Inventory and a beginning balance of $15,000 in Finished Goods Inventory. During the year, the company uses JIT costing to record the following summary transactions:

Transaction 1

Smart Touch Learning purchased $305,000 of raw materials on account.

Date	Accounts and Explanation	Debit	Credit
Trans. 1	Raw and In-Process Inventory	305,000	
	Accounts Payable		305,000

$$\left. \frac{A\uparrow}{R\&IP\uparrow} \right\} = \left\{ \frac{L\uparrow}{A/P\uparrow} + \frac{E}{} \right.$$

Transaction 2

Smart Touch Learning incurred $255,000 for labor and overhead.

Date	Accounts and Explanation	Debit	Credit
Trans. 2	Conversion Costs	255,000	
	Wages Payable, Accumulated Depreciation, etc.		255,000

$$\left. \frac{A\downarrow}{\text{Accum. Depreciation}\uparrow} \right\} = \left\{ \frac{L\uparrow}{\text{Wages Payable}\uparrow} + \frac{E\downarrow}{\text{Conversion Costs}\uparrow} \right.$$

Transaction 3

Smart Touch Learning completed 2,000 standard model tablets that it moved to Finished Goods Inventory. Recall that the standard (expected) cost of each standard model tablet is $276.75, as calculated using ABC ($150.00 direct materials + $126.75 conversion costs). The debit (increase) to Finished Goods Inventory is at standard cost of $553,500 (2,000 completed standard model tablets × $276.75 per tablet). There is no separate Work-in-Process Inventory account in JIT costing, so Smart Touch Learning credits the following:

- Raw and In-Process Inventory is credited for the direct materials, $300,000 (2,000 completed standard model tablets × $150.00 standard direct material cost per tablet).
- Conversion Costs is credited for the direct labor and indirect costs allocated to the finished tablets, $253,500 (2,000 completed standard model tablets × $126.75 standard conversion cost per tablet).

This is the key to JIT costing. The system does not track costs as the tablets move through manufacturing. Instead, *completion* of the tablets triggers the accounting system to go back and move costs from Raw and In-Process Inventory (credit), allocate Conversion Costs (credit), and attach those costs to the finished products (debit).

Date	Accounts and Explanation	Debit	Credit
Trans. 3	Finished Goods Inventory	553,500	
	Raw and In-Process Inventory		300,000
	Conversion Costs		253,500

$$\left. \frac{A\uparrow}{\begin{array}{c} R\&IP\downarrow \\ FG\uparrow \end{array}} \right\} = \left\{ \frac{L}{} + \frac{E\uparrow}{\begin{array}{c} \text{Conversion} \\ \text{Costs}\downarrow \end{array}} \right.$$

Transaction 4

Smart Touch Learning sold 1,900 tablets on account for $500 each, for a total of $950,000. The cost of goods sold is $525,825 (1,900 tablets × $276.75). The journal entries are:

$$\frac{A\uparrow}{A/R\uparrow} \Big\} = \Big\{ \quad L \quad + \quad \frac{E\uparrow}{\text{Sales Revenue}\uparrow}$$

$$\frac{A\downarrow}{FG\downarrow} \Big\} = \Big\{ \quad L \quad + \quad \frac{E\downarrow}{\text{COGS}\uparrow}$$

Date	Accounts and Explanation	Debit	Credit
Trans. 4	Accounts Receivable	950,000	
	Sales Revenue		950,000
	Cost of Goods Sold	525,825	
	Finished Goods Inventory		525,825

Exhibit 19-9 shows Smart Touch Learning's relevant accounts. Combining the Raw Materials Inventory account with the Work-in-Process Inventory account to form the single Raw and In-Process Inventory account eliminates detail and saves time and costs.

Exhibit 19-9 | **Smart Touch Learning's JIT Costing Accounts**

	BALANCE SHEET			INCOME STATEMENT
Raw and In-Process Inventory		**Finished Goods Inventory**		**Cost of Goods Sold**
Bal. 20,000		Bal. 15,000		Trans. 4 525,825
Trans. 1 305,000 / 300,000 Trans. 3	→	Trans. 3 553,500 / 525,825 Trans. 4	→	
Bal. 25,000		Bal. 42,675		
Conversion Costs				
Trans. 2 255,000 / 253,500 Trans. 3				
Unadj. Bal. 1,500				

Adjustment

You can see from Exhibit 19-9 that conversion costs are underallocated by $1,500 (actual costs of $255,000 − allocated costs of $253,500). Underallocated and overallocated Conversion Costs are treated just like underallocated and overallocated Manufacturing Overhead. The Conversion Costs account is adjusted so that it has a zero balance, and the amount underallocated is transferred to Cost of Goods Sold, as follows:

$$\frac{A}{} \Big\} = \Big\{ \quad L \quad + \quad \frac{E\uparrow\downarrow}{\substack{\text{COGS}\uparrow \\ \text{Conversion} \\ \text{Costs}\downarrow}}$$

Date	Accounts and Explanation	Debit	Credit
Adj.	Cost of Goods Sold	1,500	
	Conversion Costs		1,500

In the final analysis, Cost of Goods Sold for the year is $527,325, as shown in the T-account in Exhibit 19-10.

Exhibit 19-10 | **Adjustment for Conversion Costs**

Conversion Costs				Cost of Goods Sold		
Trans. 2	255,000	253,500	Trans. 3	Trans. 4	525,825	
Unadj. Bal.	1,500			Adj.	1,500	
		1,500	Adj.	Bal.	527,325	
Bal.	0					

If you were to go to the grocery store today, you could either buy just the ingredients you need to make dinner tonight or you could purchase enough groceries to last you two weeks. If you purchase groceries for two weeks, can you be sure you'll use all the groceries you buy, or will some of it "go bad" before you eat it? Choosing to purchase just enough groceries to get you through a short period (today) is like just-in-time costing. Companies purchase just enough raw materials for the production needs of the next day or two, rather than purchasing large amounts of raw materials that have to be stored.

Try It!

Malone Company has adopted a JIT management system and has the following transactions in August:

a. Purchased raw materials on account, $50,000.

b. Incurred labor and overhead costs, $70,000.

c. Completed 500 units with standard costs of $95 for direct materials and $150 for conversion costs.

d. Sold on account 475 units for $300 each.

10. Record the journal entries for Malone Company for August.
11. Open a T-account for Conversion Costs. Post appropriate entries to determine the amount of underallocated or overallocated overhead. Record the adjusting entry.

Check your answers online in MyAccountingLab or at http://www.pearsonhighered.com/Horngren.

For more practice, see Short Exercises S19-12 and S19-13. MyAccountingLab

HOW DO COMPANIES MANAGE QUALITY USING A QUALITY MANAGEMENT SYSTEM?

We now turn our attention to a third type of management system: quality management systems. To be profitable, companies must provide customers with quality products and services. Poor-quality items cause sales to drop as customers become aware of quality issues. Additionally, defective items must either be repaired or replaced, which increases costs. The combination of decreased revenues and increased costs can be devastating for a business.

Because just-in-time management systems have very little inventory on hand, companies are far more vulnerable to production shutdowns if they receive poor-quality or defective raw materials. For this reason, it is critical that a company's raw materials be nearly defect free. To meet this challenge, each business function monitors its activities to improve quality and eliminate defects and waste.

Learning Objective 6

Describe quality management systems (QMS) and use the four types of quality costs to make decisions

Quality Management Systems

Quality Management System (QMS)

A system that helps managers improve a business's performance by providing quality products and services.

Quality management systems (QMS) are systems that help managers improve the business's performance by providing quality products and services. There are several quality management systems currently in use, and the increased availability of software programs to assist in data collection and analysis has helped even small companies adopt these systems. The common factor in all quality management systems is the desire to improve performance, which should result in increased customer satisfaction and increased profits.

Continuous improvement is the primary goal of quality management systems, and it is monitored in many ways. For example, companies compare the cost of any changes they want to make against the benefits of the changes as one measure to aid decision making. Assume a company is considering reorganizing a work cell to improve efficiency. The reorganization costs $40,000, but the change is expected to result in a $100,000 reduction in production costs. Would the company want to implement the change considering its cost and benefits? Absolutely! Why? The change is expected to net the company an additional $60,000 in profit.

Well-designed products and production processes reduce inspections, rework, and warranty claims. Investing in research and development (R&D) can generate savings in customer service. World-class companies *design* and *build* quality into their products rather than having to *inspect* and *repair* later.

The Four Types of Quality Costs

The four types of quality-related costs are:

Prevention Costs

Costs incurred to avoid poor-quality goods or services.

Appraisal Costs

Costs incurred to detect poor-quality materials, goods, or services.

Internal Failure Costs

Costs incurred when the company corrects poor-quality goods or services before delivery to customers.

External Failure Costs

Costs incurred when the company does not detect poor-quality goods or services until after delivery to customers.

1. **Prevention costs**: costs incurred to *avoid* poor-quality goods or services.
2. **Appraisal costs**: costs incurred to *detect* poor-quality materials, goods, or services.
3. **Internal failure costs**: costs incurred when the company *corrects* poor-quality goods or services before delivery to customers.
4. **External failure costs**: costs incurred after the company *delivers* poor-quality goods or services to customers and then has to make things right with the customer.

Exhibit 19-11 gives examples of the four types of quality costs. Most prevention, appraisal, and internal failure costs ultimately become part of the cost of the finished product. External failure causes an increase in customer service costs, or it could cause lost sales due to an unhappy customer. External failure costs ultimately affect warranty expense claims or, worse, potential lawsuit liability exposure. Prevention of poor quality is much cheaper than external failure. Businesses should invest up front in prevention and appraisal costs to reduce internal and external failure costs.

Do you go to the dentist every six months to have your teeth cleaned? The cost of the cleaning is a prevention cost. By investing in the care of your teeth, not only do your teeth look nice, but you hope to prevent decay in your teeth. Preventing that decay helps you to avoid a bigger dentist bill for repairing your teeth in the future. The same is true for producing products. Money spent ensuring consistent quality standards and screening for defective products before they ship to customers is usually less than money spent on returned products and warranty claims or revenues lost from losing a customer.

Exhibit 19-11 | Four Types of Quality Costs

Prevention Costs	Appraisal Costs
• Employee training	• Inspection at various stages of production
• Evaluation of the quality of suppliers' processes	• Inspection of final products or services
• Preventive maintenance on equipment	• Product testing
Internal Failure Costs	**External Failure Costs**
• Any production problem that causes manufacturing to stop	• Lost profits due to unhappy customers
• Reworking of substandard products	• Warranty costs
• Rejected products	• Service costs at customer sites
	• Sales returns due to product defects

Quality Improvement Programs

Let's revisit Smart Touch Learning. CEO Sheena Bright is considering spending the following on a new quality improvement program:

Inspect raw materials	$ 100,000
Reengineer to improve product quality	750,000
Inspect finished goods	150,000
Preventive maintenance of equipment	100,000

Smart Touch Learning expects this quality program to reduce costs by the following amounts:

Avoid lost profits due to unhappy customers	$ 800,000
Fewer sales returns	50,000
Decrease the cost of rework	250,000
Lower warranty costs	100,000

Bright asks the controller to do the following:

1. Classify each cost into one of the four categories (prevention, appraisal, internal failure, external failure), and total the estimated costs for each category.
2. Recommend whether Smart Touch Learning should undertake the quality improvement program.

The controller completes the report shown in Exhibit 19-12 (on the next page) to compare the costs of undertaking the quality improvement program or continuing without the program.

Exhibit 19-12 | **Analysis of Smart Touch Learning's Proposed Quality Improvement Program**

Undertake the Quality Improvement Program		
Prevention		
Reengineer to improve product quality	$ 750,000	
Preventive maintenance of equipment	100,000	
Total prevention costs		$ 850,000
Appraisal		
Inspect raw materials	100,000	
Inspect finished goods	150,000	
Total appraisal costs		250,000
Total costs of undertaking the quality improvement program		$ 1,100,000
Do Not Undertake the Quality Improvement Program		
Internal Failure		
Cost of rework	$ 250,000	
Total internal failure costs		$ 250,000
External Failure		
Lost profits due to unhappy customers	800,000	
Sales returns	50,000	
Warranty costs	100,000	
Total external failure costs		950,000
Total costs of not undertaking the quality improvement program		$ 1,200,000

These estimates suggest that Smart Touch Learning would save $100,000 ($1,200,000 − $1,100,000) by undertaking the quality improvement program.

Quality costs can be hard to measure. For example, it is very hard to measure external failure costs. Lost profits due to unhappy customers do not appear in the accounting records! Therefore, quality management systems use many nonfinancial measures, such as the number of customer complaints and the volume of incoming customer-service phone calls, as a means to measure success or failure.

12. Identify the following costs as prevention, appraisal, internal failure, or external failure:

   a. Inspection of final products
   b. Sales returns of defective products
   c. Employee training
   d. Reworking defective products
   e. Working with suppliers to ensure delivery of high-quality raw materials
   f. Costs of warranty repairs
   g. Product testing

Check your answers online in MyAccountingLab or at http://www.pearsonhighered.com/Horngren.

For more practice, see Short Exercise S19-14. MyAccountingLab

REVIEW

> Things You Should Know

1. How do companies assign and allocate costs?

- Direct materials and direct labor can be easily traced to products, so they are *assigned*.
- Manufacturing overhead, an indirect cost, cannot be easily traced and is *allocated*.

$$\text{Predetermined overhead allocation rate} = \frac{\text{Total estimated overhead costs}}{\text{Total estimated quantity of the overhead allocation base}}$$

$$\text{Allocated manufacturing overhead cost} = \text{Predetermined overhead allocation rate} \times \text{Actual quantity of the allocation base used}$$

2. How is an activity-based costing system developed?

- **Step 1:** Identify activities and estimate their total indirect costs.
- **Step 2:** Identify the allocation base for each activity and estimate the total quantity of each allocation base.
- **Step 3:** Compute the predetermined overhead allocation rate for each activity.
- **Step 4:** Allocate indirect costs to the cost object.

3. How can companies use activity-based management to make decisions?

- Determining pricing and product mix
- Computing target prices and target costs

4. How can activity-based management be used in service companies?

- Activity-based costing can be used in determining the cost of services as well as products.
- Use the same four steps to develop ABC, and then use the results to make management decisions.

5. How do just-in-time management systems work?

- Just-in-time management systems are inventory management systems in which a company produces products just in time to satisfy customer needs. Suppliers deliver raw materials just in time to begin production, and finished units are completed just in time for delivery to customers.
- JIT management systems use JIT costing:
  - The Raw Materials Inventory and Work-in-Process Inventory accounts are combined into a single Raw and In-Process Inventory account.
  - Direct labor and manufacturing overhead are combined into a Conversion Costs account.
  - Summary journal entries are recorded *after* units are completed.

6. How do companies manage quality using a quality management system?

- There are four types of quality costs:
  - Prevention
  - Appraisal
  - Internal failure
  - External failure
- Businesses should invest up front in prevention and appraisal costs to reduce internal and external failure costs.

> Check Your Understanding 19-1

Check your understanding of the chapter by completing this problem and then looking at the solution. Use this practice to help identify which sections of the chapter you need to study more.

Indianapolis Auto Parts (IAP) has a Seat Assembly Department that uses activity-based costing. IAP's system has the following activities:

Activity	Allocation Base	Cost Allocation Rate
Purchasing	Number of purchase orders	$ 50.00 per purchase order
Assembling	Number of parts	$ 0.50 per part
Packaging	Number of finished seats	$ 1.00 per finished seat

Each baby seat has 20 parts. Direct materials cost per seat is $15. Direct labor cost per seat is $10. Suppose an automobile manufacturer has asked IAP for a bid on 50,000 built-in baby seats that would be installed as an option on its SUVs. IAP will use a total of 200 purchase orders if the bid is accepted.

Requirements

1. Compute the total cost IAP will incur to (a) purchase the needed materials and then (b) assemble and (c) package 50,000 baby seats. Also, compute the average cost per seat. (See Learning Objective 2)

2. For bidding, IAP adds a 30% markup to total cost. What total price will IAP bid for the entire order? (See Learning Objective 3)

3. Suppose that instead of an ABC system, IAP has a traditional product costing system that allocates indirect costs at the rate of $65 per direct labor hour. The baby seat order will require 10,000 direct labor hours. What price will IAP bid using this system's total cost assuming a 30% markup to total cost? (See Learning Objectives 1, 3)

4. Use your answers to Requirements 2 and 3 to explain how ABC can help IAP make a better decision about the bid price. (See Learning Objective 3)

> Solution

Requirement 1

Direct materials, 50,000 seats × $15.00 per seat	$ 750,000
Direct labor, 50,000 seats × $10.00 per seat	500,000
Activity costs:	
Purchasing, 200 purchase orders × $50.00 per purchase order	10,000
Assembling, 50,000 seats × 20 parts per seat × $0.50 per part	500,000
Packaging, 50,000 seats × $1.00 per seat	50,000
Total cost of order	$ 1,810,000
Divide by number of seats	÷ 50,000
Average cost per seat	$ 36.20

Requirement 2

Bid price (ABC system): $1,810,000 × 130%	$ 2,353,000

Requirement 3

Direct materials, 50,000 seats × $15.00 per seat	$ 750,000
Direct labor, 50,000 seats × $10.00 per seat	500,000
Indirect costs, 10,000 direct labor hours × $65.00 per direct labor hour	650,000
Total cost of order	$ 1,900,000

Bid price (Traditional system): $1,900,000 × 130%	$ 2,470,000

Requirement 4

IAP's bid would be $117,000 higher using the traditional system than using ABC ($2,470,000 − $2,353,000). Assuming the ABC system more accurately captures the costs caused by the order, the traditional system over-costs the order. This leads to a higher bid price and reduces IAP's chance of winning the order. The ABC system can increase IAP's chance of winning the order by bidding a lower price.

> Check Your Understanding 19-2

Check your understanding of the chapter by completing this problem and then looking at the solution. Use this practice to help identify which sections of the chapter you need to study more.

Flores Company manufactures cell phones and uses JIT costing. The standard unit cost of $30 is composed of $20 direct materials and $10 conversion costs. Raw materials purchased on account during June totaled $2,500,000. Actual conversion costs totaled $1,100,000. Flores completed 100,000 cell phones in June and sold 98,000 on account. The sales price is $55 each.

Requirements

1. Journalize these transactions. (See Learning Objective 5)

2. Prepare a T-account for the Conversion Costs account. Were conversion costs underallocated or overallocated? Explain your answer, and then make the entry to adjust the Conversion Costs account. (See Learning Objective 5)

3. What is the ending balance of the Raw and In-Process Inventory account if the beginning balance was zero? How much Cost of Goods Sold did Flores have in June after making any necessary adjustments? (See Learning Objective 5)

> Solution

Requirement 1

Date	Accounts and Explanation	Debit	Credit
	Raw and In-Process Inventory	2,500,000	
	Accounts Payable		2,500,000
	Conversion Costs	1,100,000	
	Wages Payable, Accumulated Depreciation, etc.		1,100,000
	Finished Goods Inventory	3,000,000	
	Raw and In-Process Inventory (100,000 units × $20)		2,000,000
	Conversion Costs (100,000 units × $10)		1,000,000
	Accounts Receivable (98,000 units × $55)	5,390,000	
	Sales Revenue		5,390,000
	Cost of Goods Sold (98,000 units × $30)	2,940,000	
	Finished Goods Inventory		2,940,000

Requirement 2

	Conversion Costs	
	1,100,000	1,000,000
Bal.	100,000	

Conversion costs were underallocated. Actual costs ($1,100,000) exceeded the costs allocated to Finished Goods Inventory ($1,000,000).

Date	Accounts and Explanation	Debit	Credit
	Cost of Goods Sold	100,000	
	Conversion Costs		100,000

Requirement 3

Raw and In-Process Inventory

	2,500,000	2,000,000
Bal.	500,000	

Cost of Goods Sold = $3,040,000 ($2,940,000 + $100,000)

> Key Terms

Activity (p. 1036)

Activity-Based Costing (ABC) (p. 1036)

Activity-Based Management (ABM) (p. 1036)

Appraisal Costs (p. 1054)

Conversion Costs Account (p. 1050)

External Failure Costs (p. 1054)

Full Product Cost (p. 1044)

Internal Failure Costs (p. 1054)

Just-in-Time Costing (p. 1050)

Just-in-Time (JIT) Management (p. 1048)

Predetermined Overhead Allocation Rate (p. 1030)

Prevention Costs (p. 1054)

Quality Management System (QMS) (p. 1054)

Raw and In-Process Inventory (p. 1050)

Target Cost (p. 1044)

Target Price (p. 1043)

Value Engineering (p. 1043)

> Quick Check

Learning Objective 1

1. Which statement is *false*?

   a. Using a single plantwide overhead allocation rate is the simplest method of allocating overhead costs.

   b. An allocation system that uses departmental overhead allocation rates is more refined than one that uses a plantwide overhead allocation rate.

   c. Allocation focuses on indirect costs.

   d. The predetermined overhead allocation rate is based on actual costs.

Use the following information for questions 2–4.

Compute It uses activity-based costing. Two of Compute It's production activities are *kitting* (assembling the raw materials needed for each computer in one kit) and *boxing* the completed products for shipment to customers. Assume that Compute It spends $960,000 per month on kitting and $32,000 per month on boxing. Compute It allocates the following:

- Kitting costs based on the number of parts used in the computer
- Boxing costs based on the cubic feet of space the computer requires

Suppose Compute It estimates it will use 400,000 parts per month and ship products with a total volume of 6,400 cubic feet per month.

Assume that each desktop computer requires 125 parts and has a volume of 2 cubic feet.

Learning Objective 2

2. What are the predetermined overhead allocation rates?

	Kitting	Boxing
a.	$ 0.03 per part	$ 0.05 per cubic foot
b.	$ 0.60 per part	$ 0.06 per cubic foot
c.	$ 2.40 per part	$ 5.00 per cubic foot
d.	$ 7.68 per part	$ 0.08 per cubic foot

CHAPTER 19

Learning Objective 2

3. What are the kitting and boxing costs assigned to one desktop computer?

	Kitting	Boxing
a.	$ 300.00	$ 10.00
b.	$ 30.00	$ 137.50
c.	$ 10.00	$ 9.60
d.	$ 9.60	$ 148.50

Learning Objective 2

4. Compute It contracts with its suppliers to pre-kit certain component parts before delivering them to Compute It. Assume this saves $210,000 of the kitting cost and reduces the total number of parts by 100,000 (because Compute It considers each pre-kit as one part). If a desktop now uses 90 parts, what is the new kitting cost assigned to one desktop?

a. $225.00   **b.** $300.00   **c.** $275.00   **d.** $282.00

Learning Objective 3

5. Compute It can use ABC information for what decisions?

a. Cost cutting   **c.** Product mix

b. Pricing   **d.** Items a, b, and c are all correct.

Learning Objective 4

6. Which of the following would be true for a service company?

a. ABC helps the company make more informed decisions about services.

b. Service companies use only a few activities, so a plantwide overhead allocation is always appropriate.

c. Most of the company's costs are for direct materials and direct labor. Indirect costs are a small proportion of total costs.

d. All of the above are true.

Learning Objective 5

7. Companies enjoy many benefits from using JIT. Which is *not* a benefit of adopting JIT?

a. Ability to respond quickly to changes in customer demand

b. Lower inventory carrying costs

c. Ability to continue production despite disruptions in deliveries of raw materials

d. More space available for production

Learning Objective 5

8. Which account is *not* used in JIT costing?

a. Finished Goods Inventory   **c.** Work-in-Process Inventory

b. Raw and In-Process Inventory   **d.** Conversion Costs

Learning Objective 6

9. The cost of lost future sales after a customer finds a defect in a product is which type of quality cost?

a. Prevention cost   **c.** Internal failure cost

b. Appraisal cost   **d.** External failure cost

Learning Objective 6

10. Spending on testing a product before shipment to customers is which type of quality cost?

a. External failure cost   **c.** Appraisal cost

b. Prevention cost   **d.** None of the above

Check your answers at the end of the chapter.

CHAPTER 19

ASSESS YOUR PROGRESS

> Review Questions

1. What is the formula to compute the predetermined overhead allocation rate?

2. How is the predetermined overhead allocation rate used to allocate overhead?

3. Describe how a single plantwide overhead allocation rate is used.

4. Why is using a single plantwide overhead allocation rate not always accurate?

5. Why is the use of departmental overhead allocation rates considered a refinement over the use of a single plantwide overhead allocation rate?

6. What is activity-based management? How is it different from activity-based costing?

7. How many cost pools are in an activity-based costing system?

8. What are the four steps to developing an activity-based costing system?

9. Why is ABC usually considered more accurate than traditional costing methods?

10. List two ways managers can use ABM to make decisions.

11. Define value engineering. How is it used to control costs?

12. Explain the difference between target price and target cost.

13. How can ABM be used by service companies?

14. What is a just-in-time management system?

15. Explain how the work cell manufacturing layout increases productivity.

16. What are the inventory accounts used in JIT costing?

17. How is the Conversion Costs account used in JIT costing?

18. Why is JIT costing sometimes called backflush costing?

19. Which accounts are adjusted for the underallocated or overallocated overhead in JIT costing?

20. What is the purpose of quality management systems?

21. List and define the four types of quality costs.

22. "Prevention is much cheaper than external failure." Do you agree with this statement? Why or why not?

23. What are quality improvement programs?

24. Why are some quality costs hard to measure?

> Short Exercises

S19-1 Computing single plantwide overhead allocation rates

Learning Objective 1

The Oakman Company manufactures products in two departments: Mixing and Packaging. The company allocates manufacturing overhead using a single plantwide rate with direct labor hours as the allocation base. Estimated overhead costs for the year are $810,000, and estimated direct labor hours are 360,000. In October, the company incurred 20,000 direct labor hours.

Requirements

1. Compute the predetermined overhead allocation rate. Round to two decimal places.

2. Determine the amount of overhead allocated in October.

Learning Objective 1

S19-2 Computing departmental overhead allocation rates

The Oakman Company (see Short Exercise S19-1) has refined its allocation system by separating manufacturing overhead costs into two cost pools—one for each department. The estimated costs for the Mixing Department, $510,000, will be allocated based on direct labor hours, and the estimated direct labor hours for the year are 170,000. The estimated costs for the Packaging Department, $300,000, will be allocated based on machine hours, and the estimated machine hours for the year are 40,000. In October, the company incurred 38,000 direct labor hours in the Mixing Department and 10,000 machine hours in the Packaging Department.

Requirements

1. Compute the predetermined overhead allocation rates. Round to two decimal places.

2. Determine the total amount of overhead allocated in October.

Learning Objective 2

S19-3 Using activity-based costing

Activity-based costing requires four steps. List the four steps in the order they are performed.

Learning Objectives 1, 2

S19-4 Calculating costs using traditional and activity-based systems

Bubba and Danny are college friends planning a skiing trip to Killington before the new year. They estimated the following for the trip:

	Estimated Costs	Allocation Base	Activity Allocation	
			Bubba	Danny
Food	$ 400	Pounds of food eaten	24	26
Skiing	300	Number of lift tickets	2	0
Lodging	280	Number of nights	2	2
	$ 980			

Requirements

1. Bubba suggests that the costs be shared equally. Calculate the amount each person would pay.

2. Danny does not like the idea of sharing the costs equally because he plans to stay in the room rather than ski. Danny suggests that each type of cost be allocated to each person based on the above-listed allocation bases. Using the activity allocation for each person, calculate the amount that each person would pay based on his own consumption of the activity.

CHAPTER 19

S19-5 Computing indirect manufacturing costs per unit

Learning Objective 2

Darby Corp. is considering the use of activity-based costing. The following information is provided for the production of two product lines:

Activity	Cost	Allocation Base
Setup	$ 105,000	Number of setups
Machine maintenance	60,000	Number of machine hours
Total indirect manufacturing costs	$ 165,000	

	Product A	Product B	Total
Direct labor hours	7,000	5,000	12,000
Number of setups	30	170	200
Number of machine hours	1,600	2,400	4,000

Darby plans to produce 375 units of Product A and 250 units of Product B. Compute the ABC indirect manufacturing cost per unit for each product.

S19-6 Computing indirect manufacturing costs per unit, traditional and ABC

Learning Objectives 1, 2

The following information is provided for Orbit Antenna Corp., which manufactures two products: Lo-Gain antennas and Hi-Gain antennas for use in remote areas.

Activity	Cost	Allocation Base
Setup	$ 58,000	Number of setups
Machine maintenance	30,000	Number of machine hours
Total indirect manufacturing costs	$ 88,000	

	Lo-Gain	Hi-Gain	Total
Direct labor hours	1,200	3,800	5,000
Number of setups	40	40	80
Number of machine hours	3,000	2,000	5,000

Orbit Antenna plans to produce 125 Lo-Gain antennas and 225 Hi-Gain antennas.

Requirements

1. Compute the indirect manufacturing cost per unit using direct labor hours for the single plantwide predetermined overhead allocation rate.
2. Compute the ABC indirect manufacturing cost per unit for each product.

S19-7 Using ABC to compute product costs per unit

Learning Objective 2

Jaunkas Corp. manufactures mid-fi and hi-fi stereo receivers. The following data have been summarized:

	Mid-Fi	Hi-Fi
Direct materials cost per unit	$ 400	$ 1,800
Direct labor cost per unit	600	400
Indirect manufacturing cost per unit	?	?

Indirect manufacturing cost information includes the following:

Activity	Predetermined Overhead Allocation Rate	Mid-Fi	Hi-Fi
Setup	$ 1,400 per setup	36 setups	36 setups
Inspections	$ 700 per inspection hour	35 inspection hours	20 inspection hours
Machine maintenance	$ 13 per machine hour	1,900 machine hours	1,150 machine hours

The company plans to manufacture 125 units of the mid-fi receivers and 250 units of the hi-fi receivers. Calculate the product cost per unit for both products using activity-based costing.

Learning Objective 2

S19-8 Using ABC to compute product costs per unit

Spectrum Corp. makes two products: C and D. The following data have been summarized:

	Product C	Product D
Direct materials cost per unit	$ 600	$ 2,400
Direct labor cost per unit	300	200
Indirect manufacturing cost per unit	?	?

Indirect manufacturing cost information includes the following:

Activity	Predetermined Overhead Allocation Rate	Product C	Product D
Setup	$ 1,500 per setup	35 setups	76 setups
Machine maintenance	$ 10 per MHr	1,500 MHr	3,700 MHr

The company plans to manufacture 250 units of each product. Calculate the product cost per unit for Products C and D using activity-based costing.

Note: Short Exercise S19-8 must be completed before attempting Short Exercise S19-9.

Learning Objective 3

S19-9 Using ABM to achieve target profit

Refer to Short Exercise S19-8. Spectrum Corp. desires a 25% target gross profit after covering all product costs. Considering the total product costs assigned to the Products C and D in Short Exercise S19-8, what would Spectrum have to charge the customer to achieve that gross profit? Round to two decimal places.

S19-10 Using ABM in a service company

Learning Objective 4

Haworth Company is a management consulting firm. The company expects to incur $167,500 of indirect costs this year. Indirect costs are allocated based on the following activities:

Activity	Estimated Cost	Allocation Base	Estimated Quantity of Allocation Base	Predetermined Overhead Allocation Rate
Site visits	$ 45,000	Number of visits	900 visits	$ 50 per visit
Documentation preparation	122,500	Number of pages	3,500 pages	$ 35 per page
Total indirect costs	$ 167,500			

Haworth bills clients at 120% of the direct labor costs. The company has estimated direct labor costs at $240 per hour. Last month, Haworth completed a consulting job for Client 76 and used the following resources:

Allocation Base	Client 76
Direct labor hours	60
Visits	5
Pages	50

Determine the total cost of the consulting job and the operating income earned.

Note: Short Exercise S19-10 must be completed before attempting Short Exercise S19-11.

S19-11 Using ABM in a service company

Learning Objective 4

Refer to Short Exercise S19-10. Haworth desires a 20% target operating income after covering all costs. Considering the total costs assigned to the Client 76 job in Short Exercise S19-10, what would Haworth have to charge the customer to achieve that operating income? Round to two decimal places.

S19-12 Identifying just-in-time characteristics

Learning Objective 5

Consider the following characteristics of either a JIT production system or a traditional production system. Indicate whether each is characteristic of a JIT production system or a traditional production system.

a. Products are produced in large batches.

b. Large stocks of finished goods protect against lost sales if customer demand is higher than expected.

c. Suppliers make frequent deliveries of small quantities of raw materials.

d. Employees do a variety of jobs, including maintenance and setups as well as operating machines.

e. Machines are grouped into self-contained production cells or production lines.

f. Machines are grouped according to function. For example, all cutting machines are located in one area.

g. The final operation in the production sequence "pulls" parts from the preceding operation.

h. Each employee is responsible for inspecting his or her own work.

i. Management works with suppliers to ensure defect-free raw materials.

Learning Objective 5

S19-13 Recording JIT costing journal entries

Prime Products uses a JIT management system to manufacture trading pins. The standard cost per pin is $2 for direct materials and $3 for conversion costs. Last month, Prime recorded the following data:

Number of pins completed	4,100 pins
Number of pins sold (on account at $7 each)	3,700 pins
Raw material purchases (on account)	$ 7,000
Conversion costs	$ 14,500

Use JIT costing to prepare journal entries for the month, including the entry to adjust the Conversion Costs account.

Learning Objective 6

S19-14 Matching cost-of-quality examples to categories

Stegall, Inc. manufactures motor scooters. For each of the following examples of quality costs, indicate which of the following quality cost categories each example represents: prevention costs, appraisal costs, internal failure costs, or external failure costs.

1. Preventive maintenance on machinery

2. Direct materials, direct labor, and manufacturing overhead incurred to rework a defective scooter that is detected in-house through inspection

3. Lost profits from lost sales if the company's reputation is hurt because customers previously purchased a poor-quality scooter

4. Cost of inspecting raw materials, such as chassis and wheels

5. Working with suppliers to achieve on-time delivery of defect-free raw materials

6. Cost of warranty repairs on a scooter that malfunctions at a customer's location

7. Costs of testing durability of vinyl

8. Cost to reinspect reworked scooters

> Exercises

Learning Objective 1

Basic $322,000

E19-15 Computing and using single plantwide overhead allocation rate

Koehler makes handheld calculators in two models: basic and professional. Koehler estimated $721,000 of manufacturing overhead and 515,000 machine hours for the year. The basic model actually consumed 230,000 machine hours, and the professional model consumed 285,000 machine hours.

Compute the predetermined overhead allocation rate using machine hours (MHr) as the allocation base. How much overhead is allocated to the basic model? To the professional model?

E19-16 Computing and using departmental overhead allocation rates

Learning Objective 1

Professional, total OH $477,500

Koehler (see Exercise E19-15) makes handheld calculators in two models—basic and professional—and wants to refine its costing system by allocating overhead using departmental rates. The estimated $721,000 of manufacturing overhead has been divided into two cost pools: Assembly Department and Packaging Department. The following data have been compiled:

	Assembly Department	Packaging Department	Total
Overhead costs	$ 456,500	$ 264,500	$ 721,000
Machine hours:			
Basic Model	185,000 MHr	45,000 MHr	230,000 MHr
Professional Model	230,000 MHr	55,000 MHr	285,000 MHr
Total	415,000 MHr	100,000 MHr	515,000 MHr
Direct labor hours:			
Basic Model	20,000 DLHr	50,000 DLHr	70,000 DLHr
Professional Model	105,125 DLHr	280,625 DLHr	385,750 DLHr
Total	125,125 DLHr	330,625 DLHr	455,750 DLHr

Compute the predetermined overhead allocation rates using machine hours as the allocation base for the Assembly Department and direct labor hours for the Packaging Department. How much overhead is allocated to the basic model? To the professional model? Round allocation rates to two decimal places and allocated costs to whole dollars.

Note: Exercises E19-15 and E19–16 must be completed before attempting Exercise E19-17.

E19-17 Computing and using activity-based costing overhead allocation rates

Learning Objectives 2, 3

1. Total MOH Basic $256,000

Koehler (see Exercise E19-15 and Exercise E19-16) makes handheld calculators in two models—basic and professional—and wants to further refine its costing system by allocating overhead using activity-based costing. The estimated $721,000 of manufacturing overhead has been divided into three primary activities: Materials Handling, Machine Setup, and Insertion of Parts. The following data have been compiled:

	Materials Handling	Machine Setup	Insertion of Parts	Total
Overhead costs	$ 45,000	$ 136,000	$ 540,000	$ 721,000
Allocation base	Number of parts	Number of setups	Number of parts	
Expected usage:				
Basic Model	32 parts per calculator	24 setups per year	32 parts per calculator	
Professional Model	58 parts per calculator	44 setups per year	58 parts per calculator	

Requirement 1

Koehler expects to produce 200,000 basic models and 200,000 professional models. Compute the predetermined overhead allocation rates using activity-based costing. How much overhead is allocated to the basic model? To the professional model?

Requirement 2

Compare your answers for Exercise E19-15, Exercise E19-16, and Exercise E19-17. What conclusions can you draw?

Learning Objective 2

1. POHR machine setup $310 per setup

E19-18 Computing product costs in an activity-based costing system

Franklin, Inc. uses activity-based costing to account for its chrome bumper manufacturing process. Company managers have identified four manufacturing activities: materials handling, machine setup, insertion of parts, and finishing. The budgeted activity costs for 2018 and their allocation bases are as follows:

Activity	Total Budgeted Cost	Allocation Base
Materials handling	$ 12,000	Number of parts
Machine setup	3,100	Number of setups
Insertion of parts	42,000	Number of parts
Finishing	86,000	Finishing direct labor hours
Total	$ 143,100	

Franklin expects to produce 500 chrome bumpers during the year. The bumpers are expected to use 4,000 parts, require 10 setups, and consume 1,000 hours of finishing time.

Requirements

1. Compute the predetermined overhead allocation rate for each activity.
2. Compute the expected indirect manufacturing cost of each bumper.

Learning Objective 2

2. OH cost per unit $1,685

E19-19 Computing product costs in an activity-based costing system

Turbo Champs Corp. uses activity-based costing to account for its motorcycle manufacturing process. Company managers have identified three supporting manufacturing activities: inspection, machine setup, and machine maintenance. The budgeted activity costs for 2018 and their allocation bases are as follows:

Activity	Total Budgeted Cost	Allocation Base
Inspections	$ 5,700	Number of inspections
Machine setup	22,000	Number of setups
Machine maintenance	6,000	Finishing of machine hours
Total	$ 33,700	

Turbo Champs expects to produce 20 custom-built motorcycles for the year. The motorcycles are expected to require 100 inspections, 40 setups, and 100 machine hours.

Requirements

1. Compute the predetermined overhead allocation rate for each activity.
2. Compute the expected indirect manufacturing cost of each motorcycle.

E19-20 Computing product costs in traditional and activity-based costing systems

Learning Objectives 1, 2

3. Standard $224.40

Eason Company manufactures wheel rims. The controller expects the following ABC allocation rates for 2018:

Activity	Allocation Base	Predetermined Overhead Allocation Rate
Materials handling	Number of parts	$ 4.00 per part
Machine setup	Number of setups	400.00 per setup
Insertion of parts	Number of parts	26.00 per part
Finishing	Number of finishing hours	90.00 per hour

Eason produces two wheel rim models: standard and deluxe. Expected data for 2018 are as follows:

	Standard	Deluxe
Parts per rim	4.0	7.0
Setups per 500 rims	18.0	18.0
Finishing hours per rim	1.0	5.5
Total direct hours per rim	5.0	6.0

The company expects to produce 500 units of each model during the year.

Requirements

1. Compute the total estimated indirect manufacturing cost for 2018.

2. Prior to 2018, Eason used a single plantwide overhead allocation rate system with direct labor hours as the allocation base. Compute the predetermined overhead allocation rate based on direct labor hours for 2018. Use this rate to determine the estimated indirect manufacturing cost per wheel rim for each model, to the nearest cent.

3. Compute the estimated ABC indirect manufacturing cost per unit of each model for 2018. Carry each cost to the nearest cent.

Note: Exercise E19-20 must be completed before attempting Exercise E19-21.

E19-21 Using activity-based costing to make decisions

Learning Objectives 1, 2, 3

1. Deluxe GP $120.60

Refer to Exercise E19-20. For 2019, Eason's managers have decided to use the same indirect manufacturing costs per wheel rim that they computed in 2018 using activity-based costing. In addition to the unit indirect manufacturing costs, the following data are expected for the company's standard and deluxe models for 2019:

	Standard	Deluxe
Sales price	$ 800.00	$ 940.00
Direct materials	31.00	48.00
Direct labor	45.00	52.00

Because of limited machine hour capacity, Eason can produce *either* 2,000 standard rims *or* 2,000 deluxe rims.

CHAPTER 19

Requirements

1. If Eason's managers rely on the ABC unit cost data computed in Exercise E19-20, which model will they produce? Carry each cost to the nearest cent. (Ignore selling and administrative expenses for this calculation.)

2. If the managers rely on the single plantwide overhead allocation rate cost data, which model will they produce?

3. Which course of action will yield more income for Eason?

Note: Exercises E19-20 and E19-21 must be completed before attempting Exercise E19-22.

Learning Objective 3

E19-22 Using activity-based management and target costing

OH cost per unit $524.40

Refer to Exercises E19-20 and E19-21. Controller Michael Bender is surprised by the increase in cost of the deluxe model under ABC. Market research shows that for the deluxe rim to provide a reasonable profit, Eason will have to meet a target manufacturing cost of $625.00 per rim. A value engineering study by Eason's employees suggests that modifications to the finishing process could cut finishing cost from $90.00 to $60.00 per hour and reduce the finishing direct labor hours per deluxe rim from 5.50 hours to 5.0 hours. Direct materials would remain unchanged at $48.00 per rim, as would direct labor at $52.00 per rim. The materials handling, machine setup, and insertion of parts activity costs also would remain the same.

Would implementing the value engineering recommendation enable Eason to achieve its target cost for the deluxe rim?

Learning Objectives 1, 2, 3

E19-23 Using activity-based costing to make decisions

1. Cost per collar $10.62

Treat Dog Collars uses activity-based costing. Treat's system has the following features:

Activity	Allocation Base	Predetermined Overhead Allocation Rate
Purchasing	Number of purchase orders	$ 60.00 per purchase order
Assembling	Number of parts	0.36 per part
Packaging	Number of finished collars	0.19 per collar

Each collar has three parts, direct materials cost is $5.00 per collar, and direct labor cost is $4.00 per collar. Suppose Animal Hut has asked for a bid on 30,000 dog collars. Treat will issue a total of 175 purchase orders if Animal Hut accepts Treat's bid.

Requirements

1. Compute the total estimated cost Treat will incur to purchase the needed materials and then assemble and package 30,000 dog collars. Also compute the cost per collar.

2. For bidding, Treat adds a 40% markup to total cost. What total price will the company bid for the entire Animal Hut order?

3. Suppose that instead of an ABC system, Treat has a traditional product costing system that allocates indirect costs at the rate of $9.50 per direct labor hour. The dog collar order will require 9,000 direct labor hours. What total price will Treat bid using this system's total cost?

4. Use your answers to Requirements 2 and 3 to explain how ABC can help Treat make a better decision about the bid price it will offer Animal Hut.

E19-24 Allocating indirect costs and computing income, service company

Learning Objective 4

2. Total OH cost $27,200

Western, Inc. is a technology consulting firm focused on Web site development and integration of Internet business applications. The president of the company expects to incur $640,000 of indirect costs this year, and she expects her firm to work 4,000 direct labor hours. Western's systems consultants provide direct labor at a rate of $280 per hour. Clients are billed at 160% of direct labor cost. Last month, Western's consultants spent 170 hours on Halbert's engagement.

Requirements

1. Compute Western's predetermined overhead allocation rate per direct labor hour.
2. Compute the total cost assigned to the Halbert engagement.
3. Compute the operating income from the Halbert engagement.

Note: Exercise E19-24 must be completed before attempting Exercise E19-25.

E19-25 Computing ABC allocation rates, service company

Learning Objective 4

POHR training $106 per DLHr

Refer to Exercise E19-24. The president of Western suspects that her allocation of indirect costs could be giving misleading results, so she decides to develop an ABC system. She identifies three activities: documentation preparation, information technology support, and training. She figures that documentation costs are driven by the number of pages, information technology support costs are driven by the number of software applications used, and training costs are driven by the number of direct labor hours worked. Estimates of the costs and quantities of the allocation bases follow:

Activity	Estimated Cost	Allocation Base	Estimated Quantity of Allocation Base
Documentation preparation	$ 65,850	Pages	1,317 pages
Information technology support	150,150	Applications used	715 applications
Training	424,000	Direct labor hours	4,000 hours
Total indirect costs	$ 640,000		

Compute the predetermined overhead allocation rate for each activity. Round to the nearest dollar.

Note: Exercises E19-24 and E19-25 must be completed before attempting Exercise E19-26.

E19-26 Using ABC to allocate costs and compute profit, service company

Learning Objective 4

1. Total OH cost $50,320

Refer to Exercises E19-24 and E19-25. Suppose Western's direct labor rate was $280 per hour. The Halbert engagement used the following resources last month:

Allocation Base	Halbert
Direct labor hours	170
Pages	310
Applications used	80

Requirements

1. Compute the cost assigned to the Halbert engagement, using the ABC system.
2. Compute the operating income or loss from the Halbert engagement, using the ABC system.

Note: Exercise E19-26 must be completed before attempting Exercise E19-27.

Learning Objective 4

$122,400

E19-27 Using ABC to achieve target profit, service company

Refer to Exercise E19-26. Western desires a 20% target net profit after covering all costs. Considering the total costs assigned to the Halbert engagement in Exercise E19-26, what would Western have to charge the customer to achieve that net profit? Round to two decimal places.

Learning Objective 5

1. COGS $21,780 DR

E19-28 Recording manufacturing costs in a JIT costing system

Lally, Inc. produces universal remote controls. Lally uses a JIT costing system. One of the company's products has a standard direct materials cost of $9 per unit and a standard conversion cost of $35 per unit. During January 2018, Lally produced 500 units and sold 495 units on account at $45 each. It purchased $4,800 of direct materials on account and incurred actual conversion costs totaling $14,000.

Requirements

1. Prepare summary journal entries for January.

2. The January 1, 2018, balance of the Raw and In-Process Inventory account was $70. Use a T-account to find the January 31 balance.

3. Use a T-account to determine whether conversion costs are overallocated or underallocated for the month. By how much? Prepare the journal entry to adjust the Conversion Costs account.

Learning Objective 5

1. R&IP $7,500 CR

E19-29 Recording manufacturing costs in a JIT costing system

Gateway produces electronic calculators. Suppose Gateway's standard cost per calculator is $25 for direct materials and $68 for conversion costs. The following data apply to August activities:

Direct materials purchased (on account)	$ 8,300
Conversion costs incurred	20,500
Number of calculators produced	300 calculators
Number of calculators sold (on account, at $105 each)	295 calculators

Requirements

1. Prepare summary journal entries for August using JIT costing, including the entry to adjust the Conversion Costs account.

2. The beginning balance of Finished Goods Inventory was $1,300. Use a T-account to find the ending balance of Finished Goods Inventory.

Learning Objective 6

Total external failure costs
$118,000

E19-30 Classifying quality costs

Darrel & Co. makes electronic components. Chris Darrel, the president, recently instructed Vice President Jim Bruegger to develop a total quality control program. "If we don't at least match the quality improvements our competitors are making," he told Bruegger, "we'll soon be out of business." Bruegger began by listing various "costs of quality" that Darrel incurs. The first six items that came to mind were:

a. Costs incurred by Darrel customer representatives traveling to customer sites to repair defective products, $13,000.

b. Lost profits from lost sales due to reputation for less-than-perfect products, $35,000.

c. Costs of inspecting components in one of Darrel's production processes, $40,000.

d. Salaries of engineers who are redesigning components to withstand electrical overloads, $65,000.

e. Costs of reworking defective components after discovery by company inspectors, $50,000.

f. Costs of electronic components returned by customers, $70,000.

Classify each item as a prevention cost, an appraisal cost, an internal failure cost, or an external failure cost. Then determine the total cost of quality by category.

E19-31 Classifying quality costs and using these costs to make decisions

Learning Objective 6

2. Total cost to undertake $192,000

Clason, Inc. manufactures door panels. Suppose Clason is considering spending the following amounts on a new total quality management (TQM) program:

Strength-testing one item from each batch of panels	$ 68,000
Training employees in TQM	27,000
Training suppliers in TQM	39,000
Identifying suppliers who commit to on-time delivery of perfect-quality materials	58,000

Clason expects the new program would save costs through the following:

Avoid lost profits from lost sales due to disappointed customers	$ 86,000
Avoid rework and spoilage	63,000
Avoid inspection of raw materials	57,000
Avoid warranty costs	15,000

Requirements

1. Classify each cost as a prevention cost, an appraisal cost, an internal failure cost, or an external failure cost.

2. Should Clason implement the new quality program? Give your reason.

E19-32 Classifying quality costs and using these costs to make decisions

Learning Objective 6

2. Total cost to undertake $2,305,000

Loiselle manufactures high-quality speakers. Suppose Loiselle is considering spending the following amounts on a new quality program:

Additional 20 minutes testing for each speaker	$ 625,000
Negotiating and training suppliers to obtain higher-quality materials and on-time delivery	430,000
Redesigning the speakers to make them easier to manufacture	1,250,000

Loiselle expects this quality program to save costs as follows:

Reduce warranty repair costs	$ 275,000
Avoid inspection of raw materials	580,000
Avoid rework because of fewer defective units	825,000

It also expects this program to avoid lost profits from the following:

Lost profits due to disappointed customers	$ 920,000
Lost production time due to rework	278,000

Requirements

1. Classify each of these costs into one of the four categories of quality costs (prevention, appraisal, internal failure, or external failure).
2. Should Loiselle implement the quality program? Give your reasons.

> Problems Group A

Learning Objectives 1, 2

P19-33A Comparing costs from ABC and single-rate systems

3. Travel packs $1.80

Willitte Pharmaceuticals manufactures an over-the-counter allergy medication. The company sells both large commercial containers of 1,000 capsules to health care facilities and travel packs of 20 capsules to shops in airports, train stations, and hotels. The following information has been developed to determine if an activity-based costing system would be beneficial:

Activity	Estimated Indirect Cost	Allocation Base	Estimated Quantity of Allocation Base
Materials handling	$ 95,000	Number of kilos	19,000 kilos
Packaging	200,000	Number of machine hours	5,000 hours
Quality assurance	112,500	Number of samples	1,875 samples
Total indirect costs	$ 407,500		

Actual production information includes the following:

	Commercial Containers	Travel Packs
Units produced	2,400 containers	50,000 packs
Weight in kilos	9,600	5,000
Machine hours	1,680	500
Number of samples	240	750

Requirements

1. Willitte's original single plantwide overhead allocation rate costing system allocated indirect costs to products at $81.50 per machine hour. Compute the total indirect costs allocated to the commercial containers and to the travel packs under the original system. Then compute the indirect cost per unit for each product. Round to two decimal places.
2. Compute the predetermined overhead allocation rate for each activity.
3. Use the predetermined overhead allocation rates to compute the activity-based costs per unit of the commercial containers and the travel packs. Round to two decimal places. (*Hint*: First compute the total activity-based costs allocated to each product line, and then compute the cost per unit.)
4. Compare the indirect activity-based costs per unit to the indirect costs per unit from the traditional system. How have the unit costs changed? Explain why the costs changed.

P19-34A Computing product costs in an ABC system

Learning Objective 2

1. Total activity-based costs $83.10

The Alright Manufacturing Company in Rochester, Minnesota, assembles and tests electronic components used in smartphones. Consider the following data regarding component T24 (amounts are per unit):

Direct materials cost	$ 80.00
Direct labor cost	20.00
Activity-based costs allocated	?
Total manufacturing product cost	?

The activities required to build the component follow:

Activity	Allocation Base	Cost Allocated to Each Unit				
Start station	Number of raw component chassis	4	×	$ 1.50	=	$ 6.00
Dip insertion	Number of dip insertions	?	×	0.30	=	9.60
Manual insertion	Number of manual insertions	10	×	0.50	=	?
Wave solder	Number of components soldered	4	×	1.90	=	7.60
Backload	Number of backload insertions	7	×	?	=	4.20
Test	Number of testing hours	0.43	×	90.00	=	?
Defect analysis	Number of defect analysis hours	0.15	×	?	=	12.00
Total activity-based costs						$?

Requirements

1. Complete the missing items for the two tables.
2. Why might managers favor this ABC system instead of Alright's older system, which allocated all manufacturing overhead costs on the basis of direct labor hours?

P19-35A Computing product costs in an ABC system

Learning Objectives 2, 3

1. Standard $62 per unit

Oscar, Inc. manufactures bookcases and uses an activity-based costing system. Oscar's activity areas and related data follow:

Activity	Budgeted Cost of Activity	Allocation Base	Predetermined Overhead Allocation Rate
Materials handling	$ 240,000	Number of parts	$ 1.00
Assembly	3,500,000	Number of assembling direct labor hours	17.00
Finishing	190,000	Number of finished units*	4.50

*Refers to number of units receiving the finishing activity, not the number of units transferred to Finished Goods Inventory

Oscar produced two styles of bookcases in October: the standard bookcase and an unfinished bookcase, which has fewer parts and requires no finishing. The totals for quantities, direct materials costs, and other data follow:

Product	Total Units Produced	Total Direct Materials Costs	Total Direct Labor Costs	Total Number of Parts	Total Assembling Direct Labor Hours
Standard bookcase	7,000	$ 91,000	$ 105,000	28,000	10,500
Unfinished bookcase	7,500	82,500	75,000	22,500	7,500

CHAPTER 19

Requirements

1. Compute the manufacturing product cost per unit of each type of bookcase.

2. Suppose that pre-manufacturing activities, such as product design, were assigned to the standard bookcases at $5 each and to the unfinished bookcases at $3 each. Similar analyses were conducted of post-manufacturing activities such as distribution, marketing, and customer service. The post-manufacturing costs were $20 per standard bookcase and $18 per unfinished bookcase. Compute the full product costs per unit.

3. Which product costs are reported in the external financial statements? Which costs are used for management decision making? Explain the difference.

4. What price should Oscar's managers set for unfinished bookcases to earn a net profit of $19 per bookcase?

Learning Objective 4

P19-36A Using ABC in a service company

1. Total OH cost $890

Blanchette Plant Service completed a special landscaping job for Kerry Company. Blanchette uses ABC and has the following predetermined overhead allocation rates:

Activity	Allocation Base	Predetermined Overhead Allocation Rate
Designing	Number of designs	$ 290 per design
Planting	Number of plants	$ 20 per plant

The Kerry job included $750 in plants; $1,300 in direct labor; one design; and 30 plants.

Requirements

1. What is the total cost of the Kerry job?

2. If Kerry paid $3,540 for the job, what is the operating income or loss?

3. If Blanchette desires an operating income of 30% of cost, how much should the company charge for the Kerry job?

Learning Objective 5

P19-37A Recording manufacturing costs for a JIT system

3. $6,500

Low Range produces fleece jackets. The company uses JIT costing for its JIT production system.

Low Range has two inventory accounts: Raw and In-Process Inventory and Finished Goods Inventory. On March 1, 2018, the account balances were Raw and In-Process Inventory, $9,000; Finished Goods Inventory, $1,700.

The standard cost of a jacket is $40, composed of $12 direct materials plus $28 conversion costs. Data for March's activities follow:

Number of jackets completed	15,000
Number of jackets sold (on account, for $50 each)	14,600
Direct materials purchased (on account)	$ 177,500
Conversion costs incurred	$ 521,000

Requirements

1. What are the major features of a JIT production system such as that of Low Range?

2. Prepare summary journal entries for March. Underallocated or overallocated conversion costs are adjusted to Cost of Goods Sold monthly.

3. Use a T-account to determine the March 31, 2018, balance of Raw and In-Process Inventory.

P19-38A Analyzing costs of quality

Learning Objective 6

2. Net benefit $12,620

Stella, Inc. is using a costs-of-quality approach to evaluate design engineering efforts for a new skateboard. Stella's senior managers expect the engineering work to reduce appraisal, internal failure, and external failure activities. The predicted reductions in activities over the two-year life of the skateboards follow. Also shown are the predetermined overhead allocation rates for each activity.

Activity	Predicted Reduction in Activity Units	Predetermined Overhead Allocation Rate per Unit
Inspection of incoming raw materials	390	$ 44
Inspection of finished goods	390	19
Number of defective units discovered in-house	1,200	50
Number of defective units discovered by customers	325	72
Lost profits due to dissatisfied customers	75	102

Requirements

1. Calculate the predicted quality cost savings from the design engineering work.

2. Stella spent $103,000 on design engineering for the new skateboard. What is the net benefit of this "preventive" quality activity?

3. What major difficulty would Stella's managers have in implementing this costs-of-quality approach? What alternative approach could they use to measure quality improvement?

> Problems Group B

P19-39B Comparing costs from ABC and single-rate systems

Learning Objectives 1, 2

1. Travel packs $1.40

Harcourt Pharmaceuticals manufactures an over-the-counter allergy medication. The company sells both large commercial containers of 1,000 capsules to health care facilities and travel packs of 20 capsules to shops in airports, train stations, and hotels. The following information has been developed to determine if an activity-based costing system would be beneficial:

Activity	Estimated Indirect Cost	Allocation Base	Estimated Quantity of Allocation Base
Materials handling	$ 96,000	Number of kilos	24,000 kilos
Packaging	210,000	Number of machine hours	3,000 hours
Quality assurance	114,000	Number of samples	1,900 samples
Total indirect costs	$ 420,000		

CHAPTER 19

Other production information includes the following:

	Commercial Containers	Travel Packs
Units produced	2,800 containers	51,000 packs
Weight in kilos	9,800	5,100
Machine hours	1,960	510
Number of samples	560	765

Requirements

1. Harcourt's original single plantwide overhead allocation rate system allocated indirect costs to products at $140.00 per machine hour. Compute the total indirect costs allocated to the commercial containers and to the travel packs under the original system. Then compute the indirect cost per unit for each product. Round to two decimal places.

2. Compute the predetermined overhead allocation rate for each activity.

3. Use the predetermined overhead allocation rates to compute the activity-based costs per unit of the commercial containers and the travel packs. Round to two decimal places. (*Hint:* First compute the total activity-based costs allocated to each product line, and then compute the cost per unit.)

4. Compare the indirect activity-based costs per unit to the indirect costs per unit from the traditional system. How have the unit costs changed? Explain why the costs changed as they did.

Learning Objective 2

P19-40B Computing product costs in an ABC system

1. Total activity-based costs $58.90

The Alexander Manufacturing Company in Rochester, Minnesota, assembles and tests electronic components used in smartphones. Consider the following data regarding component T24 (amounts are per unit):

Direct materials cost	$ 81.00
Direct labor cost	21.00
Activity-based costs allocated	?
Total manufacturing product cost	?

The activities required to build the component follow:

Activity	Allocation Base	Cost Allocated to Each Unit					
Start station	Number of raw component chassis	3	×	$ 1.50	=	$ 4.50
Dip insertion	Number of dip insertions	?	×	0.50	=	14.50
Manual insertion	Number of manual insertions	13	×	0.40	=	?
Wave solder	Number of components soldered	3	×	1.50	=	4.50
Backload	Number of backload insertions	7	×	?	=	2.80
Test	Number of testing hours	0.39	×	60.00	=	?
Defect analysis	Number of defect analysis hours	0.10	×	?	=	4.00
Total activity-based costs						$?

Requirements

1. Complete the missing items for the two tables.

2. Why might managers favor this ABC system instead of Alexander's older system, which allocated all manufacturing overhead costs on the basis of direct labor hours?

P19-41B Computing product costs in an ABC system

Learning Objectives 2, 3

1. Standard $72 per unit

Martin, Inc. manufactures bookcases and uses an activity-based costing system. Martin's activity areas and related data follow:

Activity	Budgeted Cost of Activity	Allocation Base	Predetermined Overhead Allocation Rate
Materials handling	$ 230,000	Number of parts	$ 1.50
Assembly	3,200,000	Number of assembling direct labor hours	16.00
Finishing	150,000	Number of finished units*	3.00

*Refers to number of units receiving the finishing activity, not the number of units transferred to Finished Goods Inventory

Martin produced two styles of bookcases in April: the standard bookcase and an unfinished bookcase, which has fewer parts and requires no finishing. The totals for quantities, direct materials costs, and other data follow:

Product	Total Units Produced	Total Direct Materials Costs	Total Direct Labor Costs	Total Number of Parts	Total Assembling Direct Labor Hours
Standard bookcase	3,000	$ 54,000	$ 67,500	9,000	4,500
Unfinished bookcase	3,500	56,000	52,500	7,000	3,500

Requirements

1. Compute the manufacturing product cost per unit of each type of bookcase.

2. Suppose that pre-manufacturing activities, such as product design, were assigned to the standard bookcases at $5 each and to the unfinished bookcases at $3 each. Similar analyses were conducted of post-manufacturing activities such as distribution, marketing, and customer service. The post-manufacturing costs were $24 per standard bookcase and $18 per unfinished bookcase. Compute the full product costs per unit.

3. Which product costs are reported in the external financial statements? Which costs are used for management decision making? Explain the difference.

4. What price should Martin's managers set for unfinished bookcases to earn a net profit of $19 per bookcase?

P19-42B Using ABC in a service company

Learning Objective 4

1. Total OH cost $890

Rennie Plant Service completed a special landscaping job for Brenton Company. Rennie uses ABC and has the following predetermined overhead allocation rates:

Activity	Allocation Base	Predetermined Overhead Allocation Rate
Designing	Number of designs	$ 290 per design
Planting	Number of plants	$ 20 per plant

The Brenton job included $1,500 in plants; $800 in direct labor; one design; and 30 plants.

Requirements

1. What is the total cost of the Brenton job?
2. If Brenton paid $3,690 for the job, what is the operating income or loss?
3. If Rennie desires an operating income of 30% of cost, how much should the company charge for the Brenton job?

Learning Objective 5

3. $2,500

P19-43B Recording manufacturing costs for a JIT system

High Mountain produces fleece jackets. The company uses JIT costing for its JIT production system.

High Mountain has two inventory accounts: Raw and In-Process Inventory and Finished Goods Inventory. On April 1, 2018, the account balances were Raw and In-Process Inventory, $10,000; Finished Goods Inventory, $2,100.

The standard cost of a jacket is $33, composed of $12 direct materials plus $21 conversion costs. Data for April's activities follow:

Number of jackets completed	19,000
Number of jackets sold (on account for $50 each)	18,600
Direct materials purchased (on account)	$ 220,500
Conversion costs incurred	$ 500,000

Requirements

1. What are the major features of a JIT production system such as that of High Mountain?
2. Prepare summary journal entries for April. Underallocated or overallocated conversion costs are adjusted to Cost of Goods Sold monthly.
3. Use a T-account to determine the April 30, 2018, balance of Raw and In-Process Inventory.

Learning Objective 6

2. Net benefit $33,025

P19-44B Analyzing costs of quality

Roxi, Inc. is using a costs-of-quality approach to evaluate design engineering efforts for a new skateboard. Roxi's senior managers expect the engineering work to reduce appraisal, internal failure, and external failure activities. The predicted reductions in activities over the two-year life of the skateboards follow. Also shown are the predetermined overhead allocation rates for each activity.

Activity	Predicted Reduction in Activity Units	Predetermined Overhead Allocation Rate per Unit
Inspection of incoming raw materials	395	$ 44
Inspection of finished goods	395	26
Number of defective units discovered in-house	1,500	54
Number of defective units discovered by customers	275	73
Lost profits due to dissatisfied customers	100	103

Requirements

1. Calculate the predicted quality cost savings from the design engineering work.
2. Roxi spent $106,000 on design engineering for the new skateboard. What is the net benefit of this "preventive" quality activity?
3. What major difficulty would Roxi's managers have in implementing this costs-of-quality approach? What alternative approach could they use to measure quality improvement?

CRITICAL THINKING

> Using Excel

P19-45 Using Excel for allocating manufacturing overhead with activity-based costing (ABC)

Download an Excel template for this problem online in MyAccountingLab or at http://www.pearsonhighered.com/Horngren.

Mt. Hood Manufacturing uses ABC to allocate manufacturing overhead costs, and has computed the following:

Activity	Allocation Base	Allocation Rate
Equipment Setup	Number of Setups	$400 per setup
Ordering	Number of Orders	$ 10 per order
Machine Maintenance	Machine Hours	$ 10 per hour
Receiving	Receiving Hours	$ 20 per hour

The company produces two models of industrial heaters, Crest and Cascade.

The quantity of each activity required by Crest and Cascade is listed below.

Allocation Base	Crest	Cascade
Number of Setups	350	250
Number of Orders	6,000	12,000
Machine Hours	24,000	18,000
Receiving Hours	3,000	7,000

Requirement

Allocate the $1,040,000 estimated manufacturing overhead between the products using activity-based costing to obtain the total manufacturing overhead cost per product. Reconcile the manufacturing overhead allocated to the two products with total manufacturing overhead.

> Continuing Problem

P19-46 Comparing costs from ABC and single-rate systems

This problem continues the Piedmont Computer Company situation from Chapter 17. Recall that Piedmont Computer Company allocated manufacturing overhead costs to jobs based on a predetermined overhead allocation rate, computed as 25% of direct labor costs. Piedmont Computer Company is now considering using an ABC system. Information about ABC costs for 2020 follows:

Activity	Allocation Base	Predetermined Overhead Allocation Rate
Assembly	Number of parts	$ 0.25
Programming	Number of direct labor hours	3.50
Testing	Number of tests	125.00

Records for two jobs appear here:

Job	Total Direct Materials Costs	Total Number of Parts	Total Direct Labor Hours	Total Number of Tests
Job 721	$ 23,400	2,500	780	8
Job 722	2,500	300	60	2

Requirements

1. Compute the total cost for each job using activity-based costing. The cost of direct labor is $25 per hour.
2. Is the job cost greater or less than that computed in Chapter 17 for each job? Why?
3. If Piedmont Computer Company wants to earn an operating income equal to 45% of the total cost, what sales price should it charge each of these two customers?

> Tying It All Together Case 19-1

Before you begin this assignment, review the Tying It All Together feature in the chapter.

PetSmart, Inc. is a large specialty pet retailer of services and solutions for the needs of pets. In addition to selling pet food and pet products, PetSmart also offers dog grooming services including bath, nail trim, teeth brushing, aromatherapy to reduce everyday stress, and nail polish and stickers. PetSmart even offers a Top Dog service that includes a premium shampoo, milk bath conditioner, scented cologne spritz, teeth brushing, and bandana or bow.

Assume PetSmart, Inc. expects to incur $380,000 of indirect costs this year. The company allocates indirect costs based on the following activities:

Activity	Estimated Cost	Allocation Base	Estimated Quantity of Allocation Base
Admission	$ 60,000	Number of admissions	20,000
Cleaning	240,000	Cleaning direct labor hours	100,000
Grooming	80,000	Grooming direct labor hours	4,000
Total indirect costs	$ 380,000		

Requirements

1. Calculate the predetermined overhead allocation rate for each activity.
2. Assume a customer brought in Sophie, a beagle, for Top Dog service. PetSmart used the following resources:

Allocation Base	Sophie, Beagle
Number of admissions	1
Cleaning direct labor hours	1
Grooming direct labor hours	0.5

Determine the total cost of the Top Dog service for Sophie assuming the total direct materials cost was $3.50 and the total direct labor cost was $12 per DLHr.

3. If PetSmart desires a 30% target operating income after covering all its costs, what would PetSmart have to charge the customer to achieve that operating income?

> Decision Cases

Decision Case 19-1

Harris Systems specializes in servers for workgroup, e-commerce, and ERP applications. The company's original job costing system has two direct cost categories: direct materials and direct labor. Overhead is allocated to jobs at the single rate of $22 per direct labor hour.

A task force headed by Harris's CFO recently designed an ABC system with four activities. The ABC system retains the current system's two direct cost categories. Overhead costs are reflected in the four activities. Pertinent data follow:

Activity	Allocation Base	Predetermined Overhead Allocation Rate
Materials handling	Number of parts	$ 0.85
Machine setup	Number of setups	500.00
Assembling	Number of assembling hours	80.00
Shipping	Number of shipments	1,500.00

Harris Systems has been awarded two new contracts, which will be produced as Job A and Job B. Budget data relating to the contracts follow:

	Job A	Job B
Number of parts	15,000	2,000
Number of setups	6	4
Number of assembling hours	1,500	200
Number of shipments	1	1
Total direct labor hours	8,000	600
Number of units produced	100	10
Direct materials cost	$ 220,000	$ 30,000
Direct labor cost	$ 160,000	$ 12,000

Requirements

1. Compute the budgeted product cost per unit for each job, using the original costing system (with two direct cost categories and a single overhead allocation rate).

2. Suppose Harris Systems adopts the ABC system. Compute the budgeted product cost per unit for each job using ABC.

3. Which costing system more accurately assigns to jobs the costs of the resources consumed to produce them? Explain.

Decision Case 19-2

Harris Systems has decided to adopt ABC. To remain competitive, Harris Systems's management believes the company must produce the type of servers produced in Job B (from Decision Case 19-1) at a target cost of $5,400. Harris Systems has just joined a B2B e-market site that management believes will enable the firm to cut direct materials costs by 10%. Harris's management also believes that a value engineering team can reduce assembly time.

Compute the assembling cost savings required per Job B-type server to meet the $5,400 target cost. (*Hint:* Begin by calculating the direct materials, direct labor, and allocated overhead costs per server.)

> Ethical Issue 19-1

Cassidy Manning is assistant controller at LeMar Packaging, Inc., a manufacturer of cardboard boxes and other packaging materials. Manning has just returned from a packaging industry conference on activity-based costing. She realizes that ABC may help LeMar meet its goal of reducing costs by 5% over each of the next three years.

LeMar Packaging's Order Department is a likely candidate for ABC. While orders are entered into a computer that updates the accounting records, clerks manually check customers' credit history and hand-deliver orders to shipping. This process occurs whether the sales order is for a dozen specialty boxes worth $80 or 10,000 basic boxes worth $8,000.

Manning believes that identifying the cost of processing a sales order would justify (1) further computerization of the order process and (2) changing the way the company processes small orders. However, the significant cost savings would arise from elimination of two positions in the Order Department. The company's sales order clerks have been with the company many years. Manning is uncomfortable with the prospect of proposing a change that will likely result in terminating these employees.

Use the IMA's ethical standards (see Chapter 16) to consider Manning's responsibility when cost savings come at the expense of employees' jobs.

> Fraud Case 19-1

Anu Ghai was a new production analyst at RHI, Inc., a large furniture factory in North Carolina. One of her first jobs was to update the predetermined overhead allocation rates for factory production costs. This was normally done once a year, by analyzing the previous year's actual data, factoring in projected changes, and calculating a new rate for the coming year. What Anu found was strange. The activity rate for "maintenance" had more than doubled in one year, and she was puzzled how that could have happened. When she spoke with Larry McAfee, the factory manager, she was told to spread the increases out over the other activity costs to "smooth out" the trends. She was a bit intimidated by Larry, an imposing and aggressive man, but she knew something wasn't quite right. Then one night she was at a restaurant and overheard a few employees who worked at RHI talking. They were joking about the work they had done fixing up Larry's home at the lake last year. Suddenly everything made sense. Larry had been using factory labor, tools, and supplies to have his lake house renovated on the weekends. Anu had a distinct feeling that if she went up against Larry on this issue, she would come out the loser. She decided to look for work elsewhere.

Requirements

1. Besides spotting irregularities, like the case above, what are some other ways that ABC cost data are useful for manufacturing companies?

2. What are some of the other options that Anu might have considered?

MyAccountingLab For a wealth of online resources, including exercises, problems, media, and immediate tutorial help, please visit http://www.myaccountinglab.com.

> Quick Check Answers

1. d **2.** c **3.** a **4.** a **5.** d **6.** a **7.** c **8.** c **9.** d **10.** c

Cost-Volume-Profit Analysis 20

Which Items Should Be Marked Down?

Charlene walks out of the summer heat into the cool, air-conditioned electronics store. She tries to envision how the store will look in a few months during the holiday season when the decorations will be up. She watches customers browsing and interacting with the sales staff. She notices which areas of the store are busy and which ones have little activity. Recent sales reports indicate touch screen computer tablets and HDTVs are the fast-moving items, and the in-store activity mirrors those reports.

Even though it is only July, Charlene has to make decisions now for the sales planned for November and December. Charlene is a buyer for the store. It is her job to ensure that the store has ample inventory to satisfy customers' needs. Charlene must decide which items should be featured on Black Friday, the day after Thanksgiving, which has become one of the busiest shopping days of the year. How low should the sales prices go for these featured items? If the sales prices are lowered, the gross profit on those items will also decrease. Will an increase in sales volume make up for the decreased gross profit per item? Will discounting certain items draw customers into the store to purchase other items that have a larger gross profit? If the company makes early buying commitments, can Charlene negotiate better deals that will decrease its costs and therefore increase profits?

Charlene's decisions could have a major impact on her company. For many retailers, the sales made in November and December determine the profitability for the year. Charlene needs a management tool, such as *cost-volume-profit analysis*, to assist her in making these planning decisions.

What Is Cost-Volume-Profit Analysis?

Have you ever wondered how companies such as **Best Buy Co., Inc.** determine which items to feature in their major sales events? How can they afford to sell certain items at such a low price on Black Friday or Cyber Monday? What effect do the sales have on overall profits?

Best Buy opened its first store in 1966 in St. Paul, Minnesota. The company now has more than 1,400 domestic stores, more than 1,700 total stores worldwide, and about 125,000 employees. Its 2015 consolidated statement of earnings reports more than $40 billion in revenues with a gross profit percentage of 22.4% and an operating income percentage of 3.6%. These percentages have been fairly consistent since 2003, although they have declined in the last 3 years. Best Buy has to consider how changes in sales prices will affect sales volume and its overall profits, which is often done by using cost-volume-profit analysis.

Cost-volume-profit analysis is not only for merchandising companies. It can also be used by manufacturing and service companies. Let's take a closer look at this powerful management tool.

Chapter 20 Learning Objectives

1 Determine how changes in volume affect costs	**4** Use CVP analysis to perform sensitivity analysis
2 Calculate operating income using contribution margin and contribution margin ratio	**5** Use CVP analysis to calculate margin of safety, operating leverage, and multiproduct breakeven points
3 Use cost-volume-profit (CVP) analysis for profit planning	

HOW DO COSTS BEHAVE WHEN THERE IS A CHANGE IN VOLUME?

Learning Objective 1

Determine how changes in volume affect costs

Some costs, such as cost of goods sold, increase as the volume of sales increases. Other costs, such as straight-line depreciation expense, are not affected by volume changes. Managers need to know how a business's costs are affected by changes in its volume of activity, such as number of products produced and sold, in order to make good decisions about the business. Let's look at three different types of costs:

- Variable costs
- Fixed costs
- Mixed costs

We will again use Smart Touch Learning, our fictitious company, to illustrate the concepts. Smart Touch Learning manufactures touch screen tablet computers that are preloaded with the company's e-learning software.

Variable Costs

Variable Cost

A cost that increases or decreases *in total* in direct proportion to increases or decreases in the volume of activity.

Variable costs are costs that increase or decrease *in total* in direct proportion to increases or decreases in the volume of activity. Volume is the measure or degree of an activity of a business action that affects costs—the more volume, the more costs incurred. Some activities that are affected by changes in volume include selling, producing, driving, and calling. The volume of activities can be measured in many different ways, such as number of units sold, number of units produced, number of miles driven by a delivery vehicle, and number of phone calls placed.

The direct materials used in the production of tablet computers are a variable cost for Smart Touch Learning. For example, each tablet computer requires a battery. If batteries cost $55 each, then the production of each tablet increases the total cost incurred by $55. The following chart shows the cost for batteries at different levels of activity:

Number of Tablets Produced	Variable Cost per Tablet	Total Variable Cost
0 tablets	$ 55	$ 0
25 tablets	55	1,375
50 tablets	55	2,750
75 tablets	55	4,125
100 tablets	55	5,500

As you can see, the total variable cost of batteries increases proportionately as the number of tablets produced increases. But the battery cost per tablet does not change. Exhibit 20-1 graphs the total variable cost for batteries as the number of tablets produced increases from 0 to 100.

Exhibit 20-1 | **Total Variable Cost of Batteries**

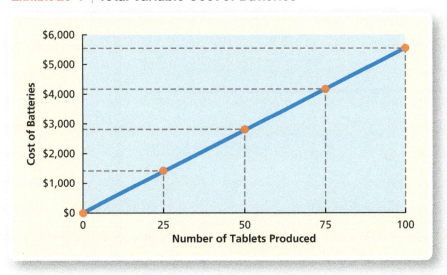

If there are no tablets manufactured, Smart Touch Learning incurs no battery cost, so the total variable cost line begins at the bottom left corner. This point is called the *origin*, and it represents zero volume and zero cost. The slope of the variable cost line is the change in total battery cost (on the vertical axis) divided by the change in the number of tablets produced (on the horizontal axis). The slope of the graph equals the variable cost per unit. In Exhibit 20-1, the slope of the variable cost line is $55 per tablet because Smart Touch Learning spends $55 on the battery for each tablet produced.

Exhibit 20-1 shows how the total variable cost of batteries varies directly with the number of tablets produced. But, again, note that the variable cost per tablet remains constant at $55.

> Remember this important fact about *variable costs:* Total variable costs fluctuate with changes in volume, but the variable cost per unit remains constant.

As shown in the preceding example, direct materials are a variable cost for a manufacturing company. Direct labor is also a variable cost. Manufacturing overhead usually includes both variable costs and fixed costs. Let's look at fixed costs next to learn how they differ from variable costs.

Fixed Costs

In contrast to variable costs, **fixed costs** are costs that do not change *in total* over wide ranges of volume of activity. Some common fixed costs include rent, salaries, property taxes, and straight-line depreciation. Smart Touch Learning's fixed costs include straight-line depreciation on the manufacturing plant and equipment. The company has these fixed costs regardless of the number of tablets produced.

Fixed Cost

A cost that remains the same *in total*, regardless of changes over wide ranges of volume of activity.

Suppose Smart Touch Learning incurs $13,500 of fixed costs each month, and the number of monthly tablets produced is between 0 and 100. Exhibit 20-2 graphs total fixed costs as a flat line that intersects the cost axis at $13,500 because Smart Touch Learning will incur the same $13,500 of fixed costs regardless of the number of tablets produced during the month.

Exhibit 20-2 | **Total Fixed Costs**

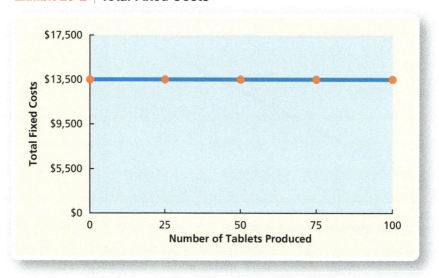

Total fixed costs do not change, as shown in Exhibit 20-2, but the *fixed cost per tablet* depends on the number of tablets produced. If Smart Touch Learning produces 25 tablets, the fixed cost per tablet is $540 ($13,500 / 25 tablets). If the number of tablets produced doubles to 50 tablets, the fixed cost per tablet is cut in half to $270 ($13,500 / 50 tablets). Therefore, the fixed cost per tablet is *inversely* related to the number of tablets produced. In other words, as the number of tablets increases, the fixed cost per tablet decreases, as follows:

Total Fixed Costs	Number of Tablets Produced	Fixed Cost per Tablet
$ 13,500	25 tablets	$ 540
13,500	50 tablets	270
13,500	75 tablets	180
13,500	100 tablets	135

Remember this important fact about fixed costs: Total fixed costs remain constant, but the fixed cost per unit is inversely related to changes in volume.

Exhibit 20-3 shows a summary of the characteristics of fixed and variable costs.

Exhibit 20-3 | **Characteristics of Variable and Fixed Costs**

	Total Cost	Cost per Unit
Variable Costs	Changes *proportionately* to changes in volume • When volume increases, total cost increases • When volume decreases, total cost decreases	Remains constant
Fixed Costs	Remains constant	Changes *inversely* to changes in volume • When volume increases, cost per unit decreases • When volume decreases, cost per unit increases

Mixed Costs

Not all costs can be classified as either fixed or variable. Costs that have both variable and fixed components are called mixed costs. For example, Smart Touch Learning's cell phone provider charges $100 per month to provide the service plus $0.10 for each minute of use. If the cell phone is used for 100 minutes, the company will bill Smart Touch Learning $110 [$100 + (100 minutes × $0.10 per minute)]. The following table shows the cost for the cell phone at different levels of activity:

Number of Minutes Used	Total Fixed Cost	Total Variable Cost	Total Mixed Cost
100 minutes	$ 100	$ 10	$ 110
200 minutes	100	20	120
300 minutes	100	30	130
400 minutes	100	40	140
500 minutes	100	50	150

Exhibit 20-4 (on the next page) shows how Smart Touch Learning can separate its cell phone bill into fixed and variable components. The $100 monthly charge is a fixed cost because it is the same no matter how many minutes the company uses the cell phone. The $0.10-per-minute charge is a variable cost that increases in direct proportion to the number of minutes of use. If Smart Touch Learning uses the phone for 100 minutes, its total variable cost is $10 (100 minutes × $0.10 per minute). If it doubles the use to 200 minutes, total variable cost also doubles to $20 (200 minutes × $0.10 per minute), and the total bill rises to $120 ($100 + $20).

Are all costs either fixed or variable?

Mixed Cost
A cost that has both fixed and variable components.

Exhibit 20-4 | **Mixed Costs**

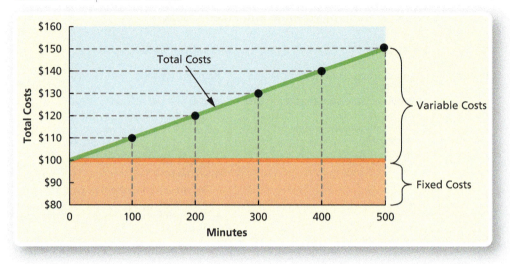

The cost you incur to operate your car is an example of a mixed cost, relative to miles driven. The more miles you drive, the more you spend on gas and oil changes, so those costs are variable. The cost you incur for insurance, however, is fixed—the amount does not change based on number of miles driven. Therefore, the total cost is mixed— it has both a variable and a fixed component.

High-Low Method

High-Low Method

A method used to separate mixed costs into their variable and fixed components, using the highest and lowest activity levels.

When companies have mixed costs, it is helpful to separate the costs into their variable and fixed components so managers can use the information to make planning and control decisions. Some mixed costs, such as the cell phone cost, are easy to separate; other costs, however, are not as easy to break down.

An easy method to separate mixed costs into variable and fixed components is the **high-low method**. This method requires you to identify the highest and lowest levels of activity over a period of time.

Let's revisit the Smart Touch Learning illustration. A summary of its manufacturing equipment maintenance costs for the past year shows the following costs for each quarter:

	Total Maintenance Cost	Number of Tablets Produced	
1st Quarter	$ 1,630	360 tablets	
2nd Quarter	1,935	415 tablets	
3rd Quarter	1,960	480 tablets ←	Highest Volume
4th Quarter	1,480	240 tablets ←	Lowest Volume

Examining the total maintenance cost each quarter, we can see that the maintenance costs are not a fixed cost because the total changes each quarter as production changes. We can also determine that the maintenance cost is not a variable cost because the cost per unit changed depending on the number of tablets produced. This must mean the maintenance cost is a mixed cost and has both fixed and variable components. We can use the high-low method, which requires three steps, to estimate Smart Touch Learning's fixed and variable costs of manufacturing equipment maintenance.

Step 1: Identify the highest and lowest levels of activity, and calculate the variable cost per unit.

The highest volume is 480 tablets produced in the third quarter of the year, and the lowest volume is 240 tablets produced in the fourth quarter.

Using the high and low volume points, find the change in costs associated with the highest and lowest volume points and divide by the change in volume of activity.

> **Variable cost per unit = Change in total cost / Change in volume of activity**
> **= (Cost associated with highest volume − Cost associated with lowest volume) /**
> **(Highest volume − Lowest volume)**
> = ($1,960 − $1,480) / (480 tablets − 240 tablets)
> = $480 / 240 tablets
> = $2 per tablet

Step 2: Calculate the total fixed cost.

> **Total fixed cost = Total mixed cost − Total variable cost**
> **= Total mixed cost − (Variable cost per unit × Number of units)**
> = $1,960 − ($2 per tablet × 480 tablets)
> = $1,960 − $960
> = $1,000

This example uses the highest volume point and its mixed cost to calculate the total fixed cost, but you can also use the lowest volume point and its mixed cost to calculate the same $1,000 total fixed cost.

> *Rework Step 2 using the lowest volume point, $1,480 total cost and 240 tablets. Verify for yourself that either point can be used!*

Remember the characteristics of variable and fixed costs: Changes in activity levels do not affect variable cost per unit or total fixed costs; both remain constant. Therefore, once the variable cost per unit is computed, either the highest or the lowest level of volume can be used to calculate the total fixed cost.

Why does Step 2 of the high-low method work with both the highest volume and the lowest volume?

Step 3: Create and use an equation to show the behavior of a mixed cost.

> **Total mixed cost = (Variable cost per unit × Number of units) + Total fixed cost**
> Total manufacturing = ($2 per tablet × Number of tablets)   + $1,000
> maintenance cost

Using this equation, the estimated manufacturing equipment maintenance cost for 400 tablets would be as follows:

> **Total manufacturing maintenance cost = ($2 per table × Number of tablets) + $1,000**
> = ($2 per tablet × 400 tablets) + $1,000
> = $1,800

This method provides a rough estimate of fixed and variable costs that can be used for planning purposes. The high and low activity volumes become the relevant range, which is discussed in the next section. Managers find the high-low method to be quick and easy, but there are other more complex methods that provide better estimates. One of these methods is regression analysis, which can be completed using spreadsheet software, such as Excel. This method is illustrated in more advanced accounting textbooks, such as cost accounting textbooks.

Relevant Range and Relativity

Relevant Range

The range of volume where total fixed costs and variable cost per unit remain constant.

The **relevant range** is the range of volume where total fixed costs remain constant and the variable cost per unit remains constant. To estimate costs, managers need to know the relevant range because of the following relationships:

- *Total* fixed costs can differ from one relevant range to another.
- The variable cost *per unit* can differ from one relevant range to another.

Exhibit 20-5 shows fixed costs for Smart Touch Learning over three different relevant ranges. If the company expects to produce 2,400 tablets next year, the relevant range is between 2,001 and 4,000 tablets, and managers will plan for fixed costs of $162,000.

Exhibit 20-5 | Relevant Range

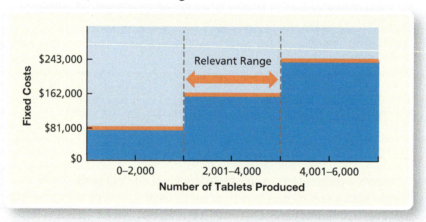

To produce more than 4,000 tablets, Smart Touch Learning will have to expand the company. This will increase total fixed costs for added rent, supervisory salaries, and equipment costs. Exhibit 20-5 shows that total fixed cost increases to $243,000 as the relevant range shifts to this higher band of volume. Conversely, if the company expects to produce fewer than 2,001 tablets, the company will budget only $81,000 of fixed costs.

Variable cost per unit can also change outside the relevant range. For example, Smart Touch Learning may get a quantity discount for batteries if it purchases more than 4,000 batteries.

We also need to remember that costs are classified as fixed or variable relative to some activity. However, if the frame of reference shifts, then the classification can shift, too. For example, Smart Touch Learning may lease cars for sales representatives to use when making sales calls. The amount of the lease is the same each month, $500. Therefore, relative to the number of tablets produced, the cost is fixed. Increasing or decreasing the number of tablets produced does not change the total amount of the lease. It remains constant at $500 per month. However, relative to the number of sales representatives, the cost is variable as it is directly proportional to the number of sales representatives. If there is one sales representative, the total cost is $500 per month. If there are two sales representatives, then two cars are required and the cost doubles to $1,000 per month. While the cost per unit remains constant, $500 per sales representative, the total cost changes with the change in volume, number of sales representatives.

For all examples and problems in this textbook, when classifying costs as fixed or variable, classify them relative to the number of units produced and sold unless told otherwise.

Following is a list of costs for a furniture manufacturer that specializes in wood tables. Classify each cost as variable, fixed, or mixed relative to the number of tables produced and sold.

1. Wood used to build tables
2. Depreciation on saws and other manufacturing equipment
3. Compensation for sales representatives paid on a salary plus commission basis
4. Supervisor's salary
5. Wages of production workers

Check your answers online in MyAccountingLab or at http://www.pearsonhighered.com/Horngren.

For more practice, see Short Exercises S20-1 through S20-3. MyAccountingLab

WHAT IS CONTRIBUTION MARGIN, AND HOW IS IT USED TO COMPUTE OPERATING INCOME?

Classifying costs as either variable or fixed is referred to as *cost behavior* because changes in volume can have an effect on how the costs behave. That is, the total cost either changes (variable costs) or remains constant (fixed costs). Let's see how managers can use cost behavior to make decisions.

Learning Objective 2

Calculate operating income using contribution margin and contribution margin ratio

Contribution Margin

Contribution margin is the difference between net sales revenue and variable costs. It is called contribution margin because it is the amount that contributes to covering the fixed costs and then to providing operating income. Contribution margin is often expressed in total. For example, if Smart Touch Learning sells 200 tablets for $500 each that incur variable costs of $275 each, then the contribution margin is:

Contribution Margin

The amount that contributes to covering the fixed costs and then to providing operating income. Net sales revenue − Variable costs.

> **Contribution margin = Net sales revenue − Variable costs**
> = ($500 per tablet × 200 tablets) − ($275 per tablet × 200 tablets)
> = $100,000 − $55,000
> = $45,000

Unit Contribution Margin

The previous example calculated contribution margin as a total amount. Contribution margin can also be expressed as a unit amount. Using the same example for Smart Touch Learning, we can express the unit contribution margin as:

> **Unit contribution margin = Net sales revenue per unit − Variable costs per unit**
> = $500 per tablet − $275 per tablet
> = $225 per tablet

The terms *unit contribution margin* and *contribution margin per unit* are used interchangeably.

Contribution Margin Ratio

Contribution Margin Ratio
The ratio of contribution margin to net sales revenue. Contribution margin / Net sales revenue.

A third way to express contribution margin is as a ratio. **Contribution margin ratio** is the ratio of contribution margin to net sales revenue. Because contribution margin is based on sales price and variable costs, which do not change per unit, the ratio can be calculated using either the total amounts or the unit amounts, as illustrated below:

Contribution margin ratio	**= Contribution margin / Net sales revenue**
	= $45,000 / $100,000
	= 45%
or	**= Unit contribution margin / Net sales revenue per unit**
	= $225 per tablet / $500 per tablet
	= 45%

Contribution Margin Income Statement

A traditional income statement classifies costs by *function*; that is, costs are classified as either product costs or period costs. Remember that *product costs* are those costs that are incurred in the purchase or production of the product sold. For a manufacturing company such as Smart Touch Learning, the product costs are direct materials, direct labor, and manufacturing overhead. These costs accumulate in the inventory accounts until the product is sold. At that point, the costs are transferred to the expense account Cost of Goods Sold. The *period costs* are the selling and administrative costs. This is the format that is required by GAAP, the Generally Accepted Accounting Principles, and the format you have been using in your accounting studies thus far.

Contribution Margin Income Statement
The income statement that groups cost by behavior—variable or fixed—and highlights the contribution margin.

The traditional income statement format does not always provide enough information for managers, so another format is used. A **contribution margin income statement** classifies cost by *behavior*; that is, costs are classified as either variable costs or fixed costs. The contribution margin income statement also highlights the contribution margin rather than the gross profit. Exhibit 20-6 illustrates the differences between the two formats.

Exhibit 20-6 | **Traditional Income Statement Versus Contribution Margin Income Statement**

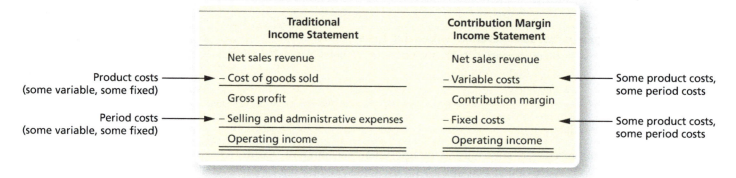

A furniture manufacturer specializes in wood tables. The tables sell for $100 per unit and incur $40 per unit in variable costs. The company has $6,000 in fixed costs per month.

6. Prepare a contribution margin income statement for one month if the company sells 200 tables.
7. What is the total contribution margin for the month when the company sells 200 tables?
8. What is the unit contribution margin?
9. What is the contribution margin ratio?

Check your answers online in MyAccountingLab or at http://www.pearsonhighered.com/Horngren.

For more practice, see Short Exercises S20-4 and S20-5.   MyAccountingLab

HOW IS COST-VOLUME-PROFIT (CVP) ANALYSIS USED?

Now that you have learned about cost behavior, let's see how managers use this information to make business decisions. **Cost-volume-profit (CVP) analysis** is a planning tool that looks at the relationships among costs and volume and how they affect profits (or losses). CVP is also sometimes referred to as *cost-volume-price analysis* because changes in sales prices also affect profits (or losses). Smart Touch Learning uses CVP analysis to estimate how changes in sales prices, variable costs, fixed costs, and volume will affect profits.

Assumptions

CVP analysis assumes the following for the relevant range:

- The price per unit does not change as volume changes. For example, Smart Touch Learning assumes that all tablets will sell for $500 each.

- Managers can classify each cost as variable, fixed, or mixed.

- The only factor that affects total costs is a change in volume, which increases or decreases total variable and mixed costs. Smart Touch Learning assumes the variable cost per tablet is $275.

- Total fixed costs do not change. Smart Touch Learning assumes fixed costs are $13,500 per month.

- There are no changes in inventory levels. Smart Touch Learning assumes the number of tablets produced equals the number of tablets sold.

    Most business conditions do not perfectly meet these general assumptions, so managers regard CVP analysis as a good approximation even though it is not exact.

Breakeven Point—Three Approaches

CVP analysis can be used to estimate the amount of sales needed to achieve the breakeven point. The **breakeven point** is the sales level at which the company does not earn a profit or a loss but has an operating income of zero. Required sales can be expressed as either a number of units or as a total dollar figure. We will look at three methods of estimating sales required to break even:

- Equation approach
- Contribution margin approach
- Contribution margin ratio approach

Learning Objective 3

Use cost-volume-profit (CVP) analysis for profit planning

Cost-Volume-Profit (CVP) Analysis

A planning tool that expresses the relationships among costs, volume, and prices and their effects on profits and losses.

Breakeven Point

The sales level at which operating income is zero. Total revenues equal total costs.

The Equation Approach

Let's start by expressing income in equation form and then breaking it down into its components:

Net sales revenue −   Total costs   = Operating income

Net sales revenue − Variable costs − Fixed costs = Operating income

Net sales revenue equals the unit sales price ($500 per tablet in this case) multiplied by the number of units (tablets) sold. Variable costs equal variable cost per unit ($275 in this case) times the number of units (tablets) sold. Smart Touch Learning's fixed costs total $13,500 per month. If the company desires to break even, then the target profit is $0. How many tablets must Smart Touch Learning sell to break even?

Net sales revenue − Variable costs − Fixed costs = Target profit
($500 per unit × Units sold) − ($275 per unit × Units sold) − $13,500 = $0
[($500 per unit − $275 per unit) × Units sold] − $13,500 = $0
$225 per unit × Units sold = $0 + $13,500
$225 per unit × Units sold = $13,500
Units sold = $13,500 / $225 per unit
Units sold = 60 units

Be sure to check your calculations. We can prove the required sales by substituting the number of units into the operating income equation and then checking to ensure that this level of sales results in $0 in profit.

Net sales revenue − Variable costs − Fixed costs = Operating income
($500 per unit × 60 units) − ($275 per unit × 60 units) − $13,500 = Operating income
$30,000 − $16,500 − $13,500 = $0

Based on these calculations, then, Smart Touch Learning must sell 60 tablets per month to achieve the breakeven point. Expressed in dollars, the company must have total sales of $30,000 per month (60 tablets × $500 per tablet).

The Contribution Margin Approach

The contribution margin approach is a shortcut method of computing the required sales in units. Notice in the previous example that the fixed costs were divided by the contribution margin per unit ($225 per unit). We can rewrite the equation approach to derive the following equation:

$$\text{Required sales in units} = \frac{\text{Fixed costs} + \text{Target profit}}{\text{Contribution margin per unit}}$$

Using this formula, we can enter the given amounts to calculate the required sales in units. Notice that the formula is dividing dollars by dollars per unit. When the dollars cancel out during the division process, the result is expressed in units.

$$\text{\textbf{Required sales in units}} = \frac{\textbf{Fixed costs} + \textbf{Target profit}}{\textbf{Contribution margin per unit}}$$
$$= \frac{(\$13,500 + \$0)}{\$225 \text{ per unit}}$$
$$= 60 \text{ units}$$

Previously, we proved our answer using the equation approach. We can also prove our answer using the contribution margin income statement format:

Net sales revenue	($500 per unit × 60 units)	$ 30,000
− Variable costs	($275 per unit × 60 units)	16,500
Contribution margin	($225 per unit × 60 units)	13,500
− Fixed costs		13,500
Operating income		$ 0

Contribution Margin Ratio Approach

Companies can use the contribution margin ratio approach to compute required sales in terms of *sales dollars* rather than in units. The formula is the same as using the contribution margin approach, except that the denominator is the contribution margin ratio rather than contribution margin per unit.

We previously computed the contribution margin ratio for Smart Touch Learning as 45%:

$$\text{Contribution margin ratio} = \text{Contribution margin / Net sales revenue}$$
$$= \$225 \text{ per tablet} / \$500 \text{ per tablet}$$
$$= 45\%$$

Notice that when we use the ratio as the denominator in the formula, we are dividing dollars by a percentage. Therefore, the result will be expressed in dollars.

$$\text{Required sales in dollars} = \frac{\text{Fixed costs} + \text{Target profit}}{\text{Contribution margin ratio}}$$
$$= \frac{(\$13,500 + \$0)}{45\%}$$
$$= \$30,000$$

Target Profit

A variation of the breakeven point calculation is the target profit calculation. **Target profit** is the operating income that results when net sales revenue minus variable and fixed costs equals management's profit goal. The same three approaches can be used. The only difference is that a company uses a target profit instead of the breakeven point of $0. Exhibit 20-7 (on the next page) shows the calculation of the target profit calculations for Smart Touch Learning using the three approaches when management's profit goal is $4,500 per month.

Target Profit
The operating income that results when net sales revenue minus variable and fixed costs equals management's profit goal.

Exhibit 20-7 | Target Profit Calculations for Smart Touch Learning

Equation Approach

Net sales revenue − Variable costs − Fixed costs = Target profit

($500 per unit × Units sold) − ($275 per unit × Units sold) − $13,500 = $4,500

[($500 per unit − $275 per unit) × Units sold] − $13,500 = $4,500

$225 per unit × Units sold = $18,000

Units sold = $18,000 / $225 per unit

Units sold = 80 units

Contribution Margin Approach

$$\text{Required sales in units} = \frac{\text{Fixed costs} + \text{Target profit}}{\text{Contribution margin per unit}}$$

$$= \frac{\$13,500 + \$4,500}{\$225 \text{ per unit}}$$

$$= 80 \text{ units}$$

Contribution Margin Ratio Approach

$$\text{Required sales in dollars} = \frac{\text{Fixed costs} + \text{Target profit}}{\text{Contribution margin ratio}}$$

$$= \frac{\$13,500 + \$4,500}{45\%}$$

$$= \$40,000$$

ETHICS

Did you check the formula?

Donna Dickerson is the assistant controller for a large manufacturing company and works directly under the supervision of the controller, Nicole Randall. While reviewing some documents Nicole prepared, Donna notices a mistake in the target profit calculations. The Excel spreadsheet used to summarize fixed costs has an error in the formula, and some of the individual costs listed are not included in the total. Donna is aware that the target profit calculations are used for planning purposes, so she brings the error to the controller's attention. Nicole doesn't seem concerned. "It doesn't really matter," says Nicole. "Those figures never show up on the financial statements, so a little mistake won't matter." Is Nicole correct? What should Donna do? What would you do?

Solution

Omitting fixed costs from the target profit calculations will understate the amount of sales required to reach the target profit. If required sales are understated, then managers might make decisions that could be detrimental to the company. Donna should convince her supervisor to admit her mistake and provide corrected estimates to managers. If Donna is unable to convince Nicole to admit her mistake, she should discuss the error and the possible consequences with Nicole's supervisor. Failure to report the error is a violation of IMA's credibility standard of ethical practice.

CVP Graph—A Graphic Portrayal

A CVP graph provides a picture that shows how changes in the levels of sales will affect profits. As in the variable, fixed, and mixed cost graphs of Exhibits 20-1, 20-2, and 20-4, the volume of units is on the horizontal axis and dollars are on the vertical axis. The five steps to graph the CVP relationships for Smart Touch Learning are illustrated in Exhibit 20-8.

Exhibit 20-8 | **Cost-Volume-Profit Graph for Smart Touch Learning**

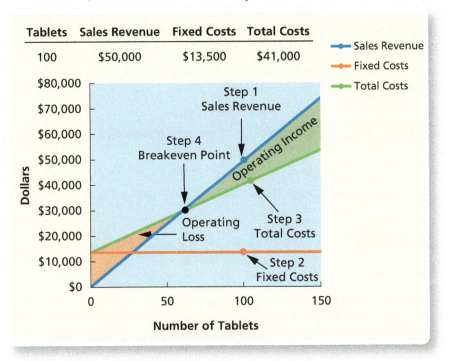

Tablets	Sales Revenue	Fixed Costs	Total Costs
100	$50,000	$13,500	$41,000

Step 1: Choose a sales volume, such as 100 tablets. Plot the point for total sales revenue at that volume: 100 tablets × $500 per tablet = $50,000. Draw the *sales revenue line* from the origin ($0) through the $50,000 point. Why start at the origin? If Smart Touch Learning sells no tablets, there is no revenue.

Step 2: Draw the *fixed cost line*, a horizontal line that intersects the dollars axis at $13,500. The fixed cost line is flat because fixed costs are the same, $13,500, no matter how many tablets are sold.

Step 3: Draw the *total cost line*. Total costs are the sum of variable costs plus fixed costs. Thus, total costs are *mixed*. The total cost line follows the form of the mixed cost line in Exhibit 20-4. Begin by computing total variable costs at the chosen sales volume: 100 tablets × $275 per tablet = $27,500. Add total variable costs to fixed costs: $27,500 + $13,500 = $41,000. Plot the total cost point of $41,000 for 100 tablets. Then draw a line through this point from the $13,500 fixed cost intercept on the dollars vertical axis. This is the *total cost line*. The total cost line starts at the fixed cost line because even if Smart Touch Learning sells no tablets, the company still incurs the $13,500 of fixed costs.

Step 4: Identify the *breakeven point*. The breakeven point is where the sales revenue line intersects the total cost line. This is where revenue exactly equals total costs—at 60 tablets, or $30,000 in sales.

Step 5: Mark the *operating loss* area on the graph. To the left of the breakeven point, total costs exceed sales revenue—leading to an operating loss, indicated by the orange zone. Mark the *operating income* area on the graph. To the right of the breakeven point, the business earns a profit because sales revenue exceeds total costs, as shown by the green zone.

Graphs like Exhibit 20-8 are helpful to managers because the managers can use the graphs to prepare a quick estimate of the profit or loss earned at different levels of sales. The three target profit formulas are also useful, but they only indicate income or loss for a single sales amount.

Try It!

A furniture manufacturer specializes in wood tables. The tables sell for $100 per unit and incur $40 per unit in variable costs. The company has $6,000 in fixed costs per month. The company desires to earn an operating profit of $12,000 per month.

10. Calculate the required sales in units to earn the target profit using the equation method.
11. Calculate the required sales in units to earn the target profit using the contribution margin method.
12. Calculate the required sales in dollars to earn the target profit using the contribution margin ratio method.
13. Calculate the required sales in units to break even using the contribution margin method.

Check your answers online in MyAccountingLab or at http://www.pearsonhighered.com/Horngren.

For more practice, see Short Exercises S20-6 through S20-11. MyAccountingLab

HOW IS CVP ANALYSIS USED FOR SENSITIVITY ANALYSIS?

Learning Objective 4
Use CVP analysis to perform sensitivity analysis

Sensitivity Analysis
A "what if" technique that estimates profit or loss results if sales price, costs, volume, or underlying assumptions change.

Managers often want to predict how changes in sales price, costs, or volume affect their profits. Managers can use CVP relationships to conduct sensitivity analysis. **Sensitivity analysis** is a "what if" technique that estimates profit or loss results if sales price, costs, volume, or underlying assumptions change. Sensitivity analysis allows managers to see how various business strategies will affect how much profit the company will make and, thus, empowers managers with better information for decision making. Let's see how Smart Touch Learning can use CVP analysis to estimate the effects of some changes in its business environment.

Changes in the Sales Price

Competition in the touch screen tablet computer business is so fierce that Smart Touch Learning believes it must cut the sales price to $475 per tablet to maintain market share. Suppose the company's variable costs remain $275 per tablet and fixed costs stay at $13,500. How will the lower sales price affect the breakeven point?

Using the contribution margin approach, the results are as follows:

$$\text{Required sales in units} = \frac{\text{Fixed costs} + \text{Target profit}}{\text{Contribution margin per unit}}$$
$$= \frac{(\$13,500 + \$0)}{(\$475 \text{ per unit} - \$275 \text{ per unit})}$$
$$= 68 \text{ units*}$$

*Actual result of 67.5 units rounded up to the next full unit as it is not possible to sell partial tablets.

With the original $500 sales price, Smart Touch Learning's breakeven point was 60 tablets. With the new lower sales price of $475 per tablet, the breakeven point increases to 68 tablets. The lower sales price means that each tablet contributes less toward fixed costs, so the company must sell more tablets to break even. Additionally, each unit sold beyond the breakeven point will contribute less to profits due to the lower contribution margin per unit.

Changes in Variable Costs

Return to Smart Touch Learning's original data, disregarding the change made in sales price in the previous example. Assume that one of the company's suppliers raises prices, which increases the variable cost for each tablet to $285 (instead of the original $275). Smart Touch Learning decides it cannot pass this increase on to its customers, so the company holds the price at the original $500 per tablet. Fixed costs remain at $13,500. How many tablets must Smart Touch Learning sell to break even after the supplier raises prices?

$$\text{Required sales in units} = \frac{\text{Fixed cost + Target profit}}{\text{Contribution margin per unit}}$$

$$= \frac{(\$13,500 + \$0)}{(\$500 \text{ per unit} - \$285 \text{ per unit})}$$

$$= 63 \text{ units}^*$$

*rounded up to next full unit

Higher variable costs per tablet reduce Smart Touch Learning's contribution margin per unit from $225 per tablet to $215 per tablet. As a result, the company must sell more tablets to break even—63 rather than the original 60. This analysis shows why managers are particularly concerned with controlling costs during an economic downturn. Increases in costs raise the breakeven point, and a higher breakeven point can lead to problems if demand falls due to a recession.

Of course, a decrease in variable costs would have the opposite effect. Lower variable costs increase the contribution margin on each tablet and, therefore, lower the breakeven point.

Changes in Fixed Costs

Return to Smart Touch Learning's original data, disregarding the changes made in the previous two examples. The company is considering spending an additional $3,000 on Web site banner ads. This would increase fixed costs from $13,500 to $16,500. If the tablets are sold at the original price of $500 each and variable costs remain at $275 per tablet, what is the new breakeven point?

$$\text{Required sales in units} = \frac{\text{Fixed costs + Target profit}}{\text{Contribution margin per unit}}$$

$$= \frac{(\$16,500 + \$0)}{(\$500 \text{ per unit} - \$275 \text{ per unit})}$$

$$= 74 \text{ units}^*$$

*rounded up to next full unit

Higher fixed costs increase the total contribution margin required to break even. In this case, increasing the fixed costs from $13,500 to $16,500 increases the breakeven point to 74 tablets (from the original 60 tablets).

Exhibit 20-9 (on the next page) shows how all of these changes affect the contribution margin per unit and the breakeven point.

Exhibit 20-9 | **Effects of Changes in Sales Price, Variable Costs, and Fixed Costs**

CAUSE	EFFECT	RESULT
Change	Contribution Margin per Unit	Breakeven Point
Sales price per unit increases	Increases	Decreases
Sales price per unit decreases	Decreases	Increases
Variable cost per unit increases	Decreases	Increases
Variable cost per unit decreases	Increases	Decreases
Total fixed cost increases	No effect	Increases
Total fixed cost decreases	No effect	Decreases

Using Sensitivity Analysis

Managers usually prefer a lower breakeven point to a higher one, but do not overemphasize this one aspect of CVP analysis. Even though Smart Touch Learning has a breakeven point of 60 units and each of the previous examples increased the breakeven point, management wants to do more than break even. Consider the following two scenarios:

	Sales Volume	Contribution Margin per Unit	Total Contribution Margin	Total Fixed Costs	Operating Income
Scenario 1	100 units	$ 15	$ 1,500	$ 1,000	$ 500
	200	15	3,000	1,000	2,000
	300	15	4,500	1,000	3,500
	400	15	6,000	1,000	5,000
Scenario 2	100 units	$ 25	$ 2,500	1,000	$ 1,500
	200	25	5,000	1,000	4,000
	300	25	7,500	1,000	6,500
	400	25	10,000	1,000	9,000

Notice how much operating income increased in Scenario 2 compared to Scenario 1 when the sales volume increased. The only difference between the two scenarios is a difference in contribution margin. Remember, contribution margin is the amount that contributes to covering the fixed costs and then to providing operating income. In both scenarios, fixed costs are covered when sales are 100 units. Therefore, in Scenario 1, each increase in sales of 100 units increased operating income by $1,500 (100 units × $15 contribution margin per unit). In Scenario 2, each increase in sales of 100 units increased operating income by $2,500 (100 units × $25 contribution margin per unit).

Managers can use contribution margin to predict the change in operating income when volume changes. In the short term, managers may not be able to reduce fixed costs to increase operating income, but they may be able to increase contribution margin. The two components of contribution margin are sales price per unit and variable costs per unit. Therefore, an increase in contribution margin can be created by an increase in sales price per unit, a decrease in variable costs per unit, or a combination of the two.

Cost Behavior Versus Management Behavior

One of the CVP assumptions mentioned earlier in the chapter is that the only factor that affects total costs is a change in volume, which increases or decreases variable and mixed costs. However, research in the last few years has shown that this is not always the case and that costs are often asymmetrical. That is, costs increase more when sales volume is increasing than costs decrease when sales volume is decreasing, a phenomenon known as **cost stickiness**. For example, as sales increase, managers will hire more workers, which increases the variable cost of labor. However, when sales decrease, managers are reluctant to lay off workers, especially if the sales decline is expected to be temporary, and instead find alternate activities for the workers. Therefore, the decrease in sales is greater than the proportionate decrease in costs. Managers need to be aware that their decisions, such as not laying off workers, may cause costs to behave differently than expected from their CVP analysis. Exhibit 20-10 illustrates an example of cost stickiness. Notice how the slope of the Total Costs line did not decrease at the same rate when sales decreased as it increased when sales increased.

Cost Stickiness
The asymmetrical change in costs when there is a decrease in the volume of activity.

Exhibit 20-10 | **Example of Cost Stickiness**

Month	Sales	Total Costs	Total Costs as a Percent of Sales
Jan.	$ 200	$ 100	50%
Feb.	400	200	50%
Mar.	600	300	50%
Apr.	800	400	50%
May	1,000	500	50%
Jun.	800	450	56%
Jul.	600	400	67%
Aug.	400	350	88%
Sep.	200	300	150%

Try It!

A furniture manufacturer specializes in wood tables. The tables sell for $100 per unit and incur $40 per unit in variable costs. The company has $6,000 in fixed costs per month. Calculate the breakeven point in units under each independent scenario.

14. Variable costs increase by $10 per unit.
15. Fixed costs decrease by $600.
16. Sales price increases by 10%.

Check your answers online in MyAccountingLab or at http://www.pearsonhighered.com/Horngren.

For more practice, see Short Exercises S20-12 and S20-13. MyAccountingLab

WHAT ARE SOME OTHER WAYS CVP ANALYSIS CAN BE USED?

Margin of Safety

The excess of expected sales over breakeven sales. The amount sales can decrease before the company incurs an operating loss.

We have learned how CVP analysis can be used for estimating target profits and breakeven points as well as sensitivity analysis. Let's look at three more applications of CVP analysis.

Margin of Safety

The **margin of safety** is the excess of expected sales over breakeven sales. The margin of safety is, therefore, the amount sales can decrease before the company incurs an operating loss. It is the *cushion* between profit and loss.

Managers use the margin of safety to evaluate the risk of both their current operations and their plans for the future. Let's apply the margin of safety to our fictitious company.

Smart Touch Learning's original breakeven point was 60 tablets. Suppose the company expects to sell 100 tablets. The margin of safety can be expressed in units, in dollars, or as a ratio. The margin of safety is:

> **Expected sales − Breakeven sales = Margin of safety in units**
> 100 tablets − 60 tablets = 40 tablets
> **Margin of safety in units × Sales price per unit = Margin of safety in dollars**
> 40 tablets × $500 per tablet = $20,000
> **Margin of safety in units / Expected sales in units = Margin of safety ratio**
> 40 tablets / 100 tablets = 40%

Sales can drop by 40 tablets, or $20,000, before Smart Touch Learning incurs a loss. This margin of safety is 40% of total expected sales. In other words, the company can lose almost half of its business before incurring an operating loss. That is a comfortable margin of safety.

Managers can use margin of safety to assess the risk to the company when there is a possibility of a large decrease in sales. For example, if a large portion of Smart Touch Learning's sales are to one customer, then losing that customer to a competitor would have a major impact on the company's profits. Realizing the magnitude of the risk helps managers make informed decisions.

Both margin of safety and target profit use CVP analysis, but from different perspectives. Margin of safety focuses on the sales part of the equation—that is, how many sales dollars the company is generating above breakeven sales dollars. Conversely, target profit focuses on how much operating income is left over from sales revenue after covering all variable and fixed costs.

> *If you have done really well on all your assignments in a particular course for the semester and currently have an A, you have created a sort of margin of safety for your grade. That is, by performing above the minimum (C, or breakeven), you have a cushion to help you maintain a passing grade even if you happen to perform poorly on a future assignment.*

Operating Leverage

The **cost structure** of a company is the proportion of fixed costs to variable costs. This relationship is important because, depending on the cost structure, small changes in the business environment could have a substantial impact on profits. Companies with higher fixed costs are at greater risk, but they also have the opportunity for greater rewards. Let's compare two companies to see how their cost structures affect their profits when there is a change in sales volume.

Two companies provide horse-drawn carriage tours in Charleston, South Carolina. This is a very competitive business, and both companies charge $25 per person for the tours. Both companies expect to provide tours to 500 passengers during September. Company A has low variable costs and high fixed costs. Company B has the opposite cost structure with high variable costs and low fixed costs. The expected contribution margin income statements for both companies are:

Cost Structure
The proportion of fixed costs to variable costs.

	Company A	Company B
Sales Revenue (500 passengers × $25 per passenger)	$ 12,500	$ 12,500
Variable Costs		
(500 passengers × $5 per passenger)	2,500	
(500 passengers × $15 per passenger)		7,500
Contribution Margin	10,000	5,000
Fixed Costs	6,000	1,000
Operating Income	$ 4,000	$ 4,000

Notice that both companies expect to earn an operating profit of $4,000 if they have 500 passengers during the month.

During September, a hurricane threatened the area and many tourists made other travel plans. Both companies had only 400 passengers during the month. Let's look at their actual income statements with this decrease in volume:

	Company A	Company B
Sales Revenue (400 passengers × $25 per passenger)	$ 10,000	$ 10,000
Variable Costs		
(400 passengers × $5 per passenger)	2,000	
(400 passengers × $15 per passenger)		6,000
Contribution Margin	8,000	4,000
Fixed Costs	6,000	1,000
Operating Income	$ 2,000	$ 3,000

Both companies experienced the same decrease in sales volume, but Company B's operating income did not decrease as much as Company A's because of its cost structure.

Operating Leverage
Effects that fixed costs have on changes in operating income when sales volume changes.

Degree of Operating Leverage
The ratio that measures the effects that fixed costs have on changes in operating income when sales volume changes. Contribution margin / Operating income.

Companies can predict the expected change in operating income due to a change in sales volume based on their cost structure. **Operating leverage** predicts the effects fixed costs have on changes in operating income when sales volume changes. The **degree of operating leverage** can be measured by dividing the contribution margin by the operating income. Let's calculate the degree of operating leverage of both companies at the 500-passenger volume:

$$\text{Degree of operating leverage} = \frac{\text{Contribution margin}}{\text{Operating income}}$$

$$\text{Company A} \quad \frac{\$10,000}{\$4,000} = 2.50$$

$$\text{Company B} \quad \frac{\$5,000}{\$4,000} = 1.25$$

The degree of operating leverage for Company A is 2.50. This means that the percentage change in operating income will be 2.50 times the percentage change in sales. For Company B, the percentage change in sales will have a lesser effect on operating income at 1.25 times the change. Let's calculate the percentage changes to verify these predictions:

		Company A		Company B
Estimated sales		$ 12,500		$ 12,500
Actual sales		(10,000)		(10,000)
Dollar change in sales		$ 2,500		$ 2,500
Percent change in sales	($2,500 / $12,500)	20%	($2,500 / $12,500)	20%
Degree of operating leverage		× 2.50		× 1.25
Predicted percent change in operating income		50%		25%
Estimated operating income		$ 4,000		$ 4,000
Actual operating income		(2,000)		(3,000)
Dollar change in operating income		$ 2,000		$ 1,000
Actual percent change in operating income	($2,000 / $4,000)	50%	($1,000 / $4,000)	25%

The chart above shows that the degree of operating leverage accurately predicted the effect on operating income when sales volume changed. Notice that Company A had higher fixed costs and, therefore, had a greater decrease in profits when sales decreased. Higher fixed costs create greater risk for the company. When there is a decrease in sales, there is also a decrease in contribution margin to cover the fixed costs and provide operating income. However, a cost structure with high fixed costs has the opposite effect when sales increase. A 20% increase in sales would have had 2.50 times that effect, or 50%, increase in operating income. Therefore, a sales increase of $2,500 ($12,500 × 20%) would have resulted in an increase in operating income of $2,000 ($4,000 × 50%).

Prepare an income statement for Company A with a 20% increase in sales. Verify for yourself that the above statement is true!

Sales Mix

Most companies sell more than one product. **Sales mix**, or *product mix*, is the combination of products that make up total sales. The same CVP formulas we used earlier can apply to a company with multiple products. Sales price and variable costs differ for each product, so each product makes a different contribution to profits. To calculate the breakeven point for the company, we must compute the *weighted-average contribution margin* of all the company's products. The sales mix provides the weights that make up total product sales. The weights equal 100% of total product sales.

For example, assume Cool Cat Furniture sold 6,000 cat beds and 4,000 scratching posts during the past year. The sales mix of 6,000 beds and 4,000 posts creates a ratio of 6,000/10,000 or 60% cat beds and 4,000/10,000 or 40% scratching posts. You could also convert this to the least common ratio, as 6/10 is the same as 3/5 cat beds and 4/10 is the same as 2/5 scratching posts. So, we say the sales mix is 3:2, or for every three cat beds sold, Cool Cat expects to sell two scratching posts. Each "package" would include five items—three cat beds and two scratching posts.

Using the sales mix, we can determine the breakeven for Cool Cat for both cat beds and scratching posts. Cool Cat's total fixed costs are $40,000. The cat bed's unit sales price is $44, and variable cost per bed is $24. The scratching post's unit sales price is $100, and variable cost per post is $30. To compute breakeven sales in units for both products, Cool Cat completes the following three steps.

Step 1: Calculate the weighted-average contribution margin per unit as follows:

	Cat Beds	Scratching Posts	Total
Sales price per unit	$ 44	$ 100	
Variable cost per unit	24	30	
Contribution margin per unit	20	70	
Sales mix in units	× 3	× 2	5 units
Contribution margin	$ 60	$ 140	$ 200
Weighted-average contribution margin per unit ($200 per unit / 5 units)			$ 40

Step 2: Calculate the breakeven point in units for the "package" of products:

$$\text{Required sales in units} = \frac{\text{Fixed costs + Target profit}}{\text{Weighted-average contribution margin per unit}}$$

$$= \frac{\$40,000 + \$0}{\$40 \text{ per unit}}$$

$$= 1,000 \text{ units}$$

Step 3: Calculate the breakeven point in units for each product in the sales mix "package." Multiply the "package" breakeven point in units by each product's proportion of the sales mix.

Breakeven sales of cat beds	(1,000 units × 3/5) = 600 cat beds
Breakeven sales of scratching posts	(1,000 units × 2/5) = 400 scratching posts

In this example, the calculations yield whole numbers. When the calculations do not yield whole numbers, round your answer up to the next whole number.

Sales Mix
The combination of products that make up total sales.

The overall breakeven point in sales dollars is $66,400:

600 cat beds at $44 sales price each	$ 26,400
400 scratching posts at $100 sales price each	40,000
Total sales revenue	$ 66,400

We can prove this breakeven point by preparing a contribution margin income statement:

	Cat Beds	Scratching Posts	Total
Sales Revenue:			
Cat beds (600 × $44)	$ 26,400		
Scratching posts (400 × $100)		$ 40,000	$ 66,400
Variable Costs:			
Cat beds (600 × $24)	14,400		
Scratching posts (400 × $30)		12,000	26,400
Contribution Margin	$ 12,000	$ 28,000	40,000
Fixed Costs			40,000
Operating Income			$ 0

If the sales mix changes, then Cool Cat can repeat this analysis using new sales mix information to find the breakeven points for each product.

In addition to finding the breakeven point, Cool Cat can also estimate the sales needed to generate a certain level of operating profit. Suppose Cool Cat would like to earn operating income of $20,000. How many units of each product must Cool Cat now sell?

$$\text{Required sales in units} = \frac{\text{Fixed costs} + \text{Target profit}}{\text{Weighted-average contribution margin per unit}}$$

$$= \frac{\$40,000 + \$20,000}{\$40 \text{ per unit}}$$

$$= 1,500 \text{ units}$$

Breakeven sales of cat beds	(1,500 units × 3/5) = 900 cat beds
Breakeven sales of scratching posts	(1,500 units × 2/5) = 600 scratching posts

We can prove this planned profit level by preparing a contribution margin income statement:

	Cat Beds	Scratching Posts	Total
Sales Revenue:			
Cat beds (900 × $44)	$ 39,600		
Scratching posts (600 × $100)		$ 60,000	$ 99,600
Variable Costs:			
Cat beds (900 × $24)	21,600		
Scratching posts (600 × $30)		18,000	39,600
Contribution Margin	$ 18,000	$ 42,000	60,000
Fixed Costs			40,000
Operating Income			$ 20,000

TYING IT ALL TOGETHER

In the chapter opener, we introduced **Best Buy Co., Inc.** Best Buy is a leading provider of technology products and services. Managers of retail companies like Best Buy have to make decisions about which products to sell, how much to charge customers for those products, and how to control costs so that the company earns a profit that is acceptable to its investors. In 2015, Best Buy incurred $711 million in advertising expenses for digital, print and television advertisements and promotional events (Notes to Consolidated Financial Statements, Note 1) and is transforming how it advertises by moving to more digital and personalized marketing (Letter to Stockholders). The company had $40,339 million in sales in 2015. Therefore, its advertising costs were less than 2% of sales ($711 million / $40,339 million = 1.76%).

When advertising expenses are classified by behavior, are they variable, fixed, or mixed costs?

Advertising expenses are fixed costs because they do not vary in total when there is a change in sales volume.

When advertising expenses are classified by function, are they product or period costs?

Advertising expenses are selling costs, part of the Selling and Administrative Expenses, which are period costs.

What would most likely happen if Best Buy increased its advertising?

An increase in advertising will increase costs, which decreases profits. However, if increased digital and personalized advertising also results in increased sales, which will increase profits, then the cost may be justified.

How might a marketing manager use CVP analysis to make decisions about increasing or decreasing advertising costs?

The marketing manager will have to predict how increased advertising will affect sales volume and complete a CVP analysis to determine if the benefit resulting from the increased advertising will be greater than the cost. A decrease in advertising will most likely result in a decrease in sales. If customers are not as exposed to the Best Buy brand and are not as aware of special deals, they may shop elsewhere. Also, if Best Buy decreases its advertising and its competitors do not, then customers may become more aware of the competitors and choose to shop there. As with the decision to increase advertising, the marketing manager will complete a CVP analysis to determine if the cost savings outweighs the profits lost due to the decrease in sales.

Try It!

A furniture manufacturer specializes in wood tables. The tables sell for $100 per unit and incur $40 per unit in variable costs. The company has $6,000 in fixed costs per month. Expected sales are 200 tables per month.

17. Calculate the margin of safety in units.
18. Determine the degree of operating leverage. Use expected sales.
19. The company begins manufacturing wood chairs to match the tables. Chairs sell for $50 each and have variable costs of $30. The new production process increases fixed costs to $7,000 per month. The expected sales mix is one table for every four chairs. Calculate the breakeven point in units for each product.

Check your answers online in MyAccountingLab or at http://www.pearsonhighered.com/Horngren.

For more practice, see Short Exercises S20-14 through S20-17.   MyAccountingLab

REVIEW

> Things You Should Know

1. How do costs behave when there is a change in volume?

- Total variable costs change in direct proportion to changes in volume, but the variable cost per unit remains unchanged.
- Total fixed costs remain unchanged with changes in volume, but the fixed cost per unit changes inversely.
- Mixed costs have a variable and fixed component.
- Mixed costs can be separated into their variable and fixed components using the high-low method.

2. What is contribution margin, and how is it used to compute operating income?

- Contribution margin = Net sales revenue − Variable costs.
- Contribution margin ratio = Contribution margin / Net sales revenue.
- The traditional income statement separates costs by function: product costs and period costs.
- The contribution margin income statement separates costs by behavior—fixed and variable—and highlights contribution margin.

3. How is cost-volume-profit (CVP) analysis used?

- Required sales to obtain the breakeven point can be calculated using three approaches:
  - Equation approach
  - Contribution margin approach
  - Contribution margin ratio approach
- Target profit is a variation of the breakeven point approaches where target profit is greater than $0.
- CVP graphs are used to make quick estimates of profit levels at various volumes of sales.

4. How is CVP analysis used for sensitivity analysis?

- Increases in sales prices increase contribution margin per unit and decrease the breakeven point.
- Decreases in sales prices decrease contribution margin per unit and increase the breakeven point.
- Increases in variable costs decrease contribution margin per unit and increase the breakeven point.
- Decreases in variable costs increase contribution margin per unit and decrease the breakeven point.
- Increases in fixed costs have no effect on contribution margin per unit and increase the breakeven point.
- Decreases in fixed costs have no effect on contribution margin per unit and decrease the breakeven point.
- Cost stickiness may cause an asymmetrical change in costs when there is a decrease in the volume of activity.

5. What are some other ways CVP analysis can be used?

- Margin of safety

  - The excess of expected sales over breakeven sales.

  - In units: Expected sales in units − Breakeven sales in units.

  - In dollars: Margin of safety in units × Sales price per unit.

  - As a ratio: Margin of safety in units / Expected sales in units.

- Operating leverage

  - Effects that fixed costs have on changes in operating income when sales volume changes.

  - Degree of operating leverage = Contribution margin / Operating income.

- Sales mix

  - Calculate the breakeven point with multiple products:

  Step 1: Calculate the weighted-average contribution margin per unit.

  Step 2: Calculate the breakeven point in units for the "package" of products.

  Step 3: Calculate the breakeven point in units for each product. Multiply the "package" breakeven point in units by each product's proportion of the sales mix.

> Check Your Understanding 20-1

Check your understanding of the chapter by completing this problem and then looking at the solution. Use this practice to help identify which sections of the chapter you need to study more.

The Sock Company buys hiking socks for $6 per pair and sells them for $10. Management budgets monthly fixed costs of $10,000 for sales volumes between 0 and 12,000 pairs of socks.

Requirements

1. Use both the equation approach and the contribution margin approach to compute the company's monthly breakeven point in units. (See Learning Objective 3)

2. Use the contribution margin ratio approach to compute the breakeven point in sales dollars. (See Learning Objective 3)

3. Compute the monthly sales level (in units) required to earn a target operating income of $6,000. Use either the equation approach or the contribution margin approach. (See Learning Objective 3)

4. Prepare a graph of The Sock Company's CVP relationships, similar to Exhibit 20-8. Draw the sales revenue line, the fixed cost line, and the total cost line. Label the axes, the breakeven point, the operating income area, and the operating loss area. (See Learning Objective 3)

> Solution

Requirement 1

Equation approach:

$$\text{Net sales revenue} - \text{Variable costs} - \text{Fixed costs} = \text{Target profit}$$

$$(\$10 \text{ per unit} \times \text{Units sold}) - (\$6 \text{ per unit} \times \text{Units sold}) - \$10{,}000 = \$0$$

$$[(\$10 \text{ per unit} - \$6 \text{ per unit}) \times \text{Units sold}] - \$10{,}000 = \$0$$

$$\$4 \text{ per unit} \times \text{Units sold} = \$10{,}000$$

$$\text{Units sold} = \$10{,}000 \, / \, \$4 \text{ per unit}$$

$$\text{Units sold} = 2{,}500 \text{ units}$$

Contribution margin approach:

$$\text{Required sales in units} = \frac{\text{Fixed costs} + \text{Target profit}}{\text{Contribution margin per unit}}$$

$$= \frac{\$10{,}000 + \$0}{\$10 \text{ per unit} - \$6 \text{ per unit}}$$

$$= 2{,}500 \text{ units}$$

Requirement 2

$$\text{Contribution margin ratio} = \frac{\text{Contribution margin}}{\text{Sales price}} = \frac{\$4}{\$10} = 40\%$$

$$\text{Required sales in dollars} = \frac{\text{Fixed costs} + \text{Target profit}}{\text{Contribution margin ratio}}$$

$$= \frac{\$10{,}000 + \$0}{40\%}$$

$$= \$25{,}000$$

This can be confirmed by multiplying the breakeven point in units (as calculated in Requirement 1) by the sales price:

$$2{,}500 \text{ pairs of socks} \times \$10 \text{ per pair of socks} = \$25{,}000$$

Requirement 3

Equation approach:

$$\text{Net sales revenue} - \text{Variable costs} - \text{Fixed costs} = \text{Target profit}$$

$$(\$10 \text{ per unit} \times \text{Units sold}) - (\$6 \text{ per unit} \times \text{Units sold}) - \$10{,}000 = \$6{,}000$$

$$[(\$10 \text{ per unit} - \$6 \text{ per unit}) \times \text{Units sold}] - \$10{,}000 = \$6{,}000$$

$$\$4 \text{ per unit} \times \text{Units sold} = \$16{,}000$$

$$\text{Units sold} = \$16{,}000 \, / \, \$4 \text{ per unit}$$

$$\text{Units sold} = 4{,}000 \text{ units}$$

Contribution margin approach:

$$\text{Required sales in units} = \frac{\text{Fixed costs } + \text{ Target profit}}{\text{Contribution margin per unit}}$$
$$= \frac{\$10,000 + \$6,000}{\$4 \text{ per unit}}$$
$$= 4,000 \text{ units}$$

Requirement 4

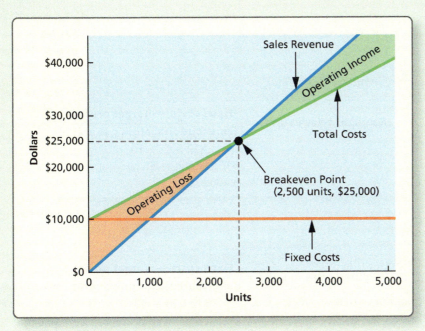

> Check Your Understanding 20-2

Check your understanding of the chapter by completing this problem and then looking at the solution. Use this practice to help identify which sections of the chapter you need to study more.

The Sock Company buys hiking socks for $6 per pair and sells them for $10. Management budgets monthly fixed costs of $12,000 for sales volumes between 0 and 12,000 pairs.

Requirements

Consider each of the following questions separately by using the foregoing information each time.

1. Calculate the breakeven point in units. (See Learning Objective 3)

2. The Sock Company reduces its sales price from $10 per pair to $8 per pair. Calculate the new breakeven point in units. (See Learning Objective 4)

3. The Sock Company finds a new supplier for the socks. Variable costs will decrease by $1 per pair. Calculate the new breakeven point in units. (See Learning Objective 4)

CHAPTER 20

4. The Sock Company plans to advertise in hiking magazines. The advertising campaign will increase total fixed costs by $2,000 per month. Calculate the new breakeven point in units. (See Learning Objective 4)

5. In addition to selling hiking socks, The Sock Company would like to start selling sports socks. The Sock Company expects to sell one pair of hiking socks for every three pairs of sports socks. The Sock Company will buy the sports socks for $4 per pair and sell them for $8 per pair. Total fixed costs will stay at $12,000 per month. Calculate the breakeven point in units for both hiking socks and sports socks. (See Learning Objective 5)

> Solution

Requirement 1

$$\text{Required sales in units} = \frac{\text{Fixed costs } + \text{ Target profit}}{\text{Contribution margin per unit}}$$
$$= \frac{\$12,000 + \$0}{\$10 \text{ per unit} - \$6 \text{ per unit}}$$
$$= 3,000 \text{ units}$$

Requirement 2

$$\text{Required sales in units} = \frac{\text{Fixed costs } + \text{ Target profit}}{\text{Contribution margin per unit}}$$
$$= \frac{\$12,000 + \$0}{\$8 \text{ per unit} - \$6 \text{ per unit}}$$
$$= 6,000 \text{ units}$$

Requirement 3

$$\text{Required sales in units} = \frac{\text{Fixed costs } + \text{ Target profit}}{\text{Contribution margin per unit}}$$
$$= \frac{\$12,000 + \$0}{\$10 \text{ per unit} - \$5 \text{ per unit}}$$
$$= 2,400 \text{ units}$$

Requirement 4

$$\text{Required sales in units} = \frac{\text{Fixed costs } + \text{ Target profit}}{\text{Contribution margin per unit}}$$
$$= \frac{\$14,000 + \$0}{\$10 \text{ per unit} - \$6 \text{ per unit}}$$
$$= 3,500 \text{ units}$$

Requirement 5

Step 1: Calculate the weighted-average contribution margin:

	Hiking	Sports	Total
Sales price per unit	$ 10	$ 8	
Variable cost per unit	6	4	
Contribution margin per unit	4	4	
Sales mix in units	× 1	× 3	4 units
Contribution margin	$ 4	$ 12	$ 16
Weighted-average contribution margin per unit ($16 per unit / 4 units)			$ 4

Step 2: Calculate the breakeven point for the "package" of products:

$$\text{Required sales in units} = \frac{\text{Fixed costs} + \text{Target profit}}{\text{Contribution margin per unit}}$$
$$= \frac{\$12,000 + \$0}{\$4 \text{ per unit}}$$
$$= 3,000 \text{ units}$$

Step 3: Calculate the breakeven point for each product:

Breakeven sales of hiking socks   (3,000 items × 1/4) = 750 pairs of hiking socks
Breakeven sales of sport socks   (3,000 items × 3/4) = 2,250 pairs of sport socks

> Key Terms

Breakeven Point (p. 1097)

Contribution Margin (p. 1095)

Contribution Margin Income Statement (p. 1096)

Contribution Margin Ratio (p. 1096)

Cost Stickiness (p. 1105)

Cost Structure (p. 1107)

Cost-Volume-Profit (CVP) Analysis (p. 1097)

Degree of Operating Leverage (p. 1108)

Fixed Cost (p. 1089)

High-Low Method (p. 1092)

Margin of Safety (p. 1106)

Mixed Cost (p. 1091)

Operating Leverage (p. 1108)

Relevant Range (p. 1094)

Sales Mix (p. 1109)

Sensitivity Analysis (p. 1102)

Target Profit (p. 1099)

Variable Cost (p. 1088)

> Quick Check

1. For Frank's Funky Sounds, straight-line depreciation on the trucks is a

   Learning Objective 1

   a. variable cost.

   b. fixed cost.

   c. mixed cost.

   d. high-low cost.

CHAPTER 20

Learning Objective 1

2. Assume Intervale Railway is considering hiring a reservations agency to handle passenger reservations. The agency would charge a flat fee of $13,000 per month, plus $3 per passenger reservation. What is the total reservation cost if 200,000 passengers take the trip next month?

    a. $613,000   **b.** $3.07   **c.** $600,000   **d.** $13,000

Learning Objective 2

3. If Intervale Railway's fixed costs total $90,000 per month, the variable cost per passenger is $45, and tickets sell for $75, what is the contribution margin per unit and contribution margin ratio?

    a. $45 per passenger; 60%   **c.** $30 per passenger; 40%

    b. $30 per passenger; 60%   **d.** $45 per passenger; 40%

Learning Objective 3

4. If Intervale Railway's fixed costs total $90,000 per month, the variable cost per passenger is $45, and tickets sell for $75, what is the breakeven point in units?

    a. 1,200 passengers   **c.** 225,000 passengers

    b. 2,000 passengers   **d.** 3,000 passengers

Learning Objective 3

5. If Intervale Railway's fixed costs total $90,000 per month, the variable cost per passenger is $45, and tickets sell for $75, how much revenue must the Railway generate to earn $120,000 in operating income per month?

    a. $350,000   **b.** $210,000   **c.** $7,000   **d.** $525,000

Learning Objective 3

6. On a CVP graph, the total cost line intersects the vertical (dollars) axis at

    a. the origin.   **c.** the breakeven point.

    b. the level of the fixed costs.   **d.** the level of the variable costs.

Learning Objective 4

7. If a company increases its sales price per unit for Product A, the new breakeven point will

    a. increase.   **c.** remain the same.

    b. decrease.   **d.** More information is needed.

Learning Objective 4

8. If a company increases its fixed costs for Product B, then the contribution margin per unit will

    a. increase.   **c.** remain the same.

    b. decrease.   **d.** More information needed.

Learning Objective 5

9. The Best Appliances had the following revenue over the past five years:

2013	$ 600,000
2014	700,000
2015	900,000
2016	800,000
2017	1,000,000

To predict revenues for 2018, The Best Appliances uses the average for the past five years. The company's breakeven revenue is $800,000 per year. What is The Best Appliances's predicted margin of safety in dollars for 2018?

    a. $800,000   **b.** $0   **c.** $200,000   **d.** $100,000

10. Rocky Mountain Waterpark sells half of its tickets for the regular price of $75. The other half go to senior citizens and children for the discounted price of $35. Variable cost per guest is $15 for both groups, and fixed costs total $60,000 per month. What is Rocky Mountain's breakeven point in total guests? Regular guests? Discount guests?

    a. 2,000; 1,000; 1,000   **c.** 750; 375; 375

    b. 800; 400; 400   **d.** 1,500; 750; 750

Check your answers at the end of the chapter.

ASSESS YOUR PROGRESS

> Review Questions

1. What is a variable cost? Give an example.
2. What is a fixed cost? Give an example.
3. What is a mixed cost? Give an example.
4. What is the purpose of using the high-low method?
5. Describe the three steps of the high-low method.
6. What is the relevant range?
7. A chain of convenience stores has one manager per store who is paid a monthly salary. Relative to Store #36 located in Atlanta, Georgia, is the manager's salary fixed or variable? Why?
8. A chain of convenience stores has one manager per store who is paid a monthly salary. Relative to the number of stores, is the manager's salary fixed or variable? Why?
9. What is contribution margin?
10. What are the three ways contribution margin can be expressed?
11. How does a contribution margin income statement differ from a traditional income statement?
12. What is cost-volume-profit analysis?
13. What are the CVP assumptions?
14. What is the breakeven point?
15. What are the three approaches to calculating the sales required to achieve the breakeven point? Give the formula for each one.
16. Of the three approaches to calculate sales required to achieve the breakeven point, which one(s) calculate the required sales in units and which one(s) calculate the required sales in dollars?
17. What is target profit?
18. Why is the calculation to determine the target profit considered a variation of the break even calculation?
19. On the CVP graph, where is the breakeven point shown? Why?
20. What is sensitivity analysis? How do managers use this tool?

21. What effect does an increase in sales price have on contribution margin? An increase in fixed costs? An increase in variable costs?

22. What is cost stickiness? Why do managers need to be aware of cost stickiness?

23. What is the margin of safety? What are the three ways it can be expressed?

24. What is a company's cost structure? How can cost structure affect a company's profits?

25. What is operating leverage? What does it mean if a company has a degree of operating leverage of 3?

26. How can CVP analysis be used by companies with multiple products?

> Short Exercises

Learning Objective 1

S20-1 Identifying variable, fixed, and mixed costs

Philadelphia Acoustics builds innovative speakers for music and home theater systems. Identify each cost as variable (V), fixed (F), or mixed (M), relative to number of speakers produced and sold.

1. Units of production depreciation on routers used to cut wood enclosures.

2. Wood for speaker enclosures.

3. Patents on crossover relays.

4. Total compensation to salesperson who receives a salary plus a commission based on meeting sales goals.

5. Crossover relays.

6. Straight-line depreciation on manufacturing plant.

7. Grill cloth.

8. Insurance on the corporate office.

9. Glue.

10. Quality inspector's salary.

Learning Objective 1

S20-2 Identifying variable, fixed, and mixed costs

Holly's Day Care has been in operation for several years. Identify each cost as variable (V), fixed (F), or mixed (M), relative to number of students enrolled.

1. Building rent.

2. Toys.

3. Compensation of the office manager, who receives a salary plus a bonus based on number of students enrolled.

4. Afternoon snacks.

5. Lawn service contract at $200 per month.

6. Holly's salary.

7. Wages of afterschool employees.

8. Drawing paper for students' artwork.

9. Straight-line depreciation on furniture and playground equipment.

10. Fee paid to security company for monthly service.

S20-3 Using the high-low method

Learning Objective 1

Mark owns a machine shop. In reviewing the shop's utility bills for the past 12 months, he found that the highest bill of $2,600 occurred in August when the machines worked 1,200 machine hours. The lowest utility bill of $2,300 occurred in December when the machines worked 600 machine hours.

Requirements

1. Use the high-low method to calculate the variable cost per machine hour and the total fixed utility cost.
2. Show the equation for determining the total utility cost for the machine shop.
3. If Mark anticipates using 800 machine hours in January, predict the shop's total utility bill using the equation from Requirement 2.

S20-4 Calculating contribution margin

Learning Objective 2

Glenn Company sells a product for $80 per unit. Variable costs are $60 per unit, and fixed costs are $800 per month. The company expects to sell 560 units in September. Calculate the contribution margin per unit, in total, and as a ratio.

S20-5 Preparing a contribution margin income statement

Learning Objective 2

Gabelman Company sells a product for $95 per unit. Variable costs are $40 per unit, and fixed costs are $2,200 per month. The company expects to sell 570 units in September. Prepare an income statement for September using the contribution margin format.

S20-6 Calculating breakeven point in units, contribution margin given

Learning Objective 3

Mackler, Inc. sells a product with a contribution margin of $50 per unit. Fixed costs are $8,000 per month. How many units must Mackler sell to break even?

S20-7 Calculating breakeven point in units, contribution margin ratio given

Learning Objective 3

Ocean Company sells a product with a contribution margin ratio of 80%. Fixed costs are $2,800 per month. What amount of sales (in dollars) must Ocean Company have to break even? If each unit sells for $30, how many units must be sold to break even?

S20-8 Computing contribution margin, units and required sales to break even, and units to achieve target profit

Learning Objectives 2, 3

Compute the missing amounts for the following table.

	A	B	C
Sales price per unit	$ 200	$ 4,000	$ 5,220
Variable costs per unit	80	1,000	2,088
Total fixed costs	73,200	660,000	3,758,400
Target profit	266,760	3,000,000	3,132,000
Calculate:			
Contribution margin per unit	_____	_____	_____
Contribution margin ratio	_____	_____	_____
Required units to break even	_____	_____	_____
Required sales dollars to break even	_____	_____	_____
Required units to achieve target profit	_____	_____	_____

Learning Objectives 2, 3

S20-9 Computing contribution margin, units and required sales to break even, units to achieve target profit

Compute the missing amounts for the following table:

	A	B	C
Sales price per unit	$ 1,400	$ (f)	$ 2,500
Variable costs per unit	(a)	2,940	1,250
Total fixed costs	273,000	1,097,600	(k)
Target profit	630,000	24,892,000	1,562,500
Contribution margin per unit	700	(g)	(l)
Contribution margin ratio	(b)	40%	(m)
Required units to break even	(c)	(h)	325 units
Required sales dollars to break even	(d)	(i)	(n)
Required units to achieve target profit	(e)	(j)	(o)

Use the following information to complete Short Exercises S20-10 through S20-15.

Funday Park competes with Cool World by providing a variety of rides. Funday Park sells tickets at $70 per person as a one-day entrance fee. Variable costs are $42 per person, and fixed costs are $170,800 per month.

Learning Objectives 2, 3

S20-10 Computing contribution margin per unit, breakeven point in sales units

Compute the contribution margin per unit and the number of tickets Funday Park must sell to break even. Perform a numerical proof to show that your answer is correct.

Learning Objectives 2, 3

S20-11 Computing contribution margin ratio, breakeven point in sales dollars

Compute Funday Park's contribution margin ratio. Carry your computation to two decimal places. Use the contribution margin ratio approach to determine the sales revenue Funday Park needs to break even.

Learning Objective 4

S20-12 Applying sensitivity analysis of changing sales price and variable cost

Using the Funday Park information presented, do the following tasks.

Requirements

1. Suppose Funday Park cuts its ticket price from $70 to $56 to increase the number of tickets sold. Compute the new breakeven point in tickets and in sales dollars.

2. Ignore the information in Requirement 1. Instead, assume that Funday Park increases the variable cost from $42 to $56 per ticket. Compute the new breakeven point in tickets and in sales dollars.

Learning Objective 4

S20-13 Applying sensitivity analysis of changing fixed costs

Refer to the original information (ignoring the changes considered in Short Exercise S20-12). Suppose Funday Park increases fixed costs from $170,800 per month to $231,000 per month. Compute the new breakeven point in tickets and in sales dollars.

S20-14 Computing margin of safety

Learning Objective 5

Refer to the original information (ignoring the changes considered in Short Exercises S20-12 and S20-13). If Funday Park expects to sell 8,100 tickets, compute the margin of safety in tickets and in sales dollars.

S20-15 Computing degree of operating leverage

Learning Objective 5

Refer to the original information (ignoring the changes considered in Short Exercises S20-12 and S20-13). If Funday Park expects to sell 8,100 tickets, compute the degree of operating leverage (round to two decimal places). Estimate the operating income if sales increase by 15%.

Use the following information to complete Short Exercises S20-16 and S20-17.

Wild Waters Swim Park sells individual and family tickets. With a ticket, each person receives a meal, three beverages, and unlimited use of the swimming pools. Wild Waters has the following ticket prices and variable costs for 2018:

	Individual	Family
Sales price per ticket	$ 50	$ 150
Variable cost per ticket	35	140

Wild Waters expects to sell one individual ticket for every four family tickets. Wild Waters's total fixed costs are $27,500.

S20-16 Calculating breakeven point for two products

Learning Objective 5

Using the Wild Waters Swim Park information presented, do the following tasks.

Requirements

1. Compute the weighted-average contribution margin per ticket.
2. Calculate the total number of tickets Wild Waters must sell to break even.
3. Calculate the number of individual tickets and the number of family tickets the company must sell to break even.

S20-17 Calculating breakeven point for two products

Learning Objective 5

For 2019, Wild Waters expects a sales mix of four individual tickets for every one family ticket.

Requirements

1. Compute the new weighted-average contribution margin per ticket.
2. Calculate the total number of tickets Wild Waters must sell to break even.
3. Calculate the number of individual tickets and the number of family tickets the company must sell to break even.

> Exercises

Learning Objectives 1, 2, 3, 4, 5

E20-18 Using terminology

Match the following terms with the correct definitions:

1. Costs that do not change in total over wide ranges of volume.	a. Breakeven point
2. Technique that estimates profit or loss results when conditions change.	b. Contribution margin
3. The sales level at which operating income is zero.	c. Cost behavior
4. Drop in sales a company can absorb without incurring an operating loss.	d. Margin of safety
5. Combination of products that make up total sales.	e. Relevant range
6. Net sales revenue minus variable costs.	f. Sales mix
7. Describes how a cost changes as volume changes.	g. Fixed costs
8. Costs that change in total in direct proportion to changes in volume.	h. Variable costs
9. The band of volume where total fixed costs and variable cost per unit remain constant.	i. Sensitivity analysis

Learning Objective 1

E20-19 Determining cost behavior

Identify each cost below as variable (V), fixed (F), or mixed (M), relative to units sold. Explain your reason.

Units Sold	25	50	75	100
a. Total phone cost	$ 150	$ 200	$ 250	$ 300
b. Materials cost per unit	35	35	35	35
c. Manager's salary	3,000	3,000	3,000	3,000
d. Depreciation cost per unit	60	30	20	15
e. Total utility cost	400	650	900	1,150
f. Total cost of goods sold	3,125	6,250	9,375	12,500

Learning Objective 1

100 units $87.50

E20-20 Determining fixed cost per unit

For each total fixed cost listed below, determine the fixed cost per unit when sales are 50, 100, and 200 units.

Store rent	$ 5,000
Manager's salary	3,000
Equipment lease	500
Depreciation on fixtures	250

Learning Objective 1

Total VC, 50 units $7,050

E20-21 Determining total variable cost

For each variable cost per unit listed below, determine the total variable cost when units produced and sold are 25, 50, and 100 units.

Direct materials	$ 40
Direct labor	80
Variable overhead	9
Sales commission	12

E20-22 Determining total mixed cost

John Street Barber Shop pays $25 per month for water for the first 8,000 gallons and $3.50 per thousand gallons above 8,000 gallons. Calculate the total water cost when the barber shop uses 7,000 gallons, 10,000 gallons, and 13,000 gallons.

Learning Objective 1

10,000 gal. $32.00

E20-23 Determining mixed costs—the high-low method

The manager of Trusty Car Inspection reviewed the monthly operating costs for the past year. The costs ranged from $4,300 for 1,300 inspections to $3,900 for 900 inspections.

Learning Objective 1

3. $4,000

Requirements

1. Use the high-low method to calculate the variable cost per inspection.

2. Calculate the total fixed costs.

3. Write the equation and calculate the operating costs for 1,000 inspections.

4. Draw a graph illustrating the total cost under this plan. Label the axes, and show the costs at 900, 1,000, and 1,300 inspections.

E20-24 Calculating contribution margin ratio, preparing contribution margin income statements

For its top managers, Worldwide Travel formats its income statement as follows:

Learning Objective 2

2. $253,000 sales level, VC $108,790

WORLDWIDE TRAVEL Contribution Margin Income Statement Three Months Ended March 31, 2018	
Net Sales Revenue	$ 316,500
Variable Costs	136,095
Contribution Margin	180,405
Fixed Costs	173,000
Operating Income	$ 7,405

Worldwide's relevant range is between sales of $253,000 and $368,000.

Requirements

1. Calculate the contribution margin ratio.

2. Prepare two contribution margin income statements: one at the $253,000 sales level and one at the $368,000 sales level. (*Hint*: The proportion of each sales dollar that goes toward variable costs is constant within the relevant range.)

CHAPTER 20

Learning Objective 2

C. CMR 70%

E20-25 Computing contribution margin in total, per unit, and as a ratio

Complete the table below for contribution margin per unit, total contribution margin, and contribution margin ratio:

	A	B	C
Number of units	1,720 units	14,920 units	4,620 units
Sales price per unit	$ 1,800	$ 4,500	$ 5,550
Variable costs per unit	720	3,600	1,665
Calculate:			
Contribution margin per unit	_____	_____	_____
Total contribution margin	_____	_____	_____
Contribution margin ratio	_____	_____	_____

Learning Objective 2

B. CMR 60%

E20-26 Computing contribution margin in total, per unit, and as a ratio

Complete the table below for the missing amounts:

	A	B	C
Number of units	2,064 units	(d)	2,570 units
Sales price per unit	$ 250	$ 125	$ (g)
Variable costs per unit	(a)	50	4,528
Contribution margin per unit	125	(e)	(h)
Total contribution margin	(b)	1,567,500	(i)
Contribution margin ratio	(c)	(f)	20%

Learning Objectives 2, 3

2. $165,600

E20-27 Computing breakeven sales

No Slip Co. produces sports socks. The company has fixed costs of $91,080 and variable costs of $0.81 per package. Each package sells for $1.80.

Requirements

1. Compute the contribution margin per package and the contribution margin ratio. (Round your answers to two decimal places.)

2. Find the breakeven point in units and in dollars using the contribution margin approach.

Learning Objectives 2, 3

1. $18,000

E20-28 Computing a change in breakeven sales

Owner Shan Mu is considering franchising her Noodles by Mu restaurant concept. She believes people will pay $10.00 for a large bowl of noodles. Variable costs are $5.00 per bowl. Mu estimates monthly fixed costs for a franchise at $9,000.

Requirements

1. Use the contribution margin ratio approach to find a franchise's breakeven sales in dollars.

2. Mu believes most locations could generate $61,500 in monthly sales. Is franchising a good idea for Mu if franchisees want a minimum monthly operating income of $21,000? Explain your answer.

E20-29 Computing breakeven sales and operating income or loss under different conditions

Learning Objectives 2, 3

Gilbert's Steel Parts produces parts for the automobile industry. The company has monthly fixed costs of $640,220 and a contribution margin of 85% of revenues.

2. $1,050,000 sales level VC $157,500

Requirements

1. Compute Gilbert's monthly breakeven sales in dollars. Use the contribution margin ratio approach.

2. Use contribution margin income statements to compute Gilbert's monthly operating income or operating loss if revenues are $500,000 and if they are $1,050,000.

3. Do the results in Requirement 2 make sense given the breakeven sales you computed in Requirement 1? Explain.

E20-30 Analyzing a cost-volume-profit graph

Learning Objective 3

Nolan Rouse is considering starting a Web-based educational business, e-Prep MBA. He plans to offer a short-course review of accounting for students entering MBA programs. The materials would be available on a password-protected Web site; students would complete the course through self-study. Rouse would have to grade the course assignments, but most of the work would be in developing the course materials, setting up the site, and marketing. Unfortunately, Rouse's hard drive crashed before he finished his financial analysis. However, he did recover the following partial CVP chart:

3. $40,000

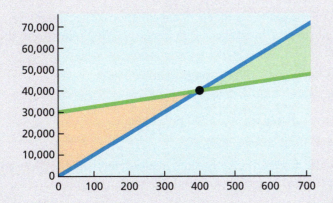

Requirements

1. Label each axis, the sales revenue line, the total costs line, the fixed costs line, the operating income area, and the breakeven point.

2. If Rouse attracts 300 students to take the course, will the venture be profitable? Explain your answer.

3. What are the breakeven sales in students and dollars?

Learning Objective 3

E20-31 Analyzing a cost-volume-profit graph

Determine how each change effects the elements of the cost-volume-profit graph by placing an X in the appropriate column(s).

CHANGE	EFFECT							
	Sales Line		Fixed Cost Line		Total Cost Line		Breakeven Point	
	Slope Increases	Slope Decreases	Shifts Up	Shifts Down	Slope Increases	Slope Decreases	Increases	Decreases
Sales Price per Unit Increases								
Sales Price per Unit Decreases								
Variable Cost per Unit Increases								
Variable Cost per Unit Decreases								
Total Fixed Cost Increases								
Total Fixed Cost Decreases								

Learning Objective 4

1b. 470 students

E20-32 Using sensitivity analysis

Mi Tierra Driving School charges $680 per student to prepare and administer written and driving tests. Variable costs of $408 per student include trainers' wages, study materials, and gasoline. Annual fixed costs of $63,920 include the training facility and fleet of cars.

Requirements

1. For each of the following independent situations, calculate the contribution margin per unit and the breakeven point in units by first referring to the original data provided:

   a. Breakeven point with no change in information.

   b. Decrease sales price to $544 per student.

   c. Decrease variable costs to $340 per student.

   d. Decrease fixed costs to $53,040.

2. Compare the impact of changes in the sales price, variable costs, and fixed costs on the contribution margin per unit and the breakeven point in units.

Learning Objective 4

$1,200

E20-33 Using sensitivity analysis

The Circle Clock Company sells a particular clock for $25. The variable costs are $13 per clock and the breakeven point is 250 clocks. The company expects to sell 300 clocks this year. If the company actually sells 400 clocks, what effect would the sale of additional 100 clocks have on operating income? Explain your answer.

Learning Objective 5

1. $38,750

E20-34 Computing margin of safety

Robbie's Repair Shop has a monthly target profit of $31,000. Variable costs are 20% of sales, and monthly fixed costs are $19,000.

Requirements

1. Compute the monthly margin of safety in dollars if the shop achieves its income goal.

2. Express Robbie's margin of safety as a percentage of target sales.

3. Why would Robbie's management want to know the shop's margin of safety?

E20-35 Computing degree of operating leverage

Following is the income statement for Marrow Mufflers for the month of June 2018:

MARROW MUFFLERS Contribution Margin Income Statement Month Ended June 30, 2018	
Net Sales Revenue (140 units × $250)	$ 35,000
Variable Costs (140 units × $50)	7,000
Contribution Margin	28,000
Fixed Costs	11,500
Operating Income	$ 16,500

Requirements

1. Calculate the degree of operating leverage. (Round to four decimal places.)

2. Use the degree of operating leverage calculated in Requirement 1 to estimate the change in operating income if total sales increase by 40% (assuming no change in sales price per unit). (Round interim calculations to four decimal places and final answer to the nearest dollar.)

3. Verify your answer in Requirement 2 by preparing a contribution margin income statement with the total sales increase of 40%.

E20-36 Calculating breakeven point for two products

Scotty's Scooters plans to sell a standard scooter for $55 and a chrome scooter for $70. Scotty's purchases the standard scooter for $30 and the chrome scooter for $40. Scotty's expects to sell one standard scooter for every three chrome scooters. Scotty's monthly fixed costs are $23,000.

Requirements

1. How many of each type of scooter must Scotty's Scooters sell each month to break even?

2. How many of each type of scooter must Scotty's Scooters sell each month to earn $25,300?

3. Suppose Scotty's expectation to sell one standard scooter for every three chrome scooters was incorrect and for every four scooters sold two are standard scooters and two are chrome scooters. Will the breakeven point of total scooters increase or decrease? Why? (Calculation not required.)

> Problems Group A

Learning Objectives 1, 2

P20-37A Calculating cost-volume-profit elements

The budgets of four companies yield the following information:

	Company			
	Beach	Lake	Mountain	Valley
Net Sales Revenue	$ 1,615,000	$ (d)	$ 1,050,000	$ (j)
Variable Costs	(a)	60,000	525,000	100,800
Fixed Costs	(b)	232,000	260,000	(k)
Operating Income (Loss)	285,600	(e)	(g)	31,500
Units Sold	170,000	10,000	(h)	(l)
Contribution Margin per Unit	$ 3.80	$ (f)	$ 75.00	$ 9.00
Contribution Margin Ratio	(c)	80%	(i)	30%

Requirements

1. Fill in the blanks for each missing value. (Round the contribution margin per unit to the nearest cent.)
2. Which company has the lowest breakeven point in sales dollars?
3. What causes the low breakeven point?

Learning Objectives 1, 2, 3

4. CM $7,962,500

P20-38A Calculating break even sales and sales to earn a target profit; preparing a contribution margin income statement

England Productions performs London shows. The average show sells 1,300 tickets at $60 per ticket. There are 175 shows per year. No additional shows can be held as the theater is also used by other production companies. The average show has a cast of 65, each earning a net average of $340 per show. The cast is paid after each show. The other variable cost is a program-printing cost of $8 per guest. Annual fixed costs total $728,000.

Requirements

1. Compute revenue and variable costs for each show.
2. Use the equation approach to compute the number of shows England Productions must perform each year to break even.
3. Use the contribution margin ratio approach to compute the number of shows needed each year to earn a profit of $5,687,500. Is this profit goal realistic? Give your reasoning.
4. Prepare England Productions's contribution margin income statement for 175 shows performed in 2018. Report only two categories of costs: variable and fixed.

P20-39A Analyzing CVP relationships

Crandall Company sells flags with team logos. Crandall has fixed costs of $583,200 per year plus variable costs of $4.80 per flag. Each flag sells for $12.00.

Learning Objectives 2, 3, 4

2. 60.00%

Requirements

1. Use the equation approach to compute the number of flags Crandall must sell each year to break even.

2. Use the contribution margin ratio approach to compute the dollar sales Crandall needs to earn $33,000 in operating income for 2018. (Round the contribution margin ratio to two decimal places.)

3. Prepare Crandall's contribution margin income statement for the year ended December 31, 2018, for sales of 70,000 flags. (Round your final answers up to the next whole number.)

4. The company is considering an expansion that will increase fixed costs by 21% and variable costs by $0.60 per flag. Compute the new breakeven point in units and in dollars. Should Crandall undertake the expansion? Give your reasoning. (Round your final answers up to the next whole number.)

P20-40A Computing breakeven sales and sales needed to earn a target profit; graphing CVP relationships; performing sensitivity analysis

Learning Objectives 2, 3, 4

1. 30 trades

National Investor Group is opening an office in Portland, Oregon. Fixed monthly costs are office rent ($8,100), depreciation on office furniture ($1,700), utilities ($2,000), special telephone lines ($1,500), a connection with an online brokerage service ($2,500), and the salary of a financial planner ($5,200). Variable costs include payments to the financial planner (9% of revenue), advertising (11% of revenue), supplies and postage (4% of revenue), and usage fees for the telephone lines and computerized brokerage service (6% of revenue).

Requirements

1. Use the contribution margin ratio approach to compute National's breakeven revenue in dollars. If the average trade leads to $1,000 in revenue for National, how many trades must be made to break even?

2. Use the equation approach to compute the dollar revenues needed to earn a monthly target profit of $12,600.

3. Graph National's CVP relationships. Assume that an average trade leads to $1,000 in revenue for National. Show the breakeven point, the sales revenue line, the fixed cost line, the total cost line, the operating loss area, the operating income area, and the sales in units (trades) and dollars when monthly operating income of $12,600 is earned.

4. Suppose that the average revenue National earns increases to $1,500 per trade. Compute the new breakeven point in trades. How does this affect the breakeven point?

Learning Objectives 2, 4, 5

2. 9,000 dz. plain & 3,000 dz. custard-filled

P20-41A Calculating breakeven point for two products, margin of safety, and operating leverage

The contribution margin income statement of Sugar Lips Donuts for August 2018 follows:

SUGAR LIPS DONUTS Contribution Margin Income Statement Month Ended August 31, 2018		
Net Sales Revenue		$ 125,000
Variable Costs:		
Cost of Goods Sold	$ 32,100	
Selling Costs	17,400	
Administrative Costs	6,750	56,250
Contribution Margin		68,750
Fixed Costs:		
Selling Costs	24,750	
Administrative Costs	8,250	33,000
Operating Income		$ 35,750

Sugar Lips sells three dozen plain donuts for every dozen custard-filled donuts. A dozen plain donuts sells for $4.00, with total variable cost of $1.80 per dozen. A dozen custard-filled donuts sells for $8.00, with total variable cost of $3.60 per dozen.

Requirements

1. Calculate the weighted-average contribution margin.

2. Determine Sugar Lips's monthly breakeven point in dozens of plain donuts and custard-filled donuts. Prove your answer by preparing a summary contribution margin income statement at the breakeven level of sales. Show only two categories of costs: variable and fixed.

3. Compute Sugar Lips's margin of safety in dollars for August 2018.

4. Compute the degree of operating leverage for Sugar Lips Donuts. Estimate the new operating income if total sales increase by 30%. (Round the degree of operating leverage to four decimal places and the final answer to the nearest dollar. Assume the sales mix remains unchanged.)

5. Prove your answer to Requirement 4 by preparing a contribution margin income statement with a 30% increase in total sales. (The sales mix remains unchanged.)

> Problems Group B

P20-42B Calculating cost-volume-profit elements

Learning Objectives 1, 2

The budgets of four companies yield the following information:

	Company			
	Blue	Red	Green	Yellow
Net Sales Revenue	$ 1,900,000	$ (d)	$ 1,500,000	$ (j)
Variable Costs	(a)	47,250	1,050,000	256,200
Fixed Costs	(b)	168,000	159,000	(k)
Operating Income (Loss)	298,500	(e)	(g)	97,800
Units Sold	190,000	9,000	(h)	(l)
Contribution Margin per Unit	$ 3.00	$ (f)	$ 75.00	$ 18.00
Contribution Margin Ratio	(c)	80%	(i)	30%

Requirements

1. Fill in the blanks for each missing value. (Round the contribution margin per unit to the nearest cent.)
2. Which company has the lowest breakeven point in sales dollars?
3. What causes the low breakeven point?

P20-43B Calculating breakeven sales and sales to earn a target profit; preparing a contribution margin income statement

Learning Objectives 1, 2, 3

3. CMR 54.67%

Famous Productions performs London shows. The average show sells 1,000 tickets at $60 per ticket. There are 175 shows a year. No additional shows can be held as the theater is also used by other production companies. The average show has a cast of 60, each earning a net average of $320 per show. The cast is paid after each show. The other variable cost is a program-printing cost of $8 per guest. Annual fixed costs total $459,200.

Requirements

1. Compute revenue and variable costs for each show.
2. Use the equation approach to compute the number of shows Famous Productions must perform each year to break even.
3. Use the contribution margin ratio approach to compute the number of shows needed each year to earn a profit of $4,264,000. Is this profit goal realistic? Give your reasoning.
4. Prepare Famous Productions's contribution margin income statement for 175 shows performed in 2018. Report only two categories of costs: variable and fixed.

Learning Objectives 2, 3, 4

3. Op. Loss $(70,200)

P20-44B Analyzing CVP relationships

White Company sells flags with team logos. White has fixed costs of $639,600 per year plus variable costs of $4.20 per flag. Each flag sells for $12.00.

Requirements

1. Use the equation approach to compute the number of flags White must sell each year to break even.

2. Use the contribution margin ratio approach to compute the dollar sales White needs to earn $32,500 in operating income for 2018. (Round the contribution margin to two decimal places.)

3. Prepare White's contribution margin income statement for the year ended December 31, 2018, for sales of 73,000 flags. (Round your final answers up to the next whole number.)

4. The company is considering an expansion that will increase fixed costs by 23% and variable costs by $0.60 per flag. Compute the new breakeven point in units and in dollars. Should White undertake the expansion? Give your reasoning. (Round your final answers up to the next whole number.)

Learning Objectives 2, 3, 4

4. 20 trades

P20-45B Computing breakeven sales and sales needed to earn a target profit; graphing CVP relationships; performing sensitivity analysis

Diversified Investor Group is opening an office in Boise, Idaho. Fixed monthly costs are office rent ($8,000), depreciation on office furniture ($1,700), utilities ($2,400), special telephone lines ($1,500), a connection with an online brokerage service ($2,500), and the salary of a financial planner ($11,900). Variable costs include payments to the financial planner (9% of revenue), advertising (11% of revenue), supplies and postage (4% of revenue), and usage fees for the telephone lines and computerized brokerage service (6% of revenue).

Requirements

1. Use the contribution margin ratio approach to compute Diversified's breakeven revenue in dollars. If the average trade leads to $800 in revenue for Diversified, how many trades must be made to break even?

2. Use the equation approach to compute the dollar revenues needed to earn a monthly target profit of $11,200.

3. Graph Diversified's CVP relationships. Assume that an average trade leads to $800 in revenue for Diversified. Show the breakeven point, the sales revenue line, the fixed cost line, the total cost line, the operating loss area, the operating income area, and the sales in units (trades) and dollars when monthly operating income of $11,200 is earned.

4. Suppose that the average revenue Diversified earns increases to $2,000 per trade. Compute the new breakeven point in trades. How does this affect the breakeven point?

P20-46B Calculating breakeven point for two products, margin of safety, and operating leverage

Learning Objectives 2, 4, 5

3. $41,000

The contribution margin income statement of Delectable Donuts for May 2018 follows:

DELECTABLE DONUTS Contribution Margin Income Statement Month Ended May 31, 2018		
Net Sales Revenue		$ 125,000
Variable Costs:		
Cost of Goods Sold	$ 32,100	
Selling Costs	17,400	
Administrative Costs	500	50,000
Contribution Margin		75,000
Fixed Costs:		
Selling Costs	37,800	
Administrative Costs	12,600	50,400
Operating Income		$ 24,600

Delectable sells five dozen plain donuts for every dozen custard-filled donuts. A dozen plain donuts sells for $4.00, with a variable cost of $1.60 per dozen. A dozen custard-filled donuts sells for $8.00, with a variable cost of $3.20 per dozen.

Requirements

1. Calculate the weighted-average contribution margin.
2. Determine Delectable's monthly breakeven point in dozens of plain donuts and custard-filled donuts. Prove your answer by preparing a summary contribution margin income statement at the breakeven level of sales. Show only two categories of costs: variable and fixed.
3. Compute Delectable's margin of safety in dollars for May 2018.
4. Compute the degree of operating leverage for Delectable Donuts. Estimate the new operating income if total sales increase by 20%. (Round the degree of operating leverage to four decimal places and the final answer to the nearest dollar. Assume the sales mix remains unchanged.)
5. Prove your answer to Requirement 4 by preparing a contribution margin income statement with a 20% increase in total sales. (The sales mix remains unchanged.)

CRITICAL THINKING

> Using Excel

P20-47 Using Excel for cost-volume-profit (CVP) analysis

Download an Excel template for this problem online in MyAccountingLab or at http://www.pearsonhighered.com/Horngren.

The Oceanside Garden Nursery buys flowering plants in four-inch pots for $1.00 each and sells them for $2.50 each. Management budgets monthly fixed costs of $2,100 for sales volumes between 0 and 5,000 plants.

Requirements

1. Use the contribution margin approach to compute the company's monthly breakeven point in units.
2. Use the contribution margin ratio approach to compute the breakeven point in sales dollars.
3. Use the contribution margin approach to compute the monthly sales level (in units) required to earn a target operating income of $5,000.
4. Prepare a graph of the company's CVP relationships. Include the sales revenue line, the fixed cost line, and the total cost line. Create a chart title and label the axes.

> Continuing Problem

P20-48 Computing breakeven sales and sales needed to earn a target profit; performing sensitivity analysis

This problem continues the Piedmont Computer Company situation from Chapter 19. Piedmont Computer Company manufactures personal computers and tablets. Based on the latest information from the cost accountant, using the current sales mix, the weighted-average sales price per unit is $750 and the weighed-average variable cost per unit is $450. The company does not expect the sales mix to vary for the next year. Average fixed costs per month are $156,000.

Requirements

1. What is the number of units that must be sold each month to reach the breakeven point?
2. If the company currently sells 945 units per month, what is the margin of safety in units and dollars?
3. If Piedmont Computer Company desires to make a profit of $15,000 per month, how many units must be sold?
4. Piedmont Computer Company thinks it can restructure some costs so that fixed costs will be reduced to $90,000 per month, but the weighted-average variable cost per unit will increase to $525 per unit. What is the new breakeven point in units? Does this increase or decrease the margin of safety? Why or why not?

COMPREHENSIVE PROBLEM

> Comprehensive Problem for Chapters 16–20

The Jacksonville Shirt Company makes two types of T-shirts: basic and custom. Basic shirts are plain shirts without any screen printing on them. Custom shirts are created using the basic shirts and then adding a custom screen printing design.

The company buys cloth in various colors and then makes the basic shirts in two departments, Cutting and Sewing. The company uses a process costing system (weighted-average method) to determine the production cost of the basic shirts. In the Cutting Department, direct materials (cloth) are added at the beginning of the process and conversion costs are added evenly through the process. In the Sewing Department, no direct materials are added. The only additional material, thread, is considered an indirect material because it cannot be easily traced to the finished product. Conversion costs are added evenly throughout the process in the Sewing Department. The finished basic shirts are sold to retail stores or are sent to the Custom Design Department for custom screen printing.

The Custom Design Department creates custom shirts by adding screen printing to the basic shirt. The department creates a design based on the customer's request and then prints the design using up to four colors. Because these shirts have the custom printing added, which is unique for each order, the additional cost incurred is determined using job order costing, with each custom order considered a separate job.

For March 2018, the Jacksonville Shirt Company compiled the following data for the Cutting and Sewing Departments:

Department	Item	Amount	Units
Cutting	Beginning balance	$ 0	0 shirts
	Started in March		1,200 shirts
	Direct materials added in March	1,920	
	Conversion costs	1,320	
	Completed and transferred to Sewing	???	1,200 shirts
	Ending balance	0	0 shirts
Sewing	Beginning balance, transferred in, $1,350; conversion costs, $650	$ 2,000	500 shirts
	Transferred in from Cutting	???	???
	Conversion costs added in March	1,196	
	Completed and transferred to Finished Goods	???	1,000 shirts
	Ending balance, 60% complete	???	???

For the same time period, the Jacksonville Shirt Company compiled the following data for the Custom Design Department:

Job	Quantity	Design Fee	Printing	Status
367	400	Yes	3 colors	Complete
368	150	No	2 colors	Complete
369	100	Yes	5 colors	Complete
370	500	Yes	4 colors	Complete

CHAPTER 20

The Jacksonville Shirt Company has previously determined that creating and programming the design cost $80 per design. This is a one-time charge. If a customer places another order with the same design, the customer is not charged a second time. Additionally, the cost to print is $0.20 per color per shirt.

Requirements

1. Complete a production cost report for the Cutting Department and the Sewing Department. What is the cost of one basic shirt?

2. Determine the total cost and the average cost per shirt for jobs 367, 368, 369, and 370. If the company set the sales price at 200% of the total cost, determine the total sales price of each job.

3. In addition to the custom jobs, the Jacksonville Shirt Company sold 1,000 basic shirts (assume the beginning balance in Finished Goods Inventory is sufficient to make these sales, and the unit cost of the basic shirts in Finished Goods Inventory is the same as the unit cost incurred this month). If the company set the sales price at 125% of the cost, determine the sales price per unit, total sales revenue, total cost of goods sold, and total gross profit for the basic shirts.

4. Calculate the total revenue, total cost of goods sold, and total gross profit for all sales, basic and custom.

5. Assume the company sold only basic shirts (no custom designs) and incurred fixed costs of $700 per month.

   a. Calculate the contribution margin per unit, contribution margin ratio, required sales in units to break even, and required sales in dollars to break even.

   b. Determine the margin of safety in units and dollars.

   c. Graph Jacksonville Shirt Company's CVP relationships. Show the breakeven point, the sales revenue line, the fixed cost line, the total cost line, the operating loss area, and the operating income area.

   d. Suppose the Jacksonville Shirt Company wants to earn an operating income of $1,000 per month. Compute the required sales in units and dollars to achieve this profit goal.

6. The Jacksonville Shirt Company is considering adding a new product line, a cloth shopping bag with custom screen printing that will be sold to grocery stores. If the current market price of cloth shopping bags is $2.25 and the company desires a net profit of 60%, what is the target cost? The company estimates the full product cost of the cloth bags will be $0.80. Should the company manufacture the cloth bags? Why or why not?

> Tying It All Together Case 20-1

Before you begin this assignment, review the Tying It All Together feature in the chapter.

Best Buy Co., Inc. is a leading provider of technology products. Customers can shop at more than 1,700 stores or online. The company is also known for its Geek Squad for technology services. Suppose Best Buy is considering a particular HDTV for a major sales item for Black Friday, the day after Thanksgiving, known as one of the busiest shopping days of the year. Assume the HDTV has a regular sales price of $900, a cost of $500, and a Black Friday proposed discounted sales price of $650. Best Buy's 2015 Annual Report states that failure to manage costs could have a material adverse effect on its profitability and that certain elements in its cost structure are largely fixed in nature. Best Buy, like most companies, wishes to maintain price competitiveness while achieving acceptable levels of profitability. (Item 1A. Risk Factors.)

Requirements

1. Calculate the gross profit of the HDTV at the regular sales price and at the discounted sales price.

2. Assume that during the November/December holiday season last year, Best Buy sold an average of 150 of this particular HDTV per store. If the HDTVs are marked down to $650, how many would each store have to sell this year to make the same total gross profit as last year?

3. Relative to Sales Revenue, what type of costs would Best Buy have that are fixed? What type of costs would be variable?

4. Because Best Buy stated that its cost structure is largely fixed in nature, what might be the impact on operating income if sales decreased? Does having a cost structure that is largely fixed in nature increase the financial risk to a company? Why or why not?

5. In the Tying It All Together feature in the chapter, we looked at the cost of advertising. Is advertising a fixed or variable cost? If the company has a small margin of safety, how would increasing advertising costs affect Best Buy's operating income? What would be the effect of decreasing advertising costs?

> Decision Case 20-1

Steve and Linda Hom live in Bartlesville, Oklahoma. Two years ago, they visited Thailand. Linda, a professional chef, was impressed with the cooking methods and the spices used in Thai food. Bartlesville does not have a Thai restaurant, and the Homs are contemplating opening one. Linda would supervise the cooking, and Steve would leave his current job to be the maître d'. The restaurant would serve dinner Tuesday through Saturday.

Steve has noticed a restaurant for lease. The restaurant has seven tables, each of which can seat four. Tables can be moved together for a large party. Linda is planning on using each table twice each evening, and the restaurant will be open 50 weeks per year.

The Homs have drawn up the following estimates:

Average revenue, including beverages and desserts	$ 45	per meal
Average cost of food	15	per meal
Chef's and dishwasher's salaries	5,100	per month
Rent (premises, equipment)	4,000	per month
Cleaning (linen, premises)	800	per month
Replacement of dishes, cutlery, glasses	300	per month
Utilities, advertising, telephone	2,300	per month

Requirements

1. Compute the *annual* breakeven number of meals and sales revenue for the restaurant.

2. Compute the number of meals and the amount of sales revenue needed to earn operating income of $75,600 for the year.

3. How many meals must the Homs serve each night to earn their target profit of $75,600?

4. What factors should the Homs consider before they make their decision as to whether to open the restaurant?

> Ethical Issue 20-1

You have just begun your summer internship at Omni Instruments. The company supplies sterilized surgical instruments for physicians. To expand sales, Omni is considering paying a commission to its sales force. The controller, Matthew Barnhill, asks you to compute: (1) the new breakeven sales figure, and (2) the operating profit if sales increase 15% under the new sales commission plan. He thinks you can handle this task because you learned CVP analysis in your accounting class.

You spend the next day collecting information from the accounting records, performing the analysis, and writing a memo to explain the results. The company president is pleased with your memo. You report that the new sales commission plan will lead to a significant increase in operating income and only a small increase in breakeven sales.

The following week, you realize that you made an error in the CVP analysis. You overlooked the sales personnel's $2,800 monthly salaries, and you did not include this fixed selling cost in your computations. You are not sure what to do. If you tell Matthew Barnhill of your mistake, he will have to tell the president. In this case, you are afraid Omni might not offer you permanent employment after your internship.

Requirements

1. How would your error affect breakeven sales and operating income under the proposed sales commission plan? Could this cause the president to reject the sales commission proposal?

2. Consider your ethical responsibilities. Is there a difference between: (a) initially making an error and (b) subsequently failing to inform the controller?

3. Suppose you tell Matthew Barnhill of the error in your analysis. Why might the consequences not be as bad as you fear? Should Barnhill take any responsibility for your error? What could Barnhill have done differently?

4. After considering all the factors, should you inform Barnhill or simply keep quiet?

> Team Project 20-1

Select a nearby company. Arrange an interview for your team with a managerial accountant, a controller, or another accounting/finance officer of the company.

Requirements

Before your team conducts the interview, research the company and answer the following questions:

1. Is this a service, merchandising, or manufacturing company? What is its primary product or service?

2. What are some possible fixed costs this company incurs?

3. What are some possible variable costs this company incurs?

4. Select one of the company's products or services. Estimate the unit contribution margin for the product or service.

At the interview, ask the above questions and compare your team's answers to the company's answers. Then ask the following questions:

5. How does the company determine the sales prices of products and services?

6. What is the company's cost structure? Does the company have relatively high or low fixed costs?

7. What is the company's sales mix? Has the sales mix changed recently? If so, what caused the change?

Your team should summarize your findings in a short paper. Provide any exhibits that enhance your explanations. Provide proper references and a works cited page.

MyAccountingLab **For a wealth of online resources, including exercises, problems, media, and immediate tutorial help, please visit** http://www.myaccountinglab.com.

> Quick Check Answers

1. b **2.** a **3.** c **4.** d **5.** d **6.** b **7.** b **8.** c **9.** b **10.** d

21 Variable Costing

Why Does the Inventory Keep Growing?

Taylor walked through the finished goods storage area toward the small office in the back. It was the end of the month and time to take inventory. Taylor worked part time at the manufacturing company while attending a local college. Most of the time, she worked in the plant office assisting the cost accountant with various accounting tasks. The work was interesting, and she was learning a lot about accounting for a manufacturing company. Also, working for a real company helped Taylor understand the concepts in her business classes.

Taylor reached the office, looked around, and sighed. There was a lot of inventory to be counted! Every month

there was more inventory, and every month the task took longer to complete. The inventory increases puzzled Taylor. Recently, she had been studying the income statements for the plant and noticed profits were increasing each month. Sales had been steady, but the gross profit percentage had been increasing because the cost of goods sold was decreasing as a percentage of sales. Taylor wondered why cost of goods sold was decreasing when inventories were increasing. And why were inventories increasing? The company was obviously producing more goods each month than it was selling. As she picked up her clipboard to start the inventory count, she decided to ask the cost accountant about the situation.

Should We Produce Extra Inventory?

Generally, companies want to keep inventory levels as low as possible. However, in some cases, it is necessary to increase the inventory levels of finished goods in order to meet seasonal customer demands. For example, **CF Industries Holdings, Inc.,** based in Deerfield, Illinois, is a global leader in nitrogen fertilizer manufacturing and distribution. CF Industries has the capacity to produce more than 15 million tons of fertilizer per year. During periods of low demand, the company produces more fertilizer than it can sell. The increased inventory levels allow the company to meet customer demand during the peak sales seasons—spring planting and fall harvesting. The company owns and leases several storage facilities to accommodate the extra inventory and has the capacity to store approximately 3 million tons of product. CF Industries uses its Forward Pricing Program (FPP) to help manage inventory levels. The FPP system allows customers to contract for future purchases at a specified price, delivery time, and volume. This allows the company to plan the production and distribution of its products.

In this chapter, we look at the effects that changing inventory levels can have on management decisions. We compare the effects of using absorption costing versus variable costing and how the allocation of manufacturing costs can create profitability distortions.

Chapter 21 Learning Objectives

1 Distinguish between variable costing and absorption costing

2 Compute operating income using variable costing and absorption costing

3 Use variable costing to make management decisions for a manufacturing business

4 Use variable costing to make management decisions for a service business

HOW DOES VARIABLE COSTING DIFFER FROM ABSORPTION COSTING?

The purpose of managerial accounting is to provide managers with information that is useful for internal decision making—for planning, directing, and controlling decisions. As you have seen, this type of information often differs from the financial accounting information provided to external users, such as investors and creditors. In this chapter, you study two methods of determining the cost of producing products and when each method is appropriate.

Learning Objective 1

Distinguish between variable costing and absorption costing

Absorption Costing

Up to this point, we have illustrated the use of absorption costing when determining the cost of products. **Absorption costing** considers direct materials costs, direct labor costs, variable manufacturing overhead costs, and fixed manufacturing overhead costs as product costs. This approach is called absorption costing because the products *absorb* all of the manufacturing costs—materials, labor, and overhead. These costs are recorded first as assets in the inventory accounts. Later, when the product is sold, the costs are transferred to the expense account Cost of Goods Sold. Absorption costing is required by the Generally Accepted Accounting Principles (GAAP) for financial statements issued to investors, creditors, and other external users. The external financial statements use the traditional income statement format with a focus on gross profit.

Absorption Costing

The product costing method that assigns direct materials, direct labor, variable manufacturing overhead, and fixed manufacturing overhead to products. Required by GAAP for external reporting.

Variable Costing

Variable costing is an alternative costing method that considers only variable manufacturing costs when determining product costs. Variable costing includes direct materials costs, direct labor costs, and variable manufacturing overhead costs as product costs. Fixed manufacturing overhead costs are considered period costs and are expensed in the period in which they are incurred, because these costs are incurred whether or not the company manufactures any goods. Variable costing cannot be used for external reporting, but it is useful to managers for planning, directing, and controlling. The internal financial statements use the contribution margin income statement format with a focus on contribution margin. **Contribution margin** is the difference between net sales revenue and variable costs. It is the amount that contributes to covering the fixed costs and then to providing operating income.

Exhibit 21-1 (on the next page) summarizes the differences between absorption costing and variable costing. Key differences between the two methods are highlighted in green.

Variable Costing

The product costing method that assigns only variable manufacturing costs to products: direct materials, direct labor, and variable manufacturing overhead. Used for internal reporting.

Contribution Margin

The amount that contributes to covering the fixed costs and then to providing operating income. Net sales revenue – Variable costs.

Exhibit 21-1 | Differences Between Absorption Costing and Variable Costing

	Absorption Costing	Variable Costing
Product Costs	Direct materials Direct labor Variable manufacturing overhead Fixed manufacturing overhead	Direct materials Direct labor Variable manufacturing overhead
Period Costs	Variable selling and administrative costs Fixed selling and administrative costs	Fixed manufacturing overhead Variable selling and administrative costs Fixed selling and administrative costs
Income Statement Format	Traditional format: Net Sales Revenue – Cost of Goods Sold Gross Profit – Selling and Administrative Costs Operating Income	Contribution margin format: Net Sales Revenue – Variable Costs Contribution Margin – Fixed Costs Operating Income

Comparison of Unit Product Costs

To illustrate the difference between absorption costing and variable costing, let's look at Smart Touch Learning. Exhibit 21-2 summarizes the company's price and cost information based on 2,000 units produced.

Exhibit 21-2 | Smart Touch Learning—Price and Cost Summary

Units produced		2,000 units
Sales price	$	500.00 per tablet
Manufacturing costs:		
Direct materials		150.00 per tablet
Direct labor		75.00 per tablet
Variable manufacturing overhead		20.00 per tablet
Fixed manufacturing overhead		111,000.00 per year
Selling and administrative costs:		
Variable selling and administrative costs		62.50 per tablet
Fixed selling and administrative costs		116,000.00 per year

The unit product cost using absorption costing will include all manufacturing costs (both variable and fixed): direct materials ($150.00), direct labor ($75.00), variable manufacturing overhead ($20.00), and fixed manufacturing overhead ($55.50 or $111,000.00 / 2,000 units). The unit product cost using variable costing will include only variable manufacturing costs: direct materials ($150.00), direct labor ($75.00), and variable manufacturing overhead ($20.00). The calculations are summarized in Exhibit 21-3.

Exhibit 21-3 | **Comparison of Unit Product Cost Computations—2,000 Units Produced**

	Absorption Costing	Variable Costing
Direct materials	$ 150.00	$ 150.00
Direct labor	75.00	75.00
Variable manufacturing overhead	20.00	20.00
Fixed manufacturing overhead ($111,000 / 2,000 units)	55.50	
Total unit product cost	$ 300.50	$ 245.00

Notice that the selling and administrative costs, both fixed and variable, are not included in the unit product cost calculations. Both costing methods consider selling and administrative costs to be period costs. Variable costing also considers fixed manufacturing overhead to be a period cost while absorption costing considers it to be a product cost.

Try It!

1. Pierce Company had the following costs:

Units produced	500 units
Manufacturing costs:	
Direct materials	$ 25 per unit
Direct labor	45 per unit
Variable manufacturing overhead	15 per unit
Fixed manufacturing overhead	5,000 per year
Selling and administrative costs:	
Variable selling and administrative costs	30 per unit
Fixed selling and administrative costs	3,200 per year

Calculate the unit product cost using absorption costing and variable costing.

Check your answer online in MyAccountingLab or at http://www.pearsonhighered.com/Horngren.

For more practice, see Short Exercises S21-1 through S21-3. MyAccountingLab

HOW DOES OPERATING INCOME DIFFER BETWEEN VARIABLE COSTING AND ABSORPTION COSTING?

Now that you know how to calculate unit product costs using variable costing and absorption costing, let's see the effects the two methods have on calculating operating income. There are three different scenarios to consider:

- Units produced equal units sold
- Units produced are more than units sold
- Units produced are less than units sold

Learning Objective 2

Compute operating income using variable costing and absorption costing

Units Produced Equal Units Sold

Let's assume that for Year 1 Smart Touch Learning has the following history:

- No beginning balance in Finished Goods Inventory
- Produced 2,000 tablet computers during the year
- Sold 2,000 tablet computers during the year

Based on these assumptions, we can also conclude that Smart Touch Learning has no ending balance in Finished Goods Inventory because the beginning balance was zero and all units produced were sold.

Exhibit 21-4 shows the income statements for Smart Touch Learning using absorption costing and variable costing. The unit costs and total fixed costs were given or calculated in Exhibits 21-2 and 21-3.

Exhibit 21-4 | Absorption and Variable Costing: Year 1—Units Produced Equal Units Sold

Absorption Costing

Net Sales Revenue	(2,000 units × $500.00 per unit)		$ 1,000,000
Cost of Goods Sold	(2,000 units × $300.50 per unit)		601,000
Gross Profit			399,000
Selling and Administrative Costs:			
Variable S&A Costs	(2,000 units × $62.50 per unit)	$ 125,000	
Fixed S&A Costs		116,000	241,000
Operating Income			$ 158,000
Finished Goods Inventory, Ending Balance			$ 0

Variable Costing

Net Sales Revenue	(2,000 units × $500.00 per unit)		$ 1,000,000
Variable Costs:			
Variable Manufacturing Costs	(2,000 units × $245.00 per unit)	$ 490,000	
Variable S&A Costs	(2,000 units × $62.50 per unit)	125,000	615,000
Contribution Margin			385,000
Fixed Costs:			
Fixed Manufacturing Costs		111,000	
Fixed S&A Costs		116,000	227,000
Operating Income			$ 158,000
Finished Goods Inventory, Ending Balance			$ 0

As shown in Exhibit 21-4, the absorption costing income statement includes all manufacturing costs (direct materials, direct labor, variable manufacturing overhead, and fixed manufacturing overhead) in the cost of goods sold. Net sales revenue less cost of goods sold determines gross profit, and then selling and administrative costs (both variable and fixed) are subtracted to determine operating income.

In the variable costing income statement, variable costs are reported separately from fixed costs. Variable costs (direct materials, direct labor, variable manufacturing overhead, and variable selling and administrative costs) are subtracted from net sales revenue to determine the contribution margin. Fixed costs (both manufacturing and selling and administrative) are then subtracted from contribution margin to determine operating income.

When all of the units produced are sold, there is no difference in operating income between the two costing methods. The reason is that all fixed costs are expensed under both methods. In other words, because the ending Finished Goods Inventory balance is zero and there are no production costs assigned to the inventory accounts, all costs incurred have been recorded as expenses and deducted from net sales revenue on the income statement.

Units Produced Are More Than Units Sold

Let's assume that for Year 2 Smart Touch Learning shows the following:

- No beginning balance in Finished Goods Inventory (Year 1 ended with a zero balance; therefore, Year 2 will start with a zero balance)
- Produced 2,500 tablet computers during the year
- Sold 2,000 tablet computers during the year
- Ending balance in Finished Goods Inventory of 500 units

Ending balance in Finished Goods Inventory = Beginning balance + Units Produced − Units sold
$$= \quad 0 \text{ units} \quad + \quad 2{,}500 \text{ units} \quad - \; 2{,}000 \text{ units}$$
$$= 500 \text{ units}$$

With the change in number of tablets produced, the unit product costs must be recalculated because fixed costs are spread over a greater number of units produced. The calculations are summarized in Exhibit 21-5. The increase in production decreased the total unit product cost from $300.50 (Exhibit 21-3) to $289.40 under absorption costing.

Exhibit 21-5 | **Comparison of Unit Product Cost Computations—2,500 Units Produced**

	Absorption Costing	Variable Costing
Direct materials	$ 150.00	$ 150.00
Direct labor	75.00	75.00
Variable manufacturing overhead	20.00	20.00
Fixed manufacturing overhead ($111,000 / 2,500 units)	44.40	
Total unit product cost	$ 289.40	$ 245.00

Suppose you invite a friend for dinner and you make an apple pie. There are only two of you, so you can each have half of the pie.

Now suppose you invite two more friends. There are four people having dinner and still only one pie. Each person can have only a fourth of the pie.

This concept also applies to fixed costs. Total fixed costs stay the same (one whole pie), so the more units produced, the smaller the amount assigned to each unit (smaller piece of pie each).

Exhibit 21-6 shows the income statements for Smart Touch Learning for Year 2 using absorption costing and variable costing. The unit costs and total fixed costs were given or calculated in Exhibits 21-2 and 21-5.

Exhibit 21-6 | **Absorption and Variable Costing: Year 2—Units Produced Are More Than Units Sold**

Absorption Costing

Net Sales Revenue	(2,000 units × $500.00 per unit)		$ 1,000,000
Cost of Goods Sold	(2,000 units × $289.40 per unit)		578,800
Gross Profit			421,200
Selling and Administrative Costs:			
Variable S&A Costs	(2,000 units × $62.50 per unit)	$ 125,000	
Fixed S&A Costs		116,000	241,000
Operating Income			$ 180,200
Finished Goods Inventory, Ending Balance	(500 units × $289.40 per unit)		$ 144,700

Variable Costing

Net Sales Revenue	(2,000 units × $500.00 per unit)		$ 1,000,000
Variable Costs:			
Variable Manufacturing Costs	(2,000 units × $245.00 per unit)	$ 490,000	
Variable S&A Costs	(2,000 units × $62.50 per unit)	125,000	615,000
Contribution Margin			385,000
Fixed Costs:			
Fixed Manufacturing Costs		111,000	
Fixed S&A Costs		116,000	227,000
Operating Income			$ 158,000
Finished Goods Inventory, Ending Balance	(500 units × $245.00 per unit)		$ 122,500

As shown in Exhibit 21-6, when more units are produced than sold, operating income is greater under absorption costing than variable costing. The reason is that with absorption costing some fixed manufacturing costs remain in ending Finished Goods Inventory on the balance sheet and have not been expensed. The difference between the operating incomes for the two methods is $22,200 ($180,200 − $158,000). This is the same difference in ending Finished Goods Inventory ($144,700 − $122,500). This difference is due to the fixed manufacturing overhead costs. Under variable costing, all of the fixed manufacturing overhead is expensed. Under absorption costing, though, $22,200 (500 units of ending inventory × $44.40 per unit fixed manufacturing overhead cost) remain in ending inventory and are therefore not expensed in the time period. This $22,200 difference results in the operating income being greater under absorption costing.

Units Produced Are Less Than Units Sold

Let's assume that for Year 3 Smart Touch Learning shows the following:

- A beginning balance in Finished Goods Inventory of 500 units that cost $144,700 under absorption costing and $122,500 under variable costing (Year 2's ending balances)
- Produced 1,500 tablet computers during the year
- Sold 2,000 tablet computers during the year

Based on the above assumptions, we can also conclude that Smart Touch has no ending balance in Finished Goods Inventory because the beginning balance was 500 units, which was increased by the 1,500 units produced and decreased by the 2,000 units sold:

Ending balance in Finished Goods Inventory	=	**Beginning balance**	+	**Units produced**	− **Units sold**
	=	500 units	+	1,500 units	− 2,000 units
	=	0 units			

With the change in number of tablets produced, the unit product costs must be recalculated. The calculations are summarized in Exhibit 21-7. The decrease in production increased the total unit product cost from $289.40 (Exhibit 21-5) to $319.00 under absorption costing because the total fixed manufacturing overhead costs were distributed among fewer units produced.

Exhibit 21-7 | **Comparison of Unit Product Cost Computations—1,500 Units Produced**

	Absorption Costing	Variable Costing
Direct materials	$ 150.00	$ 150.00
Direct labor	75.00	75.00
Variable manufacturing overhead	20.00	20.00
Fixed manufacturing overhead ($111,000 / 1,500 units)	74.00	
Total unit product cost	$ 319.00	$ 245.00

Exhibit 21-8 (on the next page) shows the income statements for Smart Touch Learning for Year 3 using absorption costing and variable costing. The unit costs and total fixed costs were given or calculated in Exhibits 21-2 and 21-7.

Exhibit 21-8 | **Absorption and Variable Costing: Year 3—Units Produced Are Less Than Units Sold**

Absorption Costing			
Net Sales Revenue	(2,000 units × $500.00 per unit)		$ 1,000,000
Cost of Goods Sold	(500 units × $289.40 per unit)	$ 144,700	
	(1,500 units × $319.00 per unit)	478,500	623,200
Gross Profit			376,800
Selling and Administrative Costs:			
Variable S&A Costs	(2,000 units × $62.50 per unit)	125,000	
Fixed S&A Costs		116,000	241,000
Operating Income			$ 135,800
Finished Goods Inventory, Ending Balance			$ 0

Variable Costing			
Net Sales Revenue	(2,000 units × $500.00 per unit)		$ 1,000,000
Variable Costs:			
Variable Manufacturing Costs	(2,000 units × $245.00 per unit)	$ 490,000	
Variable S&A Costs	(2,000 units × $62.50 per unit)	125,000	615,000
Contribution Margin			385,000
Fixed Costs:			
Fixed Manufacturing Costs		111,000	
Fixed S&A Costs		116,000	227,000
Operating Income			$ 158,000
Finished Goods Inventory, Ending Balance			$ 0

As shown in Exhibit 21-8, when more units are sold than produced, operating income is less under absorption costing than variable costing. The only way to sell more units than were produced is to sell some units that were in inventory at the beginning of the period. Notice the cost of goods sold calculation using absorption costing includes the 500 units in beginning Finished Goods Inventory at $289.40 per unit, $144,700. This is the amount shown as the ending Finished Goods Inventory for Year 2 in Exhibit 21-6. Remember that Year 2's ending inventory becomes Year 3's beginning inventory.

In variable costing, the fixed manufacturing costs for the prior year were expensed in the prior year. Because only variable costs are assigned to the units, the unit product cost is the same for all three accounting periods, $245.00 per unit. Under absorption costing, the units in beginning inventory have fixed manufacturing costs assigned to them. Therefore, the units sold under absorption costing have a higher cost per unit, which increases cost of goods sold and decreases operating income. The difference between the operating incomes for the two methods is $22,200 ($135,800 − $158,000). This difference is due to when the fixed manufacturing overhead costs are expensed. Under variable costing, all of the fixed manufacturing overhead costs from the prior period were expensed in the prior period and therefore are not shown on the current year income statement. Under absorpotion costing, the prior period fixed manufacturing costs attached to beginning inventory are expensed in the current year.

Summary

In the three years illustrated for Smart Touch Learning, the only difference was the number of tablet computers produced. In each year, the number of tablets sold (2,000 units), the sales price per unit, the variable costs per unit, and the total fixed costs were the same. Let's compare the three years to determine why many managers prefer to use variable costing for planning, directing, and controlling. Exhibit 21-9 summarizes the income statements for the three years. Notice that the total operating income for the three years ($474,000) is the same under both methods but that the operating income for each year differs under absorption costing.

Exhibit 21-9 | **Absorption and Variable Costing: 3-Year Summary—2,000 Units Sold Each Year**

Absorption Costing	Year 1	Year 2	Year 3	Total*
Net Sales Revenue	$ 1,000,000	$ 1,000,000	$ 1,000,000	$ 3,000,000
Cost of Goods Sold	601,000	578,800	623,200	1,803,000
Gross Profit	399,000	421,200	376,800	1,197,000
Selling and Administrative Costs	241,000	241,000	241,000	723,000
Operating Income	$ 158,000	$ 180,200	$ 135,800	$ 474,000
Gross Profit per Unit	$ 199.50	$ 210.60	$ 188.40	

Variable Costing	Year 1	Year 2	Year 3	Total
Net Sales Revenue	$ 1,000,000	$ 1,000,000	$ 1,000,000	$ 3,000,000
Variable Costs	615,000	615,000	615,000	1,845,000
Contribution Margin	385,000	385,000	385,000	1,155,000
Fixed Costs	227,000	227,000	227,000	681,000
Operating Income	$ 158,000	$ 158,000	$ 158,000	$ 474,000
Contribution Margin per Unit	$ 192.50	$ 192.50	$ 192.50	

*Year 1: Units Produced = Units Sold   Absorption Operating Income = Variable Operating Income
Year 2: Units Produced > Units Sold   Absorption Operating Income > Variable Operating Income
Year 3: Units Produced < Units Sold   Absorption Operating Income < Variable Operating Income

Suppose the production supervisor receives a bonus based on the amount of operating income under absorption costing. Will the supervisor increase or decrease production? Based on the summary of income statements presented in Exhibit 21-9, operating income under absorption costing was greater than operating income under variable costing in Year 2, when production exceeded sales. The production supervisor knows that absorption costing assigns fixed manufacturing overhead costs to each tablet produced. In absorption costing:

- For every tablet that is produced but not sold, absorption costing "hides" some of the fixed manufacturing overhead costs in ending Finished Goods Inventory (an asset).
- The more tablets added to ending Finished Goods Inventory, the more fixed manufacturing overhead costs are "hidden" in ending Finished Goods Inventory at the end of the month.
- The more fixed manufacturing overhead costs in ending Finished Goods Inventory, the smaller the Cost of Goods Sold and the higher the operating income.

To maximize the bonus under absorption costing, the supervisor may increase production to build up ending Finished Goods Inventory, increase operating income, and therefore increase the bonus. However, this incentive directly conflicts with the just-in-time philosophy, which emphasizes minimal inventory levels. Therefore, many managers prefer to use variable costing to make internal planning, directing, and control decisions. The use of variable costing to determine bonuses does not give the incentive to produce more products than needed.

How can using absorption costing affect production levels when determining performance-based bonuses?

TYING IT ALL TOGETHER

In the chapter opener, we introduced **CF Industries Holdings, Inc.,** one of the largest manufacturers and distributors of nitrogen fertilizer and other nitrogen products in the world. CF Industries has six nitrogen fertilizer manufacturing facilities that distribute fertilizer products throughout the United States and Canada. The company is the largest nitrogen fertilizer producer in North America selling 13,276,000 tons in 2014. The market for nitrogen fertilizer is highly seasonal with the strongest demand for fertilizer products during the spring planting season. This leads to the company building inventory levels during low demand periods to ensure there is enough product available during peak seasons.

Would CF Industries Holdings, Inc. use absorption or variable costing on the income statement included in the company's annual report?

CF Industries Holdings, Inc. would use absorption costing on the income statement included in the company's annual report because this method is required by Generally Accepted Accounting Principles.

How does an absorption costing income statement differ from a variable costing income statement?

When a company uses absorption costing, the cost of direct materials, direct labor, variable manufacturing overhead, and fixed manufacturing overhead are treated as product costs and included first in the asset account, inventory, on the balance sheet. It is only when the inventory is sold that the costs are expensed as cost

of goods sold on the income statement. An absorption income statement follows a traditional format calculating first gross profit as net sales revenue less cost of goods sold, and then operating income as gross profit less selling and administrative costs.

Alternatively, a variable costing income statement includes only variable manufacturing costs (direct labor, direct materials, and variable manufacturing overhead) when determining product costs. The fixed manufacturing overhead cost is treated as a period cost, not a product cost. A variable costing income statement follows the contribution margin format calculating first contribution margin as net sales revenue less variable costs, and then operating income as contribution margin less fixed costs.

If CF Industries Holdings, Inc. prepared a variable costing income statement instead of an absorption costing income statement would the operating income be the same?

Most likely the operating income would not be the same when using the two different methods. The only time operating income is the same under both the absorption and variable costing income statement is when units produced are equal to units sold. When units produced are different than units sold, the operating income will be different. For example, if units produced are more than units sold, the operating income is greater under absorption costing than variable costing because some fixed manufacturing costs are still in inventory and have not yet been expensed. Alternatively, if units produced are less than units sold, the operating income is less under absorption costing than variable costing.

2. Hayden Company has 50 units in Finished Goods Inventory at the beginning of the accounting period. During the accounting period, Hayden produced 150 units and sold 200 units for $150 each. All units incurred $80 in variable manufacturing costs and $20 in fixed manufacturing costs. Hayden also incurred $7,500 in Selling and Administrative Costs, all fixed. Calculate the operating income for the year using absorption costing and variable costing.

Check your answer online in MyAccountingLab or at http://www.pearsonhighered.com/Horngren.

For more practice, see Short Exercises S21-4 through S21-9. MyAccountingLab

HOW CAN VARIABLE COSTING BE USED FOR DECISION MAKING IN A MANUFACTURING COMPANY?

Learning Objective 3

Use variable costing to make management decisions for a manufacturing business

Now that you have learned about the differences between absorption costing and variable costing and how they can affect operating income, let's consider some situations where managers must make decisions. In some cases, variable costing is more appropriate for decision making, but in other cases, absorption costing is more appropriate.

Setting Sales Prices

In the long run, the sales price charged to customers must cover the full cost of the product. The full cost includes every part of the life cycle of the product: research and development, design, production, distribution, customer service, and disposal. Any fixed manufacturing costs must be included, so absorption costing is more appropriate when determining the product costs for long-term planning.

In the short run, however, variable costing should be used in some cases. For example, if a company has excess capacity and has a one-time opportunity to accept a customer order at a discounted sales price, the order should be accepted if the sales price exceeds the variable costs. In this situation, fixed costs are not relevant because they would be incurred whether or not the order is accepted. If the fixed costs are not relevant, they should not be considered when making the decision—and variable costing is an appropriate costing method to use. Short-term pricing decisions are covered in more detail in a later chapter.

Controlling Costs

We sometimes think that some costs are not controllable. For example, if the company signs a five-year lease for the manufacturing facility, the rent expense is fixed and will remain fixed for five years. However, in the long run, all costs are controllable. After five years, the company can renegotiate the lease, rent another building, or buy a building. Even though the cost of occupying the manufacturing facility is controllable, it is a decision made by upper management. The production supervisor does not control this cost. Most fixed manufacturing costs are controlled by upper management. Therefore, managers should focus on and be accountable for the costs they can control. At the production supervisor's level, the controllable costs are the variable manufacturing costs: direct materials, direct labor, and variable manufacturing overhead.

Planning Production

Production planning decisions are similar to sales price decisions: Short-term decisions should be made using variable costing, and long-term decisions should be made using absorption costing.

In the short run, production is limited by capacity. Therefore, production supervisors should produce the products with the highest contribution margin per unit, as long as there is demand for the products. Producing and selling the products with the highest contribution margin per unit generates the highest operating income. So, in the short term, variable costing is appropriate. However, in the long run, capacity can be expanded. Because expansion would affect both fixed and variable costs, absorption costing is more appropriate. Production planning decisions are covered in more detail in a later chapter.

Analyzing Profitability

We looked at profitability analysis in our study of cost-volume-profit analysis when we calculated sales needed to break even and earn a target profit. Let's expand that analysis to include decisions about products and business segments. In this type of analysis, it is helpful to use variable costing.

Products

Let's assume Smart Touch Learning sells two tablet computer models—standard and premium. The premium model has several superior features, including a larger screen, faster processor, longer-lasting battery, and specialized software programs. The premium model costs more to manufacture and has a higher sales price. The premium model is new for the company, and the sales representatives have been encouraged to promote the new model. As an incentive, their sales commission is greater for the premium model. Price and cost information for the two models are shown in Exhibit 21-10.

Exhibit 21-10 | **Standard and Premium Tablets**

	Standard	Premium
Units Sold	2,000 units	500 units
Sales Price per Unit	$ 500	$ 600
Variable Manufacturing Cost per Unit (Including direct materials, direct labor, and variable manufacturing overhead)	245	360
Sales Commissions per Unit:		
Standard: 5% of sales price	25	
Premium: 10% of sales price		60

Business Segments

Business Segment
An identifiable part of the company for which financial information is available.

Many companies divide their business into segments. A **business segment** is an identifiable part of the company for which financial information is available. Businesses can be segmented by geography (domestic and international), customer types (commercial and residential), products (motorcycles and all-terrain vehicles), or salespersons (Jane's sales territory and John's sales territory).

Let's assume that Smart Touch Learning has two business segments based on the sales territories of two sales representatives—Avila Salinas and John Carey—who are assigned specific geographic regions. During the last accounting period, both sales representatives sold 1,250 tablets each. Exhibit 21-11 shows the contribution margin income statements for both territories and determines the contribution margin ratio. As a reminder, the **contribution margin ratio** is the ratio of contribution margin to net sales revenue and can be calculated as follows:

Contribution Margin Ratio
The ratio of contribution margin to net sales revenue. Contribution margin / Net sales revenue.

Contribution margin = Net sales revenue − Variable costs
Contribution margin ratio = Contribution margin / Net sales revenue

Exhibit 21-11 | **Smart Touch Learning Contribution Margin Income Statements by Sales Territories**

	Salinas	Carey	Total
Units Sold	1,250 units	1,250 units	2,500 units
Net sales Revenue	$ 665,000	$ 635,000	$ 1,300,000
Variable Costs:			
Manufacturing	352,250	317,750	670,000
Sales Commissions	45,250	34,750	80,000
Contribution Margin	$ 267,500	$ 282,500	$ 550,000
Contribution Margin Ratio	40.23%	44.49%	42.31%

Profitability Analysis

Exhibit 21-11 shows that even though both sales representatives sold the same number of tablets, Salinas had higher revenues, whereas Carey had a higher contribution margin and contribution margin ratio. Let's look at each sales territory in more detail by examining how the sales mix affected the results. Exhibit 21-12 shows the contribution margin by products for each territory.

The more detailed statements in Exhibit 21-12 show how the sales mix of each territory affected the total contribution margin. Salinas's sales mix was 68% standard units and 32% premium units. Carey's sales mix was 92% standard units and 8% premium units. Because the standard model has a higher contribution margin ratio than the premium model, 46% compared with 30%, Carey was able to contribute more to the company's profits.

Exhibit 21-12 | **Contribution Margin by Product**

SALINAS		Standard	Premium	Total
Units Sold		850 units	400 units	1,250 units
Sales Mix		68%	32%	100%
Net Sales Revenue	(850 units × $500 per unit)	$ 425,000		
	(400 units × $600 per unit)		$ 240,000	$ 665,000
Variable Costs:				
Manufacturing	(850 units × $245 per unit)	208,250		
	(400 units × $360 per unit)		144,000	352,250
Sales Commissions	(5% of Sales Revenue)	21,250		
	(10% of Sales Revenue)		24,000	45,250
Contribution Margin		$ 195,500	$ 72,000	$ 267,500
Contribution Margin Ratio		46.00%	30.00%	40.23%

CAREY		Standard	Premium	Total
Units Sold		1,150 units	100 units	1,250 units
Sales Mix		92%	8%	100%
Net Sales Revenue	(1,150 units × $500 per unit)	$ 575,000		
	(100 units × $600 per unit)		$ 60,000	$ 635,000
Variable Costs:				
Manufacturing	(1,150 units × $245 per unit)	281,750		
	(100 units × $360 per unit)		36,000	317,750
Sales Commissions	(5% of Sales Revenue)	28,750		
	(10% of Sales Revenue)		6,000	34,750
Contribution Margin		$ 264,500	$ 18,000	$ 282,500
Contribution Margin Ratio		46.00%	30.00%	44.49%

The management of Smart Touch Learning should analyze the statements and make recommendations to the sales representatives. Questions to consider include:

- Should the sales representatives continue to focus on the premium model if it has a lower contribution margin ratio?
- Should the premium model have a higher sales commission than the standard model?
- What steps can the company take to improve the contribution margin ratio on the premium model? Increase the sales price? Decrease the sales commission? Decrease the variable cost of goods sold?

Analyzing Contribution Margin

In the previous section on profitability analysis, we analyzed the effects of sales mix on profitability. In this section, we look at the effects of changes in sales volume, sales price per unit, and variable cost per unit using a new scenario for Smart Touch Learning. This is another situation in which it is helpful to use variable costing. To do this, we will use Exhibit 21-13, which shows the income statements in contribution margin format for two accounting periods for Smart Touch Learning.

Exhibit 21-13 | **Contribution Margin Analysis—Smart Touch Learning**

	Period 1	Period 2	Difference
Units Sold	500 units	400 units	
Net Sales Revenue	$ 250,000	$ 220,000	$ (30,000)
Variable Costs:			
Manufacturing	135,000	132,000	(3,000)
Sales Commissions	20,000	17,600	(2,400)
Contribution Margin	$ 95,000	$ 70,400	$ (24,600)
Contribution Margin Ratio	38%	32%	

At first glance, it appears that it was the decrease in the number of units sold (from 500 units in Period 1 to 400 units in Period 2) that caused a decrease in contribution margin. However, that does not explain why the contribution margin ratio decreased from 38% to 32%. Remember, a change in sales volume does not affect the contribution margin per unit. So why did the contribution margin ratio decrease? Let's take the total amounts and expand them into their two components—units and amount per unit—by dividing the totals by the number of units. Exhibit 21-14 shows the expanded statements.

Exhibit 21-14 | **Expanded Contribution Margin Analysis—Smart Touch Learning**

Period 1	Total	Units	Amount per Unit	Percent of Sales
Net Sales Revenue	$ 250,000	500 units	$ 500	100%
Variable Costs:				
Manufacturing	135,000	500 units	270	54%
Sales Commissions	20,000	500 units	40	8%
Contribution Margin	$ 95,000	500 units	$ 190	38%
Contribution Margin Ratio	38%		38%	

Period 2	Total	Units	Amount per Unit	Percent of Sales
Net Sales Revenue	$ 220,000	400 units	$ 550	100%
Variable Costs:				
Manufacturing	132,000	400 units	330	60%
Sales Commissions	17,600	400 units	44	8%
Contribution Margin	$ 70,400	400 units	$ 176	32%
Contribution Margin Ratio	32%		32%	

We can now see that the change in contribution margin was the result of changes in both components—units and amount per unit. In other words, there was a volume effect and a price/cost effect. Further investigation revealed that direct materials cost increased by $60 per tablet causing variable manufacturing costs to increase from $270 to $330 per tablet. Therefore, management increased the sales price by $50 per tablet (from $500 to $550). This did not totally offset the increase in direct materials cost, but management felt the market would not bear a greater price increase. In fact, raising the sales price to $550 caused a decrease of 100 units sold, from 500 units to 400 units, which was a 20% decrease in sales (100 units / 500 units = 20%). The sales commission remained the same at 8% of sales. The contribution margin ratio decreased from 38% to 32%.

The contribution margin analysis shown here is a type of variance analysis, which will be illustrated in greater detail in a later chapter.

Summary

Exhibit 21-15 summarizes the situations in which managers must make decisions and the costing system that is more appropriate for each situation.

Exhibit 21-15 | Decision-Making Summary

Decision		Appropriate Costing Method	Reason
Setting Sales Prices	Long run	Absorption	The sales price must cover the full cost in the long run, including fixed costs.
	Short run	Variable	Fixed costs are not relevant in the short run because they usually do not change.
Controlling Costs	Upper management	Absorption	All costs, including fixed costs, are controllable by upper management in the long run.
	Lower management	Variable	Lower management usually does not have control over most fixed costs.
Planning Production	Long run	Absorption	Expansion to avoid capacity limits includes both fixed and variable costs.
	Short run	Variable	With capacity limits in the short run, products with the highest contribution margin per unit should be produced.
Analyzing Profitability	Sales mix	Variable	To increase profits, businesses should emphasize the products with the highest contribution margin per unit.
Analyzing Contribution Margin	Volume, price, variable costs	Variable	Fixed costs do not affect contribution margin.

ETHICS

How can we make the financial statements look better?

Talley, Inc. manufactures and sells cook sets consisting of three pots, two pans, and five lids. Dale Cash, the cost accountant at Talley, Inc. calculated the breakeven point for the company at 6,000 cook sets. In previous years, Talley has been profitable. This year, however, sales are down. The company expects to sell only 5,500 cook sets, and the accountant is concerned the company will have a loss for the first time in 10 years. Dale discusses the situation with the sales manager, Frank Rasmussen, and the production manager, Neil Valencia. The three men agree that fixed costs cannot be decreased in the near future, so the only way to show a profit is to sell more than 6,000 cook sets. After the meeting, Neil decides to increase production without telling the other managers. He knows that if production exceeds sales, profits will increase because a portion of the fixed costs will remain in ending Finished Goods Inventory rather than being expensed on the income statement.

Should Neil increase production when sales are down? What would you do?

Solution

Neil should not increase production just to create a profit. Not only will his actions increase inventory levels, but they could have a negative impact on cash flows and jeopardize the future of the company. If more cook sets are produced than sold, then the company is using cash to pay the variable costs associated with the increased production, including the purchase of raw materials and labor costs for the production workers. If the additional cook sets are not sold and remain in inventory, then the company is not receiving cash from customers. Cash outflows for operating activities will increase with the increase in production without an increase in cash inflows from sales and collections, which could result in the need for financing from outside sources.

Try It!

3. The Stark Company manufactures a product that is expected to incur $20 per unit in variable production costs and sell for $40 per unit. The sales commission is 10% of the sales price. Due to intense competition, Stark actually sold 200 units for $38 per unit. The actual variable production costs incurred were $23.75 per unit. Calculate the total contribution margin and contribution margin ratio at the expected price/costs and the actual price/costs. How might management use this information?

Check your answers online in MyAccountingLab or at http://www.pearsonhighered.com/Horngren.

For more practice, see Short Exercises S21-10 and S21-11. MyAccountingLab

HOW CAN VARIABLE COSTING BE USED FOR DECISION MAKING IN A SERVICE COMPANY?

Learning Objective 4

Use variable costing to make management decisions for a service business

Service companies provide services, rather than products, to their customers. Therefore, service companies do not have inventory or cost of goods sold. They do, however, have fixed and variable costs associated with providing services. Because service companies have both fixed and variable costs, variable costing can also be used in service companies.

Operating Income

Let's consider JR's Towing Services. The company owns a small fleet of tow trucks used to pick up cars involved in accidents or mechanical breakdowns. The cars are delivered to local repair shops.

JR's Towing has the following accounts:

Account	Description
Towing Revenue	Amount billed to customers for towing services
Truck Expense	Variable costs to operate tow trucks, including gas and maintenance
Driver Expense	Variable costs for drivers' wages
Depreciation Expense	Fixed costs for depreciation on the tow trucks
Shop Expense	Fixed costs for rent and utilities on the shop where trucks are stored when not in use

The income statement in contribution margin format for JR's Towing Services for 2018 is shown in Exhibit 21-16.

Exhibit 21-16 | **JR's Towing Services—Income Statement**

JR'S TOWING SERVICES Income Statement Year Ended December 31, 2018		
Towing Revenue		$ 202,500
Variable Costs:		
Truck Expense	$ 33,000	
Driver Expense	66,000	
Total Variable Costs		99,000
Contribution Margin		103,500
Fixed Costs:		
Depreciation Expense	40,000	
Shop Expense	12,000	
Total Fixed Costs		52,000
Operating Income		$ 51,500

By separating costs by behavior, fixed and variable, the company can calculate the contribution margin ratio by dividing the contribution margin by revenues:

$$\text{Contribution Margin Ratio} = \text{Contribution Margin / Towing Revenue}$$
$$= \$103{,}500 / \$202{,}500$$
$$= 51.11\%^*$$

*rounded

At the level of services provided, in 2018 the company is operating well above the breakeven point and is able to cover the fixed costs and also generate profits.

Profitability Analysis

JR's Towing Services has analyzed its data and determined it can separate the data into two business segments—city and county. Towing services provided within the city limits are shorter routes and take less time, whereas towing services provided outside the city limits are longer routes and take more time. Also, due to busier streets and more accidents, the company tows more cars within the city limits. A revised income statement by business segment is shown in Exhibit 21-17.

Exhibit 21-17 | **JR's Towing Services — Income Statement, by Business Segment**

	City	County	Total
Towing Jobs	1,500 jobs	1,200 jobs	2,700 jobs
Towing Revenue	$ 112,500	$ 90,000	$ 202,500
Variable Costs:			
Truck Expense	15,000	18,000	33,000
Driver Expense	30,000	36,000	66,000
Contribution Margin	$ 67,500	$ 36,000	$ 103,500
Fixed Costs:			
Depreciation Expense			40,000
Shop Expense			12,000
Operating Income			$ 51,500
Contribution Margin Ratio	60.00%	40.00%	51.11%

Notice that the fixed costs are listed only in the Total column. These costs are considered common costs, not segment costs. The company will incur these costs even if there are changes in the two business segments; therefore, they are not relevant to the analysis. However, by separating revenues and variable costs by business segment, we can see that the city jobs are much more profitable, with a 60% contribution margin ratio compared with 40% for county jobs. The next step is to determine why the segments have different contribution margin ratios.

Contribution Margin Analysis

To explain why the two business segments have different contribution margin ratios, let's take the total amounts and expand them into their two components—units and amount per unit—by dividing the totals by the number of units. Exhibit 21-18 shows the expanded statements.

Exhibit 21-18 | **Expanded Contribution Margin Analysis—JR's Towing Services**

CITY	Total	Jobs	Amount per Job
Towing Revenue	$ 112,500	1,500 jobs	$ 75
Variable Costs:			
Truck Expense	15,000	1,500 jobs	10
Driver Expense	30,000	1,500 jobs	20
Contribution Margin	$ 67,500	1,500 jobs	$ 45
Contribution Margin Ratio	60%		60%

COUNTY	Total	Jobs	Amount per Job
Towing Revenue	$ 90,000	1,200 jobs	$ 75
Variable Costs:			
Truck Expense	18,000	1,200 jobs	15
Driver Expense	36,000	1,200 jobs	30
Contribution Margin	$ 36,000	1,200 jobs	$ 30
Contribution Margin Ratio	40%		40%

We can now see that the change in contribution margin was the result of higher variable costs for the county jobs, which require longer trips and therefore cost more in gas and drivers' wages. The variable costs for city jobs are $30 ($10 + $20), while the variable costs for county jobs are $45 ($15 + $30). However, JR's Towing Services charges customers the same amount per job, $75. Based on this analysis, management should consider a different fee schedule for jobs outside the city limits.

4. Chaney Company provides lawn care services. Following are data for a recent week:

Service Revenue	$ 1,300
Variable Costs	780
Contribution Margin	$ 520

Chaney provided service to 25 customers during the week. Determine the average amount the company charged each customer, the variable cost per customer, and the contribution margin ratio.

Check your answers online in MyAccountingLab or at http://www.pearsonhighered.com/Horngren.

For more practice, see Short Exercise S21-12. MyAccountingLab

REVIEW

> Things You Should Know

1. How does variable costing differ from absorption costing?

- Absorption costing assigns all production costs to products: direct materials, direct labor, variable manufacturing overhead, and fixed manufacturing overhead.
- Variable costing assigns only the variable production costs to products: direct materials, direct labor, and variable manufacturing overhead. Fixed manufacturing overhead is considered a period cost.

2. How does operating income differ between variable costing and absorption costing?

- When production equals sales, the operating income is the same for both absorption costing and variable costing.
- When production exceeds sales, operating income using absorption costing is greater than when using variable costing.
- When production is less than sales, operating income using absorption costing is less than when using variable costing.

3. How can variable costing be used for decision making in a manufacturing company?

- In most short-term decisions, it is usually appropriate to use variable costing, whereas absorption costing is usually appropriate in most long-term decisions.
- Variable costing can be used in the following types of decisions:
  - Setting sales prices
  - Controlling costs
  - Planning production
  - Analyzing profitability
  - Analyzing contribution margin

4. How can variable costing be used for decision making in a service company?

- Variable costing can also be used in service companies, especially in making short-term decisions.
- In service companies, variable costing can be used for:
  - Profitability analysis
  - Contribution margin analysis

> Check Your Understanding

Check your understanding of the chapter by completing this problem and then looking at the solution. Use this practice to help identify which sections of the chapter you need to study more.

Limonade incurs the following costs for its powdered sports beverage mix in March 2018:

Direct materials cost per case	$	8.00 per case
Direct labor cost per case		3.00 per case
Variable manufacturing overhead cost per case		2.00 per case
Variable selling and administrative costs		0.50 per case
Total fixed manufacturing overhead costs		50,000.00 per month
Total fixed selling and administrative costs		25,000.00 per month
Sales price per case		25.00 per case
Cases of powdered mix produced		10,000 cases
Cases of powdered mix sold		8,000 cases

There were no beginning inventories, so Limonade has 2,000 cases of powdered mix in ending Finished Goods Inventory (10,000 cases produced − 8,000 cases sold).

Requirements

1. What is Limonade's product cost per case under absorption costing and variable costing? (See Learning Objective 1)

2. Prepare income statements for Limonade for March 2018 using absorption costing and variable costing. (See Learning Objective 2)

3. Calculate the balance in Finished Goods Inventory on March 31, 2018, using absorption costing and variable costing. (See Learning Objective 2)

4. Reconcile the differences between the operating incomes and Finished Goods Inventory balances between the two costing methods. (See Learning Objective 2)

> Solution

Requirement 1

		Absorption Costing	Variable Costing
Direct materials		$ 8.00	$ 8.00
Direct labor		3.00	3.00
Variable manufacturing overhead		2.00	2.00
Fixed manufacturing overhead	($50,000 / 10,000 cases)	5.00	
Total unit product cost		$ 18.00	$ 13.00

Requirement 2

Absorption Costing

Net Sales Revenue	(8,000 cases × $25.00 per case)	$ 200,000
Cost of Goods Sold	(8,000 cases × $18.00 per case)	144,000
Gross Profit		56,000
Selling and Administrative Costs:		
Variable S&A Costs	(8,000 cases × $0.50 per case) $ 4,000	
Fixed S&A Costs	25,000	29,000
Operating Income		$ 27,000

Variable Costing

Net Sales Revenue	(8,000 cases × $25.00 per case)	$ 200,000
Variable Manufacturing Costs	(8,000 cases × $13.00 per case) $ 104,000	
Variable S&A Costs	(8,000 cases × $0.50 per case) 4,000	108,000
Contribution Margin		92,000
Fixed Costs:		
Fixed Manufacturing Costs	50,000	
Fixed S&A Costs	25,000	75,000
Operating Income		$ 17,000

Requirement 3

Finished Goods Inventory balance, March 31, 2018:

Absorption Costing: 2,000 cases × $18.00 per case = $36,000

Variable Costing: 2,000 cases × $13.00 per case = $26,000

Requirement 4

	Absorption Costing	Variable Costing	Difference
Operating Income	$ 27,000	$ 17,000	$ 10,000
Finished Goods Inventory	36,000	26,000	10,000

The $10,000 difference is the $5 per unit of fixed manufacturing cost assigned to the unsold units and not expensed by absorption costing. $5 per unit × 2,000 unsold units = $10,000.

> Key Terms

Absorption Costing (p. 1143)

Business Segment (p. 1154)

Contribution Margin (p. 1143)

Contribution Margin Ratio (p. 1154)

Variable Costing (p. 1143)

> Quick Check

1. The primary difference between variable costing and absorption costing is
   Learning Objective 1

   a. in variable costing, fixed manufacturing overhead is a product cost.
   b. in absorption costing, fixed manufacturing overhead is a product cost.
   c. in variable costing, variable selling and administrative costs are product costs.
   d. in absorption costing, fixed selling and administrative costs are product costs.

2. Winters, Inc. is preparing financial statements to be distributed to investors and creditors. The company should prepare the income statement using
   Learning Objective 1

   a. variable costing because it is better for planning purposes.
   b. variable costing because it follows GAAP.
   c. absorption costing because it is better for controlling purposes.
   d. absorption costing because it follows GAAP.

Use the following data for questions 3–7:

Donovan Company incurred the following costs while producing 500 units: direct materials, $10 per unit; direct labor, $25 per unit; variable manufacturing overhead, $15 per unit; total fixed manufacturing overhead costs, $10,000; variable selling and administrative costs, $5 per unit; total fixed selling and administrative costs, $7,500. There are no beginning inventories.

3. What is the unit product cost using variable costing?
   Learning Objective 1

   a. $50 per unit   c. $70 per unit
   b. $55 per unit   d. $90 per unit

4. What is the unit product cost using absorption costing?
   Learning Objective 1

   a. $50 per unit   c. $70 per unit
   b. $55 per unit   d. $90 per unit

5. What is the operating income using absorption costing if 500 units are sold for $100 each?
   Learning Objective 2

   a. $500   c. $2,750
   b. $2,500   d. $5,000

6. What is the operating income using variable costing if 450 units are sold for $100 each?
   Learning Objective 2

   a. $2,750   c. $500
   b. $5,000   d. $2,500

7. What is the ending balance in Finished Goods Inventory using variable costing if 450 units are sold?
   Learning Objective 2

   a. $2,000   c. $2,750
   b. $2,500   d. $3,500

Use the following data for questions 8–9:

Sammie's Pizza sells an average of 150 pizzas per week, of which 20% are single-topping pizzas and 80% are supreme pizzas with multiple toppings. Singles sell for $8 each and incur variable costs of $2. Supremes sell for $12 each and incur variable costs of $6.

Learning Objective 3

8. The contribution margin per unit and total contribution margin for Singles and Supremes are:

	Singles		Supremes	
	Contribution Margin per Unit	Total Contribution Margin	Contribution Margin per Unit	Total Contribution Margin
a.	$6	$720	$6	$180
b.	$6	$180	$6	$720
c.	$6	$240	$6	$360
d.	$6	$180	$6	$180

Learning Objective 3

9. Which pizza should Sammie's Pizza promote to maximize profits?
   a. Singles because they contribute the highest total contribution margin.
   b. Supremes because they have the highest contribution margin ratio.
   c. Singles because they have the highest contribution margin ratio.
   d. Both should be promoted equally because they have the same contribution margin per unit.

Learning Objective 4

10. During a recent month, Cleveland Company planned to provide cleaning services to 30 customers for $25 per hour. Each job was expected to take 3 hours. The company actually served 10 more customers than expected, but the average time spent on each job was only 2.5 hours each. Cleveland's revenues for the month were
    a. $250 more than expected.
    b. $250 less than expected.
    c. $750 more than expected.
    d. Cannot be determined from data given

Check your answers at the end of the chapter.

ASSESS YOUR PROGRESS

> Review Questions

1. What is absorption costing?
2. What is variable costing?
3. How are absorption costing and variable costing the same? How are they different?
4. When units produced equal units sold, how does operating income differ between variable costing and absorption costing?
5. When units produced exceed units sold, how does operating income differ between variable costing and absorption costing? Why?
6. When units produced are less than units sold, how does operating income differ between variable costing and absorption costing? Why?
7. Explain why the fixed manufacturing overhead cost per unit changes when there is a change in the number of units produced.

8. Explain how increasing production can increase gross profit when using absorption costing.

9. When should a company use absorption costing when setting sales prices? When should it use variable costing?

10. In the long run, all costs are controllable. Is this statement true? Why or why not?

11. Why is it appropriate to use variable costing when planning production in the short term?

12. What is a business segment? Give some examples.

13. Explain how sales mix can affect the profitability of a company.

14. What are the two components that can affect contribution margin? Why is it important to investigate both?

15. How do service companies differ from manufacturing companies?

16. How can variable costing be used in service companies?

> Short Exercises

S21-1 Classifying costs

Classify each cost by placing an X in the appropriate columns. The first cost is completed as an example.

Learning Objective 1

	Absorption Costing		Variable Costing	
	Product Cost	Period Cost	Product Cost	Period Cost
a. Direct materials	X		X	
b. Direct labor				
c. Variable manufacturing overhead				
d. Fixed manufacturing overhead				
e. Variable selling and administrative costs				
f. Fixed selling and administrative costs				

Use the following information for Short Exercises S21-2 and S21-3.

Martin Company had the following costs:

Units produced	320 units
Direct materials	$ 71 per unit
Direct labor	40 per unit
Variable manufacturing overhead	13 per unit
Fixed manufacturing overhead	7,360 per year
Variable selling and administrative costs	22 per unit
Fixed selling and administrative costs	1,920 per year

S21-2 Computing unit product cost, absorption costing

Learning Objective 1

Calculate the unit product cost using absorption costing. Round your answer to the nearest cent.

Learning Objective 1

S21-3 Computing unit product cost, variable costing

Calculate the unit product cost using variable costing. Round your answer to the nearest cent.

Use the following information for Short Exercises S21-4 and S21-5.

Dracut Company reports the following information for June:

Net Sales Revenue	$ 755,000
Variable Cost of Goods Sold	240,000
Fixed Cost of Goods Sold	198,000
Variable Selling and Administrative Costs	168,000
Fixed Selling and Administrative Costs	79,000

Learning Objective 2

S21-4 Calculating contribution margin and operating income, variable costing

Calculate the contribution margin and operating income for June using variable costing.

Learning Objective 2

S21-5 Calculating gross profit and operating income, absorption costing

Calculate the gross profit and operating income for June using absorption costing.

Learning Objective 2

S21-6 Computing absorption cost per unit and variable cost per unit

Adamson, Inc. has the following cost data for Product X:

Direct materials	$	41 per unit
Direct labor		57 per unit
Variable manufacturing overhead		7 per unit
Fixed manufacturing overhead		20,000 per year

Calculate the unit product cost using absorption costing and variable costing when production is 2,000 units, 2,500 units, and 5,000 units.

Note: Short Exercise S21-6 must be completed before attempting Short Exercise S21-7.

Learning Objective 2

S21-7 Computing absorption costing gross profit

Refer to your answers to Short Exercise S21-6. Product X sells for $175 per unit. Assume no beginning inventories. Calculate the gross profit using absorption costing when Adamson:

a. Produces and sells 2,000 units.

b. Produces 2,500 units and sells 2,000 units

c. Produces 5,000 units and sells 2,000 units.

Note: Short Exercise S21-6 must be completed before attempting Short Exercise S21-8.

Learning Objective 2

S21-8 Computing variable costing contributon margin

Refer to your answers to Short Exercise S21-6. Product X sells for $175 per unit. Assume no beginning inventories. Calculate the contribution margin using variable costing when Adamson:

a. Produces and sells 2,000 units.

b. Produces 2,500 units and sells 2,000 units

c. Produces 5,000 units and sells 2,000 units.

S21-9 Computing inventory balances

Learning Objective 2

Zeng Company reports the following data:

Finished Goods Inventory:	
Beginning balance, in units	300
Units produced	2,900
Units sold	(1,600)
Ending balance, in units	1,600
Production Costs:	
Variable manufacturing costs per unit	$ 57
Total fixed manufacturing costs	26,100

Calculate the product cost per unit and the total cost of the 1,600 units in ending inventory using absorption costing and variable costing.

S21-10 Analyzing profitability

Learning Objective 3

Camden Company has divided its business into segments based on sales territories: East Coast, Midland, and West Coast. Following are financial data for 2018:

	East Coast	Midland	West Coast
Units sold	71	69	53
Sales price per unit	$ 10,300	$ 13,600	$ 12,000
Variable cost per unit	6,283	7,072	7,080

Prepare an income statement for Camden Company for 2018 using the contribution margin format assuming total fixed costs for the company were $435,000. Include columns for each business segment and a column for the total company.

Note: Short Exercise S21-10 must be completed before attempting Short Exercise S21-11.

S21-11 Analyzing profitability

Learning Objective 3

Refer to Short Exercise S21-10. Which business segment provided the greatest total contribution margin? Which business segment had the highest contribution margin ratio?

S21-12 Analyzing profitability analysis, service company

Learning Objective 4

Burlington Internet Services is an Internet service provider for commercial and residential customers. The company provided the following data for its two types of customers for the month of August:

	Commercial	Residential	Total
Number of Customers	200	600	800
Service Revenue	$ 32,000	$ 72,000	$ 104,000
Variable Costs	8,320	27,360	35,680
Contribution Margin	23,680	44,640	68,320
Fixed Costs			53,000
Operating Income			$ 15,320

For each type of customer, determine both the contribution margin per customer and the contribution margin ratio. Round to two decimal places. Which type of service is more profitable?

> Exercises

Learning Objectives 1, 2

2. CM $18,800

E21-13 Using absorption and variable costing

Meyer Company reports the following information for March:

Net Sales Revenue	$ 45,300
Variable Cost of Goods Sold	12,500
Fixed Cost of Goods Sold	11,800
Variable Selling and Administrative Costs	14,000
Fixed Selling and Administrative Costs	5,400

Requirements

1. Calculate the gross profit and operating income for March using absorption costing.
2. Calculate the contribution margin and operating income for March using variable costing.

Use the following information for Exercises E21-14 and E21-15.

Concord, Inc. has collected the following data for November (there are no beginning inventories):

Units produced and sold		500 units
Sales price	$	450 per unit
Direct materials		64 per unit
Direct labor		68 per unit
Variable manufacturing overhead		26 per unit
Fixed manufacturing overhead		7,500 per month
Variable selling and administrative costs		15 per unit
Fixed selling and administrative costs		4,400 per month

Learning Objectives 1, 2

1. $173.00

E21-14 Computing absorption costing operating income

Refer to the information for Concord, Inc.

Requirements

1. Using absorption costing, calculate the unit product cost.
2. Prepare an income statement using the traditional format.

Learning Objectives 1, 2

2. CM $138,500

E21-15 Computing variable costing operating income

Refer to the information for Concord, Inc.

Requirements

1. Using variable costing, calculate the unit product cost.
2. Prepare an income statement using the contribution margin format.

E21-16 Preparing variable costing income statements, production exceeds sales

ReVitalAde produced 13,000 cases of powdered drink mix and sold 12,000 cases in April 2018. The sales price was $29, variable costs were $12 per case ($9 manufacturing and $3 selling and administrative), and total fixed costs were $100,000 ($91,000 manufacturing overhead and $9,000 selling and administrative). The company had no beginning Finished Goods Inventory.

Requirements

1. Prepare the April income statement using variable costing.
2. Determine the product cost per unit and the total cost of the 1,000 cases in Finished Goods Inventory as of April 30.

Note: Exercise E21-16 must be completed before attempting Exercise E21-17.

E21-17 Preparing absorption costing income statements, production exceeds sales

Refer to Exercise E21-16.

Requirements

1. Prepare the April income statement using absorption costing.
2. Determine the product cost per unit and the total cost of the 1,000 cases in Finished Goods Inventory as of April 30.
3. Is the April 30 balance in Finished Goods Inventory higher or lower than variable costing? Explain why.

Note: Exercises E21-16 and E21-17 must be completed before attempting Exercise E21-18.

E21-18 Comparing variable and absorption costing

Refer to Exercises E21-16 and E21-17.

Requirements

1. Which costing method produces the highest operating income? Explain why.
2. Which costing method produces the highest April 30 balance in Finished Goods Inventory? Explain why.

Note: Exercise E21-16 must be completed before attempting Exercise E21-19.

E21-19 Preparing variable costing income statements, production less than sales

Refer to your answers to Exercise E21-16. In May 2018, ReVitalAde produced 22,000 cases of powdered drink mix and sold 23,000 cases, of which 1,000 were produced in April. The sales price was $29, variable costs were $12 per case ($9 manufacturing and $3 selling and administrative), and total fixed costs were $100,000 ($91,000 manufacturing and $9,000 selling and administrative).

Requirements

1. Prepare the May income statement using variable costing.
2. Determine the balance in Finished Goods Inventory as of May 31.

Learning Objectives 1, 2

2. FG $9,000

Learning Objectives 1, 2

1. OI $111,000

Learning Objectives 1, 2

Learning Objectives 1, 2

1. CM $391,000

Note: Exercise E21-19 must be completed before attempting Exercise E21-20.

Learning Objectives 1, 2

E21-20 Preparing absorption costing income statements, production less than sales

1. OI $284,000

Refer to Exercise E21-19.

Requirements

1. Prepare the May income statement using absorption costing.
2. Is operating income using absorption costing higher or lower than variable costing income? Explain why.
3. Determine the balance in Finished Goods Inventory as of May 31.

Learning Objective 3

E21-21 Setting sales prices

The Sweet Treats Company manufactures candy that is sold to food distributors. The company produces at full capacity for six months each year to meet peak demand during the "candy season" from Halloween through Valentine's Day. During the other six months of the year, the manufacturing facility operates at 75% of capacity. The Sweet Treats Company provides the following data for the year:

Cases of candy produced and sold	1,800,000 cases
Sales price	$ 37.00 per case
Variable manufacturing costs	20.00 per case
Fixed manufacturing costs	6,400,000 per year
Variable selling and administrative costs	2.00 per case
Fixed selling and administrative costs	3,500,000 per year

The Sweet Treats Company receives an offer to produce 13,000 cases of candy for a special event. This is a one-time opportunity during a period when the company has excess capacity. What is the minimum sales price The Sweet Treats Company should accept for the order? Explain why.

Learning Objective 3

E21-22 Analyzing profitability

Total CM $17,150

Sampler Company sells two products, Sigma and Zeta, with a sales mix of 70% and 30%, respectively. Sigma has a contribution margin per unit of $26, and Zeta has a contribution margin per unit of $21. The company sold 700 total units in September. Calculate the total amount each product contributed to the coverage of fixed costs and the total contribution margin for the company.

Note: Exercise E21-22 must be completed before attempting Exercise E21-23.

Learning Objective 3

E21-23 Analyzing profitability

Total CM $16,450

Refer to Exercise E21-22. Assume the sales mix shifted to 50% for each product. Calculate the total amount each product contributed to the coverage of fixed costs and the total contribution margin for the company.

Learning Objective 4

E21-24 Using variable costing, service company

VC at 220 Svc Calls $14,960

Henry's Helpers provides locksmith services. One type of service call is to evaluate private residences for security concerns and make recommendations for a safety plan. Use the data below to determine the company's total contribution margin, contribution margin per service call, and contribution margin ratio when 220 service calls are made in the month of June.

Service Revenue	$ 170 per service call
Variable Costs	68 per service call
Fixed Costs	21,040 per month

E21-25 Using variable costing, service company

Sherman Company provides carpet cleaning services to commercial and residential customers. Using the data below, determine the contribution margin ratio for each business segment, rounded to two decimal places:

Learning Objective 4

CMR for Residential 76%

	Commercial	Residential	Total
Service Revenue	$ 140,000	$ 240,000	$ 380,000
Variable Costs	63,000	57,600	120,600
Contribution Margin	77,000	182,400	259,400
Fixed Costs			15,000
Operating Income			$ 244,400

Note: Exercise E21-25 must be completed before attempting Exercise E21-26.

E21-26 Using variable costing, service company

Refer to Exercise E21-25. The commercial business segment provided services to 200 customers. The residential business segment provided services to 400 customers. Determine the average amount Sherman Company charged each type of customer for services, the average variable cost per customer, and the average contribution margin per customer, rounded to two decimal places. What caused the difference in contribution margin in the two segments?

Learning Objective 4

VC per Customer for Commercial $315

> Problems Group A

P21-27A Preparing variable and absorption costing income statements

Linda's Foods produces frozen meals that it sells for $7 each. The company computes a new monthly fixed manufacturing overhead allocation rate based on the planned number of meals to be produced that month. Assume all costs and production levels are exactly as planned. The following data are from Linda's Foods's first month in business:

Learning Objectives 1, 2

2b. VC $4,000

	January 2018
Units produced and sold:	
Sales	1,000 meals
Production	1,200 meals
Variable manufacturing cost per meal	$ 3
Sales commission cost per meal	1
Total fixed manufacturing overhead	660
Total fixed selling and administrative costs	500

Requirements

1. Compute the product cost per meal produced under absorption costing and under variable costing.
2. Prepare income statements for January 2018 using:
   a. absorption costing.
   b. variable costing.
3. Is operating income higher under absorption costing or variable costing in January?

Learning Objectives 1, 2

1. Absorption costing $19.00

P21-28A Preparing variable and absorption costing income statements

Game Store manufactures video games that it sells for $38 each. The company uses a fixed manufacturing overhead allocation rate of $3 per game. Assume all costs and production levels are exactly as planned. The following data are from Game Store's first two months in business during 2018:

	October	November
Sales	1,500 units	2,900 units
Production	2,800 units	2,800 units
Variable manufacturing cost per game	$ 16	$ 16
Sales commission cost per game	8	8
Total fixed manufacturing overhead	8,400	8,400
Total fixed selling and administrative costs	8,000	8,000

Requirements

1. Compute the product cost per game produced under absorption costing and under variable costing.

2. Prepare monthly income statements for October and November, including columns for each month and a total column, using these costing methods:

   a. absorption costing.

   b. variable costing.

3. Is operating income higher under absorption costing or variable costing in October? In November? Explain the pattern of differences in operating income based on absorption costing versus variable costing.

4. Determine the balance in Finished Goods Inventory on October 31 and November 30 under absorption costing and variable costing. Compare the differences in inventory balances and the differences in operating income. Explain the differences in inventory balances based on absorption costing versus variable costing.

Learning Objective 3

1. CMR for Abe 15.00%

P21-29A Analyzing profitability

Relative Furniture Company manufactures and sells oak tables and chairs. Price and cost data for the furniture follow:

	Tables	Chairs
Sales Price	$ 1,400	$ 50
Variable manufacturing costs	1,148	21
Sales commission (8%)	112	4

Relative Furniture has three sales representatives: Abe, Brett, and Corrin. Abe sold 50 tables with 4 chairs each. Brett sold 110 tables with 6 chairs each. Corrin sold 90 tables with 8 chairs each.

Requirements

1. Calculate the total contribution margin and the contribution margin ratio for each sales representative (round to two decimal places).

2. Which sales representative has the highest contribution margin ratio? Explain why.

P21-30A Using variable and absorption costing, making decisions

Learning Objectives 1, 2, 3

1. COGS absorption costing
$4,140,000

The 2018 data that follow pertain to Mike's Magnificent Eyewear, a manufacturer of swimming goggles. (Mike's Magnificent Eyewear had no beginning Finished Goods Inventory in January 2018.)

Number of goggles produced	245,000
Number of goggles sold	230,000
Sales price per unit	$ 28
Variable manufacturing cost per unit	10
Sales commission cost per unit	2
Fixed manufacturing overhead	1,960,000
Fixed selling and administrative costs	260,000

Requirements

1. Prepare both conventional (absorption costing) and contribution margin (variable costing) income statements for Mike's Magnificent Eyewear for the year ended December 31, 2018.

2. Which statement shows the higher operating income? Why?

3. Mike's Magnificent Eyewear's marketing vice president believes a new sales promotion that costs $40,000 would increase sales to 235,000 goggles. Should the company go ahead with the promotion? Give your reasoning.

P21-31A Using variable costing, service company

Learning Objective 4

2. VC per Customer for Frond $30

Professional Pool Cleaning Service provides pool cleaning services to residential customers. The company has three employees, each assigned to specific customers. The company considers each employee's territory as a business segment. The company incurs variable costs that include the employees' wages, pool chemicals, and gas for the service vans. Fixed costs include depreciation on the service vans. Following is the income statement for the month of July:

PROFESSIONAL POOL CLEANING SERVICE
Income Statement
For the Month Ended July 31, 2018

	Birman	Meech	Frond	Total
Service Revenue	$ 3,000	$ 3,500	$ 2,000	$ 8,500
Variable Costs	1,500	2,450	1,200	5,150
Contribution Margin	1,500	1,050	800	3,350
Fixed Costs				3,000
Operating Income				$ 350

Requirements

1. Calculate the contribution margin ratio for each business segment.

2. The business segments had the following numbers of customers: Birman, 60; Meech, 70; and Frond, 40. Compute the service revenue per customer, variable cost per customer, and contribution margin per customer for each business segment.

3. Which business segment was most profitable? List some possible reasons why this segment was most profitable. How might the various reasons affect the company in the long term?

> Problems Group B

Learning Objectives 1, 2

2a. OI $3,545

P21-32B Preparing variable and absorption costing income statements

Claudia's Foods produces frozen meals that it sells for $11 each. The company computes a new monthly fixed manufacturing overhead allocation rate based on the planned number of meals to be produced that month. Assume all costs and production levels are exactly as planned. The following data are from Claudia's Foods's first month in business:

	January 2018
Units produced and sold:	
Sales	850 meals
Production	1,050 meals
Variable manufacturing cost per meal	$ 5
Sales commission cost per meal	1
Total fixed manufacturing overhead	315
Total fixed selling and administrative costs	450

Requirements

1. Compute the product cost per meal produced under absorption costing and under variable costing.
2. Prepare income statements for January 2018 using:
   a. absorption costing.
   b. variable costing.
3. Is operating income higher under absorption costing or variable costing in January?

Learning Objectives 1, 2

2b. CM for Nov. $55,100

P21-33B Preparing variable and absorption costing income statements

Game Source manufactures video games that it sells for $43 each. The company uses a fixed manufacturing overhead allocation rate of $5 per game. Assume all costs and production levels are exactly as planned. The following data are from Game Source's first two months in business during 2018:

	October	November
Sales	1,500 units	2,900 units
Production	2,500 units	2,500 units
Variable manufacturing cost per game	$ 17	$ 17
Sales commission cost per game	7	7
Total fixed manufacturing overhead	12,500	12,500
Total fixed selling and administrative costs	11,500	11,500

Requirements

1. Compute the product cost per game produced under absorption costing and under variable costing.

2. Prepare monthly income statements for October and November, including columns for each month and a total column, using these costing methods:

   a. absorption costing.

   b. variable costing.

3. Is operating income higher under absorption costing or variable costing in October? In November? Explain the pattern of differences in operating income based on absorption costing versus variable costing.

4. Determine the balance in Finished Goods Inventory on October 31 and November 30 under absorption costing and variable costing. Compare the differences in inventory balances and the differences in operating income. Explain the differences in inventory balances based on absorption costing versus variable costing.

P21-34B Analyzing profitability

Father Furniture Company manufactures and sells oak tables and chairs. Price and cost data for the furniture follow:

	Tables	Chairs
Sales Price	$ 800	$ 70
Variable manufacturing costs	600	25
Sales commission (10%)	80	7

Learning Objective 3

1. CM for Caleb $33,920

Father Furniture has three sales representatives: Adam, Ben, and Caleb. Adam sold 100 tables with 6 chairs each. Ben sold 110 tables with 4 chairs each. Caleb sold 80 tables with 8 chairs each.

Requirements

1. Calculate the total contribution margin and the contribution margin ratio for each sales representative (round to two decimal places).

2. Which sales representative has the highest contribution margin ratio? Explain why.

P21-35B Using variable and absorption costing, making decisions

The 2018 data that follow pertain to Eli's Electric Eyewear, a manufacturer of swimming goggles. (Eli's Electric Eyewear had no beginning Finished Goods Inventory in January 2018.)

Learning Objectives 1, 2, 3

1. FC variable costing $1,720,000

Number of goggles produced	245,000
Number of goggles sold	215,000
Sales price per unit	$ 22
Variable manufacturing cost per unit	8
Sales commission cost per unit	5
Fixed manufacturing overhead	1,470,000
Fixed selling and administrative costs	250,000

Requirements

1. Prepare both conventional (absorption costing) and contribution margin (variable costing) income statements for Eli's Electric Eyewear for the year ended December 31, 2018.

2. Which statement shows the higher operating income? Why?

3. Eli's Electric Eyewear's marketing vice president believes a new sales promotion that costs $60,000 would increase sales to 220,000 goggles. Should the company go ahead with the promotion? Give your reasoning.

Learning Objective 4

1. CMR Moore 70%

P21-36B Using variable costing, service company

Divine Pool Cleaning Service provides pool cleaning services to residential customers. The company has three employees, each assigned to specific customers. The company considers each employee's territory as a business segment. The company incurs variable costs that include the employees' wages, pool chemicals, and gas for the service vans. Fixed costs include depreciation on the service vans. Following is the income statement for the month of August:

DIVINE POOL CLEANING SERVICE Income Statement For the Month Ended August 31, 2018				
	Byson	**Moore**	**Freeman**	**Total**
Service Revenue	$ 8,800	$ 5,500	$ 12,100	$ 26,400
Variable Costs	5,280	1,650	8,470	15,400
Contribution Margin	3,520	3,850	3,630	11,000
Fixed Costs				5,500
Operating Income				$ 5,500

Requirements

1. Calculate the contribution margin ratio for each business segment.

2. The business segments had the following number of customers: Byson, 80; Moore, 50; and Freeman, 110. Compute the service revenue per customer, variable cost per customer, and contribution margin per customer for each business segment.

3. Which business segment was most profitable? List some possible reasons why this segment was most profitable. How might the various reasons affect the company in the long term?

CRITICAL THINKING

> Using Excel

P21-37 Using Excel for variable costing

Download an Excel template for this problem online in MyAccountingLab or at http://www.pearsonhighered.com/Horngren.

Tiger Mountain Gelato incurs the following costs for its premium ice cream in May 2018:

Direct materials cost per pint	$ 2.50 per pint
Direct labor cost per pint	0.75 per pint
Variable manufacturing overhead cost per pint	0.25 per pint
Fixed manufacturing overhead costs	6,000 per month
Total fixed selling and administrative costs	5,000 per month
Sales price per pint	8.00 per pint
Pints of gelato produced	12,000 pints
Pints of gelato sold	11,500 pints

There were no beginning inventories, so Tiger Mountain Gelato has 500 pints in ending Finished Goods Inventory (12,000 pints produced less 11,500 pints sold).

Requirements

1. Calculate Tiger Mountain Gelato's product cost per pint under absorption costing and variable costing.

2. Calculate the balance in Finished Goods Inventory on May 31, 2018, using absorption costing and variable costing.

3. Prepare income statements in good form for Tiger Mountain Gelato for May 2018 using absorption costing and variable costing.

4. Reconcile the differences between operating incomes and Finished Goods Inventory balances between the two costing methods.

> Continuing Problem

P21-38 Preparing variable and absorption costing income statements

This problem continues the Piedmont Computer Problem situation from Chapter 20. Piedmont Computer Company manufactures personal computers and tablets. Based on the latest information from the cost accountant, using the current sales mix, the weighted-average sales price per unit is $750 and the weighed-average variable cost per unit is $450. The company does not expect the sales mix to vary for the next year. Assume the beginning balance in Finished Goods Inventory is $0. Additional data for the first month of 2020:

	January 2020
Units produced and sold:	
Sales	945 units
Production	1,000 units
Variable manufacturing cost per unit	$ 450
Sales commission cost per unit	25
Total fixed manufacturing overhead	93,600
Total fixed selling and administrative costs	62,400

Requirements

1. Compute the product cost per unit produced under absorption costing and under variable costing.

2. Prepare income statements for January 2020 using:

   a. absorption costing.

   b. variable costing.

3. Is operating income higher under absorption costing or variable costing in January? What causes the difference?

> Tying It All Together Case 21-1

Before you begin this assignment, review the Tying It All Together feature in the chapter.

CF Industries Holdings, Inc. is one of the largest manufacturers and distributors of nitrogen fertilizer and other nitrogen products in the world. The corporation often produces and stores large amounts of inventory during periods of low demand to ensure that there is enough product to meet the demand of peak seasons. Assume that one line of fertilizer (with no beginning Finished Goods Inventory) had the following data during a time period of low demand:

Sales price	$ 20.00 per case
Variable manufacturing costs	4.00 per case
Fixed manufacturing costs	100,000 per quarter
Variable selling and administrative costs	2.00 per case
Fixed selling and administrative costs	45,000 per quarter

Given that the time period has low demand, assume the company produced 1,000,000 cases but only sold 250,000 cases.

Requirement

1. Prepare the income statement for the quarter using variable costing.

2. Prepare the income statement for the quarter using absorption costing.

3. Why, if at all, is there a difference between operating income under the two methods?

> Decision Case 21-1

The Hurley Hat Company manufactures baseball hats. Hurley's primary customers are sporting goods stores that supply uniforms to youth baseball teams. Following is Hurley's income statement for 2018:

HURLEY HAT COMPANY Income Statement Year Ended December 31, 2018	
Net Sales Revenue	$ 1,500,000
Cost of Goods Sold	700,000
Gross Profit	800,000
Selling and Administrative Expenses	500,000
Operating Income	$ 300,000

In 2018, Hurley produced and sold 200,000 baseball hats. Of the Cost of Goods Sold, $150,000 is fixed; 80% of the Selling and Administrative Expenses are fixed. There were no beginning inventories on January 1, 2018. The company is considering two options to increase sales.

Option 1: The company is operating at 100,000 hats below full production capacity and is considering increasing advertising to increase sales to the production capacity level in 2019. The marketing director predicts that an additional $100,000 expenditure for advertising would increase sales to 300,000 hats per year.

Option 2: The sales manager has been negotiating with buyers for several national sporting goods retailers and recommends the company expand production capacity to 400,000 hats in order to secure long-term contracts beginning in 2019. The expansion is expected to increase fixed manufacturing costs by $200,000 per year. Additionally, the retailers are requesting a higher-quality hat, and the changes to the hat materials and manufacturing process would increase variable manufacturing costs by $1 per hat for the additional 200,000 hats. (The original 200,000 hats manufactured and sold would not be affected by this change.)

Requirements

1. Use the data from the 2018 income statement to prepare an income statement using variable costing. Assume no beginning or ending inventories. Calculate the contribution margin ratio. Round to two decimal places.

2. Prepare an absorption costing income statement assuming the company pursues Option 1 and increases advertising and production and sales increase to 300,000 hats.

3. Refer to the original data. Prepare an absorption costing income statement assuming the company pursues Option 2 and increases capacity and sales and production increases to 400,000 total hats.

4. Which option should the company pursue? Explain your reasoning.

> Ethical Issue 21-1

Sampson Company operates a manufacturing facility where several products are made. Each product is considered a business segment, and the product managers have the opportunity to receive a bonus based on the profit of the segment. Franco Hopper is the manager for the scissors product line. Production and sales data for the scissors product line for the past three years are shown below:

	Year 1	Year 2	Year 3
Units produced	100,000 units	125,000 units	160,000 units
Units sold	100,000 units	100,000 units	100,000 units
Sales price per unit	$ 12.00 per unit	$ 12.00 per unit	$ 12.00 per unit
Variable manufacturing cost per unit	5.00 per unit	5.00 per unit	5.00 per unit
Total fixed manufacturing costs	200,000 per year	200,000 per year	200,000 per year

Hopper's bonus is 0.5% of the gross profit of the scissors product line, based on absorption costing. Upper management is discussing changing the bonus system so that bonuses are based on operating income using variable costing. Hopper is opposed to this change and has been trying to convince the other product mangers to join him in voicing their opposition. There are no beginning inventories in Year 1.

Requirements

1. Calculate the fixed cost per unit produced for each year.
2. Prepare income statements for the three years using absorption costing.
3. Calculate Hopper's bonus based on the current plan.
4. Prepare income statements for the three years using variable costing.
5. Calculate Hopper's bonus based on the proposed plan.
6. Give possible reasons why Hopper is opposed to the proposed bonus plan. Do you think Hopper's actions have been ethical the past three years? Why or why not?

> Communication Activity 21-1

In 100 words or fewer, explain the main differences and similarities between variable costing and absorption costing.

MyAccountingLab   **For a wealth of online resources, including exercises, problems, media, and immediate tutorial help, please visit** http://www.myaccountinglab.com.

> Quick Check Answers

1. b **2.** d **3.** a **4.** c **5.** d **6.** a **7.** b **8.** b **9.** d **10.** a

Master Budgets

How Can a Budget Help My Division?

Hanna Kendall sat down at her desk with anticipation. Hanna, the newly promoted manager of her division at B&T Manufacturing, was ready to begin preparing the budget for the next year. At the last B&T division managers' meeting, most of the other managers were grumbling about the process. No one else seemed to like the task, but Hanna felt differently. She remembered from her managerial accounting class that budgeting can have many benefits. When used appropriately, budgets help managers plan, direct, and control activities for their divisions by providing guidance and benchmarks for the budgeting period. Hanna considered the budget to be a road map of sorts for her division—a way to know the direction in which the division should progress and a way to determine whether the division met its goals.

Hanna considered how to begin the process. She knew she needed to study last year's budget prepared by the previous manager, compare it to actual results to see which goals had been met, and consider outside influences such as the economic conditions for B&T's industry. Hanna also wanted to get input from her employees to ensure the goals set for the division were realistic, obtainable, and a source of motivation. Hanna had seen budgets used to punish employees when budget goals were set at an unobtainable level, but she was not that type of manager. Hanna wanted high morale in her division, with everyone working toward the same goals.

What Is a Budget?

A *budget* is a financial plan that managers use to coordinate the business's activities. All types of companies can benefit from using budgets, including nonprofit organizations such as **San Diego Zoo**, which is committed to saving species worldwide through animal care and conservation science; merchandising companies such as PetSmart, Inc., which sells pet supplies; and manufacturing companies such as Nestlé Purina PetCare Company, which manufactures pet products. There are many different types of budgets. Some are for short-term use, and others are for long-term use. Budgets help managers plan for the future, track the progress of their business segments, and take corrective action as needed. Budgeting is an extremely important management tool. In this chapter, we focus on the purposes and types of budgets and the development of one type of budget—the master budget. In later chapters, we focus on how managers can use budgets to control business activities.

Chapter 22 Learning Objectives

1 Describe budgeting objectives, benefits, and procedures and how human behavior influences budgeting

2 Define budget types and the components of the master budget

3 Prepare an operating budget for a manufacturing company

4 Prepare a financial budget for a manufacturing company

5 Prepare an operating budget for a merchandising company

6 Prepare a financial budget for a merchandising company

7 Describe how information technology can be used in the budgeting process

WHY DO MANAGERS USE BUDGETS?

Learning Objective 1

Describe budgeting objectives, benefits, and procedures and how human behavior influences budgeting

The concept of budgeting is most likely familiar to you. Financial decisions, large and small, require some type of planning. For example, as you decide whether to rent an apartment or buy a house, repair your older vehicle or buy a new one, cook at home or eat out, you are considering your financial situation. Perhaps you decide to cook at home in order to save for a down payment on a house, which indicates you have a financial plan to meet your goals. For many people, however, budgeting is not a formal process where plans are written and carefully followed. This failure to formalize the plans often results in a failure to achieve financial goals.

Companies use budgets for the same reasons as you do in your personal life—to plan, direct, and control actions and the related revenues and expenses. Companies also use budgets to meet their goals. As part of long-term planning, companies develop a corporate strategy and set goals to meet their objectives. These goals will be integrated into the budgeting process to ensure that the company achieves its long-term strategy.

Budgeting Objectives

Budget

A financial plan that managers use to coordinate a business's activities with its goals and strategies.

A **budget** is a financial plan that managers use to coordinate a business's activities with its goals and strategies. Managers use budgets in fulfilling their major responsibilities. First, they develop strategies—overall business goals, such as a goal to expand international operations or a goal to be a value leader in one market while diversifying into other markets. Companies then plan and budget for specific actions to achieve those goals. The next step is to direct the company on how to act, or, in other words, how to carry out the plans.

After acting, managers compare actual results with the budget and use the information to make control decisions. The feedback allows them to determine what, if any, corrective action to take. If, for example, the company spent more than expected in one area of operations, managers must cut other costs or increase revenues. These decisions then affect the company's future strategies and plans.

Exhibit 22-1 illustrates the process of developing strategies, planning, directing, and controlling. Notice that the process is a loop—the company begins by developing strategy to help identify the company's goals. Using those goals, the company plans the actions needed to be taken to meet its goals. The results of the actions are then compared to the plan to aid in control and provide feedback. The control step is not an end, but an input into the develop strategies step. Successful companies use current period results to help make decisions regarding the company's future.

Exhibit 22-1 | **Budgeting Objectives**

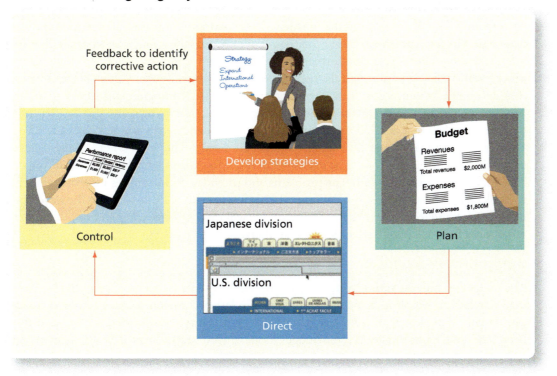

Budgeting Benefits

Budgeting requires managers to plan, promotes coordination and communication, and provides a benchmark for evaluating actual performance. The budget really represents the plan the company has in place to achieve its goals.

Planning

Budgeting requires managers to plan for the company's future. Decisions are then based on this formalized plan, which helps prevent haphazard decision making. For example, if the company plans to expand into a new market, the budget will include expected funding sources and expenditures for the expansion. Keep in mind, however, that budgets are plans for future activities and may need to be modified. If a company learns of a revenue shortfall, where actual revenues earned are less than budgeted revenues, the company has to modify its plan and devise strategies to increase revenues or cut expenses so the company can achieve its planned goals. The better the plan and the more time the company has to act on the plan, the more likely it will be to find a way to meet the target.

Coordination and Communication

The budget coordinates a company's activities. Creating a budget facilitates coordination and communication by requiring managers at different levels and in different functions across the entire value chain to work together to make a single, unified, comprehensive plan for the business. For example, a company stimulates sales by offering free shipping on orders over a specified dollar amount. If sales increase, the shipping department may have to hire additional employees to handle the increase in shipments. The budget encourages communication among managers to ensure that the extra profits from increased sales outweigh the revenue lost from not charging for shipping.

Benchmarking

Benchmarking
The practice of comparing a company with its prior performance or with best practices from other companies.

Budgets provide a benchmark that motivates employees and helps managers evaluate performance. **Benchmarking** is the practice of comparing a company with its prior performance or with best practices from other companies. Companies might compare budgeted numbers with previous year's performance or the company might compare their budgets to other leading companies through the use of industry averages. Benchmarking helps companies determine where a company can improve and helps companies plan how to meet performance goals. Through the benchmarking process, companies are able to develop budgets that present a detailed road map of how performance goals will be achieved.

Budgets should always be compared to actual results. The areas where actual results differed from the budget should be evaluated in order to explain why the amounts differed. This function helps to highlight any problems and provides opportunities for management to implement new strategies to meet its goals. In this chapter, we will focus on the development of the budget and in the next chapter, we will discuss how companies evaluate the differences between budgeted and actual numbers.

Budgeting Procedures

Participative Budget
A budgeting process where those individuals who are directly impacted by a budget are involved in the development of the budget.

The budgeting process varies from company to company. For a small company, the process may be relatively simple and somewhat informal. In larger companies, however, the process can be very complex, with a budget committee coordinating the process. To achieve the benefit of motivating employees, the budget should include input from all levels. Many companies choose to develop the budget from the bottom-up (often referred to as a *participative budget*). A **participative budget** is a budgeting process where those individuals who are directly impacted by a budget are involved in the development of the budget. This requires significant coordination among the company's various business segments. Therefore, the budgeting process usually begins several months before the beginning of the budget period.

When a company uses participative budgeting, budgets tend to be more achievable because those directly impacted by the budget help to create the plan. Preliminary budgets are developed at the departmental level and then flow up to the higher levels of the company for review by managers, vice presidents, and presidents. This bottom-up approach is better for employee morale and tends to result in more buy-in from employees as opposed to budgets that are imposed on employees by senior management.

Budgeting and Human Behavior

What is the most important part of a budgeting system? It is getting managers and employees to accept the budget so the company can benefit from the control and feedback illustrated in Exhibit 22-1.

Few people enjoy having their work monitored and evaluated. If managers use the budget as a benchmark to evaluate employees' performance, managers must first motivate employees to accept the budget's goals. Here is how they can do it:

- Managers must support the budget themselves, or no one else will.
- Managers must show employees how budgets can help them achieve better results.
- Managers must have employees participate in developing the budget so that employees feel the goals are realistic and achievable.

Budgetary Slack
Occurs when managers intentionally understate expected revenues or overstate expected expenses to increase the chances of receiving favorable performance evaluations.

Managers' performance is also evaluated by comparing actual results to the budget. When they develop the company's budget, they may be tempted to participate in budgetary "gaming" and build in budgetary slack. **Budgetary slack** occurs when managers intentionally understate expected revenues or overstate expected expenses. For example, managers might want to budget fewer sales and higher expenses than they expect. This increases the chance that their actual performance will be better than the budget and then they will receive a good evaluation. But adding slack into the budget makes it less accurate—and less useful for planning and control.

Another budgetary game is referred to as *spend it or lose it*. In many companies, if a business segment has a budgeted expense item and does not spend as much as expected for the item, there is a fear the budgeted item will have a lower amount in future budget periods. For example, if the Accounts Payable Department budget allows for $5,000 in Supplies Expense and the department only spends $3,000, then there is a fear the amount will be reduced to $3,000 in the next budget. The employees are then motivated to purchase unneeded supplies, which reduces the operating income for the company.

Try It!

Match the following statements to the appropriate budgeting objective or benefit: developing strategies, planning, directing, controlling, coordinating and communicating, and benchmarking.

1. Managers are required to think about future business activities.
2. Managers use feedback to identify corrective action.
3. Managers use results to evaluate employees' performance.
4. Managers work with managers in other divisions.

Check your answers online in MyAccountingLab or at http://www.pearsonhighered.com/Horngren.

For more practice, see Short Exercise S22-1. MyAccountingLab

WHAT ARE THE DIFFERENT TYPES OF BUDGETS?

There are many different ways that companies create budgets. Some companies will use the previous year's results and modify for expected changes. In this traditional format, managers must only justify changes to budget from the previous year's actual results. As an alternative, budgets can also be developed using a **zero-based budget**. In zero-based budgeting, all revenues and expenses must be justified for each new period. This approach assumes that operations are being started for the first time and the previous year's actual results are ignored. Zero-based budgeting is an effective way to limit the inflation of budgets and control unnecessary expenses. Because there are many different ways budgets are created and many different purposes, there are many different types of budgets. Let's look at some different types.

Strategic and Operational Budgets

The term *strategic* generally indicates a long-term goal. A company will develop strategies such as becoming the cost leader in a particular market or expanding into international markets. It may take several years to achieve these goals. A **strategic budget** is a long-term financial plan used to coordinate the activities needed to achieve the long-term goals of the company. Strategic budgets often span three to 10 years. Because of their longevity, they often are not as detailed as budgets for shorter periods.

The term *operational* generally indicates a short-term goal. After the company develops strategies and creates a strategic budget, the next step is to plan for shorter periods. An **operational budget** is a short-term financial plan used to coordinate the activities needed to achieve the short-term goals of the company. Operational budgets are generally much more detailed than strategic budgets. Operational budgets are most often one year in length (generally encompassing the fiscal year) but may also span only a week, a month, or a quarter, depending on the company's needs. Some companies develop a variation of an operational budget that maintains a continuous projection into the future.

Learning Objective 2
Define budget types and the components of the master budget

Zero-based Budget
A budget technique that requires managers to justify all revenue and expenses for each new period.

Strategic Budget
A long-term financial plan used to coordinate the activities needed to achieve the long-term goals of the company.

Operational Budget
A short-term financial plan used to coordinate the activities needed to achieve the short-term goals of the company.

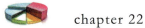

Continuous Budget
Involves continuously adding one additional month to the budget as each month goes by.

A **continuous budget** is a type of operational budget the involves continuously adding one additional month as each month goes by. When a company uses continuous budgeting, the company revises the budget by replacing the month that just ended with a month at the end so there is always a continuous 12-month period. Continuous budgeting allows a company to constantly monitor the budget and keep track of current and future amounts.

Static and Flexible Budgets

Static Budget
A budget prepared for only one level of sales volume.

A **static budget** is a budget prepared for only one level of sales volume. For example, Smart Touch Learning, the fictitious company we have used to illustrate accounting concepts throughout the textbook, may prepare a budget based on annual sales of 2,000 touch screen tablet computers. All revenue and expense calculations would be based on sales of 2,000 tablets.

Flexible Budget
A budget prepared for various levels of sales volume.

A **flexible budget** is a budget prepared for various levels of sales volume. This type of budget is useful for *what if* analysis. Smart Touch Learning may expect to sell 2,000 tablet computers, but a flexible budget showing results for selling 1,600 tablets, 1,800 tablets, 2,000 tablets, 2,200 tablets, and 2,400 tablets allows managers to plan for various sales levels. Flexible budgets are covered in detail in the next chapter.

TYING IT ALL TOGETHER

San Diego Zoo is a nonprofit organization that is committed to saving species worldwide through animal care and conservation science. The zoo was founded on October 2, 1916, and is home to more than 3,500 rare and endangered animals and more than 700,000 exotic plants. In addition, the San Diego Zoo also has a Safari Park that is an expansive wildlife sanctuary, home to more than 3,000 species including African Rhinos, Cheetahs, and Turacos (a handsome African bird). The zoo is home to one of the most valuable collections of birds in the world.

In 2003, Southern California was hit with Exotic Newcastle Disease, one of the most infectious bird diseases in the world. San Diego Zoo was forced to shut down their bird exhibits for several months and ultimately, the zoo spent half a million dollars on quarantine efforts. The great news was that no birds got sick! However, the significant cost and decrease in revenue from the exhibit being closed led the zoo to be very concerned about its bottom line.

How did the San Diego Zoo use budgeting to minimize the impact of these unbudgeted expenses?
Paula Brock, CFO of the San Diego Zoo, stated the organization used monthly budget reforecasts to find a way for the organization to still meet its bottom line even though the entity had these unexpected expenses. Monthly budget reforecast is a type of continuous budgeting that involves revising the budget based on actual data. At the San Diego Zoo, each department revised the budget within 7 to 10 days of the end of each month. This allowed the zoo to determine where other expenses could be cut and plan alternative revenue streams.

How can a nonprofit organization, such as the San Diego Zoo, help employees understand the importance of budgeting?
It's important that employees understand the link between the budget process and the organization's strategy. At the San Diego Zoo, Brock states that the budget process is like a map. It a tool that helps keep employees on track. In order to improve employee understanding of the budget process, Brock implemented budgeting that started at the department level. This allows department managers to have an understanding of how their decisions impact the organization's overall strategy and motivates employees to buy into the budgeting process.

Master Budgets

Master Budget
The set of budgeted financial statements and supporting schedules for the entire organization; includes the operating budget, capital expenditures budget, and financial budget.

The **master budget** is the set of budgeted financial statements and supporting schedules for the entire organization. Budgeted financial statements are financial statements based on budgeted amounts rather than actual amounts. The master budget is operational and static. Exhibit 22-2 shows the order in which managers prepare the components of the master budget for a manufacturing company such as Smart Touch Learning.

Exhibit 22-2 | **Master Budget Components—Manufacturing Company**

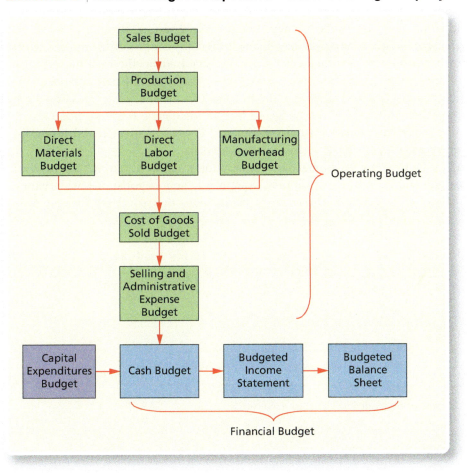

The exhibit shows that the master budget includes three types of budgets:

1. The operating budget
2. The capital expenditures budget
3. The financial budget

Note the difference between the terms operational budget and operating budget. The operational budget is a general term referring to a budget length (short-term, one year or less), whereas the operating budget is a specific part of the master budget.

The **operating budget** is the set of budgets that projects sales revenue, cost of goods sold, and selling and administrative expenses, all of which feed into the cash budget and then the budgeted financial statements. The first component of the operating budget is the sales budget, the cornerstone of the master budget. Why? Because sales affect most other components of the master budget. The company should not produce products it does not expect to sell. Additionally, variable product and period costs are projected based on sales and production levels. Therefore, the sales budget is the first step in developing the master budget.

Operating Budget
The set of budgets that projects sales revenue, cost of goods sold, and selling and administrative expenses, all of which feed into the cash budget and then the budgeted financial statements.

Capital Expenditures Budget
The budget that presents the company's plan for purchasing property, plant, equipment, and other long-term assets.

Financial Budget
The budget that includes the cash budget and the budgeted financial statements.

Cash Budget
The budget that details how the business expects to go from the beginning cash balance to the desired ending cash balance.

The second type of budget is the **capital expenditures budget**. This budget presents the company's plan for purchasing property, plant, equipment, and other long-term assets.

The third type of budget is the financial budget. The **financial budget** includes the cash budget and the budgeted financial statements. Prior components of the master budget provide information for the first element of the financial budget: the cash budget. The **cash budget** details how the business expects to go from the beginning cash balance to the desired ending cash balance and feeds into the budgeted financial statements. These budgeted financial statements include the budgeted income statement and budgeted balance sheet and look exactly like ordinary financial statements. The only difference is that they list budgeted (projected) amounts rather than actual amounts.

In creating the master budget, managers must think carefully about pricing, product lines, job assignments, needs for additional equipment, and negotiations with banks. Successful managers use this opportunity to make decisions that affect the future course of business.

Match the budget types to the definitions.

Budget Types	Definitions
5. Financial	a. Includes sales, production, and cost of goods sold budgets
6. Flexible	b. Long-term budgets
7. Operating	c. Includes only one level of sales volume
8. Operational	d. Includes various levels of sales volumes
9. Static	e. Short-term budgets
10. Strategic	f. Includes the budgeted financial statements

Check your answers online in MyAccountingLab or at http://www.pearsonhighered.com/Horngren.

For more practice, see Short Exercise S22-2. MyAccountingLab

Note to the Instructor: Learning Objectives 3 and 4 cover budgets prepared for a manufacturing company. Learning Objectives 5 and 6 cover budgets prepared for a merchandising company. You can choose to cover both manufacturing and merchandising or either. Each section is presented on a stand-alone basis.

HOW ARE OPERATING BUDGETS PREPARED FOR A MANUFACTURING COMPANY?

Learning Objective 3

Prepare an operating budget for a manufacturing company

To illustrate the preparation of the master budget, we use the fictitious company Smart Touch Learning. As you recall, the company manufactures its own brand of touch screen tablet computers that are preloaded with the company's e-learning software. The master budget is for 2021, prepared by quarter. The balance sheet for December 31, 2020, as shown in Exhibit 22-3, provides some of the data we use in preparing the master budget.

Exhibit 22-3 | **Balance Sheet**

SMART TOUCH LEARNING Balance Sheet December 31, 2020		
Assets		
Current Assets:		
Cash	$ 15,000	
Accounts Receivable	70,000	
Raw Materials Inventory	30,000	
Finished Goods Inventory	55,000	
Total Current Assets		$ 170,000
Property, Plant, and Equipment:		
Equipment	210,340	
Less: Accumulated Depreciation	(12,000)	198,340
Total Assets		$ 368,340
Liabilities		
Current Liabilities:		
Accounts Payable		$ 20,000
Stockholders' Equity		
Common Stock, no par	$ 300,000	
Retained Earnings	48,340	
Total Stockholders' Equity		348,340
Total Liabilities and Stockholders' Equity		$ 368,340

Sales Budget

The first part of the operating budget involves preparing the sales budget. The **sales budget** estimates the amount of sales revenue and is the cornerstone of the master budget because the level of sales affects production expenses and almost all other elements of the master budget. Budgeted total sales for each product equal the sales price multiplied by the expected number of units sold. The sales and marketing teams at Smart Touch Learning project that the company will sell 500 tablet computers in the first quarter of 2021, with sales increasing by 50 tablets each quarter. The tablets sell for $500 each. Exhibit 22-4 shows the sales budget for Smart Touch Learning for 2021. The total sales for the year will be carried to the budgeted income statement.

Sales Budget
The budget that estimates the amount of sales revenue.

Exhibit 22-4 | **Sales Budget**

SMART TOUCH LEARNING Sales Budget For the Year Ended December 31, 2021					
	First Quarter	**Second Quarter**	**Third Quarter**	**Fourth Quarter**	**Total**
Budgeted tablets to be sold	500	550	600	650	2,300
Sales price per unit	× $500	× $500	× $500	× $500	× $500
Total sales	$ 250,000	$ 275,000	$ 300,000	$ 325,000	$ 1,150,000

Production Budget

The **production budget** determines the number of tablets to be produced during the year to meet projected sales and is the basis for the production costs budgets: direct materials budget, direct labor budget, and manufacturing overhead budget. Additionally, the information is used to complete the cost of goods sold budget.

To calculate the number of tablets to be produced, start with the number of tablets projected to be sold. Add to this amount the desired number of tablets in ending inventory. This determines the total number of tablets needed. After determining the number of tablets needed, subtract the number of tablets in beginning inventory. The difference is the number of tablets to be produced. The calculation can be summarized as follows:

> Budgeted tablets to be sold
> + Desired tablets in ending inventory
> Total tablets needed
> − Tablets in beginning inventory
> Budgeted tablets to be produced

Keep in mind that Smart Touch Learning does not want to end the period with zero inventory; it wants to have enough tablets on hand to begin the next period. The company should have the minimum amount of inventory to be sure the company balances providing adequate amounts of goods to customers with turning over the inventory efficiently. Keeping inventory at the minimum level that meets these needs helps reduce inventory storage costs, insurance costs, and warehousing costs, and it reduces the potential for inventory to become obsolete.

Smart Touch Learning desires to have an ending inventory each quarter equal to 20% of the next quarter's sales. Using this assumption, we can determine the desired ending inventory for each quarter by multiplying the following quarter's sales by 20%. For the fourth quarter, we will need the forecasted sales for the first quarter of 2022. Assume the projected number of tablets to be sold during the first quarter of 2022 is 700, 50 more than fourth quarter 2021. Following are the calculations for desired ending inventory:

> First Quarter: Second quarter's sales × 20% = Desired ending inventory
> 550 tablets × 20% = 110 tablets
>
> Second Quarter: Third quarter's sales × 20% = Desired ending inventory
> 600 tablets × 20% = 120 tablets
>
> Third Quarter: Fourth quarter's sales × 20% = Desired ending inventory
> 650 tablets × 20% = 130 tablets
>
> Fourth Quarter: First quarter's sales (2022) × 20% = Desired ending inventory
> 700 tablets × 20% = 140 tablets

Once the calculations for desired ending inventory are determined, the company can determine the production for each quarter. Exhibit 22-5 illustrates the production budget for Smart Touch Learning. Notice that the desired ending inventory is added to the budgeted tablets to be sold to determine the total needed. The beginning inventory is then subtracted to determine the number of tablets to be produced each quarter. The beginning inventory for the first quarter is found on the December 31, 2020, balance sheet (Exhibit 22-3) which indicates the Finished Goods Inventory account has a balance of $55,000, consisting of 200 tablets at a cost of $275 each. The ending inventory of one quarter always becomes the beginning inventory of the following quarter.

Notice also in Exhibit 22-5 that the total column is not always equal to the sum of the numbers in a row. For example, both ending and beginning inventories are not totaled. Instead, the number used in the total column for desired tablets in ending inventory is the ending inventory for the fourth quarter. The number used in the total column for tablets in beginning inventory is the beginning inventory for the first quarter. The beginning inventory and ending inventory in the total column are for the year, not the sum of the four quarters.

Exhibit 22-5 | **Production Budget**

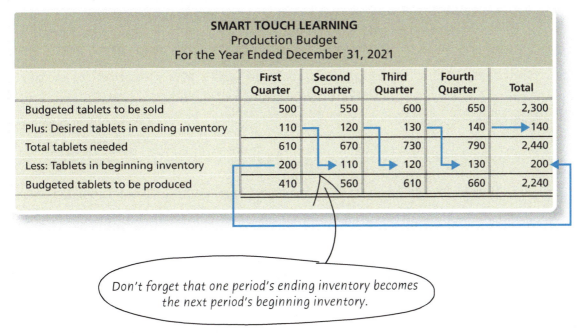

	First Quarter	Second Quarter	Third Quarter	Fourth Quarter	Total
Budgeted tablets to be sold	500	550	600	650	2,300
Plus: Desired tablets in ending inventory	110	120	130	140	140
Total tablets needed	610	670	730	790	2,440
Less: Tablets in beginning inventory	200	110	120	130	200
Budgeted tablets to be produced	410	560	610	660	2,240

SMART TOUCH LEARNING
Production Budget
For the Year Ended December 31, 2021

Don't forget that one period's ending inventory becomes the next period's beginning inventory.

Direct Materials Budget

Smart Touch Learning has determined the number of tablets to be produced each quarter in its production budget. The next step is to determine the product costs for the tablets, beginning with the **direct materials budget**. The direct materials budget estimates the amount of materials to purchase to meet the company's production needs. The purchasing department has projected that each tablet requires 3 pounds of direct materials and the expected cost of direct materials is $50 per pound. The company now needs to determine the amount of materials to purchase each quarter. The amount of indirect materials needed for the production of tablet computers has been determined to be insignificant and will therefore not be considered in the calculation. That means that the amount of materials in the Raw Materials Inventory account is assumed to be only direct materials.

Just as the Finished Goods Inventory account must be considered when calculating the amount of tablets to produce, the Raw Materials Inventory account must be considered when calculating the amount of materials to be purchased. The formula is:

Direct Materials Budget
The budget that estimates the amount of materials to purchase to meet the company's production needs.

Budgeted tablets to be produced
× Direct materials (pounds) per tablet
Direct materials needed for production
+ Desired direct materials in ending inventory (pounds)
Total direct materials needed
− Direct materials in beginning inventory (pounds)
Budgeted purchases of direct materials
× Direct materials cost per pound
Budgeted cost of direct materials purchases

The December 31, 2020, balance shown in Exhibit 22-3 places the Raw Materials Inventory balance at \$30,000 or 600 pounds (\$30,000 / \$50 per pound = 600 pounds). The company desires the ending balance in Raw Materials Inventory to be 40% of the next quarter's budgeted direct materials needed for production. The desired ending balance for the fourth quarter is 852 pounds. Following are the calculations for desired ending inventory:

First Quarter: 2nd quarter's production × 3 pounds per tablet × 40% = Desired ending inventory
560 tablets × 3 pounds per tablet × 40% = 672 pounds

Second Quarter: 3rd quarter's production × 3 pounds per tablet × 40% = Desired ending inventory
610 tablets × 3 pounds per tablet × 40% = 732 pounds

Third Quarter: 4th quarter's production × 3 pounds per tablet × 40% = Desired ending inventory
660 tablets × 3 pounds per tablet × 40% = 792 pounds

Fourth Quarter: Amount given
Desired ending inventory 852 pounds

Exhibit 22-6 illustrates the direct materials budget for Smart Touch Learning.

Exhibit 22-6 | **Direct Materials Budget**

SMART TOUCH LEARNING Direct Materials Budget For the Year Ended December 31, 2021					
	First Quarter	Second Quarter	Third Quarter	Fourth Quarter	Total
Budgeted tablets to be produced	410	560	610	660	2,240
Direct materials (pounds) per tablet	× 3	× 3	× 3	× 3	× 3
Direct materials needed for production	1,230	1,680	1,830	1,980	6,720
Plus: Desired direct materials in ending inventory (pounds)	672	732	792	852	852
Total direct materials needed	1,902	2,412	2,622	2,832	7,572
Less: Direct materials in beginning inventory (pounds)	600	672	732	792	600
Budgeted purchases of direct materials	1,302	1,740	1,890	2,040	6,972
Direct materials cost per pound	× \$50	× \$50	× \$50	× \$50	× \$50
Budgeted cost of direct materials purchases	\$ 65,100	\$ 87,000	\$ 94,500	\$ 102,000	\$ 348,600

Notice again that in the total column, the amount for ending inventory and beginning inventory is not totaled. Instead, the ending inventory is the amount of ending inventory for the fourth quarter and the beginning inventory is the amount of beginning inventory for the first quarter. The beginning inventory and ending inventory in the total column are for the year, not the sum of each quarter.

Direct Labor Budget

Direct Labor Budget
The budget that estimates the direct labor hours and related cost needed to meet the company's production needs.

The next product cost to consider is direct labor. The **direct labor budget** estimates the direct labor hours and related cost needed to support the production budget. The production manager projects that each tablet computer will require three hours of direct labor. The personnel manager projects direct labor costs to average \$25 per hour. To calculate the direct labor cost, multiply the number of tablets to be produced by the number of projected direct labor hours. Then multiply that total by the average direct labor cost per hour. Exhibit 22-7 shows the direct labor budget for Smart Touch Learning for 2021.

Exhibit 22-7 | Direct Labor Budget

SMART TOUCH LEARNING Direct Labor Budget For the Year Ended December 31, 2021					
	First Quarter	Second Quarter	Third Quarter	Fourth Quarter	Total
Budgeted tablets to be produced	410	560	610	660	2,240
Direct labor hours per unit	× 3	× 3	× 3	× 3	× 3
Direct labor hours needed for production	1,230	1,680	1,830	1,980	6,720
Direct labor cost per hour	× $25	× $25	× $25	× $25	× $25
Budgeted direct labor cost	$ 30,750	$ 42,000	$ 45,750	$ 49,500	$ 168,000

The various units used in budgeting can be confusing. Notice that the direct labor budget includes tablets produced, direct labor hours per tablet, and direct labor cost per hour. It is important to not confuse dollars (direct labor cost per hour) with the quantity of an input (direct labor hours) and units of output (budgeted tablets).

Manufacturing Overhead Budget

The last product cost to consider is manufacturing overhead. The **manufacturing overhead budget** estimates the variable and fixed manufacturing overhead needed to meet the company's production needs. The production manager worked with the cost accountant to project the variable manufacturing cost at $20 per tablet. Additionally, they project that fixed costs are $12,000 per quarter for depreciation on the manufacturing equipment and $15,440 per quarter for other fixed costs, such as utilities, insurance, and property taxes on the manufacturing facility. The manufacturing overhead budget calculates the budgeted overhead cost for the year and also the predetermined overhead allocation rate for the year. The predetermined overhead allocation rate is used to allocate the indirect overhead costs to the tablets produced. Smart Touch Learning uses direct labor hours (which is taken from the direct labor budget) as the allocation base to allocate overhead costs. As a reminder, the formula to calculate the predetermined overhead allocation rate is:

Manufacturing Overhead Budget
The budget that estimates the variable and fixed manufacturing overhead needed to meet the company's production needs.

$$\text{Predetermined Overhead Allocation Rate} = \frac{\text{Total estimated overhead costs}}{\text{Total estimated quantity of the overhead allocation base}}$$

Exhibit 22-8 (on the next page) shows the manufacturing overhead budget for Smart Touch Learning for 2021.

Exhibit 22-8 | **Manufacturing Overhead Budget**

	First Quarter	Second Quarter	Third Quarter	Fourth Quarter	Total
SMART TOUCH LEARNING Manufacturing Overhead Budget For the Year Ended December 31, 2021					
Budgeted tablets to be produced	410	560	610	660	2,240
VOH* cost per tablet	× $20	× $20	× $20	× $20	× $20
Budgeted VOH	$ 8,200	$ 11,200	$ 12,200	$ 13,200	$ 44,800
Budgeted FOH**					
Depreciation	12,000	12,000	12,000	12,000	48,000
Utilities, insurance, property taxes	15,440	15,440	15,440	15,440	61,760
Total budgeted FOH	27,440	27,440	27,440	27,440	109,760
Budgeted manufacturing overhead costs	$ 35,640	$ 38,640	$ 39,640	$ 40,640	$ 154,560
Direct labor hours (DLHr)	1,230	1,680	1,830	1,980	6,720
Predetermined overhead allocation rate ($154,560 / 6,720 DLHr)					$ 23/DLHr

*VOH – Variable Manufacturing Overhead

**FOH – Fixed Manufacturing Overhead

Cost of Goods Sold Budget

Cost of Goods Sold Budget
The budget that estimates the cost of goods sold based on the company's projected sales.

Now that the product costs have been determined, Smart Touch Learning's managers can use them to complete the **cost of goods sold budget** which estimates the cost of goods sold based on the company's projected sales. The cost of goods sold budget starts by calculating the projected cost to produce each tablet in 2021. The total projected manufacturing cost to produce each tablet in 2021 is $294, which is calculated as follows:

Direct materials cost per tablet (3 pounds per tablet × $50 per pound)	$ 150
Direct labor cost per tablet (3 DLHr per tablet × $25 per DLHr)	75
Manufacturing overhead cost per tablet (3 DLHr per tablet × $23 per DLHr)	69
Total projected manufacturing cost per tablet for 2021	$ 294

How do inventory costing methods affect the budgeting process?

Smart Touch Learning uses the first-in, first-out (FIFO) inventory costing method. The production budget illustrated in Exhibit 22-5 shows that the company starts 2021 with 200 tablets in Finished Goods Inventory, and the balance sheet in Exhibit 22-3 shows the beginning Finished Goods Inventory has a total cost of $55,000, which is $275 per tablet, the actual cost to produce the tablets in the prior period. Therefore, the first 200 tablets sold in 2021 will have a cost of $275. All other tablets sold in 2021 will assume the budgeted production cost of $294 per tablet, as calculated above.

Referring to the sales budget in Exhibit 22-4, the company projected sales of 500 tablets in the first quarter. **Therefore, the company must use the appropriate inventory costing method, FIFO, to determine the cost of each tablet sold. 200 tablets will be assigned the beginning inventory costs of $55,000 ($275 per tablet) and the remaining 300 tablets will be assigned the cost of $294 per tablet.** The cost of goods sold budget for Smart Touch Learning for 2021 is shown in Exhibit 22-9.

Exhibit 22-9 | **Cost of Goods Sold Budget**

	First Quarter	Second Quarter	Third Quarter	Fourth Quarter	Total
SMART TOUCH LEARNING					
Cost of Goods Sold Budget					
For the Year Ended December 31, 2021					
Beginning inventory, 200 tablets	$ 55,000				$ 55,000
Tablets produced and sold in 2021 @ $294 each (300, 550, 600, 650 tablets per quarter)	88,200	$ 161,700	$ 176,400	$ 191,100	617,400
Total budgeted cost of goods sold	$ 143,200	$ 161,700	$ 176,400	$ 191,100	$ 672,400

Selling and Administrative Expense Budget

The cost accountant works with the office and sales managers to develop the **selling and administrative expense budget**. The selling and administrative expense budget estimates the selling and administrative expenses needed to meet the company's projected sales. Cost behavior is also considered for this budget, with costs designated as variable or fixed. Smart Touch Learning projects the following selling and administrative costs for 2021:

Selling and Administrative Expense Budget
The budget that estimates the selling and administrative expenses needed to meet the company's projected sales.

Salaries Expense, fixed	$ 30,000 per quarter
Rent Expense, fixed	25,000 per quarter
Insurance Expense, fixed	2,500 per quarter
Depreciation Expense, fixed	1,500 per quarter
Supplies Expense, variable	1% of Sales Revenue

To calculate the projected Supplies Expense, multiply the Sales Revenue for each quarter, as calculated in the sales budget in Exhibit 22-4, by 1%.

Quarter	Sales Revenue	Supplies Expense
First	$ 250,000	$ 2,500
Second	275,000	2,750
Third	300,000	3,000
Fourth	325,000	3,250

The selling and administrative expense budget for Smart Touch Learning for 2021 is shown in Exhibit 22-10 (on the next page).

Exhibit 22-10 | **Selling and Administrative Expense Budget**

	First Quarter	Second Quarter	Third Quarter	Fourth Quarter	Total
SMART TOUCH LEARNING Selling and Administrative Expense Budget For the Year Ended December 31, 2021					
Salaries Expense	$ 30,000	$ 30,000	$ 30,000	$ 30,000	$ 120,000
Rent Expense	25,000	25,000	25,000	25,000	100,000
Insurance Expense	2,500	2,500	2,500	2,500	10,000
Depreciation Expense	1,500	1,500	1,500	1,500	6,000
Supplies Expense	2,500	2,750	3,000	3,250	11,500
Total budgeted S&A expense	$ 61,500	$ 61,750	$ 62,000	$ 62,250	$ 247,500

Try It!

11. Kendall Company projects 2019 first quarter sales to be $10,000 and increase by 5% per quarter. Determine the projected sales for 2019 by quarter and in total. Round answers to the nearest dollar.
12. Friedman Company manufactures and sells bicycles. A popular model is the XC. The company expects to sell 1,500 XCs in 2018 and 1,800 XCs in 2019. At the beginning of 2018, Friedman has 350 XCs in Finished Goods Inventory and desires to have 10% of the next year's sales available at the end of the year. How many XCs will Friedman need to produce in 2018?

Check your answers online in MyAccountingLab or at http://www.pearsonhighered.com/Horngren.

For more practice, see Short Exercises S22-3 through S22-8. MyAccountingLab

HOW ARE FINANCIAL BUDGETS PREPARED FOR A MANUFACTURING COMPANY?

Learning Objective 4

Prepare a financial budget for a manufacturing company

The financial budgets include the cash budget and the budgeted financial statements—budgeted income statement and budgeted balance sheet. However, before we can begin the cash budget, we have to complete the capital expenditures budget.

Capital Expenditures Budget

The capital expenditures budget estimates the purchases of property, plant, and equipment, such as delivery trucks, computer systems, office furniture, and manufacturing equipment. The decision to purchase these expensive, long-term assets is part of a strategic plan, and this decision-making process is covered in detail in a later chapter. For now, we will assume Smart Touch Learning plans to purchase additional manufacturing equipment on January 2, 2021. The equipment will cost $160,000 and will be paid in four equal installments during each quarter of 2021. The installment payments are included in the cash budget. A separate capital expenditures budget is not illustrated.

Cash Budget

The cash budget estimates the cash receipts and cash payments for a period of time and pulls information from the other operating budgets previously prepared. The cash budget includes three sections: cash receipts, cash payments, and short-term financing.

Cash Receipts

The primary source of cash is from customers. The sales budget illustrated in Exhibit 22-4 shows the projected sales by quarter. Smart Touch Learning projects that 30% of the sales will be cash sales, which indicates cash will be collected immediately. The remaining 70% of the sales are expected to be on account. The company expects to collect 60% of the credit sales in the quarter of the sale and 40% in the quarter following the sale. In this scenario, bad debt expense is not significant and, therefore, is not considered. The balance sheet for December 31, 2020, shows Accounts Receivable has a balance of $70,000 and this amount is expected to be collected in the first quarter of 2021. Exhibit 22-11 shows the schedule of cash receipts from customers. The total cash receipts from customers for each quarter will be carried to the cash budget. The December 31, 2021, balance in Accounts Receivable will be carried to the budgeted balance sheet.

Exhibit 22-11 | Schedule of Cash Receipts from Customers

	First Quarter	Second Quarter	Third Quarter	Fourth Quarter	Total
Total sales (from Sales Budget, Exhibit 22-4)	$ 250,000	$ 275,000	$ 300,000	$ 325,000	$ 1,150,000
	First Quarter	**Second Quarter**	**Third Quarter**	**Fourth Quarter**	**Total**
Cash Receipts from Customers:					
Accounts Receivable balance, December 31, 2020	$ 70,000				
1st Qtr.—Cash sales (30%)	75,000				
1st Qtr.—Credit sales (70%), 60% collected in 1st qtr.	105,000				
1st Qtr.—Credit sales (70%), 40% collected in 2nd qtr.		$ 70,000			
2nd Qtr.—Cash sales (30%)		82,500			
2nd Qtr.—Credit sales (70%), 60% collected in 2nd qtr.		115,500			
2nd Qtr.—Credit sales (70%), 40% collected in 3rd qtr.			$ 77,000		
3rd Qtr.—Cash sales (30%)			90,000		
3rd Qtr.—Credit sales (70%), 60% collected in 3rd qtr.			126,000		
3rd Qtr.—Credit sales (70%), 40% collected in 4th qtr.				$ 84,000	
4th Qtr.—Cash sales (30%)				97,500	
4th Qtr.—Credit sales (70%), 60% collected in 4th qtr.				136,500	
Total cash receipts from customers	$ 250,000	$ 268,000	$ 293,000	$ 318,000	$ 1,129,000
Accounts Receivable balance, December 31, 2021:					
4th Qtr.—Credit sales (70%), 40% collected in 1st qtr. 2022		$ 91,000			

Cash Payments

Smart Touch Learning has cash payments for capital expenditures, product costs (direct materials purchases, direct labor costs, and manufacturing overhead costs), and selling and administrative expenses. Therefore, the calculations for cash payments require reference to several previously developed budgets.

Direct Materials Exhibit 22-6 shows the purchases of direct materials. All direct materials purchases are on account, and Smart Touch Learning projects payments will be 75% in the quarter of the purchase and 25% in the quarter following the purchase. Reference to the

December 31, 2020, balance sheet shown in Exhibit 22-3 indicates Accounts Payable has a balance of $20,000. This amount will be paid in the first quarter of 2021.

Direct Labor Exhibit 22-7 shows the direct labor costs. Smart Touch Learning pays direct labor costs in the quarter incurred.

Manufacturing Overhead Exhibit 22-8 shows the manufacturing overhead costs. Smart Touch Learning makes cash payments for these costs in the quarter incurred. Keep in mind that we are calculating *cash payments*. Therefore, *non-cash expenses* are not included in the cash budget. The most common non-cash expense is depreciation. The cash outflow for long-term assets, such as manufacturing equipment, is at the time of purchase. Depreciation is the allocation of the asset cost to an expense account over the life of the asset. The allocation does not affect cash and is not included in the cash budget.

Selling and Administrative Expenses Exhibit 22-10 shows the selling and administrative expenses, which Smart Touch Learning pays in the quarter incurred. Again, be sure non-cash expenses, such as the depreciation on the office equipment, are not included in the cash budget.

Income Tax Expense The financial accountant at Smart Touch Learning has projected Income Tax Expense to be $70,000 for the year. Payments will be made in four equal installments during the four quarters.

Capital Expenditures The manufacturing equipment expected to be purchased on January 2, 2021, for $160,000 will be paid in four $40,000 installments in each quarter of 2021.

Exhibit 22-12 shows the schedule of cash payments. The total quarterly cash payments for each category will be carried to the cash budget. The December 31, 2021, balance in Accounts Payable will be carried to the budgeted balance sheet.

Short-term Financing

Now that we have compiled the information needed for cash receipts and cash payments, let's insert those amounts into the cash budget so we can determine the amount of short-term financing needed during 2021. Exhibit 22-13 (on page 1202) shows the partially completed cash budget for 2021. The December 31, 2020, balance sheet shown in Exhibit 22-3 shows Cash has a balance of $15,000. Smart Touch Learning's financial accountant recommends maintaining a larger cash balance in the future. The recommended minimum cash balance for 2021 is $30,000.

The company has arranged short-term financing through a local bank. The company borrows cash as needed at the beginning of each quarter, in increments of $1,000, in order to maintain the minimum cash balance. Interest is paid on any outstanding principal balance at the beginning of the following quarter at 3% per quarter. Repayments on the principal balance are also made at the beginning of the quarter, in increments of $1,000, as cash is available.

As you learned in financial accounting, percentages related to interest are usually expressed as an amount per year (annual percentage rate or APR). However, note that in this case, the interest rate is expressed as an amount per quarter.

Exhibit 22-12 | **Schedule of Cash Payments**

	First Quarter	Second Quarter	Third Quarter	Fourth Quarter	Total
Total direct materials purchases (Exhibit 22-6)	$ 65,100	$ 87,000	$ 94,500	$ 102,000	$ 348,600
	First Quarter	**Second Quarter**	**Third Quarter**	**Fourth Quarter**	**Total**
Cash Payments					
Direct Materials:					
Accounts Payable balance, December 31, 2020	$ 20,000				
1st Qtr.—Direct materials purchases (75%)	48,825				
1st Qtr.—Direct materials purchases (25%)		$ 16,275			
2nd Qtr.—Direct materials purchases (75%)		65,250			
2nd Qtr.—Direct materials purchases (25%)			$ 21,750		
3rd Qtr.—Direct materials purchases (75%)			70,875		
3rd Qtr.—Direct materials purchases (25%)				$ 23,625	
4th Qtr.—Direct materials purchases (75%)				76,500	
Total payments for direct materials	**68,825**	**81,525**	**92,625**	**100,125**	**$ 343,100**
Direct Labor (Exhibit 22-7):					
Total payments for direct labor	**30,750**	**42,000**	**45,750**	**49,500**	**168,000**
Manufacturing Overhead (Exhibit 22-8):					
Variable manufacturing overhead	8,200	11,200	12,200	13,200	44,800
Utilities, insurance, property taxes	15,440	15,440	15,440	15,440	61,760
Total payments for manufacturing overhead	**23,640**	**26,640**	**27,640**	**28,640**	**106,560**
Selling and Administrative Expenses (Exhibit 22-10):					
Salaries Expense	30,000	30,000	30,000	30,000	120,000
Rent Expense	25,000	25,000	25,000	25,000	100,000
Insurance Expense	2,500	2,500	2,500	2,500	10,000
Supplies Expense	2,500	2,750	3,000	3,250	11,500
Total payments for S&A expenses	**60,000**	**60,250**	**60,500**	**60,750**	**241,500**
Income Taxes:					
Total payments for income taxes	**17,500**	**17,500**	**17,500**	**17,500**	**70,000**
Capital Expenditures:					
Total payments for capital expenditures	**40,000**	**40,000**	**40,000**	**40,000**	**160,000**
Total cash payments (before interest)	**$ 240,715**	**$ 267,915**	**$ 284,015**	**$ 296,515**	**$ 1,089,160**

Accounts Payable balance, December 31, 2021:					
4th Qtr.—Direct materials purchases, 25% paid in 1st qtr. 2022		$ 25,500			

Exhibit 22-13 | **Cash Budget—First Quarter, Before Short-term Financing Calculations**

	First Quarter	Second Quarter	Third Quarter	Fourth Quarter	Total
SMART TOUCH LEARNING **Cash Budget** For the Year Ended December 31, 2021					
Beginning cash balance	$ 15,000				$ 15,000
Cash receipts	250,000	268,000	293,000	318,000	1,129,000
Cash available	265,000				
Cash payments:					
Capital expenditures	40,000	40,000	40,000	40,000	160,000
Purchases of direct materials	68,825	81,525	92,625	100,125	343,100
Direct labor	30,750	42,000	45,750	49,500	168,000
Manufacturing overhead	23,640	26,640	27,640	28,640	106,560
Selling and administrative expenses	60,000	60,250	60,500	60,750	241,500
Income taxes	17,500	17,500	17,500	17,500	70,000
Interest expense	0				
Total cash payments	240,715				
Ending cash balance before financing	24,285				
Minimum cash balance desired	(30,000)	(30,000)	(30,000)	(30,000)	(30,000)
Projected cash excess (deficiency)	(5,715)				
Financing:					
Borrowing					
Principal repayments					
Total effects of financing					
Ending cash balance					

Notice that the cash payment for interest expense for the first quarter is $0. The December 31, 2020, balance sheet from Exhibit 22-3 does not show Notes Payable or Interest Payable as liabilities. Therefore, no interest is owed at the beginning of the first quarter of 2021. Exhibit 22-13 shows a cash balance before financing of $24,285, which is the cash available less the cash payments ($265,000 − $240,715). This amount is less than the minimum cash balance desired and creates a cash deficiency of $5,715, which means the company needs to borrow that amount to maintain the minimum desired cash balance of $30,000. The company borrows funds in increments of $1,000, so the amount borrowed is $6,000. Smart Touch Learning will then have an ending cash balance for the first quarter of $30,285:

> **Ending cash balance before financing + Total effects of financing = Ending cash balance**
> $24,285   + $6,000   = $30,285

The ending cash balance for the first quarter, then, becomes the beginning cash balance for the second quarter. Exhibit 22-14 shows the cash budget completed for the first quarter.

Exhibit 22-14 | **Cash Budget—Second Quarter, Before Short-term Financing Calculations**

	First Quarter	Second Quarter	Third Quarter	Fourth Quarter	Total
SMART TOUCH LEARNING					
Cash Budget					
For the Year Ended December 31, 2021					
Beginning cash balance	$ 15,000	$ 30,285			$ 15,000
Cash receipts	250,000	268,000	293,000	318,000	1,129,000
Cash available	265,000	298,285			
Cash payments:					
Capital expenditures	40,000	40,000	40,000	40,000	160,000
Purchases of direct materials	68,825	81,525	92,625	100,125	343,100
Direct labor	30,750	42,000	45,750	49,500	168,000
Manufacturing overhead	23,640	26,640	27,640	28,640	106,560
Selling and administrative expenses	60,000	60,250	60,500	60,750	241,500
Income taxes	17,500	17,500	17,500	17,500	70,000
Interest expense	0				
Total cash payments	240,715				
Ending cash balance before financing	24,285				
Minimum cash balance desired	(30,000)	(30,000)	(30,000)	(30,000)	(30,000)
Projected cash excess (deficiency)	(5,715)				
Financing:					
Borrowing	6,000				
Principal repayments					
Total effects of financing	6,000				
Ending cash balance	$ 30,285				

The amount borrowed at the beginning of the first quarter accrued interest during the quarter and must be paid at the beginning of the second quarter.

> **Principal ×   Rate   × Time = Interest expense**
> $6,000 × 3% per quarter × 1 quarter = $180

In the second quarter, Smart Touch Learning does not have a cash deficiency. The company has $190 more than the required $30,000. Smart Touch Learning will not need to borrow any funds in the second quarter. Notice, though, that the company does not have enough excess cash to make a principal repayment because repayments are made in increments of $1,000. The company would only repay the loan when there is enough excess cash available. Carefully examine Exhibit 22-15, which shows the first and second quarters after financing and the third quarter before financing.

Exhibit 22-15 | **Cash Budget—Third Quarter, Before Short-term Financing Calculations**

SMART TOUCH LEARNING Cash Budget For the Year Ended December 31, 2021					
	First Quarter	Second Quarter	Third Quarter	Fourth Quarter	Total
Beginning cash balance	$ 15,000	$ 30,285	$ 30,190		$ 15,000
Cash receipts	250,000	268,000	293,000	318,000	1,129,000
Cash available	265,000	298,285	323,190		
Cash payments:					
Capital expenditures	40,000	40,000	40,000	40,000	160,000
Purchases of direct materials	68,825	81,525	92,625	100,125	343,100
Direct labor	30,750	42,000	45,750	49,500	168,000
Manufacturing overhead	23,640	26,640	27,640	28,640	106,560
Selling and administrative expenses	60,000	60,250	60,500	60,750	241,500
Income taxes	17,500	17,500	17,500	17,500	70,000
Interest expense	0	180			
Total cash payments	240,715	268,095			
Ending cash balance before financing	24,285	30,190			
Minimum cash balance desired	(30,000)	(30,000)	(30,000)	(30,000)	(30,000)
Projected cash excess (deficiency)	(5,715)	190			
Financing:					
Borrowing	6,000				
Principal repayments					
Total effects of financing	6,000				
Ending cash balance	$ 30,285	$ 30,190			

At the beginning of the third quarter, Smart Touch Learning will make an interest payment for the amount borrowed. The company owes interest for the second quarter. The calculation for the interest expense paid in the third quarter is:

> **Principal** × **Rate** × **Time** = **Interest expense**
> $6,000 × 3% per quarter × 1 quarter = $180

After the third quarter interest payment is calculated and the ending cash balance before financing is determined, Smart Touch Learning again shows a projected cash excess for the third quarter, as shown in Exhibit 22-16. The cash excess is now large enough to repay the amount previously borrowed, again in increments of $1,000.

Exhibit 22-16 shows the completed cash budget. Take time to carefully examine the document to ensure you understand the calculations. Pay special attention to the Total column of the cash budget. As with the production budget and direct materials budget, you cannot simply add across each row to determine the total amounts because this is a summary for the entire year. For example, the beginning cash balance for the year is the same as the beginning cash balance for the first quarter, and not the sum of the beginning balances for each quarter.

Exhibit 22-16 | **Completed Cash Budget**

	First Quarter	Second Quarter	Third Quarter	Fourth Quarter	Total
SMART TOUCH LEARNING Cash Budget For the Year Ended December 31, 2021					
Beginning cash balance	$ 15,000	$ 30,285	$ 30,190	$ 32,995	$ 15,000
Cash receipts	250,000	268,000	293,000	318,000	1,129,000
Cash available	265,000	298,285	323,190	350,995	1,144,000
Cash payments:					
Capital expenditures	40,000	40,000	40,000	40,000	160,000
Purchases of direct materials	68,825	81,525	92,625	100,125	343,100
Direct labor	30,750	42,000	45,750	49,500	168,000
Manufacturing overhead	23,640	26,640	27,640	28,640	106,560
Selling and administrative expenses	60,000	60,250	60,500	60,750	241,500
Income taxes	17,500	17,500	17,500	17,500	70,000
Interest expense	0	180	180	0	360
Total cash payments	240,715	268,095	284,195	296,515	1,089,520
Ending cash balance before financing	24,285	30,190	38,995	54,480	54,480
Minimum cash balance desired	(30,000)	(30,000)	(30,000)	(30,000)	(30,000)
Projected cash excess (deficiency)	(5,715)	190	8,995	24,480	24,480
Financing:					
Borrowing	6,000				6,000
Principal repayments			(6,000)		(6,000)
Total effects of financing	6,000		(6,000)		0
Ending cash balance	$ 30,285	$ 30,190	$ 32,995	$ 54,480	$ 54,480

The budgeted financial statements are the next step in the budgeting process, and the cash budget provides several amounts needed. The interest expense calculations are carried to the budgeted income statement, and the ending cash balance is carried to the budgeted balance sheet. Smart Touch Learning repaid all amounts borrowed during the year. If those amounts had not been repaid in full, the balance would be carried to the budgeted balance sheet as the balance for Notes Payable.

ETHICS

Do I have to tell my manager?

Lugo Pryor is a sales representative at Rutherford, Inc. Lugo has a reputation of always being able to exceed the sales goal set by his manager, and exceeding the sales goal results in a year-end bonus. Lugo has just received a verbal commitment from a customer for a large order to be processed in the new year. Rutherford has not yet received a purchase order from the customer, but when it arrives, it will increase Lugo's sales by approximately 10% for the year. Lugo has also received the proposed budget for the new year from his manager. Because the purchase order has not been processed, the proposed budget does not include this new order. Lugo smiles. If he can get the budget approved before the purchase order is processed, he will certainly exceed his sales goal for the next year and earn a sizable year-end bonus. Should Lugo tell his manager about the order? What would you do?

Solution

Lugo should tell his manager about the order. Budgets are used for planning decisions. Failure to let the company know about an order of this size could have negative repercussions if the production department is caught off guard and the order cannot be delivered as promised. Also, Lugo's credibility may be compromised when the truth about the order is revealed and his manager discovers the budgeting game Lugo is playing.

Budgeted Income Statement

Smart Touch Learning has now determined all amounts needed to calculate the budgeted net income for 2021. Following is a summary of the sources for these figures:

Account	Budget	Exhibit	Amount
Sales Revenue	Sales	22-4	$ 1,150,000
Cost of Goods Sold	Cost of Goods Sold	22-9	672,400
S&A Expenses	S&A Expense	22-10	247,500
Interest Expense	Cash	22-16	360
Income Tax Expense	Cash	22-16	70,000

Be sure to not confuse revenues earned with cash received from customers or expenses incurred with cash payments. The accrual based income statement reports revenues earned and expenses incurred. The cash budget reports cash receipts and cash payments.

Exhibit 22-17 shows the budgeted income statement for Smart Touch Learning for the year ended December 31, 2021.

Exhibit 22-17 | **Budgeted Income Statement**

SMART TOUCH LEARNING Budgeted Income Statement For the Year Ended December 31, 2021	
Net Sales Revenue	$ 1,150,000
Cost of Goods Sold	672,400
Gross Profit	477,600
Selling and Administrative Expenses	247,500
Operating Income	230,100
Interest Expense	360
Income before Income Taxes	229,740
Income Tax Expense	70,000
Net Income	$ 159,740

Budgeted Balance Sheet

The budgeted balance sheet for Smart Touch Learning at December 31, 2021, will pull amounts from the various budgets previously completed. One remaining calculation is for Retained Earnings. Retained Earnings is increased by the amount of net income earned and decreased by the amount of dividends declared. The net income is shown in Exhibit 22-17, and the company does not project dividends for the year. Following is a summary of the sources for the balance sheet figures:

Account	Source	Exhibit	Amount
Cash	Cash budget	22-16	$ 54,480
Accounts Receivable	Schedule of cash receipts from customers	22-11	91,000
Raw Materials Inventory	Direct materials budget	22-6	42,600
Finished Goods Inventory	Production budget	22-5	140 units
	Cost of goods sold budget	22-9	$ 294 per unit
Equipment	2020 balance sheet	22-3	210,340
	Capital expenditures budget		160,000
Accumulated Depreciation	2020 balance sheet	22-3	12,000
	Manufacturing overhead budget	22-8	48,000
	S&A expense budget	22-10	6,000
Accounts Payable	Schedule of cash payments	22-12	25,500
Common Stock	2020 balance sheet	22-3	300,000
Retained Earnings	2020 balance sheet	22-3	48,340
	Budgeted income statement	22-17	159,740

Take the time to look at each exhibit referenced above to ensure you know where each figure came from. Also, keep in mind that the balance sheet only shows the *ending balances* of each account as of December 31, 2021. The budgeted balance sheet for Smart Touch Learning for December 31, 2021, is shown in Exhibit 22-18 (on the next page).

Exhibit 22-18 | **Budgeted Balance Sheet**

SMART TOUCH LEARNING
Budgeted Balance Sheet
December 31, 2021

Assets

Current Assets:		
Cash	$ 54,480	
Accounts Receivable	91,000	
Raw Materials Inventory	42,600	
Finished Goods Inventory (140 units × $294/unit)	41,160	
Total Current Assets		$ 229,240
Property, Plant, and Equipment:		
Equipment ($210,340 + $160,000)	370,340	
Less: Accumulated Depreciation ($12,000 + $48,000 + $6,000)	(66,000)	304,340
Total Assets		$ 533,580

Liabilities

Current Liabilities:		
Accounts Payable		$ 25,500

Stockholders' Equity

Common Stock, no par	$ 300,000	
Retained Earnings ($48,340 + $159,740)	208,080	
Total Stockholders' Equity		508,080
Total Liabilities and Stockholders' Equity		$ 533,580

Try It!

13. Meeks Company has the following sales for the first quarter of 2019:

	January	February	March
Cash sales	$ 5,000	$ 5,500	$ 5,250
Sales on account	15,000	14,000	14,500
Total sales	$ 20,000	$ 19,500	$ 19,750

Sales on account are collected the month after the sale. The Accounts Receivable balance on January 1 is $12,500, the amount of December's sales on account. Calculate the cash receipts from customers for the first three months of 2019.

Check your answers online in MyAccountingLab or at http://www.pearsonhighered.com/Horngren.

For more practice, see Short Exercises S22-9 through S22-11. MyAccountingLab

HOW ARE OPERATING BUDGETS PREPARED FOR A MERCHANDISING COMPANY?

Merchandising companies purchase the products they sell rather than manufacture them. Therefore, the master budget for a merchandising company will be slightly different from the master budget for a manufacturing company. The inventory, purchases, and cost of goods sold budget replaces the production budget, direct materials budget, direct labor budget, manufacturing overhead budget, and cost of goods sold budget. Exhibit 22-19 shows the master budget components for a merchandising company.

Learning Objective 5

Prepare an operating budget for a merchandising company

Exhibit 22-19 | **Master Budget Components—Merchandising Company**

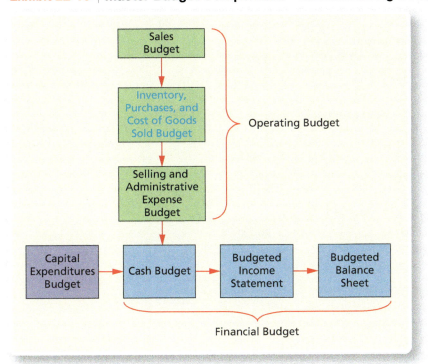

We will use Greg's Games, a fictitious company, to illustrate the preparation of the master budget. Greg's Games is a retail chain store that carries a complete line of video and board games. We will prepare the master budget for one of the retail stores for the months of April, May, June, and July, the high selling season.

Exhibit 22-20 (on the next page) shows the balance sheet for Greg's Games for March 31, 2020. The balance sheet provides some of the data that we use in preparing the master budget.

Sales Budget

In a merchandising company, just as with a manufacturing company, the forecast of sales revenue is the cornerstone of the master budget because the level of sales affects expenses and almost all other elements of the master budget. Budgeted total sales for each product equal the sales price multiplied by the expected number of units sold.

Sales in March were $40,000. The sales manager projects the following monthly sales:

April	$ 50,000
May	80,000
June	60,000
July	50,000
August	40,000

Exhibit 22-20 | **Balance Sheet**

GREG'S GAMES		
Balance Sheet		
March 31, 2020		
Assets		
Current Assets:		
Cash	$ 16,400	
Accounts Receivable	16,000	
Merchandise Inventory	48,000	
Prepaid Insurance	1,800	
Total Current Assets		$ 82,200
Property, Plant, and Equipment:		
Equipment and Fixtures	32,000	
Less: Accumulated Depreciation	(12,800)	19,200
Total Assets		$ 101,400
Liabilities		
Current Liabilities:		
Accounts Payable	$ 16,800	
Salaries and Commissions Payable	4,250	
Total Liabilities		$ 21,050
Stockholders' Equity		
Common Stock, no par	20,000	
Retained Earnings	60,350	
Total Stockholders' Equity		80,350
Total Liabilities and Stockholders' Equity		$ 101,400

Sales are 60% cash and 40% on account. Greg's Games collects all sales on account the month after the sale. The $16,000 balance in Accounts Receivable at March 31, 2020, is March's sales on account (40% of $40,000). There are no other Accounts Receivable. Uncollectible accounts are immaterial in this scenario and therefore aren't included in the master budget. Exhibit 22-21 shows the sales budget for Greg's Games for the four months. The April through July total budgeted sales of $240,000 are carried to the budgeted income statement.

Exhibit 22-21 | **Sales Budget**

GREG'S GAMES					
Sales Budget					
Four Months Ended July 31, 2020					
	April	May	June	July	Total
Cash sales (60%)	$ 30,000	$ 48,000	$ 36,000	$ 30,000	$ 144,000
Sales on account (40%)	20,000	32,000	24,000	20,000	96,000
Total budgeted sales	$ 50,000	$ 80,000	$ 60,000	$ 50,000	$ 240,000

Inventory, Purchases, and Cost of Goods Sold Budget

The **inventory, purchases, and cost of goods sold budget** estimates the cost of goods sold, ending Merchandise Inventory, and merchandise inventory purchases needed for the company's projected sales. The familiar cost of goods sold computation specifies the relations among these items:

Inventory, Purchases, and Cost of Goods Sold Budget
The budget that estimates the cost of goods sold, ending Merchandise Inventory, and merchandise inventory purchases needed for the company's projected sales.

> Beginning merchandise inventory + Purchases − Ending merchandise inventory = Cost of goods sold

Beginning merchandise inventory is known from last month's balance sheet, budgeted cost of goods sold averages 70% of sales, and budgeted ending merchandise inventory is a computed amount. Greg's Games' minimum merchandise inventory rule is as follows: Ending merchandise inventory should be equal to $20,000 plus 80% of the next month's cost of goods sold. You must solve for the budgeted purchases to calculate this figure. To do this, rearrange the previous equation to isolate purchases on the left side:

> Purchases = Cost of goods sold + Desired ending merchandise inventory − Beginning merchandise inventory

Exhibit 22-22 shows Greg's Games' merchandise inventory, purchases, and cost of goods sold budget. The beginning balance of Merchandise Inventory for April is the ending balance from the March 31 balance sheet.

Exhibit 22-22 | **Inventory, Purchases, and Cost of Goods Sold Budget**

GREG'S GAMES					
Inventory, Purchases, and Cost of Goods Sold Budget					
Four Months Ended July 31, 2020					
	April	May	June	July	Total
Cost of goods sold (70% × sales)	$ 35,000	$ 56,000	$ 42,000	$ 35,000	$ 168,000
Plus: Desired ending merchandise inventory					
$20,000 + (80% × COGS for next month)*	64,800	53,600	48,000	42,400	42,400
Total merchandise inventory required	99,800	109,600	90,000	77,400	210,400
Less: Beginning merchandise inventory	48,000	64,800	53,600	48,000	48,000
Budgeted purchases	$ 51,800	$ 44,800	$ 36,400	$ 29,400	$ 162,400

*April: $20,000 + (80% × $56,000) = $64,800
May: $20,000 + (80% × $42,000) = $53,600
June: $20,000 + (80% × $35,000) = $48,000
July: $20,000 + (80% × COGS for August) = $20,000 + (80% × (70% × $40,000)) = $42,400

Selling and Administrative Expense Budget

The selling and administrative expense budget is prepared next and estimates the selling and administrative expenses needed to meet the company's projected sales. The monthly payroll for Greg's Games is salaries of $2,500 plus sales commissions equal to 15% of sales. This is a mixed cost with both a fixed and a variable component. Other monthly expenses are as follows:

Rent Expense, fixed	$ 2,000 per month
Depreciation Expense, fixed	$ 500 per month
Insurance Expense, fixed	$ 200 per month
Miscellaneous Expense, variable	5% of Sales

The selling and administrative expense budget for Greg's Games is shown in Exhibit 22-23.

Exhibit 22-23 | **Selling and Administrative Expense Budget**

GREG'S GAMES Selling and Administrative Expense Budget Four Months Ended July 31, 2020					
	April	**May**	**June**	**July**	**Total**
Variable expenses:					
Commissions Expense (15% of sales)	$ 7,500	$ 12,000	$ 9,000	$ 7,500	$ 36,000
Miscellaneous Expenses (5% of sales)	2,500	4,000	3,000	2,500	12,000
Total variable expenses	10,000	16,000	12,000	10,000	48,000
Fixed expenses:					
Salaries Expense	2,500	2,500	2,500	2,500	10,000
Rent Expense	2,000	2,000	2,000	2,000	8,000
Depreciation Expense	500	500	500	500	2,000
Insurance Expense	200	200	200	200	800
Total fixed expenses	5,200	5,200	5,200	5,200	20,800
Total selling and administrative expenses	$ 15,200	$ 21,200	$ 17,200	$ 15,200	$ 68,800

Try It!

14. Camp Company is a sporting goods store. The company sells a tent that sleeps six people. The store expects to sell 250 tents in 2018 and 280 tents in 2019. At the beginning of 2018, Camp Company has 25 tents in Merchandise Inventory and desires to have 5% of the next year's sales available at the end of the year. How many tents will Camp Company need to purchase in 2018?

Check your answer online in MyAccountingLab or at http://www.pearsonhighered.com/Horngren.

For more practice, see Short Exercises S22-12 through S22-14. MyAccountingLab

HOW ARE FINANCIAL BUDGETS PREPARED FOR A MERCHANDISING COMPANY?

Learning Objective 6

Prepare a financial budget for a merchandising company

We continue the budgeting process for Greg's Games by preparing the capital expenditures budget, cash budget, and budgeted financial statements—budgeted income statement and budgeted balance sheet.

Capital Expenditures Budget

The capital expenditures budget estimates the purchases of property, plant, and equipment. Greg's Games plans to purchase a used delivery truck in April, paying $3,000 at the time of the purchase. Because this is the only capital expenditure, a separate budget is not illustrated. The cash payment will be shown on the cash budget.

Cash Budget

The cash budget estimates the cash receipts and cash payments for the time period. This budget pulls information from the other budgets previously prepared and has three sections: cash receipts, cash payments, and short-term financing.

Cash Receipts

The primary source of cash is from customers. The sales budget illustrated in Exhibit 22-21 shows the total sales for the period. Recall that the company's sales are 60% cash and 40% on credit. The 40% credit sales are collected the month after the sale is made. Exhibit 22-24 shows that April's budgeted cash collections consist of two parts:

1. April's cash sales from the sales budget in Exhibit 22-21 ($30,000)
2. Collections of March's credit sales ($16,000 Accounts Receivable from the March 31 balance sheet, Exhibit 22-20).

    This process is repeated for all four months.

Exhibit 22-24 | **Schedule of Cash Receipts from Customers**

GREG'S GAMES Budgeted Cash Receipts from Customers Four Months Ended July 31, 2020					
	April	**May**	**June**	**July**	**Total**
Cash sales (60%)	$ 30,000	$ 48,000	$ 36,000	$ 30,000	$ 144,000
Credit sales receipts, one month after sale (40%)	16,000*	20,000	32,000	24,000	92,000
Total cash receipts	$ 46,000	$ 68,000	$ 68,000	$ 54,000	$ 236,000

* March 31 Accounts Receivable (Exhibit 22-20)

Accounts Receivable balance, July 31:
July sales on account to be collected in August, $20,000

Cash Payments

Greg's Games pays for merchandise inventory purchases 50% during the month of purchase and 50% the month after purchase. Use the inventory, purchases, and cost of goods sold budget from Exhibit 22-22 to compute budgeted cash payments for purchases of inventory. April's cash payments for purchases consist of two parts:

1. Payment of 50% of March's purchases ($16,800 Accounts Payable balance from the March 31 balance sheet, Exhibit 22-20).
2. Payment for 50% of April's purchases (50% × $51,800 = $25,900).

This process is repeated for all four months and is illustrated in Exhibit 22-25.

Exhibit 22-25 | **Schedule of Cash Payments for Purchases**

	April	May	June	July	Total
GREG'S GAMES Budgeted Cash Payments for Purchases Four Months Ended July 31, 2020					
50% of last month's purchases	$ 16,800*	$ 25,900	$ 22,400	$ 18,200	$ 83,300
50% of this month's purchases	25,900	22,400	18,200	14,700	81,200
Total cash payments for purchases	$ 42,700	$ 48,300	$ 40,600	$ 32,900	$ 164,500

* March 31 Accounts Payable (Exhibit 22-20)

Accounts Payable balance, July 31:
50% of July purchases to be paid in August, $14,700

Use the selling and administrative expense budget (Exhibit 22-23) and Greg's Games payment information to compute cash payments for selling and administrative expenses. Greg's Games pays half the salaries and commissions in the month incurred and half in the following month. Therefore, at the end of each month, Greg's Games reports Salaries and Commissions Payable equal to half the month's payroll. The $4,250 balance in Salaries and Commissions Payable in the March 31 balance sheet in Exhibit 22-20 is half the March payroll of $8,500:

$$\text{March payroll} = \text{Salaries} + \text{Sales commissions of 15\% of sales}$$
$$= \$2,500 + (15\% \times \$40,000)$$
$$= \$2,500 + \$6,000$$
$$= \$8,500$$

Why are depreciation expense and insurance expense from the selling and administrative expense budget *excluded* from the budgeted cash payments for selling and administrative expenses?

The company's selling and administrative expenses also include $2,000 rent, $500 depreciation, $200 of insurance expense, and miscellaneous expenses of 5% of sales for the month. Greg's Games pays all those expenses in the month incurred except for insurance and depreciation. **Recall that the insurance was prepaid insurance, so the cash payment for insurance was made before this budget period; therefore, no cash payment is made for insurance during April–July. Depreciation is a non-cash expense, so it's not included in the budgeted cash payments for selling and administrative operating expenses.** April's cash payments for selling and administrative expenses consist of the following items:

Payment of 50% of March's salaries ($2,500 × 50%) (from March 31 balance sheet, Exhibit 22-20)	$ 1,250
Payment of 50% of March's commissions ($6,000 × 50%) (from March 31 balance sheet, Exhibit 22-20)	3,000
Payment of 50% of April's salaries ($2,500 × 50%) (Exhibit 22-23)	1,250
Payment of 50% of April's commissions ($7,500 × 50%) (Exhibit 22-23)	3,750
Payment of Rent Expense (Exhibit 22-23)	2,000
Payment of Miscellaneous Expenses (Exhibit 22-23)	2,500
Total April cash payments for S&A Expenses	$ 13,750

Exhibit 22-26 shows the schedule of cash payments for selling and administrative expenses for Greg's Games.

Exhibit 22-26 | Schedule of Cash Payments for Selling and Administrative Expenses

	GREG'S GAMES Budgeted Cash Payments for Selling and Administrative Expenses Four Months Ended July 31, 2020				
	April	**May**	**June**	**July**	**Total**
Variable expenses:					
50% of last month's Commissions Expense	$ 3,000	$ 3,750	$ 6,000	$ 4,500	$ 17,250
50% of this month's Commissions Expense	3,750	6,000	4,500	3,750	18,000
Miscellaneous Expenses	2,500	4,000	3,000	2,500	12,000
Total payments for variable expenses	9,250	13,750	13,500	10,750	47,250
Fixed expenses:					
50% of last month's Salaries Expense	1,250	1,250	1,250	1,250	5,000
50% of this month's Salaries Expense	1,250	1,250	1,250	1,250	5,000
Rent Expense	2,000	2,000	2,000	2,000	8,000
Total payments for fixed expenses	4,500	4,500	4,500	4,500	18,000
Total payments for S&A expenses	$ 13,750	$ 18,250	$ 18,000	$ 15,250	$ 65,250

Salaries and Commissions Payable balance, July 31:
50% of July salaries and commissions to be paid in August, $5,000

Short-term Financing

Greg's Games requires a minimum cash balance of $10,000 at the end of each month. The store can borrow cash in $1,000 increments at an annual interest rate of 12%. Management borrows no more than the amount needed to maintain the $10,000 minimum ending cash balance. Total interest expense will vary as the amount of borrowing varies from month to month. Notes payable require $1,000 installment payments of principal per month, plus monthly interest on the unpaid principal balance. This is an installment loan; therefore, payments of principal are $1,000 per month even if there is additional excess cash on hand. Borrowing and all principal and interest payments occur at the end of the month.

Now that we have compiled the information needed for cash receipts and cash payments, we are now ready to prepare the cash budget. Start with the beginning cash balance from the March 31 balance sheet (Exhibit 22-20) and add the budgeted cash receipts (Exhibit 22-24) to determine the cash available. Then subtract cash payments for purchases (Exhibit 22-25), selling and administrative expenses (Exhibit 22-26), and any capital expenditures. This yields the ending cash balance before financing. Exhibit 22-27 (on the next page) shows the partially completed cash budget.

Exhibit 22-27 | **Cash Budget**

GREG'S GAMES Cash Budget Four Months Ended July 31, 2020					
	April	**May**	**June**	**July**	**Total**
Beginning cash balance	$ 16,400				$ 16,400
Cash receipts	46,000	68,000	68,000	54,000	236,000
Cash available	62,400				
Cash payments:					
Capital expenditures	3,000	0	0	0	3,000
Purchases of merchandise inventory	42,700	48,300	40,600	32,900	164,500
Selling and administrative expenses	13,750	18,250	18,000	15,250	65,250
Interest expense	0				
Total cash payments	59,450				
Ending cash balance before financing	2,950				
Minimum cash balance desired	(10,000)	(10,000)	(10,000)	(10,000)	(10,000)
Projected cash excess (deficiency)	(7,050)				
Financing:					
Borrowing					
Principal repayments					
Total effects of financing					
Ending cash balance					

Notice that in Exhibit 22-27 April's $2,950 budgeted cash balance before financing falls $7,050 short of the minimum required ($10,000 − $2,950). To be able to access short-term financing, Greg's Games secured a line of credit with the company's bank. Securing this credit in advance is crucial to having the credit available to draw upon when cash shortages arise. Because Greg's Games borrows in $1,000 increments, the company will have to borrow $8,000 to cover April's expected shortfall. The budgeted ending cash balance equals the "ending cash balance before financing," adjusted for the total effects of the financing (an $8,000 inflow in April). Exhibit 22-28 shows that Greg's Games expects to end April with $10,950 of cash ($2,950 + $8,000).

Additionally, the amount borrowed is to be paid back in $1,000 installments plus interest at 12% annually. Note that in May, the company begins to pay the $8,000 borrowed in April. Greg's Games must also pay interest at 12%. For May, the interest paid is calculated as $8,000 owed × 12% per year × 1/12 of the year, or $80 interest. For June, the company's interest owed will change because the principal of the note has been paid down by $1,000 in May. June interest is calculated as ($8,000 − $1,000) owed × 12% per year × 1/12 of the year, or $70 interest. For July, interest is ($8,000 − $1,000 − $1,000) owed × 12% per year × 1/12 of the year, or $60 interest. Exhibit 22-28 shows the completed cash budget for April, May, June, and July.

Exhibit 22-28 | **Completed Cash Budget**

GREG'S GAMES Cash Budget Four Months Ended July 31, 2020	April	May	June	July	Total
Beginning cash balance	$ 16,400	$ 10,950	$ 11,320	$ 19,650	$ 16,400
Cash receipts	46,000	68,000	68,000	54,000	236,000
Cash available	62,400	78,950	79,320	73,650	252,400
Cash payments:					
Capital expenditures	3,000	0	0	0	3,000
Purchases of merchandise inventory	42,700	48,300	40,600	32,900	164,500
Selling and administrative expenses	13,750	18,250	18,000	15,250	65,250
Interest expense	0	80	70	60	210
Total cash payments	59,450	66,630	58,670	48,210	232,960
Ending cash balance before financing	2,950	12,320	20,650	25,440	19,440
Minimum cash balance desired	(10,000)	(10,000)	(10,000)	(10,000)	(10,000)
Projected cash excess (deficiency)	(7,050)	2,320	10,650	15,440	9,440
Financing:					
Borrowing	8,000				8,000
Principal repayments		(1,000)	(1,000)	(1,000)	(3,000)
Total effects of financing	8,000	(1,000)	(1,000)	(1,000)	5,000
Ending cash balance	$ 10,950	$ 11,320	$ 19,650	$ 24,440	$ 24,440

The cash balance at the end of July of $24,440 is the Cash balance on the July 31 budgeted balance sheet.

Budgeted Income Statement

The budgeted financial statements are the next step in the budgeting process. Following is a summary of the sources for the budgeted income statement:

Account	Budget	Exhibit	Amount
Sales Revenue	Sales	22-21	$240,000
Cost of Goods Sold	Inventory, Purchases, and Cost of Goods Sold	22-22	168,000
S&A Expenses	Selling and Administrative Expense	22-23	68,800
Interest Expense	Cash	22-28	210

Exhibit 22-29 (on the next page) shows the budgeted income statement for Greg's Games.

Exhibit 22-29 | **Budgeted Income Statement**

GREG'S GAMES Budgeted Income Statement Four Months Ended July 31, 2020		
Sales Revenue		$ 240,000
Cost of Goods Sold		168,000
Gross Profit		72,000
Selling and Administrative Expenses:		
Commissions Expense	$ 36,000	
Miscellaneous Expense	12,000	
Salaries Expense	10,000	
Rent Expense	8,000	
Depreciation Expense	2,000	
Insurance Expense	800	
Total Selling and Administrative Expenses		68,800
Operating Income		3,200
Interest Expense		210
Net Income		$ 2,990

Budgeted Balance Sheet

The budgeted balance sheet will pull amounts from the various budgets previously completed. One remaining calculation is for Retained Earnings. Retained Earnings is increased by the amount of net income earned and decreased by the amount of dividends declared. The net income is shown in Exhibit 22-29 and the company does not project any dividends. Following is a summary of the sources for the balance sheet figures:

Account	Source	Exhibit	Amount
Cash	Cash budget	22-28	$24,440
Accounts Receivable	Schedule of cash receipts from customers	22-24	20,000
Merchandise Inventory	Inventory, purchases, and COGS budget	22-22	42,400
Prepaid Insurance	March 31 balance sheet	22-20	1,800
	S&A expense budget	22-23	800
Equipment and Fixtures	March 31 balance sheet	22-20	32,000
	Capital expenditures budget		3,000
Accumulated Depreciation	March 31 balance sheet	22-20	12,800
	S&A expense budget	22-23	2,000
Accounts Payable	Schedule of cash payments for purchases	22-25	14,700
Salaries and Commissions Payable	Schedule of cash payments for S&A expenses	22-26	5,000
Notes Payable	Cash budget	22-28	5,000
Common Stock	March 31 balance sheet	22-20	20,000
Retained Earnings	March 31 balance sheet	22-20	60,350
	Budgeted income statement	22-29	2,990

Study the budgeted balance sheet in Exhibit 22-30 to make certain you understand the computation of each figure.

Exhibit 22-30 | **Budgeted Balance Sheet**

GREG'S GAMES Budgeted Balance Sheet July 31, 2020		
Assets		
Current Assets:		
Cash	$ 24,440	
Accounts Receivable	20,000	
Merchandise Inventory	42,400	
Prepaid Insurance ($1,800 − $800)	1,000	
Total Current Assets		$ 87,840
Property, Plant, and Equipment:		
Equipment and Fixtures ($32,000 + $3,000)	35,000	
Less: Accumulated Depreciation ($12,800 + $2,000)	(14,800)	20,200
Total Assets		$ 108,040
Liabilities		
Current Liabilities:		
Accounts Payable	$ 14,700	
Salaries and Commissions Payable	5,000	
Notes Payable—Short-term	5,000	
Total Liabilities		$ 24,700
Stockholders' Equity		
Common Stock, no par	20,000	
Retained Earnings ($60,350 + $2,990)	63,340	
Total Stockholders' Equity		83,340
Total Liabilities and Stockholders' Equity		$ 108,040

Try It!

15. Connor Company began operations on January 1 and has projected the following selling and administrative expenses:

Rent Expense	$ 1,000 per month, paid as incurred
Utilities Expense	500 per month, paid in month after incurred
Depreciation Expense	300 per month
Insurance Expense	100 per month, 6 months prepaid on January 1

Determine the cash payments for selling and administrative expenses for the first three months of operations.

Check your answers online in MyAccountingLab or at http://www.pearsonhighered.com/Horngren.

For more practice, see Short Exercises S22-15 through S22-17. MyAccountingLab

HOW CAN INFORMATION TECHNOLOGY BE USED IN THE BUDGETING PROCESS?

Learning Objective 7

Describe how information technology can be used in the budgeting process

Budgets require companies to complete many calculations and technology can make it more cost effective for managers to

- Conduct sensitivity analysis.
- Combine individual unit budgets to create the company wide master budget.

Sensitivity Analysis

The master budget models the company's *planned* activities. Top management pays special attention to ensure that the results of the budgeted income statement and the budgeted balance sheet support key strategies.

Actual results, however, often differ from plans. Management, therefore, wants to know how budgeted income and cash flows would change if key assumptions turned out to be incorrect. We previously defined *sensitivity analysis* as a *what if* technique that asks *what* a result will be *if* a predicted amount is not achieved or *if* an underlying assumption changes. *What if* the stock market crashes? How will this affect Smart Touch Learning's sales? Will it have to postpone a planned expansion? *What* will the company's cash balance be on June 30 *if* the period's sales are 25% cash, not 30% cash? Will Smart Touch Learning have to borrow more cash?

Many companies use computer spreadsheet programs like Excel to prepare master budget schedules and statements. Today, *what if* budget questions are easily answered within Excel with a few keystrokes.

Technology makes it cost effective to perform more comprehensive sensitivity analyses. Armed with a better understanding of how changes in sales and costs are likely to affect the company's bottom line, today's managers can react quickly if key assumptions underlying the master budget (such as sales price or quantity) turn out to be wrong. Check Your Understanding 22-1 and 22-2 (located in the review section) are examples of sensitivity analyses for Smart Touch Learning.

Budgeting Software

Companies with multiple business segments must combine the budget data from each of the segments to prepare the companywide budgeted income statement and budgeted balance sheet. This process can be difficult for companies whose business segments use different spreadsheets to prepare the budgets.

Companies often turn to budget-management software to solve this problem. Often designed as a component of the company's Enterprise Resource Planning (ERP) system, this software helps managers develop and analyze budgets.

Software also allows managers to conduct sensitivity analyses on their own segment's data. When the manager is satisfied with his or her budget, he or she can easily enter it in the companywide budget. His or her segment's budget automatically integrates with budgets from all other business segments—from around the building, around the state, around the country, or around the world.

Whether at headquarters or on the road, top executives can log into the budget system through the Internet and conduct their own sensitivity analyses on individual business segments' budgets or on the companywide budget. The result is that managers spend less time compiling and summarizing data and more time analyzing and making decisions that ensure the budget leads the company to achieve its key strategic goals.

16. Crowley Company projects the following sales:

	January	February	March
Cash sales (25%)	$ 5,000	$ 5,500	$ 6,000
Sales on account (75%)	15,000	16,500	18,000
Total sales	$ 20,000	$ 22,000	$ 24,000

Crowley collects sales on account in the month after the sale. The Accounts Receivable balance on January 1 is $13,500, which represents December's sales on account. Crowley projects the following cash receipts from customers:

	January	February	March
Cash receipts from cash sales	$ 5,000	$ 5,500	$ 6,000
Cash receipts from sales on account	13,500	15,000	16,500
Total cash receipts from customers	$ 18,500	$ 20,500	$ 22,500

Recalculate cash receipts from customers if total sales remain the same but cash sales are only 20% of the total.

Check your answers online in MyAccountingLab or at http://www.pearsonhighered.com/Horngren.

For more practice, see Short Exercises S22-18 through S22-20.   MyAccountingLab

REVIEW

> Things You Should Know

1. Why do managers use budgets?

- Budgeting objectives
  - Develop strategies—overall, long-term business goals
  - Plan—budget for specific actions to achieve goals
  - Direct—carry out the plans
  - Control—feedback to identify corrective action (if necessary)
- Budgeting benefits
  - Requires managers to plan how to increase sales and how to cut costs
  - Promotes coordination and communication, such as communicating the importance of cost-reduction goals
  - Provides a benchmark that motivates employees and helps managers evaluate how well employees contributed to the sales growth and cost-reduction goals

2. What are the different types of budgets?

- Strategic budgets—for long-term goals
- Operational budgets—for short-term goals
- Static budgets—for one level of sales volume
- Flexible budgets—for various levels of sales volumes
- Master budgets
  - Set of budgeted financial statements and supporting schedules
  - Operational and static budgets
  - Includes operating budget, capital expenditures budget, and financial budget

3. How are operating budgets prepared for a manufacturing company?

- Sales budget forecasts the sales revenue for the time period.
- Production budget determines the number of units to be produced to meet the estimated sales forecast.
  - Direct materials budget estimates the direct materials needed to meet the production budget.
  - Direct labor budget estimates the direct labor needed to meet the production budget.
  - Manufacturing overhead budget estimates both variable and fixed manufacturing overhead needed to meet the production budget.
- Cost of goods sold budget projects the total cost of goods sold based on the estimated number of units sold.
- Selling and administrative expense budget estimates the selling and administrative expense needed to meet the company's projected sales.

4. How are financial budgets prepared for a manufacturing company?

- Cash budget includes three sections:
  - Cash receipts
  - Cash payments
  - Short-term financing
- Budgeted financial statements include:
  - Budgeted income statement
  - Budgeted balance sheet

5. How are operating budgets prepared for a merchandising company?

- Operating budgets for a merchandising company are similar to a manufacturing company and include:
  - Sales budget
  - Inventory, purchases, and cost of goods sold budget estimates the cost of goods sold, ending merchandise inventory, and merchandise inventory purchases needed for the company's projected sales
  - Selling and administrative expense budget

6. **How are financial budgets prepared for a merchandising company?**

   ▪ Financial budgets for a merchandising company are similar to a manufacturing company and include:

     • Cash budget

     • Budgeted financial statements including the budgeted income statement and budgeted balance sheet

7. **How can information technology be used in the budgeting process?**

   ▪ Excel can be used to conduct sensitivity analysis—a *what if* analysis.

   ▪ Budgeting software allows business segments to integrate individual budgets into the companywide budget.

> Check Your Understanding 22-1

Check your understanding of the chapter by completing this problem and then looking at the solution. Use this practice to help identify which sections of the chapter you need to study more.

Smart Touch Learning has decided to revise its budget to show fourth quarter sales of 700 tablets due to the expectation of increased holiday sales. First quarter sales for the following year are not expected to change.

Requirements

   1. Revise the following budgets (See Learning Objective 3):

      a. Sales budget (Exhibit 22-4)

      b. Production budget (Exhibit 22-5)

   2. Describe how the following budgets will be affected (without revising the budgets) (See Learning Objective 3):

      a. Direct materials budget

      b. Direct labor budget

      c. Manufacturing overhead budget

      d. Cost of goods sold budget

      e. Selling and administrative expense budget

> Solution

Requirement 1

Revised figures appear in color for emphasis.
   a. Revised sales budget

SMART TOUCH LEARNING					
Revised Sales Budget					
For the Year Ended December 31, 2021					
	First Quarter	Second Quarter	Third Quarter	Fourth Quarter	Total
Budgeted tablets to be sold	500	550	600	700	2,350
Sales price per unit	× $500	× $500	× $500	× $500	× $500
Total sales	$ 250,000	$ 275,000	$ 300,000	$ 350,000	$1,175,000

b. Revised production budget

SMART TOUCH LEARNING Revised Production Budget For the Year Ended December 31, 2021					
	First Quarter	Second Quarter	Third Quarter	Fourth Quarter	Total
Budgeted tablets to be sold	500	550	600	700	2,350
Plus: Desired tablets in ending inventory	110	120	140*	140	140
Total tablets needed	610	670	740	840	2,490
Less: Tablets in beginning inventory	200	110	120	140	200
Budgeted tablets to be produced	410	560	620	700	2,290

*700 × 20%

Requirement 2

a. Direct materials budget: An increase in production will require more direct materials and, therefore, more purchases of materials.

b. Direct labor budget: An increase in production will require additional labor and, therefore, increase the direct labor costs.

c. Manufacturing overhead budget: An increase in production will require additional variable manufacturing overhead and, therefore, an increase in variable manufacturing overhead costs. Fixed costs will not change unless the increased production takes Smart Touch Learning out of its relevant range.

d. Cost of goods sold budget: An increase in production will decrease the production cost per unit because the fixed costs will be distributed among more units. In other words, the predetermined overhead allocation rate will decrease. The small increase in production will only have a minor effect on production costs, however, because fixed manufacturing overhead costs are a small portion of the total production cost. Therefore, total cost of goods sold will increase due to the increase in units sold.

e. Selling and administrative expense budget: If the increase in sales does not take Smart Touch Learning out of its relevant range, then fixed selling and administrative costs will not change. The variable selling and administrative cost, Supplies, will increase with the increase in sales.

> Check Your Understanding 22-2

Check your understanding of the chapter by completing this problem and then looking at the solution. Use this practice to help identify which sections of the chapter you need to study more.

Continue the revised Smart Touch Learning illustration from Check Your Understanding 22-1. Recall that the fourth quarter sales are revised to 700 tablets with the expectation of increased holiday sales.

Suppose a change in the receipt of cash from sales on account is as follows:

60% in the quarter of the sale

20% in the quarter after the sale

19% two quarters after the sale

1% never collected

Requirements

1. Revise the schedule of budgeted cash receipts (Exhibit 22-11) to include the increase in fourth quarter sales (from Check Your Understanding 22-1) and the change in the timing of customer receipts. (See Learning Objective 4)

2. How will the changes in cash receipts affect the cash budget? (See Learning Objective 4)

> Solution

Requirement 1

Revised figures appear in color for emphasis.

	First Quarter	Second Quarter	Third Quarter	Fourth Quarter	Total
Total sales (from Check Your Understanding 22-1)	$ 250,000	$ 275,000	$ 300,000	$ 350,000	$ 1,175,000

	First Quarter	Second Quarter	Third Quarter	Fourth Quarter	Total
Cash Receipts from Customers:					
Accounts Receivable balance, December 31, 2020	$ 70,000				
1st Qtr.—Cash sales (30%)	75,000				
1st Qtr.—Credit sales (70%), 60% collected in 1st qtr.	105,000				
1st Qtr.—Credit sales (70%), 20% collected in 2nd qtr.		$ 35,000			
1st Qtr.—Credit sales (70%), 19% collected in 3rd qtr.			$ 33,250		
2nd Qtr.—Cash sales (30%)		82,500			
2nd Qtr.—Credit sales (70%), 60% collected in 2nd qtr.		115,500			
2nd Qtr.—Credit sales (70%), 20% collected in 3rd qtr.			38,500		
2nd Qtr.—Credit sales (70%), 19% collected in 4th qtr.				$ 36,575	
3rd Qtr.—Cash sales (30%)			90,000		
3rd Qtr.—Credit sales (70%), 60% collected in 3rd qtr.			126,000		
3rd Qtr.—Credit sales (70%), 20% collected in 4th qtr.				42,000	
4th Qtr.—Cash sales (30%)				105,000	
4th Qtr.—Credit sales (70%), 60% collected in 4th qtr.				147,000	
Total cash receipts from customers	$ 250,000	$ 233,000	$ 287,750	$ 330,575	$ 1,101,325

Requirement 2

The decrease in cash receipts will require Smart Touch Learning to borrow more funds on the short-term note payable. Increased borrowing will increase interest expense and decrease net income for the year.

	First Quarter	Second Quarter	Third Quarter	Fourth Quarter	Total
Original budgeted cash receipts	$ 250,000	$ 268,000	$ 293,000	$ 318,000	$ 1,129,000
Revised budgeted cash receipts	250,000	233,000	287,750	330,575	1,101,325
Difference	$ 0	$ (35,000)	$ (5,250)	$ 12,575	$ (27,675)

> Key Terms

Benchmarking (p. 1186)

Budget (p. 1184)

Budgetary Slack (p. 1186)

Capital Expenditures
  Budget (p. 1190)

Cash Budget (p. 1190)

Continuous Budget (p. 1188)

Cost of Goods Sold Budget (p. 1196)

Direct Labor Budget (p. 1194)

Direct Materials Budget (p. 1193)

Financial Budget (p. 1190)

Flexible Budget (p. 1188)

Inventory, Purchases, and Cost of
  Goods Sold Budget (p. 1211)

Manufacturing Overhead
  Budget (p. 1195)

Master Budget (p. 1188)

Operating Budget (p. 1189)

Operational Budget (p. 1187)

Participative Budget (p. 1186)

Production Budget (p. 1192)

Sales Budget (p. 1191)

Selling and Administrative Expense
  Budget (p. 1197)

Static Budget (p. 1188)

Strategic Budget (p. 1187)

Zero-based Budget (p. 1187)

> Quick Check

Learning Objective 1

1. A company can expect to receive which of the following benefits when it starts its budgeting process?
   a. The budget provides managers with a benchmark against which to compare actual results for performance evaluation.
   b. The planning required to develop the budget helps managers foresee and avoid potential problems before they occur.
   c. The budget helps motivate employees to achieve sales growth and cost-reduction goals.
   d. All of the above.

Learning Objective 2

2. A company prepares a five-year budget. This budget would be considered a(n)
   a. strategic budget.
   b. operational budget.
   c. master budget.
   d. flexible budget.

Learning Objective 3

3. Which of the following is the cornerstone of the master budget?
   a. The selling and administrative expense budget
   b. The budgeted balance sheet
   c. The sales budget
   d. The production budget

Use the following information to answer questions 4 through 7.

Suppose Iron City manufactures cast iron skillets. One model is a 10-inch skillet that sells for $20. Iron City projects sales of 500 10-inch skillets per month. The production costs are $9 per skillet for direct materials, $1 per skillet for direct labor, and $2 per skillet for manufacturing overhead. Iron City has 50 10-inch skillets in inventory at the beginning of July but wants to have an ending inventory equal to 20% of the next month's sales. Selling and administrative expenses for this product line are $1,500 per month.

Learning Objective 3

4. How many 10-inch skillets should Iron City produce in July?
   a. 500 skillets
   b. 550 skillets
   c. 600 skillets
   d. 650 skillets

5. Compute the total amount budgeted for product costs for July.

    a. $6,000   **c.** $6,600

    b. $6,500   **d.** $7,200

Learning Objective 3

6. Compute the budgeted cost of goods sold for July.

    a. $6,000   **c.** $6,600

    b. $6,500   **d.** $7,200

Learning Objective 3

7. Compute the budgeted gross profit for July.

    a. $6,000   **c.** $4,000

    b. $5,000   **d.** $3,000

Learning Objective 4

8. The budgeted income statement is part of which element of the master budget?

    a. The financial budget   **c.** The capital expenditures budget

    b. The operating budget   **d.** None of the above

Learning Objective 4

9. Which of the following expenses would *not* appear in the cash budget?

    a. Depreciation expense   **c.** Interest expense

    b. Marketing expense   **d.** Wages expense

Learning Objective 4

Use the following information to answer questions 10 and 11.

Suppose Mallcentral sells 1,000 hardcover books per day at an average price of $30. Assume that Mallcentral's cost for the books is 75% of the selling price it charges retail customers. Mallcentral has no beginning inventory, but it wants to have a three-day supply of ending inventory. Assume that selling and administrative expenses are $1,000 per day.

10. Compute Mallcentral's budgeted sales for the next (seven-day) week.

    a. $157,500   **c.** $435,000

    b. $217,000   **d.** $210,000

Learning Objective 5

11. Determine Mallcentral's budgeted purchases for the next (seven-day) week.

    a. $300,000   **c.** $157,500

    b. $225,000   **d.** $75,000

Learning Objective 5

12. The budgeted balance sheet is part of which element of the master budget?

    a. Financial budget   **c.** Capital expenditures budget

    b. Operating budget   **d.** None of the above

Learning Objective 6

13. Information technology has made it easier for managers to perform all of the following tasks *except*

    a. preparing performance reports that identify variances between actual and budgeted revenues and costs.

    b. combining individual units' budgets into the companywide budget.

    c. sensitivity analyses.

    d. removing budgetary slack from the budget.

Learning Objective 7

Check your answers at the end of the chapter.

ASSESS YOUR PROGRESS

> Review Questions

1. List the four budgeting objectives.
2. One benefit of budgeting is coordination and communication. Explain what this means.
3. How is benchmarking beneficial?
4. What is budgetary slack? Why might managers try to build slack into their budgets?
5. Explain the difference between strategic and operational budgets.
6. Explain the difference between static and flexible budgets.
7. What is a master budget?
8. In a manufacturing company, what are the three types of budgets included in the master budget? Describe each type.
9. Why is the sales budget considered the cornerstone of the master budget?
10. What is the formula used to determine the number of units to be produced?
11. What is the formula used to determine the amount of direct materials to be purchased?
12. What are the two types of manufacturing overhead? How do they affect the manufacturing overhead budget calculations?
13. How is the predetermined overhead allocation rate determined?
14. What is the capital expenditures budget?
15. What are the three sections of the cash budget?
16. What are the budgeted financial statements? How do they differ from regular financial statements?
17. How does the master budget for a merchandising company differ from a manufacturing company?
18. What is the formula used to determine the amount of merchandise inventory to be purchased?
19. What budgets are included in the financial budget for a merchandising company?
20. What is sensitivity analysis? Why is it important for managers?

> Short Exercises

Learning Objective 1

S22-1 Budgeting benefits

List the three key benefits companies get from preparing a budget.

Learning Objective 2

S22-2 Budgeting types

Consider the following budgets and budget types.

Cash	Cost of Goods Sold
Flexible	Master
Operational	Sales
Static	Strategic

Which budget or budget type should be used to meet the following needs?

a. Upper management is planning for the next five years.

b. A store manager wants to plan for different levels of sales.

c. The accountant wants to determine if the company will have sufficient funds to pay expenses.

d. The CEO wants to make companywide plans for the next year.

S22-3 Preparing an operating budget—sales budget

Learning Objective 3

Brown Company manufactures luggage sets. Brown sells its luggage sets to department stores. Brown expects to sell 1,700 luggage sets for $180 each in January and 2,050 luggage sets for $180 each in February. All sales are cash only. Prepare the sales budget for January and February.

S22-4 Preparing an operating budget—production budget

Learning Objective 3

Bailey Company expects to sell 1,500 units of finished product in January and 1,750 units in February. The company has 180 units on hand on January 1 and desires to have an ending inventory equal to 80% of the next month's sales. March sales are expected to be 1,820 units. Prepare Bailey's production budget for January and February.

S22-5 Preparing an operating budget—direct materials budget

Learning Objective 3

Bell expects to produce 1,800 units in January and 2,155 units in February. The company budgets 3 pounds per unit of direct materials at a cost of $10 per pound. Indirect materials are insignificant and not considered for budgeting purposes. The balance in the Raw Materials Inventory account (all direct materials) on January 1 is 4,950 pounds. Bell desires the ending balance in Raw Materials Inventory to be 20% of the next month's direct materials needed for production. Desired ending balance for February is 4,860 pounds. Prepare Bell's direct materials budget for January and February.

S22-6 Preparing an operating budget—direct labor budget

Learning Objective 3

Baker Company expects to produce 2,050 units in January and 1,994 units in February. Baker budgets five direct labor hours per unit. Direct labor costs average $9 per hour. Prepare Baker's direct labor budget for January and February.

S22-7 Preparing an operating budget—manufacturing overhead budget

Learning Objective 3

Bennett Company expects to produce 2,030 units in January that will require 8,120 hours of direct labor and 2,210 units in February that will require 8,840 hours of direct labor. Bennett budgets $10 per unit for variable manufacturing overhead; $2,100 per month for depreciation; and $78,460 per month for other fixed manufacturing overhead costs. Prepare Bennett's manufacturing overhead budget for January and February, including the predetermined overhead allocation rate using direct labor hours as the allocation base.

S22-8 Preparing an operating budget—cost of goods sold budget

Learning Objective 3

Butler Company expects to sell 1,650 units in January and 1,550 units in February. The company expects to incur the following product costs:

Direct materials cost per unit	$ 85
Direct labor cost per unit	60
Manufacturing overhead cost per unit	55

The beginning balance in Finished Goods Inventory is 250 units at $200 each for a total of $50,000. Butler uses FIFO inventory costing method. Prepare the cost of goods sold budget for Butler for January and February.

Learning Objective 4

S22-9 Preparing a financial budget—schedule of cash receipts

Berry expects total sales of $359,000 in January and $405,000 in February. Assume that Berry's sales are collected as follows:

80% in the month of the sale

10% in the month after the sale

6% two months after the sales

4% never collected

November sales totaled $350,000, and December sales were $325,000. Prepare a schedule of cash receipts from customers for January and February. Round answers to the nearest dollar.

Learning Objective 4

S22-10 Preparing a financial budget—schedule of cash payments

Barnes Company budgeted direct materials purchases of $191,990 in January and $138,610 in February. Assume Barnes pays for direct materials purchases 60% in the month of purchase and 40% in the month after purchase. The Accounts Payable balance on January 1 is $75,000. Prepare a schedule of cash payments for purchases for January and February. Round to the nearest dollar.

Learning Objective 4

S22-11 Preparing a financial budget—cash budget

Booth has $12,500 in cash on hand on January 1 and has collected the following budget data:

	January	February
Sales	$ 529,000	$ 568,000
Cash receipts from customers	443,000	502,200
Cash payments for direct materials purchases	180,624	160,284
Direct labor costs	135,010	113,348
Manufacturing overhead costs (includes depreciation of $900 per month)	55,058	53,922

Assume direct labor costs and manufacturing overhead costs are paid in the month incurred. Additionally, assume Booth has cash payments for selling and administrative expenses including salaries of $40,000 per month plus commissions that are 1% of sales, all paid in the month of sale. The company requires a minimum cash balance of $20,000. Prepare a cash budget for January and February. Round to the nearest dollar. Will Booth need to borrow cash by the end of February?

Learning Objective 5

S22-12 Understanding the components of the master budget

The following are some of the components included in the master budget of a merchandising company.

a. Budgeted balance sheet

b. Sales budget

c. Capital expenditures budget

d. Budgeted income statement

e. Cash budget

f. Inventory, purchases, and cost of goods sold budget

g. Selling and administrative expense budget

List the items of the master budget in order of preparation.

S22-13 Preparing an operating budget—sales budget

Learning Objective 5

Trailers sells its rock-climbing shoes worldwide. Trailers expects to sell 6,500 pairs of shoes for $185 each in January and 4,000 pairs of shoes for $220 each in February. All sales are cash only. Prepare the sales budget for January and February.

S22-14 Preparing an operating budget—inventory, purchases, and cost of goods sold budget

Learning Objective 5

Brooks Company expects to sell 8,500 units for $175 each for a total of $1,487,500 in January and 2,500 units for $200 each for a total of $500,000 in February. The company expects cost of goods sold to average 70% of sales revenue, and the company expects to sell 4,700 units in March for $280 each. Brooks's target ending inventory is $20,000 plus 50% of the next month's cost of goods sold. Prepare Brooks's inventory, purchases, and cost of goods sold budget for January and February.

S22-15 Preparing a financial budget—schedule of cash receipts

Learning Objective 6

Victors expects total sales of $702,000 for January and $349,000 for February. Assume that Victors's sales are collected as follows:

50% in the month of the sale

30% in the month after the sale

16% two months after the sale

4% never collected

November sales totaled $388,000, and December sales were $407,000. Prepare a schedule of cash receipts from customers for January and February. Round answers to the nearest dollar.

S22-16 Preparing a financial budget—schedule of cash payments

Learning Objective 6

Jefferson Company has budgeted purchases of merchandise inventory of $457,500 in January and $533,250 in February. Assume Jefferson pays for inventory purchases 70% in the month of purchase and 30% in the month after purchase. The Accounts Payable balance on December 31 is $98,275. Prepare a schedule of cash payments for purchases for January and February.

S22-17 Preparing a financial budget—cash budget

Learning Objective 6

Wilson Company has $11,000 in cash on hand on January 1 and has collected the following budget data:

	January	February
Sales	$ 1,400,000	$ 710,000
Cash receipts from customers	851,420	871,800
Cash payments for merchandise inventory	561,100	532,310

Assume Wilson has cash payments for selling and administrative expenses including salaries of $55,000 plus commissions of 2% of sales, all paid in the month of sale. The company requires a minimum cash balance of $8,500. Prepare a cash budget for January and February. Will Wilson need to borrow cash by the end of February?

Note: Short Exercise S22-15 must be completed before attempting Short Exercise S22-18.

Learning Objective 7

S22-18 Using sensitivity analysis in budgeting

Refer to the Victors schedule of cash receipts from customers that you prepared in Short Exercise S22-15. Now assume that Victors's sales are collected as follows:

40% in the month of the sale

20% in the month after the sale

39% two months after the sale

1% never collected

Prepare a revised schedule of cash receipts for January and February.

Note: Short Exercise S22-9 must be completed before attempting Short Exercise S22-19.

Learning Objective 7

S22-19 Using sensitivity analysis in budgeting

Refer to the Berry's schedule of cash receipts from customers that you prepared in Short Exercise S22-9. Now assume that Berry's sales are collected as follows:

60% in the month of the sale

20% in the month after the sale

18% two months after the sale

2% never collected

Prepare a revised schedule of cash receipts for January and February.

Learning Objective 7

S22-20 Using sensitivity analysis in budgeting

Riverbed Sporting Goods Store has the following sales budget:

RIVERBED SPORTING GOODS STORE Sales Budget Four Months Ended July 31					
	April	**May**	**June**	**July**	**Total**
Cash sales (75%)	$ 39,000	$ 60,750	$ 48,750	$ 39,000	$ 187,500
Credit sales (25%)	13,000	20,250	16,250	13,000	62,500
Total sales	$ 52,000	$ 81,000	$ 65,000	$ 52,000	$ 250,000

Suppose June sales are expected to be $81,000 rather than $65,000. Revise Riverbed's sales budget.

> Exercises

E22-21 Describing master budget components

Learning Objective 2

Sarah Edwards, division manager for Pillows Plus, is speaking to the controller, Diana Rothman, about the budgeting process. Sarah states, "I'm not an accountant, so can you explain the three main parts of the master budget to me and tell me their purpose?" Answer Sarah's question.

E22-22 Preparing an operating budget—sales budget

Learning Objective 3

Jul. total sales $27,800

Yarbrough Company manufactures T-shirts printed with tourist destination logos. The following table shows sales prices and projected sales volume for the summer months:

T-Shirt Sizes	Sales Price	Projected Sales in Units		
		June	July	August
Youth	$ 7	575	500	525
Adult—regular	17	625	900	825
Adult—oversized	18	400	500	475

Prepare a sales budget for Yarbrough Company for the three months.

E22-23 Preparing an operating budget—sales and production budgets

Learning Objective 3

May pkg. produced 2,300

Lugo Company manufactures drinking glasses. One unit is a package of eight glasses, which sells for $30. Lugo projects sales for April will be 2,000 packages, with sales increasing by 250 packages per month for May, June, and July. On April 1, Lugo has 325 packages on hand but desires to maintain an ending inventory of 20% of the next month's sales. Prepare a sales budget and a production budget for Lugo for April, May, and June.

E22-24 Preparing an operating budget—direct materials, direct labor, and manufacturing overhead budgets

Learning Objective 3

3rd Qtr. OH $255.00

Grady, Inc. manufactures model airplane kits and projects production at 650, 500, 450, and 600 kits for the next four quarters. Direct materials are 4 ounces of plastic per kit and the plastic costs $1 per ounce. Indirect materials are considered insignificant and are not included in the budgeting process. Beginning Raw Materials Inventory is 850 ounces, and the company desires to end each quarter with 10% of the materials needed for the next quarter's production. Grady desires a balance of 200 ounces in Raw Materials Inventory at the end of the fourth quarter. Each kit requires 0.10 hours of direct labor at an average cost of $10 per hour. Manufacturing overhead is allocated using direct labor hours as the allocation base. Variable overhead is $0.20 per kit, and fixed overhead is $165 per quarter. Prepare Grady's direct materials budget, direct labor budget, and manufacturing overhead budget for the year. Round the direct labor hours needed for production, budgeted overhead costs, and predetermined overhead allocation rate to two decimal places. Round other amounts to the nearest whole number.

Note: Exercise E22-24 must be completed before attempting Exercise E22-25.

Learning Objective 3

3rd Qtr. COGS $550

E22-25 Preparing an operating budget—cost of goods sold budget

Refer to the budgets prepared in Exercise E22-24. Determine the cost per kit to manufacture the model airplane kits. Grady projects sales of 100, 150, 100, and 200 kits for the next four quarters. Prepare a cost of goods sold budget for the year. Grady has no kits in beginning inventory. Round amounts to two decimal places.

Learning Objectives 4, 7

1. Feb. total cash receipts
$12,080

E22-26 Preparing a financial budget—schedule of cash receipts, sensitivity analysis

Marcel Company projects the following sales for the first three months of the year: $11,200 in January; $12,300 in February; and $11,100 in March. The company expects 60% of the sales to be cash and the remainder on account. Sales on account are collected 50% in the month of the sale and 50% in the following month. The Accounts Receivable account has a zero balance on January 1. Round to the nearest dollar.

Requirements

1. Prepare a schedule of cash receipts for Marcel for January, February, and March. What is the balance in Accounts Receivable on March 31?

2. Prepare a revised schedule of cash receipts if receipts from sales on account are 60% in the month of the sale, 30% in the month following the sale, and 10% in the second month following the sale. What is the balance in Accounts Receivable on March 31?

Learning Objective 4

Mar. total cash pmts. $11,500

E22-27 Preparing a financial budget—schedule of cash payments

Marcel Company has the following projected costs for manufacturing and selling and administrative expenses:

	January	February	March
Direct materials purchases	$ 3,100	$ 3,500	$ 4,800
Direct labor costs	3,300	3,500	3,600
Depreciation on plant	550	550	550
Utilities for plant	650	650	650
Property taxes on plant	200	200	200
Depreciation on office	550	550	550
Utilities for office	250	250	250
Property taxes on office	170	170	170
Office salaries	3,500	3,500	3,500

All costs are paid in month incurred except: direct materials, which are paid in the month following the purchase; utilities, which are paid in the month after incurred; and property taxes, which are prepaid for the year on January 2. The Accounts Payable and Utilities Payable accounts have a zero balance on January 1. Prepare a schedule of cash payments for Marcel for January, February, and March. Determine the balances in Prepaid Property Taxes, Accounts Payable, and Utilities Payable as of March 31.

*Note: Exercises E22-26 and E22-27 must be completed before attempting
Exercise E22-28.*

E22-28 Preparing the financial budget—cash budget

Use the original schedule of cash receipts completed in Exercise E22-26,
Requirement 1, and the schedule of cash payments completed in Exercise E22-27 to
complete a cash budget for Marcel Company for January, February, and March.

Additional information: Marcel's beginning cash balance is $5,000, and Marcel
desires to maintain a minimum ending cash balance of $5,000. Marcel borrows
cash as needed at the beginning of each month in increments of $1,000 and repays
the amounts borrowed in increments of $1,000 at the beginning of months when
excess cash is available. The interest rate on amounts borrowed is 8% per year.
Interest is paid at the beginning of the month on the outstanding balance from the
previous month.

E22-29 Preparing the financial budget—cash budget

Hoppy Company requires a minimum cash balance of $3,500. When the company
expects a cash deficiency, it borrows the exact amount required on the first of the
month. Expected excess cash is used to repay any amounts owed. Interest owed
from the previous month's principal balance is paid on the first of the month at
14% per year. The company has already completed the budgeting process for the
first quarter for cash receipts and cash payments for all expenses except interest.
Hoppy does not have any outstanding debt on January 1. Complete the cash budget
for the first quarter for Hoppy Company. Round interest expense to the nearest
whole dollar.

Learning Objective 4

Feb. ending cash bal. $5,780

Learning Objective 4

Mar. interest expense $265

HOPPY COMPANY Cash Budget For the Three Months Ended March 31				
	January	February	March	Total
Beginning balance	3,500			
Cash receipts	19,000	27,500	42,000	88,500
Cash available	22,500			
Cash payments:				
All expenses except interest	34,000	35,000	39,000	108,000
Interest expense	0			
Total cash payments	34,000			
Ending balance before financing				
Minimum cash balance desired	(3,500)	(3,500)	(3,500)	(3,500)
Projected cash excess (deficiency)				
Financing:				
Borrowing				
Principal repayments				
Total effects of financing				
Ending cash balance				

Learning Objective 4

FG inventory $3,150

E22-30 Preparing the financial budget—budgeted balance sheet

Barker, Inc. has the following balance sheet at December 31, 2018:

BARKER, INC. Balance Sheet December 31, 2018		
Assets		
Current Assets:		
Cash	$ 2,400	
Accounts Receivable	1,400	
Raw Materials Inventory	500	
Finished Goods Inventory	1,350	
Total Current Assets		$ 5,650
Property, Plant, and Equipment:		
Equipment	16,000	
Less: Accumulated Depreciation	(1,500)	14,500
Total Assets		$ 20,150
Liabilities		
Current Liabilities:		
Accounts Payable		$ 1,000
Stockholders' Equity		
Common Stock, no par	$ 6,500	
Retained Earnings	12,650	
Total Stockholders' Equity		19,150
Total Liabilities and Stockholders' Equity		$ 20,150

Barker projects the following transactions for 2019:

Sales on account, $20,000

Cash receipts from customers from sales on account, $17,600

Purchase of raw materials on account, $7,000

Payments on account, $3,500

Total cost of completed products, $16,600, which includes the following:

Raw materials used, $7,100

Direct labor costs incurred and paid, $3,900

Manufacturing overhead costs incurred and paid, $4,800

Depreciation on manufacturing equipment, $800

Cost of goods sold, $14,800

Selling and administrative costs incurred and paid, $500

Purchase of equipment, paid in 2019, $2,000

Prepare a budgeted balance sheet for Barker, Inc. for December 31, 2019.

(*Hint:* It may be helpful to trace the effects of each transaction on the accounting equation to determine the ending balance of each account.)

E22-31 Preparing an operating budget—inventory, purchases, and cost of goods sold budget

Learning Objective 5

Qtr. ended Jun. 30 purchases $75,000

Slate, Inc. sells tire rims. Its sales budget for the nine months ended September 30, 2018, follows:

		Quarter Ended		Nine-Month Total
	March 31	June 30	September 30	
Cash sales, 20%	$ 28,000	$ 38,000	$ 33,000	$ 99,000
Credit sales, 80%	112,000	152,000	132,000	396,000
Total sales	$ 140,000	$ 190,000	$ 165,000	$ 495,000

In the past, cost of goods sold has been 40% of total sales. The director of marketing and the financial vice president agree that each quarter's ending inventory should not be below $5,000 plus 10% of cost of goods sold for the following quarter. The marketing director expects sales of $240,000 during the fourth quarter. The January 1 inventory was $38,000. Prepare an inventory, purchases, and cost of goods sold budget for each of the first three quarters of the year. Compute cost of goods sold for the entire nine-month period.

E22-32 Preparing an operating budget—selling and administrative expense budget

Learning Objective 5

Qtr. ended Mar. 31 total S&A exp. $30,800

Consider the sales budget presented in Exercise E22-31. Slate's selling and administrative expenses include the following:

Rent, $2,000 per month
Salaries, $4,000 per month
Commissions, 5% of sales
Depreciation, $1,000 per month
Miscellaneous expenses, 2% of sales

Prepare a selling and administrative expense budget for each of the three quarters of 2018 and totals for the nine-month period.

E22-33 Preparing a financial budget—schedule of cash receipts and schedule of cash payments

Learning Objective 6

b. Sep. cash recpts. $120,680

Agua Cool is a distributor of bottled water. For each of the items, compute the amount of cash receipts or payments Agua Cool will budget for September. The solution to one item may depend on the answer to an earlier item.

a. Management expects to sell equipment that cost $14,000 at a gain of $7,000. Accumulated depreciation on this equipment is $5,000.

b. Management expects to sell 7,100 cases of water in August and 9,000 cases in September. Each case sells for $14. Cash sales average 20% of total sales, and credit sales make up the rest. Three-fourths of credit sales are collected in the month of the sale, with the balance collected the following month.

c. The company pays rent and property taxes of $4,500 each month. Commissions and other selling expenses average 30% of sales. Agua Cool pays one-half of commissions and other selling expenses in the month incurred, with the balance paid the following month.

Learning Objectives 6, 7

1. Feb. ending cash bal. $10,000

E22-34 Preparing a financial budget—cash budget, sensitivity analysis

Leichter Auto Parts, a family-owned auto parts store, began January with $10,500 cash. Management forecasts that collections from credit customers will be $11,000 in January and $15,200 in February. The store is scheduled to receive $8,500 cash on a business note receivable in January. Projected cash payments include inventory purchases ($15,600 in January and $14,800 in February) and selling and administrative expenses ($2,900 each month).

Leichter Auto Parts's bank requires a $10,000 minimum balance in the store's checking account. At the end of any month when the account balance falls below $10,000, the bank automatically extends credit to the store in multiples of $1,000. Leichter Auto Parts borrows as little as possible and pays back loans in quarterly installments of $2,000, plus 4% APR interest on the entire unpaid principal. The first payment occurs three months after the loan.

Requirements

1. Prepare Leichter Auto Parts's cash budget for January and February.

2. How much cash will Leichter Auto Parts borrow in February if collections from customers that month total $14,200 instead of $15,200?

Learning Objective 6

May ending cash bal. $25,000

E22-35 Preparing a financial budget—cash budget

You recently began a job as an accounting intern at Reilly Golf Park. Your first task was to help prepare the cash budget for April and May. Unfortunately, the computer with the budget file crashed, and you did not have a backup or even a paper copy. You ran a program to salvage bits of data from the budget file. After entering the following data in the budget, you may have just enough information to reconstruct the budget.

REILLY GOLF PARK Cash Budget Two Months Ended May 31		
	April	**May**
Beginning cash balance	$ 16,700	$?
Cash receipts	?	79,900
Cash from sale of plant assets	0	2,200
Cash available	114,700	?
Cash payments:		
Purchase of inventory	?	43,000
Selling and administrative expenses	47,400	?
Interest expense	?	?
Total cash payments	98,400	?
Ending cash balance before financing	?	27,200
Minimum cash balance desired	(25,000)	(25,000)
Cash excess (deficiency)	?	?
Financing:		
Borrowing	?	?
Principal repayments	?	?
Total effects of financing	?	?
Ending cash balance	?	?

Reilly Golf Park eliminates any cash deficiency by borrowing the exact amount needed from First Street Bank, where the current interest rate is 6% per year. Reilly Golf Park first pays interest on its outstanding debt at the end of each month. The company then repays all borrowed amounts at the end of the month with any excess cash above the minimum required but after paying monthly interest expenses. Reilly does not have any outstanding debt on April 1.

Complete the cash budget. Round interest expense to the nearest whole dollar.

E22-36 Preparing a financial budget—budgeted balance sheet

Use the following June actual ending balances and July 31, 2018, budgeted amounts for Omas to prepare a budgeted balance sheet for July 31, 2018.

a. June 30 Merchandise Inventory balance, $17,770

b. July purchase of Merchandise Inventory, $4,400, paid in cash

c. July payments of Accounts Payable, $8,400

d. June 30 Accounts Payable balance, $10,700

e. June 30 Furniture and Fixtures balance, $34,100; Accumulated Depreciation balance, $29,880

f. June 30 total stockholders' equity balance, $28,020

g. July Depreciation Expense, $500

h. Cost of Goods Sold, 60% of sales

i. Other July expenses, including income tax, $2,000, paid in cash

j. June 30 Cash balance, $11,600

k. July budgeted sales, all on account, $12,600

l. June 30 Accounts Receivable balance, $5,130

m. July cash receipts from collections on account, $14,700

(*Hint:* It may be helpful to trace the effects of each transaction on the accounting equation to determine the ending balance of each account.)

E22-37 Using sensitivity analysis

Rucker Company prepared the following budgeted income statement for 2019:

Learning Objective 6

Cash $11,500

Learning Objective 7

1. Op. Inc. at 1,700 units
$306,000

RUCKER COMPANY Budgeted Income Statement For the Year Ended December 31, 2019	
Unit Sales	1,300
Sales Revenue ($400 per unit)	$ 520,000
Cost of Goods Sold (45% of sales)	234,000
Gross Profit	286,000
Selling and Administrative Expenses (10% of sales)	52,000
Operating Income	$ 234,000

Requirements

1. Prepare a budgeted income statement with columns for 700 units, 1,300 units, and 1,700 units sold.

2. How might managers use this type of budgeted income statement?

3. How might spreadsheet software such as Excel assist in this type of analysis?

> Problems Group A

Learning Objective 3

3. POHR $10
4. Adult bats COGS $72,540

P22-38A Preparing an operating budget—sales, production, direct materials, direct labor, overhead, COGS, and S&A expense budgets

The Langley Batting Company manufactures wood baseball bats. Langley's two primary products are a youth bat, designed for children and young teens, and an adult bat, designed for high school and college-aged players. Langley sells the bats to sporting goods stores, and all sales are on account. The youth bat sells for $40; the adult bat sells for $65. Langley's highest sales volume is in the first three months of the year as retailers prepare for the spring baseball season. Langley's balance sheet for December 31, 2018, follows:

LANGLEY BATTING COMPANY Balance Sheet December 31, 2018		
Assets		
Current Assets:		
Cash	$ 30,000	
Accounts Receivable	16,700	
Raw Materials Inventory	6,000	
Finished Goods Inventory	21,300	
Total Current Assets		$ 74,000
Property, Plant, and Equipment:		
Equipment	130,000	
Less: Accumulated Depreciation	(50,000)	80,000
Total Assets		$ 154,000
Liabilities		
Current Liabilities:		
Accounts Payable		$ 15,200
Stockholders' Equity		
Common Stock, no par	$ 90,000	
Retained Earnings	48,800	
Total Stockholders' Equity		138,800
Total Liabilities and Stockholders' Equity		$ 154,000

Other data for Langley Batting Company for the first quarter of 2019:

a. Budgeted sales are 1,200 youth bats and 2,600 adult bats.

b. Finished Goods Inventory on December 31, 2018, consists of 300 youth bats at $14 each and 950 adult bats at $18 each.

c. Desired ending Finished Goods Inventory is 350 youth bats and 300 adult bats; FIFO inventory costing method is used.

d. Direct materials requirements are 48 ounces of wood per youth bat and 56 ounces of wood per adult bat. The cost of wood is $0.25 per ounce.

e. Raw Materials Inventory of December 31, 2018, consists of 24,000 ounces of wood at $0.25 per ounce.

f. Desired ending Raw Materials Inventory is 24,000 ounces (indirect materials are insignificant and not considered for budgeting purposes).

g. Each bat requires 0.7 hours of direct labor; direct labor costs average $18 per hour.

h. Variable manufacturing overhead is $0.30 per bat.

i. Fixed manufacturing overhead includes $1,300 per quarter in depreciation and $20,140 per quarter for other costs, such as insurance and property taxes.

j. Fixed selling and administrative expenses include $9,000 per quarter for salaries; $2,500 per quarter for rent; $1,000 per quarter for insurance; and $200 per quarter for depreciation.

k. Variable selling and administrative expenses include supplies at 2% of sales.

Requirements

1. Prepare Langley's sales budget for the first quarter of 2019.

2. Prepare Langley's production budget for the first quarter of 2019.

3. Prepare Langley's direct materials budget, direct labor budget, and manufacturing overhead budget for the first quarter of 2019. Round the predetermined overhead allocation rate to two decimal places. The overhead allocation base is direct labor hours.

4. Prepare Langley's cost of goods sold budget for the first quarter of 2019.

5. Prepare Langley's selling and administrative expense budget for the first quarter of 2019.

P22-39A Preparing a financial budget—schedule of cash receipts, schedule of cash payments, cash budget

Puckett Company has provided the following budget information for the first quarter of 2018:

Total sales	$ 216,000
Budgeted purchases of direct materials	40,600
Budgeted direct labor cost	36,800
Budgeted manufacturing overhead costs:	
Variable manufacturing overhead	1,025
Depreciation	1,000
Insurance and property taxes	6,650
Budgeted selling and administrative expenses:	
Salaries expense	14,000
Rent expense	2,500
Insurance expense	2,000
Depreciation expense	350
Supplies expense	4,320

Learning Objective 4

1. Total cash pmts. $194,095
2. Ending Cash bal. $14,505

Additional data related to the first quarter of 2018 for Puckett Company:

a. Capital expenditures include $41,000 for new manufacturing equipment to be purchased and paid in the first quarter.

b. Cash receipts are 75% of sales in the quarter of the sale and 25% in the quarter following the sale.

c. Direct materials purchases are paid 50% in the quarter purchased and 50% in the next quarter.

d. Direct labor, manufacturing overhead, and selling and administrative costs are paid in the quarter incurred.

e. Income tax expense for the first quarter is projected at $49,000 and is paid in the quarter incurred.

f. Puckett Company expects to have adequate cash funds and does not anticipate borrowing in the first quarter.

g. The December 31, 2017, balance in Cash is $25,000, in Accounts Receivable is $21,600, and in Accounts Payable is $16,500.

Requirements

1. Prepare Puckett Company's schedule of cash receipts from customers and schedule of cash payments for the first quarter of 2018.

2. Prepare Puckett Company's cash budget for the first quarter of 2018.

Learning Objective 4

1. NI $166,100
2. FG inventory $3,150

P22-40A Preparing a financial budget—budgeted income statement and balance sheet

Bradley Company has the following post-closing trial balance on December 31, 2018:

BRADLEY COMPANY Post-Closing Trial Balance December 31, 2018		
Account	Debit	Credit
Cash	$ 15,000	
Accounts Receivable	23,200	
Raw Materials Inventory	11,000	
Finished Goods Inventory	25,900	
Equipment	125,000	
Accumulated Depreciation		$ 35,000
Accounts Payable		13,600
Common Stock		150,000
Retained Earnings		1,500
Totals	$ 200,100	$ 200,100

The company's accounting department has gathered the following budgeting information for the first quarter of 2019:

Budgeted total sales, all on account	$ 305,000
Budgeted direct materials to be purchased and used	32,000
Budgeted direct labor cost	12,500
Budgeted manufacturing overhead costs:	
Variable manufacturing overhead	2,100
Depreciation	1,300
Insurance and property taxes	1,350
Budgeted cost of goods sold	72,000
Budgeted selling and administrative expenses:	
Salaries expense	7,000
Rent expense	2,000
Insurance expense	1,100
Depreciation expense	550
Supplies expense	15,250
Budgeted cash receipts from customers	263,500
Budgeted income tax expense	41,000
Budgeted purchase and payment for capital expenditures (additional equipment)	43,000

Additional information:

a. Direct materials purchases are paid 70% in the quarter purchased and 30% in the next quarter.

b. Direct labor, manufacturing overhead, selling and administrative costs, and income tax expense are paid in the quarter incurred.

c. Accounts payable at December 31, 2018 are paid in the first quarter of 2019.

Requirements

1. Prepare Bradley Company's budgeted income statement for the first quarter of 2019.

2. Prepare Bradley Company's budgeted balance sheet as of March 31, 2019.

Learning Objectives 3, 4

1. 3rd Qtr. DM purchases $34,680
4th Qtr. total cash pmts. (before
interest) $87,159

P22-41A Completing a comprehensive budgeting problem—manufacturing company

The Gerard Tire Company manufactures racing tires for bicycles. Gerard sells tires for $90 each. Gerard is planning for the next year by developing a master budget by quarters. Gerard's balance sheet for December 31, 2018, follows:

GERARD TIRE COMPANY		
Balance Sheet		
December 31, 2018		
Assets		
Current Assets:		
Cash	$ 56,000	
Accounts Receivable	20,000	
Raw Materials Inventory	5,100	
Finished Goods Inventory	9,900	
Total Current Assets		$ 91,000
Property, Plant, and Equipment:		
Equipment	194,000	
Less: Accumulated Depreciation	(42,000)	152,000
Total Assets		$ 243,000
Liabilities		
Current Liabilities:		
Accounts Payable		$ 8,000
Stockholders' Equity		
Common Stock, no par	$ 120,000	
Retained Earnings	115,000	
Total Stockholders' Equity		235,000
Total Liabilities and Stockholders' Equity		$ 243,000

Other data for Gerard Tire Company:

a. Budgeted sales are 1,500 tires for the first quarter and expected to increase by 200 tires per quarter. Cash sales are expected to be 10% of total sales, with the remaining 90% of sales on account.

b. Finished Goods Inventory on December 31, 2018, consists of 300 tires at $33 each.

c. Desired ending Finished Goods Inventory is 30% of the next quarter's sales; first quarter sales for 2020 are expected to be 2,300 tires. FIFO inventory costing method is used.

d. Raw Materials Inventory on December 31, 2018, consists of 600 pounds of rubber compound used to manufature the tires.

e. Direct materials requirements are 2 pounds of a rubber compound per tire. The cost of the compound is $8.50 per pound.

f. Desired ending Raw Materials Inventory is 40% of the next quarter's direct materials needed for production; desired ending inventory for December 31, 2019 is 600 pounds; indirect materials are insignificant and not considered for budgeting purposes.

g. Each tire requires 0.4 hours of direct labor; direct labor costs average $12 per hour.

h. Variable manufacturing overhead is $4 per tire.

i. Fixed manufacturing overhead includes $6,000 per quarter in depreciation and $16,770 per quarter for other costs, such as utilities, insurance, and property taxes.

j. Fixed selling and administrative expenses include $12,500 per quarter for salaries; $3,000 per quarter for rent; $450 per quarter for insurance; and $2,000 per quarter for depreciation.

k. Variable selling and administrative expenses include supplies at 2% of sales.

l. Capital expenditures include $15,000 for new manufacturing equipment, to be purchased and paid in the first quarter.

m. Cash receipts for sales on account are 70% in the quarter of the sale and 30% in the quarter following the sale; December 31, 2018, Accounts Receivable is received in the first quarter of 2019; uncollectible accounts are considered insignificant and not considered for budgeting purposes.

n. Direct materials purchases are paid 60% in the quarter purchased and 40% in the following quarter; December 31, 2018, Accounts Payable is paid in the first quarter of 2019.

o. Direct labor, manufacturing overhead, and selling and administrative costs are paid in the quarter incurred.

p. Income tax expense is projected at $1,500 per quarter and is paid in the quarter incurred.

q. Gerard desires to maintain a minimum cash balance of $55,000 and borrows from the local bank as needed in increments of $1,000 at the beginning of the quarter; principal repayments are made at the beginning of the quarter when excess funds are available and in increments of $1,000; interest is 6% per year and paid at the beginning of the quarter based on the amount outstanding from the previous quarter.

Requirements

1. Prepare Gerard's operating budget and cash budget for 2019 by quarter. Required schedules and budgets include: sales budget, production budget, direct materials budget, direct labor budget, manufacturing overhead budget, cost of goods sold budget, selling and administrative expense budget, schedule of cash receipts, schedule of cash payments, and cash budget. Manufacturing overhead costs are allocated based on direct labor hours. Round all calculations to the nearest dollar.

2. Prepare Gerard's annual financial budget for 2019, including budgeted income statement and budgeted balance sheet.

1246 chapter 22

Learning Objective 5

2. May purchases $102,500
3. Apr. total S&A exp. $19,300

P22-42A Preparing an operating budget—sales budget; inventory, purchases and COGS budget; and S&A expense budget

Burton Office Supply's March 31, 2018, balance sheet follows:

BURTON OFFICE SUPPLY Balance Sheet March 31, 2018		
Assets		
Current Assets:		
Cash	$ 32,000	
Accounts Receivable	12,000	
Merchandise Inventory	40,000	
Prepaid Insurance	1,600	
Total Current Assets		$ 85,600
Property, Plant, and Equipment:		
Equipment and Fixtures	40,000	
Less: Accumulated Depreciation	(12,000)	28,000
Total Assets		$ 113,600
Liabilities		
Current Liabilities:		
Accounts Payable	$ 16,000	
Salaries and Commissions Payable	2,700	
Total Liabilities		$ 18,700
Stockholders' Equity		
Common Stock, no par	25,000	
Retained Earnings	69,900	
Total Stockholders' Equity		94,900
Total Liabilities and Stockholders' Equity		$ 113,600

The budget committee of Burton Office Supply has assembled the following data:

a. Sales in April are expected to be $200,000. Burton forecasts that monthly sales will increase 2% over April sales in May. June's sales will increase by 4% over April sales. July sales will increase 20% over April sales.

b. Burton maintains inventory of $15,000 plus 25% of the cost of goods sold budgeted for the following month. Cost of goods sold equal 50% of sales revenue.

c. Monthly salaries amount to $7,000. Sales commissions equal 5% of sales for that month.

d. Other monthly expenses are as follows:

- Rent: $2,000

- Depreciation: $200

- Insurance: $100

- Income tax: $2,200

Requirements

1. Prepare Burton's sales budget for April and May 2018. Round all calculations to the nearest dollar.

2. Prepare Burton's inventory, purchases, and cost of goods sold budget for April and May.

3. Prepare Burton's selling and administrative expense budget for April and May.

P22-43A Preparing a financial budget—schedule of cash receipts, schedule cash payments, cash budget

Baxter Company's budget committee provides the following information:

Learning Objective 6

1. Jan. total cash recpts. $83,800
3. Feb. total pmts. for S&A exp. $9,977

December 31, 2017, account balances:		
Cash		$ 26,000
Accounts Receivable		19,000
Merchandise Inventory		25,000
Accounts Payable		11,000
Salaries and Commissions Payable		2,950
Budgeted amounts for 2018:	January	February
Sales, all on account	$ 81,000	$ 82,800
Purchases, all on account	40,600	41,500
Commissions Expense	4,050	4,140
Salaries Expense	3,500	3,500
Rent Expense	2,400	2,400
Depreciation Expense	900	900
Insurance Expense	300	300
Income Tax Expense	2,400	2,400

Requirements

1. Prepare the schedule of cash receipts from customers for January and February 2018. Assume cash receipts are 80% in the month of the sale and 20% in the month following the sale.

2. Prepare the schedule of cash payments for purchases for January and February 2018. Assume purchases are paid 60% in the month of purchase and 40% in the month following the purchase.

3. Prepare the schedule of cash payments for selling and administrative expenses for January and February 2018. Assume 40% of the accrual for Salaries and Commissions Payable is for commissions and 60% is for salaries. The December 31 balance will be paid in January. Salaries and commissions are paid 30% in the month incurred and 70% in the following month. Rent and income tax expenses are paid as incurred. Insurance expense is an expiration of the prepaid amount.

4. Prepare the cash budget for January and February 2018. Assume no financing took place.

Learning Objective 6

2. RE $111,610

P22-44A Preparing a financial budget—budgeted income statement and balance sheet

Ball Company has the following post-closing trial balance on December 31, 2018:

BALL COMPANY Post-Closing Trial Balance December 31, 2018		
Account	Debit	Credit
Cash	$ 23,000	
Accounts Receivable	32,000	
Merchandise Inventory	15,500	
Prepaid Insurance	2,400	
Equipment and Fixtures	60,000	
Accumulated Depreciation		$ 10,000
Accounts Payable		24,000
Salaries and Commissions Payable		6,600
Common Stock		18,000
Retained Earnings		74,300
Totals	$ 132,900	$ 132,900

The company's accounting department has gathered the following budgeting information for the first quarter of 2019:

Budgeted total sales, all on account	$ 121,800
Budgeted purchases of merchandise inventory, all on account	60,400
Budgeted cost of goods sold	60,900
Budgeted selling and administrative expenses:	
Commissions expense	6,090
Salaries expense	7,000
Rent expense	4,100
Depreciation expense	600
Insurance expense	400
Budgeted cash receipts from customers	125,840
Budgeted cash payments for merchandise inventory	67,775
Budgeted cash payments for salaries and commissions	14,822
Budgeted income tax expense	5,400

Additional information:

Rent and income tax expenses are paid as incurred. Insurance expense is an expiration of the prepaid amount.

Requirements

1. Prepare a budgeted income statement for the quarter ended March 31, 2019.
2. Prepare a budgeted balance sheet as of March 31, 2019.

P22-45A Completing a comprehensive budgeting problem—merchandising company

Learning Objectives 5, 6

6. Total cash pmts. $79,200
7. NI $6,500

Alliance Printing Supply of Baltimore has applied for a loan. Its bank has requested a budgeted income statement for April 2018 and a balance sheet at April 30, 2018. The March 31, 2018, balance sheet follows:

ALLIANCE PRINTING SUPPLY
Balance Sheet
March 31, 2018

Assets

Current Assets:		
Cash	$ 50,700	
Accounts Receivable	15,500	
Merchandise Inventory	12,000	
Total Current Assets		$ 78,200
Property, Plant, and Equipment:		
Equipment and Fixtures	80,500	
Less: Accumulated Depreciation	(12,900)	67,600
Total Assets		$ 145,800

Liabilities

Current Liabilities:		
Accounts Payable		$ 8,600

Stockholders' Equity

Common Stock, no par	$ 38,000	
Retained Earnings	99,200	
Total Stockholders' Equity		137,200
Total Liabilities and Stockholders' Equity		$ 145,800

As Alliance Printing Supply's controller, you have assembled the following additional information:

a. April dividends of $7,000 were declared and paid.

b. April capital expenditures of $16,300 budgeted for cash purchase of equipment.

c. April depreciation expense, $1,000.

d. Cost of goods sold, 40% of sales.

e. Desired ending inventory for April is $22,400.

f. April selling and administrative expenses include salaries of $37,000, 30% of which will be paid in cash and the remainder paid next month.

g. Additional April selling and administrative expenses also include miscellaneous expenses of 10% of sales, all paid in April.

h. April budgeted sales, $89,000, 80% collected in April and 20% in May.

i. April cash payments of March 31 liabilities incurred for March purchases of inventory, $8,600.

j. April purchases of inventory, $8,600 for cash and $37,400 on account. Half the credit purchases will be paid in April and half in May.

Requirements

1. Prepare the sales budget for April.

2. Prepare the inventory, purchases, and cost of goods sold budget for April.

3. Prepare the selling and administrative expense budget for April.

4. Prepare the schedule of cash receipts from customers for April.

5. Prepare the schedule of cash payments for selling and administrative expenses for April.

6. Prepare the cash budget for April. Assume the company does not use short-term financing to maintain a minimum cash balance.

7. Prepare the budgeted income statement for April.

8. Prepare the budgeted balance sheet at April 30, 2018.

Learning Objective 7

1. Option 2 Feb. NI $1,400

P22-46A Using sensitivity analysis

Caputo Company prepared the following budgeted income statement for the first quarter of 2018:

CAPUTO COMPANY Budgeted Income Statement For the Quarter Ended March 31, 2018				
	January	February	March	Total
Net Sales Revenue (20% increase per month)	$ 10,000	$ 12,000	$ 14,400	$ 36,400
Cost of Goods Sold (50% of sales)	5,000	6,000	7,200	18,200
Gross Profit	5,000	6,000	7,200	18,200
S&A Expenses ($3,000 + 5% of sales)	3,500	3,600	3,720	10,820
Operating Income	1,500	2,400	3,480	7,380
Income Tax Expense (30% of operating income)	450	720	1,044	2,214
Net Income	$ 1,050	$ 1,680	$ 2,436	$ 5,166

Caputo Company is considering two options. Option 1 is to increase advertising by $1,100 per month. Option 2 is to use better-quality materials in the manufacturing process. The better materials will increase the cost of goods sold to 55% but will provide a better product at the same sales price. The marketing manager projects either option will result in sales increases of 25% per month rather than 20%.

Requirements

1. Prepare budgeted income statements for both options, assuming both options begin in January and January sales remain $10,000. Round all calculations to the nearest dollar.

2. Which option should Caputo choose? Explain your reasoning.

> Problems **Group B**

Learning Objective 3

3. POHR $11
4. Adult bats COGS $65,450

P22-47B Preparing an operating budget—sales, production, direct materials, direct labor, overhead, COGS, and S&A expense budgets

The Irwin Batting Company manufactures wood baseball bats. Irwin's two primary products are a youth bat, designed for children and young teens, and an adult bat, designed for high school and college-aged players. Irwin sells the bats to sporting goods stores, and all sales are on account. The youth bat sells for $35; the adult bat sells for $50. Irwin's highest sales volume is in the first three months of the year as retailers prepare for the spring baseball season. Irwin's balance sheet for December 31, 2018, follows:

IRWIN BATTING COMPANY Balance Sheet December 31, 2018		
Assets		
Current Assets:		
Cash	$ 20,000	
Accounts Receivable	18,500	
Raw Materials Inventory	9,000	
Finished Goods Inventory	16,000	
Total Current Assets		$ 63,500
Property, Plant, and Equipment:		
Equipment	130,000	
Less: Accumulated Depreciation	(70,000)	60,000
Total Assets		$ 123,500
Liabilities		
Current Liabilities:		
Accounts Payable		$ 11,600
Stockholders' Equity		
Common Stock, no par	$ 90,000	
Retained Earnings	21,900	
Total Stockholders' Equity		111,900
Total Liabilities and Stockholders' Equity		$ 123,500

Other data for Irwin Batting Company for the first quarter of 2019:

a. Budgeted sales are 1,400 youth bats and 3,300 adult bats.

b. Finished Goods Inventory on December 31, 2018, consists of 700 youth bats at $15 each and 550 adult bats at $10 each.

c. Desired ending Finished Goods Inventory is 220 youth bats and 300 adult bats; FIFO inventory costing method is used.

d. Direct materials requirements are 40 ounces of wood for youth bats and 70 ounces of wood for adult bats. The cost of wood is $0.10 per ounce.

e. Raw Materials Inventory on December 31, 2018, consists of 90,000 ounces of wood at $0.10 per ounce.

f. Desired ending Raw Materials Inventory is 90,000 ounces (indirect materials are insignificant and not considered for budgeting purposes).

g. Each bat requires 0.4 hours of direct labor; direct labor costs average $26 per hour.

h. Variable manufacturing overhead is $0.30 per bat.

i. Fixed manufacturing overhead includes $1,300 per quarter in depreciation and $14,977 per quarter for other costs, such as insurance and property taxes.

j. Fixed selling and administrative expenses include $13,000 per quarter for salaries; $3,500 per quarter for rent; $1,400 per quarter for insurance; and $450 per quarter for depreciation.

k. Variable selling and administrative expenses include supplies at 1% of sales.

Requirements

1. Prepare Irwin's sales budget for the first quarter of 2019.

2. Prepare Irwin's production budget for the first quarter of 2019.

3. Prepare Irwin's direct materials, direct labor budget, and manufacturing overhead budget for the first quarter of 2019. Round the predetermined overhead allocation rate to two decimal places. The overhead allocation base is direct labor hours.

4. Prepare Irwin's cost of goods sold budget for the first quarter of 2019.

5. Prepare Irwin's selling and administrative expense budget for the first quarter of 2019.

Learning Objective 4

1. Total cash pmts. $176,980
2. Ending Cash bal. $30,320

P22-48B **Preparing a financial budget—schedule of cash receipts, schedule of cash payments, cash budget**

Haney Company has provided the following budget information for the first quarter of 2018:

Total sales	$214,000
Budgeted purchases of direct materials	40,300
Budgeted direct labor cost	37,200
Budgeted manufacturing overhead costs:	
Variable manufacturing overhead	1,150
Depreciation	1,200
Insurance and property taxes	6,600
Budgeted selling and administrative expenses:	
Salaries expense	13,000
Rent expense	2,500
Insurance expense	1,100
Depreciation expense	350
Supplies expense	4,280

Additional data related to the first quarter of 2018 for Haney Company:

a. Capital expenditures include $38,000 for new manufacturing equipment, to be purchased and paid in the first quarter.

b. Cash receipts are 65% of sales in the quarter of the sale and 35% in the quarter following the sale.

c. Direct materials purchases are paid 50% in the quarter purchased and 50% in the next quarter.

d. Direct labor, manufacturing overhead, and selling and administrative costs are paid in the quarter incurred.

e. Income tax expense for the first quarter is projected at $44,000 and is paid in the quarter incurred.

f. Haney Company expects to have adequate cash funds and does not anticipate borrowing in the first quarter.

g. The December 31, 2017, balance in Cash is $45,000, in Accounts Receivable is $23,200, and in Accounts Payable is $9,000.

Requirements

1. Prepare Haney Company's schedule of cash receipts from customers and schedule of cash payments for the first quarter of 2018.

2. Prepare Haney Company's cash budget for the first quarter of 2018.

P22-49B Preparing a financial budget—budgeted income statement and balance sheet

Ballentine Company has the following post-closing trial balance on December 31, 2018:

Learning Objective 4

1. NI $174,295
2. FG inventory $11,600

BALLENTINE COMPANY Post-Closing Trial Balance December 31, 2018		
Account	Debit	Credit
Cash	$ 45,000	
Accounts Receivable	17,900	
Raw Materials Inventory	7,000	
Finished Goods Inventory	25,900	
Equipment	120,000	
Accumulated Depreciation		$ 20,000
Accounts Payable		17,300
Common Stock		85,000
Retained Earnings		93,500
Totals	$ 215,800	$ 215,800

The company's accounting department has gathered the following budgeting information for the first quarter of 2019:

Budgeted total sales, all on account	$ 305,500
Budgeted direct materials to be purchased and used	40,000
Budgeted direct labor cost	12,500
Budgeted manufacturing overhead costs:	
Variable manufacturing overhead	2,600
Depreciation	800
Insurance and property taxes	1,100
Budgeted cost of goods sold	71,300
Budgeted selling and administrative expenses:	
Salaries expense	7,000
Rent expense	3,500
Insurance expense	2,000
Depreciation expense	350
Supplies expense	3,055
Budgeted cash receipts from customers	263,500
Budgeted income tax expense	44,000
Budgeted purchase and payment for capital expenditures (additional equipment)	34,000

Additional information:

a. Direct materials purchases are paid 50% in the quarter purchased and 50% in the next quarter.

b. Direct labor, ma following budgeted income statement nufacturing overhead, selling and administrative costs, and income tax expense are paid in the quarter incurred.

c. Accounts payable at December 31, 2018 are paid in the first quarter of 2019.

Requirements

1. Prepare Ballentine Company's budgeted income statement for the first quarter of 2019.

2. Prepare Ballentine Company's budgeted balance sheet as of March 31, 2019.

Learning Objectives 3, 4

1. 3rd Qtr. DM purchases $15,600
4th Qtr. total cash pmts. (before interest) $60,810

P22-50B Completing a comprehensive budgeting problem—manufacturing company

The Gavin Tire Company manufactures racing tires for bicycles. Gavin sells tires for $70 each. Gavin is planning for the next year by developing a master budget by quarters. Gavin's balance sheet for December 31, 2018, follows:

GAVIN TIRE COMPANY Balance Sheet December 31, 2018		
Assets		
Current Assets:		
Cash	$ 20,000	
Accounts Receivable	30,000	
Raw Materials Inventory	3,000	
Finished Goods Inventory	10,800	
Total Current Assets		$ 63,800
Property, Plant, and Equipment:		
Equipment	168,000	
Less: Accumulated Depreciation	(39,000)	129,000
Total Assets		$ 192,800
Liabilities		
Current Liabilities:		
Accounts Payable		$ 16,000
Stockholders' Equity		
Common Stock, no par	$ 130,000	
Retained Earnings	46,800	
Total Stockholders' Equity		176,800
Total Liabilities and Stockholders' Equity		$ 192,800

Other data for Gavin Tire Company:

a. Budgeted sales are 1,000 tires for the first quarter and expected to increase by 200 tires per quarter. Cash sales are expected to be 10% of total sales, with the remaining 90% of sales on account.

b. Finished Goods Inventory on December 31, 2018, consists of 300 tires at $36 each.

c. Desired ending Finished Goods Inventory is 40% of the next quarter's sales; first quarter sales for 2020 are expected to be 1,800 tires; FIFO inventory costing method is used.

d. Raw Materials Inventory on December 31, 2018 consists of 750 pounds of rubber compound used to manufacture the tires.

e. Direct materials requirements are 2.5 pounds of rubber compound per tire. The cost of the compound Is $4 per pound.

f. Desired ending Raw Materials Inventory is 40% of the next quarter's direct materials needed for production; desired ending inventory for December 31, 2019 is 750 pounds; indirect materials are insignificant and not considered for budgeting purposes.

g. Each tire requires 0.30 hours of direct labor; direct labor costs average $20 per hour.

h. Variable manufacturing overhead is $3 per tire.

i. Fixed manufacturing overhead includes $6,000 per quarter in depreciation and $10,860 per quarter for other costs, such as utilities, insurance, and property taxes.

j. Fixed selling and administrative expenses include $8,000 per quarter for salaries; $4,800 per quarter for rent; $1,950 per quarter for insurance; and $2,000 per quarter for depreciation.

k. Variable selling and administrative expenses include supplies at 2% of sales.

l. Capital expenditures include $25,000 for new manufacturing equipment, to be purchased and paid in the first quarter.

m. Cash receipts for sales on account are 70% in the quarter of the sale and 30% in the quarter following the sale; December 31, 2018, Accounts Receivable is received in the first quarter of 2019; uncollectible accounts are considered insignificant and not considered for budgeting purposes.

n. Direct materials purchases are paid 50% in the quarter purchased and 50% in the following quarter; December 31, 2018, Accounts Payable is paid in the first quarter of 2019.

o. Direct labor, manufacturing overhead, and selling and administrative costs are paid in the quarter incurred.

p. Income tax expense is projected at $3,500 per quarter and is paid in the quarter incurred.

q. Gavin desires to maintain a minimum cash balance of $20,000 and borrows from the local bank as needed in increments of $1,000 at the beginning of the quarter; principal repayments are made at the beginning of the quarter when excess funds are available and in increments of $1,000; interest is 12% per year and paid at the beginning of the quarter based on the amount outstanding from the previous quarter.

Requirements

1. Prepare Gavin's operating budget and cash budget for 2019 by quarter. Required schedules and budgets include: sales budget, production budget, direct materials budget, direct labor budget, manufacturing overhead budget, cost of goods sold budget, selling and administrative expense budget, schedule of cash receipts, schedule of cash payments, and cash budget. Manufacturing overhead costs are allocated based on direct labor hours. Round all calculations to the nearest dollar.

2. Prepare Gavin's annual financial budget for 2019, including budgeted income statement and budgeted balance sheet.

Learning Objective 5

2. May purchases $82,000
3. Apr. total S&A exp. $15,500

P22-51B Preparing an operating budget—sales budget; inventory, purchases and COGS budget; and S&A expense budget

Ballard Office Supply's March 31, 2018, balance sheet follows:

BALLARD OFFICE SUPPLY Balance Sheet March 31, 2018		
Assets		
Current Assets:		
Cash	$ 35,000	
Accounts Receivable	14,000	
Merchandise Inventory	27,000	
Prepaid Insurance	1,200	
Total Current Assets		$ 77,200
Property, Plant, and Equipment:		
Equipment and Fixtures	35,000	
Less: Accumulated Depreciation	(18,000)	17,000
Total Assets		$ 94,200
Liabilities		
Current Liabilities:		
Accounts Payable	$ 19,000	
Salaries and Commissions Payable	3,325	
Total Liabilities		$ 22,325
Stockholders' Equity		
Common Stock, no par	18,000	
Retained Earnings	53,875	
Total Stockholders' Equity		71,875
Total Liabilities and Stockholders' Equity		$ 94,200

The budget committee of Ballard Office Supply has assembled the following data.

a. Sales in April are expected to be $160,000. Ballard forecasts that monthly sales will increase 2% over April sales in May. June's sales will increase by 4% over April sales. July sales will increase 20% over April sales.

b. Ballard maintains inventory of $7,000 plus 25% of the cost of goods sold budgeted for the following month. Cost of goods sold equal 50% of sales revenue.

c. Monthly salaries amount to $3,000. Sales commissions equal 5% of sales for that month.

d. Other monthly expenses are as follows:

- Rent: $3,400

- Depreciation: $800

- Insurance: $300

- Income tax: $1,500

Requirements

1. Prepare Ballard's sales budget for April and May 2018. Round all calculations to the nearest dollar.

2. Prepare Ballard's inventory, purchases, and cost of goods sold budget for April and May.

3. Prepare Ballard's selling and administrative expense budget for April and May.

P22-52B Preparing a financial budget—schedule of cash receipts, schedule of cash payments, cash budget

Beasley Company's budget committee provides the following information:

Learning Objective 6

1. Feb. total cash recpts. $84,320
3. Feb. total pmts. for S&A exp. $11,414

December 31, 2017, account balances:		
Cash		$ 32,000
Accounts Receivable		19,000
Merchandise Inventory		16,000
Accounts Payable		15,000
Salaries and Commissions Payable		2,900
Budgeted amounts for 2018:	**January**	**February**
Sales, all on account	$ 84,000	$ 84,400
Purchases, all on account	41,000	41,600
Commissions Expense	4,200	4,220
Salaries Expense	5,000	5,000
Rent Expense	2,200	2,200
Depreciation Expense	500	500
Insurance Expense	200	200
Income Tax Expense	1,900	1,900

Requirements

1. Prepare the schedule of cash receipts from customers for January and February 2018. Assume cash receipts are 80% in the month of the sale and 20% in the month following the sale.

2. Prepare the schedule of cash payments for purchases for January and February 2018. Assume purchases are paid 70% in the month of purchase and 30% in the month following the purchase.

3. Prepare the schedule of cash payments for selling and administrative expense for January and February 2018. Assume 25% of the accrual for Salaries and Commissions Payable is for commissions and 75% is for salaries. The December 31 balance will be paid in January. Salaries and commissions are paid 70% in the month incurred and 30% in the following month. Rent and income tax expenses are paid as incurred. Insurance expense is an expiration of the prepaid amount.

4. Prepare the cash budget for January and February. Assume no financing took place.

Learning Objective 6

2. RE $64,965

P22-53B Preparing a financial budget—budgeted income statement and balance sheet

Buncomb Company has the following post-closing trial balance on December 31, 2018:

BUNCOMB COMPANY Post-Closing Trial Balance December 31, 2018		
Account	**Debit**	**Credit**
Cash	$ 22,000	
Accounts Receivable	20,000	
Merchandise Inventory	15,500	
Prepaid Insurance	2,400	
Equipment and Fixtures	30,000	
Accumulated Depreciation		$ 20,000
Accounts Payable		26,000
Salaries and Commissions Payable		6,700
Common Stock		14,000
Retained Earnings		23,200
Totals	$ 89,900	$ 89,900

The company's accounting department has gathered the following budgeting information for the first quarter of 2019:

Budgeted total sales, all on account	$ 121,700
Budgeted purchases of merchandise inventory, all on account	61,200
Budgeted cost of goods sold	60,850
Budgeted selling and administrative expenses:	
Commissions expense	6,085
Salaries expense	3,000
Rent expense	4,100
Depreciation expense	900
Insurance expense	300
Budgeted cash receipts from customers	126,450
Budgeted cash payments for merchandise inventory	67,925
Budgeted cash payments for salaries and commissions	14,836
Budgeted income tax expense	4,700

Additional information:

Rent and income tax expenses are paid as incurred. Insurance expense is an expiration of the prepaid amount.

Requirements

1. Prepare a budgeted income statement for the quarter ended March 31, 2019.
2. Prepare a budgeted balance sheet as of March 31, 2019.

P22-54B Completing a comprehensive budgeting problem—merchandising company

Learning Objectives 5, 6

6. Total cash pmts. $88,200
7. NI $300

Belton Printing Company of Baltimore has applied for a loan. Its bank has requested a budgeted income statement for the month of April 2018 and a balance sheet at April 30, 2018. The March 31, 2018, balance sheet follows:

BELTON PRINTING COMPANY Balance Sheet March 31, 2018		
Assets		
Current Assets:		
Cash	$ 51,100	
Accounts Receivable	13,600	
Merchandise Inventory	12,000	
Total Current Assets		$ 76,700
Property, Plant, and Equipment:		
Equipment and Fixtures	81,100	
Less: Accumulated Depreciation	(12,400)	68,700
Total Assets		$ 145,400
Liabilities		
Current Liabilities:		
Accounts Payable		$ 8,300
Stockholders' Equity		
Common Stock, no par	$ 35,000	
Retained Earnings	102,100	
Total Stockholders' Equity		137,100
Total Liabilities and Stockholders' Equity		$ 145,400

As Belton Printing's controller, you have assembled the following additional information:

a. April dividends of $7,000 were declared and paid.

b. April capital expenditures of $17,000 budgeted for cash purchase of equipment.

c. April depreciation expense, $800.

d. Cost of goods sold, 55% of sales.

e. Desired ending inventory for April is $24,800.

f. April selling and administrative expenses includes salaries of $29,000, 20% of which will be paid in cash and the remainder paid next month.

g. Additional April selling and administrative expenses also include miscellaneous expenses of 10% of sales, all paid in April.

h. April budgeted sales, $86,000, 80% collected in April and 20% in May.

i. April cash payments of March 31 liabilities incurred for March purchases of inventory, $8,300.

j. April purchases of inventory, $22,900 for cash and $37,200 on account. Half the credit purchases will be paid in April and half in May.

Requirements

1. Prepare the sales budget for April.
2. Prepare the inventory, purchases, and cost of goods sold budget for April.
3. Prepare the selling and administrative expense budget for April.
4. Prepare the schedule of cash receipts from customers for April.
5. Prepare the schedule of cash payments for selling and administrative expenses for April.
6. Prepare the cash budget for April. Assume the company does not use short-term financing to maintain a minimum cash balance.
7. Prepare the budgeted income statement for April.
8. Prepare the budgeted balance sheet at April 30, 2018.

Learning Objective 7

1. Option 2 Feb. NI $1,876

P22-55B Using sensitivity analysis

Holly Company prepared the following budgeted income statement for the first quarter of 2018:

HOLLY COMPANY Budgeted Income Statement For the Quarter Ended March 31, 2018					
		January	February	March	Total
Net Sales Revenue	(20% increase per month)	$ 8,000	$ 9,600	$ 11,520	$ 29,120
Cost of Goods Sold	(40% of sales)	3,200	3,840	4,608	11,648
Gross Profit		4,800	5,760	6,912	17,472
S&A Expenses	($2,000 + 10% of sales)	2,800	2,960	3,152	8,912
Operating Income		2,000	2,800	3,760	8,560
Income Tax Expense	(30% of operating income)	600	840	1,128	2,568
Net Income		$ 1,400	$ 1,960	$ 2,632	$ 5,992

Holly Company is considering two options. Option 1 is to increase advertising by $700 per month. Option 2 is to use better-quality materials in the manufacturing process. The better materials will increase the cost of goods sold to 45% but will provide a better product at the same sales price. The marketing manager projects either option will result in sales increases of 30% per month rather than 20%.

Requirements

1. Prepare budgeted income statements for both options, assuming both options begin in January and January sales remain $8,000. Round all calculations to the nearest dollar.
2. Which option should Holly choose? Explain your reasoning.

CRITICAL THINKING

> Using Excel

P22-56 Using Excel for to prepare an operating budeget (manufacturing company)

Download an Excel template for this problem online in MyAccountingLab or at http://www.pearsonhighered.com/Horngren.

Thunder Creek Company is preparing budgets for the first quarter of 2018. All relevant information is presented on the Excel template.

Requirements

1. Prepare a Sales Budget.

2. Prepare a Production Budget.

3. Prepare a Direct Materials Budget.

4. Prepare a Direct Labor Budget.

5. Prepare a Manufacturing Overhead Budget.

6. Prepare a Cost of Goods Sold Budget

7. Prepare a Selling and Administrative Expense Budget.

> Continuing Problem

P22-57 Preparing a financial budget

This problem continues the Piedmont Computer Company situation from Chapter 21. Assume Piedmont Computer began January with $15,000 cash. Management forecasts that cash receipts from credit customers will be $48,000 in January and $51,000 in February. Projected cash payments include equipment purchases ($20,000 in January and $41,000 in February) and selling and administrative expenses ($2,000 each month).

Piedmont Computer Company's bank requires a $26,000 minimum balance in the firm's checking account. At the end of any month when the account balance falls below $26,000, the bank automatically extends credit to the firm in multiples of $5,000. Piedmont Computer Company borrows as little as possible and pays back loans each month in $1,000 increments, plus 12% interest on the entire unpaid principal. The first payment occurs one month after the loan.

Requirements

1. Prepare Piedmont Computer Company's cash budget for January and February 2020.

2. How much cash will Piedmont Computer Company borrow in February if cash receipts from customers that month total $41,000 instead of $51,000?

> Tying It All Together Case 22-1

Before you begin this assignment, read the article, "Budgeting in the Real World" found at http://ww2.cfo.com/strategy/2005/07/. Answer the following questions based on your reading.

Requirements

1. How did the **San Diego Zoo** use technology to make the budget process easier?

2. How can companies hold managers more accountable?

3. What is the greatest contribution of software to the budgeting process?

> Decision Case 22-1

Each autumn, as a hobby, Anne Magnuson weaves cotton place mats to sell through a local craft shop. The mats sell for $20 per set of four. The shop charges a 10% commission and remits the net proceeds to Magnuson at the end of December. Magnuson has woven and sold 25 sets each year for the past two years. She has enough cotton in inventory to make another 25 sets. She paid $7 per set for the cotton. Magnuson uses a four-harness loom that she purchased for cash exactly two years ago. It is depreciated at the rate of $10 per month. The Accounts Payable balance relates to the cotton inventory and is payable by September 30.

Magnuson is considering buying an eight-harness loom so that she can weave more intricate patterns in linen. The new loom costs $1,000 and would be depreciated at $20 per month. Her bank has agreed to lend her $1,000 at 18% interest per year, with $200 payment of principal, plus accrued interest payable each December 31. Magnuson believes she can weave 15 linen place mat sets in time for the Christmas rush if she does not weave any cotton mats. She predicts that each linen set will sell for $50. Linen costs $18 per set. Magnuson's supplier will sell her linen on credit, payable December 31.

Magnuson plans to keep her old loom whether or not she buys the new loom. The balance sheet for her weaving business at August 31, 2018, is as follows:

ANNE MAGNUSON, WEAVER Balance Sheet August 31, 2018			
Assets		**Liabilities**	
Current Assets:		Current Liabilities:	
Cash	$ 25	Account Payable	$ 74
Inventory of cotton	175		
Total Current Assets	200		
Property, Plant, and Equipment:		**Stockholders' Equity**	
Loom	500	Stockholders' Equity	386
Less: Accumulated Depreciation	(240)		
Total PP&E	260		
Total Assets	$ 460	Total Liabilities and Stockholders' Equity	$ 460

Requirements

1. Prepare a cash budget for the four months ending December 31, 2018, for two alternatives: weaving the place mats in cotton using the existing loom and weaving the place mats in linen using the new loom. For each alternative, prepare a budgeted income statement for the four months ending December 31, 2018, and a budgeted balance sheet at December 31, 2018.

2. On the basis of financial considerations only, what should Magnuson do? Give your reason.

3. What nonfinancial factors might Magnuson consider in her decision?

> Ethical Issue 22-1

Southeast Suites operates a regional hotel chain. Each hotel is operated by a manager and an assistant manager/controller. Many of the staff who run the front desk, clean the rooms, and prepare the breakfast buffet work part time or have a second job, so employee turnover is high.

Assistant Manager/Controller Terry Dunn asked the new bookkeeper to help prepare the hotel's master budget. The master budget is prepared once a year and is submitted to company headquarters for approval. Once approved, the master budget is used to evaluate the hotel's performance. These performance evaluations affect hotel managers' bonuses, and they also affect company decisions on which hotels deserve extra funds for capital improvements.

When the budget was almost complete, Dunn asked the bookkeeper to increase amounts budgeted for labor and supplies by 15%. When asked why, Dunn responded that hotel manager Clay Murry told her to do this when she began working at the hotel. Murry explained that this budgetary cushion gave him flexibility in running the hotel. For example, because company headquarters tightly controls capital improvement funds, Murry can use the extra money budgeted for labor and supplies to replace broken televisions or pay "bonuses" to keep valued employees. Dunn initially accepted this explanation because she had observed similar behavior at the hotel where she worked previously.

Requirements

Put yourself in Dunn's position. In deciding how to deal with the situation, answer the following questions:

1. What is the ethical issue?

2. What are the options?

3. What are the possible consequences?

4. What should you do?

> Fraud Case 22-1

Patrick works for McGill's Computer Repair, owned and operated by Frank McGill. As a computer technician, Patrick has grown accustomed to friends and family members asking for assistance with their personal computers. In an effort to increase his income, Patrick started a personal computer repair business that he operates out of his home on a part-time basis, working evenings and weekends. Because Patrick is doing this "on the side" for friends and family, he does not want to charge as much as McGill's charges its customers. When Frank McGill assigned Patrick the task of developing the budget for his department, Patrick increased the amount budgeted for computer parts. When the budget was approved, Patrick purchased as many parts as the budget allowed, even when they were not needed. He then took the extra parts home to use in his personal business in an effort to keep his costs down and profits up. So far, no one at McGill's has asked about the parts expense because Patrick has not allowed the actual amount spent to exceed the budgeted amount.

Requirements

1. Why would Patrick's actions be considered fraudulent?

2. What can a company do to protect against this kind of business risk?

MyAccountingLab **For a wealth of online resources, including exercises, problems, media, and immediate tutorial help, please visit** http://www.myaccountinglab.com.

> Quick Check Answers

1. d **2.** a **3.** c **4.** b **5.** c **6.** a **7.** c **8.** a **9.** a **10.** d **11.** b **12.** a **13.** d

Flexible Budgets and Standard Cost Systems

23

Why Are We Not Meeting Our Budget?

Ritchie Billings owns a small food-processing plant in the Midwest. The company specializes in producing flour by processing grains grown by local farmers. The product list includes oat, wheat, soy, and corn flour. Ritchie is looking at the income statement for the past six months and comparing it to the budget. There is a difference between the budgeted operating income and the actual operating income, but Ritchie is having a hard time figuring out why.

Ritchie knows he has been paying the farmers more for grain this year, which has increased the direct materials cost. Also, he has hired some really good workers lately. He is paying them more than expected, and they have been so efficient he did not have to replace one employee who quit. Shouldn't the savings from having one less employee offset the increased wages paid to the other employees? Ritchie also recently replaced a manufacturing machine. The new machine is much more efficient, using less electricity and requiring less maintenance. Where are those cost savings on the income statement?

Ritchie needs a system that will allow him to better analyze the costs his company incurs so he can better understand the effects his decisions have on operating income.

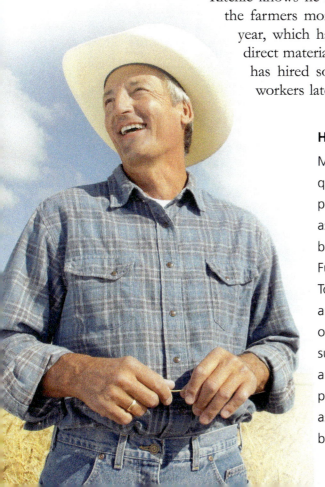

How Much Corn Is in Corn Flakes?

Most production companies have manufacturing standards for both costs and quantities of inputs. For example, consider the **Kellogg Company**. Kellogg Company manufactures and markets ready-to-eat cereal and convenience foods, such as All-Bran, Cocoa Krispies, Special K, and Corn Flakes. More than 100 years ago, brothers W. K. Kellogg and Dr. John Harvey Kellogg accidentally flaked wheat berry. Further experimentation led to flaked corn and the recipe for Kellogg's Corn Flakes. Today, the Kellogg Company uses corn, wheat, potato flakes, soy bean oil, sugar, and cocoa as their principal raw materials. When the company produces a batch of Corn Flakes, the company expects to use a certain quantity of milled corn and sugar. Additionally, the company has expectations about the cost of the milled corn and sugar. Even small changes in these expectations can have a significant effect on profits, so they are closely monitored. In this chapter, you learn how companies such as Kellogg Company can use flexible budgets and standard cost systems to control business activities and take corrective action when needed.

Chapter 23 Learning Objectives

1 Prepare flexible budgets and performance reports using static and flexible budgets

2 Identify the benefits of a standard cost system and understand how standards are set

3 Compute the standard cost variances for direct materials and direct labor

4 Compute the standard cost variances for manufacturing overhead

5 Describe the relationship among and responsibility for the product cost variances

6 Record transactions in a standard cost system and prepare a standard cost income statement

Previously, you learned how managers use budgets for planning, directing, and controlling business activities. Exhibit 23-1 illustrates budgeting objectives.

Exhibit 23-1 | Budgeting Objectives

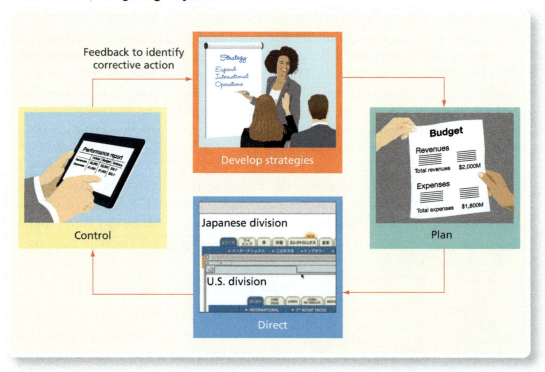

The master budget focuses on the planning step. In this chapter, we focus on the directing and controlling steps as we look at the decisions managers make during and after the budgeting period, based on the actual results. Managers may ask:

- Did my division meet its sales goals?
- Have costs increased?
- Sales have dropped, so how do we need to adjust spending?

Businesses often have to make hard decisions. An economic downturn or increased competition may cause a decrease in sales. If that happens, spending must also decrease in order for the company to remain profitable. A budget *variance* is the difference between an *actual* amount and a *budgeted* amount. This chapter shows how managers use variances to direct and control business activities. It is important to know *why* actual amounts differ from the budget. This enables managers to identify problems and decide what action to take.

HOW DO MANAGERS USE BUDGETS TO CONTROL BUSINESS ACTIVITIES?

To illustrate the concepts, we will use Cheerful Colors, a fictitious crayon manufacturer. The company begins the manufacturing process by combining direct materials, such as heated liquid paraffin wax and dry pigments. The heated mixture is then poured into molds. After the molds cool, the crayons are removed, inspected, and boxed in bulk. The crayons are then shipped to another facility where paper wrappers are added to each crayon and the crayons are boxed to meet individual customers' needs. Cheerful Colors uses molds that make 100 crayons each and considers each batch of 100 crayons to be one unit for sales and costing purposes.

Performance Reports Using Static Budgets

Before the beginning of the year, Cheerful Colors's managers prepared a master budget. The master budget is a **static budget,** which means that it is prepared for only *one* level of sales volume. The static budget does not change after it is developed.

    Exhibit 23-2 (on the next page) shows a static budget performance report for Cheerful Colors for 2019. A **budget performance report** is a report that summarizes the actual results, budgeted amounts, and the differences. The static budget performance report shows that Cheerful Colors's actual operating income for 2019 is $36,320. This is $2,570 higher than expected from the static budget. This is a $2,570 favorable variance for 2019 operating income. A **variance** is the difference between an actual amount and the budgeted amount. The variances are presented in the third column of Exhibit 23-2. Variances can be either favorable or unfavorable as follows:

- Favorable (F) if an actual amount *increases* operating income
  - Actual revenue > Budgeted revenue
  - Actual expense < Budgeted expense

- Unfavorable (U) if an actual amount *decreases* operating income
  - Actual revenue < Budgeted revenue
  - Actual expense > Budgeted expense

The variances in Exhibit 23-2 are called **static budget variances**. A static budget variance is the difference between actual results and the expected results in the static budget. Cheerful Colors's static budget variance for operating income is favorable primarily because Cheerful Colors sold 52,000 batches of crayons rather than the 50,000 batches it budgeted to sell during 2019. But there is more to this story. A static budget performance report is useful in evaluating a manager's effectiveness when the actual level of sales closely approximates the budgeted amount. It is also useful in evaluating the manager's ability to control fixed manufacturing costs and fixed selling and administrative expenses. A static budget performance report, though, is not helpful in evaluating variable costs because as production changes, variable costs should change accordingly. Cheerful Colors needs a better tool to examine budgeted income at different sales levels.

Exhibit 23-2 | **Static Budget Performance Report**

CHEERFUL COLORS Static Budget Performance Report For the Year Ended December 31, 2019			
	Actual Results	Static Budget	Static Budget Variance
Units (Batches of 100)	52,000	50,000	2,000 F
Sales Revenue	$ 384,800	$ 375,000	$ 9,800 F
Variable Costs:			
Manufacturing:			
Direct Materials	104,000	87,500	16,500 U
Direct Labor	145,600	150,000	4,400 F
Variable Overhead	30,160	37,500	7,340 F
Selling and Administrative:			
Supplies	19,200	18,750	450 U
Total Variable Costs	298,960	293,750	5,210 U
Contribution Margin	85,840	81,250	4,590 F
Fixed Costs:			
Manufacturing	23,920	25,000	1,080 F
Selling and Administrative	25,600	22,500	3,100 U
Total Fixed Costs	49,520	47,500	2,020 U
Operating Income	$ 36,320	$ 33,750	$ 2,570 F

Performance Reports Using Flexible Budgets

The report in Exhibit 23-2 is hard to analyze because the static budget is based on 50,000 batches of crayons, but the actual results are for 52,000 batches of crayons. This report raises more questions than it answers—for example:

- Why did the $16,500 unfavorable direct materials variance occur?
- Did workers waste materials?
- Did the cost of materials suddenly increase?
- How much of the additional expense arose because Cheerful Colors sold 52,000 batches rather than 50,000 batches?

We need a flexible budget to help answer these questions.

Preparing Flexible Budgets

Flexible Budget
A budget prepared for various levels of sales volume.

A **flexible budget** summarizes revenues and expenses for various levels of sales volume within a relevant range. A flexible budget is simply a series of budgets at different levels of activity. Flexible budgets are useful because they show operating income at several different levels of activity. Flexible budgets are also useful because they help to isolate how variable costs change based on different levels of activity. To create a flexible budget, you need to know the following:

- Budgeted selling price per unit
- Budgeted variable cost per unit
  - Budgeted product costs
    - Budgeted direct materials
    - Budgeted direct labor
    - Budgeted variable manufacturing overhead costs
  - Budgeted variable selling and administrative expenses
- Total budgeted fixed costs
  - Budgeted fixed manufacturing overhead costs
  - Budgeted fixed selling and administrative expenses
- Different volume levels within the relevant range

Exhibit 23-3 is a flexible budget for Cheerful Colors's revenues and expenses that predicts what will happen if sales reach 48,000 batches, 50,000 batches, or 52,000 batches of crayons during 2019. The budgeted sales price per batch is $7.50. Budgeted variable costs are $1.75 for direct materials, $3.00 for direct labor, $0.75 for variable manufacturing overhead, and 5% of sales revenue for selling and administrative supplies. Budgeted fixed costs are $25,000 for manufacturing overhead and $22,500 for selling and administrative.

Exhibit 23-3 | **Flexible Budget**

CHEERFUL COLORS Flexible Budget For the Year Ended December 31, 2019				
	Budget Amounts per Unit			
Units (Batches of 100)		48,000	50,000	52,000
Sales Revenue	$ 7.50	$ 360,000	$ 375,000	$ 390,000
Variable Costs:				
Manufacturing:				
Direct Materials	1.75	84,000	87,500	91,000
Direct Labor	3.00	144,000	150,000	156,000
Variable Overhead	0.75	36,000	37,500	39,000
Selling and Administrative:				
Supplies	5% of sales	18,000	18,750	19,500
Total Variable Costs		282,000	293,750	305,500
Contribution Margin		78,000	81,250	84,500
Fixed Costs:				
Manufacturing		25,000	25,000	25,000
Selling and Administrative		22,500	22,500	22,500
Total Fixed Costs		47,500	47,500	47,500
Operating Income		$ 30,500	$ 33,750	$ 37,000

Notice in Exhibit 23-3 that sales revenue, variable costs, and contribution margin increase as more batches of crayons are sold, but fixed costs remain constant regardless of the number of crayons sold within the relevant range of 48,000 to 52,000 batches. This is an important distinction to remember about flexible budgets. Because total fixed costs remain constant within a specific relevant range of output, fixed costs will not change on a flexible budget. Variable costs, in total, will.

Budget Variances

It is not enough to know that a variance occurred. Managers must know *why* a variance occurred in order to pinpoint problems and take corrective action. As you can see in Exhibit 23-2, the static budget underestimated both sales and total variable costs. These differences are caused by two primary factors: There is a difference in prices or costs, and/or there is a difference in volume. To develop more useful information, managers divide the static budget variance into two broad categories:

Flexible Budget Variance
The difference between actual results and the expected results in the flexible budget for the *actual* units sold.

Sales Volume Variance
The difference between the expected results in the flexible budget for the *actual* units sold and the static budget.

- **Flexible budget variance**—the difference between actual results and the expected results in the flexible budget for the *actual* units sold. The variance arises because the company had different revenues and/or costs than expected for the *actual* units sold. The flexible budget variance occurs because sales price per unit, variable cost per unit, and/or total fixed costs were different than planned on in the static budget.

- **Sales volume variance**—the difference between expected results in the flexible budget for the *actual* units sold and the static budget. This variance arises because the actual number of units sold differed from the number of units on which the static budget was based. Sales volume variance is the volume difference between actual sales and budgeted sales.

Exhibit 23-4 diagrams these variances.

Exhibit 23-4 | **Static Budget Variances**

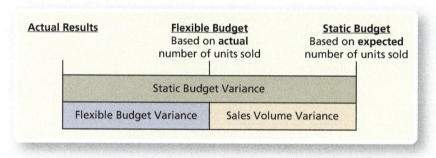

Following are the formulas for computing the two variances for Cheerful Colors:

Flexible budget variance = Actual results (based on 52,000 units sold) − Flexible budget (based on 52,000 units sold)
Sales volume variance = Flexible budget (based on 52,000 units sold) − Static budget (based on 50,000 units sold)

We have seen that Cheerful Colors budgeted (planned to sell) 50,000 batches of crayons during 2019. Actual sales were 52,000 batches. We need to compute the flexible budget variance and the sales volume variance for Cheerful Colors. Exhibit 23-5 is Cheerful Colors's flexible budget performance report for 2019. Recall that the variances in the second and fourth columns of Exhibit 23-5 are:

- Favorable (F) if an actual amount increases operating income.

- Unfavorable (U) if an actual amount decreases operating income.

Column 1 of the performance report shows the actual results—based on the 52,000 batches of crayons actually sold. These amounts were originally shown in Exhibit 23-2 and are not based on the budget amounts per unit, but are the actual operating revenues and expenses for the period. Actual operating income is $36,320 for 2019.

Column 3 is Cheerful Colors's flexible budget (as shown in Exhibit 23-3) for the 52,000 batches actually sold. Operating income should have been $37,000 based on that level of sales.

Exhibit 23-5 | **Flexible Budget Performance Report**

	1		2 (1) – (3)	3	4 (3) – (5)	5
CHEERFUL COLORS Flexible Budget Performance Report For the Year Ended December 31, 2019						
	Budget Amounts per Unit	Actual Results	Flexible Budget Variance	Flexible Budget	Sales Volume Variance	Static Budget
Units (Batches of 100)		52,000		52,000		50,000
Sales Revenue	$ 7.50	$ 384,800	$ 5,200 U	$ 390,000	$ 15,000 F	$ 375,000
Variable Costs:						
Manufacturing:						
Direct Materials	1.75	104,000	13,000 U	91,000	3,500 U	87,500
Direct Labor	3.00	145,600	10,400 F	156,000	6,000 U	150,000
Variable Overhead	0.75	30,160	8,840 F	39,000	1,500 U	37,500
Selling and Administrative:						
Supplies	5% of sales	19,200	300 F	19,500	750 U	18,750
Total Variable Costs		298,960	6,540 F	305,500	11,750 U	293,750
Contribution Margin		85,840	1,340 F	84,500	3,250 F	81,250
Fixed Costs:						
Manufacturing		23,920	1,080 F	25,000	0	25,000
Selling and Administrative		25,600	3,100 U	22,500	0	22,500
Total Fixed Costs		49,520	2,020 U	47,500	0	47,500
Operating Income		$ 36,320	$ 680 U	$ 37,000	$ 3,250 F	$ 33,750

Flexible Budget Variance
$ 680 U

Sales Volume Variance
$ 3,250 F

Static Budget Variance
$ 2,570 F

Column 5 (originally shown in Exhibit 23-2) gives the static budget for the 50,000 batches expected to have been sold in 2019. Cheerful Colors budgeted earnings of $33,750 before the budgeting period began.

Column 2 is the flexible budget variance and shows operating income is $680 less than Cheerful Colors expected for 52,000 batches of crayons. Managers want to know why operating income did not match the flexible budget.

- Sales revenue was $5,200 less than expected for 52,000 batches.
- Total variable costs were $6,540 less than expected for 52,000 batches.
- Total fixed costs were $2,020 higher than expected for 52,000 batches.

Overall, expenses decreased by $4,520 ($6,540 decrease in total variable expenses minus $2,020 increase in total fixed expenses) below the flexible budget, and sales revenue decreased by $5,200, resulting in the overall $680 unfavorable flexible budget variance for operating income.

Managers need to focus on why costs are higher than expected to determine whether the increase is controllable, which means it can be managed, or uncontrollable due to some abnormal or isolated event. Managers also focus on why costs are lower than expected to determine whether, for example, poorer-quality materials were used or standards need to be updated.

Column 4 is the sales volume variance, which is the difference between column 3 and column 5. The differences between the static budget and the flexible budget—column 4—arise only because Cheerful Colors sold 52,000 batches of crayons rather than the 50,000 batches it planned to sell. Sales revenue is $15,000 more than Cheerful Colors planned (2,000 more batches sold at $7.50 budgeted sales price). Total variable expenses are $11,750 higher (unfavorable) than planned for the same reason—2,000 more batches sold. Fixed costs are the same for both budgets as the units were within the relevant range. Overall, operating income is favorable by $3,250 because Cheerful Colors sold more crayons than it planned to sell (52,000 batches rather than the 50,000 batches budgeted). Notice that this is also the planned contribution margin difference of $3,250.

The next step is to look deeper into the flexible budget variances to better understand what caused the variances so managers can take corrective action as needed.

1. Garland Company expects to sell 600 wreaths in December 2018, but wants to plan for 100 more and 100 less than expected. The wreaths sell for $5.00 each and have variable costs of $2.00 each. Fixed costs are expected to be $500 for the month. Prepare a flexible budget for 500, 600, and 700 wreaths.

Check your answer online in MyAccountingLab or at http://www.pearsonhighered.com/Horngren.

For more practice, see Short Exercises S23-1 through S23-3. MyAccountingLab

WHY DO MANAGERS USE A STANDARD COST SYSTEM TO CONTROL BUSINESS ACTIVITIES?

Learning Objective 2

Identify the benefits of a standard cost system and understand how standards are set

Standard

A price, cost, or quantity that is expected under normal conditions.

Standard Cost System

An accounting system that uses standards for product costs— direct materials, direct labor, and manufacturing overhead.

Most companies use standards to develop budgets. A **standard** is the price, cost, or quantity that is expected under normal conditions. For example, based on Exhibit 23-5, Cheerful Colors expects the direct materials to cost $1.75 per batch of 100 crayons. Therefore, the standard cost for direct materials is $1.75, and that was the amount used to develop both the static and flexible budgets. The terms *standard* and *budget* are sometimes used interchangeably. However, a budget amount generally indicates a total amount, whereas a standard amount is a per unit amount. In the case of direct materials, the standard is $1.75 per batch, and the budgeted amount for 52,000 batches is $91,000 ($1.75 per batch × 52,000 batches).

Cheerful Colors uses a **standard cost system**, which is an accounting system that uses standards for product costs—direct materials, direct labor, and manufacturing overhead. A standard cost system allows management to determine how much a product should cost. Each input has both a cost standard and an efficiency standard. For example, Cheerful Colors has a standard for the following:

- Cost it pays per pound of paraffin wax (this determines the cost standard)

- Amount of wax it uses for making the crayons (this determines the efficiency standard)

Let's see how managers set these cost and efficiency standards.

Setting Standards

Setting standards can be the most difficult part of using a standard cost system. Setting standards requires coordination and communication among different divisions and functions. For example, the cost standard for direct materials starts with the base purchase cost of each unit of Raw Materials Inventory. Accountants help purchasing managers set a cost standard for materials after considering purchase discounts, freight in, and receiving costs. Companies can work with reliable vendors to build relationships that ensure quality and on-time delivery of materials at an affordable cost.

For direct labor, accountants work with human resources managers to determine the cost standard for direct labor. They must consider basic pay rates, payroll taxes, and fringe benefits. Job descriptions reveal the level of experience needed for each task. A big part of this process is ensuring that employees receive training for the job and are paid fairly for the job.

Accountants work with production managers to estimate manufacturing overhead costs. Production managers identify an appropriate allocation base such as direct labor hours or direct labor cost, or they allocate overhead using activity-based costing. Accountants then compute the standard overhead allocation rates. Exhibit 23-6 summarizes the setting of standard costs.

Exhibit 23-6 | Standard Setting Issues

	Cost Standards	Efficiency Standards
Direct Materials	Responsibility: Purchasing manager	Responsibility: Production manager and engineers
	Factors: Purchase cost, discounts, delivery requirements, credit policies	Factors: Product specifications, spoilage, production scheduling
Direct Labor	Responsibility: Human resources manager	Responsibility: Production manager and engineers
	Factors: Wage rate based on experience requirements, payroll taxes, fringe benefits	Factors: Time requirements for the production level and employee experience needed
Manufacturing Overhead	Responsibility: Production manager	
	Factors: Nature and amount of resources needed to support activities, such as moving materials, maintaining equipment, and product inspection	

Let's see how Cheerful Colors might determine its production cost standards for materials, labor, and manufacturing overhead.

Cost Standards

The manager in charge of purchasing for Cheerful Colors indicates that the purchase price, net of discounts, is $1.65 per pound of paraffin. Delivery, receiving, and inspection add an average of $0.10 per pound. Cheerful Colors's hourly wage for workers is $10.00, and payroll taxes, and fringe benefits total $2.00 per direct labor hour. Variable manufacturing overhead will total $37,500 based on 50,000 batches of crayons (static budget), fixed manufacturing overhead is $25,000, and overhead is allocated based on 12,500 estimated direct labor hours. Exhibit 23-7 (on the next page) computes Cheerful Colors's cost standards for direct materials, direct labor, and manufacturing overhead based on the static budget of 50,000 batches of crayons.

Exhibit 23-7 | **Standard Cost Calculations**

Direct materials cost standard for paraffin:		
Purchase price, net of discounts	$ 1.65 per pound	
Delivery, receiving, and inspection	0.10 per pound	
Total standard cost per pound of paraffin	$ 1.75 per pound	
Direct labor cost standard:		
Hourly wage	$ 10.00 per direct labor hour	
Payroll taxes and fringe benefits	2.00 per direct labor hour	
Total standard cost per direct labor hour	$ 12.00 per direct labor hour	

Variable overhead cost standard:

$$\frac{\text{Estimated variable overhead cost}}{\text{Estimated quantity of allocation base}} = \frac{\$37{,}500}{12{,}500 \text{ direct labor hours}} = \$ 3.00 \text{ per direct labor hour}$$

Fixed overhead cost standard:

$$\frac{\text{Estimated fixed overhead cost}}{\text{Estimated quantity of allocation base}} = \frac{\$25{,}000}{12{,}500 \text{ direct labor hours}} = \$ 2.00 \text{ per direct labor hour}$$

Efficiency Standards

Production managers and engineers set direct materials and direct labor efficiency standards. Efficiency standards are also called *quantity standards* or *usage standards* because they are a measure of how much *input* should be put into the manufacturing process. In other words, if employees are working efficiently, without spilling or otherwise wasting materials, how much paraffin should Cheerful Colors put into each batch of crayons, the *output*? That amount is the direct materials efficiency standard.

> Be careful to not confuse inputs and outputs. Inputs are what go into making the product and include materials, labor, and overhead. Outputs are the finished products—in this case, crayons. Another way to think about it: Inputs are what go into the factory, and outputs are what come out of the factory.

To set labor standards, companies can analyze every movement in the production process and then take steps to eliminate inefficiencies. For example, to eliminate unnecessary work, machines can be rearranged for better work flow and less materials handling. Another way companies set labor standards is to utilize continuous improvement which allow companies to review historical data-based standards and tighten these standards incrementally over a period of time. Companies can also conduct time-and-motion studies to streamline various tasks. For example, a plant can install a conveyer at waist height to minimize bending and lifting.

Companies often develop efficiency standards based on *best practices*. This is often called *benchmarking*. The best practice may be an internal benchmark from other plants or divisions within the company, or it may be an external benchmark from other companies. Internal benchmarks are easy to obtain, but managers can also purchase external benchmark data.

Cheerful Colors has analyzed the manufacturing process and has set the following efficiency standards:

- Direct materials efficiency standard: 1.00 pound of paraffin per batch of crayons
- Direct labor efficiency standard: 0.25 direct labor hours per batch of crayons

Manufacturing overhead is allocated based on direct labor hours, and the efficiency standard for expected direct labor hours has been established, so no additional efficiency standards are required for manufacturing overhead.

Standard Cost System Benefits

The use of standard cost systems is widespread in manufacturing companies in the United States and around the world. Using a standard cost system helps managers:

- Prepare the master budget
- Set target levels of performance for flexible budgets
- Identify performance standards
- Set sales prices of products and services
- Decrease accounting costs

Standard cost systems might appear to be expensive. Indeed, the company must invest up front to develop the standards, and the standards must be updated on a regular basis—at least once per year. But standards can save accounting costs. When integrated with the company's Enterprise Resource Planning (ERP) system, businesses can easily keep track of inventory costs, determine cost and efficiency variances, and make real-time decisions.

Variance Analysis for Product Costs

Once standards are established, managers can use the standards to assign costs to production. At least once per year, managers will compare the actual production costs to the standard costs to locate variances.

A **cost variance** measures how well the business keeps unit costs of material and labor inputs within standards. As the name suggests, the cost variance is the *difference in costs* (actual cost per unit − standard cost per unit) of an input, multiplied by the *actual quantity* used of the input:

Cost Variance

Measures how well the business keeps unit costs of material and labor inputs within standards.

> Cost variance = (Actual Cost × Actual Quantity) − (Standard Cost × Actual Quantity)
> = (Actual Cost − Standard Cost) × Actual Quantity
> = (AC − SC) × AQ

An **efficiency variance** measures how well the business uses its materials or human resources. The efficiency variance measures the *difference in quantities* (actual quantity of input used − standard quantity of input allowed for the actual number of units produced), multiplied by the *standard cost per unit* of the input:

Efficiency Variance

Measures how well the business uses its materials or human resources.

> Efficiency variance = (Standard Cost × Actual Quantity) − (Standard Cost × Standard Quantity)
> = (Actual Quantity − Standard Quantity) × Standard Cost
> = (AQ − SQ) × SC

Exhibit 23-8 (on the next page) shows the formulas for computing the cost and efficiency variances. Exhibit 23-9 (on the next page) shows the relationship among variances and how to separate total flexible budget variances for materials and labor into cost and efficiency variances.

Exhibit 23-8 | **Cost and Efficiency Variances**

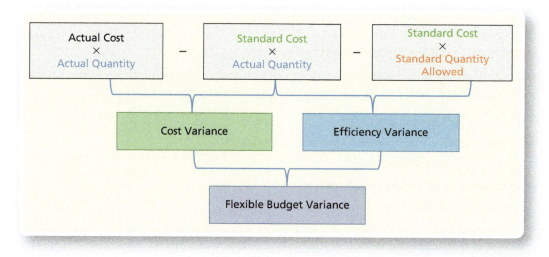

Exhibit 23-9 emphasizes two points:

- First, the cost and efficiency variances add up to the flexible budget variance.
- Second, static budgets play no role in the cost and efficiency variances.

The static budget is used only to compute the sales volume variance, the variance caused because the company sold a different quantity than it thought it would sell when it created the static budget. It is never used to compute the flexible budget variance or the cost and efficiency variances for materials and labor.

Exhibit 23-9 | **Variance Relationships**

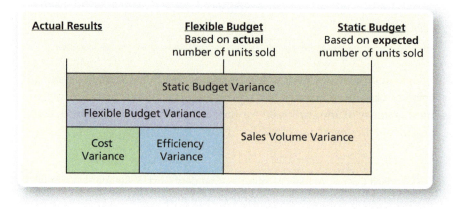

DECISIONS

How much time should employees report?

Will Crocker is an accountant at Southeast Accounting, a regional accounting firm headquartered in Charlotte, North Carolina. Accounting personnel at Southeast Accounting are required to report time spent working on clients' accounts. The actual reported time is used to estimate the labor time required for similar jobs for other clients and for subsequent jobs for the same client. Therefore, the reported time has two primary purposes. It is used to determine engagement fees—the amount the client will be charged for the job. It is also used to evaluate personnel efficiency—whether or not the employee is able to complete the job in the expected time.

Will has recently completed an engagement at a client's location. Will's actual time on the engagement was 70 hours, but the engagement was budgeted for 50 hours. Will is reluctant to report the 70 hours actually worked because it will create an unfavorable direct labor efficiency variance. Accountants at Southeast Accounting often report actual engagement time at or just slightly above the budgeted time even if the actual time is substantially more. Should Will report the actual time spent on the engagement or under-report the time to avoid an unfavorable variance?

Solution

Will should report the actual time spent on each engagement. Management, not aware that engagements are taking longer than expected, is routinely underestimating the time needed for the engagements in subsequent years. The employees' actions are causing a never-ending loop—budgeted hours are too low, employees fail to report the actual higher amounts, and, therefore, subsequent budgeted hours are also too low. To help solve the problem, management needs to emphasize the need for accurate figures for budgeting purposes. By continually using inaccurate amounts, the firm is underestimating the cost to complete the engagements, which also causes it to undercharge the clients. This can create serious profitability issues.

Management also needs to work to erase the climate of fear at the firm, where employees feel threatened by the variance system and the impact unfavorable variances could have on their jobs. Variances should be used to investigate and make changes, not punish employees. In the current environment, it is improbable management will collect accurate information from the employees.

Match the variance to the correct definition.

Variance	Definition
2. Cost variance	a. The difference between the expected results in the flexible budget for the *actual* units sold and the static budget.
3. Efficiency variance	b. The difference between actual results and the expected results in the flexible budget for the *actual* units sold.
4. Flexible budget variance	c. Measures how well the business keeps unit costs of material and labor inputs within standards.
5. Sales volume variance	d. The difference between actual results and the expected results in the static budget.
6. Static budget variance	e. Measures how well the business uses its materials or human resources.

Check your answers online in MyAccountingLab or at http://www.pearsonhighered.com/Horngren.

For more practice, see Short Exercises S23-4 and S23-5. MyAccountingLab

HOW ARE STANDARD COSTS USED TO DETERMINE DIRECT MATERIALS AND DIRECT LABOR VARIANCES?

Now we'll return to our Cheerful Colors example. Exhibit 23-5, the flexible budget performance report, showed several substantial flexible budget variances, including a $13,000 unfavorable variance for direct materials and a $10,400 favorable variance for direct labor. Exhibit 23-10 (on the next page) summarizes the flexible budget variances for the production costs.

Learning Objective 3

Compute the standard cost variances for direct materials and direct labor

Exhibit 23-10 | Flexible Budget Variances for Production Costs

	Budget Amounts per Unit	Actual Results	Flexible Budget Variance	Flexible Budget
Units (Batches of 100)		52,000		52,000
Variable Costs:				
Direct Materials	$ 1.75	$ 104,000	$ 13,000 U	$ 91,000
Direct Labor	3.00	145,600	10,400 F	156,000
Variable Overhead	0.75	30,160	8,840 F	39,000
Fixed Costs:				
Fixed Overhead		23,920	1,080 F	25,000
Totals		$ 303,680	$ 7,320 F	$ 311,000

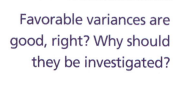

Favorable variances are good, right? Why should they be investigated?

Sometimes managers think that only unfavorable variances should be evaluated, but both favorable and unfavorable variances should be investigated, if substantial, to determine their causes. **For example, suppose a company avoided routine maintenance on machinery which caused a favorable cost variance in the current period. In a later period, the company could have a major breakdown that could have been avoided if the machinery had been properly maintained. The breakdown could require not only a substantial repair bill, but also a halt in production that could lead to lost sales.** Therefore, managers should look at any variance that is significant.

Let's look at the flexible budget variances for direct materials and direct labor and separate them into their two components—cost and efficiency.

Direct Materials Variances

The flexible budget variance for direct materials is $13,000 unfavorable. Additional data concerning direct materials follow, including standards discussed in the previous section:

Direct materials cost standard	$1.75 per pound of paraffin
Direct materials efficiency standard	1.00 pound of paraffin per batch of crayons
Actual amount of paraffin purchased and used	65,000 pounds
Actual cost of paraffin purchased and used	$104,000

Direct Materials Cost Variance

Direct Materials Cost Variance
The difference between the amount actually paid for direct materials (actual cost) and what should have been paid (standard cost). (AC − SC) × AQ.

Using the above information, we can determine the **direct materials cost variance** which measures the difference between the amount actually paid for direct materials (actual cost) and the amount that should have been paid (standard cost). This variance measures how well the business keeps unit costs of direct materials within standards. Notice, first, that Cheerful Colors paid less than expected for the paraffin. The actual cost per pound of paraffin is $1.60 ($104,000 / 65,000 pounds = $1.60 per pound). Using the formula, the direct materials cost variance is $9,750 favorable. The calculation follows:

> **Direct Materials Cost Variance = (AC − SC) × AQ**
> $= (\$1.60 \text{ per pound} - \$1.75 \text{ per pound}) \times 65,000 \text{ pounds}$
> $= \$9,750 \text{ F}$

The direct materials cost variance is *favorable* because the purchasing department paid *less* for paraffin than the standard cost.

Direct Materials Efficiency Variance

The **direct materials efficiency variance** measures the difference between the direct materials actually used (actual quantity) and the direct materials that should have been used for the actual output (standard quantity). This variance measures how well the business uses its materials. To calculate the direct materials efficiency variance, the standard quantity of inputs has to be determined. The standard quantity of inputs is the *quantity that should have been used* for the actual units produced. For Cheerful Colors, the standard quantity of inputs (paraffin) that workers should have used for the actual number of crayon batches produced is 52,000 pounds (1.00 pound per batch × 52,000 batches). The direct materials efficiency variance is as follows:

> **Direct Materials Efficiency Variance**
>
> The difference between the direct materials actually used (actual quantity) and the direct materials that should have been used for the actual output (standard quantity). (AQ − SQ) × SC.

> **Direct Materials Efficiency Variance = (AQ − SQ) × SC**
> = (65,000 pounds − 52,000 pounds) × $1.75 per pound
> = $22,750 U

The direct materials efficiency variance is *unfavorable* because workers used *more* paraffin than was planned (budgeted) for 52,000 batches of crayons.

Exhibit 23-11 | **Direct Materials Variances**

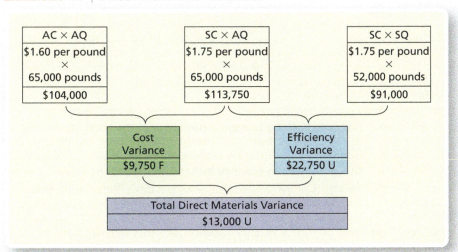

Favorable and unfavorable variances are netted together in the same way debits and credits are. Favorable variances are added together to create a total favorable variance. Unfavorable variances are added together to create a total unfavorable variance. But if a favorable and an unfavorable variance exist, the variances are subtracted from each other. The variance is determined to be favorable or unfavorable based on which one is the larger amount.

Summary of Direct Materials Variances

Exhibit 23-11 summarizes how Cheerful Colors divides the $13,000 unfavorable direct materials flexible budget variance into its cost and efficiency components.

In summary, Cheerful Colors spent $13,000 more than it should have for paraffin used in production because:

- Workers used 13,000 pounds of paraffin more than expected. The inefficient use of the paraffin reduced profits by $22,750, as shown by the unfavorable efficiency variance.
- Cheerful Colors paid $1.60 per pound of paraffin instead of the standard rate of $1.75 per pound—for a favorable cost variance.

Let's consider why each variance may have occurred and who may be responsible.

1. The purchasing manager is in the best position to explain the favorable cost variance. Cheerful Colors's purchasing manager may have negotiated a lower cost for paraffin.
2. The production manager in charge of making crayons can explain why workers used so much paraffin to make the 52,000 batches of crayons. Was the paraffin of lower quality that caused crayons to be rejected? Did workers waste materials? Did the production equipment malfunction? Cheerful Colors's top management needs this information to decide what corrective action to take.

These variances raise questions that can help pinpoint problems. But be careful! A favorable variance does not always mean that a manager did a good job, nor does an unfavorable variance mean that a manager did a bad job. Perhaps Cheerful Colors's purchasing manager got a lower cost by purchasing inferior-quality materials. This could lead to wasted materials and poor-quality crayons. If so, the purchasing manager's decision hurt the company. This illustrates why good managers use variances as a guide for investigation, rather than merely to assign blame, and investigate favorable as well as unfavorable variances.

TYING IT ALL TOGETHER

Kellogg Company was founded in 1906 and manufactures and markets ready-to-eat cereal and convenience foods. The company's brands include Apple Jacks, Corn Pops, Mueslix, and Rice Krispies Treats. The company also custom-bakes cookies for the Girl Scouts of the U.S.A. The primary raw materials used by Kellogg Company include corn, wheat, potato flakes, soy bean oil, sugar, and cocoa. The cost of these agricultural commodities could fluctuate from budgeted costs due to government policy, weather conditions, and unforeseen circumstances. For example, over the last five years the cost of soy bean oil has decreased from $1,255.67 per metric ton to $748.53 per metric ton.

What is the financial impact if actual commodity costs are different from budgeted commodity costs?

When actual costs are different from budgeted costs, a variance occurs. Understanding variances are important because they help companies, such as Kellogg Company, understand why a company's operating income is higher or lower than expected. Variances can be either favorable (have a positive impact on operating income) or unfavorable (have a negative impact on operating income). Suppose that Kellogg had budgeted the cost of soy bean oil at $1,255.67 per metric ton instead of $748.53. Kellogg would experience a cost variance because the actual cost would be less than the standard cost. This would create a significant favorable variance that would have a positive impact on operating income.

Suppose Kellogg Company noticed that the total actual cost of soy bean oil was significantly different than the total budgeted amount. How could Kellogg Company investigate this difference in order to better understand the cause?

Kellogg Company should investigate this difference by determining the total direct materials variance. The total direct materials variance is comprised of two parts: the cost variance and the efficiency variance. The cost variance determines the difference in actual cost compared to standard cost. The efficiency variance looks at the quantity used to produce the cereal and is the difference in actual quantity used compared to the standard quantity. Kellogg Company must investigate both the cost variance and the efficiency variance in order to understand why the total direct materials cost varied from the total budgeted amount.

Direct Labor Variances

Cheerful Colors uses a similar approach to analyze the direct labor flexible budget variance. The flexible budget variance for direct labor is $10,400 favorable, as shown in Exhibit 23-10. Additional data concerning direct labor follow, including standards discussed in the previous section:

Direct labor cost standard	$12.00 per DLHr
Direct labor efficiency standard	0.25 DLHr per batch of crayons
Actual amount of direct labor hours	10,400 DLHr
Actual cost of direct labor	$145,600

Direct Labor Cost Variance

Using the prior information, we can calculate the **direct labor cost variance**, which measures the difference between the actual amount paid for direct labor (actual cost) and the amount that should have been paid (standard cost). This variance measures how well the business keeps its unit costs of labor input within standards. Notice that Cheerful Colors paid more than expected for direct labor. The actual cost per hour of direct labor is $14.00 ($145,600 / 10,400 DLHr = $14.00 per DLHr) and the standard cost per hour of direct labor is $12.00. Using the formula, the direct labor cost variance is $20,800 unfavorable. The calculation follows:

> **Direct Labor Cost Variance = (AC − SC) × AQ**
> = ($14.00 per DLHr − $12.00 per DLHr) × 10,400 DLHr
> = $20,800 U

The $20,800 direct labor cost variance is *unfavorable* because Cheerful Colors paid workers $2.00 *more* per hour than budgeted ($14.00 actual cost − $12.00 standard cost).

Direct Labor Efficiency Variance

Now let's see how efficiently Cheerful Colors used its labor. The **direct labor efficiency variance** measures the difference between the actual labor hours (actual quantity) and the labor hours that should have been used (standard quantity). This variance measures how well the business uses its human resources. The standard quantity of direct labor hours that workers *should have used* to make 52,000 batches of crayons is 0.25 direct labor hours each, or 13,000 total direct labor hours (52,000 batches × 0.25 DLHr per batch). The direct labor efficiency variance is as follows:

> **Direct Labor Efficiency Variance = (AQ − SQ) × SC**
> = (10,400 DLHr − 13,000 DLHr) × $12.00 per DLHr
> = $31,200 F

The $31,200 direct labor efficiency variance is *favorable* because laborers actually worked 2,600 *fewer* hours than the flexible budget called for to produce 52,000 batches of crayons.

Summary of Direct Labor Variances

Exhibit 23-12 summarizes how Cheerful Colors divides the $10,400 favorable direct labor flexible budget variance into its cost and efficiency components.

Exhibit 23-12 | Direct Labor Variances

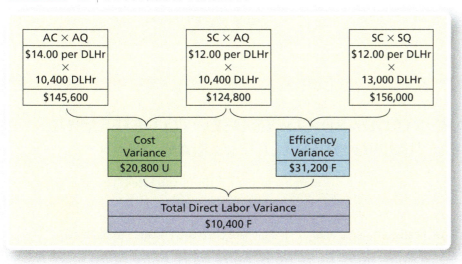

Direct Labor Cost Variance
The difference between the actual amount paid for direct labor (actual cost) and the amount that should have been paid (standard cost). (AC − SC) × AQ.

Direct Labor Efficiency Variance
The difference between the actual labor hours (actual quantity) and the labor hours that should have been used (standard quantity). (AQ − SQ) × SC.

The $10,400 favorable direct labor variance suggests that total labor costs were significantly less than expectations. To manage Cheerful Colors's labor costs, we need to gain more insight:

- Workers made 52,000 batches of crayons in 10,400 hours instead of the budgeted 13,000 hours—for a favorable efficiency variance.
- Cheerful Colors paid its employees an average of $14.00 per hour in 2019 instead of the standard rate of $12.00—for an unfavorable cost variance.

This situation reveals a trade-off. Perhaps Cheerful Colors hired more experienced, and thus more expensive, workers and had an unfavorable cost variance. However, due to more advanced skills, experience, and/or motivation, the workers turned out more work than expected, and the strategy was successful. The overall effect on profits was favorable. This possibility reminds us that managers should take care in using variances to evaluate performance. Managers should always carefully analyze the data before taking action.

Tipton Company manufactures shirts. During June, Tipton made 1,200 shirts and gathered the following additional data:

Direct materials cost standard	$6.00 per yard of fabric
Direct materials efficiency standard	1.50 yards per shirt
Actual amount of fabric purchased and used	1,680 yards
Actual cost of fabric purchased and used	$10,500
Direct labor cost standard	$15.00 per DLHr
Direct labor efficiency standard	2.00 DLHr per shirt
Actual amount of direct labor hours	2,520 DLHr
Actual cost of direct labor	$36,540

Calculate the following variances:

7. Direct materials cost variance
8. Direct materials efficiency variance
9. Total direct materials variance
10. Direct labor cost variance
11. Direct labor efficiency variance
12. Total direct labor variance

Check your answers online in MyAccountingLab or at http://www.pearsonhighered.com/Horngren.

For more practice, see Short Exercises S23-6 through S23-8. MyAccountingLab

HOW ARE STANDARD COSTS USED TO DETERMINE MANUFACTURING OVERHEAD VARIANCES?

Learning Objective 4

Compute the standard cost variances for manufacturing overhead

In this section, we will evaluate the manufacturing overhead variances. The total overhead variance is the difference between:

Actual overhead cost	and	Standard overhead allocated to production

Exhibit 23-10 shows that Cheerful Colors incurred $30,160 in variable overhead costs and $23,920 in fixed overhead costs. Therefore, total overhead costs incurred are $54,080 ($30,160 + $23,920). The next step is to see how Cheerful Colors allocates overhead in a standard cost system.

Allocating Overhead in a Standard Cost System

In a standard cost system, the manufacturing overhead allocated to production is as follows:

$$\text{Overhead allocated to production} = \text{Standard overhead allocation rate} \times \text{Standard quantity of the allocation base allowed for actual output}$$

In a standard cost system, the *standard* overhead allocation rate replaces the *predetermined* overhead allocation rate illustrated in previous chapters, but the concept is the same. It is a rate calculated during the budgeting process when other standards are determined.

Let's begin by computing Cheerful Colors's standard variable and fixed overhead allocation rates. Cheerful Colors allocates overhead based on direct labor hours. The static budget that was presented in Exhibit 23-2 indicated expected production would be 50,000 batches of crayons. At that level of production and using the direct labor efficiency standard of 0.25 direct labor hours per batch, Cheerful Colors expected to incur 12,500 direct labor hours, which is calculated as follows:

$$\text{Budgeted allocation base} = 50{,}000 \text{ batches} \times 0.25 \text{ direct labor hours per batch} = 12{,}500 \text{ DLHr}$$

The static budget also shows budgeted variable overhead at $37,500 and budgeted fixed overhead at $25,000. We are using *static budget* amounts here because standards are set *before* the budgeting period, so the accountants at Cheerful Colors did not yet know the actual production levels for the year when the standards were set.

The standard overhead allocation rate is calculated as follows:

$$\text{Standard overhead allocation rate} = \frac{\text{Budgeted overhead cost}}{\text{Budgeted allocation base}}$$

$$= \frac{\text{Budgeted VOH*}}{\text{Budgeted allocation base}} + \frac{\text{Budgeted FOH*}}{\text{Budgeted allocation base}}$$

$$\text{Standard overhead allocation rate} = \frac{\$37{,}500}{12{,}500 \text{ DLHr}} + \frac{\$25{,}000}{12{,}500 \text{ DLHr}}$$

$$= \$3.00 \text{ per DLHr} + \$2.00 \text{ per DLHr}$$

$$= \$5.00 \text{ per DLHr}$$

*VOH = Variable overhead; FOH = Fixed overhead

Cheerful Colors used a $3.00 per direct labor hour rate to allocate variable overhead to batches and $2.00 per direct labor hour rate to allocate fixed overhead to batches in 2019. Now, let's analyze the variances for variable and fixed overhead.

Variable Overhead Variances

Cheerful Colors uses a similar approach to analyze the variable overhead flexible budget variance as it did to analyze the direct materials and direct labor variances. Remember, direct materials and direct labor are also variable costs, so the approach is similar.

According to Exhibit 23-10, Cheerful Colors has an $8,840 favorable variable overhead flexible budget variance, which means the company spent less than budgeted. To analyze the favorable variance, Cheerful Colors computes the variable overhead cost and efficiency variances. Recall that the standard cost for variable overhead is $3.00 per direct labor hour, and 13,000 direct labor hours were budgeted for 52,000 batches of crayons in the flexible budget (0.25 DLHr per batch × 52,000 batches). However, actual variable overhead cost was $30,160, and it took 10,400 direct labor hours to make 52,000 batches. To summarize the data for variable overhead:

Variable overhead cost standard	$3.00 per DLHr
Variable overhead efficiency standard	0.25 DLHr per batch of crayons
Actual amount of direct labor hours	10,400 DLHr
Actual cost of variable overhead	$30,160

Variable Overhead Cost Variance

Variable Overhead Cost Variance
The difference between the actual variable overhead (actual cost) and the standard variable overhead for the actual allocation base incurred (standard cost). (AC − SC) × AQ.

Using the above information, we can calculate the **variable overhead cost variance** which measures the difference between the actual variable overhead (actual cost) and the standard variable overhead for the actual allocation base incurred (standard cost). This variance measures how well the business keeps unit costs of variable overhead inputs within standards. Notice that Cheerful Colors paid less than expected for variable overhead. The actual cost of variable overhead per hour of direct labor is $2.90 ($30,160 / 10,400 DLHr = $2.90 per DLHr) and the standard cost is $3.00 per DLHr. Using the formula, the variable overhead cost variance is $1,040 favorable. The calculation follows:

> **Variable Overhead Cost Variance = (AC − SC) × AQ**
> = ($2.90 per DLHr − $3.00 per DLHr) × 10,400 DLHr
> = $1,040 F

The $1,040 variable overhead cost variance is *favorable* because Cheerful Colors spent $0.10 *less* per hour than budgeted ($2.90 actual cost − $3.00 standard cost).

Variable Overhead Efficiency Variance

Variable Overhead Efficiency Variance
The difference between the actual allocation base (actual quantity) and the amount of the allocation base that should have been used (standard quantity). (AQ − SQ) × SC.

Now let's see how efficiently Cheerful Colors used its variable overhead. The **variable overhead efficiency variance** measures the difference in the actual allocation base (actual quantity) and the amount of the allocation base that should have been used (standard quantity). This variance measures how well the business uses its variable overhead inputs. Because variable overhead is allocated based on direct labor hours used, this variance will also be favorable, as the direct labor efficiency variance was favorable. The *standard quantity of direct labor hours* that workers should have used to make 52,000 batches of crayons is 13,000 total direct labor hours (52,000 batches × 0.25 DLHr per batch). The variable overhead efficiency variance is as follows:

> **Variable Overhead Efficiency Variance = (AQ − SQ) × SC**
> = (10,400 DLHr − 13,000 DLHr) × $3.00 per DLHr
> = $7,800 F

The $7,800 variable overhead efficiency variance is *favorable* because laborers actually worked 2,600 *fewer* hours than the flexible budget called for to produce 52,000 batches of crayons, and variable overhead is allocated based on direct labor hours.

Summary of Variable Overhead Variances

Exhibit 23-13 summarizes how Cheerful Colors divides the $8,840 favorable variable overhead flexible budget variance into its cost and efficiency components.

Exhibit 23-13 | Variable Overhead Variances

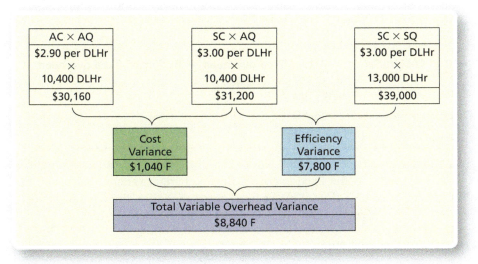

The $8,840 favorable variable overhead variance indicates that variable overhead costs were less than expected. To manage Cheerful Colors's variable overhead costs, we need to get more insight:

- Cheerful Colors incurred $1,040 less than anticipated actual variable overhead costs—for a favorable cost variance.
- Workers made 52,000 batches of crayons in 10,400 hours instead of the budgeted 13,000 hours—for a favorable efficiency variance.

Management may decide that the variable overhead cost variance is sufficiently small and does not warrant investigation. However, the company may want to investigate the variance further to determine if the reduction in costs was controllable or if the cost standard needs to be updated.

Fixed Overhead Variances

The three production costs analyzed so far were variable costs, so the analysis was similar for direct materials, direct labor, and variable overhead. However, Cheerful Colors uses a slightly different approach to analyze the fixed overhead variances. Remember that fixed costs are not expected to change *in total* within the relevant range, but they do change *per unit* when there is a change in volume. To analyze fixed overhead costs, we will need three amounts:

- Actual fixed overhead costs incurred
- Budgeted fixed overhead costs
- Allocated fixed overhead costs

Keep in mind that the budgeted amount for fixed overhead is the same in both the static budget and the flexible budget because fixed costs are not expected to change in total when there is a change in volume within the relevant range. Refer to Exhibit 23-5, Flexible Budget Performance Report, to review this concept.

Fixed Overhead Cost Variance

The **fixed overhead cost variance** measures the difference between *actual* fixed overhead and *budgeted* fixed overhead to determine the controllable portion of total fixed overhead variance. This variance measures how well the business keeps fixed overhead within standard.

Fixed Overhead Cost Variance
Determines the cost associated with the difference between actual fixed overhead and budgeted fixed overhead.
Actual fixed overhead − Budgeted fixed overhead

Both of these amounts, the actual fixed overhead and the budgeted fixed overhead, are given in Exhibit 23-2, Static Budget Performance Report, and Exhibit 23-5, Flexible Budget Performance Report.

> **Fixed Overhead Cost Variance = Actual fixed overhead − Budgeted fixed overhead**
> = $23,920 − $25,000
> = $1,080 F

The $1,080 fixed overhead cost variance is *favorable* because Cheerful Colors actually spent less than budgeted for fixed overhead. Notice that the fixed overhead cost variance calculated above is the same as the fixed overhead flexible budget variance calculated in Exhibit 23-5. Changes in volume do not affect fixed costs; therefore, there is only a cost effect and not an efficiency effect in the fixed overhead flexible budget variance.

Fixed Overhead Volume Variance

Fixed Overhead Volume Variance
Determines the cost associated with the difference between budgeted fixed overhead and the amount of fixed overhead allocated to actual output. Budgeted fixed overhead − Allocated fixed overhead.

The **fixed overhead volume variance** measures the difference between the budgeted fixed overhead and the amount of fixed overhead allocated to actual output. This variance measures how fixed overhead is allocated when actual volume is not equal to budgeted volume. Using the standard overhead allocation rate for fixed overhead previously calculated, fixed overhead is allocated at $2.00 per direct labor hour and each batch of crayons has an efficiency standard of 0.25 direct labor hours per batch. Therefore, the amount of fixed overhead allocated is $26,000, as shown below:

> **Overhead allocated to production = Standard overhead allocation rate × Standard quantity of the allocation base allowed for *actual* output**
> = $2.00 per DLHr × (0.25 DLHr per batch × 52,000 batches)
> = $2.00 per DLHr × 13,000 DLHr
> = $26,000

The fixed overhead volume variance is as follows:

> **Fixed Overhead Volume Variance = Budgeted fixed overhead − Allocated fixed overhead**
> = $25,000 − $26,000
> = $1,000 F

The $1,000 fixed overhead volume variance is *favorable* because Cheerful Colors produced more batches than budgeted and, therefore, allocated more overhead to crayon batches than the $25,000 budgeted fixed overhead amount. In other words, based on the standard for fixed overhead, Cheerful Colors has overallocated fixed overhead by $1,000. When overhead is adjusted at the end of the accounting period, the adjustment for the overal-location of overhead will decrease Cost of Goods Sold. Because the adjustment is a decrease to an expense, the fixed overhead volume variance is favorable.

The fixed overhead volume variance is not a *cost* variance—it is a *volume* variance—and explains why fixed overhead is overallocated or underallocated. Exhibit 23-14 graphs the fixed overhead volume variance for Cheerful Colors. The small blue triangle bordered by the lines representing budgeted fixed overhead, standard fixed overhead allocated, and standard direct labor hours lines represents the favorable fixed overhead volume variance for this example.

Exhibit 23-14 | **Fixed Overhead Volume Variance**

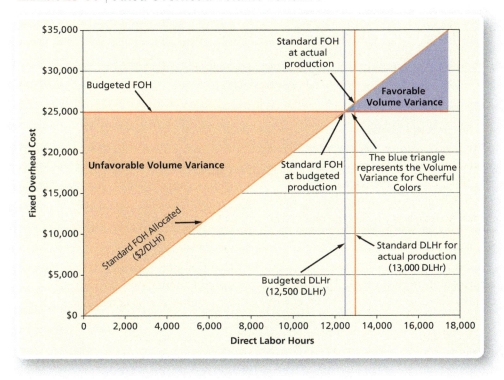

Summary of Fixed Overhead Variances

Exhibit 23-15 summarizes the fixed overhead variances.

To manage Cheerful Colors's fixed overhead costs, we need to get more insight:

- Cheerful Colors incurred $1,080 less than anticipated in fixed overhead costs for a favorable cost variance.
- Workers made 52,000 batches of crayons, which was 2,000 batches more than budgeted and resulted in a $1,000 favorable volume variance.

Management may decide that the fixed overhead cost variance is sufficiently small and does not warrant investigation. However, they may want to investigate the variance further to determine if the reduction in costs was controllable or if the cost standard needs to be updated.

Exhibit 23-15 | **Fixed Overhead Variances**

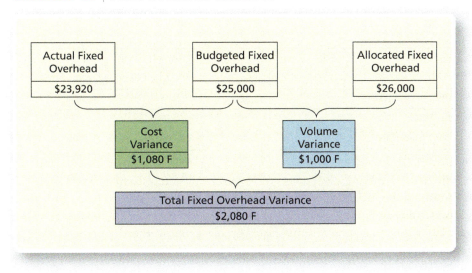

Try It!

This Try It! continues the previous Try It! for Tipton Company, a shirt manufacturer. During June, Tipton made 1,200 shirts but had budgeted production at 1,400 shirts. Tipton gathered the following additional data:

Variable overhead cost standard	$0.50 per DLHr
Direct labor efficiency standard	2.00 DLHr per shirt
Actual amount of direct labor hours	2,520 DLHr
Actual cost of variable overhead	$1,512
Fixed overhead cost standard	$0.25 per DLHr
Budgeted fixed overhead	$700
Actual cost of fixed overhead	$750

Calculate the following variances:

13. Variable overhead cost variance
14. Variable overhead efficiency variance
15. Total variable overhead variance
16. Fixed overhead cost variance
17. Fixed overhead volume variance
18. Total fixed overhead variance

Check your answers online in MyAccountingLab or at http://www.pearsonhighered.com/Horngren.

For more practice, see Short Exercises S23-9 and S23-10. MyAccountingLab

WHAT IS THE RELATIONSHIP AMONG THE PRODUCT COST VARIANCES, AND WHO IS RESPONSIBLE FOR THEM?

Learning Objective 5

Describe the relationship among and responsibility for the product cost variances

Now that we have looked at the individual product cost variances, let's look at the big picture. Exhibit 23-10 showed the flexible budget variances for the product costs—direct materials, direct labor, and manufacturing overhead. They are duplicated here for easier reference:

	Budget Amounts per Unit	Actual Results	Flexible Budget Variance	Flexible Budget
Units (Batches of 100)		52,000		52,000
Variable Costs:				
Direct Materials	$ 1.75	$ 104,000	$ 13,000 U	$ 91,000
Direct Labor	3.00	145,600	10,400 F	156,000
Variable Overhead	0.75	30,160	8,840 F	39,000
Fixed Costs:				
Fixed Overhead		23,920	1,080 F	25,000
Totals		$ 303,680	$ 7,320 F	$ 311,000

The individual variances are summarized here:

Direct materials cost variance	$ 9,750 F
Direct materials efficiency variance	22,750 U
Direct labor cost variance	20,800 U
Direct labor efficiency variance	31,200 F
Variable overhead cost variance	1,040 F
Variable overhead efficiency variance	7,800 F
Fixed overhead cost variance	1,080 F
Fixed overhead volume variance	1,000 F

Variance Relationships

Exhibit 23-16 illustrates the relationships among the various product cost variances. Take time to carefully study the diagram.

Exhibit 23-16 | Product Cost Variance Relationships

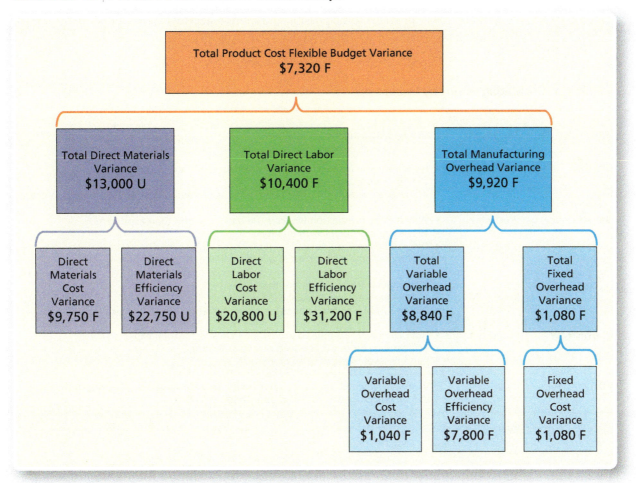

Notice that the fixed overhead volume variance is not included in the diagram. As previously stated, this variance is not a flexible budget variance but a volume variance. It shows how allocating fixed costs on a per unit basis causes a difference between budgeted fixed overhead and allocated fixed overhead. The allocation causes the overallocation or underallocation of fixed manufacturing overhead.

Variance Responsibilities

Management by Exception

When managers concentrate on results that are outside the accepted parameters.

Now that all the variances are summarized, Cheerful Colors can investigate the variances it feels are significant. This is called **management by exception** because managers concentrate on results that are outside the accepted parameters. In other words, managers focus on the exceptions. Variances can be expressed as a percentage of a budgeted amount or a dollar amount. Many companies use a combination of percentages and dollar amounts. For example, a company may investigate any variances greater than 10% of the budgeted amount and/or $10,000 or more.

Cheerful Colors investigates any variances greater than $5,000. Therefore, Cheerful Colors will look into the following variances:

Direct materials cost variance	$ 9,750 F
Direct materials efficiency variance	22,750 U
Direct labor cost variance	20,800 U
Direct labor efficiency variance	31,200 F
Variable overhead efficiency variance	7,800 F

Exhibit 23-17 provides some possible questions Cheerful Colors's upper management may want to ask.

Exhibit 23-17 | **Management by Exception**

Variance	Manager	Possible Questions
DM cost	Purchasing	• How were you able to purchase paraffin at such a reduced cost? • Did you compromise on quality? • Will you be able to continue purchasing at this amount or was it a one-time deal?
DM efficiency	Production	• Why did the production workers use more paraffin than expected? • Was there a problem with quality? • Did you have inexperienced workers that caused excessive waste? • Was there some event, such as a large spillage, that caused the variance?
DL cost	Human Resources	• Why were workers paid more than expected? • Did the workers hired have advanced skills? • Did an increase in fringe benefits cause the labor cost to increase?
DL efficiency	Production	• How were workers able to produce batches faster than expected? • Are workers more experienced or better trained? • Can this level of production continue?
VOH efficiency	Production	• VOH was allocated on direct labor hours. Therefore, the possible questions for the DL efficiency variance also apply here.

Match the product cost variance with the manager most probably responsible. Some answers may be used more than once. Some answers may not be used.

Variance	Manager
19. Variable overhead cost variance	a. Human resources
20. Direct materials efficiency variance	b. Purchasing
21. Direct labor cost variance	c. Production
22. Fixed overhead cost variance	
23. Direct materials cost variance	

Check your answers online in MyAccountingLab or at http://www.pearsonhighered.com/Horngren.

For more practice, see Short Exercise S23-11. MyAccountingLab

HOW DO JOURNAL ENTRIES DIFFER IN A STANDARD COST SYSTEM?

Using a standard cost system simplifies the recording process because entries are made at standard costs. Let's look at the various journal entries.

Journal Entries

Management needs to know about variances to address each problem. Therefore, Cheerful Colors records variances from standards as soon as possible. This means that Cheerful Colors records direct materials cost variances when materials are purchased. It also means that Work-in-Process Inventory is debited at standard input quantities and standard costs as crayons are manufactured. However, because our chapter example for Cheerful Colors was for the year 2019, we will record summary entries.

Transaction 1—Direct Materials Purchased

The journal entry to record direct materials purchased has an emphasis on the *cost* of the materials. Transaction 1 records the debit to Raw Materials Inventory, which is recorded at the actual quantity of paraffin purchased (65,000 pounds) at the *standard cost* ($1.75 per pound). In contrast, the credit to Accounts Payable is for the actual quantity of paraffin purchased (65,000 pounds) at the *actual cost* ($1.60 per pound). This is the actual amount owed to the vendor. Maintaining Raw Materials Inventory at the $1.75 *standard cost* allows Cheerful Colors to record the direct materials cost variance at the time of purchase. Recall that Cheerful Colors's direct materials cost variance was $9,750 favorable. A favorable variance means less expense has been incurred than planned and would have a credit balance. If the variance account has a credit balance, it is considered a *contra expense*. An unfavorable variance means more expense has been incurred than planned and would have a debit balance.

Learning Objective 6
Record transactions in a standard cost system and prepare a standard cost income statement

> When recording variances, favorable variances are credited and unfavorable variances are debited. Remember that variances are considered favorable if they increase operating income—and operating income is increased with credits (like revenues). Variances are considered unfavorable if they decrease operating income—and operating income is decreased with debits (like expenses).

$$\frac{A\uparrow}{RM\uparrow} \Big\} = \Big\{ \frac{L\uparrow}{A/P\uparrow} + \frac{E\uparrow}{DM\ Cost\ Var.\uparrow}$$

Date	Accounts and Explanation	Debit	Credit
Trans. 1	Raw Materials Inventory (65,000 pounds × $1.75/pound)	113,750	
	Direct Materials Cost Variance		9,750
	Accounts Payable (65,000 pounds × $1.60/pound)		104,000
	Purchased direct materials.		

Transaction 2—Direct Materials Usage

The journal entry to record the direct materials usage has an emphasis on the *quantity* of the materials used. In Transaction 2, Cheerful Colors debits Work-in-Process Inventory for the standard cost at the *standard quantity* of 52,000 pounds of direct materials that should have been used to make 52,000 batches of crayons. This maintains Work-in-Process Inventory at standard cost. Raw Materials Inventory is credited for the *actual quantity* of materials put into production (65,000 pounds) at the standard cost ($1.75 per pound). Cheerful Colors's direct materials efficiency variance was $22,750 unfavorable. An unfavorable variance means more expenses have been incurred than budgeted so the variance will be recorded as a debit, which increases expenses and decreases profits.

$$\frac{A\downarrow}{\genfrac{}{}{0pt}{}{WIP\uparrow}{RM\downarrow}} \Big\} = \Big\{ \underline{\ L\ } + \frac{E\downarrow}{DM\ Eff.\ Var.\downarrow}$$

Date	Accounts and Explanation	Debit	Credit
Trans. 2	Work-in-Process Inventory (1 lb./batch × $1.75/lb.× 52,000 batches)	91,000	
	Direct Materials Efficiency Variance	22,750	
	Raw Materials Inventory (65,000 pounds × $1.75/pound)		113,750
	Used direct materials.		

> Direct materials were put into Raw Materials Inventory at actual quantity *purchased* times standard cost, and they are transferred out at actual quantity *used* times standard cost.

Transaction 3—Direct Labor

In Transaction 3, Work-in-Process Inventory is debited for the $12.00 per hour *standard cost* of the 13,000 direct labor hours that should have been used for 52,000 batches, the *standard quantity*. Wages Payable is credited for the *actual cost* (the *actual* hours worked at the *actual* wage rate) because this is the amount Cheerful Colors must pay the workers. The direct labor cost variance is $20,800 unfavorable, a debit amount. The direct labor efficiency variance is credited for the $31,200 favorable variance. This maintains Work-in-Process Inventory at standard cost.

Date	Accounts and Explanation	Debit	Credit
Trans. 3	Work-in-Process Inventory (0.25 DLHr/batch × $12/DLHr × 52,000 batches)	156,000	
	Direct Labor Cost Variance	20,800	
	Direct Labor Efficiency Variance		31,200
	Wages Payable (10,400 DLHr × $14.00/DLHr)		145,600
	Direct labor costs incurred.		

$$\left.\frac{A\uparrow}{WIP\uparrow}\right\} = \left\{\frac{L\uparrow}{\substack{Wages \\ Pay.\uparrow}} + \frac{E\uparrow}{\substack{DL\ Cost\ Var.\downarrow \\ DL\ Eff.\ Var.\uparrow}}\right.$$

Transaction 4—Overhead Incurred

Transaction 4 records Cheerful Colors's actual overhead costs for 2019. Manufacturing Overhead is debited for the actual overhead costs: $30,160 actual variable overhead plus $23,920 actual fixed overhead equals $54,080 total manufacturing overhead. Various Accounts is a fictitious account used here to simplify the illustration and may include accounts such as Cash, Accounts Payable, Accumulated Depreciation, Prepaid Insurance, or other accounts related to incurring overhead costs.

Date	Accounts and Explanation	Debit	Credit
Trans. 4	Manufacturing Overhead ($30,160 + $23,920)	54,080	
	Various Accounts		54,080
	Manufacturing overhead costs incurred.		

$$\left.\frac{A\downarrow}{\substack{Accum. \\ Deprn.\uparrow \\ Cash\downarrow \\ Prepaid \\ Ins.\downarrow}}\right\} = \left\{\frac{L\uparrow}{A/P\uparrow} + \frac{E\downarrow}{Mfg.\ OH\uparrow}\right.$$

Transaction 5—Overhead Allocated

Transaction 5 shows the overhead allocated to Work-in-Process Inventory computed as:

$$\begin{array}{c} \text{Standard overhead} \\ \text{allocation rate} \end{array} \times \begin{array}{c} \text{Standard quantity of the allocation} \\ \text{base for actual output} \end{array}$$
$$\$5.00/\text{DLHr} \times (0.25\ \text{DLHr/batch} \times 52,000\ \text{batches})$$

Date	Accounts and Explanation	Debit	Credit
Trans. 5	Work-in-Process Inventory ($5.00/DLHr × 0.25 DLHr/batch × 52,000 batches)	65,000	
	Manufacturing Overhead		65,000
	Manufacturing overhead costs allocated.		

$$\left.\frac{A\uparrow}{WIP\uparrow}\right\} = \left\{\frac{L}{} + \frac{E\uparrow}{Mfg.\ OH\downarrow}\right.$$

Transaction 6—Completed Goods

Transaction 6 transfers the standard cost of the 52,000 batches of crayons completed during 2019 from Work-in-Process Inventory to Finished Goods Inventory. The amount transferred is the total standard costs for the 52,000 batches: direct materials ($91,000), direct labor ($156,000), and manufacturing overhead ($65,000).

$$\left.\begin{array}{c} A\uparrow\downarrow \\ \hline FG\uparrow \\ WIP\downarrow \end{array}\right\} = \left\{\begin{array}{c} L + E \\ \hline \end{array}\right.$$

Date	Accounts and Explanation	Debit	Credit
Trans. 6	Finished Goods Inventory	312,000	
	Work-in-Process Inventory		312,000
	Completed goods transferred.		

Transaction 7—Cost of Goods Sold

Transaction 7 transfers the cost of goods sold of the 52,000 batches completed at the standard cost of $6.00 per batch ($312,000 from Transaction 6 divided by 52,000 batches). This transaction assumes all batches produced during 2019 were sold in 2019. The sales journal entry has not been presented for simplicity purposes.

$$\left.\begin{array}{c} A\downarrow \\ \hline FG\downarrow \end{array}\right\} = \left\{\begin{array}{c} L + E\downarrow \\ \hline COGS\uparrow \end{array}\right.$$

Date	Accounts and Explanation	Debit	Credit
Trans. 7	Cost of Goods Sold	312,000	
	Finished Goods Inventory		312,000
	Cost of sales at standard cost.		

Transaction 8—Adjust Manufacturing Overhead

Transaction 8 adjusts the Manufacturing Overhead account and records the overhead variances. All of the manufacturing overhead variances are favorable, so they are all credited. The debit to Manufacturing Overhead indicates that the actual overhead costs debited to the account were less than the allocated amounts credited to the account, and overhead was overallocated. The account, therefore, had a credit balance and has to be debited to bring it to a zero balance. When overhead is underallocated, then the adjustment to Manufacturing Overhead is a credit, and the net amount of the overhead variances is unfavorable.

$$\left.\begin{array}{c} A \\ \hline \\ \\ \\ \\ \end{array}\right\} = \left\{\begin{array}{c} L + E\uparrow\downarrow \\ \hline MOH\uparrow \\ VOH\ Cost\ Var.\uparrow \\ VOH\ Eff.\ Var.\uparrow \\ FOH\ Cost\ Var.\uparrow \\ FOH\ Vol.\ Var.\uparrow \end{array}\right.$$

Date	Accounts and Explanation	Debit	Credit
Trans. 8	Manufacturing Overhead	10,920	
	Variable Overhead Cost Variance		1,040
	Variable Overhead Efficiency Variance		7,800
	Fixed Overhead Cost Variance		1,080
	Fixed Overhead Volume Variance		1,000
	To adjust Manufacturing Overhead.		

Exhibit 23-18 shows the relevant Cheerful Colors accounts after posting these entries.

Exhibit 23-18 | Flow of Costs in a Standard Cost System

Raw Materials Inventory			
Trans. 1	113,750	113,750	Trans. 2
Bal.	0		

Work-in-Process Inventory			
Trans. 2	91,000	312,000	Trans. 6
Trans. 3	156,000		
Trans. 5	65,000		
Bal.	0		

Finished Goods Inventory			
Trans. 6	312,000	312,000	Trans. 7
Bal.	0		

Manufacturing Overhead			
Trans. 4	54,080	65,000	Trans. 5
Trans. 8	10,920		
Bal.	0		

Cost of Goods Sold	
Trans. 7	312,000

Accounts Payable		
	104,000	Trans. 1

Direct Materials Cost Variance		
	9,750	Trans. 1

Direct Materials Efficiency Variance	
Trans. 2	22,750

Wages Payable		
	145,600	Trans. 3

Direct Labor Cost Variance	
Trans. 3	20,800

Direct Labor Efficiency Variance		
	31,200	Trans. 3

Various Accounts		
	54,080	Trans. 4

Variable Overhead Cost Variance		
	1,040	Trans. 8

Variable Overhead Efficiency Variance		
	7,800	Trans. 8

Fixed Overhead Cost Variance		
	1,080	Trans. 8

Fixed Overhead Volume Variance		
	1,000	Trans. 8

Notice that the inventory accounts have a zero balance at the end of 2019. That is because we assumed Cheerful Colors used all materials purchased, completed all units started, and sold all units completed.

Standard Cost Income Statement

Cheerful Colors's top management needs to know about the company's cost variances. Exhibit 23-19 (on the next page) shows a standard cost income statement that highlights the variances for management.

First, notice that the operating income shown in Exhibit 23-19 is the same as that shown in Exhibit 23-5, Flexible Budget Performance Report. The standard cost income statement doesn't alter the actual operating income—it simply emphasizes the variances from standard.

The statement starts with sales revenue at standard and subtracts the unfavorable sales revenue variance of $5,200 (from Exhibit 23-5) to yield actual sales revenue. (A favorable sales revenue variance would be added.) Next, the statement shows Cost of Goods Sold at standard cost. Then, the statement separately lists each manufacturing cost variance, followed by Cost of Goods Sold at actual cost. The variances with credit balances are shown in parentheses because they are contra expenses and therefore decrease the expense Cost of Goods Sold.

At the end of the period, all the variance accounts, which are temporary accounts, are closed to zero out their balances.

Exhibit 23-19 | **Standard Cost Income Statement**

CHEERFUL COLORS Standard Cost Income Statement For the Year Ended December 31, 2019		
Sales Revenue at standard (52,000 batches @ $7.50)		$ 390,000
Sales Revenue Variance*		(5,200)
Sales Revenue at actual		384,800
Cost of Goods Sold at standard cost (52,000 batches @ $6.00)	$ 312,000	
Manufacturing Cost Variances:		
Direct Materials Cost Variance	$ (9,750)	
Direct Materials Efficiency Variance	22,750	
Direct Labor Cost Variance	20,800	
Direct Labor Efficiency Variance	(31,200)	
Variable Overhead Cost Variance	(1,040)	
Variable Overhead Efficiency Variance	(7,800)	
Fixed Overhead Cost Variance	(1,080)	
Fixed Overhead Volume Variance	(1,000)	
Total Manufacturing Cost Variances	(8,320)	
Cost of Goods Sold at actual cost		303,680
Gross Profit		81,120
Selling and Administrative Expenses**		44,800
Operating Income		$ 36,320

*From Exhibit 23-5

**$19,200 + $25,600 from Exhibit 23-5

The income statement shows that the net effect of all the manufacturing cost variances is $8,320 favorable. Therefore, 2019's operating income is $8,320 more than it would have been if all the actual manufacturing costs had been equal to their standard costs.

Gunter Company reported the following manufacturing overhead variances.

Variable overhead cost variance	$ 320 F
Variable overhead efficiency variance	458 U
Fixed overhead cost variance	667 U
Fixed overhead volume variance	625 F

24. Record the journal entry to adjust Manufacturing Overhead.

25. Was Manufacturing Overhead overallocated or underallocated?

Check your answers online in MyAccountingLab or at http://www.pearsonhighered.com/Horngren.

For more practice, see Short Exercises S23-12 through S23-14. MyAccountingLab

REVIEW

> Things You Should Know

1. How do managers use budgets to control business activities?

- Variances are differences between budgeted amounts and actual amounts.
  - Favorable (F) variances increase operating income.
  - Unfavorable (U) variances decrease operating income.
- A static budget performance report shows the differences between the static budget and actual results.
- Flexible budgets help managers plan for various levels of sales.
- A flexible budget performance report shows the following:
  - Flexible budget variance—the differences between the actual results and the flexible budget.
  - Sales volume variance—the differences between the flexible budget and the static budget.

2. Why do managers use a standard cost system to control business activities?

- A standard is a price, cost, or quantity that is expected under normal conditions.
- A standard cost system uses standards for product costs—direct materials, direct labor, and manufacturing overhead.
- Managers must establish both cost and efficiency standards.
- Standard cost systems allow managers to efficiently record transactions related to production.
- The flexible budget variance can be further broken down into its two components:

$$
\begin{aligned}
\text{Cost Variance} &= (\text{Actual Cost} \times \text{Actual Quantity}) - (\text{Standard Cost} \times \text{Actual Quantity}) \\
&= (\text{Actual Cost} - \text{Standard Cost}) \times \text{Actual Quantity} \\
&= (AC - SC) \times AQ
\end{aligned}
$$

$$
\begin{aligned}
\text{Efficiency Variance} &= (\text{Standard Cost} \times \text{Actual Quantity}) - (\text{Standard Cost} \times \text{Standard Quantity}) \\
&= (\text{Actual Quantity} - \text{Standard Quantity}) \times \text{Standard Cost} \\
&= (AQ - SQ) \times SC
\end{aligned}
$$

- A cost variance measures the difference in actual and standard costs based on the actual amount used.
- An efficiency variance measures the difference in the actual amount used and the standard amount based on the standard cost.

3. How are standard costs used to determine direct materials and direct labor variances?

- Direct materials cost variance—measures how well the business keeps unit costs of material inputs within standards. $(AC - SC) \times AQ$

- Direct materials efficiency variance—measures how well the business uses its materials. $(AQ - SQ) \times SC$
- Direct labor cost variance—measures how well the business keeps unit costs of labor inputs within standards. $(AC - SC) \times AQ$
- Direct labor efficiency variance—measures how well the business uses its human resources. $(AQ - SQ) \times SC$

4. How are standard costs used to determine manufacturing overhead variances?

- Manufacturing overhead costs are allocated using the standard overhead allocation rate:

$$\text{Standard overhead allocation rate} = \frac{\text{Budgeted overhead cost}}{\text{Budgeted allocation base}}$$

$$= \frac{\text{Budgeted VOH*}}{\text{Budgeted allocation base}} + \frac{\text{Budgeted FOH*}}{\text{Budgeted allocation base}}$$

*VOH = Variable overhead; FOH = Fixed overhead

- Variable overhead cost variance—measures how well the business keeps unit costs of variable overhead inputs within standards. $(AC - SC) \times AQ$
- Variable overhead efficiency variance—measures how well the business uses its variable overhead inputs. $(AQ - SQ) \times SC$
- Fixed overhead cost variance—measures how well the business keeps fixed overhead within standards. Actual fixed overhead − Budgeted fixed overhead
- Fixed overhead volume variance—measures how fixed overhead is allocated when actual volume is not equal to budgeted volume. Budgeted fixed overhead − Allocated fixed overhead

5. What is the relationship among the product cost variances, and who is responsible for them?

- The net amount of the product variances (except the fixed overhead volume variance) equals the total product cost flexible budget variance.
- The fixed overhead volume variance is not a cost variance but a volume variance.
- Various managers are responsible for the variances. Sometimes decisions by one manager may affect variances for another manager (for example, purchasing cheaper materials may cause problems in production).

6. How do journal entries differ in a standard cost system?

- Raw Materials Inventory—actual quantity at standard cost.
- Work-in-Process Inventory, Finished Goods Inventory, and Cost of Goods Sold—standard quantity of inputs allowed for actual outputs, at the standard cost of inputs.
- Favorable variances are credited because they increase operating income.
- Unfavorable variances are debited because they decrease operating income.
- The manufacturing overhead variances account for the difference between the actual costs debited to Manufacturing Overhead and the standard costs allocated by a credit to Manufacturing Overhead.
- A standard cost income statement highlights the variances for management.

> Check Your Understanding 23-1

Check your understanding of the chapter by completing this problem and then looking at the solution. Use this practice to help identify which sections of the chapter you need to study more.

Sutherland Company manufactures book bags and has provided the following information for June 2018:

	Actual Results	Static Budget
Units	7,000	8,000
Sales Revenue	$ 87,500	$ 96,000
Variable Expenses	57,400	64,000
Contribution Margin	30,100	32,000
Fixed Expenses	19,000	20,000
Operating Income	$ 11,100	$ 12,000

Requirements

1. Prepare a flexible budget performance report using Exhibit 23-5 as a guide. (*Hint:* You will need to calculate the flexible budget amounts for 7,000 units.) (See Learning Objective 1)

2. As the company owner, which employees would you praise or criticize after you analyze this performance report? (See Learning Objective 1)

> Solution

Requirement 1

SUTHERLAND COMPANY
Flexible Budget Performance Report
For the Month Ended June 30, 2018

	Budget Amounts per Unit	Actual Results	Flexible Budget Variance (1) – (3)	Flexible Budget	Sales Volume Variance (3) – (5)	Static Budget
	1		2	3	4	5
Units		7,000		7,000		8,000
Sales Revenue	$ 12.00	$ 87,500	$ 3,500 F	$ 84,000	$12,000 U	$ 96,000
Variable Costs	8.00	57,400	1,400 U	56,000	8,000 F	64,000
Contribution Margin		30,100	2,100 F	28,000	4,000 U	32,000
Fixed Costs		19,000	1,000 F	20,000	0	20,000
Operating Income		$ 11,100	$ 3,100 F	$ 8,000	$ 4,000 U	$ 12,000

Flexible Budget Variance
$ 3,100 F

Sales Volume Variance
$ 4,000 U

Static Budget Variance
$ 900 U

Requirement 2

More information is needed to determine which employees to praise or criticize. As the company owner, you should determine the *causes* of the variances before praising or criticizing employees. It is especially important to determine whether the variance is due to factors the manager can control. For example:

- The $1,000 favorable flexible budget variance for fixed costs could be due to a reduction in insurance premiums. Or the savings might have come from delaying a scheduled overhaul of equipment that decreased fixed expenses in the short term but could increase the company's costs in the long run.
- The $4,000 unfavorable sales volume variance for operating income could be due to an ineffective sales staff, or it could be due to a natural disaster that made it difficult for employees to get to work, bringing work to a standstill.

Wise managers use variances to raise questions and direct attention, not to fix blame.

> Check Your Understanding 23-2

Check your understanding of the chapter by completing this problem and then looking at the solution. Use this practice to help identify which sections of the chapter you need to study more.

Sutherland Company produced 7,000 book bags in June, and *actual* amounts were as follows:

Direct materials (cloth)	7,400 yards @ $2.00 per yard
Direct labor	2,740 hours @ $10.00 per hour
Variable overhead	$ 5,400
Fixed overhead	11,900

Sutherland's *standards* were as follows:

Direct materials (cloth)	1 yard per book bag @ $2.00 per yard
Direct labor	0.40 direct labor hours per book bag @ $10.50 per direct labor hour
Variable overhead	0.40 direct labor hours per book bag @ $2.00 per direct labor hour
Fixed overhead	$9,600 (0.40 direct labor hours per book bag @ $3.00 per direct labor hour)

Requirements

1. Compute cost and efficiency variances for direct materials, direct labor, and variable overhead. (See Learning Objectives 3 and 4)
2. Compute the cost and volume variances for fixed overhead. (See Learning Objective 4)

> Solution

Requirement 1

Direct Materials Variances

Standard materials allowed = 1 yard per book bag × 7,000 book bags = 7,000 yards

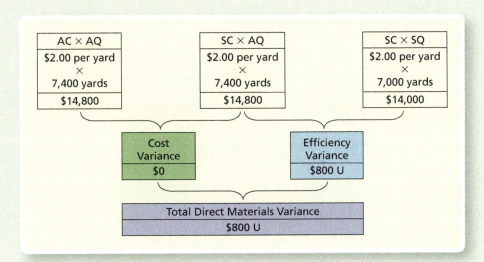

Direct Labor Variances

Standard labor allowed = 0.40 direct labor hours per book bag × 7,000 book bags = 2,800 direct labor hours

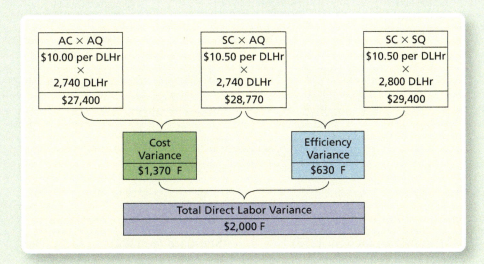

Variable Overhead Variances

Standard labor allowed = 0.40 direct labor hours per book bag × 7,000 book bags = 2,800 direct labor hours

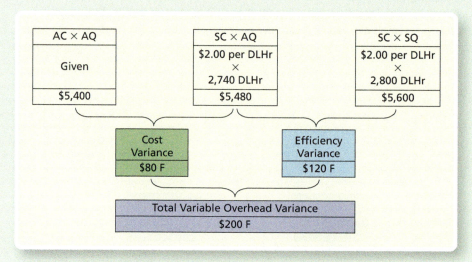

Requirement 2

Fixed Overhead Variances

Fixed overhead allocation = 0.40 direct labor hours per book bag × $3.00 per book bag × 7,000 book bags = $8,400

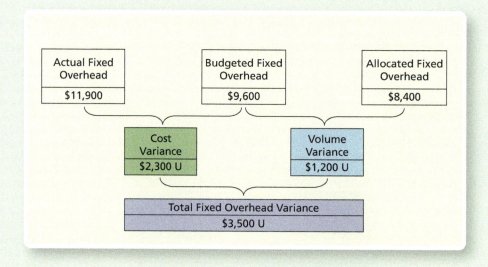

> Key Terms

> Quick Check

Questions 1–4 rely on the following data.

MajorNet Systems is a start-up company that makes connectors for high-speed Internet connections. The company has budgeted variable costs of $145 for each connector and fixed costs of $7,500 per month. MajorNet's static budget predicted production and sales of 100 connectors in August, but the company actually produced and sold only 84 connectors at a total cost of $21,000.

1. MajorNet's total flexible budget cost for 84 connectors per month is

   a. $14,500.   **c.** $19,680.
   b. $12,180.   **d.** $21,000.

   Learning Objective 1

2. MajorNet's sales volume variance for total costs is

   a. $1,320 U.   **c.** $2,320 U.
   b. $1,320 F.   **d.** $2,320 F.

   Learning Objective 1

3. MajorNet's flexible budget variance for total costs is

   a. $1,320 U.   **c.** $2,320 U.
   b. $1,320 F.   **d.** $2,320 F.

   Learning Objective 1

4. MajorNet Systems's managers could set direct labor standards based on

   a. time-and-motion studies.   **c.** benchmarking.
   b. continuous improvement.   **d.** All of the above.

   Learning Objective 2

Questions 5–6 rely on the following data.

MajorNet Systems has budgeted three hours of direct labor per connector, at a standard cost of $17 per hour. During August, technicians actually worked 189 hours completing 84 connectors. All 84 connectors actually produced were sold. MajorNet paid the technicians $17.80 per hour.

5. What is MajorNet's direct labor cost variance for August?

   a. $67.20 U   **c.** $201.60 U
   b. $151.20 U   **d.** $919.80 U

   Learning Objective 3

6. What is MajorNet's direct labor efficiency variance for August?

   a. $919.80 F   **c.** $1,121.40 F
   b. $1,071.00 F   **d.** $3,364.20 F

   Learning Objective 3

Questions 7–9 rely on the following data.

FrontGrade Systems allocates manufacturing overhead based on machine hours. Each connector should require 11 machine hours. According to the static budget, FrontGrade expected to incur the following:

   1,100 machine hours per month (100 connectors × 11 machine hours per connector)

   $5,500 in variable manufacturing overhead costs

   $8,250 in fixed manufacturing overhead costs

During August, FrontGrade actually used 1,000 machine hours to make 110 connectors and spent $5,600 in variable manufacturing costs and $8,300 in fixed manufacturing overhead costs.

Learning Objective 4

7. FrontGrade's standard *variable* manufacturing overhead allocation rate is
   - **a.** $5.00 per machine hour.
   - **b.** $5.50 per machine hour.
   - **c.** $7.50 per machine hour.
   - **d.** $12.50 per machine hour.

Learning Objective 4

8. Calculate the variable overhead cost variance for FrontGrade.
   - **a.** $450 F
   - **b.** $600 U
   - **c.** $1,050 F
   - **d.** $1,650 F

Learning Objective 4

9. Calculate the variable overhead efficiency variance for FrontGrade.
   - **a.** $450 F
   - **b.** $600 U
   - **c.** $1,050 F
   - **d.** $1,650 F

Learning Objective 5

10. The person probably most responsible for the direct labor efficiency variance is
    - **a.** the marketing manager.
    - **b.** the production manager.
    - **c.** the human resources manager.
    - **d.** the purchasing manager.

Learning Objective 6

11. MajorNet Systems's static budget predicted production of and sales of 100 connectors in August, but the company actually produced and sold only 84 connectors. Direct materials were budgeted at $95 per connector. The company purchased and used direct materials that cost $8,148. What is the journal entry for the direct materials purchased?

Date	Accounts and Explanation	Debit	Credit
a.	Raw Materials Inventory	7,980	
	Direct Materials Cost Variance	168	
	Accounts Payable		8,148
b.	Raw Materials Inventory	7,980	
	Direct Materials Efficiency Variance	168	
	Accounts Payable		8,148
c.	Work-in-Process Inventory	7,980	
	Direct Materials Cost Variance	168	
	Raw Materials Inventory		8,148
d.	Work-in-Process Inventory	7,980	
	Direct Materials Efficiency Variance	168	
	Raw Materials Inventory		8,148

Check your answers at the end of the chapter.

ASSESS YOUR PROGRESS

> Review Questions

1. What is a variance?

2. Explain the difference between a favorable and an unfavorable variance.

3. What is a static budget performance report?

4. How do flexible budgets differ from static budgets?

5. How is a flexible budget used?

6. What are the two components of the static budget variance? How are they calculated?

7. What is a flexible budget performance report?

8. What is a standard cost system?

9. Explain the difference between a cost standard and an efficiency standard. Give an example of each.

10. Give the general formulas for determining cost and efficiency variances.

11. How does the static budget affect cost and efficiency variances?

12. List the direct materials variances, and briefly describe each.

13. List the direct labor variances, and briefly describe each.

14. List the variable overhead variances, and briefly describe each.

15. List the fixed overhead variances, and briefly describe each.

16. How is the fixed overhead volume variance different from the other variances?

17. What is management by exception?

18. List the eight product variances and the manager most likely responsible for each.

19. Briefly describe how journal entries differ in a standard cost system.

20. What is a standard cost income statement?

> Short Exercises

S23-1 Matching terms

Learning Objective 1

Match each term to the correct definition.

Terms

a. Flexible budget

b. Flexible budget variance

c. Sales volume variance

d. Static budget

e. Variance

Definitions

1. A summarized budget for several levels of volume that separates variable costs from fixed costs.

2. A budget prepared for only one level of sales.

3. The difference between an actual amount and the budgeted amount.

4. The difference arising because the company actually earned more or less revenue, or incurred more or less cost, than expected for the actual level of output.

5. The difference arising only because the number of units actually sold differs from the static budget units.

CHAPTER 23

Learning Objective 1

S23-2 Preparing flexible budgets

Moje, Inc. manufactures travel locks. The budgeted selling price is $19 per lock, the variable cost is $9 per lock, and budgeted fixed costs are $13,000 per month. Prepare a flexible budget for output levels of 4,000 locks and 11,000 locks for the month ended April 30, 2018.

Learning Objective 1

S23-3 Calculating flexible budget variances

Complete the flexible budget variance analysis by filling in the blanks in the partial flexible budget performance report for 9,000 travel locks for Grant, Inc.

GRANT, INC.
Flexible Budget Performance Report (partial)
For the Month Ended April 30, 2018

	Actual Results	Flexible Budget Variance		Flexible Budget
Units	9,000	(a)		9,000
Sales Revenue	$ 126,000	(b)	(c)	$ 108,000
Variable Costs	52,300	(d)	(e)	50,300
Contribution Margin	73,700	(f)	(g)	57,700
Fixed Costs	16,100	(h)	(i)	14,900
Operating Income	$ 57,600	(j)	(k)	$ 42,800

Learning Objective 2

S23-4 Matching terms

Match each term to the correct definition.

Terms

a. Benchmarking
b. Efficiency variance
c. Cost variance
d. Standard

Definitions

1. Measures whether the quantity of materials or labor used to make the actual number of outputs is within the standard allowed for the number of outputs.

2. Uses standards based on best practice.

3. Measures how well the business keeps unit costs of materials and labor inputs within standards.

4. A price, cost, or quantity that is expected under normal conditions.

Learning Objective 2

S23-5 Identifying the benefits of standard costs

Setting standards for a product may involve many employees of the company. Identify some of the employees who may be involved in setting the standard costs, and describe what their role might be in setting those standards.

S23-6 Calculating materials variances

Learning Objective 3

Martin, Inc. is a manufacturer of lead crystal glasses. The standard direct materials quantity is 1.0 pound per glass at a cost of $0.50 per pound. The actual result for one month's production of 6,500 glasses was 1.2 pounds per glass, at a cost of $0.30 per pound. Calculate the direct materials cost variance and the direct materials efficiency variance.

S23-7 Calculating labor variances

Learning Objective 3

Martin, Inc. manufactures lead crystal glasses. The standard direct labor time is 0.5 hours per glass, at a cost of $18 per hour. The actual results for one month's production of 6,500 glasses were 0.2 hours per glass, at a cost of $11 per hour. Calculate the direct labor cost variance and the direct labor efficiency variance.

Note: Short Exercises S23-6 and S23-7 must be completed before attempting Short Exercise S23-8.

S23-8 Interpreting material and labor variances

Learning Objective 3

Refer to your results from Short Exercises S23-6 and S23-7.

Requirements

1. For each variance, who in Martin's organization is most likely responsible?

2. Interpret the direct materials and direct labor variances for Martin's management.

S23-9 Computing standard overhead allocation rates

Learning Objective 4

The following information relates to Morgan, Inc.'s overhead costs for the month:

Static budget variable overhead	$7,800
Static budget fixed overhead	$3,900
Static budget direct labor hours	1,300 hours
Static budget number of units	5,200 units

Morgan allocates manufacturing overhead to production based on standard direct labor hours. Compute the standard variable overhead allocation rate and the standard fixed overhead allocation rate.

Note: Short Exercise S23-9 must be completed before attempting Short Exercise S23-10.

S23-10 Computing overhead variances

Learning Objective 4

Refer to the Morgan, Inc. data in Short Exercise S23-9. Last month, Morgan reported the following actual results: actual variable overhead, $10,800; actual fixed overhead, $2,770; actual production of 7,000 units at 0.20 direct labor hours per unit. The standard direct labor time is 0.25 direct labor hours per unit (1,300 static direct labor hours / 5,200 static units).

Requirements

1. Compute the overhead variances for the month: variable overhead cost variance, variable overhead efficiency variance, fixed overhead cost variance, and fixed overhead volume variance.

2. Explain why the variances are favorable or unfavorable.

Learning Objective 5

S23-11 Understanding variance relationships

Complete the table below for the missing variances.

Total Flexible Budget Product Cost Variance					
(a)					
Total Direct Materials Variance		Total Direct Labor Variance		Total Manufacturing Overhead Variance	
(b)		(c)		(d)	
Direct Materials Cost Variance	Direct Materials Efficiency Variance	Direct Labor Cost Variance	Direct Labor Efficiency Variance	Total Variable Overhead Variance	Total Fixed Overhead Variance
$310 F	$165 U	$160 U	$415 F	(e)	(f)
				Variable Overhead Cost Variance	Variable Overhead Efficiency Variance	Fixed Overhead Cost Variance
				$525 U	$575 F	$50 F

Learning Objective 6

S23-12 Journalizing materials entries

The following direct materials variance analysis was performed for Moore.

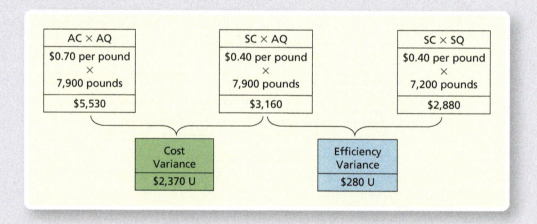

Requirements

1. Record Moore's direct materials journal entries. Assume purchases were made on account.
2. Explain what management will do with this variance information.

S23-13 Journalizing labor entries

Learning Objective 6

The following direct labor variance analysis was performed for Morris.

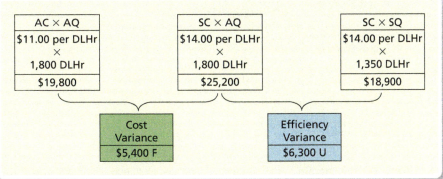

Requirements

1. Record Morris's direct labor journal entry (use Wages Payable).
2. Explain what management will do with this variance information.

S23-14 Preparing a standard cost income statement

Learning Objective 6

Use the following information to prepare a standard cost income statement for Mitchell Company for 2018.

Cost of Goods Sold (at standard)	$ 366,000	Direct Labor Efficiency Variance	$ 19,500 F
Sales Revenue (at standard)	570,000	Variable Overhead Efficiency Variance	3,300 U
Direct Materials Cost Variance	7,200 U	Fixed Overhead Volume Variance	12,500 F
Direct Materials Efficiency Variance	2,700 U	Selling and Administrative Expenses	71,000
Direct Labor Cost Variance	42,000 U	Variable Overhead Cost Variance	1,700 F
Fixed Overhead Cost Variance	2,100 F		

> Exercises

E23-15 Preparing a flexible budget

Learning Objective 1

$229,500 Op. Inc. for 55,000 units

Office Plus sells its main product, ergonomic mouse pads, for $13 each. Its variable cost is $5.10 per pad. Fixed costs are $205,000 per month for volumes up to 65,000 pads. Above 65,000 pads, monthly fixed costs are $250,000. Prepare a monthly flexible budget for the product, showing sales revenue, variable costs, fixed costs, and operating income for volume levels of 45,000, 55,000, and 75,000 pads.

Learning Objective 1

E23-16 Preparing a flexible budget performance report

Murphy Company managers received the following incomplete performance report:

MURPHY COMPANY Flexible Budget Performance Report For the Year Ended July 31, 2018					
	Actual Results	Flexible Budget Variance	Flexible Budget	Sales Volume Variance	Static Budget
Units	35,000	(a)	35,000	5,000 F	(g)
Sales Revenue	$ 219,000	(b)	$ 219,000	$ 27,000 F	(h)
Variable Expenses	85,000	(c)	84,000	13,000 U	(i)
Contribution Margin	134,000	(d)	135,000	14,000 F	(j)
Fixed Expenses	105,000	(e)	100,000	0	(k)
Operating Income	$ 29,000	(f)	$ 35,000	$ 14,000 F	(l)

Complete the performance report. Identify the employee group that may deserve praise and the group that may be subject to criticism. Give your reasoning.

Learning Objective 1

Flex. Bud. Var. for Op. Inc.
$31,040 F

E23-17 Preparing a flexible budget performance report

Top managers of Marshall Industries predicted 2018 sales of 14,800 units of its product at a unit price of $9.50. Actual sales for the year were 14,600 units at $12.00 each. Variable costs were budgeted at $2.00 per unit, and actual variable costs were $2.10 per unit. Actual fixed costs of $48,000 exceeded budgeted fixed costs by $4,000.

Prepare Marshall's flexible budget performance report. What variance contributed most to the year's favorable results? What caused this variance?

Learning Objectives 2, 3

2. DM Eff. Var. $675 F

E23-18 Defining the benefits of setting cost standards and calculating materials and labor variances

Murry, Inc. produced 1,000 units of the company's product in 2018. The standard quantity of direct materials was three yards of cloth per unit at a standard cost of $1.35 per yard. The accounting records showed that 2,500 yards of cloth were used and the company paid $1.40 per yard. Standard time was two direct labor hours per unit at a standard rate of $10.00 per direct labor hour. Employees worked 1,700 hours and were paid $9.50 per hour.

Requirements

1. What are the benefits of setting cost standards?
2. Calculate the direct materials cost variance and the direct materials efficiency variance as well as the direct labor cost and efficiency variances.

E23-19 Calculating materials and labor variances

Learning Objective 3

DL Eff. Var. $2,400 F

Matthews Fender, which uses a standard cost system, manufactured 20,000 boat fenders during 2018, using 143,000 square feet of extruded vinyl purchased at $1.30 per square foot. Production required 400 direct labor hours that cost $16.00 per hour. The direct materials standard was seven square feet of vinyl per fender, at a standard cost of $1.35 per square foot. The labor standard was 0.028 direct labor hour per fender, at a standard cost of $15.00 per hour.

Compute the cost and efficiency variances for direct materials and direct labor. Does the pattern of variances suggest Matthews Fender's managers have been making trade-offs? Explain.

E23-20 Computing overhead variances

Learning Objective 4

1. FOH Vol. Var. $3,000 U

Mason Fender is a competitor of Matthews Fender from Exercise E23-19. Mason Fender also uses a standard cost system and provides the following information:

Static budget variable overhead	$ 2,300
Static budget fixed overhead	$ 23,000
Static budget direct labor hours	575 hours
Static budget number of units	23,000 units
Standard direct labor hours	0.025 hours per fender

Mason Fender allocates manufacturing overhead to production based on standard direct labor hours. Mason Fender reported the following actual results for 2018: actual number of fenders produced, 20,000; actual variable overhead, $5,350; actual fixed overhead, $26,000; actual direct labor hours, 460.

Requirements

1. Compute the overhead variances for the year: variable overhead cost variance, variable overhead efficiency variance, fixed overhead cost variance, and fixed overhead volume variance.

2. Explain why the variances are favorable or unfavorable.

E23-21 Calculating overhead variances

Learning Objective 4

1. VOH Cost Var. $1,600 U

Mills, Inc. is a competitor of Murry, Inc. from Exercise E23-18. Mills also uses a standard cost system and provides the following information:

Static budget variable overhead	$ 1,200
Static budget fixed overhead	$ 1,600
Static budget direct labor hours	800 hours
Static budget number of units	400 units
Standard direct labor hours	2 hours per unit

Mills allocates manufacturing overhead to production based on standard direct labor hours. Mills reported the following actual results for 2018: actual number of units produced, 1,000; actual variable overhead, $4,000; actual fixed overhead, $3,100; actual direct labor hours, 1,600.

Requirements

1. Compute the variable overhead cost and efficiency variances and fixed overhead cost and volume variances.

2. Explain why the variances are favorable or unfavorable.

Learning Objective 6

GP $270,700

E23-22 Preparing a standard cost income statement

The May 2018 revenue and cost information for McDonald Outfitters, Inc. follows:

Sales Revenue (at standard)	$ 610,000
Cost of Goods Sold (at standard)	348,000
Direct Materials Cost Variance	1,500 F
Direct Materials Efficiency Variance	6,600 F
Direct Labor Cost Variance	4,200 U
Direct Labor Efficiency Variance	2,700 F
Variable Overhead Cost Variance	2,800 U
Variable Overhead Efficiency Variance	1,100 U
Fixed Overhead Cost Variance	2,300 U
Fixed Overhead Volume Variance	8,300 F

Prepare a standard cost income statement for management through gross profit. Report all standard cost variances for management's use. Has management done a good or poor job of controlling costs? Explain.

Learning Objective 6

MOH Adj. $1,000 DR

E23-23 Preparing journal entries

Marsh Company uses a standard cost system and reports the following information for 2018:

Standards:
3 yards of cloth per unit at $1.05 per yard
2 direct labor hours per unit at $10.50 per hour
Overhead allocated at $5.00 per direct labor hour
Actual:
2,600 yards of cloth were purchased at $1.10 per yard
Employees worked 1,800 hours and were paid $10.00 per hour
Actual variable overhead was $1,700
Actual fixed overhead was $7,300

Marsh Company reported the following variances:

Direct materials cost variance	$ 130 U
Direct materials efficiency variance	420 F
Direct labor cost variance	900 F
Direct labor efficiency variance	2,100 F
Variable overhead cost variance	1,500 U
Variable overhead efficiency variance	1,500 F
Fixed overhead cost variance	600 U
Fixed overhead volume variance	1,600 F

Marsh produced 1,000 units of finished product in 2018. Record the journal entries to record direct materials, direct labor, variable overhead, and fixed overhead, assuming all expenditures were on account and there were no beginning or ending balances in the inventory accounts (all materials purchased were used in production, and all goods produced were sold). Record the journal entries to record the transfer to Finished Goods Inventory and Cost of Goods Sold (omit the journal entry for Sales Revenue). Adjust the Manufacturing Overhead account.

E23-24 Preparing a standard cost income statement

McCarthy Fender, which uses a standard cost system, manufactured 20,000 boat fenders during 2018. The 2018 revenue and cost information for McCarthy follows:

Learning Objective 6

GP $1,097,480

Sales Revenue	$ 1,300,000
Cost of Goods Sold (at standard)	196,800
Direct materials cost variance	7,150 F
Direct materials efficiency variance	5,950 U
Direct labor cost variance	400 U
Direct labor efficiency variance	530 F
Variable overhead cost variance	650 U
Variable overhead efficiency variance	360 F
Fixed overhead cost variance	2,350 U
Fixed overhead volume variance	4,410 U

Assume each fender produced was sold for the standard price of $65, and total selling and administrative costs were $250,000. Prepare a standard cost income statement for 2018 for McCarthy Fender.

> Problems Group A

P23-25A Preparing a flexible budget performance report

Cell One Technologies manufactures capacitors for cellular base stations and other communications applications. The company's July 2018 flexible budget shows output levels of 6,000, 7,500, and 9,500 units. The static budget was based on expected sales of 7,500 units.

Learning Objective 1

3. Static Bud. Var. for Op. Inc.
$22,900 F

CELL ONE TECHNOLOGIES
Flexible Budget
For the Month Ended July 31, 2018

	Budget Amount per Unit	6,000	7,500	9,500
Units		6,000	7,500	9,500
Sales Revenue	$ 21	$ 126,000	$ 157,500	$ 199,500
Variable Expenses	10	60,000	75,000	95,000
Contribution Margin		66,000	82,500	104,500
Fixed Expenses		55,000	55,000	55,000
Operating Income		$ 11,000	$ 27,500	$ 49,500

The company sold 9,500 units during July, and its actual operating income was as follows:

CELL ONE TECHNOLOGIES
Income Statement
For the Month Ended July 31, 2018

Sales Revenue	$ 206,500
Variable Expenses	100,100
Contribution Margin	106,400
Fixed Expenses	56,000
Operating Income	$ 50,400

Requirements

1. Prepare a flexible budget performance report for July.

2. What was the effect on Cell One's operating income of selling 2,000 units more than the static budget level of sales?

3. What is Cell One's static budget variance for operating income?

4. Explain why the flexible budget performance report provides more useful information to Cell One's managers than the simple static budget variance. What insights can Cell One's managers draw from this performance report?

Learning Objectives 1, 2, 3, 4

2. VOH Eff. Var. $1,368 U

P23-26A Preparing a flexible budget computing standard cost variances

Morton Recliners manufactures leather recliners and uses flexible budgeting and a standard cost system. Morton allocates overhead based on yards of direct materials. The company's performance report includes the following selected data:

		Static Budget (1,000 recliners)	Actual Results (980 recliners)
Sales	(1,000 recliners × $505 each)	$ 505,000	
	(980 recliners × $480 each)		$ 470,400
Variable Manufacturing Costs:			
Direct Materials	(6,000 yds. @ $8.60/yd.)	51,600	
	(6,143 yds. @ $8.40/yd.)		51,601
Direct Labor	(10,000 DLHr @ $9.20/DLHr)	92,000	
	(9,600 DLHr @ $9.30/DLHr)		89,280
Variable Overhead	(6,000 yds. @ $5.20/yd.)	31,200	
	(6,143 yds. @ $6.60/yd.)		40,544
Fixed Manufacturing Costs:			
Fixed Overhead		60,600	62,600
Total Cost of Goods Sold		235,400	244,025
Gross Profit		$ 269,600	$ 226,375

Requirements

1. Prepare a flexible budget based on the actual number of recliners sold.
2. Compute the cost variance and the efficiency variance for direct materials and for direct labor. For manufacturing overhead, compute the variable overhead cost, variable overhead efficiency, fixed overhead cost, and fixed overhead volume variances. Round to the nearest dollar.
3. Have Morton's managers done a good job or a poor job controlling materials, labor, and overhead costs? Why?
4. Describe how Morton's managers can benefit from the standard cost system.

P23-27A Computing standard cost variances and reporting to management

Hear Smart manufactures headphone cases. During September 2018, the company produced and sold 105,000 cases and recorded the following cost data:

Learning Objectives 3, 4, 5

1. DM Eff. Var. $150 F

Standard Cost Information

	Quantity	Cost
Direct Materials	2 parts	$ 0.15 per part
Direct Labor	0.02 hours	8.00 per hour
Variable Manufacturing Overhead	0.02 hours	10.00 per hour

Fixed Manufacturing Overhead ($28,500 for static budget volume of 95,000 units and 1,900 hours, or $15 per hour)

Actual Cost Information

Direct Materials	(209,000 parts @ $0.20 per part)	$ 41,800
Direct Labor	(1,600 hours @ $8.15 per hour)	13,040
Variable Manufacturing Overhead		9,000
Fixed Manufacturing Overhead		26,000

Requirements

1. Compute the cost and efficiency variances for direct materials and direct labor.

2. For manufacturing overhead, compute the variable overhead cost and efficiency variances and the fixed overhead cost and volume variances.

3. Hear Smart's management used better quality materials during September. Discuss the trade-off between the two direct material variances.

Learning Objectives 3, 4, 5, 6

3. VOH Cost Var. $985 F

P23-28A Computing and journalizing standard cost variances

Moss manufactures coffee mugs that it sells to other companies for customizing with their own logos. Moss prepares flexible budgets and uses a standard cost system to control manufacturing costs. The standard unit cost of a coffee mug is based on static budget volume of 59,800 coffee mugs per month:

Direct Materials (0.2 lbs. @ $0.25 per lb.)		$ 0.05
Direct Labor (3 minutes @ $0.11 per minute)		0.33
Manufacturing Overhead:		
Variable (3 minutes @ $0.06 per minute)	$ 0.18	
Fixed (3 minutes @ $0.13 per minute)	0.39	0.57
Total Cost per Coffee Mug		$ 0.95

Actual cost and production information for July 2018 follows:

a. There were no beginning or ending inventory balances. All expenditures were on account.

b. Actual production and sales were 62,500 coffee mugs.

c. Actual direct materials usage was 11,000 lbs. at an actual cost of $0.17 per lb.

d. Actual direct labor usage was 197,000 minutes at a total cost of $25,610.

e. Actual overhead cost was $10,835 variable and $29,765 fixed.

f. Selling and administrative costs were $95,000.

Requirements

1. Compute the cost and efficiency variances for direct materials and direct labor.

2. Journalize the purchase and usage of direct materials and the assignment of direct labor, including the related variances.

3. For manufacturing overhead, compute the variable overhead cost and efficiency variances and the fixed overhead cost and volume variances.

4. Journalize the actual manufacturing overhead and the allocated manufacturing overhead. Journalize the movement of all production costs from Work-in-Process Inventory. Journalize the adjusting of the Manufacturing Overhead account.

5. Moss intentionally hired more highly skilled workers during July. How did this decision affect the cost variances? Overall, was the decision wise?

Note: Problem P23-28A must be completed before attempting Problem P23-29A.

Learning Objective 6

COGS at actual $68,080

P23-29A Preparing a standard cost income statement

Review your results from Problem P23-28A. Moss's standard and actual sales price per mug is $3. Prepare the standard cost income statement for July 2018.

> Problems Group B

P23-30B Preparing a flexible budget performance report

Cell Plus Technologies manufactures capacitors for cellular base stations and other communication applications. The company's July 2018 flexible budget shows output levels of 8,500, 10,000, and 12,000 units. The static budget was based on expected sales of 10,000 units.

Learning Objective 1

3. Static Bud. Var. for Op. Inc. $22,900 F

CELL ONE TECHNOLOGIES Flexible Budget For the Month Ended July 31, 2018				
	Budget Amounts per Unit			
Units		8,500	10,000	12,000
Sales Revenue	$ 24	$ 204,000	$ 240,000	$ 288,000
Variable Expenses	13	110,500	130,000	156,000
Contribution Margin		93,500	110,000	132,000
Fixed Expenses		57,000	57,000	57,000
Operating Income		$ 36,500	$ 53,000	$ 75,000

The company sold 12,000 units during July, and its actual operating income was as follows:

CELL ONE TECHNOLOGIES Income Statement For the Month Ended July 31, 2018	
Sales Revenue	$ 295,000
Variable Expenses	161,100
Contributions Margin	133,900
Fixed Expenses	58,000
Operating Income	$ 75,900

Requirements

1. Prepare a flexible budget performance report for July 2018.
2. What was the effect on Cell Plus's operating income of selling 2,000 units more than the static budget level of sales?
3. What is Cell Plus's static budget variance for operating income?
4. Explain why the flexible budget performance report provides more useful information to Cell Plus's managers than the simple static budget variance. What insights can Cell Plus's managers draw from this performance report?

P23-31B Preparing a flexible budget and computing standard cost variances

McKnight Recliners manufactures leather recliners and uses flexible budgeting and a standard cost system. McKnight allocates overhead based on yards of direct materials. The company's performance report includes the following selected data:

Learning Objectives 1, 2, 3, 4

2. VOH Eff. Var. $1,377 U

		Static Budget (1,025 recliners)	Actual Results (1,005 recliners)
Sales	(1,025 recliners × $500 each)	$ 512,500	
	(1,005 recliners × $495 each)		$ 497,475
Variable Manufacturing Costs:			
Direct Materials	(6,150 yds. @ $8.50/yard)	52,275	
	(6,300 yds. @ $8.30/yard)		52,290
Direct Labor	(10,250 DLHr @ $9.20/DLHr)	94,300	
	(9,850 DLHr @ $9.40/DLHr)		92,590
Variable Overhead	(6,150 yds. @ $5.10/yard)	31,365	
	(6,300 yds. @ $6.50/yard)		40,950
Fixed Manufacturing Costs:			
Fixed Overhead		62,730	64,730
Total Cost of Goods Sold		240,670	250,560
Gross Profit		$ 271,830	$ 246,915

Requirements

1. Prepare a flexible budget based on the actual number of recliners sold.
2. Compute the cost variance and the efficiency variance for direct materials and for direct labor. For manufacturing overhead, compute the variable overhead cost, variable overhead efficiency, fixed overhead cost, and fixed overhead volume variances. Round to the nearest dollar.
3. Have McKnight's managers done a good job or a poor job controlling materials, labor, and overhead costs? Why?
4. Describe how McKnight's managers can benefit from the standard cost system.

Learning Objectives 3, 4, 5

1. DM Eff. Var. $480 F

P23-32B Computing standard cost variances and reporting to management

Headset manufactures headphone cases. During September 2018, the company produced 106,000 cases and recorded the following cost data:

Standard Cost Information

	Quantity	Cost
Direct Materials	2 parts	$ 0.16 per part
Direct Labor	0.02 hours	8.00 per hour
Variable Manufacturing Overhead	0.02 hours	11.00 per hour
Fixed Manufacturing Overhead ($30,720 for static budget volume of 96,000 units and 1,920 hours, or $16 per hour)		

Actual Information

Direct Materials	(209,000 parts @ $0.21 per part)	$ 43,890
Direct Labor	(1,620 hours @ $8.10 per hour)	13,122
Variable Manufacturing Overhead		9,000
Fixed Manufacturing Overhead		30,000

Requirements

1. Compute the cost and efficiency variances for direct materials and direct labor.

2. For manufacturing overhead, compute the variable overhead cost and efficiency variances and the fixed overhead cost and volume variances.

3. Headset's management used better-quality materials during September. Discuss the trade-off between the two direct material variances.

P23-33B Computing and journalizing standard cost variances

Learning Objectives 3, 4, 5, 6

3. VOH Cost Var. $985 F

Middleton manufactures coffee mugs that it sells to other companies for customizing with their own logos. Middleton prepares flexible budgets and uses a standard cost system to control manufacturing costs. The standard unit cost of a coffee mug is based on static budget volume of 59,800 coffee mugs per month:

Direct Materials (0.2 lbs. @ $0.25 per lb.)		$ 0.05
Direct Labor (3 minutes @ $0.14 per minute)		0.42
Manufacturing Overhead:		
Variable (3 minutes @ $0.06 per minute)	$ 0.18	
Fixed (3 minutes @ $0.13 per minute)	0.39	0.57
Total Cost per Coffee Mug		$ 1.04

Actual cost and production information for July 2018 follows:

a. There were no beginning or ending inventory balances. All expenditures were on account.

b. Actual production and sales were 62,500 coffee mugs.

c. Actual direct materials usage was 11,000 lbs. at an actual cost of $0.17 per lb.

d. Actual direct labor usage of 197,000 minutes at a cost of $33,490.

e. Actual overhead cost was $10,835 variable and $29,965 fixed.

f. Selling and administrative costs were $130,000.

Requirements

1. Compute the cost and efficiency variances for direct materials and direct labor.

2. Journalize the purchase and usage of direct materials and the assignment of direct labor, including the related variances.

3. For manufacturing overhead, compute the variable overhead cost and efficiency variances and the fixed overhead cost and volume variances.

4. Journalize the actual manufacturing overhead and the allocated manufacturing overhead. Journalize the movement of all production from Work-in-Process Inventory. Journalize the adjusting of the Manufacturing Overhead account.

5. Middleton intentionally hired more highly skilled workers during July. How did this decision affect the cost variances? Overall, was the decision wise?

Note: Problem P23-33B must be completed before attempting Problem P23-34B.

P23-34B Preparing a standard cost income statement

Learning Objective 6

COGS at actual $76,160

Review your results from Problem P23-33B. Middleton's actual and standard sales price per mug is $5. Prepare the standard cost income statement for July 2018.

CRITICAL THINKING

> Using Excel

P23-35 Using Excel to prepare a flexible budget performance report

Download an Excel template for this problem online in MyAccountingLab or at http://www.pearsonhighered.com/Horngren.

Pilchuck Company manufactures tote bags and has provided the following information for September 2018:

	Actual Results	Static Budget
Units	11,000	12,000
Sales Revenue	$368,000	$384,000
Variable Costs	183,000	198,000
Contribution Margin	185,000	186,000
Fixed Costs	76,000	77,184
Operating Income	$109,000	$108,816

Requirements

1. Prepare a flexible budget performance report, including the heading. Use the ABS function when calculating variances, and use the drop-down selections for F or U when describing the variances.

2. Calculate the Static Budget Variance for operating income, and label it as a F (favorable) or U (unfavorable) variance.

> Continuing Problem

P23-36 Preparing a flexible budget and performance report

This continues the Piedmont Computer Company situation from Chapter 22. Assume Piedmont Computer Company has created a standard cost card for the PCC model tablet computer, with overhead allocated based on direct labor hours:

Direct materials	$ 300 per tablet
Direct labor	3 hours per tablet at $26 per hour
Variable overhead	3 hours per tablet at $5 per hour
Fixed overhead	$54,000 per month

During the month of September, Piedmont Computer Company incurred the following costs while manufacturing 1,100 PCC model tablets:

Direct materials	$ 341,000
Direct labor	88,000
Variable overhead	17,600
Fixed overhead	56,320

Requirements

1. Prepare a flexible budget for September for 900, 1,000, and 1,100 PCC model tablets. The tablet has a standard sales price of $675. List variable costs separately.

2. Using 1,000 PCC model tablets for the static budget, prepare a flexible budget performance report for September. Total sales revenue for the month was $767,800. The company sold 1,100 tablets.

3. What insights can the management of Piedmont Computer Company draw from the performance report?

> Tying It All Together Case 23-1

Before you begin this assignment, review the Tying It All Together feature in the chapter.

Kellogg Company manufacturers and markets ready-to-eat cereal and convenience foods including Raisin Bran, Pop Tarts, Rice Krispies Treats, and Pringles. In addition to the raw materials used when producing its products, Kellogg Company also has significant labor costs associated with the products. As of January 2, 2016, Kellogg Company had approximately 33,577 employees. A shortage in the labor pool, regulatory measures, and other pressures could increase the company's labor cost, having a negative impact on the company's operating income.

Requirements

1. Suppose Kellogg Company noticed an increase in its actual direct labor costs compared to the budgeted amount. How could Kellogg Company investigate this?

2. What is the direct labor cost variance and how would a company calculate this variance?

3. What is the direct labor efficiency variance and how would a company calculate this variance?

4. Suppose that Kellogg Company found an unfavorable total direct labor variance that was due completely to the direct labor cost variance. What measures could Kellogg Company take to control this variance?

5. Suppose that Kellogg Company found an unfavorable total direct labor variance that was due completely to the direct labor efficiency variance. What measures could Kellogg Company take to control this variance?

> Decision Case 23-1

Suppose you manage the local Scoopy's ice cream parlor. In addition to selling ice cream cones, you make large batches of a few flavors of milk shakes to sell throughout the day. Your parlor is chosen to test the company's "Made-for-You" system. This new system enables patrons to customize their milk shakes by choosing different flavors.

Customers like the new system and your staff appears to be adapting, but you wonder whether this new made-to-order system is as efficient as the old system in which you just made a few large batches. Efficiency is a special concern because your performance is evaluated in part on the restaurant's efficient use of materials and labor. Your superiors consider efficiency variances greater than 5% to be unacceptable.

You decide to look at your sales for a typical day. You find that the parlor used 390 pounds of ice cream and 72 hours of direct labor to produce and sell 2,000 shakes. The standard quantity allowed for a shake is 0.2 pound of ice cream and 0.03 hour of direct labor. The standard costs are $1.50 per pound for ice cream and $8 per hour for labor.

Requirements

1. Compute the efficiency variances for direct labor and direct materials.

2. Provide likely explanations for the variances. Do you have reason to be concerned about your performance evaluation? Explain.

3. Write a memo to Scoopy's national office explaining your concern and suggesting a remedy.

> Fraud Case 23-1

Drew Castello, general manager of Sunflower Manufacturing, was frustrated. He wanted the budgeted results, and his staff was not getting them to him fast enough. Drew decided to pay a visit to the accounting office, where Jeff Hollingsworth was supposed to be working on the reports. Jeff had recently been hired to update the accounting system and speed up the reporting process.

"What's taking so long?" Drew asked. "When am I going to get the variance reports?" Jeff sighed and attempted to explain the problem. "Some of the variances appear to be way off. We either have a serious problem in production, or there is an error in the spreadsheet. I want to recheck the spreadsheet before I distribute the report." Drew pulled up a chair, and the two men went through the spreadsheet together. The formulas in the spreadsheet were correct and showed a large unfavorable direct labor efficiency variance. It was time for Drew and Jeff to do some investigating.

After looking at the time records, Jeff pointed out that it was unusual that every employee in the production area recorded exactly eight hours each day in direct labor. Did they not take breaks? Was no one ever five minutes late getting back from lunch? What about clean-up time between jobs or at the end of the day?

Drew began to observe the production laborers and noticed several disturbing items. One employee was routinely late for work, but his time card always showed him clocked in on time. Another employee took 10- to 15-minute breaks every hour, averaging about $1\frac{1}{2}$ hours each day, but still reported eight hours of direct labor each day. Yet another employee often took an extra 30 minutes for lunch, but his time card showed him clocked in on time. No one in the production area ever reported any "down time" when they were not working on a specific job, even though they all took breaks and completed other tasks such as doing clean-up and attending department meetings.

Requirements

1. How might the observed behaviors cause an unfavorable direct labor efficiency variance?

2. How might an employee's time card show the employee on the job and working when the employee was not present?

3. Why would the employees' activities be considered fraudulent?

> Team Project 23-1

Lynx Corp. manufactures windows and doors. Lynx has been using a standard cost system that bases cost and efficiency standards on Lynx's historical long-run average performance. Suppose Lynx's controller has engaged your team of management consultants to advise him or her whether Lynx should use some basis other than historical performance for setting standards.

Requirements

1. List the types of variances you recommend that Lynx compute (for example, direct materials cost variance for glass). For each variance, what specific standards would Lynx need to develop? In addition to cost standards, do you recommend that Lynx develop any nonfinancial standards?

2. There are many approaches to setting standards other than simply using long-run average historical costs and quantities.

   a. List three alternative approaches that Lynx could use to set standards, and explain how Lynx could implement each alternative.

   b. Evaluate each alternative method of setting standards, including the pros and cons of each method.

   c. Write a memo to Lynx's controller detailing your recommendations. First, should Lynx retain its historical data-based standard cost approach? If not, which of the alternative approaches should it adopt?

> Communication Activity 23-1

In 75 words or fewer, explain what a cost variance is and describe its potential causes.

MyAccountingLab   **For a wealth of online resources, including exercises, problems, media, and immediate tutorial help, please visit** http://www.myaccountinglab.com.

> Quick Check Answers

1. c   2. d   3. a   4. d   5. b   6. b   7. a   8. b   9. c   10. b   11. a

24

Responsibility Accounting and Performance Evaluation

How Do I Control What I Can't See?

Pierre Simons founded his beverage company, Drake Drink Company, a few years ago, and the company is now expanding. Pierre is making plans to add another soft drink bottling facility. So far, all operations have been in one area, with the corporate office attached to the bottling facility. The new plant, however, will be about 200 miles from the current location. Pierre believes the new location will help the company expand into new markets and decrease shipping costs. The problem is control. How will Pierre oversee operations at a plant 200 miles away?

The Drake Drink Company has reached the point where one person can no longer oversee all of the day-to-day operations. Pierre has to find competent employees to manage the new plant. He also has to develop a system that will allow him to clearly communicate the company's goals to the new managers and monitor the progress at the new plant. Pierre, as a business owner, has profitability goals, but he is also concerned with other aspects of the business. How will he ensure that his new customers are satisfied, proper procedures are followed to ensure safe products are produced, and employees are motivated?

How Is Success Measured?

As companies grow and expand, the management of day-to-day operations has to be delegated—one person cannot continue to oversee every aspect of the business. Consider **PepsiCo, Inc.** Pepsi-Cola was created in the late 1890s by Caleb Bradham, a New Bern, North Carolina, pharmacist. PepsiCo, Inc. was founded in 1965 with the merger of Pepsi-Cola and Frito-Lay. Through expansion and acquisitions, PepsiCo now has annual revenue of approximately $63 billion and more than 263,000 employees worldwide. How does upper management track the progress of the company? PepsiCo reports the operations of six business segments in its annual report distributed to the public, but internally it has a significant number of subunits that report on their progress. The company has to have a system to ensure that each manager is making decisions that are in the best interest of the whole company, not just his or her department. In this chapter, we look at ways companies can track the progress of each business segment.

Chapter 24 Learning Objectives

1 Explain why companies decentralize and use responsibility accounting

2 Describe the purpose of performance evaluation systems and how the balanced scorecard helps companies evaluate performance

3 Use responsibility reports to evaluate cost, revenue, and profit centers

4 Use return on investment (ROI) and residual income (RI) to evaluate investment centers

5 Determine how transfer pricing affects decentralized companies

The previous two chapters have focused on using budgets for planning, directing, and controlling business activities. In the planning stage, companies look forward to future accounting periods and set goals. In the directing stage, managers coordinate the company's day-to-day activities, including purchasing, manufacturing, and selling. In the controlling stage, companies compare actual performance with the goals and take action as needed. In this chapter, we again look at budgets, but in a slightly different context. We consider how different types of business units need to be evaluated in different ways. We also consider the use of nonfinancial measures for measuring performance.

WHY DO DECENTRALIZED COMPANIES NEED RESPONSIBILITY ACCOUNTING?

In a small company, the owner or top executives often make all planning, directing, and controlling decisions. Small companies are most often considered to be **centralized companies** because centralized decision making is easier due to the smaller scope of their operations. However, when a company grows, it is impossible for a single person to manage the entire organization's daily operations. Therefore, most companies decentralize as they grow. **Decentralized companies** split their operations into different segments, such as departments or divisions. Top management delegates decision-making responsibility to the segment managers. Top management determines the type of decentralization that best suits the company's strategy. For example, decentralization may be based on geographic area (domestic and international), customer base (commercial and residential), product line (motorcycles and all-terrain vehicles), business function (sales and service), or some other business characteristic.

Advantages of Decentralization

Decentralization offers several advantages to large companies, including the following:

- **Frees top management time.** By delegating responsibility for daily operations to business segment managers, top management can concentrate on long-term strategic planning and higher-level decisions that affect the entire company.

- **Supports use of expert knowledge.** Decentralization allows top management to hire the expertise each business segment needs to excel in its own specific operations. For example, decentralizing by state allows companies to hire managers with specialized knowledge of consumer demand for products or services, demographics, or the laws in each state. Such specialized knowledge can help segment managers make better decisions

Learning Objective 1
Explain why companies decentralize and use responsibility accounting

Centralized Company
A company in which major planning, directing, and controlling decisions are made by top executives.

Decentralized Company
A company that is divided into business segments, with segment managers making planning, directing, and controlling decisions for their segments.

than could the company's top managers about product and business improvements within the business segment.

- **Improves customer relations.** Segment managers focus on just one segment of the company. Therefore, they can maintain closer contact with important customers than can upper management. Thus, decentralization often leads to improved customer relations and quicker customer response time.

- **Provides training.** Decentralization also provides segment managers with training and experience necessary to become effective top managers. For example, companies often choose CEOs based on their past performance as division managers.

- **Improves motivation and retention.** Empowering segment managers to make decisions increases managers' motivation and retention. This improves job performance and satisfaction.

Disadvantages of Decentralization

Despite its advantages, decentralization can also cause potential problems, including the following:

- **Duplication of costs.** Decentralization may cause the company to duplicate certain costs or assets. For example, each business segment may hire its own payroll department and purchase its own payroll software. Companies can often avoid such duplications by providing centralized services. For example, a hotel chain might segment its business by property, yet each property might share one centralized reservations office and one centralized Web site.

Goal Congruence
Aligning the goals of business segment managers and other subordinates with the goals of top management.

- **Problems achieving goal congruence.** Goal congruence occurs when segment managers' goals align with top management's goals. Decentralized companies often struggle to achieve goal congruence. Segment managers may not fully understand the "big picture" of the company. They may make decisions that are good for their division but could harm another division or the rest of the company. For example, a division that makes component parts of the company's product might use cheaper components to decrease product costs. However, cheaper components might hurt the product line's quality. As a result, the company's brand, *as a whole*, might suffer. Later in this chapter, we see how managerial accountants can design performance evaluation systems that encourage goal congruence.

Although we've discussed some disadvantages of decentralization, it's important to note that the advantages of decentralization usually outweigh the disadvantages.

TYING IT ALL TOGETHER

PepsiCo was incorporated in Delaware in 1919 and was reincorporated after the merger with Frito Lay in 1986. The company is well known for its varied brands including Frito-Lay, Gatorade, Pepsi-Cola, Quaker, and Tropicana. PepsiCo makes, markets, distributes, and sells a wide variety of beverages and snacks to customers in more than 200 countries and territories.

How does PepsiCo decentralize its operations?

PepsiCo decentralizes its operations geographically and also in North America by product line. On its 2015 annual report, PepsiCo reported six different divisions: Frito-Lay North America, Quaker Foods North America, North America Beverages, Latin America, Europe Sub-Saharan Africa, and Asia, Middle East and North Africa. It is also likely that PepsiCo would further decentralize each division.

Why do companies, such as PepsiCo, choose to decentralize their operations?

Companies as large as PepsiCo will benefit in many ways from decentralization. Decentralization allows companies to monitor results for each division separately. In addition, top management can delegate decision-making authority to division managers. For example, at PepsiCo, Indra Nooyi, the Chairman of the Board and Chief Executive Officer, would delegate decision-making authority to division managers such as Thomas Greco (CEO Frito-Lay North America) and Laxman Narasimhan (CEO Latin America). PepsiCo also utilizes decentralization to meet the eating habits and cultural differences of the many different countries and regions the company operates in. PepsiCo offers different chips and drinks based on regional preferences.

Responsibility Accounting

Decentralized companies delegate responsibility for specific decisions to each subunit, creating responsibility centers. A **responsibility center** is a part of the organization for which a manager has decision-making authority and accountability for the results of those decisions. We again use the fictitious company Smart Touch Learning. As you recall, Smart Touch Learning manufactures its own brand of touch screen tablet computers that are preloaded with the company's e-learning software. The e-learning software is also sold independently.

Each manager is responsible for planning, directing, and controlling some part of the company's activities. Lower-level managers are often responsible for budgeting, directing, and controlling costs of a single value chain function. For example, one manager is responsible for planning, directing, and controlling the *production* of Smart Touch Learning's tablet computers at the plant, while another manager is responsible for planning, directing, and controlling the *distribution* of the product to customers. Lower-level managers report to higher-level managers, who have broader responsibilities. Managers in charge of production and distribution report to senior managers responsible for profits earned by an entire product line.

Responsibility Centers

Decentralized companies need a way to evaluate their various responsibility centers. A **responsibility accounting system** is a system for evaluating the performance of each responsibility center and its manager. The goal of the system's performance reports is to provide relevant information to the managers empowered to make decisions. There are four types of responsibility centers:

- Cost center
- Revenue center
- Profit center
- Investment center

Cost Center In a **cost center**, the manager is only responsible for controlling costs. Manufacturing operations, such as the tablet computer production line at Smart Touch Learning, are cost centers. The line foreman controls costs by monitoring materials costs, repair and maintenance costs, employee costs, and employee efficiency. The foreman is *not* responsible for generating revenues because he or she is not involved in selling the product. The plant manager evaluates the foreman on his or her ability to control *costs* by comparing actual costs to budgeted costs. Responsibility reports for cost centers include only costs.

Revenue Center In a **revenue center**, the manager is only responsible for generating revenues. A kiosk that sells sunglasses at a local mall is an example of a revenue center. The business is a part of a chain, so the local manager does not control costs. The merchandise inventory is purchased by a central purchasing department, and rent paid to the mall is negotiated by the corporate office. Company procedures indicate only one employee should be in the booth, so the local manager has little control over wages expense. The primary responsibility of the manager is to generate revenues by selling sunglasses. Therefore, the kiosk is considered a revenue center. Responsibility reports for a revenue center include only revenues.

Profit Center In a **profit center**, the manager is responsible for generating revenues and controlling costs and, therefore, profits. The manager responsible for a grocery store is accountable for increasing sales revenue *and* controlling costs to achieve the profit goals. The manager controls costs by ordering sufficient merchandise inventory to meet sales

Responsibility Center
A part of the organization for which a manager has decision-making authority and accountability for the results of those decisions.

Responsibility Accounting System
A system for evaluating the performance of each responsibility center and its manager.

Cost Center
A responsibility center whose manager is only responsible for controlling costs.

Revenue Center
A responsibility center whose manager is only responsible for generating revenue.

Profit Center
A responsibility center whose manager is responsible for generating revenue and controlling costs and, therefore, profits.

demand without having excessive spoilage from outdated food products and scheduling workers to have sufficient customer service without paying more than necessary in wages. Profit center responsibility reports include both revenues and expenses to show the profit center's operating income.

Investment Center In an **investment center**, the manager is responsible for generating profits and efficiently managing the center's invested capital. Managers of investment centers, for example division managers of a chain of stores, are responsible for (1) generating sales, (2) controlling expenses, (3) managing the amount of investment in capital expenditures required to earn the income, and (4) planning future investments for growth and expansion of the company. The division manager has limited funds and has to decide which store will receive a renovation and when a new computerized inventory system will be installed. These long-term investments, also called *capital investments* and *invested capital*, are purchased with the intent to increase profits, so the investment center manager is evaluated on how well the center uses the investments to generate profits. Investment center responsibility reports include profits as well as return on investment (ROI) and residual income (RI) measures, which are covered later in the chapter.

Exhibit 24-1 summarizes the types of responsibility centers, their managers' responsibilities, and their responsibility reports.

> **Investment Center**
> A responsibility center whose manager is responsible for generating profits and efficiently managing the center's invested capital.

Exhibit 24-1 | Responsibility Centers

Responsibility Center	Manager's Responsibility	Responsibility Report
Cost Center	Controlling costs	Compares actual costs to budgeted costs
Revenue Center	Generating revenues	Compares actual revenues to budgeted revenues
Profit Center	Producing profits through generating revenues and controlling costs	Compares actual revenues and costs to budgeted revenues and costs
Investment Center	Producing profits and efficiently managing the center's invested capital	Compares actual profits to budgeted profits and measures return on investment and residual income

Responsibility Reports

Exhibit 24-2 shows how an organization like Smart Touch Learning might assign responsibility.

At the top level, the President—Chief Executive Officer (CEO) oversees each of the two vice presidents. The Vice President—Chief Operating Officer (COO) oversees two divisions. Division managers, such as the tablet computer division manager, generally have broad responsibility, including deciding how to use assets to maximize return on investment. Most companies classify divisions as *investment centers*.

Each division manager supervises all the activities in that division. Exhibit 24-2 shows that the Tablet Computer Division manager oversees the production of two product lines—standard tablets and premium tablets. Product lines are generally considered *profit centers*. Thus, the manager of the standard tablets product line is responsible for evaluating lower-level managers of both:

- Cost centers—such as plants that make standard tablets
- Revenue centers—such as managers responsible for selling standard tablets

Exhibit 24-2 | **Smart Touch Learning Organization Chart (Partial)**

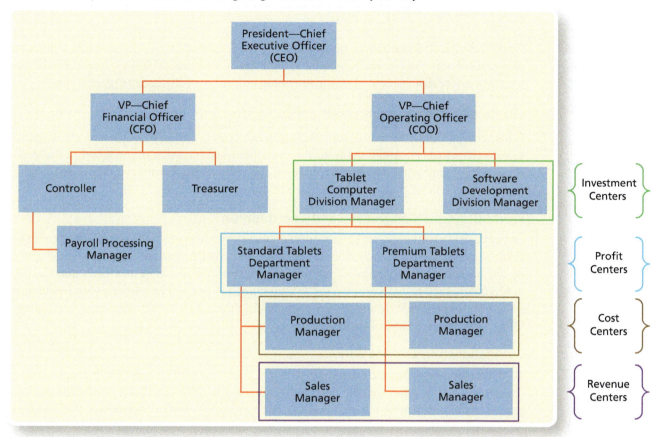

Try It!

Fill in the blanks with the phrase that best completes the sentence. Some phrases may be used more than once and some not at all.

Phrases:

cost center	revenue center
investment center	lower
profit center	higher
responsibility center	

1. The maintenance department at the local zoo is a(n) _____.
2. The gift shop at the local zoo is a(n) _____.
3. The menswear department of a department store, which is responsible for buying and selling merchandise, is a(n) _____.
4. The production line at a manufacturing plant is a(n) _____.
5. A(n) _____ is any segment of the business whose manager is accountable for specific activities.
6. A division of a beverage manufacturing company responsible for a particular brand of soft drink is a(n) _____.
7. The sales manager in charge of a shoe company's northwest sales territory oversees a(n) _____.
8. Managers of cost and revenue centers are at _____ levels of the organization than are managers of profit and investment centers.

Check your answers online in MyAccountingLab or at http://www.pearsonhighered.com/Horngren.

For more practice, see Short Exercises S24-1 and S24-2. MyAccountingLab

WHAT IS A PERFORMANCE EVALUATION SYSTEM, AND HOW IS IT USED?

Learning Objective 2
Describe the purpose of performance evaluation systems and how the balanced scorecard helps companies evaluate performance

Performance Evaluation System
A system that provides top management with a framework for maintaining control over the entire organization.

Once a company decentralizes operations, top management is no longer involved in running the subunits' day-to-day operations. Performance evaluation systems provide top management with a framework for maintaining control over the entire organization.

Goals of Performance Evaluation Systems

When companies decentralize, top management needs a system to communicate its goals to subunit managers. Additionally, top management needs to determine whether the decisions being made at the subunit level are effectively meeting company goals. Let's look at the primary goals of performance evaluation systems.

Promoting Goal Congruence and Coordination

As previously mentioned, decentralization increases the difficulty of achieving goal congruence. Segment managers may not always make decisions consistent with the overall goals of the organization. A company will be able to achieve its goals only if each unit moves, in a synchronized fashion, toward the overall company goals. The performance evaluation system should provide incentives for coordinating the subunits' activities and direct them toward achieving the overall company goals.

Communicating Expectations

To make decisions that are consistent with the company's goals, segment managers must know the goals and the specific part their unit plays in attaining those goals. The performance evaluation system should spell out the unit's most critical objectives. With a clear picture of what upper management expects, segment managers can direct their daily operating decisions so those expectations are met.

Motivating Segment Managers

Segment managers are usually motivated to make decisions that will help to achieve top management's expectations. For additional motivation, upper management may offer bonuses to segment managers who meet or exceed performance targets. Top management must exercise extreme care in setting performance targets. For example, managers measured solely by their ability to control costs may take whatever actions are necessary to achieve that goal, including sacrificing quality or customer service. Such actions would *not* be in the best interests of the company as a whole. Therefore, upper management must consider the ramifications of the performance targets it sets for segment managers.

Providing Feedback

As noted previously, in decentralized companies, top management is not involved in the day-to-day operations of each subunit. Performance evaluation systems provide upper management with the feedback it needs to maintain control over the entire organization, even though it has delegated responsibility and decision-making authority to segment managers. If targets are not met at the unit level, upper management will take corrective actions, ranging from modifying unit goals (if the targets were unrealistic) to replacing the segment manager (if the targets were achievable but the manager failed to reach them).

Benchmarking

Performance evaluation results are often used for benchmarking, which is the practice of comparing the company's achievements against the best practices in the industry. Companies also benchmark performance against the subunit's past performance. Historical trend data (measuring performance over time) help managers assess whether their decisions are improving, having no effect on, or adversely affecting subunit performance. Some companies also benchmark performance against other subunits with similar characteristics. Comparing results against industry benchmarks, however, is often more revealing than comparing results against budgets or past performance. To survive, a company must keep up with its competitors. Benchmarking helps the company determine whether it is performing at least as well as its competitors.

Limitations of Financial Performance Measurement

In the past, performance measurement revolved almost entirely around *financial* performance. On the one hand, this focus makes sense because the ultimate goal of a company is to generate profit. On the other hand, *current* financial performance tends to reveal the results of *past* actions rather than indicate *future* performance. For this reason, financial measures tend to be **lag indicators** (after the fact) rather than **lead indicators** (future predictors). Management needs to know the results of past decisions, but it also needs to know how current decisions may affect the future. To adequately assess the company, managers need both lead indicators and lag indicators.

Lag Indicator
A performance measure that indicates past performance.

Lead Indicator
A performance measure that forecasts future performance.

Another limitation of financial performance measures is that they tend to focus on the company's short-term achievements rather than on long-term performance because financial reports are prepared on a monthly, quarterly, or annual basis. To remain competitive, top management needs clear signals that assess and predict the company's performance over longer periods of time.

Due to the limitations of financial performance measures, companies need to also use operational performance measures, such as customer satisfaction, in their performance evaluation systems. **Operational performance measures** are nonfinancial measures that evaluate a firm's performance on the basis of effectiveness and efficiency to ensure all segments of the business are working together to achieve the company's goals.

Operational Performance Measure
A nonfinancial performance measure that evaluates effectiveness and efficiency to ensure all segments of the business are working together to achieve the company's goals.

The Balanced Scorecard

In the early 1990s, Robert Kaplan and David Norton introduced the **balanced scorecard**.[1] The balanced scorecard is a performance evaluation system that requires management to consider *both* financial performance measures (lag indicators) and operational performance measures (lead indicators) when judging the performance of a company and its subunits. These measures should be linked with the company's goals and its strategy for achieving those goals. The balanced scorecard represents a major shift in corporate performance measurement. Rather than treating financial indicators as the sole measure of performance, companies recognize that they are only one measure among a broader set. Keeping score of operating measures *and* traditional financial measures gives management a "balanced" view of the organization because management needs to consider other critical factors, such as customer satisfaction, operational efficiency, and employee excellence. Management uses *key performance indicators*— such as customer satisfaction ratings and revenue growth—to measure critical factors that affect the success of the company. **Key performance indicators (KPIs)** are summary performance measures that help managers assess whether the company is achieving its goals.

Balanced Scorecard
The performance evaluation system that requires management to consider both financial performance measures and operational performance measures when judging the performance of a company and its subunits.

Key Performance Indicator (KPI)
A summary performance measure that helps managers assess whether the company is achieving its goals.

The balanced scorecard views the company from four different perspectives, each of which evaluates a specific aspect of organizational performance:

- Financial perspective
- Customer perspective
- Internal business perspective
- Learning and growth perspective

[1]Robert Kaplan and David Norton, "The Balanced Scorecard—Measures That Drive Performance," *Harvard Business Review on Measuring Corporate Performance* (Boston: Harvard Business School Press, 1998): 123–145; Robert Kaplan and David Norton, *Translating Strategy into Action: The Balanced Scorecard* (Boston: Harvard Business School Press, 1996).

The company's strategy affects and, in turn, is affected by all four perspectives. There is a cause-and-effect relationship linking the four perspectives.

Companies that adopt the balanced scorecard usually have specific goals they wish to achieve within each of the four perspectives. Once management clearly identifies the goals, it develops KPIs that can assess how well the goals are being achieved. That is, it measures actual results of KPIs against goal KPIs. The difference is the variance. Management can focus attention on the most critical variances and prevent information overload. Management should take care to use only a few KPIs for each perspective. Let's look at each of the perspectives and discuss the links among them.

Financial Perspective

This perspective helps managers answer the question "How do we look to investors and creditors?" The ultimate goal of for-profit companies is to generate income. Therefore, company strategy revolves around increasing the company's profits through increasing revenue growth and productivity. Companies grow revenue by introducing new products, gaining new customers, and increasing sales to existing customers. Companies increase productivity through reducing costs and using the company's assets more efficiently. The financial perspective focuses management's attention on KPIs that assess financial objectives, such as revenue growth and cost cutting. The latter portion of this chapter discusses the most commonly used financial perspective KPIs in detail.

Customer Perspective

This perspective helps managers evaluate the question "How do customers see us?" Evaluating customer satisfaction is critical to achieving the company's financial goals outlined in the financial perspective of the balanced scorecard. Customers are typically concerned with four specific product or service attributes: (1) the product's price, (2) the product's quality, (3) the product's performance and service, and (4) the product's delivery time. Because each of these attributes is critical to making the customer happy, most companies have specific objectives for each of these attributes.

Internal Business Perspective

This perspective helps managers address the question "At what business processes must we excel to meet customer and financial objectives?" The answer to this question incorporates three factors: innovation, operations, and post-sales service. All three factors critically affect customer satisfaction, which will affect the company's financial success.

Satisfying customers once does not guarantee future success, which is why the first important factor of the internal business perspective is innovation. Customers' needs and wants constantly change. Just a few years ago, self-driving cars and 3-D printers did not exist. Companies must continually improve existing products and develop new products to succeed in the future.

The second important factor of the internal business perspective is operations. Lean and effective internal operations allow the company to meet customers' needs and expectations and remain competitive.

The third factor of the internal business perspective is post-sales service. Claims of excellent post-sales service help to generate more sales.

Learning and Growth Perspective

This perspective helps managers assess the question "How can we continue to improve and create value?" The learning and growth perspective focuses on three factors: (1) employee capabilities, (2) information system capabilities, and (3) the company's "climate for action." The learning and growth perspective lays the foundation needed to improve internal business operations, sustain customer satisfaction, and generate financial success. Without skilled employees, updated technology, and a positive corporate culture, the company will not be able to meet the objectives of the other perspectives.

Let's consider each of these factors. First, because most routine work is automated, employees are freed up to be critical and creative thinkers who, therefore, can help achieve the company's goals. The learning and growth perspective measures employees' skills, knowledge, motivation, and empowerment. Second, employees need timely and accurate information on customers, internal processes, and finances; therefore, KPIs measure the maintenance and improvement of the company's information system. Finally, management must create a corporate culture that supports and encourages communication, change, and growth. For example, a company may use the balanced scorecard to communicate strategy to every employee and to show each employee how his or her daily work contributes to company success. Exhibit 24-3 summarizes the balanced scorecard and gives examples of KPIs for each perspective.

Exhibit 24-3 | Balanced Scorecard

Perspective	Strategy	Common Key Performance Indicators (KPIs)
Financial	Increase company profits through increasing revenue growth and productivity	• Net income • Sales revenue growth • Gross margin growth • Cash flow • Return on investment • Residual income
Customer	Improve customer satisfaction for long-term success	• Customer satisfaction ratings • Percentage of market share • Increase in number of customers • Number of repeat customers • Number of customer complaints • Rate of on-time deliveries • Percentage of sales returns

Internal Business	Improve internal efficiency and effectiveness to achieve profitability and customer satisfaction through:
	   • Innovation
	   • Operations
	   • Post-sales service
		• Number of new products developed
		• New-product development time
		• Manufacturing cycle time
		• Defect rate
		• Number of units produced per hour
		• Number of warranty claims received
		• Average repair time
		• Average wait time for a customer service representative

Learning and Growth	Retain skilled employees, update technology, and create a positive corporate culture to provide a foundation for improved internal operations, sustain customer satisfaction, and generate financial success	• Hours of employee training • Number of cross-trained employees • Percentage of computer downtime • Percentage of processes with real-time feedback on quality, cycle time, and cost • Employee satisfaction • Employee turnover • Number of employee suggestions implemented

So far, we have looked at why companies decentralize, why they need to measure subunit performance, and how the balanced scorecard can help provide key operational measures. In the second half of the chapter, we focus on how companies measure the financial perspective of the balanced scorecard.

Try It!

Classify each key performance indicator according to the balanced scorecard perspective it addresses. Choose from the following: financial perspective, customer perspective, internal business perspective, or learning and growth perspective.

9. Number of repeat customers
10. Employee turnover
11. Revenue growth
12. Number of on-time deliveries
13. Number of defects found during the manufacturing process

Check your answers online in MyAccountingLab or at http://www.pearsonhighered.com/Horngren.

For more practice, see Short Exercises S24-3 and S24-4. MyAccountingLab

HOW DO COMPANIES USE RESPONSIBILITY ACCOUNTING TO EVALUATE PERFORMANCE IN COST, REVENUE, AND PROFIT CENTERS?

Learning Objective 3
Use responsibility reports to evaluate cost, revenue, and profit centers

In this part of the chapter, we take a more detailed look at how companies measure the financial perspective of the balanced scorecard for different business segments of the company. We focus now on the financial performance measurement of each type of responsibility center.

Responsibility reports are performance reports that capture the financial performance of cost, revenue, and profit centers with a focus on responsibility and control. Recall that performance reports compare *actual* results with *budgeted* amounts and display a variance, or difference, between the two amounts. Because *cost centers* are only responsible for controlling costs, their performance reports include only information on actual costs versus budgeted *costs*. Likewise, performance reports for *revenue centers* contain only actual revenue versus budgeted *revenue*. However, *profit centers* are responsible for both controlling costs and generating revenue. Therefore, their performance reports contain actual and budgeted information on both their *revenues and costs*.

Responsibility Report
Performance report that captures the financial performance of cost, revenue, and profit centers with a focus on responsibility and controllability.

A unique factor of responsibility reports is the focus on *responsibility* and *controllability*. Because the responsibility reports are used for performance evaluation, the focus is only on what the manager has responsibility for and control over. It is not logical to evaluate a manager on items he or she cannot control or is not responsible for.

Controllable Versus Noncontrollable Costs

Controllable Cost
A cost that a manager has the power to influence by his or her decisions.

A **controllable cost** is one that the manager has the power to influence by his or her decisions. All costs are ultimately controllable at the upper levels of management, but controllability decreases as responsibility decreases. That means lower-level management has responsibility for a limited amount of costs. Responsibility accounting attempts to associate costs with the manager who has control over the costs. Results are shown on a responsibility report, sometimes called a *responsibility accounting performance report*. Responsibility reports are completed for each manager of a business segment.

Let's consider the production manager at Smart Touch Learning. This manager is responsible for efficiently and cost-effectively producing quality products. The production manager is, therefore, responsible for controlling the direct materials usage by properly training production workers, thus avoiding waste. On the other hand, the production manager does not make investment decisions, such as the decision to replace older, inefficient manufacturing equipment with new equipment. That type of decision is made at a higher level of management. Therefore, a responsibility report for the production manager would not include depreciation expense on the manufacturing equipment because that cost is beyond his or her control. Likewise, the manager does not control his or her own salary, so that item would also not be listed on the report.

Responsibility Reports

Let's look at responsibility reports for cost, revenue, and profit centers.

Cost Centers

Cost center responsibility reports typically focus on the *flexible budget variance*—the difference between actual results and the flexible budget. Recall that a flexible budget uses standard (budgeted) costs at the actual level of activity. Therefore, the flexible budget variance highlights the differences caused by changes in cost, not by changes in sales or production volume. Exhibit 24-4 illustrates the difference between a *performance report* and *responsibility report* for a cost center using the regional payroll processing department of Smart Touch Learning. Because the payroll processing department only incurs costs and does not generate revenue, it is classified as a cost center.

Exhibit 24-4 | **Performance Report Versus Responsibility Report—Cost Center**

SMART TOUCH LEARNING
Payroll Processing Department Performance Report
For the Month Ended July 31, 2020

	Actual Results	Flexible Budget	Flexible Budget Variance	% Variance*
Salaries	$ 3,000	$ 3,000	$ 0	0.0%
Wages	15,500	15,000	500 U	3.3% U
Payroll Benefits	6,100	5,000	1,100 U	22.0% U
Equipment Depreciation	3,000	3,000	0	0.0%
Supplies	1,850	2,000	150 F	7.5% F
Other Expenses	1,900	2,000	100 F	5.0% F
Total Expenses	$ 31,350	$ 30,000	$ 1,350 U	4.5% U

* % Variance = Flexible Budget Variance / Flexible Budget

SMART TOUCH LEARNING
Payroll Processing Department Responsibility Report
For the Month Ended July 31, 2020

	Actual Results	Flexible Budget	Flexible Budget Variance	% Variance*
Wages	$ 15,500	$ 15,000	$ 500 U	3.3% U
Supplies	1,850	2,000	150 F	7.5% F
Other Expenses	1,900	2,000	100 F	5.0% F
Total Expenses	$ 19,250	$ 19,000	$ 250 U	1.3% U

* % Variance = Flexible Budget Variance / Flexible Budget

Notice that the 1.3% variance for Total Expenses is not the net of the % Variance for each expense: (3.3%) + 7.5% + 5.0% ≠ 1.3%. This is an example of a horizontal analysis, which is the difference between two amounts divided by the base amount. In this case, the difference is the Flexible Budget Variance and the base amount is the Flexible Budget.

The performance report shows all costs incurred by the department. The salaries, wages, and payroll benefits are the costs related to the employees of the Regional Payroll Processing Department. The other expenses listed on the reports are direct costs of that department. This report is useful when management needs to know the full cost of operating the department. For example, if Smart Touch Learning is considering outsourcing the payroll function and eliminating the department, then management needs the full cost information to make the decision. (This type of decision is covered later in the short-term business decisions chapter.) However, if Smart Touch Learning wants to evaluate the performance of the department manager, then the responsibility report is more useful. Notice the items that are included in the performance report but are *not* included in the responsibility report:

- Salaries—The department manager does not control his or her own salary.
- Payroll Benefits—Costs such as health insurance are determined at a higher level and are not controlled by the department manager. Other payroll costs, such as payroll taxes, are determined by law and also are not controlled by the department manager.
- Equipment Depreciation—The department manager does not have the authority to make investment decisions and, therefore, is not held responsible for the cost.

Managers use *management by exception* to determine which variances in the responsibility report are worth investigating. Management by exception directs management's attention to important differences between actual and budgeted amounts. For example, management may investigate only variances that exceed a certain dollar amount (for example, more than $1,000) or a certain percentage of the budgeted figure (for example, more than 10%). Using percentage variances help highlight the proportion of the variance by showing the relative change between the budgeted and actual amounts. For example, the flexible budget variance for wages was $500 unfavorable which is only a 3.3% unfavorable variance ($500 / $15,000). However, for supplies, the flexible budget variance is only $150 favorable but is a 7.5% favorable variance ($150 / $2,000). Variances expressed as percentages help managers identify which variances need investigation. Smaller variances signal that operations are close to target and do not require management's immediate attention. Companies that use standard costs can compute cost and efficiency variances to better understand why significant flexible budget variances occurred.

Revenue Centers

Revenue center responsibility reports often highlight both the flexible budget variance and the sales volume variance. The responsibility report for the Premium Tablet Sales Department of Smart Touch Learning might look similar to Exhibit 24-5, with detailed sales volume and revenue shown for each type of premium tablet computer sold. The Sales Department is part of the Premium Tablet Department (for simplicity, the exhibit shows volume and revenue for only one item).

Exhibit 24-5 | **Responsibility Report—Revenue Center**

SMART TOUCH LEARNING Premium Tablet Sales Department Responsibility Report For the Month Ended July 31, 2020					
	Actual Sales	Flexible Budget Variance	Flexible Budget	Sales Volume Variance	Static Budget
Number of Premium Tablets	90	0	90	10 F	80
Net Sales Revenue	$ 47,250	$ 2,250 F	$ 45,000	$ 5,000 F	$ 40,000

Recall that the sales volume variance is due strictly to volume differences—selling more or fewer units than originally planned. The flexible budget variance, however, is due strictly to differences in the sales price—selling units for a higher or lower price than originally planned. The budgeted sales price is $500 per tablet ($45,000 / 90 tablets). However, the actual sales price was $525 per tablet ($47,250 / 90 tablets) which resulted in a $2,250 favorable flexible budget variance. Both the sales volume variance and the flexible budget variance help revenue center managers understand why they have exceeded or fallen short of budgeted revenue.

Profit Centers

Managers of profit centers are responsible for both generating revenue and controlling costs, so their performance reports include both revenues and expenses. Exhibit 24-6 shows an example of a profit center *performance* report for the Standard Tablet Computer Department.

Exhibit 24-6 | **Performance Report—Profit Center**

	Actual	Flexible Budget	Flexible Budget Variance	% Variance
SMART TOUCH LEARNING				
Standard Tablet Department Performance Report				
For the Month Ended July 31, 2020				
Net Sales Revenue	$ 5,243,600	$ 5,000,000	$ 243,600 F	4.9% F
Variable Expenses	4,183,500	4,000,000	183,500 U	4.6% U
Contribution Margin	1,060,100	1,000,000	60,100 F	6.0% F
Traceable Fixed Expenses	84,300	75,000	9,300 U	12.4% U
Department Segment Margin	$ 975,800	$ 925,000	$ 50,800 F	5.5% F

Notice how this profit center performance report contains a line called "Traceable Fixed Expenses." Recall that one drawback of decentralization is that subunits may duplicate costs or assets. Many companies avoid this problem by providing centralized service departments where several subunits, such as profit centers, share assets or costs. For example, the payroll processing cost center shown in Exhibit 24-4 serves all of Smart Touch Learning. In addition to centralized payroll departments, companies often provide centralized human resources departments, legal departments, and information systems departments.

When subunits share centralized services, management must decide how to allocate those costs to the various segments that utilize their services. If the costs are not allocated, the subunit's performance report will *not* include any charge for using those services. However, if they are allocated, the performance report will show a charge for the traceable portion of those expenses, as shown in Exhibit 24-6.

Most companies charge subunits for their use of centralized services because the subunit would incur a cost to buy those services on its own. For example, if Smart Touch Learning did not operate a centralized payroll department, the Standard Tablet Department would have to hire its own payroll processing personnel and purchase computers, payroll software, and supplies necessary to process the department's payroll. As an alternative, it could outsource payroll to an outside company. In either event, the department would incur a cost for processing payroll. It only seems fair that the department is charged for using the centralized payroll processing department.

Keep in mind, however, that even if the department is charged for the services, the charge would most likely be included in the department's *performance* report but not be included in the department's *responsibility* report. Responsibility accounting holds the manager with the most influence for the cost accountable for the cost. The manager for the Standard Tablet Department would most likely not have any control over cost decisions made for the payroll processing department. Exhibit 24-7 shows the responsibility report for the department. Notice that the traceable fixed expenses are not included.

Exhibit 24-7 | **Responsibility Report—Profit Center**

SMART TOUCH LEARNING Standard Tablet Department Responsibility Report For the Month Ended July 31, 2020				
	Actual	Flexible Budget	Flexible Budget Variance	% Variance
Net Sales Revenue	$ 5,243,600	$ 5,000,000	$ 243,600 F	4.9% F
Variable Expenses	4,183,500	4,000,000	183,500 U	4.6% U
Contribution Margin	$ 1,060,100	$ 1,000,000	$ 60,100 F	6.0% F

DECISIONS

Am I responsible for what I can't control?

Fraser Marrero is the sales representative for the northwest territory of Tidwell, Inc. Tidwell considers each sales territory a business segment. The company provides each sales representative with a monthly income statement for his or her territory, and sales representatives are evaluated based on these statements. Tidwell also has a bonus system. Year-end bonuses for sales representatives are determined based on the success of the sales territory.

Fraser is taking some time to analyze his income statements for the first nine months of the fiscal year. Fraser has worked hard to build better relationships with existing customers while also adding new customers. The sales revenue for his territory has been steadily increasing. Unfortunately, the operating income for the territory has not shown much improvement. Fraser has had some increases in travel costs, but they have been in line with the increases in sales. Other costs, however, have increased significantly. The income statements show the allocation of corporate administrative costs such as salaries for office personnel and depreciation on office equipment.

"How am I ever going to earn a bonus with all these additional costs?" Fraser wondered. "I don't have any control over them, but I still seem to be held responsible for them. I need to talk to the sales manager."

Fraser schedules a meeting with the sales manager, Tony Voss. How should the sales manager respond?

Solution

All employees need to understand the goals of the company and work toward achieving them. Tony should explain why Fraser is being evaluated the way that he is so he can work to improve his performance, which should also benefit the company as a whole. The sales manager should explain that sales territories are expected to generate enough sales to cover their own territory's costs, a portion of the corporate overhead costs, and also contribute toward companywide profits. Fraser receives benefits from the corporate office, such as payroll processing, customer order processing, and collections of accounts receivable from his customers. Therefore, it is appropriate for a portion of the corporate costs to be allocated to his territory. The current reporting system allows upper management to determine which territories are achieving the company's overall profitability goals.

Alternate Solution

Fraser has a right to question the sales manager about the evaluation system. Fraser should be evaluated only on those items that he has control over, which is a key component of responsibility accounting. If the corporate office installs a new computer system, which increases depreciation, the current system allocates a portion to his territory, causing an increase in expenses and a decrease in operating income. Fraser, however, has no control over this decision and should not be held responsible for it. Fraser should request that Tidwell, Inc. not only provide the performance reports it is currently generating, but also responsibility reports for each territory. The responsibility reports should include only those items the sales representatives have significant control over and are able to influence. Performance evaluations and bonuses should be based on the responsibility reports.

Summary

Regardless of the type of responsibility center, responsibility reports should focus on information, not blame. Analyzing budget variances helps managers understand the underlying reasons for the unit's performance. Once management understands these reasons, it may be able to take corrective actions. Some variances are, however, uncontrollable. For example, the 2010 BP oil spill in the Gulf of Mexico caused damage to many businesses along the coast as well as environmental damage to the wetlands and wildlife. Consequently, the cost of seafood from the Gulf of Mexico increased because of the decreased supply. These cost increases resulted in unfavorable cost variances for many restaurants and seafood retailers. Managers should not be held accountable for conditions they cannot control. Responsibility accounting can help managers identify the causes of variances, thereby allowing them to determine what was controllable and what was not.

We have just looked at the detailed financial information presented in responsibility reports. In addition to these *detailed* reports, upper management often uses *summary* measures—financial KPIs—to assess the financial performance of cost, revenue, and profit centers. Examples include the *cost per unit of output* (for cost centers), *revenue growth* (for revenue centers), and *gross margin growth* (for profit centers). KPIs such as these are used to address the financial perspective of the balanced scorecard for cost, revenue, and profit centers. In the next section, we look at the most commonly used KPIs for investment centers.

Match the responsibility center to the correct responsibility report.

Responsibility Centers	Responsibility Reports
14. Cost center	**a.** Includes flexible budget variances for revenues and costs.
15. Revenue center	**b.** Includes flexible budget variances for costs.
16. Profit center	**c.** Includes flexible budget variances and sales volume variances for revenues.

Check your answers online in MyAccountingLab or at http://www.pearsonhighered.com/Horngren.

For more practice, see Short Exercise S24-5. MyAccountingLab

HOW DOES PERFORMANCE EVALUATION IN INVESTMENT CENTERS DIFFER FROM OTHER CENTERS?

Investment centers are typically large divisions of a company. The duties of an investment center manager are similar to those of a CEO. The CEO is responsible for maximizing income, in relation to the company's invested capital, by using company assets efficiently. Likewise, investment center managers are responsible for not only generating profit, but also making the best use of the investment center's assets.

For example, an investment center manager has the authority to open new stores or close existing stores. The manager may also decide how much inventory to hold, what types of investments to make, how aggressively to collect accounts receivable, and whether to invest in new equipment. In other words, the manager has decision-making responsibility over all of the center's assets, both current and long-term.

Learning Objective 4

Use return on investment (ROI) and residual income (RI) to evaluate investment centers

Companies cannot evaluate investment centers the way they evaluate profit centers, based only on operating income, because operating income does not indicate how *efficiently* the segment is using its assets. The financial evaluation of investment centers must measure two factors: (1) how much operating income the segment is generating and (2) how efficiently the segment is using its assets.

Consider Smart Touch Learning. In addition to its Tablet Computer Division, it also has an online e-Learning Division. Operating income, average total assets, and net sales revenue for the two divisions for July follow:

	e-Learning Division	Tablet Computer Division
Operating income	$ 450,000	$ 975,800
Average total assets	2,500,000	6,500,000
Net sales revenue	7,500,000	5,243,600

Based on operating income alone, the Tablet Computer Division (with operating income of $975,800) appears to be more profitable than the e-Learning Division (with operating income of $450,000). However, this comparison is misleading because it does not consider the assets invested in each division. The Tablet Computer Division has more assets than does the e-Learning Division.

To adequately evaluate an investment center's financial performance, companies need summary performance measures—or KPIs—that include *both* the division's operating income *and* its assets. In the next sections, we discuss two commonly used performance measures: return on investment (ROI) and residual income (RI). Both measures incorporate both the division's assets and its operating income. For simplicity, we leave the term *divisional* or *investment center* out of the equations. However, keep in mind that all of the equations use investment center data when evaluating an investment center's performance. Also, each ratio has been rounded to the nearest full percentage.

Return on Investment (ROI)

Return on Investment (ROI)
A measure of profitability and efficiency. Operating income / Average total assets.

Return on investment (ROI) is one of the most commonly used KPIs for evaluating an investment center's financial performance. ROI is a measure of profitability and efficiency. Companies typically define ROI as follows:

$$\text{ROI} = \frac{\text{Operating income}}{\text{Average total assets}}$$

ROI measures the amount of operating income an investment center earns relative to the amount of its average total assets. The ROI formula focuses on how well the average total assets were utilized to generate operating income (before considering other income and expense items, such as interest expense). Each division's ROI is calculated as follows:

$$\text{e-Learning Division's ROI} = \frac{\$450,000}{\$2,500,000} = 0.18 = 18\%$$

$$\text{Tablet Computer Division's ROI} = \frac{\$975,800}{\$6,500,000} = 0.15 = 15\%$$

Although the Tablet Computer Division has a higher operating income than the e-Learning Division, the Tablet Computer Division is actually *less* profitable than the e-Learning Division when we consider that the Tablet Computer Division does not utilize its average total assets as efficiently.

In addition to comparing ROI across divisions, management also compares a division's ROI across time to determine whether the division is becoming more or less profitable in relation to its average total assets. Additionally, management often benchmarks divisional ROI with other companies in the same industry to determine how each division is performing compared to its competitors.

To determine what is driving a division's ROI, management often restates the ROI equation in its expanded form. Notice that net sales revenue is incorporated in the denominator of the first term and in the numerator of the second term. When the two terms are multiplied together, net sales revenue cancels out, leaving the original ROI formula.

$$ROI = \frac{Operating\ income}{Net\ sales\ revenue} \times \frac{Net\ sales\ revenue}{Average\ total\ assets} = \frac{Operating\ income}{Average\ total\ assets}$$

Expanding the equation this way helps managers better understand how they can improve their ROI. The first term in the expanded equation is called the **profit margin ratio**:

$$Profit\ margin\ ratio = \frac{Operating\ income}{Net\ sales\ revenue}$$

Why do managers rewrite the ROI formula this way?

The profit margin ratio shows how much operating income the division earns on every $1.00 of sales, so this term focuses on profitability. Each division's profit margin ratio is calculated as follows:

$$\frac{e\text{-Learning Division's}}{profit\ margin\ ratio} = \frac{Operating\ income}{Net\ sales\ revenue} = \frac{\$450,000}{\$7,500,000} = 0.06 = 6\%$$

$$\frac{Tablet\ Computer\ Division's}{profit\ margin\ ratio} = \frac{Operating\ income}{Net\ sales\ revenue} = \frac{\$975,800}{\$5,243,600} = 0.19 = 19\%$$

Profit Margin Ratio
A profitability measure that shows how much operating income is earned on every dollar of net sales revenue. Operating income / Net sales revenue.

The e-Learning Division has a profit margin ratio of 6%, meaning that it earns operating income of $0.06 on every $1.00 of sales. The Tablet Computer Division, however, is much more profitable with a profit margin ratio of 19%, earning $0.19 on every $1.00 of sales.

Asset turnover ratio is the second term of the expanded ROI equation:

$$Asset\ turnover\ ratio = \frac{Net\ sales\ revenue}{Average\ total\ assets}$$

Asset Turnover Ratio
Measures how efficiently a business uses its average total assets to generate sales. Net sales revenue / Average total assets.

The asset turnover ratio shows how efficiently a division uses its average total assets to generate sales. Rather than focusing on profitability, the asset turnover ratio focuses on efficiency. Each division's asset turnover ratio is calculated as follows:

$$\frac{e\text{-Learning Division's}}{asset\ turnover\ ratio} = \frac{Net\ sales\ revenue}{Average\ total\ assets} = \frac{\$7,500,000}{\$2,500,000} = 3.00$$

$$\frac{Tablet\ Computer\ Division's}{asset\ turnover\ ratio} = \frac{Net\ sales\ revenue}{Average\ total\ assets} = \frac{\$5,243,600}{\$6,500,000} = 0.81$$

The e-Learning Division has an asset turnover ratio of 3. This means that the e-Learning Division generates $3.00 of sales with every $1.00 of average total assets. The Tablet Computer Division's asset turnover ratio is only 0.81. The Tablet Computer Division generates only $0.81 of sales with every $1.00 of average total assets. The e-Learning Division uses its average total assets much more efficiently in generating sales than the Tablet Computer Division.

Putting the two terms back together in the expanded ROI equation gets the following:

	Profit margin ratio	×	Asset turnover ratio	=	ROI
e-Learning Division	6%	×	3.00	=	18%
Tablet Computer Division	19%	×	0.81	=	15%

As you can see, the expanded ROI equation gives management more insight into the division's ROI. Management can now see that the Tablet Computer Division is more profitable on its sales (profit margin ratio of 19%) than the e-Learning Division (profit margin ratio of 6%), but the e-Learning Division is doing a better job of generating sales with its average total assets (asset turnover ratio of 3.00) than the Tablet Computer Division (asset turnover ratio of 0.81). Therefore, the e-Learning Division has a higher ROI of 18%.

If managers are not satisfied with their division's asset turnover ratio, how can they improve it? They might try to eliminate nonproductive assets, for example, by being more aggressive in collecting accounts receivables, by decreasing inventory levels, or by disposing of unnecessary plant assets. Or they might decide to change the retail store layout to increase sales.

What if management is not satisfied with the current profit margin ratio? To increase the profit margin ratio, management must increase the operating income earned on every dollar of sales. Management may cut product costs or selling and administrative costs, but it needs to be careful when trimming costs. Cutting costs in the short term can hurt long-term ROI. For example, sacrificing quality or cutting back on research and development could decrease costs in the short run but may hurt long-term sales. The balanced scorecard helps management carefully consider the consequences of cost-cutting measures before acting on them.

ROI has one major drawback. Evaluating division managers based solely on ROI gives them an incentive to adopt *only* projects that will maintain or increase their current ROI. Suppose that top management has set a companywide target ROI of 16%. Both divisions are considering investing in in-store video display equipment that shows customers how to use featured products. This equipment would increase sales because customers would be more likely to buy the products when they see the infomercials. The equipment would cost each division $100,000 and is expected to provide each division with $17,000 of annual operating income. The *equipment's* ROI is as follows:

$$\text{Equipment ROI} = \frac{\$17,000}{\$100,000} = 0.17 = 17\%$$

Upper management would want the divisions to invest in this equipment because the equipment will provide a 17% ROI, which is higher than the 16% target rate. But what will the managers of the divisions do? Because the Tablet Computer Division currently has an ROI of 15%, the new equipment (with its 17% ROI) will *increase* the division's *overall* ROI. Therefore, the Tablet Computer Division manager will buy the equipment.

However, the e-Learning Division currently has an ROI of 18%. If the e-Learning Division invests in the equipment, its *overall* ROI will *decrease*. Therefore, the manager of the e-Learning Division will probably turn down the investment. In this case, goal congruence is *not* achieved—only one division will invest in equipment. Yet top management wants both divisions to invest in the equipment because the equipment return exceeds the 16% target ROI.

Next, we will discuss a performance measure that managers can use to help overcome this problem with ROI.

Residual Income (RI)

Residual income (RI) is another commonly used KPI for evaluating an investment center's financial performance. Similar to ROI, RI considers both the division's operating income and its average total assets. RI measures the division's profitability and the efficiency with which the division uses its average total assets. RI also incorporates another piece of information: top management's target rate of return (such as the 16% target rate of return in the previous example). The target rate of return is the minimum acceptable rate of return that top management expects a division to earn with its average total assets. You will learn how to calculate target rate of return in your finance class. For now, we provide the target rate of return for you.

RI compares the division's actual operating income with the minimum operating income expected by top management *given the size of the division's average total assets*. RI is the *extra* operating income above the minimum operating income. A positive RI means that the division's operating income exceeds top management's target rate of return. A negative RI means the division is not meeting the target rate of return. Let's look at the RI equation and then calculate the RI for both divisions using the 16% target rate of return from the previous example.

> RI = Operating income − Minimum acceptable operating income
> RI = Operating income − (Target rate of return × Average total assets)

In this equation, the minimum acceptable operating income is defined as top management's target rate of return multiplied by the division's average total assets. Therefore,

> e-Learning Division's RI = $450,000 − (16% × $2,500,000)
> = $450,000 − $400,000
> = $50,000

The positive RI indicates that the e-Learning Division exceeded top management's 16% target rate of return expectations. The RI calculation also confirms what we learned about the e-Learning Division's ROI. Recall that the e-Learning Division's ROI was 18%, which is higher than the target rate of return of 16%.

Now let's calculate the RI for the Tablet Computer Division:

> Tablet Computer Division's RI = $975,800 − (16% × $6,500,000)
> = $975,800 − $1,040,000
> = $(64,200)

The Tablet Computer Division's RI is negative. This means that the Tablet Computer Division did not use its average total assets as effectively as top management expected. Recall that the Tablet Computer Division's ROI of 15% fell short of the target rate of return of 16%.

A company may prefer to use RI over ROI for performance evaluation because RI is more likely to lead to goal congruence than ROI. Consider the video display equipment that both divisions could buy. In both divisions, the equipment is expected to generate a 17% return which is above management's target rate of return of 16%. Management would encourage the divisions to buy the equipment. But, if the divisions used ROI

Residual Income (RI)
A measure of profitability and efficiency computed as actual operating income less a specified minimum acceptable operating income.

Why would a company prefer to use RI over ROI for performance evaluation?

as the evaluation tool, we learned that the Tablet Computer Division would buy the equipment because it would increase the division's ROI. The e-Learning Division, on the other hand, probably would not buy the equipment because it would lower the division's ROI.

However, if management evaluates divisions based on RI rather than ROI, what would the divisions do? The answer depends on whether the project yields a positive or negative RI. Recall that the equipment would cost each division $100,000 but would provide $17,000 of operating income each year. The RI provided by *just* the equipment would be as follows:

$$
\begin{aligned}
\text{Equipment RI} &= \$17{,}000 - (16\% \times \$100{,}000) \\
&= \$17{,}000 - \$16{,}000 \\
&= \$1{,}000
\end{aligned}
$$

If purchased, this equipment would *improve* each division's current RI by $1,000 each year. As a result, both divisions would be motivated to invest in the equipment. Goal congruence is achieved because both divisions would take the action that top management desires. That is, both divisions would invest in the equipment.

Another benefit of RI is that management may set different target returns for different divisions. For example, management might require a higher target rate of return from a division operating in a riskier business environment. If the tablet computer industry were riskier than the e-learning industry, top management might decide to set a higher target rate of return—perhaps 17%—for the Tablet Computer Division.

Exhibit 24-8 summarizes the KPIs for investment centers.

Exhibit 24-8 | Investment Center KPIs

Return on Investment	
Equation	ROI = Profit margin ratio × Asset turnover ratio $$= \dfrac{\text{Operating income}}{\text{Net sales revenue}} \times \dfrac{\text{Net sales revenue}}{\text{Average total assets}} = \dfrac{\text{Operating income}}{\text{Average total assets}}$$
Advantages	• The expanded equation provides management with additional information on profitability and efficiency. • Management can compare ROI across divisions and with other companies. • ROI is useful for resource allocation.
Residual Income	
Equation	RI = Operating income – (Average total assets × Target rate of return)
Advantages	• RI promotes goal congruence better than ROI. • The equation incorporates management's target rate of return. • Management can use different target rates of return for divisions with different levels of risk.

Limitations of Financial Performance Measures

We have looked at two KPIs (ROI and RI) commonly used to evaluate the financial performance of investment centers. As discussed in the following sections, all of these measures have drawbacks that management should keep in mind when evaluating the financial performance of investment centers.

Measurement Issues

The ROI and RI calculations appear to be very straightforward; however, management must make some decisions before these measures can be calculated. For example, both use the term *average total assets*. Recall that total assets is a balance sheet amount, which means that it is a snapshot at any given point in time. Because the total assets amount will be *different* at the beginning of the period and at the end of the period, most companies choose to use a simple average of the two amounts in their ROI and RI calculations.

Management must also decide if it really wants to include *all* assets in the average total asset calculation. Many large businesses are continually buying land on which to build future retail outlets. Until those stores are built and opened, the land (including any construction in progress) is a nonproductive asset, which is not adding to the company's operating income. Including nonproductive assets in the average total asset calculation drives down the ROI and RI results. Therefore, some companies do not include nonproductive assets in these calculations.

Another asset measurement issue is whether to use the gross book value of assets (the historical cost of the assets) or the net book value of assets (historical cost less accumulated depreciation). Many companies use the net book value of assets because the amount is consistent with and easily pulled from the balance sheet. Because depreciation expense factors into the company's operating income, the net book value concept is also consistent with the measurement of operating income. However, using the net book value of assets has a definite drawback. Over time, the net book value of assets decreases because accumulated depreciation continues to grow until the assets are fully depreciated. Therefore, ROI and RI get *larger* over time *because of depreciation* rather than because of actual improvements in operations. In addition, the rate of this depreciation effect depends on the depreciation method used.

In general, calculating ROI based on the net book value of assets gives managers an incentive to continue using old, outdated equipment because its low net book value results in a higher ROI. However, top management may want the division to invest in new technology to create operational efficiency (internal business perspective of the balanced scorecard) or to enhance its information systems (learning and growth perspective). The long-term effects of using outdated equipment may be devastating, as competitors use new technology to produce at lower costs and sell at lower prices. Therefore, to create *goal congruence*, some firms prefer calculating ROI based on the gross book value of assets. The same general rule holds true for RI calculations: All else being equal, using net book value increases RI over time.

Short-term Focus

One serious drawback of financial performance measures is their short-term focus. Companies usually prepare responsibility reports and calculate ROI and RI figures over a one-year time frame or less. If upper management uses a short time frame, division managers have an incentive to take actions that will lead to an immediate increase in these measures, even if such actions may not be in the company's long-term interest (such as cutting back on R&D or advertising). On the other hand, some potentially positive actions considered by subunit managers may take longer than one year to generate income at the targeted level. Many product life cycles start slowly, even incurring losses in the early stages, before generating profit. If managers are measured on short-term financial performance only, they may not introduce new products because they are not willing to wait several years for the positive effect to show up in their financial performance measures.

As a potential remedy, management can measure financial performance using a longer time horizon, such as three to five years. Extending the time frame gives subunit managers the incentive to think long term, rather than short term, and make decisions that will positively affect the company over the next several years.

The limitations of financial performance measures reinforce the importance of the balanced scorecard. The deficiencies of financial measures can be overcome by taking a broader view of performance—including KPIs from all four balanced scorecard perspectives rather than concentrating on only the financial measures.

Padgett Company has compiled the following data:

Net sales revenue	$ 1,000,000
Operating income	60,000
Average total assets	400,000
Management's target rate of return	12%

Calculate the following amounts for Padgett:

17. Profit margin ratio
18. Asset turnover ratio
19. Return on investment
20. Residual income

Check your answers online in MyAccountingLab or at http://www.pearsonhighered.com/Horngren.

For more practice, see Short Exercises S24-6 through S24-9. MyAccountingLab

HOW DO TRANSFER PRICES AFFECT DECENTRALIZED COMPANIES?

Learning Objective 5

Determine how transfer pricing affects decentralized companies

Transfer Price

The transaction amount of one unit of goods when the transaction occurs between divisions within the same company.

When companies decentralize, one responsibility center may transfer goods to another responsibility center within the company. For example, the e-Learning Division at Smart Touch Learning transfers e-Learning software to the Tablet Computer Division. When this happens, a transaction must be recorded for each division, and the company must determine the amount of the transaction. The **transfer price** is the transaction amount of one unit of goods when the transaction occurs between divisions within the same company. The challenge is determining the amount of the transfer price.

Objectives in Setting Transfer Prices

The primary objective in setting transfer prices is to achieve goal congruence by selecting a price that will maximize overall company profits. A secondary objective is to evaluate the managers of the responsibility centers involved. Achieving these objectives can be challenging because the managers have different objectives for their divisions. The manager of the division selling the product wants the highest transfer price in order to increase revenues for that division, which will increase division profits. The manager of the purchasing division wants the lowest transfer price in order to decrease costs, which will increase profits for that division. If one manager wants the highest transfer price and the other manager wants the lowest transfer price, there is a conflict.

In many cases, the amount of the transfer price does not affect overall company profits because it is revenue for one division and an expense for the other division. Therefore, when profits for all divisions are consolidated, the amounts offset each other and the net effect is zero. In other cases, however, the amount of the transfer price does affect overall profits, so the company needs to have an established system that encourages goal congruence. Let's look at some different scenarios to understand how transfer prices should be determined.

Setting Transfer Prices

The e-Learning Division of Smart Touch Learning develops and sells online courses in accounting, economics, marketing, and management. The courses sell for $100 each; therefore, the market price is $100. Based on current production, the total cost of production is $80, of which $60 is variable cost and $20 is fixed cost. Therefore, the contribution margin per unit is $40 as shown below:

Sales Price per Unit	$ 100
Variable Cost per Unit	60
Contribution Margin per Unit	$ 40

The Tablet Computer Division of Smart Touch Learning loads the courses on the tablet computers prior to selling them. The two divisions are investment centers, so each division records transactions independently. Therefore, the transfer of courses from one division to the other is a sale for the e-Learning Division and a purchase for the Tablet Computer Division. How much should the Tablet Computer Division pay for the courses?

The transfer price should be an amount between the market price of $100 and the variable cost of $60. The Tablet Computer Division would not be willing to pay more than $100 as that is the amount the product can be purchased for in the market (making the assumption that similar courses can be purchased from other vendors and Smart Touch Learning is willing to load courses from other vendors on its tablets). The e-Learning Division would not be willing to sell for less than $60 because any amount less than that will cause a negative contribution margin. The range of $60 to $100 is the negotiable range for the transfer price. Exhibit 24-9 illustrates the negotiable range.

Exhibit 24-9 | Transfer Price Negotiable Range

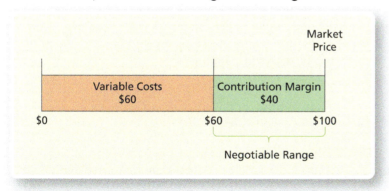

Operating at Capacity

If the e-Learning Division is operating at capacity, it is producing and selling all the courses it is capable of without expanding the facility and adding more employees and/or equipment. In this case, the division has to make a choice about whom to sell to: customers outside the company or the Tablet Computer Division. Because the division has a choice of customers, the transfer price should be a **market-based transfer price**—the sales price Smart Touch Learning charges customers outside the company, which is the market price. If the e-Learning Division sells for less than the market price, then it will have a decrease in contribution margin and company profits will decrease. The lost contribution margin becomes an opportunity cost for the division. An **opportunity cost** is the benefit given up by choosing an alternative course of action.

Market-Based Transfer Price
A transfer price based on the current market value of the goods.

Opportunity Cost
The benefit given up by choosing an alternative course of action.

Operating Below Capacity

If the e-Learning Division is operating below capacity, then it should be willing to sell courses to the Tablet Computer Division at any amount equal to or above the variable cost of $60. Selling at any price above $60 will create more contribution margin for the division to help cover fixed costs and thereafter increase profits. A **cost-based transfer price** considers the cost of the goods when determining the price. In this situation, the managers can negotiate a transfer price that is satisfactory to both divisions. The price could be the variable cost, the full cost including the variable cost and the fixed cost, or the cost plus a markup.

> **Cost-Based Transfer Price**
> A transfer price based on the cost of producing the goods.

If Smart Touch Learning allows the division managers to negotiate a cost-based transfer price, the company should consider using *standard* costs rather than *actual* costs. Otherwise, the selling division has no motivation to control costs. For example, if the negotiated price is the actual variable cost plus a 10% markup, the e-Learning Division will always report a positive contribution margin because the sales price will always be more than the variable cost. There is no incentive for the division to monitor and control the costs of materials, labor, or variable overhead. However, if the transfer price is based on standard costs, the e-Learning Division has an incentive to control costs. Failure to control costs may result in losses for the division and a poor evaluation for the division manager.

Other Issues

There are other issues involved with transfer costs that are beyond the scope of this course. For example, international companies must consider the income tax consequences if tax rates vary between the divisions involved in the transfer. There are legal and ethical issues involved when companies attempt to evade paying income taxes by using transfer prices that shift profits to the division based in the country with the lowest tax rate.

In some cases, it is difficult to determine a market price. For example, if a division of a company manufactures a component of a product that is used only in the company's own products, then there is no outside source to purchase from or an outside market to sell to. A cost-based transfer price would have to be used.

Other issues are nonfinancial. For example, a division may decide to purchase from an outside vendor rather than another division within the company. In that case, the product may be of lower quality or there may be delays in shipping.

Sheffield Company manufactures power tools. The Electric Drill Division (an investment center) can purchase the motors for the drills from the Motor Division (another investment center) or from an outside vendor. The cost to purchase from the outside vendor is $20. The Motor Division also sells to outside customers. The motor needed by the Electric Drill Division sells for $25 to outside customers and has a variable cost of $15. The Motor Division has excess capacity.

21. If Sheffield Company allows division managers to negotiate transfer prices, what is the minimum amount the manager of the Motor Division should consider?
22. What is the maximum transfer price the manager of the Electric Drill Division should consider?

Check your answers online in MyAccountingLab or at http://www.pearsonhighered.com/Horngren.

For more practice, see Short Exercise S24-10 MyAccountingLab

REVIEW

> Things You Should Know

1. Why do decentralized companies need responsibility accounting?

- Decentralized companies are divided into segments with segment managers making planning, directing, and controlling decisions for their segments.
- Advantages of decentralization
  - Frees top management time
  - Supports use of expert knowledge
  - Improves customer relations
  - Provides training
  - Improves motivation and retention
- Disadvantages of decentralization
  - Duplication of costs
  - Problems achieving goal congruence
- Responsibility accounting systems evaluate the performance of each responsibility center and its manager.
- Responsibility centers
  - Cost centers—responsible for controlling costs
  - Revenue centers—responsible for generating revenue
  - Profit centers—responsible for controlling costs and generating revenue
  - Investment centers—responsible for controlling costs, generating revenue, and efficiently managing the division's invested capital

2. What is a performance evaluation system, and how is it used?

- Performance evaluation system—a system that provides a framework for maintaining control over the entire organization
- Goals of performance evaluation systems
  - Promoting goal congruence and coordination
  - Communicating expectations
  - Motivating segment managers and other employees
  - Providing feedback
  - Benchmarking
- The balanced scorecard measures both financial and operational performance measures within four perspectives:
  - Financial perspective
  - Customer perspective
  - Internal business perspective
  - Learning and growth perspective

CHAPTER 24

3. **How do companies use responsibility accounting to evaluate performance in cost, revenue, and profit centers?**

- Managers should be evaluated based only on controllable costs—those they have the power to influence by their decisions.
- Responsibility reports
  - Cost centers—focus on the flexible budget variances of controllable costs
  - Revenue centers—focus on flexible budget variances and sales volume variances of revenues
  - Profit centers—focus on flexible budget variances of revenues and controllable costs

4. **How does performance evaluation in investment centers differ from other centers?**

- Evaluated on both profitability and efficiency
  - Profitability—ability to generate operating income
  - Efficiency—use of assets
- Return on investment (ROI) = Operating income / Average total assets
- ROI can be expanded into two components
  - Profit margin ratio = Operating income / Net sales revenue
  - Asset turnover ratio = Net sales revenue / Average total assets
  - ROI = Profit margin ratio × Asset turnover ratio
- Residual income (RI) = Operating income − Minimum acceptable operating income
- Residual income (RI) = Operating income − (Target rate of return × Average total assets)
- Limitations of financial performance measures
  - Measurement issues—determining the amount to use for average total assets
  - Short-term focus—may cause managers to make decisions that increase measures in the short term but hurt the company in the long term

5. **How do transfer prices affect decentralized companies?**

- The transfer price is the transaction amount of one unit of goods when the transaction occurs between divisions within the same company.
- Transfer prices should be set to achieve goal congruence.
- Market-based transfer prices are appropriate when the selling division is operating at capacity.
- Cost-based transfer prices are appropriate when the selling division is operating below capacity.
- The transfer price negotiable range is the variable cost to the market price.

> Check Your Understanding 24-1

Check your understanding of the chapter by completing this problem and then looking at the solution. Use this practice to help identify which sections of the chapter you need to study more.

The balanced scorecard gives performance perspective from four different viewpoints.

Requirements

1. Each of the following describes a key performance indicator. Determine which of the balanced scorecard perspectives is being addressed (financial, customer, internal business, or learning and growth) (See Learning Objective 2):

   a. Employee turnover

   b. Earnings per share

   c. Percentage of on-time deliveries

   d. Revenue growth rate

   e. Percentage of defects discovered during manufacturing

   f. Number of warranty claims

   g. New product development time

   h. Number of repeat customers

   i. Number of employee suggestions implemented

2. Read the following company initiatives, and determine which of the balanced scorecard perspectives is being addressed (financial, customer, internal business, or learning and growth) (See Learning Objective 2):

   a. Purchasing efficient production equipment

   b. Providing employee training

   c. Updating retail store lighting

   d. Paying quarterly dividends to stockholders

   e. Updating the company's information system

> Solution

Requirement 1

    a. Learning and growth

    b. Financial

    c. Customer

    d. Financial

    e. Internal business

    f. Internal business

    g. Internal business

    h. Customer

    i. Learning and growth

Requirement 2

    a. Internal business

    b. Learning and growth

    c. Customer

    d. Financial

    e. Learning and growth

> Check Your Understanding 24-2

Check your understanding of the chapter by completing this problem and then looking at the solution. Use this practice to help identify which sections of the chapter you need to study more.

Swift Company has three divisions and expects each division to earn a 16% target rate of return. The company had the following results last year:

Division	Profit margin ratio	Asset turnover ratio	ROI
1	7.2%	2.737	19.7%
2	11.7%	1.584	18.5%

Division 3 reported the following data:

Operating income	$ 1,450,000
Average total assets	16,100,000
Net sales revenue	26,500,000

Requirements

1. Compute Division 3's profit margin ratio, asset turnover ratio, and ROI. Round your results to three decimal places. Interpret the results in relation to the other two divisions. (See Learning Objective 4)

2. Compute and interpret Division 3's RI. (See Learning Objective 4)

3. What can you conclude based on the financial performance KPIs? (See Learning Objective 4)

> Solution

Requirement 1

$$\frac{\text{Division 3's}}{\text{profit margin ratio}} = \frac{\text{Operating income}}{\text{Net sales revenue}} = \frac{\$1,450,000}{\$26,500,000} = 0.055 = 5.5\%$$

$$\frac{\text{Division 3's}}{\text{asset turnover ratio}} = \frac{\text{Net sales revenue}}{\text{Average total assets}} = \frac{\$26,500,000}{\$16,100,000} = 1.646$$

$$\text{Division 3's ROI} = \text{Profit margin ratio} \times \text{Asset turnover ratio}$$
$$= 5.5\% \times 1.646 = 9.1\%$$

Division 3 is far from meeting top management's expectations. Its ROI is only 9.1%. The profit margin ratio of 5.5% is significantly lower than the other two divisions. Additionally, the asset turnover ratio (1.646) is much lower than Division 1's but slightly higher than Division 2's. This means that Division 3 is not generating sales from its average total assets as efficiently as Division 1 but it is more efficient than Division 2. Division management needs to consider ways to increase the efficiency with which it uses divisional average total assets and increase profitability.

Requirement 2

> RI = Operating income − (Target rate of return × Average total assets)
>   = $1,450,000 − (16% × $16,100,000)
>   = $1,450,000 − $2,576,000
>   = $(1,126,000)

The negative RI confirms the ROI results: The division is not meeting management's target rate of return.

Requirement 3

Both investment center financial performance KPIs (ROI and RI) point to the same conclusion: Division 3 is not meeting financial expectations. Either top management's and stakeholders' expectations are unrealistic or the division is not *currently* performing up to par. Recall, however, that financial performance measures tend to be lag indicators—measuring the results of decisions made in the past. The division's manager may currently be implementing new initiatives to improve the division's future profitability. Lead indicators should be used to project whether such initiatives are pointing the division in the right direction.

> Key Terms

Asset Turnover Ratio (p. 1341)
Balanced Scorecard (p. 1331)
Centralized Company (p. 1325)
Controllable Cost (p. 1334)
Cost-Based Transfer Price (p. 1348)
Cost Center (p. 1327)
Decentralized Company (p. 1325)
Goal Congruence (p. 1326)
Investment Center (p. 1328)

Key Performance Indicator
  (KPI) (p. 1331)
Lag Indicator (p. 1331)
Lead Indicator (p. 1331)
Market-Based Transfer Price (p. 1347)
Operational Performance
  Measure (p. 1331)
Opportunity Cost (p. 1347)
Performance Evaluation System
  (p. 1330)

Profit Center (p. 1327)
Profit Margin Ratio (p. 1341)
Residual Income (RI) (p. 1343)
Responsibility Accounting
  System (p. 1327)
Responsibility Center (p. 1327)
Responsibility Report (p. 1334)
Return on Investment (ROI) (p. 1340)
Revenue Center (p. 1327)
Transfer Price (p. 1346)

> Quick Check

1. Which is *not* one of the potential advantages of decentralization?

   Learning Objective 1

   a. Improves motivation and retention
   b. Supports use of expert knowledge
   c. Improves customer relations
   d. Increases goal congruence

2. The Quaker Foods division of PepsiCo is most likely treated as a(n)

   Learning Objective 1

   a. revenue center.
   b. cost center.
   c. investment center.
   d. profit center.

Learning Objective 2

3. Which of the following is *not* a goal of performance evaluation systems?

    a. Promoting goal congruence and coordination

    b. Communicating expectations

    c. Providing feedback

    d. Reprimanding unit managers

Learning Objective 2

4. Which of the following balanced scorecard perspectives essentially asks, "Can we continue to improve and create value?"

    a. Customer   c. Financial

    b. Learning and growth   d. Internal business

Learning Objective 3

5. The performance evaluation of a cost center is typically based on its

    a. sales volume variance.   c. static budget variance.

    b. ROI.   d. flexible budget variance.

The following data apply to questions 6 through 9.

Assume the Residential Division of Kipper Faucets had the following results last year:

Net sales revenue	$ 4,160,000
Operating income	1,040,000
Average total assets	5,200,000
Management's target rate of return	18%

Learning Objective 4

6. What is the division's profit margin ratio?

    a. 400%   c. 25%

    b. 20%   d. 80%

Learning Objective 4

7. What is the division's asset turnover ratio?

    a. 0.20   c. 1.25

    b. 0.80   d. 0.25

Learning Objective 4

8. What is the division's ROI?

    a. 20%   c. 500%

    b. 25%   d. 80%

Learning Objective 4

9. What is the division's RI?

    a. $(140,000)   c. $140,000

    b. $104,000   d. $(104,000)

Learning Objective 5

10. Penn Company has a division that manufactures a component that sells for $50 and has variable costs of $25 and fixed costs of $10. Another division wants to purchase the component. What is the minimum transfer price if the division is operating at capacity?

    a. $10   c. $35

    b. $25   d. $50

Check your answers at the end of the chapter.

ASSESS YOUR PROGRESS

> Review Questions

1. Explain the difference between a centralized company and a decentralized company.
2. List the advantages of decentralization.
3. List the disadvantages of decentralization.
4. What is goal congruence?
5. Usually, which outweighs the other in decentralization—advantages or disadvantages?
6. What is the purpose of a responsibility accounting system?
7. What is a responsibility center?
8. List the four types of responsibility centers, and briefly describe each.
9. What is a performance evaluation system?
10. What are the goals of a performance evaluation system?
11. Explain the difference between a lag indicator and a lead indicator.
12. How is the use of a balanced scorecard as a performance evaluation system helpful to companies?
13. What is a key performance indicator?
14. What are the four perspectives of the balanced scorecard? Briefly describe each.
15. Explain the difference between a controllable and a noncontrollable cost.
16. What is the typical focus of responsibility reports for cost centers, revenue centers, and profit centers?
17. What are two key performance indicators used to evaluate investment centers?
18. Describe the two ways ROI can be calculated.
19. What does ROI measure?
20. What is the biggest disadvantage of using ROI to evaluate investment centers?
21. How is RI calculated?
22. What does RI measure?
23. What is the biggest advantage of using RI to evaluate investment centers?
24. What are some limitations of financial performance measures?
25. What is a transfer price?
26. Explain the difference between market-based transfer prices and cost-based transfer prices.
27. How does capacity affect transfer pricing decisions?

> Short Exercises

S24-1 Explaining decentralization

Learning Objective 1

Decentralization divides company operations into various reporting units. Most decentralized subunits can be described as one of four different types of responsibility centers.

Requirements

1. Explain why companies decentralize. Describe some typical methods of decentralization.

2. List the four most common types of responsibility centers, and describe their responsibilities.

Learning Objective 1

S24-2 Classifying responsibility centers

Each of the following managers works for a national chain of hotels and has been given certain decision-making authority. Classify each of the managers according to the type of responsibility center he or she probably manages.

a. Manager of the Central Reservation Office

b. Managers of various corporate-owned hotel locations

c. Managers of the Northeast and Southeast Corporate Divisions

d. Manager of the Housekeeping Department at one hotel

e. Manager of the complimentary breakfast buffet at one hotel

Learning Objective 2

S24-3 Explaining why companies use performance evaluation systems

Well-designed performance evaluation systems accomplish many goals. Consider the following actions, and state which goal is being achieved by the action:

a. Comparing targets to actual results

b. Providing subunit managers with performance targets

c. Comparing actual results with industry standards

d. Providing bonuses to subunit managers who achieve performance targets

e. Aligning subunit performance targets with company strategy

f. Comparing actual results of competitors

g. Taking corrective actions

h. Using the adage "you get what you measure" when designing the performance evaluation system

Learning Objective 2

S24-4 Describing the balanced scorecard and identifying key performance indicators for each perspective

Consider the following key performance indicators, and classify each according to the balanced scorecard perspective it addresses. Choose from financial perspective, customer perspective, internal business perspective, or learning and growth perspective.

a. Number of employee suggestions implemented

b. Revenue growth

c. Number of on-time deliveries

d. Percentage of sales force with access to real-time inventory levels

e. Customer satisfaction ratings

f. Number of defects found during manufacturing

g. Number of warranty claims

h. Return on investment

i. Variable cost per unit

j. Percentage of market share

k. Number of hours of employee training

l. Number of new products developed

m. Yield rate (number of units produced per hour)

n. Average repair time

o. Employee satisfaction

p. Number of repeat customers

S24-5 Using performance reports to evaluate cost, revenue, and profit centers

Learning Objective 3

Management by exception is a term often used in performance evaluation. Describe management by exception and how it is used in the evaluation of cost, revenue, and profit centers.

S24-6 Evaluating investment centers

Learning Objective 4

Consider the following data, and determine which of the corporate divisions is more profitable. Explain your reasoning.

	Domestic	International
Operating income	$ 10,000,000	$ 11,000,000
Average total assets	24,000,000	32,000,000

S24-7 Using ROI and RI to evaluate investment centers

Learning Objective 4

XTreme Sports Company makes snowboards, downhill skis, cross-country skis, skateboards, surfboards, and inline skates. The company has found it beneficial to split operations into two divisions based on the climate required for the sport: Snow Sports and Non-snow Sports. The following divisional information is available for the past year:

	Net Sales Revenue	Operating Income	Average Total Assets	ROI
Snow Sports	$ 5,500,000	$ 990,000	$ 4,100,000	24.1%
Non-snow Sports	8,500,000	1,530,000	6,100,000	25.1%

XTreme's management has specified a 13% target rate of return. Calculate each division's profit margin ratio. Interpret your results.

Note: Short Exercise S24-7 must be completed before attempting Short Exercise S24-8.

S24-8 Using ROI and RI to evaluate investment centers

Learning Objective 4

Refer to the information in Short Exercise S24-7.

Requirements

1. Compute each division's asset turnover ratio (round to two decimal places). Interpret your results.

2. Use your answers to Requirement 1, along with the profit margin ratio, to recalculate ROI using the expanded formula. Do your answers agree with the basic ROI in Short Exercise S24-7?

Note: Short Exercise S24-7 must be completed before attempting Short Exercise S24-9.

Learning Objective 4

S24-9 Using ROI and RI to evaluate investment centers

Refer to the information in Short Exercise S24-7. Compute each division's RI. Interpret your results. Are your results consistent with each division's ROI?

Learning Objective 5

S24-10 Transfer pricing

Henderson Company manufactures electronics. The Calculator Division (an investment center) manufactures handheld calculators. The division can purchase the batteries used in the calculators from the Battery Division (another investment center) or from an outside vendor. The cost to purchase batteries from the outside vendor is $5. The transfer price to purchase from the Battery Division is $6. The Battery Division also sells to outside customers. The sales price is $6, and the variable cost is $3. The Battery Division has excess capacity.

Requirements

1. Should the Calculator Division purchase from the Battery Division or the outside vendor?

2. If Henderson Company allows division managers to negotiate transfer prices, what is the maximum transfer price the manager of the Calculator Division should consider?

3. What is the minimum transfer price the manager of the Battery Division should consider?

4. Does your answer to Requirement 3 change if the Battery Division is operating at capacity?

> Exercises

Learning Objective 1

E24-11 Identifying responsibility centers after decentralization

Grandpa Jim's Cookie Company sells homemade cookies made with organic ingredients. His sales are strictly Web based. The business is taking off more than Grandpa Jim ever expected, with orders coming from across the country from both consumers and corporate event planners. Grandpa decides to decentralize and hires a full-time baker who will manage production and product costs and a Web site designer/sales manager who will focus on increasing sales through the Web site. Grandpa Jim can no longer handle the business on his own, so he hires a business manager to work with the other employees to ensure the company is best utilizing its assets to produce profit. Grandpa will then have time to focus on new product development.

Now that Grandpa Jim's Cookie Company has decentralized, identify the type of responsibility center that each manager is managing.

Learning Objective 2

E24-12 Explaining why companies use performance evaluation systems

Financial performance is measured in many ways.

Requirements

1. Explain the difference between lag and lead indicators.

2. The following is a list of financial measures. Indicate whether each is a lag or a lead indicator:

   a. Income statement shows net income of $100,000

   b. Listing of next week's orders of $50,000

    c. Trend showing that average hits on the redesigned Web site are increasing at 5% per week

    d. Price sheet from vendor reflecting that cost per pound of sugar for the next month is $2

    e. Contract signed last month with large retail store that guarantees a minimum shelf space for Grandpa's Overloaded Chocolate Cookies for the next year

E24-13 Explaining why companies use performance evaluation systems

Learning Objective 2

Well-designed performance evaluation systems accomplish many goals. Describe the potential benefits performance evaluation systems offer.

E24-14 Describing the balanced scorecard and identifying key performance indicators for each perspective

Learning Objective 2

Consider the following key performance indicators, and classify each indicator according to the balanced scorecard perspective it addresses. Choose from the financial perspective, customer perspective, internal business perspective, and the learning and growth perspective.

    a. Number of customer complaints

    b. Number of information system upgrades completed

    c. Residual income

    d. New product development time

    e. Employee turnover rate

    f. Percentage of products with online help manuals

    g. Customer retention

    h. Percentage of compensation based on performance

    i. Percentage of orders filled each week

    j. Gross margin growth

    k. Number of new patents

    l. Employee satisfaction ratings

    m. Manufacturing cycle time (average length of production process)

    n. Earnings growth

    o. Average machine setup time

    p. Number of new customers

    q. Employee promotion rate

    r. Cash flow from operations

    s. Customer satisfaction ratings

    t. Machine downtime

    u. Finished products per day per employee

    v. Percentage of employees with access to upgraded system

    w. Wait time per order prior to start of production

E24-15 Using responsibility reports to evaluate cost, revenue, and profit centers

Learning Objective 3

One subunit of Harris Sports Company had the following financial results last month:

1. Direct Materials 8.11% U

Harris—Subunit X	Actual Results	Flexible Budget	Flexible Budget Variance (F or U)	% Variance (F or U)
Direct Materials	$ 28,000	$ 25,900		
Direct Labor	13,000	13,800		
Indirect Labor	26,400	23,100		
Utilities	12,300	11,300		
Depreciation	25,000	25,000		
Repairs and Maintenance	4,600	5,600		
Total	$ 109,300	$ 104,700		

Requirements

1. Complete the performance evaluation report for this subunit. Enter the variance percent as a percentage of the budgeted amount rounded to two decimal places.

2. Based on the data presented, what type of responsibility center is this subunit?

3. Which items should be investigated if part of management's decision criteria is to investigate all variances exceeding $2,500 or 10%?

4. Should only unfavorable variances be investigated? Explain.

Learning Objective 3

E24-16 Using responsibility reports to evaluate cost, revenue, and profit centers

The accountant for a subunit of Speed Sports Company went on vacation before completing the subunit's monthly responsibility report. This is as far as she got:

Speed—Subunit X Revenue by Product	Actual Results	Flexible Budget Variance	Flexible Budget	Sales Volume Variance	Static Budget
Downhill-RI	$ 321,000	(a)	(b)	$ 17,000 F	$ 295,000
Downhill-RII	151,000	(c)	$ 161,000	(d)	145,000
Cross-EXI	285,000	$ 3,000 U	288,000	(e)	303,000
Cross-EXII	259,000	(f)	255,000	16,500 U	271,500
Snow-LXI	425,000	2,000 F	(g)	(h)	404,000
Total	$ 1,441,000	(i)	(j)	(k)	$ 1,418,500

Requirements

1. Complete the responsibility report for this subunit.

2. Based on the data presented, what type of responsibility center is this subunit?

3. Which items should be investigated if part of management's decision criteria is to investigate all variances exceeding $12,000?

Learning Objective 4

1. Residential's ROI 34.00%

E24-17 Using ROI and RI to evaluate investment centers

Zims, a national manufacturer of lawn-mowing and snow-blowing equipment, segments its business according to customer type: professional and residential. The following divisional information was available for the past year:

	Net Sales Revenue	Operating Income	Average Total Assets
Residential	$ 550,000	$ 65,280	$ 192,000
Professional	1,090,000	164,820	402,000

Management has a 26% target rate of return for each division.

Requirements

1. Calculate each division's ROI. Round all of your answers to four decimal places.

2. Calculate each division's profit margin ratio. Interpret your results.

3. Calculate each division's asset turnover ratio. Interpret your results.

4. Use the expanded ROI formula to confirm your results from Requirement 1. What can you conclude?

Note: Exercise E24-17 must be completed before attempting Exercise E24-18.

E24-18 Using ROI and RI to evaluate investment centers

Refer to the data in Exercise E24-17. Calculate each division's RI. Interpret your results.

Learning Objective 4

Professional's RI $60,300

E24-19 Determining transfer pricing

The Watkins Company is decentralized, and divisions are considered investment centers. Watkins specializes in sports equipment, and one division manufactures netting that is used for basketball hoops, soccer goals, and other sports equipment. The Netting Division reports the following information for a heavy-duty basketball hoop net:

Learning Objective 5

Sales Price per Unit	$ 18
Variable Cost per Unit	6
Contribution Margin per Unit	$ 12

The Basketball Equipment Division can purchase a similar heavy-duty net from an outside vendor for $15.

Requirements

1. Determine the negotiable range for the transfer price.

2. What is the minimum transfer price the Netting Division should consider if operating at capacity? Below capacity?

3. What is the maximum transfer price the Basketball Equipment Division should consider?

> Problems Group A

P24-20A Integrating decentralization and performance evaluation systems

One subunit of Racer Sports Company had the following financial results last month:

Learning Objectives 1, 2, 3

1. Sales $25,000 F

Subunit X	Actual Results	Flexible Budget	Flexible Budget Variance (F or U)	% Variance (F or U)
Net Sales Revenue	$ 476,000	$ 451,000		
Variable Expenses	261,000	251,000		
Contribution Margin	215,000	200,000		
Traceable Fixed Expenses	40,000	26,000		
Divisional Segment Margin	$ 175,000	$ 174,000		

Requirements

1. Complete the performance evaluation report for this subunit (round to two decimal places).

2. Based on the data presented and your knowledge of the company, what type of responsibility center is this subunit?

3. Which items should be investigated if part of management's decision criteria is to investigate all variances equal to or exceeding $8,000 *and* exceeding 10% (both criteria must be met)?

4. Should only unfavorable variances be investigated? Explain.

5. Is it possible that the variances are due to a higher-than-expected sales volume? Explain.

6. Will management place equal weight on each of the variances exceeding $8,000? Explain.

7. Which balanced scorecard perspective is being addressed through this performance report? In your opinion, is this performance report a lead or a lag indicator? Explain.

8. List one key performance indicator for the three other balanced scorecard perspectives. Make sure to indicate which perspective is being addressed by the indicators you list.

Learning Objective 4

3. Asset turnover ratio 7.00

P24-21A Using ROI and RI to evaluate investment centers

Consider the following condensed financial statements of Forever Free, Inc. The company's target rate of return is 40%.

FOREVER FREE, INC. Income Statement For the Year Ended December 31, 2018	
Net Sales Revenue	$ 3,500,000
Cost of Goods Sold	2,200,000
Gross Profit	1,300,000
Operating Expenses	950,000
Operating Income	350,000
Other Income and (Expenses):	
Interest Expense	(27,000)
Income Before Income Tax Expense	323,000
Income Tax Expense	113,050
Net Income	$ 209,950

FOREVER FREE, INC. Comparative Balance Sheet As of December 31, 2018 and 2017		
	2018	**2017**
Assets		
Cash	$ 64,000	$ 52,000
Accounts Receivable	49,200	17,800
Supplies	1,000	400
Property, Plant, and Equipment, net	331,800	229,800
Patents, net	135,000	119,000
Total Assets	$ 581,000	$ 419,000
Liabilities and Stockholders' Equity		
Accounts Payable	$ 17,000	$ 19,000
Short-term Notes Payable	136,000	42,000
Long-term Notes Payable	184,000	114,500
Common Stock, no Par	232,000	242,000
Retained Earnings	12,000	1,500
Total Liabilities and Stockholders' Equity	$ 581,000	$ 419,000

Requirements

1. Calculate the company's ROI. Round all of your answers to four decimal places.

2. Calculate the company's profit margin ratio. Interpret your results.

3. Calculate the company's asset turnover ratio. Interpret your results.

4. Use the expanded ROI formula to confirm your results from Requirement 1. Interpret your results.

5. Calculate the company's RI. Interpret your results.

P24-22A   Using ROI and RI to evaluate investment centers

Learning Objective 4

4. Paint Stores's ROI 34.49%

Wolf Paints is a national paint manufacturer and retailer. The company is segmented into five divisions: Paint Stores (branded retail locations), Consumer (paint sold through home improvement stores), Automotive (sales to auto manufacturers), International, and Administration. The following is selected divisional information for its two largest divisions: Paint Stores and Consumer.

	Net Sales Revenue	Operating Income	Average Total Assets
Paint Stores	$ 3,980,000	$ 476,000	$ 1,380,000
Consumer	1,315,000	195,000	1,600,000

Management has specified a 21% target rate of return.

Requirements

1. Calculate each division's ROI. Round all of your answers to four decimal places.
2. Calculate each division's profit margin ratio. Interpret your results.
3. Calculate each division's asset turnover ratio. Interpret your results.
4. Use the expanded ROI formula to confirm your results from Requirement 1. Interpret your results.
5. Calculate each division's RI. Interpret your results, and offer a recommendation for any division with negative RI.
6. Describe some of the factors that management considers when setting its minimum target rate of return.

P24-23A Determining transfer pricing

Learning Objective 5

2. Total CM $24,000

The Harris Company is decentralized, and divisions are considered investment centers. Harris has one division that manufactures oak dining room chairs with upholstered seat cushions. The Chair Division cuts, assembles, and finishes the oak chairs and then purchases and attaches the seat cushions. The Chair Division currently purchases the cushions for $22 from an outside vendor. The Cushion Division manufactures upholstered seat cushions that are sold to customers outside the company. The Chair Division currently sells 800 chairs per quarter, and the Cushion Division is operating at capacity, which is 800 cushions per quarter. The two divisions report the following information:

Chair Division		Cushion Division	
Sales Price per Chair	$ 85	Sales Price per Cushion	$ 32
Variable Cost (other than cushion)	42	Variable Cost per Cushion	13
Variable Cost (cushion)	22		
Contribution Margin per Chair	$ 21	Contribution Margin per Cushion	$ 19

Requirements

1. Determine the total contribution margin for Harris Company for the quarter.
2. Assume the Chair Division purchases the 800 cushions needed from the Cushion Division at its current sales price. What is the total contribution margin for each division and the company?

3. Assume the Chair Division purchases the 800 cushions needed from the Cushion Division at its current variable cost. What is the total contribution margin for each division and the company?

4. Review your answers for Requirements 1, 2, and 3. What is the best option for Harris Company?

5. Assume the Cushion Division has capacity of 1,600 cushions per quarter and can continue to supply its outside customers with 800 cushions per quarter and also supply the Chair Division with 800 cushions per quarter. What transfer price should Harris Company set? Explain your reasoning. Using the transfer price you determined, calculate the total contribution margin for the quarter.

> Problems Group B

Learning Objectives 1, 2, 3

1. CM $13,000 F

P24-24B Integrating decentralization and performance evaluation systems

One subunit of Track Sports Company had the following financial results last month:

Subunit X	Actual Results	Flexible Budget	Flexible Budget Variance (F or U)	% Variance (F or U)
Net Sales Revenue	$ 474,000	$ 455,000		
Variable Expenses	261,000	255,000		
Contribution Margin	213,000	200,000		
Traceable Fixed Expenses	38,000	29,000		
Divisional Segment Margin	$ 175,000	$ 171,000		

Requirements

1. Complete the performance evaluation report for this subunit (round to two decimal places).

2. Based on the data presented and your knowledge of the company, what type of responsibility center is this subunit?

3. Which items should be investigated if part of management's decision criteria is to investigate all variances equal to or exceeding $8,000 *and* exceeding 10% (both criteria must be met)?

4. Should only unfavorable variances be investigated? Explain.

5. Is it possible that the variances are due to a higher-than-expected sales volume? Explain.

6. Will management place equal weight on each of the variances exceeding $8,000? Explain.

7. Which balanced scorecard perspective is being addressed through this performance report? In your opinion, is this performance report a lead or a lag indicator? Explain.

8. List one key performance indicator for the three other balanced scorecard perspectives. Make sure to indicate which perspective is being addressed by the indicators you list.

P24-25B Using ROI and RI to evaluate investment centers

Learning Objective 4

Consider the following condensed financial statements of Pure Life, Inc. The company's target rate of return is 30%.

2. Profit margin ratio 5.00%

PURE LIFE, INC. Income Statement For the Year Ended December 31, 2018	
Net Sales Revenue	$ 6,000,000
Cost of Goods Sold	3,700,000
Gross Profit	2,300,000
Operating Expenses	2,000,000
Operating Income	300,000
Other Income and (Expenses):	
Interest Expense	(34,000)
Income Before Income Tax Expense	266,000
Income Tax Expense	93,100
Net Income	$ 172,900

PURE LIFE, INC. Comparative Balance Sheet As of December 31, 2018 and 2017	2018	2017
Assets		
Cash	$ 76,000	$ 62,000
Accounts Receivable	61,400	26,800
Supplies	600	200
Property, Plant, and Equipment, net	305,000	204,000
Patents, net	163,000	101,000
Total Assets	$ 606,000	$ 394,000
Liabilities and Stockholders' Equity		
Accounts Payable	$ 29,000	$ 31,000
Short-term Notes Payable	148,000	52,000
Long-term Notes Payable	196,000	126,500
Common Stock, no Par	205,500	169,000
Retained Earnings	27,500	15,500
Total Liabilities and Stockholders' Equity	$ 606,000	$ 394,000

Requirements

1. Calculate the company's ROI. Round all of your answers to four decimal places.
2. Calculate the company's profit margin ratio. Interpret your results.
3. Calculate the company's asset turnover ratio. Interpret your results.
4. Use the expanded ROI formula to confirm your results from Requirement 1. Interpret your results.
5. Calculate the company's RI. Interpret your results.

P24-26B Using ROI and RI to evaluate investment centers

Learning Objective 4

Tiger Paints is a national paint manufacturer and retailer. The company is segmented into five divisions: Paint Stores (branded retail locations), Consumer (paint sold through home improvement stores), Automotive (sales to auto manufacturers), International, and Administration. The following is selected divisional information for its two largest divisions: Paint Stores and Consumer:

3. Consumer's asset turnover ratio 0.8202

	Net Sales Revenue	Operating Income	Average Total Assets
Paint Stores	$ 4,000,000	$ 476,000	$ 1,420,000
Consumer	1,300,000	196,000	1,585,000

Management has specified a 19% target rate of return.

Requirements

1. Calculate each division's ROI. Round all of your answers to four decimal places.

2. Calculate each division's profit margin ratio. Interpret your results.

3. Calculate each division's asset turnover ratio. Interpret your results.

4. Use the expanded ROI formula to confirm your results from Requirement 1. Interpret your results.

5. Calculate each division's RI. Interpret your results, and offer a recommendation for any division with negative RI.

6. Describe some of the factors that management considers when setting its minimum target rate of return.

Learning Objective 5

3. Total CM $48,600

P24-27B Determining transfer pricing

The Hernandez Company is decentralized, and divisions are considered investment centers. Hernandez has one division that manufactures oak dining room chairs with upholstered seat cushions. The Chair Division cuts, assembles, and finishes the oak chairs and then purchases and attaches the seat cushions. The Chair Division currently purchases the cushions for $32 from an outside vendor. The Cushion Division manufactures upholstered seat cushions that are sold to customers outside the company. The Chair Division currently sells 1,800 chairs per quarter, and the Cushion Division is operating at capacity, which is 1,800 cushions per quarter. The two divisions report the following information:

Chair Division		Cushion Division	
Sales Price per Chair	$ 95	Sales Price per Cushion	$ 34
Variable Cost (other than cushion)	56	Variable Cost per Cushion	12
Variable Cost (cushion)	32		
Contribution Margin per Chair	$ 7	Contribution Margin per Cushion	$ 22

Requirements

1. Determine the total contribution margin for Hernandez Company for the quarter.

2. Assume the Chair Division purchases the 1,800 cushions needed from the Cushion Division at its current sales price. What is the total contribution margin for each division and the company?

3. Assume the Chair Division purchases the 1,800 cushions needed from the Cushion Division at its current variable cost. What is the total contribution margin for each division and the company?

4. Review your answers for Requirements 1, 2, and 3. What is the best option for Hernandez Company?

5. Assume the Cushion Division has capacity of 3,600 cushions per quarter and can continue to supply its outside customers with 1,800 cushions per quarter and also supply the Chair Division with 1,800 cushions per quarter. What transfer price should Hernandez Company set? Explain your reasoning. Using the transfer price you determined, calculate the total contribution margin for the quarter.

CRITICAL THINKING

> Using Excel

P24-28 Using Excel to calculate key performance indicators (KPIs)

Download an Excel template for this problem online in MyAccountingLab or at http://www.pearsonhighered.com/Horngren.

The US Solar Company has data for the four divisions for the year, and wants the results for the three specified key performance indicators (KPIs).

Division	Operating Income	Average Total Assets	Net Sales Revenue	Profit Margin Ratio	Asset Turnover Ratio	Return on Investment (ROI)
East	$ 1,580,000.00	$ 12,000,750.00	$ 25,900,000.00			
North	650,000.00	4,875,000.00	6,337,500.00			
South	275,050.00	995,090.00	855,770.00			
West	2,300,000.00	13,800,000.00	9,200,000.00			

Requirements

1. Create an Excel table from the data.
2. Rename the table as Solar_KPI
3. Select another table style for the table.
4. Use table arithmetic for the formulas (rounded to three decimal places) for
   a. Profit Margin Ratio
   b. Asset Turnover Ratio
   c. Return on Investment (ROI)

> Continuing Problem

P24-29 Using ROI and RI to evaluate investment centers

This problem continues the Piedmont Computer Company situation from Chapter 23. Piedmont Computer Company reported 2020 sales of $3,600,000 and operating income of $183,600. Average total assets during 2020 were $600,000. Piedmont Computer Company's target rate of return is 16%.

Calculate Piedmont Computer Company's profit margin ratio, asset turnover ratio, ROI, and RI for 2020. Comment on the results.

COMPREHENSIVE PROBLEM

Comprehensive Problem for Chapters 22–24

The Trolley Toy Company manufactures toy building block sets for children. Trolley is planning for 2019 by developing a master budget by quarters. Trolley's balance sheet for December 31, 2018, follows:

TROLLEY TOY COMPANY
Balance Sheet
December 31, 2018

Assets

Current Assets:		
Cash	$ 58,000	
Accounts Receivable	22,000	
Raw Materials Inventory	1,200	
Finished Goods Inventory	5,400	
Total Current Assets		$ 86,600
Property, Plant, and Equipment:		
Equipment	142,000	
Less: Accumulated Depreciation	(47,000)	95,000
Total Assets		$ 181,600

Liabilities

Current Liabilities:		
Accounts Payable		$ 8,000

Stockholders' Equity

Common Stock, no par	$ 120,000	
Retained Earnings	53,600	
Total Stockholders' Equity		173,600
Total Liabilities and Stockholders' Equity		$ 181,600

Other budget data for Trolley Toy Company:

a. Budgeted sales are 1,400 sets for the first quarter and expected to increase by 150 sets per quarter. Cash sales are expected to be 30% of total sales, with the remaining 70% of sales on account. Sets are budgeted to sell for $90 per set.

b. Finished Goods Inventory on December 31, 2018, consists of 200 sets at $27 each.

c. Desired ending Finished Goods Inventory is 40% of the next quarter's sales; first quarter sales for 2020 are expected to be 2,000 sets. FIFO inventory costing method is used.

d. Raw Materials Inventory on December 31, 2018, consists of 600 pounds. Direct materials requirement is 3 pounds per set. The cost is $2 per pound.

e. Desired ending Raw Materials Inventory is 10% of the next quarter's direct materials needed for production; desired ending inventory for December 31, 2019, is 600 pounds; indirect materials are insignificant and not considered for budgeting purposes.

f. Each set requires 0.30 hours of direct labor; direct labor costs average $12 per hour.

g. Variable manufacturing overhead is $3.60 per set.

h. Fixed manufacturing overhead includes $7,000 per quarter in depreciation and $2,585 per quarter for other costs, such as utilities, insurance, and property taxes.

i. Fixed selling and administrative expenses include $11,000 per quarter for salaries; $1,500 per quarter for rent; $1,350 per quarter for insurance; and $1,500 per quarter for depreciation.

j. Variable selling and administrative expenses include supplies at 2% of sales.

k. Capital expenditures include $45,000 for new manufacturing equipment, to be purchased and paid for in the first quarter.

l. Cash receipts for sales on account are 40% in the quarter of the sale and 60% in the quarter following the sale; Accounts Receivable balance on December 31, 2018, is expected to be received in the first quarter of 2019; uncollectible accounts are considered insignificant and not considered for budgeting purposes.

m. Direct materials purchases are paid 90% in the quarter purchased and 10% in the following quarter; Accounts Payable balance on December 31, 2018, is expected to be paid in the first quarter of 2019.

n. Direct labor, manufacturing overhead, and selling and administrative costs are paid in the quarter incurred.

o. Income tax expense is projected at $3,500 per quarter and is paid in the quarter incurred.

p. Trolley desires to maintain a minimum cash balance of $55,000 and borrows from the local bank as needed in increments of $1,000 at the beginning of the quarter; principal repayments are made at the beginning of the quarter when excess funds are available and in increments of $1,000; interest is 10% per year and paid at the beginning of the quarter based on the amount outstanding from the previous quarter.

Requirements

1. Prepare Trolley's operating budget and cash budget for 2019 by quarter. Required schedules and budgets include: sales budget, production budget, direct materials budget, direct labor budget, manufacturing overhead budget, cost of goods sold budget, selling and administrative expense budget, schedule of cash receipts, schedule of cash payments, and cash budget. Manufacturing overhead costs are allocated based on direct labor hours.

2. Prepare Trolley's annual financial budget for 2019, including budgeted income statement and budgeted balance sheet.

3. Trolley sold 7,000 sets in 2019, and its actual operating income was as follows:

TROLLEY TOY COMPANY
Income Statement
For the Year Ended December 31, 2019

Net Sales Revenue		$ 630,000
Cost of Goods Sold:		
Variable	$ 94,890	
Fixed	36,540	131,430
Gross Profit		498,570
Selling and Administrative Expenses:		
Variable	12,600	
Fixed	61,400	74,000
Operating Income		424,570
Other Income and (Expenses):		
Interest Expense		(425)
Income Before Income Taxes		424,145
Income Tax Expense		22,000
Net Income		$ 402,145

Prepare a flexible budget performance report through operating income for 2019. Show product costs separately from selling and administrative costs. To simplify the calculations due to sets in beginning inventory having a different cost than those produced and sold in 2019, assume the following product costs:

	Variable	Fixed	Total
Static budget	$ 84,240	$ 38,340	$ 122,580
Flexible budget	93,940	38,340	132,280

4. What was the effect on Trolley's operating income of selling 500 sets more than the static budget level of sales?

5. What is Trolley's static budget variance for operating income?

6. Explain why the flexible budget performance report provides more useful information to Trolley's managers than the static budget performance report. What insights can Trolley's managers draw from this performance report?

7. During 2019, Trolley recorded the following cost data:

Standard Cost Information

	Quantity	Cost
Direct materials	3 pounds per set	$ 2.00 per pound
Direct labor	0.30 hours per set	$ 12.00 per hour
Variable manufacturing overhead	0.30 hours per set	$ 12.00 per hour
Fixed manufacturing overhead Static budget amount: $38,340	0.30 hours per set	$ 21.00 per hour

Actual Cost Information

Direct materials	(20,700 pounds @ $2.50 per pound)	$ 51,750
Direct labor	(2,060 hours @ $12.40 per hour)	25,544
Variable manufacturing overhead	(2,060 hours @ $11.60 per hour)	23,896
Fixed manufacturing overhead		36,540

Compute the cost and efficiency variances for direct materials and direct labor.

8. For manufacturing overhead, compute the variable overhead cost and efficiency variances and the fixed overhead cost and volume variances.

9. Prepare the standard cost income statement for 2019.

10. Calculate Trolley's ROI for 2019. To calculate average total assets, use the December 31, 2018, balance sheet for the beginning balance and the budgeted balance sheet for December 31, 2019, for the ending balance. Round all of your answers to four decimal places.

11. Calculate Trolley's profit margin ratio for 2019. Interpret your results.

12. Calculate Trolley's asset turnover ratio for 2019. Interpret your results.

13. Use the expanded ROI formula to confirm your results from Requirement 10. Interpret your results.

14. Trolley's management has specified a 30% target rate of return. Calculate Trolley's RI for 2019. Interpret your results.

> **Tying It All Together Case 24-1**

Before you begin this assignment, review the Tying It All Together feature in the chapter. It will also be helpful if you review PepsiCo's 2015 annual report (https://www.sec.gov/Archives/edgar/data/77476/000007747616000066/pepsico201510-k.htm).

PepsiCo, Inc. a leading global food and beverage company, organizes itself into six reportable segments or divisions: Frito-Lay North America (FLNA), Quaker Foods North America (QFNA), North America Beverages (NAB), Latin America (LA), Europe Sub-Saharan Africa (ESSA), and Asia, Middle East and North Africa (AMENA).

Requirements

1. Review the 2015 annual report for PepsiCo and provide a brief summary about each of the different segments. See Part I, Item 1, Our Operations.

2. What are some advantages that PepsiCo has from decentralization?

3. What are some disadvantages that PepsiCo has from decentralization?

4. Review the 2015 annual report for PepsiCo, and determine the amount of operating profit in each of the different segments for 2015. Use Notes to Consolidated Financial Statements, Note 1.

5. Review the 2015 annual report for PepsiCo, and calculate the return on investment (ROI) for the 6 segments for 2015. Use Notes to Consolidated Financial Statements, Note 1.

6. In terms of ROI, rank the 6 segments from most profitable to less profitable. How does this ranking compare to the ranking by operating income?

> Decision Case 24-1

Colgate-Palmolive Company operates two product segments. Go to https://www.sec.gov/Archives/edgar/data/21665/000162828016011343/cl-12312015x10k.htm. The necessary information will be in the Notes to Consolidated Financial Statements, Note 15: Segment Information.

Requirements

1. What are the two product segments? Gather data about each segment's net sales revenue, operating income, and identifiable assets for 2015.

2. Calculate ROI for each segment for 2015.

3. Which segment has the highest ROI? Explain why.

4. If you were on the top management team and could allocate extra funds to only one division, which division would you choose? Why?

> Ethical Issue 24-1

Dixie Irwin is the department manager for Religious Books, a manufacturer of religious books that are sold through Internet companies. Irwin's bonus is based on reducing production costs.

Irwin has identified a supplier, Cheap Paper, that can provide paper products at a 10% cost reduction. The paper quality is not the same as that of the current paper used in production. If Irwin uses the supplier, she will certainly achieve her personal bonus goals; however, other company goals may be in jeopardy. What is the ethical issue? Identify the key performance issues at risk, and recommend a plan of action for Irwin.

> Fraud Case 24-1

Everybody knew Ed McAlister was a brilliant businessman. He had taken a small garbage collection company in Kentucky and built it up to be one of the largest and most profitable waste management companies in the Midwest. But when he was convicted of a massive financial fraud, what surprised everyone was how crude and simple the scheme was. To keep the earnings up and the stock prices soaring, he and his coworkers came up with an almost foolishly simple scheme: First, they doubled the useful lives of the dumpsters. That allowed them to cut depreciation expense in half. The following year, they simply increased the estimated salvage value of the dumpsters, allowing them to further reduce depreciation expense. With thousands of dumpsters spread over 14 states, these simple adjustments gave the company an enormous boost to the bottom line. When it all came tumbling down, McAlister had to sell everything he owned to pay for his legal costs and was left with nothing.

Requirements

1. If an asset has either too long a useful life or too high an estimated salvage value, what happens, from an accounting perspective, when that asset is worn out and has to be disposed of?

2. Do the rules of GAAP (Generally Accepted Accounting Principles) mandate specific lives for different types of assets?

3. How might either too long a useful life or too high an estimated salvage value affect key performance indicators such as return on investment and residual income?

> Team Project 24-1

Each group should identify one public company's product to evaluate. The team should gather all the information it can about the product.

Requirement

Develop a list of key performance indicators for the product.

> Communication Activity 24-1

In 150 words or fewer, list each of the four perspectives of the balanced scorecard. Give an example of one KPI from each of the perspectives, and explain what measure the KPI provides for a retailing business.

MyAccountingLab **For a wealth of online resources, including exercises, problems, media, and immediate tutorial help, please visit** http://www.myaccountinglab.com.

> Quick Check Answers

1. d **2.** c **3.** d **4.** b **5.** d **6.** c **7.** b **8.** a **9.** b **10.** d

Short-Term Business Decisions

Will Someone Clean Up This Mess?

Woody Styles looked at his apartment. It was a mess. Attending college full time and working part time didn't leave much time for cleaning. The "dust bunnies" were threatening to take over, and the kitchen floor was rather sticky. Woody didn't like his living conditions, but he also didn't want to use his scheduled study time to clean the apartment. Woody decided the best choice was to outsource the cleaning by hiring a cleaning company to come in every couple of weeks.

Woody was familiar with the concept of outsourcing from his brother Allen, the design manager at Abraham Airplane Company. Allen's job includes analyzing the prototypes of newly created airplanes and gliders to determine which parts should be manufactured in Abraham's manufacturing facilities and which ones should be outsourced to a third-party vendor. Allen has to decide whether Abraham's employees have the expertise to make the part and whether Abraham's equipment is adequate. Often, it is more economical to contract with another company to produce the parts, such as the tires on the landing gear, than it is to buy the needed equipment and train employees to use it efficiently and effectively.

Woody decided to analyze his outsourcing decision. He researched the cost of a cleaning service and compared it to the hours he would have to work at his part-time job to pay for the service. Woody decided the best short-term decision was to clean the apartment himself, but he looked forward to outsourcing the job when he graduated and began working full time.

How Do Managers Make Decisions?

Managers have to make business decisions every day, such as whom to sell to, how much to charge, which products to make, and when it is better to buy a product or service rather than producing it in-house. **The Boeing Company** is the world's largest aerospace company and the leading manufacturer of commercial airplanes and defense, space, and security systems. The company employs more than 160,000 people in more than 65 countries. Recently, the Boeing Commercial Airline division has focused its new product development on the Boeing 787 Dreamliner, which has had record-breaking customer orders. The first customer delivery was in September 2011. On January 16, 2013, the Federal Aviation Administration (FAA) issued an emergency airworthiness directive ordering all U.S.-based airlines to ground their Boeing 787s due to the risk of a battery overheating or catching fire. The batteries were outsourced and produced by a third-party vendor. Boeing made modifications to the batteries, and the planes were flying again in about three months. The decision to outsource can have a lasting impact on a company's reputation and overall profitability, but Boeing's response was quick—and hopefully the company will not experience any long-term negative effects. These are the types of decisions that we will evaluate in this chapter.

Chapter 25 Learning Objectives

1   Identify information that is relevant for making short-term decisions

2   Make regular and special pricing decisions

3   Make decisions about dropping a product, product mix, and sales mix

4   Make outsourcing and processing further decisions

In previous chapters, we saw how managers use cost behavior to determine a company's breakeven point, estimate the sales volume needed to achieve target profits, prepare budgets, and evaluate performance. In this chapter, we see how managers use their knowledge of cost behavior to make short-term business decisions, such as whether to accept an order with special pricing or drop an unprofitable product. The decisions we discuss in this chapter pertain to short periods of time, usually one year or less. In the next chapter, we discuss longer-term decisions. Before we look at some typical short-term decisions in detail, let's consider a manager's decision-making process and the information managers need to evaluate their options.

HOW IS RELEVANT INFORMATION USED TO MAKE SHORT-TERM DECISIONS?

Learning Objective 1

Identify information that is relevant for making short-term decisions

Exhibit 25-1 illustrates how managers make decisions among alternative courses of action. Managerial accountants help with the third step: gather and analyze *relevant information* to compare alternatives.

Exhibit 25-1 | **How Managers Make Decisions**

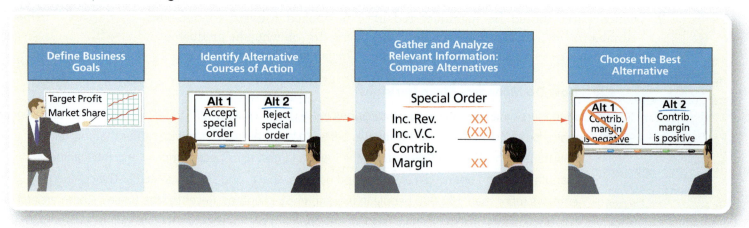

Relevant Information

Relevant Information
Expected future data that differ among alternatives.

Relevant Cost
A cost that is relevant to a particular decision because it is a future cost and differs among alternatives.

When managers make decisions, they focus on information that is relevant to the decisions. **Relevant information** is expected *future* data that *differ* among alternatives. **Relevant costs** are costs that are relevant to a particular decision. To illustrate, if the fictitious company Smart Touch Learning was considering purchasing a new delivery truck and was choosing between two different models, the cost of the trucks, the sales tax, and the insurance premium costs would all be relevant because these costs are *future* costs (after Smart Touch

Learning decides which truck to buy) and *differ between alternatives* (each truck model has a different invoice price, sales tax, and insurance premium). These costs are *relevant* because they can affect the decision of which truck to purchase.

Irrelevant costs are costs that do *not* affect the decision because they are not in the future or do not differ among alternatives. For example, if the two truck models have similar fuel efficiency and maintenance ratings, we do not expect the truck operating costs to differ between those two alternatives. Because these future costs do not differ, they do not affect Smart Touch Learning's decision. In other words, they are *irrelevant* to the decision.

Sunk costs are costs that were incurred in the *past* and cannot be changed regardless of which future action is taken. Sunk costs are always irrelevant to the decision. This does not mean we cannot learn from past decisions—managers should always consider the results of past decisions when making future decisions. However, because sunk costs are already spent, the cost is not relevant to future decision making. For example, perhaps Smart Touch Learning wants to trade in its current truck when the company buys the new truck. The amount Smart Touch Learning paid for the current truck—which the company bought for $15,000 a year ago—is a sunk cost. No decision made *now* can alter the sunk costs spent in the past. All the company can do *now* is keep the current truck, trade it in, or sell it for the best price the company can get—even if that price is substantially less than what Smart Touch Learning originally paid for the truck.

What *is* relevant is the amount Smart Touch Learning can receive if it sells the truck in the future. Suppose that one dealership offers an $8,000 trade-in value for the truck, but another dealership offers $10,000. Because the amounts differ and the transaction will take place in the future, the trade-in value *is* relevant to Smart Touch Learning's decision. The same principle applies to all situations—*only relevant data affect decisions*.

Relevant Nonfinancial Information

Nonfinancial, or qualitative, factors also play a role in managers' decisions and, as a result, can be relevant. For example, closing manufacturing plants and laying off employees can seriously hurt employee morale. The decision to buy or subcontract a product or service rather than produce it in-house can reduce control over delivery time or product quality. Offering discounted prices to select customers can upset regular customers and tempt them to take their business elsewhere. **Managers must always consider the potential quantitative *and* qualitative effects of their decisions.**

Managers who ignore qualitative factors can make serious mistakes. For example, the City of Nottingham, England, spent $1.6 million on 215 solar-powered parking meters after seeing how well the parking meters worked in countries along the Mediterranean Sea. However, they did not consider that British skies are typically overcast. The result was that the meters did not always work because of the lack of sunlight. The city *lost* money because people parked for free! Relevant qualitative information has the same characteristics as relevant financial information. The qualitative effect occurs in the *future* and *differs* between alternatives. In the parking meter example, the amount of *future* sunshine required by the meters *differed* between the alternatives. The mechanical meters did not require any sunshine, but the solar-powered meters needed a lot of sunshine.

Differential Analysis

A common approach to making short-term business decisions is called **differential analysis**. In this approach, the emphasis is on the difference in operating income between the alternative approaches. Differential analysis is also sometimes called *incremental analysis*. Instead of looking at the company's *entire* income statement under each decision alternative, we just look at how operating income would *differ* under each alternative. Using this approach, we leave

---

Irrelevant Cost
A cost that does not affect the decision because it is not in the future or does not differ among alternatives.

Sunk Cost
A cost that was incurred in the past and cannot be changed regardless of which future action is taken.

Is relevant information always financial?

Differential Analysis
A method that looks at how operating income would differ under each decision alternative; leaves out irrelevant information.

out irrelevant information—the revenues and costs that will not differ between alternatives. In this chapter, we consider several kinds of short-term business decisions:

- Regular and special pricing
- Dropping unprofitable products and segments, product mix, and sales mix
- Outsourcing and processing further

As you study these decisions, keep in mind the two keys in analyzing short-term business decisions:

1. **Focus on relevant revenues, costs, and profits.** Irrelevant information only clouds the picture and creates information overload.
2. **Use a contribution margin approach that separates variable costs from fixed costs.** Because fixed costs and variable costs behave differently, they must be analyzed separately. Traditional income statements, which blend fixed and variable costs together, can mislead managers. Contribution margin income statements, which isolate costs by behavior (variable or fixed), help managers gather the cost behavior information they need. Keep in mind that manufacturing costs per unit are mixed costs, too—so they can also mislead managers. If you use manufacturing costs per unit in your analysis, be sure to first separate the unit cost into its fixed and variable portions.

We use these two keys in each decision.

Doherty Company is considering replacing the individual printers each employee in the corporate office currently uses with a network printer located in a central area. The network printer is more efficient and would, therefore, cost less to operate than the individual printers. However, most of the office staff think having to use a centralized printer would be inconvenient. They prefer to have individual printers located at each desk. Identify the following information as financial or nonfinancial and relevant or irrelevant. The first item has been completed as an example.

	Financial	Nonfinancial	Relevant	Irrelevant
1. Amount paid for current printers	✓			✓
2. Resale value of current printers				
3. Cost of new printer				
4. Operating costs of current printers				
5. Operating costs of new printer				
6. Employee morale				

Check your answers online in MyAccountingLab or at http://www.pearsonhighered.com/Horngren.

For more practice, see Short Exercise S25-1. MyAccountingLab

HOW DOES PRICING AFFECT SHORT-TERM DECISIONS?

We start our discussion on decision making by looking at regular pricing decisions and special pricing decisions. In the past, managers did not consider pricing to be a short-term decision. However, product life cycles are getting shorter in most industries. Companies often sell products for only a few months before replacing them with an updated model, even if the updating is small. The clothing and technology industries have always had short life cycles. Even auto and housing styles change frequently. Pricing has become a shorter-term decision than it was in the past.

Learning Objective 2
Make regular and special pricing decisions

Setting Regular Prices

There are three basic questions managers must answer when setting regular prices for their products or services:

- What is the company's target profit?
- How much will customers pay?
- Is the company a price-taker or a price-setter for this product or service?

The answers to these questions are complex and ever changing. Stockholders expect the company to achieve certain profits. Economic conditions, historical company earnings, industry risk, competition, and new business developments all affect the level of profit that stockholders expect. Stockholders usually tie their profit expectations to the amount of assets invested in the company. For example, stockholders may expect a 10% annual return on investment (ROI). A company's stock price tends to decline if it does not meet target profits, so managers must keep costs low while generating enough revenue to meet target profits.

This leads to the second question: How much will customers pay? Managers cannot set prices above what customers are willing to pay, or sales volume will decline. The amount customers will pay depends on supply and demand, which is influenced by the competition, the product's uniqueness, the effectiveness of marketing campaigns, general economic conditions, and so forth.

To address the third pricing question, whether a company is a price-taker or a price-setter, imagine a horizontal line with price-takers at one end and price-setters at the other end. A company falls somewhere along this line for each of its products and services. Companies are **price-takers** when they have little or no control over the prices of their products or services and *take* the price set by the market. This occurs when their products and services are *not* unique or when competition is intense. Examples include food commodities (milk and corn), natural resources (oil and lumber), and generic consumer products and services (paper towels, dry cleaning, and banking).

Companies are **price-setters** when they have more control over pricing—in other words, they can *set the price* to some extent. Companies are price-setters when their products are unique, which results in less competition. Unique products, such as original art and jewelry, specially manufactured machinery, patented perfume scents, and the latest technological gadget, can command higher prices.

Obviously, managers would rather be price-setters than price-takers. To gain more control over pricing, companies try to differentiate their products. They want to make their products unique in terms of features, service, or quality or at least make the buyer *think* their product is unique or somehow better. Companies achieve this differentiation partly through their advertising efforts. Consider Nike's athletic shoes, Starbucks's coffee, Kleenex's tissues, Tylenol's acetaminophen, Capital One's credit cards, Shell's gas, Abercrombie and Fitch's jeans—the list goes on and on. Are these products really better or significantly different from their lower-priced competitors? It is possible. If these companies can make customers *believe* that this is true, they will gain more control over their pricing because customers

Price-Taker
A company that has little control over the prices of its products and services because its products and services are not unique or competition is intense.

Price-Setter
A company that has control over the prices of its products and services because its products and services are unique and there is little competition.

are willing to pay *more* for their product or service. What is the downside? These companies must charge higher prices or sell more just to cover their advertising costs.

A company's approach to pricing depends on whether it is on the price-taking or price-setting side of the spectrum. Price-takers emphasize a target-pricing approach. Price-setters emphasize a cost-plus pricing approach. Keep in mind that most companies provide many products and services; a company may be a price-taker for some products and a price-setter for other products. Therefore, managers tend to use both approaches to some extent. Exhibit 25-2 summarizes the difference between price-takers and price-setters.

Exhibit 25-2 | **Price-Takers Versus Price-Setters**

Companies Are Price-Takers for a Product When:	Companies Are Price-Setters for a Product When:
• Product lacks uniqueness	• Product is more unique
• Intense competition	• Less competition
• Pricing approach emphasizes target pricing	• Pricing approach emphasizes cost-plus pricing

Target Pricing

Target Pricing
A method to manage costs and profits by determining the target full product cost. Revenue at market price − Desired profit = Target full product cost.

Target Full Product Cost
The full cost to develop, produce, and deliver the product or service.

When a company is a price-taker, it emphasizes a target-pricing approach to managing costs and profits. **Target pricing** starts with the market price of the product (the price customers are willing to pay) and then subtracts the company's desired profit to determine the maximum allowed **target full product cost**—the *full* cost to develop, produce, and deliver the product or service. Target pricing is sometimes called *target costing* because the desired target cost is derived from the target price. The target pricing formula is:

$$
\begin{array}{l}
\text{Revenue at market price} \\
-\ \text{Desired profit} \\
\hline
\text{Target full product cost}
\end{array}
$$

How will I know the revenue at market price?

In this relationship, the sales price is *taken* from the market. It is the amount set by the market—the maximum amount customers are willing to pay. The company has no control over this amount and, therefore, must focus on controlling costs to obtain the desired profit. Recall that a product's *full* cost contains all elements from the value chain—both product costs (direct materials, direct labor, and manufacturing overhead) and period costs (selling and administrative costs). Both product costs and period costs include fixed and variable costs. If the product's current cost is higher than the target full product cost, the company must find ways to reduce the product's cost or it will not meet its profit goals. Managers often use activity-based costing along with value engineering (as discussed in a previous chapter) to find ways to cut costs.

Let's return to Smart Touch Learning, a fictitious company that manufactures tablet computers. Assume Smart Touch Learning determines the current market price is $500 per tablet. Exhibit 25-3 shows the expected operating income for Smart Touch Learning for 2019 for 2,400 tablets.

Exhibit 25-3 | **Smart Touch Learning's Budgeted Income Statement**

SMART TOUCH LEARNING Budgeted Income Statement Year Ended December 31, 2019		
Net Sales Revenue		$ 1,200,000
Variable Costs:		
Manufacturing	$ 588,000	
Selling and Administrative	150,000	738,000
Contribution Margin		462,000
Fixed Costs:		
Manufacturing	110,000	
Selling and Administrative	116,000	226,000
Operating Income		$ 236,000

Because there is intense competition, Smart Touch Learning will emphasize a target-pricing approach. Assume the company's stockholders expect a 10% annual return on the company's assets (ROI). If the company has $2,500,000 average assets, the desired profit is $250,000 ($2,500,000 × 10%). The target full product cost at the current sales volume of 2,400 tablets is calculated as follows:

Revenue at market price	(2,400 tablets @ $500 each, from Exhibit 25-3)	$ 1,200,000
Less: Desired profit	(calculated above)	250,000
Target full product cost		$ 950,000

Once we know the target full product cost, we can analyze the fixed and variable cost components separately. Can Smart Touch Learning make and sell 2,400 tablets at a full product cost of $950,000? We know from Smart Touch Learning's contribution margin income statement (Exhibit 25-3) that the company's variable costs are $307.50 per unit ($738,000 / 2,400 tablets). This variable cost per unit includes both manufacturing costs and selling and administrative costs. We also know the company incurs $226,000 in fixed costs in its current relevant range. Again, some fixed costs stem from manufacturing and some from selling and administrative activities. *In setting regular sales prices, companies must cover **all** of their costs—whether the costs are product or period, fixed or variable.*

Making and selling 2,400 tablets currently cost the company $964,000 [(2,400 units × $307.50 variable cost per unit) + $226,000 of fixed costs], which is $14,000 more than the target full product cost of $950,000. What options does Smart Touch Learning have?

1. Accept the lower operating income of $236,000, which is a 9.44% return on investment ($236,000 operating income / $2,500,000 average assets), not the 10% target return required by stockholders.
2. Reduce fixed costs by $14,000 or more.
3. Reduce variable costs by $14,000 or more.
4. Attempt to increase sales volume. If the company has excess manufacturing capacity, making and selling more units would only affect variable costs; however, it would mean that current fixed costs are spread over more units. Therefore, total cost per unit would decrease and profits would increase.

5. Change or add to its product mix (covered later in this chapter).
6. Attempt to differentiate its tablet computer from the competition to gain more control over sales prices (become a price-setter).
7. A combination of the above strategies that would increase revenues and/or decrease costs by $14,000.

Smart Touch Learning's managers can use cost-volume-profit (CVP) analysis, as you learned in a previous chapter, to determine how many tablets the company would have to sell to achieve its target profit. The company would have to consider how to increase demand for the tablets and the additional costs that would be incurred, such as advertising costs. Managers do not have an easy task when the current cost exceeds the target full product cost. Sometimes companies just cannot compete given the current market price. If that is the case, they may have no other choice than to quit making that product. (This decision is also covered later in the chapter.)

Cost-Plus Pricing

Cost-Plus Pricing
A method to manage costs and profits by determining the price. Full product cost + Desired profit = Cost-plus price.

When a company is a price-setter, it emphasizes a cost-plus approach to pricing. This pricing approach is essentially the *opposite* of the target-pricing approach. **Cost-plus pricing** starts with the company's full product costs (as a given) and *adds* its desired profit to determine a cost-plus price.

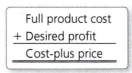

Full product cost
+ Desired profit
Cost-plus price

As you can see, it is the basic profit calculation rearranged to solve for the revenue figure—price.

When the product is unique, the company has more control over pricing—but the company still needs to make sure that the cost-plus price is not higher than what customers are willing to pay. Let's go back to our Smart Touch Learning example. This time, assume the tablet computers benefit from brand recognition due to the company's preloaded e-learning software so the company has some control over the price it charges for its tablets. Using a cost-plus pricing approach, assuming the current level of sales, and a desired profit of 10% of average assets, the cost-plus price is $506, calculated as follows:

Current variable costs	($307.50 per tablet × 2,400 tablets)	$ 738,000
Plus: Fixed costs		226,000
Full product cost		964,000
Plus: Desired profit	(10% × $2,500,000 average assets)	250,000
Target revenue		$ 1,214,000
Divided by number of tablets		÷ 2,400 units
Cost-plus price per tablet		$ 506 per unit*

*rounded

If the current market price for generic tablet computers is $500, as we assumed earlier, can Smart Touch Learning sell its brand-name tablet computers for $506 or more? Probably. The answer depends on how well the company has been able to differentiate its product or brand name. The company may use focus groups or marketing surveys to find out how customers would respond to its cost-plus price. The company may find out that its cost-plus price is too high, or it may find that it could set the price even higher without losing sales.

Notice how pricing decisions (1) focus on relevant information and (2) use a contribution margin approach that separates variable costs from fixed costs—our two keys to decision making. In pricing decisions, all cost information is relevant because the company must cover *all* costs along the value chain before it can generate a profit. However, we still need to consider variable costs and fixed costs separately because they behave differently at different volumes.

To maximize the effectiveness of pricing decisions, our pricing decision rule is as follows:

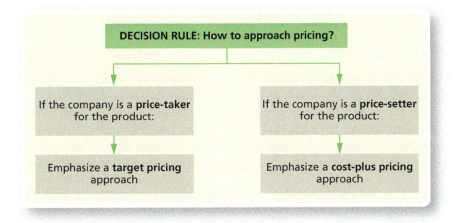

Special Pricing

A special pricing decision occurs when a customer requests a one-time order at a *reduced* sales price. Before agreeing to the special deal, management must consider the following questions:

- Does the company have the excess capacity available to fill the order?
- Will the reduced sales price be high enough to cover the *differential* costs of filling the order?
- Will the special order affect regular sales in the long run?

First, managers must consider available manufacturing capacity. If the company is already using all its existing manufacturing capacity and selling all units made at its *regular* sales price, it would not be as profitable to fill a special order at a *reduced* sales price. Therefore, available excess capacity is a necessity for accepting a special order. This is true for service firms as well as manufacturers.

Second, managers need to consider whether the special reduced sales price is high enough to cover the *differential* costs of filling the special order. Differential costs are the costs that are different if the alternative is chosen. The special price *must* be greater than the variable costs of filling the order or the company will incur a loss on the deal. In other words, the special order must provide a *positive* contribution margin.

Additionally, the company must consider differential fixed costs. If the company has excess capacity, fixed costs probably will not be affected by producing more units (or delivering more service). However, in some cases, management may have to incur some other fixed costs to fill the special order, such as additional insurance premiums or the purchase of special equipment. If so, they need to consider whether the special order sales price is high enough to generate a positive contribution margin *and* cover the additional fixed costs.

Finally, managers need to consider whether the special order will affect regular sales in the long run. Will regular customers find out about the special order and demand a lower price? Will the special order customer come back *again and again*, asking for the same reduced price? Will the special order price start a price war with competitors? Managers should determine the answers to these questions and consider how customers will respond. Managers may decide that any profit from the special sales order is not worth these risks.

Let's consider a special pricing example. Smart Touch Learning normally sells its tablet computers for $500 each. Assume that a company has offered Smart Touch Learning $68,750 for 250 tablets, or $275 per tablet. The special pricing requested is substantially less than the regular sales price. Additional information about this sale includes:

- Production will use manufacturing capacity that would otherwise be idle (excess capacity).
- No change in fixed costs.
- No additional variable *nonmanufacturing* expenses (because no extra selling or administrative costs are incurred with this special order).
- No effect on regular sales.

We have addressed every consideration except one: Is the special sales price high enough to cover the variable *manufacturing* costs associated with the order?

Suppose Smart Touch Learning expects to make and sell 2,400 tablets before considering the special order. Exhibit 25-4 shows Smart Touch Learning's budgeted income statement using the traditional income statement on the left side of Exhibit 25-4 and the contribution margin income statement on the right (as previously shown in Exhibit 25-3).

Exhibit 25-4 | **Smart Touch Learning's Budgeted Income Statement—Traditional and Contribution Margin Formats**

SMART TOUCH LEARNING						
Budgeted Income Statement						
Year Ended December 31, 2019						
Traditional Format			**Contribution Margin Format**			
Net Sales Revenue		$ 1,200,000	Net Sales Revenue			$ 1,200,000
Cost of Goods Sold		698,000	Variable Costs:			
Gross Profit		502,000	Manufacturing		$ 588,000	
Selling and Administrative Expenses		266,000	Selling & Administrative		150,000	738,000
Operating Income		$ 236,000	Contribution Margin			462,000
			Fixed Costs:			
			Manufacturing		110,000	
			Selling & Administrative		116,000	226,000
			Operating Income			$ 236,000

The traditional format income statement shows product cost of $290.83 per tablet ($698,000 COGS / 2,400 tablets = $290.83 per tablet, rounded). A manager who does not examine these numbers carefully may believe that Smart Touch Learning should *not* accept the special order at a sales price of $275.00 because each tablet costs $290.83 to manufacture. But appearances can be deceiving! Recall that the manufacturing cost per unit for the tablet is a *mixed* cost, containing both fixed and variable cost components. To correctly answer our question, we need to find only the *variable* portion of the manufacturing unit cost. This requires the manager to focus on the relevant data and use a contribution margin approach that separates variable costs from fixed costs.

The right side of Exhibit 25-4 shows the contribution margin income statement that separates variable expenses from fixed expenses. The contribution margin income statement allows us to see that the *variable* manufacturing cost per tablet is only $245 ($588,000 / 2,400 tablets = $245 per tablet). The special sales price of $275 per tablet is *higher* than the variable manufacturing cost of $245. Therefore, the special order will provide a positive contribution margin of $30 per tablet ($275 − $245). Because the special order is for 250 tablets, Smart Touch Learning's total contribution margin should increase by $7,500 (250 tablets × $30 per tablet) if it accepts this order.

Using a differential analysis approach, Smart Touch Learning compares the additional revenues from the special order with the additional expenses to see if the special order will contribute to profits. These are the amounts that will be different if the order is accepted. Exhibit 25-5 shows that the special sales order will increase revenue by $68,750 (250 tablets × $275) but will also increase variable manufacturing costs by $61,250 (250 tablets × $245). As a result, Smart Touch Learning's contribution margin will increase by $7,500, as previously shown. The other costs shown in Exhibit 25-4 are not relevant to the decision. Variable selling and administrative expenses will be the same whether or not Smart Touch Learning accepts the special order because Smart Touch Learning made no special efforts to acquire this sale. Fixed manufacturing costs will not change because Smart Touch Learning has enough idle capacity to produce 250 extra tablets without needing additional facilities. Fixed selling and administrative expenses will not be affected by this special order, either. Because there are no additional fixed costs, the total increase in contribution margin flows directly to operating income. As a result, the special sales order will increase operating income by $7,500.

Exhibit 25-5 | **Differential Analysis of Special Pricing Decision**

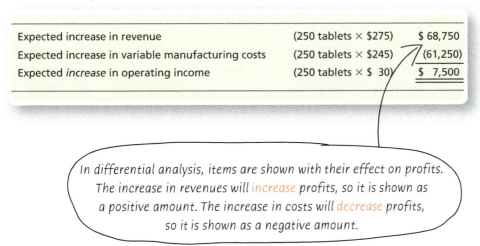

Expected increase in revenue	(250 tablets × $275)	$ 68,750
Expected increase in variable manufacturing costs	(250 tablets × $245)	(61,250)
Expected *increase* in operating income	(250 tablets × $ 30)	$ 7,500

In differential analysis, items are shown with their effect on profits. The increase in revenues will *increase* profits, so it is shown as a positive amount. The increase in costs will *decrease* profits, so it is shown as a negative amount.

Notice that the analysis follows the two keys to making short-term business decisions discussed earlier: (1) Focus on relevant data (revenues and costs that *will change* if Smart Touch Learning accepts the special order) and (2) use of a contribution margin approach that separates variable costs from fixed costs.

To summarize, for special pricing decisions, the decision rule is as follows:

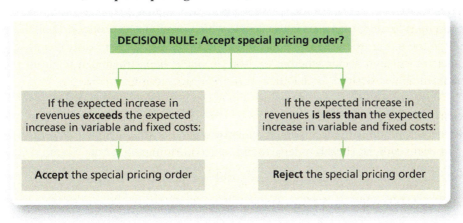

DECISION RULE: Accept special pricing order?

If the expected increase in revenues **exceeds** the expected increase in variable and fixed costs:	If the expected increase in revenues **is less than** the expected increase in variable and fixed costs:
Accept the special pricing order	**Reject** the special pricing order

DECISIONS

Should we accept this order?

Jeff Sylvester is a sales representative for Angelfish to Zebras, a manufacturer of stuffed animals. The company sells the stuffed animals to retailers, such as department stores and toy stores. Jeff enjoys his job—he's a good salesman, and he likes selling a product that makes children happy. Jeff recently received a request from a new customer for a special promotion. The store wants Angelfish to Zebras to manufacture a teddy bear wearing a shirt with the store's logo. The store will sell the bears only during a three-week period coinciding with the store's 25th anniversary and will provide the shirts. The store has asked for a special price on the bears, 20% less than Angelfish to Zebras's regular price. The store has justified its request by stating it is a one-time deal because the store does not usually sell stuffed animals and Angelfish to Zebras will not incur any selling costs. Jeff needs to decide whether to accept the sales order. The bears would be made during the company's slow period, after the rush of the holiday season, so capacity is not a problem. Should Jeff accept the order?

Solution

Based on the information given, it appears fixed costs would not change if the order is accepted because the order is for a current product and the manufacturing facility has excess capacity. Additionally, there would be no change in selling and administrative costs. Therefore, the only differential costs would be the variable manufacturing costs. If the reduced sales price is greater than the variable manufacturing costs, then Jeff should accept the order.

Alternative Solution

The marketing manager may have another perspective. The company should carefully consider its existing customers. What if Angelfish to Zebras's other customers find out about the deal? Would they expect the same low sales price? If so, can the company afford to sell to regular customers at such a low price? These questions should be answered before a final decision is made.

Thomas Company makes a product that regularly sells for $12.50 per unit. The product has variable manufacturing costs of $8.50 per unit and fixed manufacturing costs of $2.00 per unit (based on $200,000 total fixed costs at current production of 100,000 units). Therefore, the total production cost is $10.50 per unit. Thomas Company receives an offer from Wesley Company to purchase 5,000 units for $9.00 each. Selling and administrative costs and future sales will not be affected by the sale, and Thomas does not expect any additional fixed costs.

7. If Thomas Company has excess capacity, should it accept the offer from Wesley? Show your calculations.
8. Does your answer change if Thomas Company is operating at capacity? Why or why not?

Check your answers online in MyAccountingLab or at http://www.pearsonhighered.com/Horngren.

For more practice, see Short Exercises S25-2 and S25-3. MyAccountingLab

HOW DO MANAGERS DECIDE WHICH PRODUCTS TO PRODUCE AND SELL?

Learning Objective 3

Make decisions about dropping a product, product mix, and sales mix

Deciding which products to produce and sell is a major managerial decision. If manufacturing capacity is limited, managers must decide which products to produce. If shelf space is limited in the stores, then managers must decide which products to display and sell. Also, managers must often decide whether to drop products, departments, or territories that are not as profitable as desired. Let's look at how these decisions are made.

Dropping Unprofitable Products and Segments

Some of the questions managers must consider when deciding whether to drop a product or a business segment, such as a department or territory, include:

• Does the product or segment provide a positive contribution margin?

• Will fixed costs continue to exist, even if the company drops the product or segment?

- Are there any direct fixed costs that can be avoided if the company drops the product or segment?
- Will dropping the product or segment affect sales of the company's other products?
- What would the company do with the freed manufacturing capacity or store space?

Once again, we follow the two key guidelines for short-term business decisions: (1) Focus on relevant data and (2) use a contribution margin approach. The relevant financial data are still the changes in revenues and expenses, but now we are considering a *decrease* in volume rather than an *increase*, as we did in the special pricing decision. In the following example, we consider how managers decide to drop a product. Managers would use the same process in deciding whether to drop a business segment, such as a department or territory.

Earlier, we focused on one of Smart Touch Learning's products—the Standard Tablet. Now we focus on two of its products—the Standard Tablet and the Premium Tablet. Exhibit 25-6 shows the company's budgeted contribution margin income statement by product, assuming fixed costs are shared by both products. The middle column shows the income for the Standard Tablets, as previously shown in Exhibit 25-4. Because the Premium Tablet product line, as shown in the third column, has an operating *loss* of $5,000, management is considering dropping the product.

Exhibit 25-6 | **Budgeted Income Statement by Product**

	Total	Standard Tablets	Premium Tablets
SMART TOUCH LEARNING Budgeted Income Statement Year Ended December 31, 2019			
Net Sales Revenue	$ 1,430,000	$ 1,200,000	$ 230,000
Variable Costs:			
Manufacturing	706,000	588,000	118,000
Selling & Administrative	172,000	150,000	22,000
Total Variable Costs	878,000	738,000	140,000
Contribution Margin	552,000	462,000	90,000
Fixed Costs:			
Manufacturing	180,000	110,000	70,000
Selling & Administrative	141,000	116,000	25,000
Total Fixed Costs	321,000	226,000	95,000
Operating Income (Loss)	$ 231,000	$ 236,000	$ (5,000)

The first question management should ask is "Does the product provide a positive contribution margin?" If the product has a negative contribution margin, then the product is not even covering its variable costs. Therefore, the company should drop the product. However, if the product has a positive contribution margin, then it is *helping* to cover some of the company's fixed costs. In Smart Touch Learning's case, the Premium Tablets provide a positive contribution margin of $90,000. Smart Touch Learning's managers now need to consider fixed costs.

The Effect of Fixed Costs

Smart Touch Learning could allocate fixed costs in many different ways, and each way would allocate a different amount of fixed costs to each product. For example, fixed costs could be allocated using a traditional method with direct labor hours as the allocation base, by using activity-based costing, or by using some other method. However, in the short term, many fixed costs remain unchanged in total regardless of how they are allocated to products or other cost objects. Therefore, allocated fixed costs are *irrelevant* except for any amounts that will change because of the decision that is made. What is relevant are the following:

1. Will the fixed costs continue to exist *even if* the product is dropped?
2. Are there any *direct* fixed costs of the Premium Tablets that can be avoided if the product is dropped?

Let's consider various assumptions when dropping products.

Fixed Costs Will Continue to Exist and Will Not Change Fixed costs that will continue to exist even after a product is dropped are often called *unavoidable* fixed costs. Unavoidable fixed costs are *irrelevant* to the decision because they *will not change* if the company drops the product. Let's assume that all of Smart Touch Learning's total fixed costs of $321,000 will continue to exist even if the company drops the Premium Tablets. Also assume that Smart Touch Learning makes the Premium Tablets in the same plant using the same machinery as the Standard Tablets. Thus, only the contribution margin the Premium Tablets provide is relevant. If Smart Touch Learning drops the Premium Tablets, it will lose the $90,000 contribution margin.

The differential analysis shown in Exhibit 25-7 verifies the loss. If Smart Touch Learning drops the Premium Tablets, revenue will decrease by $230,000, but variable expenses will decrease by only $140,000, resulting in a net $90,000 decrease in operating income. Because fixed costs are unaffected, they are not included in the analysis. This analysis suggests that management should *not* drop Premium Tablets. It is actually more beneficial for Smart Touch Learning to lose $5,000 on the product line than to drop the Premium Tablets and lose $90,000 in total operating income.

Exhibit 25-7 | **Differential Analysis of Dropping a Product When Fixed Costs Will *Not* Change**

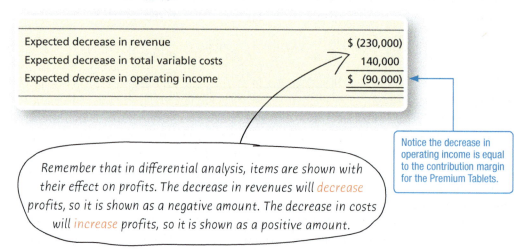

Expected decrease in revenue	$ (230,000)
Expected decrease in total variable costs	140,000
Expected *decrease* in operating income	$ (90,000)

Remember that in differential analysis, items are shown with their effect on profits. The decrease in revenues will *decrease* profits, so it is shown as a negative amount. The decrease in costs will *increase* profits, so it is shown as a positive amount.

Notice the decrease in operating income is equal to the contribution margin for the Premium Tablets.

Direct Fixed Costs Will Change In this scenario, instead assume Smart Touch Learning manufactures the Premium Tablets in a separate facility. If the product line is dropped, the lease on the facility can be terminated and the company will be able to avoid all fixed costs except $3,000. In this situation, $92,000 of the fixed costs belong *only* to the Premium

Tablet product line ($95,000 total fixed costs − $3,000 unavoidable fixed costs = $92,000 avoidable fixed costs). These would be direct fixed costs of the Premium Tablets only.[1] Therefore, $92,000 of fixed costs are avoidable fixed costs and *are relevant* to the decision because they would change (go away) if the product line were dropped.

Exhibit 25-8 shows that, in this situation, operating income will *increase* by $2,000 if Smart Touch Learning drops the Premium Tablets. Revenues will decline by $230,000, but expenses will decline even more—by $232,000. The result is a net increase to operating income of $2,000. This analysis suggests that management should drop the Premium Tablets.

Exhibit 25-8 | Differential Analysis of Dropping a Product When Fixed Costs *Will* Change

Expected decrease in revenue		$ (230,000)
Expected decrease in total variable costs	$ 140,000	
Expected decrease in fixed costs	92,000	
Expected decrease in total costs		232,000
Expected *increase* in operating income		$ 2,000

Other Considerations

Management must also consider whether dropping the product or segment would hurt other product sales. In the examples given so far, we assumed that dropping the Premium Tablets would not affect Smart Touch Learning's other product sales. However, think about a grocery store. Even if the produce department is not profitable, would managers drop it? Probably not, because if they did, they would lose customers who want one-stop shopping. In such situations, managers must also include the loss of contribution margin from *other* departments affected by the change when deciding whether to drop a department. Another example is a company that manufactures dining room tables and chairs. If the company dropped the tables, there would be a definite effect on chairs as most customers want to purchase chairs that match the table.

Management should also consider what it could do with freed manufacturing capacity. In the first Smart Touch Learning example, we assumed that the company produces both Standard Tablets and Premium Tablets using the same manufacturing equipment. If Smart Touch Learning drops the Premium Tablets, could it make and sell another product using the freed machine hours? Is product demand strong enough that Smart Touch Learning could make and sell more of the Standard Tablets? Managers should consider whether using the machinery to produce a different product or expanding existing product lines would be more profitable than using the machinery to produce Premium Tablets.

Short-term business decisions should take into account all costs affected by the choice of action. Managers must ask the following questions: What total costs—variable and fixed—will change? Are there additional environmental costs (for example, waste water disposal) that should be considered? As Exhibits 25-7 and 25-8 show, the key to deciding whether to drop products or segments is to compare the lost revenue against the costs that

---

[1]To aid in decision making, companies should separate direct fixed costs from indirect fixed costs on their contribution margin income statements. Companies should *assign direct fixed costs* to the appropriate product and *not allocate indirect fixed costs* among products.

can be saved and to consider what would be done with the freed capacity. The decision rule is as follows:

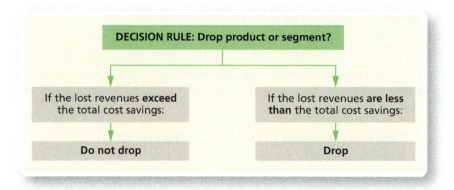

Product Mix

Constraint
A factor that restricts the production or sale of a product.

Companies do not have unlimited resources. **Constraints** that restrict the production or sale of a product vary from company to company. For a manufacturer like Smart Touch Learning, the production constraint may be labor hours, machine hours, or available materials. For a merchandiser, the primary constraint is display space. Other companies are constrained by sales demand. Competition may be stiff, and so the company may be able to sell only a limited number of units. In such cases, the company produces only as much as it can sell. However, if a company can sell all the units it can produce, which products should it emphasize? For which items should production be increased? Companies facing constraints consider the following questions:

- What constraints would stop the company from making (or displaying) all the units the company can sell?
- Which products offer the highest contribution margin per unit of the constraint?
- Would emphasizing one product over another affect fixed costs?

Let's return to our Smart Touch Learning example. Assume the company can sell all the Standard Tablets and Premium Tablets it produces, but it has only 19,500 machine hours of manufacturing capacity, and the company uses the same machines to make both types of tablets. In this case, machine hours are the constraint. The data in Exhibit 25-9 suggest that Premium Tablets are more profitable than Standard Tablets as the Premium Tablets have a higher contribution margin per unit and a higher contribution margin ratio.

Exhibit 25-9 | **Smart Touch Learning's Contribution Margin per Unit**

	Standard Tablet	Premium Tablet
Sales price per tablet	$ 500.00	$ 575.00
Variable costs per tablet	307.50	350.00
Contribution margin per tablet	$ 192.50	$ 225.00
Contribution margin ratio:		
Standard: $192.50 / $500.00	38.50%	
Premium: $225.00 / $575.00		39.13%*

*rounded

However, in order to determine which product to emphasize, we cannot make the decision based only on contribution margin per unit. Instead, we must determine which product has the highest contribution margin per unit of the constraint. To determine which product to emphasize, follow the decision rule:

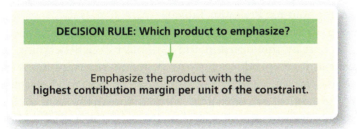

Because *machine hours* are the constraint, Smart Touch Learning needs to figure out which product has the *highest contribution margin per machine hour.* Assume that Standard Tablets require 7.5 machine hours to produce, and Premium Tablets require 10.0 machine hours to produce. Exhibit 25-10 illustrates the calculation for the contribution margin per machine hour for each product.

Exhibit 25-10 | **Smart Touch Learning's Contribution Margin per Machine Hour**

	Standard Tablet	Premium Tablet
(1) Hours required to produce one tablet	7.5000	10.0000
(2) Tablets produced per hour [1 hour / (1)]	0.1333*	0.1000
(3) Contribution margin per tablet	$ 192.50	$ 225.00
Contribution margin per machine hour [(2) × (3)]	$ 25.66*	$ 22.50

*rounded

Standard Tablets have a higher contribution margin per machine hour, $25.66, than Premium Tablets, $22.50. Smart Touch Learning will earn more profit by producing Standard Tablets. Why? Because even though Standard Tablets have a lower contribution margin per tablet, Smart Touch Learning can make more Standard Tablets than Premium Tablets in the 19,500 available machine hours and generate more total contribution margin. Exhibit 25-11 proves that Smart Touch Learning earns more total profit by making Standard Tablets. Multiplying the contribution margin per machine hour by the available number of machine hours shows that Smart Touch Learning can earn $500,370 of contribution margin by producing only Standard Tablets but only $438,750 by producing only Premium Tablets.

Exhibit 25-11 | **Total Contribution Margin with Machine Hour Constraint**

	Standard Tablet	Premium Tablet
Contribution margin per machine hour	$ 25.66*	$ 22.50
Available capacity—number of machine hours	× 19,500	× 19,500
Total contribution margin at full capacity	$ 500,370	$ 438,750

*rounded

To maximize profits, Smart Touch Learning should make 2,600 Standard Tablets (19,500 machine hours available / 7.5 machine hours required per Standard Tablet) and zero Premium Tablets. Smart Touch Learning should not make Premium Tablets because for every machine hour spent making Premium Tablets, Smart Touch Learning would give up $3.16 of contribution margin ($25.66 per machine hour for Standard Tablets versus $22.50 per machine hour for Premium Tablets).

We made two assumptions here: (1) Smart Touch Learning's sales of other products will not be hurt by this decision and (2) Smart Touch Learning can sell as many Standard Tablets as it can produce. Let's challenge these assumptions. First, how could making only Standard Tablets hurt sales of other products? The retailers who display Smart Touch Learning tablet computers in their stores may want a choice in products so customers can compare and choose the tablet that best suits their needs. If Smart Touch Learning produces only one type of tablet, retailers may be reluctant to display the brand. Sales of Standard Tablets might fall if Smart Touch Learning no longer offers Premium Tablets.

Let's challenge our second assumption. Smart Touch Learning had only budgeted sales of 2,400 Standard Tablets and has the capacity to produce 2,600 (19,500 machine hours available / 7.5 machine hours required per Standard Tablet). Suppose that a new competitor has decreased the demand for Smart Touch Learning's Standard Tablets and now the company expects to sell only 2,000 Standard Tablets. Smart Touch Learning should only make as many Standard Tablets as it can sell and use the remaining machine hours to produce Premium Tablets. How will this constraint in sales demand change profitability?

Recall from Exhibit 25-11 that Smart Touch Learning will make $500,370 of contribution margin by using all 19,500 machine hours to produce Standard Tablets. However, if Smart Touch Learning makes only 2,000 Standard Tablets, it will use only 15,000 machine hours (2,000 Standard Tablets × 7.5 machine hours required per Standard Tablet). That leaves 4,500 machine hours (19,500 machine hours − 15,000 machine hours) available for making Premium Tablets, which will allow the company to make 450 Premium Tablets (4,500 machine hours / 10.0 machine hours required per Premium Tablet). Smart Touch Learning's new contribution margin will be $486,150, as shown in Exhibit 25-12.

Exhibit 25-12 | **Total Contribution Margin with Machine Hour Constraint and Limited Market**

	Standard Tablet	Premium Tablet	Total
Contribution margin per machine hour	$ 25.66*	$ 22.50	
Machine hours devoted to product	× 15,000	× 4,500	19,500
Total contribution margin at full capacity	$ 384,900	$ 101,250	$ 486,150

*rounded

Because of the change in product mix, Smart Touch Learning's total contribution margin will fall from $500,370 to $486,150, a $14,220 decrease. Smart Touch Learning had to give up $3.16 of contribution margin per machine hour ($25.66 − $22.50) on the 4,500 hours it spent producing Premium Tablets rather than Standard Tablets. However, Smart Touch Learning had no choice—the company would have incurred an *actual loss* from producing Standard Tablets that it could not sell. If Smart Touch Learning had produced 2,600 Standard Tablets but sold only 2,000, the company would have spent $184,500 to make the unsold tablets (600 Standard Tablets × $307.50 variable cost per Standard Tablet) yet received no sales revenue from them.

What about fixed costs? In most cases, changing the product mix emphasis in the short run will not affect fixed costs, so fixed costs are irrelevant. However, it is possible that fixed costs could differ by emphasizing a different product mix. What if Smart Touch Learning had a month-to-month lease on a production machine used only for making Premium Tablets? If Smart Touch Learning made only Standard Tablets, it could *avoid* the production equipment cost. However, if Smart Touch Learning makes any Premium Tablets, it needs the equipment. In this case, the fixed costs become relevant because they differ between alternative product mixes (Premium Tablets only versus Standard Tablets only versus both products).

Notice that the analysis again follows the two guidelines for short-term business decisions: (1) Focus on relevant data (only those revenues and costs that differ) and (2) use a contribution margin approach, which separates variable costs from fixed costs.

Sales Mix

The previous illustrations focused on production constraints for a manufacturing company. Merchandising companies also have constraints, with display space as the most common constraint. Merchandisers are constrained by the size of their stores, and managers must choose which products to display.

Because Smart Touch Learning's Standard and Premium Tablets require the same amount of shelf space, let's consider Bragg Company, a fictitious company that operates gift shops in airports. Airport gift shops are fairly small, and Bragg has only 48 linear feet of bookshelves in each store. The following chart shows the *average* sales price, cost of purchasing the books, which is a variable cost, and contribution margin for hardcover and paperback books:

	Hardcover Books	Paperback Books
Sales Price	$ 28.00	$ 12.00
Variable Cost	19.60	7.20
Contribution Margin	$ 8.40	$ 4.80

Fixed costs are not affected by the choice of products to display. Based only on this information, it is apparent that hardcover books have a higher contribution margin per unit and should be the product emphasized. However, managers also have to consider the constraint of limited shelf space. Management at Bragg has determined that each linear foot of bookshelves can display 10 hardcover books or 20 paperback books. Remember that the decision rule for constraints is to *emphasize the product with the highest contribution margin per unit of the constraint.* Exhibit 25-13 shows the total contribution margin with the display space constraint.

Exhibit 25-13 | **Total Contribution Margin with Display Space Constraint**

	Hardcover Books	Paperback Books
Contribution margin per book	$ 8.40	$ 4.80
Books per linear foot of display space	× 10	× 20
Total contribution margin per linear foot of display space	$ 84.00	$ 96.00

Bragg can generate more profits per foot of shelving if paperback books are displayed. Therefore, the company should emphasize paperback books. However, Bragg should also consider the market—what do airport shoppers want? Bragg can display twice as many paperback books than hardcover books. Will the increased variety of titles displayed increase sales and inventory turnover? Will it lose sales if only paper-back books are displayed? Other factors must also be considered when making sales mix decisions.

Try It!

McCollum Company manufactures two products. Both products have the same sales price, and the volume of sales is equivalent. However, due to the difference in production processes, Product A has higher variable costs and Product B has higher fixed costs. Management is considering dropping Product B because that product line has an operating loss.

McCOLLUM COMPANY Income Statement Month Ended June 30, 2018			
	Total	Product A	Product B
Net Sales Revenue	$ 150,000	$ 75,000	$ 75,000
Variable Costs	90,000	55,000	35,000
Contribution Margin	60,000	20,000	40,000
Fixed Costs	50,000	5,000	45,000
Operating Income/(Loss)	$ 10,000	$ 15,000	$ (5,000)

9. If fixed costs cannot be avoided, should McCollum drop Product B? Why or why not?
10. If 50% of Product B's fixed costs are avoidable, should McCollum drop Product B? Why or why not?

Check your answers online in MyAccountingLab or at http://www.pearsonhighered.com/Horngren.

For more practice, see Short Exercises S25-4 and S25-5. MyAccountingLab

HOW DO MANAGERS MAKE OUTSOURCING AND PROCESSING FURTHER DECISIONS?

Learning Objective 4

Make outsourcing and processing further decisions

Now let's consider some short-term management decisions regarding how products are produced, such as whether the company should outsource a component of the finished product or sell a product as it is or process it further.

Outsourcing

Many companies choose to outsource products or services. For example, a hotel chain may outsource its reservation system. This allows the company to concentrate on its primary function—serving the needs of its guests—rather than purchasing and operating an extensive computerized reservation system. By outsourcing, the hotel chain is taking advantage of another company's expertise, which allows it to focus on its core business functions. Outsourcing decisions are often called *make-or-buy decisions* because managers must decide whether to buy a component product or service or produce it in-house. The heart of these decisions is *how best to use available resources.*

Smart Touch Learning is deciding whether to make the casings for its tablet computers in-house or to outsource them to Crump Casings, a company that specializes in producing casings for computers, cell phones, and other electronic products. Smart Touch Learning's cost to produce 2,400 casings is as follows:

Direct materials	$ 15,600
Direct labor	7,200
Variable manufacturing overhead	13,200
Fixed manufacturing overhead	19,200
Total manufacturing cost	$ 55,200
Number of casings	÷ 2,400
Cost per casing	$ 23

Crump Casings offers to sell Smart Touch Learning the casings for $21 each. Should Smart Touch Learning make the casings or buy them from Crump Casings? Smart Touch Learning's $23 cost per unit to make the casing is $2 higher than the cost of buying it from Crump Casings. Initially, it seems that Smart Touch Learning should outsource the casings, but the correct answer is not so simple because manufacturing costs per unit contain both fixed and variable components. In deciding whether to outsource, managers must assess fixed and variable costs separately. Some of the questions managers must consider when deciding whether to outsource include:

- How do the company's variable costs compare with the outsourcing costs?
- Are any fixed costs avoidable if the company outsources?
- What could the company do with the freed manufacturing capacity?

How do these considerations apply to Smart Touch Learning? By purchasing the casings, Smart Touch Learning can avoid all variable manufacturing costs—$15,600 of direct materials, $7,200 of direct labor, and $13,200 of variable manufacturing overhead. In total, the company will save $36,000 in variable manufacturing costs, or $15 per casing ($36,000 / 2,400 casings). However, Smart Touch Learning will have to pay the variable outsourcing cost of $21 per unit, or $50,400 for the 2,400 casings. Based only on variable costs, the lower cost alternative is to manufacture the casings in-house. However, managers must still consider fixed costs.

Assume, first, that Smart Touch Learning cannot avoid any of the fixed costs by outsourcing. In this case, the company's fixed costs are irrelevant to the decision because Smart Touch Learning would continue to incur $19,200 of fixed costs either way (the fixed costs do not differ between alternatives). Smart Touch Learning should continue to make its own casings because the variable cost of outsourcing the casings, $50,400, exceeds the variable cost of making the casings, $36,000. Exhibit 25-14 (on the next page) shows the differential analysis for the outsourcing decision.

Exhibit 25-14 | **Differential Analysis for Outsourcing Decision When Fixed Costs Will *Not* Change**

Casing Costs	Make Casings	Outsource Casings	Difference (Make – Outsource)
Variable costs:			
Direct materials	$ 15,600		$ 15,600
Direct labor	7,200		7,200
Variable manufacturing overhead	13,200		13,200
Purchase cost ($21 × 2,400 casings)		$ 50,400	(50,400)
Total differential cost of casings	$ 36,000	$ 50,400	$ (14,400)

The Difference column shows the effect on profits. If Smart Touch Learning buys the casings, it will save (not spend, avoid) the variable manufacturing costs. If the company saves costs, that will increase profits, so the difference is shown as a positive amount. The amount spent to buy the casings is a cost that will decrease profits, so it is shown as a negative amount.

However, what if Smart Touch Learning can avoid some fixed costs by outsourcing the casings? Assume that management can reduce fixed overhead cost by $12,000 by outsourcing the casings. Smart Touch Learning will still incur $7,200 of fixed overhead ($19,200 − $12,000) if it outsources the casings. In this case, fixed costs become relevant to the decision because they differ between alternatives. Exhibit 25-15 shows the differential analysis when fixed costs will change.

Exhibit 25-15 | **Differential Analysis for Outsourcing Decision When Fixed Costs *Will* Change**

Casing Costs	Make Casings	Outsource Casings	Difference (Make – Outsource)
Variable costs:			
Direct materials	$ 15,600		$ 15,600
Direct labor	7,200		7,200
Variable manufacturing overhead	13,200		13,200
Fixed manufacturing overhead costs	12,000		12,000
Purchase cost ($21 × 2,400 casings)		$ 50,400	(50,400)
Total differential cost of casings	$ 48,000	$ 50,400	$ (2,400)

Another way to think about it: Should Smart Touch Learning spend $50,400 in order to save $48,000? Absolutely not!

Exhibit 25-15 shows that even with the $12,000 reduction in fixed costs, it would still cost Smart Touch Learning less to make the casings than to buy them from Crump Casings. The net savings from making the casings is $2,400. Exhibit 25-15 also shows that outsourcing decisions follow our two key guidelines for short-term business decisions: (1) Focus on relevant data (differences in costs in this case) and (2) use a contribution margin approach that separates variable costs from fixed costs.

Note how the unit cost—which does *not* separate costs according to behavior—can be deceiving. If Smart Touch Learning's managers made their decision by comparing the total manufacturing cost per casing ($23) to the outsourcing unit cost per casing ($21), they would have incorrectly decided to outsource. Recall that the manufacturing unit cost ($23) contains both fixed and variable components, whereas the outsourcing cost ($21) is strictly variable. To make the correct decision, Smart Touch Learning had to separate the two cost components and analyze them separately.

Our decision rule for outsourcing is as follows:

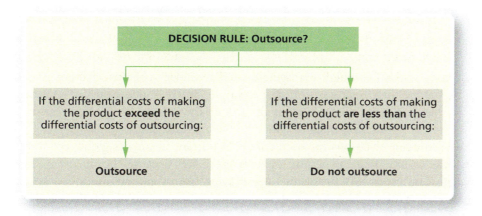

We have not considered what Smart Touch Learning could do with the freed manufacturing capacity it would have if it outsourced the casings. The analysis in Exhibit 25-15 assumes there is no other use for the production facilities if Smart Touch Learning buys the casings from Crump Casings. But suppose Smart Touch Learning has an opportunity to use its freed-up facilities to make another product, which has an expected profit of $30,000. Now, Smart Touch Learning must consider its **opportunity cost**—the benefit given up by choosing an alternative course of action. In this case, Smart Touch Learning's opportunity cost of making the casings is the $30,000 profit it gives up if it does not free its production facilities to make the new product.

Smart Touch Learning's managers must now consider three alternatives:

1. Use the facilities to make the casings.
2. Buy the casings and leave facilities idle (continue to assume $12,000 of avoidable fixed costs from outsourcing casings).
3. Buy the casings and use facilities to make the new product (continue to assume $12,000 of avoidable fixed costs from outsourcing casings).

The alternative with the lowest *net* cost is the best use of Smart Touch Learning's facilities. Exhibit 25-16 (on the next page) compares the three alternatives.

In this scenario, Smart Touch Learning should buy the casings from Crump Casings and use the freed manufacturing capacity to make the new product. If Smart Touch Learning makes the casings or if it buys the casings from Crump Casings but leaves its production facilities idle, it will give up the opportunity to earn an additional $30,000.

Opportunity Cost
The benefit given up by choosing an alternative course of action.

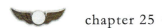

Exhibit 25-16 | **Differential Analysis for Outsourcing Decision When Fixed Costs *Will* Change and Opportunity Cost Exists**

	Make Casings	Outsource Casings	
		Facilities Idle	Make New Product
Expected cost of 2,400 casings (from Exhibit 25-15)	$ 48,000	$ 50,400	$ 50,400
Expected *profit* from new product			(30,000)
Expected *net cost* of obtaining 2,400 casings	$ 48,000	$ 50,400	$ 20,400

This analysis shows the net cost of the three alternatives. The $30,000 of expected profit from using the freed manufacturing space will increase overall profits if the company chooses to buy the casings, thereby decreasing net costs.

Smart Touch Learning's managers should consider qualitative factors as well as net cost in making their final decision. For example, Smart Touch Learning's managers may believe they can better control quality by making the casings themselves. This is an argument for Smart Touch Learning to continue making the casings.

Outsourcing decisions are increasingly important in today's global economy. In the past, make-or-buy decisions often ended up as "make" because coordination, information exchange, and paperwork problems made buying from suppliers too inconvenient. Now, companies can use the Internet to tap into information systems of suppliers and customers located around the world. Paperwork vanishes, and the information required to satisfy the strictest JIT delivery schedule is available in real time. As a result, companies are focusing on their core competencies and are outsourcing more functions.

TYING IT ALL TOGETHER

The Boeing Company is one of the world's major aerospace firms and operates under five principal segments: Commercial Airplanes, Boeing Military Aircraft, Network & Space Systems, Global Services & Support, and Boeing Capital. In the company's financial statements, Boeing states that many of its major components and product equipment items are subcontracted with a number of companies.

Why do companies, such as Boeing, choose to outsource some its components?

Companies, such as Boeing, choose to outsource because it can result in lower product costs and allows the company to focus on its core business processes. In addition, outsourcing enables companies to tap into global knowledge and frees up internal resources that could be used for other purposes. Sometimes

companies choose to outsource to gain access to resources not available internally. Outsourcing also can help companies expand and gain access to new territories.

Are there disadvantages to outsourcing?

As we discussed in the chapter opener, there can be significant disadvantages to outsourcing. One disadvantage might be the risk associated with having a third-party manufacturer produce substandard components. Another risk might be the loss of control over the manufacturing process, such as where the product is made. There could also be a concern with being able to meet commitments to customers if a subcontractor experiences delays or other performance problems. Sometimes the decision to outsource can bring about negative publicity and negatively impact employee morale.

Sell or Process Further

At what point in processing should a company sell its product? Many companies, especially in the food processing and natural resource industries, face this business decision. Companies in these industries process a raw material (milk, corn, livestock, crude oil, and lumber, to name a few) to a point before it is saleable. For example, a dairy processor pasteurizes raw milk before it is saleable. The company must then decide whether it should sell the pasteurized milk as is or process it further into other dairy products, such as reduced-fat milk, butter, sour cream, cheese, and other dairy products. Some questions managers consider when deciding whether to sell as is or process further include:

- How much revenue will the company receive if it sells the product as is?
- How much revenue will the company receive if it sells the product after processing it further?
- How much will it cost to process the product further?

Consider one of Smart Touch Learning's sell or process further decisions. Suppose Smart Touch Learning can sell its tablet computers as is or add front-accessible USB ports to the tablets. The cost to add the USB ports is $5. This cost includes the cost of the modified casing, the USB component, and the labor to add the component. This feature is very popular with customers, and tablets with this feature sell for $20 more than tablets without the feature. Exhibit 25-17 shows the differential analysis for this decision.

Exhibit 25-17 | **Differential Analysis for Sell or Process Further Decision**

		Sell	Process Further	Difference
Expected revenue from selling	(2,400 tablets × $500 each)	$ 1,200,000		
Expected revenue from selling	(2,400 tablets × $520 each)		$ 1,248,000	$ 48,000
Additional costs of processing	(2,400 tablets × $5 each)		(12,000)	(12,000)
Total net revenue		$ 1,200,000	$ 1,236,000	$ 36,000

Notice that Smart Touch Learning's managers do *not* consider the other costs incurred in producing the tablets, $964,000 as shown in Exhibit 25-3 ($738,000 variable costs + $226,000 fixed costs). These costs are **joint costs**—costs of a production process that yields multiple products. (In this case, the multiple products are the tablets without the feature and the tablets with the feature.) Joint costs are *sunk* costs. Recall from our previous discussion that a sunk cost is a past cost that cannot be changed regardless of which future action the company takes. Smart Touch Learning has incurred the joint costs, regardless of whether it sells the tablets as is or processes them further by adding the front-accessible USB ports. Therefore, the joint costs are *not* relevant to the decision. Exhibit 25-18 illustrates joint costs.

Joint Cost
A cost of a production process that yields multiple products.

Exhibit 25-18 | **Joint Costs**

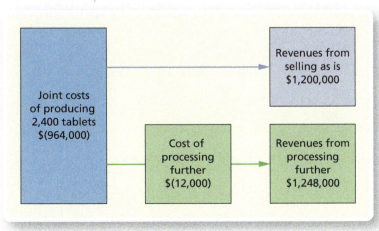

By analyzing only the relevant costs in Exhibit 25-17, managers see that they can increase profit by $36,000 if they add the USB ports. The $48,000 additional revenue ($1,248,000 − $1,200,000) outweighs the additional $12,000 cost of the extra processing. Thus, the decision rule is as follows:

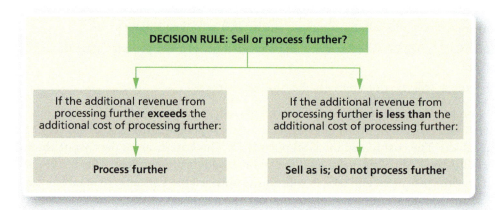

Recall that our keys to decision making include: (1) Focusing on relevant information and (2) using a contribution margin approach that separates variable costs from fixed costs. The analysis in Exhibit 25-17 includes only those *future* costs and revenues that *differ* between alternatives. We assumed Smart Touch Learning already has the equipment and labor necessary to add the additional feature to the tablets. Because fixed costs would not differ between alternatives, they were irrelevant. However, if Smart Touch Learning has to acquire equipment to add the feature, the extra fixed costs would be relevant. Once again, we see that fixed costs are relevant only if they *differ* between alternatives.

Try It!

Grimm Company makes decorative wedding cakes. The company is considering buying the cakes rather than baking them, which will allow it to concentrate on decorating. The company averages 100 wedding cakes per year and incurs the following costs from baking wedding cakes:

Direct materials	$ 500
Direct labor	1,000
Variable manufacturing overhead	200
Fixed manufacturing overhead	1,200
Total manufacturing cost	$ 2,900
Number of cakes	÷ 100
Cost per cake	$ 29

Fixed costs are primarily the depreciation on kitchen equipment such as ovens and mixers. Grimm expects to retain the equipment. Grimm can buy the cakes for **$25**.

11. Should Grimm make the cakes or buy them? Why?

12. If Grimm decides to buy the cakes, what are some qualitative factors that Grimm should also consider?

Check your answers online in MyAccountingLab or at http://www.pearsonhighered.com/Horngren.

For more practice, see Short Exercises S25-6 through S25-8. MyAccountingLab

REVIEW

> Things You Should Know

1. How is relevant information used to make short-term decisions?

- Decision making is a four-step process:
  - Define business goals.
  - Identify alternative courses of action.
  - Gather and analyze relevant information; compare alternatives.
  - Choose the best alternative.
- Relevant information is expected *future* data that *differ* among alternatives.
- Sunk costs occurred in the past and cannot be changed; therefore, they are irrelevant in making decisions.
- Qualitative factors are nonfinancial and can also be relevant.
- Differential analysis emphasizes the differences in operating income under each alternative.
- Two keys in analyzing short-term business decisions are:
  - Focus on relevant revenues, costs, and profits.
  - Use a contribution margin approach that separates variable costs from fixed costs.

2. How does pricing affect short-term decisions?

- When setting *regular* prices, managers should consider the following:
  - What is the company's target profit?
  - How much will customers pay?
  - Is the company a price-taker or a price-setter for this product or service?
- Price-takers have little control over the prices of their products and services because they are not unique or competition is intense.
  - Price-takers must "take" the market price.
  - The pricing approach emphasizes target pricing where:

    Revenue at market price − Desired profit = Target full product cost.
- Price-setters have more control over the prices of their products because they are unique and there is little competition.
  - Price-setters can "set" the market price.
  - The pricing approach emphasizes cost-plus pricing where:

    Full product cost + Desired profit = Cost-plus price.
- When considering special orders at reduced prices, managers should consider the following:
  - Does the company have the excess capacity available to fill the order?
  - Will the reduced sales price be high enough to cover the *differential* costs of filling the order?
  - Will the special order affect regular sales in the long run?

- Remember the special pricing decision rule:
  - If the expected increase in revenues *exceeds* the expected increase in variable and fixed costs, *accept* the special pricing order.
  - If the expected increase in revenues *is less than* the expected increase in variable and fixed costs, *reject* the special pricing order.

3. How do managers decide which products to produce and sell?

- When deciding whether to drop a product or a business segment, such as a department or territory, questions managers should answer include the following:
  - Does the product or segment provide a positive contribution margin?
  - Will fixed costs continue to exist even if the company drops the product or segment?
  - Are there any direct fixed costs that can be avoided if the company drops the product or segment?
  - Will dropping the product or segment affect sales of the company's other products?
  - What would the company do with the freed manufacturing capacity or store space?
- Remember the decision rule for dropping a product or segment:
  - If the lost revenues *exceed* the total cost savings, *do not drop* the product or segment.
  - If the lost revenues *are less than* the total cost savings, *drop* the product or segment.
- Companies facing constraints consider the following questions:
  - What constraint(s) stop(s) the company from making (or displaying) all the units the company can sell?
  - Which products offer the highest contribution margin per unit of the constraint?
  - Would emphasizing one product over another affect fixed costs?
- Remember the decision rule for which product to emphasize: Emphasize the product with the highest contribution margin per unit of the constraint.
- For merchandising companies, display space is often the most common constraint.

4. How do managers make outsourcing and processing further decisions?

- Some of the questions managers must consider when deciding whether to outsource include the following:
  - How do the company's variable costs compare with the outsourcing costs?
  - Are any fixed costs avoidable if the company outsources?
  - What could the company do with the freed manufacturing capacity?
- Remember the outsourcing decision rule:
  - If the differential costs of making the product *exceed* the differential costs of outsourcing, *outsource*.
  - If the differential costs of making the product *are less than* the differential costs of outsourcing, *do not outsource*.

- Some questions managers consider when deciding whether to sell as is or process further include:

  - How much revenue will the company receive if it sells the product as is?
  - How much revenue will the company receive if it sells the product after processing it further?
  - How much will it cost to process the product further?

- Joint costs, the cost of production that yields multiple products, are sunk costs and, therefore, are not relevant to the decision of processing further.

- Remember the sell or process further decision rule:

  - If the additional revenue from processing further *exceeds* the additional cost of processing further, *process further.*
  - If the additional revenue from processing further *is less than* the additional cost of processing further, *sell—do not process further.*

> Check Your Understanding 25-1

Check your understanding of the chapter by completing this problem and then looking at the solution. Use this practice to help identify which sections of the chapter you need to study more.

MC Alexander Industries makes tennis balls. Its only plant can produce as many as 2,500,000 cans of tennis balls per year. Current production is 2,000,000 cans. Annual manufacturing, selling, and administrative fixed costs total $700,000. The variable cost of making and selling each can of tennis balls is $1.00. Stockholders expect a 12% annual return on the company's $3,000,000 of assets.

Requirements

1. What is MC Alexander's current full product cost of making and selling 2,000,000 cans of tennis balls? What is the current full *unit* product cost of each can of tennis balls? (See Learning Objective 2)

2. Assume MC Alexander is a price-taker, and the current market price is $1.45 per can of tennis balls (the price at which manufacturers sell to retailers). What is the *target* full product cost of producing and selling 2,000,000 cans of tennis balls? Given MC Alexander's current costs, will the company reach the stockholders' profit goals? (See Learning Objective 2)

3. If MC Alexander cannot change its fixed costs, what is the target variable cost per can of tennis balls? (See Learning Objective 2)

4. Suppose MC Alexander could spend an extra $100,000 on advertising to differentiate its product so that it could be a price-setter. Assuming the original volume and costs, plus the $100,000 of new advertising costs, what cost-plus price will MC Alexander want to charge for a can of tennis balls? (See Learning Objective 2)

5. Nelson, Inc. has just asked MC Alexander to supply the company with 400,000 cans of tennis balls at a special order price of $1.20 per can. Nelson wants MC Alexander to package the tennis balls under the Nelson label (MC Alexander will imprint the Nelson logo on each tennis ball and can). MC Alexander will have to spend $10,000 to change the packaging machinery. Assuming the original volume and costs, should MC Alexander accept this special order? (Assume MC Alexander will incur variable selling costs as well as variable manufacturing costs related to this order.) (See Learning Objective 2)

> Solution

Requirement 1

The full product cost per unit is as follows:

Fixed costs	$ 700,000
Plus: Total variable costs (2,000,000 cans × $1.00 per can)	2,000,000
Total full product costs	$ 2,700,000
Divided by the number of cans	÷ 2,000,000
Full product cost per can	$ 1.35

Requirement 2

The target full product cost is as follows:

Revenue at market price	(2,000,000 cans × $1.45 per can)	$ 2,900,000
Less: Desired profit	(12% × $3,000,000 of assets)	360,000
Target full product cost		$ 2,540,000

MC Alexander's current total full product costs ($2,700,000 from Requirement 1) are $160,000 higher than the target full product cost ($2,540,000). If MC Alexander cannot reduce product costs, it will not be able to meet stockholders' profit expectations.

Requirement 3

Assuming MC Alexander cannot reduce its fixed costs, the target variable cost per can is as follows:

Target full product cost (from Requirement 2)	$ 2,540,000
Less: Fixed costs	700,000
Target total variable costs	$ 1,840,000
Divided by the number of cans	÷ 2,000,000
Target variable cost per can	$ 0.92

Because MC Alexander cannot reduce its fixed costs, it needs to reduce variable costs by $0.08 per can ($1.00 − $0.92) to meet its profit goals. This would require an 8% cost reduction, which may not be possible.

Requirement 4

If MC Alexander can differentiate its tennis balls, it will gain more control over pricing. The company's new cost-plus price would be as follows:

Current total costs (from Requirement 1)	$ 2,700,000
Plus: Additional cost of advertising	100,000
Plus: Desired profit (from Requirement 2)	360,000
Target revenue	$ 3,160,000
Divided by the number of cans	2,000,000
Cost-plus price per can	$ 1.58

MC Alexander must study the market to determine whether retailers would pay $1.58 per can of tennis balls.

Requirement 5

Nelson's special order price ($1.20) is less than the current full product cost of each can of tennis balls ($1.35 from Requirement 1). However, this should not influence management's decision. MC Alexander could fill Nelson's special order using existing excess capacity. MC Alexander takes a differential analysis approach to its decision, comparing the extra revenue with the differential costs of accepting the order. Variable costs will increase if MC Alexander accepts the order, so the variable costs are relevant. Only the *additional* fixed costs of changing the packaging machine ($10,000) are relevant because all other fixed costs will remain unchanged.

Revenue from special order	(400,000 cans × $1.20 per can)	$ 480,000
Less: Variable costs of special order	(400,000 cans × $1.00 per can)	400,000
Contribution margin from special order		80,000
Less: Additional fixed costs of special order		10,000
Operating income provided by special order		$ 70,000

MC Alexander should accept the special order because it will increase operating income by $70,000. However, MC Alexander also needs to consider whether its regular customers will find out about the special order price and demand lower prices, too.

> Check Your Understanding 25-2

Check your understanding of the chapter by completing this problem and then looking at the solution. Use this practice to help identify which sections of the chapter you need to study more.

Shelly's Shades produces standard and deluxe sunglasses:

	Standard	Deluxe
Sales price per pair	$ 20	$ 30
Variable expenses per pair	16	21

The company has 15,000 machine hours available. In one machine hour, Shelly's can produce 70 pairs of the standard model or 30 pairs of the deluxe model.

Requirements

1. Which model should Shelly's emphasize? (See Learning Objective 3)

2. Shelly's also produces a third product: sport sunglasses. Shelly's incurs the following costs for 20,000 pairs of its sport sunglasses:

Direct materials	$ 20,000
Direct labor	80,000
Variable manufacturing overhead	40,000
Fixed manufacturing overhead	80,000
Total manufacturing cost	$ 220,000
Divided by number of pairs	÷ 20,000
Cost per pair	$ 11

Another manufacturer has offered to sell similar sunglasses to Shelly's for $10 per unit, a total purchase cost of $200,000. If Shelly's outsources *and* leaves its plant idle, it can save $50,000 of fixed overhead costs. Or it can use the freed manufacturing facilities to make other products that will contribute $70,000 to profits. In this case, the company will not be able to avoid any fixed costs. Identify and analyze the alternatives. What is the best course of action? (See Learning Objective 4)

> Solution

Requirement 1

	Standard	Deluxe
Sales price per pair	$ 20	$ 30
Less: Variable expenses per pair	16	21
Contribution margin per pair	$ 4	$ 9
Units produced each machine hour	× 70	× 30
Contribution margin per machine hour	$ 280	$ 270
Capacity—number of machine hours	× 15,000	× 15,000
Total contribution margin at full capacity	$ 4,200,000	$ 4,050,000

Decision: Emphasize the standard model because it has the higher contribution margin per unit of the constraint—machine hours.

Requirement 2

	Make Sunglasses	Buy Sunglasses Facilities Idle	Buy Sunglasses Make Other Products
Relevant Costs:			
Direct materials	$ 20,000		
Direct labor	80,000		
Variable overhead	40,000		
Fixed overhead	50,000		$ 50,000
Purchase cost (20,000 pairs × $10 per pair)		$ 200,000	200,000
Total cost of obtaining sunglasses	190,000	200,000	250,000
Profit from other products			(70,000)
Net cost of obtaining sunglasses	$ 190,000	$ 200,000	$ 180,000

Decision: Shelly's should buy the sunglasses from the outside supplier and use the freed manufacturing facilities to make other products.

> Key Terms

> Quick Check

1. In making short-term business decisions, what should you do?

   a. Use a traditional costing approach.

   b. Focus on total costs.

   c. Separate variable from fixed costs.

   d. Focus only on quantitative factors.

   Learning Objective 1

2. Which of the following is relevant to Kitchenware.com's decision to accept a special order at a lower sales price from a large customer in China?

   a. The cost of shipping the order to the customer

   b. The cost of Kitchenware.com's warehouses in the United States

   c. Founder Eric Crowley's salary

   d. Kitchenware.com's investment in its Web site

   Learning Objective 1

3. Which of the following costs are irrelevant to business decisions?

   a. Avoidable costs

   b. Costs that differ between alternatives

   c. Sunk costs

   d. Variable costs

   Learning Objective 1

4. When making decisions, managers should consider

   a. revenues that differ between alternatives.

   b. costs that do not differ between alternatives.

   c. only variable costs.

   d. sunk costs in their decisions.

   Learning Objective 1

5. When pricing a product or service, managers must consider which of the following?

   a. Only period costs

   b. Only manufacturing costs

   c. Only variable costs

   d. All costs

   Learning Objective 2

6. When companies are price-setters, their products and services

   a. are priced by managers using a target-pricing emphasis.

   b. tend to have a lot of competitors.

   c. tend to be commodities.

   d. tend to be unique.

   Learning Objective 2

7. In deciding whether to drop its electronics product line, Smith Company should consider

   a. how dropping the electronics product line would affect sales of its other products.

   b. the costs it could save by dropping the product line.

   c. the revenues it would lose from dropping the product line.

   d. All of the above.

   Learning Objective 3

8. In deciding which product lines to emphasize when a production constraint exists, the company should focus on the product line that has the highest

   a. contribution margin per unit of product.

   b. contribution margin per unit of the constraint.

   c. profit per unit of product.

   d. contribution margin ratio.

   Learning Objective 3

Learning Objective 4

9. When making outsourcing decisions, which of the following is true?

   a. Expected use of the freed capacity is irrelevant.

   b. The variable cost of producing the product in-house is relevant.

   c. The total manufacturing unit cost of making the product in-house is relevant.

   d. Avoidable fixed costs are irrelevant.

Learning Objective 4

10. When deciding whether to sell as is or process a product further, managers should ignore which of the following?

    a. The costs of processing the product thus far

    b. The cost of processing further

    c. The revenue if the product is sold as is

    d. The revenue if the product is processed further

Check your answers at the end of the chapter.

ASSESS YOUR PROGRESS

> Review Questions

1. List the four steps in short-term decision making. At which step are managerial accountants most involved?

2. What makes information relevant to decision making?

3. What makes information irrelevant to decision making?

4. What are sunk costs? Give an example.

5. When is nonfinancial information relevant?

6. What is differential analysis?

7. What are the two keys in short-term decision making?

8. What questions should managers answer when setting regular prices?

9. Explain the difference between price-takers and price-setters.

10. What is target pricing? Who uses it?

11. What does the target full product cost include?

12. What is cost-plus pricing? Who uses it?

13. What questions should managers answer when considering special pricing orders?

14. When completing a differential analysis, when are the differences shown as positive amounts? As negative amounts?

15. When should special pricing orders be accepted?

16. What questions should managers answer when considering dropping a product or segment?

17. Explain why a segment with an operating loss can cause the company to have a decrease in total operating income if the segment is dropped.

18. What is a constraint?

19. What questions should managers answer when facing constraints?

20. What is the decision rule concerning products to emphasize when facing a constraint?

21. What is the most common constraint faced by merchandisers?

22. What is outsourcing?

23. What questions should managers answer when considering outsourcing?

24. What questions should managers answer when considering selling a product as is or processing further?

25. What are joint costs? How do they affect the sell or process further decision?

26. What is the decision rule for selling a product as is or processing it further?

> Short Exercises

S25-1 Describing and identifying information relevant to business decisions

Learning Objective 1

You are trying to decide whether to trade in your inkjet printer for a more recent model. Your usage pattern will remain unchanged, but the old and new printers use different ink cartridges.

Indicate if the following items are relevant or irrelevant to your decision:

a. The price of the new printer

b. The price paid for the old printer

c. The trade-in value of the old printer

d. Paper cost

e. The difference between ink cartridges' costs

S25-2 Making pricing decisions

Learning Objective 2

Skiable Acres operates a Rocky Mountain ski resort. The company is planning its lift ticket pricing for the coming ski season. Investors would like to earn a 10% return on investment on the company's $270,000,000 of assets. The company primarily incurs fixed costs to groom the runs and operate the lifts. Skiable Acres projects fixed costs to be $31,000,000 for the ski season. The resort serves about 725,000 skiers and snowboarders each season. Variable costs are about $8 per guest. Currently, the resort has such a favorable reputation among skiers and snowboarders that it has some control over the lift ticket prices.

Requirements

1. Would Skiable Acres emphasize target pricing or cost-plus pricing? Why?

2. If other resorts in the area charge $85 per day, what price should Skiable Acres charge?

Note: Short Exercise S25-2 must be completed before attempting Short Exercise S25-3.

S25-3 Making pricing decisions

Learning Objective 2

Refer to details about Skiable Acres from Short Exercise S25-2. Assume that Skiable Acres's reputation has diminished and other resorts in the vicinity are charging only $85 per lift ticket. Skiable Acres has become a price-taker and will not be able to charge more than its competitors. At the market price, Skiable Acres managers believe they will still serve 725,000 skiers and snowboarders each season.

Requirements

1. If Skiable Acres cannot reduce its costs, what profit will it earn? State your answer in dollars and as a percent of assets. Will investors be happy with the profit level?

2. Assume Skiable Acres has found ways to cut its fixed costs to $30,000,000. What is its new target variable cost per skier/snowboarder?

Learning Objective 3

S25-4 Making dropping a product or segment decisions

Edna Fashions operates three departments: Men's, Women's, and Accessories. Departmental operating income data for the third quarter of 2018 are as follows:

	Men's	Women's	Accessories	Total
EDNA FASHIONS Income Statement For the Quarter Ended September 30, 2018				
	Department			
	Men's	Women's	Accessories	Total
Net Sales Revenue	$ 101,000	$ 59,000	$ 102,000	$ 262,000
Variable Costs	65,000	35,000	91,000	191,000
Contribution Margin	36,000	24,000	11,000	71,000
Fixed Costs	27,000	19,000	29,000	75,000
Operating Income (Loss)	$ 9,000	$ 5,000	$ (18,000)	$ (4,000)

Assume that the fixed costs assigned to each department include only direct fixed costs of the department:

- Salary of the department's manager
- Cost of advertising directly related to that department

If Edna Fashions drops a department, it will not incur these fixed costs. Under these circumstances, should Edna Fashions drop any of the departments? Give your reasoning.

Learning Objective 3

S25-5 Making product mix decisions

StoreAll produces plastic storage bins for household storage needs. The company makes two sizes of bins: large (50 gallon) and regular (35 gallon). Demand for the products is so high that StoreAll can sell as many of each size as it can produce. The company uses the same machinery to produce both sizes. The machinery can be run for only 3,300 hours per period. StoreAll can produce 10 large bins every hour, whereas it can produce 17 regular bins in the same amount of time. Fixed costs amount to $115,000 per period. Sales prices and variable costs are as follows:

	Regular	Large
Sales price per unit	$ 8.00	$ 10.40
Variable costs per unit	3.50	4.40

Requirements

1. Which product should StoreAll emphasize? Why?

2. To maximize profits, how many of each size bin should StoreAll produce?

3. Given this product mix, what will the company's operating income be?

S25-6 Making outsourcing decisions

Learning Objective 4

Suppose Roasted Pepper restaurant is considering whether to (1) bake bread for its restaurant in-house or (2) buy the bread from a local bakery. The chef estimates that variable costs of making each loaf include $0.52 of ingredients, $0.27 of variable overhead (electricity to run the oven), and $0.79 of direct labor for kneading and forming the loaves. Allocating fixed overhead (depreciation on the kitchen equipment and building) based on direct labor, Roasted Pepper assigns $0.96 of fixed overhead per loaf. None of the fixed costs are avoidable. The local bakery would charge $1.78 per loaf.

Requirements

1. What is the full product unit cost of making the bread in-house?
2. Should Roasted Pepper bake the bread in-house or buy from the local bakery? Why?
3. In addition to the financial analysis, what else should Roasted Pepper consider when making this decision?

S25-7 Making outsourcing decisions

Learning Objective 4

Priscilla Smiley manages a fleet of 250 delivery trucks for Daniels Corporation. Smiley must decide whether the company should outsource the fleet management function. If she outsources to Fleet Management Services (FMS), FMS will be responsible for maintenance and scheduling activities. This alternative would require Smiley to lay off her five employees. However, her own job would be secure; she would be Daniels's liaison with FMS. If she continues to manage the fleet, she will need fleet-management software that costs $9,500 per year to lease. FMS offers to manage this fleet for an annual fee of $300,000. Smiley performed the following analysis:

	Retain In-House	Outsource to FMS	Difference
Annual leasing fee for software	$ 9,500		$ 9,500
Annual maintenance of trucks	147,000		147,000
Total annual salaries of five laid-off employees	185,000		185,000
Fleet Management Service's annual fee		$ 300,000	(300,000)
Total differential cost of outsourcing	$ 341,500	$ 300,000	$ 41,500

Requirements

1. Which alternative will maximize Daniels's short-term operating income?
2. What qualitative factors should Daniels consider before making a final decision?

S25-8 Making sell or process further decisions

Learning Objective 4

Heavenly Dessert processes cocoa beans into cocoa powder at a processing cost of $9,700 per batch. Heavenly Dessert can sell the cocoa powder as is, or it can process the cocoa powder further into either chocolate syrup or boxed assorted chocolates. Once processed, each batch of cocoa beans would result in the following sales revenue:

Cocoa powder	$ 14,500
Chocolate syrup	103,000
Boxed assorted chocolates	204,000

The cost of transforming the cocoa powder into chocolate syrup would be $72,000. Likewise, the company would incur a cost of $183,000 to transform the cocoa powder into boxed assorted chocolates. The company president has decided to make boxed assorted chocolates due to their high sales value and to the fact that the cocoa bean processing cost of $9,700 eats up most of the cocoa powder profits.

Has the president made the right or wrong decision? Explain your answer. Be sure to include the correct financial analysis in your response.

> Exercises

Learning Objective 1

E25-9 Describing and identifying information relevant to business decisions

Dan Jacobs, production manager for GreenLife, invested in computer-controlled production machinery last year. He purchased the machinery from Superior Design at a cost of $3,000,000. A representative from Superior Design has recently contacted Dan because the company has designed an even more efficient piece of machinery. The new design would double the production output of the year-old machinery but would cost GreenLife another $4,500,000. Jacobs is afraid to bring this new equipment to the company president's attention because he convinced the president to invest $3,000,000 in the machinery last year.

Explain what is relevant and irrelevant to Jacobs's dilemma. What should he do?

Learning Objective 2

1. $5,600

E25-10 Making special pricing decisions

Suppose the Baseball Hall of Fame in Cooperstown, New York, has approached Collector-Cardz with a special order. The Hall of Fame wishes to purchase 56,000 baseball card packs for a special promotional campaign and offers $0.38 per pack, a total of $21,280. Collector-Cardz's total production cost is $0.58 per pack, as follows:

Variable costs:	
Direct materials	$ 0.11
Direct labor	0.09
Variable overhead	0.08
Fixed overhead	0.30
Total cost	$ 0.58

Collector-Cardz has enough excess capacity to handle the special order.

Requirements

1. Prepare a differential analysis to determine whether Collector-Cardz should accept the special sales order.

2. Now assume that the Hall of Fame wants special hologram baseball cards. Collector-Cardz will spend $5,700 to develop this hologram, which will be useless after the special order is completed. Should Collector-Cardz accept the special order under these circumstances, assuming no change in the special pricing of $0.38 per pack?

E25-11 Making special pricing decisions

Learning Objective 2

Newtown Sunglasses sell for about $154 per pair. Suppose that the company incurs the following average costs per pair:

1. $340,000

Direct materials	$ 39
Direct labor	15
Variable manufacturing overhead	6
Variable selling expenses	3
Fixed manufacturing overhead	20*
Total cost	$ 83

* $2,050,000 Total fixed manufacturing overhead / 102,500 Pairs of sunglasses

Newtown has enough idle capacity to accept a one-time-only special order from Water Shades for 17,000 pairs of sunglasses at $80 per pair. Newtown will not incur any variable selling expenses for the order.

Requirements

1. How would accepting the order affect Newtown's operating income? In addition to the special order's effect on profits, what other (longer-term qualitative) factors should Newtown's managers consider in deciding whether to accept the order?

2. Newtown's marketing manager, Peter Kyler, argues against accepting the special order because the offer price of $80 is less than Newtown's $83 cost to make the sunglasses. Kyler asks you, as one of Newtown's staff accountants, to explain whether his analysis is correct. What would you say?

E25-12 Making pricing decisions

Learning Objective 2

Johnson Builders builds 1,500-square-foot starter tract homes in the fast-growing suburbs of Atlanta. Land and labor are cheap, and competition among developers is fierce. The homes are a standard model, with any upgrades added by the buyer after the sale. Johnson Builders's costs per developed sublot are as follows:

3. Desired profit $28,840

Land	$ 50,000
Construction	123,000
Landscaping	9,000
Variable selling costs	8,000

Johnson Builders would like to earn a profit of 14% of the variable cost of each home sold. Similar homes offered by competing builders sell for $207,000 each. Assume the company has no fixed costs.

Requirements

1. Which approach to pricing should Johnson Builders emphasize? Why?

2. Will Johnson Builders be able to achieve its target profit levels?

3. Bathrooms and kitchens are typically the most important selling features of a home. Johnson Builders could differentiate the homes by upgrading the bathrooms and kitchens. The upgrades would cost $16,000 per home but would enable Johnson Builders to increase the sales prices by $28,000 per home.

CHAPTER 25

(Kitchen and bathroom upgrades typically add about 175% of their cost to the value of any home.) If Johnson Builders makes the upgrades, what will the new cost-plus price per home be? Should the company differentiate its product in this manner?

Learning Objective 3

E25-13 Making decisions about dropping a product

1. $(33,000)

Top managers of Video Avenue are alarmed by their operating losses. They are considering dropping the DVD product line. Company accountants have prepared the following analysis to help make this decision:

VIDEO AVENUE Income Statement For the Year Ended December 31, 2018			
	Total	Blu-ray Discs	DVD Discs
Net Sales Revenue	$ 437,000	$ 308,000	$ 129,000
Variable Costs	250,000	154,000	96,000
Contribution Margin	187,000	154,000	33,000
Fixed Costs:			
Manufacturing	132,000	76,000	56,000
Selling and Administrative	65,000	51,000	14,000
Total Fixed Expenses	197,000	127,000	70,000
Operating Income (Loss)	$ (10,000)	$ 27,000	$ (37,000)

Total fixed costs will not change if the company stops selling DVDs.

Requirements

1. Prepare a differential analysis to show whether Video Avenue should drop the DVD product line.
2. Will dropping DVDs add $37,000 to operating income? Explain.

Note: Exercise E25-13 must be completed before attempting Exercise E25-14.

Learning Objective 3

E25-14 Making decisions about dropping a product

$6,000

Refer to Exercise E25-13. Assume that Video Avenue can avoid $39,000 of direct fixed costs by dropping the DVD product line.

Prepare a differential analysis to show whether Video Avenue should stop selling DVDs.

E25-15 Making product mix decisions

Learning Objective 3

2. CM per MHr, Regular $441

Tread Light produces two types of exercise treadmills: regular and deluxe. The exercise craze is such that Tread Light could use all its available machine hours to produce either model. The two models are processed through the same production departments. Data for both models are as follows:

	Per Unit	
	Deluxe	**Regular**
Sales price	$ 1,030	$ 610
Costs:		
Direct materials	320	130
Direct labor	88	180
Variable manufacturing overhead	270	90
Fixed manufacturing overhead*	102	34
Variable operating expenses	121	63
Total costs	901	497
Operating income	$ 129	$ 113

*allocated on the basis of machine hours

Requirements

1. What is the constraint?
2. Which model should Tread Light produce? (*Hint:* Use the allocation of fixed manufacturing overhead to determine the proportion of machine hours used by each product.)
3. If Tread Light should produce both models, compute the mix that will maximize operating income.

E25-16 Making sales mix decisions

Learning Objective 3

CM per sq. ft., Designer $3.20

Moore Company sells both designer and moderately priced fashion accessories. Top management is deciding which product line to emphasize. Accountants have provided the following data:

	Per Item	
	Designer	**Moderately Priced**
Average sales price	$ 185	$ 87
Average variable costs	105	22
Average contribution margin	80	65
Average fixed costs (allocated)	20	10
Average operating income	$ 60	$ 55

The Moore Company store in Grand Junction, Colorado, has 14,000 square feet of floor space. If Moore Company emphasizes moderately priced goods, it can display 840 items in the store. If Moore Company emphasizes designer wear, it can display only 560 designer items. These numbers are also the average monthly sales in units.

Prepare an analysis to show which product the company should emphasize.

CHAPTER 25

Learning Objective 3

1. CM per linear ft., Licious-Ade
12-oz. can $7.20

E25-17 Making sales mix decisions

Each morning, Max Smith stocks the drink case at Max's Beach Hut in Myrtle Beach, South Carolina. The drink case has 120 linear feet of refrigerated drink space. Each linear foot can hold either six 12-ounce cans or three 20-ounce bottles.

Max's Beach Hut sells three types of cold drinks:

1. Licious-Ade in 12-oz. cans for $1.40 per can
2. Licious-Ade in 20-oz. bottles for $1.90 per bottle
3. Pep-Cola in 20-oz. bottles for $2.20 per bottle

Max's Beach Hut pays its suppliers:

1. $0.20 per 12-oz. can of Licious-Ade
2. $0.35 per 20-oz. bottle of Licious-Ade
3. $0.55 per 20-oz. bottle of Pep-Cola

Max's Beach Hut's monthly fixed costs include:

Hut rental	$ 355
Refrigerator rental	65
Max's salary	1,700
Total fixed costs	$ 2,120

Max's Beach Hut can sell all the drinks stocked in the display case each morning.

Requirements

1. What is Max's Beach Hut's constraining factor? What should Max stock to maximize profits?
2. Suppose Max's Beach Hut refuses to devote more than 80 linear feet to any individual product. Under this condition, how many linear feet of each drink should Max's stock? How many units of each product will be available for sale each day?

Learning Objective 4

Differential cost $(1.00)

E25-18 Making outsourcing decisions

Cool Systems manufactures an optical switch that it uses in its final product. The switch has the following manufacturing costs per unit:

Direct materials	$ 5.00
Direct labor	3.00
Variable overhead	6.00
Fixed overhead	7.00
Manufacturing product cost	$ 21.00

Another company has offered to sell Cool Systems the switch for $15.00 per unit. If Cool Systems buys the switch from the outside supplier, the idle manufacturing facilities cannot be used for any other purpose, yet none of the fixed costs are avoidable.

Prepare an outsourcing analysis to determine whether Cool Systems should make or buy the switch.

Note: Exercise E25-18 must be completed before attempting Exercise E25-19.

Learning Objective 4

1. Outsource and make new
product $960,000

E25-19 Making outsourcing decisions

Refer to Exercise E25-18. Cool Systems needs 79,000 optical switches. By outsourcing them, Cool Systems can use its idle facilities to manufacture another product that will contribute $225,000 to operating income.

Requirements

1. Identify the expected net costs that Cool Systems will incur to acquire 79,000 switches under three alternative plans: make the switches, buy the switches and leave facilities idle, buy the switches and use the idle facilities to make another product.

2. Which plan makes the best use of Cool System's facilities? Support your answer.

E25-20 Making sell or process further decisions

Learning Objective 4

Total net rev. difference $910

NaturalMaid processes organic milk into plain yogurt. NaturalMaid sells plain yogurt to hospitals, nursing homes, and restaurants in bulk, one-gallon containers. Each batch, processed at a cost of $840, yields 300 gallons of plain yogurt. NaturalMaid sells the one-gallon tubs for $5 each and spends $0.14 for each plastic tub. Natural-Maid has recently begun to reconsider its strategy. NaturalMaid wonders if it would be more profitable to sell individual-size portions of fruited organic yogurt at local food stores. NaturalMaid could further process each batch of plain yogurt into 6,400 individual portions (3/4 cup each) of fruited yogurt. A recent market analysis indicates that demand for the product exists. NaturalMaid would sell each individual portion for $0.58. Packaging would cost $0.10 per portion, and fruit would cost $0.11 per portion. Fixed costs would not change.

Should NaturalMaid continue to sell only the gallon-size plain yogurt (sell as is) or convert the plain yogurt into individual-size portions of fruited yogurt (process further)? Why?

> Problems Group A

P25-21A Identifying relevant information and making pricing decisions

Learning Objectives 1, 2

2. $55,200

Sea Blue manufactures flotation vests in Charleston, South Carolina. Sea Blue's contribution margin income statement for the month ended December 31, 2018, contains the following data:

SEA BLUE Income Statement For the Month Ended December 31, 2018	
Sales in Units	32,000
Net Sales Revenue	$ 608,000
Variable Costs:	
Manufacturing	96,000
Selling and Administrative	108,000
Total Variable Costs	204,000
Contribution Margin	404,000
Fixed Costs:	
Manufacturing	124,000
Selling and Administrative	94,000
Total Fixed Costs	218,000
Operating Income	$ 186,000

Suppose Overboard wishes to buy 4,600 vests from Sea Blue. Sea Blue will not incur any variable selling and administrative expenses on the special order. The Sea Blue plant has enough unused capacity to manufacture the additional vests. Overboard has offered $15 per vest, which is below the normal sales price of $19.

CHAPTER 25

Requirements

1. Identify each cost in the income statement as either relevant or irrelevant to Sea Blue's decision.

2. Prepare a differential analysis to determine whether Sea Blue should accept this special sales order.

3. Identify long-term factors Sea Blue should consider in deciding whether to accept the special sales order.

P25-22A Making pricing decisions

Snappy Plants operates a commercial plant nursery where it propagates plants for garden centers throughout the region. Snappy Plants has $5,100,000 in assets. Its yearly fixed costs are $650,000, and the variable costs for the potting soil, container, label, seedling, and labor for each gallon-size plant total $1.90. Snappy Plants's volume is currently 500,000 units. Competitors offer the same plants, at the same quality, to garden centers for $4.25 each. Garden centers then mark them up to sell to the public for $9 to $12, depending on the type of plant.

Requirements

1. Snappy Plants's owners want to earn a 11% return on investment on the company's assets. What is Snappy Plants's target full product cost?

2. Given Snappy Plants's current costs, will its owners be able to achieve their target profit?

3. Assume Snappy Plants has identified ways to cut its variable costs to $1.75 per unit. What is its new target fixed cost? Will this decrease in variable costs allow the company to achieve its target profit?

4. Snappy Plants started an aggressive advertising campaign strategy to differentiate its plants from those grown by other nurseries. Snappy Plants does not expect volume to be affected, but it hopes to gain more control over pricing. If Snappy Plants has to spend $105,000 this year to advertise and its variable costs continue to be $1.75 per unit, what will its cost-plus price be? Do you think Snappy Plants will be able to sell its plants to garden centers at the cost-plus price? Why or why not?

P25-23A Making decisions about dropping a product

Learning Objective 3

2b. $(41,000)

Members of the board of directors of Security Check have received the following operating income data for the year ended May 31, 2018:

	Product Line		
SECURITY CHECK Income Statement For the Year Ended May 31, 2018			
	Industrial Systems	Household Systems	Total
Net Sales Revenue	$ 360,000	$ 380,000	$ 740,000
Cost of Goods Sold:			
Variable	37,000	47,000	84,000
Fixed	260,000	63,000	323,000
Total Cost of Goods Sold	297,000	110,000	407,000
Gross Profit	63,000	270,000	333,000
Selling and Administrative Expenses:			
Variable	64,000	73,000	137,000
Fixed	44,000	26,000	70,000
Total Selling and Administrative Expenses	108,000	99,000	207,000
Operating Income (Loss)	$ (45,000)	$ 171,000	$ 126,000

Members of the board are surprised that the industrial systems product line is not profitable. They commission a study to determine whether the company should drop the line. Company accountants estimate that dropping industrial systems will decrease fixed cost of goods sold by $80,000 and decrease fixed selling and administrative expenses by $12,000.

Requirements

1. Prepare a differential analysis to show whether Security Check should drop the industrial systems product line.
2. Prepare contribution margin income statements to show Security Check's total operating income under the two alternatives: (a) with the industrial systems line and (b) without the line. Compare the *difference* between the two alternatives' income numbers to your answer to Requirement 1.
3. What have you learned from the comparison in Requirement 2?

P25-24A Making product mix decisions

Learning Objective 3

2. CM, Deluxe $2,310

Brinn, located in Port St. Lucie, Florida, produces two lines of electric toothbrushes: deluxe and standard. Because Brinn can sell all the toothbrushes it can produce, the owners are expanding the plant. They are deciding which product line to emphasize. To make this decision, they assemble the following data:

	Per Unit	
	Deluxe Toothbrush	Standard Toothbrush
Sales price	$ 86	$ 56
Variable costs	20	18
Contribution margin	$ 66	$ 38
Contribution margin ratio	76.7%	67.9%

CHAPTER 25

After expansion, the factory will have a production capacity of 4,100 machine hours per month. The plant can manufacture either 50 standard electric toothbrushes or 35 deluxe electric toothbrushes per machine hour.

Requirements

1. Identify the constraining factor for Brinn.

2. Prepare an analysis to show which product line to emphasize.

Learning Objective 4

1. $(6,380)

P25-25A Making outsourcing decisions

Snow Ride manufactures snowboards. Its cost of making 1,900 bindings is as follows:

Direct materials	$ 17,590
Direct labor	3,200
Variable overhead	2,080
Fixed overhead	6,300
Total manufacturing costs for 1,900 bindings	$ 29,170

Suppose Livingston will sell bindings to Snow Ride for $13 each. Snow Ride would pay $3 per unit to transport the bindings to its manufacturing plant, where it would add its own logo at a cost of $0.50 per binding.

Requirements

1. Snow Ride's accountants predict that purchasing the bindings from Livingston will enable the company to avoid $2,100 of fixed overhead. Prepare an analysis to show whether Snow Ride should make or buy the bindings.

2. The facilities freed by purchasing bindings from Livingston can be used to manufacture another product that will contribute $3,100 to profit. Total fixed costs will be the same as if Snow Ride had produced the bindings. Show which alternative makes the best use of Snow Ride's facilities: (a) make bindings, (b) buy bindings and leave facilities idle, or (c) buy bindings and make another product.

Learning Objective 4

3. $18,420

P25-26A Making sell or process further decisions

Oak Petroleum has spent $202,000 to refine 63,000 gallons of petroleum distillate, which can be sold for $6.00 per gallon. Alternatively, Oak can process the distillate further and produce 58,000 gallons of cleaner fluid. The additional processing will cost $1.80 per gallon of distillate. The cleaner fluid can be sold for $9.10 per gallon. To sell the cleaner fluid, Oak must pay a sales commission of $0.12 per gallon and a transportation charge of $0.19 per gallon.

Requirements

1. Diagram Oak's decision alternatives, using Exhibit 25-18 as a guide.

2. Identify the sunk cost. Is the sunk cost relevant to Oak's decision?

3. Should Oak sell the petroleum distillate or process it into cleaner fluid? Show the expected net revenue difference between the two alternatives.

> Problems Group B

P25-27B Identifying relevant information and making pricing decisions

Nautical manufactures flotation vests in Tampa, Florida. Nautical's contribution margin income statement for the month ended December 31, 2018, contains the following data:

NAUTICAL Income Statement For the Month Ended December 31, 2018	
Sales in Units	29,000
Net Sales Revenue	$ 551,000
Variable Costs:	
Manufacturing	116,000
Selling and Administrative	111,000
Total Variable Costs	227,000
Contribution Margin	324,000
Fixed Costs:	
Manufacturing	123,000
Selling and Administrative	92,000
Total Fixed Expenses	215,000
Operating Income	$ 109,000

Suppose Water Works wishes to buy 4,800 vests from Nautical. Nautical will not incur any variable selling and administrative expenses on the special order. The Nautical plant has enough unused capacity to manufacture the additional vests. Water Works has offered $15 per vest, which is below the normal sales price of $19.

Requirements

1. Identify each cost in the income statement as either relevant or irrelevant to Nautical's decision.

2. Prepare a differential analysis to determine whether Nautical should accept this special sales order.

3. Identify long-term factors Nautical should consider in deciding whether to accept the special sales order.

P25-28B Making pricing decisions

Green Thumb operates a commercial plant nursery, where it propagates plants for garden centers throughout the region. Green Thumb has $5,300,000 in assets. Its yearly fixed costs are $625,000, and the variable costs for the potting soil, container, label, seedling, and labor for each gallon-size plant total $1.70. Green Thumb's volume is currently 490,000 units. Competitors offer the same plants, at the same quality, to garden centers for $4.00 each. Garden centers then mark them up to sell to the public for $9 to $12, depending on the type of plant.

Requirements

1. Green Thumb's owners want to earn an 10% return on the company's assets. What is Green Thumb's target full product cost?

2. Given Green Thumb's current costs, will its owners be able to achieve their target profit?

3. Assume Green Thumb has identified ways to cut its variable costs to $1.55 per unit. What is its new target fixed cost? Will this decrease in variable costs allow the company to achieve its target profit?

4. Green Thumb started an aggressive advertising campaign strategy to differentiate its plants from those grown by other nurseries. Green Thumb does not expect volume to be affected, but it hopes to gain more control over pricing. If Green Thumb has to spend $135,000 this year to advertise and its variable costs continue to be $1.55 per unit, what will its cost-plus price be? Do you think Green Thumb will be able to sell its plants to garden centers at the cost-plus price? Why or why not?

Learning Objective 3

2b. $(33,000)

P25-29B Making decisions about dropping a product

Members of the board of directors of Security Team have received the following operating income data for the year ended March 31, 2018:

	SECURITY TEAM Income Statement For the Month Ended March 31, 2018		
	Product Line		
	Industrial Systems	**Household Systems**	**Total**
Net Sales Revenue	$ 300,000	$ 330,000	$ 630,000
Cost of Goods Sold:			
Variable	35,000	42,000	77,000
Fixed	210,000	63,000	273,000
Total Cost of Goods Sold	245,000	105,000	350,000
Gross Profit	55,000	225,000	280,000
Selling and Administrative Expenses:			
Variable	66,000	77,000	143,000
Fixed	39,000	28,000	67,000
Total Selling and Administrative Expenses	105,000	105,000	210,000
Operating Income (Loss)	$ (50,000)	$ 120,000	$ 70,000

Members of the board are surprised that the industrial systems product line is losing money. They commission a study to determine whether the company should drop the line. Company accountants estimate that dropping industrial systems will decrease fixed cost of goods sold by $81,000 and decrease fixed selling and administrative expenses by $15,000.

Requirements

1. Prepare a differential analysis to show whether Security Team should drop the industrial systems product line.

2. Prepare contribution margin income statements to show Security Team's total operating income under the two alternatives: (a) with the industrial systems line and (b) without the line. Compare the *difference* between the two alternatives' income numbers to your answer to Requirement 1.

3. What have you learned from this comparison in Requirement 2?

P25-30B Making product mix decisions

Learning Objective 3

2. CM, Standard $2,340

Brik, located in San Antonio, Texas, produces two lines of electric toothbrushes: deluxe and standard. Because Brik can sell all the toothbrushes it can produce, the owners are expanding the plant. They are deciding which product line to emphasize. To make this decision, they assemble the following data:

	Per Unit	
	Deluxe Toothbrush	**Standard Toothbrush**
Sales price	$ 88	$ 54
Variable expense	22	18
Contribution margin	$ 66	$ 36
Contribution margin ratio	75.0%	66.7%

After expansion, the factory will have a production capacity of 4,900 machine hours per month. The plant can manufacture either 65 standard electric toothbrushes or 27 deluxe electric toothbrushes per machine hour.

Requirements

1. Identify the constraining factor for Brik.
2. Prepare an analysis to show which product line the company should emphasize.

P25-31B Making outsourcing decisions

Learning Objective 4

1. $(12,530)

Cold Sports manufactures snowboards. Its cost of making 2,000 bindings is as follows:

Direct materials	$ 17,510
Direct labor	2,600
Variable overhead	2,060
Fixed overhead	7,000
Total manufacturing costs for 2,000 bindings	$ 29,170

Suppose Topnotch will sell bindings to Cold Sports for $15 each. Cold Sports would pay $3 per unit to transport the bindings to its manufacturing plant, where it would add its own logo at a cost of $0.50 per binding.

Requirements

1. Cold Sports's accountants predict that purchasing the bindings from Topnotch will enable the company to avoid $2,300 of fixed overhead. Prepare an analysis to show whether Cold Sports should make or buy the bindings.
2. The facilities freed by purchasing bindings from Topnotch can be used to manufacture another product that will contribute $3,100 to profit. Total fixed costs will be the same as if Cold Sports had produced the bindings. Show which alternative makes the best use of Cold Sports's facilities: (a) make bindings, (b) buy bindings and leave facilities idle, or (c) buy bindings and make another product.

Learning Objective 4

3. $18,620

P25-32B Making sell or process further decisions

Elm Petroleum has spent $204,000 to refine 61,000 gallons of petroleum distillate, which can be sold for $6.30 per gallon. Alternatively, Elm can process the distillate further and produce 58,000 gallons of cleaner fluid. The additional processing will cost $1.80 per gallon of distillate. The cleaner fluid can be sold for $9.10 per gallon. To sell the cleaner fluid, Elm must pay a sales commission of $0.10 per gallon and a transportation charge of $0.16 per gallon.

Requirements

1. Diagram Elm's decision alternatives, using Exhibit 25-18 as a guide.

2. Identify the sunk cost. Is the sunk cost relevant to Elm's decision?

3. Should Elm sell the petroleum distillate or process it into cleaner fluid? Show the expected net revenue difference between the two alternatives.

CRITICAL THINKING

> Using Excel

P25-33 Using Excel to calculate optimum product mix

Download an Excel template for this problem online in MyAccountingLab or at http://www.pearsonhighered.com/Horngren.

Magnolia Company produces leather shoes in three models: Medina, Ballard, and Fremont. Currently, Magnolia is manufacturing 4,000 pairs of Medina, 6,000 pairs of Ballard, and 1,500 pairs of Fremont during the year, for a total contribution margin of $2,242,500. However, some of the resources used in the manufacturing process are underutilized, leading the manager to believe that there could be an alternative product mix for shoes that would increase the total contribution margin. Magnolia can sell all shoes produced.

The current product mix is:

	Shoe			Total Contribution Margin
	Medina	Ballard	Fremont	
Pairs of shoes	4,000	6,000	1,500	
Sales price per pair	$ 385	$ 250	$ 180	
Variable costs per pair	175	50	45	
Contribution margin per pair	210	200	135	$ 2,242,500
Contribution margin ratio	55%	80%	75%	

Magnolia has the following manufacturing constraints:

	Machine hours required per pair of shoes			Total machine hours used	Total machine hours available
Process	Medina	Ballard	Fremont		
Cutting	0.15	0.15	0.20	0	1,800
Sewing	0.25	0.10	0.10	0	2,100
Packaging	0.25	0.10	0.10	0	2,400

Requirements

1. Using the formula in the cell for Total Contribution Margin on the Product Mix template, create the formulas in the blue shaded cells for
   a. Total contribution margin using SUMPRODUCT
   b. Machine hours used using SUMPRODUCT

2. The objective and constraints headings are the green shaded cells. Create formulas in the blue shaded cells.

3. Use Excel's Solver to compute the number of pairs of shoes for each of the three models in order to maximize the contribution margin, given the constraints.

> Continuing Problem

P25-34 Making outsourcing decisions

This problem continues the Piedmont Computer Company situation from Chapter 24. Piedmont Computer Company's payroll accountant has submitted her resignation and will be leaving the company in two weeks. The company must decide if it will hire a replacement or outsource the payroll position. The current employee earns a salary of $40,000. Medical insurance, employer payroll taxes, and contributions to the pension plan for this position cost $7,600. The company has already invested $22,000 in payroll software. Required annual updates to remain in compliance with all state and federal laws are $495. The company also spends $1,750 per year in professional development for this position to ensure the employee stays up-to-date with payroll changes.

Piedmont Computer Company pays its employees weekly. Payroll Professionals will process the company's weekly payroll for $1,000 per week. This fee also includes preparing all necessary payroll tax returns, reports, and W-2s.

Requirements

1. Prepare a differential analysis to determine if Piedmont Computer Company should replace the employee or outsource the payroll function.

2. What other factors should Piedmont Computer Company consider in making this decision?

> Tying It All Together Case 25-1

Before you begin this assignment, review the Tying It All Together feature in the chapter.

The Boeing Company manufacturers many different types of planes including the 737, 747, 767, 777, and 787. The Boeing 747 is a wide-body commercial jet airliner and cargo aircraft known for its distinctive "hump" upper deck along the forward part of the aircraft. The 747 can accommodate up to 660 passengers although it typically seats only 410 passengers in a three-class configuration. The 747-8 Intercontinental is inspired by the Boeing 787 Dreamliner and includes a sculpted ceiling, LED dynamic lighting, larger bins, and a new staircase design. In the company's 2015 annual report, Boeing reported reduced orders and demand for new freighter aircraft (747-8) and plans to reduce production rates on its 747 program.

Requirements

1. How would a company, such as Boeing, evaluate the dropping of a product?

2. What type of income statement would a company use to evaluate business decisions such as dropping a product? Why?

> Ethical Issue 25-1

Mary Tan is the controller for Duck Associates, a property management company in Portland, Oregon. Each year, Tan and payroll clerk Toby Stock meet with the external auditors about payroll accounting. This year, the auditors suggest that Tan consider outsourcing Duck Associates's payroll accounting to a company specializing in payroll processing services. This would allow Tan and her staff to focus on their primary responsibility: accounting for the properties under management. At present, payroll requires 1.5 employee positions—payroll clerk Toby Stock and a bookkeeper who spends half her time entering payroll data in the system.

Tan considers this suggestion, and she lists the following items relating to outsourcing payroll accounting:

a. The current payroll software that was purchased for $4,000 three years ago would not be needed if payroll processing were outsourced.

b. Duck Associates's bookkeeper would spend half her time preparing the weekly payroll input form that is given to the payroll processing service. She is paid $450 per week.

c. Duck Associates would no longer need payroll clerk Toby Stock, whose annual salary is $42,000.

d. The payroll processing service would charge $2,000 per month.

Requirements

1. Would outsourcing the payroll function increase or decrease Duck Associates's operating income?

2. Tan believes that outsourcing payroll would simplify her job, but she does not like the prospect of having to lay off Stock, who has become a close personal friend. She does not believe there is another position available for Stock at his current salary. Can you think of other factors that might support keeping Stock, rather than outsourcing payroll processing? How should each of the factors affect Tan's decision if she wants to do what is best for Duck Associates and act ethically?

> Team Project 25-1

Ledfords is a chain of home improvement stores. Suppose Ledfords is trying to decide whether to produce its own line of Formica countertops, cabinets, and picnic tables. Assume Ledford would incur the following unit costs in producing its own product lines:

	Countertops	Cabinets	Picnic Tables
Direct materials per unit	$ 15	$ 10	$ 25
Direct labor per unit	10	5	15
Variable manufacturing overhead per unit	5	2	6

Rather than making these products, assume that Ledfords could buy them from outside suppliers. Suppliers would charge Ledfords $40 per countertop, $25 per cabinet, and $65 per picnic table. Whether Ledfords makes or buys these products, assume that the company expects the following annual sales:

- Countertops—487,200 at $130 each
- Cabinets—150,000 at $75 each
- Picnic tables—100,000 at $225 each

Assume that Ledfords has a production facility with excess capacity that could be used to produce these products with no additional fixed costs. If making is sufficiently more profitable than outsourcing, Ledfords will start production of the new line of products. The president of Ledfords has asked your consulting group for a recommendation.

Requirements

1. Are the following items relevant or irrelevant in Ledfords's decision to use its plant to manufacture its own products?

    a. The unit sales prices of the countertops, cabinets, and picnic tables (the sales prices that Ledfords charges its customers)

    b. The prices outside suppliers would charge Ledfords for the three products if Ledfords decides to outsource the products rather than make them

    c. The direct materials, direct labor, and variable overhead Ledfords would incur to manufacture the three product lines

    d. The president's salary

2. Determine whether Ledfords should make or outsource the countertops, cabinets, and picnic tables. In other words, what is the annual difference in operating income if Ledfords decides to make rather than outsource each of these three products?

3. Write a memo giving your recommendation to Ledfords's president. The memo should clearly state your recommendation, along with a brief summary of the reasons for your recommendation.

> Quick Check Answers

1. c   **2.** a   **3.** c   **4.** a   **5.** d   **6.** d   **7.** d   **8.** b   **9.** b   **10.** a

CHAPTER 25

26 Capital Investment Decisions

If I Build It, Will They Buy?

Cody Thacker stands in the parking lot of the newest location of Thacker's C-Store, watching the new customers coming in for their first visit to his 10th store. Cody is pleased with the volume of traffic at the new convenience store. Opening a new store is a large investment and somewhat of a gamble. The previous new store, Store #9, is not doing well. Cody got a great deal on the land but failed to fully evaluate the market. Store #9 does not have the customer volume it needs to make it a profitable location, the workforce is limited, and employee turnover is a huge problem.

Fortunately, Cody learned from the mistake and was more careful when selecting this latest location. Before making the final decision on the location of Store #10, Cody considered the area's population to ensure the store would have the needed customer volume and workforce. He also analyzed the other types of stores in the area, paying particular attention to the locations of competitors' convenience stores, which could affect his ability to attract customers and workers. So far, he is not having problems getting qualified, reliable workers. Morale is high, and the employees are cheerful. The gas pumps are busy, and the traffic inside at the food and beverage counters is brisk. Cody feels his investment in land, building, equipment, and inventory at this C-Store is going to generate a good return. He hopes the profits from his current stores will allow him to open Store #11 within the next year.

Where Should We Expand?

All companies have to make investment decisions, such as deciding when to expand, replace equipment, and upgrade technology. Making wise decisions concerning investments in long-term assets is crucial to the long-term success of businesses. **TravelCenters of America LLC** operate and franchise 456 travel center and convenience store locations under the brand names TravelCenters of America (TA) and Petro Stopping Centers. The company offers a broad range of products and services, including diesel fuel and gasoline, truck repair, full service restaurants, and other driver amenities. In 2015, the company entered agreements to acquire 24 convenience stores for a purchase price of $32.8 million and 53 restaurant locations for a total of $250 million. TravelCenters has a stated goal of taking care of all highway travelers in the finest full-service facilities on the road. To obtain this goal, TravelCenters has to be selective in its expansion. Each potential location has to be carefully evaluated, and the company has to have a selection process in place to determine new locations.

The focus of this chapter is on learning methods of analyzing potential investment opportunities so the investments chosen meet a company's needs and provide the best return on investment.

Chapter 26 Learning Objectives

1. Describe the importance of capital investments and the capital budgeting process

2. Use the payback and the accounting rate of return methods to make capital investment decisions

3. Use the time value of money to compute the future and present values of lump sums and annuities

4. Use discounted cash flow methods to make capital investment decisions

WHAT IS CAPITAL BUDGETING?

In financial accounting, you learned how to account for **capital assets**—the operational assets businesses use for long periods of time. Examples include buildings, manufacturing equipment, and office furniture. The assets are considered *operational* assets because they are used in the day-to-day operations of the business in its efforts to generate revenues. They are called *capital assets* because they are *capitalized*, which means they are recorded as long-term assets when acquired and, except for land, depreciated over their useful lives. Remember that depreciation is the allocation of a capital asset's cost over its useful life. Depreciation for capital assets used in production, such as manufacturing equipment and the factory building, is accumulated in Manufacturing Overhead. The cost is transferred through the inventory accounts and eventually to Cost of Goods Sold, which is an expense account. Depreciation for the capital assets not used in production, such as office furniture and the corporate office building, is recorded as Depreciation Expense, a selling and administrative expense. Either way, the cost is expensed over the useful life of the asset.

When a capital asset is acquired, by purchase or construction, the company is making a **capital investment**. The focus of this chapter is on how companies make capital investment decisions. The process of making capital investment decisions is often referred to as **capital budgeting**, which is planning for investments in long-term assets in a way that returns the most profitability to the company. Capital budgeting is critical to the business because these investments affect operations for many years and usually require large sums of cash.

Capital investment decisions affect all businesses as they try to become more efficient by automating production and implementing new technologies. Grocers and retailers have invested in expensive checkout machines that allow customers to self-scan their purchases, and airlines have invested in kiosks that allow passengers to self-check-in. These new technologies require substantial cash investments. How do managers decide whether these expansions in plant and equipment will be good investments? They use capital investment analysis. Some large companies employ staff solely dedicated to capital budgeting analysis. They spend thousands of hours per year determining which capital investments to pursue.

The Capital Budgeting Process

Previously, when you learned how to complete the master budget, we discussed the budgeting objectives: to develop strategy, plan, direct, and control. The same objectives apply to capital budgeting, but the planning process is more involved due to the long-term nature of the assets. Exhibit 26-1 (on the next page) illustrates the capital budgeting process.

Learning Objective 1
Describe the importance of capital investments and the capital budgeting process

Capital Asset
An operational asset used for a long period of time.

Capital Investment
The acquisition of a capital asset.

Capital Budgeting
The process of planning to invest in long-term assets in a way that returns the most profitability to the company.

Exhibit 26-1 | **Capital Budgeting Process**

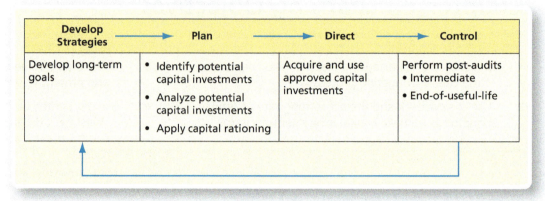

The first step in the capital budgeting process is to develop strategies. These are the long-term goals of the business, such as expanding international operations or being a value leader in one market while diversifying into other markets. This step is the same for all budgeting—short-term, intermediate, and long-term. After companies develop strategies, the next steps are to plan and budget for specific actions to achieve those goals.

The second step in the capital budgeting process is the planning process, which has three substeps. The first is to identify potential capital investments—for example, new technology and equipment that may make the company more efficient, competitive, and/or profitable. Employees, consultants, and outside vendors often offer capital investment proposals to management. After identifying potential capital investments, the second substep is to analyze the investments using one or more capital budgeting methods. In this chapter, we discuss four popular methods of analyzing potential capital investments:

1. Payback
2. Accounting rate of return (ARR)
3. Net present value (NPV)
4. Internal rate of return (IRR)

The first two methods, payback and accounting rate of return, are fairly quick and easy, and they work well for capital investments that have a relatively short life span, such as computer equipment and software that may have a useful life of only three to five years. Payback and accounting rate of return are also used to screen potential investments from those that are less desirable. Payback provides management with valuable information on how fast the cash invested will be recouped. The accounting rate of return shows the effect of the investment on the company's accrual-based income.

However, these two methods are inadequate if the capital investments have a longer life span because these methods do not consider the time value of money, which is the recognition that money earns interest over time. The last two methods, net present value and internal rate of return, factor in the time value of money so they are more appropriate for longer-term capital investments, such as Smart Touch Learning's expansion to manufacturing tablet computers. Management often uses a combination of methods to make final capital investment decisions.

Capital budgeting is not an exact science. Although the calculations these methods require may appear precise, remember that they are based on estimates—predictions about an uncertain future. These estimates must consider many unknown factors, such as changing consumer preferences, competition, the state of the economy, and government regulations. The further into the future the decision extends, the more likely that actual results will differ from predictions. This makes long-term decisions riskier than short-term decisions.

The analysis of capital investments sometimes involves a two-stage process. In the first stage, managers screen the potential capital investments using one or both of the methods that do *not* incorporate the time value of money—payback and accounting rate of return. These simple methods quickly weed out undesirable investments. Potential capital investments that pass Stage 1 go on to a second stage of analysis. In the second stage, managers further analyze the potential investments using the net present value and/or internal rate of return methods. Because these methods consider the time value of money, they provide more accurate information about the potential investment's profitability.

Some companies can pursue all of the potential investments that meet or exceed their decision criteria. However, because of limited resources, most companies must engage in capital rationing, which is the third substep in the planning process. **Capital rationing** is the process of ranking and choosing among alternative capital investments based on the availability of funds. Managers must determine if and when to make specific capital investments, so capital rationing occurs when the company has limited cash available to invest in long-term assets. For example, management may decide to wait three years to buy a certain piece of equipment because it considers other investments more important. In the intervening three years, the company will reassess whether it should still invest in the equipment. Perhaps technology has changed and even better equipment is available. Perhaps consumer tastes have changed so the company no longer needs the equipment. Because of changing factors, long-term capital budgets are usually revised from year to year.

The third step in the capital budgeting process is to direct—acquire and use the capital assets selected in the capital rationing process. The assets are used to generate revenues and contribute to company profits and managers must direct the use of the assets.

The fourth step in the capital budgeting process is control. In the short-term operational budgeting process, the control step is called *variance analysis*. Capital budgeting has a similar process. After acquiring and using the capital assets, companies compare the actual results from the investments to the projected results. The comparisons are called **post-audits**, and they help companies determine whether the investments are going as planned and deserve continued support or whether they should abandon the projects and dispose of the assets. Post-audits should be routinely performed during the life of the project, not just at the end of the project's life span. The intermediate post-audits allow managers to make adjustments to the projects during their lifetimes. Managers also use feedback from post-audits to better estimate projections for future projects. If managers expect routine post-audits, they will more likely submit realistic estimates with their capital investment proposals.

Notice in Exhibit 26-1 that the control step loops back to the first step: develop strategies. The post-audits help mangers learn from their decisions and make adjustments as needed. The adjustments are then considered when developing new strategies. Also, keep in mind that capital investments are long-term investments and managers must monitor multiple, overlapping investments. For example, the decision to build a new manufacturing facility may be a 30-year project, whereas the manufacturing equipment needed in the new facility may be projected to last only 15 years. Meanwhile, the computer system may need to be upgraded every two to three years and replaced every five or six years. Capital budgeting is a complex process.

Focus on Cash Flows

Generally Accepted Accounting Principles (GAAP) are based on accrual accounting, but capital budgeting focuses on cash flows. The desirability of a capital asset depends on its ability to generate *net cash inflows*—that is, cash inflows in excess of cash outflows—over the asset's useful life. Recall that operating income based on accrual accounting contains

Capital Rationing
The process of ranking and choosing among alternative capital investments based on the availability of funds.

Post-Audit
The comparison of the actual results of capital investments to the projected results.

non-cash expenses, such as depreciation expense and bad debts expense. These expenses decrease operating income but do not require a cash outlay. The capital investment's net cash inflows, therefore, will differ from its operating income. Of the four capital budgeting methods covered in this chapter, only the accounting rate of return method uses accrual-based accounting income. The other three methods use the investment's projected net cash inflows.

Cash *inflows* include future cash revenue generated from the investment, any future savings in ongoing cash operating costs resulting from the investment, and any future residual value of the asset. Cash inflows are projected by employees from production, marketing, materials management, accounting, and other departments to aid managers in estimating the projected cash flows. Good estimates are a critical part of making the best decisions.

What do the projected net cash inflows include?

To determine the investment's net cash inflows, the cash inflows are *netted* against the investment's future cash outflows, such as the investment's ongoing cash operating costs and cash paid for refurbishment, repairs, and maintenance costs. The initial investment itself is also a significant cash outflow. However, in our calculations, *we will always consider the amount of the investment separately from all other cash flows related to the investment.* The projected net cash inflows are given in our examples and in the assignment material. In reality, much of capital investment analysis revolves around projecting these figures as accurately as possible using input from employees throughout the organization—production, marketing, and so forth—depending on the type of capital investment. Exhibit 26-2 summarizes the common cash inflows and outflows from capital investments.

Exhibit 26-2 | **Capital Investment Cash Flow**

Cash Inflows	Cash Outflows
Revenue generated from investment	Initial investment (acquisition cost)
Savings in operating costs	Additional operating costs
Residual value	Refurbishment, repairs, and maintenance

Exhibit 26-3 illustrates the life cycle of capital investments, with the time line representing multiple years.

Exhibit 26-3 | **Life Cycle of Capital Investments**

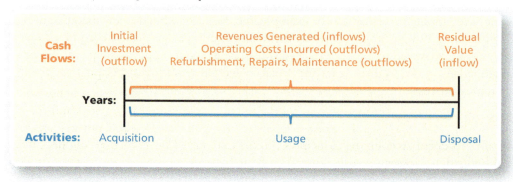

Try It!

Match the following business activities to the steps in capital budgeting process.

Steps in the capital budgeting process:

a. Develop strategies
b. Plan
c. Direct
d. Control

Business activities:

1. A manager evaluates progress one year into the project.
2. Employees submit suggestions for new investments.
3. The company builds a new factory.
4. Top management attends a retreat to set long-term goals.
5. Proposed investments are analyzed.
6. Proposed investments are ranked.
7. New equipment is purchased.

Check your answers online in MyAccountingLab or at http://www.pearsonhighered.com/Horngren.

For more practice, see Short Exercise S26-1. MyAccountingLab

HOW DO THE PAYBACK AND ACCOUNTING RATE OF RETURN METHODS WORK?

The primary focus of the rest of the chapter is learning how to analyze potential capital investments. We begin with two capital investment analysis methods that companies use to evaluate shorter capital investment choices (three to five years) and initially screen longer capital investment choices—payback and accounting rate of return.

> **Learning Objective 2**
>
> Use the payback and the accounting rate of return methods to make capital investment decisions

Payback

Payback is a capital investment analysis method that measures the length of time it takes to recover, in net cash inflows, the cost of the initial investment. The initial investment is also called the *capital outlay*. All else being equal, the shorter the payback period, the more attractive the asset. Computing the payback depends on whether net cash inflows are equal each year or differ over time. We consider each, in turn.

> **Payback**
>
> A capital investment analysis method that measures the length of time it takes to recover, in net cash inflows, the cost of the initial investment.

Payback with Equal Annual Net Cash Inflows

Smart Touch Learning is considering investing $240,000 in hardware and software to provide a business-to-business (B2B) portal. Employees throughout the company will use the B2B portal to access company-approved suppliers. Smart Touch Learning expects the portal to save $60,000 per year for each of the six years of its useful life. The savings will arise from reducing the number of purchasing personnel the company employs and from reduced costs on the goods and services purchased. Net cash inflows arise from an increase in revenues, a decrease in expenses, or both. In Smart Touch Learning's case, the net cash inflows result from lower expenses.

When net cash inflows are equal each year, managers compute the payback with the following formula:

$$\text{Payback} = \frac{\text{Amount invested}}{\text{Expected annual net cash inflow}}$$

Smart Touch Learning computes the investment's payback as follows:

$$\text{Payback for B2B portal} = \frac{\$240,000}{\$60,000 \text{ per year}} = 4 \text{ years}$$

Smart Touch Learning expects to recoup the $240,000 investment in the B2B portal by the end of year 4, when the accumulated net cash inflows total $240,000.

Smart Touch Learning is also considering whether to, instead, invest $240,000 to upgrade its Web site. The company expects the upgraded Web site to generate $80,000 in net cash inflows each year of its three-year life. The payback is computed as follows:

$$\text{Payback for Web site upgrade} = \frac{\$240,000}{\$80,000 \text{ per year}} = 3 \text{ years}$$

Smart Touch Learning will recoup the $240,000 investment for the Web site upgrade by the end of year 3, when the accumulated net cash inflows total $240,000. The Web site upgrade project has a shorter payback period than the B2B project—three years compared with four years. Therefore, based on this method of analysis, the Web site upgrade is a more attractive project. Exhibit 26-4 summarizes the payback calculations.

Exhibit 26-4 | Payback—Equal Annual Net Cash Inflows

	Net Cash Outflows	Net Cash Inflows			
		B2B Portal		Web Site Upgrade	
Year	Amount Invested	Annual	Accumulated	Annual	Accumulated
0	$ 240,000				
1		$ 60,000	$ 60,000	$ 80,000	$ 80,000
2		60,000	120,000	80,000	160,000
3		60,000	180,000	80,000	240,000
4		60,000	240,000		
5		60,000	300,000		
6		60,000	360,000		

Payback with Unequal Net Cash Inflows

The payback equation only works when net cash inflows are the same each period. When periodic cash flows are unequal, you must total net cash inflows until the amount invested is recovered. Assume that Smart Touch Learning is considering an alternate investment, the Z80 portal. The Z80 portal differs from the B2B portal and the Web site upgrade in two respects: (1) It has *unequal* net cash inflows during its life, and (2) it has a $30,000 residual value at the end of its life. The Z80 portal will generate net cash inflows of $100,000 in year 1, $80,000 in year 2, $50,000 each year in years 3 and 4, $40,000 each in years 5 and 6, and $30,000 in residual value when the equipment is sold at the end of the project's useful life. Exhibit 26-5 shows the payback schedule for these unequal annual net cash inflows.

Exhibit 26-5 | Payback—Unequal Annual Net Cash Inflows

Net Cash Outflows		Net Cash Inflows Z80 Portal	
Year	Amount Invested	Annual	Accumulated
0	$ 240,000		
1		$ 100,000	$ 100,000
2		80,000	180,000
3		50,000	230,000
4		50,000	280,000
5		40,000	320,000
6		40,000	360,000
6 (Residual value)		30,000	390,000

By the end of year 3, the company has recovered $230,000 of the $240,000 initially invested, so it is only $10,000 short of payback. Because the expected net cash inflow in year 4 is $50,000, by the end of year 4 the company will have recovered *more* than the initial investment. Therefore, the payback is somewhere between three and four years. Assuming that the cash flow occurs evenly throughout the fourth year, the payback is calculated as follows:

$$\text{Payback for Z80 portal} = 3 \text{ years} + \frac{\$10,000 \text{ (amount needed to complete recovery in year 4)}}{\$50,000 \text{ (net cash inflow in year 4)}} = 3.2 \text{ years}$$

Based on the payback method alone, the projects would be ranked as follows:

Rank	Project	Payback Period
1	Web site upgrade	3.0 years
2	Z80 portal	3.2 years
3	B2B portal	4.0 years

Criticism of Payback

A major criticism of the payback method is that it focuses only on time to recover the initial investment, not on profitability. The payback considers only those cash flows that occur *during* the payback period. This method ignores any cash flows that occur *after* that period. For example, Exhibit 26-4 shows that the B2B portal will continue to generate net cash inflows for two years after its payback. These additional net cash inflows amount to $120,000 ($60,000 × 2 years), yet the payback method ignores this extra cash. A similar situation occurs with the Z80 portal. As shown in Exhibit 26-5, the Z80 portal will provide an additional $150,000 of net cash inflows ($390,000 total accumulated cash inflows − $240,000 amount invested), including residual value, after its payback of 3.2 years. However, the Web site upgrade's useful life, as shown in Exhibit 26-4, is the same as its payback (three years). No cash flows are ignored, yet the Web site will merely cover its cost and provide no profit. Because this is the case, the company has no financial reason to invest in the Web site.

Exhibit 26-6 compares the payback of the three investments. As the exhibit illustrates, the payback method does not consider the asset's profitability. The method only tells management how quickly it will recover the cash invested. Even though the Web site upgrade has the shortest payback, both the B2B portal and the Z80 portal are better investments because they provide profit. The key point is that the investment with the shortest payback is best *only if all other factors are the same* and if the payback is less than or equal to the useful life of the asset. **Therefore, managers usually use the payback method as a screening device to eliminate investments that will take too long to recoup the initial investment. They rarely use payback as the sole method for deciding whether to invest in the asset.** Managers also use accounting rate of return, net present value, and internal rate of return to evaluate capital investments.

Exhibit 26-6 | **Comparing Payback Periods Between Investments**

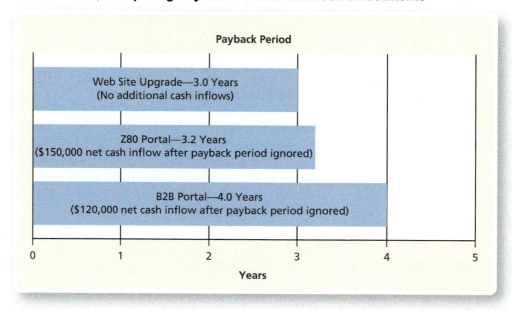

When using the payback method, managers are guided by the following decision rule:

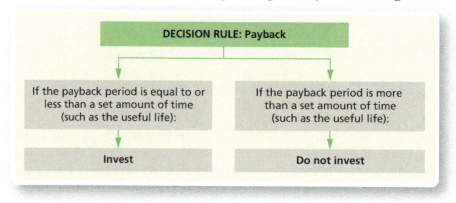

Accounting Rate of Return (ARR)

Accounting Rate of Return (ARR)
A capital investment analysis method that measures the profitability of an investment. Average annual operating income / Average amount invested.

Companies are in business to earn profits. The **accounting rate of return (ARR)** is a capital investment analysis method that measures the profitability of an investment. The formula for calculating ARR is:

$$ARR = \frac{\text{Average annual operating income}}{\text{Average amount invested}}$$

Notice that ARR focuses on the *operating income,* not the net cash inflow, that an asset generates. ARR measures the average annual rate of return over the asset's entire life, so it is sometimes called *average rate of return* or *annual rate of return.* Also, notice the similarity to ROI—return on investment—used to evaluate investment centers. The primary difference is ARR is used to evaluate the lifetime return of an investment and ROI is used to evaluate an annual return.

Let's first consider investments with no residual value. Recall the B2B portal, which costs $240,000, has equal annual net cash inflows of $60,000, a six-year useful life, and no (zero) residual value.

Let's look at the average annual operating income in the numerator first. The average annual operating income of an asset is simply the asset's total operating income over the course of its operating life divided by its lifespan (number of years). Operating income is based on *accrual accounting.* Therefore, any non-cash expenses, such as depreciation expense, must be subtracted from the asset's net cash inflows to arrive at its operating income. Exhibit 26-7 displays the formula for calculating average annual operating income.

Exhibit 26-7 | **Calculating Average Annual Income from Capital Investment**

Total net cash inflows during operating life of the asset	A
Less: Total depreciation during operating life of the asset (Cost – Residual Value)	B
Total operating income during operating life	(A – B)
Divide by: Asset's operating life in years	C
Average annual operating income from asset	[(A – B) / C]

The B2B portal's average annual operating income is as follows:

Total net cash inflows during operating life of the asset ($60,000 per year × 6 years)	$ 360,000
Less: Total depreciation during operating life of the asset ($240,000 – $0)	240,000
Total operating income during operating life	120,000
Divide by: Asset's operating life in years	÷ 6 years
Average annual operating income from asset	$ 20,000

Now let's look at the denominator of the ARR equation. The *average* amount invested in an asset is its book value at the beginning of the asset's useful life plus the book value at the end of the asset's useful life divided by 2. Another way to say that is the asset's initial cost plus the asset's residual value divided by 2. Remember that book value is cost less accumulated depreciation. Therefore, the book value of the asset decreases each year because of the annual depreciation.

Because the B2B portal does not have a residual value, the *average* amount invested is $120,000:

> **Average amount invested** = **(Amount invested + Residual value) / 2**
> = ($240,000 + $0) / 2
> = $120,000

We calculate the B2B portal's ARR as follows:

$$\text{ARR of B2B portal} = \frac{\text{Average annual operating income}}{\text{Average amount invested}}$$
$$= \frac{\$20{,}000}{\$120{,}000} = 0.167 = 16.7\%$$

Now consider the Z80 portal. Recall that the Z80 portal differed from the B2B portal only in that it had unequal net cash inflows during its life and a $30,000 residual value at the end of its life. Its average annual operating income is calculated as follows:

Total net cash inflows during operating life of the asset*	$ 360,000
Less: Total depreciation during operating life of the asset ($240,000 − $30,000)	210,000
Total operating income during operating life	150,000
Divide by: Asset's operating life in years	÷ 6 years
Average annual operating income from asset	$ 25,000

*Add cash inflows from each year, not including residual value

Notice that the Z80 portal's average annual operating income of $25,000 is higher than the B2B portal's average annual operating income of $20,000. Because the Z80 portal has a residual value at the end of its life, less depreciation is expensed each year, leading to a higher average annual operating income.

Now let's calculate the denominator of the ARR equation, the average amount invested in the asset. For the Z80 portal, the average asset investment is as follows:

$$\textbf{Average amount invested} = \textbf{(Amount invested + Residual value) / 2}$$
$$= (\$240,000 + \$30,000) / 2$$
$$= \$135,000$$

We calculate the Z80 portal's ARR as follows:

$$\textbf{ARR of Z80 portal} = \frac{\textbf{Average annual operating income}}{\textbf{Average amount invested}}$$
$$= \frac{\$25,000}{\$135,000} = 0.185 = 18.5\%$$

Companies that use the ARR method set a minimum required accounting rate of return. If Smart Touch Learning requires an ARR of at least 20%, then its managers would not approve an investment in the B2B portal or the Z80 portal because the ARR for both investments is less than 20%.

The decision rule is as follows:

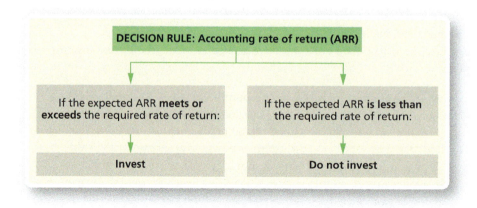

DECISIONS

Where did these numbers come from?

The management team at Browne and Browne (BnB) is deep in the budgeting process. Strategic goals have been finalized, and capital investments are being evaluated. Every department within BnB can submit potential investments. Predicted future cash flows and initial investment figures are given to the accounting department for evaluation using various capital investment analysis methods. Then the department representatives can present the proposals to the management team.

Daryl Baez is a new manager at BnB and just completed his presentation for replacing some aging equipment. He felt prepared and did not expect many questions, but the team members had several. Their primary concern is the calculations for future net cash inflows. Daryl explained that the vendor provided the figures for reduced operating costs based on the efficiency of the new equipment. Should the management team be concerned about the predictions? What should Daryl do? What would you do?

Solution

Capital investments involve large sums of cash, and decisions affect operations for many years. Therefore, the management team should be concerned about the validity of the predictions. Inaccurate predictions could have a long-term, negative impact on profits. If Daryl's only source is the sales representative trying to make the sale, the figures may not be accurate. Daryl should conduct his own research. He could contact current users of the equipment and ask for their feedback. He could look for reviews in trade magazines. Diligence on his part before the purchase will ensure the figures are accurate, satisfy the management team, and help BnB generate higher returns on investments.

Lockwood Company is considering a capital investment in machinery:

Initial investment	$ 600,000
Residual value	50,000
Expected annual net cash inflows	100,000
Expected useful life	8 years
Required rate of return	12%

8. Calculate the payback.
9. Calculate the ARR. Round the percentage to two decimal places.
10. Based on your answers to the above questions, should Lockwood invest in the machinery?

Check your answers online in MyAccountingLab or at http://www.pearsonhighered.com/Horngren.

For more practice, see Short Exercises S26-2 through S26-8. MyAccountingLab

WHAT IS THE TIME VALUE OF MONEY?

A dollar received today is worth more than a dollar to be received in the future because you can invest today's dollar and earn additional interest so you'll have more cash in the future. The fact that invested cash earns interest over time is called the **time value of money**. This concept explains why we would prefer to receive cash sooner rather than later. The time value of money means that the timing of capital investments' net cash inflows is important. Two methods of capital investment analysis incorporate the time value of money: the net present value (NPV) and internal rate of return (IRR). This

Learning Objective 3

Use the time value of money to compute the future and present values of lump sums and annuities

Time Value of Money

Recognition that money earns interest over time.

section reviews the time value of money to make sure you have a firm foundation for discussing these two methods.

Time Value of Money Concepts

The time value of money depends on several key factors:

1. The principal amount (p)
2. The number of periods (n)
3. The interest rate (i)

The principal (p) refers to the amount of the investment or borrowing. Because this chapter deals with capital investments, we will primarily discuss the principal in terms of investments. However, the same concepts apply to borrowings, such as mortgages payable and bonds payable, which we covered in the financial accounting chapters. We state the principal as either a single lump sum or an annuity. For example, if you win the lottery, you have the choice of receiving all the winnings now (a single lump sum) or receiving a series of equal payments for a period of time in the future (an annuity). An **annuity** is a stream of *equal cash payments* made at *equal time intervals*.[1] For example, $100 cash received per month for 12 months is an annuity. Capital investments also have lump sums and annuities. For example, consider the Smart Touch Learning's Web site upgrade project from the previous section of the chapter. The amount initially invested in the project, $240,000, is a lump sum because it is a one-time payment. However, the annual cash inflows of $80,000 per year for three years is an annuity. We consider both types of cash flows in capital investment decisions.

The number of periods (n) is the length of time from the beginning of the investment until termination. All else being equal, the shorter the investment period, the lower the total amount of interest earned. If you withdraw your savings after four years rather than five years, you will earn less interest. In this chapter, the number of periods is stated in years.[2]

The interest rate (i) is the annual percentage earned on the investment. Interest can be computed as either simple interest or compound interest.

Simple Interest Versus Compound Interest

Simple interest means that interest is calculated *only* on the principal amount. **Compound interest** means that interest is calculated on the principal *and* on all previously earned interest. *Compound interest assumes that all interest earned will remain invested and earn additional interest at the same interest rate.* Exhibit 26-8 compares simple interest of 6% on a five-year, $10,000 investment with interest compounded yearly (rounded to the nearest dollar). As you can see, the amount of compound interest earned yearly grows as the base on which it is calculated (principal plus cumulative interest to date) grows. Over the life of this investment, the total amount of compound interest is more than the total amount of simple interest. Most investments yield compound interest, so we assume compound interest, rather than simple interest, for the rest of this chapter.

Annuity
A stream of equal cash payments made at equal time intervals.

Simple Interest
Interest calculated only on the principal amount.

Compound Interest
Interest calculated on the principal and on all previously earned interest.

---

[1] An *ordinary annuity* is an annuity in which the installments occur at the *end* of each period. An *annuity due* is an annuity in which the installments occur at the beginning of each period. Throughout this chapter, we use ordinary annuities because they are better suited to capital budgeting cash flow assumptions.

[2] The number of periods can also be stated in days, months, or quarters. If one of these methods is used, the interest rate needs to be adjusted to reflect the number of time periods in the year.

Exhibit 26-8 | **Simple Interest Versus Compound Interest—$10,000 at 6% for 5 Years**

Year	Simple Interest Calculation	Simple Interest	Compound Interest Calculation	Compound Interest
1	$10,000 × 6%	$ 600	$10,000 × 6%	$ 600
2	$10,000 × 6%	600	($10,000 + $600) × 6%	636
3	$10,000 × 6%	600	($10,000 + $600 + $636) × 6%	674*
4	$10,000 × 6%	600	($10,000 + $600 + $636 + $674) × 6%	715
5	$10,000 × 6%	600	($10,000 + $600 + $636 + $674 + $715) × 6%	758
	Total interest	$ 3,000	Total interest	$ 3,383

*all calculations rounded to the nearest dollar for the rest of this chapter

Future Value and Present Value Factors

The future value or present value of an investment simply refers to the value of an investment at different points in time. We can calculate the future value or the present value of any investment by knowing (or assuming) information about the three factors we listed earlier: (1) the principal amount, (2) the number of periods, and (3) the interest rate. For example, in Exhibit 26-8, we calculated the interest that would be earned on (1) a $10,000 principal, (2) invested for five years, (3) at 6% interest. The **future value** of the investment is simply its worth at the end of a specific time frame (e.g., five years) or the original principal *plus* the interest earned. In our example, the future value of the investment is as follows:

Future Value
The value of an investment at the end of a specific time frame.

> **Future value = Principal + Interest earned**
> = $10,000 + $3,383
> = $13,383

If we invest $10,000 *today*, its *present value* is simply $10,000. **Present value** is the value of an investment today. So another way of stating the future value is as follows:

Present Value
The value of an investment today.

> Future value = Present value + Interest earned

If we know the future value and want to find the present value, we can rearrange the equation as follows:

> **Present value = Future value − Interest earned**
> $10,000 = $13,383 − $3,383

The only difference between present value and future value is the amount of interest that is earned in the intervening time span.

Calculating each period's compound interest, as we did in Exhibit 26-8, and then adding it to the present value to determine the future value (or subtracting it from the future value to determine the present value) is tedious. Fortunately, mathematical formulas have been developed that specify future values and present values for unlimited combinations of interest rates (*i*) and time periods (*n*). Separate formulas exist for single lump sum investments and annuities.

These formulas are programmed into most business calculators, so the user only needs to correctly enter the principal amount, interest rate, and number of time periods to find present or future values. These formulas are also programmed into spreadsheet functions in Microsoft Excel. In this section of the chapter, we use present value tables. (The Excel formulas are illustrated later in the chapter. Note that because the table values are rounded, the Excel results will differ slightly.) The present value tables contain the results of the formulas for various interest rate and time period combinations.

The formulas and resulting tables are shown in Appendix A at the end of this book:

1. Present Value of $1 (Appendix A, Table A-1)—used to calculate the value today of one future amount (a lump sum).
2. Present Value of Ordinary Annuity of $1 (Appendix A, Table A-2)—used to calculate the value today of a series of equal future amounts (annuities).
3. Future Value of $1 (Appendix A, Table A-3)—used to calculate the value in the future of one present amount (a lump sum).
4. Future Value of Ordinary Annuity of $1 (Appendix A, Table A-4)—used to calculate the value in the future of a series of equal future amounts (annuities).

Take a moment to look at these tables because we are going to use them throughout the rest of the chapter. Note that the columns are interest rates (i) and the rows are periods (n).

The numbers in each table, known as present value factors (PV factors) and future value factors (FV factors), are for an investment (or loan) of $1. For example, in Appendix A, Table A-1, the PV factor for an interest rate of 6% ($i = 6\%$) and 5 periods ($n = 5$) is 0.747. To find the present value of an amount other than $1, multiply the PV factor by the future amount. To find the future value of an amount other than $1, multiply the FV factor by the present amount.

The annuity tables are derived from the lump sum tables. For example, the Annuity PV factors (in the Present Value of Ordinary Annuity of $1 table) are the *sums* of the PV factors found in the Present Value of $1 tables for a given number of time periods. The annuity tables allow us to perform one-step calculations rather than separately computing the present value of each annual cash installment and then summing the individual present values or future values.

Present Value of a Lump Sum

The process for calculating present values is often called *discounting future cash flows* because future amounts are discounted (interest removed) to their present value. Let's consider the investment in Exhibit 26-8. The future value of the investment is $13,383. So the question is, "How much would I have to invest today (in the present time) to have $13,383 five years in the future if I invested at 6%?" Let's calculate the present value using PV factors.

> Present value = Future value × PV factor for $i = 6\%, n = 5$

We determine the PV factor from the table labeled Present Value of $1 (Appendix A, Table A-1). We use this table for lump sum amounts. We look down the 6% column and across the 5 periods row and find the PV factor is 0.747. We finish our calculation as follows:

> **Present value = Future value × PV factor for $i = 6\%, n = 5$**
> = $13,383 × 0.747
> = $9,997

Notice the calculation is off by $3 due to rounding ($10,000 − $9,997). The PV factors are rounded to three decimal places, so the calculations may not be exact. Also, the interest calculations in Exhibit 26-8 were rounded to the nearest dollar. Therefore, there are two rounding issues in this exhibit. However, we do have the answer to our question: If approximately $10,000 is invested today at 6% for five years, at the end of five years, the investment will grow to $13,383. Or, conversely, if we expect to receive $13,383 five years from now, its equivalent (discounted) value today is approximately $10,000. In other words, we need to invest approximately $10,000 today at 6% to have $13,383 five years from now.

Present Value of an Annuity

Let's now assume that instead of receiving a lump sum at the end of the five years, you will receive $2,000 at the end of each year. This is a series of equal payments ($2,000) over equal intervals (years), so it is an annuity. How much would you have to invest today to receive these payments, assuming an interest rate of 6%?

We determine the annuity PV factor from the table labeled Present Value of Ordinary Annuity of $1 (Appendix A, Table A-2). We use this table for annuities. We look down the 6% column and across the 5 periods row and find the annuity PV factor is 4.212. We finish our calculation as follows:

> **Present value = Amount of each cash inflow × Annuity PV factor for i = 6%, n = 5**
> = $2,000 × 4.212
> = $8,424

This means that an investment today of $8,424 at 6% will yield $2,000 per year for the next five years, or total payments of $10,000 over five years ($2,000 per year × 5 years). The reason is that interest is being earned on principal that is left invested each year. Let's verify the calculation.

Year	[1] Beginning Balance Previous [4]	[2] Interest [1] × 6%	[3] Withdrawal $2,000	[4] Ending Balance [1] + [2] − [3]
0				$ 8,424
1	$ 8,424	$ 505	$ 2,000	6,929
2	6,929	416	2,000	5,345
3	5,345	321	2,000	3,666
4	3,666	220	2,000	1,886
5	1,886	114*	2,000	0

*rounded up by $1

The chart shows that the initial investment of $8,424 is invested for one year, earning $505 in interest. At the end of that period, the first withdrawal of $2,000 takes place, leaving a balance of $6,929 ($8,424 + $505 − $2,000). At the end of the five years, the ending balance is $0, proving that the present value of the $2,000 annuity is $8,424.

Present Value Examples

Let's assume you have just won the lottery after purchasing one $5 lottery ticket. The state offers you the following three payout options for your after-tax prize money:

> Option 1: $1,000,000 now
> Option 2: $150,000 at the end of each year for the next 10 years ($1,500,000 total)
> Option 3: $2,000,000 at the end of 10 years

Which alternative should you take? You might be tempted to wait 10 years to "double" your winnings. You may be tempted to take the cash now and spend it. However, assume you plan to prudently invest all money received—no matter when you receive it—so that you have financial flexibility in the future (for example, for buying a house, retiring early, or taking exotic vacations). How can you choose among the three payment alternatives, when the total amount of each option varies ($1,000,000 versus $1,500,000 versus $2,000,000) and the timing of the cash flows varies (now versus some each year versus later)? Comparing these three options is like comparing apples to oranges—we just cannot do it—unless we find some common basis for comparison. Our common basis for comparison will be the prize-money's worth at a certain point in time—namely, today. In other words, if we convert each payment option to its *present value*, we can compare apples to apples.

We already know the principal amount and timing of each payment option, so the only assumption we will have to make is the interest rate. The interest rate will vary, depending on the amount of risk you are willing to take with your investment. Riskier investments (such as stock investments) command higher interest rates; safer investments (such as FDIC-insured bank deposits) yield lower interest rates. Let's say that after investigating possible investment alternatives, you choose an investment contract with an 8% annual return. We already know that the present value of Option #1 is $1,000,000 because we would receive that $1,000,000 today. Let's convert the other two payment options to their present values so that we can compare them. We will need to use the Present Value of Ordinary Annuity of $1 table (Appendix A, Table A-2) to convert payment Option #2 (because it is an annuity—a series of equal cash payments made at equal intervals) and the Present Value of $1 table (Appendix A, Table A-1) to convert payment Option #3 (because it is a lump sum). To obtain the PV factors, we will look down the 8% column and across the 10 periods row. Then we finish the calculations as follows:

Option 2:
Present value = Amount of each cash inflow × Annuity PV factor for i = 8%, n = 10
= $150,000 × 6.710
= $1,006,500

Option 3:
Present value = Future Value × PV factor for i = 8%, n = 10
= $2,000,000 × 0.463
= $926,000

Exhibit 26-9 shows that we have converted each payout option to a common basis—its worth *today*—so we can make a valid comparison among the options. Based on this comparison, you should choose Option #2 because its worth, in today's dollars, is the highest of the three options.

Exhibit 26-9 | **Present Value of Lottery Payout Options**

Payment Options	Present Value of Lottery Payout (i = 8%, n = 10)
Option #1	$ 1,000,000
Option #2	1,006,500
Option #3	926,000

The lottery problem is a good example of how businesses use discounted cash flows to analyze capital investments. Companies make initial investments. The initial investment is already in present value, similar to Lottery Option 1. The purpose of the investment is to increase cash flows in the future, but those future cash flows have to be discounted back to their present value in order to compare them to the initial investment already in present value, similar to Lottery Option 2. Some investments also have a residual value, meaning the company can sell the assets at the end of their useful lives and receive a lump sum cash inflow in the future, similar to Lottery Option 3.

Future Value of a Lump Sum

Let's now use the tables to calculate the future value of a lump sum considering the investment in Exhibit 26-8. Instead of calculating present value, though, we will change the scenario to evaluate the future value. "If I invested $10,000 today (in the present time), how much would I have in five years at an interest rate of 6%?" We will calculate the future value using FV factors.

> Future value = Present value × FV factor for i = 6%, n = 5

We determine the FV factor from the table labeled Future Value of $1 (Appendix A, Table A-3). We use this table for lump sum amounts. We look down the 6% column and across the 5 periods row and find the FV factor is 1.338. We finish our calculation as follows:

> **Future value = Present value × FV factor for i = 6%, n = 5**
> = $10,000 × 1.338
> = $13,380

Notice the calculation is off by $3 due to rounding ($13,380 − $13,383). The FV factors are rounded to three decimal places, so the calculations may not be exact. Also, the interest calculations in Exhibit 26-8 were rounded to the nearest dollar. Therefore, there are two rounding issues in this exhibit. However, we do have the answer to our question: If $10,000 is invested today at 6% for five years, at the end of five years, the investment will grow to $13,380.

Future Value of an Annuity

Let's now calculate the future value of an annuity assuming that you will receive $2,000 at the end of each year. This is a series of equal payments ($2,000) over equal intervals (years), so it is an annuity. How much would these payments be worth five years from now, assuming an interest rate of 6%?

We determine the annuity FV factor from the table labeled Future Value of Ordinary Annuity of $1 (Appendix A, Table A-4). We use this table for annuities. We look down the 6% column and across the 5 periods row and find the annuity FV factor is 5.637. We finish our calculation as follows:

> **Future value = Amount of each cash inflow × Annuity FV factor for i = 6%, n = 5**
> = $2,000 × 5.637
> = $11,274

This means investing $2,000 per year for five years at 6% will yield $11,274. The reason is that interest is being earned on principal that is left invested each year.

Now that you have reviewed time value of money concepts, in the next section we discuss the two capital investment analysis methods that incorporate the time value of money: net present value (NPV) and internal rate of return (IRR).

Calculate the present value of the following future cash flows, rounding all calculations to the nearest dollar.

11. $5,000 received in three years with interest of 10%

12. $5,000 received in each of the following three years with interest of 10%

13. Payments of $2,000, $3,000, and $4,000 received in years 1, 2, and 3, respectively, with interest of 7%

Check your answers online in MyAccountingLab or at http://www.pearsonhighered.com/Horngren.

For more practice, see Short Exercises S26-9 and S26-11. MyAccountingLab

HOW DO DISCOUNTED CASH FLOW METHODS WORK?

Learning Objective 4

Use discounted cash flow methods to make capital investment decisions

Neither payback nor ARR recognizes the time value of money. That is, these methods fail to consider the *timing* of the net cash inflows an asset generates. *Discounted cash flow methods*—the net present value (NPV) and the internal rate of return (IRR) methods—overcome this weakness. These methods incorporate compound interest by assuming that companies will reinvest future cash flows when they are received. Many service, merchandising, and manufacturing firms use discounted cash flow methods to make capital investment decisions.

The NPV and IRR methods rely on present value calculations to compare the amount of the investment (the investment's initial cost) with its expected net cash inflows. If the present value of the investment's net cash inflows exceeds the initial cost of the investment, that's a good investment. Recall that an investment's *net cash inflows* include all *future* cash flows related to the investment, such as future increased sales or cost savings, netted against the investment's cash operating costs. Because the cash outflow for the investment occurs *now*, but the net cash inflows from the investment occur in the *future*, companies can make only valid "apple-to-apple" comparisons if they convert the cash flows to the *same point in time*—namely the present value. Companies use the present value to make the comparison (rather than the future value) because the investment's initial cost is already stated at its present value.[3] Let's begin our discussion of discounted cash flow methods by taking a closer look at the NPV method.

Net Present Value (NPV)

Smart Touch Learning is considering expanding production to include laptop computers and desktop computers, with each product considered a separate potential capital investment project. The projects each require the purchase of one specialized machine. Each machine costs $1,000,000, has a five-year life, and has zero residual value. The two projects have different patterns of predicted net cash inflows, as shown in Exhibit 26-10.

---

[3]If the investment is to be purchased through lease payments, rather than a current cash outlay, we would still use the current cash price of the investment as its initial cost. If no current cash price is available, we would discount the future lease payments back to their present value to estimate the investment's current cash price.

Exhibit 26-10 | Expected Cash Inflows for Two Projects

	Annual Net Cash Inflows	
Year	Laptop Computers	Desktop Computers
1	$ 305,450	$ 500,000
2	305,450	350,000
3	305,450	300,000
4	305,450	250,000
5	305,450	40,000
Total	$ 1,527,250	$ 1,440,000

The laptop project generates more net cash inflows, but the desktop project brings in cash sooner. To decide how attractive each investment is, we find its net present value. **Net present value (NPV)** is a capital investment analysis method that measures the *net difference* between the present value of the investment's net cash inflows and the investment's initial cost. We *discount* the net cash inflows—just as we did in the lottery example—using Smart Touch Learning's minimum required rate of return. This rate is called the **discount rate** because it is the interest rate used for the present value calculations. The discount rate is the interest rate that discounts or reduces future amounts to their lesser value in the present (today). It is also called the *required rate of return* or *hurdle rate* because the investment must meet or exceed this rate to be acceptable. The discount rate depends on the riskiness of investments. The higher the risk, the higher the discount rate. Smart Touch Learning's discount rate for these investments is 14%.

Net Present Value (NPV)
A capital investment analysis method that measures the net difference between the present value of the investment's net cash inflows and the investment's cost.

Discount Rate
Management's minimum desired rate of return on a capital investment.

> To help you understand what a discount (hurdle) rate is, visualize a runner jumping over a hurdle at a track—the hurdle is the minimum height the runner must jump. The hurdle rate is the minimum rate that the investment must achieve.

Next we compare the present value of the net cash inflows to the investment's initial cost to decide which projects meet or exceed management's minimum desired rate of return. In other words, management is deciding whether the $1,000,000 investment is worth more (because the company would give it up now to invest in the project) or whether the project's future net cash inflows are worth more. Management can make a valid comparison only between the two sums of money by comparing them at the *same* point in time—namely, at their present value.

NPV with Equal Periodic Net Cash Inflows

Smart Touch Learning expects the laptop project to generate $305,450 of net cash inflows each year for five years. Because these cash flows are equal in amount and occur every year, they are an annuity. Therefore, we use the Present Value of Ordinary Annuity of $1 table (Appendix A, Table A-2) to find the appropriate Annuity PV factor for $i = 14\%$, $n = 5$.

The present value of the net cash inflows from Smart Touch Learning's laptop project is as follows:

Present value = Amount of each cash inflow × Annuity PV factor for $i = 14\%$, $n = 5$
= $305,450 × 3.433
= $1,048,610

Next we simply subtract the investment's initial cost of $1,000,000 from the present value of the net cash inflows of $1,048,610. The difference of $48,610 is the *net* present value (NPV), as shown below:

Years		Net Cash Inflow	Annuity PV Factor ($i = 14\%$, $n = 5$)	Present Value
1–5	Present value of annuity	$305,450	3.433	$ 1,048,610
0	Initial investment			(1,000,000)
	Net present value of the laptop project			$ 48,610

A *positive* NPV means that the project earns *more than* the required rate of return. A negative NPV means that the project earns *less than* the required rate of return. This leads to the following decision rule:

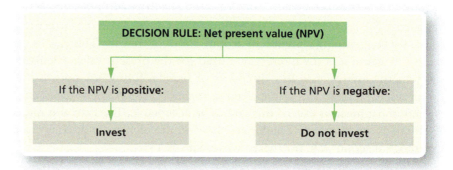

In Smart Touch Learning's case, the laptop project is an attractive investment. The $48,610 positive NPV means that the laptop project earns *more than* Smart Touch Learning's 14% required rate of return.

Another way managers can use present value analysis is to start the capital budgeting process by computing the total present value of the net cash inflows from the project to determine the *maximum* amount the company can invest in the project and still earn the required rate of return. For Smart Touch Learning, the present value of the net cash inflows is $1,048,610. This means that Smart Touch Learning can invest a maximum of $1,048,610 and still earn the 14% target rate of return. (If Smart Touch Learning invests $1,048,610, the NPV will be $0 and the return will be exactly 14%.) Because Smart Touch Learning's managers believe they can undertake the project for $1,000,000, the project is an attractive investment.

NPV with Unequal Periodic Net Cash Inflows

In contrast to the laptop project, the net cash inflows of the desktop project are unequal—$500,000 in year 1, $350,000 in year 2, and so on—because the company expects to have higher sales volume in the early years of the project than in later years. Because these amounts vary by year, Smart Touch Learning's managers *cannot* use the annuity table to compute the present value of the desktop project. They must compute the present value of each individual year's net cash inflows *separately* (as separate lump sums received in different years), using the Present Value of $1 table (Appendix A, Table A-1). The net cash inflow received in year 1 is discounted using a PV factor of $i = 14\%$, $n = 1$, while the $350,000 net cash inflow received in year 2 is discounted using a PV factor of $i = 14\%$, $n = 2$, and so forth. After separately discounting each of the five years' net cash inflows, we add each result to find that the *total* present value of the desktop project's net cash inflows is $1,078,910. Finally, we subtract the investment's cost of $1,000,000 to arrive at the desktop project's NPV: $78,910.

Years		Net Cash Inflow	PV Factor (i = 14%)	Present Value
	Present value of each year's inflow:			
1	(n = 1)	$ 500,000	0.877	$ 438,500
2	(n = 2)	350,000	0.769	269,150
3	(n = 3)	300,000	0.675	202,500
4	(n = 4)	250,000	0.592	148,000
5	(n = 5)	40,000	0.519	20,760
	Total PV of cash inflows			1,078,910
0	Initial investment			(1,000,000)
	Net present value of the desktop project			$ 78,910

Because the NPV is positive, Smart Touch Learning expects the desktop project to earn more than the 14% required rate of return, making this an attractive investment.

Our calculations show that both the laptop and desktop projects have positive NPVs. Therefore, both are attractive investments. Because resources are limited, companies are not always able to invest in all capital assets that meet their investment criteria. As mentioned earlier, this is called *capital rationing*. For example, Smart Touch Learning may not have the funds to invest in both the desktop and laptop projects at this time. In this case, Smart Touch Learning should choose the desktop project because it yields a higher NPV. The desktop project should earn an additional $78,910 beyond the 14% required rate of return, while the laptop project returns an additional $48,610 and both projects require the same investment of $1,000,000.

This example illustrates an important point. The laptop project promises more *total* net cash inflows. But the *timing* of the desktop cash flows—loaded near the beginning of the project—gives the desktop investment a higher NPV. The desktop project is more attractive because of the time value of money. Its dollars, which are received sooner, are worth more now than the more distant dollars of the laptop project.

NPV of a Project with Residual Value

Many assets yield cash inflows at the end of their useful lives because they have residual value. Companies discount an investment's residual value to its present value when determining the *total* present value of the project's net cash inflows. The residual value is discounted as a single lump sum—not an annuity—because it will be received only once, when the asset is sold. In short, it is just another type of cash inflow of the project.

Suppose Smart Touch Learning expects that the laptop project equipment will be worth $100,000 at the end of its five-year life. To determine the laptop project's NPV, we discount the residual value of $100,000 using the Present Value of $1 table ($i = 14\%$, $n = 5$) located in Appendix A, Table A-1. We then *add* its present value of $51,900 to the present value of the laptop project's other net cash inflows we calculated previously ($1,048,610). This gives the new net present value calculation as shown here:

Years		Net Cash Inflow	Annuity PV Factor ($i = 14\%$, $n = 5$)	PV Factor ($i = 14\%$, $n = 5$)	Present Value
1–5	Present value of annuity	$305,450	3.433		$ 1,048,610
5	Present value of residual value	100,000		0.519	51,900
	Total PV of cash inflows				1,100,510
0	Initial investment				(1,000,000)
	Net present value of the laptop project				$ 100,510

Because of the expected residual value, the laptop project is now more attractive than the desktop project. If Smart Touch Learning could pursue only the laptop or desktop project because of capital rationing, Smart Touch Learning would now choose the laptop project because its NPV of $100,510 is higher than the desktop project's NPV of $78,910 and both projects require the same investment of $1,000,000.

Profitability Index

If Smart Touch Learning had to choose between the laptop and desktop project, the company would choose the desktop project in the first scenario because it yields a higher NPV ($78,910) and the laptop project in the second scenario because it yields a higher NPV when the residual value is considered ($100,510). However, comparing the NPV of the two projects is *only* valid because both projects require the same initial cost—$1,000,000. In contrast, Exhibit 26-11 summarizes three capital investment options faced by Smart Touch Learning. Each capital project requires a different initial investment. All three projects are attractive because each yields a positive NPV. Assuming Smart Touch Learning can invest in only one project at this time, which one should it choose? Project B yields the highest NPV, but it also requires a larger initial investment than the alternatives.

Exhibit 26-11 | Smart Touch Learning Capital Investment Options

Cash Flows	Project A	Project B	Project C
Present value of net cash inflows	$ 150,000	$ 238,000	$ 182,000
Initial investment	(125,000)	(200,000)	(150,000)
Net present value (NPV)	$ 25,000	$ 38,000	$ 32,000

Profitability Index

Computes the number of dollars returned for every dollar invested, with all calculations performed in present value dollars. Present value of net cash inflows / Initial investment.

To choose among the projects, Smart Touch Learning computes the profitability index (also known as the *present value index*). The **profitability index** computes the number of dollars returned for every dollar invested, *with all calculations performed in present value dollars.* The profitability index is computed as follows:

> Profitability index = Present value of net cash inflows / Initial investment

The profitability index allows us to compare alternative investments in present value terms (like the NPV method), but it also considers differences in the investments' initial cost. Let's compute the profitability index for all three alternatives.

Project	Present value of net cash inflows	/	Initial investment	=	Profitability index
A	$ 150,000	/	$ 125,000	=	1.20
B	238,000	/	200,000	=	1.19
C	182,000	/	150,000	=	1.21

The profitability index shows that Project C is the best of the three alternatives because it returns $1.21 (in present value dollars) for every $1.00 invested. Projects A and B return slightly less.

Let's also compute the profitability index for Smart Touch Learning's laptop and desktop projects (using the first scenario, without the residual value for the laptop project):

Project	Present value of net cash inflows	/	Initial investment	=	Profitability index
Laptop	$ 1,048,610	/	$ 1,000,000	=	1.049
Desktop	1,078,910	/	1,000,000	=	1.079

The profitability index confirms our prior conclusion that the desktop project is more profitable than the laptop project. The desktop project returns $1.079 (in present value dollars) for every $1.00 invested. We did not need the profitability index to determine that the desktop project was preferable because both projects required the same investment ($1,000,000). Because Smart Touch Learning chose the desktop project over the laptop project, the NPV of the laptop project is the opportunity cost. The *opportunity cost* is the benefit foregone by choosing an alternative course of action.

Internal Rate of Return (IRR)

Another discounted cash flow method for capital budgeting is the internal rate of return. The **internal rate of return (IRR)** is the rate of return, based on discounted cash flows, of a capital investment. *It is the interest rate that makes the NPV of the investment equal to zero.*

Let's look at this concept in another light by assuming NPV equals zero:

NPV = Present value of net cash inflows – Initial investment
If:
NPV = 0
then:
Initial investment = Present value of net cash inflows

Internal Rate of Return (IRR)
The rate of return, based on discounted cash flows, of a capital investment. The interest rate that makes the NPV of the investment equal to zero.

When NPV is calculated, the PV factor is selected using the company's required rate of return. If the NPV is positive, then you know the actual rate of return is greater than the required rate of return and it is an acceptable project. However, you do not know the actual rate of return, only that it is greater than the required rate. If the NPV is zero, then you know the actual rate is equal to the required rate. The actual rate of return is called the *internal rate of return*. In other words, the IRR is the *interest rate* that makes the initial cost of the investment equal to the present value of the investment's net cash inflows, which means the NPV is zero. The IRR is compared to the required rate of return to determine if the project is acceptable.

IRR with Equal Periodic Net Cash Inflows

Let's first consider Smart Touch Learning's laptop project, which would cost $1,000,000 and result in five equal yearly net cash inflows of $305,450. We compute the IRR of an investment with equal periodic cash flows (annuity) by taking the following steps:

1. The IRR is the interest rate that makes the cost of the investment *equal to* the present value of the investment's net cash inflows, so we set up the following equation:

> Initial investment = PV of net cash inflows
> Initial investment = Amount of each cash inflow × Annuity PV factor (i = ?, n = given)

2. Next we plug in the information we do know—the investment cost, $1,000,000, the equal annual net cash inflows, $305,450, but assume there is no residual value, and the number of periods (five years):

> **Initial investment = Amount of each cash inflow × Annuity PV factor (i = ?, n = given)**
> $1,000,000 = $305,450 × Annuity PV factor (i = ?, n = 5)

3. We then rearrange the equation and solve for the Annuity PV factor (i = ?, n = 5):

> **Annuity PV factor (i = ?, n = 5) = Initial investment / Amount of each cash inflow**
> = $1,000,000 / $305,450
> = 3.274

4. Finally we find the interest rate that corresponds to this Annuity PV factor. Turn to the Present Value of Ordinary Annuity of $1 table (Appendix A, Table A-2). Scan the row corresponding to the project's expected life—five years, in our example. Choose the column(s) with the number closest to the Annuity PV factor you calculated in step 3. The 3.274 annuity PV factor is in the 16% column. Therefore, the IRR of the laptop project is 16%. Smart Touch Learning expects the project to earn an internal rate of return of 16% over its life. We can confirm this result by using a 16% discount rate to calculate the project's NPV and prove the amount is zero. In other words, 16% is the discount rate that makes the investment cost equal to the present value of the investment's net cash inflows.

Years		Net Cash Inflow	Annuity PV Factor (i = 16%, n = 5)	Present Value
1–5	Present value of annuity	$305,450	3.274	$ 1,000,000*
0	Initial investment			(1,000,000)
	Net present value of the laptop project			$ 0

*slight rounding of $43

To decide whether the project is acceptable, compare the IRR with the minimum desired rate of return. The decision rule is as follows:

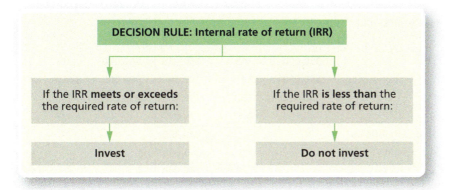

DECISION RULE: Internal rate of return (IRR)

If the IRR **meets or exceeds** the required rate of return:

Invest

If the IRR **is less than** the required rate of return:

Do not invest

Recall that Smart Touch Learning's required rate of return, or discount rate, is 14%. Because the laptop project's IRR (16%) is higher than the hurdle rate (14%), Smart Touch Learning would invest in the project.

In the laptop project, the exact Annuity PV factor (3.274) appears in the Present Value of an Ordinary Annuity of $1 table (Appendix A, Table A-2). Many times, the exact factor will not appear in the table. For example, let's find the IRR of Smart Touch Learning's B2B portal from Exhibit 26-4. Recall the B2B portal had a six-year life with annual net cash inflows of $60,000. The investment costs $240,000. We find its Annuity PV factor using the same steps:

Annuity PV factor (i = ?, n = 6) = Initial investment / Amount of each cash inflow
= $240,000 / $60,000
= 4.000

Now look in the Present Value of Ordinary Annuity of $1 table in the row marked 6 periods (Appendix A, Table A-2). You will not see 4.00 under any column. The closest two factors are 3.889 (at 14%) and 4.111 (at 12%). Thus, the B2B portal's IRR must be somewhere between 12% and 14%. If we need a more precise figure, we could interpolate, or use a business calculator or Microsoft Excel, to find the portal's exact IRR of 12.978%. Since Smart Touch Learning had a 14% required rate of return, it would *not* invest in the B2B portal because the portal's IRR is less than 14%.

IRR with Unequal Periodic Net Cash Flows

Because the desktop project has unequal cash inflows, Smart Touch Learning cannot use the Present Value of Ordinary Annuity of $1 table to find the asset's IRR. Rather, Smart Touch Learning must use a trial-and-error procedure to determine the discount rate making the project's NPV equal to zero. For example, because the company's minimum required rate of return is 14%, Smart Touch Learning might start by calculating whether the desktop project earns at least 14%. Recall from the NPV calculation that the desktop's NPV using a 14% discount rate is $78,910. Because the NPV is *positive*, the IRR must be *higher* than 14%. Smart Touch Learning continues the trial-and-error process using *higher* discount rates until the company finds the rate that brings the net present value of the desktop project to *zero*. The table on the next page shows the NPV calculations using discount rates of 16% and 18%. At 18%, the NPV is $3,980, which is very close to zero. Thus, the IRR must be slightly higher than 18%.

Years		Net Cash Inflow	PV Factor ($i = 16\%$)	Present Value	Net Cash Inflow	PV Factor ($i = 18\%$)	Present Value
	PV of each year's inflow:						
1	($n = 1$)	$ 500,000	0.862	$ 431,000	$ 500,000	0.847	$ 423,500
2	($n = 2$)	350,000	0.743	260,050	350,000	0.718	251,300
3	($n = 3$)	300,000	0.641	192,300	300,000	0.609	182,700
4	($n = 4$)	250,000	0.552	138,000	250,000	0.516	129,000
5	($n = 5$)	40,000	0.476	19,040	40,000	0.437	17,480
	Total PV of cash inflows			1,040,390			1,003,980
0	Initial investment			(1,000,000)			(1,000,000)
	NPV			$ 40,390			$ 3,980

The desktop's internal rate of return is higher than Smart Touch Learning's 14% required rate of return, so the desktop project is acceptable.

Comparing Capital Investment Analysis Methods

We have discussed four capital budgeting methods commonly used by companies to make capital investment decisions. Two of these methods do not incorporate the time value of money: payback and ARR. The discounted cash flow methods are superior because they consider both the time value of money and profitability. These methods compare an investment's initial cost with its future net cash inflows—all converted to the *same point in time*—the present value. Profitability is built into the discounted cash flow methods because they consider *all* cash inflows and outflows over the project's life. Exhibit 26-12 compares the four methods of capital investment analysis.

Exhibit 26-12 | **Comparison of Capital Investment Analysis Methods**

	Payback	Accounting Rate of Return (ARR)	Net Present Value (NPV)	Internal Rate of Return (IRR)
Focus	The time it takes to recover the company's initial cash investment	How the investment will affect operating income	The difference between the PV of the net cash inflows and the initial cash investment	The rate of return, based on discounted cash flows, of a capital investment
Strengths	• Simple to compute • Highlights risks of investments with longer cash recovery periods	• The only method that uses accrual accounting figures • Measures the profitability of the asset over its entire life	• Incorporates the time value of money • Considers the asset's net cash flows over its entire life • Indicates whether the asset will earn the company's minimum required rate of return	• Incorporates the time value of money • Considers the asset's net cash flows over its entire life • Computes the project's unique rate of return • No additional steps needed for capital rationing decisions
Weaknesses	• Ignores the time value of money • Ignores any cash flows occurring after the payback period, including any residual value	• Ignores the time value of money	• The profitability index should be computed for capital rationing decisions when the assets require different initial investments	• Difficult to calculate accurately without a business calculator or computer software

Managers often use more than one method to gain different perspectives on risks and returns. For example, Smart Touch Learning could decide to pursue capital projects with positive NPVs, provided that those projects have a payback of less than or equal to four years.

TYING IT ALL TOGETHER

TravelCenters of America LLC is the largest full-service travel center company in the United States, serving both professional drivers and motorists. Since 2011, the company's growth strategy has been to acquire additional travel center and convenience center locations. In 2015, TravelCenters announced its acquisition of Quaker Steak & Lube, a casual dining restaurant brand. In the company's annual report, the company states, "We currently intend to continue our efforts to selectively acquire additional properties and businesses and to otherwise grow our business."

What are some capital investment analysis methods that companies, such as TravelCenters of America LLC, might use to evaluate its capital investment choices?

There are several different methods that companies can use to evaluate its capital investment choices. For example, the payback method measures the length of time it would take for a company to recover, in net cash inflows, its initial investment. Another analysis method, the accounting rate of return, measures the profitability of an investment.

While the payback method and accounting rate of return method can be useful, neither method recognizes the time value of method. Which methods might TravelCenters of America LLC use if they wanted to factor in the timing of the net cash flows an investment generates?

TravelCenters of America LLC could use either the net present value (NPV) or internal rate of return (IRR) method to evaluate a potential investment and the timing of the net cash flows it generates. The net present value method evaluates the difference between the present value of the net cash inflows and the initial cash investment. This analysis indicates if a company will earn the company's minimum rate or return. The internal rate of return method is useful in determining the actual rate of return of a capital investment but can be difficult to calculate without using software such as Excel.

Sensitivity Analysis

The examples of capital investment analysis methods illustrated in the chapter used the present value tables located in Appendix A. These calculations can also be completed using a business calculator with NPV and IRR functions. Using computer spreadsheet software, such as Microsoft Excel, can be more beneficial, however, because it allows for easy manipulation of the figures to perform sensitivity analysis. Remember that sensitivity analysis is a *what if* technique that shows how results differ when underlying assumptions change. Capital budgeting decisions affect cash flows far into the future. Smart Touch Learning managers might want to know whether their decision would be affected by any of their major assumptions. Examples include changing the discount rate from 14% to 12% or 16% or increasing or decreasing the net cash inflows by 10%. After reviewing the basic information for NPV analysis, managers perform sensitivity analyses to recalculate and review the results.

Let's use Excel to calculate the NPV and IRR of the two projects Smart Touch Learning is considering: laptop computers and desktop computers. Recall that both projects require an initial investment of $1,000,000 and have no residual value. Their annual net cash inflows are:

	Annual Net Cash Inflows	
Year	Laptop Computers	Desktop Computers
1	$ 305,450	$ 500,000
2	305,450	350,000
3	305,450	300,000
4	305,450	250,000
5	305,450	40,000
Total	$ 1,527,250	$ 1,440,000

One method of setting up Excel spreadsheets is to have areas of the spreadsheet designated for inputs and outputs. Cells for entering the inputs are at the top of the spreadsheet. Cells with formulas to calculate the outputs are in a section below the inputs. All outputs are calculated by Excel based on the formulas entered, which reference the cells with the inputs. This method of setup allows the user to make changes to any input cell and have Excel automatically recalculate the outputs. Exhibit 26-13 shows the Excel spreadsheet set up in this manner with Smart Touch Learning's capital investment analysis for the two projects.

Exhibit 26-13 | Capital Investment Analysis Using Excel

	A	B	C	D	E	F
1	Smart Touch Learning					
2	Capital Investment Analysis					
3						
4	Project:	Laptops		Desktops		
5						
6	INPUTS:					
7	Useful Life (in years)	5		5		
8	Discount rate	14%		14%		
9						
10	Initial Investment	$ (1,000,000)		$ (1,000,000)		
11	Cash Inflows:					
12	Year 1	305,450		500,000		
13	Year 2	305,450		350,000		
14	Year 3	305,450		300,000		
15	Year 4	305,450		250,000		
16	Year 5	305,450		40,000		
17	Totals	$ 1,527,250		$ 1,440,000		
18						
19	OUTPUTS:					
20	NPV	$48,635		$79,196		
21	IRR	16.01%		18.23%		
22						

Notice that the initial investment is entered as a negative amount because it is a cash outflow and the cash inflows are entered as positive amounts. In the output section, Excel calculated the NPV for both projects at a slightly different amount than the amounts calculated using the PV tables. The difference between the Excel calculation and the calculation using the PV tables is because the PV factors in the tables are rounded to three decimal places.

Exhibit 26-14 shows the formulas used to calculate the NPV and IRR of the two projects.

Exhibit 26-14 | Excel Formulas

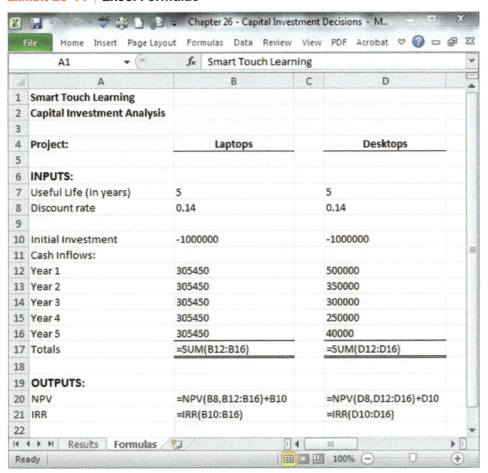

The formula to calculate NPV is = NPV(rate, value1, value2, ...). For the laptop project, the discount rate is entered in cell B8 and the cash inflows are in cells B12 through B16. Notice that the initial investment amount in cell B10 is added. Excel calculated the PV of the cash inflows and then added the negative amount of the cash outflow to determine the NPV:

$$= \text{NPV(B8, B12: B16)} + \text{B10}$$

The IRR formula includes the range of all the cash flows, including the initial investment. Keep in mind that it is imperative to list the cash flows in the proper order! The time value of money considers the timing of the cash flows, and Excel is calculating the NPV and IRR based on the order of the entries.

Now that the spreadsheet is set up, Smart Touch Learning can easily change any amounts in the input section to complete a sensitivity analysis. Also, the spreadsheet can be used to analyze any other projects by simply changing the inputs. If other projects have longer lives, then rows can be inserted to accommodate the additional cash inflows and then the formulas adjusted to include those rows.

Try setting up the spreadsheet as shown. Then change some inputs—such as the discount rate—to see how the results change.

Capital Rationing

We have mentioned capital rationing several times, but it is worthwhile to revisit the topic. Most companies have limited resources and have to make hard decisions about which projects to pursue and which ones to delay or reject. These decisions are not just based on the quantitative factors of payback, ARR, NPV, and IRR. Qualitative factors must also be considered. For example, a company may choose manufacturing equipment with a lower NPV because it is more environmentally friendly or accept a project that is not profitable but adds value to the community. Companies should also consider the opportunity costs of rejecting certain projects and the possibility of lost business if there is a negative public perception of the company's choices. Exhibit 26-15 shows a decision tree for capital rationing.

Exhibit 26-15 | Decision Tree for Capital Rationing

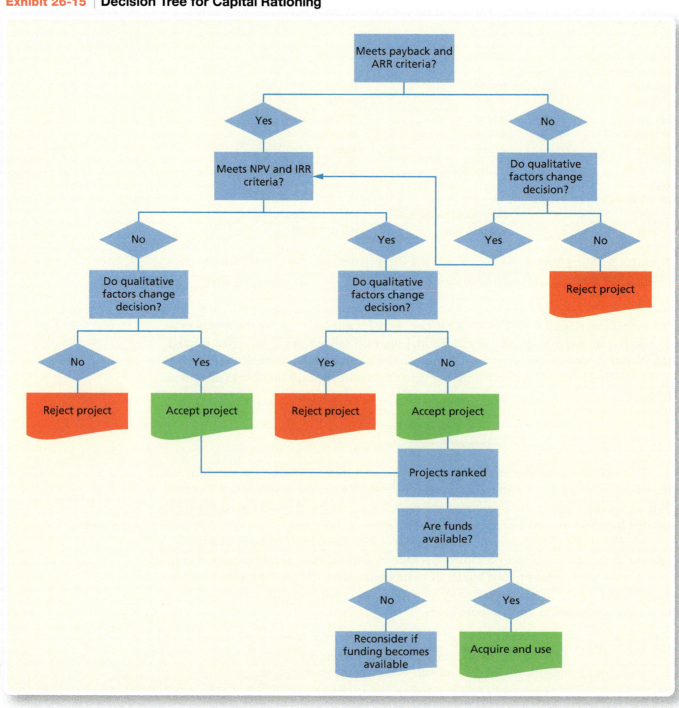

Cornell Company is considering a project with an initial investment of $596,500 that is expected to produce cash inflows of $125,000 for nine years. Cornell's required rate of return is 12%.

14. What is the NPV of the project?
15. What is the IRR of the project?
16. Is this an acceptable project for Cornell?

Check your answers online in MyAccountingLab or at http://www.pearsonhighered.com/Horngren.

For more practice, see Short Exercises S26-12 through S26-15. MyAccountingLab

REVIEW

> Things You Should Know

1. What is capital budgeting?

- Capital assets are long-term, operational assets.

- Capital investments are acquisitions of capital assets.

- Capital budgeting is planning to invest in capital assets in a way that returns the most profitability to the company.

- Capital budgeting decisions typically require large investments and affect operations for several years.

- The capital budgeting process involves the following steps: develop strategies, plan, direct, control.

- Capital rationing is the process of ranking and choosing among alternative capital investments based on the availability of funds.

- Capital budgeting has a focus on cash flows.

  - Cash inflows include:
    - Revenue generated from the investment
    - Savings in operating costs
    - Residual value

  - Cash outflows include:
    - Initial investment (acquisition cost)
    - Additional operating costs
    - Refurbishment, repairs, and maintenance

CHAPTER 26

2. How do the payback and accounting rate of return methods work?

■ Payback is a capital investment analysis method that measures the length of time it takes to recover, in net cash inflows, the cost of the initial investment.

- If net cash inflows are equal:

$$\text{Payback} = \frac{\text{Amount invested}}{\text{Expected annual net cash inflow}}$$

- If net cash inflows are unequal:
  - Add accumulated net cash inflows for full years before complete recovery, then:

$$\text{Payback} = \text{Full years} + \frac{\text{Amount needed to complete recovery in next year}}{\text{Net cash inflow in next year}}$$

- Criticisms of payback:
  - Focus is on time, not profitability
  - Ignores cash flows after payback period
- Decision rule: If the payback period is equal to or less than a set amount of time (such as the useful life), invest in the asset.

■ Accounting rate of return (ARR) is a capital investment analysis method that measures the profitability of an investment.

$$\text{ARR} = \frac{\text{Average annual operating income}}{\text{Average amount invested}}$$

- Uses operating income rather than cash flows.
- Decision rule: If the expected ARR *meets or exceeds* the required rate of return, invest in the asset.

3. What is the time value of money?

■ The fact that invested money earns interest over time is called the *time value of money*. This concept explains why we would prefer to receive cash sooner rather than later.

■ Lump sum payments are one-time cash payments.

■ Annuities are streams of equal cash payments made at equal time intervals.

■ Simple interest means that interest is calculated *only* on the principal amount.

■ Compound interest means that interest is calculated on the principal *and* on all previously earned interest.

■ To calculate the present value of a lump sum, use the following equation:

$$\text{Present value} = \text{Future value} \times \text{PV factor for } i = ?, n = ?$$

■ To calculate the present value of an annuity, use this equation:

$$\text{Present value} = \text{Amount of each cash inflow} \times \text{Annuity PV factor for } i = ?, n = ?$$

- To calculate the future value of a lump sum, use the following equation:

> Future value = Present value × FV factor for i = ?, n = ?

- To calculate the future value of an annuity, use this equation:

> Future value = Amount of each cash inflow × Annuity FV factor for i = ?, n = ?

4. How do discounted cash flow methods work?

- Discounted cash flow methods incorporate compound interest and make comparisons by converting all cash flows to the *same point in time*—namely the present value.
- Net Present Value (NPV) analysis is a capital investment analysis method that measures the net difference between the present value of the investment's net cash inflows and the investment's cost.
  - Discount rate is management's minimum desired rate of return on a capital investment and is used to select the present value factors used when calculating the net present value of a project.
  - Decision rule: If the NPV is *positive*, invest in the capital asset.
  - The profitability index computes the number of dollars returned for every dollar invested, *with all calculations performed in present value dollars*. It is useful to rank projects of different sizes.

> Profitability index = Present value of net cash inflows / Initial investment

- Internal rate of return (IRR) is the rate of return, based on discounted cash flows, of a capital investment. *It is the interest rate that makes the NPV of the investment equal to zero.*
  - If net cash inflows are equal:
    - Determine the annuity PV factor using this equation:

> Annuity PV factor (i = ?, n = given) = Initial investment / Amount of each cash inflow

  - Use the Present Value of an Ordinary Annuity of $1 table to find the factor closest to the result to estimate the IRR.
  - If net cash inflows are unequal, use the following methods:
    - A trial-and-error method can be used to estimate the IRR.
    - To find an exact IRR, use a business calculator or spreadsheet software, such as Excel.
    - Decision rule: If the IRR *meets or exceeds* the required rate of return, invest in the asset.
- Review Exhibit 26-12 for a comparison of the four capital investment analysis methods.
- Sensitivity analysis allows managers to evaluate differences when underlying assumptions change.
- Using spreadsheet software, such as Excel, allows for quicker, more precise analysis and easier sensitivity analysis.
- Capital rationing occurs when funds for capital investments are limited.
  - Quantitative and qualitative factors should be considered.
  - Review Exhibit 26-15 for a capital rationing decision tree.

> Check Your Understanding 26-1

Check your understanding of the chapter by completing this problem and then looking at the solution. Use this practice to help identify which sections of the chapter you need to study more.

Dyno-max is considering buying a new water treatment system for its plant in Austin, Texas. The company screens its potential capital investments using the payback and accounting rate of return methods. If a potential investment has a payback of less than four years and a minimum 12% accounting rate of return, it will be considered further. The data for the water treatment system follow:

Cost of water treatment system	$ 48,000
Estimated residual value	0
Estimated annual net cash inflow (each year for 5 years) from anticipated environmental cleanup savings	13,000
Estimated useful life	5 years

Requirements

1. Compute the water treatment system's payback. (See Learning Objective 2)
2. Compute the water treatment system's ARR. (See Learning Objective 2)
3. Should Dyno-max turn down this investment proposal or consider it further? (See Learning Objective 2)

> Solution

Requirement 1

$$\text{Payback} = \frac{\text{Amount invested}}{\text{Expected annual net cash inflow}}$$

$$= \frac{\$48,000}{\$13,000} = 3.7 \text{ years (rounded)}$$

Requirement 2

Total net cash inflows during operating life of the asset ($13,000 per year × 5 years)	$ 65,000
Less: Total depreciation during operating life of the asset ($48,000 − $0)	48,000
Total operating income during operating life	17,000
Divide by: Asset's operating life in years	÷5 years
Average annual operating income from asset	$ 3,400

$$\text{ARR} = \frac{\$3,400}{(\$48,000 + \$0) / 2} = \frac{\$3,400}{\$24,000} = 0.142 = 14.2\%$$

Requirement 3

Decision: The water treatment system proposal passes both initial screening tests. The payback is slightly less than four years, and the accounting rate of return is higher than 12%. Dyno-max should further analyze the proposal using a method that incorporates the time value of money.

> Check Your Understanding 26-2

Check your understanding of the chapter by completing this problem and then looking at the solution. Use this practice to help identify which sections of the chapter you need to study more.

Recall from Check Your Understanding 26-1 that Dyno-max is considering buying a new water treatment system. The investment proposal passed the initial screening tests (payback and accounting rate of return) so the company now wants to analyze the proposal using the discounted cash flow methods. Recall that the water treatment system costs $48,000, has a five-year life, and has no residual value. The estimated net cash inflows from environmental cleanup savings are $13,000 per year over its life. The company's required rate of return is 16%.

Requirements

1. Compute the water treatment system's NPV. (See Learning Objective 4)

2. Find the water treatment system's IRR (exact percentage is not required). (See Learning Objective 4)

3. Should Dyno-max buy the water treatment system? Why? (See Learning Objective 4)

> Solution

Requirement 1

Years		Net Cash Inflow	Annuity PV Factor (*i* = 16%, *n* = 5)	Present Value
1–5	Present value of annuity	$13,000	3.274	$ 42,562
0	Initial investment			(48,000)
	Net present value			$ (5,438)

Requirement 2

Annuity PV factor (*i* = ?, *n* = 5) = Initial investment / Amount of each cash inflow
= $48,000 / $13,000
= 3.692

Because the cash flows occur for five years, we look for the PV factor 3.692 in the row marked *n* = 5 on the Present Value of Ordinary Annuity of $1 table (Appendix A, Table A-2). The PV factor is 3.605 at 12% and 3.791 at 10%. Therefore, the water treatment system has an IRR that falls between 10% and 12%. (*Optional:* Using a business calculator or Excel, we find an 11.04% internal rate of return.)

Requirement 3

Decision: Dyno-max should not buy the water treatment system. It has a negative NPV, and its IRR falls below the company's required rate of return. Both methods consider profitability and the time value of money. Because the savings came mainly from the estimated environmental cleanup savings, the company may want to study this issue further to ensure all environmental savings, both short-term and long-term, were considered in the initial evaluation.

> Key Terms

Accounting Rate of Return
(ARR) (p. 1434)
Annuity (p. 1438)
Capital Asset (p. 1427)
Capital Budgeting (p. 1427)
Capital Investment (p. 1427)
Capital Rationing (p. 1429)

Compound Interest (p. 1438)
Discount Rate (p. 1445)
Future Value (p. 1439)
Internal Rate of Return (IRR)
(p. 1449)
Net Present Value (NPV)
(p. 1445)

Payback (p. 1431)
Post-Audit (p. 1429)
Present Value (p. 1439)
Profitability Index (p. 1448)
Simple Interest (p. 1438)
Time Value of Money (p. 1437)

> Quick Check

Learning Objective 1

1. What is the second step of capital budgeting?
   a. Gathering the money for the investment
   b. Identifying potential projects
   c. Getting the accountant involved
   d. All of the above

Learning Objective 2

2. Which of the following methods does not consider the investment's profitability?
   a. ARR   b. Payback   c. NPV   d. IRR

Learning Objective 2

3. Suppose Francine Dunkelberg's Sweets is considering investing in warehouse-management software that costs $550,000, has $75,000 residual value, and should lead to cost savings of $130,000 per year for its five-year life. In calculating the ARR, which of the following figures should be used as the equation's denominator (average amount invested in the asset)?
   a. $275,000   b. $237,500   c. $625,000   d. $312,500

Learning Objective 3

4. Your rich aunt has promised to give you $2,000 per year at the end of each of the next four years to help you pay for college. Using a discount rate of 12%, the present value of the gift can be stated as
   a. $PV = \$2,000$ (PV factor, $i = 4\%, n = 12$).
   b. $PV = \$2,000$ (Annuity PV factor, $i = 12\%, n = 4$).
   c. $PV = \$2,000$ (Annuity FV factor, $i = 12\%, n = 4$).
   d. $PV = \$2,000 \times 12\% \times 4$.

Learning Objective 3

5. Which of the following affects the present value of an investment?
   a. The type of investment (annuity versus single lump sum)
   b. The number of time periods (length of the investment)
   c. The interest rate
   d. All of the above

Learning Objective 4

6. Which of the following is true regarding capital rationing decisions?
   a. Companies should always choose the investment with the highest NPV.
   b. Companies should always choose the investment with the highest ARR.
   c. Companies should always choose the investment with the shortest payback.
   d. None of the above

7. In computing the IRR on an expansion at Mountain Creek Resort, Vernon Valley would consider all of the following *except*

Learning Objective 4

    a. present value factors.

    b. depreciation on the assets built in the expansion.

    c. predicted cash inflows over the life of the expansion.

    d. the cost of the expansion.

8. The IRR is

Learning Objective 4

    a. the interest rate at which the NPV of the investment is zero.

    b. the firm's hurdle rate.

    c. the same as the ARR.

    d. None of the above

9. Which of the following is the most reliable method for making capital budgeting decisions?

Learning Objective 4

    a. ARR method   **c.** NPV method

    b. Post-audit method   **d.** Payback method

10. Ian Corp. is considering two expansion projects. The first project streamlines the company's warehousing facilities. The second project automates inventory utilizing bar code scanners. Both projects generate positive NPV, yet Ian Corp. only chooses the bar coding project. Why?

Learning Objective 4

    a. The payback is greater than the warehouse project's life.

    b. The internal rate of return of the warehousing project is less than the company's required rate of return for capital projects.

    c. The company is practicing capital rationing.

    d. All of the above are true.

Check your answers at the end of the chapter.

ASSESS YOUR PROGRESS

> Review Questions

1. Explain the difference between capital assets, capital investments, and capital budgeting.

2. Describe the capital budgeting process.

3. What is capital rationing?

4. What are post-audits? When are they conducted?

5. List some common cash inflows from capital investments.

6. List some common cash outflows from capital investments.

7. What is the payback method of analyzing capital investments?

8. How is payback calculated with equal net cash inflows?

9. How is payback calculated with unequal net cash inflows?

10. What is the decision rule for payback?

11. What are some criticisms of the payback method?

12. What is the accounting rate of return?

13. How is ARR calculated?

14. What is the decision rule for ARR?

15. Why is it preferable to receive cash sooner rather than later?

16. What is an annuity? How does it differ from a lump sum payment?

17. How does compound interest differ from simple interest?

18. Explain the difference between the present value factor tables—Present Value of $1 and Present Value of Ordinary Annuity of $1.

19. How is the present value of a lump sum determined?

20. How is the present value of an annuity determined?

21. Why are net present value and internal rate of return considered discounted cash flow methods?

22. What is net present value?

23. What is the decision rule for NPV?

24. What is the profitability index? When is it used?

25. What is the internal rate of return?

26. How is IRR calculated with equal net cash inflows?

27. How is IRR calculated with unequal net cash inflows?

28. What is the decision rule for IRR?

29. How can spreadsheet software, such as Excel, help with sensitivity analysis?

30. Why should both quantitative and qualitative factors be considered in capital investment decisions?

> Short Exercises

Learning Objective 1

S26-1 Outlining the capital budgeting process

Review the following activities of the capital budgeting process:

a. Budget capital investments.

b. Project investments' cash flows.

c. Perform post-audits.

d. Make investments.

e. Use feedback to reassess investments already made.

f. Identify potential capital investments.

g. Screen/analyze investments using one or more of the methods discussed.

Place the activities in sequential order as they occur in the capital budgeting process.

Learning Objective 2

S26-2 Using payback to make capital investment decisions

Carter Company is considering three investment opportunities with the following payback periods:

	Project A	Project B	Project C
Payback period	2.7 years	6.4 years	3.8 years

Use the decision rule for payback to rank the projects from most desirable to least desirable, all else being equal.

S26-3 Using accounting rate of return to make capital investment decisions

Learning Objective 2

Carter Company is considering three investment opportunities with the following accounting rates of return:

	Project X	Project Y	Project Z
ARR	13.25%	6.58%	10.47%

Use the decision rule for ARR to rank the projects from most desirable to least desirable. Carter Company's required rate of return is 8%.

S26-4 Using the payback and accounting rate of return methods to make capital investment decisions

Learning Objective 2

Consider how Hunter Valley Snow Park Lodge could use capital budgeting to decide whether the $11,000,000 Snow Park Lodge expansion would be a good investment. Assume Hunter Valley's managers developed the following estimates concerning the expansion:

Number of additional skiers per day	121 skiers
Average number of days per year that weather conditions allow skiing at Hunter Valley	142 days
Useful life of expansion (in years)	7 years
Average cash spent by each skier per day	$ 241
Average variable cost of serving each skier per day	83
Cost of expansion	11,000,000
Discount rate	10%

Assume that Hunter Valley uses the straight-line depreciation method and expects the lodge expansion to have a residual value of $600,000 at the end of its seven-year life.

Requirements

1. Compute the average annual net cash inflow from the expansion.
2. Compute the average annual operating income from the expansion.

Note: Short Exercise S26-4 must be completed before attempting Short Exercise S26-5.

S26-5 Using the payback method to make capital investment decisions

Learning Objective 2

Refer to the Hunter Valley Snow Park Lodge expansion project in Short Exercise S26-4. Compute the payback for the expansion project. Round to one decimal place.

Note: Short Exercise S26-4 must be completed before attempting Short Exercise S26-6.

S26-6 Using the ARR method to make capital investment decisions

Learning Objective 2

Refer to the Hunter Valley Snow Park Lodge expansion project in Short Exercise S26-4. Calculate the ARR. Round to two decimal places.

CHAPTER 26

Note: Short Exercises S26-4, S26-5, and S26-6 must be completed before attempting Short Exercise S26-7.

Learning Objective 2

S26-7 Using the payback and ARR methods to make capital investment decisions

Refer to the Hunter Valley Snow Park Lodge expansion project in Short Exercise S26-4 and your calculations in Short Exercises S26-5 and S26-6. Assume the expansion has zero residual value.

Requirements

1. Will the payback change? Explain your answer. Recalculate the payback if it changes. Round to one decimal place.

2. Will the project's ARR change? Explain your answer. Recalculate ARR if it changes. Round to two decimal places.

3. Assume Hunter Valley screens its potential capital investments using the following decision criteria:

Maximum payback period	5.0 years
Minimum accounting rate of return	18.00%

Will Hunter Valley consider this project further or reject it?

Learning Objective 2

S26-8 Using the payback and ARR methods to make capital investment decisions

Suppose Hunter Valley is deciding whether to purchase new accounting software. The payback for the $30,050 software package is two years, and the software's expected life is three years. Hunter Valley's required rate of return for this type of project is 10.0%. Assuming equal yearly cash flows, what are the expected annual net cash savings from the new software?

Learning Objective 3

S26-9 Determining present value

Use the Present Value of $1 table (Appendix A, Table A-1) to determine the present value of $1 received one year from now. Assume a 8% interest rate. Use the same table to find the present value of $1 received two years from now. Continue this process for a total of five years. Round to three decimal places.

Requirements

1. What is the *total* present value of the cash flows received over the five-year period?
2. Could you characterize this stream of cash flows as an annuity? Why or why not?
3. Use the Present Value of Ordinary Annuity of $1 table (Appendix A, Table A-2) to determine the present value of the same stream of cash flows. Compare your results to your answer to Requirement 1.
4. Explain your findings.

Learning Objective 3

S26-10 Determining present value

Your grandfather would like to share some of his fortune with you. He offers to give you money under one of the following scenarios (you get to choose):

1. $7,250 per year at the end of each of the next eight years
2. $49,650 (lump sum) now
3. $98,650 (lump sum) eight years from now

Requirements

1. Calculate the present value of each scenario using an 8% discount rate. Which scenario yields the highest present value? Round to nearest whole dollar.

2. Would your preference change if you used a 10% discount rate?

S26-11 Determining future value

Learning Objective 3

David is entering high school and is determined to save money for college. David feels he can save $6,000 each year for the next four years from his part-time job. If David is able to invest at 7%, how much will he have when he starts college?

Note: Short Exercise S26-4 must be completed before attempting Short Exercise S26-12.

S26-12 Using NPV to make capital investment decisions

Learning Objective 4

Refer to the Hunter Valley Snow Park Lodge expansion project in Short Exercise S26-4. What is the project's NPV (round to nearest dollar)? Is the investment attractive? Why or why not?

Note: Short Exercise S26-4 must be completed before attempting Short Exercise S26-13.

S26-13 Using NPV to make capital investment decisions

Learning Objective 4

Refer to Short Exercise S26-4. Assume the expansion has no residual value. What is the project's NPV (round to nearest dollar)? Is the investment attractive? Why or why not?

Note: Short Exercise S26-4 must be completed before attempting Short Exercise S26-14.

S26-14 Using IRR to make capital investment decisions

Learning Objective 4

Refer to Short Exercise S26-4. Continue to assume that the expansion has no residual value. What is the project's IRR? Is the investment attractive? Why or why not?

S26-15 Using NPV to make capital investment decisions

Learning Objective 4

Hicks Company is considering an investment opportunity with the following expected net cash inflows: Year 1, $235,000; Year 2, $195,000; Year 3, $125,000. The company uses a discount rate of 6%, and the initial investment is $365,000. Calculate the NPV of the investment. Should the company invest in the project? Why or why not?

> Exercises

E26-16 Defining capital investments and the capital budgeting process

Learning Objectives 1, 2, 4

Match each capital budgeting method with its definition.

Methods

1. Accounting rate of return
2. Internal rate of return
3. Net present value
4. Payback

Definitions

a. Is only concerned with the time it takes to get cash outflows returned.

b. Considers operating income but not the time value of money in its analyses.

c. Compares the present value of cash outflows to the present value of cash inflows to determine investment worthiness.

d. The true rate of return an investment earns.

Learning Objectives 1, 2, 4

E26-17 Defining capital investment terms

Fill in each statement with the appropriate capital investment analysis method: Payback, ARR, NPV, or IRR. Some statements may have more than one answer.

a. _____ is(are) more appropriate for long-term investments.

b. _____ highlights risky investments.

c. _____ shows the effect of the investment on the company's accrual-based income.

d. _____ is the interest rate that makes the NPV of an investment equal to zero.

e. _____ requires management to identify the discount rate when used.

f. _____ provides management with information on how fast the cash invested will be recouped.

g. _____ is the rate of return, using discounted cash flows, a company can expect to earn by investing in the asset.

h. _____ does not consider the asset's profitability.

i. _____ uses accrual accounting rather than net cash inflows in its computation.

Learning Objective 2

E26-18 Using payback to make capital investment decisions

Consider the following three projects. All three have an initial investment of $800,000.

	Net Cash Inflows					
	Project L		Project M		Project N	
Year	Annual	Accumulated	Annual	Accumulated	Annual	Accumulated
1	$ 100,000	$ 100,000	$ 200,000	$ 200,000	$ 400,000	$ 400,000
2	100,000	200,000	250,000	450,000	400,000	800,000
3	100,000	300,000	350,000	800,000		
4	100,000	400,000	400,000	1,200,000		
5	100,000	500,000	500,000	1,700,000		
6	100,000	600,000				
7	100,000	700,000				
8	100,000	800,000				

Requirements

1. Determine the payback period of each project. Rank the projects from most desirable to least desirable based on payback.

2. Are there other factors that should be considered in addition to the payback period?

Learning Objective 2

3.7 yrs.

E26-19 Using payback to make capital investment decisions

Henry Co. is considering acquiring a manufacturing plant. The purchase price is $1,200,000. The owners believe the plant will generate net cash inflows of $325,000 annually. It will have to be replaced in six years. Use the payback method to determine whether Henry should purchase this plant. Round to one decimal place.

E26-20 Using payback to make capital investment decisions

Henry Hardware is adding a new product line that will require an investment of $1,512,000. Managers estimate that this investment will have a 10-year life and generate net cash inflows of $310,000 the first year, $270,000 the second year, and $240,000 each year thereafter for eight years. Compute the payback period. Round to one decimal place.

Note: Exercise S26-20 must be completed before attempting Exercise S26-21.

E26-21 Using ARR to make capital investment decisions

Refer to the Henry Hardware information in Exercise E26-20. Assume the project has no residual value. Compute the ARR for the investment. Round to two places.

E26-22 Using the time value of money

Helen wants to take the next four years off work to travel around the world. She estimates her annual cash needs at $31,000 (if she needs more, she will work odd jobs). Helen believes she can invest her savings at 10% until she depletes her funds.

Requirements

1. How much money does Helen need now to fund her travels?

2. After speaking with a number of banks, Helen learns she will only be able to invest her funds at 6%. How much does she need now to fund her travels?

E26-23 Using the time value of money

Congratulations! You have won a state lottery. The state lottery offers you the following (after-tax) payout options:

Option #1:	$12,000,000 after five years
Option #2:	$2,150,000 per year for five years
Option #3:	$10,000,000 after three years

Assuming you can earn 6% on your funds, which option would you prefer?

E26-24 Using NPV to make capital investment decisions

Holmes Industries is deciding whether to automate one phase of its production process. The manufacturing equipment has a six-year life and will cost $910,000. Projected net cash inflows are as follows:

Year 1	$ 262,000
Year 2	254,000
Year 3	222,000
Year 4	215,000
Year 5	200,000
Year 6	175,000

Requirements

1. Compute this project's NPV using Holmes's 14% hurdle rate. Should Holmes invest in the equipment?

Learning Objective 2

5.9 yrs.

Learning Objective 2

13.07%

Learning Objective 3

2. $107,415

Learning Objective 3

Option #2 $9,055,800

Learning Objective 4

2. Equip. with refurb. $(18,794) NPV

CHAPTER 26

2. Holmes could refurbish the equipment at the end of six years for $104,000. The refurbished equipment could be used one more year, providing $77,000 of net cash inflows in year 7. Additionally, the refurbished equipment would have a $55,000 residual value at the end of year 7. Should Holmes invest in the equipment and refurbish it after six years? (*Hint:* In addition to your answer to Requirement 1, discount the additional cash outflow and inflows back to the present value.)

Learning Objective 4

1. Project B $40,050 NPV

E26-25 Using NPV and profitability index to make capital investment decisions

Use the NPV method to determine whether Hawkins Products should invest in the following projects:

- *Project A*: Costs $285,000 and offers seven annual net cash inflows of $55,000. Hawkins Products requires an annual return of 14% on investments of this nature.
- *Project B*: Costs $395,000 and offers 10 annual net cash inflows of $77,000. Hawkins Products demands an annual return of 12% on investments of this nature.

Requirements

1. What is the NPV of each project? Assume neither project has a residual value. Round to two decimal places.
2. What is the maximum acceptable price to pay for each project?
3. What is the profitability index of each project? Round to two decimal places.

Learning Objective 4

Project A 8%–9% IRR

E26-26 Using IRR to make capital investment decisions

Refer to the data regarding Hawkins Products in Exercise E26-25. Compute the IRR of each project, and use this information to identify the better investment.

Learning Objective 4

E26-27 Using capital rationing to make capital investment decisions

Hudson Manufacturing is considering three capital investment proposals. At this time, Hudson only has funds available to pursue one of the three investments.

	Equipment A	Equipment B	Equipment C
Present value of net cash inflows	$ 1,647,351	$ 1,969,888	$ 2,064,830
Initial investment	(1,484,100)	(1,641,573)	(1,764,812)
NPV	$ 163,251	$ 328,315	$ 300,018

Which investment should Hudson pursue at this time? Why?

Learning Objective 4

E26-28 Using capital rationing to make capital investment decisions

Mountain Manufacturing is considering the following capital investment proposals. Mountain's requirement criteria include a maximum payback period of five years and a required rate of return of 12.5%. Determine if each investment is acceptable or should be rejected (ignore qualitative factors). Rank the acceptable investments in order from most desirable to least desirable.

Project	A	B	C	D	E
Payback	3.15 years	4.20 years	2.00 years	3.25 years	5.00 years
NPV	$ 10,250	$ 42,226	$ (10,874)	$ 36,251	$ 0
IRR	13.0%	14.2%	8.5%	14.0%	12.5%
Profitability Index	1.54	1.92	0.75	2.86	1.00

> Problems Group A

P26-29A Using the time value of money

Learning Objective 3

1. $2,102,485

You are planning for a very early retirement. You would like to retire at age 40 and have enough money saved to be able to withdraw $215,000 per year for the next 40 years (based on family history, you think you will live to age 80). You plan to save by making 10 equal annual installments (from age 30 to age 40) into a fairly risky investment fund that you expect will earn 10% per year. You will leave the money in this fund until it is completely depleted when you are 80 years old.

Requirements

1. How much money must you accumulate by retirement to make your plan work? (*Hint:* Find the present value of the $215,000 withdrawals.)

2. How does this amount compare to the total amount you will withdraw from the investment during retirement? How can these numbers be so different?

P26-30A Using payback, ARR, NPV, IRR, and profitability index to make capital investment decisions

Learning Objectives 2, 4

1. 25.6% ARR; 1.35 profitability index

Splash Nation is considering purchasing a water park in Atlanta, Georgia, for $1,910,000. The new facility will generate annual net cash inflows of $483,000 for eight years. Engineers estimate that the facility will remain useful for eight years and have no residual value. The company uses straight-line depreciation, and its stockholders demand an annual return of 10% on investments of this nature.

Requirements

1. Compute the payback, the ARR, the NPV, the IRR, and the profitability index of this investment.

2. Recommend whether the company should invest in this project.

P26-31A Using payback, ARR, NPV, IRR, and profitability index to make capital investment decisions

Learning Objectives 2, 4

1. Plan A 1.09 profitability index; Plan B $(1,793,250) NPV

Hill Company operates a chain of sandwich shops. The company is considering two possible expansion plans. Plan A would open eight smaller shops at a cost of $8,700,000. Expected annual net cash inflows are $1,550,000 for 10 years, with zero residual value at the end of 10 years. Under Plan B, Hill Company would open three larger shops at a cost of $8,340,000. This plan is expected to generate net cash inflows of $990,000 per year for 10 years, the estimated useful life of the properties. Estimated residual value for Plan B is $1,200,000. Hill Company uses straight-line depreciation and requires an annual return of 10%.

Requirements

1. Compute the payback, the ARR, the NPV, and the profitability index of these two plans.

2. What are the strengths and weaknesses of these capital budgeting methods?

3. Which expansion plan should Hill Company choose? Why?

4. Estimate Plan A's IRR. How does the IRR compare with the company's required rate of return?

Learning Objectives 2, 4

1. Refurbish $19,810 NPV;
Purchase 2.7 years payback

P26-32A Using payback, ARR, and NPV with unequal cash flows

Henderson Manufacturing, Inc. has a manufacturing machine that needs attention. The company is considering two options. Option 1 is to refurbish the current machine at a cost of $1,200,000. If refurbished, Henderson expects the machine to last another eight years and then have no residual value. Option 2 is to replace the machine at a cost of $4,600,000. A new machine would last 10 years and have no residual value. Henderson expects the following net cash inflows from the two options:

Year	Refurbish Current Machine	Purchase New Machine
1	$ 350,000	$ 3,780,000
2	340,000	510,000
3	270,000	440,000
4	200,000	370,000
5	130,000	300,000
6	130,000	300,000
7	130,000	300,000
8	130,000	300,000
9		300,000
10		300,000
Total	$ 1,680,000	$ 6,900,000

Henderson uses straight-line depreciation and requires an annual return of 10%.

Requirements

1. Compute the payback, the ARR, the NPV, and the profitability index of these two options.

2. Which option should Henderson choose? Why?

Learning Objective 4

1. Plan Beta 12.94 IRR
3. Plan Alpha $105,379 NPV

P26-33A Using Excel to solve for NPV and IRR

Hayes Company is considering two capital investments. Both investments have an initial cost of $10,000,000 and total net cash inflows of $17,000,000 over 10 years. Hayes requires a 12% rate of return on this type of investment. Expected net cash inflows are as follows:

Year	Plan Alpha	Plan Beta
1	$ 1,700,000	$ 1,700,000
2	1,700,000	2,300,000
3	1,700,000	2,900,000
4	1,700,000	2,300,000
5	1,700,000	1,700,000
6	1,700,000	1,600,000
7	1,700,000	1,200,000
8	1,700,000	800,000
9	1,700,000	400,000
10	1,700,000	2,100,000
Total	$ 17,000,000	$ 17,000,000

Requirements

1. Use Excel to compute the NPV and IRR of the two plans. Which plan, if any, should the company pursue?

2. Explain the relationship between NPV and IRR. Based on this relationship and the company's required rate of return, are your answers as expected in Requirement 1? Why or why not?

3. After further negotiating, the company can now invest with an initial cost of $9,500,000 for both plans. Recalculate the NPV and IRR. Which plan, if any, should the company pursue?

> Problems Group B

P21-34B Using the time value of money

Learning Objective 3

1. $2,476,760

You are planning for an early retirement. You would like to retire at age 40 and have enough money saved to be able to withdraw $220,000 per year for the next 30 years (based on family history, you think you will live to age 70). You plan to save by making 20 equal annual installments (from age 20 to age 40) into a fairly risky investment fund that you expect will earn 8% per year. You will leave the money in this fund until it is completely depleted when you are 70 years old.

Requirements

1. How much money must you accumulate by retirement to make your plan work? (*Hint:* Find the present value of the $220,000 withdrawals.)

2. How does this amount compare to the total amount you will withdraw from the investment during retirement? How can these numbers be so different?

P26-35B Using payback, ARR, NPV, IRR, and profitability index to make capital investment decisions

Learning Objectives 2, 4

1. 24.2% ARR; 1.22 profitability index

Water City is considering purchasing a water park in Omaha, Nebraska, for $1,920,000. The new facility will generate annual net cash inflows of $472,000 for eight years. Engineers estimate that the facility will remain useful for eight years and have no residual value. The company uses straight-line depreciation, and its stockholders demand an annual return of 12% on investments of this nature.

Requirements

1. Compute the payback, the ARR, the NPV, the IRR, and the profitability index of this investment.

2. Recommend whether the company should invest in this project.

P26-36B Using payback, ARR, NPV, IRR, and profitability index to make capital investment decisions

Learning Objectives 2, 4

1. Plan A 1.39 profitability index; Plan B $(187,580) NPV

Howard Company operates a chain of sandwich shops. The company is considering two possible expansion plans. Plan A would open eight smaller shops at a cost of $8,500,000. Expected annual net cash inflows are $1,600,000 for 10 years, with zero residual value at the end of 10 years. Under Plan B, Howard Company would open three larger shops at a cost of $8,100,000. This plan is expected to generate net cash inflows of $1,000,000 per year for 10 years, which is the estimated useful life of the properties. Estimated residual value for Plan B is $990,000. Howard Company uses straight-line depreciation and requires an annual return of 6%

Requirements

1. Compute the payback, the ARR, the NPV, and the profitability index of these two plans.

2. What are the strengths and weaknesses of these capital budgeting methods?

3. Which expansion plan should Howard Company choose? Why?

4. Estimate Plan A's IRR. How does the IRR compare with the company's required rate of return?

Learning Objectives 2, 4

1. Refurbish $257,880 NPV; Purchase 2.8 years payback

P26-37B Using payback, ARR, and NPV with unequal cash flows

Hughes Manufacturing, Inc. has a manufacturing machine that needs attention. The company is considering two options. Option 1 is to refurbish the current machine at a cost of $2,600,000. If refurbished, Hughes expects the machine to last another eight years and then have no residual value. Option 2 is to replace the machine at a cost of $3,800,000. A new machine would last 10 years and have no residual value. Hughes expects the following net cash inflows from the two options:

Year	Refurbish Current Machine	Purchase New Machine
1	$ 1,760,000	$ 2,970,000
2	440,000	490,000
3	360,000	410,000
4	280,000	330,000
5	200,000	250,000
6	200,000	250,000
7	200,000	250,000
8	200,000	250,000
9		250,000
10		250,000
Total	$ 3,640,000	$ 5,700,000

Hughes uses straight-line depreciation and requires an annual return of 10%.

Requirements

1. Compute the payback, the ARR, the NPV, and the profitability index of these two options.

2. Which option should Hughes choose? Why?

P26-38B Using Excel to solve for NPV and IRR

Hamilton Company is considering two capital investments. Both investments have an initial cost of $7,000,000 and total net cash inflows of $16,000,000 over 10 years. Hamilton requires a 20% rate of return on this type of investment. Expected net cash inflows are as follows:

Learning Objective 4

1. Plan Beta 22.89% IRR
3. Plan Alpha $207,955 NPV

Year	Plan Alpha	Plan Beta
1	$ 1,600,000	$ 1,600,000
2	1,600,000	2,200,000
3	1,600,000	2,800,000
4	1,600,000	2,200,000
5	1,600,000	1,600,000
6	1,600,000	1,500,000
7	1,600,000	1,300,000
8	1,600,000	1,100,000
9	1,600,000	900,000
10	1,600,000	800,000
Total	$ 16,000,000	$ 16,000,000

Requirements

1. Use Excel to compute the NPV and IRR of the two plans. Which plan, if any, should the company pursue?

2. Explain the relationship between NPV and IRR. Based on this relationship and the company's required rate of return, are your answers as expected in Requirement 1? Why or why not?

3. After further negotiating, the company can now invest with an initial cost of $6,500,000. Recalculate the NPV and IRR. Which plan, if any, should the company pursue?

CRITICAL THINKING

> Using Excel

P26-39 Using Excel for capital budgeting calculations

Download an Excel template for this problem online in MyAccountingLab or at http://www.pearsonhighered.com/Horngren.

Glacier Creek Textiles is planning to purchase new manufacturing equipment. The equipment has an acquisition cost of $100,000, an estimated useful life of five years and no residual value. The company uses a 12% rate of return to evaluate capital projects. The cash flows for the five years are:

Year	Net Cash Outflows	Net Cash Inflows
0	$(100,000)	
1		25,000
2		29,000
3		26,000
4		28,000
5		35,000

Requirements

1. Compute the accounting rate of return.
2. Compute the net present value of the investment using Excel's PV function.
3. Compute the net present value of the investment using Excel's NPV function.
4. Compute the profitability index, rounded to two decimal places.
5. Compute the internal rate of return of the investment using Excel's IRR function. Display to two decimal places, but do not round.

> Continuing Problem

P26-40 Using payback, ARR, NPV, and IRR to make capital investment decisions

This problem continues the Piedmont Computer Company situation from Chapter 25. Piedmont Computer Company is considering purchasing two different types of servers. Server A will generate net cash inflows of $25,000 per year and have a zero residual value. Server A's estimated useful life is three years, and it costs $45,000.

Server B will generate net cash inflows of $25,000 in year 1, $15,000 in year 2, and $5,000 in year 3. Server B has a $5,000 residual value and an estimated useful life of three years. Server B also costs $45,000. Piedmont Computer Company's required rate of return is 14%.

Requirements

1. Calculate payback, accounting rate of return, net present value, and internal rate of return for both server investments. Use Microsoft Excel to calculate NPV and IRR.
2. Assuming capital rationing applies, which server should Piedmont Computer Company invest in?

COMPREHENSIVE PROBLEM

> Comprehensive Problem for Chapters 25 and 26

Darren Dillard, majority stockholder and president of Dillard, Inc., is working with his top managers on future plans for the company. As the company's managerial accountant, you've been asked to analyze the following situations and make recommendations to the management team.

Requirements

1. Division A of Dillard, Inc. has $5,250,000 in assets. Its yearly fixed costs are $557,000, and the variable costs of its product line are $1.90 per unit. The division's volume is currently 500,000 units. Competitors offer a similar product, at the same quality, to retailers for $4.25 each. Dillard's management team wants to earn a 12% return on investment on the division's assets.

   a. What is Division A's target full product cost?

   b. Given the division's current costs, will Division A be able to achieve its target profit?

   c. Assume Division A has identified ways to cut its variable costs to $1.75 per unit. What is its new target fixed cost? Will this decrease in variable costs allow the division to achieve its target profit?

   d. Division A is considering an aggressive advertising campaign strategy to differentiate its product from its competitors. The division does not expect volume to be affected, but it hopes to gain more control over pricing. If Division A has to spend $120,000 next year to advertise and its variable costs continue to be $1.75 per unit, what will its cost-plus price be? Do you think Division A will be able to sell its product at the cost-plus price? Why or why not?

2. The division manager of Division B received the following operating income data for the past year:

DIVISION B OF DILLARD, INC. Income Statement For the Year Ended December 31, 2018			
	Product Line		
	T205	B179	Total
Net Sales Revenue	$ 310,000	$ 360,000	$ 670,000
Cost of Goods Sold:			
Variable	31,000	44,000	75,000
Fixed	275,000	67,000	342,000
Total Cost of Goods Sold	306,000	111,000	417,000
Gross Profit	4,000	249,000	253,000
Selling and Administrative Expenses:			
Variable	68,000	80,000	148,000
Fixed	47,000	27,000	74,000
Total Selling and Administrative Expenses	115,000	107,000	222,000
Operating Income (Loss)	$ (111,000)	$ 142,000	$ 31,000

The manager of the division is surprised that the T205 product line is not profitable. The division accountant estimates that dropping the T205 product line will decrease fixed cost of goods sold by $75,000 and decrease fixed selling and administrative expenses by $10,000.

a. Prepare a differential analysis to show whether Division B should drop the T205 product line.

b. What is your recommendation to the manager of Division B?

3. Division C also produces two product lines. Because the division can sell all of the product it can produce, Dillard is expanding the plant and needs to decide which product line to emphasize. To make this decision, the division accountant assembled the following data:

	Per Unit	
	K707	**G582**
Sales price	$ 84	$ 50
Variable costs	24	21
Contribution margin	$ 60	$ 29
Contribution margin ratio	71.4%	58.0%

After expansion, the factory will have a production capacity of 4,700 machine hours per month. The plant can manufacture either 40 units of K707s or 62 units of G582s per machine hour.

a. Identify the constraining factor for Division C.

b. Prepare an analysis to show which product line to emphasize.

4. Division D is considering two possible expansion plans. Plan A would expand a current product line at a cost of $8,600,000. Expected annual net cash inflows are $1,525,000, with zero residual value at the end of 10 years. Under Plan B, Division D would begin producing a new product at a cost of $8,000,000. This plan is expected to generate net cash inflows of $1,100,000 per year for 10 years, the estimated useful life of the product line. Estimated residual value for Plan B is $980,000. Division D uses straight-line depreciation and requires an annual return of 10%.

a. Compute the payback, the ARR, the NPV, and the profitability index for both plans.

b. Compute the estimated IRR of Plan A.

c. Use Excel to verify the NPV calculations in Requirement 4(a) and the actual IRR for the two plans. How does the IRR of each plan compare with the company's required rate of return?

d. Division D must rank the plans and make a recommendation to Dillard's top management team for the best plan. Which expansion plan should Division D choose? Why?

> Tying It All Together Case 26-1

Before you begin this assignment, review the Tying It All Together feature in the chapter. It will also be helpful if you review TravelCenters of America LLC's 2015 annual report (https://www.sec.gov/Archives/edgar/data/1378453/000137845316000040/a2015123110k.htm).

TravelCenters of America LLC is the largest full-service travel center company in the United States, serving both professional drivers and motorists. Since 2011, the company's growth strategy has been to acquire additional travel center and convenience center locations. In addition to agreements entered into in 2015, the company acquired 3 travel centers and 170 convenience centers for a total purchase price of $320.3 million.

Requirements

1. Using the payback method, suppose TravelCenters of America expects to receive annual net cash inflow of $32.03 million per year. How many years would it take to payback the initial investment?

2. What are some disadvantages to using the payback method? Why would a company, such as TravelCenters of America, not use the payback method as their sole method for making capital investment decisions?

> Ethical Issue 26-1

Spencer Wilkes is the marketing manager at Darby Company. Last year, Spencer recommended the company approve a capital investment project for the addition of a new product line. Spencer's recommendation included predicted cash inflows for five years from the sales of the new product line. Darby Company has been selling the new products for almost one year. The company has a policy of conducting annual post-audits on capital investments, and Spencer is concerned about the one-year post-audit because sales in the first year have been lower than he estimated. However, sales have been increasing for the last couple of months, and Spencer expects that by the end of the second year, actual sales will exceed his estimates for the first two years combined.

Spencer wants to shift some sales from the second year of the project into the first year. Doing so will make it appear that his cash flow predictions were accurate. With accurate estimates, he will be able to avoid a poor performance evaluation. Spencer has discussed his plan with a couple of key sales representatives, urging them to report sales in the current month that will not be shipped until a later month. Spencer has justified this course of action by explaining that there will be no effect on the annual financial statements because the project year does not coincide with the fiscal year—by the time the accounting year ends, the sales will have actually occurred.

Requirements

1. What is the fundamental ethical issue? Who are the affected parties?

2. If you were a sales representative at Darby Company, how would you respond to Spencer's request? Why?

3. If you were Spencer's manager and you discovered his plan, how would you respond?

4. Are there other courses of action Spencer could take?

> Fraud Case 26-1

John Johnson is the majority stockholder in Johnson's Landscape Company, owning 52% of the company's stock. John asked his accountant to prepare a capital investment analysis for the purchase of new mowers. John used the analysis to persuade a loan officer at the local bank to loan the company $100,000. Once the loan was secured, John used the cash to remodel his home, updating the kitchen and bathrooms, installing new flooring, and adding a pool.

Requirements

1. Are John's actions fraudulent? Why or why not? Does John's percentage of ownership affect your answer?

2. What steps could the bank take to prevent this type of activity?

> Team Project 26-1

Assume you are preparing to move into a new neighborhood. You are considering renting or buying. Divide your team into two groups.

Requirements

1. Group 1 will analyze the renting option. A suitable rental is available for $500 per month, and you expect rent to increase by $50 per month per year. Prepare a schedule showing rent payments for the next 15 years. To simplify the problem, assume rent is paid annually. Using 5% as the discount rate, determine the present value of the rent payments. Round present value amounts to the nearest dollar.

2. Group 2 will analyze the buying option. A suitable purchase will require financing $105,876 at 5%. Annual payments for 15 years will be $10,200 (annual payments assumed to simplify the problem). Calculate the present value of the payments. Additionally, using Excel with appropriate formulas, prepare a payment schedule with the following columns (Year 1 is completed as an example):

Year	Beginning Balance	Payment	Applied to Interest	Applied to Principal	Ending Balance
0					$ 105,876
1	$ 105,876	$ 10,200	$ 5,294	$ 4,906	100,970

3. After each group has prepared its schedule, meet as a full team to discuss the analyses. What is the total cash paid out for each option? What is the present value of the cash paid out for each option? Explain the implications of the previous two answers. Are there other factors that should be considered before deciding to rent or buy?

> Communication Activity 26-1

In 100 words or fewer, explain the difference between NPV and IRR.

MyAccountingLab For a wealth of online resources, including exercises, problems, media, and immediate tutorial help, please visit http://www.myaccountinglab.com.

> Quick Check Answers

1. b **2.** b **3.** d **4.** b **5.** d **6.** d **7.** b **8.** a **9.** c **10.** c

Appendix A

Present Value Tables

Appendix A

Table A-1 | **Present Value of $1**

Present Value

Periods	1%	2%	3%	4%	5%	6%	7%	8%	9%	10%	12%	14%	15%	16%	18%	20%
1	0.990	0.980	0.971	0.962	0.952	0.943	0.935	0.926	0.917	0.909	0.893	0.877	0.870	0.862	0.847	0.833
2	0.980	0.961	0.943	0.925	0.907	0.890	0.873	0.857	0.842	0.826	0.797	0.769	0.756	0.743	0.718	0.694
3	0.971	0.942	0.915	0.889	0.864	0.840	0.816	0.794	0.772	0.751	0.712	0.675	0.658	0.641	0.609	0.579
4	0.961	0.924	0.888	0.855	0.823	0.792	0.763	0.735	0.708	0.683	0.636	0.592	0.572	0.552	0.516	0.482
5	0.951	0.906	0.863	0.822	0.784	0.747	0.713	0.681	0.650	0.621	0.567	0.519	0.497	0.476	0.437	0.402
6	0.942	0.888	0.837	0.790	0.746	0.705	0.666	0.630	0.596	0.564	0.507	0.456	0.432	0.410	0.370	0.335
7	0.933	0.871	0.813	0.760	0.711	0.665	0.623	0.583	0.547	0.513	0.452	0.400	0.376	0.354	0.314	0.279
8	0.923	0.853	0.789	0.731	0.677	0.627	0.582	0.540	0.502	0.467	0.404	0.351	0.327	0.305	0.266	0.233
9	0.914	0.837	0.766	0.703	0.645	0.592	0.544	0.500	0.460	0.424	0.361	0.308	0.284	0.263	0.225	0.194
10	0.905	0.820	0.744	0.676	0.614	0.558	0.508	0.463	0.422	0.386	0.322	0.270	0.247	0.227	0.191	0.162
11	0.896	0.804	0.722	0.650	0.585	0.527	0.475	0.429	0.388	0.350	0.287	0.237	0.215	0.195	0.162	0.135
12	0.887	0.788	0.701	0.625	0.557	0.497	0.444	0.397	0.356	0.319	0.257	0.208	0.187	0.168	0.137	0.112
13	0.879	0.773	0.681	0.601	0.530	0.469	0.415	0.368	0.326	0.290	0.229	0.182	0.163	0.145	0.116	0.093
14	0.870	0.758	0.661	0.577	0.505	0.442	0.388	0.340	0.299	0.263	0.205	0.160	0.141	0.125	0.099	0.078
15	0.861	0.743	0.642	0.555	0.481	0.417	0.362	0.315	0.275	0.239	0.183	0.140	0.123	0.108	0.084	0.065
16	0.853	0.728	0.623	0.534	0.458	0.394	0.339	0.292	0.252	0.218	0.163	0.123	0.107	0.093	0.071	0.054
17	0.844	0.714	0.605	0.513	0.436	0.371	0.317	0.270	0.231	0.198	0.146	0.108	0.093	0.080	0.060	0.045
18	0.836	0.700	0.587	0.494	0.416	0.350	0.296	0.250	0.212	0.180	0.130	0.095	0.081	0.069	0.051	0.038
19	0.828	0.686	0.570	0.475	0.396	0.331	0.277	0.232	0.194	0.164	0.116	0.083	0.070	0.060	0.043	0.031
20	0.820	0.673	0.554	0.456	0.377	0.312	0.258	0.215	0.178	0.149	0.104	0.073	0.061	0.051	0.037	0.026
21	0.811	0.660	0.538	0.439	0.359	0.294	0.242	0.199	0.164	0.135	0.093	0.064	0.053	0.044	0.031	0.022
22	0.803	0.647	0.522	0.422	0.342	0.278	0.226	0.184	0.150	0.123	0.083	0.056	0.046	0.038	0.026	0.018
23	0.795	0.634	0.507	0.406	0.326	0.262	0.211	0.170	0.138	0.112	0.074	0.049	0.040	0.033	0.022	0.015
24	0.788	0.622	0.492	0.390	0.310	0.247	0.197	0.158	0.126	0.102	0.066	0.043	0.035	0.028	0.019	0.013
25	0.780	0.610	0.478	0.375	0.295	0.233	0.184	0.146	0.116	0.092	0.059	0.038	0.030	0.024	0.016	0.010
26	0.772	0.598	0.464	0.361	0.281	0.220	0.172	0.135	0.106	0.084	0.053	0.033	0.026	0.021	0.014	0.009
27	0.764	0.586	0.450	0.347	0.268	0.207	0.161	0.125	0.098	0.076	0.047	0.029	0.023	0.018	0.011	0.007
28	0.757	0.574	0.437	0.333	0.255	0.196	0.150	0.116	0.090	0.069	0.042	0.026	0.020	0.016	0.010	0.006
29	0.749	0.563	0.424	0.321	0.243	0.185	0.141	0.107	0.082	0.063	0.037	0.022	0.017	0.014	0.008	0.005
30	0.742	0.552	0.412	0.308	0.231	0.174	0.131	0.099	0.075	0.057	0.033	0.020	0.015	0.012	0.007	0.004
40	0.672	0.453	0.307	0.208	0.142	0.097	0.067	0.046	0.032	0.022	0.011	0.005	0.004	0.003	0.001	0.001
50	0.608	0.372	0.228	0.141	0.087	0.054	0.034	0.021	0.013	0.009	0.003	0.001	0.001	0.001		

Table A-2   **Present Value of Ordinary Annuity of $1**

Present Value

Periods	1%	2%	3%	4%	5%	6%	7%	8%	9%	10%	12%	14%	15%	16%	18%	20%
1	0.990	0.980	0.971	0.962	0.952	0.943	0.935	0.926	0.917	0.909	0.893	0.877	0.870	0.862	0.847	0.833
2	1.970	1.942	1.913	1.886	1.859	1.833	1.808	1.783	1.759	1.736	1.690	1.647	1.626	1.605	1.566	1.528
3	2.941	2.884	2.829	2.775	2.723	2.673	2.624	2.577	2.531	2.487	2.402	2.322	2.283	2.246	2.174	2.106
4	3.902	3.808	3.717	3.630	3.546	3.465	3.387	3.312	3.240	3.170	3.037	2.914	2.855	2.798	2.690	2.589
5	4.853	4.713	4.580	4.452	4.329	4.212	4.100	3.993	3.890	3.791	3.605	3.433	3.352	3.274	3.127	2.991
6	5.795	5.601	5.417	5.242	5.076	4.917	4.767	4.623	4.486	4.355	4.111	3.889	3.784	3.685	3.498	3.326
7	6.728	6.472	6.230	6.002	5.786	5.582	5.389	5.206	5.033	4.868	4.564	4.288	4.160	4.039	3.812	3.605
8	7.652	7.325	7.020	6.733	6.463	6.210	5.971	5.747	5.535	5.335	4.968	4.639	4.487	4.344	4.078	3.837
9	8.566	8.162	7.786	7.435	7.108	6.802	6.515	6.247	5.995	5.759	5.328	4.946	4.772	4.607	4.303	4.031
10	9.471	8.983	8.530	8.111	7.722	7.360	7.024	6.710	6.418	6.145	5.650	5.216	5.019	4.833	4.494	4.192
11	10.368	9.787	9.253	8.760	8.306	7.887	7.499	7.139	6.805	6.495	5.938	5.453	5.234	5.029	4.656	4.327
12	11.255	10.575	9.954	9.385	8.863	8.384	7.943	7.536	7.161	6.814	6.194	5.660	5.421	5.197	4.793	4.439
13	12.134	11.348	10.635	9.986	9.394	8.853	8.358	7.904	7.487	7.103	6.424	5.842	5.583	5.342	4.910	4.533
14	13.004	12.106	11.296	10.563	9.899	9.295	8.745	8.244	7.786	7.367	6.628	6.002	5.724	5.468	5.008	4.611
15	13.865	12.849	11.938	11.118	10.380	9.712	9.108	8.559	8.061	7.606	6.811	6.142	5.847	5.575	5.092	4.675
16	14.718	13.578	12.561	11.652	10.838	10.106	9.447	8.851	8.313	7.824	6.974	6.265	5.954	5.669	5.162	4.730
17	15.562	14.292	13.166	12.166	11.274	10.477	9.763	9.122	8.544	8.022	7.120	6.373	6.047	5.749	5.222	4.775
18	16.398	14.992	13.754	12.659	11.690	10.828	10.059	9.372	8.756	8.201	7.250	6.467	6.128	5.818	5.273	4.812
19	17.226	15.678	14.324	13.134	12.085	11.158	10.336	9.604	8.950	8.365	7.366	6.550	6.198	5.877	5.316	4.844
20	18.046	16.351	14.877	13.590	12.462	11.470	10.594	9.818	9.129	8.514	7.469	6.623	6.259	5.929	5.353	4.870
21	18.857	17.011	15.415	14.029	12.821	11.764	10.836	10.017	9.292	8.649	7.562	6.687	6.312	5.973	5.384	4.891
22	19.660	17.658	15.937	14.451	13.163	12.042	11.061	10.201	9.442	8.772	7.645	6.743	6.359	6.011	5.410	4.909
23	20.456	18.292	16.444	14.857	13.489	12.303	11.272	10.371	9.580	8.883	7.718	6.792	6.399	6.044	5.432	4.925
24	21.243	18.914	16.936	15.247	13.799	12.550	11.469	10.529	9.707	8.985	7.784	6.835	6.434	6.073	5.451	4.937
25	22.023	19.523	17.413	15.622	14.094	12.783	11.654	10.675	9.823	9.077	7.843	6.873	6.464	6.097	5.467	4.948
26	22.795	20.121	17.877	15.983	14.375	13.003	11.826	10.810	9.929	9.161	7.896	6.906	6.491	6.118	5.480	4.956
27	23.560	20.707	18.327	16.330	14.643	13.211	11.987	10.935	10.027	9.237	7.943	6.935	6.514	6.136	5.492	4.964
28	24.316	21.281	18.764	16.663	14.898	13.406	12.137	11.051	10.116	9.307	7.984	6.961	6.534	6.152	5.502	4.970
29	25.066	21.844	19.188	16.984	15.141	13.591	12.278	11.158	10.198	9.370	8.022	6.983	6.551	6.166	5.510	4.975
30	25.808	22.396	19.600	17.292	15.372	13.765	12.409	11.258	10.274	9.427	8.055	7.003	6.566	6.177	5.517	4.979
40	32.835	27.355	23.115	19.793	17.159	15.046	13.332	11.925	10.757	9.779	8.244	7.105	6.642	6.234	5.548	4.997
50	39.196	31.424	25.730	21.482	18.256	15.762	13.801	12.233	10.962	9.915	8.304	7.133	6.661	6.246	5.554	4.999

Future Value Tables

Table A-3 | **Future Value of $1**

Future Value

Periods	1%	2%	3%	4%	5%	6%	7%	8%	9%	10%	12%	14%	15%
1	1.010	1.020	1.030	1.040	1.050	1.060	1.070	1.080	1.090	1.100	1.120	1.140	1.150
2	1.020	1.040	1.061	1.082	1.103	1.124	1.145	1.166	1.188	1.210	1.254	1.300	1.323
3	1.030	1.061	1.093	1.125	1.158	1.191	1.225	1.260	1.295	1.331	1.405	1.482	1.521
4	1.041	1.082	1.126	1.170	1.216	1.262	1.311	1.360	1.412	1.464	1.574	1.689	1.749
5	1.051	1.104	1.159	1.217	1.276	1.338	1.403	1.469	1.539	1.611	1.762	1.925	2.011
6	1.062	1.126	1.194	1.265	1.340	1.419	1.501	1.587	1.677	1.772	1.974	2.195	2.313
7	1.072	1.149	1.230	1.316	1.407	1.504	1.606	1.714	1.828	1.949	2.211	2.502	2.660
8	1.083	1.172	1.267	1.369	1.477	1.594	1.718	1.851	1.993	2.144	2.476	2.853	3.059
9	1.094	1.195	1.305	1.423	1.551	1.689	1.838	1.999	2.172	2.358	2.773	3.252	3.518
10	1.105	1.219	1.344	1.480	1.629	1.791	1.967	2.159	2.367	2.594	3.106	3.707	4.046
11	1.116	1.243	1.384	1.539	1.710	1.898	2.105	2.332	2.580	2.853	3.479	4.226	4.652
12	1.127	1.268	1.426	1.601	1.796	2.012	2.252	2.518	2.813	3.138	3.896	4.818	5.350
13	1.138	1.294	1.469	1.665	1.886	2.133	2.410	2.720	3.066	3.452	4.363	5.492	6.153
14	1.149	1.319	1.513	1.732	1.980	2.261	2.579	2.937	3.342	3.798	4.887	6.261	7.076
15	1.161	1.346	1.558	1.801	2.079	2.397	2.759	3.172	3.642	4.177	5.474	7.138	8.137
16	1.173	1.373	1.605	1.873	2.183	2.540	2.952	3.426	3.970	4.595	6.130	8.137	9.358
17	1.184	1.400	1.653	1.948	2.292	2.693	3.159	3.700	4.328	5.054	6.866	9.276	10.76
18	1.196	1.428	1.702	2.026	2.407	2.854	3.380	3.996	4.717	5.560	7.690	10.58	12.38
19	1.208	1.457	1.754	2.107	2.527	3.026	3.617	4.316	5.142	6.116	8.613	12.06	14.23
20	1.220	1.486	1.806	2.191	2.653	3.207	3.870	4.661	5.604	6.728	9.646	13.74	16.37
21	1.232	1.516	1.860	2.279	2.786	3.400	4.141	5.034	6.109	7.400	10.80	15.67	18.82
22	1.245	1.546	1.916	2.370	2.925	3.604	4.430	5.437	6.659	8.140	12.10	17.86	21.64
23	1.257	1.577	1.974	2.465	3.072	3.820	4.741	5.871	7.258	8.954	13.55	20.36	24.89
24	1.270	1.608	2.033	2.563	3.225	4.049	5.072	6.341	7.911	9.850	15.18	23.21	28.63
25	1.282	1.641	2.094	2.666	3.386	4.292	5.427	6.848	8.623	10.83	17.00	26.46	32.92
26	1.295	1.673	2.157	2.772	3.556	4.549	5.807	7.396	9.399	11.92	19.04	30.17	37.86
27	1.308	1.707	2.221	2.883	3.733	4.822	6.214	7.988	10.25	13.11	21.32	34.39	43.54
28	1.321	1.741	2.288	2.999	3.920	5.112	6.649	8.627	11.17	14.42	23.88	39.20	50.07
29	1.335	1.776	2.357	3.119	4.116	5.418	7.114	9.317	12.17	15.86	26.75	44.69	57.58
30	1.348	1.811	2.427	3.243	4.322	5.743	7.612	10.06	13.27	17.45	29.96	50.95	66.21
40	1.489	2.208	3.262	4.801	7.040	10.29	14.97	21.72	31.41	45.26	93.05	188.9	267.9
50	1.645	2.692	4.384	7.107	11.47	18.42	29.46	46.90	74.36	117.4	289.0	700.2	1,084

Table A-4 | Future Value of Ordinary Annuity of $1

						Future Value						
Periods	**1%**	**2%**	**3%**	**4%**	**5%**	**6%**	**7%**	**8%**	**9%**	**10%**	**12%**	**14%**	**15%**
1	1.000	1.000	1.000	1.000	1.000	1.000	1.000	1.000	1.000	1.000	1.000	1.000	1.000
2	2.010	2.020	2.030	2.040	2.050	2.060	2.070	2.080	2.090	2.100	2.120	2.140	2.150
3	3.030	3.060	3.091	3.122	3.153	3.184	3.215	3.246	3.278	3.310	3.374	3.440	3.473
4	4.060	4.122	4.184	4.246	4.310	4.375	4.440	4.506	4.573	4.641	4.779	4.921	4.993
5	5.101	5.204	5.309	5.416	5.526	5.637	5.751	5.867	5.985	6.105	6.353	6.610	6.742
6	6.152	6.308	6.468	6.633	6.802	6.975	7.153	7.336	7.523	7.716	8.115	8.536	8.754
7	7.214	7.434	7.662	7.898	8.142	8.394	8.654	8.923	9.200	9.487	10.09	10.73	11.07
8	8.286	8.583	8.892	9.214	9.549	9.897	10.26	10.64	11.03	11.44	12.30	13.23	13.73
9	9.369	9.755	10.16	10.58	11.03	11.49	11.98	12.49	13.02	13.58	14.78	16.09	16.79
10	10.46	10.95	11.46	12.01	12.58	13.18	13.82	14.49	15.19	15.94	17.55	19.34	20.30
11	11.57	12.17	12.81	13.49	14.21	14.97	15.78	16.65	17.56	18.53	20.65	23.04	24.35
12	12.68	13.41	14.19	15.03	15.92	16.87	17.89	18.98	20.14	21.38	24.13	27.27	29.00
13	13.81	14.68	15.62	16.63	17.71	18.88	20.14	21.50	22.95	24.52	28.03	32.09	34.35
14	14.95	15.97	17.09	18.29	19.60	21.02	22.55	24.21	26.02	27.98	32.39	37.58	40.50
15	16.10	17.29	18.60	20.02	21.58	23.28	25.13	27.15	29.36	31.77	37.28	43.84	47.58
16	17.26	18.64	20.16	21.82	23.66	25.67	27.89	30.32	33.00	35.95	42.75	50.98	55.72
17	18.43	20.01	21.76	23.70	25.84	28.21	30.84	33.75	36.97	40.54	48.88	59.12	65.08
18	19.61	21.41	23.41	25.65	28.13	30.91	34.00	37.45	41.30	45.60	55.75	68.39	75.84
19	20.81	22.84	25.12	27.67	30.54	33.76	37.38	41.45	46.02	51.16	63.44	78.97	88.21
20	22.02	24.30	26.87	29.78	33.07	36.79	41.00	45.76	51.16	57.28	72.05	91.02	102.4
21	23.24	25.78	28.68	31.97	35.72	39.99	44.87	50.42	56.76	64.00	81.70	104.8	118.8
22	24.47	27.30	30.54	34.25	38.51	43.39	49.01	55.46	62.87	71.40	92.50	120.4	137.6
23	25.72	28.85	32.45	36.62	41.43	47.00	53.44	60.89	69.53	79.54	104.6	138.3	159.3
24	26.97	30.42	34.43	39.08	44.50	50.82	58.18	66.76	76.79	88.50	118.2	158.7	184.2
25	28.24	32.03	36.46	41.65	47.73	54.86	63.25	73.11	84.70	98.35	133.3	181.9	212.8
26	29.53	33.67	38.55	44.31	51.11	59.16	68.68	79.95	93.32	109.2	150.3	208.3	245.7
27	30.82	35.34	40.71	47.08	54.67	63.71	74.48	87.35	102.7	121.1	169.4	238.5	283.6
28	32.13	37.05	42.93	49.97	58.40	68.53	80.70	95.34	113.0	134.2	190.7	272.9	327.1
29	33.45	38.79	45.22	52.97	62.32	73.64	87.35	104.0	124.1	148.6	214.6	312.1	377.2
30	34.78	40.57	47.58	56.08	66.44	79.06	94.46	113.3	136.3	164.5	241.3	356.8	434.7
40	48.89	60.40	75.40	95.03	120.8	154.8	199.6	259.1	337.9	442.6	767.1	1,342	1,779
50	64.46	84.58	112.8	152.7	209.3	290.3	406.5	573.8	815.1	1,164	2,400	4,995	7,218

Appendix B
Accounting Information Systems

What Should I Do with All This Paperwork?

Sara Faraday stared at the stack of papers on her desk. It was early January, and her accountant had called to remind her that she needed to submit the business's accounting information so that the tax return could be prepared. Sara is a stockholder and manager of a successful gourmet kitchen store that sells specialty food and kitchen products and also offers cooking classes and workshops. Sara loves interacting with her customers, whether she's helping them find the perfect kitchen product or teaching them a new technique. What she doesn't like about her business is the overwhelming amount of paperwork required to keep the business records. When she first started her business, she kept track of sales to customers and bills paid in a notebook. Now, though, her business has grown so much that it is no longer efficient to keep track of her accounting records in this manner.

Sara is considering asking her accountant to help her set up a more efficient accounting information system. She wants a system that will save her time and make the recordkeeping process easier. In addition, she would like to find a way to record all of her transactions on the computer so that her business's information is easily accessible. Sara also wants a system that will produce reports, such as financial statements, that can help her make business decisions. She knows that there has to be an easier way to record the transactions than what she is currently doing.

Is There a More Efficient Way?

Before the invention of computers, businesses had to handle all of their accounting transactions manually—that is, one journal entry at a time using paper and pencil. As computer technology progressed, more and more accounting information was processed using an automated system. Now, most businesses use some form of computerized accounting software. It might be a very basic system that handles only accounting information, or it might be a very advanced system that stores not only accounting information, but also information about human resources, production, and customer services. For example, **McCormick & Company, Incorporated** started with a desire to be the global leader in flavor. The company manufactures, markets, and distributes spices, seasoning mixes, condiments, and other flavorful products. In 1889, founder Willoughby M. McCormick sold flavors and extracts door to door. As the business has grown into the multinational company, McCormick & Company had to find a way to keep track of all of the business's accounting information. The company uses a specialized computerized system that integrates all of its lines of business. In this appendix, we explore how accounting information systems, such as the one that McCormick & Company uses, can help a business run more efficiently and effectively.

Appendix **B** Learning Objectives

1 Describe an effective accounting information system

2 Journalize and post sales and cash receipts in a manual accounting information system using special journals and subsidiary ledgers

3 Journalize and post purchases, cash payments, and other transactions in a manual accounting information system using special journals and subsidiary ledgers

4 Describe how transactions are recorded in a computerized accounting information system

WHAT IS AN ACCOUNTING INFORMATION SYSTEM?

Learning Objective 1

Describe an effective accounting information system

Accounting Information System (AIS)

A system that collects, records, stores, and processes accounting data to produce information that is useful for decision makers.

An **accounting information system (AIS)** collects, records, stores, and processes accounting data to produce information that is useful for decision makers. Businesses must have a way to collect and store data for a large number of transactions and then use that data to produce reports that investors, creditors, and managers can use to make decisions. Exhibit B-1 shows examples of business transactions and activities that are completed when using an accounting information system.

Exhibit B-1 | **Business Transactions and AIS Activities**

Business Transactions	AIS Activities
Sell merchandise inventory	Receipt of customer order Approval of credit sale Check availability of merchandise inventory Shipment of inventory to customer Processing of sales invoice Receipt of customer payment
Purchase of goods or services	Request for purchase of goods or services Approval of vendor Receipt of goods or services Processing of vendor invoice Payment for goods or services
Payroll	Approval of new employees Collection of time records Preparation and payment of payroll Preparation and payment of payroll taxes

Effective Accounting Information Systems

An effective accounting information system provides the following:

- Control
- Compatibility
- Flexibility
- Relevance
- Positive cost/benefit relationship

Control

An accounting information system must provide adequate controls of the business's assets and data. Internal controls can safeguard a business's assets and reduce the likelihood of fraud and errors. For example, a business needs procedures for making cash payments. An accounting information system creates the structure to encourage adherence to management's procedures.

Compatibility

A compatible system works smoothly with the business's employees and organizational structure. A small business doesn't need a big accounting information system. It could handle its accounting with an entry-level software package such as QuickBooks® or Sage® 50 Accounting (formerly called *Peachtree*). But a large company needs a different system—one that can manage multiple branches and track revenues and expenses in all divisions of the business.

Flexibility

An accounting information system must be flexible to accommodate changes in a business over time. Businesses might start selling some new products, or they might expand to new locations. This will require a more complicated accounting information system.

Relevance

An effective accounting information system provides information that is relevant. In other words, it improves decision making and reduces uncertainty. The information produced must be useful to the business in achieving its overall goals.

Positive Cost/Benefit Relationship

Control, compatibility, flexibility, and relevance can be expensive. A business needs a system that gives the most benefit for the least cost. A relatively inexpensive system, such as QuickBooks, may be the most economical way for a business to do its accounting. Or it may be necessary for a business to invest a large amount of cash in a more complicated system. In addition, the business must consider the cost of training employees to use the system and time spent on entering data into the system. The business must invest only in an accounting information system in which the benefits received outweigh the cost of the system.

An accounting information system can be either manual (completed using paper and pencil) or computerized. All the previously discussed features are needed whether the accounting information system is computerized or manual.

Components of an Accounting Information System

An accounting information system has three basic components:

- Source documents and input devices
- Processing and storage
- Outputs

Source Documents and Input Devices

All data must come from **source documents**, which provide the evidence for accounting transactions. Examples of source documents include purchase invoices, bank checks, and sales invoices. Many businesses have paper source documents that require employees to transfer data from the paper source document into the accounting information system. This can be done either by data entry procedures using a keyboard and computer or by using computerized scanning equipment.

Source Document
Provides the evidence and data for accounting transactions.

Most businesses now are using computerized accounting information systems to create electronic source documents and capture the data in electronic format. Examples include an electronic invoice and an electronic receiving report.

Source documents also provide control and reliability in an accounting information system. Standardized source documents that require specific data to be input ensure that each transaction is recorded accurately and completely. In addition, prenumbered source documents provide necessary control in a system by automatically assigning a sequential number to each new transaction.

Processing and Storage

Once data has been input into the system, it must be processed. In a manual accounting information system, processing includes journalizing transactions and posting to the accounts. A computerized system, on the other hand, uses software to process transactions. This software reads and edits transaction data. It allows businesses to process transactions without actually requiring employees to journalize and post to the accounts.

A business's data must also be stored. In a manual system, data are contained in paper documents that are often stored in filing cabinets and off-site document warehouses. Computerized systems now allow businesses to keep data on a main computer, called a

Server
The main computer where data are stored, which can be accessed from many different computers.

server, that often allows employees to access information from anywhere in the world. The protection and security of a business's data have become increasingly important. Businesses must be aware of threats to their data such as hacking (unauthorized access) and malware (viruses and spyware). Companies are spending increasingly large amounts of cash to ensure that their data and information are secure.

Outputs

Outputs are the reports used for decision making, including the financial statements. In a manual system, reports and financial statements must be created using Word documents, Excel spreadsheets, PowerPoint presentations, or other software applications. In a computerized system, the accounting software can generate reports instantaneously that can be easily formatted and used to make business decisions.

TYING IT ALL TOGETHER

McCormick & Company, Incorporated is a global leader in flavor that manufactures, markets, and distributes spices, seasoning mixes, condiments, and other flavorful products. The company's brands include McCormick, Lawry's, and Club House. In addition, the company also markets authentic ethnic brands, such as Zatarain's, Thai Kitchen, and Simply Asia. (You can find McCormick & Company's annual report at http://phx.corporate-ir.net/phoenix.zhtml?c=65454&p=irol-sec&control_symbol=#14157537.)

How do companies, such as McCormick & Company, rely on information technology systems?

In the annual report, McCormick & Company state that the company relies on its information technology systems to operate its business efficiently. Information technology systems allow companies to manage their business data, communications, supply chain, order entry and fulfillment, and other business processes.

What would happen if McCormick & Company's information technology systems fail to perform adequately?

McCormick & Company state, in its annual report, that a failure in its information technology system could disrupt its business and could result in transaction errors, processing inefficiencies, and the loss of sales and customers. Ultimately, the failure could cause McCormick & Company's business and results of operations to suffer.

Try It!

Match the benefit of an effective accounting information system with the definition.

Benefit	Definition
1. Control	a. Works smoothly with the business's employees and organization structure
2. Relevance	b. Can accommodate changes in the business over time
3. Flexibility	c. Provides safeguards for a business's assets and reduces the likelihood of fraud and errors
4. Compatibility	d. Benefits received outweigh the cost of the system
5. Positive cost/benefit relationship	e. Provides information that will improve decision making and reduce uncertainty

Check your answers online in MyAccountingLab or at http://www.pearsonhighered.com/Horngren.

For more practice, see Short Exercises SB-1 and SB-2. MyAccountingLab

HOW ARE SALES AND CASH RECEIPTS RECORDED IN A MANUAL ACCOUNTING INFORMATION SYSTEM?

We will begin by reviewing how transactions are recorded in a manual accounting information system. You may be wondering why we cover manual accounting information systems when many businesses have computerized systems. There are three main reasons:

1. Learning a manual system equips you to work with both manual and computerized systems. The accounting is the same regardless of the system.
2. Few small businesses have computerized all their accounting. Even companies that use QuickBooks or Sage 50 Accounting, two popular entry-level accounting information systems, keep some manual accounting records.
3. Learning a manual system helps you master accounting.

> **Learning Objective 2**
>
> Journalize and post sales and cash receipts in a manual accounting information system using special journals and subsidiary ledgers

Special Journals

In a manual system, transactions are classified by type. It is inefficient to record all transactions in the general journal, so businesses use special journals. A **special journal** is an accounting journal designed to record a specific type of transaction. Sales on account, cash receipts, purchases on account, and cash payments are treated as four separate categories and, therefore, create the four special journals. For example:

> **Special Journal**
>
> An accounting journal designed to record one specific type of transaction.

- Sales on account are recorded in a *sales journal*.
- Cash receipts are recorded in a *cash receipts journal*.
- Purchases of inventory and other assets on account are recorded in a *purchases journal*.
- Cash payments are recorded in a *cash payments journal*.
- Transactions that do not fit in any of the special journals, such as adjusting entries, are recorded in the *general journal*, which serves as the "journal of last resort."

The five types of transactions, the related journal, and the posting abbreviations used in a manual system are summarized in Exhibit B-2.

Exhibit B-2 | **Manual Accounting Information System**

Transaction	Journal	Posting Abbreviation
Sale on account	Sales journal	S
Cash receipt	Cash receipts journal	CR
Purchase on account	Purchases journal	P
Cash payment	Cash payments journal	CP
All others	General journal	J

Subsidiary Ledgers

Subsidiary Ledger
Record of accounts that provides supporting details on individual balances, the total of which appears in a general ledger account.

In addition to special journals, an accounting information system also uses subsidiary ledgers. A **subsidiary ledger** holds individual accounts that support a general ledger account. There are two common subsidiary ledgers: accounts receivable subsidiary ledger and accounts payable subsidiary ledger.

Accounts Receivable Subsidiary Ledger

Accounts Receivable Subsidiary Ledger
A subsidiary ledger that includes an accounts receivable account for each customer that contains detailed information such as the amount sold, received, and owed.

The **accounts receivable subsidiary ledger** includes a receivable account for each customer. The customer name and account balance is detailed in the subsidiary ledger. In addition, the subsidiary ledger contains detailed information such as the amount sold, received, and still due for each customer. The total of the accounts in the accounts receivable subsidiary ledger must equal the Accounts Receivable balance in the general ledger. This is demonstrated in Exhibit B-3. The Accounts Receivable balance of $4,319 in the general ledger equals the sum of the accounts in the accounts receivable subsidiary ledger ($935 + $907 + $694 + $1,783).

Exhibit B-3 | **Accounts Receivable Subsidiary Ledger**

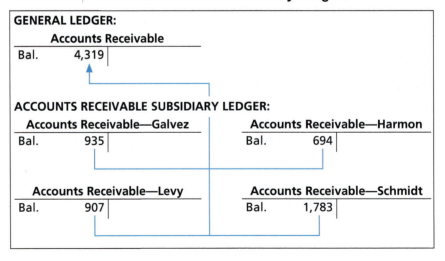

The Accounts Receivable account in the general ledger is called a **control account**. A control account's balance equals the sum of the balances of the accounts in a subsidiary ledger.

Control Account
An account whose balance equals the sum of the balances in a group of related accounts in a subsidiary ledger.

Accounts Payable Subsidiary Ledger

To pay debts on time, a company must know how much it owes each supplier. Accounts Payable in the general ledger shows only a single total for the amount owed on account. It does not indicate the amount owed to each vendor. Companies keep an accounts payable subsidiary ledger that is similar to the accounts receivable subsidiary ledger.

The **accounts payable subsidiary ledger** lists vendors in alphabetical order, along with amounts purchased from the vendors, amounts paid to the vendors, and the remaining amounts owed to them. The total of the individual balances in the subsidiary ledger equals the Accounts Payable (control account) balance in the general ledger.

Accounts Payable Subsidiary Ledger
A subsidiary ledger that includes an accounts payable account for each vendor that contains detailed information such as the amount purchased, paid, and owed.

> *Don't confuse the terms* customers *and* vendors. *Remember that a company sells to customers and purchases from vendors.*

The Sales Journal

Most merchandisers sell merchandise inventory on account. These credit sales are entered in the **sales journal**. The sales journal is used when recording the sale of merchandise inventory *on account*. The sale of merchandise inventory for cash is not recorded in the sales journal, but instead, it is recorded in the cash receipts journal. In addition, credit sales of assets other than merchandise inventory—for example, buildings—occur infrequently and are not recorded in the sales journal. They are, instead, recorded in the general journal.

Sales Journal
Special journal used to record credit sales.

Recording Transactions

Exhibit B-4 (on the next page) illustrates a sales journal (Panel A) and the related posting to the ledgers (Panel B). When a business completes a sale, the accountant enters the following information in the sales journal:

- Date
- Invoice number
- Customer name
- Transaction amount

Exhibit B-4 | **Sales Journal with Posting**

PANEL A—Sales Journal:

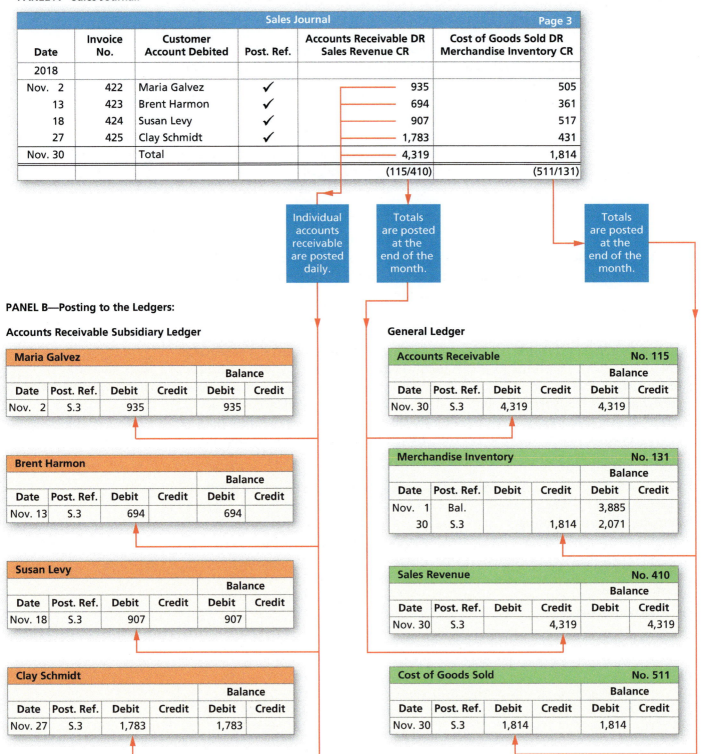

		Sales Journal				Page 3
Date	Invoice No.	Customer Account Debited	Post. Ref.	Accounts Receivable DR Sales Revenue CR	Cost of Goods Sold DR Merchandise Inventory CR	
2018						
Nov. 2	422	Maria Galvez	✓	935	505	
13	423	Brent Harmon	✓	694	361	
18	424	Susan Levy	✓	907	517	
27	425	Clay Schmidt	✓	1,783	431	
Nov. 30		Total		4,319	1,814	
				(115/410)	(511/131)	

Individual accounts receivable are posted daily.

Totals are posted at the end of the month.

Totals are posted at the end of the month.

PANEL B—Posting to the Ledgers:

Accounts Receivable Subsidiary Ledger

Maria Galvez

				Balance	
Date	Post. Ref.	Debit	Credit	Debit	Credit
Nov. 2	S.3	935		935	

Brent Harmon

				Balance	
Date	Post. Ref.	Debit	Credit	Debit	Credit
Nov. 13	S.3	694		694	

Susan Levy

				Balance	
Date	Post. Ref.	Debit	Credit	Debit	Credit
Nov. 18	S.3	907		907	

Clay Schmidt

				Balance	
Date	Post. Ref.	Debit	Credit	Debit	Credit
Nov. 27	S.3	1,783		1,783	

General Ledger

Accounts Receivable   **No. 115**

				Balance	
Date	Post. Ref.	Debit	Credit	Debit	Credit
Nov. 30	S.3	4,319		4,319	

Merchandise Inventory   **No. 131**

				Balance	
Date	Post. Ref.	Debit	Credit	Debit	Credit
Nov. 1	Bal.			3,885	
30	S.3		1,814	2,071	

Sales Revenue   **No. 410**

				Balance	
Date	Post. Ref.	Debit	Credit	Debit	Credit
Nov. 30	S.3		4,319		4,319

Cost of Goods Sold   **No. 511**

				Balance	
Date	Post. Ref.	Debit	Credit	Debit	Credit
Nov. 30	S.3	1,814		1,814	

Consider the first transaction in Panel A. On November 2, the business sold merchandise inventory on account, terms 15/20, n/30, to Maria Galvez for $1,100 with a cost of $505. The invoice number is 422. In Chapter 5, you learned that this transaction was recorded as follows when using the general journal:

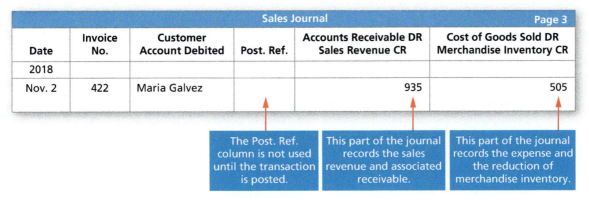

Date	Accounts and Explanation	Debit	Credit
Nov. 2	Accounts Receivable	935	
	Sales Revenue ($1,100 − ($1,100 × 0.15))		935
	Sale on account less discount.		
2	Cost of Goods Sold	505	
	Merchandise Inventory		505
	Recorded the cost of goods sold.		

$$\frac{A\uparrow}{\substack{\text{Accounts}\\\text{Receivable}\uparrow}} \Big\} = \Big\{ \quad L \quad + \quad \frac{E\uparrow}{\substack{\text{Sales}\\\text{Revenue}\uparrow}}$$

$$\frac{A\downarrow}{\substack{\text{Merchandise}\\\text{Inventory}\downarrow}} \Big\} = \Big\{ \quad L \quad + \quad \frac{E\downarrow}{\substack{\text{Cost of}\\\text{Goods Sold}\uparrow}}$$

When using special journals, instead of recording this transaction in the general journal, the business records the transaction in the sales journal. All of the information related to the sale appears on a single line in the sales journal as follows:

Sales Journal					Page 3
Date	Invoice No.	Customer Account Debited	Post. Ref.	Accounts Receivable DR Sales Revenue CR	Cost of Goods Sold DR Merchandise Inventory CR
2018					
Nov. 2	422	Maria Galvez		935	505

The Post. Ref. column is not used until the transaction is posted.	This part of the journal records the sales revenue and associated receivable.	This part of the journal records the expense and the reduction of merchandise inventory.

The entry records the sales revenue and associated accounts receivable by entering the net amount of the sale, $935, in the Accounts Receivable DR, Sales Revenue CR column. The entry also records the expense of the sale and the reduction of merchandise inventory by recording the cost of the sale, $505, in the Cost of Goods Sold DR, Merchandise Inventory CR column. By using a sales journal, the recording of sales is streamlined, thus saving a significant amount of time.

It's important to remember that a transaction is recorded in either the general journal or a special journal, but not in both. We are illustrating the general journal entry as a teaching tool to help you understand how the entry is recorded in the special journal. Transactions are not recorded in both journals. To do so would be to record the entry twice.

This business, like most other companies, uses a perpetual inventory system. Throughout this appendix, we illustrate the perpetual inventory system. When recording a sale, the business must record the Cost of Goods Sold and the decrease in Merchandise Inventory. If the business, instead, used a periodic inventory system, the sales journal would not need the last column (Cost of Goods Sold DR, Merchandise Inventory CR) because there is no entry recorded to Cost of Goods Sold and Merchandise Inventory at the time of the sale.

In the sales journal that we are using in this example, there are only two columns used for dollar amounts. One column records the sales revenue and accounts receivable, and the other column records the expense of the sale. Businesses that collect sales tax would need to modify the sales journal shown to include an additional column for Sales Taxes Payable. The modified sales journal would have the following headings:

				Sales Journal			Page 3
Date	Invoice No.	Customer Account Debited	Post. Ref.	Accounts Receivable DR	Sales Taxes Payable CR	Sales Revenue CR	Cost of Goods Sold DR Merchandise Inventory CR

Each business will modify its sales journal to fit the types of sales it makes. Remember, though, that only sales on account are recorded in the sales journal.

Posting

Entries in the sales journal are posted to both the accounts receivable subsidiary ledger and the general ledger.

Posting to the Accounts Receivable Subsidiary Ledger Individual accounts receivable are posted daily from the sales journal to the accounts receivable subsidiary ledger. For example, on November 2, the accountant posts the $935 receivable to the individual accounts receivable for Maria Galvez. Entries in the Accounts Receivable DR, Sales Revenue CR column in the sales journal are posted daily to the subsidiary ledger to keep a current record of the amount receivable from each customer.

After posting to the subsidiary ledger, the accountant enters a check mark in the posting reference column of the sales journal (see Exhibit B-4). That lets the business know that the transaction was posted to Galvez's account.

Posting to the General Ledger At the end of the month, the accountant totals (commonly called *footing*) the Accounts Receivable DR, Sales Revenue CR, and Cost of Goods Sold DR, Merchandise Inventory CR columns. The totals of these columns are posted from the sales journal to the general ledger.

In Exhibit B-4 (Panel A), November's credit sales total $4,319. The $4,319 is posted to the Accounts Receivable and Sales Revenue accounts in the general ledger. The account numbers of each account are then printed beneath the total in the sales journal. In Panel B of Exhibit B-4, the account number for Accounts Receivable is 115 and the account number for Sales Revenue is 410. Entering these account numbers in the sales journal shows that the $4,319 has been posted to the two accounts.

The debit to Cost of Goods Sold and the credit to Merchandise Inventory for the monthly total of $1,814 are also posted at the end of the month. After posting, these accounts' numbers are entered beneath the total to show that Cost of Goods Sold and Merchandise Inventory have been updated.

As the accountant posts to the ledgers, the journal page number and journal name abbreviation are entered in the ledger account to show the source of the data. All transaction data in Exhibit B-4 originated on page 3 of the sales journal, so all posting references are S.3. "S" indicates sales journal. After posting, the Accounts Receivable balance in the general ledger should equal the sum of the individual customer balances in the subsidiary ledger.

Trace all the postings in Exhibit B-4. The way to learn an accounting information system is to study the flow of data. The arrows indicate the direction of the information.

The Cash Receipts Journal

Cash Receipts Journal
Special journal used to record cash receipts.

All businesses have lots of cash transactions, and therefore a **cash receipts journal** comes in handy. The cash receipts journal is a special journal that is used to record cash receipts.

Exhibit B-5 illustrates the cash receipts journal. Every transaction recorded in this journal is a cash receipt.

Exhibit B-5 | **Cash Receipts Journal with Posting**

PANEL A—Cash Receipts Journal:

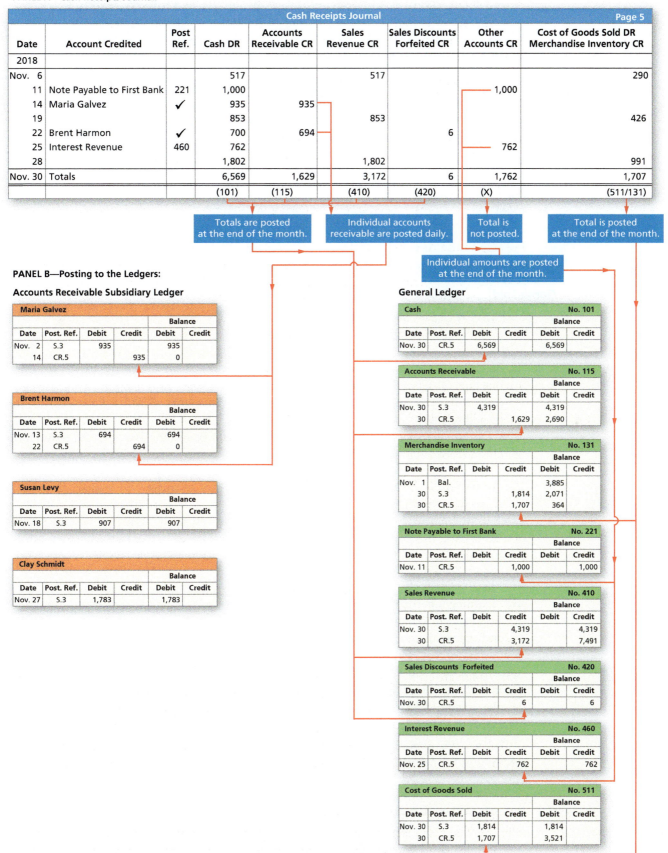

PANEL B—Posting to the Ledgers:

The main sources of cash are collections on account and cash sales. Collections on account are recorded in the Accounts Receivable CR column and the Cash DR column. Cash sales are recorded in the Sales Revenue CR column, the Cash DR column, and Cost of Goods Sold DR, Merchandise Inventory CR column. The cash receipts journal also has an Other Accounts CR column that is used to record miscellaneous cash receipt transactions and a Sales Discounts Forfeited CR column used to record sales discounts forfeited.

Recording Transactions

In Exhibit B-5, the first cash receipt occurred on November 6 and was a cash sale for $517 (cost of goods sold, $290). If the transaction had been recorded in the general journal, the following entries would have been recorded:

$$\frac{A\uparrow}{Cash\uparrow} \bigg\} = \bigg\{ \quad L \quad + \quad \frac{E\uparrow}{Sales\ Revenue\uparrow}$$

$$\frac{A\downarrow}{Merchandise\ Inventory\downarrow} \bigg\} = \bigg\{ \quad L \quad + \quad \frac{E\downarrow}{Cost\ of\ Goods\ Sold\uparrow}$$

Date	Accounts and Explanation	Debit	Credit
Nov. 6	Cash	517	
	Sales Revenue		517
	Cash sale.		
6	Cost of Goods Sold	290	
	Merchandise Inventory		290
	Recorded the cost of goods sold.		

By recording the transaction in the cash receipts journal instead, the entries can be recorded on one line. Observe the debit to Cash and the credit to Sales Revenue ($517) and the debit to Cost of Goods Sold and credit to Merchandise Inventory ($290) for the cost of the merchandise sold.

On November 11, the business borrowed $1,000 from First Bank. If the transaction had been recorded in the general journal, the following entry would have been made:

$$\frac{A\uparrow}{Cash\uparrow} \bigg\} = \bigg\{ \frac{L\uparrow}{Notes\ Payable\uparrow} + \ \underline{\quad E \quad}$$

Date	Accounts and Explanation	Debit	Credit
Nov. 11	Cash	1,000	
	Note Payable to First Bank		1,000
	Received cash in exchange for note.		

By recording it in the cash receipts journal instead, the accountant would record the $1,000 in the Cash DR column. The Other Accounts CR column is used for the Notes Payable credit because there is no specific credit column for borrowings. For this transaction, the account title, Note Payable to First Bank, is entered in the Account Credited column. The Other Accounts CR column is used when a transaction involves a credit entry that is not listed in the headings (columns) of the cash receipts journal. The entry on November 25 is another example. On November 25, the business received $762 cash of interest revenue. The cash receipts journal does not include a column for credits to interest revenue; therefore, the Other Accounts CR column must be used and the credit account must be written in the Account Credited column.

On November 14, the business collected $935 from Maria Galvez. Back on November 2, the business sold $1,100 of merchandise to Galvez, terms 15/20, n/30 and recorded the net sale in the sales journal. This credit sale allowed a $165 discount for prompt payment, and Galvez paid within the discount period. The business records this cash receipt in the cash receipts journal by debiting Cash for $935 and by crediting Accounts Receivable for $935. The customer's name appears in the Account Credited column.

The business does not have to deal with the sales discount associated with the Galvez sale because the sale was recorded net of discount at the time of sale. Only when a customer does not take advantage of the discount will the business use the Sales Discounts Forfeited CR column. Let's look at Brent Harmon as an example. On November 22, the business collected $700 from Brent Harmon representing the $694 he owed plus $6 sales discounts forfeited. Because Harmon did not pay within the discount period, he must pay more than the amount of the receivable. The transaction is recorded in the cash receipts journal as a $700 Cash DR, $694 Accounts Receivable CR, and $6 Sales Discounts Forfeited CR.

Posting

As with the sales journal, entries in the cash receipts journal are posted daily to the accounts receivable subsidiary ledger and monthly to the general ledger.

Posting to the Accounts Receivable Subsidiary Ledger Amounts from the cash receipts journal are posted to the accounts receivable subsidiary ledger daily. The postings are credits. Trace the $935 credit to Maria Galvez's account. It reduces her balance to zero. The receipt from Brent Harmon reduces his balance to $0. After posting, the accountant enters a check mark in the posting reference column of the cash receipts journal and shows the CR.5 posting reference in the subsidiary ledger. CR.5 signifies that the posting is transferred from the cash receipts journal, page 5.

> The posting reference CR.5 should not be confused with the abbreviation for credit, CR. The posting reference for the cash receipts journal always includes a page reference while the abbreviation for credit does not.

Posting to the General Ledger At the end of the month, each column in the cash receipts journal is totaled. The equality of the debits and credits is verified by comparing the sum of all debit columns to the sum of all credit columns.

Debit Columns		Credit Columns	
Cash	$ 6,569	Accounts Receivable	$ 1,629
Cost of Goods Sold	1,707	Sales Revenue	3,172
		Sales Discounts Forfeited	6
		Other Accounts	1,762
		Merchandise Inventory	1,707
Total	$ 8,276		$ 8,276

All columns, except for the Other Accounts CR column, are posted in total to the general ledger. For example, the total for Cash ($6,569) is posted as a debit in the Cash account in the general ledger. After posting, the account number is printed below the column total in the cash receipts journal. The account number for Cash (101) appears below the column total, and likewise for the other column totals. The journal reference (CR) and page number (5) are shown in the general ledger as reference of the posting. Follow the arrows in Exhibit B-5, which track the posted amounts.

The column total for Other Accounts CR is *not* posted. Instead, these credits are posted individually. In Exhibit B-5, the November 11 transaction reads "Note Payable to First Bank." This $1,000 credit entry will need to be posted individually to the Note Payable to First Bank account in the general ledger. The account number (221) in the Post. Ref. column shows that the transaction amount was posted individually. The letter X below the column means that the column total was *not* posted.

After posting, the sum of the individual ending balances in the accounts receivable subsidiary ledger equals the ending balance of Accounts Receivable in the general ledger, as follows:

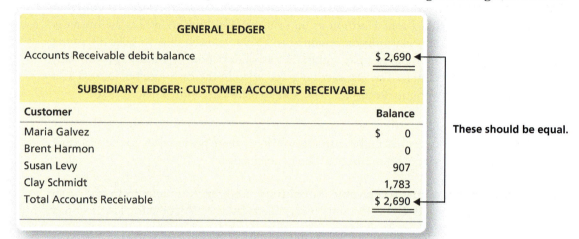

GENERAL LEDGER	
Accounts Receivable debit balance	$ 2,690

SUBSIDIARY LEDGER: CUSTOMER ACCOUNTS RECEIVABLE	
Customer	**Balance**
Maria Galvez	$ 0
Brent Harmon	0
Susan Levy	907
Clay Schmidt	1,783
Total Accounts Receivable	$ 2,690

These should be equal.

Try It!

6. Evenson Co. sold merchandise inventory on account, terms n/30, to Brain Crain, $300. The cost of the goods sold was $240. What special journal should the transaction be recorded in, and what is the column used for the $300?

Check your answer online in MyAccountingLab or at http://www.pearsonhighered.com/Horngren.

For more practice, see Short Exercises SB-3 through SB-7. MyAccountingLab

HOW ARE PURCHASES, CASH PAYMENTS, AND OTHER TRANSACTIONS RECORDED IN A MANUAL ACCOUNTING INFORMATION SYSTEM?

Learning Objective 3

Journalize and post purchases, cash payments, and other transactions in a manual accounting information system using special journals and subsidiary ledgers

Purchases Journal

Special journal used to record all purchases of merchandise inventory, office supplies, and other assets on account.

In the previous section, you learned that when using a manual accounting information system, sales on account are recorded in the sales journal and cash receipts are recorded in the cash receipts journal. We now turn our attention to purchases and cash payments.

The Purchases Journal

A merchandising business purchases merchandise inventory and other items, such as office supplies, equipment, and furniture, on account. The **purchases journal** handles these transactions plus other purchases incurred *on account*. Cash purchases are not recorded in the purchases journal; instead, they are recorded in the cash payments journal.

Exhibit B-6 illustrates a purchases journal (Panel A) and posting to the ledgers (Panel B). The purchases journal has special columns for:

• Credits to Accounts Payable

• Debits to Merchandise Inventory, Office Supplies, and Other Accounts

The Other Accounts DR columns are used for purchases on account of items other than merchandise inventory and office supplies. This business uses a perpetual inventory system. In a periodic inventory system, the Merchandise Inventory DR column would be replaced with a column titled Purchases DR.

Exhibit B-6 | Purchases Journal with Posting

PANEL A—Purchases Journal:

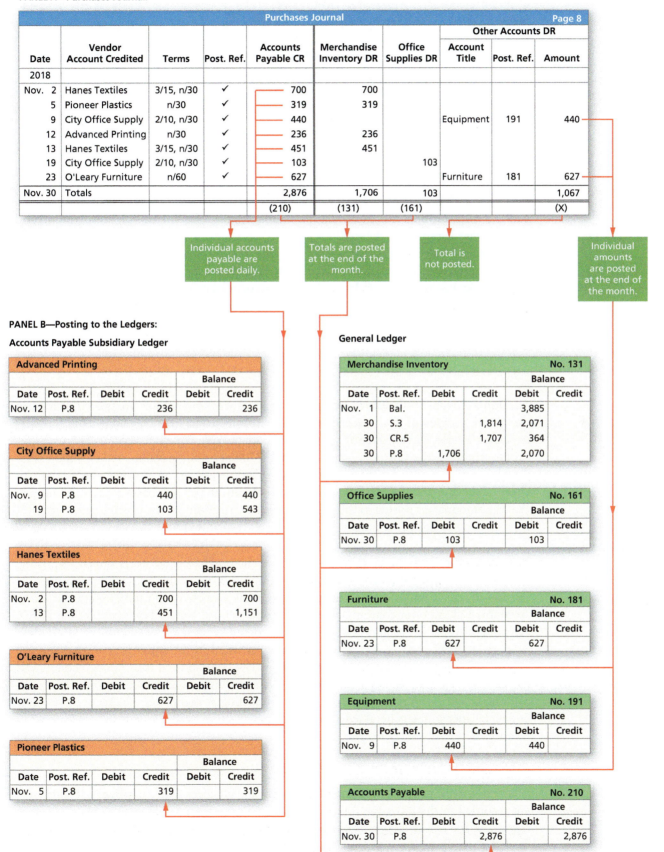

							Other Accounts DR		
Date	Vendor Account Credited	Terms	Post. Ref.	Accounts Payable CR	Merchandise Inventory DR	Office Supplies DR	Account Title	Post. Ref.	Amount
2018									
Nov. 2	Hanes Textiles	3/15, n/30	✓	700	700				
5	Pioneer Plastics	n/30	✓	319	319				
9	City Office Supply	2/10, n/30	✓	440			Equipment	191	440
12	Advanced Printing	n/30	✓	236	236				
13	Hanes Textiles	3/15, n/30	✓	451	451				
19	City Office Supply	2/10, n/30	✓	103		103			
23	O'Leary Furniture	n/60	✓	627			Furniture	181	627
Nov. 30	Totals			2,876	1,706	103			1,067
				(210)	(131)	(161)			(X)

Individual accounts payable are posted daily.

Totals are posted at the end of the month.

Total is not posted.

Individual amounts are posted at the end of the month.

PANEL B—Posting to the Ledgers:

Accounts Payable Subsidiary Ledger

General Ledger

Advanced Printing

Date	Post. Ref.	Debit	Credit	Balance Debit	Balance Credit
Nov. 12	P.8		236		236

City Office Supply

Date	Post. Ref.	Debit	Credit	Balance Debit	Balance Credit
Nov. 9	P.8		440		440
19	P.8		103		543

Hanes Textiles

Date	Post. Ref.	Debit	Credit	Balance Debit	Balance Credit
Nov. 2	P.8		700		700
13	P.8		451		1,151

O'Leary Furniture

Date	Post. Ref.	Debit	Credit	Balance Debit	Balance Credit
Nov. 23	P.8		627		627

Pioneer Plastics

Date	Post. Ref.	Debit	Credit	Balance Debit	Balance Credit
Nov. 5	P.8		319		319

Merchandise Inventory   No. 131

Date	Post. Ref.	Debit	Credit	Balance Debit	Balance Credit
Nov. 1	Bal.			3,885	
30	S.3		1,814	2,071	
30	CR.5		1,707	364	
30	P.8	1,706		2,070	

Office Supplies   No. 161

Date	Post. Ref.	Debit	Credit	Balance Debit	Balance Credit
Nov. 30	P.8	103		103	

Furniture   No. 181

Date	Post. Ref.	Debit	Credit	Balance Debit	Balance Credit
Nov. 23	P.8	627		627	

Equipment   No. 191

Date	Post. Ref.	Debit	Credit	Balance Debit	Balance Credit
Nov. 9	P.8	440		440	

Accounts Payable   No. 210

Date	Post. Ref.	Debit	Credit	Balance Debit	Balance Credit
Nov. 30	P.8		2,876		2,876

Recording Transactions

Let's begin by looking at the first transaction. On November 2, the business purchased merchandise inventory costing $700 from Hanes Textiles on account. If the transaction had been recorded in the general journal, the following entry would have been recorded:

$$\frac{A\uparrow}{\text{Merchandise Inventory}\uparrow} \bigg\} = \bigg\{ \frac{L\uparrow}{\text{Accounts Payable}\uparrow} + \frac{E}{}$$

Date	Accounts and Explanation	Debit	Credit
Nov. 2	Merchandise Inventory	700	
	Accounts Payable		700
	Purchased inventory on account.		

By recording the entry in the purchases journal, the transaction can be recorded on one line. The vendor's name (Hanes Textiles) is entered in the Vendor Account Credited column. The purchase terms of 3/15, n/30 are also entered to show the due date and the discount available. Accounts Payable is credited for the transaction amount, and Merchandise Inventory is debited.

Note the November 9 purchase of equipment on account from City Office Supply. The purchases journal holds no column for equipment, so the business uses the Other Accounts DR columns. Because this was a credit purchase, the accountant enters the vendor name (City Office Supply) in the Vendor Account Credited column and Equipment in the Account Title column.

Posting

Entries from the purchases journal are posted daily to the accounts payable subsidiary ledger and monthly to the general ledger.

Accounts Payable Subsidiary Ledger Individual accounts payable are posted daily from the purchases journal to the accounts payable subsidiary ledger. This allows the business to always have a current record of the accounts payable for each vendor. For example, on November 2, the business would post the $700 accounts payable credit to the Hanes Textiles account in the accounts payable subsidiary ledger. After posting, the accountant enters a check mark in the posting reference column of the purchases journal to indicate that the amount was posted in the subsidiary ledger. In addition, the posting reference (P.8) is printed in the subsidiary ledger.

Posting to the General Ledger Posting from the purchases journal is similar to posting from the other special journals. Exhibit B-6, Panel B, illustrates the posting process. At the end of each month, each column in the journal is totaled. All totals, except the Other Accounts DR Amount column, are posted to the general ledger. For example, the $2,876 Accounts Payable CR total is posted to the Accounts Payable account in the general ledger as a credit. After posting, the account number is listed in the purchases journal and the posting reference is listed in the general ledger. The column total for Other Accounts DR Amount is *not* posted. Instead, these debits are posted individually to the specific accounts, as done in the cash receipts journal. After all posting is complete, the Accounts Payable ending balance in the general ledger should equal the sum of the individual vendor ending balances in the subsidiary ledger.

The Cash Payments Journal

Cash Payments Journal

Special journal used to record cash payments by check and currency.

Businesses make most cash payments by check, and all checks (and payments of currency) are recorded in the **cash payments journal**. This special journal is also called the *check register* and the *cash disbursements journal*. Exhibit B-7 shows the cash payments journal, with the ledgers in Panel B.

Exhibit B-7 | Cash Payments Journal with Posting

PANEL A–Cash Payments Journal:

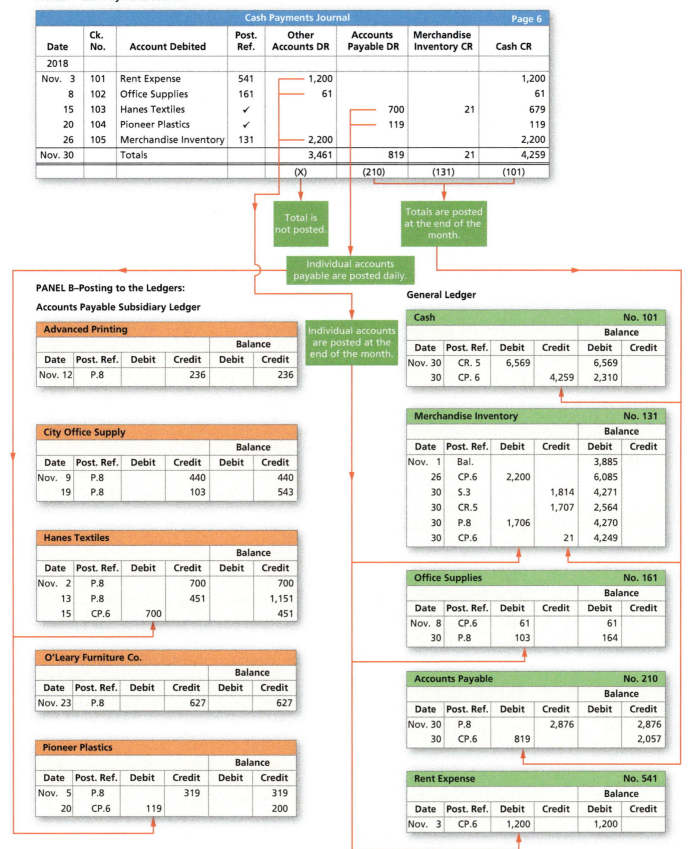

Cash Payments Journal							Page 6
Date	Ck. No.	Account Debited	Post. Ref.	Other Accounts DR	Accounts Payable DR	Merchandise Inventory CR	Cash CR
2018							
Nov. 3	101	Rent Expense	541	1,200			1,200
8	102	Office Supplies	161	61			61
15	103	Hanes Textiles	✓		700	21	679
20	104	Pioneer Plastics	✓		119		119
26	105	Merchandise Inventory	131	2,200			2,200
Nov. 30		Totals		3,461	819	21	4,259
				(X)	(210)	(131)	(101)

Total is not posted.

Totals are posted at the end of the month.

Individual accounts payable are posted daily.

PANEL B–Posting to the Ledgers:

Individual accounts are posted at the end of the month.

Accounts Payable Subsidiary Ledger

General Ledger

Advanced Printing

Date	Post. Ref.	Debit	Credit	Balance Debit	Balance Credit
Nov. 12	P.8		236		236

Cash No. 101

Date	Post. Ref.	Debit	Credit	Balance Debit	Balance Credit
Nov. 30	CR. 5	6,569		6,569	
30	CP. 6		4,259	2,310	

City Office Supply

Date	Post. Ref.	Debit	Credit	Balance Debit	Balance Credit
Nov. 9	P.8		440		440
19	P.8		103		543

Merchandise Inventory No. 131

Date	Post. Ref.	Debit	Credit	Balance Debit	Balance Credit
Nov. 1	Bal.			3,885	
26	CP.6	2,200		6,085	
30	S.3		1,814	4,271	
30	CR.5		1,707	2,564	
30	P.8	1,706		4,270	
30	CP.6		21	4,249	

Hanes Textiles

Date	Post. Ref.	Debit	Credit	Balance Debit	Balance Credit
Nov. 2	P.8		700		700
13	P.8		451		1,151
15	CP.6	700			451

Office Supplies No. 161

Date	Post. Ref.	Debit	Credit	Balance Debit	Balance Credit
Nov. 8	CP.6	61		61	
30	P.8	103		164	

O'Leary Furniture Co.

Date	Post. Ref.	Debit	Credit	Balance Debit	Balance Credit
Nov. 23	P.8		627		627

Accounts Payable No. 210

Date	Post. Ref.	Debit	Credit	Balance Debit	Balance Credit
Nov. 30	P.8		2,876		2,876
30	CP.6	819			2,057

Pioneer Plastics

Date	Post. Ref.	Debit	Credit	Balance Debit	Balance Credit
Nov. 5	P.8		319		319
20	CP.6	119			200

Rent Expense No. 541

Date	Post. Ref.	Debit	Credit	Balance Debit	Balance Credit
Nov. 3	CP.6	1,200		1,200	

The cash payments journal has two debit columns—one for Other Accounts and one for Accounts Payable. It has two credit columns—one for Merchandise Inventory (for purchase discounts) and one for Cash. This special journal also has columns for the date and check number of each cash payment and the account debited.

Recording Transactions

Let's review the first transaction listed in the cash payments journal. On November 3, the business paid cash of $1,200 for rent. This payment of cash is recorded in the cash payments journal by entering $1,200 in the Cash CR column and the Other Accounts DR column. The Other Accounts DR column is used to record debits to accounts for which no special column exists. The business enters the name of the other account used, Rent Expense, in the Account Debited column. The Other Accounts DR column was also used on November 8 for the purchase of office supplies for cash and on November 26 for the purchase of Merchandise Inventory with cash.

On November 15, the business paid the vendor, Hanes Textiles, on account, with credit terms of 3/15, n/30 (for details, see the first transaction in the purchases journal, Exhibit B-6). Paying within the discount period allowed a 3% discount ($21), and the business paid the remaining $679 ($700 less the $21 discount). If the business had recorded the transaction in the general journal, the following would have been recorded:

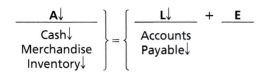

Date	Accounts and Explanation	Debit	Credit
Nov. 15	Accounts Payable	700	
	Cash		679
	Merchandise Inventory		21
	Paid within discount period.		

Instead, the business will record the transaction in the cash payments journal. The entry will be recorded by entering the $679 in the Cash CR column. The Accounts Payable DR column will be recorded for $700, and the discount of $21 will be entered into the Merchandise Inventory CR column. All transactions involving cash payments are recorded in the cash payments journal.

Posting

Entries in the cash payments journal are posted daily to the accounts payable subsidiary ledger and monthly to the general ledger.

Posting to the Accounts Payable Subsidiary Ledger Posting from the cash payments journal is similar to posting from the cash receipts journal. Individual vendor amounts (accounts payable) are posted daily to the accounts payable subsidiary ledger. The postings are debits and reduce the balance in the individual accounts payable account. Trace the $700 debit to Hanes Textiles's Accounts Payable. The $700 reduces the balance in the Hanes's subsidiary account to $451. After posting, a check mark is entered in the cash payments journal and the posting reference (CP.6) is printed in the subsidiary ledger.

Posting to the General Ledger At the end of the month, each column is totaled. The totals, except for the Other Accounts DR column, are posted to the specific general ledger accounts. After posting, the account number is printed below the column total in the cash payments journal and the posting reference is printed in the general ledger.

Amounts in the Other Accounts DR column are posted individually (for example, Rent Expense—debit $1,200). When each Other Account DR is posted to the general ledger, the account number is printed in the Post. Ref. column. The letter X below the Other Accounts DR column signifies that the total is *not* posted.

To review accounts payable, companies list individual vendor ending balances in the accounts payable subsidiary ledger. The general ledger and subsidiary ledger totals should agree.

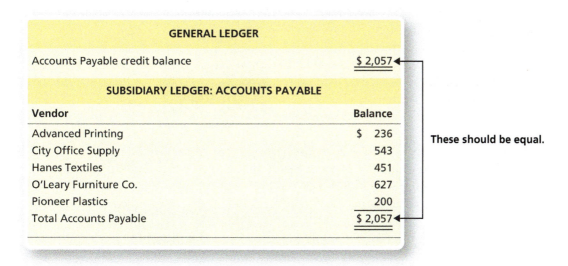

GENERAL LEDGER	
Accounts Payable credit balance	$ 2,057

SUBSIDIARY LEDGER: ACCOUNTS PAYABLE	
Vendor	Balance
Advanced Printing	$ 236
City Office Supply	543
Hanes Textiles	451
O'Leary Furniture Co.	627
Pioneer Plastics	200
Total Accounts Payable	$ 2,057

These should be equal.

The General Journal

Special journals save time recording repetitive transactions. But some transactions don't fit a special journal. Examples include the adjusting entries for depreciation, the expiration of prepaid insurance, and the accrual of salaries payable at the end of the period. Companies also use the general journal for sales returns and allowances and purchase returns and allowances not involving cash receipts or cash payments. All accounting information systems need a general journal. The adjusting entries and the closing entries are recorded in the general journal, along with other nonroutine transactions.

As we have seen, a manual accounting information system involves five journals: sales journal, cash receipts journal, purchases journal, cash payments journal, and the general journal. It's important to remember that transactions are recorded in either one of the special journals or in the general journal, but not both. Exhibit B-8 (on the next page) provides a summary of all five journals that will help you decide which journal to use when recording transactions in a manual system.

Exhibit B-8 | **Recording Transactions in Special Journals**

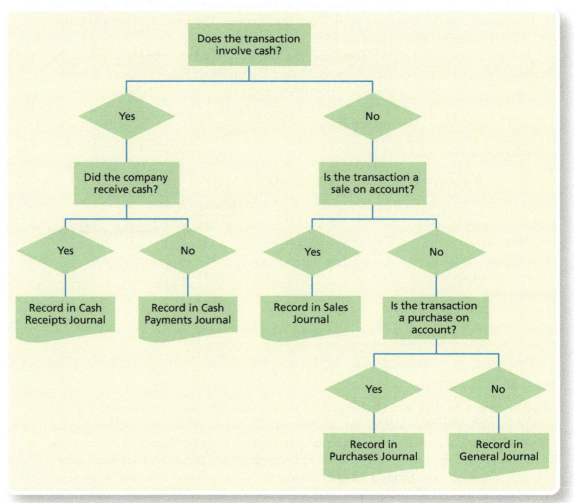

7. Fiscella Co. paid monthly rent of $2,000. What special journal should the transaction be recorded in? What columns will be used?

Check your answer online in MyAccountingLab or at http://www.pearsonhighered.com/Horngren.

For more practice, see Short Exercises SB-8 through SB-12.   MyAccountingLab

HOW ARE TRANSACTIONS RECORDED IN A COMPUTERIZED ACCOUNTING INFORMATION SYSTEM?

A computerized accounting information system has two basic components:

- Hardware
- Software

Hardware is the electronic equipment: computers, monitors, printers, and the network that connects them. Most systems require a network to link computers. In a networked system, the server stores the program and the data.

Software is the set of programs that drives the computer. Accounting software reads, edits, and stores transaction data. It also generates the reports that businesses can use to make decisions. Many software packages are flexible. For example, a small cleaning business may be only partly computerized. This small business may use the computer for employee payrolls, but other parts of the accounting information system may be manual.

Entry-Level Software

With increased availability of affordable computerized accounting information systems, more and more businesses are completing all of their accounting on the computer. Two popular entry-level software packages are QuickBooks and Sage 50 Accounting. Both of these programs allow businesses to enter sales of services and merchandise inventory. In addition, these programs can record expenses and produce reports such as financial statements. These computerized accounting information systems are relatively easy to use, often requiring little knowledge of accounting or GAAP. Computerized accounting software allows businesses to organize finances, track sales and expenses, and complete recordkeeping. QuickBooks and Sage 50 Accounting, though, work best for small businesses. As businesses grow and expand, they need a software system that can handle more advanced processes and transactions.

Enterprise Resource Planning (ERP) Systems

Larger companies will often use an enterprise resource planning (ERP) system to manage their data. ERP systems such as SAP® and Oracle® can integrate all company data into a single database. ERP feeds the data into software for all company activities—from purchasing to production and customer service.

Advantages of ERP systems include:

- Reduce operating costs.
- Help companies adjust to changes.
- Replace separate software systems, such as sales and payroll.

Disadvantages of ERP systems include:

- ERP is expensive. Major installations can cost millions of dollars.
- Implementation also requires a large commitment of time and people.

Many ERP systems and entry-level systems can be offered in the "cloud." Cloud computing refers to purchasing software and data storage from a third party. In cloud computing, the software and data are stored on the third-party server instead of by the business. Employees access the software and data via the Internet by using a Web browser. Cloud computing can reduce costs by a significant amount for many businesses.

Learning Objective 4

Describe how transactions are recorded in a computerized accounting information system

Hardware

Electronic equipment that includes computers, monitors, printers, and the network that connects them.

Network

The system of electronic linkages that allows different computers to share the same information.

Software

Set of programs or instructions that drives the computer to perform the work desired.

Enterprise Resource Planning (ERP)

Software system that can integrate all of a company's functions, departments, and data into a single system.

Cloud Computing

Software and data are stored on a third-party server instead of by the business and can be accessed by employees via the Internet.

QuickBooks

One way to understand how computerized accounting software works is to view how transactions are handled in this type of system. We are now going to look at a common entry-level system, QuickBooks. Although your instructor might not have you complete any assignments using QuickBooks, it will be helpful to view the way QuickBooks handles common accounting entries.

Most computerized accounting information systems are organized by function or task. A user can select a function, such as creating an invoice, from a menu. (A menu is a list of options for choosing computer functions.) QuickBooks uses a navigation panel located on the left-hand side of the screen that allows users to select from a menu of options such as Customers, Vendors, Employees, Transactions, and Reports. The tabs (Customers, Vendors, Employees, Transactions, and Reports) on the navigation panel handle all transactions that a company would use. Transactions involving customers, including invoices (accounts receivable), receipt of payments, and sales returns, would be recorded on the Customers tab. The Vendors tab handles transactions involving vendors, including entering bills (accounts payable), paying bills, and processing refunds. The financial reports of a business such as the income statement and balance sheet are also accessible from the navigation panel.

ETHICS

Should I change the transaction?

Girmanesh Landin is responsible for recording all of the transactions for Marshall's Home Care. This is Girmanesh's first job as a staff accountant, and she wants to do a good job. Last week, she recorded several cash payments for bills in the computerized accounting information system. She now realizes that she selected the incorrect cash account. She selected the savings account instead of the checking account. Girmanesh knows that she could go back into each transaction and make the correction without anyone knowing that she made the mistake, but she is unsure of what to do. Should Girmanesh make the correction?

information system before she changes each transaction. Attempting to hide her mistakes could cause her integrity to be questioned because it would appear that she was trying to cover up things rather than ask for clarification and help. Most businesses will prefer that Girmanesh make a separate correcting entry instead of going back in and changing the incorrect transaction. This procedure allows for businesses to have a record of the original transaction and then the correcting entry. It is generally never a good idea to change transactions that have already been recorded, and many software systems will not allow such actions as a method to prevent fraud.

Solution

Because Girmanesh is new to the job, she should find out the procedure for making corrections in the accounting

Creating a Sales Invoice

Suppose on June 23, Smart Touch Learning performed $3,000 of services for Richard Michura on account. To record this transaction in QuickBooks, Smart Touch Learning would need to create an invoice for Richard. Exhibit B-9 shows the invoice the company created. Notice that there are no debits and credits on the invoice. In a computerized accounting information system, the business does not have to record the transaction in debit and credit format. Instead, by creating the invoice, the software knows automatically to record a debit to Accounts Receivable—Michura and a credit to Sales Revenue. After creating the invoice, the software posts the transaction to the appropriate general ledger accounts. There is no need for the business to manually post the transaction; the software takes care of the posting process.

Exhibit B-9 | Invoice

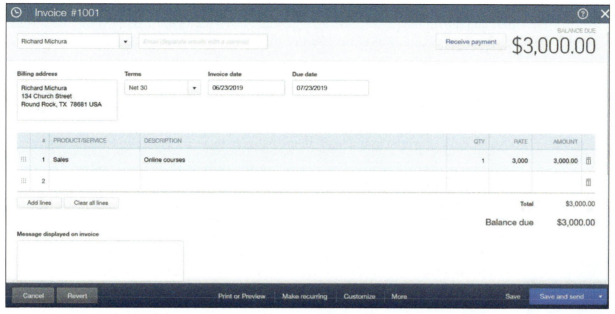

When Smart Touch Learning receives the $3,000 from the customer, the accounting clerk will enter the transaction in the Customers tab of QuickBooks by locating the customer's invoice and selecting the "Receive payment" action. By doing this, QuickBooks identifies that the invoice has been paid and that Richard Michura has no further outstanding balance.

Entering Bills

When a business needs to record a bill received, it will use the Vendors tab of QuickBooks. Suppose that on June 25, Smart Touch Learning receives a $580 bill for utilities. Exhibit B-10 shows the bill that the company will record in QuickBooks. When Smart Touch Learning saves the bill, the software will automatically record a debit to Utilities Expense and credit to Accounts Payable—Smart Energy.

Exhibit B-10 | Bill

On July 5, when Smart Touch Learning makes payment on the bill, it will enter the payment in the Vendors tab of QuickBooks. The accounting clerk will select the bill to be paid and record the payment by selecting the "Make payment" action. Again, the software takes care of recording the journal entry and posting to the ledger accounts.

Viewing Financial Statements

QuickBooks has the ability to produce numerous reports such as the income statement (called *Profit & Loss* in QuickBooks), balance sheet, and statement of cash flows. The software can also be used to create accounts receivable and accounts payable aging schedules. Exhibit B-11 shows an example of an income statement for Smart Touch Learning.

Exhibit B-11 | **Income Statement**

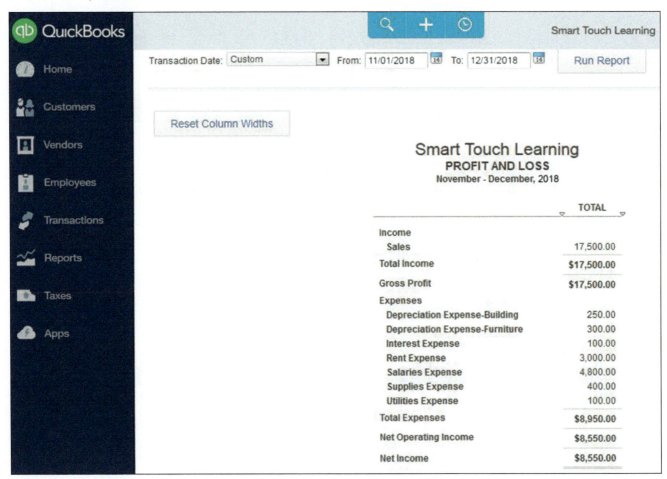

One of the many benefits of using a computerized accounting information system is the ease with which reports are created. For most reports needed, the software includes prebuilt templates that can be used. In addition, the software automatically transfers the amounts from the general ledger to the financial statements. The only thing the accountant needs to do is set the correct time period and review the financial statements for accuracy.

Try It!

8. Fill in the missing information.

    a. _____ is the set of programs that drives the computer.

    b. Most systems require a(n) _____ to link computers.

    c. _____ is the electronic equipment used in a computerized accounting information system.

Check your answers online in MyAccountingLab or at http://www.pearsonhighered.com/Horngren.

For more practice, see Short Exercise SB-13. MyAccountingLab

REVIEW

> Things You Should Know

1. What is an accounting information system?

- An accounting information system (AIS) collects, records, stores, and processes accounting data to produce information that is useful for decision makers.

- An effective accounting information system provides control, compatibility, flexibility, relevance, and a positive cost/benefit relationship.

- An accounting information system has three basic components:
  - Source documents and input devices
  - Processing and storage
  - Outputs

2. How are sales and cash receipts recorded in a manual accounting information system?

- In a manual system, businesses use special journals that are designed to record a specific type of transaction. The four special journals and their uses are:
  - Sales journal—records sales on account
  - Cash receipts journal—records cash receipts
  - Purchases journal—records purchases on account
  - Cash payments journal—records cash payments

- Subsidiary ledgers are used to hold individual accounts that support a general ledger account. Two common subsidiary ledgers are the accounts receivable subsidiary ledger and accounts payable subsidiary ledger.

- Credit sales are recorded in the sales journal, which uses two columns—Accounts Receivable DR, Sales Revenue CR and Cost of Goods Sold DR, Merchandise Inventory CR.

- Cash receipts are recorded in the cash receipts journal, which includes a Cash DR column and various other debit and credit columns.

3. **How are purchases, cash payments, and other transactions recorded in a manual accounting information system?**

- Purchases on account are recorded in the purchases journal, which includes an Accounts Payable CR column and various other debit columns.

- Cash payments are recorded in the cash payments journal, which includes a Cash CR column and various other debit and credit columns.

- The general journal is used for transactions that aren't recorded in one of the special journals, such as adjusting and closing entries.

4. **How are transactions recorded in a computerized accounting information system?**

- A computerized accounting information system has two basic components:

  - Hardware—the electronic equipment
  - Software—the set of programs that drives the computer

- Entry-level software, such as QuickBooks and Sage 50 Accounting, is often used by small businesses.

- Larger companies use an enterprise resource planning (ERP) system to manage their data.

> Check Your Understanding Problem

Check your understanding of the chapter by completing this problem and then looking at the solution. Use this practice to help identify which sections of the chapter you need to study more.

Houlihan Company completed the following selected transactions during March 2019:

Mar. 4	Received $500 for a cash sale of merchandise inventory to a customer (cost, $319).
6	Received $65 on account, terms n/30, from Brady Lee.
9	Received $1,080 on a note receivable from Beverly Mann. This amount includes the $1,000 note receivable plus interest revenue.
15	Received $800 for a cash sale of merchandise inventory to a customer (cost, $522).
24	Borrowed $2,200 by signing a note payable to Interstate Bank.
27	Received $1,200 on account from Lance Albert. Collection was received after the discount period and included $20 of sales discounts forfeited.

Requirements

The general ledger showed the following balances at February 28: Cash, $1,117; Accounts Receivable, $2,790; Note Receivable—Beverly Mann, $1,000; and Merchandise Inventory, $1,819. The accounts receivable subsidiary ledger at February 28 contained debit balances as follows: Lance Albert, $1,840; Melinda Fultz, $885; Brady Lee, $65.

1. Record the transactions in the cash receipts journal, page 7. (See Learning Objective 2)

2. Compute column totals at March 31. (See Learning Objective 2)

3. Post from the cash receipts journal to the general ledger and the accounts receivable subsidiary ledger. Use four-column accounts. Use complete posting references, including the following account numbers: Cash, 11; Accounts Receivable, 12; Note Receivable—Beverly Mann, 13; Merchandise Inventory, 14; Note Payable—Interstate Bank,

22; Sales Revenue, 41; Sales Discounts Forfeited, 42; Interest Revenue, 46; and Cost of Goods Sold, 51. Insert a check mark (√) in the posting reference column for each February 28 account balance. (See Learning Objective 2)

4. Balance the Accounts Receivable subsidiary ledger with the Accounts Receivable account in the general ledger. (See Learning Objective 2)

> Solution

Requirements 1 and 2

Cash Receipts Journal								Page 7
Date	Account Credited	Post. Ref.	Cash DR	Accounts Receivable CR	Sales Revenue CR	Sales Discounts Forfeited CR	Other Accounts CR	Cost of Goods Sold DR Merchandise Inventory CR
2019								
Mar. 4			500		500			319
6	Brady Lee	✓	65	65				
9	Note Receivable-Beverly Mann	13	1,080				1,000	
	Interest Revenue	46					80	
15			800		800			522
24	Note Payable-Interstate Bank	22	2,200				2,200	
27	Lance Albert	✓	1,200	1,180			20	
31			5,845	1,245	1,300	20	3,280	841
			(11)	(12)	(41)	(42)	(X)	(51/14)

Requirement 3

ACCOUNTS RECEIVABLE SUBSIDIARY LEDGER

Lance Albert

Date	Post. Ref.	Debit	Credit	Balance Debit	Balance Credit
Feb. 28	✓			1,840	
Mar. 27	CR.7		1,180	660	

Melinda Fultz

Date	Post. Ref.	Debit	Credit	Balance Debit	Balance Credit
Feb. 28	✓			885	

Brady Lee

Date	Post. Ref.	Debit	Credit	Balance Debit	Balance Credit
Feb. 28	✓			65	
Mar. 6	CR.7		65	0	

GENERAL LEDGER

Cash					No. 11
				Balance	
Date	Post. Ref.	Debit	Credit	Debit	Credit
Feb. 28	✓			1,117	
Mar. 31	CR.7	5,845		6,962	

Accounts Receivable					No. 12
				Balance	
Date	Post. Ref.	Debit	Credit	Debit	Credit
Feb. 28	✓			2,790	
Mar. 31	CR.7		1,245	1,545	

Note Receivable—Beverly Mann					No. 13
				Balance	
Date	Post. Ref.	Debit	Credit	Debit	Credit
Feb. 28	✓			1,000	
Mar. 9	CR.7		1,000	0	

Merchandise Inventory					No. 14
				Balance	
Date	Post. Ref.	Debit	Credit	Debit	Credit
Feb. 28	✓			1,819	
Mar. 31	CR.7		841	978	

Note Payable—Interstate Bank					No. 22
				Balance	
Date	Post. Ref.	Debit	Credit	Debit	Credit
Mar. 24	CR.7		2,200		2,200

Sales Revenue					No. 41
				Balance	
Date	Post. Ref.	Debit	Credit	Debit	Credit
Mar. 31	CR.7		1,300		1,300

Sales Discounts Forfeited					No. 42
				Balance	
Date	Post. Ref.	Debit	Credit	Debit	Credit
Mar. 31	CR.7		20		20

Interest Revenue					No. 46
				Balance	
Date	Post. Ref.	Debit	Credit	Debit	Credit
Mar. 9	CR.7		80		80

Cost of Goods Sold					No. 51
				Balance	
Date	Post. Ref.	Debit	Credit	Debit	Credit
Mar. 31	CR.7	841		841	

Requirement 4

GENERAL LEDGER	
Accounts Receivable debit balance	$ 1,545
SUBSIDIARY LEDGER: CUSTOMER ACCOUNTS RECEIVABLE	
Customer	Balance
Lance Albert	$ 660
Melinda Fultz	885
Brady Lee	0
Total Accounts Receivable	$ 1,545

> Key Terms

Accounting Information System (AIS) (p. B-2)

Accounts Payable Subsidiary Ledger (p. B-7)

Accounts Receivable Subsidiary Ledger (p. B-6)

Cash Payments Journal (p. B-16)

Cash Receipts Journal (p. B-10)

Cloud Computing (p. B-21)

Control Account (p. B-7)

Enterprise Resource Planning (ERP) (p. B-21)

Hardware (p. B-21)

Network (p. B-21)

Purchases Journal (p. B-14)

Sales Journal (p. B-7)

Server (p. B-4)

Software (p. B-21)

Source Document (p. B-3)

Special Journal (p. B-5)

Subsidiary Ledger (p. B-6)

> Quick Check

1. Which of the following benefits of an effective accounting information system provides safeguards for a business's assets and reduces the likelihood of fraud and errors?

   Learning Objective 1

   a. Flexibility

   b. Relevance

   c. Control

   d. Compatibility

2. The outputs of a computerized accounting information system are called

   Learning Objective 1

   a. reports.

   b. software.

   c. processing.

   d. purchase invoices.

3. Which of the following is not a special journal?

   Learning Objective 2

   a. Sales journal

   b. General journal

   c. Cash receipts journal

   d. Purchases journal

4. Mountain Day Spa sold merchandise inventory on credit, terms n/30, to Marvin Smith, $400. Cost of goods sold was $250. When using a manual accounting information system, where should Mountain record this transaction, and what is the appropriate column in which to record the $250?

   Learning Objective 2

   a. Sales journal; Accounts Receivable DR, Sales Revenue CR

   b. Cash receipts journal; Cash DR, Sales Revenue CR

   c. Sales journal; Cost of Goods Sold DR, Merchandise Inventory CR

   d. Cash receipts journal; Cash DR, Accounts Receivable CR

5. Which of the following correctly describes the posting of transactions from the sales journal?

   Learning Objective 2

   a. Individual accounts receivable are posted daily to the general ledger.

   b. At the end of the month, the totals of the columns are posted to the general ledger.

   c. Transactions are posted daily to the general ledger.

   d. The total of the Accounts Receivable DR, Sales Revenue CR column is posted to the accounts receivable subsidiary ledger.

Learning Objective 3

6. Centex Sound Systems purchased merchandise inventory costing $8,000 from Flower Co. on account. Where should Centex record this transaction, and what account is credited?

   a. Cash payments journal; credit Cash

   b. Sales journal; credit Sales Revenue

   c. Purchases journal; credit Accounts Payable

   d. General journal; credit Merchandise Inventory

Learning Objective 3

7. Every transaction recorded in the cash payments journal includes a

   a. credit to Cash.

   b. debit to Accounts Receivable.

   c. debit to Sales Discounts.

   d. debit to Cash.

Learning Objective 3

8. When using a manual accounting information system, which of the following transactions would be recorded in the general journal?

   a. Depreciation of office furniture

   b. Cash payment of rent

   c. Sale of merchandise inventory on account

   d. Purchase of merchandise inventory on account

Learning Objective 4

9. Which is a disadvantage of an enterprise resource planning (ERP) system?

   a. Helps companies adjust to changes

   b. Can replace separate software systems

   c. Can reduce operating costs

   d. Implementation requires a large commitment of time and people

Check your answers at the end of the chapter.

ASSESS YOUR PROGRESS

> Review Questions

1. What is an accounting information system (AIS)?

2. What does an effective accounting information system provide?

3. Explain the three basic components of an accounting information system.

4. What is a special journal?

5. What is the purpose of a subsidiary ledger?

6. What is a control account?

7. List the four special journals often used in a manual accounting information system. What types of transactions are recorded in each of the special journals?

8. Explain the posting process of the sales journal.

9. Provide some examples of transactions that would be recorded in the Other Accounts CR column of the cash receipts journal.

10. What are the columns that are typically used in the purchases journal?

11. Explain the posting process of the cash payments journal.

12. When is the general journal used in a manual accounting information system? Provide some examples of transactions that would be recorded in the general journal.

13. Explain the two components of a computerized accounting information system.

14. What are two common entry-level accounting software systems used by small businesses?

15. What is an enterprise resource planning (ERP) system? What are the advantages and disadvantages of using an ERP?

16. How is QuickBooks organized?

17. How would a business record a sale of services on account in QuickBooks?

18. How would a business record a bill received in QuickBooks?

> Short Exercises

SB-1 Evaluating features of an effective accounting information system

Learning Objective 1

In Vogue, a T-shirt business, is growing fast and needs a better accounting information system. Consider the features of an effective system. Which features are most important? Why? Which feature must you consider if your financial resources are limited?

SB-2 Defining components of an accounting information system

Learning Objective 1

Match each example with a component of a computerized accounting information system. Components may be used more than once.

Example	Component
1. Server	a. Source documents and input devices
2. Bank checks	b. Processing and storage
3. Reports	c. Outputs
4. Keyboard	
5. Software	
6. Financial statements	
7. Bar code scanner	

SB-3 Identifying special journals

Learning Objective 2

Use the following abbreviations to indicate the journal in which you would record transactions a through n.

- J = General journal
- S = Sales journal
- CR = Cash receipts journal
- P = Purchases journal
- CP = Cash payments journal

Transactions:

- ___ **a.** Cash purchase of merchandise inventory
- ___ **b.** Collection of dividend revenue earned on an investment
- ___ **c.** Prepayment of insurance
- ___ **d.** Borrowing money on a long-term note payable
- ___ **e.** Purchase of equipment on account

___ **f.** Cost of goods sold along with a credit sale

___ **g.** Cash sale of merchandise inventory

___ **h.** Payment of rent

___ **i.** Depreciation of computer equipment

___ **j.** Purchase of merchandise inventory on account

___ **k.** Collection of accounts receivable

___ **l.** Expiration of prepaid insurance

___ **m.** Sale on account

___ **n.** Payment on account

Learning Objective 2

SB-4 Recording transactions in a sales journal

Jun. 1	Sold merchandise inventory on account to Fran Jack, $1,220. Cost of goods, $980. Invoice no. 101.
8	Sold merchandise inventory on account to Ireland Frank, $2,025. Cost of goods, $1,640. Invoice no. 102.
13	Sold merchandise inventory on account to Jake Thompson, $420. Cost of goods, $210. Invoice no. 103.
28	Sold merchandise inventory on account to Gabe West, $820. Cost of goods, $620. Invoice no. 104.

Use the following sales journal to record the preceding transactions. All credit sales are terms of n/30.

Sales Journal					Page 1
Date	Invoice No.	Customer Account Debited	Post. Ref.	Accounts Receivable DR Sales Revenue CR	Cost of Goods Sold DR Merchandise Inventory CR
2018					

Note: Short Exercise SB-4 must be completed before attempting Short Exercise SB-5.

Learning Objective 2

SB-5 Posting transactions from a sales journal to a subsidiary ledger and general ledger

Review your results from Short Exercise SB-4.

Requirements

1. Total each column of the sales journal.

2. Open the following four-column accounts in the accounts receivable subsidiary ledger: Accounts Receivable—Frank; Accounts Receivable—Jack; Accounts Receivable—Thompson; Accounts Receivable—West. Post the transactions to the accounts receivable subsidiary ledger.

3. Open the following selected four-column accounts in the general ledger: Accounts Receivable (112); Merchandise Inventory (118), Bal. $5,000; Sales Revenue (411); Cost of Goods Sold (511). Post the total of each column to the general ledger.

4. Balance the total of the customer ending balances in the accounts receivable subsidiary ledger against Accounts Receivable in the general ledger.

SB-6 Recording transactions in a cash receipts journal

Learning Objective 2

Jul. 5 Sold merchandise inventory for cash, $1,700. Cost of goods, $1,400.

　12 Collected interest revenue of $2,050.

　18 Received cash from Heidi Next, $1,200, on account. There was no discount.

　29 Received $5,300 from Mitch Dylan in full settlement of his account receivable including sales discounts forfeited of $20.

Use the following cash receipts journal to record the preceding transactions.

| | | | | Cash Receipts Journal | | | | Page 3 |
Date	Account Credited	Post. Ref.	Cash DR	Accounts Receivable CR	Sales Revenue CR	Sales Discounts Forfeited CR	Other Accounts CR	Cost of Goods Sold DR Merchandise Inventory CR
2018								

Note: Short Exercise SB-6 must be completed before attempting Short Exercise SB-7.

SB-7 Posting transactions from a cash receipts journal to a subsidiary ledger and general ledger

Learning Objective 2

Review your results from Short Exercise SB-6.

Requirements

1. Total each column of the cash receipts journal.

2. Open the following four-column accounts in the accounts receivable subsidiary ledger: Accounts Receivable—Dylan, Bal. $5,280; Accounts Receivable—Next, Bal. $2,250. Post the transactions to the accounts receivable subsidiary ledger.

3. Open the following selected four-column accounts in the general ledger: Cash (111), Bal. $4,550; Accounts Receivable (112), Bal. $7,530; Merchandise Inventory (118), Bal. $3,250; Sales Revenue (411), Bal. $25,000; Sales Discounts Forfeited (412); Interest Revenue (419); Cost of Goods Sold (511), Bal. $14,500. Post the total of each column to the general ledger. Also, post the Other Accounts column to the general ledger.

4. Balance the total of the customer ending balances in the accounts receivable subsidiary ledger against Accounts Receivable in the general ledger.

Learning Objective 3

SB-8 Recording transactions in a purchases journal

Oct. 1	Purchased merchandise inventory on account with credit terms of 4/10, n/30 from Mayer Co., $2,200.
11	Purchased office supplies on account from Bird Co., $600. Terms were n/EOM.
24	Purchased furniture on account with credit terms of 3/10, n/60 from Silly Co., $900.

Use the following purchases journal to record the preceding transactions.

							Other Accounts DR		
Date	Vendor Account Credited	Terms	Post. Ref.	Accounts Payable CR	Merchandise Inventory DR	Office Supplies DR	Account Title	Post Ref.	Amount
2018									

Note: Short Exercise SB-8 must be completed before attempting Short Exercise SB-9.

Learning Objective 3

SB-9 Posting transactions from a purchases journal to a subsidiary ledger and general ledger

Review your results from Short Exercise SB-8.

Requirements

1. Total each column of the purchases journal.
2. Open the following four-column accounts in the accounts payable subsidiary ledger: Accounts Payable—Bird Co.; Accounts Payable—Mayer Co.; Accounts Payable—Silly Co. Post the transactions to the accounts payable subsidiary ledger.
3. Open the following selected four-column accounts in the general ledger: Merchandise Inventory (115); Office Supplies (116); Furniture (151); Accounts Payable (211). Post the total of each column to the general ledger. Also, post the Other Accounts column to the general ledger.
4. Balance the total of the vendor ending balances in the accounts payable subsidiary ledger against Accounts Payable in the general ledger.

Learning Objective 3

SB-10 Recording transactions in a cash payments journal

Jan. 5	Issued check no. 430 to purchase equipment for cash, $1,700.
7	Purchased merchandise inventory for cash, $450, issuing check no. 431.
18	Paid Kat Co. amount owed, $775, less $100 discount. Issued check no. 432.
28	Issued check no. 433 to pay utilities, $260. The bill was just received, and there is no liability recorded.

Use the following cash payments journal to record the preceding transactions.

						Cash Payments Journal			Page 8
Date	Ck. No.	Account Debited	Post. Ref.	Other Accounts DR	Accounts Payable DR	Merchandise Inventory CR	Cash CR
2018							

Note: Short Exercise SB-10 must be completed before attempting Short Exercise SB-11.

SB-11 Posting transactions from a cash payments journal to a subsidiary ledger and general ledger

Learning Objective 3

Review your results from Short Exercise SB-10.

Requirements

1. Total each column of the cash payments journal.

2. Open the following four-column accounts in the accounts payable subsidiary ledger: Accounts Payable—Kat Co., Bal. $1,900. Post the transactions to the accounts payable subsidiary ledger.

3. Open the following selected four-column accounts in the general ledger: Cash (111), Bal. $5,000; Merchandise Inventory (118), $2,100; Equipment (150), $9,900; Accounts Payable (211), $1,900; Utilities Expense (541). Post the total of each column to the general ledger. Also, post the Other Accounts column to the general ledger.

4. Balance the total of the vendor ending balances in the accounts payable subsidiary ledger against Accounts Payable in the general ledger.

SB-12 Recording transactions in a general journal

Learning Objective 3

Mar. 2	Sold merchandise inventory on account, terms n/30, to B. Kelp, issuing invoice no. 501 for $1,000 (cost, $680).
6	Issued credit memo to B. Kelp for $1,000 for merchandise returned to the business by the customer. Also accounted for receipt of the merchandise inventory at cost.
21	Purchased merchandise inventory on credit terms of 3/10, n/30 from Pond Co., $600.
28	Returned damaged merchandise inventory to Pond Co., issuing a debit memo for $600.

Journalize the above transactions that should be recorded in the general journal. If a transaction should not be recorded in the general journal, identify the special journal that should be used. Assume the company uses the perpetual inventory system.

Learning Objective 4

SB-13 Understanding components of a computerized accounting information system

Ned Timmons, engineer, is considering using a computerized accounting system for his professional engineering business. Ned has asked that you help him understand the components of a computerized accounting information system by answering the following questions:

Requirements

1. What are the two basic components of a computerized accounting information system?
2. Provide examples of each component.
3. If Ned were interested in an entry-level software system, what software might you recommend?

> Exercises

Learning Objective 2

Accounts Receivable DR, Sales Revenue CR column total $1,550

EB-14 Recording transactions—sales journal

Feb. 1	Sold merchandise inventory on account, terms n/30, to Cole Co., $1,050. Cost of goods, $860. Invoice no. 401.
6	Sold merchandise inventory for cash, $950 (cost, $750).
12	Collected interest revenue of $170.
15	Received cash from Cole Co. in full settlement of its account receivable.
20	Sold merchandise inventory on account, terms n/30, to Dump Co., issuing invoice no. 402 for $500 (cost, $325).
22	Sold merchandise inventory for cash, $600 (cost $530).
26	Sold office supplies to an employee for cash of $150.
28	Received $500 from Dump Co. in full settlement of its account receivable.

Requirements

1. Prepare headings for a sales journal. Journalize the transactions that should be recorded in the sales journal. Assume the company uses the perpetual inventory system.
2. Total each column of the sales journal.

Learning Objective 2

Accounts Receivable CR column total $1,550

EB-15 Recording transactions—cash receipts journal

Refer to information in Exercise EB-14.

Requirements

1. Prepare headings for a cash receipts journal. Journalize the transactions that should be recorded in the cash receipts journal.
2. Total each column of the cash receipts journal.

EB-16 Using the sales and cash receipts journals

The sales and cash receipts journals of Caverly Office Products include the following entries:

				Sales Journal	Page 1
Date	Invoice No.	Customer Account Debited	Post. Ref.	Accounts Receivable DR Sales Revenue CR	Cost of Goods Sold DR Merchandise Inventory CR
2018					
May 7	601	L. Ebert	✓	110	63
10	602	T. Ross	✓	65	33
10	603	E. Loop	✓	95	37
12	604	B. Goebel	✓	120	76
May 31		Total		390	209

						Cash Receipts Journal		Page 5
Date	Account Credited	Post. Ref.	Cash DR	Accounts Receivable CR	Sales Revenue CR	Sales Discounts Forfeited CR	Other Accounts CR	Cost of Goods Sold DR Merchandise Inventory CR
2018								
May 16	L. Ebert	✓						
19	E. Loop	✓						
24			320		320			250
30	T. Ross	✓						
May 31	Total							

Identify the missing information in the cash receipts journal for those transactions listed. All credit sales are terms n/30. Assume all the accounts are paid in full. Also, total the columns in the cash receipts journal and show that total debits equal total credits.

EB-17 Analyzing postings from the cash receipts journal

The cash receipts journal of Silver Plastics follows:

						Cash Receipts Journal		Page 7
Date	Account Credited	Post. Ref.	Cash DR	Accounts Receivable CR	Sales Revenue CR	Sales Discounts Forfeited CR	Other Accounts CR	Cost of Goods Sold DR Merchandise Inventory CR
2018								
Jan. 2	Awesome, Corp.	(g)	830	810		20		
9	King, Inc.	(h)	490	490				
19	Note Receivable	(i)	4,480				4,000	
	Interest Revenue	(j)					480	
30	J. T. Folk	(k)	330	320		10		
31			4,230		4,230			3,500
Jan. 31	Total		10,360	1,620	4,230	30	4,480	3,500
			(a)	(c)	(d)	(b)	(e)	(f)

Silver's general ledger includes the following selected accounts, along with their account numbers:

Number	Account
110	Cash
115	Accounts Receivable
118	Merchandise Inventory
125	Notes Receivable
510	Sales Revenue
512	Sales Discounts Forfeited
520	Interest Revenue
611	Cost of Goods Sold

Indicate whether each posting reference (a) through (k) should be a

- Check mark (✓) for a posting to a customer account in the accounts receivable subsidiary ledger.
- Account number for a posting to an account in the general ledger. If so, give the account number.
- Letter (X) for an amount not posted.

Learning Objective 2

EB-18 Identifying transactions in the accounts receivable subsidiary ledger

A customer account in the accounts receivable subsidiary ledger of Leger Old Company follows:

JOSH WILLOW					
				Balance	
Date	Post. Ref.	Debit	Credit	Debit	Credit
Nov. 1				400	
9	S.5	1,180		1,580	
18	J.8		190	1,390	
30	CR.9		700	690	

Describe the three posted transactions.

Learning Objective 3

Accounts Payable CR column total $4,800

EB-19 Recording transactions—purchases journal

Apr. 2	Purchased merchandise inventory on credit terms of 3/10, n/60 from Vanderbilt Co., $2,400.
5	Issued check no. 820 to purchase equipment for cash, $3,600.
11	Purchased merchandise inventory for cash, $750, issuing check no. 821.
12	Issued check no. 822 to pay Vanderbilt Co. net amount owed from Apr. 2.
19	Purchased office supplies on account from Downing Supplies, $500. Terms were n/EOM.
24	Purchased merchandise inventory on credit terms of net 30 from Wilmington Sales, $1,900.
28	Issued check no. 823 to pay for insurance coverage, debiting Prepaid Insurance for $1,000.
29	Issued check no. 824 to pay rent for the month, $1,250.

Requirements

1. Prepare headings for a purchases journal. Journalize the transactions that should be recorded in the purchases journal. The company uses the perpetual inventory system.

2. Total each column of the purchases journal.

EB-20 Recording transactions—cash payments journal

Refer to information in Exercise EB-19.

Requirements

1. Prepare headings for a cash payments journal. Journalize the transactions that should be recorded in the cash payments journal.

2. Total each column of the cash payments journal.

EB-21 Posting from the purchases journal; balancing the ledgers

The purchases journal of Southeastern Publishing Company follows:

							Other Accounts DR		
Date	**Vendor Account Credited**	**Terms**	**Post. Ref.**	**Accounts Payable CR**	**Merchandise Inventory DR**	**Office Supplies DR**	**Account Title**	**Post. Ref.**	**Amount**
2018									
Sep. 2	Leap Tech	n/30		830	830				
5	Jell Supply	n/30		155		155			
13	Leap Tech	5/10, n/30		1,470	1,470				
26	Fallon Equipment	n/30		880			Equipment		880
Sep. 30	Total								

Purchases Journal — Page 7

Requirements

1. Total each column of the purchases journal.

2. Open four-column ledger accounts for Merchandise Inventory (118), Office Supplies (120), Equipment (150), and Accounts Payable (211). Post to these accounts from the purchases journal. Use dates and posting references in the accounts.

3. Open four-column accounts in the accounts payable subsidiary ledger for Fallon Equipment, Jell Supply, and Leap Tech. Post from the purchases journal. Use dates and posting references in the ledger accounts.

4. Balance the Accounts Payable control account in the general ledger with the total of the ending balances in the accounts payable subsidiary ledger.

EB-22 Identifying transactions in the accounts payable subsidiary ledger

A vendor account in the accounts payable subsidiary ledger of Frost Company follows.

LARRY CARPENTER

				Balance	
Date	Post. Ref.	Debit	Credit	Debit	Credit
Dec. 1					1,800
12	P.4		2,340		4,140
20	J.10	200			3,940
29	CP.6	1,500			2,440

Learning Objective 3

Cash CR column total $8,928

Learning Objective 3

Merchandise Inventory DR column total $2,300

Learning Objective 3

Describe the three posted transactions.

Learning Objectives 2, 3

EB-23 Identifying errors in special journals

Transaction	Recording
a. Henry Associates paid $490 on account for an earlier purchase of merchandise inventory.	Purchases journal
b. Recorded depreciation expense for the month.	Cash payments journal
c. Collected interest revenue.	Cash receipts journal
d. Sold merchandise inventory on account.	Cash receipts journal
e. Issued check no. 535 for purchase of merchandise inventory.	Purchases journal
f. Returned damaged inventory that was purchased on account.	Purchases journal
g. Sold merchandise inventory for cash.	Sales journal

For each transaction listed, identify the recording error and indicate the journal that should have been used.

> Problems Group A

All problems can be completed manually or by using either MyAccountingLab General Ledger or QuickBooks.

Learning Objectives 2, 3

Cash Receipts Journal, Accounts Receivable CR column total $11,600

PB-24A Using the sales, cash receipts, and general journals

Assume Sparkling Springs Glass Company uses the perpetual inventory system. The general ledger of Sparkling Springs Glass Company includes the following selected accounts, along with their account numbers:

Number	Account	Number	Account
11	Cash	18	Equipment
12	Accounts Receivable	19	Land
13	Notes Receivable	41	Sales Revenue
15	Merchandise Inventory	51	Cost of Goods Sold
16	Office Supplies		

Sales and cash receipts transactions in July were as follows:

Jul. 2	Sold merchandise inventory on credit, terms n/30, to Intel, Inc., $1,500 (cost, $200).
3	Sold office supplies to an employee at cost, $80, receiving cash.
7	Cash sales for the week totaled $2,300 (cost, $1,500).
9	Sold merchandise inventory on account, terms n/30, to A. B. Miller, $7,700 (cost, $5,200).
10	Sold land that cost $10,000 for cash of the same amount.
11	Sold merchandise inventory on account, terms n/30, to Speedy Electric, $5,400 (cost, $3,350).
12	Received cash from Intel in full settlement of its account receivable from July 2.
14	Cash sales for the week were $2,600 (cost, $1,700).
15	Sold merchandise inventory on credit, terms n/30, to the partnership of William & Bill, $3,400 (cost, $2,400).
20	Sold merchandise inventory on account, terms n/30, to Speedy Electric, $500 (cost, $250).
21	Cash sales for the week were $980 (cost, $640).
22	Received $4,000 cash from A. B. Miller in partial settlement of his account receivable.
25	Received cash from William & Bill for its account receivable from July 15.
25	Sold merchandise inventory on account, terms n/30, to Oscar Co., $1,520 (cost, $1,000).
27	Collected $5,000 on a note receivable. There was no interest earned.
28	Cash sales for the week totaled $3,710 (cost, $2,450).
29	Sold merchandise inventory on account, terms n/30, to R. O. Bart, $200 (cost, $100).
31	Received $2,700 cash on account from A. B. Miller.

Requirements

1. Use the appropriate journal to record the preceding transactions in a sales journal (omit the Invoice No. column) and a cash receipts journal (omit the Sales Discounts Forfeited column).

2. Total each column of the sales journal and the cash receipts journal. Show that total debits equal total credits.

3. Show how postings would be made by writing the account numbers and check marks in the appropriate places in the journals.

PB-25A Using the purchases, cash payments, and general journals

The general ledger of Shiny Lake Golf Shop includes the following selected accounts, along with their account numbers:

Number	Account	Number	Account
111	Cash	181	Equipment
131	Merchandise Inventory	211	Accounts Payable
161	Prepaid Insurance	564	Rent Expense
171	Office Supplies	583	Utilities Expense

Transactions in December that affected purchases and cash payments follow:

Dec. 2	Purchased merchandise inventory on credit from Tomas, $4,500. Terms were 1/10, n/30.
3	Paid monthly rent, debiting Rent Expense for $2,300.
5	Purchased office supplies on credit terms of 1/10, n/30 from Right Supply, $440.
8	Received and paid electricity utility bill, $580.
9	Purchased equipment on account from Ace Equipment, $6,600. Payment terms were n/30.
10	Returned the equipment to Ace Equipment. It was damaged.
11	Paid Tomas the amount owed on the purchase of December 2.
12	Purchased merchandise inventory on account from Callahan Golf, $4,000. Terms were 3/10, n/30.
13	Purchased merchandise inventory for cash, $600.
14	Paid a semiannual insurance premium, debiting Prepaid Insurance, $1,400.
16	Paid its account payable to Right Supply from December 5.
18	Received and paid gas and water utility bills, $200.
21	Purchased merchandise inventory on credit terms of 2/10, n/45 from Dormer, Inc., $3,400.
21	Paid its account payable to Callahan Golf from December 12.
22	Purchased office supplies on account from Office World, Inc., $600. Terms were n/30.
26	Returned to Dormer, Inc. $1,000 of the merchandise inventory purchased on December 21.
31	Paid Dormer, Inc. the net amount owed from December 21 less the return on December 26.

Requirements

1. Shiny Lake Golf Shop records purchase returns in the general journal. Use the appropriate journal to record the transactions in a purchases journal, a cash payments journal (omit the Check No. column), and a general journal. The company uses the perpetual inventory system.

2. Total each column of the special journals. Show that total debits equal total credits in each special journal.

3. Show how postings would be made from the journals by writing the account numbers and check marks in the appropriate places in the journals.

PB-26A Using all journals, posting, and balancing the ledgers

Learning Objectives 2, 3

Trial balance, total debits $48,600

Tulsa Computer Security uses the perpetual inventory system and makes all credit sales on terms of n/30. Tulsa completed the following transactions during May:

May 2	Issued invoice no. 913 for sale on account to K. D. King, $2,200 (cost, $1,500).
3	Purchased merchandise inventory on credit terms of 3/10, n/60 from Henderson Co., $2,900.
5	Sold merchandise inventory for cash, $1,800 (cost, $350).
5	Issued check no. 532 to purchase furniture for cash, $2,950.
8	Collected interest revenue of $1,350.
9	Issued invoice no. 914 for sale on account to Berkner Co., $5,700 (cost, $2,000).
10	Purchased merchandise inventory for cash, $1,000, issuing check no. 533.
12	Received cash from K. D. King in full settlement of her account receivable from the sale on May 2.
13	Issued check no. 534 to pay Henderson Co. the net amount owed from May 3. Round to the nearest dollar.
13	Purchased office supplies on account from Magyar, Inc., $500. Terms were n/EOM.
15	Sold merchandise inventory on account to M. O. Small, issuing invoice no. 915 for $850 (cost, $400).
18	Issued invoice no. 916 for credit sale to K. D. King, $300 (cost, $150).
19	Received cash from Berkner Co. in full settlement of its account receivable from May 9.
20	Purchased merchandise inventory on credit terms of n/30 from Silva Distributing, $2,100.
22	Purchased furniture on credit terms of 3/10, n/60 from Henderson Co., $500.
22	Issued check no. 535 to pay for insurance coverage, debiting Prepaid Insurance for $1,400.
24	Sold office supplies to an employee for cash of $125, which was Tulsa's cost.
25	Received bill and issued check no. 536 to pay utilities, $550.
28	Purchased merchandise inventory on credit terms of 2/10, n/30 from Magyar, Inc., $575.
29	Returned damaged merchandise inventory to Magyar, Inc., issuing a debit memo for $575.
29	Sold merchandise inventory on account to Berkner Co., issuing invoice no. 917 for $2,400 (cost, $1,400).
30	Issued check no. 537 to pay Magyar, Inc. in full for May 13 purchase.
31	Received cash in full from K. D. King on credit sale of May 18.
31	Issued check no. 538 to pay monthly salaries of $2,250.

Requirements

1. Open four-column general ledger accounts using Tulsa's account numbers and balances as of May 1, 2018, that follow. All accounts have normal balances.

Number	Account	Bal.
111	Cash	$ 15,000
112	Accounts Receivable	1,700
114	Merchandise Inventory	7,000
116	Office Supplies	600
117	Prepaid Insurance	0
151	Furniture	2,200
211	Accounts Payable	900
311	Common Stock	10,000
314	Retained Earnings	11,400
411	Sales Revenue	7,800
419	Interest Revenue	1,300
511	Cost of Goods Sold	2,800
531	Salaries Expense	1,900
541	Utilities Expense	200

2. Open four-column accounts in the subsidiary ledgers with beginning balances as of May 1, if any. Accounts receivable subsidiary ledger—Balakrishnan Co., $1,700; Berkner Co., $0; M. O. Small, $0; and K. D. King, $0. Accounts payable subsidiary ledger—Henderson Co., $0; Magyar, Inc., $0; Silva Distributing, $0; and White Co., $900.

3. Enter the transactions in a sales journal (page 7), a cash receipts journal (page 5, omit Sales Discounts Forfeited column), a purchases journal (page 10), a cash payments journal (page 8), and a general journal (page 6), as appropriate.

4. Post daily to the accounts receivable subsidiary ledger and to the accounts payable subsidiary ledger.

5. Total each column of the special journals. Show that total debits equal total credits in each special journal. On May 31, post to the general ledger.

6. Prepare a trial balance as of May 31, 2018, to verify the equality of the general ledger. Balance the total of the customer account ending balances in the accounts receivable subsidiary ledger against Accounts Receivable in the general ledger. Do the same for the accounts payable subsidiary ledger and Accounts Payable in the general ledger.

> Problems Group B

All problems can be completed manually or by using either MyAccountingLab General Ledger or QuickBooks.

PB-27B Using the sales, cash receipts, and general journals

Assume Peaceful Spring Company uses the perpetual inventory system. The general ledger of Peaceful Springs Company includes the following selected accounts, along with their account numbers:

Learning Objectives 2, 3

Cash Receipts Journal, Accounts Receivable CR column total $11,800

Number	Account	Number	Account
11	Cash	18	Equipment
12	Accounts Receivable	19	Land
13	Notes Receivable	41	Sales Revenue
15	Merchandise Inventory	51	Cost of Goods Sold
16	Office Supplies		

Sales and cash receipts transactions in November were as follows:

Nov. 2	Sold merchandise inventory on credit, terms n/30, to Intelysis, Inc., $2,200 (cost, $400).
6	Sold office supplies to an employee at cost, $85, receiving cash.
6	Cash sales for the week totaled $2,400 (cost, $1,400).
8	Sold merchandise inventory on account, terms n/30, to A. Z. Morris, $7,500 (cost, $5,000).
9	Sold land that cost $9,000 for cash of the same amount.
11	Sold merchandise inventory on account, terms n/30, to Sloan Electric, $5,000 (cost, $3,450).
11	Received cash from Intelysis in full settlement of its account receivable from November 2.
13	Cash sales for the week were $2,200 (cost, $1,750).
15	Sold merchandise inventory on credit, terms n/30, to West and Michael, $3,000 (cost, $2,200).
19	Sold merchandise inventory on account, terms n/30, to Sloan Electric, $700 (cost, $200).
20	Cash sales for the week were $940 (cost, $640).
21	Received $4,400 cash from A. Z. Morris in partial settlement of its account receivable.
22	Received cash from West and Michael for its account receivable from November 15.
22	Sold merchandise inventory on account, terms n/30, to Olivia Co., $1,510 (cost, $980).
25	Collected $5,800 on a note receivable. There was no interest earned.
27	Cash sales for the week totaled $3,780 (cost, $2,430).
27	Sold merchandise inventory on account, terms n/30, to R. A. Brown, $230 (cost, $110).
30	Received $2,200 cash on account from A. Z. Morris.

Requirements

1. Use the appropriate journal to record the preceding transactions in a sales journal (omit the Invoice No. column) and a cash receipts journal (omit the Sales Discounts Forfeited column).

2. Total each column of the sales journal and the cash receipts journal. Determine that total debits equal total credits.

3. Show how postings would be made from the journals by writing the account numbers and check marks in the appropriate places in the journals.

Learning Objective 3

Purchases Journal, Accounts Payable CR column total $19,470

PB-28B Using the purchases, cash payments, and general journals

The general ledger of Finnish Lake Golf Shop includes the following selected accounts, along with their account numbers:

Number	Account	Number	Account
111	Cash	181	Equipment
131	Merchandise Inventory	211	Accounts Payable
161	Prepaid Insurance	564	Rent Expense
171	Office Supplies	583	Utilities Expense

Transactions in December that affected purchases and cash payments were as follows:

Dec. 2	Purchased merchandise inventory on credit from Tighe, $4,100. Terms were 3/10, n/30.
3	Paid monthly rent, debiting Rent Expense for $2,200.
5	Purchased office supplies on credit terms of 3/10, n/30 from Rapid Supply, $470.
8	Received and paid electricity utility bill, $510.
9	Purchased equipment on account from A-1 Equipment, $6,900. Payment terms were net 30.
10	Returned the equipment to A-1 Equipment. It was damaged.
11	Paid Tighe the amount owed on the purchase of December 2.
12	Purchased merchandise inventory on account from Crystal Golf, $4,900. Terms were 1/10, n/30.
13	Purchased merchandise inventory for cash, $660.
14	Paid a semiannual insurance premium, debiting Prepaid Insurance, $1,200.
16	Paid its account payable to Rapid Supply from December 5.
18	Received and paid gas and water utility bills, $500.
21	Purchased merchandise inventory on credit terms of 1/10, n/45 from Devin, Inc., $3,000.
21	Paid its account payable to Crystal Golf from December 12.
22	Purchased office supplies on account from Office Stuff, Inc., $100. Terms were n/30.
26	Returned to Devin, Inc. $1,000 of the merchandise inventory purchased on December 21.
31	Paid Devin, Inc. the net amount owed from December 21 less the return on December 26.

Requirements

1. Use the appropriate journal to record the preceding transactions in a purchases journal, a cash payments journal (omit the Check No. column), and a general journal. Finnish Lake Golf Shop records purchase returns in the general journal. The company uses the perpetual inventory system.

2. Total each column of the special journals. Show that total debits equal total credits in each special journal.

3. Show how postings would be made from the journals by writing the account numbers and check marks in the appropriate places in the journals.

PB-29B Using all journals, posting, and balancing the ledgers

Atlanta Computer Security uses the perpetual inventory system and makes all credit sales on terms of n/30. During March, Atlanta completed these transactions:

Learning Objectives 2, 3

Trial balance, total debits $47,950

Mar. 2	Issued invoice no. 191 for sale on account to L. E. Kingston, $3,000 (cost, $800).
3	Purchased merchandise inventory on credit terms of 3/10, n/60 from High, $2,500.
4	Sold merchandise inventory for cash, $1,100 (cost, $300).
5	Issued check no. 473 to purchase furniture for cash $2,450.
8	Collected interest revenue of $1,150.
9	Issued invoice no. 192 for sale on account to Common Co., $5,700 (cost, $2,200).
10	Purchased merchandise inventory for cash, $1,400, issuing check no. 474.
12	Received cash from L. E. Kingston in full settlement of her account receivable from the sale of March 2.
13	Issued check no. 475 to pay High net amount owed from March 3. Round to the nearest dollar.
13	Purchased office supplies on account from Mann Corp., $350. Terms were n/EOM.
15	Sold merchandise inventory on account to Suarez Co., issuing invoice no. 193 for $700 (cost, $250).
18	Issued invoice no. 194 for credit sale to L. E. Kingston, $400 (cost, $200).
19	Received cash from Common Co. in full settlement of its account receivable from March 9.
20	Purchased merchandise inventory on credit terms of n/30 from James Swenson, $2,200.
22	Purchased furniture on credit terms of 3/10, n/60 from High, $400.
22	Issued check no. 476 to pay for insurance coverage, debiting Prepaid Insurance for $1,800.
24	Sold office supplies to an employee for cash of $100, which was Atlanta's cost.
25	Received bill and issued check no. 477 to pay utilities, $550.
28	Purchased merchandise inventory on credit terms of 2/10, n/30 from Mann Corp., $550.
29	Returned damaged merchandise inventory to Mann Corp., issuing a debit memo for $550.
29	Sold merchandise inventory on account to Common Co., issuing invoice no. 195 for $2,800 (cost, $1,400).
30	Issued check no. 478 to pay Mann Corp. in full for March 13 purchase.
31	Received cash in full from L. E. Kingston on credit sale of March 18.
31	Issued check no. 479 to pay monthly salaries of $1,550.

Requirements

1. Open four-column general ledger accounts using Atlanta Computer Security's account numbers and balances as of March 1, 2018, that follow. All accounts have normal balances.

Number	Account	Bal.
111	Cash	$ 15,800
112	Accounts Receivable	1,900
114	Merchandise Inventory	6,500
116	Office Supplies	600
117	Prepaid Insurance	0
151	Furniture	2,000
211	Accounts Payable	900
311	Common Stock	14,000
314	Retained Earnings	6,600
411	Sales Revenue	7,600
419	Interest Revenue	1,400
511	Cost of Goods Sold	2,100
531	Salaries Expense	1,300
541	Utilities Expense	300

2. Open four-column accounts in the subsidiary ledgers with beginning balances as of March 1, if any. Accounts receivable subsidiary ledger: Arrundel Co., $1,900; Common Co., $0; L. E. Kingston, $0; and Suarez, $0. Accounts payable subsidiary ledger: High, $0; Mann Corp, $0; James Swenson, $0; and Young Co., $900.

3. Enter the transactions in a sales journal (page 8), a cash receipts journal (page 3, omit Sales Discounts Forfeited column), a purchases journal (page 6), a cash payments journal (page 9), and a general journal (page 4), as appropriate.

4. Post daily to the accounts receivable subsidiary ledger and to the accounts payable subsidiary ledger.

5. Total each column of the special journals. Show that total debits equal total credits in each special journal. On March 31, post to the general ledger.

6. Prepare a trial balance as of March 31, 2018, to verify the equality of the general ledger. Balance the total of the customer account ending balances in the accounts receivable subsidiary ledger against Accounts Receivable in the general ledger. Do the same for the accounts payable subsidiary ledger and Accounts Payable in the general ledger.

CRITICAL THINKING

> Continuing Problem

PB-30 Using all journals

This problem continues the Canyon Canoe Company situation from Chapter 4. At the beginning of the new year, Canyon Canoe Company decided to carry and sell T-shirts with its logo printed on them. Canyon Canoe Company uses the perpetual inventory system to account for the inventory. During January 2019, Canyon Canoe Company completed the following merchandising transactions:

Jan. 1	Purchased 10 T-shirts at $4 each and paid cash.
2	Sold 6 T-shirts for $10 each, total cost of $24. Received cash.
3	Purchased 50 T-shirts on account at $5 each. Terms 2/10, n/30.
7	Paid the supplier for the T-shirts purchased on January 3, less discount.
8	Realized 4 T-shirts from the January 1 order were printed wrong and returned them for a cash refund.
10	Sold 40 T-shirts on account for $10 each, total cost of $200. Terms 3/15, n/45.
12	Received payment for the T-shirts sold on account on January 10, less discount.
14	Purchased 100 T-shirts on account at $4 each. Terms 4/15, n/30.
18	Canyon Company called the supplier from the January 14 purchase and told them that some of the T-shirts were the wrong color. The supplier offered a $50 purchase allowance.
20	Paid the supplier for the T-shirts purchased on January 14, less the allowance and discount.
21	Sold 60 T-shirts on account for $10 each, total cost of $220. Terms 2/20, n/30.
23	Received a payment on account for the T-shirts sold on January 21, less discount.
25	Purchased 320 T-shirts on account at $5 each. Terms 2/10, n/30, FOB shipping point.
27	Paid freight associated with the January 25 purchase, $48.
29	Paid for the January 25 purchase, less discount.
30	Sold 275 T-shirts on account for $10 each, total cost of $1,300. Terms 2/10, n/30.
31	Received payment for the T-shirts sold on January 30, less discount.

Requirements

1. Enter the transactions in a sales journal (page 2), a cash receipts journal (page 5, omit Sales Discounts Forfeited column), a purchases journal (page 7), a cash payments journal (page 6), and a general journal (page 4), as appropriate.

2. Total each column of the special journals. Show that total debits equal total credits in each special journal.

> Practice Set

PB-31 Using all journals

This problem continues the Crystal Clear Cleaning practice set begun in Chapter 2 and continued through Chapters 3 and 4.

Crystal Clear Cleaning has decided that, in addition to providing cleaning services, it will sell cleaning products. Crystal Clear uses the perpetual inventory system. During December 2018, Crystal Clear completed the following transactions:

Dec. 2	Purchased 1,000 units of inventory for $4,000 on account from Sparkle Company on terms, 5/10, n/20.
5	Purchased 1,200 units of inventory from Borax on account with terms 4/10, n/30. The total invoice was for $6,000, which included a $300 freight charge.
7	Returned 300 units of inventory to Sparkle from the December 2 purchase (cost $1,200).
9	Paid Borax.
11	Sold 500 units of goods to Happy Maids for $5,500 on account with terms n/30. Crystal Clear's cost of the goods was $2,000.
12	Paid Sparkle.
15	Received 100 units with a retail price of $1,100 back from customer Happy Maids. The goods cost Crystal Clear $400.
21	Received payment from Happy Maids, settling the amount due in full.
28	Sold 500 units of goods to Bridget, Inc. on account for $6,500 (cost $2,022). Terms 1/15, n/30.
29	Paid cash for utilities of $550.
30	Paid cash for Sales Commission Expense of $214.
31	Received payment from Bridget, Inc., less discount.

Requirements

1. Use the appropriate journal to record the preceding transactions in a sales journal (omit the Invoice No. column), a cash receipts journal (omit Sales Discounts Forfeited column), a purchases journal, a cash payments journal (omit the Check No. column), and a general journal.

2. Total each column of the special journals. Show that total debits equal total credits in each special journal.

COMPREHENSIVE PROBLEM

> Comprehensive Problem for Appendix B

Completing the Accounting Cycle for a Merchandising Entity—Using Special Journals

Amherst Networking Systems adjusts and closes its books and then prepares financial statements monthly. Amherst uses the perpetual inventory system and all sales on credit have terms of n/30. The company completed the following transactions during August:

Aug. 1	Issued check no. 682 for August office rent of $1,300.
2	Issued check no. 683 to pay the salaries payable of $1,300 from July 31.
2	Issued invoice no. 503 for sale on account to R. T. Loeb, $700. Amherst's cost of this merchandise inventory was $210.
3	Purchased merchandise inventory on credit terms of 1/15, n/60 from Goldner, Inc., $1,400.
4	Received cash on account from Friend Company, $2,400.
4	Sold merchandise inventory for cash, $370 (cost, $111).
5	Issued check no. 684 to purchase office supplies for cash, $730.
7	Issued invoice no. 504 for sale on account to K. D. Sanders, $2,100 (cost, $630).
8	Issued check no. 685 to pay Filter Company $2,500 of the amount owed at July 31. This payment occurred after the end of the discount period.
11	Issued check no. 686 to pay Goldner, Inc. the net amount owed from August 3.
12	Received cash from R. T. Loeb in full settlement of her account receivable from August 2.
16	Issued check no. 687 to pay salaries expense of $1,290.
19	Purchased merchandise inventory for cash, $850, issuing check no. 688.
22	Purchased furniture on credit terms of 3/15, n/60 from Bradford Corporation, $510.
23	Sold merchandise inventory on account to Friend Company, issuing invoice no. 505 for $9,000 (cost, $2,700).
24	Received half the July 31 amount receivable from K. D. Sanders.
26	Purchased office supplies on credit terms of 2/10, n/30 from Filter Company, $240.
30	Returned damaged merchandise inventory to the company from whom Amherst made the cash purchase on August 19, receiving cash of $850.
31	Purchased merchandise inventory on credit terms of 1/10, n/30 from Seacrest Supply, $8,000.
31	Issued check no. 689 to stockholders, for dividends, $600.

Requirements

1. Open these four-column accounts with their account numbers and July 31 balances in the various ledgers.

General Ledger

Nbr.	Account Name	Debit	Credit
101	Cash	$ 5,020	
102	Accounts Receivable	22,490	
105	Merchandise Inventory	41,300	
109	Office Supplies	1,680	
117	Prepaid Insurance	2,600	
160	Furniture	37,000	
161	Accumulated Depreciation—Furniture		$ 10,000
201	Accounts Payable		12,700
204	Salaries Payable		1,300
220	Note Payable, Long-term		25,000
301	Common Stock		20,000
305	Retained Earnings		41,090
310	Dividends		
400	Income Summary		
401	Sales Revenue		
501	Cost of Goods Sold		
510	Salaries Expense		
513	Rent Expense		
514	Depreciation Expense—Furniture		
516	Insurance Expense		
519	Supplies Expense		

Accounts Receivable Subsidiary Ledger: Friend Company $2,400; R. T. Loeb, $0; Parker, Inc., $11,300; and K. D. Sanders, $8,790.

Accounts Payable Subsidiary Ledger: Bradford Corporation, $0; Filter Company, $12,700; Goldner, Inc., $0; and Seacrest Supply, $0.

2. Journalize the August transactions using a sales journal (page 4), a cash receipts journal (page 11, omit Sales Discounts Forfeited column), a purchases journal (page 8), a cash payments journal (page 5), and a general journal (page 9).

3. Post daily to the accounts receivable subsidiary ledger and the accounts payable subsidiary ledger. On August 31, post to the general ledger.

4. Prepare an unadjusted trial balance for the month ended August 31.

5. Journalize and post the following adjusting entries:
   a. Office supplies on hand, $1,000.
   b. Prepaid insurance expired, $350.
   c. Depreciation expense on furniture, $250.
   d. Accrued salaries expense, $1,060.

6. Prepare an adjusted trial balance.

7. Prepare a multistep income statement, statement of retained earnings, and classified balance sheet.

8. Journalize closing entries and post.

9. Prepare a post-closing trial balance.

> Tying It All Together Case

Before you begin this assignment, review the Tying It All Together feature in the chapter. It will also be helpful if you review McCormick & Company, Incorporated's 2015 annual report (http://phx.corporate-ir.net/phoenix.zhtml?c=65454&p=irol-sec&control_symbol=#14157537).

McCormick & Company Incorporated, is a global leader in flavor that manufactures, markets, and distributes spices, seasoning mixes, condiments, and other flavorful products. The company's brands include McCormick, Lawry's, and Club House. In addition, the company also markets authentic ethnic brands such as Zatarain's, Thai Kitchen, and Simply Asia.

Requirements

1. Review Item 1A (Risk Factors) of the Notes to the Financial Statements. How does McCormick & Company, Incorporated minimize the risks associated with data breaches or cyber attacks?

2. Perform a web search on ways businesses can prevent security breaches. What are some security solutions that McCormick & Company might use?

> Decision Case B-1

A fire destroyed certain accounting records of Green Books. The controller, Marilyn Green, asks your help in reconstructing the records. All of the sales are on account, with credit terms of n/30. The only accounting record preserved from the fire is the accounts receivable subsidiary ledger, which follows.

Requirements

1. Determine the beginning and ending balances of Accounts Receivable.
2. Determine the sales on account in the month of April.
3. Determine total cash receipts on account from customers during April.

Garcia Sales

Date	Post. Ref.	Debit	Credit	Balance Debit	Balance Credit
Apr. 1				450	
3	CR.8		450	0	
25	S.6	3,600		3,600	
29	S.6	1,100		4,700	

Leewright, Inc.

Date	Post. Ref.	Debit	Credit	Balance Debit	Balance Credit
Apr. 1				2,800	
15	S.6	2,600		5,400	
29	CR.8		1,500	3,900	

Sally Jones

Date	Post. Ref.	Debit	Credit	Balance Debit	Balance Credit
Apr. 1				1,100	
5	CR.8		1,100	0	
11	S.6	400		400	
21	CR.8		400	0	
24	S.6	2,000		2,000	

APPENDIX B

Jacques LeHavre					
				Balance	
Date	Post. Ref.	Debit	Credit	Debit	Credit
Apr. 1				0	
8	S.6	2,400		2,400	
16	S.6	900		3,300	
18	CR.8		2,400	900	
19	J.5		200	700	
27	CR.8		700	0	

> Fraud Case B-1

Didrikson Rubin, the auditor of Red Barn Farm Equipment, was verifying cash payments to vendors for the past several months. She noticed that several checks had been paid to a specific vendor, but she couldn't find a record of the transactions in the computerized system. Didrikson suspects that an employee is issuing checks to a fictitious "vendor" and then deleting the transactions from the computerized system. How might Didrikson investigate the suspected fraud?

> Team Project B-1

Ace Moving is considering investing in an entry-level computerized accounting information system. Ace needs a system that can record customer invoices and cash receipts. In addition, it would like to track all of its bills and cash payments. As a team, investigate the two common entry-level accounting software products: QuickBooks and Sage 50 Accounting. Prepare a PowerPoint presentation that summarizes the similarities and differences between the two software systems.

> Communication Activity B-1

In 150 words or fewer, explain what an accounting information system is and describe an effective system.

MyAccountingLab   **For a wealth of online resources, including exercises, problems, media, and immediate tutorial help, please visit** http://www.myaccountinglab.com.

> Quick Check Answers

1. c **2.** a **3.** b **4.** c **5.** b **6.** c **7.** a **8.** a **9.** d

Appendix C
The Statement of Cash Flows

Why Doesn't the Business Have Any Cash?

David National reviewed his company's income statement with a confused look on his face. The statement reported a net profit of $20,000 for the past quarter. David knew that sales had been increasing in his small sporting equipment retail shop, and he expected this trend to continue through the end of the year. But David didn't understand why the income statement showed a profit. The company's payroll clerk had called him earlier in the day and told him that there wasn't enough cash in the bank to pay the employees's monthly salaries.

It didn't make sense to David that the company could report a $20,000 profit on the income statement but not have enough cash to pay the payroll. He figured that the newly hired accountant, Mark Maloney, must have made a mistake.

David picked up the phone to call Mark. He had several questions to ask him. Why didn't the company have any cash in the bank? How was the company using its cash? How could the company report a $20,000 profit but not have that much cash in the bank? Where did the cash received from customers go?

After speaking with his accountant, David learned that the profit reported on the income statement didn't represent cash and that it was important that he review the company's statement of cash flows. The statement of cash flows, Mark told him, reports the cash receipts and cash payments of the business. It shows the sources and uses of cash and helps answer the question "Where did the cash go?"

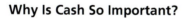

Why Is Cash So Important?

You can probably answer that question from your own experience. It takes cash to pay bills and to generate future income for a business. Businesses, such as **Amazon.com, Inc.,** a retail Web site that sells everything from sporting equipment to household goods, closely monitors cash. Amazon.com is interested in where its cash came from (receipts) and how its cash is spent (payments). One way for Amazon.com to monitor its cash receipts and payments is by preparing a statement of cash flows. For example, on Amazon.com's 2015 statement of cash flows, the corporation reported that it paid $4.5 million purchasing property and equipment and that it paid $273 million cash for income taxes (net of refunds). It also reported that from 2014 to 2015 the corporation had an increase in cash of $1,333 million, even though net income was only $596 million. In this chapter, you learn what a statement of cash flows is and why it is useful to a business. In addition, you learn how to prepare the statement and understand why companies and investors carefully monitor the statement of cash flows.

Appendix C Learning Objectives

1 Identify the purposes of the statement of cash flows and distinguish among operating, investing, and financing cash flows

2 Prepare the statement of cash flows by the indirect method

3 Use free cash flow to evaluate business performance

4 Prepare the statement of cash flows by the direct method (Appendix 14A)

5 Prepare the statement of cash flows by the indirect method using a spreadsheet (Appendix 14B)

WHAT IS THE STATEMENT OF CASH FLOWS?

Learning Objective 1

Identify the purposes of the statement of cash flows and distinguish among operating, investing, and financing cash flows

Up to this point, you have learned about three financial statements—the income statement, the statement of retained earnings, and the balance sheet. Each of these financial statements reports specific items about a company. The income statement reports net income or net loss for the time period. The statement of retained earnings reports the changes in retained earnings during the time period, and the balance sheet reports a company's financial position. None of these statements reports specifically on the changes in cash.

When a comparative balance sheet for two periods is presented, it shows whether cash increased or decreased. But the balance sheet does not show *why* cash increased or decreased. We need the statement of cash flows for that. The **statement of cash flows** reports on a business's cash receipts and cash payments for a specific period. This statement does the following:

Statement of Cash Flows
Reports on a business's cash receipts and cash payments for a specific period.

Cash Flows
Cash receipts and cash payments of a business.

- Reports on the **cash flows** of a business—where cash came from (receipts) and how cash was spent (payments).

- Reports why cash increased or decreased during the period.

- Covers a span of time and is dated the same as the income statement—"Year Ended December 31, 2018," for example.

Purpose of the Statement of Cash Flows

The statement of cash flows explains why net income as reported on the income statement does not equal the change in the cash balance. In essence, the statement of cash flows is the link between the accrual-based income statement and the cash reported on the balance sheet.

How do people use cash flow information? The statement of cash flows helps do the following:

- **Predict future cash flows.** Past cash receipts and payments help predict future cash flows.

- **Evaluate management.** Wise investment decisions help the business prosper, while unwise decisions cause the business to have problems. Investors and creditors use cash flow information to evaluate managers' decisions.

- **Predict ability to pay debts and dividends.** Lenders want to know whether they will collect on their loans. Stockholders want dividends on their investments. The statement of cash flows helps make these predictions.

Classification of Cash Flows

There are three basic types of cash flow activities, and the statement of cash flows has a section for each:

- Operating activities
- Investing activities
- Financing activities

Each section reports cash inflows (cash receipts coming into the company) and cash outflows (cash payments going out of the company) based on these three divisions.

Operating Activities

Operating activities is the first section on the statement of cash flows and is often the most important category. The **operating activities** section reports on activities that create revenue or expense in the entity's business. It reflects the day-to-day operations of the business such as cash receipts (cash inflows) from customers for the sales of merchandise inventory and services and the cash payments (cash outflows) for purchases of merchandise inventory or payment of operating expenses. The operating activities section also includes cash receipts (cash inflows) for interest revenue and dividend income and cash payments (cash outflows) for interest expense and income tax expense.

Operating Activities
Activities that create revenue or expense in the entity's business; a section of the statement of cash flows.

Investing Activities

Investing activities is the second category listed on the statement of cash flows. This section reports cash receipts and cash payments that increase or decrease long-term assets such as property, plant, equipment, notes receivable, and investments. It includes the cash inflow from selling and the cash outflow for the purchase of these long-term assets. In addition, it includes the lending (cash outflow) and collection (cash inflow) of long-term notes receivable.

Investing Activities
Activities that increase or decrease long-term assets; a section of the statement of cash flows.

Financing Activities

The last category on the statement of cash flows is **financing activities**. Financing activities include cash inflows and outflows involved in long-term liabilities and equity. This includes issuing stock, paying dividends, and buying and selling treasury stock. It also includes borrowing money and paying off long-term liabilities such as notes payable, bonds payable, and mortgages payable.

Each section of the statement of cash flows affects a different part of the balance sheet. The operating activities section reports on how cash flows affect the current accounts—current assets and current liabilities. Investing activities affect the long-term assets. And the financing activities affect long-term liabilities and equity. Exhibit C-1 shows the relationship between operating, investing, and financing cash flows and the various parts of the balance sheet.

Financing Activities
Activities that increase or decrease long-term liabilities and equity; a section of the statement of cash flows.

Exhibit C-1 | Operating, Investing, and Financing Cash Flows and the Balance Sheet Accounts

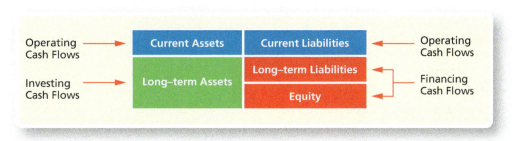

Non-cash Investing and Financing Activities
Investing and financing activities that do not involve cash.

Under IFRS, interest revenue and dividend income may be reported either as an operating activity or as an investing activity. Interest expense and dividends paid may be reported either as an operating activity or as a financing activity.

Non-cash Investing and Financing Activities

The three sections of the statement of cash flows report only activities that involve cash. Companies do make investments that do not require cash. They also obtain financing that does not involve cash. Such transactions are called **non-cash investing and financing activities**. Examples of these activities include the purchase of equipment financed by a long-term note payable or the contribution of equipment by a stockholder in exchange for common stock. These activities are not included in the statement of cash flows. Instead, they appear either as a separate schedule at the bottom of the statement or in the notes to the financial statements.

Exhibit C-2 summarizes the different sections on the statement of cash flows.

Exhibit C-2 | **Sections of the Statement of Cash Flows**

Operating Activities	Cash Inflows: • From customers for the sales of merchandise inventory and services • For interest revenue and dividend income Cash Outflows: • For the purchase of merchandise inventory and payment of operating expenses • For interest expense and income tax expense
Investing Activities	Cash Inflows: • From the sale of property, plant, equipment, and investments • From the collection of long-term notes receivable Cash Outflows: • To purchase property, plant, equipment, and investments • For loans made to borrowers
Financing Activities	Cash Inflows: • From issuance of stock and selling treasury stock • From receipt of borrowing money Cash Outflows: • For payment of dividends and buying treasury stock • For repayments of loans
Non-cash Investing and Financing Activities	A separate schedule that includes investing and financing activities that *do not* include cash

The statement of cash flows reports only activities that involve either the receipt of cash or the payment of cash. If a transaction does not involve cash, it will not be included in the operating, investing, or financing sections of the statement of cash flows.

Two Formats for Operating Activities

There are two ways to format the operating activities section of the statement of cash flows:

- The **indirect method** starts with net income and adjusts it to net cash provided by operating activities.
- The **direct method** restates the income statement in terms of cash. The direct method shows all the cash receipts and all the cash payments from operating activities.

The indirect and direct methods use different computations but produce the same amount of net cash flow from operating activities. Both methods present investing activities and financing activities in exactly the same format. Only the *operating activities* section is presented differently between the two methods.

We begin with the indirect method because most companies use it. To focus on the direct method, review Appendix CA, located at the end of this chapter.

Indirect Method
A format of the operating activities section of the statement of cash flows; starts with net income and reconciles to net cash provided by operating activities.

Direct Method
A format of the operating activities section of the statement of cash flows; lists the operating cash receipts and cash payments.

IFRS permits the use of either the direct or indirect method.

Identify each item as operating (O), investing (I), financing (F), or non-cash (N).

1. Cash receipt from the sale of equipment
2. Cash payment for salaries
3. Cash receipt from the collection of long-term notes receivable
4. Purchase of equipment in exchange for notes payable
5. Cash receipt from the issuance of common stock

Check your answers online in MyAccountingLab or at http://www.pearsonhighered.com/Horngren.

For more practice, see Short Exercises SC-1 and SC-2. MyAccountingLab

HOW IS THE STATEMENT OF CASH FLOWS PREPARED USING THE INDIRECT METHOD?

To prepare the statement of cash flows, you need the income statement for the current year, as well as the balance sheets from the current and prior years. In addition, you need to review the transactions for some additional information. For illustrative purposes, we will use Shop-Mart, Inc., a fictitious retail store that sells electronics, home furnishings, home supplies, and more. ShopMart's comparative balance sheet is shown in Exhibit C-3 (on the next page), and

Learning Objective 2
Prepare the statement of cash flows by the indirect method

its income statement is shown in Exhibit C-4. Additional information provided by Shop-Mart includes the following:

- Purchased $310,000 in plant assets by paying cash.
- Sold plant assets with a cost of $55,000 and accumulated depreciation of $15,000, yielding a gain of $10,000.
- Received $90,000 cash from issuance of notes payable.
- Paid $10,000 cash to retire notes payable.
- Received $120,000 cash from issuing shares of common stock.
- Paid $20,000 cash for purchase of shares of treasury stock.

Exhibit C-3 | **Comparative Balance Sheet**

SHOPMART, INC. Comparative Balance Sheet December 31, 2018 and 2017			
	2018	2017	Increase (Decrease)
Assets			
Current Assets:			
Cash	$ 22,000	$ 42,000	$ (20,000)
Accounts Receivable	90,000	73,000	17,000
Merchandise Inventory	143,000	145,000	(2,000)
Long-term Assets:			
Plant Assets	507,000	252,000	255,000
Accumulated Depreciation—Plant Assets	(47,000)	(42,000)	(5,000)
Total Assets	$ 715,000	$ 470,000	$ 245,000
Liabilities			
Current Liabilities:			
Accounts Payable	$ 90,000	$ 50,000	$ 40,000
Accrued Liabilities	5,000	10,000	(5,000)
Long-term Liabilities:			
Notes Payable	160,000	80,000	80,000
Total Liabilities	255,000	140,000	115,000
Stockholders' Equity			
Common Stock, no par	370,000	250,000	120,000
Retained Earnings	110,000	80,000	30,000
Treasury Stock	(20,000)	0	(20,000)
Total Stockholders' Equity	460,000	330,000	130,000
Total Liabilities and Stockholders' Equity	$ 715,000	$ 470,000	$ 245,000

Exhibit C-4 | **Income Statement**

SHOPMART, INC. Income Statement Year Ended December 31, 2018		
Net Sales Revenue		$ 286,000
Cost of Goods Sold		156,000
Gross Profit		130,000
Operating Expenses:		
Salaries and Wages Expense	$ 56,000	
Depreciation Expense—Plant Assets	20,000	
Other Operating Expense	16,000	
Total Operating Expenses		92,000
Operating Income		38,000
Other Income and (Expenses):		
Interest Revenue	12,000	
Dividend Revenue	9,000	
Gain on Disposal of Plant Assets	10,000	
Interest Expense	(15,000)	
Total Other Income and (Expenses)		16,000
Income Before Income Taxes		54,000
Income Tax Expense		14,000
Net Income		$ 40,000

To prepare the statement of cash flows by the indirect method, we follow Steps 1–5:

Step 1: Complete the cash flows from operating activities section using net income and adjusting for increases or decreases in current assets (other than cash) and current liabilities. Also adjust for gains or losses from long-term assets and non-cash expenses such as depreciation expense.

Step 2: Complete the cash flows from investing activities section by reviewing the long-term assets section of the balance sheet.

Step 3: Complete the cash flows from financing activities section by reviewing the long-term liabilities and equity sections of the balance sheet.

Step 4: Compute the net increase or decrease in cash during the year. The change in cash is the key reconciling figure for the statement of cash flows and must match the change in cash reported on the comparative balance sheet.

Step 5: Prepare a separate schedule reporting any non-cash investing and financing activities.

Let's apply these steps to show the operating activities of ShopMart. Exhibit C-5 presents the completed statement of cash flows.

Exhibit C-5 | **Statement of Cash Flows—Indirect Method**

SHOPMART, INC. Statement of Cash Flows Year Ended December 31, 2018			
Cash Flows from Operating Activities:			
Net Income		$ 40,000	
Adjustments to Reconcile Net Income to Net Cash Provided by Operating Activities:			
Depreciation Expense—Plant Assets	$ 20,000		Step 1: Operating Activities
Gain on Disposal of Plant Assets	(10,000)		
Increase in Accounts Receivable	(17,000)		
Decrease in Merchandise Inventory	2,000		
Increase in Accounts Payable	40,000		
Decrease in Accrued Liabilities	(5,000)	30,000	
Net Cash Provided by Operating Activities		70,000	
Cash Flows from Investing Activities:			
Cash Payment for Acquisition of Plant Assets	(310,000)		Step 2: Investing Activities
Cash Receipt from Disposal of Plant Assets	50,000		
Net Cash Used for Investing Activities		(260,000)	
Cash Flows from Financing Activities:			
Cash Receipt from Issuance of Notes Payable	90,000		
Cash Payment of Notes Payable	(10,000)		Step 3: Financing Activities
Cash Receipt from Issuance of Common Stock	120,000		
Cash Payment for Purchase of Treasury Stock	(20,000)		
Cash Payment of Dividends	(10,000)		
Net Cash Provided by Financing Activities		170,000	
Net Increase (Decrease) in Cash		(20,000)	Step 4: Net Increase (Decrease) in Cash
Cash Balance, December 31, 2017		42,000	
Cash Balance, December 31, 2018		$ 22,000	

Cash Flows from Operating Activities

When using the indirect method, the statement of cash flows operating activities section begins with net income (or net loss) because revenues and expenses, which affect net income, produce cash receipts and cash payments. Revenues bring in cash receipts, and expenses must be paid. But net income as shown on the income statement is accrual-based, and the cash flows (cash basis net income) do not always equal the accrual basis revenues and expenses. For example, sales *on account* generate revenues that increase net income, but the company has not yet collected cash from those sales. Accrued expenses decrease net income, but the company has not paid cash *if the expenses are accrued*.

To go from net income to net cash flow from operating activities, we must make some adjustments to net income on the statement of cash flows. These additions and subtractions follow net income and are labeled *Adjustments to Reconcile Net Income to Net Cash Provided by Operating Activities*.

Depreciation, Depletion, and Amortization Expenses

These adjustments include adding back non-cash expenses such as depreciation, depletion, and amortization expenses. These expenses are added back to net income to reconcile net income to net cash flow from operating activities. Let's see why this occurs. Depreciation is recorded as follows:

Date	Accounts and Explanation	Debit	Credit
	Depreciation Expense—Plant Assets	20,000	
	Accumulated Depreciation—Plant Assets		20,000

$$\underbrace{\frac{A\downarrow}{\text{Accumulated Depreciation}\uparrow}}_{} = \begin{cases} \underline{L} + \underline{\text{Depreciation Expense}\uparrow} \\ E\downarrow \end{cases}$$

You can see that depreciation does not affect cash as there is no Cash account in the journal entry. Depreciation is a non-cash expense. The cash outflow related to depreciation occurred when the asset was purchased, not as it is depreciated. However, depreciation, like all the other expenses, decreases net income. Therefore, to go from net income to net cash flows, we must remove depreciation by adding it back to net income.

SHOPMART, INC.
Statement of Cash Flows (Partial)
Year Ended December 31, 2018

Cash Flows from Operating Activities:		
Net Income		$ 40,000
Adjustments to Reconcile Net Income to Net Cash Provided by Operating Activities:		
Depreciation Expense—Plant Assets	$ 20,000	

Suppose you had only two transactions during the period:

- Cash sale of $60,000
- Depreciation expense of $20,000

Accrual basis net income is $40,000 ($60,000 − $20,000), but net cash flow from operations is $60,000. To reconcile from net income, depreciation of $20,000 must be added to net income, $40,000, to determine net cash flow from operations, $60,000. We would also add back any depletion and amortization expenses because they are non-cash expenses, similar to depreciation.

Gains and Losses on the Disposal of Long-term Assets

Disposals of long-term assets such as land and buildings are investing activities, and these disposals usually create a gain or a loss. The gain or loss is included in net income, which is already in the operating activities section of the statement of cash flows. The gain or loss must be removed from net income on the statement of cash flows so the total cash receipts from the sale of the asset can be shown in the investing activities section.

Exhibit C-4, ShopMart's income statement, includes a gain on disposal of plant assets. During 2018, ShopMart sold equipment, and there was a gain of $10,000 on the sale. The gain was included in the calculation of net income on the income statement, so the gain must be removed from operating cash flows. The gain increased net income, so it is subtracted in the operating activities section.

SHOPMART, INC. Statement of Cash Flows (Partial) Year Ended December 31, 2018		
Cash Flows from Operating Activities:		
Net Income		$ 40,000
Adjustments to Reconcile Net Income to Net Cash Provided by Operating Activities:		
Depreciation Expense—Plant Assets	$ 20,000	
Gain on Disposal of Plant Assets	(10,000)	

What if there is a loss on disposal of plant assets?

On the other hand, a loss on the disposal of plant assets would decrease net income on the income statement, so the amount of the loss would be reversed to determine the net cash provided by operating activities on the statement of cash flows. For example, a $5,000 loss on disposal of plant assets would be a $5,000 addition to net income on the statement of cash flows to determine net cash provided by operating activities.

Changes in Current Assets and Current Liabilities

Most current assets and current liabilities result from operating activities. For example:

- Accounts receivable result from sales.
- Merchandise inventory relates to cost of goods sold, and so on.

Changes in the current asset and current liability accounts create adjustments to net income on the statement of cash flows, as follows:

- **An increase in a current asset other than cash causes a decrease adjustment to net income.** If Accounts Receivable, Merchandise Inventory, or Prepaid Expenses increases, then the adjustment to net income is a decrease. For example, ShopMart's balance sheet in Exhibit C-3 shows that Accounts Receivable increased by $17,000. Accounts Receivable is increased when the company makes sales on account and decreases when the company collects cash from customers. Therefore, there were more sales on account (revenue earned and reported on the income statement) than cash collections, the amount we want to reflect on the statement of cash flows. Because the indirect method of accounting for operating activities begins with net income, subtract the $17,000 increase in the current asset Accounts Receivable to adjust accrual-based net income to net cash flows provided by operating activities.

- **A decrease in a current asset other than cash causes an increase adjustment to net income.** Decreases in current assets will have the opposite effect as illustrated above. ShopMart's Merchandise Inventory decreased by $2,000. What caused the decrease? ShopMart must have sold more merchandise inventory than it purchased. Therefore, we add the decrease in Merchandise Inventory of $2,000 to net income on the statement of cash flows.

- **An increase in a current liability causes an increase adjustment to net income.** ShopMart's Accounts Payable increased by $40,000. This means there were more purchases on account than cash paid for the purchases, resulting in an increase to the liability. Accordingly, even though net income was reduced by the expense, cash was not reduced as much. Therefore, an increase in a current liability is *added* to net income in the statement of cash flows.

- **A decrease in a current liability causes a decrease adjustment to net income.** Decreases in current liabilities have the opposite effect of increases. The payments of the current liabilities were more than the accrual of the expenses. Therefore, we subtract decreases in current liabilities from net income to get net cash flow from operating activities. ShopMart's Accrued Liabilities decreased by $5,000. That change shows up as a $5,000 decrease adjustment to net income.

SHOPMART, INC. Statement of Cash Flows (Partial) Year Ended December 31, 2018		
Cash Flows from Operating Activities:		
Net Income		$ 40,000
Adjustments to Reconcile Net Income to Net Cash Provided by Operating Activities:		
Depreciation Expense—Plant Assets	$ 20,000	
Gain on Disposal of Plant Assets	(10,000)	
Increase in Accounts Receivable	(17,000)	
Decrease in Merchandise Inventory	2,000	
Increase in Accounts Payable	40,000	
Decrease in Accrued Liabilities	(5,000)	30,000

DECISIONS

What can be done to create a positive cash flow?

Meggie Mohamed, CEO, knew that the bank would carefully review her company's most recent statement of cash flows before determining if it would approve the loan needed for expansion. The bank loan officer had told her that it is important that the business show strong operating cash flows. Meggie knows that her company's operating cash flow for this past quarter will most likely be negative. Although the company recorded significant revenue, most of the revenue was recorded as receivables. Meggie expects that the cash will come in soon, but not in time to report a positive operating cash flow. What should Meggie do? What would you do?

Solution

Meggie could explain to the bank officer that her company is expecting to collect a significant amount of cash in the near future on outstanding receivables. She could provide detailed collection information including the estimated time frame of collection and the amount expected. Meggie also has another option. She could look into selling the receivables to another business, often called a factor. By selling the receivables, the company will be able to decrease its accounts receivable balance, increase its cash balance, and report a positive balance in operating cash flows.

Evaluating Cash Flows from Operating Activities

During 2018, ShopMart's operating activities provided a net cash inflow of $70,000 ($40,000 + $30,000), so the amount is labeled Net Cash *Provided by* Operating Activities. If this amount were a net cash outflow, ShopMart would report Net Cash *Used for* Operating Activities.

SHOPMART, INC. Statement of Cash Flows (Partial) Year Ended December 31, 2018		
Cash Flows from Operating Activities:		
Net Income		$ 40,000
Adjustments to Reconcile Net Income to Net Cash Provided by Operating Activities:		
Depreciation Expense—Plant Assets	$ 20,000	
Gain on Disposal of Plant Assets	(10,000)	
Increase in Accounts Receivable	(17,000)	
Decrease in Merchandise Inventory	2,000	
Increase in Accounts Payable	40,000	
Decrease in Accrued Liabilities	(5,000)	30,000
Net Cash Provided by Operating Activities		70,000

The operating activities section (indirect method) always starts with accrual basis net income. Adjustments are then made to determine the cash basis net income. Exhibit C-6 summarizes the adjustments made to reconcile net income to net cash provided by operating activities.

Exhibit C-6 | Adjustments Made to Reconcile Net Income to Net Cash Provided by Operating Activities

Item	Adjustment to Net Income on Statement of Cash Flows
Depreciation, Depletion, and Amortization Expense	Increase
Gains on Disposal of Long-term Assets	Decrease
Losses on Disposal of Long-term Assets	Increase
Increases in Current Assets other than Cash	Decrease
Decreases in Current Assets other than Cash	Increase
Increases in Current Liabilities	Increase
Decreases in Current Liabilities	Decrease

Cash Flows from Investing Activities

Investing activities affect long-term assets, such as Plant Assets, Investments, and Notes Receivable. These are shown on ShopMart's balance sheet (Exhibit C-3). Now, let's see how to compute the investing cash flows.

When computing investing cash flows, it is helpful to evaluate the T-accounts for each long-term asset. The T-account will show if there was an acquisition or disposal that happened during the year. Let's look at the Plant Assets and Accumulated Depreciation accounts for ShopMart.

Plant Assets

12/31/2017	252,000		
Acquisitions	310,000	55,000	Disposals
12/31/2018	507,000		

Accumulated Depreciation—Plant Assets

		42,000	12/31/2017
Disposals	15,000	20,000	Depr. Exp.
		47,000	12/31/2018

> Depreciation Expense is from the income statement.

The beginning and ending balances for each account are taken directly from the comparative balance sheet. Depreciation expense has been included in the Accumulated Depreciation account, and this was taken from the income statement. The acquisition and disposal information came from the additional information provided when we introduced the example:

- Purchased $310,000 in plant assets by paying cash.
- Sold plant assets with a cost of $55,000 and accumulated depreciation of $15,000, yielding a gain of $10,000.

We now know that ShopMart paid $310,000 cash to purchase plant assets. This item is listed first in the investing activities section and shown as an outflow of cash, as indicated by the parentheses.

Next we need to determine the amount of cash received for the disposal of plant assets. Using the information provided, we can recreate the journal entry for the disposal and solve for the missing cash amount.

Date	Accounts and Explanation	Debit	Credit
	Cash	?	
	Accumulated Depreciation—Plant Assets	15,000	
	Gain on Disposal of Plant Assets		10,000
	Plant Assets		55,000

$$A\uparrow \begin{cases} \text{Cash}\uparrow \\ \text{Accumulated} \\ \text{Depreciation}\downarrow \\ \text{Plant Assets}\downarrow \end{cases} = \quad L \quad + \quad E\uparrow \text{ Gain on Disposal}\uparrow$$

We compute the cash receipt from the disposal as follows:

> Cash received = Cost − Accumulated Depreciation + Gain − Loss
> = $55,000 − $15,000 + $10,000
> = $50,000

The cash receipt from the sale of plant assets of $50,000 is shown next in the investing activities section. As there are no other changes to long-term assets, the net cash from investing activities is determined. Notice that this is a net cash outflow, as indicated by the parentheses, and is reported as Net Cash *Used for* Investing Activities.

In this partial statement, we are showing only the investing activities section of the statement of cash flows. Remember that the investing activities section is reported after the operating activities section.

SHOPMART, INC.
Statement of Cash Flows (Partial)
Year Ended December 31, 2018

Cash Flows from Investing Activities:		
Cash Payment for Acquisition of Plant Assets	(310,000)	
Cash Receipt from Disposal of Plant Assets	50,000	
Net Cash Used for Investing Activities		(260,000)

Cash Flows from Financing Activities

Financing activities affect the long-term liability and equity accounts, such as Long-term Notes Payable, Bonds Payable, Common Stock, and Retained Earnings. To determine the cash flows from financing activities, we need to review each of these account types.

Long-term Liabilities

The T-account for ShopMart's Notes Payable is shown below. Additional information concerning notes payable is also provided by the company as follows:

- Received $90,000 cash from issuance of notes payable.
- Paid $10,000 cash to retire notes payable.

Notes Payable			
		80,000	12/31/2017
Payment	10,000	90,000	Issuance
		160,000	12/31/2018

The beginning and ending balances of Notes Payable are taken from the comparative balance sheet. For ShopMart, a new issuance of notes payable is known to be a $90,000 cash receipt and is shown by the following journal entry:

$$\frac{A\uparrow}{Cash\uparrow} \Big\} = \Big\{ \frac{L\uparrow}{Notes\ Payable\uparrow} + E$$

Date	Accounts and Explanation	Debit	Credit
	Cash	90,000	
	Notes Payable		90,000

In addition, ShopMart paid $10,000 cash to retire notes payable.

$$\frac{A\downarrow}{Cash\downarrow} \Big\} = \Big\{ \frac{L\downarrow}{Notes\ Payable\downarrow} + E$$

Date	Accounts and Explanation	Debit	Credit
	Notes Payable	10,000	
	Cash		10,000

The cash inflow and cash outflow associated with these notes payable are listed first in the cash flows from financing activities section.

SHOPMART, INC.
Statement of Cash Flows (Partial)
Year Ended December 31, 2018

Cash Flows from Financing Activities:	
Cash Receipt from Issuance of Notes Payable	90,000
Cash Payment of Notes Payable	(10,000)

Common Stock and Treasury Stock

Cash flows for financing activities are also determined by analyzing the stock accounts. For example, the amount of new issuances of stock is determined by analyzing the stock accounts and reviewing the additional information provided:

- Received $120,000 cash from issuing shares of common stock.
- Paid $20,000 cash for purchase of shares of treasury stock.

ShopMart's stock T-accounts are as follows:

Common Stock

		250,000	12/31/2017
Retirement	0	120,000	Issuance
		370,000	12/31/2018

Treasury Stock

12/31/2017	0		
Purchase	20,000	0	Disposal
12/31/2018	20,000		

The common stock account shows a new stock issuance of $120,000 and would be recorded by the following journal entry:

Date	Accounts and Explanation	Debit	Credit
	Cash	120,000	
	Common Stock		120,000

$$\left. \begin{array}{c} A\uparrow \\ Cash\uparrow \end{array} \right\} = \left\{ \begin{array}{ccc} L & + & E\uparrow \\ & & Common \\ & & Stock\uparrow \end{array} \right.$$

This is shown as $120,000 cash inflow in the financing activities section of the statement.

Treasury stock also changed on ShopMart's balance sheet. The T-account is showing an acquisition of treasury stock that would be recorded as follows:

Date	Accounts and Explanation	Debit	Credit
	Treasury Stock	20,000	
	Cash		20,000

$$\left. \begin{array}{c} A\downarrow \\ Cash\downarrow \end{array} \right\} = \left\{ \begin{array}{ccc} L & + & E\downarrow \\ & & Treasury \\ & & Stock\uparrow \end{array} \right.$$

The $20,000 is shown as a cash outflow in the financing section of the statement of cash flows for the purchase of treasury stock.

SHOPMART, INC. Statement of Cash Flows (Partial) Year Ended December 31, 2018	
Cash Flows from Financing Activities:	
Cash Receipt from Issuance of Notes Payable	90,000
Cash Payment of Notes Payable	(10,000)
Cash Receipt from Issuance of Common Stock	120,000
Cash Payment for Purchase of Treasury Stock	(20,000)

Computing Dividend Payments

The amount of dividend payments can be computed by analyzing the Retained Earnings account. First, we input the balances from the balance sheet:

Retained Earnings			
		80,000	12/31/2017
Net Loss	?	?	Net Income
Dividends	?		
		110,000	12/31/2018

Retained Earnings increases when companies earn net income. Retained Earnings decreases when companies have a net loss and when they declare dividends. We know that ShopMart earned net income of $40,000 from the income statement in Exhibit 14-4.

Retained Earnings			
		80,000	12/31/2017
Net Loss	?	40,000	Net Income
Dividends	?		
		110,000	12/31/2018

Net Income is from the income statement.

ShopMart can't have both net income and net loss for the same period; therefore, the missing value must be the amount of dividends ShopMart declared. Solving for the dividends follows:

Ending Retained Earnings = Beginning Retained Earnings + Net income − Net loss − Dividends
$110,000 = $80,000 + $40,000 − $0 − Dividends
Dividends = $80,000 + $40,000 − $0 − $110,000
Dividends = $10,000

So our final Retained Earnings T-account shows the following:

Retained Earnings			
		80,000	12/31/2017
		40,000	Net Income
Dividends	10,000		
		110,000	12/31/2018

In order for the cash dividends to be reported on the statement of cash flows, the company must have paid the dividends. In this case, we know the cash dividends are paid because there are no dividends payable reported on ShopMart's balance sheet. Companies can also distribute stock dividends. A stock dividend has *no* effect on Cash and is *not* reported in the financing activities section of the statement of cash flows. ShopMart had no stock dividends, only cash dividends, which will be shown as an outflow in the financing activities section of the statement of cash flows.

SHOPMART, INC. Statement of Cash Flows (Partial) Year Ended December 31, 2018		
Cash Flows from Financing Activities:		
Cash Receipt from Issuance of Notes Payable	$ 90,000	
Cash Payment of Notes Payable	(10,000)	
Cash Receipt from Issuance of Common Stock	120,000	
Cash Payment for Purchase of Treasury Stock	(20,000)	
Cash Payment of Dividends	(10,000)	
Net Cash Provided by Financing Activities		170,000

TYING IT ALL TOGETHER

Amazon.com, Inc. opened its virtual doors on the internet in July 1995 and completed an initial public offering in May 1997. The company serves customers through its retail Web sites selling millions of unique products. In addition, the company manufactures and sells electronic devices including Kindle e-readers and Fire tablets. Amazon.com also offers Amazon Prime, a membership program that includes unlimited free shipping on items and access to unlimited streaming of movies and TV episodes. (You can find Amazon.com, Inc.'s annual report at http://phx.corporate-ir.net/phoenix.zhtml?c=97664&p=irol-reportsAnnual)

What format does Amazon.com, Inc. use for its statement of cash flows?

Amazon.com, Inc. uses an indirect method statement of cash flows. This method starts with net income and adjusts net income to net cash provided by operating activities.

On Amazon.com, Inc.'s statement of cash flows, the company reports cash provided by operating activities

for the year ended December 31, 2015, of $11,920 million. What were the operating cash flows a result of?

Cash flows from operating activities reports on activities that create revenue or expense in the company's business. This section reflects the day-to-day operations. Amazon.com reports that the company's operating cash flows result primarily from cash received from customers, advertising agreements, and co-branded credit card agreements. The cash inflows are offset by cash payments for products and services, employee compensation, and interest payments on long-term obligations.

Did Amazon.com, Inc. pay a cash dividend in 2015? How would an investor know?

Amazon.com did not pay a cash dividend in 2015. An investor could easily tell if a company paid a cash dividend by reviewing the financing activities section of the statement of cash flows. This section reports cash inflows and outflows associated with long-term liabilities and equity, including the payment of cash dividends.

Net Change in Cash and Cash Balances

To complete the statement of cash flows, the net change in cash and its effect on the beginning cash balance must be shown. This represents the total change in cash for the period and reconciles the statement of cash flows. First, the net increase or decrease in cash is computed by combining the cash provided by or used for operating, investing, and financing activities. In the case of ShopMart, there is a net decrease in the cash balance of $20,000 for the year and is calculated as follows:

> Net increase (decrease) in cash = Net cash provided by operating activities − Net cash used for investing activities + Net cash provided by financing activities
> = $70,000 − $260,000 + $170,000
> = $(20,000)

Next, the beginning cash from December 31, 2017, is listed at $42,000, as shown on the comparative balance sheet. The net decrease of $20,000 is subtracted from beginning cash of $42,000, which equals the ending cash balance on December 31, 2018, of $22,000. This is the key to the statement of cash flows—it explains why the cash balance for ShopMart decreased by $20,000, even though the company reported net income for the year.

SHOPMART, INC. Statement of Cash Flows (Partial) Year Ended December 31, 2018	
Net Cash Provided by Operating Activities	$ 70,000
Net Cash Used for Investing Activities	(260,000)
Net Cash Provided by Financing Activities	170,000
Net Increase (Decrease) in Cash	(20,000)
Cash Balance, December 31, 2017	42,000
Cash Balance, December 31, 2018	$ 22,000

Before moving on, take a moment to review the completed Statement of Cash Flows shown earlier in Exhibit C-5.

Non-cash Investing and Financing Activities

The last step in preparing the statement of cash flows is to prepare the non-cash investing and financing activities section. This section appears as a separate schedule of the statement of cash flows or in the notes to the financial statements. Our ShopMart example did not include transactions of this type because the company did not have any non-cash transactions during the year. So, to illustrate them, let's consider three non-cash transactions for another fictitious company, The Outdoors, Inc. How would they be reported? First, we gather the non-cash activities for the company:

1. Acquired $300,000 building by issuing common stock.
2. Acquired $70,000 land by issuing notes payable.
3. Retired $100,000 notes payable by issuing common stock.

Now, we consider each transaction individually.

1. The Outdoors issued common stock of $300,000 to acquire a building. The journal entry to record the purchase would be as follows:

Date	Accounts and Explanation	Debit	Credit
	Building	300,000	
	Common Stock		300,000

$$\left.\frac{A\uparrow}{\text{Building}\uparrow}\right\} = \left\{\frac{L}{} + \frac{E\uparrow}{\text{Common Stock}\uparrow}\right.$$

This transaction would not be reported on the statement of cash flows because no cash was paid or received. But the building and the common stock are important. The purchase of the building is an investing activity. The issuance of common stock is a financing activity. Taken together, this transaction is a *non-cash investing and financing activity*.

2. The second transaction listed indicates that The Outdoors acquired $70,000 of land by issuing a note. The journal entry to record the purchase would be as follows:

Date	Accounts and Explanation	Debit	Credit
	Land	70,000	
	Notes Payable		70,000

$$\left.\frac{A\uparrow}{\text{Land}\uparrow}\right\} = \left\{\frac{L\uparrow}{\substack{\text{Notes}\\\text{Payable}\uparrow}} + \frac{E}{}\right.$$

This transaction would not be reported on the statement of cash flows because no cash was paid or received. But the land and the notes payable are important. The purchase of the land is an investing activity. The issuance of the note is a financing activity. Taken together, this transaction is a *non-cash investing and financing activity*.

3. The third transaction listed indicates that The Outdoors retired $100,000 of debt by issuing common stock. The journal entry to record the transaction would be as follows:

Date	Accounts and Explanation	Debit	Credit
	Notes Payable	100,000	
	Common Stock		100,000

$$\left.\frac{A}{}\right\} = \left\{\frac{L\downarrow}{\substack{\text{Notes}\\\text{Payable}\downarrow}} + \frac{E\uparrow}{\substack{\text{Common}\\\text{Stock}\uparrow}}\right.$$

This transaction would not be reported on the statement of cash flows because no cash was paid or received. But the notes payable and the stock issuance are important. The retirement of the note and the issuance of the common stock are both financing activities. Taken together, this transaction, even though it is two financing transactions, is reported in the *non-cash investing and financing activities*.

Non-cash investing and financing activities are reported in a separate part of the statement of cash flows. Exhibit C-7 (on the next page) illustrates non-cash investing and financing activities for The Outdoors. This information is either reported as a separate schedule following the statement of cash flows or can be disclosed in a note.

Exhibit C-7 | **Non-cash Investing and Financing Activities**

THE OUTDOORS, INC. Statement of Cash Flows (Partial) Year Ended December 31, 2018	
Non-cash Investing and Financing Activities:	
Acquisition of building by issuing common stock	$ 300,000
Acquisition of land by issuing notes payable	70,000
Retirement of notes payable by issuing common stock	100,000
Total Non-cash Investing and Financing Activities	$ 470,000

Try It!

6. Owl, Inc.'s accountants have assembled the following data for the year ended December 31, 2018:

Cash receipt from sale of equipment	$ 20,000
Depreciation expense	12,000
Cash payment of dividends	4,000
Cash receipt from issuance of common stock	12,000
Net income	30,000
Cash purchase of land	25,000
Increase in current liabilities	10,000
Decrease in current assets other than cash	8,000

Prepare Owl's statement of cash flows using the indirect method for the year ended December 31, 2018. Assume beginning and ending Cash are $12,000 and $75,000 respectively.

Check your answer online in MyAccountingLab or at http://www.pearsonhighered.com/Horngren.

For more practice, see Short Exercises SC-3 through SC-9. MyAccountingLab

---

Learning Objective 3

Use free cash flow to evaluate business performance

Free Cash Flow

The amount of cash available from operating activities after paying for planned investments in long-term assets and after paying dividends to shareholders. Net cash provided by operating activities − Cash payments planned for investments in long-term assets − Cash dividends.

HOW DO WE USE FREE CASH FLOW TO EVALUATE BUSINESS PERFORMANCE?

Throughout this chapter, we have focused on cash flows from operating, investing, and financing activities. Some investors want to know how much cash a company can "free up" for new opportunities. **Free cash flow** is the amount of cash available from operating activities after paying for planned investments in long-term assets and after paying cash dividends to shareholders. Free cash flow can be computed as follows:

> Free cash flow = Net cash provided by operating activities − Cash payments planned for investments in long-term assets − Cash dividends

Many companies use free cash flow to estimate the amount of cash that would be available for unexpected opportunities. Suppose ShopMart expects net cash provided by operations of $200,000. Assume the company plans to spend $160,000 to modernize its retail facilities and pays $15,000 in cash dividends. In this case, ShopMart's free cash flow would be $25,000 ($200,000 − $160,000 − $15,000). If a good investment opportunity comes along, the company should have $25,000 cash available to invest.

> 7. Kalapono Company expects the following for 2018:
>
> - Net cash provided by operating activities of $100,000.
> - Net cash provided by financing activities of $10,000.
> - Net cash used for investing activities of $20,000 (no sales of long-term assets).
> - Cash dividends paid to stockholders was $2,000.
>
> How much free cash flow does Kalapono expect for 2018?
>
> **Check your answer online in MyAccountingLab or at http://www.pearsonhighered.com/Horngren.**
>
> For more practice, see Short Exercises SC-10.   MyAccountingLab

APPENDIX CA: Preparing the Statement of Cash Flows by the Direct Method

HOW IS THE STATEMENT OF CASH FLOWS PREPARED USING THE DIRECT METHOD?

The Financial Accounting Standards Board (FASB) prefers the direct method of reporting cash flows from operating activities. The direct method provides clearer information about the sources and uses of cash than does the indirect method. However, very few non-public companies use the direct method because it takes more computations than the indirect method. Investing and financing cash flows are exactly the same presentation under both direct and indirect methods. Because only the preparation of the operating activities section differs, it is all we discuss in this appendix.

To illustrate how the operating activities section of the statement of cash flows differs for the direct method, we use the ShopMart data we used within the main chapter.

Learning Objective 4

Prepare the statement of cash flows by the direct method

Cash Flows from Operating Activities

In the indirect method, we start with accrual basis net income and then adjust it to cash basis through a series of adjusting items. When using the direct method, we take each line item of the income statement and convert it from accrual to cash basis. So, in essence, the operating activities section of the direct-method cash flows statement is really just a cash-basis income statement. Now let's apply this information to ShopMart.

Cash Collections from Customers

The first item on the income statement shown in Exhibit C-4 is Net Sales Revenue. Net Sales Revenue represents the total of all sales, whether for cash or on account. The balance sheet account related to Net Sales Revenue is Accounts Receivable. Accounts Receivable went from $73,000 at December 31, 2017, to $90,000 at December 31, 2018, an increase of $17,000. Net Sales Revenue can be converted to cash receipts from customers as follows:

Cash receipts from customers = Net Sales Revenue + Beginning Accounts Receivable − Ending Accounts Receivable
= $286,000 + $73,000 − $90,000
= $269,000

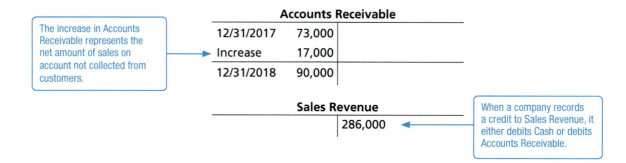

The increase in Accounts Receivable represents the net amount of sales on account not collected from customers.

Accounts Receivable

12/31/2017	73,000	
Increase	17,000	
12/31/2018	90,000	

Sales Revenue

	286,000

When a company records a credit to Sales Revenue, it either debits Cash or debits Accounts Receivable.

So, the cash ShopMart received from customers is $269,000. This is the first item in the operating activities section of the direct-method statement of cash flows.

SHOPMART, INC.
Statement of Cash Flows (Partial)
Year Ended December 31, 2018

Cash Flows from Operating Activities:	
Receipts:	
Collections from Customers	$ 269,000

Had ShopMart had a decrease in Accounts Receivable, the amount of cash collections from customers would be higher than Net Sales Revenue.

Cash Receipts of Interest Revenue

The income statement reports interest revenue of $12,000. The balance sheet account related to Interest Revenue is Interest Receivable. Because there is no Interest Receivable account on the balance sheet, the interest revenue must have all been received in cash. So, the statement of cash flows shows interest received of $12,000.

SHOPMART, INC.
Statement of Cash Flows (Partial)
Year Ended December 31, 2018

Cash Flows from Operating Activities:	
Receipts:	
Collections from Customers	$ 269,000
Interest Revenue Received	12,000

Cash Receipts of Dividend Revenue

The income statement reports dividend revenue of $9,000. The balance sheet account related to Dividend Revenue is Dividends Receivable. As with the interest, there is no Dividends Receivable account on the balance sheet. Therefore, the dividend revenue must have all been received in cash. So, the statement of cash flows shows cash received from dividends of $9,000.

SHOPMART, INC. Statement of Cash Flows (Partial) Year Ended December 31, 2018		
Cash Flows from Operating Activities:		
Receipts:		
Collections from Customers	$ 269,000	
Interest Revenue Received	12,000	
Dividends Received on Investments	9,000	
Total Cash Receipts		$ 290,000

Payments to Suppliers

Payments to suppliers include all payments for the following:

- Merchandise inventory
- Operating expenses except employee compensation, interest, and income taxes

Suppliers, also called *vendors*, are those entities that provide the business with its merchandise inventory and essential services. The accounts related to supplier payments for merchandise inventory are Cost of Goods Sold, Merchandise Inventory, and Accounts Payable. Cost of Goods Sold on the income statement was $156,000. Merchandise Inventory decreased from $145,000 at December 31, 2017, to $143,000 at December 31, 2018. Accounts Payable increased from $50,000 at December 31, 2017, to $90,000 at December 31, 2018. We can calculate the cash paid for inventory as follows:

Cash paid for merchandise inventory = Cost of Goods Sold − Beginning Merchandise Inventory + Ending Merchandise Inventory
+ Beginning Accounts Payable − Ending Accounts Payable
= $156,000 − $145,000 + $143,000 + $50,000 − $90,000
= $114,000

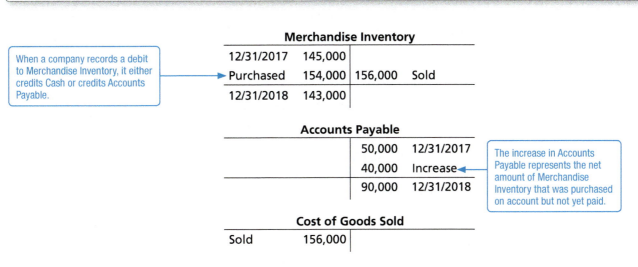

Merchandise Inventory

When a company records a debit to Merchandise Inventory, it either credits Cash or credits Accounts Payable.

12/31/2017	145,000		
Purchased	154,000	156,000	Sold
12/31/2018	143,000		

Accounts Payable

	50,000	12/31/2017
	40,000	Increase
	90,000	12/31/2018

The increase in Accounts Payable represents the net amount of Merchandise Inventory that was purchased on account but not yet paid.

Cost of Goods Sold

Sold	156,000	

The accounts related to supplier payments for operating expenses are Other Operating Expense and Accrued Liabilities. Other operating expenses on the income statement were $16,000. Accrued Liabilities decreased from $10,000 at December 31, 2017, to $5,000 at December 31, 2018. Cash paid for operating expenses can be calculated as follows:

Cash paid for other operating expenses = Other Operating Expense + Beginning Accrued Liabilities − Ending Accrued Liabilities
= $16,000 + $10,000 − $5,000
= $21,000

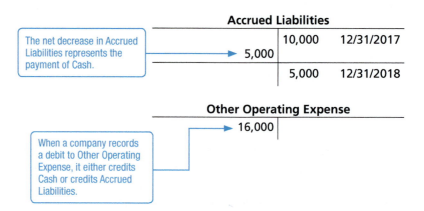

Adding the cash paid for merchandise inventory and the cash paid for other operating expenses together, we get total cash paid to suppliers of $135,000 ($114,000 + $21,000).

SHOPMART, INC. Statement of Cash Flows (Partial) Year Ended December 31, 2018		
Cash Flows from Operating Activities:		
Receipts:		
Collections from Customers	$ 269,000	
Interest Revenue Received	12,000	
Dividends Received on Investments	9,000	
Total Cash Receipts		$ 290,000
Payments:		
To Suppliers	(135,000)	

Payments to Employees

This category includes payments for salaries, wages, and other forms of employee compensation. Accrued amounts are not cash flows because they have not yet been paid. The accounts related to employee payments are Salaries and Wages Expense from the income statement and Salaries and Wages Payable from the balance sheet. Because there is not a Salaries and Wages Payable account on the balance sheet, the Salaries and Wages Expense account must represent all amounts paid in cash to employees. So, the statement of cash flows shows cash payments to employees of $56,000.

SHOPMART, INC.
Statement of Cash Flows (Partial)
Year Ended December 31, 2018

Cash Flows from Operating Activities:		
Receipts:		
Collections from Customers	$ 269,000	
Interest Revenue Received	12,000	
Dividends Received on Investments	9,000	
Total Cash Receipts		$ 290,000
Payments:		
To Suppliers	(135,000)	
To Employees	(56,000)	

Payments for Interest Expense and Income Tax Expense

These cash payments are reported separately from the other expenses. The accounts related to interest payments are Interest Expense from the income statement and Interest Payable from the balance sheet. Because there is no Interest Payable account on the balance sheet, the Interest Expense account from the income statement must represent all amounts paid in cash for interest. So, the statement of cash flows shows cash payments for interest of $15,000.

The accounts related to income tax payments are Income Tax Expense from the income statement and Income Tax Payable from the balance sheet. Because there is no Income Tax Payable account on the balance sheet, the Income Tax Expense account from the income statement must represent all amounts paid in cash for income tax. So, the statement of cash flows shows cash payments for income tax of $14,000.

SHOPMART, INC.
Statement of Cash Flows (Partial)
Year Ended December 31, 2018

Cash Flows from Operating Activities:		
Receipts:		
Collections from Customers	$ 269,000	
Interest Revenue Received	12,000	
Dividends Received on Investments	9,000	
Total Cash Receipts		$ 290,000
Payments:		
To Suppliers	(135,000)	
To Employees	(56,000)	
For Interest	(15,000)	
For Income Tax	(14,000)	
Total Cash Payments		(220,000)

Are depreciation expense and gain or loss on disposal of plant assets included in the operating activities section when using the direct method?

Non-cash Expenses and Gains or Losses on Disposal of Long-term Assets

Non-cash expenses and gains or losses on disposal of long-term assets are reported on the income statement but are not included in the operating activities when using the direct method. Non-cash expenses are not reported because these items do not affect cash. The cash received from the disposal of long-term assets is reported in the investing activities section, not the operating activities section.

Net Cash Provided by Operating Activities

To calculate net cash provided by operating activities using the direct method, we add all the cash receipts and cash payments described previously and find the difference. For ShopMart, total cash receipts were $290,000. Total cash payments were $220,000. So, net cash provided by operating activities is $70,000. If you refer back to the indirect method statement of cash flows shown in Exhibit C-5, you will find that it showed the same $70,000 for net cash provided by operating activities. The amount is the same, only the method by which it was calculated was different.

The remainder of ShopMart's statement of cash flows is exactly the same as what we calculated using the indirect method. Exhibit CA-1 shows the completed statement of cash flows using the direct method for operating activities.

Exhibit CA-1 | **Statement of Cash Flows—Direct Method**

SHOPMART, INC. Statement of Cash Flows Year Ended December 31, 2018		
Cash Flows from Operating Activities:		
Receipts:		
Collections from Customers	$ 269,000	
Interest Revenue Received	12,000	
Dividends Received on Investments	9,000	
Total Cash Receipts		$ 290,000
Payments:		
To Suppliers	(135,000)	
To Employees	(56,000)	
For Interest	(15,000)	
For Income Tax	(14,000)	
Total Cash Payments		(220,000)
Net Cash Provided by Operating Activities		70,000
Cash Flows from Investing Activities:		
Cash Payment for Acquisition of Plant Assets	(310,000)	
Cash Receipt from Disposal of Plant Assets	50,000	
Net Cash Used for Investing Activities		(260,000)
Cash Flows from Financing Activities:		
Cash Receipt from Issuance of Notes Payable	90,000	
Cash Payment of Notes Payable	(10,000)	
Cash Receipt from Issuance of Common Stock	120,000	
Cash Payment for Purchase of Treasury Stock	(20,000)	
Cash Payment of Dividends	(10,000)	
Net Cash Provided by Financing Activities		170,000
Net Increase (Decrease) in Cash		(20,000)
Cash Balance, December 31, 2017		42,000
Cash Balance, December 31, 2018		$ 22,000

8A. Big Island, Inc. began 2018 with cash of $40,000. During the year, Big Island earned revenue of $200,000 and collected $120,000 from customers. Expenses for the year totaled $160,000, of which Big Island paid $65,000 in cash to suppliers and $80,000 in cash to employees. The company received $2,000 cash for interest revenue and paid $10,000 for income taxes. Big Island also paid $35,000 to purchase equipment and a cash dividend of $15,000 to its stockholders during 2018. Prepare the company's operating activities section of the statement of cash flows for the year ended December 31, 2018. Use the direct method.

Check your answer online in MyAccountingLab or at http://www.pearsonhighered.com/Horngren.

For more practice, see Short Exercises Short Exercises SCA-11 through Short Exercises SCA-14. MyAccountingLab

APPENDIX CB: Preparing the Indirect Statement of Cash Flows Using a Spreadsheet

HOW IS THE STATEMENT OF CASH FLOWS PREPARED USING THE INDIRECT METHOD AND A SPREADSHEET?

This chapter discussed the uses of the statement of cash flows in decision making and showed how to prepare the statement using T-accounts. The T-account approach works well as a learning device. In practice, however, most companies face complex situations. In these cases, a spreadsheet can help in preparing the statement of cash flows.

The spreadsheet starts with the beginning balance sheet and concludes with the ending balance sheet. Two middle columns—one for debit amounts and the other for credit amounts—complete the spreadsheet. These columns, labeled "Transaction Analysis," hold the data for the statement of cash flows. Accountants can prepare the statement directly from the lower part of the spreadsheet. This appendix is based on the ShopMart data used in this chapter. We illustrate this approach only with the indirect method for operating activities. This method could be used for the direct method as well.

The *indirect* method reconciles accrual basis net income to net cash provided by operating activities. Exhibit CB-1 (on the next page) is the spreadsheet for preparing the statement of cash flows by the *indirect* method. Panel A shows the transaction analysis, and Panel B gives the information to prepare the statement of cash flows.

Learning Objective 5

Prepare the statement of cash flows by the indirect method using a spreadsheet

Exhibit CB-1 | **Spreadsheet for Statement of Cash Flows—Indirect Method**

	A	B	C	D	E	F	G
1	SHOPMART, INC.						
2	Spreadsheet for Statement of Cash Flows						
3	Year Ended December 31, 2018						
4							
5	**Panel A—Balance Sheet:**	**Balance 12/31/2017**		**Transaction Analysis**			**Balance 12/31/2018**
6				**DEBIT**	**CREDIT**		
7	Cash	$ 42,000			20,000	(n)	$ 22,000
8	Accounts Receivable	73,000	(d)	17,000			90,000
9	Merchandise Inventory	145,000			2,000	(e)	143,000
10	Plant Assets	252,000	(h)	310,000	55,000	(c)	507,000
11	Accumulated Depreciation—Plant Assets	(42,000)	(c)	15,000	20,000	(b)	(47,000)
12	Total Assets	$ 470,000					$ 715,000
13							
14	Accounts Payable	50,000			40,000	(f)	90,000
15	Accured Liabilities	10,000	(g)	5,000			5,000
16	Notes Payable	80,000	(j)	10,000	90,000	(i)	160,000
17	Total Liabilities	140,000					255,000
18							
19	Common Stock, no par	250,000			120,000	(k)	370,000
20	Retained Earnings	80,000	(m)	10,000	40,000	(a)	110,000
21	Treasury Stock	0	(l)	20,000			(20,000)
22	Total Liabilities and Stockholders' Equity	$ 470,000		$ 387,000	$ 387,000		$ 715,000
23							
24	**Panel B—Statement of Cash Flows:**						
25	Cash Flows from Operating Activities:						
26	Net Income		(a)	40,000			
27	Adjustments to Reconcile Net Income to Net Cash Provided by Operating Activities:						
28	Depreciation Expense—Plant Assets		(b)	20,000			
29	Gain on Disposal of Plant Assets				10,000	(c)	
30	Increase in Accounts Receivable				17,000	(d)	
31	Decrease in Merchandise Inventory		(e)	2,000			
32	Increase in Accounts Payable		(f)	40,000			
33	Decrease in Accrued Liabilities				5,000	(g)	
34	Net Cash Provided by Operating Activities						
35	Cash Flows from Investing Activities:						
36	Cash Payment for Acquisition of Plant Assets				310,000	(h)	
37	Cash Receipt from Disposal of Plant Assets		(c)	50,000			
38	Net Cash Used for Investing Activities						
39	Cash Flows from Financing Activities:						
40	Cash Receipt from Issuance of Notes Payable		(i)	90,000			
41	Cash Payment of Notes Payable				10,000	(j)	
42	Cash Receipt from Issuance of Common Stock		(k)	120,000			
43	Cash Payment for Purchase of Treasury Stock				20,000	(l)	
44	Cash Payment of Dividends				10,000	(m)	
45	Net Cash Provided by Financing Activities						
46	Net Increase (Decrease) in Cash		(n)	20,000			
47	Total			$ 382,000	$ 382,000		
48							

The following is a listing of the transaction analysis provided on the spreadsheet using the indirect method:

a. Net income of $40,000 is the first operating cash inflow. Net income is entered on the spreadsheet (Panel B) as a debit to Net Income under Cash Flows from Operating Activities and as a credit to Retained Earnings on the balance sheet (Panel A).

b. Next come the adjustments to net income, starting with depreciation of $20,000— transaction (b)—which is debited to Depreciation Expense—Plant Assets and credited to Accumulated Depreciation—Plant Assets.

c. This transaction is the sale of plant assets. The $10,000 gain on the sale is entered as a credit to Gain on Disposal of Plant Assets—a subtraction from net income—under operating cash flows. This credit removes the $10,000 gain from operating activities because the cash proceeds from the sale were $50,000, not $10,000. The $50,000 sale amount is then entered on the spreadsheet under investing activities. Entry (c) is completed by crediting the plant assets' cost of $55,000 to the Plant Assets account and debiting Accumulated Depreciation—Plant Assets for $15,000.

d. Entry (d) debits Accounts Receivable for its $17,000 increase during the year. This amount is credited to Increase in Accounts Receivable under operating cash flows.

e. This entry credits Merchandise Inventory for its $2,000 decrease during the year. This amount is debited to Decrease in Merchandise Inventory under operating cash flows.

f. This entry credits Accounts Payable for its $40,000 increase during the year. Then it is debited to show as Increase in Accounts Payable under operating cash flows.

g. This entry debits Accrued Liabilities for its $5,000 decrease during the year. Then it is credited to show as Decrease in Accrued Liabilities under operating cash flows.

h. This entry debits Plant Assets for the purchase of $310,000 and credits Cash Payment for Acquisition of Plant Assets under investing cash flows.

i. This entry is represented by a credit to Notes Payable and a debit under cash flows from financing activities of $90,000 (Cash Receipt from Issuance of Notes Payable).

j. This entry is the opposite of (i). It is represented by a debit (reduction) of $10,000 to Notes Payable and a credit under Cash Flows from Financing Activities for Cash Payment of Notes Payable.

k. This entry debits Cash Receipts from Issuance of Common Stock of $120,000 under financing cash flows. The offsetting credit is to Common Stock.

l. The purchase of treasury stock debited the Treasury Stock account on the balance sheet $20,000. The corresponding cash flow entry Cash Payment for Purchase of Treasury Stock credits $20,000 to reduce cash flow.

m. The $10,000 reduction (debit) to the Retained Earnings account is the result of dividends declared and paid by the company. So, we show Cash Payment of Dividends as a credit in the financing section.

n. The final item in Exhibit CB-1 is the Net Increase (Decrease) in Cash. It is shown as a credit to Cash and a debit to Net Increase (Decrease) in Cash of $20,000.

In Panel B of Exhibit CB-1, the debits represent increases (or inflows) of cash and the credits represent decreases (or outflows). This is because debits increase Cash and credits decrease Cash.

Try It!

9B. Muench, Inc.'s accountant has partially completed the spreadsheet for the statement of cash flows. Fill in the remaining missing information.

	A	B	C	D	E	F	G
1	MUENCH, INC.						
2	Spreadsheet for Statement of Cash Flows						
3	Year Ended December 31, 2018						
4							
5	**Panel A—Balance Sheet:**	**Balance 12/31/2017**		**Transaction Analysis**			**Balance 12/31/2018**
6				**DEBIT**	**CREDIT**		
7	Cash	$ 16,000					$ 20,000
8	Accounts Receivable	3,250					5,000
9	Plant Assets	14,000		1,000			15,000
10	Accumulated Depreciation	(100)			100		(200)
11	Total Assets	$ 33,150					$ 39,800
12							
13	Accounts Payable	5,000					3,500
14							
15	Common Stock, no par	24,150			5,850		30,000
16	Retained Earnings	4,000		5,700			6,300
17	Total Liabilities and Stockholders' Equity	$ 33,150					$ 39,800
18							
19	**Panel B—Statement of Cash Flows:**						
20	Cash Flows from Operating Activities:						
21	Net Income						
22	Adjustments to Reconcile Net Income to Net Cash Provided by Operating Activities:						
23	Depreciation Expense—Plant Assets			100			
24	Increase in Accounts Receivable						
25	Decrease in Accounts Payable						
26	Net Cash Provided by Operating Activities						
27	Cash Flows from Investing Activities:						
28	Cash Payment for Acquisition of Plant Assets				1,000		
29	Net Cash Used for Investing Activities						
30	Cash Flows from Financing Activities:						
31	Cash Receipt from Issuance of Common Stock			5,850			
32	Cash Payment of Dividends				5,700		
33	Net Cash Provided by Financing Activities						
34	Net Increase (Decrease) in Cash						
35							

Check your answer online in MyAccountingLab or at http://www.pearsonhighered.com/Horngren.

For more practice, see Short Exercise SCB-15. MyAccountingLab

REVIEW

> Things You Should Know

1. What is the statement of cash flows?

- The statement of cash flows reports on a business's cash receipts and cash payments for a specific period.
- There are three basic types of cash flow activities:
  - Operating activities—Reports on activities that create revenue or expense in the entity's business.
  - Investing activities—Reports cash receipts and cash payments that increase or decrease long-term assets.
  - Financing activities—Includes cash receipts and cash payments involved in long-term liabilities and equity.
- Non-cash investing and financing activities are not included in the statement of cash flows but appear either as a separate schedule at the bottom of the statement or in the notes to the financial statements.
- There are two ways to format operating activities on the statement of cash flows:
  - Indirect method—Starts with net income and adjusts it to net cash provided by operating activities.
  - Direct method—Restates the income statement in terms of cash.

2. How is the statement of cash flows prepared using the indirect method?

- **Step 1:** Complete the cash flows from operating activities section using net income and adjusting for increases or decreases in current assets (other than cash) and current liabilities. Also adjust for gains or losses on long-term assets and non-cash expenses.
- **Step 2:** Complete the cash flows from investing activities section by reviewing the long-term assets section of the balance sheet.
- **Step 3:** Complete the cash flows from financing activities section by reviewing the long-term liabilities and equity sections of the balance sheet.
- **Step 4:** Compute the net increase or decrease in cash during the year.
- **Step 5:** Prepare a separate schedule reporting any non-cash investing and financing activities.

3. How do we use free cash flow to evaluate business performance?

- Free cash flow is the amount of cash available from operating activities after paying for planned investments in long-term assets and after paying cash dividends to shareholders.
- Free cash flow = Net cash provided by operating activities − Cash payments planned for investments in long-term assets − Cash dividends.

4. How is the statement of cash flows prepared using the direct method? (Appendix CA)

- The operating activities section is the only section that differs between the direct and indirect methods.
- When using the direct method, each line item on the income statement is converted from accrual basis to cash basis.

5. **How is the statement of cash flows prepared using the indirect method and a spreadsheet? (Appendix CB)**

   ▪ A spreadsheet can be used to help in preparing the statement of cash flows.

   ▪ The spreadsheet helps accountants analyze the changes in balance sheet accounts.

> Check Your Understanding

Check your understanding of the chapter by completing this problem and then looking at the solution. Use this practice to help identify which sections of the chapter you need to study more.

The Adams Corporation reported the following income statement for 2018 and comparative balance sheet for 2018 and 2017, along with transaction data for 2018:

ADAMS CORPORATION Comparative Balance Sheet December 31, 2018 and 2017			
	2018	2017	Increase (Decrease)
Assets			
Current Assets:			
Cash	$ 22,000	$ 3,000	$ 19,000
Accounts Receivable	22,000	23,000	(1,000)
Merchandise Inventory	35,000	34,000	1,000
Long-term Assets:			
Plants Assets	153,200	97,200	56,000
Accumulated Depreciation—Plant Assets	(27,200)	(25,200)	(2,000)
Total Assets	$ 205,000	$ 132,000	$ 73,000
Liabilities			
Current Liabilities:			
Accounts Payable	$ 35,000	$ 26,000	$ 9,000
Accrued Liabilities	7,000	9,000	(2,000)
Income Tax Payable	10,000	10,000	0
Long-term Liabilities:			
Bonds Payable	84,000	53,000	31,000
Total Liabilities	136,000	98,000	38,000
Stockholders' Equity			
Common Stock, no par	52,000	20,000	32,000
Retained Earnings	27,000	19,000	8,000
Treasury Stock	(10,000)	(5,000)	(5,000)
Total Stockholders' Equity	69,000	34,000	35,000
Total Liabilities and Stockholders' Equity	$ 205,000	$ 132,000	$ 73,000

ADAMS CORPORATION
Income Statement
Year Ended December 31, 2018

Net Sales Revenue		$ 662,000
Cost of Goods Sold		560,000
Gross Profit		102,000
Operating Expenses:		
Salaries and Wages Expense	$ 46,000	
Depreciation Expense—Plant Assets	10,000	
Rent Expense	2,000	
Total Operating Expenses		58,000
Operating Income		44,000
Other Income and (Expenses):		
Loss on Disposal of Plant Assets	(2,000)	
Total Other Income and (Expenses)		(2,000)
Net Income Before Income Taxes		42,000
Income Tax Expense		16,000
Net Income		$ 26,000

Transaction data for 2018

Cash paid for purchase of equipment	$140,000
Cash payment of dividends	18,000
Issuance of common stock to retire bonds payable	13,000
Issuance of bonds payable to borrow cash	44,000
Cash receipt from issuance of common stock	19,000
Cash receipt from sale of equipment	74,000
(Cost, $84,000; Accumulated Depreciation, $8,000)	
Cash paid for purchase of treasury stock	5,000

Prepare Adams Corporation's statement of cash flows for the year ended December 31, 2018. Format cash flows from operating activities by the indirect method. (See Learning Objective 2)

> Solution

ADAMS CORPORATION Statement of Cash Flows Year Ended December 31, 2018		
Cash Flows from Operating Activities:		
Net Income		$ 26,000
Adjustments to Reconcile Net Income to Net Cash Provided by Operating Activities:		
Depreciation Expense—Plant Assets	$ 10,000	
Loss on Disposal of Plant Assets	2,000	
Decrease in Accounts Receivable	1,000	
Increase in Merchandise Inventory	(1,000)	
Increase in Accounts Payable	9,000	
Decrease in Accrued Liabilities	(2,000)	19,000
Net Cash Provided by Operating Activities		45,000
Cash Flows from Investing Activities:		
Cash Payment for Acquisition of Plant Assets	(140,000)	
Cash Receipt from Disposal of Plant Assets	74,000	
Net Cash Used for Investing Activities		(66,000)
Cash Flows from Financing Activities:		
Cash Receipt from Issuance of Bonds Payable	44,000	
Cash Receipt from Issuance of Common Stock	19,000	
Cash Payment for Purchase of Treasury Stock	(5,000)	
Cash Payment of Dividends	(18,000)	
Net Cash Provided by Financing Activities		40,000
Net Increase (Decrease) in Cash		19,000
Cash Balance, December 31, 2017		3,000
Cash Balance, December 31, 2018		$ 22,000
Non-cash Investing and Financing Activities:		
Issuance of Common Stock to Retire Bonds Payable		$ 13,000
Total Non-cash Investing and Financing Activities		$ 13,000

Relevant T-accounts:

Plant Assets

12/31/2017	97,200		
Acquisitions	140,000	84,000	Disposals
12/31/2018	153,200		

Accumulated Depreciation—Plant Assets

		25,200	12/31/2017
Disposals	8,000	10,000	Depr. Exp.
		27,200	12/31/2018

Bonds Payable

		53,000	12/31/2017
Retirement	13,000	44,000	Issuance
		84,000	12/31/2018

Common Stock

		20,000	12/31/2017
Retirement	0	13,000	Issuance
		19,000	Issuance
		52,000	12/31/2018

Treasury Stock

12/31/2017	5,000		
Purchase	5,000	0	Disposal
12/31/2018	10,000		

Retained Earnings

		19,000	12/31/2017
		26,000	Net Income
Dividends	18,000		
		27,000	12/31/2018

> Key Terms

Cash Flows (p. C-2)

Direct Method (p. C-5)

Financing Activities (p. C-3)

Free Cash Flow (p. C-20)

Indirect Method (p. C-5)

Investing Activities (p. C-3)

Non-cash Investing and Financing Activities (p. C-4)

Operating Activities (p. C-3)

Statement of Cash Flows (p. C-2)

> Quick Check

Learning Objective 1

1. The purposes of the statement of cash flows are to
   a. evaluate management decisions.
   b. determine ability to pay debts and dividends.
   c. predict future cash flows.
   d. All of the above

Learning Objective 1

2. The main categories of cash flow activities on the statement of cash flows are
   a. direct and indirect.
   b. current and long-term.
   c. non-cash investing and financing.
   d. operating, investing, and financing.

Learning Objective 1

3. Operating activities are most closely related to
   a. long-term assets.
   b. current assets and current liabilities.
   c. long-term liabilities and stockholders' equity.
   d. dividends and treasury stock.

Learning Objective 2

4. Which item does *not* appear on a statement of cash flows prepared by the indirect method?
   a. Collections from customers
   b. Depreciation expense
   c. Net income
   d. Gain on sale of land

Learning Objective 2

5. Leather Shop earned net income of $57,000 after deducting depreciation of $5,000 and all other expenses. Current assets decreased by $4,000, and current liabilities increased by $8,000. How much was Leather Shop's net cash provided by operating activities (indirect method)?
   a. $40,000   b. $66,000   c. $48,000   d. $74,000

Learning Objective 2

6. The Plant Assets account and Accumulated Depreciation—Plant Assets account of Star Media show the following:

Plant Assets			
12/31/2017	100,000		
Acquisitions	428,000	52,500	Disposals
12/31/2018	475,500		

Accumulated Depreciation—Plant Assets			
		20,000	12/31/2017
Disposals	10,500	34,000	Depr. Exp.
		43,500	12/31/2018

Star Media sold plant assets at an $11,000 loss. Where on the statement of cash flows should Star Media report the sale of plant assets? How much should the business report for the sale?

a. Financing cash flows—cash receipt of $42,000
b. Investing cash flows—cash receipt of $53,000
c. Investing cash flows—cash receipt of $31,000
d. Investing cash flows—cash receipt of $42,000

7. Mountain Water Corp. issued common stock of $28,000 to pay off long-term notes payable of $28,000. In what section(s) would these transactions be recorded?

Learning Objective 2

   a. Financing activities payment of note, $(28,000)
   b. Financing activities cash receipt, $28,000
   c. Non-cash investing and financing activities, $28,000
   d. Both a and b are correct.

8. Holmes, Inc. expects net cash flow from operating activities to be $160,000, and the company plans purchases of equipment of $83,000 and repurchases of stock of $24,000. What is Holmes's free cash flow?

Learning Objective 3

   a. $53,000   b. $160,000   c. $77,000   d. $83,000

9A. Maxwell Furniture Center had accounts receivable of $20,000 at the beginning of the year and $54,000 at year-end. Revenue for the year totaled $116,000. How much cash did the business collect from customers?

Learning Objective 4
Appendix 14A

   a. $150,000   b. $62,000   c. $116,000   d. $82,000

10B. If accrued liabilities increased during the year, which of the following is correct when using a spreadsheet to complete the statement of cash flows (indirect method)?

Learning Objective 5
Appendix CB

   a. Increase in Accrued Liabilities would be debited
   b. Increase in Accrued Liabilities would be credited
   c. Accrued Liabilities would be debited
   d. None of the above is correct.

Check your answers at the end of the chapter.

ASSESS YOUR PROGRESS

> Review Questions

1. What does the statement of cash flows report?
2. How does the statement of cash flows help users of financial statements?
3. Describe the three basic types of cash flow activities.
4. What types of transactions are reported in the non-cash investing and financing activities section of the statement of cash flows?
5. Describe the two formats for reporting operating activities on the statement of cash flows.
6. Describe the five steps used to prepare the statement of cash flows by the indirect method.
7. Explain why depreciation expense, depletion expense, and amortization expense are added to net income in the operating activities section of the statement of cash flows when using the indirect method.
8. If a company experienced a loss on disposal of long-term assets, how would this be reported in the operating activities section of the statement of cash flows when using the indirect method? Why?

9. If current assets other than cash increase, what is the effect on cash? What about a decrease in current assets other than cash?

10. If current liabilities increase, what is the effect on cash? What about a decrease in current liabilities?

11. What accounts on the balance sheet must be evaluated when completing the investing activities section of the statement of cash flows?

12. What accounts on the balance sheet must be evaluated when completing the financing activities section of the statement of cash flows?

13. What should the net change in cash section of the statement of cash flows always reconcile with?

14. What is free cash flow, and how is it calculated?

15A. How does the direct method differ from the indirect method when preparing the operating activities section of the statement of cash flows?

16B. Why might a spreadsheet be helpful when completing the statement of cash flows?

> Short Exercises

Learning Objective 1

SC-1 Describing the purposes of the statement of cash flows

Financial statements all have a goal. The statement of cash flows does as well. Describe how the statement of cash flows helps investors and creditors perform each of the following functions:

a. Predict future cash flows.

b. Evaluate management decisions.

c. Predict the ability to make debt payments to lenders and pay dividends to stockholders.

Learning Objective 1

SC-2 Classifying items on the statement of cash flows

Cash flow items must be categorized into one of four categories. Identify each item as operating (O), investing (I), financing (F), or non-cash (N).

a. Cash purchase of merchandise inventory

b. Cash payment of dividends

c. Cash receipt from the collection of long-term notes receivable

d. Cash payment for income taxes

e. Purchase of equipment in exchange for notes payable

f. Cash receipt from the sale of land

g. Cash received from borrowing money

h. Cash receipt for interest income

i. Cash receipt from the issuance of common stock

j. Cash payment of salaries

SC-3 Classifying items on the indirect statement of cash flows

Learning Objectives 1, 2

Destiny Corporation is preparing its statement of cash flows by the *indirect* method. Destiny has the following items for you to consider in preparing the statement:

a. Increase in accounts payable

b. Payment of dividends

c. Decrease in accrued liabilities

d. Issuance of common stock

e. Gain on sale of building

f. Loss on sale of land

g. Depreciation expense

h. Increase in merchandise inventory

i. Decrease in accounts receivable

j. Purchase of equipment

Identify each item as a(n):

- Operating activity—addition to net income (O+) or subtraction from net income (O−)

- Investing activity—cash inflow (I+) or cash outflow (I−)

- Financing activity—cash inflow (F+) or cash outflow (F−)

- Activity that is not used to prepare the indirect statement of cash flows (N)

SC-4 Computing cash flows from operating activities—indirect method

Learning Objective 2

DVR Equipment, Inc. reported the following data for 2018:

Income Statement:	
Net Income	$ 43,000
Depreciation Expense	6,000
Balance Sheet:	
Increase in Accounts Receivable	6,000
Decrease in Accounts Payable	2,000

Compute DVR's net cash provided by operating activities—indirect method.

SC-5 Computing cash flows from operating activities—indirect method

Learning Objective 2

Winding Road Cellular accountants have assembled the following data for the year ended April 30, 2018:

Cash receipt from sale of land	$ 27,000	Net income	$ 55,000
Depreciation expense	2,000	Cash purchase of equipment	44,000
Cash payment of dividends	5,800	Decrease in current liabilities	20,000
Cash receipt from issuance of common stock	17,000	Increase in current assets other than cash	27,000

Prepare the *operating* activities section using the indirect method for Winding Road Cellular's statement of cash flows for the year ended April 30, 2018.

Note: Short Exercise SC-5 must be completed before attempting Short Exercise SC-6.

SC-6 Computing cash flows from investing and financing activities

Learning Objective 2

Use the data in Short Exercise SC-5 to complete this exercise. Prepare Winding Road Cellular's statement of cash flows using the indirect method for the year ended April 30, 2018. Assume beginning and ending Cash are $48,000 and $52,200, respectively.

Learning Objective 2

SC-7 Computing investing and financing cash flows

Preston Media Corporation had the following income statement and balance sheet for 2018:

PRESTON MEDIA CORPORATION
Income Statement
Year Ended December 31, 2018

Sales Revenue	$ 80,000
Depreciation Expense—Plant Assets	11,000
Other Expenses	50,000
Net Income	$ 19,000

PRESTON MEDIA CORPORATION
Comparative Balance Sheet
December 31, 2018 and 2017

	2018	2017
Assets		
Current Assets:		
Cash	$ 5,000	$ 3,900
Accounts Receivable	9,600	5,100
Long-term Assets:		
Plants Assets	105,350	84,350
Accumulated Depreciation—Plant Assets	(29,350)	(18,350)
Total Assets	$ 90,600	$ 75,000
Liabilities		
Current Liabilities:		
Accounts Payable	$ 8,000	$ 4,500
Long-term Liabilities:		
Notes Payable	9,000	12,000
Total Liabilities	17,000	16,500
Stockholders' Equity		
Common Stock, no par	27,000	23,000
Retained Earnings	46,600	35,500
Total Stockholders' Equity	73,600	58,500
Total Liabilities and Stockholders' Equity	$ 90,600	$ 75,000

Requirements

1. Compute the acquisition of plant assets for Preston Media Corporation during 2018. The business sold no plant assets during the year. Assume the company paid cash for the acquisition of plant assets.

2. Compute the payment of a long-term note payable. During the year, the business issued a $4,400 note payable.

Note: Short Exercise SC-7 must be completed before attempting Short Exercise SC-8.

SC-8 Preparing the statement of cash flows—indirect method

Learning Objective 2

Use the Preston Media Corporation data in Short Exercise S14-7 and the results you calculated from the requirements. Prepare Preston Media's statement of cash flows—indirect method—for the year ended December 31, 2018.

SC-9 Computing the change in cash; identifying non-cash transactions

Learning Objective 2

Jennifer's Wedding Shops earned net income of $27,000, which included depreciation of $16,000. Jennifer's acquired a $119,000 building by borrowing $119,000 on a long-term note payable.

Requirements

1. How much did Jennifer's cash balance increase or decrease during the year?

2. Were there any non-cash transactions for the company? If so, show how they would be reported in the statement of cash flows.

SC-10 Computing free cash flow

Learning Objective 3

Julie Lopez Company expects the following for 2018:

- Net cash provided by operating activities of $148,000.
- Net cash provided by financing activities of $56,000.
- Net cash used for investing activities of $77,000 (no sales of long-term assets).
- Cash dividends paid to stockholders of $7,000.

How much free cash flow does Lopez expect for 2018?

SCA-11 Preparing a statement of cash flows using the direct method

Learning Objective 4
Appendix CA

Jelly Bean, Inc. began 2018 with cash of $58,000. During the year, Jelly Bean earned revenue of $595,000 and collected $614,000 from customers. Expenses for the year totaled $427,000, of which Jelly Bean paid $212,000 in cash to suppliers and $205,000 in cash to employees. Jelly Bean also paid $148,000 to purchase equipment and a cash dividend of $57,000 to its stockholders during 2018. Prepare the company's statement of cash flows for the year ended December 31, 2018. Format operating activities by the direct method.

SCA-12 Preparing operating activities using the direct method

Learning Objective 4
Appendix CA

Amy's Learning Center has assembled the following data for the year ended June 30, 2018:

Payments to suppliers	$ 115,000
Cash payment for purchase of equipment	39,000
Payments to employees	66,000
Payment of notes payable	34,000
Payment of dividends	7,500
Cash receipt from issuance of stock	22,000
Collections from customers	188,000
Cash receipt from sale of land	58,000
Cash balance, June 30, 2017	41,000

Prepare the *operating* activities section of the business's statement of cash flows for the year ended June 30, 2018, using the direct method.

Note: Short Exercise SCA-12 must be completed before attempting Short Exercise SCA-13.

Learning Objective 4
Appendix CA

SCA-13 Preparing the direct method statement of cash flows

Use the data in Short Exercise S14A-12 and your results. Prepare the business's complete statement of cash flows for the year ended June 30, 2018, using the *direct* method for operating activities.

Learning Objective 4
Appendix CA

SCA-14 Preparing the direct method statement of cash flows

Red Toy Company reported the following comparative balance sheet:

RED TOY COMPANY Comparative Balance Sheet December 31, 2018 and 2017		
	2018	**2017**
Assets		
Current Assets:		
Cash	$ 21,000	$ 17,000
Accounts Receivable	53,000	42,000
Merchandise Inventory	76,000	88,000
Prepaid Expenses	3,100	2,100
Long-term Assets:		
Plants Assets, Net	221,000	185,000
Investments	77,000	91,000
Total Assets	$ 451,100	$ 425,100
Liabilities		
Current Liabilities:		
Accounts Payable	$ 42,000	$ 38,000
Salaries Payable	25,000	20,000
Accrued Liabilities	7,000	16,000
Long-term Liabilities:		
Notes Payable	61,000	69,000
Total Liabilities	135,000	143,000
Stockholders' Equity		
Common Stock, no par	45,000	40,000
Retained Earnings	271,100	242,100
Total Stockholders' Equity	316,100	282,100
Total Liabilities and Stockholders' Equity	$ 451,100	$ 425,100

Requirements

1. Compute the collections from customers during 2018 for Red Toy Company. Sales Revenue totaled $134,000.

2. Compute the payments for inventory during 2018. Cost of Goods Sold was $79,000.

**SCB-15 Using a spreadsheet to complete the statement of cash flows—
indirect method**

Learning Objective 5
Appendix CB

Companies can use a spreadsheet to complete the statement of cash flows. Each item that follows is recorded in the transaction analysis columns of the spreadsheet.

a. Net income

b. Increases in current assets (other than Cash)

c. Decreases in current liabilities

d. Cash payment for acquisition of plant assets

e. Cash receipt from issuance of common stock

f. Depreciation expense

Identify each as being recorded by a Debit or Credit in the *statement of cash flows section* of the spreadsheet.

> Exercises

EC-16 Classifying cash flow items

Learning Objective 1

Consider the following transactions:

a. Purchased equipment for $130,000 cash.

b. Issued $14 par preferred stock for cash.

c. Cash received from sales to customers of $35,000.

d. Cash paid to vendors, $17,000.

e. Sold building for $19,000 gain for cash.

f. Purchased treasury stock for $28,000.

g. Retired a notes payable with 1,250 shares of the company's common stock.

Identify the category of the statement of cash flows in which each transaction would be reported.

Learning Objective 1

EC-17 Classifying transactions on the statement of cash flows—indirect method

Consider the following transactions:

Date	Accounts and Explanation	Debit	Credit
a.	Cash	72,000	
	Common Stock		72,000
b.	Treasury Stock	16,500	
	Cash		16,500
c.	Cash	88,000	
	Sales Revenue		88,000
d.	Land	103,000	
	Cash		103,000
e.	Depreciation Expense—Equipment	6,800	
	Accumulated Depreciation—Equipment		6,800
f.	Dividends Payable	19,500	
	Cash		19,500
g.	Land	22,000	
	Notes Payable		22,000
h.	Cash	9,600	
	Equipment		9,600
i.	Bonds Payable	51,000	
	Cash		51,000
j.	Building	137,000	
	Notes Payable		137,000
k.	Loss on Disposal of Equipment	1,800	
	Accumulated Depreciation—Equipment	200	
	Equipment		2,000

Identify the category of the statement of cash flows, indirect method, in which each transaction would be reported.

Learning Objectives 1, 2

EC-18 Classifying items on the indirect statement of cash flows

The statement of cash flows categorizes like transactions for optimal reporting.

Identify each item as a(n):

- Operating activity—addition to net income (O+) or subtraction from net income (O−)
- Investing activity—cash inflow (I+) or cash outflow (I−)
- Financing activity—cash inflow (F+) or cash outflow (F−)
- Non-cash investing and financing activity (NIF)
- Activity that is not used to prepare the indirect statement of cash flows (N)

The *indirect* method is used to report cash flows from operating activities.

a. Loss on sale of land.

b. Acquisition of equipment by issuance of note payable.

c. Payment of long-term debt.

d. Acquisition of building by issuance of common stock.

e. Increase in Salaries Payable.

f. Decrease in Merchandise Inventory.

g. Increase in Prepaid Expenses.

h. Decrease in Accrued Liabilities.

i. Cash sale of land (no gain or loss).

j. Issuance of long-term note payable to borrow cash.

k. Depreciation Expense.

l. Purchase of treasury stock.

m. Issuance of common stock.

n. Increase in Accounts Payable.

o. Net income.

p. Payment of cash dividend.

EC-19 Computing operating activities cash flow—indirect method

The records of Vintage Color Engraving reveal the following:

Learning Objective 2

Net Cash Prov. by Op. Act. $16,000

Net income	$ 36,000	Depreciation expense	$ 5,000
Sales revenue	53,000	Decrease in current liabilities	19,000
Loss on sale of land	4,000	Increase in current assets other than cash	10,000
Acquisition of land	35,000		

Compute cash flows from operating activities by the indirect method for year ended December 31, 2018.

EC-20 Computing operating activities cash flow—indirect method

The accounting records of CD Sales, Inc. include the following accounts:

Learning Objective 2

Net Cash Prov. by Op. Act. $49,500

Account	Beginning Balance	Ending Balance
Cash	$ 7,500	$ 6,500
Accounts Receivable	21,000	17,500
Merchandise Inventory	20,000	30,000
Accounts Payable	15,000	19,000

Accumulated Depreciation—Equipment		
	56,000	Jul. 1
	2,000	Depr. Exp.
	58,000	Jul. 31

Retained Earnings			
Dividends 15,000	63,000	Jul. 1	
	50,000	Net Inc.	
	98,000	Jul. 31	

Compute CD's net cash provided by (used for) operating activities during July 2018. Use the indirect method.

Learning Objective 2

Net Cash Prov. by Op.
Act. $98,000

EC-21 Preparing the statement of cash flows—indirect method

The income statement of Boost Plus, Inc. follows:

BOOST PLUS, INC. Income Statement Year Ended September 30, 2018		
Net Sales Revenue		$ 231,000
Cost of Goods Sold		94,000
Gross Profit		137,000
Operating Expenses:		
Salaries Expense	$ 54,000	
Depreciation Expense—Plant Assets	27,000	
Total Operating Expenses		81,000
Net Income Before Income Taxes		56,000
Income Tax Expense		3,000
Net Income		$ 53,000

Additional data follow:

a. Acquisition of plant assets is $124,000. Of this amount, $108,000 is paid in cash and $16,000 by signing a note payable.

b. Cash receipt from sale of land totals $20,000. There was no gain or loss.

c. Cash receipts from issuance of common stock total $36,000.

d. Payment of notes payable is $15,000.

e. Payment of dividends is $5,000.

f. From the balance sheet:

	September 30	
	2018	**2017**
Cash	$ 39,000	$ 13,000
Accounts Receivable	46,000	61,000
Merchandise Inventory	94,000	88,000
Land	82,000	102,000
Plant Assets	214,000	90,000
Accumulated Depreciation	(61,000)	(34,000)
Accounts Payable	32,000	15,000
Accrued Liabilities	12,000	20,000
Notes Payable (long-term)	16,000	15,000
Common Stock, no par	40,000	4,000
Retained Earnings	314,000	266,000

Prepare Boost Plus's statement of cash flows for the year ended September 30, 2018, using the indirect method. Include a separate section for non-cash investing and financing activities.

EC-22 Computing cash flows for investing and financing activities

Learning Objective 2

Consider the following facts for Java Jolt:

2. Book Value on Plant Assets Sold $7,000

a. Beginning and ending Retained Earnings are $45,000 and $70,000, respectively. Net income for the period is $60,000.

b. Beginning and ending Plant Assets are $124,500 and $134,500, respectively.

c. Beginning and ending Accumulated Depreciation—Plant Assets are $21,500 and $26,500, respectively.

d. Depreciation Expense for the period is $17,000, and acquisitions of new plant assets total $29,000. Plant assets were sold at a $5,000 gain.

Requirements

1. How much are cash dividends?

2. What was the amount of the cash receipt from the sale of plant assets?

EC-23 Computing the cash effect

Learning Objective 2

Rouse Exercise Equipment, Inc. reported the following financial statements for 2018:

2. Payment: $8,000
4. Dividends $47,000

ROUSE EXERCISE EQUIPMENT, INC.		
Income Statement		
Year Ended December 31, 2018		
Net Sales Revenue		$ 713,000
Cost of Goods Sold		342,000
Gross Profit		371,000
Operating Expenses:		
Depreciation Expense	$ 54,000	
Other Operating Expenses	210,000	
Total Operating Expenses		264,000
Net Income		$ 107,000

ROUSE EXERCISE EQUIPMENT, INC.
Comparative Balance Sheet
December 31, 2018 and 2017

	2018	2017
Assets		
Current Assets:		
Cash	$ 17,000	$ 16,000
Accounts Receivable	57,000	46,000
Merchandise Inventory	79,000	90,000
Long-term Assets:		
Plants Assets	260,500	216,400
Accumulated Depreciation—Plant Assets	(38,500)	(32,400)
Investments	96,000	73,000
Total Assets	$ 471,000	$ 409,000
Liabilities		
Current Liabilities:		
Accounts Payable	$ 72,000	$ 71,000
Salaries Payable	3,000	5,000
Long-term Liabilities:		
Notes Payable	61,000	69,000
Total Liabilities	136,000	145,000
Stockholders' Equity		
Common Stock, no par	45,000	34,000
Retained Earnings	290,000	230,000
Total Stockholders' Equity	335,000	264,000
Total Liabilities and Stockholders' Equity	$ 471,000	$ 409,000

Requirements

1. Compute the amount of Rouse Exercise's acquisition of plant assets. Assume the acquisition was for cash. Rouse Exercise disposed of plant assets at book value. The cost and accumulated depreciation of the disposed asset was $47,900. No cash was received upon disposal.

2. Compute new borrowing or payment of long-term notes payable, with Rouse Exercise having only one long-term notes payable transaction during the year.

3. Compute the issuance of common stock with Rouse Exercise having only one common stock transaction during the year.

4. Compute the payment of cash dividends.

Note: Exercise EC-23 must be completed before attempting Exercise EC-24.

Learning Objective 2

Net Cash Prov. by Op. Act. $160,000

EC-24 Preparing the statement of cash flows—indirect method

Use the Rouse Exercise Equipment data in Exercise EC-23. Prepare the company's statement of cash flows—indirect method—for the year ended December 31, 2018. Assume investments are purchased with cash.

EC-25 Identifying and reporting non-cash transactions

Learning Objective 2

Total Non-cash Inv. and Fin.
Act. $153,000

Dirtbikes, Inc. identified the following selected transactions that occurred during the year ended December 31, 2018:

a. Issued 750 shares of $3 par common stock for cash of $17,000.

b. Issued 5,100 shares of $3 par common stock for a building with a fair market value of $96,000.

c. Purchased new truck with a fair market value of $29,000. Financed it 100% with a long-term note.

d. Retired short-term notes of $28,000 by issuing 1,900 shares of $3 par common stock.

e. Paid long-term note of $10,500 to Bank of Tallahassee. Issued new long-term note of $23,000 to Bank of Trust.

Identify any non-cash transactions that occurred during the year, and show how they would be reported in the non-cash investing and financing activities section of the statement of cash flows.

EC-26 Analyzing free cash flow

Learning Objective 3

Use the Rouse Exercise Equipment data in Exercises E14-23 and E14-24. Rouse plans to purchase a truck for $23,000 and a forklift for $125,000 next year. In addition, it plans to pay cash dividends of $3,500. Assuming Rouse plans similar activity for 2019, what would be the amount of free cash flow?

ECA-27 Preparing operating activities cash flow—direct method

**Learning Objective 4
Appendix CA**

Net Cash Prov. by Op. Act. $3,000

The accounting records of Four Seasons Parts reveal the following:

Payment of salaries and wages	$ 34,000	Net income	$ 21,000
Depreciation expense	10,000	Payment of income tax	16,000
Payment of interest	17,000	Collection of dividend revenue	5,000
Payment of dividends	5,000	Payment to suppliers	51,000
Collections from customers	116,000		

Compute cash flows from operating activities using the *direct* method for the year ended December 31, 2018.

Learning Objective 4
Appendix CA

Net Cash Prov. by Op.
Act. $76,000

ECA-28 Preparing the statement of cash flows—direct method

The income statement and additional data of Value Corporation follow:

VALUE CORPORATION Income Statement Year Ended June 30, 2018		
Net Sales Revenue		$ 233,000
Cost of Goods Sold		104,000
Gross Profit		129,000
Operating Expenses:		
Salaries Expense	$ 48,000	
Depreciation Expense—Plant Assets	21,000	
Advertising Expense	12,000	
Total Operating Expenses		81,000
Operating Income		48,000
Other Income and (Expenses):		
Dividend Revenue	7,000	
Interest Expense	(2,500)	
Total Other Income and (Expenses)		4,500
Net Income Before Income Taxes		52,500
Income Tax Expense		7,500
Net Income		$ 45,000

a. Collections from customers are $13,000 more than sales.

b. Dividend revenue, interest expense, and income tax expense equal their cash amounts.

c. Payments to suppliers are the sum of cost of goods sold plus advertising expense.

d. Payments to employees are $3,000 more than salaries expense.

e. Cash payment for the acquisition of plant assets is $102,000.

f. Cash receipts from sale of land total $29,000.

g. Cash receipts from issuance of common stock total $38,000.

h. Payment of long-term notes payable is $10,000.

i. Payment of dividends is $9,000.

j. Cash balance at June 30, 2017, was $21,000; at June 30, 2018, it was $43,000.

Prepare Value Corporation's statement of cash flows for the year ended June 30, 2018. Use the *direct* method.

Learning Objective 4
Appendix CA

ECA-29 Computing cash flow items—direct method

Consider the following facts:

1. Cash Receipts from
Cust. $72,000

a. Beginning and ending Accounts Receivable are $24,000 and $20,000, respectively. Credit sales for the period total $68,000.

b. Cost of goods sold is $77,000.

c. Beginning Merchandise Inventory balance is $29,000, and ending Merchandise Inventory balance is $26,000.

d. Beginning and ending Accounts Payable are $12,000 and $16,000, respectively.

Requirements

1. Compute cash collections from customers.
2. Compute cash payments for merchandise inventory.

ECA-30 Computing cash flow items—direct method

A-One Mobile Homes reported the following in its financial statements for the year ended December 31, 2018:

Learning Objective 4
Appendix CA

2. Cash Paid for Merchandise Inventory $18,542
7. Dividends $374

	2018	2017
Income Statement		
Net Sales Revenue	$ 25,118	$ 21,893
Cost of Goods Sold	18,074	15,501
Depreciation Expense	271	234
Other Operating Expenses	4,632	4,277
Income Tax Expense	530	482
Net Income	$ 1,611	$ 1,399
Balance Sheet		
Cash	$ 21	$ 19
Accounts Receivable	798	615
Merchandise Inventory	3,483	2,832
Property, Plant, and Equipment, net	4,351	3,437
Accounts Payable	1,547	1,364
Accrued Liabilities	938	851
Long-term Liabilities	477	461
Common Stock, no par	670	443
Retained Earnings	5,021	3,784

Requirements

1. Compute the collections from customers.
2. Compute payments for merchandise inventory.
3. Compute payments of other operating expenses.
4. Compute the acquisitions of property, plant, and equipment (no sales of property during 2018).
5. Compute the amount of borrowing, with A-One paying no long-term liabilities.
6. Compute the cash receipt from issuance of common stock.
7. Compute the payment of cash dividends.

ECB-31 Using a spreadsheet to prepare the statement of cash flows—indirect method

Learning Objective 5
Appendix CB

Use the Boost Plus, Inc. data in Exercise EC-21 to prepare the spreadsheet for the 2018 statement of cash flows. Format cash flows from operating activities by the indirect method.

> Problems Group A

Learning Objectives 1, 2

2. Net Income $266,400
4. Net Cash Used by Op.
Act. $(48,000)

PC-32A Identifying the purpose and preparing the statement of cash flows—indirect method

American Rare Coins (ARC) was formed on January 1, 2018. Additional data for the year follow:

a. On January 1, 2018, ARC issued no par common stock for $450,000.

b. Early in January, ARC made the following cash payments:

    1. For store fixtures, $53,000

    2. For merchandise inventory, $340,000

    3. For rent expense on a store building, $20,000

c. Later in the year, ARC purchased merchandise inventory on account for $239,000. Before year-end, ARC paid $139,000 of this accounts payable.

d. During 2018, ARC sold 2,400 units of merchandise inventory for $275 each. Before year-end, the company collected 85% of this amount. Cost of goods sold for the year was $250,000, and ending merchandise inventory totaled $329,000.

e. The store employs three people. The combined annual payroll is $96,000, of which ARC still owes $3,000 at year-end.

f. At the end of the year, ARC paid income tax of $17,000. There are no income taxes payable.

g. Late in 2018, ARC paid cash dividends of $44,000.

h. For store fixtures, ARC uses the straight-line depreciation method, over five years, with zero residual value.

Requirements

1. What is the purpose of the statement of cash flows?

2. Prepare ARC's income statement for the year ended December 31, 2018. Use the single-step format, with all revenues listed together and all expenses listed together.

3. Prepare ARC's balance sheet at December 31, 2018.

4. Prepare ARC's statement of cash flows using the indirect method for the year ended December 31, 2018.

Learning Objective 2

Net Cash Used for Inv.
Act. $(15,500)

PC-33A Preparing the statement of cash flows—indirect method

Accountants for Morganson, Inc. have assembled the following data for the year ended December 31, 2018:

	2018	2017
Current Assets:		
Cash	$ 99,400	$ 25,000
Accounts Receivable	64,100	69,700
Merchandise Inventory	83,000	75,000
Current Liabilities:		
Accounts Payable	57,600	55,200
Income Tax Payable	14,800	16,800

Transaction Data for 2018:

Issuance of common stock for cash	$ 38,000	Payment of notes payable	$ 46,100
Depreciation expense	24,000	Payment of cash dividends	50,000
Purchase of equipment with cash	74,000	Issuance of notes payable to borrow cash	62,000
Acquisition of land by issuing long-term notes payable	119,000	Gain on sale of building	4,500
Book value of building sold	54,000	Net income	68,500

Prepare Morganson's statement of cash flows using the indirect method. Include an accompanying schedule of non-cash investing and financing activities.

PC-34A Preparing the statement of cash flows—indirect method with non-cash transactions

The 2018 income statement and comparative balance sheet of Rolling Hills, Inc. follow:

Learning Objective 2

Net Cash Prov. by Op.
Act. $125,100

ROLLING HILLS, INC.
Income Statement
Year Ended December 31, 2018

Net Sales Revenue		$ 440,000
Cost of Goods Sold		209,200
Gross Profit		230,800
Operating Expenses:		
Salaries Expense	$ 77,400	
Depreciation Expense—Plant Assets	14,400	
Other Operating Expenses	10,200	
Total Operating Expenses		102,000
Operating Income		128,800
Other Income and (Expenses):		
Interest Revenue	8,700	
Interest Expense	(21,100)	
Total Other Income and (Expenses)		(12,400)
Net Income Before Income Taxes		116,400
Income Tax Expense		20,000
Net Income		$ 96,400

ROLLING HILLS, INC. Comparative Balance Sheet December 31, 2018 and 2017		
	2018	2017
Assets		
Current Assets:		
Cash	$ 26,900	$ 15,700
Accounts Receivable	26,500	25,400
Merchandise Inventory	79,800	91,500
Long-term Assets:		
Land	35,100	14,000
Plant Assets	124,840	114,650
Accumulated Depreciation—Plant Assets	(18,940)	(17,950)
Total Assets	$ 274,200	$ 243,300
Liabilities		
Current Liabilities:		
Accounts Payable	$ 35,700	$ 30,400
Accrued Liabilities	28,700	30,300
Long-term Liabilities:		
Notes Payable	79,000	108,000
Total Liabilities	143,400	168,700
Stockholders' Equity		
Common Stock, no par	88,900	64,500
Retained Earnings	41,900	10,100
Total Stockholders' Equity	130,800	74,600
Total Liabilities and Stockholders' Equity	$ 274,200	$ 243,300

Additionally, Rolling Hills purchased land of $21,100 by financing it 100% with long-term notes payable during 2018. During the year, there were no sales of land, no retirements of stock, and no treasury stock transactions. A plant asset was disposed of for $0. The cost and the accumulated depreciation of the disposed asset was $13,410. The plant acquisition was for cash.

Requirements

1. Prepare the 2018 statement of cash flows, formatting operating activities by the *indirect* method.

2. How will what you learned in this problem help you evaluate an investment?

PC-35A Preparing the statement of cash flows—indirect method, evaluating cash flows, and measuring free cash flows

Learning Objectives 2, 3

1. Net Cash Used for Inv. Act. $(152,700)

The comparative balance sheet of Jackson Educational Supply at December 31, 2018, reported the following:

	2018	2017
Current Assets:		
Cash	$ 87,700	$ 23,500
Accounts Receivable	15,300	22,000
Merchandise Inventory	62,600	60,400
Current Liabilities:		
Accounts Payable	28,100	26,100
Accrued Liabilities	10,600	11,300

Jackson's transactions during 2018 included the following:

Payment of cash dividends	$ 16,200	Depreciation expense	$ 16,700
Purchase of equipment with cash	54,700	Purchase of building with cash	98,000
Issuance of long-term notes payable to borrow cash	48,000	Net income	57,600
Issuance of common stock for cash	105,000		

Requirements

1. Prepare the statement of cash flows of Jackson Educational Supply for the year ended December 31, 2018. Use the indirect method to report cash flows from operating activities.

2. Evaluate Jackson's cash flows for the year. Mention all three categories of cash flows, and give the reason for your evaluation.

3. If Jackson plans similar activity for 2019, what is its expected free cash flow?

PCA-36A Preparing the statement of cash flows—direct method

Learning Objective 4
Appendix CA

2. Total Assets $1,051,400
3. Net Cash Prov. by Op. Act. $308,500

Boundary Rare Coins (BRC) was formed on January 1, 2018. Additional data for the year follow:

a. On January 1, 2018, BRC issued no par common stock for $475,000.

b. Early in January, BRC made the following cash payments:

   1. For store fixtures, $53,000
   2. For merchandise inventory, $260,000
   3. For rent expense on the store building, $13,000

c. Later in the year, BRC purchased merchandise inventory on account for $240,000. Before year-end, BRC paid $160,000 of this accounts payable.

d. During 2018, BRC sold 2,200 units of merchandise inventory for $450 each. Before year-end, the company collected 85% of this amount. Cost of goods sold for the year was $330,000, and ending merchandise inventory totaled $170,000.

e. The store employs three people. The combined annual payroll is $80,000, of which BRC still owes $4,000 at year-end.

f. At the end of the year, BRC paid income tax of $24,000. There are no income taxes payable.

g. Late in 2018, BRC paid cash dividends of $40,000.

h. For store fixtures, BRC uses the straight-line depreciation method, over five years, with zero residual value.

Requirements

1. Prepare BRC's income statement for the year ended December 31, 2018. Use the single-step format, with all revenues listed together and all expenses listed together.

2. Prepare BRC's balance sheet at December 31, 2018.

3. Prepare BRC's statement of cash flows for the year ended December 31, 2018. Format cash flows from operating activities by the *direct* method.

Learning Objective 4
Appendix CA

1. Net Cash Prov. by Op.
Act. $125,100
Collections from Cust. $438,900

PCA-37A Preparing the statement of cash flows—direct method

Use the Rolling Hills, Inc. data from Problem P14-34A.

Requirements

1. Prepare the 2018 statement of cash flows by the direct method.

2. How will what you learned in this problem help you evaluate an investment?

Learning Objective 5
Appendix CB

Cash Pmt. of Div. $28,300
Cash Pmt. for Acq. of
Land $25,200

PCB-38A Using a spreadsheet to prepare the statement of cash flows— indirect method

The 2018 comparative balance sheet and income statement of Appleton Group, Inc. follow. Appleton disposed of a plant asset at book value during 2018.

APPLETON GROUP, INC. Income Statement Year Ended December 31, 2018		
Net Sales Revenue		$ 443,000
Cost of Goods Sold		205,800
Gross Profit		237,200
Operating Expenses:		
Salaries Expense	$ 76,800	
Depreciation Expense—Plant Assets	15,400	
Other Operating Expenses	49,300	
Total Operating Expenses		141,500
Operating Income		95,700
Other Income and (Expenses):		
Interest Revenue	11,600	
Interest Expense	(24,400)	
Total Other Income and (Expenses)		(12,800)
Net Income Before Income Taxes		82,900
Income Tax Expense		16,200
Net Income		$ 66,700

APPLETON GROUP, INC.
Comparative Balance Sheet
December 31, 2018 and 2017

	2018	2017
Assets		
Current Assets:		
Cash	$ 14,700	$ 15,900
Accounts Receivable	42,200	43,900
Merchandise Inventory	97,600	93,900
Long-term Assets:		
Land	42,200	17,000
Plant Assets	121,950	110,750
Accumulated Depreciation—Plant Assets	(20,250)	(16,450)
Total Assets	$ 298,400	$ 265,000
Liabilities		
Current Liabilities:		
Accounts Payable	$ 25,900	$ 26,900
Accrued Liabilities	24,500	22,700
Long-term Liabilities:		
Notes Payable	51,000	65,000
Total Liabilities	101,400	114,600
Stockholders' Equity		
Common Stock, no par	138,900	130,700
Retained Earnings	58,100	19,700
Total Stockholders' Equity	197,000	150,400
Total Liabilities and Stockholders' Equity	$ 298,400	$ 265,000

Prepare the spreadsheet for the 2018 statement of cash flows. Format cash flows from operating activities by the indirect method. A plant asset was disposed of for $0. The cost and accumulated depreciation of the disposed asset was $11,600. There were no sales of land, no retirement of common stock, and no treasury stock transactions. Assume plant asset and land acquisitions were for cash.

> Problems Group B

PC-39B Identifying the purpose and preparing the statement of cash flows—indirect method

Learning Objectives 1, 2

2. Net Income $492,800
4. Net Cash Prov. by Op. Act. $359,500

Classic Rare Coins (CRC) was formed on January 1, 2018. Additional data for the year follow:

a. On January 1, 2018, CRC issued no par common stock for $525,000.

b. Early in January, CRC made the following cash payments:

1. For store fixtures, $51,000
2. For merchandise inventory, $240,000
3. For rent expense on a store building, $18,000

c. Later in the year, CRC purchased merchandise inventory on account for $243,000. Before year-end, CRC paid $153,000 of this accounts payable.

d. During 2018, CRC sold 2,800 units of merchandise inventory for $325 each. Before year-end, the company collected 95% of this amount. Cost of goods sold for the year was $290,000, and ending merchandise inventory totaled $193,000.

e. The store employs three people. The combined annual payroll is $82,000, of which CRC still owes $5,000 at year-end.

f. At the end of the year, CRC paid income tax of $17,000. There was no income taxes payable.

g. Late in 2018, CRC paid cash dividends of $38,000.

h. For store fixtures, CRC uses the straight-line depreciation method, over five years, with zero residual value.

Requirements

1. What is the purpose of the statement of cash flows?

2. Prepare CRC's income statement for the year ended December 31, 2018. Use the single-step format, with all revenues listed together and all expenses listed together.

3. Prepare CRC's balance sheet at December 31, 2018.

4. Prepare CRC's statement of cash flows using the indirect method for the year ended December 31, 2018.

Learning Objective 2

PC-40B Preparing the statement of cash flows—indirect method

Accountants for Benson, Inc. have assembled the following data for the year ended December 31, 2018:

Net Cash Prov. by Op. Act. $85,700

	2018	2017
Current Assets:		
Cash	$ 105,100	$ 18,000
Accounts Receivable	64,400	68,900
Merchandise Inventory	86,000	82,000
Current Liabilities:		
Accounts Payable	58,000	56,100
Income Tax Payable	14,700	16,900

Transaction Data for 2018:			
Issuance of common stock for cash	$ 37,000	Payment of notes payable	$ 47,100
Depreciation expense	24,000	Payment of cash dividends	53,000
Purchase of equipment with cash	69,000	Issuance of notes payable to borrow cash	68,000
Acquisition of land by issuing long-term notes payable	123,000	Gain on sale of building	4,500
Book value of building sold	61,000	Net income	66,000

Prepare Benson's statement of cash flows using the indirect method. Include an accompanying schedule of non-cash investing and financing activities.

PC-41B Preparing the statement of cash flows—indirect method with non-cash transactions

Learning Objective 2

1. Net Cash Prov. by Op. Act. $136,300

The 2018 income statement and comparative balance sheet of Sweet Valley, Inc. follow:

SWEET VALLEY, INC. Income Statement Year Ended December 31, 2018		
Net Sales Revenue		$ 445,000
Cost of Goods Sold		203,200
Gross Profit		241,800
Operating Expenses:		
Salaries Expense	$ 77,400	
Depreciation Expense—Plant Assets	14,500	
Other Operating Expenses	10,100	
Total Operating Expenses		102,000
Operating Income		139,800
Other Income and (Expenses):		
Interest Revenue	8,200	
Interest Expense	(21,100)	
Total Other Income and (Expenses)		(12,900)
Net Income Before Income Taxes		126,900
Income Tax Expense		19,400
Net Income		$ 107,500

SWEET VALLEY, INC.
Comparative Balance Sheet
December 31, 2018 and 2017

	2018	2017
Assets		
Current Assets:		
Cash	$ 26,300	$ 15,400
Accounts Receivable	26,400	25,100
Merchandise Inventory	79,300	91,300
Long-term Assets:		
Land	34,900	14,000
Plant Assets	115,790	108,330
Accumulated Depreciation—Plant Assets	(19,890)	(18,630)
Total Assets	$ 262,800	$ 235,500
Liabilities		
Current Liabilities:		
Accounts Payable	$ 35,600	$ 30,100
Accrued Liabilities	28,900	30,800
Long-term Liabilities:		
Notes Payable	78,000	105,000
Total Liabilities	142,500	165,900
Stockholders' Equity		
Common Stock, no par	88,200	64,800
Retained Earnings	32,100	4,800
Total Stockholders' Equity	120,300	69,600
Total Liabilities and Stockholders' Equity	$ 262,800	$ 235,500

Additionally, Sweet Valley purchased land of $20,900 by financing it 100% with long-term notes payable during 2018. During the year, there were no sales of land, no retirements of stock, and no treasury stock transactions. A plant asset was disposed of for $0. The cost and the accumulated depreciation of the disposed asset was $13,240. Plant asset was acquired for cash.

Requirements

1. Prepare the 2018 statement of cash flows, formatting operating activities by the *indirect* method.

2. How will what you learned in this problem help you evaluate an investment?

PC-42B Preparing the statement of cash flows—indirect method, evaluating cash flows, and measuring free cash flows

Learning Objectives 2, 3

The comparative balance sheet of Robeson Educational Supply at December 31, 2018, reported the following:

1. Net Cash Used for Inv. Act. $(157,400)

	2018	2017
Current Assets:		
Cash	$ 83,900	$ 20,500
Accounts Receivable	14,500	21,800
Merchandise Inventory	61,800	60,400
Current Liabilities:		
Accounts Payable	29,600	28,100
Accrued Liabilities	10,500	11,900

Robeson's transactions during 2018 included the following:

Payment of cash dividends	$ 21,200	Depreciation expense	$ 17,400
Purchase of equipment with cash	54,400	Purchase of building with cash	103,000
Issuance of long-term notes payable to borrow cash	44,000	Net income	63,600
Issuance of common stock for cash	111,000		

Requirements

1. Prepare the statement of cash flows of Robeson Educational Supply for the year ended December 31, 2018. Use the indirect method to report cash flows from operating activities.

2. Evaluate Robeson's cash flows for the year. Mention all three categories of cash flows, and give the reason for your evaluation.

3. If Robeson plans similar activity for 2018, what is its expected free cash flow?

PCA-43B Preparing the statement of cash flows—direct method

Learning Objective 4
Appendix CA

Diversion Rare Coins (DRC) was formed on January 1, 2018. Additional data for the year follow:

2. Total Assets $1,118,800
3. Collections from Cust. $918,000

a. On January 1, 2018, DRC issued no par common stock for $450,000.

b. Early in January, DRC made the following cash payments:

1. For store fixtures, $46,000
2. For merchandise inventory, $310,000
3. For rent expense on a store building, $18,000

c. Later in the year, DRC purchased merchandise inventory on account for $238,000. Before year-end, DRC paid $138,000 of this accounts payable.

d. During 2018, DRC sold 2,700 units of merchandise inventory for $400 each. Before year-end, the company collected 85% of this amount. Cost of goods sold for the year was $340,000, and ending merchandise inventory totaled $208,000.

e. The store employs three people. The combined annual payroll is $97,000, of which DRC still owes $6,000 at year-end.

f. At the end of the year, DRC paid income tax of $18,000. There was no income taxes payable.

g. Late in 2018, DRC paid cash dividends of $35,000.

h. For store fixtures, DRC uses the straight-line depreciation method, over five years, with zero residual value.

Requirements

1. Prepare DRC's income statement for the year ended December 31, 2018. Use the single-step format, with all revenues listed together and all expenses listed together.

2. Prepare DRC's balance sheet at December 31, 2018.

3. Prepare DRC's statement of cash flows for the year ended December 31, 2018. Format cash flows from operating activities by the direct method.

Learning Objective 4
Appendix CA

1. Net Cash Prov. by Op.
Act. $136,300
Collections from Cust. $443,700

PCA-44B Preparing the statement of cash flows—direct method

Use the Sweet Valley data from Problem P14-41B.

Requirements

1. Prepare the 2018 statement of cash flows by the direct method.

2. How will what you learned in this problem help you evaluate an investment?

Learning Objective 5
Appendix CB

Cash Pmt. of Div. $28,200
Cash Pmt. of N/P $13,000

PCB-45B Using a spreadsheet to prepare the statement of cash flows—indirect method

The 2018 comparative balance sheet and income statement of Attleboro Group, Inc. follow. Attleboro disposed of a plant asset at book value in 2018.

ATTLEBORO GROUP, INC. Income Statement Year Ended December 31, 2018		
Net Sales Revenue		$ 441,000
Cost of Goods Sold		205,400
Gross Profit		235,600
Operating Expenses:		
Salaries Expense	$ 76,300	
Depreciation Expense	15,300	
Other Operating Expenses	49,600	
Total Operating Expenses		141,200
Operating Income		94,400
Other Income and (Expenses):		
Interest Revenue	11,500	
Interest Expense	(24,400)	
Total Other Income and (Expenses)		(12,900)
Net Income Before Income Taxes		81,500
Income Tax Expense		16,200
Net Income		$ 65,300

ATTLEBORO GROUP, INC.
Comparative Balance Sheet
December 31, 2018 and 2017

	2018	2017
Assets		
Current Assets:		
Cash	$ 14,000	$ 15,500
Accounts Receivable	42,000	43,700
Merchandise Inventory	96,800	93,300
Long-term Assets:		
Land	36,400	11,000
Plant Assets	121,250	112,850
Accumulated Depreciation—Plant Assets	(20,350)	(18,650)
Total Assets	$ 290,100	$ 257,700
Liabilities		
Current Liabilities:		
Accounts Payable	$ 24,500	$ 26,000
Accrued Liabilities	23,900	22,600
Long-term Liabilities:		
Notes Payable	56,000	69,000
Total Liabilities	104,400	117,600
Stockholders' Equity		
Common Stock, no par	129,500	121,000
Retained Earnings	56,200	19,100
Total Stockholders' Equity	185,700	140,100
Total Liabilities and Stockholders' Equity	$ 290,100	$ 257,700

Prepare the spreadsheet for the 2018 statement of cash flows. Format cash flows from operating activities by the indirect method. A plant asset was disposed of for $0. The cost and accumulated depreciation of the disposed asset was $13,600. There were no sales of land, no retirement of common stock, and no treasury stock transactions. Assume plant asset and land acquisitions were for cash.

CRITICAL THINKING

> Using Excel

PC-46 Using Excel to prepare the statement of cash flows, indirect method

Download an Excel template for this problem online in MyAccountingLab or at http://www.pearsonhighered.com/Horngren.

The James Island Clothing Company began operations on July 1, 2018. The adjusted trial balance as of December 31, 2018, appears below, along with transaction data for 2018

James Island Clothing Company
Adjusted Trial Balance
December 31, 2018

Account Title	Balance Debit	Balance Credit
Cash	$ 95,700	
Accounts Receivable	12,000	
Inventory	4,400	
Office Equipment	26,000	
Truck	18,000	
Accumulated Depreciation—Plant Assets		$ 6,000
Accounts Payable		5,500
Note Payable (Short-term)		10,000
Note Payable (Long-term)		33,000
Common Stock		100,000
Retained Earnings		
Dividends	1,000	
Sales Revenue		15,000
Cost of Goods Sold	3,600	
Rent Expense	2,000	
Advertising Expense	800	
Depreciation Expense	6,000	
	$ 169,500	$ 169,500

Transaction data for 2018

Cash paid for purchase of office equipment	$ 6,000
Cash paid for purchase of truck	5,000
Acquisition of plant assets with a long-term notes payable	33,000
Cash payment of dividends	1,000
Cash receipt from issuance of common stock	100,000

Requirements

1. Complete the worksheet for the James Island Clothing Company, filling in the Transaction Analysis columns. Note: Some of the input cells marked in blue may not require entries.

2. Prepare the James Island Clothing Company statement of cash flows for the year ended December 31, 2018. Use the indirect method.

> Continuing Problem

PC-47 Preparing the statement of cash flows—indirect method

Canyon Canoe Company's comparative balance sheet is shown below. 2019 amounts are assumed, but include several transactions from prior chapters.

CANYON CANOE COMPANY Comparative Balance Sheet December 31, 2018 and 2019		
	2019	2018
Assets		
Current Assets:		
Cash	$ 523,693	$ 12,125
Short-term Investments, net	23,840	0
Accounts Receivable, net	2,422	7,600
Merchandise Inventory	355	0
Office Supplies	60	165
Prepaid Rent	0	2,000
Property, Plant, and Equipment:		
Land	155,000	85,000
Building	610,000	35,000
Canoes	12,000	12,000
Office Furniture and Equipment	150,000	0
Accumulated Depreciation—PP&E	(35,180)	(850)
Total Assets	**$ 1,442,190**	**$ 153,040**
Liabilities		
Current Liabilities:		
Accounts Payable	$ 5,195	$ 3,050
Utilities Payable	745	295
Telephone Payable	700	325
Wages Payable	4,250	1,250
Notes Payable	15,000	0
Interest Payable	350	50
Unearned Revenue	500	350
Long-term Liabilities:		
Notes Payable	7,200	7,200
Mortgage Payable	405,000	0
Bonds Payable	210,000	0
Discount on Bonds Payable	(1,270)	0
Total Liabilities	**647,670**	**12,520**
Stockholders' Equity		
Paid-In Capital:		
Preferred Stock	60,000	0
Paid-In Capital in Excess of Par—Preferred	10,000	0
Common Stock	186,000	136,000
Paid-In Capital in Excess of Par—Common	150,000	0
Retained Earnings	388,520	4,520
Total Stockholders' Equity	**794,520**	**140,520**
Total Liabilities and Stockholders' Equity	**$ 1,442,190**	**$ 153,040**

Additional data follow:

1. The income statement for 2019 included the following items:

   a. Net income, $417,000.

   b. Depreciation expense for the year, $34,330.

   c. Amortization on the bonds payable, $254.

2. There were no disposals of property, plant and equipment during the year. All acquisitions of PP&E were for cash except the land, which was acquired by issuing preferred stock.

3. The company issued bonds payable with a face value of $210,000, receiving cash of $208,476.

4. The company distributed 4,000 shares of common stock in a stock dividend when the market value was $4.50 per share. All other dividends were paid in cash.

5. The common stock, except for the stock dividend, was issued for cash.

6. The cash receipt from the notes payable in 2019 is considered a financing activity because it does not relate to operations.

Requirement

Prepare the statement of cash flows for the year ended December 31, 2019, using the indirect method.

> Tying It All Together Case

Before you begin this assignment, review the Tying It All Together feature in the chapter. It will also be helpful if you review Amazon.com, Inc.'s 2015 annual report (http://phx.corporate-ir.net/phoenix.zhtml?c=97664&p=irol-reportsAnnual).

Amazon.com, Inc. serves its customers through its retail Web sites, selling millions of unique products. In addition, the company manufactures and sells electronic devices including Kindle e-readers and Fire tablets. Amazon.com also offers Amazon Prime, a membership program that includes unlimited free shipping on items and access to unlimited streaming of movies and TV episodes.

Requirements

1. Review Item 7 (Management's Discussion and Analysis of Financial Condition and Results of Operations) included in the 2015 Annual Report. What does Amazon.com, Inc. state is the company's financial focus? What are free cash flows and how does Amazon.com plan to increase its free cash flows?

2. Review the statement of cash flows for Amazon.com, Inc. What type of noncash adjustments to net income did Amazon.com report in 2015?

3. Review the 2015 statement of cash flows for Amazon.com, Inc. What was the net cash provided (used) for investing activities? What were the cash inflows and outflows related to this section?

4. Review the 2015 statement of cash flows for Amazon.com, Inc. What was the net cash provided (used) for financing activities? What were the cash inflows and outflows related to this section?

> Decision Case C-1

Theater by Design and Show Cinemas are asking you to recommend their stock to your clients. Because Theater by Design and Show Cinemas earn about the same net income and have similar financial positions, your decision depends on their statement of cash flows, summarized as follows:

	Theater by Design		Show Cinemas	
Net Cash Provided by Operating Activities		$ 30,000		$ 70,000
Cash Provided by (Used for) Investing Activities:				
Purchase of Plant Assets	$ (20,000)		$ (100,000)	
Sale of Plant Assets	40,000	20,000	10,000	(90,000)
Cash Provided by (Used for) Financing Activities:				
Issuance of Common Stock		0		30,000
Payment of Long-term Debt		(40,000)		0
Net Increase (Decrease) in Cash		$ 10,000		$ 10,000

Based on their cash flows, which company looks better? Give your reasons.

> Ethical Issue C-1

Moss Exports is having a bad year. Net income is only $60,000. Also, two important overseas customers are falling behind in their payments to Moss, and Moss's accounts receivable are ballooning. The company desperately needs a loan. The Moss Exports Board of Directors is considering ways to put the best face on the company's financial statements. Moss's bank closely examines cash flow from operating activities. Daniel Peavey, Moss's controller, suggests reclassifying the receivables from the slow-paying clients as long-term. He explains to the board that removing the $80,000 increase in accounts receivable from current assets will increase net cash provided by operations. This approach may help Moss get the loan.

Requirements

1. Using only the amounts given, compute net cash provided by operations, both without and with the reclassification of the receivables. Which reporting makes Moss look better?

2. Under what condition would the reclassification of the receivables be ethical? Unethical?

> Financial Statement Case C-1

Details about a company's cash flows appear in a number of places in the annual report. Use **Target Corporation's** Fiscal 2015 Annual Report to answer the following questions. Visit **http://www.pearsonhighered.com/Horngren** to view a link to Target Corporation's Fiscal 2015 Annual Report.

Requirements

1. Which method does Target use to report net cash flows from *operating* activities? How can you tell?

2. Target earned net income during 2015. Did operations *provide* cash or *use* cash during 2015? Give the amount. How did net cash provided by (used for) operations during 2015 compare with net income in 2015?

3. For the year ended January 30, 2016 (fiscal year 2015), did Target pay cash dividends? If so, how much?

4. For the year ended January 30, 2016, did Target use cash to purchase property, plant, and equipment? If so, how much?

MyAccountingLab   **For a wealth of online resources, including exercises, problems, media, and immediate tutorial help, please visit** http://www.myaccountinglab.com.

> Quick Check Answers

1. d   **2.** d   **3.** b   **4.** a   **5.** d   **6.** c   **7.** c   **8.** c   **9A.** d   **10B.** a

Appendix D
Financial Statement Analysis

What Companies Should I Invest In?

Clara Wu misses her mom, Sylvia, a lot these days. Her mom always knew just the right words to say when Clara came to visit after a long hard day at work, and her mom's chocolate cookies always worked magic in making her feel better. Since her mom passed away six months ago, Clara has had to make a lot of decisions on her own. As executor of her mom's estate, she was responsible for helping the accountant and attorney finalize the financial details and the estate paperwork. Clara knew that once the estate was settled, she would be receiving a large amount of cash. She knew that deciding what to do with the cash would be a very important decision.

When Clara met with her financial planner, she shared her goals of paying off her student loans and other personal debt and then saving toward her retirement. She wanted to take the cash remaining after paying off her debts and invest it in the stock market. Clara was worried, though. She tried to stay current on the financial markets by reading the business section of the newspaper and listening to the financial news, but she wasn't sure how to decide which companies would be the best investment choices. Clara's financial planner advised her that there are a number of tools that she could use to evaluate companies and determine which company is more profitable. Other tools will be helpful in helping her determine trends across a period of time. Clara knew that with help from her financial planner and these tools she could make sense out of companies' financial statements and invest with a confidence that would make her mom proud.

What Are the Tools That Help Users Analyze a Business?

In this chapter, you learn about tools that allow users to see beyond the pure numbers on the financial statements and translate them into meaningful analysis. So far you have learned some of what it takes to prepare financial statements; now you will learn how to use financial statements to help manage a company effectively, make wise investments, and compare one company to another. Certified financial planners who work for companies, such as **Raymond James Financial, Inc.,** a financial services holding company that operates a full-service brokerage and investment firm headquartered in Florida, analyze financial statements to compare a company's performance across several periods of time. This comparison helps investors determine how a company is performing over time. In addition, financial planners use another tool, called *ratio analysis*, to measure one company against other companies in the same industry. Whether you will be an investor, an employee, or a manager of a company, knowing how to evaluate a company's performance accurately will help you make smart business decisions.

Appendix D Learning Objectives

1   Explain how financial statements are used to analyze a business

2   Perform a horizontal analysis of financial statements

3   Perform a vertical analysis of financial statements

4   Compute and evaluate the standard financial ratios

HOW ARE FINANCIAL STATEMENTS USED TO ANALYZE A BUSINESS?

Learning Objective 1

Explain how financial statements are used to analyze a business

In this chapter, we use what you have learned about financial statements to analyze Smart Touch Learning. We will determine if it was profitable, as well as its overall financial health.

Purpose of Analysis

Investors and creditors cannot evaluate a company by examining only one year's data. That is why most financial statements cover at least two periods. In fact, most financial analyses cover trends over three to five years. This chapter shows you how to use some of the analytical tools for charting a company's progress through time. These tools can be used by small business owners to measure performance, by financial analysts to analyze stock investments, by auditors to obtain an overall sense of a company's financial health, by creditors to determine credit risk, or by any other person wanting to compare financial data in relevant terms.

To accurately determine the financial performance of a company, such as Smart Touch Learning, we need to compare its performance in the following ways:

- from year to year
- with a competing company
- with the same industry as a whole

After this comparison, we will have a better idea of how to judge the company's present situation and predict what might happen in the near future.

Tools of Analysis

There are three main ways to analyze financial statements:

- Horizontal analysis provides a year-to-year comparison of a company's performance in different periods.
- Vertical analysis provides a way to compare different companies.
- Ratio analysis can be used to provide information about a company's performance. It is used most effectively to measure a company against other companies in the same industry and to denote trends within the company.

Corporate Financial Reports

Before we discuss the different tools available for financial statement analysis, let's review corporate financial reports.

Publicly traded corporations have their stock listed on public stock exchanges, such as the New York Stock Exchange or the NASDAQ. They are required by the Securities and Exchange Commission (SEC) to file annual and quarterly reports (also called a *Form 10-K* and *Form 10-Q*). An **annual report** provides information about a company's financial condition. These reports help investors make informed investment decisions.

Annual Report
Provides information about a company's financial condition.

Business Overview

A typical annual report begins with an overview of the business—including the industry the company is in, its growth strategy, and an overview of the company's brands. It also often discusses the company's competitors and the risks related to the company's business.

Management's Discussion and Analysis of Financial Condition and Results of Operations

Another part of the annual report is **management's discussion and analysis of financial condition and results of operations (MD&A).** This section of the annual report is intended to help investors understand the results of operations and the financial condition of the company. It is important to realize that this section is written by the company and could present a biased view of the company's financial condition and results. This section of the report is the company's attempt to explain its financial statements and to discuss its performance.

The MD&A section is of interest to investors, though, because it often contains information that is not found in the financial data. Such information might include how a company is planning to spend its cash during the next year for property, plant, and equipment or whether significant changes are expected to occur that would cause revenue or expenses to increase or decrease in the future. This section often provides forward-looking information that can be useful to investors who are trying to estimate what future earnings will be for the company.

Management's Discussion and Analysis of Financial Condition and Results of Operations (MD&A)
The section of the annual report that is intended to help investors understand the results of operations and the financial condition of the company.

Report of Independent Registered Public Accounting Firm

A report of the independent registered public accounting firm (often referred to as the *auditor's report*) is included in an annual report. The audit report attests to the fairness of the presentation of the financial statements and states whether the financial statements are presented in accordance with Generally Accepted Accounting Principles (GAAP). This report is prepared by an independent external auditor who has performed an audit on the financial statements. In addition, the external auditor is responsible for assessing the effectiveness of the company's internal controls.

Most audit reports have *unqualified opinions*, which means that the financial statements are presented fairly, in all material respects. A *qualified opinion* might be issued if the financial statements include a departure from GAAP. If the auditor finds that the financial statements are not represented fairly, an *adverse opinion* would be given.

DECISIONS

Should an unqualified opinion be issued?

Patty Schneider was performing the independent audit for Drake Storage, Inc. Patty was reviewing the work that her staff auditors had completed, and she had several concerns about the company's financial statements. Patty's staff had determined that Drake had underreported its cost of goods sold in order to overstate net income. Patty had spoken to Drake Storage's audit committee and discussed her concerns. The audit committee disagreed with the accounting firm's findings. What should Patty do?

Solution

Patty's accounting firm should issue either a qualified opinion or an adverse opinion. To issue an unqualified opinion stating that the financial statements are presented fairly in all material respects would be misleading to investors and creditors. As an independent auditor, Patty's primary responsibility is to report on the fairness of the financial statements and assure the public that the financial statements are presented in accordance with GAAP. If they are not, her firm has a responsibility to issue either a qualified or adverse opinion.

Financial Statements

An annual report contains the four basic financial statements you have learned in this text-book: the balance sheet (sometimes referred to as *statement of financial position*), the income statement (or *statement of operations*), the statement of stockholders' equity, and the statement of cash flows. Corporations are required to report multiple-period information for all financial statements. For example, the **Kohl's Corporation** 2015 Annual Report presents financial data for the past three fiscal periods (2015, 2014, and 2013).

Notes to Financial Statements

Immediately following the financial statements are the notes to the financial statements. These notes include a summary of significant accounting policies and explanations of specific items on the financial statements. These notes are an important part of the financial statements and are often referred to by investors to understand the information included in the financial statements.

Match the different parts of the annual report with the appropriate description.

1. Includes the income statement, balance sheet, statement of stockholders' equity, and statement of cash flows.

2. Attests to the fairness of the presentation of the financial statements.

3. Includes a summary of significant accounting policies and explanations of specific items on the financial statements.

4. Is written by the company to help investors understand the results of operations and the financial condition of the company.

a. Notes to financial statements

b. Report of independent registered public accounting firm

c. Management's discussion and analysis of financial condition and results of operations (MD&A)

d. Financial statements

Check your answers online in MyAccountingLab or at http://www.pearsonhighered.com/Horngren.

For more practice, see Short Exercise SD-1.   MyAccountingLab

HOW DO WE USE HORIZONTAL ANALYSIS TO ANALYZE A BUSINESS?

Learning Objective 2

Perform a horizontal analysis of financial statements

Many decisions hinge on whether the numbers—sales, expenses, and net income, for example—are increasing or decreasing. For example, have sales and other revenues risen from last year? By how much?

Sales may have increased, but considered in isolation, this fact is not very helpful. The *percentage change* in sales over time is more relative and, therefore, more helpful. For example, if a company had sales of $100,000 one year and sales increased by $50,000 the next year, that would be a significant increase. However, if the company had sales of $1 billion and sales increased by $50,000, that would not be significant. Therefore, it is often more relevant to know the percentage increase than the dollar increase.

The study of percentage changes in line items from comparative financial statements is called **horizontal analysis**. Horizontal analysis compares the change in each financial statement item from one year to the next. Computing a percentage change in comparative statements requires two steps:

1. Compute the dollar amount of the change in a line item from the earlier period to the later period.
2. Divide the dollar amount of change by the earlier period amount, and multiply by 100. We call the earlier period the base period.

Horizontal Analysis
The study of percentage changes in line items from comparative financial statements. (Dollar amount of change / Base period amount) × 100.

Horizontal analysis is illustrated for Smart Touch Learning as:

	2020	2019	Increase (Decrease)	
			Amount	Percentage
Net Sales Revenue	$858,000	$803,000	$55,000	6.8%

Smart Touch Learning's net sales revenue increased by 6.8% during 2020, computed as follows:

Step 1: Compute the dollar amount of change in sales from 2019 to 2020:

Dollar amount of change = Later period amount − Earlier period amount
= $858,000 − $803,000
= $55,000

Step 2: Divide the dollar amount of change by the base period amount and multiply by 100. This computes the percentage change for the period:

Horizontal analysis % = (Dollar amount of change / Base period amount) × 100
= ($55,000 / $803,000) × 100
= 6.8%*

*All percentage calculations are rounded to the nearest tenth for the rest of this chapter.

Horizontal Analysis of the Income Statement

The horizontal analysis of Smart Touch Learning's income statement is shown in Exhibit D-1 (on the next page). This comparative income statement reveals a significant amount of growth during 2020. Net sales revenue increased by 6.8% while Cost of Goods Sold increased by only 0.8%, resulting in a 17.3% increase in gross profit. Additionally, Smart Touch Learning was able to control its operating expenses, creating a 77.2% growth in operating income.

Two items on Smart Touch Learning's income statement with the slowest growth rates are Cost of Goods Sold and Administrative Expenses. Cost of Goods Sold increased by only 0.8%, and administrative expenses decreased by 4.1%. On the bottom line, net income grew by an incredible 84.6%. That is real progress!

Exhibit D-1 | **Comparative Income Statement—Horizontal Analysis**

SMART TOUCH LEARNING Income Statement Years Ended December 31, 2020 and 2019			Increase (Decrease)	
	2020	**2019**	**Amount**	**Percentage**
Net Sales Revenue	$ 858,000	$ 803,000	$ 55,000	6.8%
Cost of Goods Sold	513,000	509,000	4,000	0.8
Gross Profit	345,000	294,000	51,000	17.3
Operating Expenses:				
Selling Expenses	126,000	114,000	12,000	10.5
Administrative Expenses	118,000	123,000	(5,000)	(4.1)
Total Operating Expenses	244,000	237,000	7,000	3.0
Operating Income	101,000	57,000	44,000	77.2
Other Income and (Expenses):				
Interest Revenue	4,000	0	4,000	—
Interest Expense	(24,000)	(14,000)	10,000	71.4
Total Other Income and (Expenses)	(20,000)	(14,000)	6,000	42.9
Income Before Income Taxes	81,000	43,000	38,000	88.4
Income Tax Expense	33,000	17,000	16,000	94.1
Net Income	$ 48,000	$ 26,000	$ 22,000	84.6%

Horizontal Analysis of the Balance Sheet

Horizontal analysis of Smart Touch Learning's comparative balance sheet is shown in Exhibit D-2. This analysis also shows growth in assets, with total assets increasing by 22.2%. Notice that both Cash and Cash Equivalents and Prepaid Expenses decreased during the year, but these decreases were offset by increases in other assets.

Smart Touch Learning's total liabilities also grew. Total liabilities increased by 33.0% but notice that Accrued Liabilities decreased by 12.9%, as indicated by the percentage in parentheses. This is another indicator of positive growth for Smart Touch Learning because it implies the corporation is using debt to grow the company. Accrued liabilities actually decreased, as indicated by the liability figures in parentheses.

Exhibit D-2 | **Comparative Balance Sheet—Horizontal Analysis**

SMART TOUCH LEARNING Balance Sheet December 31, 2020 and 2019				
	2020	**2019**	**Increase (Decrease)**	
			Amount	**Percentage**
Assets				
Current Assets:				
Cash and Cash Equivalents	$ 29,000	$ 32,000	$ (3,000)	(9.4)%
Accounts Receivable, Net	114,000	85,000	29,000	34.1
Merchandise Inventory	113,000	111,000	2,000	1.8
Prepaid Expenses	6,000	8,000	(2,000)	(25.0)
Total Current Assets	262,000	236,000	26,000	11.0
Property, Plant, and Equipment, Net	507,000	399,000	108,000	27.1
Long-term Investments	18,000	9,000	9,000	100.0
Total Assets	$ 787,000	$ 644,000	$ 143,000	22.2%
Liabilities				
Current Liabilities:				
Accounts Payable	$ 73,000	$ 68,000	$ 5,000	7.4%
Accrued Liabilities	27,000	31,000	(4,000)	(12.9)
Notes Payable	42,000	27,000	15,000	55.6
Total Current Liabilities	142,000	126,000	16,000	12.7
Long-term Liabilities	289,000	198,000	91,000	46.0
Total Liabilities	431,000	324,000	107,000	33.0
Stockholders' Equity				
Common Stock, no par	186,000	186,000	0	0.0
Retained Earnings	170,000	134,000	36,000	26.9
Total Stockholders' Equity	356,000	320,000	36,000	11.3
Total Liabilities and Stockholders' Equity	$ 787,000	$ 644,000	$ 143,000	22.2%

Trend Analysis

Trend analysis is a form of horizontal analysis. Trend percentages indicate the direction a business is taking. For example, how have sales changed over a five-year period? What trend does net income show? These questions can be answered by trend analysis over a period, such as three to five years.

Trend analysis percentages are computed by selecting a base period (for example, the earliest year). The base period amounts are set equal to 100%. The amounts for each subsequent year are expressed as a percentage of the base amount. To compute trend analysis percentages, we divide each item for the following years by the base period amount and multiply by 100.

> **Trend Analysis**
> A form of horizontal analysis in which percentages are computed by selecting a base period as 100% and expressing amounts for following periods as a percentage of the base period amount. (Any period amount / Base period amount) × 100.

Trend % = (Any period amount / Base period amount) × 100

Assume Smart Touch Learning's Net Sales Revenue were $750,000 in 2016 and rose to $858,000 in 2020. To illustrate trend analysis, review the trend of net sales revenue during 2016–2020. The base year is 2016, the earliest year, so that year's percentage is set equal to 100.

	2020	2019	2018	2017	2016
Net Sales Revenue	$ 858,000	$ 803,000	$ 780,000	$ 748,000	$ 750,000
Trend Percentages	114.4%	107.1%	104.0%	99.7%	100.0%

We want percentages for the five-year period 2016–2020. We compute these by dividing each year's net sales revenue amount by the 2016 net sales revenue amount and multiply by 100. For example, the trend percentage for 2017 is calculated as follows:

$$\text{Trend \%} = (\text{Any period amount} / \text{Base period amount}) \times 100$$
$$= (\$748,000 / \$750,000) \times 100$$
$$= 99.7\%$$

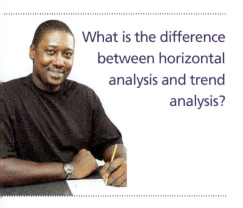

What is the difference between horizontal analysis and trend analysis?

Notice that net sales revenue decreased slightly in 2017, and then the rate of growth increased from 2018–2020. You can perform a trend analysis on any one or multiple item(s) you consider important. Trend analysis is widely used to predict the future health of a company.

Trend analysis and horizontal analysis are very similar, but they can be used to indicate different things for a company. **Horizontal analysis allows a company to see the percentage change from one year to the next. Trend analysis shows the percentage change from a base year forward to determine whether the trend in net sales revenue, for example, is positive or negative over a longer period of time.**

Try It!

5. Freedom Corp. reported the following on its comparative income statement:

(*In millions*)	2019	2018
Net Sales Revenue	$ 10,000	$ 8,000
Cost of Goods Sold	4,500	3,000

Prepare a horizontal analysis of net sales revenue, cost of goods sold, and gross profit—both in dollar amounts and in percentages.

Check your answers online in MyAccountingLab or at http://www.pearsonhighered.com/Horngren.

For more practice, see Short Exercises SD-2 and SD-3.   MyAccountingLab

HOW DO WE USE VERTICAL ANALYSIS TO ANALYZE A BUSINESS?

Learning Objective 3

Perform a vertical analysis of financial statements

As you have seen, horizontal analysis and trend analysis percentages highlight changes in an item from year to year, or over *time*. But no single technique gives a complete picture of a business, so we also need vertical analysis.

Vertical analysis of a financial statement shows the relationship of each item to its base amount, which is the 100% figure. Every other item on the statement is then reported as a percentage of that base. For the income statement, net sales revenue is the base. For the balance sheet, total assets is the base.

Vertical Analysis
An analysis of a financial statement that reveals the relationship of each statement item to its base amount, which is the 100% figure. (Specific item / Base amount) × 100.

> Vertical analysis % = (Specific item / Base amount) × 100

Vertical Analysis of the Income Statement

Exhibit D-3 shows the completed vertical analysis of Smart Touch Learning's 2020 and 2019 comparative income statement.

Exhibit D-3 | **Comparative Income Statement—Vertical Analysis**

SMART TOUCH LEARNING Income Statement Years Ended December 31, 2020 and 2019				
	2020	Percent of Total	2019	Percent of Total
Net Sales Revenue	$ 858,000	100.0%	$ 803,000	100.0%
Cost of Goods Sold	513,000	59.8	509,000	63.4
Gross Profit	345,000	40.2	294,000	36.6
Operating Expenses:				
Selling Expenses	126,000	14.7	114,000	14.2
Administrative Expenses	118,000	13.8	123,000	15.3
Total Operating Expenses	244,000	28.4	237,000	29.5
Operating Income	101,000	11.8	57,000	7.1
Other Income and (Expenses):				
Interest Revenue	4,000	0.5	0	0.0
Interest Expense	(24,000)	(2.8)	(14,000)	(1.7)
Total Other Income and (Expenses)	(20,000)	(2.3)	(14,000)	(1.7)
Income Before Income Taxes	81,000	9.4	43,000	5.4
Income Tax Expense	33,000	3.8	17,000	2.1
Net Income	$ 48,000	5.6%	$ 26,000	3.2%

The vertical analysis percentage for Smart Touch Learning's cost of goods sold is 59.8% of net sales revenue (($513,000 / $858,000) × 100 = 59.8%) in 2020 and 63.4% (($509,000 / $803,000) × 100 = 63.4%) in 2019. This means that for every $1 in net sales revenue, almost $0.60 in 2020 and approximately $0.63 in 2019 is spent on cost of goods sold. This percentage decrease in cost of goods sold helps explain the percentage increase in gross profit as calculated in the horizontal analysis in Exhibit 15-1. Smart Touch Learning was able to decrease the cost of goods sold by more than $0.03 for every $1 of net sales revenue.

Smart Touch Learning's net income is 5.6% of net sales revenue in 2020 and 3.2% of net sales revenue in 2019. That improvement from 2019 to 2020 is extremely good. Suppose under normal conditions a company's net income is 10% of revenues. A drop to 4% may cause the investors to be alarmed and sell their stock.

Vertical Analysis of the Balance Sheet

Exhibit D-4 depicts the vertical analysis of Smart Touch Learning's balance sheet. The base amount (100%) is total assets. The base amount is also total liabilities and stockholders' equity because they are exactly the same number (remember the accounting equation); in 2020, that's $787,000.

Exhibit D-4 | **Comparative Balance Sheet—Vertical Analysis**

SMART TOUCH LEARNING				
Balance Sheet				
December 31, 2020 and 2019				
	2020	**Percent of Total**	**2019**	**Percent of Total**
Assets				
Current Assets:				
Cash and Cash Equivalents	$ 29,000	3.7%	$ 32,000	5.0%
Accounts Receivable, Net	114,000	14.5	85,000	13.2
Merchandise Inventory	113,000	14.4	111,000	17.2
Prepaid Expenses	6,000	0.8	8,000	1.2
Total Current Assets	262,000	33.3	236,000	36.6
Property, Plant, and Equipment, Net	507,000	64.4	399,000	62.0
Long-term Investments	18,000	2.3	9,000	1.4
Total Assets	$ 787,000	100.0%	$ 644,000	100.0%
Liabilities				
Current Liabilities:				
Accounts Payable	$ 73,000	9.3%	$ 68,000	10.6%
Accrued Liabilities	27,000	3.4	31,000	4.8
Notes Payable	42,000	5.3	27,000	4.2
Total Current Liabilities	142,000	18.0	126,000	19.6
Long-term Liabilities	289,000	36.7	198,000	30.7
Total Liabilities	431,000	54.8	324,000	50.3
Stockholders' Equity				
Common Stock, no par	186,000	23.6	186,000	28.9
Retained Earnings	170,000	21.6	134,000	20.8
Total Stockholders' Equity	356,000	45.2	320,000	49.7
Total Liabilities and Stockholders' Equity	$ 787,000	100.0%	$ 644,000	100.0%

The vertical analysis of Smart Touch Learning's balance sheet reveals several interesting things:

- Current assets make up 33.3% of total assets in 2020 and 36.6% of total assets in 2019. This is typical for most companies with current assets representing close to 30% of total assets.
- Total liabilities are 54.8% of total assets in 2020, increasing slightly from 2019, 50.3%.
- Stockholders' equity makes up 45.2% of total assets in 2020 and 49.7% of total assets in 2019. The percentage share of total assets was nearly equally distributed between total liabilities and total equity for both years.

Common-Size Statements

Horizontal analysis and vertical analysis provide much useful data about a company. As we have seen, Smart Touch Learning's percentages depict a very successful company. But the data apply only to one business.

To compare Smart Touch Learning to another company, we can use a common-size statement. A **common-size statement** reports only percentages—the same percentages that appear in a vertical analysis. By only reporting percentages, it removes dollar value bias when comparing one company to another company. **Dollar value bias** is the bias one sees from comparing numbers in absolute (dollars) rather than relative (percentage) terms. For us, $1 million seems like a large number. For some large companies, it is immaterial.

We could prepare common-size statements for Smart Touch Learning from year to year; however, we will start by preparing common-size income statements for Smart Touch Learning and Learning School, another fictitious company, both of which compete in the same industry. Which company earns a higher percentage of revenues as profits for its shareholders? Exhibit D-5 gives both companies' common-size income statements for 2020 so that we can compare them on a relative, not absolute, basis.

Common-Size Statement
A financial statement that reports only percentages (no dollar amounts).

Dollar Value Bias
The bias one sees from comparing numbers in absolute (dollars) rather than relative (percentage) terms.

Exhibit D-5 | **Common-Size Income Statement—Smart Touch Learning Versus Learning School**

SMART TOUCH LEARNING Versus LEARNING SCHOOL Common-Size Income Statement Year Ended December 31, 2020	Smart Touch Learning	Learning School
Net Sales Revenue	100.0%	100.0%
Cost of Goods Sold	59.8	36.3
Gross Profit	40.2	63.7
Operating Expenses:		
Selling Expenses	14.7	21.8
Administrative Expenses	13.8	7.3
Total Operating Expenses	28.4	29.1
Operating Income	11.8	34.6
Other Income and (Expenses):		
Interest Revenue	0.5	11.5
Interest Expense	(2.8)	(10.3)
Total Other Income and (Expenses)	(2.3)	1.2
Income Before Income Taxes	9.4	35.8
Income Tax Expense	3.8	12.3
Net Income	5.6%	23.5%

Exhibit D-5 shows that Learning School was more profitable than Smart Touch Learning in 2020. Learning School's gross profit percentage is 63.7%, compared with Smart Touch Learning's 40.2%. This means that Learning School is earning more gross profit from every dollar of revenue than Smart Touch Learning is earning. And, most importantly, Learning School's percentage of net income to revenues is 23.5%. That means almost one-fourth of Learning School's revenues result in profits for the company's stockholders. Smart Touch

Learning's percentage of net income to revenues, on the other hand, is 5.6%, significantly lower than Learning School's. Smart Touch Learning's lower net income is directly attributable to its larger percentage of cost of goods sold to net sales revenue. Smart Touch Learning's cost of goods sold represents 59.8% of net sales revenue, whereas Learning School's cost of goods sold is only 36.3%.

Benchmarking

Benchmarking
The practice of comparing a company's performance with best practices from other companies.

Benchmarking is the practice of comparing a company's performance with best practices from other companies. It often uses the common-size percentages in a graphical manner to highlight differences. There are two main types of benchmarks in financial statement analysis: benchmarking against a key competitor and benchmarking against the industry average.

Benchmarking Against a Key Competitor

Exhibit D-5 uses a key competitor, Learning School, to compare Smart Touch Learning's profitability. The two companies compete in the same industry, so Learning School serves as an ideal benchmark for Smart Touch Learning. The charts in Exhibit D-6 highlight the profitability difference between the companies. Focus on the segments of the graphs showing cost of goods sold and net income. Learning School is clearly more profitable than Smart Touch Learning, primarily because its cost of goods sold is significantly lower.

Exhibit D-6 | **Graphical Analysis of Common-Size Income Statement—Smart Touch Learning Versus Learning School**

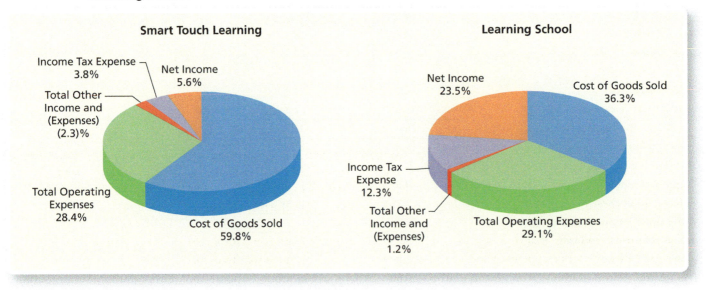

Benchmarking Against the Industry Average

The industry average can also serve as a very useful benchmark for evaluating a company. An industry comparison would show how Smart Touch Learning is performing alongside the average for the e-learning industry. *Annual Statement Studies*, published by the Risk Management Association, provides common-size statements for most industries. To compare Smart Touch Learning to the industry average, we would simply insert the industry-average common-size income statement in place of Learning School in Exhibit D-5.

As you are taking classes toward your degree, how do you know how quickly you can complete your studies? If you knew the average credit hours taken each semester was 12 credit hours, then 12 credit hours would be your benchmark. Comparing the number of classes you take to the average of 12 credit hours a semester is the same concept as benchmarking. Maybe you are taking 15 credit hours a semester. Then you'd be completing your degree faster than the average student. Maybe you take only 3 credit hours in the spring so you can work a part-time job. Then you'd be completing classes at a slower pace than average.

Try It!

6. Monroe Corp. reported the following amounts on its balance sheet at December 31, 2018 and 2017:

	2018	2017
Cash and Receivables	$ 35,000	$ 40,000
Merchandise Inventory	20,000	15,000
Property, Plant, and Equipment, Net	80,000	60,000
Total Assets	$ 135,000	$ 115,000

Prepare a vertical analysis of Monroe Corp. for 2018 and 2017.

Check your answers online in MyAccountingLab or at http://www.pearsonhighered.com/Horngren.

For more practice, see Short Exercises SD-4 and SD-5. MyAccountingLab

HOW DO WE USE RATIOS TO ANALYZE A BUSINESS?

Online financial databases, such as LexisNexis and the Dow Jones, provide data on thousands of companies. Suppose you want to compare some companies' recent earnings histories. You might want to compare companies' returns on stockholders' equity. You could use a computer to search the databases and give you the names of the 20 companies with the highest return on equity. You can use any ratio to search for information that is relevant to a particular decision.

Learning Objective 4
Compute and evaluate the standard financial ratios

Remember, however, that no single ratio tells the whole picture of any company's performance. Different ratios explain different aspects of a company. The ratios we discuss in this chapter may be classified and used for the following purposes:

- Evaluating the ability to pay current liabilities
- Evaluating the ability to sell merchandise inventory and collect receivables
- Evaluating the ability to pay long-term debt
- Evaluating profitability
- Evaluating stock as an investment

We will use the comparative income statement and balance sheet of Smart Touch Learning, shown in Exhibit D-7, to discuss the ratios that can be used to evaluate a company. Let's begin by discussing ratios that can be used to evaluate a company's ability to pay its current liabilities.

Exhibit D-7 | Comparative Financial Statements

SMART TOUCH LEARNING Balance Sheet December 31, 2020 and 2019		
	2020	2019
Assets		
Current Assets:		
Cash and Cash Equivalents	$ 29,000	$ 32,000
Accounts Receivable, Net	114,000	85,000
Merchandise Inventory	113,000	111,000
Prepaid Expenses	6,000	8,000
Total Current Assets	262,000	236,000
Property, Plant, and Equipment, Net	507,000	399,000
Long-term Investments	18,000	9,000
Total Assets	$ 787,000	$ 644,000
Liabilities		
Current Liabilities:		
Accounts Payable	$ 73,000	$ 68,000
Accrued Liabilities	27,000	31,000
Notes Payable	42,000	27,000
Total Current Liabilities	142,000	126,000
Long-term Liabilities	289,000	198,000
Total Liabilities	431,000	324,000
Stockholders' Equity		
Common Stock, no par	186,000	186,000
Retained Earnings	170,000	134,000
Total Stockholders' Equity	356,000	320,000
Total Liabilities and Stockholders' Equity	$ 787,000	$ 644,000

SMART TOUCH LEARNING Income Statement Years Ended December 31, 2020 and 2019		
	2020	2019
Net Sales Revenue	$ 858,000	$ 803,000
Cost of Goods Sold	513,000	509,000
Gross Profit	345,000	294,000
Operating Expenses:		
Selling Expenses	126,000	114,000
Administrative Expenses	118,000	123,000
Total Operating Expenses	244,000	237,000
Operating Income	101,000	57,000
Other Income and (Expenses):		
Interest Revenue	4,000	0
Interest Expense	(24,000)	(14,000)
Total Other Income and (Expenses)	(20,000)	(14,000)
Income Before Income Taxes	81,000	43,000
Income Tax Expense	33,000	17,000
Net Income	$ 48,000	$ 26,000

Evaluating the Ability to Pay Current Liabilities

In this section, we discuss one equation and three ratios that measure a company's ability to pay current liabilities.

Working Capital

Working Capital
A measure of a business's ability to meet its short-term obligations with its current assets. Current assets – Current liabilities.

Determining a company's working capital is a good starting place to evaluate a company's ability to pay its current liabilities. **Working capital** measures the ability to meet short-term obligations with current assets. Working capital is defined as follows:

Working capital = Current assets − Current liabilities

Smart Touch Learning's working capital at December 31, 2020 and 2019, is calculated as follows:

Working capital = Current assets − Current liabilities
2020: $262,000 − $142,000 = $120,000
2019: $236,000 − $126,000 = $110,000

Smart Touch Learning's working capital is positive, indicating that the company has more current assets than current liabilities, but additional information would be helpful. Three additional decision tools based on working capital are the cash ratio, acid-test ratio, and current ratio.

Cash Ratio

Cash is an important part of every business. Without an adequate supply of available cash, businesses cannot continue to operate. Businesses, therefore, monitor cash very carefully. One measure that can be used to calculate a company's liquidity is the cash ratio. The cash ratio helps to determine a company's ability to meet its short-term obligations and is calculated as cash plus cash equivalents divided by total current liabilities.

Cash Ratio
A measure of a company's ability to pay current liabilities from cash and cash equivalents: (Cash + Cash equivalents) / Total current liabilities.

Notice that the cash ratio includes cash and cash equivalents. As a reminder, cash equivalents are highly liquid investments that can be converted into cash in three months or less. Examples of cash equivalents are money-market accounts and investments in U.S. government securities.

The cash ratios of Smart Touch Learning, at December 31, 2020 and 2019, along with the average for the industry are as follows:

$$\text{Cash ratio} = \frac{\text{Cash + Cash equivalents}}{\text{Total current liabilities}}$$

$$2020: \frac{\$29,000}{\$142,000} = 0.20$$

$$2019: \frac{\$32,000}{\$126,000} = 0.25$$

$$\text{Industry average} = 0.40$$

The cash ratio has decreased slightly from 2019 to 2020 due to a decrease in available cash and cash equivalents and an increase in total current liabilities. This ratio is the most conservative valuation of liquidity because it looks at only cash and cash equivalents, leaving out other current assets such as merchandise inventory and accounts receivable. Notice that for both years, the cash ratio was below 1.0. Having a cash ratio below 1.0 is a good thing. A cash ratio above 1.0 might signify that the company has an unnecessarily large amount of cash supply. This cash could be used to generate higher profits or be distributed as dividends to stockholders. However, a very low ratio doesn't send a strong message to investors and creditors that the company has the ability to repay its short-term debt.

Acid-Test (or Quick) Ratio

The acid-test ratio (sometimes called the *quick ratio*) tells us whether a company could pay all its current liabilities if they came due immediately. That is, could the company pass the acid test? The acid-test ratio is not as stringent as the cash ratio because it includes more assets in the calculation.

Acid-Test Ratio
The ratio of the sum of cash, cash equivalents, short-term investments, and net current receivables to total current liabilities. The ratio tells whether the entity could pay all its current liabilities if they came due immediately. (Cash including cash equivalents + Short-term investments + Net current receivables) / Total current liabilities.

To compute the acid-test ratio, we add cash and cash equivalents, short-term investments (those that may be sold in the next 12 months or the business operating cycle, whichever is longer), and net current receivables (accounts receivable and notes receivable, net of allowances) and divide this sum by total current liabilities. Merchandise inventory and prepaid expenses are *not* included in the acid-test ratio because they are the least-liquid current assets. Smart Touch Learning's acid-test ratios for 2020 and 2019 follow:

$$\text{Acid-test ratio} = \frac{\text{Cash including cash equivalents} + \text{Short-term investments} + \text{Net current receivables}}{\text{Total current liabilities}}$$

$$2020: \frac{\$29,000 + \$0 + \$114,000}{\$142,000} = 1.01$$

$$2019: \frac{\$32,000 + \$0 + \$85,000}{\$126,000} = 0.93$$

$$\text{Industry average} = 0.46$$

The company's acid-test ratio improved during 2020 and is significantly better than the industry average. The norm for the acid-test ratio ranges from 0.20 for shoe retailers to 1.20 for manufacturers of equipment, as reported by the Risk Management Association. An acid-test ratio of 0.90 to 1.00 is acceptable in most industries.

Current Ratio

Current Ratio

Measures the company's ability to pay current liabilities from current assets. Total current assets / Total current liabilities.

The most widely used ratio is the **current ratio,** which is calculated as the total current assets divided by total current liabilities. The current ratio measures a company's ability to pay its current liabilities with its current assets. It is less stringent than the acid-test ratio and the cash ratio because it includes all current assets in the calculation.

The current ratios of Smart Touch Learning, at December 31, 2020 and 2019, along with the average for the industry, are as follows:

$$\text{Current ratio} = \frac{\text{Total current assets}}{\text{Total current liabilities}}$$

$$2020: \frac{\$262,000}{\$142,000} = 1.85$$

$$2019: \frac{\$236,000}{\$126,000} = 1.87$$

$$\text{Industry average} = 0.60$$

A high current ratio indicates that the business has sufficient current assets to maintain normal business operations. Compare Smart Touch Learning's current ratio of 1.85 for 2020 with the industry average of 0.60.

What is an acceptable current ratio? The answer depends on the industry. The norm for companies in most industries is around 1.50, as reported by the Risk Management Association. Smart Touch Learning's current ratio of 1.85 is strong. Keep in mind that we would not want to see a current ratio that is too high, say 2.5. This would indicate that the company is too liquid and, therefore, is not using its current assets effectively. For example, the company may need to reduce merchandise inventory levels so as not to tie up available resources.

ETHICS

Should the debt be reclassified?

Victor Brannon, senior accountant for Moose Corporation, was preparing the latest financial ratios. He knew that the ratios were watched carefully by Moose Corporation's lenders due to strict loan agreements that required the corporation to maintain a minimum current ratio of 1.5. Victor knew that the past quarter's financial ratios would not meet the lenders' requirements. His boss, Cara Romano, suggested that Victor classify a note payable due in 11 months as a long-term liability. What should Victor do? What would you do?

Solution

Liabilities are classified as current if they will be settled within one year or the operating cycle, whichever is longer. The classification between current and long-term is clear. Victor should not classify the note payable as a long-term liability. It should be classified as current even though the corporation will not meet the lenders' requirements.

Evaluating the Ability to Sell Merchandise Inventory and Collect Receivables

In this section, we discuss five ratios that measure a company's ability to sell merchandise inventory and collect receivables.

Inventory Turnover

The **inventory turnover** ratio measures the number of times a company sells its average level of merchandise inventory during a year. A high rate of turnover indicates ease in selling merchandise inventory; a low rate indicates difficulty. A value of 4 means that the company sold its average level of merchandise inventory four times—once every three months—during the year.

To compute inventory turnover, we divide cost of goods sold by the average merchandise inventory for the period. We use the cost of goods sold—not sales—because both cost of goods sold and inventory are stated *at cost*. Sales at *sales price* are not comparable with merchandise inventory *at cost*.

Smart Touch Learning's inventory turnover for 2020 is as follows:

Inventory Turnover
Measures the number of times a company sells its average level of merchandise inventory during a period. Cost of goods sold / Average merchandise inventory.

$$\text{Inventory turnover} = \frac{\text{Cost of goods sold}}{\text{Average merchandise inventory}}$$

$$2020: \frac{\$513,000}{[(\$111,000 + \$113,000)/2]} = 4.58$$

$$\text{Industry average} = 27.70$$

Cost of goods sold comes from the income statement (Exhibit D-7). Average merchandise inventory is figured by adding the beginning merchandise inventory of $111,000 to the ending inventory of $113,000 and dividing by 2. (See the balance sheet, Exhibit D-7. Remember that 2019's ending balances become 2020's beginning balances.)

Inventory turnover varies widely with the nature of the business. For example, most manufacturers of farm machinery have an inventory turnover close to three times a year. In contrast, companies that remove natural gas from the ground hold their merchandise inventory for a very short period of time and have an average turnover of 30. Smart Touch Learning's turnover of 4.58 times a year means, on average, the company has enough inventory to handle sales for almost 80 days (365 / 4.58 times). The inventory turnover is very low for this industry, which has an average turnover of 27.70 times per year. This ratio has identified an area in which Smart Touch Learning needs to improve.

Days' Sales in Inventory

Another key measure is the **days' sales in inventory** ratio. This measures the average number of days merchandise inventory is held by the company. Smart Touch Learning's days' sales in inventory for 2020 is as follows:

Days' Sales in Inventory
Measures the average number of days that inventory is held by a company. 365 days / Inventory turnover.

$$\text{Days' sales in inventory} = \frac{365 \text{ days}}{\text{Inventory turnover}}$$

$$2020: \frac{365 \text{ days}}{4.58} = 79.7 \text{ days}$$

$$\text{Industry average} = 13 \text{ days}$$

Days' sales in inventory varies widely, depending on the business. Smart Touch Learning's days' sales in inventory of 79.7 days is too high for its industry, which has an average days' sales in inventory ratio of only 13 days. This ratio has identified an area in which Smart Touch Learning needs to improve. Smart Touch Learning should focus on reducing average merchandise inventory held. By decreasing average merchandise inventory, the company can increase inventory turnover and lower the average days' sales in merchandise inventory. Smart Touch Learning will also be able to reduce its merchandise inventory storage and insurance costs as well as reduce the risk of holding obsolete merchandise inventory.

Gross Profit Percentage

Gross Profit Percentage
Measures the profitability of each sales dollar above the cost of goods sold. Gross profit / Net sales revenue.

Gross profit (sometimes called *gross margin*) is net sales revenue minus the cost of goods sold. Merchandisers strive to increase the **gross profit percentage** (also called the *gross margin percentage*). This ratio measures the profitability of each net sales dollar above the cost of goods sold and is computed as gross profit divided by net sales revenue.

The gross profit percentage is one of the most carefully watched measures of profitability. It reflects a business's ability to earn a profit on the merchandise inventory. The gross profit earned on merchandise inventory must be high enough to cover the remaining operating expenses and to earn net income. A small increase in the gross profit percentage from last year to this year may signal an important rise in income. Conversely, a small decrease from last year to this year may signal trouble.

Smart Touch Learning's gross profit percentage for 2020 is as follows:

$$\text{Gross profit percentage} = \frac{\text{Gross profit}}{\text{Net sales revenue}}$$

$$2020: \frac{\$345,000}{\$858,000} = 0.402 = 40.2\%$$

$$\text{Industry average} = 43\%$$

Gross profit percentage varies widely, depending on the business. Smart Touch Learning's gross profit percentage is 40.2%, which is slightly lower than the industry average of 43%. This ratio has identified an area in which Smart Touch Learning needs to improve. To increase gross profit percentage, Smart Touch Learning needs to decrease the cost of the merchandise inventory and/or increase revenue (sales price). Additionally, addressing Smart Touch Learning's inventory turnover issues will probably help Smart Touch Learning to increase its gross profit percentage.

Accounts Receivable Turnover Ratio

Accounts Receivable Turnover Ratio
A ratio that measures the number of times the company collects the average accounts receivable balance in a year. Net credit sales / Average net accounts receivable.

The **accounts receivable turnover ratio** measures the number of times the company collects the average receivables balance in a year. The higher the ratio, the faster the cash collections. However, a receivable turnover that is too high may indicate that credit is too tight, causing the loss of sales to good customers. To compute accounts receivable turnover, we divide net credit sales (assuming all Smart Touch Learning's sales from Exhibit 15-7 are on account) by average net accounts receivable.

Smart Touch Learning's accounts receivable turnover ratio for 2020 is computed as follows:

$$\text{Accounts receivable turnover ratio} = \frac{\text{Net credit sales}}{\text{Average net accounts receivable}}$$

$$2020: \frac{\$858,000}{[(\$85,000 + \$114,000) / 2]} = 8.6$$

$$\text{Industry average} = 29.1$$

Net credit sales, assumed to equal net sales, comes from the income statement (Exhibit D-7). Average net accounts receivable is figured by adding the beginning Accounts Receivable of $85,000 to the ending Accounts Receivable of $114,000 and dividing by 2. (See the balance sheet, Exhibit D-7.)

Smart Touch Learning's accounts receivable turnover ratio of 8.6 times per year is much slower than the industry average of 29.1. Why the difference? Smart Touch Learning is a fairly new business that sells to established people who pay their accounts over time. Further, this turnover coincides with the lower-than-average inventory turnover. So, Smart Touch Learning may achieve a higher accounts receivable turnover by increasing its inventory turnover ratio.

Days' Sales in Receivables

Days' sales in receivables, also called the *collection period*, indicates how many days it takes to collect the average level of receivables and is computed as 365 days divided by the accounts receivable turnover ratio. The number of days in average accounts receivable should be close to the number of days customers are allowed to make payment. The shorter the collection period, the more quickly the organization can use its cash. The longer the collection period, the less cash is available for operations.

To compute this ratio for Smart Touch Learning for 2020, we divide 365 days by the accounts receivable turnover ratio we previously calculated:

$$\text{Days' Sales in Receivables} = \frac{365 \text{ days}}{\text{Accounts receivable turnover ratio}}$$

$$2020: \frac{365 \text{ days}}{8.6} = 42.4 \text{ days}$$

$$\text{Industry average} = 25 \text{ days}$$

Smart Touch Learning's ratio tells us that 42.4 average days' sales remain in Accounts Receivable and need to be collected. The company's days' sales in receivables ratio is much higher (worse) than the industry average of 25 days. We need to determine the company's credit terms to assess this ratio. Smart Touch Learning might give its customers a longer time to pay, such as 45 days versus 30 days. Alternatively, Smart Touch Learning's credit department may need to review the criteria it uses to evaluate individual customers' credit. Without the customers' good paying habits, the company's cash flow would suffer.

Evaluating the Ability to Pay Long-term Debt

The ratios discussed so far yield insight into current assets and current liabilities. They help us measure ability to sell merchandise inventory, collect receivables, and pay current liabilities. Most businesses also have long-term debt. Three key indicators of a business's ability to pay long-term liabilities are the debt ratio, the debt to equity ratio, and the times-interest-earned ratio.

Debt Ratio

The relationship between total liabilities and total assets—called the **debt ratio**—shows the proportion of assets financed with debt and is calculated by dividing total liabilities by total assets. If the debt ratio is 100%, then all the assets are financed with debt. A debt ratio of 50% means that half the assets are financed with debt, and the other half are financed by the owners of the business. The higher the debt ratio, the higher the company's financial risk. The debt ratio can be used to evaluate a business's ability to pay its debts.

The debt ratios for Smart Touch Learning at the end of 2020 and 2019 follow:

$$\text{Debt ratio} = \frac{\text{Total liabilities}}{\text{Total assets}}$$

$$2020: \frac{\$431,000}{\$787,000} = 0.548 = 54.8\%$$

$$2019: \frac{\$324,000}{\$644,000} = 0.503 = 50.3\%$$

Industry average = 69%

Both total liabilities and total asset amounts are from the balance sheet, presented in Exhibit D-7. Smart Touch Learning's debt ratio in 2020 of 54.8% is not very high. The Risk Management Association reports that the average debt ratio for most companies ranges from 57% to 67%, with relatively little variation from company to company. Smart Touch Learning's debt ratio indicates a fairly low-risk position compared with the industry average debt ratio of 69%.

Debt to Equity Ratio

Debt to Equity Ratio
A ratio that measures the proportion of total liabilities relative to total equity. Total liabilities / Total equity.

The relationship between total liabilities and total equity—called the **debt to equity ratio**—shows the proportion of total liabilities relative to total equity. Thus, this ratio measures financial leverage. If the debt to equity ratio is greater than 1, then the company is financing more assets with debt than with equity. If the ratio is less than 1, then the company is financing more assets with equity than with debt. The higher the debt to equity ratio, the greater the company's financial risk.

The debt to equity ratios for Smart Touch Learning at the end of 2020 and 2019 follow:

$$\text{Debt to equity ratio} = \frac{\text{Total liabilities}}{\text{Total equity}}$$

$$2020: \frac{\$431,000}{\$356,000} = 1.21$$

$$2019: \frac{\$324,000}{\$320,000} = 1.01$$

Industry average = 2.23

Smart Touch Learning's debt to equity ratio in 2020 of 1.21 is not very high. Smart Touch Learning's debt to equity ratio indicates a fairly low-risk position compared with the industry average debt to equity ratio of 2.23.

Times-Interest-Earned Ratio

Times-Interest-Earned Ratio
Evaluates a business's ability to pay interest expense. (Net income + Income tax expense + Interest expense) / Interest expense.

The debt ratio and debt to equity ratio say nothing about the ability to pay interest expense. Analysts and investors use the **times-interest-earned ratio** to evaluate a business's ability to pay interest expense. This ratio measures the number of times earnings before interest and taxes (EBIT) can cover (pay) interest expense. This ratio is also called the *interest-coverage ratio*. A high times-interest-earned ratio indicates a business's ease in paying interest expense; a low ratio suggests difficulty. The times-interest-earned ratio is calculated as EBIT (Net income + Income tax expense + Interest expense) divided by interest expense.

Calculation of Smart Touch Learning's times-interest-earned ratio follows:

$$\text{Times-interest-earned ratio} = \frac{\text{Net income} + \text{Income tax expense} + \text{Interest expense}}{\text{Interest expense}}$$

$$2020: \frac{\$48,000 + \$33,000 + \$24,000}{\$24,000} = 4.38$$

$$2019: \frac{\$26,000 + \$17,000 + \$14,000}{\$14,000} = 4.07$$

$$\text{Industry average} = 7.80$$

The company's times-interest-earned ratios of 4.38 for 2020 and 4.07 for 2019 are significantly lower than the industry average of 7.80 times, but it is slightly better than the ratio for the average U.S. business. The norm for U.S. business, as reported by the Risk Management Association, falls in the range of 2.0 to 3.0. When you consider Smart Touch Learning's debt ratio and its times-interest-earned ratio, Smart Touch Learning appears to have little difficulty paying its liabilities.

Evaluating Profitability

The fundamental goal of business is to earn a profit. Ratios that measure profitability often are reported in the business press. Let's examine five profitability measures.

Profit Margin Ratio

The **profit margin ratio** shows the percentage of each net sales dollar earned as net income. In other words, the profit margin ratio shows how much net income a business earns on every $1.00 of sales. This ratio focuses on the profitability of a business and is calculated as net income divided by net sales revenue.

Smart Touch Learning's profit margin ratio follows:

Profit Margin Ratio
A profitability measure that shows how much net income is earned on every dollar of net sales. Net income / Net sales revenue.

$$\text{Profit margin ratio} = \frac{\text{Net income}}{\text{Net sales revenue}}$$

$$2020: \frac{\$\ 48,000}{\$858,000} = 0.056 = 5.6\%$$

$$2019: \frac{\$\ 26,000}{\$803,000} = 0.032 = 3.2\%$$

$$\text{Industry average} = 1.7\%$$

Both net income and net sales revenue amounts are from the income statement presented in Exhibit D-7. Companies strive for a high profit margin. The higher the profit margin, the more sales dollars end up as profit. The increase in Smart Touch Learning's profit margin ratio from 2019 to 2020 is significant and identifies the company as more successful than the average e-learning providers, whose profit margin ratio is 1.7%.

Rate of Return on Total Assets

The **rate of return on total assets** measures a company's success in using its assets to earn a profit. There are two ways that a company can finance its assets:

Rate of Return on Total Assets
A ratio that measures the success a company has in using its assets to earn income. (Net income + Interest expense) / Average total assets.

- Debt—A company can borrow cash from creditors to purchase assets. Creditors earn interest on the money that is loaned.

- Equity—A company receives cash or other assets from stockholders. Stockholders invest in the company and hope to receive a return on their investment.

Rate of return on total assets is calculated by adding interest expense to net income and dividing by average total assets. Interest expense is added back to net income to determine the real return on the assets regardless of the corporation's financing choices (debt or equity).

Computation of the rate of return on total assets ratio for Smart Touch Learning follows:

$$\text{Rate of return on total assets} = \frac{\text{Net income + Interest expense}}{\text{Average total assets}}$$

$$2020: \frac{\$48,000 + \$24,000}{[(\$644,000 + \$787,000) / 2]} = 0.101 = 10.1\%$$

$$\text{Industry average} = 6.0\%$$

Net income and interest expense come from the income statement (Exhibit D-7). Average total assets is figured by adding the beginning total assets of $644,000 to the ending total assets of $787,000 and dividing by 2. (See the balance sheet, Exhibit D-7.) Smart Touch Learning's rate of return on total assets ratio of 10.1% is much better than the industry average of 6.0%.

Asset Turnover Ratio

Asset Turnover Ratio
Measures how efficiently a business uses its average total assets to generate sales. Net sales revenue / Average total assets.

The **asset turnover ratio** measures the amount of net sales revenue generated for each average dollar of total assets invested. This ratio measures how well a company is using its assets to generate sales revenues. To compute this ratio, we divide net sales revenue by average total assets.

Smart Touch Learning's 2020 asset turnover ratio is as follows:

$$\text{Asset turnover ratio} = \frac{\text{Net sales revenue}}{\text{Average total assets}}$$

$$2020: \frac{\$858,000}{[(\$644,000 + \$787,000) / 2]} = 1.20 \text{ times}$$

$$\text{Industry average} = 3.52 \text{ times}$$

Smart Touch Learning's asset turnover ratio of 1.20 is much lower than the industry average of 3.52 times, indicating that Smart Touch Learning is generating less net sales revenue for each average dollar of total assets invested. Recall that Smart Touch Learning's gross profit percentage was lower than the industry's also. Normally, companies with high gross profit percentages will have low asset turnover. Companies with low gross profit percentages will have high asset turnover ratios. This is another area in which Smart Touch Learning's management must consider options to increase sales and decrease its average total assets to improve this ratio.

Rate of Return on Common Stockholders' Equity

Rate of Return on Common Stockholders' Equity
Shows the relationship between net income available to common stockholders and their average common equity invested in the company. (Net income − Preferred dividends) / Average common stockholders' equity.

A popular measure of profitability is **rate of return on common stockholders' equity**, often shortened to *return on equity*. This ratio shows the relationship between net income available to common stockholders and their average common equity invested in the company. The rate of return on common stockholders' equity shows how much income is earned for each $1 invested by the common shareholders.

To compute this ratio, we first subtract preferred dividends from net income to get net income available to the common stockholders. (Smart Touch Learning does not have any preferred stock issued, so preferred dividends are zero.) Then we divide net income available to common stockholders by average common stockholders' equity during the year. Common equity is total stockholders' equity minus preferred equity. Average common stockholders' equity is the average of the beginning and ending common stockholders' equity balances.

The 2020 rate of return on common stockholders' equity for Smart Touch Learning follows:

$$\text{Rate of return on common stockholders' equity} = \frac{\text{Net income} - \text{Preferred dividends}}{\text{Average common stockholders' equity}}$$

$$2020: \frac{\$48,000 - \$0}{[(\$320,000 + \$356,000) / 2]} = 0.142 = 14.2\%$$

$$\text{Industry average} = 10.5\%$$

Smart Touch Learning's rate of return on common stockholders' equity of 14.2% is higher than its rate of return on total assets of 10.1%. This difference results from borrowing at one rate—say, 8%—and investing the money to earn a higher rate, such as the firm's 14.2% return on equity. This practice is called **trading on the equity**, or using *leverage*. It is directly related to the debt ratio. The higher the debt ratio, the higher the leverage. Companies that finance operations with debt are said to *leverage* their positions.

During good times, leverage increases profitability. But leverage can have a negative impact on profitability as well. Therefore, leverage is a double-edged sword, increasing profits during good times but compounding losses during bad times. Compare Smart Touch Learning's rate of return on common stockholders' equity with the industry average of 10.5%. Once again, Smart Touch Learning is performing much better than the average company in its industry. A rate of return on common stockholders' equity of 15% to 20% year after year is considered good in most industries. At 14.2%, Smart Touch Learning is doing well.

Trading on the Equity
Earning more income on borrowed money than the related interest expense, thereby increasing the earnings for the owners of the business.

Earnings per Share (EPS)

Earnings per share (EPS) is perhaps the most widely quoted of all financial statistics. EPS is the only ratio that must appear on the financial statements. Earnings per share reports the amount of net income (loss) for each share of the company's *outstanding common stock*. Earnings per share is calculated as net income minus preferred dividends divided by the weighted average number of common shares outstanding. Preferred dividends are subtracted from net income because the preferred stockholders have the first claim to dividends. The computation for the weighted average number of common shares outstanding is covered in advanced accounting courses. For simplicity, we will determine earnings per share on the average number of shares outstanding, calculated as the beginning balance plus ending balance divided by two.

FASB requires that earnings per share appear on the income statement. Corporations report a separate EPS figure for each element of income, which was shown in more detail in the stockholders' equity chapter.

Smart Touch Learning's EPS for 2020 and 2019 follow. (Note that Smart Touch Learning had 10,000 shares of common stock outstanding throughout both years.)

Earnings per Share (EPS)
Amount of a company's net income (loss) for each share of its outstanding common stock. (Net income − Preferred dividends) / Weighted average number of common shares outstanding.

$$\text{Earnings per share} = \frac{\text{Net income} - \text{Preferred dividends}}{\text{Weighted average number of common shares outstanding}}$$

$$2020: \frac{\$48,000 - \$0}{10,000 \text{ shares}} = \$4.80 \text{ per share}$$

$$2019: \frac{\$26,000 - \$0}{10,000 \text{ shares}} = \$2.60 \text{ per share}$$

$$\text{Industry average} = \$9.76 \text{ per share}$$

Smart Touch Learning's EPS increased significantly in 2020 (by almost 85%). Its stockholders should not expect this big a boost in EPS every year. Most companies strive to increase EPS by 10% to 15% annually, and leading companies do so. But even the most successful companies have an occasional bad year. EPS for the industry at $9.76 is a little more than twice Smart Touch Learning's 2020 EPS. Therefore, Smart Touch Learning needs to work on continuing to increase EPS by increasing its net income so that it is more competitive with other companies in its industry.

Evaluating Stock as an Investment

Investors purchase stock to earn a return on their investment. This return consists of two parts: (1) gains (or losses) from selling the stock at a price above (or below) purchase price and (2) dividends. The ratios we examine in this section help analysts evaluate stock investments.

Price/Earnings Ratio

Price/Earnings Ratio
The ratio of the market price of a share of common stock to the company's earnings per share. Measures the value that the stock market places on $1 of a company's earnings. Market price per share of common stock / Earnings per share.

The **price/earnings ratio** is the ratio of the market price of a share of common stock to the company's earnings per share. The price/earnings ratio shows the market price of $1 of earnings. This ratio, abbreviated P/E, appears in many print or online stock listings and measures the value that the stock market places on a company's earnings.

Calculations for the P/E ratios of Smart Touch Learning follow. The market prices of common stock for real companies can be obtained from a financial Web site, a stockbroker, or the company's Web site. The market price for Smart Touch Learning's common stock was $60 at the end of 2020 and $35 at the end of 2019. The earnings per share values were calculated immediately before the P/E ratio.

$$\text{Price/earnings ratio} = \frac{\text{Market price per share of common stock}}{\text{Earnings per share}}$$

$$2020: \frac{\$60 \text{ per share}}{\$4.80 \text{ per share}} = 12.50$$

$$2019: \frac{\$35 \text{ per share}}{\$2.60 \text{ per share}} = 13.46$$

$$\text{Industry average} = 17.79$$

Smart Touch Learning's P/E ratio for 2020 of 12.50 means that the company's stock is selling at 12.5 times one year's earnings per share. Smart Touch Learning would like to see this ratio increase in future years in order to be more in line with the industry average P/E of 17.79.

Dividend Yield

Dividend Yield
Ratio of annual dividends per share of stock to the stock's market price per share. Measures the percentage of a stock's market value that is returned annually as dividends to stockholders. Annual dividend per share / Market price per share.

Dividend yield is the ratio of annual dividends per share to the stock's market price per share. This ratio measures the percentage of a stock's market value that is returned annually as dividends to shareholders. *Preferred* stockholders, who invest primarily to receive dividends, pay special attention to dividend yield.

Assume Smart Touch Learning paid annual cash dividends of $1.20 per share of common stock in 2020 and $1.00 in 2019. As noted previously, market prices of the company's common stock were $60 in 2020 and $35 in 2019. The firm's dividend yields on common stock follow:

$$\text{Dividend yield} = \frac{\text{Annual dividend per share}}{\text{Market price per share}}$$

$$2020: \frac{\$1.20 \text{ per share}}{\$60 \text{ per share}} = 0.020 = 2.0\%$$

$$2019: \frac{\$1.00 \text{ per share}}{\$35 \text{ per share}} = 0.029 = 2.9\%$$

$$\text{Industry average} = 3.6\%$$

In this calculation, we are determining the dividend yield for common stock. Dividend yield can also be calculated for preferred stock.

An investor who buys Smart Touch Learning's common stock for $60 can expect to receive 2.0% of the investment annually in the form of cash dividends. The industry, however, is paying out 3.6% annually. An investor might be willing to accept lower dividends (cash now) if the stock's market price is growing (cash later when the stock is sold).

Dividend Payout

Dividend payout is the ratio of annual dividends declared per common share relative to the earnings per share of the company. This ratio measures the percentage of earnings paid annually to common shareholders as cash dividends.

Recall that Smart Touch Learning paid annual cash dividends of $1.20 per share of common stock in 2020 and $1.00 in 2019. Earnings per share were calculated as $4.80 per share for 2020 and $2.60 for 2019. So, Smart Touch Learning's dividend payout yields are as follows:

Dividend Payout
The ratio of dividends declared per common share relative to the earnings per share of the company. Annual dividend per share / Earnings per share.

$$\text{Dividend payout} = \frac{\text{Annual dividend per share}}{\text{Earnings per share}}$$

$$2020: \frac{\$1.20 \text{ per share}}{\$4.80 \text{ per share}} = 0.25 = 25\%$$

$$2019: \frac{\$1.00 \text{ per share}}{\$2.60 \text{ per share}} = 0.38 = 38\%$$

$$\text{Industry average} = 63\%$$

Smart Touch Learning's dividend payout ratios of 25% in 2020 and 38% in 2019 are less than the industry average of 63%. Smart Touch Learning, being a fairly new company, might be retaining more of its earnings for growth and expansion. An investor who buys Smart Touch Learning's common stock may predict annual cash dividends to be about 25% of earnings, based on the 2020 dividend payout ratio. This investor would want to see higher market prices and higher asset turnover for Smart Touch Learning in the future for Smart Touch Learning to stay competitive.

Red Flags in Financial Statement Analyses

Analysts look for *red flags* in financial statements that may signal financial trouble. Recent accounting scandals highlight the importance of these red flags. The following conditions may reveal that the company is too risky:

- **Movement of sales, merchandise inventory, and receivables.** Sales, merchandise inventory, and receivables generally move together. Increased sales lead to higher receivables and may require more merchandise inventory (or higher inventory turnover) to meet demand. Unexpected or inconsistent movements among sales, merchandise inventory, and receivables make the financial statements look suspect.

- **Earnings problems.** Has net income decreased significantly for several years in a row? Did the company report net income in previous years but now is reporting a net loss? Most companies cannot survive losses year after year.

- **Decreased cash flow.** Cash flow validates net income. Is net cash flow from operating activities consistently lower than net income? If so, the company is in trouble. Are the sales of plant assets a major source of cash? If so, the company may face a cash shortage.

- **Too much debt.** How does the company's debt ratio compare to that of major competitors? If the debt ratio is too high, the company may be unable to pay its debts.

- **Inability to collect receivables.** Are days' sales in receivables growing faster than for competitors? If so, a cash shortage may be looming.

- **Buildup of merchandise inventories.** Is inventory turnover too slow? If so, the company may be unable to sell goods, or it may be overstating merchandise inventory.

Do any of these red flags apply to Smart Touch Learning from the analyses we did in the chapter? Although the financial statements depict a strong and growing company, the analysis pointed out several areas of weakness for Smart Touch Learning that include low inventory turnover, low accounts receivable turnover, low gross profit margin, low times interest earned, low asset turnover, and low earnings per share. Smart Touch Learning should continue to carefully monitor its financial statements as it continues to grow. Exhibit D-8 summarizes the financial ratios that you have learned in this chapter.

Exhibit D-8 | Using Ratios in Financial Statement Analysis

Ratio	Computation	Information Provided
Evaluating the ability to pay current liabilities:		
Working capital	Current assets − Current liabilities	A business's ability to meet its short-term obligations with its current assets.
Cash ratio	$\dfrac{\text{Cash} + \text{Cash equivalents}}{\text{Total current liabilities}}$	The company's ability to pay current liabilities from cash and cash equivalents.
Acid-test ratio	$\dfrac{\text{Cash including cash equivalents} + \text{Short-term investments} + \text{Net current receivables}}{\text{Total current liabilities}}$	The company's ability to pay all its current liabilities if they came due immediately.
Current ratio	$\dfrac{\text{Total current assets}}{\text{Total current liabilities}}$	The company's ability to pay current liabilities from current assets.

(Continued on next page)

Exhibit D-8 | **Using Ratios in Financial Statement Analysis (Continued)**

Ratio	Computation	Information Provided
Evaluating the ability to sell merchandise inventory and collect receivables:		
Inventory turnover	$\dfrac{\text{Cost of goods sold}}{\text{Average merchandise inventory}}$	The number of times a company sells its average level of merchandise inventory during a period.
Days' sales in inventory	$\dfrac{365 \text{ days}}{\text{Inventory turnover}}$	The average number of days that inventory is held by a company.
Gross profit percentage	$\dfrac{\text{Gross profit}}{\text{Net sales revenue}}$	The profitability of each sales dollar above the cost of goods sold.
Accounts receivable turnover ratio	$\dfrac{\text{Net credit sales}}{\text{Average net accounts receivable}}$	The number of times the company collects the average receivables balance in a year.
Days' sales in receivables	$\dfrac{365 \text{ days}}{\text{Accounts receivable turnover ratio}}$	The number of days it takes to collect the average level of receivables.
Evaluating the ability to pay long-term debt:		
Debt ratio	$\dfrac{\text{Total liabilities}}{\text{Total assets}}$	The proportion of assets financed with debt.
Debt to equity ratio	$\dfrac{\text{Total liabilities}}{\text{Total equity}}$	The proportion of total liabilities relative to total equity.
Times-interest-earned ratio	$\dfrac{\text{Net income} + \text{Income tax expense} + \text{Interest expense}}{\text{Interest expense}}$	A business's ability to pay interest expense.
Evaluating profitability:		
Profit margin ratio	$\dfrac{\text{Net income}}{\text{Net sales revenue}}$	How much net income is earned on every dollar of net sales revenue.
Rate of return on total assets	$\dfrac{\text{Net income} + \text{Interest expense}}{\text{Average total assets}}$	The success a company has in using its assets to earn income.
Asset turnover ratio	$\dfrac{\text{Net sales revenue}}{\text{Average total assets}}$	How efficiently a business uses its average total assets to generate sales.
Rate of return on common stockholders' equity	$\dfrac{\text{Net income} - \text{Preferred dividends}}{\text{Average common stockholders' equity}}$	The relationship between net income available to common stockholders and their average common equity invested in the company.
Earnings per share	$\dfrac{\text{Net income} - \text{Preferred dividends}}{\text{Weighted average number of common shares outstanding}}$	Amount of a company's net income (loss) for each share of its outstanding common stock.
Evaluating stock as an investment:		
Price/earnings ratio	$\dfrac{\text{Market price per share of common stock}}{\text{Earnings per share}}$	The value the stock market places on $1 of a company's earnings.
Dividend yield	$\dfrac{\text{Annual dividend per share}}{\text{Market price per share}}$	The percentage of a stock's market value that is returned annually as dividends to stockholders.
Dividend payout	$\dfrac{\text{Annual dividend per share}}{\text{Earnings per share}}$	Ratio of dividends declared per common share relative to the earnings per share of the company.

Try It!

The financial statements of Ion Corporation include the following items:

	Current Year	Preceding Year
Balance Sheet:		
Cash	$ 6,000	$ 8,000
Short-term Investments	4,400	10,700
Net Accounts Receivable	21,600	29,200
Merchandise Inventory	30,800	27,600
Prepaid Expenses	6,000	3,600
Total Current Assets	68,800	79,100
Total Current Liabilities	53,200	37,200
Income Statement:		
Net Sales Revenue	$ 184,800	
Cost of Goods Sold	126,000	

Compute the following ratios for the current year:

7. Current ratio
8. Acid-test ratio
9. Inventory turnover
10. Gross profit percentage

Check your answers online in MyAccountingLab or at http://www.pearsonhighered.com/Horngren.

For more practice, see Short Exercises SD-6 through SD-12.   MyAccountingLab

REVIEW

> Things You Should Know

1. How are financial statements used to analyze a business?

- There are three main ways to analyze financial statements:
  - Horizontal analysis
  - Vertical analysis
  - Ratio analysis
- Annual reports provide information about a company's financial condition and include the following:
  - Business overview
  - Management's discussion and analysis of financial condition and results of operations (MD&A)

- Report of independent registered public accounting firm
- Financial statements
- Notes to the financial statements

2. How do we use horizontal analysis to analyze a business?

- Horizontal analysis is the study of percentage changes in line items from comparative financial statements. It compares one year to the next. (Dollar amount of change / Base period amount) $\times$ 100.

- Trend analysis is a form of horizontal analysis in which percentages are computed by selecting a base year as 100% and expressing the amounts for following periods as a percentage of the base period amount. (Any period amount / Base period amount) $\times$ 100.

3. How do we use vertical analysis to analyze a business?

- Vertical analysis reveals the relationship of each statement item to its base amount, which is the 100% figure. (Specific item / Base amount) $\times$ 100.
  - For the income statement, net sales revenue is the base.
  - For the balance sheet, total assets is the base.
- Common-size statements are financial statements that report only percentages—the same percentages that appear in vertical analysis.
- Benchmarking is the practice of comparing a company's performance with its prior performance or with best practices from other companies.

4. How do we use ratios to analyze a business?

- Ratios can be used to evaluate a company's:
  - ability to pay current liabilities
  - ability to sell merchandise inventory and collect receivables
  - ability to pay long-term debt
  - profitability
  - stock as an investment
- Exhibit D-8 summarizes common ratios that can be used to analyze a business.

> Check Your Understanding D-1

Check your understanding of the chapter by completing this problem and then looking at the solution. Use this practice to help identify which sections of the chapter you need to study more.

Kimball Corporation makes cell phone covers and has the following comparative income statement for the years ended December 31, 2019 and 2018:

KIMBALL CORPORATION Income Statement Years Ended December 31, 2019 and 2018		
	2019	2018
Revenues:		
Net Sales Revenue	$ 300,000	$ 250,000
Other Revenues	0	1,000
Total Revenues	300,000	251,000
Expenses:		
Cost of Goods Sold	214,200	170,000
Engineering, Selling, and Administrative Expenses	54,000	48,000
Interest Expense	6,000	5,000
Income Tax Expense	9,000	3,000
Other Expenses	2,700	0
Total Expenses	285,900	226,000
Net Income	$ 14,100	$ 25,000

Requirement

Perform a horizontal analysis and a vertical analysis of Kimball Corporation. State whether 2019 was a good year or a bad year, and give your reasons. (See Learning Objectives 2 and 3)

> Solution

KIMBALL CORPORATION Income Statement Years Ended December 31, 2019 and 2018				
			Increase (Decrease)	
	2019	2018	Amount	Percentage
Revenues:				
Net Sales Revenue	$ 300,000	$ 250,000	$ 50,000	20.0%
Other Revenues	0	1,000	(1,000)	—
Total Revenues	300,000	251,000	49,000	19.5
Expenses:				
Cost of Goods Sold	214,200	170,000	44,200	26.0
Engineering, Selling, and Administrative Expenses	54,000	48,000	6,000	12.5
Interest Expense	6,000	5,000	1,000	20.0
Income Tax Expense	9,000	3,000	6,000	200.0
Other Expenses	2,700	0	2,700	—
Total Expenses	285,900	226,000	59,900	26.5
Net Income	$ 14,100	$ 25,000	$ (10,900)	(43.6)%

The horizontal analysis shows that net sales revenue increased 20.0%. Total expenses increased by 26.5%, and net income decreased 43.6%. So, even though Kimball's net sales revenue increased, the company's expenses increased by a larger percentage, netting an overall 43.6% reduction in net income between the years. That indicates that 2019 was a bad year in comparison to 2018. This analysis identifies areas in which management should review more data. For example, cost of goods sold increased 26.0%. Managers would want to know why this increase occurred to determine whether the company can implement cost-saving strategies (such as purchasing from other, lower-cost vendors).

KIMBALL CORPORATION
Income Statement
Years Ended December 31, 2019 and 2018

	2019	Percent	2018	Percent
Revenues:				
Net Sales Revenue	$ 300,000	100.0%	$ 250,000	100.0%
Other Revenues	0	0.0	1,000	0.4
Total Revenues	300,000	100.0	251,000	100.4
Expenses:				
Cost of Goods Sold	214,200	71.4	170,000	68.0
Engineering, Selling, and Administrative Expenses	54,000	18.0	48,000	19.2
Interest Expense	6,000	2.0	5,000	2.0
Income Tax Expense	9,000	3.0	3,000	1.2
Other Expenses	2,700	0.9	0	0
Total Expenses	285,900	95.3	226,000	90.4
Net Income	$ 14,100	4.7%	$ 25,000	10.0%

The vertical analysis shows changes in the line items as percentages of net sales revenue. A few notable items are:

• Cost of Goods Sold increased from 68.0% to 71.4%;

• Engineering, Selling, and Administrative Expenses decreased from 19.2% to 18.0%.

These two items are Kimball's largest dollar expenses, so their percentage changes are important. This indicates that cost controls need to be improved, especially for COGS.

The 2019 net income declined to 4.7% of sales, compared with 10.0% the preceding year. Kimball's increase in cost of goods sold is the biggest factor in the overall decrease in net income as a percentage of sales.

> Check Your Understanding D-2

Check your understanding of the chapter by completing this problem and then looking at the solution. Use this practice to help identify which sections of the chapter you need to study more.

JAVA, INC. Four-Year Selected Financial Data Years Ended January 31, 2019–2016				
Operating Results:	**2019**	**2018**	**2017**	**2016**
Net Sales Revenue	$ 13,848	$ 13,673	$ 11,635	$ 9,054
Cost of Goods Sold	9,704	8,599	6,775	5,318
Interest Expense	109	75	45	46
Income from Operations	338	1,455	1,817	1,333
Income Tax Expense	100	263	338	247
Net Income (Net Loss)	(8)	877	1,127	824
Cash Dividends on Common Stock	76	75	76	77
Financial Position:				
Merchandise Inventory	1,677	1,904	1,462	1,056
Total Assets	7,591	7,012	5,189	3,963
Current Ratio	1.48:1	0.95:1	1.25:1	1.20:1
Stockholders' Equity	3,010	2,928	2,630	1,574
Average Number of Shares of Common Stock Outstanding	860	879	895	576

Requirements

Using the financial data presented above, compute the following ratios and evaluate Java's results for 2019–2017 (See Learning Objective 4):

1. Profit margin ratio
2. Earnings per share
3. Inventory turnover
4. Times-interest-earned ratio
5. Rate of return on common stockholders' equity
6. Gross profit percentage

> Solution

	2019	2018	2017
1. Profit margin ratio	$\dfrac{\$(8)}{\$13,848} = (0.06\%)$	$\dfrac{\$877}{\$13,673} = 6.4\%$	$\dfrac{\$1,127}{\$11,635} = 9.7\%$
2. Earnings per share	$\dfrac{\$(8)}{860 \text{ shares}} = \$(0.01) \text{ per share}$	$\dfrac{\$877}{879 \text{ shares}} = \$1.00 \text{ per share}$	$\dfrac{\$1,127}{895 \text{ shares}} = \$1.26 \text{ per share}$
3. Inventory turnover	$\dfrac{\$9,704}{(\$1,904 + \$1,677)\,/\,2} = 5.4 \text{ times}$	$\dfrac{\$8,599}{(\$1,462 + \$1,904)\,/\,2} = 5.1 \text{ times}$	$\dfrac{\$6,775}{(\$1,056 + \$1,462)\,/\,2} = 5.4 \text{ times}$
4. Times-interest-earned ratio	$\dfrac{[\$(8) + \$100 + \$109]}{\$109} = 1.8 \text{ times}$	$\dfrac{(\$877 + \$263 + \$75)}{\$75} = 16.2 \text{ times}$	$\dfrac{(\$1,127 + \$338 + \$45)}{\$45} = 33.6 \text{ times}$
5. Rate of return on common stockholders' equity	$\dfrac{\$(8)}{(\$2,928 + \$3,010)\,/\,2} = (0.3\%)$	$\dfrac{\$877}{(\$2,630 + \$2,928)\,/\,2} = 31.6\%$	$\dfrac{\$1,127}{(\$1,574 + \$2,630)\,/\,2} = 53.6\%$
6. Gross profit percentage	$\dfrac{(\$13,848 - \$9,704)}{\$13,848} = 29.9\%$	$\dfrac{(\$13,673 - \$8,599)}{\$13,673} = 37.1\%$	$\dfrac{(\$11,635 - \$6,775)}{\$11,635} = 41.8\%$

Evaluation: During this period, Java's operating results deteriorated on all these measures except inventory turnover. The times-interest-earned ratio and rate of return on common stockholders' equity percentages are down sharply. From these data, it is clear that Java could sell its coffee, but not at the markups the company enjoyed in the past. The final result, in 2019, was a net loss for the year.

> Key Terms

Accounts Receivable Turnover Ratio (p. D-18)
Acid-Test Ratio (p. D-15)
Annual Report (p. D-3)
Asset Turnover Ratio (p. D-22)
Benchmarking (p. D-12)
Cash Ratio (p. D-15)
Common-Size Statement (p. D-11)
Current Ratio (p. D-16)
Days' Sales in Inventory (p. D-17)
Days' Sales in Receivables (p. D-19)
Debt Ratio (p. D-19)

Debt to Equity Ratio (p. D-20)
Dividend Payout (p. D-25)
Dividend Yield (p. D-24)
Dollar Value Bias (p. D-11)
Earnings per Share (EPS) (p. D-23)
Gross Profit Percentage (p. D-18)
Horizontal Analysis (p. D-5)
Inventory Turnover (p. D-17)
Management's Discussion and Analysis of Financial Condition and Results of Operations (MD&A) (p. D-3)

Price/Earnings Ratio (p. D-24)
Profit Margin Ratio (p. D-21)
Rate of Return on Common Stockholders' Equity (p. D-22)
Rate of Return on Total Assets (p. D-21)
Times-Interest-Earned Ratio (p. D-20)
Trading on the Equity (p. D-23)
Trend Analysis (p. D-7)
Vertical Analysis (p. D-9)
Working Capital (p. D-14)

> Quick Check

Liberty Corporation reported the following financial statements:

LIBERTY CORPORATION Comparative Balance Sheet December 31, 2019 and 2018		
	2019	**2018**
Assets		
Current Assets:		
Cash and Cash Equivalents	$ 2,450	$ 2,094
Accounts Receivable	1,813	1,611
Merchandise Inventory	1,324	1,060
Prepaid Expenses	1,709	2,120
Total Current Assets	7,296	6,885
Other Assets	18,500	15,737
Total Assets	$ 25,796	$ 22,622
Liabilities		
Current Liabilities	$ 7,230	$ 8,467
Long-term Liabilities	4,798	3,792
Total Liabilities	12,028	12,259
Stockholders' Equity		
Common Stock, no par	6,568	4,363
Retained Earnings	7,200	6,000
Total Stockholders' Equity	13,768	10,363
Total Liabilities and Stockholders' Equity	$ 25,796	$ 22,622

LIBERTY CORPORATION Income Statement Year Ended December 31, 2019	
Net Sales Revenue	$ 20,941
Cost of Goods Sold	7,055
Gross Profit	13,886
Operating Expenses	7,065
Operating Income	6,821
Interest Expense	210
Income Before Income Taxes	6,611
Income Tax Expense	2,563
Net Income	$ 4,048

1. What part of the Liberty's annual report is written by the company and could present a biased view of financial conditions and results?

   Learning Objective 1

   a. Balance Sheet
   b. Management's Discussion and Analysis of Financial Condition and Results of Operations (MD&A)
   c. Auditor's Report
   d. Income Statement

2. Horizontal analysis of Liberty's balance sheet for 2019 would report

   Learning Objective 2

   a. Cash as 9.50% of total assets.
   b. a 17% increase in Cash and Cash Equivalents.
   c. a current ratio of 1.01.
   d. inventory turnover of 6 times.

3. Vertical analysis of Liberty's balance sheet for 2019 would report

   Learning Objective 3

   a. Cash as 9.50% of total assets.   c. a current ratio of 1.01.
   b. inventory turnover of 6 times.   d. a 17% increase in Cash.

4. Which statement best describes Liberty's acid-test ratio for 2019?

   Learning Objective 4

   a. Greater than 1   c. Less than 1
   b. Equal to 1   d. None of the above

5. Liberty's inventory turnover during 2019 was (amounts rounded)

   Learning Objective 4

   a. 6 times.   c. 8 times.
   b. 7 times.   d. not determinable from the data given.

6. Assume all sales are on credit. During 2019, Liberty's days' sales in receivables ratio was (amounts rounded)

   Learning Objective 4

   a. 34 days.   b. 30 days.   c. 32 days.   d. 28 days.

7. Which measure expresses Liberty's times-interest-earned ratio? (amounts rounded)

   Learning Objective 4

   a. 54.7%   b. 19 times   c. 34.5%   d. 32 times

8. Liberty's rate of return on common stockholders' equity can be described as

   Learning Objective 4

   a. weak.   b. normal.   c. strong.   d. average.

9. The company has 2,500 shares of common stock outstanding. What is Liberty's earnings per share?

   Learning Objective 4

   a. $1.62   b. $1.75   c. $2.73   d. 2.63 times

10. The company has 2,500 shares of common stock outstanding and the market price is $20 per share. What is Liberty's price/earnings ratio?

    Learning Objective 4

    a. 0.08   b. $0.08   c. 12.35   d. 12.35 times

Check your answers at the end of the chapter.

ASSESS YOUR PROGRESS

> Review Questions

1. What are the three main ways to analyze financial statements?
2. What is an annual report? Briefly describe the key parts of the annual report.
3. What is horizontal analysis, and how is a percentage change computed?
4. What is trend analysis, and how does it differ from horizontal analysis?
5. What is vertical analysis? What item is used as the base for the income statement? What item is used as the base for the balance sheet?
6. Describe a common-size statement and how it might be helpful in evaluating a company.
7. What is benchmarking, and what are the two main types of benchmarks in financial statement analysis?
8. Briefly describe the ratios that can be used to evaluate a company's ability to pay current liabilities.
9. Briefly describe the ratios that can be used to evaluate a company's ability to sell merchandise inventory and collect receivables.
10. Briefly describe the ratios that can be used to evaluate a company's ability to pay long-term debt.
11. Briefly describe the ratios that can be used to evaluate a company's profitability.
12. Briefly describe the ratios that can be used to evaluate a company's stock as an investment.
13. What are some common red flags in financial statement analysis?

> Short Exercises

Learning Objective 1

SD-1 Explaining financial statements

Caleb King is interested in investing in Orange Corporation. What types of tools should Caleb use to evaluate the company?

Learning Objective 2

SD-2 Performing horizontal analysis

Verifine Corp. reported the following on its comparative income statement:

(In millions)	2019	2018	2017
Revenue	$ 9,890	$ 9,690	$ 9,135
Cost of Goods Sold	6,250	6,000	5,890

Prepare a horizontal analysis of revenues and gross profit—both in dollar amounts and in percentages—for 2019 and 2018.

Learning Objective 2

SD-3 Calculating trend analysis

Muscateer Corp. reported the following revenues and net income amounts:

(In millions)	2019	2018	2017	2016
Revenue	$ 9,610	$ 9,355	$ 9,050	$ 8,950
Net Income	7,290	6,790	5,020	4,300

Requirements

1. Calculate Muscateer's trend analysis for revenues and net income. Use 2016 as the base year, and round to the nearest percent.

2. Which measure increased at a higher rate during 2017–2019?

SD-4 Performing vertical analysis

Learning Objective 3

Great Value Optical Company reported the following amounts on its balance sheet at December 31, 2018 and 2017:

	2018	2017
Cash and Receivables	$ 80,640	$ 80,575
Merchandise Inventory	56,840	54,450
Property, Plant, and Equipment, Net	142,520	139,975
Total Assets	$ 280,000	$ 275,000

Prepare a vertical analysis of Great Value's assets for 2018 and 2017.

SD-5 Preparing common-size income statement

Learning Objective 3

Data for Connor, Inc. and Alto Corp. follow:

	Connor	Alto
Net Sales Revenue	$ 13,000	$ 22,000
Cost of Goods Sold	7,917	15,730
Other Expenses	4,342	5,170
Net Income	$ 741	$ 1,100

Requirements

1. Prepare common-size income statements.

2. Which company earns more net income?

3. Which company's net income is a higher percentage of its net sales revenue?

Use the following information for Short Exercises SD-6 through SD-10.

Accel's Companies, a home improvement store chain, reported the following summarized figures:

ACCEL'S COMPANIES Income Statement Years Ended May 31, 2018 and 2017		
	2018	2017
Net Sales Revenue	$ 40,600	$ 40,500
Cost of Goods Sold	28,400	30,600
Interest Expense	600	570
All Other Expenses	4,300	8,200
Net Income	$ 7,300	$ 1,130

ACCEL'S COMPANIES						
Balance Sheet						
May 31, 2018 and 2017						
Assets				**Liabilities**		
	2018	**2017**			**2018**	**2017**
Cash	$ 2,400	$ 900		Total Current Liabilities	$ 28,000	$ 13,200
Short-term Investments	28,000	9,000		Long-term Liabilities	13,900	10,300
Accounts Receivable	7,500	5,200		Total Liabilities	41,900	23,500
Merchandise Inventory	6,900	8,600		**Stockholders' Equity**		
Other Current Assets	8,000	1,500		Common Stock	11,000	11,000
Total Current Assets	52,800	25,200		Retained Earnings	29,900	19,700
All Other Assets	30,000	29,000		Total Equity	40,900	30,700
Total Assets	$ 82,800	$ 54,200		Total Liabilities and Equity	$ 82,800	$ 54,200

Accel's has 10,000 common shares outstanding during 2018.

Learning Objective 4

SD-6 Evaluating current ratio

Requirements

1. Compute Accel's Companies' current ratio at May 31, 2018 and 2017.
2. Did Accel's Companies' current ratio improve, deteriorate, or hold steady during 2018?

Learning Objective 4

SD-7 Computing inventory, gross profit, and receivables ratios

Requirements

1. Compute the inventory turnover, days' sales in inventory, and gross profit percentage for Accel's Companies for 2018.
2. Compute days' sales in receivables during 2018. Round intermediate calculations to three decimal places. Assume all sales were on account.
3. What do these ratios say about Accel's Companies' ability to sell inventory and collect receivables?

Learning Objective 4

SD-8 Measuring ability to pay liabilities

Requirements

1. Compute the debt ratio and the debt to equity ratio at May 31, 2018, for Accel's Companies.
2. Is Accel's ability to pay its liabilities strong or weak? Explain your reasoning.

Learning Objective 4

SD-9 Measuring profitability

Requirements

1. Compute the profit margin ratio for Accel's Companies for 2018.
2. Compute the rate of return on total assets for 2018.
3. Compute the asset turnover ratio for 2018.
4. Compute the rate of return on common stockholders' equity for 2018.
5. Are these rates of return strong or weak? Explain your reasoning.

SD-10 Computing EPS and P/E ratio

Learning Objective 4

Requirements

1. Compute earnings per share (EPS) for 2018 for Accel's. Round to the nearest cent.

2. Compute Accel's Companies' price/earnings ratio for 2018. The market price per share of Accel's stock is $12.50.

3. What do these results mean when evaluating Accel's Companies' profitability?

SD-11 Using ratios to reconstruct an income statement

Learning Objective 4

Old Mills's income statement appears as follows (amounts in thousands):

OLD MILLS Income Statement Year Ended December 31, 2018	
Net Sales Revenue	$ 6,900
Cost of Goods Sold	(a)
Selling and Administrative Expenses	1,710
Interest Expense	(b)
Other Expenses	120
Income Before Income Taxes	1,150
Income Tax Expense	(c)
Net Income	(d)

Use the following ratio data to complete Old Mills's income statement:

1. Inventory turnover is 3.70 (beginning Merchandise Inventory was $810; ending Merchandise Inventory was $770).

2. Profit margin ratio is 14%.

SD-12 Using ratios to reconstruct a balance sheet

Learning Objective 4

Traditional Mills's balance sheet appears as follows (amounts in thousands):

TRADITIONAL MILLS Balance Sheet December 31, 2018			
Assets		**Liabilities**	
Cash	$ 45	Total Current Liabilities	$ 2,500
Accounts Receivables	(a)	Long-term Note Payable	(e)
Merchandise Inventory	800	Other Long-term Liabilities	760
Prepaid Expenses	(b)	Total Liabilities	(f)
Total Current Assets	(c)		
Plant Assets, Net	(d)	**Stockholders' Equity**	
Other Assets	2,490	Stockholders' Equity	2,450
Total Assets	$ 7,000	Total Liabilities and Stockholders' Equity	$ (g)

Use the following ratio data to complete Traditional Mills's balance sheet.

1. Current ratio is 0.72.
2. Acid-test ratio is 0.36.

> Exercises

Learning Objective 2

1. Net Income 34.7%

ED-13 Performing horizontal analysis—income statement

Data for Mulberry Designs, Inc. follow:

MULBERRY DESIGNS, INC. Comparative Income Statement Years Ended December 31, 2018 and 2017		
	2018	2017
Net Sales Revenue	$ 431,000	$ 372,350
Expenses:		
Cost of Goods Sold	203,850	186,000
Selling and Administrative Expenses	99,000	93,250
Other Expenses	9,000	4,650
Total Expenses	311,850	283,900
Net Income	$ 119,150	$ 88,450

Requirements

1. Prepare a horizontal analysis of the comparative income statement of Mulberry Designs, Inc. Round percentage changes to one decimal place.
2. Why did 2018 net income increase by a higher percentage than net sales revenue?

Learning Objective 2

1. 2019 Net Income 153%

ED-14 Computing trend analysis

Grand Oaks Realty's net revenue and net income for the following five-year period, using 2015 as the base year, follow:

	2019	2018	2017	2016	2015
Net Revenue	$ 1,360,000	$ 1,180,000	$ 1,147,000	$ 1,008,000	$ 1,044,000
Net Income	127,000	120,000	87,000	75,000	83,000

Requirements

1. Compute a trend analysis for net revenue and net income. Round to the nearest full percent.
2. Which grew faster during the period, net revenue or net income?

ED-15 Performing vertical analysis of a balance sheet

Learning Objective 3

2018 Current Assets: 12.5%

Theta Designs, Inc. has the following data:

THETA DESIGNS, INC. Comparative Balance Sheet December 31, 2018 and 2017		
	2018	**2017**
Assets		
Total Current Assets	$ 25,000	$ 73,440
Property, Plant, and Equipment, Net	153,600	168,300
Other Assets	21,400	64,260
Total Assets	**$ 200,000**	**$ 306,000**
Liabilities		
Total Current Liabilities	$ 27,600	$ 49,266
Long-term Debt	72,400	208,998
Total Liabilities	100,000	258,264
Stockholders' Equity		
Total Stockholders' Equity	100,000	47,736
Total Liabilities and Stockholders' Equity	**$ 200,000**	**$ 306,000**

Perform a vertical analysis of Theta Designs's balance sheet for each year.

ED-16 Preparing common-size income statements

Learning Objective 3

1. 2018 Net Income 27.6%

Refer to the data presented for Mulberry Designs, Inc. in Exercise E15-13.

Requirements

1. Prepare a comparative common-size income statement for Mulberry Designs, Inc. using the 2018 and 2017 data. Round percentages to one-tenth percent (three decimal places).

2. To an investor, how does 2018 compare with 2017? Explain your reasoning.

ED-17 Computing working capital changes

Learning Objective 4

2019 Working Capital $255,000

Data for Research Enterprises follows:

	2019	**2018**	**2017**
Total Current Assets	$ 490,000	$ 320,000	$ 230,000
Total Current Liabilities	235,000	160,000	115,000

Compute the dollar amount of change and the percentage of change in Research Enterprises's working capital each year during 2019 and 2018. What do the calculated changes indicate?

Learning Objective 4

e. 89 days

ED-18 Computing key ratios

The financial statements of Valerie's Natural Foods include the following items:

	Current Year	Preceding Year
Balance Sheet:		
Cash	$ 16,000	$ 26,000
Short-term Investments	19,000	28,000
Net Accounts Receivable	60,000	92,000
Merchandise Inventory	78,000	74,000
Prepaid Expenses	17,000	6,000
Total Current Assets	190,000	226,000
Total Current Liabilities	136,000	82,000
Income Statement:		
Net Credit Sales	$ 476,000	
Cost of Goods Sold	312,000	

Compute the following ratios for the current year:

a. Current ratio

b. Cash ratio

c. Acid-test ratio

d. Inventory turnover

e. Days' sales in inventory

f. Days' sales in receivables

g. Gross profit percentage

Learning Objective 4

d. 2018: 61.9%

ED-19 Analyzing the ability to pay liabilities

Big Beautiful Photo Shop has asked you to determine whether the company's ability to pay current liabilities and total liabilities improved or deteriorated during 2018. To answer this question, you gather the following data:

	2018	2017
Cash	$ 58,000	$ 47,000
Short-term Investments	34,000	0
Net Accounts Receivable	140,000	124,000
Merchandise Inventory	217,000	272,000
Total Assets	530,000	565,000
Total Current Liabilities	288,000	205,000
Long-term Notes Payable	40,000	50,000
Income from Operations	165,000	158,000
Interest Expense	55,000	41,000

Compute the following ratios for 2018 and 2017, and evaluate the company's ability to pay its current liabilities and total liabilities:

a. Current ratio

b. Cash ratio

c. Acid-test ratio

d. Debt ratio

e. Debt to equity ratio

ED-20 Analyzing profitability

Micatin, Inc.'s comparative income statement follows. The 2017 data are given as needed.

Learning Objective 4

1. 2019: 13.0%

MICATIN INC. Comparative Income Statement Years Ended December 31, 2019 and 2018			
Dollars in thousands	2019	2018	2017
Net Sales Revenue	$ 181,000	$ 160,000	
Cost of Goods Sold	93,500	86,500	
Selling and Administrative Expenses	45,000	40,500	
Interest Expense	8,000	12,000	
Income Tax Expense	11,000	10,500	
Net Income	$ 23,500	$ 10,500	
Additional data:			
Total Assets	$ 209,000	$ 187,000	$ 167,000
Common Stockholders' Equity	96,000	91,500	80,500
Preferred Dividends	2,000	2,000	0
Common Shares Outstanding During the Year	15,000	15,000	10,000

Requirements

1. Calculate the profit margin ratio for 2019 and 2018.
2. Calculate the rate of return on total assets for 2019 and 2018.
3. Calculate the asset turnover ratio for 2019 and 2018.
4. Calculate the rate of return on common stockholders' equity for 2019 and 2018.
5. Calculate the earnings per share for 2019 and 2018.
6. Calculate the 2019 dividend payout on common stock. Assume dividends per share for common stock are equal to $1.13 per share.
7. Did the company's operating performance improve or deteriorate during 2019?

ED-21 Evaluating a stock as an investment

Data for Oxford State Bank follow:

Learning Objective 4

Dividend Yield 2018: 1.4%

	2018	2017
Net Income	$ 71,900	$ 64,300
Dividends—Common	22,000	22,000
Dividends—Preferred	16,800	16,800
Total Stockholders' Equity at Year-End (includes 95,000 shares of common stock)	770,000	610,000
Preferred Stock	200,000	200,000
Market Price per Share of Common Stock	$ 16.50	$ 10.00

Evaluate the common stock of Oxford State Bank as an investment. Specifically, use the three stock ratios to determine whether the common stock has increased or decreased in attractiveness during the past year. Round to two decimal places.

Learning Objective 4

Total Assets $2,800,000

ED-22 Using ratios to reconstruct a balance sheet

The following data are adapted from the financial statements of Bridget's Shops, Inc.:

Total Current Assets	$ 1,216,000
Accumulated Depreciation	2,000,000
Total Liabilities	1,540,000
Preferred Stock	0
Debt Ratio	55%
Current Ratio	1.60

Prepare Bridget's condensed balance sheet as of December 31, 2018.

> Problems Group A

Learning Objectives 2, 4

2. 2019: 16.7%

PD-23A Computing trend analysis and return on common equity

Net sales revenue, net income, and common stockholders' equity for Eyesight Mission Corporation, a manufacturer of contact lenses, follow for a four-year period.

	2019	2018	2017	2016
Net Sales Revenue	$ 766,000	$ 708,00	$ 644,000	$ 664,000
Net Income	60,000	38,000	36,000	44,000
Ending Common Stockholders' Equity	368,000	352,000	326,000	296,000

Requirements

1. Compute trend analyses for each item for 2017–2019. Use 2016 as the base year, and round to the nearest whole percent.
2. Compute the rate of return on common stockholders' equity for 2017–2019, rounding to three decimal places.

Learning Objective 3

1. Net Income 11.3%

PD-24A Performing vertical analysis

The Klein Department Stores, Inc. chief executive officer (CEO) has asked you to compare the company's profit performance and financial position with the averages for the industry. The CEO has given you the company's income statement and balance sheet as well as the industry average data for retailers.

KLEIN DEPARTMENT STORES, INC.
Income Statement Compared with Industry Average
Year Ended December 31, 2018

	Klein	Industry Average
Net Sales Revenue	$ 778,000	100.0%
Cost of Goods Sold	524,372	65.8
Gross Profit	253,628	34.2
Operating Expenses	159,490	19.7
Operating Income	94,138	14.5
Other Expenses	6,224	0.4
Net Income	$ 87,914	14.1%

KLEIN DEPARTMENT STORES, INC.
Balance Sheet Compared with Industry Average
December 31, 2018

	Klein	Industry Average
Current Assets	$ 339,000	70.9%
Property, Plant, and Equipment, Net	130,000	23.6
Intangible Assets, Net	7,000	0.8
Other Assets	24,000	4.7
Total Assets	$ 500,000	100.0%
Current Liabilities	$ 232,000	48.1%
Long-term Liabilities	111,000	16.6
Total Liabilities	343,000	64.7
Stockholders' Equity	157,000	35.3
Total Liabilities and Stockholders' Equity	$ 500,000	100.0%

Requirements

1. Prepare a vertical analysis for Klein for both its income statement and balance sheet.
2. Compare the company's profit performance and financial position with the average for the industry.

Note: Problem PD-24A must be completed before attempting Problem PD-25A.

PD-25A **Preparing common-size statements, analysis of profitability and financial position, comparison with the industry, and using ratios to evaluate a company**

Consider the data for Klein Department Stores presented in Problem PD-24A.

Requirements

1. Prepare a common-size income statement and balance sheet for Klein. The first column of each statement should present Klein's common-size statement, and the second column, the industry averages.
2. For the profitability analysis, compute Klein's (a) gross profit percentage and (b) profit margin ratio. Compare these figures with the industry averages. Is Klein's profit performance better or worse than the industry average?
3. For the analysis of financial position, compute Klein's (a) current ratio and (b) debt to equity ratio. Compare these ratios with the industry averages. Assume the current ratio industry average is 1.47, and the debt to equity industry average is 1.83. Is Klein's financial position better or worse than the industry averages?

Learning Objectives 3, 4

2. Gross Profit Percentage 32.6%

PD-26A **Determining the effects of business transactions on selected ratios**

Financial statement data of *Style Traveler Magazine* include the following items:

Cash	$ 23,000
Accounts Receivable, Net	81,000
Merchandise Inventory	185,000
Total Assets	635,000
Accounts Payable	99,000
Accrued Liabilities	37,000
Short-term Notes Payable	51,000
Long-term Liabilities	224,000
Net Income	68,000
Common Shares Outstanding	20,000 shares

Learning Objective 4

1. Current Ratio 1.55

Requirements

1. Compute *Style Traveler*'s current ratio, debt ratio, and earnings per share. Round all ratios to two decimal places, and use the following format for your answer:

Current Ratio	Debt Ratio	Earnings per Share

2. Compute the three ratios after evaluating the effect of each transaction that follows. Consider each transaction *separately*.

   a. Purchased merchandise inventory of $49,000 on account.

   b. Borrowed $127,000 on a long-term note payable.

c. Issued 2,000 shares of common stock, receiving cash of $107,000.

d. Received cash on account, $5,000.

Learning Objective 4

1. 2018: e. 48.9%

PD-27A Using ratios to evaluate a stock investment

Comparative financial statement data of Sanfield, Inc. follow:

SANFIELD, INC. Comparative Income Statement Years Ended December 31, 2018 and 2017		
	2018	**2017**
Net Sales Revenue	$ 462,000	$ 430,000
Cost of Goods Sold	236,000	213,000
Gross Profit	226,000	217,000
Operating Expenses	135,000	133,000
Income from Operations	91,000	84,000
Interest Expense	8,000	12,000
Income Before Income Tax	83,000	72,000
Income Tax Expense	18,000	22,000
Net Income	$ 65,000	$ 50,000

SANFIELD, INC. Comparative Balance Sheet December 31, 2018 and 2017			
	2018	**2017**	**2016***
Assets			
Current Assets:			
Cash	$ 99,000	$ 97,000	
Accounts Receivable, Net	109,000	117,000	$ 100,000
Merchandise Inventory	142,000	164,000	207,000
Prepaid Expenses	15,000	5,000	
Total Current Assets	365,000	383,000	
Property, Plant, and Equipment, Net	215,000	177,000	
Total Assets	$ 580,000	$ 560,000	$ 599,000
Liabilities			
Total Current Liabilities	$ 222,000	$ 244,000	
Long-term Liabilities	113,000	92,000	
Total Liabilities	335,000	336,000	
Stockholders' Equity			
Preferred Stock, 4%	92,000	92,000	
Common Stockholders' Equity, no par	153,000	132,000	85,000
Total Liabilities and Stockholders' Equity	$ 580,000	$ 560,000	

* Selected 2016 amounts

1. Market price of Sanfield's common stock: $51.48 at December 31, 2018, and $37.08 at December 31, 2017.

2. Common shares outstanding: 16,000 on December 31, 2018 and 15,000 on December 31, 2017 and 2016.

3. All sales are on credit.

Requirements

1. Compute the following ratios for 2018 and 2017:

    a. Current ratio

    b. Cash ratio

    c. Times-interest-earned ratio

    d. Inventory turnover

    e. Gross profit percentage

    f. Debt to equity ratio

    g. Rate of return on common stockholders' equity

    h. Earnings per share of common stock

    i. Price/earnings ratio

2. Decide (a) whether Sanfield's ability to pay debts and to sell inventory improved or deteriorated during 2018 and (b) whether the investment attractiveness of its common stock appears to have increased or decreased.

PD-28A Using ratios to decide between two stock investments

Learning Objective 4

1. Digitalized e. $4.25

Assume that you are purchasing an investment and have decided to invest in a company in the digital phone business. You have narrowed the choice to Digitalized Corp. and Every Zone, Inc. and have assembled the following data.

Selected income statement data for the current year:

	Digitalized	Every Zone
Net Sales Revenue (all on credit)	$ 423,035	$ 493,845
Cost of Goods Sold	210,000	260,000
Interest Expense	0	19,000
Net Income	51,000	72,000

Selected balance sheet and market price data at the *end* of the current year:

	Digitalized	Every Zone
Current Assets:		
Cash	$ 24,000	$ 17,000
Short-term Investments	40,000	14,000
Accounts Receivable, Net	40,000	48,000
Merchandise Inventory	66,000	97,000
Prepaid Expenses	23,000	12,000
Total Current Assets	$ 193,000	$ 188,000
Total Assets	$ 266,000	$ 323,000
Total Current Liabilities	105,000	96,000
Total Liabilities	105,000	128,000
Common Stock:		
$1 par (12,000 shares)	12,000	
$1 par (17,000 shares)		17,000
Total Stockholders' Equity	161,000	195,000
Market Price per Share of Common Stock	76.50	114.48
Dividends Paid per Common Share	1.10	1.00

Selected balance sheet data at the *beginning* of the current year:

	Digitalized	Every Zone
Balance Sheet:		
Accounts Receivable, net	$ 41,000	$ 54,000
Merchandise Inventory	81,000	87,000
Total Assets	261,000	272,000
Common Stock:		
$1 par (12,000 shares)	12,000	
$1 par (17,000 shares)		17,000

Your strategy is to invest in companies that have low price/earnings ratios but appear to be in good shape financially. Assume that you have analyzed all other factors and that your decision depends on the results of ratio analysis.

Requirements

1. Compute the following ratios for both companies for the current year:
   a. Acid-test ratio
   b. Inventory turnover
   c. Days' sales in receivables
   d. Debt ratio
   e. Earnings per share of common stock
   f. Price/earnings ratio
   g. Dividend payout

2. Decide which company's stock better fits your investment strategy.

Learning Objectives 2, 4

3. 2018: Inventory turnover 8.04

PD-29A Completing a comprehensive financial statement analysis

In its annual report, ABC Athletic Supply, Inc. includes the following five-year financial summary:

ABC ATHLETIC SUPPLY, INC.

Five-Year Financial Summary (Partial; adapted)

(Dollar amounts in thousands except per share data)	2018	2017	2016	2015	2014	2013
Net Sales Revenue	$ 250,000	$ 216,000	$ 191,000	$ 161,000	$ 134,000	
Net Sales Revenue Increase	16%	13%	19%	20%	17%	
Domestic Comparative Store Sales Increase	5%	6%	4%	7%	9%	
Other Income—Net	2,110	1,840	1,760	1,690	1,330	
Cost of Goods Sold	189,250	164,592	148,216	126,385	106,396	
Selling and Administrative Expenses	41,210	36,330	31,620	27,440	22,540	
Interest:						
Interest Expense	(1,080)	(1,380)	(1,400)	(1,020)	(830)	
Interest Income	125	165	155	235	190	
Income Tax Expense	4,470	3,900	3,700	3,320	2,700	
Net Income	16,225	11,803	7,979	4,760	3,054	
Per Share of Common Stock:						
Net Income	1.60	1.30	1.20	1.00	0.78	
Dividends	0.40	0.38	0.34	0.30	0.26	
Financial Position						
Current Assets, Excluding Merchandise Inventory	$ 30,700	$ 27,200	$ 26,700	$ 24,400	$ 21,500	
Merchandise Inventory	24,500	22,600	21,700	19,000	17,500	$ 16,700
Property, Plant, and Equipment, Net	51,400	45,200	40,000	35,100	25,600	
Total Assets	106,600	95,000	88,400	78,500	64,600	
Current Liabilities	32,300	28,000	28,300	25,000	16,500	
Long-term Debt	23,000	21,500	17,600	19,100	12,000	
Stockholders' Equity	51,300	45,500	42,500	34,400	36,100	
Financial Ratios						
Acid-Test Ratio	1.0	1.0	0.9	1.0	1.3	
Rate of Return on Total Assets	17.2%	14.4%	11.2%	8.1%	7.1%	
Rate of Return on Common Stockholders' Equity	33.5%	26.8%	20.8%	13.5%	13.0%	

Requirements

Analyze the company's financial summary for the fiscal years 2014–2018 to decide whether to invest in the common stock of ABC. Include the following sections in your analysis.

1. Trend analysis for net sales revenue and net income (use 2014 as the base year).
2. Profitability analysis.
3. Evaluation of the ability to sell merchandise inventory.
4. Evaluation of the ability to pay debts.
5. Evaluation of dividends.
6. Should you invest in the common stock of ABC Athletic Supply, Inc.? Fully explain your final decision

> Problems Group B

PD-30B Computing trend analysis and return on common equity

Net sales revenue, net income, and common stockholders' equity for Azbel Mission Corporation, a manufacturer of contact lenses, follow for a four-year period.

Learning Objectives 2, 4

2. 2018: 11.9%

	2019	2018	2017	2016
Net Sales Revenue	$ 758,000	$ 701,000	$ 639,000	$ 659,000
Net Income	59,000	40,000	39,000	42,000
Ending Common Stockholders' Equity	360,000	346,000	324,000	302,000

Requirements

1. Compute trend analyses for each item for 2017–2019. Use 2016 as the base year, and round to the nearest whole percent.
2. Compute the rate of return on common stockholders' equity for 2017–2019, rounding to three decimal places.

PD-31B Performing vertical analysis

The Randall Department Stores, Inc. chief executive officer (CEO) has asked you to compare the company's profit performance and financial position with the averages for the industry. The CEO has given you the company's income statement and balance sheet as well as the industry average data for retailers.

Learning Objective 3

1. Net Income 10.9%

RANDALL DEPARTMENT STORES, INC.
Income Statement Compared with Industry Average
Year Ended December 31, 2018

	Randall	Industry Average
Net Sales Revenue	$ 783,000	100.0%
Cost of Goods Sold	527,742	65.8
Gross Profit	255,258	34.2
Operating Expenses	163,647	19.7
Operating Income	91,611	14.5
Other Expenses	6,264	0.4
Net Income	$ 85,347	14.1%

RANDALL DEPARTMENT STORES, INC.
Balance Sheet Compared with Industry Average
December 31, 2018

	Randall	Industry Average
Current Assets	$ 310,040	70.9%
Property, Plant, and Equipment, Net	119,600	23.6
Intangible Assets, Net	7,360	0.8
Other Assets	23,000	4.7
Total Assets	$ 460,000	100.0%
Current Liabilities	$ 210,680	48.1%
Long-term Liabilities	103,960	16.6
Total Liabilities	314,640	64.7
Stockholders' Equity	145,360	35.3
Total Liabilities and Stockholders' Equity	$ 460,000	100.0%

Requirements

1. Prepare a vertical analysis for Randall for both its income statement and balance sheet.

2. Compare the company's profit performance and financial position with the average for the industry.

Note: Problem PD-31B must be completed before attempting Problem PD-32B.

Learning Objectives 3, 4

1. Current Assets 67.4%

PD-32B Preparing common-size statements, analysis of profitability and financial position, comparison with the industry, and using ratios to evaluate a company

Consider the data for Randall Department Stores presented in Problem PD-31B.

Requirements

1. Prepare a common-size income statement and balance sheet for Randall. The first column of each statement should present Randall's common-size statement, and the second column, the industry averages.

2. For the profitability analysis, compute Randall's (a) gross profit percentage and (b) profit margin ratio. Compare these figures with the industry averages. Is Randall's profit performance better or worse than the industry average?

3. For the analysis of financial position, compute Randall's (a) current ratio and (b) debt to equity ratio. Compare these ratios with the industry averages. Assume the current ratio industry average is 1.47, and the debt to equity industry average is 1.83. Is Randall's financial position better or worse than the industry averages?

Learning Objective 4

1. Earnings per Share $1.38

PD-33B Determining the effects of business transactions on selected ratios

Financial statement data of *Modern Traveler's Magazine* include the following items:

Cash	$ 19,000
Accounts Receivable, Net	82,000
Merchandise Inventory	183,000
Total Assets	638,000
Accounts Payable	102,000
Accrued Liabilities	35,000
Short-term Notes Payable	50,000
Long-term Liabilities	221,000
Net Income	69,000
Common Shares Outstanding	50,000 shares

Requirements

1. Compute *Modern Traveler's* current ratio, debt ratio, and earnings per share. Round all ratios to two decimal places, and use the following format for your answer:

Current Ratio	Debt Ratio	Earnings per Share

2. Compute the three ratios after evaluating the effect of each transaction that follows. Consider each transaction *separately*.

   a. Purchased merchandise inventory of $42,000 on account.

   b. Borrowed $121,000 on a long-term note payable.

   c. Issued 5,000 shares of common stock, receiving cash of $103,000.

   d. Received cash on account, $5,000.

PD-34B Using ratios to evaluate a stock investment

Comparative financial statement data of Garfield, Inc. follow:

Learning Objective 4

1. 2017: e. 50.2%

GARFIELD, INC.
Comparative Income Statement
Years Ended December 31, 2018 and 2017

	2018	2017
Net Sales Revenue	$ 461,000	$ 424,000
Cost of Goods Sold	241,000	211,000
Gross Profit	220,000	213,000
Operating Expenses	137,000	135,000
Income from Operations	83,000	78,000
Interest Expense	9,000	13,000
Income Before Income Tax	74,000	65,000
Income Tax Expense	18,000	24,000
Net Income	$ 56,000	$ 41,000

GARFIELD, INC.
Comparative Balance Sheet
December 31, 2018 and 2017

	2018	2017	2016*
Assets			
Current Assets:			
Cash	$ 99,000	$ 98,000	
Accounts Receivable, Net	108,000	114,000	$ 107,000
Merchandise Inventory	146,000	164,000	202,000
Prepaid Expenses	20,000	9,000	
Total Current Assets	373,000	385,000	
Property, Plant, and Equipment, Net	211,000	181,000	
Total Assets	$ 584,000	$ 566,000	$ 602,000
Liabilities			
Total Current Liabilities	$ 227,000	$ 246,000	
Long-term Liabilities	117,000	100,000	
Total Liabilities	344,000	346,000	
Stockholders' Equity			
Preferred Stock, 3%	98,000	98,000	
Common Stockholders' Equity, no par	142,000	122,000	89,000
Total Liabilities and Stockholders' Equity	$ 584,000	$ 566,000	

* Selected 2016 amounts

1. Market price of Garfield's common stock: $69.36 at December 31, 2018, and $38.04 at December 31, 2017.

2. Common shares outstanding: 14,000 on December 31, 2018 and 12,000 on December 31, 2017 and 2016.

3. All sales are on credit.

Requirements

1. Compute the following ratios for 2018 and 2017:

   a. Current ratio

   b. Cash ratio

   c. Times-interest-earned ratio

   d. Inventory turnover

   e. Gross profit percentage

   f. Debt to equity ratio

   g. Rate of return on common stockholders' equity

   h. Earnings per share of common stock

   i. Price/earnings ratio

2. Decide (a) whether Garfield's ability to pay debts and to sell inventory improved or deteriorated during 2018 and (b) whether the investment attractiveness of its common stock appears to have increased or decreased.

Learning Objective 4

1c. Green Zone 38 days

PD-35B Using ratios to decide between two stock investments

Assume that you are purchasing an investment and have decided to invest in a company in the digital phone business. You have narrowed the choice to All Digital Corp. and Green Zone, Inc. and have assembled the following data.

Selected income statement data for the current year:

	All Digital	Green Zone
Net Sales Revenue (all on credit)	$ 417,925	$ 493,115
Cost of Goods Sold	209,000	258,000
Interest Expense	0	14,000
Net Income	58,000	72,000

Selected balance sheet and market price data at the *end* of the current year:

	All Digital	Green Zone
Current Assets:		
Cash	$ 23,000	$ 18,000
Short-term Investments	37,000	17,000
Accounts Receivable, Net	39,000	49,000
Merchandise Inventory	64,000	102,000
Prepaid Expenses	21,000	17,000
Total Current Assets	$ 184,000	$ 203,000
Total Assets	$ 263,000	$ 326,000
Total Current Liabilities	105,000	99,000
Total Liabilities	105,000	134,000
Common Stock:		
$1 par (10,000 shares)	10,000	
$2 par (14,000 shares)		28,000
Total Stockholders' Equity	158,000	192,000
Market Price per Share of Common Stock	92.80	128.50
Dividends Paid per Common Share	1.20	0.90

Selected balance sheet data at the *beginning* of the current year:

	All Digital	Green Zone
Balance Sheet:		
Accounts Receivable, Net	$ 41,000	$ 54 000
Merchandise Inventory	81,000	89,000
Total Assets	258,000	277,000
Common Stock:		
$1 par (10,000 shares)	10,000	
$2 par (14,000 shares)		28,000

Your strategy is to invest in companies that have low price/earnings ratios but appear to be in good shape financially. Assume that you have analyzed all other factors and that your decision depends on the results of ratio analysis.

Requirements

1. Compute the following ratios for both companies for the current year:

   a. Acid-test ratio

   b. Inventory turnover

   c. Days' sales in receivables

   d. Debt ratio

   e. Earnings per share of common stock

   f. Price/earnings ratio

   g. Dividend payout

2. Decide which company's stock better fits your investment strategy.

Learning Objectives 2, 4

3. 2018: Inventory turnover 8.86

PD-36B Completing a comprehensive financial statement analysis

In its annual report, XYZ Athletic Supply, Inc. includes the following five-year financial summary:

XYZ ATHLETIC SUPPLY, INC.
Five-Year Financial Summary (Partial; adapted)

(Dollar amounts in thousands except per share data)	2018	2017	2016	2015	2014	2013
Net Sales Revenue	$ 275,000	$ 222,000	$ 199,000	$ 171,000	$ 131,000	
Net Sales Revenue Increase	24%	12%	16%	31%	17%	
Domestic Comparative Store Sales Increase	6%	6%	5%	8%	10%	
Other Income—Net	2,090	1,780	1,770	1,700	1,310	
Cost of Goods Sold	208,725	169,386	154,822	134,235	103,883	
Selling and Administrative Expenses	41,280	36,340	31,670	27,450	22,540	
Interest:						
Interest Expense	(1,070)	(1,370)	(1,330)	(1,100)	(800)	
Interest Income	140	155	150	230	140	
Income Tax Expense	4,420	3,900	3,610	3,390	2,730	
Net Income	21,735	12,939	9,488	6,755	2,497	
Per Share of Common Stock:						
Net Income	1.10	0.80	0.70	0.50	0.28	
Dividends	0.45	0.43	0.39	0.35	0.31	
Financial Position						
Current Assets, Excluding Merchandise Inventory	$ 30,900	$ 27,200	$ 26,800	$ 24,400	$ 21,800	
Merchandise Inventory	24,700	22,400	21,600	19,300	17,000	$ 16,800
Property, Plant, and Equipment, Net	51,600	46,200	40,500	35,000	25,200	
Total Assets	107,200	95,800	88,900	78,700	64,000	
Current Liabilities	32,600	27,800	28,800	25,600	17,000	
Long-term Debt	23,000	21,200	16,800	18,600	12,900	
Stockholders' Equity	51,600	46,800	43,300	35,500	34,100	
Financial Ratios						
Acid-Test Ratio	0.9	1.0	0.9	1.0	1.3	
Rate of Return on Total Assets	22.5%	15.5%	12.8%	10.9%	9.9%	
Rate of Return on Common Stockholders' Equity	44.2%	28.7%	24.1%	19.4%	18.9%	

Requirements

Analyze the company's financial summary for the fiscal years 2014–2018 to decide whether to invest in the common stock of XYZ. Include the following sections in your analysis.

1. Trend analysis for net sales revenue and net income (use 2014 as the base year).
2. Profitability analysis.
3. Evaluation of the ability to sell merchandise inventory.
4. Evaluation of the ability to pay debts.
5. Evaluation of dividends.
6. Should you invest in the common stock of XYZ Athletic Supply, Inc.? Fully explain your final decision

CRITICAL THINKING

> Using Excel

PD-37 Using Excel for financial statement analysis

Download an Excel template for this problem online in MyAccountingLab or at http://www.pearsonhighered.com/Horngren.
Riverside Sweets, a retail candy store chain, reported the following figures:

RIVERSIDE SWEETS Balance Sheet June 30, 2018 and 2019		
	2019	**2018**
Assets		
Current Assets:		
Cash	$ 125,000	$ 119,000
Short-term Investments	685,000	650,000
Accounts Receivable	225,000	198,000
Merchandise Inventory	65,000	70,000
Other Current Assets	195,000	191,000
Total Current Assets	1,295,000	1,228,000
Property, Plant, and Equipment, Net	875,000	832,000
Total Assets	$ 2,170,000	$ 2,060,000
Liabilities		
Current Liabilities:		
Accounts Payable	$ 265,000	$ 251,750
Accrued Liabilities	641,000	725,523
Total Current Liabilities	906,000	977,273
Long-term Liabilities		
Bonds Payable	250,000	150,000
Mortgage Payable	150,000	175,000
Total Long-term Liabilities	400,000	325,000
Total Liabilities	1,306,000	1,302,273
Stockholders' Equity		
Common Stock, $1 par, 225,000 shares		
issued and outstanding	225,000	225,000
Paid-In Capital in Excess of Par	58,000	58,000
Retained Earnings	581,000	474,727
Total Stockholders' Equity	864,000	757,727
Total Liabilities and Stockholders' Equity	$ 2,170,000	$ 2,060,000

RIVERSIDE SWEETS	
Income Statement	
Year Ended June 30, 2019	
Net Sales Revenue	$ 2,800,000
Cost of Goods Sold	1,551,600
Gross Profit	1,248,400
Operating Expenses	450,540
Operating Income	797,860
Other Income and (Expenses):	
Interest Expense	(15,000)
Income Before Income Taxes	782,860
Income Tax Expense	153,529
Net Income	$ 629,331

Additional financial information:

a. 75% of net sales revenue are on account.

b. Market price of stock is $36 per share on June 30, 2019.

c. Annual dividend for 2019 was $1.50 per share.

d. All short-term investments are cash equivalents.

Requirements

1. Perform a horizontal analysis on the balance sheet for 2018 and 2019.

2. Perform a vertical analysis on the income statement.

3. Compute the following ratios:

a. Working Capital	**k.** Debt to Equity Ratio
b. Current Ratio	**l.** Times-Interest-Earned Ratio
c. Acid-Test (Quick) Ratio	**m.** Profit Margin Ratio
d. Cash Ratio	**n.** Rate of Return on Total Assets
e. Accounts Receivable Turnover	**o.** Asset Turnover Ratio
f. Days' Sales in Receivables	**p.** Rate of Return on Common Stockholders' Equity
g. Inventory Turnover	**q.** Earnings per Share (EPS)
h. Days' Sales in Inventory	**r.** Price/Earnings Ratio
i. Gross Profit Percentage	**s.** Dividend Yield
j. Debt Ratio	**t.** Dividend Payout

> Continuing Problem

PD-38 Using ratios to evaluate a stock investment

This problem continues the Canyon Canoe Company situation from Appendix C. The company wants to invest some of its excess cash in trading securities and is considering two investments, The Paddle Company (PC) and Recreational Life Vests (RLV). The income statement, balance sheet, and other data for both companies follow for 2019 and 2018, as well as selected data for 2017:

	THE PADDLE COMPANY Comparative Financial Statements Years Ended December 31			RECREATIONAL LIFE VESTS Comparative Financial Statements Years Ended December 31		
Income Statement	2019	2018	2017	2019	2018	2017
Net Sales Revenue	$ 430,489	$ 425,410		$ 410,570	$ 383,870	
Cost of Goods Sold	258,756	256,797		299,110	280,190	
Gross Profit	171,733	168,613		111,460	103,680	
Operating Expenses	153,880	151,922		78,290	70,830	
Operating Income	17,853	16,691		33,170	32,850	
Interest Expense	865	788		2,780	2,980	
Income before Income Tax	16,988	15,903		30,390	29,870	
Income Tax Expense	5,137	4,809		8,780	8,630	
Net Income	$ 11,851	$ 11,094		$ 21,610	$ 21,240	
Balance Sheet						
Assets						
Cash & Cash Equivalents	$ 69,159	$ 70,793		$ 65,730	$ 55,270	
Accounts Receivable	44,798	44,452	$ 44,104	39,810	38,650	$ 36,460
Merchandise Inventory	79,919	66,341	76,363	68,500	65,230	59,930
Other Current Assets	15,494	16,264		24,450	37,630	
Total Current Assets	209,370	197,850		198,490	196,780	
Long-term Assets	89,834	90,776		116,760	116,270	
Total Assets	$ 299,204	$ 288,626	$ 276,482	$ 315,250	$ 313,050	$ 310,640
Liabilities						
Current Liabilities	$ 69,554	$ 60,232		$ 90,810	$ 90,010	
Long-term Liabilities	31,682	29,936		96,310	105,890	
Total Liabilities	101,236	90,168		187,120	195,900	
Stockholders' Equity						
Common Stock	72,795	80,885		111,530	102,480	
Retained Earnings	125,173	117,573		16,600	14,670	
Total Stockholders' Equity	197,968	198,458	197,668	128,130	117,150	103,840
Total Liabilities and Stockholder's Equity	$ 299,204	$ 288,626		$ 315,250	$ 313,050	
Other Data						
Market price per share	$ 21.38	$ 33.82		$ 46.37	$ 51.64	
Annual dividend per share	0.32	0.30		0.53	0.45	
Weighted average number of shares outstanding	9,000	8,000		9,000	8,000	

Requirements

1. Using the financial statements given, compute the following ratios for both companies for 2019 and 2018. Assume all sales are credit sales. Round all ratios to two decimal places.

   a. Current ratio
   b. Cash ratio
   c. Inventory turnover
   d. Accounts receivable turnover
   e. Gross profit percentage
   f. Debt ratio
   g. Debt to equity ratio

   h. Profit margin ratio
   i. Asset turnover ratio
   j. Rate of return on common stockholders' equity
   k. Earnings per share
   l. Price/earnings ratio
   m. Dividend yield
   n. Dividend payout

2. Compare the companies' performance for 2019 and 2018. Make a recommendation to Canyon Canoe Company about investing in these companies. Which company would be a better investment, The Paddle Company or Recreational Life Vests? Base your answer on ability to pay current liabilities, ability to sell merchandise and collect receivables, ability to pay long-term debt, profitability, and attractiveness as an investment.

> Decision Case D-1

Lance Berkman is the controller of Saturn, a dance club whose year-end is December 31. Berkman prepares checks for suppliers in December, makes the proper journal entries, and posts them to the appropriate accounts in that month. However, he holds on to the checks and mails them to the suppliers in January.

Requirements

1. What financial ratio(s) is(are) most affected by the action to hold onto the checks until January?
2. What is Berkman's purpose in undertaking this activity?

> Ethical Issue D-1

Ross's Lipstick Company's long-term debt agreements make certain demands on the business. For example, Ross may not purchase treasury stock in excess of the balance of retained earnings. Also, long-term debt may not exceed stockholders' equity, and the current ratio may not fall below 1.50. If Ross fails to meet any of these requirements, the company's lenders have the authority to take over management of the company.

Changes in consumer demand have made it hard for Ross to attract customers. Current liabilities have mounted faster than current assets, causing the current ratio to fall to 1.47. Before releasing financial statements, Ross's management is scrambling to improve the current ratio. The controller points out that an investment can be classified as either long-term or short-term, depending on management's intention. By deciding to convert an investment to cash within one year, Ross can classify the investment as short-term—a current asset. On the controller's recommendation, Ross's board of directors votes to reclassify long-term investments as short-term.

Requirements

1. What effect will reclassifying the investments have on the current ratio? Is Ross's true financial position stronger as a result of reclassifying the investments?
2. Shortly after the financial statements are released, sales improve; so, too, does the current ratio. As a result, Ross's management decides not to sell the investments it had reclassified as short-term. Accordingly, the company reclassifies the investments as long-term. Has management behaved unethically? Give the reasoning underlying your answer.

> Financial Statement Case D-1

Use **Target Corporation**'s Fiscal 2015 Annual Report to answer the following questions. Visit **http://www.pearsonhighered.com/Horngren** to view a link to the Target Corporation Annual Report.

Requirements

1. Compute trend analyses for Sales and Net earnings / (loss). Use 2013 as the base year. What is the most notable aspect of these data?

2. Perform a vertical analysis for Target Corporation's balance sheet as of January 31, 2016 (fiscal year 2015), and January 31, 2015 (fiscal year 2014). Include only these main categories:

   Assets:
   Total current assets
   Property and equipment, net
   Noncurrent assets of discontinued operations
   Other noncurrent assets
   Total assets
   Liabilities and shareholders' investment:
   Total current liabilities
   Total noncurrent liabilities
   Total shareholders' investment
   Total liabilities and shareholders' investment

> Team Projects

Team Project D-1

Select an industry you are interested in, and pick any company in that industry to use as the benchmark. Then select two other companies in the same industry. For each category of ratios, compute all the ratios for the three companies. Write a two-page report that compares the two companies with the benchmark company.

Team Project D-2

Select a company and obtain its financial statements. Convert the income statement and the balance sheet to common size, and compare the company you selected to the industry average. The Risk Management Association's *Annual Statement Studies* and Dun & Bradstreet's *Industry Norms & Key Business Ratios* publish common-size statements for most industries.

MyAccountingLab   **For a wealth of online resources, including exercises, problems, media, and immediate tutorial help, please visit http://www.myaccountinglab.com.**

Quick Check Answers

1. b   **2.** b   **3.** a   **4.** c   **5.** a   **6.** b   **7.** d   **8.** c   **9.** a   **10.** c

Glossary

Absorption Costing The product costing method that assigns direct materials, direct labor, variable manufacturing overhead, and fixed manufacturing overhead to products. Required by GAAP for external reporting. (p. 1143)

Accelerated Depreciation Method A depreciation method that expenses more of the asset's cost near the start of its useful life and less at the end of its useful life. (p. 498)

Account A detailed record of all increases and decreases that have occurred in an individual asset, liability, or equity during a specific period. (p. 57)

Accounting The information system that measures business activities, processes the information into reports, and communicates the results to decision makers. (p. 2)

Accounting Cycle The process by which companies produce their financial statements for a specific period. (p. 201)

Accounting Equation The basic tool of accounting, measuring the resources of the business (what the business owns or has control of) and the claims to those resources (what the business owes to creditors and to the owners). Assets = Liabilities + Equity (p. 11)

Accounting Information System (AIS) A system that collects, records, stores, and processes accounting data to produce information that is useful for decision makers. (p. 2)

Accounting Rate of Return (ARR) A capital investment analysis method that measures the profitability of an investment. Average annual operating income / Average amount invested. (p. 1434)

Account Number On a check, the number that identifies the account upon which the payment is drawn. (p. 396)

Accounts Payable A short-term liability that will be paid in the future. (p. 15)

Accounts Payable Subsidiary Ledger A subsidiary ledger that includes an accounts payable account for each vendor that contains detailed information such as the amount purchased, paid, and owed. (p. B-7)

Accounts Receivable Subsidiary Ledger A subsidiary ledger that includes an accounts receivable account for each customer that contains detailed information such as the amount sold, received, and owed. (p. B-6)

Accounts Receivable The right to receive cash in the future from customers for goods sold or for services performed. (pp. 16, 433)

Accounts Receivable Turnover Ratio A ratio that measures the number of times the company collects the average accounts receivable balance in a year. Net credit sales / Average net accounts receivable. (pp. 457, 817)

Accrual Basis Accounting Accounting method that records revenues when earned and expenses when incurred. (p. 120)

Accrued Expense An expense that the business has incurred but has not yet paid. (p. 132)

Accrued Liability A liability for which the business knows the amount owed but the bill has not been paid. (p. 58)

Accrued Revenue A revenue that has been earned but for which the cash has not yet been collected. (p. 136)

Accumulated Depreciation The sum of all the depreciation expense recorded to date for a depreciable asset. (p. 129)

Acid-Test Ratio The ratio of the sum of cash, cash equivalents, short-term investments, and net current receivables to total current liabilities. The ratio tells whether the entity could pay all its current liabilities if they came due immediately. (pp. 456, 814)

Activity A task, operation, or procedure. (p. 1036)

Activity-Based Costing (ABC) Focuses on the costs of activities as the building blocks for allocating indirect costs to products and services. (p. 1036)

Activity-Based Management (ABM) Using activity-based cost information to make decisions that improve customer satisfaction while also increasing profits. (p. 1036)

Adjunct Account An account that is directly related to another account. Adjunct accounts have the same normal balance as the related account and are added to the related account on the balance sheet. (p. 632)

Adjusted Trial Balance A list of all the accounts with their adjusted balances. (p. 140)

Adjusting Entry An entry made at the end of the accounting period that is used to record revenues to the period in which they are earned and expenses to the period in which they occur. (p. 125)

Administrative Expenses Expenses incurred that are not related to marketing the company's goods and services. (p. 271)

Aging-of-Receivables Method A method of estimating uncollectible receivables by determining the balance of the Allowance for Bad Debts account based on the age of individual accounts receivable. (p. 446)

Allocation Base A denominator that links indirect costs to cost objects. Ideally, the allocation base is the primary cost driver of the indirect costs. (p. 919)

Allowance for Bad Debts A contra asset account, related to accounts receivable, that holds the estimated amount of uncollectible accounts. (p. 439)

Allowance Method A method of accounting for uncollectible receivables in which the company estimates bad debts expense instead of waiting to see which customers the company will not collect from. (p. 439)

Amortization Schedule A schedule that details each loan payment's allocation between principal and interest and the beginning and ending loan balances. (p. 620)

Amortization The process by which businesses spread the allocation of an intangible asset's cost over its useful life. (p. 512)

Annual Report Provides information about a company's financial condition. (p. 802)

Annuity A stream of equal cash payments made at equal time intervals. (pp. 640, 1438)

Appraisal Costs Costs incurred to detect poor-quality materials, goods, or services. (p. 1054)

Appropriation of Retained Earnings Restriction of a portion of retained earnings that is recorded by a journal entry. (p. 696)

Assets Economic resources that are expected to benefit the business in the future. Something the business owns or has control of. (p. 12)

Asset Turnover Ratio Measures how efficiently a business uses its average total assets to generate sales. Net sales revenue / Average total assets. (pp. 416, 821, 1341)

Audit An examination of a company's financial statements and records. (p. 10)

Authorized Stock The maximum number of shares of stock that the corporate charter allows the corporation to issue. (p. 673)

Available-for-Sale (AFS) Debt Investment A debt security that isn't a trading debt investment or a held-to-maturity debt investment. (p. 548)

Bad Debts Expense The cost to the seller of extending credit. It arises from the failure to collect from some credit customers. (p. 437)

Balanced Scorecard The performance evaluation system that requires management to consider both financial performance measures and operational performance measures when judging the performance of a company and its subunits. (p. 1331)

Balance Sheet Reports on the assets, liabilities, and stockholders' equity of the business as of a specific date. (p. 21)

Bank Reconciliation A document explaining the reasons for the difference between a depositor's cash records and the depositor's cash balance in its bank account. (p. 398)

Bank Statement A document from the bank that reports the activity in the customer's account. It shows the bank account's beginning and ending balances and lists the month's cash transactions conducted through the bank account. (p. 397)

Benchmarking The practice of comparing a company's performance with best practices from other companies. (pp. 811, 1186)

Board of Directors Elected by the stockholders and responsible for developing the strategic goals of a corporation. (p. 861)

Bond Payable A long-term debt issued to multiple lenders called bondholders, usually in increments of $1,000 per bond. (p. 623)

Book Value A depreciable asset's cost minus accumulated depreciation. (pp. 130, 496)

Breakeven Point The sales level at which operating income is zero. Total revenues equal total costs. (p. 1097)

Budget A financial plan that managers use to coordinate a business's activities with its goals and strategies. (p. 1184)

Budgetary Slack Occurs when managers intentionally understate expected revenues or overstate expected expenses to increase the chances of receiving favorable performance evaluations. (p. 1186)

Budget Performance Report A report that summarizes the actual results, budgeted amounts, and the differences. (p. 1267)

Business Segment An identifiable part of the company for which financial information is available. (p. 1154)

Callable Bonds Bonds that the issuer may call and pay off at a specified price whenever the issuer wants. (p. 635)

Canceled Checks Physical or scanned copies of the maker's cashed (paid) checks. (p. 397)

Capital Asset An operational asset used for a long period of time. (p. 1427)

Capital Budgeting The process of planning to invest in long-term assets in a way that returns the most profitability to the company. (p. 1427)

Capital Expenditure An expenditure that increases the capacity or efficiency of a plant asset or extends its useful life. Capital expenditures are debited to an asset account. (p. 493)

Capital Expenditures Budget The budget that presents the company's plan for purchasing property, plant, equipment, and other long-term assets. (p. 1190)

Capital Investment The acquisition of a capital asset. (p. 1427)

Capitalize Recording the acquisition of land, building, or other assets by debiting (increasing) an asset account. (p. 491)

Capital Rationing The process of ranking and choosing among alternative capital investments based on the availability of funds. (p. 1429)

Capital Stock Represents the individual's ownership of the corporation's capital. (p. 673)

Carrying Amount of Bonds A bond payable *minus* the discount account current balance

or *plus* the premium account current balance. (p. 630)

Cash Basis Accounting Accounting method that records revenues only when cash is received and expenses only when cash is paid. (p. 120)

Cash Budget The budget that details how the business expects to go from the beginning cash balance to the desired ending cash balance. (p. 1190)

Cash Equivalent A highly liquid investment that can be converted into cash in three months or less. (p. 403)

Cash Flows Cash receipts and cash payments of a business. (p. 733)

Cash Payments Journal Special journal used to record cash payments by check and currency. (p. B-16)

Cash Ratio A measure of a company's ability to pay current liabilities from cash and cash equivalents: (pp. 403, 814)

Cash Receipts Journal Special journal used to record cash receipts. (p. B-10)

Centralized Company A company in which major planning, directing, and controlling decisions are made by top executives. (p. 1325)

Certified Management Accountants (CMAs) Certified professionals who specialize in accounting and financial management knowledge. They typically work for a single company. (p. 4)

Certified Public Accountants (CPAs) Licensed professional accountants who serve the general public. (p. 4)

Chart of Accounts A list of all of a company's accounts with their account numbers. (p. 59)

Check A document that instructs a bank to pay the designated person or business a specified amount of money. (p. 396)

Chief Executive Officer (CEO) Officer of a company that has ultimate responsibility for implementing the company's short and long-term plans. (p. 861)

Classified Balance Sheet A balance sheet that places each asset and each liability into a specific category. (p. 188)

Closing Entries Entries that transfer the revenues, expenses, and Dividends balances to the Retained Earnings account to prepare the company's books for the next period. (p. 194)

Closing Process A step in the accounting cycle that occurs at the end of the period. The closing process consists of journalizing and posting the closing entries to set the balances of the revenues, expenses, Income Summary, and Dividends accounts to zero for the next period. (p. 193)

Cloud Computing Software and data are stored on a third-party server instead of by the business and can be accessed by employees via the Internet. (p. B-21)

Collusion Two or more people working together to circumvent internal controls and defraud a company. (p. 385)

Commercial Substance A characteristic of a transaction that causes a change in future cash flows. (p. 517)

Committee of Sponsoring Organizations (COSO) A committee that provides thought leadership related to enterprise risk management, internal control, and fraud deterrence. (p. 381)

Common-Size Statement A financial statement that reports only percentages (no dollar amounts). (p. 810)

Common Stock Represents the basic ownership of a corporation. (pp. 12, 674)

Compound Interest Interest calculated on the principal and on all previously earned interest. (pp. 640, 1438)

Compound Journal Entry A journal entry that is characterized by having multiple debits and/or multiple credits. (p. 70)

Comprehensive Income A company's change in total stockholders' equity from all sources other than owners' investments and dividends. (p. 557)

Conservatism A business should report the least favorable figures in the financial statements when two or more possible options are presented. (p. 328)

Consistency Principle A business should use the same accounting methods and procedures from period to period. (p. 327)

Consolidated Statements Financial statements that combine the balance sheets, income statements, and statements of cash flow of the parent company with those of its controlling interest affiliates. (p. 554)

Consolidation Accounting The way to combine the financial statements of two or more companies that have the same owners. (p. 554)

Constraint A factor that restricts the production or sale of a product. (p. 1388)

Contingent Liability A potential liability that depends on some future event. (p. 594)

Continuous Budget Involves continuously adding one additional month to the budget as each month goes by. (p. 1188)

Contra Account An account that is paired with, and is listed immediately after, its related account in the chart of accounts and associated financial statement and whose normal balance is the opposite of the normal balance of the related account. (p. 129)

Contributed Capital Owner contributions to a corporation. (p. 12)

Contribution Margin The amount that contributes to covering the fixed costs and then to providing operating income. Net sales revenue – Variable costs. (pp. 1095, 1143)

Contribution Margin Income Statement The income statement that groups cost by behavior—variable or fixed—and highlights the contribution margin. (p. 1096)

Contribution Margin Ratio The ratio of contribution margin to net sales revenue. Contribution margin / Net sales revenue. (pp. 1096, 1154)

Control Account An account whose balance equals the sum of the balances in a group of related accounts in a subsidiary ledger. (p. B-7)

Controllable Cost A cost that a manager has the power to influence by his or her decisions. (p. 1334)

Controlling Interest Equity Investment An equity security in which the investor owns more than 50% of the investee's voting stock. (p. 548)

Controlling Monitoring operations and keeping the company on track. (p. 862)

Conversion Costs Account A temporary account used in JIT management systems to accumulate direct labor and manufacturing overhead costs and then allocate the costs as units are completed. (p. 1050)

Conversion Costs The cost to convert direct materials into finished goods: Direct labor plus manufacturing overhead. (p. 867)

Conversion Costs The cost to convert direct materials into finished goods: Direct labor plus manufacturing overhead. (p. 967)

Copyright Exclusive right to reproduce and sell a book, musical composition, film, other work of art, or intellectual property. (p. 513)

Corporation A business organized under state law that is a separate legal entity. (p. 7)

Corporation A business organized under state law that is a separate legal entity. (p. 672)

Cost Accounting System An accounting system that measures, records, and reports product costs. (p. 908)

Cost-Based Transfer Price A transfer price based on the cost of producing the goods. (p. 1348)

Cost Center A responsibility center whose manager is only responsible for controlling costs. (p. 1327)

Cost Driver The primary factor that causes a cost to increase or decrease. (p. 919)

Cost Object Anything for which managers want a separate measurement of cost. (p. 866)

Cost of Goods Available for Sale The total cost spent on inventory that was available to be sold during a period. (p. 332)

Cost of Goods Manufactured The manufacturing costs of the goods that finished the production process in a given accounting period. (p. 872)

Cost of Goods Sold Budget The budget that estimates the cost of goods sold based on the company's projected sales. (p. 1196)

Cost of Goods Sold (COGS) The cost of the merchandise inventory that the business has sold to customers. (p. 251)

Cost-Plus Pricing A method to manage costs and profits by determining the price. (p. 1380)

Cost Pool An accumulation of individual costs. (p. 971)

Cost Principle A principle that states that acquired assets and services should be recorded at their actual cost. (pp. 9, 490)

Cost Stickiness The asymmetrical change in costs when there is a decrease in the volume of activity. (p. 1105)

Cost Structure The proportion of fixed costs to variable costs. (p. 1107)

Cost Variance Measures how well the business keeps unit costs of material and labor inputs within standards. (p. 1275)

Cost-Volume-Profit (CVP) Analysis A planning tool that expresses the relationships among costs, volume, and prices and their effects on profits and losses. (p. 1097)

Credit The right side of a T-account. (p. 61)

Credit Memorandum An increase in a bank account. (p. 399)

Creditor Any person or business to whom a business owes money. (p. 4)

Credit Terms The payment terms of purchase or sale as stated on the invoice. (p. 255)

Cumulative Preferred Stock Preferred stock whose owners must receive all dividends in arrears plus the current year dividend before the corporation pays dividends to the common stockholders. (p. 687)

Current Asset An asset that is expected to be converted to cash, sold, or used up during the next 12 months or within the business's normal operating cycle if the cycle is longer than a year. (p. 189)

Current Liability A liability that must be paid with cash or with goods and services within one year or within the entity's operating cycle if the cycle is longer than a year. (pp. 189, 579)

Current Portion of Notes Payable The amount of the principal that is payable within one year of the balance sheet date. (p. 583)

Current Ratio Measures the company's ability to pay current liabilities from current assets. Total current assets / Total current liabilities. (pp. 203, 815)

Days' Sales in Inventory Measures the average number of days that inventory is held by a company. 365 days / Inventory turnover. (pp. 346, 816)

Days' Sales in Receivables The ratio of average net accounts receivable to one day's sales. The ratio tells how many days it takes to collect the average level of accounts receivable. 365 days / Accounts receivable turnover ratio. (pp. 457, 818)

Debentures Unsecured bonds backed only by the credit worthiness of the bond issuer. (p. 625)

Debit The left side of a T-account. (p. 61)

Debit Memorandum A decrease in a bank account. (p. 399)

Debtor The party to a credit transaction who takes on an obligation/payable. (p. 433)

Debt Ratio Shows the proportion of assets financed with debt. Total liabilities / Total assets. (pp. 81, 818)

Debt Security Investment in notes or bonds payable issued by another company. (p. 546)

Debt to Equity Ratio A ratio that measures the proportion of total liabilities relative to total equity. Total liabilities / Total equity. (pp. 638, 819)

Decentralized Company A company that is divided into business segments, with segment managers making planning, directing, and controlling decisions for their segments. (p. 1325)

Deferred Expense An asset created when a business makes advance payments of future expenses. (p. 125)

Deferred Revenue A liability created when a business collects cash from customers in advance of completing a service or delivering a product. (p. 131)

Deficit Debit balance in the Retained Earnings account. (p. 695)

Degree of Operating Leverage The ratio that measures the effects that fixed costs have on changes in operating income when sales volume changes. Contribution margin / Operating income. (p. 1108)

Depletion The process by which businesses spread the allocation of a natural resource's cost over its usage. (p. 511)

Deposit in Transit A deposit recorded by the company but not yet by its bank. (p. 398)

Deposit Ticket A bank form that is completed by the customer and shows the amount of each deposit. (p. 396)

Depreciable Cost The cost of a plant asset minus its estimated residual value. (p. 495)

Depreciation The process by which businesses spread the allocation of a plant asset's cost over its useful life. (pp. 127, 489)

Differential Analysis A method that looks at how operating income would differ under each decision alternative; leaves out irrelevant information. (p. 1375)

Direct Cost Cost that can be easily and cost-effectively traced to a cost object. (p. 866)

Directing Running the day-to-day operations of a business. (p. 862)

Direct Labor Budget The budget that estimates the direct labor hours and related cost needed to meet the company's production needs. (p. 1194)

Direct Labor Cost Variance The difference between the actual amount paid for direct labor (actual cost) and the amount that should have been paid (standard cost). (p. 1281)

Direct Labor (DL) The cost of wages and salaries of employees who convert raw materials into finished products. (p. 866)

Direct Labor Efficiency Variance The difference between the actual labor hours (actual quantity) and the labor hours that should have been used (standard quantity). (p. 1281)

Direct Materials Budget The budget that estimates the amount of materials to purchase to meet the company's production needs. (p. 1193)

Direct Materials Cost Variance The difference between the amount actually paid for direct materials (actual cost) and what should have been paid (standard cost). (p. 1278)

Direct Materials (DM) The cost of raw materials that are converted into the finished product and are easily traced to the product. (p. 866)

Direct Materials Efficiency Variance The difference between the direct materials actually used (actual quantity) and the direct materials that should have been used for the actual output (standard quantity). (p. 1279)

Direct Method A format of the operating activities section of the statement of cash flows; lists the operating cash receipts and cash payments. (p. 736)

Direct Write-off Method A method of accounting for uncollectible receivables in which the company records bad debts expense when a customer's account receivable is uncollectible. (p. 437)

Disclosure Principle A business's financial statements must report enough information for outsiders to make knowledgeable decisions about the company. (p. 327)

Discount on Bonds Payable Occurs when a bond's issue price is less than face value. (p. 625)

Discount Rate Management's minimum desired rate of return on a capital investment. (p. 1445)

Dishonor a Note Failure of a note's maker to pay a note receivable at maturity. (p. 454)

Dividend A distribution of a corporation's earnings to stockholders. (pp. 12, 674)

Dividend in Arrears A preferred stock dividend is in arrears if the dividend has not been paid for the year and the preferred stock is cumulative. (p. 687)

Dividend Payout The ratio of dividends declared per common share relative to the earnings per share of the company. Annual dividend per share / Earnings per share. (p. 824)

Dividend Yield Ratio of annual dividends per share of stock to the stock's market price per share. Measures the percentage of a stock's market value that is returned annually as dividends to stockholders. Annual dividend per share / Market price per share. (p. 823)

Dollar Value Bias The bias one sees from comparing numbers in absolute (dollars) rather than relative (percentage) terms. (p. 810)

Double-Declining-Balance Method An accelerated depreciation method that computes annual depreciation by multiplying the depreciable asset's decreasing book value by a constant percent that is two times the straight-line depreciation rate. (p. 498)

Double-Entry System A system of accounting in which every transaction affects at least two accounts. (p. 61)

Earnings per Share (EPS) Amount of a company's net income (loss) for each share of its outstanding common stock. (Net income – Preferred dividends) / Weighted average number of common shares outstanding. (pp. 694, 822)

Economic Entity Assumption An organization that stands apart as a separate economic unit. (p. 6)

Effective-Interest Amortization Method An amortization model that calculates interest expense based on the current carrying amount of the bond and the market interest rate at issuance, and then amortizes the difference between the cash interest payment and calculated interest expense as a decrease to the discount or premium. (p. 646)

Efficiency Variance Measures how well the business uses its materials or human resources. (p. 1275)

Electronic Data Interchange (EDI) A streamlined process that bypasses paper documents altogether. Computers of customers communicate directly with the computers of suppliers to automate routine business transactions. (p. 389)

Electronic Funds Transfer (EFT) A system that transfers cash by electronic communication rather than by paper documents. (p. 397)

Encryption Rearranging plain-text messages by a mathematical process—the primary method of achieving security in e-commerce. (p. 384)

Enterprise Resource Planning (ERP) Software system that can integrate all of a company's functions, departments, and data into a single system. (pp. 877, B-21)

Equity The owners' claims to the assets of the business. (p. 12)

Equity Security Investment in stock ownership in another company that sometimes pays cash dividends or issues stock dividends. (p. 546)

Equivalent Units of Production (EUP) Used to measure the direct materials, direct labor, and manufacturing overhead incurred on partially completed units and expressed in terms of fully completed units. (p. 967)

Evaluated Receipts Settlement (ERS) A procedure that compresses the payment approval process into a single step by comparing the receiving report to the purchase order. (p. 389)

Expenses The costs of selling goods or services. (p. 12)

External Auditor An outside accountant, completely independent of the business, who evaluates the controls to ensure that the financial statements are presented fairly in accordance with GAAP. (p. 383)

External Failure Costs Costs incurred when the company does not detect poor-quality goods or services until after delivery to customers. (p. 1054)

Extraordinary Repair Repair work that generates a capital expenditure because it extends the asset's life past the normal expected life. (p. 493)

Face Value The amount a borrower must pay back to the bondholders on the maturity date. (p. 624)

Fair Value The price that would be used if the investments were sold on the market. (p. 554)

Faithful Representation Providing information that is complete, neutral, and free from error. (p. 6)

Federal Insurance Contributions Act (FICA) The federal act that created the Social Security tax that provides retirement, disability, and medical benefits. (p. 585)

Financial Accounting The field of accounting that focuses on providing information for external decision makers. (pp. 3, 860)

Financial Accounting Standards Board (FASB) The private organization that oversees the creation and governance of accounting standards in the United States. (p. 6)

Financial Budget The budget that includes the cash budget and the budgeted financial statements. (p. 1190)

Financial Leverage Occurs when a company earns more income on borrowed money than the related interest expense. (p. 628)

Financial Statements Business documents that are used to communicate information needed to make business decisions. (p. 19)

Financing Activities Activities that increase or decrease long-term liabilities and equity; a section of the statement of cash flows. (p. 734)

Finished Goods Inventory (FG) Completed goods that have not yet been sold. (p. 865)

Firewall A device that enables members of a local network to access the network, while keeping nonmembers out of the network. (p. 384)

First-In, First-Out (FIFO) Method An inventory costing method in which the first costs into inventory are the first costs out to cost of goods sold. Ending inventory is based on the costs of the most recent purchases. (p. 332)

First-In, First-Out Method (for Process Costing) Determines the cost of equivalent units of production by accounting for beginning inventory costs separately from current period costs. It assumes the first units started in the production process are the first units completed and sold. (p. 988)

Fiscal Year An accounting year of any 12 consecutive months that may or may not coincide with the calendar year. (p. 122)

Fixed Cost A cost that remains the same *in total*, regardless of changes over wide ranges of volume of activity. (p. 1089)

Fixed Overhead Cost Variance Determines the cost associated with the difference between actual fixed overhead and budgeted fixed overhead. (p. 1285)

Fixed Overhead Volume Variance Determines the cost associated with the difference between budgeted fixed overhead and the amount of fixed overhead allocated to actual output. (p. 1286)

Flexible Budget A budget prepared for various levels of sales volume. (pp. 1188, 1268)

Flexible Budget Variance The difference between actual results and the expected results in the flexible budget for the *actual* units sold. (p. 1270)

FOB Destination Situation in which the buyer takes ownership (title) to the goods at the delivery destination point and the seller typically pays the freight. (p. 258)

FOB Shipping Point Situation in which the buyer takes ownership (title) to the goods after the goods leave the seller's place of business (shipping point) and the buyer typically pays the freight. (p. 258)

Franchise Privilege granted by a business to sell a product or service under specified conditions. (p. 514)

Free Cash Flow The amount of cash available from operating activities after paying for planned investments in long-term assets and after paying dividends to shareholders. Net cash provided by operating payments planned for investments in long-term dividends. (p. 751)

Freight In The transportation cost to ship goods into the purchaser's warehouse; therefore, it is freight on purchased goods. (p. 258)

Freight Out The transportation cost to ship goods out of the seller's warehouse; therefore, it is freight on goods sold to a customer. (p. 258)

Full Product Cost The cost to develop, produce, and deliver the product or service. (p. 1044)

Future Value The value of an investment at the end of a specific time frame. (pp. 626, 1439)

Generally Accepted Accounting Principles (GAAP) Accounting guidelines, currently formulated by the Financial Accounting Standards Board (FASB); the main U.S. accounting rule book. (p. 6)

Goal Congruence Aligning the goals of business segment managers and other subordinates with the goals of top management. (p. 1326)

Going Concern Assumption Assumes that the entity will remain in operation for the foreseeable future. (p. 10)

Goodwill Excess of the cost of an acquired company over the sum of the market values of its net assets (assets minus liabilities). (p. 514)

Gross Pay The total amount of salary, wages, commissions, and any other employee compensation before taxes and other deductions. (p. 584)

Gross Profit Excess of Net Sales Revenue over Cost of Goods Sold. (p. 252)

Gross Profit Percentage Measures the profitability of each sales dollar above the cost of goods sold. Gross profit / Net sales revenue. (pp. 272, 817)

Hardware Electronic equipment that includes computers, monitors, printers, and the network that connects them. (p. B-21)

Held-to-Maturity (HTM) Debt Investment A debt security the investor intends to hold and has the ability to hold until it matures. (p. 547)

High-Low Method A method used to separate mixed costs into their variable and fixed components, using the highest and lowest activity levels. (p. 1092)

Horizontal Analysis The study of percentage changes in line items from comparative financial statements. (p. 804)

Impairment A permanent decline in asset value. (p. 512)

Imprest System A way to account for petty cash by maintaining a constant balance in the petty cash account. At any time, cash plus petty cash tickets must total the amount allocated to the petty cash fund. (p. 391)

Income Statement Reports the *net income* or *net loss* of the business for a specific period. (p. 20)

Income Summary A temporary account into which revenues and expenses are transferred prior to their final transfer into the Retained Earnings account. Summarizes net income (or net loss) for the period. (p. 194)

Income Tax Expense Expense incurred by a corporation related to federal and state income taxes. (p. 271)

Income Tax Withholding Income tax deducted from an employee's gross pay. (p. 585)

Indirect Cost Cost that cannot be easily or cost-effectively traced to a cost object. (p. 866)

Indirect Labor The cost of wages and salaries in the factory for persons not directly producing the product and cannot be conveniently traced directly to specific finished products or are not large enough to justify tracing to the specific product. (p. 867)

Indirect Materials The cost of raw materials that cannot be conveniently traced directly to specific finished products or are not large enough to justify tracing to the specific product. (p. 867)

Indirect Method A format of the operating activities section of the statement of cash flows; starts with net income and reconciles to net cash provided by operating activities. (p. 736)

Intangible Asset An asset with no physical form that is valuable because of the special rights it carries. (pp. 189, 512)

Interest The revenue to the payee for loaning money—the expense to the debtor. (p. 449)

Interest Period The period of time during which interest is computed. It extends from the original date of the note to the maturity date. (p. 450)

Interest Rate The percentage rate of interest specified by the note. (p. 450)

Internal Auditor An employee of the business who ensures the company's employees are following company policies, that the company meets all legal requirements, and that operations are running efficiently. (p. 383)

Internal Control The organizational plan and all the related measures adopted by an entity to safeguard assets, encourage employees to follow company policies, promote operational efficiency, and ensure accurate and reliable accounting records. (p. 381)

Internal Control Report A report by management describing its responsibility for and the adequacy of internal controls over financial reporting. (p. 382)

Internal Failure Costs Costs incurred when the company corrects poor-quality goods or services before delivery to customers. (p. 1054)

Internal Rate of Return (IRR) The rate of return, based on discounted cash flows, of a capital investment. The interest rate that makes the NPV of the investment equal to zero. (p. 1449)

International Accounting Standards Board (IASB) The private organization that oversees the creation and governance of International Financial Reporting Standards (IFRS). (p. 10)

International Financial Reporting Standards (IFRS) A set of global accounting guidelines, formulated by the International Accounting Standards Board (IASB). (p. 10)

Inventory Costing Method A method of approximating the flow of inventory costs in a business that is used to determine the amount of cost of goods sold and ending merchandise inventory. (p. 331)

Inventory, Purchases, and Cost of Goods Sold Budget The budget that estimates the cost of goods sold, ending Merchandise Inventory, and merchandise inventory purchases needed for the company's projected sales. (p. 1211)

Inventory Shrinkage The loss of inventory that occurs because of theft, damage, and errors. (p. 265)

Inventory Turnover Measures the number of times a company sells its average level of merchandise inventory during a period. Cost of goods sold / Average merchandise inventory. (pp. 346, 816)

Investee The corporation that issued the bond or stock to the investor. (p. 546)

Investing Activities Activities that increase or decrease long-term assets; a section of the statement of cash flows. (p. 734)

Investment Center A responsibility center whose manager is responsible for generating profits and efficiently managing the center's invested capital. (p. 1328)

Investor The owner of a bond or stock of a corporation. (p. 546)

Invoice A seller's request for payment from the purchaser. (p. 253)

Irrelevant Cost A cost that does not affect the decision because it is not in the future or does not differ among alternatives. (p. 1375)

Issued Stock Stock that has been issued but may or may not be held by stockholders. (p. 673)

Issue Price The amount that the corporation receives from issuing stock. (p. 676)

Job The production of a single unique product or specialized service, or a batch of unique products. (p. 908)

Job Cost Record A document that shows the direct materials, direct labor, and manufacturing overhead costs for an individual job. (p. 909)

Job Order Costing System An accounting system that accumulates costs by job. Used by companies that manufacture unique products or provide specialized services. (pp. 908, 962)

Joint Cost A cost of a production process that yields multiple products. (p. 1397)

Journal A record of transactions in date order. (p. 65)

Just-in-Time Costing A costing system that starts with output completed and then assigns manufacturing costs to units sold and to inventories. (p. 1050)

Just-in-Time (JIT) Management A cost management system in which a company produces products just in time to satisfy needs. Suppliers deliver materials just in time to begin

production, and finished units are completed just in time for delivery to the customer. (p. 877)

Just-in-Time (JIT) Management A cost management system in which a company produces products just in time to satisfy needs. Suppliers deliver materials just in time to begin production, and finished units are completed just in time for delivery to the customer. (p. 1048)

Key Performance Indicator (KPI) A summary performance measure that helps managers assess whether the company is achieving its goals. (p. 1331)

Labor Time Record A record used to assign direct labor cost to specific jobs. (p. 914)

Lag Indicator A performance measure that indicates past performance. (p. 1331)

Land Improvement A depreciable improvement to land, such as fencing, sprinklers, paving, signs, and lighting. (p. 490)

Large Stock Dividend A stock dividend greater than 20% to 25% of the issued and outstanding stock. (p. 689)

Last-In, First-Out (LIFO) Method An inventory costing method in which the last costs into inventory are the first costs out to cost of goods sold. The method leaves the oldest costs—those of beginning inventory and the earliest purchases of the period—in ending inventory. (p. 333)

Lead Indicator A performance measure that forecasts future performance. (p. 1331)

Ledger The record holding all the accounts of a business, the changes in those accounts, and their balances.

Legal Capital The portion of stockholders' equity that cannot be used for dividends. (p. 685)

Liabilities Debts that are owed to creditors. (pp. 12, 579)

License Privilege granted by a government to use public property in performing services. (p. 514)

Limited-Liability Company (LLC) A company in which each member is only liable for his or her own actions. (p. 7)

Line Position Job that is directly involved in providing goods or services to customers. (p. 862)

Liquidity A measure of how quickly an item can be converted to cash. (p. 189)

Lock-Box System A system in which customers send their checks to a post office box that belongs to a bank. A bank employee empties the box daily and records the deposits into the company's bank account. (p. 387)

Long-term Asset An asset that will not be converted to cash or used up within the business's operating cycle or one year, whichever is greater. (p. 189)

Long-term Investment Investments in bonds (debt securities) or stocks (equity securities) in which the company intends to hold the investment for longer than one year. (p. 189)

Long-term Investment An investment in debt and equity securities that the investor intends to hold for longer than one year. (p. 547)

Long-term Liability A liability that does not need to be paid within one year or within the entity's operating cycle, whichever is longer. (pp. 189, 579, 620)

Lower-of-Cost-or-Market (LCM) Rule Rule that merchandise inventory should be reported in the financial statements at whichever is lower—its historical cost or its market value. (p. 341)

Maker The party who issues the check. (p. 396)

Management by Exception When managers concentrate on results that are outside the accepted parameters. (p. 1290)

Management's Discussion and Analysis of Financial Condition and Results of Operations (MD&A) The section of the annual report that is intended to help investors understand the results of operations and the financial condition of the company. (p. 802)

Managerial Accounting The field of accounting that focuses on providing information for internal decision makers. (pp. 3, 860)

Manufacturing Company A company that uses labor, equipment, supplies, and facilities to convert raw materials into finished products. (p. 865)

Manufacturing Overhead Budget The budget that estimates the variable and fixed manufacturing overhead needed to meet the company's production needs. (p. 1195)

Manufacturing Overhead (MOH) Manufacturing costs that cannot be easily and cost-effectively traced to a cost object. Includes all manufacturing costs except direct materials and direct labor. (p. 866)

Margin of Safety The excess of expected sales over breakeven sales. The amount sales can decrease before the company incurs an operating loss. (p. 1106)

Market-Based Transfer Price A transfer price based on the current market value of the goods. (p. 1347)

Market Interest Rate The interest rate that investors demand in order to loan their money. (p. 627)

Master Budget The set of budgeted financial statements and supporting schedules for the entire organization; includes the operating budget, capital expenditures budget, and financial budget. (p. 1188)

Matching Principle Guides accounting for expenses, ensures that all expenses are recorded when they are incurred during the period, and matches those expenses against the revenues of the period. (p. 123)

Materiality Concept A company must perform strictly proper accounting only for items that are significant to the business's financial situation. (p. 328)

Materials Requisition A document that requests the transfer of raw materials to the production floor. (p. 912)

Maturity Date The date when a note is due. (p. 433)

Maturity Value The sum of the principal plus interest due at maturity. (p. 450)

Memorandum Entry An entry in the journal that notes a significant event, but has no debit or credit amount. (p. 692)

Merchandise Inventory The merchandise that a business sells to customers. (p. 250)

Merchandiser A business that sells merchandise, or goods, to customers. (p. 250)

Merchandising Company A company that resells products previously bought from suppliers. (p. 865)

Mixed Cost A cost that has both fixed and variable components. (p. 1091)

Modified Accelerated Cost Recovery System (MACRS) A depreciation method that is used for tax purposes. (p. 500)

Monetary Unit Assumption The assumption that requires the items on the financial statements to be measured in terms of a monetary unit. (p. 10)

Mortgages Payable Long-term debts that are backed with a security interest in specific property. (p. 621)

Multi-Step Income Statement Income statement format that contains subtotals to highlight significant relationships. In addition to net income, it reports gross profit and operating income. (p. 270)

Natural Resource An asset that comes from the earth and is consumed. (p. 511)

Net Income The result of operations that occurs when total revenues are greater than total expenses. (p. 13)

Net Loss The result of operations that occurs when total expenses are greater than total revenues. (p. 13)

Net Pay Gross pay minus all deductions. The amount of compensation that the employee actually takes home. (p. 584)

Net Present Value (NPV) A capital investment analysis method that measures the net difference between the present value of the investment's net cash inflows and the investment's cost. (p. 1445)

Net Purchases Purchases less purchase returns and allowances less purchase discounts. (p. 276)

Net Realizable Value The net value a company expects to collect from its accounts receivable. Accounts Receivable less Allowance for Bad Debts. (p. 439)

Network The system of electronic linkages that allows different computers to share the same information. (p. B-21)

Non-cash Investing and Financing Activities Investing and financing activities that do not involve cash. (p. 735)

Noncumulative Preferred Stock Preferred stock whose owners do not receive passed dividends. (p. 687)

Nonsufficient Funds (NSF) Check A check for which the maker's bank account has insufficient money to pay the check. (p. 399)

No-Par Stock Stock that has no amount (par) assigned to it. (p. 675)

Normal Balance The balance that appears on the increase side of an account. (p. 62)

No Significant Influence Equity Investment An equity security in which the investor lacks the ability to participate in the decisions of the investee company. (p. 548)

Notes Payable A *written* promise made by the business to pay a debt, usually involving *interest*, in the future. (p. 58)

Notes Receivable A written promise that a customer will pay a fixed amount of principal plus interest by a certain date in the future. (pp. 58, 433)

Obsolete An asset is considered obsolete when a newer asset can perform the job more efficiently. (p. 495)

Operating Activities Activities that create revenue or expense in the entity's business; a section of the statement of cash flows. (p. 734)

Operating Budget The set of budgets that projects sales revenue, cost of goods sold, and selling and administrative expenses, all of which feed into the cash budget and then the budgeted financial statements. (p. 1189)

Operating Cycle The time span during which cash is paid for goods and services, which are then sold to customers from whom the business collects cash. (p. 189)

Operating Expenses Expenses, other than Cost of Goods Sold, that are incurred in the entity's major ongoing operations. (p. 252)

Operating Income Measures the results of the entity's major ongoing activities. Gross profit minus operating expenses. (p. 271)

Operating Leverage Effects that fixed costs have on changes in operating income when sales volume changes. (p. 1108)

Operational Budget A short-term financial plan used to coordinate the activities needed to achieve the short-term goals of the company. (p. 1187)

Operational Performance Measure A nonfinancial performance measure that evaluates effectiveness and efficiency to ensure all segments of the business are working together to achieve the company's goals. (p. 1331)

Operational Planning Focuses on short-term actions dealing with a company's day-to-day operations. (p. 862)

Opportunity Cost The benefit given up by choosing an alternative course of action. (pp. 1347, 1395)

Organizational Chart Shows the relationship between departments and divisions and managers responsible for each section. (p. 861)

Other Income and Expenses Revenues or expenses that are outside the normal, day-to-day operations of a business, such as a gain or loss on the sale of plant assets or interest expense. (p. 271)

Outstanding Check A check issued by a company and recorded on its books but not yet paid by its bank. (p. 398)

Outstanding Stock Issued stock in the hands of stockholders. (p. 674)

Overallocated Overhead Occurs when the actual manufacturing overhead costs are less than allocated manufacturing overhead costs. (p. 923)

Paid-In Capital Represents amounts received from the stockholders of a corporation in exchange for stock. (p. 675)

Paid-In Capital in Excess of Par Represents amounts received from stockholders in excess of par value. (p. 677)

Parent Company A company that owns a controlling interest in another company. (p. 554)

Participative Budget A budgeting process where those individuals who are directly impacted by a budget are involved in the development of the budget. (p. 1186)

Partnership A business with two or more owners and not organized as a corporation. (p. 7)

Par Value An amount assigned by a company to a share of its stock. (p. 675)

Patent An intangible asset that is a federal government grant conveying an exclusive 20-year right to produce and sell a process, product, or formula. (p. 512)

Payback A capital investment analysis method that measures the length of time it takes to recover, in net cash inflows, the cost of the initial investment. (p. 1431)

Payee The individual or business to whom the check is paid. (p. 396)

Payroll Register A schedule that summarizes the earnings, withholdings, and net pay for each employee. (p. 587)

Pension Plan A plan that provides benefits to retired employees. (p. 592)

Percent-of-Receivables Method A method of estimating uncollectible receivables by determining the balance of the Allowance for

Bad Debts account based on a percentage of accounts receivable. (p. 443)

Percent-of-Sales Method A method of estimating uncollectible receivables that calculates bad debts expense based on a percentage of net credit sales. (p. 442)

Performance Evaluation System A system that provides top management with a framework for maintaining control over the entire organization. (p. 1330)

Period Cost Operating cost that is expensed in the accounting period in which it is incurred. (p. 868)

Periodic Inventory System An inventory system that requires businesses to obtain a physical count of inventory to determine quantities on hand. (p. 252)

Permanent Account An account that is *not* closed at the end of the period—the asset, liability, Common Stock, and Retained Earnings accounts. (p. 193)

Perpetual Inventory System An inventory system that keeps a running computerized record of merchandise inventory. (p. 252)

Petty Cash A fund containing a small amount of cash that is used to pay for minor expenditures. (p. 390)

Physical Units Actual units that the company will account for during the period. (p. 969)

Planning Choosing goals and deciding how to achieve them. (p. 862)

Post-Audit The comparison of the actual results of capital investments to the projected results. (p. 1429)

Post-Closing Trial Balance A list of the accounts and their balances at the end of the period after journalizing and posting the closing entries. It should include only permanent accounts. (p. 200)

Posting Transferring data from the journal to the ledger. (p. 65)

Predetermined Overhead Allocation Rate Estimated overhead cost per unit of the allocation base, calculated at the beginning of the accounting period. Total estimated overhead costs / Total estimated quantity of the overhead allocation base. (pp. 918, 1030)

Preemptive Right Stockholder's right to maintain his or her proportionate ownership in the corporation. (p. 674)

Preferred Stock Stock that gives its owners certain advantages over common stockholders, such as the right to receive dividends before the common stockholders and the right to receive assets before the common stockholders if the corporation liquidates. (p. 675)

Premium on Bonds Payable Occurs when a bond's issue price is more than face value. (p. 625)

Premium The amount above par at which a stock is issued. (p. 677)

Prepaid Expense A payment of an expense in advance. (p. 58)

Present Value The value of an investment today. (pp. 626, 1439)

Prevention Costs Costs incurred to avoid poor-quality goods or services. (p. 1054)

Price/Earnings Ratio The ratio of the market price of a share of common stock to the company's earnings per share. Measures the value that the stock market places on $1 of a company's earnings. Market price per share of common stock / Earnings per share. (pp. 698, 823)

Price-Setter A company that has control over the prices of its products and services because its products and services are unique and there is little competition. (p. 1377)

Price-Taker A company that has little control over the prices of its products and services because its products and services are not unique or competition is intense. (p. 1377)

Prime Costs The direct costs of the manufacturing process: Direct materials plus direct labor. (p. 867)

Principal The amount loaned out by the payee and borrowed by the maker of the note. (p. 449)

Prior-Period Adjustment A correction to Retained Earnings for an error of an earlier period. (p. 696)

Process One of a series of steps in manufacturing production; usually associated with making large quantities of similar items. (p. 962)

Process Costing System An accounting system that accumulates costs by process. Used by companies that manufacture identical units through a series of uniform production steps or processes. (pp. 909, 962)

Product Cost The cost of purchasing or making a product. The cost is recorded as an asset (inventory) and then expensed (Cost of Goods Sold) when the product is sold. (p. 868)

Production Budget The budget that determines the number of units to be produced to meet projected sales. (p. 1192)

Production Cost Report A report prepared by a processing department for equivalent units of production, production costs, and the assignment of those costs to the completed and in process units. (p. 968)

Profitability Index Computes the number of dollars returned for every dollar invested, with all calculations performed in present value dollars. Present value of net cash inflows / Initial investment. (p. 1448)

Profit Center A responsibility center whose manager is responsible for generating revenue and controlling costs and, therefore, profits. (p. 1327)

Profit Margin Ratio A profitability measure that shows how much net income is earned

on every dollar of net sales. Net income / Net sales revenue. (p. 820)

Profit Margin Ratio A profitability measure that shows how much operating income is earned on every dollar of net sales revenue. Operating income / Net sales revenue. (p. 1341)

Property, Plant, and Equipment Long-lived, tangible assets, such as land, buildings, and equipment, used in the operation of a business. (p. 127)

Property, Plant, and Equipment Long-lived, tangible assets, such as land, buildings, and equipment, used in the operation of a business. (p. 189)

Property, Plant, and Equipment (PP&E) Long-lived, tangible assets, such as land, buildings, and equipment, used in the operation of a business. (p. 489)

Public Company A company that sells its stock to the general public. (p. 381)

Purchase Allowance An amount granted to the purchaser as an incentive to keep goods that are not "as ordered." (p. 256)

Purchase Discount A discount that businesses offer to purchasers as an incentive for early payment. (p. 255)

Purchase Return A situation in which sellers allow purchasers to return merchandise that is defective, damaged, or otherwise unsuitable. (p. 256)

Purchases Journal Special journal used to record all purchases of merchandise inventory, office supplies, and other assets on account. (p. B-14)

Quality Management System (QMS) A system that helps managers improve a business's performance by providing quality products and services. (p. 1054)

Rate of Return on Common Stockholders' Equity Shows the relationship between net income available to common stockholders and their average common equity invested in the company. (Net income − Preferred dividends) / Average common stockholders' equity. (pp. 698, 821)

Rate of Return on Total Assets A ratio that measures the success a company has in using its assets to earn income. (pp. 560, 820)

Raw and In-Process Inventory A combined account for Raw Materials Inventory and Work-in-Process Inventory used in JIT management systems. (p. 1050)

Raw Materials Inventory (RM) Materials converted through the manufacturing process into a finished product. (p. 865)

Receivable A monetary claim against a business or an individual. (p. 433)

Relative-Market-Value Method A method of allocating the total cost (100%) of multiple assets purchased at one time. Total cost is divided among the assets according to their relative market values. (p. 492)

Relevant Cost A cost that is relevant to a particular decision because it is a future cost and differs among alternatives. (p. 1374)

Relevant Information Expected future data that differ among alternatives. (p. 1374)

Relevant Range The range of volume where total fixed costs and variable cost per unit remain constant. (p. 1094)

Remittance Advice An optional attachment to a check that tells the business the reason for the payment. (p. 387)

Residual Income (RI) A measure of profitability and efficiency computed as actual operating income less a specified minimum acceptable operating income. (p. 1343)

Residual Value The expected value of a depreciable asset at the end of its useful life. (pp. 128, 495)

Responsibility Accounting System A system for evaluating the performance of each responsibility center and its manager. (p. 1327)

Responsibility Center A part of the organization for which a manager has decision-making authority and accountability for the results of those decisions. (p. 1327)

Responsibility Report Performance report that captures the financial performance of cost, revenue, and profit centers with a focus on responsibility and controllability. (p. 1334)

Retailer A type of merchandiser who buys merchandise either from a manufacturer or a wholesaler and then sells those goods to consumers. (p. 250)

Retained Earnings Equity earned by profitable operations of a corporation that is not distributed to stockholders. (pp. 12, 675)

Return on Assets (ROA) Measures how profitably a company uses its assets. Net income / Average total assets. (p. 24)

Return on Investment (ROI) A measure of profitability and efficiency. Operating income / Average total assets. (p. 1340)

Revenue Center A responsibility center whose manager is only responsible for generating revenue. (p. 1327)

Revenue Expenditure An expenditure that does not increase the capacity or efficiency of an asset or extend its useful life. Revenue expenditures are debited to an expense account. (p. 493)

Revenue Recognition Principle Requires companies to record revenue when (or as) the entity satisfies each performance obligation. (p. 122)

Revenues Amounts earned from delivering goods or services to customers. (p. 12)

Reversing Entry A special journal entry that eases the burden of accounting for transactions in the next period. Such entries are the exact opposite of a prior adjusting entry. (p. 206)

Routing Number On a check, the 9-digit number that identifies the bank upon which the payment is drawn. (p. 396)

Sales Budget The budget that estimates the amount of sales revenue. (p. 1191)

Sales Discounts Reduction in the amount of revenue earned on sales for early payment. (p. 262)

Sales Journal Special journal used to record credit sales. (p. 7)

Sales Mix The combination of products that make up total sales. (p. 1109)

Sales Returns and Allowances Customer's return of merchandise or an allowance granted to the customer. (p. 263)

Sales Revenue The amount that a merchandiser earns from selling its inventory. (p. 261)

Sales Volume Variance The difference between the expected results in the flexible budget for the *actual* units sold and the static budget. (p. 1270)

Sarbanes-Oxley Act (SOX) Requires management to review internal control and take responsibility for the accuracy and completeness of their financial reports. (p. 11)

Sarbanes-Oxley Act (SOX) Requires companies to review internal control and take responsibility for the accuracy and completeness of their financial reports. (p. 382)

Secured Bonds Bonds that give bondholders the right to take specified assets of the issuer if the issuer fails to pay principal or interest. (p. 625)

Securities and Exchange Commission (SEC) U.S. governmental agency that oversees the U.S. financial markets. (p. 6)

Security A share or interest representing financial value. (p. 546)

Selling and Administrative Expense Budget The budget that estimates the selling and administrative expenses needed to meet the company's projected sales. (p. 1197)

Selling Expenses Expenses related to marketing and selling the company's goods and services. (p. 271)

Sensitivity Analysis A "what if" technique that estimates profit or loss results if sales price, costs, volume, or underlying assumptions change. (p. 1102)

Separation of Duties Dividing responsibilities between two or more people to limit fraud and promote accuracy of accounting records. (p. 383)

Serial Bonds Bonds that mature in installments at regular intervals. (p. 625)

Server The main computer where data are stored, which can be accessed from many different computers. (p. B-4)

Service Company A company that sells services—time, skills, and knowledge—instead of products. (p. 865)

Short-term Investment An investment in debt and equity securities that the investor intends to sell in one year or less. (p. 547)

Short-term Note Payable A written promise made by the business to pay a debt, usually involving interest, within one year or less. (p. 581)

Signature Card A card that shows each authorized person's signature for a bank account. (p. 396)

Significant Influence Equity Investment An equity security in which the investor has the ability to exert influence over operating and financial decisions of the investee company. (p. 548)

Simple Interest Interest calculated only on the principal amount. (p. 640)

Simple Interest Interest calculated only on the principal amount. (p. 1438)

Single-Step Income Statement Income statement format that groups all revenues together and then lists and deducts all expenses together without calculating any subtotals. (p. 269)

Small Stock Dividend A stock dividend of less than 20% to 25% of the issued and outstanding stock. (p. 689)

Social Security (FICA) Tax Federal Insurance Contributions Act (FICA) tax, which is withheld from employees' pay and matched by the employer. (p. 585)

Software Set of programs or instructions that drives the computer to perform the work desired. (p. B-21)

Sole Proprietorship A business with a single owner. (p. 7)

Source Document Provides the evidence and data for accounting transactions. (pp. 64, B-3)

Special Journal An accounting journal designed to record one specific type of transaction. (p. B-5)

Specific Identification Method An inventory costing method based on the specific cost of particular units of inventory. (p. 331)

Staff Position Job that provides support for line positions. (p. 862)

Standard A price, cost, or quantity that is expected under normal conditions. (p. 1272)

Standard Cost System An accounting system that uses standards for product costs—direct materials, direct labor, and manufacturing overhead. (p. 1272)

Stated Interest Rate The interest rate that determines the amount of cash interest the borrower pays and the investor receives each year. (p. 625)

Stated Value Stock No-par stock that has been assigned an amount similar to par value. (p. 675)

Statement of Cash Flows Reports on a business's cash receipts and cash payments for a specific period. (pp. 22, 733)

Statement of Retained Earnings Reports how the company's retained earnings balance changed from the beginning to the end of the period. (p. 20)

Static Budget A budget prepared for only one level of sales volume. (pp. 1188, 1267)

Static Budget Variance The difference between actual results and the expected results in the static budget. (p. 1267)

Stock Certificate Paper evidence of ownership in a corporation. (p. 673)

Stock Dividend A distribution by a corporation of its own stock to its stockholders. (p. 688)

Stockholder A person who owns stock in a corporation. (p. 7)

Stockholders' Equity A corporation's equity that includes paid-in capital and retained earnings. (p. 675)

Stock Split An increase in the number of issued and outstanding shares of stock coupled with a proportionate reduction in the par value of the stock. (p. 692)

Straight-Line Amortization Method An amortization method that allocates an equal amount of bond discount or premium to each interest period over the life of the bond. (p. 630)

Straight-Line Method A depreciation method that allocates an equal amount of depreciation each year. (Cost – Residual value) / Useful life. (pp. 128, 496)

Strategic Budget A long-term financial plan used to coordinate the activities needed to achieve the long-term goals of the company. (p. 1187)

Strategic Planning Involves developing long-term strategies to achieve a company's goals. (p. 862)

Subsidiary Company A company that is controlled by another corporation. (p. 554)

Subsidiary Ledger Record of accounts that provides supporting details on individual balances, the total of which appears in a general ledger account. (p. B-6)

Sunk Cost A cost that was incurred in the past and cannot be changed regardless of which future action is taken. (p. 1375)

T-Account A summary device that is shaped like a capital *T* with debits posted on the left side of the vertical line and credits on the right side of the vertical line. (p. 61)

Target Cost The maximum cost to develop, produce, and deliver the product or service *and* earn the desired net profit. Target sales price minus desired net profit. (p. 1044)

Target Full Product Cost The full cost to develop, produce, and deliver the product or service. (p. 1378)

Target Price The amount customers are willing to pay for a product or service. (p. 1043)

Target Pricing A method to manage costs and profits by determining the target full product cost. Revenue at (p. 1378)

Target Profit The operating income that results when net sales revenue minus variable and fixed costs equals management's profit goal. (p. 1099)

Temporary Account An account that relates to a particular accounting period and is closed at the end of that period—the revenues, expenses, Income Summary, and Dividends accounts. (p. 193)

Term Bonds Bonds that all mature at the same time. (p. 625)

Time Period Concept Assumes that a business's activities can be sliced into small time segments and that financial statements can be prepared for specific periods, such as a month, quarter, or year. (p. 122)

Times-Interest-Earned Ratio Evaluates a business's ability to pay interest expense. (pp. 596, 1437)

Time Value of Money Recognition that money earns interest over time. (pp. 626, 1437)

Timing Difference Difference that arises between the balance on the bank statement and the balance on the company's books because of a time lag in recording transactions. (p. 398)

Total Quality Management (TQM) A philosophy designed to integrate all organizational areas in order to provide customers with superior products and services, while meeting organizational goals throughout the value chain. (p. 877)

Trademark An asset that represents distinctive identifications of a product or service. (p. 514)

Trading Debt Investment A debt security that the investor plans to sell in the very near future. (p. 547)

Trading on the Equity Earning more income on borrowed money than the related interest expense, thereby increasing the earnings for the owners of the business. (p. 822)

Transaction An event that affects the financial position of the business and can be measured with faithful representation. (p. 13)

Transfer Price The transaction amount of one unit of goods when the transaction occurs between divisions within the same company. (p. 1346)

Transferred In Costs Costs that were incurred in a previous process and brought into a later process as part of the product's cost. (p. 975)

Treasury Stock A corporation's own stock that it has previously issued and later reacquired. (p. 681)

Trend Analysis A form of horizontal analysis in which percentages are computed by selecting a base period as 100% and expressing amounts for following periods as a percentage of the base period amount. (p. 806)

Trial Balance A list of all ledger accounts with their balances at a point in time. (p. 79)

Triple Bottom Line Evaluating a company's performance by its economic (profits), social (people), and environmental (planet) impact. (p. 878)

Underallocated Overhead Occurs when the actual manufacturing overhead costs are more than allocated manufacturing overhead costs. (p. 923)

Underwriter A firm that handles the issuance of a company's stock to the public, usually assuming some of the risk by agreeing to buy the stock if the firm cannot sell all of the stock to its clients. (p. 676)

Unearned Revenue A liability created when a business collects cash from customers in advance of providing services or delivering goods. (p. 58)

Unemployment Compensation Taxes Payroll tax paid by employers to the government, which uses the cash to pay unemployment benefits to people who are out of work. (p. 589)

Units-of-Production Method A depreciation method that allocates a varying amount of depreciation each year based on an asset's usage. (p. 497)

Useful Life Length of the service period expected from an asset. May be expressed in time or usage. (p. 495)

Value Chain Includes all activities that add value to a company's products and services. (p. 878)

Value Engineering Reevaluating activities to reduce costs while satisfying customer needs. (p. 1043)

Variable Cost A cost that increases or decreases *in total* in direct proportion to increases or decreases in the volume of activity. (p. 1088)

Variable Costing The product costing method that assigns only variable manufacturing costs to products: direct materials, direct labor, and variable manufacturing overhead. Used for internal reporting. (p. 1143)

Variable Overhead Cost Variance The difference between the actual variable overhead (actual cost) and the standard variable overhead for the actual allocation base incurred (standard cost). (p. 1284)

Variable Overhead Efficiency Variance The difference between the actual allocation base (actual quantity) and the amount of the allocation base that should have been used (standard quantity). (p. 1284)

Variance The difference between an actual amount and the budgeted amount; labeled as favorable if it increases operating income and unfavorable if it decreases operating income. (p. 1267)

Vendor The individual or business from whom a company purchases goods. (p. 251)

Vertical Analysis An analysis of a financial statement that reveals the relationship of each statement item to its base amount, which is the 100% figure. (p. 808)

Warranty An agreement that guarantees a company's product against defects. (p. 592)

Weighted-Average Method An inventory costing method based on the weighted-average cost per unit of inventory that is calculated after each purchase. Weighted-average cost per unit is determined by dividing the cost of goods available for sale by the number of units available. (p. 335)

Weighted-Average Method (for Process Costing) Determines the average cost of equivalent units of production by combining beginning inventory costs with current period costs. (p. 971)

Wholesaler A type of merchandiser who buys goods from manufacturers and then sells them to retailers. (p. 250)

Working Capital A measure of a business's ability to meet its short-term obligations with its current assets. Current assets − Current liabilities. (p. 813)

Work-in-Process Inventory (WIP) Goods that have been started in the manufacturing process but are not yet complete. (p. 865)

Worksheet An internal document that helps summarize data for the preparation of financial statements. (p. 144)

Zero-based Budget A budget technique that requires managers to justify all revenue and expenses for each new period. (p. 1187)

Subject Index

Company Index

Photo Credits

Appendix C

Page C-1: (top) Nielskliim/Shutterstock; (middle right) Kongsky/Shutterstock; (bottom left) HomeArt/Shutterstock; page C-2: (top left) Aaron Amat/Shutterstock; (middle right) Sean Gladwell/Shutterstock; page C-10: Iodrakon/Shutterstock; page C-25: michaeljung/Shutterstock

Appendix D

Page D-1: (top) Get4net/Fotolia; (middle right) Rangizzz/Fotolia; (bottom left) Imagemore Co. Ltd./Alamy; page D-2: (middle right) Pokomeda/Shutterstock; page D-8: Lisa F. Young/Shutterstock